Foreign & Commonwealth Office

D1809431

The Diplomatic Service List 2005

FORTIETH EDITION

London: TSO

Published by The Stationery Office and available from:

Online
www.tso.co.uk/bookshop

Mail, Telephone, Fax & E-mail
TSO
PO Box 29. Norwich NR3 IGN
Telephone orders/General enquiries: 0870 600 5522
Fax orders: 0870 600 5533
E-mail: book.orders@tso.co.uk
Textphone: 0870 240 3701

TSO Shops
123 Kingsway. London WC2B 6PQ
020 7242 6393 Fax 020 7242 6394
68 69 Bull Street, Birmingham B4 6AD
0121 236 9696 Fax 0121 236 9699
9-21 Princess Street, Manchester M60 8AS
0161834 7201 Fax 0161 833 0634
16 Arthur Street Belfast BT 1 4GD
028 9023 8451 Fax 028 9023 5401
18 19 High Street, Cardiff CF1 2BZ
029 2039 5548 Fax 029 2038 4347
71 Lothian Road, Edinburgh EH3 9AZ
0870 606 5566 Fax 0870 606 5588

TSO Accredited Agents
(see Yellow Pages)

and through good booksellers

ISBN 0 11 591781 0

Preface

Her Majesty's Diplomatic Service provides the staffs of British Diplomatic and Consular posts overseas in Commonwealth and Foreign countries, as well as in the Foreign & Commonwealth Office in London.

The organisation of the Service and the careers of its members are described in this List, which will be published each year. It is based on information available in August 2004 but includes details of some later changes.

The Diplomatic Service was established on 1 January, 1965, by the merger of the former Foreign, Commonwealth and Trade Commissioner Services. Subsequently, it incorporated the staffs of the Colonial Office in London, which merged with the Commonwealth Relations Office on 1 August, 1966, to form the Commonwealth Office.

The Foreign Office and Commonwealth Office continued as separate Departments of State responsible to separate Secretaries of State until 17 October, 1968. On that day they combined to form the Foreign and Commonwealth Office responsible to one Secretary of State. The Permanent Under-Secretary of the Office and the Head of the Diplomatic Service is Sir Michael Jay, KCMG.

Representatives of Commonwealth countries and foreign states serving in London are shown in a separate publication, the London Diplomatic List, published by The Stationery Office every six months.

Every effort has been made to ensure that the information given in this edition is correct at the time of going to press. Human Resources Directorate will continue to provide the Editor with information on staff movements for Part IV. However, it will be the officer's responsibility to provide information about changes in personal family details such as new marriages, births, dissolved marriages etc. Please refer to re-issued circular 127-03 dated 25th June 2003 for further details.

Amendments and new entries for the 2006 edition of the Diplomatic Service List should be sent to the Editor to arrive no later than Friday, 19th August 2005:-

> Lisa T. Gamandi (Editor)
> Foreign and Commonwealth Office
> Publications Section
> Room WH. MZ. 11,
> King Charles St,
> LONDON SW1A 2AH.

November 2004.

Table of Contents

Home Departments

List of Ministers, Senior Officers and
Home Departments in the
Foreign Commonwealth Office

Part I: Home Departments

ACCOMMODATION

Ministers, Senior Officers and most geographical departments are accommodated in the Main Building, Downing Street, London SW1. Departments are also accommodated in other buildings.

Foreign and Commonwealth Office, Downing Street (West) SW1A 2AL	020 7008 1500
Foreign and Commonwealth Office, Downing Street (East) SW1A 2AL	020 7008 1500
Foreign and Commonwealth Office, Whitehall SW1A 2AP	020 7008 1500
Foreign and Commonwealth Office, King Charles St SW1A 2AH	020 7008 1500
Old Admiralty Building, Whitehall, London SW1A 2PA	020 7008 1500
UK Visas, 89 Albert Embankment, London SE1 7TP	020 7008 8438
Vauxhall Cross, 85 Albert Embankment, London SE1 7TP	020 7008 4440
Apollo House, 36 Wellesley Road, Croydon CR0 9YA	020 8686 5622
Hanslope Park, Hanslope, Milton Keynes MK19 7BH	01908 510444
UK Trade & Investment, Kingsgate House, 66-74 Victoria Street. London SW1E 6SW	020 7215 5000

TELEPHONE ENQUIRIES
If the number, department or building is not known, callers should ring 020 7270 3000 and ask to be connected to the Central Enquiry point.

TELEGRAPHIC ADDRESS
PRODROME LONDON

TELEX 297711 (a/b PRODROME G)

Internet World Wide Web Address: www.fco.gov.uk

The Foreign and Commonwealth Office provides, through its staff in the UK and through its diplomatic missions abroad, the means of communication between the British Government and other governments and international governmental organisations on all matters falling within the field of international relations. It is responsible for alerting the British Government to the implications of developments overseas; for promoting British interests overseas; for protecting British citizens abroad; for explaining British policies to, and cultivating relationships with, governments overseas; for the discharge of British responsibilities to the overseas territories; for entry clearance (through UK Visas, with the Home Office); and for promoting British business overseas (jointly with the Department of Trade and Industry through UK Trade and Investment).

MINISTERS AND THEIR STAFFS

Secretary of State for Foreign & Commonwealth Affairs
The Rt Hon Jack Straw MP
Team Parliamentary Private Secretary: Roger Casale MP
Principal Private Secretary: Geoffrey Adams CMG
Telephone: 020 7008 2059
GTN: 7008 2059
Private Secretaries: Jonathan Sinclair, Kara Owen
Telephone: 020 7008 2069
Telephone: 020 7008 2070
GTN: 7008 2069
GTN: 7008 2070
Enquiries: 020 7008 2079 *(Diary Enquiries)*
GTN: 7008 2079
Enquiries: 020 7008 2057 *(Clerical Enquiries)*
GTN: 7008 2057
Special Advisers: Ed Owen, Dr Michael Williams
Telephone: 020 7008 2112
Telephone: 020 7008 2117
GTN: 7008 2112
GTN: 7008 2117

Minister of State for Europe
Dr Denis MacShane MP
Parliamentary Private Secretary:
Phyllis Starkey MP
Private Secretary: Peter Boxer
Telephone: 020 7008 8294
GTN: 7008 8294
Assistant Private Secretary: Stuart Templar
Telephone: 020 7008 8032
GTN: 7008 8032
Office Manager: Venetia Smith
Telephone: 020 7008 8033
GTN: 7008 8033

Minister of State for the Middle East
The Rt Hon Baroness Symons of Vernham Dean
Parliamentary Private Secretary: Mark Todd MP
Private Secretary: Emma Wade
Telephone: 020 7008 2090
GTN: 7008 2090
Assistant Private Secretaries: Jennifer Townson
Tracey McLelland
Telephone: 020 7008 2091
Telephone: 020 7008 2092
GTN: 020 7008 2091
GTN: 020 7008 2092

Minister of State for Trade, Investment and Foreign Affairs
Douglas Alexander MP
Parliamentary Private Secretary: Eric Joyce MP
Private Secretary: Peter Elder
Assistant Private Secretaries: Alison Keeling
Bradley Jones
Telephone: 020 7008 2127
Telephone: 020 7008 2128
GTN: 7008 2127
GTN: 7008 2128

Parliamentary Under-Secretary of State
Bill Rammell MP
Private Secretary: David Whineray
Telephone: 020 7008 3367
GTN: 7008 3367
Assistant Private Secretary: Lisa Glover
Telephone: 020 7008 3371
GTN: 7008 3371
Diary Co-ordinator: Claire Bruce
Telephone: 020 7008 3365
GTN: 7008 3365
Personal Assistant: Catherine Bassa
Telephone: 020 7008 3362
GTN: 7008 3362
Correspondence Clerks: Salma Siddiqi, Dean Barrett
Telephone: 020 7008 3362
Telephone: 020 7008 3364
GTN: 7008 3362
GTN: 7008 3364

Parliamentary Under-Secretary of State
Chris Mullin MP
Private Secretary: Bharat Joshi
Telephone: 020 7008 2173
GTN: 7008 2173
Assistant Private Secretaries: Caron Rohsler, Nicky Wilbrey
Telephone: 020 7008 2172
Telephone: 020 7008 3363
GTN: 7008 2172
GTN: 7008 3363
Diary Secretary: Vaishali Patel
Telephone: 020 7008 2520
GTN: 7008 2520
Parliamentary Clerk: Jeremy Hill
Telephone: 020 7008 4005
GTN: 7008 4005

SENIOR OFFICERS AND THEIR STAFFS

Permanent Under-Secretary of State and Head of the Diplomatic Service
Sir Michael Jay KCMG
Private Secretary: Menna Rawlings
Assistant Private Secretaries: Nicola Friel, Andrea McGlone
Diary Secretaries: Esther Hartless, Karen Shanks
Telephone: 020 7008 2150
GTN: 7008 2150

Group Chief Executive UK Trade and Investment
Sir Stephen Brown KCVO
Telephone: 020 7215 4643
GTN: 7215 4643
Private Secretary: Simon Cooper
Telephone: 020 7215 4300
GTN: 215 4300

DIRECTORS GENERAL
Dickie Stagg CMG *(Corporate Affairs)*
John Sawers CMG *(Political)*
Nicola Brewer CMG *(EU Policy)*
David Richmond *(Defence/Intelligence)*
Martin Donnelly *(Economic)*

DIRECTORS
James Bevan *(Africa)*
Robert Culshaw MVO *(Americas/Overseas Territories)*
Edward Oakden *(Defence and Strategic Threats)*
Stephen Pattison *(International Security)*
Dominick Chilcott *(EU Bilateral, Resources & Mediterranean)*
Paul Sizeland *(Consular Services)*
Robin Barnett *(UK Visas)*
Stephen Sage *(Chief Executive, FCO Services)*
Philippa Drew *(Global Issues)*
Peter Gooderham *(Middle East/North Africa)*
Dominic Asquith *(Iraq)*
Anne Pringle CMG *(Strategy and Information)*
John Williams *(Communications)*
Nigel Cox *(Asia and Pacific)*
Tom Phillips CMG *(South Asia and Afghanistan)*
Darren Warren *(Human Resources)*
Ric Todd *(Finance)*
Creon Butler *(Chief Economist) (Economic Policy)*

SPECIAL REPRESENTATIVES
Alan Goulty CMG *(UK Special Representative for Sudan)*
Tom Phillips CMG *(UK Special Representative for Afghanistan)*
Sir Brian Fall KCMG *(UK Special Representative for Georgia)*

DEPARTMENTS IN THE FOREIGN AND COMMONWEALTH OFFICE
The FCO Organisation Project is having a major effect on the structure of FCO Home Departments which will continue until March 2005. Whilst every effort has been made to reflect the changes that have taken effect up to the time of printing it will not be possible to include all of them until the next edition.

Afghanistan Group
The Mission of the Afghanistan Unit is to help Afghanistan achieve stability, security and prosperity, to the benefit of the Afghan people, the United Kingdom and the world community.

Whitehall,
LONDON SW1A 2AH
Enquiries: 020 7008 2866
Enquiries: 020 7008 2995
GTN: 7008 2866
GTN: 7008 2995
UK Special Representative: Tom Phillips CMG
Head of Unit: Jan Thompson
Deputy Head of Unit: Charles Longsdale

Africa Department (Equatorial)
Political and economic relations with Nigeria, Ghana, Sierra Leone, The Gambia, Kenya, Tanzania, Uganda, Ethiopia, Eritrea, Somalia, Djibouti, Liberia, Senegal, Guinea, Mali, Burkina Faso, Ivory Coast (Cote d'Ivoire), Togo, Benin, Niger, Chad, Cameroon, Gabon, Central African Republic, Equatorial Guinea, Guinea Bissau, Cape Verde, Economic Community of West African States (ECOWAS) and East African Community (EAC), Africa Union, Inter-Governmental Authority for Development (IGAD).

King Charles Street,
LONDON SW1A 2AH
Enquiries: 020 7008 2903
GTN: 7008 2903
Superintending Director: James Bevan
Head of Department: Tim Hitchens
Deputy Heads of Department: Patrick Moody

Africa Department (Southern)
Political and economic relations with Angola, Botswana, Burundi, The Comoros, Congo, Democratic Republic of Congo, Lesotho, Madagascar, Malawi, Mauritius, Mozambique, Namibia, Rwanda, Sao Tomé and Principe, Seychelles, South Africa, Swaziland, Zambia and Zimbabwe; Southern African Development Community (SADC).

King Charles Street,
LONDON SW1A 2AH
Enquiries: 020 7008 2552
GTN: 7008 2552
Superintending Director: James Bevan
Head of Department: Andrew Lloyd
Deputy Heads of Department: Fergus Cochrane-Dyet, Nigel Bowie

Association of South East Asian Nations and Oceania Group
Political and economic relations with Australia, Brunei, Burma, Cambodia, East Timor, Indonesia, Laos, Malaysia, New Zealand, Philippines, Singapore, South Pacific, Thailand and Vietnam; ASEAN, ASEM, ARF and COASI.

FCO,
Whitehall,
LONDON SW1A 2AH
Enquiries: 020 7008 2600
GTN: 7008 2600
Superintending Director: Nigel Cox
Head of Group: Michael Reilly
Deputy Head of Group: Valerie Brownridge

Climate Change and Energy Group
Delivery of HMG international Energy and Climate Change objectives: International energy policy and collaboration; multilateral and bilateral producer-consumer dialogue; promotion of international action and policies and measures to combat Climate Change; nuclear power (including reprocessing and shipments); physical security of energy infrastructure; energy sector investment and governance; oil, gas, coal, renewables, and new energy technologies; energy efficiency, sustainable energy and low carbon energy solutions; carbon sequestration; electricity; pipelines and interconnectors.

King Charles Street,
LONDON SW1A 2AH
Enquiries: 020 7008 2621
GTN: 7008 2621
Superintending Director: Philippa Drew
Head of Group: (Vacant)

Deputy Heads of Group: Simon Banks, Shaun Cleary (until Dec 04)

Commonwealth Co-ordination Department
Policy, procedures and practices relating to the Commonwealth as a whole. Commonwealth Heads of Government Meetings. Commonwealth Ministerial Action Group meetings. Liaison with the Commonwealth Secretariat, Commonwealth Foundation, and a wide range of pan-Commonwealth NGOs professional associations, organisations and societies. Commonwealth constitutional questions.

Whitehall,
LONDON SW1A 2AL
Enquiries: 020 7008 2943
GTN: 7008 2943
Superintending Director: Philippa Drew
Head of Department: Asif Ahmad
Deputy Head of Department: Tony Humphries OBE

Consular Directorate
Consular Directorate comprises 5 Groups: Assistance; Crisis; Passports and Documentary Services; Policy, Communications and Training; Resources. Correspondence and enquiries should be directed to the relevant Group, and copies to the Director.
Director of Consular Services: Paul Sizeland

CONSULAR ASSISTANCE GROUP:
Help given to individual cases of Britons in distress overseas; policy related to the human rights of Britons in distress overseas.

Old Admiralty Building,
LONDON SW1A 2PA
Enquiries: 020 7008 0223
GTN: 7008 0223
Head of Group: Janet Douglas

CONSULAR CRISIS GROUP:
Provides consular assistance to British nationals affected by major incidents overseas. Publishes FCO Travel Advice (www.fco.gov.uk/travel)for British nationals travelling overseas. Undertakes consular emergency and contingency planning, including management of Rapid Deployment Teams.

Old Admiralty Building,
LONDON SW1A 2PA
Enquiries: 020 7008 0225
GTN: 7008 0225
Head of Group: Ralph Publicover

PASSPORTS AND DOCUMENTARY SERVICES GROUP:
FCO passport policy and co-ordination of Posts' passport operations; birth and death registration and marriages abroad; advise on nationality and passport matters; overseas document searches. Civil matters; coroners requests; notarial acts; claims for compensation from other Governments in respect of loss, injury or damage suffered overseas by individuals or companies; legalisation of documents in the UK and overseas.

Modernisation of Consular work using latest IT advancements; projects include GenIE secure digital passports and biometric passports.

Downing Street (East),
King Charles Street,
LONDON SW1A 2AH
Enquiries: 020 7008 1967
GTN: 7008 1967
Head of Group: David Clegg MVO

POLICY, COMMUNICATION AND TRAINING GROUP:
Consular assistance policy (non-human rights related), the Consular Strategy 2004-07, best practice and information handling, including access requests under the Data Protection Act and Freedom of Information Act from January 2005. Manages the "Know Before You Go" consular awareness campaign (www.fco.gov.uk/knowbeforeyougo), and consular publications. Responsible for training within the global consular operation.

Old Admiralty Building,
LONDON SW1A 2PA
Enquiries: 020 7008 0083
GTN: 7008 0083
Head of Group: Tim Flear MVO

CONSULAR RESOURCES GROUP:
Resource management of worldwide consular operations. Funding, planning, deployment and monitoring of staff and resources to achieve best value. Forecasting and monitoring of consular income, costs and expenditure. Measurement of performance against Public Service Agreement targets. Information management and staffing reviews.

Old Admiralty Building,
LONDON SW1A 2PA
Enquiries: 020 7008 0218
GTN: 7008 0218
Head of Group: David Popplestone

Counter-Proliferation Department
Nuclear non-proliferation issues, including the Nuclear Non-Proliferation Treaty, CTBT, IAEA and Nuclear Suppliers Group. Missile proliferation issues and MTCR. Chemical and Biological Weapons Conventions, Australia Group and CW/BW proliferation issues. Policy on conventional arms sales, MANPADS and exports of Dual-Use Goods. UN Arms Register. Wassenaar Arrangement. Arms Control and Disarmament Research Unit.

Downing Street (West),
King Charles Street
LONDON SW1A 2AH
Enquiries: 020 7008 2261
Enquiries: 020 7008 2751
GTN: 7008 2261
GTN: 7008 2751
Superintending Director: Edward Oakden
Head of Department: David Landsman
Deputy Heads of Department: Sarah Price, Trevor Moore

Counter Terrorism Policy Department
Counter-terrorism policy, bilaterally and in
international fora. Crisis management.

King Charles Street,
LONDON SW1A 2AH
Enquiries: 020 7008 2583
GTN: 7008 2583
Superintending Director: Edward Oakden
Head of Department: Philip Parham
Deputy Head of Department: Martyn Warr

Diplomatic Service Families Association
Works with the Administration on 'best practice
family-friendly policy'. Promotes the interests and
welfare of UK diplomatic families, spouses and
partners, at home and abroad, in issues including
career development, child education, special needs
and disabilities, matters affecting foreign-born
spouses/partners, and other welfare and social
matters.

FCO,
Old Admiralty Building,
LONDON SW1A 2PA
Enquiries: 020 7008 0286
GTN: 7008 0286
DSFA Chairwoman: Emilie Salvesen
Vice-Chairwoman and Education/Sponsorship
Scheme Adviser: Marianne Gass
Executive Secretary: Christine Easter

Drugs and International Crime Department
International aspects of UK activity against drug
trafficking, human trafficking, money laundering
and other international organised crime.

King Charles Street,
LONDON SW1A 2AH
Enquiries: 020 7008 1833
Enquiries: 020 7008 1808
GTN: 7008 1833
GTN: 7008 1808
Superintending Director: Edward Oakden
Head of Department: Lesley Pallett
Deputy Head of Department: Rowan Laxton

Eastern Adriatic Department
Relations with Croatia, Serbia and Montenegro
(including Kosovo), Bosnia and Herzegovina,
Macedonia and Albania.

Downing Street West,
LONDON SW1A 2AL
Enquiries: 020 7008 2756
Enquiries: 020 7008 2372
Enquiries: 020 7008 3433
Enquiries: 020 7008 3459
GTN: 7008 2756
GTN: 7008 2372
GTN: 7008 3433
GTN: 7008 3459
Superintending Director: Linda Duffield
Head of Department: Karen Pierce cvo
Deputy Head of Department: Paul Fox

Eastern Department
Policy on Russia, the Caucasus (Armenia,
Azerbaijan, Georgia), Central Asia (Kazakhstan,
Kyrgyzstan, Tajikistan, Turkmenistan, Uzbekistan)
and Caspian energy issues.

Downing Street West,
LONDON SW1A 2AL
Enquiries: 020 7008 2427
Enquiries: 020 7008 2423
Enquiries: 020 7008 3831
GTN: 7008 2427
GTN: 7008 2423
GTN: 7008 3831
Director General: John Sawer
Head of Department: Simon Smith
Deputy Head of Department: Dominic Schroeder

Economic Policy Directorate
Economic Policy Directorate's principal task is the
pursuit of FCO Strategic Priority No 5: Promotion
of UK economic interests in an open and
expanding global economy. The Directorate's work
also makes a strong contribution in support of
other Strategic Priorities, particularly No 6
(Sustainable Development).

FCO,
Whitehall,
LONDON SW1A 2AH
Enquiries: 020 7008 2732
GTN: 7008 2732
Director General: Martin Donnelly
Director and Chief Economist: Creon Butler

GLOBAL ECONOMY GROUP
The performance of the UK economy increasingly
relies on a stable and prosperous international
economic environment. The Global Economy
Group (GEG), and its network of economic
officers, will support this through promoting the
economic development and stability of other
nations, and engaging with key multilateral
institutions. There are three main areas where GED
will support Strategic Priority 5: Working with
multilateral institutions to promote global stability
and prosperity; Promotion of UK economic
interests, Promotion of good economic governance
and reform in key countries (excluding EU)
Head of Group: Hasan Bakhshi

GLOBAL BUSINESS GROUP
The business sector is crucial to delivery of
Strategic Priority 5. The core business of Global
Business Group (GBG) will be to help build
conditions to maximise the potential of the
business sector to contribute to UK economic
interests through sustainable global economic
prosperity. In particular, GBG are working to:
promote a secure and positive environment for
investment; promote a secure and positive
environment for UK business in the transport
sector; promote a commitment by business
(particularly UK business) to socially responsible
behaviour.
Head of Group: Graham Minter

G8 PRESIDENCY TEAM

This team leads within Whitehall on preparation for the UK's presidency of the G8 in 2005 and co-ordinates the UK's participation in the G8 processes.
Head of Team: Charles Hay

SCIENCE AND INNOVATION GROUP

Co-ordination of global Science and Technology Network and advising of issues within the Foreign and Commonwealth Office.
Head of Group: Fiona Clouder Richards

INTERNATIONAL TRADE TEAM

The Team's objective is to provide FCO input on the World Trade Organisation (WTO) Trade Round (the Doha Development Agenda) and other trade issues, working closely with the Department of Trade and Industry, UKRep, UKMis Geneva and other government departments.
International Trade Team, reporting via Simon Manley in European Union (Internal) to Creon Butler. This team is jointly owned by Economic Policy Directorate and EU Directorate General.
Environment Policy Department
International environment policy; environmental dimensions of sustainable development and globalisation; EU environment policy; climate change; biodiversity; environmental security.
Details at www.fco.gov.uk/environment.

FCO,
King Charles Street,
LONDON SW1A 2AH
Enquiries: 020 7008 4131
Enquiries: 020 7008 4112
GTN: 7008 4131
GTN: 7008 4112
Superintending Director: Philippa Drew
Head of Department: Valerie Caton
Deputy Head of Department: Dominic Meiklejohn

Estate Strategy Unit

Formulation and implementation of strategy for the FCO's estate in the UK and overseas.

Apollo House,
36 Wellesley Road,
CROYDON CR0 9YA
Enquiries: 020 8253 6358
Enquiries: 020 8253 6353
GTN: 3822 6358
GTN: 3822 6353
Director General: Dickie Stagg CMG
Head of Unit: Julian Metcalfe
Deputy Head of Unit: Jeremy Neate

European Union (External) Assistant Directorate

Comprises of three teams: EU Northern Europe and International Team; Common Foreign and Security Policy Team; EU Enlargement and Wider Europe Team.

Downing Street East,
LONDON SW1A 2AL
Enquiries: 020 7008 3812
Enquiries: 020 7008 4266

GTN: 7008 3812
GTN: 7008 4266
Director General: Nicola Brewer CMG
Assistant Director EU-E: Tim Barrow LVO MBE

COMMON FOREIGN AND SECURITY POLICY TEAM:
Co-ordination of foreign policy among EU member states and implementation of Common Foreign and Security Policy.

Downing Street (East),
LONDON SW1A 2AH
Enquiries: 020 7008 2807
GTN: 7008 2807
Team Leader: James Morrison

EU NORTHERN EUROPE AND INTERNATIONAL TEAM:
Relations between the European Union, Accession States, third countries, Ukraine, Belarus and Moldova; international trade and development matters.

Downing Street (East),
LONDON SW1A 2AH
Enquiries: 020 7008 3018
GTN: 7008 3018
Team Leader: Andrew Key

EU ENLARGEMENT AND WIDER EUROPE TEAM:
Relations between the European Union and third countries; international trade and development matters; enlargement of the Union.

Downing Street (East),
LONDON SW1A 2AH
Enquiries: 020 7008 3018
GTN: 7008 3018
Team Leader: Charles Garrett

European Union (Internal)

The internal economic and institutional policies of the European Union.
Downing Street (East),

LONDON SW1A 2AL
Enquiries: 020 7008 3388
GTN: 7008 3388
Director General: Nicola Brewer CMG
Assistant Director: David Frost
Team Leaders: Simon Manley *(Economic/Central Europe Team)*, Mara Goldstein *(JHA/Germany Team)*, Tom Drew *(IGC Unit)*
Head of Convention Unit: Catherine Royle

European Union - Mediterranean

Political and bilateral relations with Turkey, Cyprus, Greece, Italy. Holy See, Malta, Spain, Portugal and Andorra. UK policy towards the UN-sponsored discussions on the future of Cyprus. External relations and some aspects of internal administration of Gibraltar.

King Charles Street,
LONDON SW1A 2AH
Enquiries: 020 7008 2011
GTN: 7008 2011
Superindending Director: Dominick Chilcott
Team Leaders: Rob Fenn *(Eastern Mediterranean)*, Wendy Wyver *(Western Mediterranean)*.

Far East Group
Relations between the United Kingdom and China, including the Hong Kong Special Administrative Region, Japan, Democratic People's Republic of Korea, Republic of Korea and Mongolia,.

FCO,
Whitehall,
LONDON SW1A 2AP
Enquiries: 020 7008 3074
GTN: 7008 3074
Superintending Director: Nigel Cox
Head of Group: Denis Keefe
Deputy Heads of Group: Geoff Cole, David Ellis

Financial Planning and Performance Department
Resource planning, budgeting and allocation, expenditure monitoring and performance measurement, fees and charging.

Old Admiralty Building,
LONDON SW1A 2PA
Enquiries: 020 7008 1085
GTN: 7008 1085
Superintending Director: Ric Todd
Head of Department: Tristan Price
Deputy Heads of Department: Matthew Owen, Noel Langley, James Tansley

FCO Association
Old Admiralty Building,
LONDON SW1A 2PA
Enquiries: 020 7008 0967
GTN: 7008 0967
Chairman: Roger Westbrook CMG
Hon Secretary: Maureen Howley MBE

FCO Services
FCO Services provides the main support services for the FCO at home and overseas. FCO Services is based at the following locations:

King Charles Street,
LONDON SW1A 2AH

Old Admiralty Building,
Whitehall,
LONDON SW1A 2PA

Apollo House,
Wellesley Road,
CROYDON CR0 9YA
Hanslope Park,
Hanslope,
MILTON KEYNES MK19 7BH

Enquiries: 01908 515165 (Customer Services)
GTN: 3905 5165
Chief Executive: Stephen Sage

CLIENT SERVICES:
The first point of contact for all customers. Accounts managers, sales and marketing, strategic planning.

Enquiries: 01908 515165
GTN: 3905 5165
Head of Client Services: Joy Herring

FACILITIES SERVICE DELIVERY GROUP:
Property and estate management services for the diplomatic estate at home and overseas. Technical and protective security measures.

Enquiries: 020 8253 6247 (Overseas Estate)
Enquiries: 020 7008 8007 (Home Estate)
Enquiries: 01908 515524 (Technical Security)
Enquiries: 01908 516889 (Protective Security)
GTN: 3822 6247 (Overseas Estate)
GTN: 7008 8007 (Home Estate)
GTN: 3905 5524 (Technical Security)
GTN: 3905 6889 (Protective Security)
Head of Service Delivery Group: Nigel Morris

ICT SERVICE DELIVERY GROUP:
Installation and support of the FCO's ICT infrastructure.

Enquiries: 020 7008 2976 (Communications Centre)
Enquiries: 01908 515506 (FTN world-wide communications network)
Enquiries: 01908 516571 (IT)
GTN: 7008 2976 (Communications Centre)
GTN: 3905 5506 (FTN world-wide communications network)
GTN: 3905 6571 (IT)
Head of Service Delivery Group: Patrick Cullen

PEOPLE AND BEST PRACTICE SERVICE DELIVERY GROUP:
The following services are provided: Technical training; IT Training; language training; language testing and examinations; security clearance; management consultancy; information systems consultancy.

Enquiries: 01908 515641 (Technical Training)
Enquiries: 020 7008 0455 (IT Training)
Enquiries: 020 7008 0300 (Language Training)
Enquiries: 020 7008 0440 (Translation and Interpreting)
Enquiries: 020 7008 0304 (Testing and Examinations)
Enquiries: 020 7008 0013 (Management Consultancy Services)
Enquiries: 020 7008 1261 (Vetting)
Enquiries: 01908 515933 (IS Consultancy)
GTN: 3905 5641 (Technical Training)
GTN: 7008 0455 (IT Training)
GTN: 7008 0300 (Language Training)
GTN: 7008 0440 (Translation and Interpreting)
GTN: 7008 0304 (Testing and Examinations)
GTN: 7008 0013 (Management Consultancy)
GTN: 7008 1261 (Vetting)
GTN: 3905 5933 (IS Consultancy)
Head of Service Delivery Group: Dr Vanessa L Davies

POSITIVE IMAGE UK SERVICE DELIVERY GROUP:
Organisation of conference visits, production of publications and films, printing services and management of the Fine Rooms.

Enquiries: 020 7008 8101 (Conferences and Visits)
Enquiries: 020 7008 3233 (Crystal Print)
Enquiries: 020 7008 6050 (Creative Services)

GTN: 7008 8101 (Conference and Services)
GTN: 7008 3233 (Crystal Print)
GTN: 7008 6050 (Creative Services)
Head of Service Delivery Group: John Elgie

SUPPLY CHAIN SERVICE DELIVERY GROUP:
Procurement, purchasing and logistics.

Enquiries: 01908 515788 (Logistics)
Enquiries: 020 8253 6434 (Supply Solutions)
Enquiries: 01908 516744 (Purchasing)
GTN: 3905 5788 (Logistics)
GTN: 3822 6434 (Supply Solutions)
GTN: 3905 6744 (Purchasing)
Head of Service Delivery Group: Rod Peters

FINANCE GROUP:
Financial management.
Enquiries: 01908 516876
GTN: 3905 6876
Head of Finance Group: Kerry Simmonds

HUMAN RESOURCES GROUP:
Personnel management and developmental training.

Enquiries: 01908 515007 (Personnel)
Enquiries: 01908 515641 (Training)
GTN: 3905 5007 (Personnel)
GTN: 3905 5641 (Training)
Head of Human Resources Group: Elaine Kennedy

Government Diamonds Office
See under United Nations Department.

Human Resources Directorate
The purpose of the Human Resource Directorate is to recruit, develop, deploy, motivate and support FCO staff to meet the FCO's objectives.

Old Admiralty Building,
LONDON SW1A 2PA
Superintending Director and Head of HR Directorate: David Warren

HR DIRECT:
A one stop shop service for HR enquiries from staff throughout the FCO.
Manager of HR Direct: Andrew Heyn

HEALTH AND WELFARE POLICY TEAM:
Health, safety and welfare of staff at home and overseas.
Assistant Director: Andrew George

LEGAL POLICY TEAM:
Human resource policy and management questions including implementation of employment legislation and relations with the trade union side, organisation and structure of the FCO's personnel, conduct and discipline, diplomatic status, diversity and equal opportunities.
Assistant Directors: Diane Corner, Carole Sweeney

PAY AND BENEFITS POLICY TEAM:
Pay, pensions, allowances, conditions of service.
Head of Team: David Powell

PROFESSIONAL DEVELOPMENT:
All aspects of staff performance management and development, including career development advice, training, learning and development, mentoring, core competences, staff appraisal and assessment, promotion competitions and Assessment and Development Centres. Individual staff records.
Assistant Directors: Howard Drake *(Career Development and Senior Management Structure)*, Richard Tauwhare *(Learning and Development)*, Gerry Reffo *(Performance Assessment and Development)*.

WORKFORCE PLANNING TEAM:
Human resource planning, personnel statistics; individual personnel movements, appointments, probation, promotions, sick absence, recruitment; transfers, secondments and loans to and from other services.
Assistant Director: Simon Pease

Human Rights, Democracy and Governance Group
The FCO point of advice on human rights policy questions in all international organisations, including obligations and commitments at the UN, Council of Europe, OSCE and Commonwealth. Responsible, in co-operation with geographical departments, for: developing and co-ordinating HMG's human rights policy and ensuring consistency of application in the UK's overseas bilateral relations; liaison with Department for International Development on human rights aspects of bilateral and multilateral development policy; liaison with Whitehall departments, ensuring that the development of domestic policy takes account of HMG's international human rights obligations and objectives; supervision of UK and Overseas Territory periodic reports under international treaty obligations; FCO point of contact and liaison for NGOs and other bodies on general (i.e. non-country specific) human rights matters. Manages FCO's Human Rights Project Fund and produces the Human Rights Annual Report.

King Charles Street,
LONDON SW1A 2AH
Enquiries: 020 7008 3616
GTN: 7008 3616
Superintending Director: Philippa Drew
Head of Department: Jon Benjamin
Deputy Head of Department: Chris Trott

Information Management Group
Information Policy & Access: Freedom of Information, Data Protection, EIRs; Records Management: registry, records custody, e-archiving, review and release; Treaty information and publication; Historical advice; publication of Documents on British Policy Overseas; Library & Information Services.

Old Admiralty Building,
LONDON SW1A 2PA
Enquiries: 020 7008 1128
GTN: 7008 1128
Superintending Director: Anne Pringle CMG

Head of Department: Heather Yasamee
Information Policy & Access: Richard Barr
Records Management: Penny Prior
Treaty: Paul Barnett
Historian: Gill Bennett OBE
Chief Librarian: Vacant

Internal Audit Department
King Charles Street,
LONDON SW1A 2AH
Enquiries: 020 7008 8010
GTN: 7008 8010
Superintending Director: Ric Todd
Head of Department: Jon Hews
Deputy Head of Department: Trevor Jarvis
Head of Financial Compliance Unit: David Major
Audit Manager: Richard Clark

IT Strategy Unit
Responsible for ICT investment policy and budgets
and co-ordination with central government
Departments on ICT issues.

Old Admiralty Building,
Whitehall,
LONDON SW1A 2PA
Enquiries: 020 7008 0524
GTN: 7008 0524
Director General: Dickie Stagg CMG
Head of Unit: Nick Westcott
Deputy Head of Unit: Nick Clouting

Latin America and Caribbean Department
Political and economic bilateral relations with all
Latin American and independent Caribbean
countries, and Latin American and Caribbean
regional organisations.

FCO,
King Charles Street,
LONDON SW1A 2AH
Enquiries: 020 7008 2481
GTN: 7008 2481
Superintending Director: Robert Culshaw MVO
Head of Department: Stephen Williams
Deputy Head of Department: Andrew Allen

Legal Advisers
Advice on international, EU and UK law and
practice in connection with HMG's foreign
relations, including treaties and international
litigation, and with the work of the FCO generally.
Legal advice concerning the governance of UK
overseas territories.

King Charles Street,
LONDON SW1A 2AH
Enquiries: 020 7008 3080
Enquiries: 020 7008 3081
GTN: 7008 3080
GTN: 7008 3081
Legal Adviser: Sir Michael Wood KCMG
Deputy Legal Advisers: Ian Hendry CMG,
Christopher Whomersley, John Grainger

Middle East Department
Relations with Bahrain, Iran, Iraq, Kuwait, Oman,
Qatar, Republic of Yemen, Saudi Arabia, United
Arab Emirates.

Downing Street West,
LONDON SW1A 2AL
Enquiries: 020 7008 2997
GTN: 7008 2997
King Charles Street,
LONDON SW1A 2AH
Superintending Director: Peter Gooderham
Head of Department: Charles Gray CMG
Deputy Head of Department: Jolyon Welsh

Near East and North Africa Department
Relations with Algeria, Egypt, the Palestinian
Authority, Israel, Jordan, Lebanon, Mauritania,
Libya, Morocco, Sudan, Syria and Tunisia. HMG's
interests in the Middle East peace process and the
EU's Barcelona process.

Downing Street West and King Charles Street,
LONDON SW1A 2AL
Enquiries: 020 7008 3751
GTN: 7008 3751
Superintending Director: Peter Gooderham
Head of Department: Nicholas Archer
Deputy Head of Department: Rosemary Waugh

North America Team
Relations with Canada and the United States
(including the US Virgin Islands and Puerto Rico).

FCO,
Whitehall,
LONDON SW1A 2AP
Enquiries: 020 7008 2663
GTN: 7008 2663
Superintending Director: Robert Culshaw MVO
Team Leader: Martin Rickerd OBE MVO
Deputy Team Leader: Anne Jarrett

Organisation for Security and Co-operation in Europe (OSCE) and the Council of Europe Department
UK Policy on the Organisation for Security and
Co-operation in Europe and on the Council of
Europe.

Whitehall,
LONDON SW1A 2AH
Enquiries: 020 7008 2426
GTN: 7008 2426
Superintending Director: Linda Duffield
Head of Department: Peter January
Deputy Head of Department: Anneli Conroy

Overseas Territories Department
Management of HMG's responsibilities for the
Overseas Territories of Anguilla, Bermuda, the
British Antarctic Territory, the British Indian Ocean
Territory, the British Virgin Islands, the Cayman
Islands, the Falkland Islands, Montserrat, Pitcairn,
South Georgia and the South Sandwich Islands, St
Helena and Ascension and Tristan da Cunha and
the Turks and Caicos Islands. Co-ordination of UK
policy on the Overseas Territories and organisation

of the annual Overseas Territories Consultative Council; and liaison on South Atlantic matters. Also includes Polar Regions Unit, which leads on HMG's responsibilities under the Antarctic Treaty and represents the UK at Arctic Council.

King Charles Street,
LONDON SW1A 2AH
Enquiries: 020 7008 2643
GTN: 7008 2643
Superintending Director: Robert Culshaw MVO
Head of Department: Tony Crombie OBE
Deputy Heads of Department: Fraser Wilson, Sarah Booker
Head of Polar Regions Unit: Dr Mike Richardson

Parliamentary Relations and Devolution Department

Advice and guidance to FCO Ministers and officials on parliamentary practice and procedure. Monitoring of all parliamentary business of interest to the FCO. Contact with Select Committees of both Houses of Parliament. Liaison with the British Group of the Inter-Parliamentary Union. Liaison with the Parliamentary Commissioner for Administration. Responsibility for FCO relations with the devolved administrations and legislatures in Scotland, Wales and Northern Ireland.

King Charles Street,
LONDON SW1A 2AH
Enquiries: 020 7008 2236
Enquiries: 020 7008 2235
Enquiries: 020 7008 2234
GTN: 7008 2236
GTN: 7008 2235
GTN: 7008 2234
Superintending Director: Anne Pringle CMG
Head of Department: Matthew Hamlyn
Deputy Head of Department: Sue Breeze
Parliamentary Clerk: Jeremy Hill

Press Office

Advises the Secretary of State, Foreign Office Ministers and departments of the FCO on questions of presentation relating to the British Government's foreign policy. It is the authorised contact between the FCO and the British media.

Downing Street West,
LONDON SW1A 2AH
Enquiries: 020 7008 3100
GTN: 7008 3100
Superintending Director & Press Secretary: John Williams
Head of Newsroom & Deputy Head of Department: Peter Reid

Prism Programme

Prism is a business change management programme. Prism will provide the FCO with a global on-line management information system (covering personnel, pay, finance and procurement), which will enable better decision making.

Old Admiralty Building,
Whitehall,

LONDON SW1A 2PA
Superintending Director: Ric Todd
Programme Manager (FCO): Andy Tucker
Deputy Programme Managers: Giles Whitaker, Roger Seager

Procurement Policy Department

Advice and guidance to FCO departments and posts overseas on best practice in the purchase of goods and services; sponsorship and selling into wider markets; operational environmental issues; Programme and project management best practice.

Old Admiralty Building,
LONDON SW1A 2PA
Enquiries: 020 7008 0924
GTN: 7008 0924
Superintending Director: Ric Todd
Head of Department: Michael Gower
Deputy Head of Department: Charles Sime

Protocol Division

Diplomatic Missions: Policy on handling of appointments, privileges, immunities and security of the Diplomatic Corps and International Organisations in Britain. Diplomatic and International Organisations lists. Organisation of ceremonial events, and policy and advice on protocol and precedence. Honours Secretariat: FCO aspects of honours policy. Diplomatic Service and Overseas Honours Lists, British honorary awards, Foreign and Commonwealth honours for British citizens. Investitures, presentation of insignia. Royal Households Secretariat: Co-ordination between the FCO and Royal Households, especially on overseas visits by the Royal Family. Royal Visits Committee.

Old Admiralty Building,
Whitehall,
LONDON SW1A 2PA
Head of Division and Vice Marshal of the Diplomatic Corps: Charles de Chassiron CVO
Deputy Head of Division and Assistant Marshal of the Diplomatic Corps: Chris Osborne
Director General: Dickie Stagg CMG

Public Diplomacy Group

Strategic guidance on public diplomacy to Foreign and Commonwealth Office Directorates and Posts overseas. Co-ordination of major public diplomacy campaigns. Advice on polling and evaluation of public diplomacy projects and campaigns. Administration of the grants-in-aid to, and policy on, the BBC World Service and the British Council. Responsibility for the Wilton Park Executive Agency. Bilateral and multilateral cultural relations, other than EU; FCO Chevening and Commonwealth scholarship programmes for overseas students. Aspects of international education and international sport.

King Charles Street,
LONDON SW1A 2AH
Enquiries: 020 7008 1618
GTN: 7008 1618
Superintending Director: Anne Pringle CMG

Head of Group: Tim Livesey
Deputy Head of Group: Charles Winnington-Ingram

Research Analysts
Contributes to the formulation of foreign policy through objective, policy relevant research and analysis based on specialist expertise.

King Charles Street,
Whitehall,
LONDON SW1A 2AH
Enquiries: 020 7008 5942
GTN: 7008 5942
Director: Anne Pringle CMG
Head of Research Analysts: Robin Hoggard
Heads of Research Groups: Dr Clare Thomas *(African Research Group)*
Patrick Holdich: *(Americas Research Group)*
Duncan Allan: *(Eastern Research Group)*
Vacant: *(Europe Research Group)*
Paul Bentall: *(International Security and Global Issues Research Group)*
Greg Shapland: *(Middle East and North Africa Research Group)*
Peter Clark: *(Northern Asia/Pacific Research Group)*
Kathleen Kazer: *(South and South East Asia Research Group)*

Resource Accounting Department
Preparation of Resource Accounts. Accounting Policy and advice. Payment of invoices. Debtor control, maintenance and development of Fixed Asset Register and Management Accounts. Funding of FCO posts overseas. Accounting systems and financial training.

Old Admiralty Building,
LONDON SW1A 2PA
Enquiries: 020 7008 1063
GTN: 7008 1063
Hanslope Park,
MILTON KEYNES MK19 7BH
Enquiries: 01908 515531
GTN: 3905 5531
Finance Director: Ric Todd
Head of Department and Chief Accountant: Iain Morgan

Security Policy Group
NATO and EU security and defence policy issues; the foreign policy implications of British defence policy as regards Transatlantic and European defence, including nuclear weapons issues; nuclear and conventional arms control and disarmament; missile defence issues; UN disarmament fora; armaments policy and defence equipment procurement including collaborative projects; conflict prevention; UK defence attachés.

Downing Street East,
LONDON SW1A 2AH
Enquiries: 020 7008 3131
GTN: 7008 3131
Superintending Director: Stephen Pattison
Head of Department: Paul Johnston

Deputy Head of Department: Jennifer Anderson

Security Strategy Unit
Formulation of FCO security policy and co-ordination of physical, technical and personnel counter measures, and security education training.

Old Admiralty Building,
LONDON SW1A 2PA
Enquiries: 020 7008 1153
GTN: 7008 1153
Director General: Dickie Stagg CMG
Head of Unit: Peter Millett
Deputy Head of Unit: Julian Chandler

South Asian Group
Relations with India, Pakistan, Bangladesh, Sri Lanka, Nepal, Bhutan, the Maldives.

Whitehall,
LONDON SW1A 2AL
Enquiries: 020 7008 2388
GTN: 7008 2388
Superintending Director: Tom Phillips
Head of Department: Stephen Smith
Deputy Head of Department: James Dauris

Strategy Group
Support for FCO Board and Directors Committee, lead responsibility for the FCO Strategy, promotion of strategic policy thinking. Co-ordination of FCO's programme of change and innovation. Internal communication and policy.

King Charles Street,
LONDON SW1A 2AH
Enquiries: 020 7008 2911
GTN: 7008 2911
Director: Anne Pringle CMG
Assistant Director: Vivien Life

Sudan Unit
Joint FCO/DFID Unit set up in April 2002 to work on the peace process, humanitarian aid and development projects in Sudan.

King Charles Street,
LONDON SW1A 2AH
Telephone: 020 7008 3947
GTN: 7008 3947
UK Special Representative for Sudan: Alan Goulty CMG
Head of Unit: Dr Alastair McPhail

Trade Union Side (of the Diplomatic Service Whitley Council)
Collective Bargaining (pay, terms and conditions of service) on behalf of approximately 5,800 Diplomatic Service and Home Civil Service FCO staff.

Trade Union Side,
FCO,
King Charles Street,
LONDON SW1A 2AH
Enquiries: 020 7008 1708
GTN: 7008 1708
TUS Chair: Stephen Watson

TUS Deputy Chairs: Penny Miller, Robert Streeton
TUS Vice-Chairs: Pauline Abrams, Rod Baker,
Michael Carbine, Sandra Davis, Patrick Holdich,
John Hudson-Peat
TUS Secretary: Pam Chapman
TUS Assistant Secretary: Davy Evans

UK Outreach Team
Widening and deepening the FCO's engagement
with key organisations and communities in
strategic policy areas: improving the projection of
the FCO to its key audiences.

King Charles Street,
LONDON SW1A 2AH
Telephone: 020 7008 6063
GTN: 7008 6063
Web: http://www.pndu.net
Superintending Director: Anne Pringle CMG
Head of Unit: Fraser Wheeler
Faith Groups and Ethnic Minorities Adviser:
Mockbul Ali

UK Trade and Investment
The Foreign and Commonwealth Office and
Department of Trade and Industry trade support
services are operated by UK Trade and Investment.
Kingsgate House,

66-74 Victoria Street,
LONDON SW1E 6SW
Enquiries: 020 7215 8000
Minicom: 020 7215 2471
Joint Board Chairmen: Douglas Alexander MP
Group Chief Executive: Sir Stephen Brown KCVO
Deputy Group Chief Executive: Ian Jones
Head of International Sectors Group: Peter Tibber
Group Director International Trade Development:
Ian Fletcher
*Group Director Strategy and Communications
Group*: John Reynolds

UK Visas (Joint FCO/Home Office Directorate)
Management of the visa operation at British
missions overseas in accordance with UK
Immigration Rules. Liaison with other FCO and
Home Office departments on policy and matters
arising from the visa operation overseas. Replies to
letters from MPs and members of the public on
individual visa cases.

Correspondence Address:
King Charles Street,
LONDON SW1A 2AH
Enquiries: 020 7008 8438
GTN: 7008 8438
Web: http://www.ukvisas.gov.uk/enquiries
Directors General: Dickie Stagg CMG – *Corporate
Affairs,* Bill Jeffrey – *Immigration & Nationality
Directorate (Home Office)*
Director UKvisas: Robin Barnett
Head of Directorate: Mandie Campbell
Deputy Heads of Directorate: Nick Astbury, Sue
Davidson, Paul Sherar

United Nations Department
Policy towards the United Nations, particularly
Security Council, General Assembly; Counter-
Terrorism Committee; United Nations peace-
keeping operations; International Policing Unit;
sanctions; conflict prevention; International
humanitarian law (including Geneva Conventions);
Red Cross/Crescent issues; War Crimes;
International Criminal Tribunals for former
Yugoslavia and Rwanda; International Criminal
Court; humanitarian mine action; migration/refugee
policy; UN finance, development and reform;
general aspects of policy towards the UN
specialised agencies; Government Diamonds
Office.

King Charles Street,
LONDON SW1A 2AH
Enquiries: 020 7008 3583
Enquiries: 020 7008 2487
GTN: 7008 3583
GTN: 7008 2487
Superintending Director: Philippa Drew
Head of Department: Alistair Harrison CVO
Head of Conflict Prevention Unit: Joan Link
Deputy Heads of Department: Helen Taylor *(War
Crimes; UN finance, development and reform)*,
Sarah Macintosh *(Security Council issues;
Sanctions; Peacekeeping)*
Head of Government Diamonds Office: Clive
Wright

Whitehall Liaison Department
General co-ordination duties and responsibility for
liaison with the Cabinet Office and other
government departments.

Downing Street West,
LONDON SW1A 2AH
Enquiries: 020 7008 2350
GTN: 7008 2350
Vauxhall Cross,
85 Albert Embankment,
LONDON SE1 7TP
Director General: David Richmond
Head of Department: Matthew Kidd
Deputy Head of Department: Iain Kelly

Wilton Park
Wilton Park Conferences, lasting up to a maximum
of three and a half days, examine current
international challenges, especially EU issues,
security policy, European and Atlantic relations;
Russia, Central Europe, the Caspian, South Asia,
North East and Central Asia; and Africa; areas of
conflict in the developing world and global
economic policies. Conference participants are
experts on the conference topic drawn from
different professions and from all over the world.
Wiston House is also available for conferences
organised by other institutions.

Wilton Park,
Wiston House,
STEYNING,
West Sussex BN44 3DZ
Telephone: 01903 817772
Fax: 01903 816373
Email: lorraine.jones@wiltonpark.org.uk
Web: http://www.wiltonpark.org.uk
Chief Executive: Colin Jennings

**Lists of British Representatives in
Commonwealth and Foreign Countries
and in Ireland**

British Missions Overseas (addresses and
contact Numbers of Missions and Consulates
etc.)

PART II. Embassies, High Commissions, Deputy High Commissions and Consular Posts.

AFGHANISTAN

Kabul
British Embassy
Ambassador: Dr Rosalind M Marsden, CMG
Deputy Head of Mission: Mr Tim Gurney
Counsellor (Political): Mr Steve J A Brooking, OBE
First Secretary (Political): Ms Fiona M Morrison
First Secretary (Management): Mr Steve Smith
Second Secretary (Political): Mr Tom R Young
Second Secretary (Political): Mr David Pinson
Second Secretary (Political): Mr Benjamin White

ALBANIA

Tirana (SP - see page 120)
British Embassy
Rruga Skenderbeg 12
Tirana
FTN Code - 8385 followed by 4 digit extn number
Telephone: (00) (355) (42) 34973/4/5
Facsimile: (00) (355) (42) 47697
Airtech: (00) (355) (42) 25455
Office Hours (GMT): Winter: Mon-Thurs: 07 30 - 16 00
Fri: 07 30 - 13 30
Summer: Mon-Thurs: 06 30 - 15 00
Fri: 06 30 - 12 30
Ambassador: Mr Richard Jones
Deputy Head of Mission: Mr Joe Preston
Defence Attaché:
Lieutenant Colonel Philip G Cox, OBE
First Secretary (Cultural) (British Council Director): Ms Joan Barry
First Secretary (Political): Mr Nicholas Turnbull
First Secretary (resides in Budapest):
Ms Sandra Agnew
Second Secretary (Management Officer and Consul): Mr Julian Pearson
Second Secretary (resides in Rome):
Mr Dennis Norman
Second Secretary (resides in Rome):
Mr Graham Dempsey
Second Secretary (resides in Budapest):
Mr Steve Brown
Second Secretary (resides in Athens):
Mr Paul Weldon
Third Secretary (Political/PPA): Ms Louise Taylor
Third Secretary (Political): Mrs Sandra Preston
Third Secretary (Immigration): Mrs Julie Beard
Staff Assistant to Defence Attaché:
Staff Sergeant Darren J Chantler
Attaché: Ms Teresa McDonough

Attaché: Mrs Wendy Pitchford

ALGERIA

Algiers (SP - see page 120)
British Embassy
7th Floor
Hilton Hotel Alger
Pins Maritimes
Palais des Expositions
El Mohammadia
Algiers
FTN Code – 8388 + extn number
Telephone: (00) (213) (21) 23 00 68
Facsimile: (00) (213) (21) 23 00 67
23 01 83 Chancery
Airtech: (00) (213) (21) 23 00 69
Office Hours (GMT): Sun - Thurs: 07 00 - 14 00
Ambassador: Mr Brian E Stewart
Deputy Head of Mission: Mr Nicholas D Low
Defence Attaché (Resides in London):
Commander Matt P Briers, RN
Second Secretary (Management Officer/Consul):
Mr Terry O'Connell
Second Secretary: Mr Benedict Lyons
Third Secretary (Immigration):
Mr Tony Mesarowicz
General Registry: (Vacant)

ANDORRA

British Embassy
Ambassador (resides at Madrid):
Mr Stephen John L Wright, CMG
Consul-General (resides at Barcelona):
Mr Geoffrey S Cowling
e-mail: bcon@cyberbcn.com
N.B Consular and Commercial Enquiries should be addressed to Barcelona
British Honorary Consulate
Casa Jacint Pons, 3/2
La Massana
Principality of Andorra
Telephone: (00) (376) 839 840
Facsimile: (00) (376) 839 840
e-mail: britconand@mypic.ad
Honorary Consul: Mr Hugh Garner

ANGOLA

Luanda
British Embassy
Rua Diogo Cao, 4

Caixa Postal 1244, Luanda
FTN Code – 8501 + extn number
Telephone: (00) (244) (2) 334582, 334583,
          392991, 387681
Facsimile: (00) (244) (2) 333331 (U/C)
Satellite Fax: 00 871 144 5140 (Airtech)
e-mail: postmaster.luanda@fco.gov.uk
Office hours (GMT): Mon and Fri 07 00 - 13 00
Tue-Thur 07 00 - 11 30 and 13 00 - 16 00
Ambassador: Mr John Thompson, MBE
Deputy Head of Mission and Consul:
Mr Ross Denny
Defence Attaché:
Lieutenant Colonel The Lord Crofton
First Secretary (Development):
Mr Martin Johnston
Second Secretary (Political/PPA): Mr Adrian Lee
Second Secretary (Commercial):
Mr Steven Graham
Third Secretary (Management) and Vice-Consul:
Mr Peter Ford
Registrar and PA to HMA: Ms Pauline Shodeke
Defence Attaché's Assistant:
Staff Sergeant Tony Stead

ANTIGUA AND BARBUDA

St. John's
British High Commission
P.O. Box 483, Price Waterhouse Centre,
11, Old Parham Road, St. John's
FTN Code – 8481 + extn number
Telephone: (00) (1) (268) 462 0008/9, 463 0010
Facsimile: (00) (1) (268) 562 2124
Airtech: (00) (1) (268) 462 2806
e-mail: britishc@candw.ag
Office Hours (GMT): Mon - Thurs: 12 00 – 20 00
and Fri: 12 00 - 17 00 (only)
Open to the Public: Mon - Fri: 12 00 – 16 30
*High Commissioner: Mr John White
Resident British Commissioner:
Miss Jean Sharpe, OBE
*Deputy Resident British Commissioner:
Mr Paul Lawrence
Deputy High Commissioner: Mr Rob Holland
*Defence Adviser: Captain Steve G Wilson, RN
*First Secretary (Chancery): Mr Graham Honey
*First Secretary (Management): Mrs Ros Day
*Second Secretary (Chancery): Mr Rick Gomez
*Second Secretary (Chancery/Information):
Mr Nick J Pyle, MBE
*Third Secretary (Immigration): Mr Mark Harrison
*Resides at Bridgetown

ARGENTINA

Buenos Aires
British Embassy
Dr. Luis Agote 2412/52, 1425 Capital Federal,
Buenos Aires
FTN Code – 8502 + extn number
Telephone: (00) (54) (11) 4808 2200 Switchboard
          4808 + Direct Extension Access
Facsimile: (00) (54) (11) 4808 2274 Management
          4808 2283 Commercial

4808 2228 Political and Public
  Diplomacy
4808 2316 Chancery
4808 2221 Defence Section
4808 2235 Consular
Airtech: (00) (54) (11) 4808 2211 Chancery
Office Hours (GMT): Mon-Thurs: 11 45 – 16 00
and 17 00 – 20 30 (Mar-Dec)
Fri: 11 45 – 17 00
Mon-Fri: 11 45 – 17 30 (Jan, Feb)
Ambassador (Ext 2202): Dr John Hughes
Minister and Deputy Head of Mission (Ext 2204):
Mrs Catherine Royle
Counsellor: (Ext. 2209): Mr John Lewis
Defence, Naval and Military Attaché (Ext 2218):
Captain Chris J Hyldon, RN
Air Attaché (Ext 2218):
Group Captain Ian Capewell, RAF
First Secretary (Head of Political/Economic
Section) (Ext 2205): Mr Owen Jenkins
First Secretary (Commercial) (Ext 2251):
Mr Dave Prodger
Cultural Attaché (British Council Director)
(Tel: 4311 9814 Ext 140): Mr Martin Fryer
First Secretary (Management) (Ext 2255):
Miss Christine E McEwen
First Secretary (Technical Works Officer) (Ext
2291): Mr Ronnie Clarke
Second Secretary (Political) (Ext 2207):
Mr Mal Green
Second Secretary (Political) (Ext 2275):
Mr Alex Brown
Second Secretary (Political) (Ext 2268):
Mr Ian Duddy
Second Secretary (Political) (Ext 2312):
Ms Alison Laird
Second Secretary (Technical) (Ext 2215):
Mr Stuart Moss
Second Secretary (Consul) (Ext 2294):
Mr Jim Edwards
Assistant Cultural Attaché (Deputy Director British
Council) (Tel: 4311 9814 Ext 142):
Ms Lena Milosevic
Third Secretary (Management) (Ext 2210):
Mr Matthew Withers

Mendoza
Honorary Consulate
Emilio Civit 778
Mendoza
Telephone: (00) (54) (261) 4238529/4238514
Facsimile: (00) (54) (261) 4238565
Office Hours: Mon-Fri 08 30 – 13 00 and
17 00 – 20 30
Honorary Consul: Mr Carlos Alberto Pulenta

Córdoba
Honorary Consulate
Chacabuco 716
Córdoba
Telephone: (00) (54) (351) 4208293
Facsimile: (00) (54) (351) 4208201/4208259
Office Hours: Mon-Fri 09 00 – 13 00 and
16.30 – 20 30
Honorary Consul: Mr Fulvio Pagani

Santa Fe
Honorary Consulate
Av Pte J D Perón 8101
Rosario
Telephone/Fax: (00) (54) (341) 4590206
Office Hours: Mon-Fri 09 00 – 13 00
and 14 30 – 17 30
Honorary Consul: Mr Alberto C Gollan

ARMENIA

Yerevan (SP - see page 120)
British Embassy
34 Baghramyan Ave, Yerevan 375019
FTN Code - 8339 + 4 digit extn number
Telephone: (00) 3741 264301
Facsimile: (00) 3741 264318 (Unclassified)
            070 9238 3796 (Efax)
Airtech: (00) 3741 264327
e-mail: britemb@arminco.com
(Commercial/General/Other Enquiries)
dfidhead@netsys.am DFID
dfidassist@netsys.am DFID
Officer's:- firstname.lastname@fco.gov.uk
Office Hours (GMT): 05 00 - 09 00
and 10 00 - 13 00
Ambassador: Miss Thorda Abbott-Watt
Deputy Head of Mission: Mr Roy Wilson
Third Secretary (Management and Vice Consul):
Ms Stephanie L Bee, MBE
Third Secretary (Political/PPAS):
Ms Sarah L Murrell
Defence Attaché (resides at Tbilisi):
Lieutenant Colonel Chris J Nunn, OBE, RM
TMO's (reside at HP): Mr Bob Fletcher
Cultural Attaché: Dr Roger Budd
Attaché: Mr Chris Skinn

AUSTRALIA

Canberra
British High Commission
Commonwealth Avenue, Yarralumla
Canberra, ACT 2600
FTN Code – 8471 + extn number
Telephone: (00) (61) (2) 6270 6666
Facsimile: (00) (61) (2) 6273 3236 General
            6273 4360 Economic
            6270 6653 Chancery
e-mail: bhc.canberra@uk.emb.gov.au
Consular Section:
39 Brindabella Crt, Brindabella Business Park,
Canberra Airport, ACT 2609
Telephone: (00) (61) (2) 1902 941 555
Passports/Entry Clearances
(3) 9414 5517 Passports/Entry Clearances
Facsimile: (00) (61) (2) 1902 941 600
e-mail: bhc.consular@uk.emb.gov.au
Office Hours (GMT): Apr-Oct 22 45 - 02 30 and
03 30 - 07 00,
Nov-Mar 21 45 - 01 30 and 02 30 - 06 00
High Commissioner: Sir Alastair Goodlad, KCMG
Deputy High Commissioner: Mr Robert Court
Counsellor (Multilateral): Mr Andrew Dean
Defence and Naval Adviser and Head BDLS:
Commodore Bob J Love, RN, CBE

Counsellor (Police Liaison): Mr Nicholas O'Brien
Military and Air Adviser:
Group Captain Steven Duffill, RAF
First Secretary (Political): Mrs Jean Harrod, MBE
First Secretary (External Affairs): Mr Jeff Harrod
First Secretary (Management): Mr Alan Gee
*First Secretary (Defence/Research) Head of the
British Defence Research and Supply Staff:*
Dr David Watson
First Secretary (Defence Equipment Cooperation):
Mr Roger Matthews
First Secretary (Information/Economic):
Ms Imogen Wiles
First Secretary: Mr Martin Short
First Secretary: Dr Robert Vickery
First Secretary (Technical Management):
Mr Rod Bronson
First Secretary (Technical Security):
Mr Liam Brennan
First Secretary (TWO): Mr Brien Hooker
Second Secretary (Consular): Mr Stan Blake
Second Secretary: Miss Janice Black
Third Secretary (External Affairs):
Miss Jacqui Richards
Third Secretary (Passports): Mr Darren Cogger

Adelaide
British Consulate
Level 22, 25 Grenfell Street
Adelaide SA 5000
Telephone: (00) (61) (8) 8212 7280
Facsimile: (00) (61) (8) 8212 7282
Airtech: (00) (61) (8) 8212 7283
e-mail: bc.adelaide@mail.uk.emb.gov.au
Consul: Mr Vic S Warrington

Brisbane
British Consulate-General
Level 26, Waterfront Place
1 Eagle Street, Brisbane, Queensland, 4000
Telephone: (00) (61) (7) 3223 3200
            General/Consular
            3223 3206/7 Commercial Section
Facsimile: (00) (61) (7) 3236 2576
Airtech: (00) (61) (7) 3236 1668
e-mail: bcgbris1@mail.uk.emb.gov.au
(All information, visa and routine passport work is
centralised in Canberra).
Office Hours (GMT): 23 00 - 07 00
Consul-General: Mr Donald H Cairns
Deputy Consul General: Ms Caroline A Saunders
Vice Consul: Mrs Megan M Hunt, MBE

Melbourne
British Consulate-General
17th Floor, 90 Collins Street
Melbourne, Victoria 3000
Telephone: (00) (61) (3) 9652 1670 Commercial
1600 Consular
Facsimile: (00) (61) (3) 9650 2990
Airtech: (00) (61) (3) 9650 2716
e-mail: bcgmelb1@mail.uk.emb.gov.au
Office Hours (GMT): Apr-Oct 23 00 - 07 30
Nov-Mar 22 00 - 06 30
Consul-General: Mr Peter West
Deputy Consul-General: Mr David Seddon
Vice-Consul: Mr Philip J Mudie

Perth
British Consulate-General
Level 26, Allendale Square
77 St. George's Terrace
Perth, Western Australia 6000
Telephone: (00) (61) (8) 9224 4700
Facsimile: (00) (61) (8) 9224 4720 Consular and
		Management
		9224 4719 Commercial
		9224 4718 Airtech
e-mail: bcgperth@mail.uk.emb.gov.au
Issue of all general information about the UK, UK
visas/entry clearances, and passports, centralised at
Canberra
Office Hours (GMT): 01 00-05 00, 06 00-09 00
(Public counter 01 00-06 00)
Consul-General: Mr Stuart Gregson
Deputy Consul-General: Mr John Makin

Sydney
British Consulate-General &
Directorate of Trade and Investment Promotion
Level 16, The Gateway
1 Macquarie Place, Sydney NSW, 2000
Telephone: (00) (61) (2) 9247 7521 (8 lines)
Facsimile: (00) (61) (2) 9233 1826 Commercial
		9251 6201 Consular, Management,
e-mail: bcgsyd2@mail.uk.emb.gov.au
(Commercial)
bcgsyd1@mail.uk.emb.gov.au (Press and Public
Affairs/Consular)
Offices Hours (GMT): Apr-Oct 23 00 - 02 30 and
03 30 - 07 00
Nov-Mar 22 00 - 01 30 and 02 30 - 06 00
Consul-General: Mr Timothy Holmes
*Director of Trade Promotion and Deputy Consul
General:* Mr Chris Glynn
Director of Investment and Consul:
Mr Jamie Banks
British Council Director: Mr Simon Gammell
Vice-Consul (Commercial): Mrs A Ross McDowell
Management Officer: Mrs Heather Halliwell
Consular/Admin Officer: Mr Les Tod
Press and Public Affairs Manager: Mr R Swift

Tasmania
British Honorary Consulate
1a Brisbane St
Hobart TAS 7000
Telephone: (00) (61) (3) 6213 3310
Facsimile: (00) (61) (3) 6231 1139
e-mail: djmotors@onaustralia.com.au
Office Hours (GMT): Apr - Oct: 23 00 - 07 30
Nov - Mar: 22 00 - 06 30
Honorary Consul: Mr Michael Johns

AUSTRIA

Vienna
British Embassy
Jaurèsgasse 12, 1030 Vienna
FTN Code – 8310 + extn number
Telephone: (00) (43) (1) 716 130
Facsimile: (00) (43) (1) 71613 2999 Chancery
		71613 6900 Commercial
		71613 2900 Management
Airtech:	(00) (43) (1) 71613 2310

e-mail: press@britishembassy.at (Press and Public
Affairs Section)
commerce@britishembassy.at (Commercial
Section)
chancery@britishembassy.at (Chancery)
visa-consular@britishembassy.at (Consular
Section)
Website: www.britishembassy.at
Consular Section
Jaurèsgasse 10, 1030 Vienna
FTN Code – 8310 + extn number
Telephone: (00) (43) (1) 71613 5151
		or 00 43 1 71613 followed by
		individual extn number
Facsimile: (00) (43) (1) 71613 5900
(All mail should be addressed to the British
Embassy)
Office Hours (GMT): Winter: Mon - Fri 08 00 -
12 00 and 13 00 - 16 00
Summer: Mon - Fri 07 00 - 11 00 and 12 00 -
15 00
Ambassador (2202): Mr John Macgregor, cvo
*Counsellor, Consul-General, Dep. Head of Mission
(2204):* Dr Piers Baker
Counsellor (Chancery) (2211):
Mr M Adrian Gamble
Counsellor (Labour) (resides at Berlin):
Miss Elaine Trewartha
Defence Attaché (2216):
Lieutenant Colonel Len W Chapman
First Secretary (Management) and Consul (2261):
Mr Eric M Jones
First Secretary (Technical Works) (2264):
Mr John Sweeney
First Secretary (Commercial) (6148): Mr John Hall
First Secretary (FLO) (2318): Mr Nicholas Hamill
British Council Director: Dr Simon Cole
Second Secretary (2219): Miss Stella Burch
Second Secretary (EU Affairs) (2343):
Mr Andrew Ayre
Second Secretary (Chancery) (2220):
Mr William Gatward
Second Secretary (Chancery) (2224):
Miss Clare Glackin
Second Secretary (2210): Mr Ian Purvis
Second Secretary (DLO) (2256):
Mr David N Hollingbery
Second Secretary (ILO) (2225): Mr Martin J Reeve
Attaché and Vice-Consul (ECO) (5330):
Mr Jonathan O'Shaughnessy
Third Secretary (Management) (2260):
Miss Jan H Richardson
Third Secretary (2272): Mr Gordon J Winter
Vice-Consul (5332): Mr Harald De Soye

**Vienna United Kingdom Mission to the United
Nations in Vienna, see Missions and Delegations
page 113**
**Vienna United Kingdom Delegation to the
Organisation for Security and Cooperation in
Europe (OSCE), see Missions and Delegations
page 113**

Bregenz
British Consulate
Bundesstrasse 110

A-6923 Lauterach/Bregenz
Telephone: (00) (43) (5574) 78586
Facsimile: (00) (43) (5574) 70928
Office Hours (GMT): Winter 08 00 - 11 00
Summer 07 00 - 10 00
Honorary Consul: Dipl-Ing P Senger-Weiss

Graz
British Consulate
Schmiedgasse 12, A-8010 Graz
Telephone: (00) (43) (316) 8216 1621
Facsimile: (00) (43) (316) 8216 1645
Office Hours (GMT): Winter: Mon - Thurs 08 00 -
11 00 and 13 30 - 15 00; Fri 08 00 - 11 00
Summer: Mon - Thurs 07 00 - 10 00 and 12 30 -
14 00; Fri 07 00 - 10 00
Honorary Consul: Mr K D Bruhl, CBE
Honorary Vice-Consul: Ms Eva Bruhl
Secretary: Ms C Casati / Ms B Tatschl

Innsbruck
British Consulate
Kaiserjagerstrasse 1/Top B9
A-6020 Innsbruck
Telephone: (00) (43) (512) 588320
Facsimile: (00) (43) (512) 5799738
Office Hours (GMT): Winter 08 00 - 11 00,
Summer 07 00 - 10 00
Honorary Consul: Ing Hellmut Buchroithner
Honorary Vice-Consul: Dr Ivo Rungg
Secretary: Ms Stefanie Gapp

Salzburg
British Consulate
Alter Markt 4, A-5020 Salzburg
Telephone: (00) (43) (662) 848133
Facsimile: (00) (43) (662) 845563
Office Hours (GMT): Winter 08 00 - 11 00,
Summer 07 00 - 10 00
Honorary Consul: Mr M M Kaindl, OBE
Honorary Pro-Consul: Mrs Helga Danmayr

AZERBAIJAN

Baku (SP - see page 120)
British Embassy
45, Khagani Street
Baku AZ1000
FTN Code – 8483 + extn number
Telephone: (00) (99 412) 975188/89/90
Facsimile: (00) (99 412) 922739, 972474
(Commercial Section)
Airtech: (00) (99 412) 975893
e-mail: office@britemb.baku.a
office@ukemb.baku.az (Commercial Section)
Website: www.britishhembassy.gov.uk/azerbaijan
Office Hours (GMT): Mon - Fri: 05 00 - 09 00 and
10 00 - 13 00
Ambassador: Dr Lawrence S C Bristow
Deputy Head of Mission: Miss Paula Nobes
Defence Attaché (resides at Tbilisi):
Lieutenant Colonel Christopher J Nunn, OBE, RM
Cultural Attaché (British Council):
Ms Margaret S Jack
First Secretary (Political): Mr Lachlan Forbes
Second Secretary (Commercial): Mr Chris Gotch
Second Secretary (Political): Mr Sean Melbourne

Vice-Consul: Mr Derek Lavery
Third Secretary (Management): Miss Carol Wright
Third Secretary (Political): Mr David Proudfoot
Attaché: Mr Jamal Williams

BAHAMAS, THE

Nassau (SP - see page 120)
British High Commission
Ansbacher House (3rd Floor)
East Street, P.O. Box N7516, Nassau
FTN Code – 8467 + extn number
Telephone: (00) (1) (242) 325 7471 Switchboard
Facsimile: (00) (1) (242) 323 3871
Airtech: (00) (1) (242) 325 7474
e-mail: bhcnassau@fco.gov.uk
Website:
www.britishhighcommission.gov.uk/bahamas
Office Hours (GMT): Mon – Thurs: 13 30 - 18 00,
18 30 - 21 30 Fri: 13 30 - 18 30
High Commissioner: Mr Roderick Gemmell, OBE
Deputy High Commissioner: Mr Steve Firstbrook
Defence Adviser (resides at Kingston):
Colonel Charles G Le Brun
First Secretary (resides at Miami):
Mr Geoffrey Chalder
Second Secretary (resides at Miami):
Mr Jamie W Cox

BAHRAIN

Bahrain
British Embassy
21 Government Avenue, Manama 306
P.O. Box 114
FTN Code – 8484 + extn number
Telephone: (00) (973)574100
            574167 Information
Telegrams: PRODROME, BAHRAIN
Facsimile: (00) (973) 574161 Chancery
            574138 Consular/Management
            574101 Commercial
            574121 Visa
            574140 Registry (Comms)
            574135 Airtech
e-mail: britemb@batelco.com.bh
Website: www.ukembassy.gov.bh
Office Hours (GMT): Sat - Wed 04 30 - 11 30
Ambassador and Consul-General:
Mr Robin D Lamb
*Deputy Head of Mission and Head of Political
Section:* Mr Simon C H Wilson
Defence Attaché: Commander Nigel P Smith, RN
First Secretary (Political): Mr David London
*First Secretary (Regional Expert, Engaging with
the Arab World):* Mrs Jacky Perkins
British Council Director: Ms Sandra Hamrouni
Second Secretary (Commercial):
Ms Isabel Mulvaney
Second Secretary (Consul/ECM/MO):
Mr Iain Kingston
Airline Liaison Officer: Mr A Martin
*Third Secretary (Political, Press and Public
Affairs):* Mrs Karen Williams
Third Secretary (ECO): Mrs J Allan

BANGLADESH

Dhaka
British High Commission
United Nations Road, Baridhara Dhaka
Postal address: P.O. Box 6079, Dhaka-1212
FTN Code - 8511 + extn number
Telephone: (00) (880) (2) 8822705 (5 lines)
       followed by individual extension
       number
       8821273 DHC Direct line
Facsimile: (00) (880) (2) 8826181 High
       Commissioner's Office
       8816135 Chancery
       8823437 Management
       8823666 Immigration
       9882819 Consular
e-mail: Dhaka.Commercial@fco.gov.uk
(Commercial Section)
Dhaka.Consular@fco.gov.uk (Consular)
Dhaka.Immigration@fco.gov.uk (Immigration)
Dhaka.Management@fco.gov.uk (Management)
Dhaka.Press@fco.gov.uk (Press and Public Affairs)
Clodhaka@fco.gov.uk (Community Liaison
Officer)
Website: www.ukinbangladesh.org
Office Hours (GMT): Sun to Wed: 02 00 – 10 00
and Thur 02 00 – 08 00
High Commissioner (2201): Mr Anwar Choudhury
*Deputy High Commissioner and Commercial
Counsellor (2203):* Mr Robert Gibson
Defence Adviser (resides in New Delhi):
Brigadier Ian D O Rees
First Secretary (Medical Officer):
Dr Jacqueline Howell
*First Secretary (Senior Management Officer)
(2230):* Mr Mike Stevenson
First Secretary (Immigration/Consular) (2302):
Mr Lawson Ross
*First Secretary (Drug Liaison) (resides in
Mumbai):* Mr Simon Sutcliffe
British Council Director: Ms June Rollinson
Second Secretary (Airline Liaison Officer) (2212):
Mr Paul Kramer
*Second Secretary (Commercial/Press and Public
Affairs) (2209):* Ms Millie Sen-Gupta
Second Secretary (Commercial) (2313):
Mr Andrew McAllister
Second Secretary (Immigration) (2354):
Mrs Claire Shaw
Second Secretary (Immigration) (2453):
Ms Meena Joshi
Second Secretary (Immigration) (2300):
Mr Nick Bostin
Second Secretary (Management) (2231):
Mrs Sally Oulmi
Second Secretary (Political) (2210): Mr Alan Shaw
Vice Consul (2305): Ms Amanda Cooper
*International Pensions Service Officer (IPSO)
(2317):* Mr Iqubal Makati
Registrar (2217): Mr Simon Mitchell

Dhaka
Department for International Development
(DFIDB)
United House, 10 Gulshan Avenue

Gulshan, Dhaka 1212
FTN Code - 8775 + extn number
Telephone: (00) (880) (2) 881 0800 (hunting
       number)
Facsimile: (00) (880) (2) 882 4661 / 882 3181
Head of DFID Bangladesh (3113):
Mr Paul Ackroyd
Deputy Head (3127): Dr Mehtab Currey
First Secretary (Management Unit) (3112):
Mrs Jean Forrest
Estate Manager (1052): Ms Marina Negri
Transport Manager: Mr Frank Ward
Economic Adviser (2123): Mr Reaz Islam
Economic Adviser (2110): Mrs Joanna McGowan
Enterprise Development Adviser (2133):
Mr Frank Matsaert
Senior Engineering Adviser (2001):
Mr Peregrine Swann
Assistant Engineering Adviser (2012):
Mr Asufta Alam
Water and Sanitation Manager (2028):
Mr Rodney Dyer
Senior Rural Livelihood Adviser (2064):
Mr Martin Leach
*Natural Resources and Environment Adviser
(2057):* Mr Tim Robertson
Rural Livelihoods Manager (2053):
Mr Duncan King
Senior Governance Adviser (2114):
Ms Sheelagh Stewart
Governance Adviser (2137): Mr Chris Murgatroyd
Justice Sector Co-ordinator (2129): Ms Bea Parkes
Health and Population Adviser (3064):
Dr Neil Squires
Education Adviser (3007): Ms Kate Wesson
Health Adviser (3018): Mr Dinesh Nair
Senior Social Development Adviser (2079):
Mr Eric Hanley
Programme Manager (GGR) (2105):
Mr Donald Couper
*Deputy Programme Manager (Human
Development) (3024):* Mr Chris Allen
Deputy Programme Manager (GGR) (2082):
Mr Mick McGill
Human Resources Manager (3093):
Mrs Sue McGill
Finance and Contract Manager (3133):
Mr Jim Brady
Deputy Programme Manager (GGR) (2097):
Ms Sarah White
Deputy Programme Manager (IUDT/RL) (2029):
Ms Paula Barrett
Programme Officer (2026): Ms Alexandra Tighe
(Ms Christine Marsh – Temporarily)

BARBADOS

Bridgetown
British High Commission
Lower Collymore Rock (P.O. Box 676),
Bridgetown
FTN Code – 8512 + extn number
Telephone: (00) (1) (246) 430 7800
Facsimile: (00) (1) (246) 430 7851 Chancery
       430 7860 Management/Consular
       430 7826 Commercial/Information

Airtech: (00) (1) (246) 430 7845
e-mail: britishhc@sunbeach.net
Office Hours (GMT): 12 00 – 20 00 Monday to
Thursday 12 00 – 17 00 Friday
High Commissioner: Mr John White
Also High Commissioner (Non Resident) To
Antigua & Barbuda, Commonwealth of Dominica,
Grenada, St Kitts & Nevis, St Lucia and St Vincent
and the Grenadines.
Deputy High Commissioner: Mr Rob Holland
Defence Adviser: Captain Steve G Wilson, RN
First Secretary (Chancery): Mr Graham Honey
First Secretary (Management): Ms Ros Day
Second Secretary (Chancery/Information):
Mr Nick J Pyle, MBE
Second Secretary (Chancery): Mr Andy Danton
Second Secretary (Chancery): Mr Rick Gomez
Third Secretary (Management/ Consular):
Mr Jim Collins
Third Secretary (Technical Works): Mr Phil Barker
Third Secretary (Immigration): Mr Mark Harrison
Head of Commercial Section:
Mr Hadford S Howell, MBE
Overseas Territories Advisers
First Secretary (Financial Services Adviser):
Mr Kevin Mann

**Department for International Development
Caribbean**
Chelsea House, Chelsea Road
(P.O. Box 167), St Michael
Telephone: (00) (1) (246) 430 7900
Facsimile: (00) (1) (246) 430 7959
Office Hours (GMT): 12 00 – 20 00
Head of DFID (C): Ms Joanne Alston
Senior Governance Adviser: Mr David Biggs
Private Sector Development Adviser:
Mr Kevin Quinlan
Senior Social Development Adviser:
Ms Miranda Munro
Governance Adviser: Ms Kathy Higgins
Economic Adviser: Mr Paul Mullard
Economic Assistant: Ms Weyinmi Omamuli
Human Resources/Finance Manager:
Mr Robert Bateson
Regional IS Manager: Ms Denise Niles
Head of Regional Unit: Ms Jane Armstrong
Programme Officer: Ms Cherianne Clarke
Executive Support and Programme Officer:
Ms Sandee Layne

BELARUS

Minsk (SP - see page 120)
British Embassy
37 Karl Marx Street, 220030 Minsk
Telephone: (00) (375) (172) 105920 (Switchboard)
                 292310 (Visa and Consular – Recorded
                 Information)
Facsimile: (00) (375) (172) 292306 (General)
                 292311 (Visa Section)
Airtech: 292315
e-mail: britinfo@nsys.by
Office Hours (GMT): Summer: Mon-Thur 06 00 -
10 00 and 11 00 - 14 30; Fri 06 00 - 12 00

Winter: Mon-Thur 07 00 - 11 00 and 12 00 -
15 30; Fri 07 00 - 13 00
Ambassador and Consul-General:
Mr Brian Bennett
Deputy Head of Mission: Mr James Quinn
Defence Attaché (resides at Moscow):
Colonel Colin A Bulleid
Assistant Defence Attaché (resides at Moscow):
Squadron Leader Sean T O'Brien, RAF
*First Secretary (Technical Works) (resides in
Vienna):* Mr Ian Sweeney
Second Secretary (ILO) (resides in Kiev):
Mr Chris Lain
*Second Secretary (Technical. Management)
(resides in Warsaw):* Mr Simon Lochmuller
Third Secretary (Immigration) and Vice Consul: Mr
Martin Child
Attaché: Miss Amanda Lissenden

BELGIUM

Brussels
British Embassy
Rue D'Arlon/Aarlenstraat 85
B-1040 Brussels
Telephone: (00) (32) (2) 287 6211
Facsimile: (00) (32) (2) 287 6250 HMA's and
                 DHM's Offices
                 6355 Political
                 6270 Consular
                 6240 Commercial
                 6360 Press and Public Affairs
Airtech: 6380
e-mail: firstname.surname@fco.gov.uk
Website: www.britishembassy.gov.uk/belgium
Office Hours (GMT): Summer: 07 00 – 11 00 and
12 00 – 15 00
Winter: 08 00 – 12 00 and 13 00 – 16 00
Ambassador: Mr Richard Kinchen, MVO
Deputy Head of Mission and Consul-General:
Mr Matthew J Rous
Counsellor (Global and Regional Affairs):
Ms Christine A MacQueen
Defence Attaché (Resides in The Hague):
Captain A Robin Davies, RN
Cultural Counsellor (British Council):
Dr Ray Thomas
First Secretary (Head of Political Section):
Mr John McManus
First Secretary (Political): Mr Paul S R Norman
First Secretary (Political): Mr Jules Irens
First Secretary (Economic and Social Affairs):
Ms Elisabeth Boyles
First Secretary (Commercial): Mr Guy A Harrison
First Secretary (Technical): Mr Stephen Roseblade
Second Secretary (PPA/Economic): Ms Lucy Joyce
Second Secretary (Consul):
Miss Catherine F Armstrong
Second Secretary (Technical): Mr Robert Bruton
Second Secretary (Technical): Mr Neil Sturgess
Third Secretary (Political): Mr Mark O'Reilly
Third Secretary (Political): Mr Richard Brown
Third Secretary (PA/HMA): (Vacant)
Third Secretary (Global and Regional Affairs):
Mrs Rebecca Murray

Brussels
British Embassy
Joint Management Office
Rue d'Arlon/Aarlenstraat 85
1040 Brussels
Telephone: (00) (32) (2) 287 6211
Facsimile: (00) (32) (2) 287 6320
Counsellor (Head of Joint Management Office):
Mr Roger A Cambridge, MVO
First Secretary: Ms Janice Sweid
Second Secretary: Mr Derek L Walker
Third Secretary: Mr Stuart W Gardner

**Brussels United Kingdom Delegation to NATO,
see Missions and Delegations page 114
Brussels Office of the United Kingdom
Permanent Representative to the European
Union, see Missions and Delegations page 115**

Antwerp
British Honorary Consulate-General
Postbox 580
Groenplaats
2000 Antwerp 1
Telephone: (00) (32) (3) 213 2125
Facsimile: (00) (32) (3) 213 2991
e-mail: cgantwerp@unicall.be
Office Hours: Callers are advised to telephone for
an appointment.
Honorary Consul-General: Baron Paul Buysse, CBE
Pro-Consul: Mrs Mary Ann Marinus

Ghent
British Honorary-Consulate
c/o Meyvaert Glass Engineering NV
Dok Noord 3
9000 Ghent
Telephone: (00) (32) (9) 235 7221 / 225 5427
Facsimile: (00) (32) (9) 222 8127
e-mail: british.consul@meyvaert.be
Office Hours: Callers are advised to telephone for
an appointment.
Honorary Consul: Mr Paul Meyvaert

Liège
British Honorary-Consulate
Quai de Maastricht 14, 4000 Liège
Telephone: (00) (32) (4) 232 9797
Facsimile: (00) (32) (4) 223 1109
e-mail: info@liege.port-autonome.be
Office Hours: Callers are advised to telephone for
an appointment.
Honorary Consul: Mme Marie-Dominique Simonet

BELIZE

Belmopan (SP - see page 120)
British High Commission
P. O. Box 91 Belmopan or B.F.P.O 12
FTN Code - 8494 + 1000 for switchboard
Telephone: (00) (501) 822 2146
Facsimile: (00) (501) 822 2761
Airtech: (00) (501) 822 3694
e-mail: brithicom@btl.net
Website: www.britishhighbze.com
Office Hours (GMT): Mon-Thurs: 14 00 – 18 00
and 19 00 – 22 00. Fri: 14 00 – 20 00

High Commissioner: Mr Alan Jones
Deputy High Commissioner:
Mr Howard Lattin-Rawstrone
Defence Adviser (resides in Kingston):
Colonel Charles G Le Brun
Second Secretary (resides in Panama):
Mr Alan Pamplin
Second Secretary (Consular/Management):
Mr Carl Mackerras
Second Secretary (Development):
Mrs Sonia Warner
Third Secretary (Chancery): Mr Simon Mustard

BENIN

Cotonou
British Embassy (all staff resident in Nigeria)
Ambassador: Mr Richard Gozney, CMG
Consul: Mr Maurice Harper
Second Secretary (Commercial): Mr John Wales

BOLIVIA

La Paz (SP - see page 120)
British Embassy
Avenida Arce No.2732
Casilla (PO Box) 694
FTN Code – 8504+ extn number
Telephone: (00) (591) (2) 2433424 (connects to 9
          lines)
Facsimile: (00) (591) (2) 2431073
Airtech: (00) (591) (2) 2432301
Duty Officer: (00) (591) 772 92311
e-mail: ppa@megalink.com (Embassy)
Website: www.britishembassy.gov.uk/bolivia
Office Hours (GMT): Monday – Thursday 12:30 –
16:30 and 17:30 to 21:00. Friday 12:30 – 17:30
Ambassador: Mr William Sinton, OBE
Deputy Head of Mission and HM Consul:
Mr Chris Poole
Defence Attaché (resides in Santiago):
Colonel Iain S Campbell
Second Secretary and Vice Consul (Management):
Mr Peter Cartwright
*Third Secretary (Technical Management) (resides
in Brasilia):* Mr Alan Barnes
Commercial Officer: Mr Eduardo Suarez

**Department for International Development
(Bolivia)**
Av. Arce No. 2799,
Esquina Cordero,
Edificio Fortaleza,
Piso 14
Telephone: (00) (591) (2) 243 5000
Facsimile: (00) (591) (2) 243 4306
Head of Development Co-operation:
Mr Sam Bickersteth
Social Inclusion Adviser: Ms Pipa Bird
Human Rights and Health Adviser: Silke Seco

BOSNIA AND HERZEGOVINA

Sarajevo
British Embassy
Tina Ujevica 8, Sarajevo, Bosnia and Herzegovina

Telephone: (00 387 33) (28) 2200 Main
        switchboard
        (28) 2235 Consular/Visa
Facsimile: (00 387 33) (28) 2203 Chancery;
        Management
        (20) 4780 Commercial; DfID;
        Consular/Visa
Airtech: (28) 2223
e-mail: PoliticalEnquiries.Sarajevo@fco.gov.uk
CommercialEnquiries.Sarajevo@fco.gov.uk
DFIDEnquiries.Sarajevo@fco.gov.uk
ConsularEnquiries.Sarajevo@fco.gov.uk
VisaEnquiries.Sarajevo@fco.gov.uk
britemb@bih.net.ba
Website: www.britishembassy.ba
Office Hours (GMT): April-October: Mon-Thurs
06 30 - 15 00; Fri 06 30 - 13 30
November-March: Mon-Thurs 07 30 - 16 00; Fri
07 30 - 14 30
Ambassador (2214): Mr Ian Cliff, OBE
Deputy Head of Mission (2211): Mr Daniel Fearn
First Secretary (Chancery) (2216):
Mr Alistair Sommerlad
First Secretary (British Council Director):
Mr Chris Rawlings
*First Secretary (Director of Commercial and
Economic Affairs) (2233):* Mr Richard Salt
*First Secretary (Management and HM Consul)
(2232):* Mr John Ellis
Second Secretary (DfID) (2248):
Ms Mary Shockledge
Second Secretary (Political/PPA) (2244):
Ms Alex Cole
Second Secretary (Political) (2215):
Mr Alistair Bridgwood
Second Secretary (Political) (2216):
Mr Stephen Burdes
Third Secretary (Political):
Miss Philippa Chatterton
Vice-Consul (2245): Mr James Hudson

Banja Luka
British Embassy Office
Simeuna Dzaka 8, Banja Luka,
Bosnia and Herzegovina
Tel/Fax: (00 387 51) 212 395/216 842
Mobile: (00 387 65) 512 698
e-mail: BLOffice.Sarajevo@fco.gov.uk
Head of Office: Mr Robert Contractor

BOTSWANA

Gaborone (SP - see page 120)
British High Commission
Private Bag 0023, Gaborone
FTN Code – 8515 + extn number
Telephone: (00) (267) 395 2841
Facsimile: (00) (267) 395 6105
Airtech: (00) (267) 395 2650
e-mail: bhc@botsnet.bw
Website:
www.britishhighcommission.gov.uk/botswana
Office Hours (GMT): Mon - Thurs: 06 00 - 10 30
and 11 30 - 14 30. Fri: 06 00 - 11 00
High Commissioner: Mr David B Merry, CMG
Deputy High Commissioner: Mr John L Smith

Defence Adviser (resides at Harare):
Colonel Bob J Griffiths, MBE
British Council Director: Mr David Knox
Second Secretary (Development/Regional Affairs):
Mr John L Riley
Third Secretary (Consular and Management):
Mr Michael J Redden

BRAZIL

Brasilia
British Embassy
Setor de Embaixadas Sul, Quadra 801, Conjunto K,
CEP 70.408-900, Brasilia – DF, Brazil
FTN Code - 8516 + extn number
Telephone: (00) (55) (61) 329 2300
Facsimile: (00) (55) (61) 329 2369
Airtech: (00) (55) (61) 329 2343
e-mail: contact@reinounido.org.br
Website: www.reinounido.org.br
Office Hours (GMT): Mon - Thurs: 11 30 – 20 30
Fri: 11 30 – 15 30
Ambassador (2353): Dr Peter Collecott, CMG
Deputy Head of Mission (2305): Mr Hugo Shorter
Defence, Military and Air Attaché (2351):
Group Captain Ralph Ashenhurst, RAF
Naval Attaché (2324):
Commander R A Harry Harrison, RN
*First Secretary (Economic and Commercial/Trade
Policy) (2337):* Mr Matthew Lownds
First Secretary (Management) and Consul (2319):
Mr Neil Storey
First Secretary (2356): Mr Francis A Dick
British Council Director: Dr David Cooke
DfID Director: Mr Bo Sundstrom
Second Secretary (Economic) (2333):
Mr Paul Rennie
Second Secretary (Political) (2309):
Mr Richard Barlow
Second Secretary (Political) (2336):
Mr Robert Luke
Second Secretary (Technical Management) (2345):
Mr Alan Barnes
*Third Secretary (Management) and Vice-Consul
(2314):* Ms Aileen Carrick

**Department for International Development
(Brazil)**
Ed. Centro Empresarial Varig Scn,
Quadra 4, Bloco B,
2o Andar, Sala 202
CEP 70.710-926, Brasilia - DF, Brazil
Telephone: (00) (55) (61) 327 7230
Facsimile: (00) (55) (61) 326 8918

British Council (Brazil)
Ed. Centro Empresarial Varig Scn,
Quadra 4, Bloco B,
Torre Ouest, Conjunto 202
CEP 70.710-926, Brasilia - DF, Brazil
Telephone: (00) (55) (61) 2106 7500
Facsimile: (00) (55) (61) 2106 7599
e-mail: brasilia@britishcouncil.org.br
Website: www.britishcouncil.org.br

Belém
British Consulate

Av. Governador Malcher, 815 Ed Palladium Center
Conj. 410/411
Belém – Para
CEP 66.035-900
Caixa Postal 98
Telephone: (00) (55) (91) 222 5074, 223 0990
Facsimile: (00) (55) (91) 212 0274
Honorary Consul: Dr A M dos Santos

Manáus
British Consulate
Swedish Match da Amazonia S.A
Rua Poraque 240
Distrito Industrial
Manáus – Am
CEP 69075 –180
Telephone: (00) (55) (92) 613 1819
Facsimile: (00) (55) (92) 613 1420
Honorary Consul: Mr V J Brown

Rio de Janeiro
British Consulate-General
Praia do Flamengo, 284/2 andar,
Rio de Janeiro - RJ, CEP 22210-030
FTN Code – 8456 + extn number
Telephone: (00) (55) (21) 2555 9600
            (Switchboard)
            9640 (Consular Section)
Facsimile: (00) (55) (21) 25559672 (Management)
            9604 (Chancery)
            9670 (Commercial)
            9671 (Consular)
Airtech: (00) (55) (21) 2555 9608
e-mail: britishconsulaterio@terra.com.br (General)
consular.section@fco.gov.uk (Consular Section)
Office Hours (GMT): Mon - Fri: March -
November: 11 30 - 20 00
December - February: 10 00 - 19 00
Consul-General: Mr Paul Yaghmourian
Deputy Consul-General and Consul (Commercial):
Mr Tim Dearden
British Council Director: Mr Sital Dhillon
Vice-Consul (Commercial): Ms Janet Fullard
Vice-Consul (Management): Mrs Sharon Ganney
Vice-Consul (Consular/Immigration):
Mr Andy Cole
Pro-Consul: Mr Murilo Veiga
Pro-Consul: Ms Marina Zelenoy

Belo Horizonte
British Consulate
Rua dos Inconfidentes, 1075, Sala 1302
Belo Horizonte – MG – 30140 120
Savassi
Telephone: (00) (31) 3261 2072
Facsimile: (00) (31) 3261 0226
e-mail: belohorizonte@gra-bretanha.org.br
Honorary Consul: Mr Roger A Gough, MBE
Commercial Officer: Mr Rogerio Pacheco, MBE

Fortaleza
British Consulate
c/o Grupo Edson Queiroz, Praca da Imprensa s/n,
Aldeota, Fortaleza - CE, CEP 60135-900
Telephone: (00) (55) (85) 466 8580/8582
Facsimile: (00) (55) (85) 261 8763
e-mail: annette@edsonqueiroz.com.br

Honorary Consul:
Mrs Annette T Reeves de Castro

Recife
Av. Conselheiro Aguiar, 2941/3°
Boa Viagem
Recife-PE, CEP 51020-020
Telephone: (00) (55) (81) 3465 0230
Facsimile: (00) (55) (81) 3465 0247
e-mail: recife@gra-bretanha.org.br
Honorary Consul: Mr Alan E Fiore
Commercial Officer: Mr Chris Cobb

Salvador
British Consulate
Av. Estados Unidos, No 18-B
8 Andar-Comercio, Ed-Estados Unidos
CEP 40010 - 020, Salvador - BA
Telephone: (00) (55) (71) 243 7399
Facsimile: (00) (55) (71) 242 7293/243 7856
e-mail: adcos@allways.com.br
Honorary Consul: Mr Nigel Lee

São Paulo
British Consulate-General
Centro Brasileiro Britanico
Rua Ferreira de Araujo, 2 Andar
Pinheiros
05428-002-São Paulo-SP
FTN Code - 8463 + extn number
Telephone: (00) (55) (11) 3094 2700
Facsimile: (00) (55) (11) 3094 2717 (Commercial)
3094 2750 (Management)
Airtech: (00) (55) (11)3816 4887
e-mail: saopaulo@gra-bretanha.org.br
Website: www.gra-bretanha.org.br
Office Hours (GMT): Mon - Thurs: 11 30 - 19 45,
Fri 11 30 - 19 30 (UK Summer)
Mon - Thurs: 10 30 - 18 45, Fri 10 30 - 18 30 (UK
Winter)
Consul-General and Director of Trade and
Investment Brazil (ext 2707,
PA's ext 2710): Mr Andy Henderson
Deputy Consul-General and Deputy Director of
Trade and Investment (ext 2713): Mr Pat Ashworth
British Council Director: Mr Mike Winter
Vice-Consul (Consular/Management) (ext 2714):
Mr David Paginton
Vice-Consul (Commercial) (ext 2735):
Mr Andy Burch
Vice-Consul (Customs) (ext 2701):
Mr Nick Freeman
Pro-Consul (Consular/Management) (ext 2727):
Ms Lisa Evely
Pro-Consul (Consular/Management) (ext 2756):
Ms Ana Armond

Curitiba
British Trade Office and British Consulate
Rusa Presidente Faria, 51, 2 andar,
CJ.705 - Curitiba, PR CEP 80020-290
Telephone: (00) (55) (41) 322 1202
Facsimile: (00) (55) (41) 322 3537
e-mail: curitiba@gra-bretanha.org.br
Commercial Officer and Honorary Consul:
Mr Peter ter Poorten

Porto Alegre
British Consulate
Edificio Montreal, Rua Itapeva,
110 Conjunto 505, Passo D'Areia
91350-080 Porto Alegre - RS
Telephone: (00) (55) (51) 341 0720
Facsimile: (00) (55) (51) 341 0720
e-mail: britpec@mailbr.com.br
Honorary Consul: Mr Geoffrey Powell

Porto Alegre
British Commercial Office
Rua Antenor Lemos 57 Cj 403,
Bairro Menino Deus, 90850-100,
Porto Alegre -RS
Telephone: (00) (55) (51) 232 141
Facsimile: (00) (55) (51) 231 6094
e-mail: portoalegre@gra-bretanha.org.br
Commercial Officer: Mrs Denise Pellin

Rio Grande
British Consulate
Wilson Sons, Rua Riachuelo, 201 terreo,
CEP 96200-390, Rio Grande - RS
Porto Alegre - RS
Telephone: (00) (55) (53) 233 7700
Facsimile: (00) (55) (53) 233 7701
(00) (55) (53) 231 1530
e-mail: rjg@wilson.com.br
Honorary Consul: Mr Richard Grantham

Santos
British Consulate
Rua Tuiuti 58, 2 andar, Caixa Postal 204,
11101-220-220, Santos
Telephone: (00) (55) (13) 3211 2300, Direct: (55)
(13) 3219 4659
Mobile: (55) (13) 9972 1622
Facsimile: (00) (55) (13) 3210 3840
(55) (13) 3219 5250
e-mail: daw@wilson.com.br
Honorary Consul: Mr David A Walton

BRUNEI

Bandar Seri Begawan
British High Commission
PO Box 2197
Bandar Seri Begawan 8674
FTN Code – 8359 + extn number or 1000 for
switchboard
Telephone: (00) (673) (2) 222231/223121
(switchboard)
226001 Consular/Visa (FTN: 8359 2500)
Facsimile: (00) (673) (2) 234315 (FTN: 8359
2245)
Airtech: (00) (673) (2) 234316 (FTN: 8359
2231)
e-mail: brithc@brunet.bn
Website:
www.britishhighcommission.gov.uk/brunei
Office Hours (GMT): Mon to Thurs 00 30 - 04 45
and 06 00 - 09 00. Fri 00 30 - 04 30
High Commissioner (ext 2211):
Mr Andrew J F Caie
Deputy High Commissioner (ext 2213):
Mr Martin Walley

Defence Adviser (2230 + direct ext 2219):
Captain Paddy H Watson, RN
First Secretary (Defence Cooperation) (ext 2214):
Mr Colin Britteon
Third Secretary (Trade and Investment) (ext 2226):
Mr Brian Price
*Third Secretary (Management/Consular) (ext
2220):* Mrs Lisa Jennians
Attaché (ext 2212): Miss Tina Nickels
Attaché (ext 2217): Mr Samuel Hayes

BULGARIA

Sofia
British Embassy
9 Moskovska Street, Sofia
FTN Code - 8477 + extn number
Telephone: (00) (359) (2) 933 9222
Facsimile: 933 9219 (Chancery)
9250 (Management)
9289 (Defence)
9279 (Commercial)
9263 (Visa/Consular)
9233 (DFID)
9265 (Airtech)
942 4344 (British Council)
e-mail: Officer's firstname.surname@fco.gov.uk
Website: www.british-embassy.bg
Office Hours (GMT): Mon – Thurs 06 30 – 15 30,
Fri 06 30 – 11 00
Ambassador: Mr Jeremy Hill (2203)
Deputy Head of Mission:
Mr Laurence Broyd (2204)
Counsellor: Mr Ian Woods (2206)
Defence Attaché: Colonel John R C Saville (2214)
Cultural Attaché (British Council Director):
Mr Ian Stewart
First Secretary (Commercial):
Mrs Christine McNeil (2228)
Deputy Defence Attaché:
Lieutenant Commander Ken M Smith, RN (2212)
Second Secretary (Management):
Ms Sheila Towe (2238)
Second Secretary (Political/Press):
Mr Iain Stewart (2207)
Second Secretary (EU/Economic):
Mr Richard Shackleton (2299)
Second Secretary (Political): Mr Rob Finley (2301)
Second Secretary: Mr Lee Williams (2282)
Second Secretary: Mr Adrian Barnard (2303)
Second Secretary (Consul and ECM):
Miss Hilary Arthur (2260)
*Assistant Cultural Attaché (British Council Deputy
Director):* Ms Lisa McManus
Head of DFID Section:
Mrs Toni Grancharova (2226)
Third Secretary (Political):
Mr Karl Tluczek (2223)
Attaché (Immigration and Vice Consul):
Mr Ramesh Jogiya (2262)
Attaché (Immigration and Vice Consul):
Mr Ian Hollis (2287)
Attaché (Immigration): Mr Cris Ashworth (2261)
Chaplain: Rev James Ramsay

Varna
British Consulate
40 Graf Igantiev Street
PO Box 229
Varna
Telephone: (00) (359) (52) 6655 555
Facsimile: 6655 755
e-mail: bozhilov@unimasters.bg
Honorary Consul: Mr Nikolai Bozhilov

BURKINA

Ouagadougou
British Embassy (all staff reside at Abidjan)
Ambassador: Mr D Coates
First Secretary (Commercial), Consul and Deputy Head of Mission: (Vacant)
Second Secretary (Political/Information):
Ms K Miller, MBE
Second Secretary (Management): (Vacant)
Third Secretary and Vice- Consul (Passports and Visas): (Vacant)

British Honorary Consulate
Hotel Yibi
10 BP 13593
Ouagadougou
Telephone: (00) (226) 30 73 23
Facsimile: (00) (226) 30 59 00
e-mail: ypi@cenatrin.bf
Honorary Consul: Mr Y Pichot

BURMA (SP - see page 120)

Rangoon (Yangon)
British Embassy
80 Strand Road (P.O. Box 638), Rangoon
FTN Code – 8412 + extn number
Telephone: (00) (95) (1) 256918, 380322,
370863-5, 370867, 371852-3, 254657,
254659, 256438
Facsimile: (00) (95) (1) 370866
Airtech: (00) (95) (1) 380321
Office Hours (GMT): 01 30 - 10 00
Except Wed 01 30 - 06 30
Ambassador: Ms Victoria J Bowman
Deputy Head of Mission and HM Consul:
Mr Martin Garrett, MVO
Cultural Attaché, British Council Director (Tel: 256290 ext:312): Mr Marcus Milton
First Secretary (Technical) (resides at Bangkok):
Miss Teresa Hyman
Second Secretary (Political):
Miss Angela M E Macro
Second Secretary (Management) and Vice-Consul:
Mr Nick J Enescott
Third Secretary (Technical) (resides at Bangkok):
Mr David Ellis
Third Secretary (Political): Mr Nigel P Blackwood
Attaché: Mrs Karen D H Sowerby

BURUNDI

Bujumbura
British Embassy (all staff resident in Kigali)
Ambassador: Mr J J Macadie
Deputy Head of Mission: Mr C W Frean

Defence Attaché (resides at Kampala):
Lieutenant Colonel C J A Wilton
Third Secretary (Political): Ms C Vaudrey

British Embassy Liaison Office
Bujumbura
Burundi
Telephone: (00) (257) 827 602
Facsimile: (00) (257) 246 479
e-mail: BELO@cbinf.com
Liaison Officer: Mr M Nzigamasabo

CAMBODIA

Phnom Penh (SP - see page 120)
British Embassy
27-29 Street 75, Phnom Penh
FTN Code - 8393 + 1000 for switchboard
Telephone: (00) (855 23) 427124, 428295
Facsimile: (00) (855 23) 427125
Airtech: (00) (855 23) 427390
e-mail: BRITEMB@bigpond.com.kh
Consular@phnompenh.mail.fco.gov.uk
Office Hours (GMT): Mon - Thurs: 01 00 - 10 00,
Fri: 01 00 - 06 00
Ambassador: Mr David G Reader
Second Secretary and Deputy Head of Mission:
Mr John Mitchell
Third Secretary and Vice Consul: Mr Gary Benham
Attaché: Siân Martin

Department for International Development (Cambodia)
34 Monivong Boulevard
Phnom Penh
Telephone: (00) (855 23) 430240
Facsimile: (00) (855 23) 430254
e-mail: c-khieu@dfid.gov.uk
Head of Office and Governance Adviser:
Dr Daniel Arghiros
Rural Livelihoods Adviser: Mr Chris Price
Health Adviser: Ms Elizabeth Smith
Deputy Programme Manager:
Ms Phillipa Hoffman

CAMEROON

Yaoundé
British High Commission
Avenue Winston Churchill
BP 547, Yaoundé
FTN Code – 8394 + extn number
Telephone: (00) (237) 2 22 05 45/2 22 07 96
Facsimile: (00) (237) 2 22 01 48
Airtech: (00) (237) 2 22 91 55
Duty Officer Mobile: (00) (237) 7 713 053
e-mail: BHC.yaounde@fco.gov.uk
Office Hours (GMT): Mon- Thu: 06 45 - 14 45
Fri: 06 45 - 12 45
High Commissioner: Mr Richard Wildash, LVO
Deputy High Commissioner: Mr David Williams
British Council Director: Ms Jenny Scott
Second Secretary: Mr Nick Baker
Third Secretary (MO/Vice-Consul): Mr Steve Auld
Third Secretary (Entry Clearance): Ms Jo Parry
Attaché: Ms Brenda Thurston

Douala
British Consulate
Standard Chartered Bank Cameroon SA,
Boulevard de la Liberté
BP 1784, Douala
Telephone: (00) (237) 3 42 21 77/3 42 81 45
Facsimile: (00) (237) 3 42 88 96
Office Hours (GMT): Mon: 06 30 - 13 30
Tues-Fri: 06 30 - 13 00
Commercial/Political/Consular Officer:
Ms Emma Denans

CANADA

Ottawa
British High Commission
80 Elgin Street, Ottawa, Ontario K1P 5K7
FTN Code – 8421 + extn number
Telephone: (00) (1) (613) 237 1530
Voicemail and Direct Lines: (00) (1) (613) 237
1542 - (key in extension shown by name)
Facsimile: (00) (1) (613) 237 7980
         232 0738 Management
         232 2533 Visa
         237 5211 Economic
         237 6537 Passport
         567 8045 Political
e-mail: BHC@fco.gov.uk
management@fco.gov.uk
information@fco.gov.uk
chancery@fco.gov.uk
consular@fco.gov.uk
trade-econ@fco.gov.uk
Website: www.britain-in-canada.org
Office Hours (GMT): 13 00 - 21 00
High Commissioner:
Mr David N Reddaway, CMG, MBE
Deputy High Commissioner (2343):
Mr Julian A Evans
Counsellor (Trade/Economic) (2324):
Mr Neil R Chrimes
Counsellor: Mr Clive Newell
*Counsellor (Cultural Affairs) (British Council
Director) (2318):* Mr Peter Chenery
Defence and Military Adviser (2369):
Brigadier Christopher J R Day
Naval and Air Adviser (2384):
Group Captain Tim P Brewer, OBE, RAF
*First Secretary (Head of Political/Information
Section) (2274):* Mr C O'Connor
First Secretary (Science and Technology) (2360):
Ms Julia Hinde
First Secretary (Management) (2326):
Mr Richard Sharp
*First Secretary (Head of Media and Public Affairs)
(2262):* Mr Patrick O'Brien
First Secretary (2214): Mr Ben Lowater
Second Secretary (Economic) (2247):
Mr Alan Richmond
Second Secretary (Trade) (2282): Mr M Dolan
Assistant Naval Adviser B.D.L.S. (2234):
Lieutenant Commander John R Cunane, RN
Second Secretary (Consular) (2320):
Mr Chris Smart
Third Secretary (Political) (2228):
Mrs Katherine Hickey

Third Secretary (Economic) (2331):
Mr Gavin Crockard

Montreal
British Consulate-General
Suite 4200, 1000 De La Gauchetiere West
Montreal, Quebec
H3B 4W5
Telephone: (00) (1) (514) 866-5863
Direct Line - see individual officers
Facsimile: (00) (1) (514) 866 0202
Airtech: (00) (1) (514) 866 4867
Office Hours (GMT): 14 00 - 22 00
Consul-General (233): Ms Sarah Gillett, MVO
Deputy Consul-General (230): Mr Philip Hagger
Consul (Commercial) (225): Mrs Debbie J Fern

**Montreal United Kingdom Representative on
the Council of the International Civil Aviation
Organisation, see Missions and Delegations page
117**

Toronto
British Consulate-General
British Trade and Investment Office
777 Bay Street, Suite 2800, College Park
Toronto, Ontario M5G 2G2
FTN Code – 8423 + extn number
Telephone: (00) (1) 416 593 1290
Facsimile: (00) (1) 416 593 1229
Airtech: (00) (1) 416 593 1425
e-mail: britcon2@gta.igs.net
Office Hours (GMT): 12 30 - 21 00
*Consul-General and Director, Trade and
Investment:* Mr Geoffrey Berg, MVO
*Deputy Consul-General and Deputy Director Trade
(2236):* Mr Mike Upton
Consul (Inward Investment) (2234):
Mr Mike Moon
Consul (Commercial) (2231): Ms Jonathan Drew
Vice-Consul/Management Officer (2227):
Miss Jo Bowyer

Vancouver
British Consulate-General
1111 Melville Street, Suite 800
Vancouver, British Colombia, V6E 3V6
FTN Code – 8422 + extn number
Telephone: (00) (1) (604) 683 4421
Direct Lines - see individual officers
Facsimile: (00) (1) (604) 681 0693
Airtech: (00) (1) (604) 683 7768
Office Hours (GMT): 16 30 - 00 30
Consul-General (1-2205): Mr James Rawlinson
Deputy Consul-General (1-2208):
Mr Andy Newlands

Calgary
British Trade Office
Suite 1500, Bow Valley Square IV
250-6th Avenue S.W.
Calgary, Alberta T2P 3H7
Telephone: (00) (1) (403) 705 1755
Facsimile: (00) (1) (403) 264 1262
Office Hours (GMT): 15 30 – 23 30
Director: Mr Rob Elgie

Commercial Assistant: Ms Tara Meinhardt

Halifax/Dartmouth
British Consulate
1, Canal Street, P.O. Box 605
Dartmouth, Nova Scotia B2Y 3Y9
Telephone: (00) (1) (902) 461 1381
Facsimile: (00) (1) (902) 465 2578
Honorary Consul: Mr A A Smithers

St. John's
British Consulate
113 Topsail Road, St. John's
Newfoundland A1E 2A9
Telephone: (00) (1) (709) 579 2002
Facsimile: (00) (1) (709) 579 0475
Honorary Consul: Mr F D Smith

Winnipeg
British Consulate
229, Athlone Drive, Winnipeg,
Manitoba, R3J 3L6
Telephone: (00) (1) (204) 896 1380
Facsimile: (00) (1) (204) 269 3025
Honorary Consul: Mr R M Hill

Quebec City
British Consulate
Le Complexe St-Amable
700 - 1150 Claire-Fontaine, Quebec City
Quebec, G1R 5G4
Telephone: (00) (1) (418) 521 3000
Facsimile: (00) (1) (418) 521 3099
Honorary Consul: Mr R Drouin

CAPE VERDE

Praia
British Embassy (all staff resident at Dakar)
Ambassador: Mr Peter Newall
Deputy Head of Mission and Consul:
Mr Derek Levoir
Vice-Consul/ECO: Ms Christine Johnson
Management Officer: Mr Nick Faulkner

Sao Vincente
British Honorary Consulate
Shell Cabo Verde, Avenue Amilcar Cabral CP4,
Mindelo, Sao Vincente
Telephone: (00) (238) 232 66 25/26/27
Facsimile: (00) (238) 232 66 29
Please note that all mobile telephone numbers are
to be prefixed by the number 9
e-mail: antonio.a.canuto@scv.simis.com
Honorary Consul: Mr Antonio Canuto (Hon) MBE

CENTRAL AFRICAN REPUBLIC

Bangui
British Embassy (all staff reside at Yaoundé)
Ambassador and Consul-General:
Mr Richard Wildash, LVO
First Secretary and Consul: Mr David Williams

CHAD

Ndjamena
British Embassy (all staff reside at Yaoundé)

Ambassador: Mr Richard Wildash, LVO
First Secretary and Consul: Mr David Williams

Ndjamena
British Consulate
BP1060
Ndjamena
Tel/Fax: (00) (235) 52 39 70
Mobile: (00) (235) 841 11 02
e-mail: econsit@hotmail.com
Honorary Consul: Mrs Ermanna Delacroix

CHILE

Santiago
British Embassy
Av. El Bosque 0125, Casilla 72-D
or Casilla 16552, Santiago
FTN Code – 8524+ extn number
Telephone: (00) (56) (2) 370 4100
Facsimile: (00) (56) (2) 370 4180 Commercial
4170 Consulate
4160 Management
4140 Chancery
335 5988 Information
235 7375 British Council
e-mail: chancery.santiago@fco.gov.uk
commercial.santiago@fco.gov.uk
consular.santiago@fco.gov.uk
defence.santiago@fco.gov.uk
Website: www.britemb.cl
Office Hours (GMT): (October - March): Mon-
Thurs: 12 00 - 20 30 Fri: 12 00 – 16 00
(March - October): Mon-Thurs: 13 00 - 21.30 Fri:
13 00 – 17 00
Ambassador: Mr Richard Wilkinson, CVO
Deputy Head of Mission:
Mr James de Waal (Ext 4112)
Defence Attaché:
Colonel Iain S Campbell (Ext 4120)
Counsellor - Defence Export Services:
Mrs Jackie Callcut (Ext 4149)
Counsellor (Political):
Mr Ian Anderson (Ext 4123)
First Secretary (Commercial):
Mr Paul Taylor (Ext 4174)
Second Secretary (Management) and Consul:
Mr Kevin Brind, MBE (Ext 4138)
Second Secretary: Mr Ned Holborn (Ext 4114)
Third Secretary: Miss Maria Knapp (Ext 4124)

British Council
Av. Eliodoro Yañez 831
Providencia – Santiago
Telephone: (00) (56) (2) 410 6900
Facsimile: (00) (56) (2) 410 6929
Cultural Attaché (British Council Director):
Mr John Knagg, OBE (Ext 6955)

Valparaíso
British Consulate
Blanco 1199 Piso 5
Casilla 68 – V
Valparaíso
Telephone/ Facsimile: (00) (56) (32) 213063
e-mail: con.britanico@entelchile.net
Honorary Consul: Mr Iain Hardy

Punta Arenas
British Consulate
Cataratas del Niagara 01325, Punta Arenas
Casilla 22-D
Telephone: (00) (56) (61) 211535
Facsimile: (00) (56) (61) 239880
e-mail: reesking@tie.cl
Honorary Consul: Mr John Rees

CHINA

Beijing
British Embassy
Main Building
11 Guang Hua Lu, Jian Guo Men Wai, Beijing
100600
FTN Code – 8403 + 4 and individuals extn number
Telephone: (00) (86) (10) 5192 4000
            (Main Switchboard)
            6532 6895
Facsimile: (00) (86) (10) 6532 1937
e-mail: commercialmail.beijing@fco.gov.uk (UK
Trade and Investment Section)
info@britishcentre.co.uk (UK Trade and
Investment Information Resources)
s.t.beijing@fco.gov.uk (Science and Technology)
Office Hours (GMT): 00 30 – 04 00 and
05 30 – 09 00

Consular/Visa Section:
Kerry Centre, 21st Floor, 1 Guang Hua Lu, Beijing
100600
FTN Code – 8465 + extn number
Telephone: (00) (86) (10) 8529 6600, 6075, 6084
            (extension numbers given)
            6532 1961, 6750 (Out of Hours)
            8529 6600 (24hr Recorded Information
            Service)
Facsimile: (00) (86) (10) 8529 6081 (Consular)
            8529 6080 (Visa Section)
e-mail: visamail@beijing.mail.fco.gov.uk
            (Visa Enquiries)
consularmail@beijing.mail.fco.gov.uk
(Consular Enquiries)
Office Hours (GMT): 00 30 – 04 00 and 05 00 –
08 30

DFID China:
30th Floor, South Tower, Beijing Kerry Centre, 1
Guang Hua Lu, Beijing100020
Telephone: (00) (86) (10) 8529 6882 (extension
            numbers given)
Facsimile: (00) (86) (10) 8529 6002/3/4/5
e-mail: dfid@beijing.mail.fco.gov.uk
f.mcconnon@dfid.gov.uk
Office Hours (GMT): 00 30 – 04 00 and
05 30 – 09 00

Cultural and Education Section:
4th Floor Landmark Building, Tower 1, 8 North
Dongsanhuan Road,
Chaoyang District, Beijing 100004
Telephone: (00) (86) (10) 6590 6903 (extension
            numbers given)
Facsimile: (00) (86) (10) 6590 0977
e-mail: enquiry@britishcouncil.org.cn

Office Hours (GMT): 00 30 – 04 00 and 05 30 –
09 00
Ambassador (PA ext. 231):
Sir Christopher Hum, KCMG
*Minister, Consul General and Deputy Head of
Mission (PA ext. 254):* Mr John Dennis
*Counsellor (Director of Trade and Investment) (ext.
256):* Mr Charles Haswell
Counsellor (Political/Economic) (ext. 253):
Ms Barbara Woodward
Counsellor (Science and Technology) (ext.338):
Mr Robin Porter
Counsellor (Global Issues) (ext. 368):
Mr Peter Wood
Counsellor (British Council Director) (ext. 219):
Mr Michael O'Sullivan
Counsellor (Development) (ext. 2002):
Mr Adrian Davis
Defence, Military and Air Attaché (PA ext. 423):
Brigadier Archie J Miller-Bakewell
Naval and Air Attaché (ext. 246):
Group Captain Keith J Parkes, MBE, RAF
First Secretary (Political) (ext. 232):
Mr Ian Seckington
First Secretary (Political) (ext. 309):
Mr John Fox
First Secretary (Political) (ext. 345):
Mr David McFarlane
First Secretary (Economic) (ext. 322):
Mr Nick Bridge
First Secretary (Economic) (ext. 227):
Ms Nicola Willey
First Secretary (Trade and Investment) (ext. 205):
Mr Steve Buckley
First Secretary (Trade and Investment) (ext. 339):
Mr Gareth Hoar
First Secretary (Trade and Investment) (ext. 320):
Mrs Terry Evans
First Secretary (Chevening/Financial):
Mr Simon Goya-Brown
First Secretary (Management) (ext. 228):
Mr Phil Robinson
First Secretary (Technical Management) (ext. 259):
Mr John Thornton
*First Secretary (Regional Technical Works) (ext.
435):* Mr Carl Gray
*First Secretary (Clinical Nursing Officer) (ext.
290):* Ms Jayne Senior, MBE
First Secretary (HM Consul) (ext. 3301/2):
Ms Sue Morrell
*First Secretary (British Council Deputy Director)
(ext. 237):* Mr Keith Davies
*First Secretary (Education) (British Council) (ext.
238):* Mr Andrew Disbury
*First Secretary (Cultural) (British Council) (ext.
221):* Mr Paul Clementson
*First Secretary (Finance) (British Council) (ext.
228):* Ms Lucy Watkins
First Secretary (Development) (ext. 2023):
Dr Chris Athayde
First Secretary (Development) (ext. 2044):
Mr Peter Shelley
First Secretary (Development) (ext. 2007):
Mr Gordon Wilson
First Secretary (Development) (ext. 2024):
Mr John Warburton

First Secretary (Development) (ext. 2004):
Ms Fiona McConnon
First Secretary (Development) (ext. 2006):
Ms Susan Milner
First Secretary (Development) (ext. 2043):
Ms Clare Roberts
First Secretary (Development) (ext. 2036):
Ms Catherine Martin
First Secretary (Development) (ext. 2022):
Mr Martin Taylor
First Secretary (Development) (ext. 2012):
Ms Jillian Popkins
First Secretary (Development) (ext. 2033):
Ms Jane Jamieson
First Secretary (Development) (ext. 2011):
Mr Rahul Malhotra
Second Secretary (Economic) (ext. 437):
Ms Gillian Cull
Second Secretary (Political) (ext. 216):
Ms Claire Filshie
Second Secretary (Political) (ext. 315):
Ms Liz Wilson
Second Secretary (Political/Information) (ext. 233):
Mr Alex Pinfield
Second Secretary (Trade and Investment) (ext. 220): Mr Ben Ladd
Second Secretary (Trade and Investment) (ext. 308): Mrs Kirstie Cranshaw
Second Secretary (Trade and Investment) (ext. 311): Mr Ian Cranshaw
Second Secretary (Trade and Investment) (ext. 285): Mr David Spires
Second Secretary (Inward Investment) (ext.439):
Ms Claire West
Second Secretary (Management) (ext. 219):
Mr Steve Mitchell
Second Secretary (Technical Management) (ext. 234): Mr Simon Moseley
Second Secretary (Security) (ext. 270):
Mr Colin Gingell
Second Secretary (Immigration) (ext. 3340):
Mr Malcolm Whatley
Second Secretary (Immigration) (ext. 3351):
Mr David Rolls
Second Secretary (Airport Liaison Officer) (ext. 3304): Mr Rupert Montgomery
Second Secretary (Arts and Science) (British Council) (ext. 220): Mr Richard Cotton
Second Secretary (Governance) (British Council) (ext. 232): Mr Gary Hallsworth
Second Secretary (EU – China Project) (British Council) (Tel. 8527 5155 ext.33):
Mr Stephen Forbes
Second Secretary (Development) (ext. 2017):
Ms Vina Malloo
Second Secretary (Development) (ext. 2010):
Mr Matthew Perkins
Second Secretary (Development) (ext. 2018):
Mr Strahan Spencer
Second Secretary (Development) (ext. 2034):
Mr Kevin Leitch
Third Secretary (Vice-Consul) (ext. 3303):
Mrs Gail Johnson
Third Secretary (Immigration) (ext. 3316):
Mr Yatin Madlani

Third Secretary (Immigration) (ext. 3341):
Mr Adrian Mapperley
Third Secretary (Immigration) (ext. 3344):
Mrs Sam Schinkel
Third Secretary (Immigration) (ext. 3345):
Mrs Susannah Richmond
Third Secretary (Immigration) (ext. 3380):
Mrs Lindy Beach
Third Secretary (Immigration) (ext. 3346):
Mr Mark Richmond
Third Secretary (Immigration) (ext. 3347):
Ms Karen Dyball
Third Secretary (Immigration) (ext. 3342):
Mr Paul Kingford
Third Secretary (Immigration) (ext. 3380):
Ms Wendy Shepherd
Third Secretary (Immigration) (ext. 3319):
Mr Mike Berry
Third Secretary (Technical Works) (ext. 266):
Mr Gavin Caldwell
Third Secretary (Visits) (ext. 222):
Mr Edmund Marler
Third Secretary (Development) (ext. 2037):
Ms Teresa Kondratowicz
Third Secretary (Development) (ext. 2045):
Mr Kebur Azbaha
Defence Attaché (ext. 215): W.O. Brian Joyce
Defence Attaché (ext. 226): Sergeant Del Marx
Attaché (PA to Ambassador) (ext. 231):
Mrs Avril Chassels
Attaché (PA to Minister and Deputy Head of Mission): Mrs Lucy Cleaver
Attaché (319): Mr Matthew Haslett
Attaché (241): Mr John Moriarty
Attaché (236): Mrs Lesley McAllister
Attaché (229): Mr Richard Reilly

Shanghai
British Consulate-General
Suite 301, Shanghai Centre
1376 Nan Jing Xi Lu
Shanghai 200040
Telephone: (00) (86) (21) 6279 7650
Facsimile: (00) (86) (21) 6279 7651 (General)
6279 7388 (Commercial)
e-mail: britishconsulate@shanghai.mail.fco.gov.uk
firstname.lastname@fco.gov.uk
Website: www.britishconsulate.sh.cn
Office Hours (GMT): 00 30 - 09 00 (Mon - Thu)
00 30 - 07 30 (Fri)

Visa Section
Suite 751, Shanghai Centre
1376 Nan Jing Xi Lu
Shanghai 200040
Telephone: (00) (86) (21) 6279 8130
Facsimile: (00) (86) (21) 6279 8254
e-mail: visa@shanghai.mail.fco.gov.uk
Office Hours (GMT): 00 30 - 09 00 (Mon - Thu)
00 30 - 07 30 (Fri)

British Council
1 Floor Pidemco Tower
318 Fu Zhou Lu
Shanghai 200001
Telephone: (00) (86) (21) 6391 2626
Facsimile: (00) (86) (21) 6391 2121
e-mail: bc.shanghai@britishcouncil.org.cn
firstname.lastname@britishcouncil.org.cn
Website: www.britishcouncil.org.cn
Office Hours (GMT): 00 30 - 09 00
Consul-General: Ms Sue Bishop
Deputy Consul-General: Mr Philip Mani
Head of Commercial: Mr Douglas Barrett
Head of Science and Technology: Mr Nick Khosla
Consul (Commercial): Mr Bob Shead
Consul (Commercial): Mr Barry Nicholson
Consul (Commercial): Mr Tim Standbrook
Consul (Economic/Press and Public Affairs):
Mr Mark Gooding
*Consul - British Council Director (Cultural and
Education):* Mr Jeff Streeter
*Consul - British Council Deputy Director
(Cultural):* Mr Jim Hollington
*Consul - British Council Assistant Director
(Education):* Mr Richard Everitt
*Consul - Examinations Services Manager
(Education):* Ms Sarah Deverall
Consul (Entry Clearance Manager):
Mr Ian Sargeant
Vice-Consul (Management): Mrs Angela Tokalau
Vice-Consul (Visa): Miss Emily Graham
Vice-Consul (Visa): Miss Norah Finlay
Vice-Consul (Visa): Mr Nigel Rennison
Pro-Consul (Consular): Mrs Emma Nicholson

Guangzhou
British Consulate-General
2nd Floor Guangdong International Hotel
(Visa/Consular/Management Sections)
7th Floor Guangdong International Hotel
(Commercial/Political/Economic Sections)
339 Huanshi Dong Lu
Guangzhou 510098
Telephone: (00) (86) (20) 8335 1354 General
8335 1316 British Council
Facsimile: (00) (86) (20) 8331 2799
               Management/Consular
               8333 6485 Commercial
               8332 7509 Visa
               8335 1321 British Council
e-mail: guangzhou.commercial@fco.gov.uk
(Commercial)
guangzhou.consular@fco.gov.uk (Consular)
guangzhou.visas@fco.gov.uk (Visas)
bc.guangzhou@britishcouncil.org.cn (British
Council)
Office Hours (GMT): Mon-Fri: 01 00 - 04 30 and
05 30 - 09 00
Consul-General: Mr Christopher Wood
Deputy Consul General: Mr Sanjay Wadvani
Consul (Political/Economic):
Miss Claire Lawrence
Consul (Commercial): Mr Haden Spicer
Consul (Commercial): Mr Paul Wills
Consul (Consular/Management): Ms Claire Lawley
Consul (Visas): Mr Richard Burns

Consul (Cultural and Education):
Ms Christine Skinner
Vice-Consul (Visa): Mr Andrew Bartholomeou
Vice-Consul (Visa): Mr Daniel Jones
Vice-Consul (Visa): Mr Mark Gee
Vice-Consul (Visa): Mr Simon Burton
Attaché: Miss Sarah Pratt

Chongqing
British Consulate-General
Suite 2801, Metropolitan Tower
68 Zourong Road
Chongqing 40010
Telephone: (00) (86) (23) 6381 0321
Facsimile: (00) (86) (23) 6381 0322
Airtech: (00) (86) (23) 6381 0320
e-mail: bcgchq@public.cta.cq.cn
Office Hours (GMT): Mon - Fri 01 00 - 04 00 and
05 00 - 09 00
Consul General: Miss Carma Elliot
Consul: Mr Scott Strain
British Council Director: Ms Joanne Speakman

Hong Kong Special Administrative Region
British Consulate-General
No. 1 Supreme Court Road
Central, Hong Kong
PO Box 528
Telephone: (00) (852) 2901 3000
Facsimile: (00) (852) 2901 3066 Commercial
               3007 Management
               3008 Press and Public Affairs
               3204 Consular
               3347 Visa
               3420 Fiscal and Drugs Liaison Office
               3143 BC Passport
               3195 Passport
               3034 Airport Liaison Office
e-mail: political@britishconsulate.org.hk (Political
and Economic)
commercial@britishconsulate.org.hk (Commercial)
management@britishconsulate.org.hk
(Management)
press@britishconsulate.org.hk (Press and Public
Affairs)
consular@britishconsulate.org.hk (Consular)
visa@britishconsulate.org.hk (Visa)
passport@britishconsulate.org.hk (Passport)
Website: www.britishconsulate.org.hk
Office Hours (GMT): Mon - Fri: 00 30 - 09 15
Consul-General: Mr Stephen Bradley
Deputy Head of Mission: Mr Adam Noble
*Deputy Consul-General and Director of Trade and
Investment:* Mr Bob Rayner
*Deputy Consul-General (Security and Regional
Affairs):* Mr Christopher Sykes
Consul (Management): Mr Peter Phelan, OBE
Consul (Trade Commissioner): Mr Philip Tissot
HM Consul: Mr Bill Ridout
Fiscal and Drugs Liaison Officer:
Mr Andy Lawson
Consul (Passports): Mr John Geoghegan
Consul (Deputy Trade Commissioner):
Mr Timothy Hanson
Airline Liaison Officer: Mr Andrew Gray
Airline Liaison Officer: Mr Philip Boyle

British Council Director: Ms Ruth Gee
Vice-Consul (Political/Economic):
Mr Daniel Chugg
Vice-Consul (Management):
Mr Simon Drew
Vice-Consul (Technical Management):
Mr Glyn Griffiths
Vice-Consul (IT Management):
Mr Paul Francis
Vice-Consul (Security Management):
Mr John Vowles, MBE
Vice Consul (Political/Economic):
Mr Brian Simpson
Vice-Consul (Economic/Finance):
Ms Kate Harrisson
Vice-Consul (Political/Economic): Ms Amy Owen
Vice-Consul (Political/Economic):
Miss Clare Jackson
Vice-Consul (Security and Regional Affairs):
Mr Martin Lerigo
Vice Consul (Visas): Mr Colin Green
Vice Consul (Visas): Mr Craig Hiden
Vice-Consul (Passports): Mrs Sarah Taylor
Vice-Consul (Consular): Mr Alan Morrison
*Vice-Consul (Executive Assistant to Consul
General):* Miss Alyson Garden
Attaché (PA to Consul General):
Mrs Kate Livingston
Attaché (Political/Economic): Miss Catriona Souter
Attaché (Political/Economic): Mr Chris Naylor
Attaché (Chancery): Mr Gary Davies
Attaché (Chancery): Ms Claire Scarratt
Attaché (Passports): Mrs Ann Cooke

**UK Trade and Investment – Inward Investment
Regional Office**
British Consulate-General, No 1 Supreme Court
Road,
Central, Hong Kong
Telephone: (00) (852) 2901 3367
Facsimile: (00) (852) 2901 3155
e-mail: ukinvestmentap@fco.gov.uk
Website: www.uktradeinvest.gov.uk
Regional Director: Mr Paul Grey

FCO Supply Solutions Hong Kong
7/F, 3 Supreme Court Road, Hong Kong
Telephone: (00) (852) 2901 3488
Facsimile: (00) (852) 2901 3477
e-mail sales@fco.gov.uk
Office Hours (GMT): Mon-Fri 00 15 - 09 30
General Manager: Mr Robert Thursfield

Macao
British Consulate-General
No. 1 Supreme Court Rd, Central, Hong Kong
Telephone: (00) (852) 2901 3000
Facsimile: (00) (852) 2901 3066
Consul-General (Resides at Hong Kong):
Mr Stephen Bradley
Deputy Head of Mission (Resides at Hong Kong):
Mr Adam Noble
*Deputy Consul-General and Director of Trade and
Investment (Resides at Hong Kong):*
Mr Bob Rayner
HM Consul (Resides at Hong Kong):
Mr Bill Ridout

Consul (Commercial) (Resides at Hong Kong):
Mr Philip Tissot
Vice-Consul (Resides at Hong Kong):
Mr Alan Morrison
*Vice-Consul (Political/Economic) (Resides at Hong
Kong):* Miss Clare Jackson

Macao
PO Box 1148
Macao SAR
Telephone: (00) (853) 6850886
Facsimile: (00) (853) 810222
e-mail: honbcmo@yahoo.co.uk
Honorary Consul: Mr Glenn McCartney

COLOMBIA

Bogotá
British Embassy
Edificio ING Barings
Carrera 9 No 76 - 49 Piso 9
Bogotá
FTN Code – 8530 + extn number or 8530 1000
(switchboard)
Telephone: (00) (57) (1) 326 8300
Facsimile: (00) (57) (1) 326 8302 (Management
              Section)
              326 8305 (Commercial Section)
              326 8298 (Political Section)
              326 5303 (Visa/Consular Section)
Airtech: 326 8280
e-mail: britain@cable.net.co
Office Hours (GMT): Mon-Thurs: 13 30 - 17 30
and 18 30 – 21 30, Fri: 13 30 – 18 30
Ambassador (5202): Sir Thomas Duggin
Counsellor and Deputy Head of Mission (5203):
Mrs S J le Jeune d'Allegeershecque
Counsellor (5214): Mr Nicholas Busvine, OBE
Counsellor (Cultural: British Council Director):
Mr Charles Nuttall
Defence Attaché (5210): Colonel Mike E Wilcox
First Secretary (5218): Mr Andrew Gay
First Secretary (Works) (resides at Buenos Aires):
Mr Ronnie Clarke
First Secretary (Management) (5212):
Mr Alan Marshall
First Secretary (5208): Mr Steve Reynolds
First Secretary (Trade and Investment) (5268):
Mr Gary Soper
Second Secretary (5220): Miss Moira Allan
Second Secretary (5316): Mr Philip Sheriff
Second Secretary (Immigration/Consular) (5221):
Mr Brian Hefford
Second Secretary (Technical Management) (5200):
Mr Nick Moss-Norbury
Second Secretary (5209): Mr Chris Marshall
Second Secretary (5207): Ms Rebecca Brown
Second Secretary (Cultural: British Council):
Mr Richard Everitt
Second Secretary (Cultural: British Council):
Mr Carl Rhymer
Second Secretary (5206): Mr Andy Bonsey
Second Secretary (5336): Mrs Jackie Brown
Second Secretary (5240): Mr Steve Morgan
Second Secretary (5211): Mr Andy Bridges
Second Secretary (5204): Mr Graham Partington

Second Secretary (5213): Mr Mark O'Hagan
Second Secretary (5310): Mr Jack Dodds
Third Secretary (Management) (5247):
Mr Brendan Gill
Third Secretary (5217): Mr David Brough
Third Secretary (Immigration) (5270):
Ms Caroline Wise
Third Secretary (Immigration) (5285):
Mrs Julie Clarke-Soper
Third Secretary (Immigration) (5265):
Mr Mike Saunders
Assistant Defence Attaché (5320):
Mr Allan Dawson
Assistant Defence Attaché (5212): Mr Jamie Lucas
Assistant Defence Attaché (5216):
Mr Wayne Arden
Assistant Defence Attaché (5216):
Mr Kenny Wonnacott
Assistant Defence Attaché (5211):
Mr Greig Gilchrist
Assistant Defence Attaché: Mr Tom Palmer
Attaché (Security) (5241): Mr Tony Neal

Cali
British Consulate
Calle 25 No 1N – 65 (Air Mail Box 1326)
Cali
Telephone/Facsimile: (00) (57) (2) 653 6089
e-mail: Britaincali@uniweb.net.co
Honorary Consul: Mr Peter Laurence
Consular Assistant: Ms Constanza Diez

Medellín
British Consulate
Carrera 42 No 53-26
Itagui, Medellín
Telephone: (00) (57) (4) 377 9966
Facsimile: (00) (57) (4) 377 9787
e-mail: Embajadabr@geo.net.co
Honorary Consul: Mr Fernando Osorio, MBE
Consular Assistant: Ms Maria Mercedes Botero

COMOROS

Moroni
British Embassy (all staff resident in Madagascar)
Ambassador: Mr B Donaldson
Deputy Head of Mission: Ms R M Owens

Moroni
British Consulate - vacant

CONGO (DEMOCRATIC REPUBLIC)

Kinshasa (SP – see page 120)
British Embassy
83 Avenue du Roi Baudouin,
Kinshasa
FTN Code – 8706 + extn number
Telephone: (00) (243) 98169100, 98169111,
98169200
Facsimile: (00) (243) 8846102
Duty Officer: (00) (243) 9906129
DHM: (00) (243) 9951429
e-mail: ambrit@ic.cd
Office Hours (GMT): Mon -Thurs 06 30 - 13 30;
Fri 06 30 - 13 00

Ambassador: Mr Andrew Sparkes
Consul and Deputy Head of Mission:
Mr Mark Bensberg
Defence Attaché:
Lieutenant Colonel James R Charlesworth
Second Secretary: Miss Rachel Brass
Third Secretary (Consular/Management):
Mr Mark Douglas-Hiley
Attaché (Immigration): Vacant

CONGO

Brazzaville
British Embassy (all staff reside in Kinshasa)
Ambassador: Mr Andrew Sparkes
Consul and Deputy Head of Mission:
Mr Mark Bensberg
Defence Attaché:
Lieutenant Colonel James R Charlesworth

Brazzaville
Ets LISA (à côté de DHL)
Avenue Fosch, Brazzaville
Telephone: (00) (242) 620893
Facsimile: (00) (242) 838543
e-mail: yorick@congonet.cg
Honorary Consul: Mr Dominique Picard, MBE

COSTA RICA

San José (SP – see page 120)
British Embassy
Apartado 815, Edificio Centro Colon
(11th Floor), San José 1007
FTN Code – 8399 + extn number
Telephone: (00) (506) 258 2025
Facsimile: (00) (506) 233 9938
Airtech: (00) (506) 258 5537
e-mail: britemb@racsa.co.cr
Website: www.britishembassycr.com
Office Hours (GMT) Mon-Thurs 14 00 - 22 00,
Fri 14 00 - 19 00
Ambassador and Consul-General:
Ms Georgina Susan Butler
Deputy Head of Mission: Mr Oriel Willock
First Secretary (Resides in Panama City):
Mr Alan David Pamplin
Second Secretary (Resides in Panama City):
Mr Gary Foster

CÔTE D'IVOIRE see IVORY COAST

CROATIA

Zagreb
British Embassy
UI Ivana Lucica 4, Zagreb
FTN Code – 8384 + extn number
Telephone: (00) (385) (1) 600 9100 (Switchboard)
615 6621/6623/6624/6625 (Visa and
Consular)
Facsimile: (00) (385) (1) 600 9111
615 6628/6629 (Visa and Consular)
466 4379 (Political Section)
455 6304 (Commercial)
466 4090 (Development Section)
Airtech: 600 9210

e-mail: british.embassyzagreb@fco.gov.uk
commercial.section@zg.htnet.hr
Office Hours (GMT): Summer: 06 30 - 15 00
Mon-Thur, 06 30 - 12 00 Fri
Winter: 07 30 - 16 00 Mon-Thur, 07 30 - 13 00 Fri
Ambassador: Mr Nicholas R Jarrold
Deputy Head of Mission: Mr Edward Mason
Defence Attaché:
Lieutenant Colonel Mark D Wentworth
First Secretary (Commercial): Mr Jim T Fraser
First Secretary (Political): Mr Gareth Lungley
British Council Director: Mr Roy Cross
Second Secretary (Immigration/Consular):
Mr Bob Hunter
Second Secretary (Development):
Mr Richard A O Jones
Second Secretary (Management): Mr Paul Robbins
Second Secretary (Immigration Liaison):
Mr Tom Attwood
Third Secretary (Political/PPA):
Ms Elizabeth Ryan
Third Secretary (Political): Mr Philip Shone
Third Secretary (Vice-Consul): Ms Fiona Mason
Third Secretary (Immigration):
Mr Richard Mindang
Assistant Defence Attaché:
Sergeant Steve M Marshall
Assistant Management Officer: Mr Ian Morley

Split
British Consulate
Obala Hrvatskog Narodnog Preporoda 10/III
21000 Split
Telephone: (00) (385) (21) 341 464
Facsimile: (00) (385) (21) 362 905
e-mail: british-consulat-st@st.tel.hr
Office Hours (GMT): Summer: 06 30 - 13 30
Mon-Thur, 06 30 - 11 00 Fri
July, August: 05 30 - 12 30 Mon-Fri
Winter: 07 30 - 14 30 Mon-Thur, 07 30 - 12 00 Fri
Honorary Consul: Captain Ante Roje
Pro Consul: Mrs Sarina Kalebota

Dubrovnik
British Consulate
Buniceva Poljana 3, 20000 Dubrovnik
Telephone/Facsimile: (00) (385) (20) 324 597
e-mail: honcons.dubrovnik@inet.hr
Office Hours (GMT): Summer: 08 00 - 11 00 Mon,
Tue, Thurs and Fri
Winter: 09 00 - 12 00 Mon, Tue, Thurs and Fri
Honorary Consul: Mrs Sara Marojica, MBE

CUBA

Havana
British Embassy
Calle 34 No. 702/4 entre 7ma Avenida y 17
Miramar, Havana
FTN Code – 8533+ extn number
Telephone: (00) (53) (7) 204 1771 Switchboard
Facsimile: (00) (53) (7) 204 8104
           Management/Consular/Immigration
           204 1049 Commercial/Information
           204 9214 Chancery
e-mail: embrit@ceniai.inf.cu (Embassy)
britcoun@ip.etecsa.cu (British Council)

Office Hours (GMT): Summer: 12 00 - 19 30
Winter: 13 00 - 20 30
Ambassador: Mr John Dew
First Secretary and Deputy Head of Mission:
Mr Nigel Baker
Defence Attaché (resides at Caracas):
Group Captain Willie G S Dobson, RAF
First Secretary (Commercial/Economic):
Mr Chris S George
First Secretary (Management) and Consul:
Mr John Farrand
*First Secretary (Science/Culture, British Council
Director):* Mr William Edmundson
First Secretary (resides at Kingston): Mr Jim Day
Second Secretary (Political/Information):
Miss Susannah Payne
Second Secretary (resides at Kingston):
Mr Keith Wiggins
Second Secretary (resides at Mexico City):
Mr Ian Taylor
Third Secretary (Commercial/Immigration):
Mr Alan Dacey
Attaché (Chief Security Officer): (Vacant)
Attaché: Miss Rebecca Jones
Attaché: Miss Melanie Cook
Attaché (Technical Works): Mr Tam O'Donnell

CYPRUS

Nicosia
British High Commission
Alexander Pallis Street (PO Box 21978), 1587
Nicosia or BFPO 567
FTN Code – 8534 + extn number
Telephone: (00) (357) (22) 861100
Facsimile: (00) (357) (22) 861125 Information
           861315 Chancery
           861175 Management
           861200 Consular
           861150 Commercial
Airtech: 861287
e-mail: infobhc@cylink.com.cy
Office Hours (GMT): Mon - Fri 05 30 - 12 30
High Commissioner: Mr Lyn Parker
Counsellor and Deputy High Commissioner:
Mr Philip Barton, OBE
Defence Adviser:
Colonel Tom M Fitzalan Howard, CBE
Counsellor (Political): Mr Charles Parton
British Council Director: Mr Peter Skelton
First Secretary (Consular):
Mr Gordon MacLeod (tel: 22861360)
First Secretary (Commercial):
Mr David Brown (tel: 22861340)
First Secretary (Chancery):
Mr Mick Bispham (tel: 22861250)
First Secretary (Chancery):
Mr Alex Parsons (tel: 22861220)
First Secretary (Management):
Mr Roger Davies (tel: 22861350)
Second Secretary (Chancery):
Mr Alex Miller (tel: 22861251)
Second Secretary (Political):
Ms Jill Morris (tel: 22861230)
Second Secretary (Economic):
Mr Anthony Ellis (tel: 22861231)

Second Secretary (EU/Economic):
Ms Kristina Hill (tel: 22861339)
Second Secretary (Chancery/Information):
Mr Nigel Bond (tel: 22862380)
Second Secretary (resides in Tel Aviv):
Mr John Walker
Attaché (Consular):
Mr Daniel Barker (tel: 22861362)
Attaché (Consular):
Ms Claire Dorrian (tel: 22861363)
Attaché (Consular):
Mr Robert Sylvester (tel: 22861361)
Attaché (Chancery):
Mr Ian Hirchfield (tel: 22861331)

Zygi
British East Mediterranean Relay Station
PO Box 54912, Limassol
Telephone: (00) (357) (24) 332511, 332341
Facsimile: (00) (357) (24) 332595, 332180
Office Hours (GMT): Mon - Fri 05 50 - 12 40
First Secretary (Management) (Resides in Nicosia):
Mr Roger Davies

CZECH REPUBLIC

Prague
British Embassy
Thunovska 14
118 00 Prague 1
FTN Code – 8334 + extn number
Telephone: (00) (420) 2 5740 2111
Facsimile: (00) (420) 2 5740 2296
e-mail: info@britain.cz
Airtech: (00) (420) 2 5740 2249

Trade and Investment Section
Palac Myslbek
Na Prikope 21
117 19 Prague 1
FTN Code – 8363 + extn number
Telephone: (00) (420) 2 2224 0021/2/3
Facsimile: (00) (420) 2 2224 3625
e-mail: tradeinvest.PRAGC@fco.gov.uk

British Council
Bredovsky dvůr, Politickych vězňu 13
110 00 Prague 1
Telephone: (00) (420) 2 2199 1162
Facsimile: (00) (420) 2 2493 3847
Telex: 122097 (a/b BCCZ C)
e-mail: Forename.Surname@britishcouncil.cz
Office Hours (GMT): end Mar - end Oct: 06 30 -
15 00 (local 08.30 – 17 00)
Ambassador: Ms Linda J Duffield, CMG
*Counsellor and Deputy Head of Mission (ext
2253):* Mr Michael Tatham
Defence Attaché (ext 2261):
Colonel Simon C Newton
Cultural Attaché (British Council Director):
Mrs Mandy Johnson
First Secretary (Commercial): Mrs Karen Stanton
First Secretary (EU/Economic) (ext 2315):
Mrs Judith Gardiner
First Secretary (Management/Consul) (ext 2226):
Mr Dick Coleman

First Secretary (Political/External) (ext 2258):
Mr Alexander Martin
First Secretary (TWO) (resides in Vienna):
Mr John Sweeney
British Council Assistant Director:
Ms Elizabeth White
Assistant Defence Attaché (ext 2240):
Squadron Leader Euan C Alexander, RAF
*Second Secretary (Political/Press and Public
Affairs) (ext 2245):* Mr Peter Wickenden
Second Secretary (Commercial): Mr Andrew Wells
Second Secretary/DLO: Mr Steven Hemsley
Second Secretary/TMO (resides in Vienna):
Mr Ian Purvis
Second Secretary/ALO (resides in Budapest):
Mr Stephen Brown
Third Secretary and Vice-Consul (ext 2205):
Mrs Maggie Yarunina
Third Secretary (Political) (ext 2259):
Mr James Armstrong
Third Secretary (Political/EU) (ext 2237):
Mr Alan Caughey
Third Secretary (Management) (ext 2223):
Mrs Julie B Jackson

DENMARK

Copenhagen
British Embassy
Kastelsvej 36/38/40, DK-2100 Copenhagen Ø
FTN Code – 8320 + extn number
Telephone: (00) (45) 35 44 52 00
Facsimile: (00) (45) 35 44 52 93
    Information Section
    52 14 Political Section
    52 46 Commercial Department
    52 53 Consular
    52 59 Management
e-mail: info@britishembassy.dk
Website: www.britishembassy.dk
Office Hours (GMT): end Mar - end Oct 07 00 -
15 00 and end Oct - end Mar 08 00 - 16 00

Consular/Visa Section:
Consular: end Mar - end Oct 07 00 - 10 30 and 11
30 - 13 00
end Oct - end Mar 08 00 - 11 30 and 12 30 - 14 00
Visa: end Mar - end Oct 07 00 - 09 00
end Oct - end Mar 08 00 - 10 00
Commercial: end Mar - end Oct 06 30 - 10 30 and
11 30 - 14 30
end Oct - end Mar 07 30 - 11 30 and 12 30 - 15 30

British Council (Cultural Section
Director: Dr Michael Sorensen-Jones
Gammel Mønt 12. 3. 1117 Copenhagen K
Telephone: (00) (45) 33 36 94 00
(Tel. Hours: 09 00 - 12 00, 13 00 - 15 30)
Educational Enquiries:
Telephone: (00) (45) 33 36 94 04
(Tel. Hours: 12 30 - 15 30)
e-mail: british.council@britishcouncil.dk
Ambassador: Sir Nicholas W Browne, KBE, CMG
Counsellor: Mr T S A Folliss
Defence Attaché:
Commander Charlie D Wilson, OBE, RN
First Secretary (Commercial): Ms P Balkin

First Secretary (Political): Ms C Powers
First Secretary (Management) and Consul:
Mr S Puryer
Second Secretary (Political): Mr A Campbell
Second Secretary (Political): Ms K Brooking
Second Secretary (Technical/Management):
Mr J Preston
Third Secretary (Political): Mr G Crockard
Attaché (AMO/Vice-Consul): Mr N Jones
Vice-Consul: Mrs J T Christoffersen
Vice-Consul: Mrs S Oxfeldt Jensen

Aabenraa
British Consulate
Turistchef
c/o Turistbureauet
H.P. Hanssens Gade 5
6200 Aabenraa
Telephone: (00) (45) 74 62 35 00
Facsimile: (00) (45) 74 63 07 44
e-mail: aabtur@post3.tele.dk
Office Hours (GMT): 06 30 - 14 30
Honorary Consul: Mr William Klinker (Danish)

Aalborg
British Consulate
Hasserisvej 112
Postboks 23
9100 Aalborg
Telephone: 98 11 34 99
Facsimile: 98 11 56 99
e-mail: jbh.as@mail.dk
Office Hours (GMT): 05 30 - 13 30
Honorary Consul: Mr Jørgen Bladt (Danish)

Aarhus
British Consulate
c/o SCANAD A/S
Skolegade 19B, 8100 Aarhus C
Telephone: 87 30 77 77
             87 30 77 15 (Assistant direct)
Facsimile: 87 30 77 07
e-mail: ch@scanad.dk
Office Hours (GMT): 06 30 - 14 30
Honorary Consul: Mr Claus R Herluf (Danish)

Esbjerg
British Consulate
Kanalen 1, 6700 Esbjerg
Telephone: 79 11 19 00
Facsimile: 79 11 19 01
e-mail: britishconsulate@danbor.dk or
iw@danbor.dk
Office Hours (GMT): 06 30 - 14 00
Honorary Consul: Mr Gert Kragelund (Danish)

Fredericia
British Consulate
Vesthavnen, P O Box 235
7000 Fredericia
Telephone: 75 92 20 00
Facsimile: 76 20 29 80
e-mail: pia raun rasmussen@rahbek.dk
Office Hours (GMT): 06 00 - 14 30
Honorary Consul:
Mr Morten Rahbek Hansen (Danish)

Herning
British Consulate
Aage Damgaard ApS
Lundvej 8, 7400 Herning
Telephone: 96 27 73 00
Facsimile: 97 12 48 58
e-mail: lars@aage-damgaard.dk
Office Hours (GMT): 06 30 - 14 30
Honorary Consul: Mr Lars Damgaard (Danish)

Odense
British Consulate
Albanitorv 4, Postboks 308
5100 Odense C
Telephone: 66 14 47 14
Facsimile: 66 14 61 30
Office Hours (GMT): 06 00 - 14 00
Honorary Consul: Mr Frits Niegel, MBE (Danish)

Rønne (Bornholm) - closed

Tórshavn, Faroe Islands
British Consulate
P/F Damfar, P O Box 1154
Niels Finsensgøta 5
FR-110 Tórshavn
Faroe Islands
Telephone: 298 35 99 77
Facsimile: 298 35 99 80
e-mail: damfar@post.olivant.fo
Office Hours (GMT): 09 00 - 17 00
Honorary Consul: Mr Tummas H Dam

DJIBOUTI

British Embassy
(All staff resident at Addis Ababa)
Ambassador: Mr R Dewar
First Secretary (Management and Consul):
Miss A Marriott, MBE
Second Secretary: Mr O Richards

British Consulate
PO Box 169, Rue de Djibouti
Djibouti
Telephone (00) (253) 25 09 17
Facsimile: (00) (253) 35 78 15
e-mail: british.consulate@intnet.dj
Honorary Consul (Resident in Djibouti):
Mr A Martinet

DOMINICA

Roseau
British High Commission
Lower Collymore Rock (PO Box 676)
Bridgetown, Barbados
Telephone: (00) (1) (246) 430 7800
Facsimile: (00) (1) (246) 430 7851 Chancery
             (246) 430 7860 Management/Consular
             (246) 430 7826 Commercial/
             Information
e-mail: britishhc@sunbeach.net
Office Hours (GMT) 12 00 – 16 30
and 17 30 – 20 00
(All staff reside at Bridgetown)
High Commissioner: Mr John White
Deputy High Commissioner: Mr Rob Holland

Defence Adviser: Captain Steve G Wilson, RN
First Secretary (Chancery): Mr Graham Honey
First Secretary (Management): Ms Ros Day
High Commissioner's Special Representative:
Mr Nick J Pyle, MBE
Second Secretary (Chancery): Mr Rick Gomez
Third Secretary (Immigration): Mr Mark Harrison

Roseau
British Consulate
Office of the Honorary British Consul
c/o Courts (Dominica) Ltd
PO Box 2269, Roseau
Telephone: Office: (1 767) 448 7655 or 448 0166
Facsimile: (1 767) 448 7817
e-mail: smaynard@courts.co.dm
Honorary Consul: Mr Simon Maynard

DOMINICAN REPUBLIC

Santo Domingo (SP – see page 120)
British Embassy
Ave 27 de Febrero No 233
Edificio Corominas Pepín
Santo Domingo, Dominican Republic
Telephone: (00) (1) (809) 472 7111
          472 7905 (Commercial)
          472 7373/7671 (Consular)
Facsimile: (00) (1) (809) 472 7190
          (Chancery/Commerial)
          472 7574 (Consular/Management)
e-mail: brit.emb.sadom@codetel.net.do
Office Hours (GMT): Mon-Thurs 12 00 - 20 30
Fri 12 00 - 17:00
Ambassador: Mr Andy Ashcroft
Deputy Head of Mission: Mr Kevin Shaughnessy
Defence Attaché (Resides at Caracas):
Group Captain Willie G S Dobson, RAF

Puerto Plata
British Consulate
Calle Beller No.51
Puerto Plata, R.D.
Telephone: (00) (1) (809) 586-4244 / 8464
Facsimile: (00) (1) (809) 586-3096
Honorary Consul: Mrs Cindy Salem
Consular Agent: Mr Genny Mendez

EAST TIMOR

Dili (SP – see page 120)
British Embassy
Pantai Kelapa (Avenida de Portugal)
Dili
(Postal Address: PO Box 194, The Post Office,
Dili, East Timor)
FTN Code – 8445 + extn
Telephone: (00) (670) 332 2838
          (00) (670) 723 1600 (HM Ambassador)
          (00) (670) 723 1601 (DHM)
Facsimile: (00) (670) 331 2652
Airtech: (00) (670) 332 2837
e-mail: herminia.freitas@fco.gov.uk
Office Hours (GMT): Mon-Fri 00 30 – 08 00
Ambassador: Ms Tina S Redshaw
Deputy Head of Mission: Mr Lee Jackson, MBE

Defence Attaché (resides at Jakarta):
Colonel Alan J Roberts
First Secretary (Technical) (resides at Singapore):
Mr Richard Hardy
*Second Secretary (Technical) (resides at
Singapore):* Mr Nick Folker

ECUADOR

Quito (SP – see page 120)
British Embassy
Citiplaza Building
Naciones Unidas Ave and República de El Salvador
14th Floor
(Consular Section 12th Floor)
FTN Code – 8537 + extn number
Telephone: (00) (593) (2) 2 970 800 / 970 801
Facsimile: (00) (593) (2) 2 970 807 Consular
          2 970 809 Commercial
          2 970 810 Management
          2 970 811 Chancery
Airtech: 2 970 812
P.O. Box: 17 – 17 - 830
e-mail: britembq@interactive.net.ec
Office Hours (GMT): Mon – Thur 13 30 - 17 30
and 18 30 - 22 00, Fri 13 30 - 18 30
Ambassador: Mr Richard G Lewington
Consul and Deputy Head of Mission:
Mr Peter Evans
Defence Attaché (resides at Caracas):
Group Captain William G S Dobson, RAF
Second Secretary (TC/Chancery):
Mr Robin J Shackell
Second Secretary: Mr Brian Corbett, MBE
Third Secretary (Management):
Miss Rachel Brazier
Third Secretary (Vice-Consul): Miss Sofie Deeks
Vice-Consul: Mr Uwe Roepke

Guayaquil
British Consulate
c/o Agripac
General Córdova 623 y Padre Solano
PO Box 09-10-8598, Guayaquil
Telephone: (00) (593) (4) 2 560400, ext 318
Facsimile: (00) (593) (4) 2 562641
e-mail: carmstrong@agripac.com.ec or
rtorres@agripac.com.ec
Office Hours (GMT): 14 30 - 18 00
and 20 00 - 23 00
Honorary Consul: Mr Colin R Armstrong, OBE
Honorary Vice-Consul: Mrs Rocio Torres

Guayaquil
British Embassy - Trade Office
Torres del Norte Building,
Torre A, 5th Floor, Office 503
Kennedy Norte, Av. Miguel H. Alcivar, Manzana
506
Telephone: (00) (593) (4) 2 687112
Facsimile: (00) (593) (4) 2 687113
e-mail: britembg@interactive.net.ec
Office Hours (GMT): Mon-Thurs: 13 30 - 17 30
and 18 30 - 22 00, Fri: 13 30 - 18 30
Commercial Officer: Miss Irene Lertora
Commercial Assistant:
Miss Monica Ingarévalo

Galápagos
British Consulate
c/o Etica Office, Barrio Estrada,
Puerto Ayora, Isla Santa Cruz, Galápagos
Telephone: (00) (593) (5) 526157 / 526159
Facsimile: (00) (593) (5) 526591
e-mail: dbalfour@eticapa.com.ec
Office Hours (GMT): 13 00 - 17 00
and 19 00 - 23 00
Honorary Consul: Mr David Balfour, MBE

EGYPT

Cairo
British Embassy
7, Ahmed Ragheb Street, Garden City, Cairo
FTN Code – 8538 + extn number
Telephone: (00) (20) (2) 794 0850, 794 0852/8
Facsimile: 796 1458 Political,
794 3065 Consular and Information
794 0859 Commercial
796 3222 Management
795 1235 Visa
Airtech: 8538 2215
e-mail: info@britishembassy.org.eg
Website: www.britishembassy.org.eg
Office Hours (GMT): Sunday - Wednesday:
Chancery, Commercial sections work: 06 30 –
14 00
Defence: 06 00 – 14 00 (including lunch)
Consular, Visa, Management: 06 00 – 13 30
Office Hours (GMT): Thursday:
Chancery, Commercial: 06 30 – 12 30
Defence: 06 00 – 12 30
Consular, Visa, Managament: 06 00 – 12 00
Ambassador: Sir Derek Plumbly, KCMG
Counsellor and Deputy of Mission:
Mr Michael Davenport
Defence Attaché: Captain Philip W Holihead, RN
Cultural Counsellor (British Council Director):
Dr John Grote, OBE
Counsellor (Regional Affairs):
Mr Edmund Fitton-Brown
First Secretary (Commercial): Mr Simon Fisher
*First Secretary and Head of Political and
Economic Section:* Mr Tim Stew, MBE
First Secretary (Political): Mr David Kilby
*First Secretary (Cultural) and British Council
Deputy Director:* Ms Sally Goggin
First Secretary and Consul: Mr Mark Rakestraw
First Secretary (Cultural): Mr Steven Murrell
First Secretary (Technical Works Officer):
Mr John Warrener
First Secretary (Management): Mr Shaun Flaherty
*First Secretary (Regional Expert, Arab World
Projects):* Mr Nicholas Abbott
Second Secretary (Aid): Mr Ian Ruff
Second Secretary (Commercial):
Mr Stephen Townsend
Second Secretary (Technical Management):
Mr Andrew Higham
Second Secretary (Immigration):
Mr Rupert Montgomery
Second Secretary (Press and Public Affairs):
Ms Caroline Alcock

Second Secretary (Cultural):
Miss Samantha Harvey
Deputy Management Officer: Mr Gordon Horne
Attaché and Vice-Consul: Mr Jason Lambert
Attaché and Vice-Consul: Mr Richard Postill
Attaché and Vice-Consul: Mrs Debbie Hare
Attaché: Mr Roger Williams
Attaché: Mrs Jacqui Glen
Attaché: Ms Caroline Begley
Attaché: Mr Adam Harris
Attaché: Mrs Ruth Whelan
Attaché: Ms Aurea Marshall

Alexandria (SP)
British Consulate-General
3 Mina Street, Kafr Abdou, Roushdi,
Ramley Alexandria, 21529
Telephone: (00) (20) (3) 5467001, 5467002,
5223717, 5220507
Facsimile: (00) (20) (3) 5467177
Office Hours (GMT): Sun - Wed: 06 00 - 13 30,
Thurs: 06 00 - 13 00
Consul-General: Mr Alan Cobden

Suez
British Consulate
HS Supply Co.
9 El-Galaa Street, Suez
Telephone: (00) (20) (62) 334102 (Consulate), (00)
(20) (62) 313872 (Office), 314055 (Home)
Telex: 66112 DRHSS UN
Facsimile: (00) (20) (62) 320729
Mobile: 012 210 1343
Honorary Consul: Dr Hussein Samir

Luxor
British Honorary Consular Agent
Gaddis Hotel
Khaled Ibn El Walid St.
Luxor
Telephone: (00) (20) (95) 382838 (Consulate and
Office), 374814 (Home)
Facsimile: (00) (20) (95) 380814, 382837
Mobile: 012 210 5456
Honorary Consular Agent: Mr Ehab Gaddis

EL SALVADOR

San Salvador (SP – see page 120)
British Embassy (except where shown all staff
reside at Guatemala City)
Ambassador: Mr Richard D Lavers
First Secretary and Deputy Head of Mission:
Mr Kevin A Garvey
Defence Attaché: Colonel Ian Blair-Pilling, OBE
First Secretary (DLO) (resides at Panama City):
Mr Alan Pamplin
Second Secretary (Management) and Consul:
Mr Colin Gracey
Second Secretary (Chancery): Mrs Susie Kitchens
Assistant Defence Attaché:
W.O. Eugene J McCran, RAF
Second Secretary (DLO) (resides at Panama City):
Mr Gary Foster
Third Secretary: Mr Amar Shazad

San Salvador
British Consulate
PO Box 242
San Salvador
Telephone: (00) (503) 281 5555 or 271 1050
Telefax: (00) (503) 271 1026
Honorary Consul: Mr George Chippendale, MBE

EQUATORIAL GUINEA

Malabo
British Embassy (all staff reside at Yaoundé)
Ambassador and Consul-General:
Mr Richard Wildash, LVO
First Secretary and Consul: Mr David Williams

ERITREA

Asmara
British Embassy
66-68 Mariam Ghimbi Street
PO Box 5584 Asmara
Telephone: (00) (291) 1 12 01 45
Facsimile: (00) (291) 1 12 01 04
Airtech: (00) (291) 1 20 28 39
e-mail: Asmara.Enquiries@fco.gov.uk
Office Hours (GMT): Mon-Thurs 05 00 – 10 30
and 11 30 – 13 30, Fri 05 00 – 10 30
Ambassador: Mr M T Murray
Defence Attaché (Resides in Nairobi):
Colonel A D K Inkster
Third Secretary (Management/Immigration/Vice-Consul and Deputy Head of Mission):
Mrs A L Taylor

ESTONIA (SP – see page 120)

Tallinn
British Embassy
Wismari 6
10136 Tallinn
FTN Code – 8321 + extn number
Telephone: (00) (372) 667 4700 (Switchboard)
Facsimile: (00) (372) 667 4755
            (Political/HMA/DHM)
            4724 (Commercial)
            4756 (Management/Defence)
            4725 (Consular/Visa)
e-mail: information@britishembassy.ee
Website: www.britishembassy.ee
Office Hours (GMT): Summer: 06 00 – 14 00
Winter: 07 00 – 15 00
Ambassador (4703): Mr Nigel R Haywood
Deputy Head of Mission (4713):
Mr William Elliott
Defence Attaché (resides at Riga):
Lieutenant Colonel Glen A B Grant
First Secretary (British Council Director):
Ms Kyllike Tohver
First Secretary (Political) (4704): Mr Will Evans
Second Secretary (Technical Management) (resides at Helsinki): Mr Tim Goode
Third Secretary (Management) and Consul (4728):
Miss Tiiu Morris
Third Secretary (Political) (4722): Mr Stuart Peters
Third Secretary (Regional Affairs) (4744):
Mr Simon Shaw

UKTI Officer (4736): Miss Ketevan Moseshvili
Vice Consul and ECO (4706): Mr Paul Jordan
Political Attaché (4715): Mr Daniel Garlick
Press Officer (4719): Miss Kaire Kroos

ETHIOPIA

Addis Ababa
British Embassy
Fikre Mariam Abatechan Street
PO Box 858
Addis Ababa
FTN Code - 8539 + 1000 for switchboard
Telephone: (00) (251) 1 61 23 54
Facsimile: (00) (251) 1 61 05 88
            (00) (251) 1 61 41 54
            (Visa/Consular Section)
e-mail: BritishEmbassy.AddisAbaba@fco.gov.uk
Office Hours (GMT): Mon-Thurs: 05 00 - 13 30
Fri: 05 00 - 10 00
Consular/Visa Section Public Opening Hours: Mon - Fri: 05 30 - 09 00
Ambassador: Mr Robert Dewar
Deputy Head of Mission: Ms Deborah Fisher
Defence Attaché: Colonel David S Charters
First Secretary (Conflict Prevention):
Mr Jeremy Astill Brown
First Secretary (British Council Director):
Mr Michael Moore
First Secretary (Management/Consul):
Mr Doug Winter
First Secretary (British Council):
Mr Simon Winetroube
Second Secretary (Political): Mr Daniel Drake
Second Secretary (Political/Economic/Information): Miss Holly Tett
Second Secretary (Technical Management Officer):
Mr Peter Waterhouse
Third Secretary (Immigration/Vice Consul):
Ms Carole Jarvie
Third Secretary (Management/Security):
Mr Glyn Cartmell

Department for International Development (DFID) Ethiopia
British Embassy Compound
PO Box.858
Addis Ababa
Telephone: (00) (251) 1 61 23 54
Facsimile: (00) (251) 1 62 24 32
Head of Office: Mr Paul Ackroyd
Deputy Head of Office (Programme):
Mr Anthony Way
Deputy Head of Office (Management):
Mr Toby Weaver
Social Development Adviser: Ms Claudia Fumo
Education Adviser: Ms Laure Beaufils
Food Security Adviser: Mr Tim Robertson
Food Security Adviser: Ms Melkamnesh Alemu
Governance Adviser: Mr Rupert Bladon
HIV/AIDS Adviser: Ms Marion Kelly
Peace and Security Adviser: Ms Lu Ecclestone
Economic Adviser: Ms Vanessa Head
Food Security Adviser (EU): Mr Tim Waites
Rural Development Adviser (WB):
Ms Michelle Philips

Deputy Programme Manager: Ms Carol Norman
Deputy Programme Manager: Ms Helen Winterton
Office Manager: Mr John Hawkes
IT Manager: Ms Sara Green

FIJI

Suva (SP – see page 120)
British High Commission
Victoria House
Gladstone Road
Suva (PO Box 1355)
FTN Code – 8443 + extn number
Telephone: (00) (679) 3229100
Facsimile: (00) (679) 3229132 (General)
3229140 (Chancery)
Airtech: (00) (679) 3229139
e-mail: Public Affairs:
publicdiplomacysuva@fco.gov.uk
Commercial Office:
tradeinvestmentsuva@fco.gov.uk
e-mail for individual officers – insert:
firstname.surname + @fco.gov.uk
Website:
http://www.britishhighcommission.gov.uk/fiji
Office Hours (GMT): Sun -Wed 20 15 - 01 00 and
02 00 - 05 00, Thurs 20 15 - 01 00
*High Commissioner, also Alternate Representative
for Pitcairn; South Pacific Commission;
non-resident High Commissioner to Nauru,
Kiribati and Tuvalu:* Mr Charles F Mochan
(Ext 2120)
*Deputy High Commissioner. Also non-resident
Ambassador to Micronesia, Marshall Islands and
Palau; Deputy High Commissioner to Nauru,
Kiribati and Tuvalu:* Mr Ian Powell (ext 2122)
Defence Adviser (resides at Wellington):
Colonel Alec A Peebles
*Second Secretary (Political, Press and Public
Affairs); Deputy Head of Mission and Consul to
Micronesia Marshall Islands and Palau:*
Mr Stephen Tarry (ext 2110)
*Third Secretary
(Management/Consular/Immigration):*
Mr Andrew Osborn (Ext 2105)

FINLAND

Helsinki
British Embassy
Itainen Puistotie 17, 00140
Helsinki
FTN Code - 8322 + 1000 for switchboard
Telephone: (00) (358) (9) 2286 5100
Telefax: Political Section (00) (358) (9) 2286
5284
All other Sections (00) (358) (9) 2286 5262, 5272
e-mail: info@britishembassy.fi
Website: www.britishembassy.fi
Office Hours (GMT): Sep-June: 07 00 - 15 00,
June-Aug: 06 30 - 13 00
Ambassador: Mr Matthew Kirk (5222)
Counsellor and Deputy Head of Mission:
Mr Richard Powell (5234)
Counsellor (Political/PPAS): Mr Brian Olley
(5264)

Counsellor (Regional Affairs):
Mr Richard Knowlton (5207)
Defence Attaché:
Lieutenant Colonel Rick M Andrews (5246)
Head of UK Trade and Investment Services:
Mr John Slate (5219)
*Regional Director of Inward Investment Services
(Resident in Stockholm):* Mr Adrian Pinder
HM Consul and First Secretary (Management):
Mr Roger Woodward (5221)
British Council Director: Ms Tuija Talvitie
*Deputy Head of UK Trade and Investment
Services:* Mr Silvano Rebecchi (5229)
Second Secretary (Political/EU):
Mr Andy Pryce (5240)
Second Secretary (Management/Technical):
Mr Tim Goode (5244)
Vice-Consul/Deputy Management Officer:
Mr Steven M Anderson (5238)
Attaché (Political): Mr Les Jay (5277)
Chaplain: Rev. Rupert Moreton

Jyväskylä
British Consulate
Telephone: (00) (358) (14) 446 9211
Telefax: (00) (358) (14) 446 9216
Honorary Consul: Mr Risto Jamsen (Finnish)

Kotka
British Consulate
Telephone: (00) (358) (5) 234 4281
Telefax: (00) (358) (5) 218 1375
Honorary Consul: Mr K Näski (Finnish)

Kuopio
British Consulate
70100 Kuopio
Telephone: (00) (358) (17) 265 7777
Telefax: (00) (358) (17) 261 1085
Honorary Consul: Mr H A Palsola (Finnish)

Åland Islands
British Consulate
Telephone: (00) (358) (18) 13591,47720
Telefax: (00) (358) (18) 13196
Honorary Consul: Mr B H Olofsson (Finnish)

Oulu
British Consulate
Telephone: (00) (358) (83) 310 7117
Telefax: (00) (358) (83) 310 7133
Honorary Consul: Mr P Koskela (Finnish)

Rovaniemi
British Consulate
Telephone: (00) (358) (16) 317 831
Honorary Consul: Mr L Pitkanen (Finnish)

Tampere
British Consulate
Telephone: (00) (358) (3) 256 5701
Telefax: (00) (358) (3) 256 5739
Honorary Consul: Mrs R K Varpe (Finnish)

Turku
British Consulate
Telephone: (00) (358) (2) 274 3410
Telefax: (00) (358) (2) 274 3440

Honorary Consul: Mr Jari Lähteenmäki (Finnish)

Vaasa
British Consulate
Telephone: (00) (358) (6) 2822 000
Telefax: (00) (358) (6) 2822 055
Honorary Consul: Mr R Grönblom (Finnish)

FRANCE

Paris
British Embassy
35 rue du Faubourg St. Honoré
75383 Paris Cedex 08
FTN Code – 8330 + extn number
Telephone: (00) (33) (1) 44 51 31 00
Facsimile: (00) (33) (1) 44 51 34 83
               Ambassadors Office/Chancery
               32 88 Management
               34 01 Commercial
               34 85 Political/Economic
               32 34 Press and Public Affairs
               34 40 Defence/Global Issues
               31 27 Consular
               31 28 Visa
Telephone: (00) (33) (1) 49 55 73 00
               British Council
Facsimile: (00) (33) (1) 47 05 77 02
               British Council
Website: http://www.amb-grandebretagne.fr
Office Hours (GMT): Summer 08 30 – 12 00 and
13 30 – 17 00. Winter 09 30 – 13 00
and 14 30 – 18 00
Ambassador: Sir John Holmes, GCVO, KBE, CMG
Minister: Mr Giles Paxman, LVO
Defence/Air Attaché:
Air Commodore Christopher J Blencowe, RAF
Naval Attaché: Captain Didier Lombard, RN
Military Attaché: Brigadier Timothy J Gregson, MBE
Counsellor (Trade, Development and Investment):
Mr John Duncan, OBE
Counsellor (Global Issues): Mr Hugh Elliott
Counsellor (EU/Economic): Mr Nicholas Hopton
Counsellor (Political): Mr Peter McQuibban
Counsellor (Cultural) (British Council Director):
Mr John Tod, OBE
Counsellor (Management): Mr Richard White, MBE
First Secretary (Press and Public Affairs):
Mr Nicholas Allan
First Secretary and Consul-General:
Mr Jeffrey Thomas
First Secretary (Global Issues):
Dr Helen Dickinson
First Secretary (Global Issues):
Ms Victoria Courtney
First Secretary (EU/Economic):
Mr Andrew Gregory
First Secretary (EU/Economic): Ms Shona Riach
First Secretary (EU/Economic):
Ms Joanna Kuenssberg
First Secretary (EU/Economic):
Mrs Helen Pennant
First Secretary (Political): Mr Angus Lapsley
First Secretary (Political): Mr Jeremy Legge
First Secretary (Political): (Vacant)
First Secretary (Political): Mr Andrew Page

First Secretary (Political): Ms Cathy Ward, LVO
First Secretary (Defence Procurement):
Mrs Jennifer Grogan
First Secretary (Management): Mr Peter Duffy
First Secretary (Estate Manager):
Mr John Darlington
First Secretary (Technical): Mr Brian Farnham
First Secretary (Commercial): Mr Philip Shaw
First Secretary (Commercial):
Mr John Greengrass, MBE
*Cultural Attaché (British Council Deputy
Director):* Mr David Kirwan
First Secretary and Consul: Mr Brian West
Assistant Air Attaché:
Wing Commander Graham August, RAF
Second Secretary (Global Issues):
Miss Kirsteen Hall
Second Secretary (EU/Economic):
Dr Kay Williams
Second Secretary (EU/Economic):
Ms Frances Hooper
Second Secretary (Political):
Miss Alexandra Martens
Second Secretary (Political): Ms Cecily Newby
Second Secretary (Technical): Mr Martin Price
Second Secretary (Press and Public Affairs):
Mr Sujeevan Satheesan
Private Secretary: Miss Joanna Samuels-Watson
Third Secretary (Management):
Mr Christopher Daltrey
Third Secretary (Passports): Mr Ian Gallacher
Third Secretary (Immigration):
Mr Michael Kearney
Third Secretary (Political) Visits Officer:
Mrs Marina Pettigrew, MVO
Third Secretary (Commercial): Mr Kevin Brant

**Paris British Consulate General (see entry
under Paris below)**
**Paris United Kingdom Delegation to OECD, see
Missions and Delegations page 114**
**Paris United Kingdom Delegation to UNESCO,
see Missions and Delegations page 113**
**Strasbourg United Kingdom Delegation to
Council of Europe, see Missions and Delegations
page 116**

Bordeaux
British Consulate-General
353 Boulevard du President Wilson
33073 Bordeaux Cedex
Telephone: (00) (33) (5) 57 22 21 10
Facsimile: (00) (33) (5) 56 08 33 12
Office Hours (GMT): Summer 07 00 – 10 30 and
12 00 – 15 30. Winter 08 00 – 11 30
and 13 00 – 16 30
Consul-General: Mr Thomas Kennedy, LVO
Consul (Commercial): Mr Alastair Roberts
Vice-Consul: Mr Paul Dixon, MBE

Toulouse
British Consulate
Telephone: (00) (33) (5) 61 15 02 02
Facsimile: (00) (33) (5) 61 15 08 92
Honorary Consul: Mr Roger Virnuls, MBE

Biarritz
Honorary British Consulate - Vacant

Lille
British Consulate-General
11 Square Dutilleul
59000 Lille
Telephone: (00) (33) (3) 20 12 82 72
Facsmilie: (00) (33) (3) 20 54 88 16
Airtech: (00) (33) (3) 20 54 46 15
Office Hours (GMT): Summer 07 30 – 10 30 and
12 00 – 15 00. Winter 08 30 – 11 30
and 13 00 – 16 00
Consul-General: Mr Clive Alderton
Vice-Consul (Commercial): Mr David Hinchliffe
Vice-Consul (Commercial): Mr John Gleave
Vice-Consul: Mrs Carol Vorobieff, MBE

Amiens
British Consulate
Telephone: (00) (33) (3) 22 72 08 48
Facsimile: (00) (33) (3) 22 82 23 01
Office Hours (GMT): Summer 06 30 – 10 30 and
12 00 – 16 00. Winter 07 30 – 11 30
and 13 00 – 17 00
Honorary British Consul: Mr Roger Davis

Boulogne-sur-Mer
British Consulate
Telephone: (00) (33) (3) 21 87 16 80
Facsimile: (00) (33) (3) 21 91 30 30
Office Hours (GMT) Summer 06 00 – 10 00 and
12 00 – 16 00. Winter 07 00 – 11 00
and 13 00 – 17 00
Honorary Consul: Mr Gerard Barron, MBE

Calais
British Consulate
Telephone: (00) (33) (3) 21 96 33 76
Facsimile: (00) (33) (3) 21 19 43 69
Office Hours (GMT) Summer 06 30 – 16 00.
Winter 07 30 – 17 00
Honorary Consul: Mr Jean-Michel Inglis, MBE

Dunkirk
British Consulate
Telephone: (00) (33) (3) 28 66 11 98
Facsimile: (00) (33) (3) 28 59 09 99
Office Hours (GMT): Summer 06 30 – 10 00 and
12 00 – 16 00. Winter 07 30 – 11 00
and 13 00 – 17 00
Honorary Consul: Mr Christopher R Baker, MBE

Lyon
British Consulate-General
24 rue Childebert, 69002 Lyon
Telephone: (00) (33) (4) 72 77 81 70
Facsimile: (00) (33) (4) 72 77 81 79
Airtech: (00) (33) (4) 78 38 27 77
Office Hours (GMT): Summer 07 00 – 10 30 and
12 00 – 15 30. Winter 08 00 – 11 30
and 13 00 – 16 30
Consul-General: Mr Colin C Bright
Consul (Commercial): Miss Miranda Knaggs
Vice-Consul: Mrs Jeanie Labaye

Clermont Ferrand
British Consul

Telephone: (00) (33) (4) 73 34 24 29
Honorary Consul: Mr Dominique Martinie

Marseille
British Consulate-General
24 Avenue de Prado, 13006 Marseilles
Telephone: (00) (33) (4) 91 15 72 10
Facsimile: (00) (33) (4) 91 37 47 06
Office Hours (GMT): Summer 07 00 – 10 30 and
12 00 – 15 30. Winter 08 00 – 11 30
and 13 00 – 16 30
Consul-General (also for Monaco):
Mr Simon Lever
Vice-Consul: Ms Donna Faure

Nice
By appointment only, please contact British
Consulate-General Marseille
Honorary Consul: Mrs Simone Paissoni

Montpellier (HC)
British Consulate
Telephone/Facsimile: (00) (33) (4) 67 15 52 07
Honorary Consul: Mr Norman J Paget

Paris
British Consulate-General
18bis rue d'Anjou 75008 Paris
(All mail should be sent to the British Embassy,
Paris)
Telephone: (00) (33) (1) 44 51 31 00
Facsimile: (00) (33) (1) 44 51 31 27
            (00) (33) (1) 44 51 31 28 (Visas)
Office Hours (GMT): Summer 07 30 – 11 00 and
12 30 – 16 00. Winter 08 30 – 12 00
and 13 30 – 17 00
Consul-General: Mr Jeffrey Thomas
Consul: Mr Brian West
Vice-Consul: Mr Stephen J Donnelly, MBE
Vice-Consul (Passport Officer): Mr Ian Gallacher
Vice-Consul (Immigration): Mr Michael Kearney
Vice-Consul (Immigration): Mrs Suzanne Groves
Vice-Consul (Immigration):
Mr Frederick Cracknell
Vice-Consul: Mr Simon M Taylor
Vice-Consul: Mr Mark Pettigrew

Cherbourg
British Consulate
Telephone: (00) (33) (2) 33 88 65 60
Facsimile: (00) (33) (2) 33 88 67 07
Honorary Consul: Mr Gérard R Caron, MBE

French Guiana (Cayenne)
British Consulate
Telephone: (00) (594) 31 10 34
Facsimile: (00) (594) 30 40 94
Honorary Consul: Mr Joseph G Nouh-Chaia MBE

French Polynesia (Papeete)
British Consulate
Telephone: (00) (689) 70 63 82
Facsimile: (00) (689) 42 00 50
Honorary Consul: Mr Marc Allain

Nantes
British Consulate
B P 22026

44020 NANTES
Telephone: (00) (33) (2) 51 72 72 60
Facsimile: (00) (33) (2) 40 47 36 92
Office Hours (GMT): 07 00 - 10 15 and
12 00 - 15 00
Honorary Consul: Mrs Angela M Stokes

Le Havre
British Consulate
B.P. 10515
76058 LE HAVRE
Telephone: (00) (33) (2) 35 19 78 88
Facsimile: (00) (33) (2) 35 19 78 98
Honorary Consul: Mme Nadine H Corbel

Lorient
British Consulate
Telephone: (00) (33) (2) 97 87 36 20
Facsimile: (00) (33) (2) 97 87 36 49
Honorary Consul: Mr Anthony M Le Saffre

Fort de France, Martinique
British Consulate
Telephone: (00) (596) 61 88 92
Facsimile: (00) (596) 61 33 89
Honorary Consul: Mme Alison J Ernoult

Guadeloupe
British Consulate
Telephone: (00) (590) 82 57 57
Facsimile: (00) (590) 82 89 33
Honorary Consul: Mr David A Wood

La Réunion
British Consulate
Telephone: (00) (33) (2) 62 34 75 76
Honorary Consul: Mr Gordon Smith

New Caledonia
British Consulate
Telephone: (00) (687) 27 36 27 or 28 21 53
Facsimile: (00) (687) 28 51 44
Honorary Consul: Mr Maxwell Shekleton

Saumur
British Consulate
Telephone: (00) (33) (2) 41 52 90 54
Facsimile: (00) (33) (2) 41 52 99 92
Consular Agent: Mr Khrisna C Lester

St Malo-Dinard
British Consulate
Telephone: (00) (33) (2) 23 18 30 30
Facsimile: (00) (33) (2) 99 40 64 42
Honorary Consul: Mrs Veronique Rondel

Tours
British Consulate
Telephone/Facsimile: (00) (33) (2) 47 43 50 58
Honorary Consul: Mr Brian J Cordery, OBE

GABON

Libreville
British Embassy (except where shown all staff
reside at Yaoundé)
Ambassador and Consul-General: Mr Richard
Wildash, LVO
First Secretary and Consul: Mr David Williams

Defence Attaché (resides at Kinshasa):
Lieutenant Colonel James R Charlesworth

British Consulate
c/o Brossette, BP 486,
Libreville
Telephone: (00) (241) 76 22 00/74 20 41
Facsimile: (00) (241) 76 57 89
Mobile: (00) (241) 75 86 36
Honorary Consul: Mr David Harwood, MBE

GAMBIA, THE

Banjul (SP – see page 120)
British High Commission
48 Atlantic Road, Fajara (PO Box 507), Banjul
FTN Code – 8540 + extn number
Telephone: (00) (220) 4495133, 4495134
Facsimile: (00) (220) 4496134
Airtech: (00) (220) 4494505
e-mail: bhcbanjul@gamtel.gm
Office Hours (GMT): Mon-Thurs 08 00 - 15 00
and Fri 08 00 - 13 00
High Commissioner: Mr E Jenkinson, OBE
Deputy High Commissioner: Mr R Rimmer
Defence Adviser (resides at Rabat):
Lieutenant Colonel S J A Lloyd, MBE
Third Secretary (Management/Consular):
Mr B Bulling
Third Secretary (Immigration): Mrs C Dogan
Third Secretary (Immigration): Mr N Hackett

**Department for International Development
Office**
c/o British High Commission
Banjul
Telephone: (00) (220) 4497537, 4495578
Facsimile: (00) (220) 4494127
e-mail: r-watt.dfid@qanet.gm
Head of DFID Office: Mr R Watt

GEORGIA

Tbilisi (SP – see page 120)
British Embassy
Sheraton Metechi Palace Hotel,
380003 Tbilisi
Telephone: (00) (995 32) 955497, 998447, 988796
Facsimile: (00) (995 32) 001065
Airtech: (00) (995 32) 775030
e-mail: british.embassy@caucasus.net
Office Hours (GMT): Mon-Fri 05 00 - 13 00
Ambassador: Mr Donald MacLaren
Deputy Head of Mission: Mr Rod MacKenna
Defence Attaché:
Lieutenant Colonel Christopher J Nunn, OBE, RM
First Secretary (Cultural): Ms Jo Bakowski
*First Secretary (Technical Management) (based in
Ankara):* Mr Paul Holmes
First Secretary (Political): Mr Michael W Seaman
Third Secretary (Political): Mr William Robinson
Third Secretary (Political): Mr Darren Woodcock
Third Secretary (Management/Vice Consul):
Mr Garth Robinson
Attaché (Immigration): Ms Karen Hennessy
Defence Assistant: Staff Sergeant Rob Hamling

GERMANY

Berlin
British Embassy
Wilhelmstrasse 70
10117 Berlin
FTN Code – 8340 + extn number
Telephone: (00) (49) (30) 20457 0
Facsimile: (00) (49) (30) 20457 571 (Ambassador)
20457 572 (DHM's Office)
20457 573 (Political)
20457 574 (Media)
20457 594 (Public Relations)
20457 575 (EU and Economics)
20457 576 (Labour, Social Affairs and Environment)
20457 577 (Commercial)
20457 578 (Management)
20457 579 (Consular)
20457 581 (Defence)
20457 582 (Defence Supply)
20457 347 (Agriculture)
20457 346 (Research/Technology)
Website: http://www.britischebotschaft.de
Office Hours (GMT): 08 00 – 12 00 and 13 00 – 16 30
Ambassador: Sir Peter Torry KCMG (101)
Deputy Head of Mission and Head of Political, Media and Public Affairs:
Mr Jeremy Cresswell CVO (151)
Counsellor (Research and Technology):
Mr Steve Plater (Resides Munich)
Counsellor and Head of EU and Economic Section: Ms Pamela Major (301)
Defence Attaché:
Brigadier Robert Pridham, OBE (401)
Counsellor (Labour): Miss Elaine Trewartha (310)
Political Counsellor: Mr David Woods(451)
First Secretary (Political External):
Mr Nick Alexander(223)
First Secretary (Economic): Mr Mike Bolton(321)
First Secretary and Head of Media:
Mr Jonathan Brenton (251)
First Secretary (Technical Management):
Mr Colin Buswell(521)
First Secretary (Agriculture): Mr Craig Egner(335)
Naval Attaché:
Captain Stephen R Gosden, RN (403)
First Secretary (Political External):
Mr Nigel Ingram(222)
First Secretary (Political Internal):
Mr John Kraus(211)
First Secretary (European Union):
Mr Paul Heardman(331)
First Secretary (Research and Technology):
Ms Helen Hughes McKay (338)
Air Attaché:
Group Captain John P Moloney, RAF (405)
First Secretary (Defence Supply):
Mr Ed O'Donnell(421)
First Secretary and Head of Public Relations:
Mr Paul O'Connor(223)
Military Attaché: Colonel Mike C Parish, OBE (407)
First Secretary (Technical Works Officer):
Mr Steve Pink(559)

First Secretary and Head of Management:
Mr Mike Purves (501)
First Secretary (Environment):
Ms Lynn Sheppard (341)
First Secretary (Fiscal Liaison Officer):
Mr Mike Stevens(241)
First Secretary (Political External):
Mr Paul Williams(221)
First Secretary and Head of Trade and Investment:
Mr Ian Worthington OBE (451)
British Council Director: Mrs Kathryn Board
Second Secretary (European Union):
Mrs Sophie Goodrick (332)
Second Secretary (Drugs Liaison Officer):
Mr Chris Humphrey (407)
Second Secretary (Political):
Mr Philip Owen (227)
Second Secretary (Technical Management):
Mr Denis Price (522)
Second Secretary (PS/Ambassador):
Mr Simon Ferrand (102)
Second Secretary (Management/Consular):
Miss Rita Wisker(531)
Third Secretary (Consular/Management):
Mrs Trudy Curry (541)

Fiscal Liaison Office
Kaiser-Friedrich Strasse 19
53113 Bonn
Telephone: (00) (49) (228) 24 99 211/212
Facsimile: (00) (49) (228) 24 99 222
Office Hours (GMT): 08 00 – 12 00 and 13 00 – 16 30
Second Secretary (Fiscal Liaison Officer):
Mr Steve Pope

Leipzig
British Trade Office
Gohliser Str 7
0-04105 Leipzig
Telephone: (00) (49) 0341 564 9672, 564 9674
Facsimile: (00) (49) 0341 564 9673
Commercial Officer: Frau K Rath
Commercial Assistant: Frau Pia Mann

Düsseldorf
British Consulate-General
Yorckstrasse 19, 40476 Düsseldorf
(Only mail from United Kingdom can be sent to Box 2002, BFPO 105)
Telephone: (00) (49) (211) 9448-0 (9448 + Ext – see entries)
Direct Lines: 9448 226 Passport Section
9448 289 Visa Section
9448 222 Commercial Section
9448 245 Press and Public Affairs
Facsimile: (00) (49) (211) 48 63 59 Commercial and Investment Sections
48 81 90 Press, Passport, Consular and Management
48 86 03 Visa Section
Airtech: 94 48 242
e-mail: Consular.Section@fco.gov.uk (Passport Section)
Visa.Section@fco.gov.uk (Visa Section)
Commercial.Section@fco.gov.uk (Commercial Section)

Website: www.britischebotschaft.de (for British
Nationals resident in Germany) / (Visa enquiries)
www.uktradeinvest.de (trade development in
Germany)
www.investuk.de (Investment promotion in
Germany)
Office Hours (GMT): Winter: Mon-Thurs: 07 30 -
11 30 and 12 30 - 16 00. Fri: 07 30 - 11 30
and 12 30 - 15 30. Summer: Mon-Thurs: 06 30 -
10 30 and 11 30 - 15 00, Fri: 06 30 - 10 30
and 11 30 - 14 30
*Consul-General and Director of Trade and
Investment in Germany (201):*
Mr W Boyd McCleary
*Deputy Consul-General and Deputy Director for
Trade and Investment in Germany (202):*
Mr Tim Brownbill
Consul (Management) (231): Mr John K Hague
Consul (Investment) (207): Mr Peter Ivey
Consul (Commercial) (203): Mr Bill Kelly
Consul (Consular/Immigration) (260):
Ms Creena M Lavery
Vice-Consul (Commercial) (208):
Mr Scott Melling
Vice-Consul (Immigration) (264):
Mrs Caroline Boyce
Vice-Consul (Consular/Passports) (234):
Ms Tracey Caulfield
Vice-Consul (Consular) (255): Mr David Kelly
Commercial Officer (CCU) (219):
Mrs Sylvia A Tunmore
Commercial Officer (209): Mr Dirk Mokwinski
Commercial Officer (213): Mr Peter Foster
Inward Investment (205): Mr Christian Fehling
Inward Investment (182): Mr Georg H Rehberg
PR and Marketing (153): Ms Tanja Ziemus
Press and Public Affairs (223): Mr Thomas Wittek

Frankfurt
British Consulate-General
Triton Haus
Bockenheimer Landstrasse 42
60323 Frankfurt-am-Main
Mail from United Kingdom only should be
addressed:
British Consulate-General, Frankfurt
PO Box 2009, BFPO 10
FTN Code - 8345 + extn number
Telephone: (00) (49) (69) 17 000 20
Facsimile: (00) (49) (69) 72 95 53
Office Hours (GMT): Mon-Thurs: 07 30 - 12 00
and 13 00 - 16 00
Fri: 07 30 - 12 00 and 12 30 - 14 30
Consul-General: Mr Neil C Paterson (2250)
Consul (Consular/Management):
Mrs Carol A Schumann (2222)
Vice-Consul: Mrs Christine Townsend (2225)
Trade Officer: Herr Rudolf Schneider (2237)
Trade Officer: Frau Sabine Schnurbusch (2239)
Press and Public Affairs Officer:
Dr Wolfgang Dobler (2235)
Attaché: Mr David Connelly (2236)
Attaché: Mr David Hollingberry (2228)
Attaché: Mr Robert Barber (2257)
(Visa and Passport work is centralised in
Dusseldorf.)

Hamburg
British Consulate-General
Harvestehuder Weg 8a, 20148 Hamburg
FTN Code - 8343 + extn number
Telephone: (00) (49) (40) 448 0320
Facsimile: (00) (49) (40) 410 7259
Airtech: (00) (49) (40) 448 032 31
Office Hours (GMT): 07 30 - 11 30
and 12 30 - 16 00
Consul-General: Mr Timothy Collard (2011)
Consul (Management/Consular):
Mr Anthony J Hackett (2030)
Vice-Consul (Consular):
Mrs Mary Sanderson (2035)
Commercial Officer: Herr Thomas Siems (2033)
Commercial Officer: Mr John Holway (2022)
Commercial Officer: Herr Bernd Klein (2023)
Press and Public Affairs Officer:
Ms Jo Dawes (2039)
(Visa and Passport work is centralised in
Dusseldorf.)

Bremen
British Consulate
Herrlichkeiten 6, Postfach 10 38 60, 28199 Bremen
Telephone: (00) (49) (421) 590708
Facsimile: (00) (49) (421) 5907109
Office Hours (GMT): 07 30 - 11 30
and 13 30 - 14 30
Honorary Consul: Herr H-C Enge

Hanover
British Consulate
Hannover Ruchversicherungs AG
Karl-Wiechart-Allee 50
30625 Hannover
Telephone: (00) (511) 3883808
Facsimile: (00) (511) 5604690
Office Hours (GMT): 06 30 - 10 00 and
10 30 - 12 00
Honorary Consul: Herr W Zeller

Kiel
British Consulate
United Canal Agency GmbH
Schleuse, Maklerstrasse 11-14, 24159 Kiel
Telephone: (00) (49) 431 331971
Facsimile: (00) (49) 431 3053746
Telex: 299829 (a/b UBCK D)
Office (GMT): 06 30 - 11 00 and 12 00 - 15 00
Honorary Consul: Herr J Petersen

Munich
British Consulate-General
Bürkleinstrasse 10
D - 80538 München
(Mail from United Kingdom only should be
addressed:
British Consulate-General, Munich
PO Box 2010, BFPO 105)
Telephone: (00) (49) (89) 211090
Facsimile: 21109 166 Consul-General
21109 166 Press andPublic Affairs
21109 166 Research and Technology
Section
21109 155 Commercial Section
21109 155 Investment Section

21109 144 Management Section
21109 144 Consular Section
Office Hours (GMT): 07 30 - 11 00 and
12 00 - 16 00
Consul-General and Counsellor R and T:
Mr Steve Plater
Consul (Trade and Investment) and DHM:
Mr Hugh Taylor
Consul: Mr Geoff Deane
Consul (Consular/Management): Mrs Milli Timsit
Vice-Consul (Trade): Mr Charles Pattinson
Press and Public Affairs Officer:
Mrs Birgit Dammert
Trade Officer: Dr Astrid Ritter Heinrich
Investment Officer: Ms Heike Bieber
Vice-Consul (Consular): Mrs Christine Ruhstorfer
Research and Technology Officer:
Ms Muzinée Kistenfeger
(Visa and Passport work is centralised in
Dusseldorf.)

Nuremburg

British Consulate
M Schmitt and Sohn GmbH and Co
Hadermuhle 9-15
D - 90402 Nuremburg
Telephone: (00) (49) (911) 2404-303
Facsimile: (00) (49) (911) 2404-111
Honorary Consul: Dr J Schmitt

Stuttgart

British Consulate-General
Breite Strasse 2, 70173
Stuttgart
Telephone: (00) (49) (711) 16 26 9-0
Facsimile: (00) (49) (711) 16 26 9-30
Office Hours (GMT): As Frankfurt
Consul-General: Mr Mark P Twigg
Commercial Officer: Frau A Seidler
Commercial Officer: Frau B Koch
Pro-Consul: Mrs M Braun

GHANA

Accra

British High Commission
Osu Link, off Gamel Abdul Nasser Avenue
(PO Box 296), Accra
FTN Code – 8541 + extn number
Telephone: (00) (233) (21) 7010650, 221665
          (24 hours)
          7010721 Immigration Section
Facsimile: (00) (233) (21) 7010655
          221715 Immigration Section
Airtech: (00) (233) (21)242936
e-mail: high.commission.accra@fco.gov.uk
Website: www.britishhighcommission.gov.uk/ghana
Office Hours (GMT): 07 45 - 14 45
Immigration Section Public Hours 07 30 - 10 30
Consular Section Public Hours 07 30 - 13 30
High Commissioner: Mr Gordon Wetherell
Deputy High Commissioner: Mr Robert Gwynn
Defence Adviser:
Lieutenant Colonel Jonathan A F Howard
First Secretary (Commercial): Ms Sarah Stevenson
First Secretary (Senior Management Officer):
Mr David Jones

First Secretary (Immigration): Mr Andy Holden
British Council Director: Mr John Payne
*Second Secretary (Political, Press and Public
Affairs):* Mr Gary Nicholls
Second Secretary (Environment): Ms Farida Shaikh
Second Secretary (Immigration/Consular):
Mrs Caroline Cross
Second Secretary (Immigration):
Mrs Margaret Brown
Second Secretary (Immigration): Mrs Gillian Elliot
Second Secretary (Airline Liaison Officer):
Mr Julian Kennett
Second Secretary (Technical Management Officer):
Mr Roger Russell
Third Secretary (Deputy Management Officer):
Mr Bernie Andrews
Third Secretary (Immigration): Ms Stacey Nichols
Third Secretary (Immigration):
Mr Andrew Brimacombe
Third Secretary (Immigration): Ms Fiona Hayward
Third Secretary (Immigration): Mr Ian Abbott
Third Secretary (Immigration): Mr Steve Scott
Third Secretary (Immigration): Mr Rob Tait
Third Secretary (Immigration): Mrs Angela Walters
Third Secretary (Immigration): (Vacant)
Third Secretary (Immigration): Mrs Fiona McPhail
Third Secretary (Immigration):
Mrs Karen Simpson
Third Secretary (Immigration): Mr Rob Dixon
Third Secretary (Immigration): Mr Tim Galvin

Department for International Development (DFID) Ghana

Masida House
Sankara Interchange
PO Box 296, Accra
FTN Code - 8774 + extn number
Telephone: (00) (233) (21) 253243
Facsimile: (00) (233) (21) 253244
Head of DFID Ghana: Mr John Winter
Deputy Head: Ms Emma Spicer
Office Manager: Mr Neil Mullin
Economic Adviser: Mr Paul Walters
Education Adviser: Mr Charles Kirkcaldy
Engineering Adviser: Ms Amanda Duff
Governance Adviser: Karijn de Jong
Health Adviser: Sandy Baldwin
HIV/AIDS Adviser: Mr Victor Bampoe
Private Sector Development Adviser:
Ms Mavis Owusu-Gyamfi
Rural Livelihoods Adviser: Mr Ben Davies
Social Development Adviser: Ms Kirsty Mason
Deputy Programme Manager: Ms Denise Hill
Deputy Programme Manager: Mr Rex Quaye
Deputy Programme Manager:
Ms Galina Okartei-Akko
Deputy Programme Manager: Ms Kate Alexander
Assistant Programme Manager (UK based):
Mr Yoland Bewick

GREECE

Athens

British Embassy
1 Ploutarcou Street, 106 75 Athens
FTN Code - 8542 + extn number (switchboard:
8542 1000)

Telephone: (00) (30) 210 727 2600
          Night (RSO): (00) (30) 210 723 7727
          724 1331
Facsimile: (00) (30) 210 727 2734 Political and
          Commercial Section
          2720 Consular Section
          2876 Management Section
          2723 Chancery/Political
          2743 Press and Public Affairs
          2750 Olympic Section
          2725 Residence
          2727 Fiscal and Drugs Liaison Section
Airtech: (00) (30) 210 722 7122
e-mail: information.athens@fco.gov.uk
Website: http://www.british-embassy.gr
Office Hours (GMT): 06 00 - 13 00
Ambassador: Mr Simon L Gass, CMG, CVO
*Counsellor, Consul-General and Deputy Head of
Mission:* Mr Andrew J Noble, LVO
Counsellor: Mr Nicholas Langman
Defence and Naval Attaché:
Captain John R Wills, RN
Military and Air Attaché:
Colonel Mark Blatherwick, MBE, GM
Counsellor (Cultural) (British Council Director):
Mr Desmond Lauder
First Secretary (Economic): Mr David S Gordon-
MacLeod
First Secretary (Political, Press and Public Affairs):
Mrs Francesca J G Flessati, OBE
First Secretary (External): Mr Daniel Tarshish
First Secretary (Defence Supply): Mr John Bewley
First Secretary (Management):
Mr Keith McMahon, MBE
First Secretary (Commercial): Mr Frank Jones
First Secretary and Consul: Mr Donald Holder
First Secretary (Cultural Affairs): (Vacant)
Fiscal Liaison Officer: Mr Matthew Clark
Drugs Liaison Officer: Mr Nick Jepson
Olympic *Attaché:* Ms Adele Taylor, MBE
Second Secretary and Vice-Consul:
Mr Simon Batty
Second Secretary (Political/Information): Ms
Lynda Burns
Second Secretary: Mr Paul Weldon
Second Secretary (Economic):
Miss Margaret M Belof
Third Secretary (Political): Mr Rex Amos
Third Secretary (Management):
Ms Joanne Crabtree
Third Secretary and Vice-Consul:
Mrs Patsy McQuilton

Corfu
British Vice-Consulate
Menekratous 1, 491 00 Corfu
Telephone: (00) (30) 26610 30055
Facsimile: (00) (30) 26610 37995
e-mail: corfu@british-consulate.gr
Vice-Consul: Ms Lucy Steele

Heraklion (Crete)
British Consulate
16 Papa-Alexandrou Street
712 02 Heraklion
Telephone: (00) (30) 2810 224012

Facsimile: (00) (30) 2810 243935
e-mail: crete@british-consulate.gr
Consul: Mrs Marion R Tzanaki, MBE

Kos
British Vice-Consulate
8, Annetas Laoumtzi Street,
853 00 Kos
Telephone: (00) (30) 22420 21549
Facsimile: (00) (30) 22420 25948
e-mail: kos@british-consulate.gr
Honorary Vice-Consul: Mr Konstantinos Kourounis

Patras
British Vice-Consulate
Votsi 2
262 21 Patras
Telephone: (00) (30) 2610 277329
Facsimile: (00) (30) 2610 225334
Honorary Vice-Consul:
Mrs Marie Jeanne Morphy-Karatza, MBE

Rhodes
British Consulate
Pavlou Mela 3
PO Box 47
851 00 Rhodes
Telephone: (00) (30) 22410 27247 or 22005
Facsimile: (00) (30) 22410 22615
e-mail: rhodes@british-consulate.gr
Honorary Consul:
Mr Dimitrios E Demetriades, MBE

Thessaloniki
British Consulate
21 Aristotelous Street
546 24 Thessaloniki
Telephone: (00) (30) 2310 278006
Facsimile: (00) (30) 2310 283868
e-mail: salonika@british-consulate.gr
Consul: Mrs Sarah Edwards-Economidi

Syros
British Vice-Consulate
8 Akti Petrou Ralli,
Hermoupolis
841 00 Syros
Telephone: (00) (30) 22810 82232 or 88922
Facsimile: (00) (30) 22810 83293
Honorary Vice-Consul: Mrs Virginia Parissi-
Thermou

Zakynthos
British Vice-Consulate
5 Foskolos Street
291 00 Zakynthos
Telephone: (00) (30) 26950 22906 or 48030
Facsimile: (00) (30) 26950 23769
e-mail: zakynthos@british-consulate.gr
Honorary Vice-Consul:
Mrs Evridiki (Vicky) Vitsou-Kotsoni

GRENADA

St George's (SP – see page 120)
British High Commission, Netherlands Building,
Grand Anse,
St George's, Grenada

Telephone: (00) (1) (473) 440 3536, 440 3222
Facsimile: (00) (1) (473) 440 4939
e-mail: bhcgrenada@caribsurf.com
Office Hours (GMT): Mon - Thurs: 12 00 - 17 00
and 17 30 - 20 00. Fri: 12 00 - 17 00
* *High Commissioner:* Mr John White
Resident British Commissioner: Mr Vic Wallis
* *Deputy High Commissioner:* Mr Rob Holland
* *Defence Adviser:* Captain Steve G Wilson, RN
* *First Secretary (Chancery):* Mr Graham Honey
* *First Secretary (Management):* Ms Ros Day
* *Second Secretary (Chancery/Information):*
Mr Nick J Pyle, MBE
** *Second Secretary (Technical Works):*
Mr David Holmes
* *Second Secretary (Chancery):* Mr Rick Gomez
* *Third Secretary:* Mr Philip Barker
* *Third Secretary (Immigration):*
Mr Mark Harrison
**Resides at Bridgetown*
***Resides at Mexico City*

GUATEMALA

Guatemala City (SP – see page 120)
British Embassy
16 Calle 00-55, Zona 10
Edificio Torre Internacional, Nivel 11
Guatemala City
FTN Code - 8459 + 1000 (Receptionist)
2011 (PA to HMA and DHM)
2019 (Commercial)
2009 (PPA and Development)
2020 (Management)
2012 (Consular and Visa)
Telephone: (00) (502) 367 5425-29
Facsimile: (00) (502) 367 5430
e-mail: embassy@intelnett.com
Office Hours (GMT): Mon-Thurs 14 30 – 18 30
and 19 30 - 2300. Fri 14 30 – 18 30
Ambassador (also Ambassador (Non Resident) to
El Salvador and Tegucigalpa):
Mr Richard D Lavers (2032)
First Secretary, Consul and Deputy Head of
Mission: Mr Kevin A Garvey (2031)
Defence Attaché:
Colonel Ian Blair-Pilling, OBE (2016)
First Secretary (DLO) (resides at Panama City):
Mr Alan Pamplin
Second Secretary (Management/Consular):
Mr Colin Gracey (2013)
Second Secretary (Chancery):
Mrs Susie Kitchens (2036)
Second Secretary (DLO) (resides at Panama City):
Mr Gary Foster
Third Secretary: Mr Amar Shazad (2017)

GUINEA

Conakry
British Embassy (Resident at the BHC, Freetown)
Ambassador: Miss Helen M Horn, MBE
Defence Attaché:
Lieutenant Colonel Desmond J A Bergin, OBE
Second Secretary (Management): Mr Jem Convery

Conakry
British Consulate-General
BP 834 Conakry
Telephone: (00) (224) 45 58 07 / 45 60 20 (Office)
(224) 45 29 59 (Home)
Facsimile: (00) (224) 45 60 20
Satellite Phone: 00 874 762 471260
Satellite Fax: 00 874 762 471262
e-mail: britcon.oury@biasy.net
(Resident in Conakry)
Consul: Mr Les Hartley
Commercial Officer/Press Assistant:
Mr George Tounkara
Consular/Management Assistant: Mr Oury Barry

GUINEA-BISSAU

Bissau
British Embassy (all staff resident in Dakar)
Ambassador: Mr Peter Newall
Deputy Head of Mission and Consul:
Mr Derek Levoir
Vice-Consul/ECO: Ms Christine Johnson
Management Officer: Mr Nick Faulkner

Bissau
British Honorary Consulate
Mavegro Int., CP100, Bissau
Telephone: (00) (245) 20 12 24/20 12 16 (Office)
(00) (245) 20 16 07 (Home)
Facsimile: (00) (245) 20 12 65
e-mail: mavegro@gttelecom.gw
mavegro@hotmail.com
Honorary Consul: Mr Jan Van Maanen

GUYANA

Georgetown (SP – see page 120)
British High Commission
44 Main Street, (PO Box 10849), Georgetown
FTN Code – 8543 + extn number
Telephone: (00) (592) (22) 65881/2/3/4
Facsimile: 53555
Management/Commercial/Development
50671 Immigration and Consular
37321 Chancery
68818 (Airtech)
e-mail: firstname.surname@fco.gov.uk
Office Hours (GMT): 11 30 - 18 30
High Commissioner: Mr Steve J Hiscock
Deputy High Commissioner: Mr Malcolm Kirk
Defence Adviser (resides at Bridgetown):
Lieutenant Commander Steve G Wilson, RN
First Secretary (Development): Mr Jonathan Baxter
Second Secretary (Management): Mr Graham Birse
Second Secretary (Development):
Mrs Lynn MacAulay
Second Secretary (Chancery) (resides in Port of
Spain): Mr Tony Reader
Second Secretary (Chancery/Commercial):
Mr Richard Cox
Third Secretary (Immigration/Consular):
Mr Neil Frape
Third Secretary (Technical Management) (resides
at Bridgetown): Mr Phil Barker
Personal Assistant to High Commissioner:
Mr Matthew Nottingham

HAITI

Port-au-Prince
British Embassy
Ambassador: (resides in Santo Domingo):
Mr Andrew R Ashcroft
Second Secretary and Consul: (resides in Santo Domingo): Mr Kevin Shaughnessy

Port-au Prince
British Consulate
Hotel Montana (PO Box 1302), Port-au-Prince
Telephone: (00) (509) 257 3969
Facsimile: (00) (509) 257 4048
e-mail: britcon@transnethaiti.com
Office Hours (GMT): 13 00 - 18 00
Vice-Consul: Mrs Allison Insley-Madsen

HOLY SEE

British Embassy (SP – see page 120)
91 Via dei Condotti, I-00187, Rome
Telephone: (00) (39) (06) 699 23561
Facsimile: (00) (39) (06) 6994 0684
Office Hours (GMT): All Year: 08 00 - 12 00 and
13 00 - 16 00
Except:- Jul-Aug 07 00 - 13 00
Ambassador: Mrs K F Colvin

HONDURAS

Tegucigalpa
British Embassy Closed
(Please refer to Guatemala City)

British Consulate
Honorary Consul: (To be confirmed)

British Development Office in Honduras
DFID Office
Colonia Palmira
Avenida Republica de Mexico #2402
Tegucigalpa MDC
Telephone: (00) (504) 221 2109, 2126, 2547, 2588
Facsimile: (00) (504) 221 1959
e-mail: v-heard@dfid.gov.uk
Office Hours: Mon-Fri 08 00 – 17 00
Head of British Development Office: Mr Vic Heard

San Pedro Sula
British Consulate
2° Calle, 18 y 19 Ave. N.O. Casa # 182
Colonia Moderna
Apartado Postal No. 63
San Pedro Sula, Cortés
Telephone: (00) (504) 550 2337
Facsimile: (00) (504) 550-2486
Office Hours (GMT): 08 00 - 11 30
14 00 - 16 00 (local time) – Monday to Friday
inclusive
Honorary Consul: Mr Edgardo Dumas

HUNGARY

Budapest
British Embassy, Harmincad u. 6., Budapest 1051
FTN Code - 8478 + extn or 1000 for switchboard
Telephone: (00) (36) (1) 266 2888

Facsimile: (00) (36) (1) 266 0907
Management/PPA/Programmes (FTN - 8478 6221),
429 6360 Consular/Visa/Commercial (FTN - 8478
6360), 429 6301 Political (FTN - 8478 6301)
Airtech: (00) (36) (1) 429 6299
e-mail: info@britemb.hu
Website: http://www.britishembassy.hu
Office Hours (GMT): Summer 07 00 - 1500,
Winter 08 00 - 16 00
Ambassador: Mr John Nichols (6211)
Counsellor and Deputy Head of Mission:
Mr Michael Ward (6212)
Defence Attaché:
Colonel Anthony Patrick Burnside (6220)
Cultural Attaché: (British Council Director)
(Tel. 478 4700): Mr Jim McGrath
First Secretary (Commercial):
Miss Debbie Goldthorpe, LVO (6250)
First Secretary (Political): Mr Robert Dear (6203)
First Secretary (Political):
Mr Simon Wilson, OBE (6225)
First Secretary (Management/HM Consul):
Mr Mike Goodwin (6230)
First Secretary (Political):
Mr Mark Morgan, MBE (6205)
First Secretary (Technical Works Officer):
Ms Sandra Agnew (6327)
First Secretary (Cultural) (Tel. 478 4700):
Mr Paul Clementson
First Secretary (Cultural) (Tel. 478 4700):
Mr Nigel Bellingham
Assistant Defence Attaché:
Squadron Leader Alan Fisher (6227)
Second Secretary (PPA and Political):
Mr Jason Moore (6350)
Second Secretary (Commercial):
Ms Jane Sanders (6287)
Second Secretary (Political):
Mr Nick Catsaras (6204)
Second Secretary (Technical Management):
Mr Paul Davies (6215)
Second Secretary (Technical Management):
Mr Terry Wiltshire (6216)
Second Secretary (Airline Liaison Officer):
Mr Steve Brown (6249)
Second Secretary (Organised Crime Liaison Officer): Mr Steve Bosanquet (6377)
Vice-Consul and Entry Clearance Officer:
Mr Mark Rush (6240)
Third Secretary (Management):
Mr Richard Homer (6231)

ICELAND

Reykjavik (SP – see page 120)
British Embassy
Laufasvegur 31, 101 Reykjavik
Postal Address: PO Box 460, 121 Reykjavik
Telephone: (00) (354) 550 5100
Facsimile: (00) (354) 550 5105
Airtech: (00) (354) 550 5104
e-mail: britemb@centrum.is
Office Hours (GMT): Mon-Thurs 08 30 - 16 00,
Fri 08 30 - 15 30
Ambassador and Consul-General:
Mr Alp Mehmet, MVO

Deputy Head of Mission and Consul:
Mr Simon Minshull
Trade and Investment Officer:
Mrs Elsa Einarsdottir
First Secretary (Inward Investment) (resides in Stockholm): Mr Adrian Pinder

Akureyri
British Vice-Consulate
Central Hospital (Fjordungssjukrahusid a Akureyri)
v/Eyrarlandsveg PO Box 380
IS-602 Akureyri
Telephone: (00) (354) 463 0102
Facsimile: (00) (354) 462 4621
Office Hours (GMT): 09 00 - 12 00
and 13 00 - 17 00
Honorary Vice-Consul: Mr Halldor Jonsson

INDIA

New Delhi
British High Commission
Chanakyapuri, New Delhi 110021
FTN Code – 8414 + extn number
Telephone: (00) (91) (11) 2687 2161
Facsimile: (00) (91) (11) 2687 2882
　　　　Management Dept
　　　　2687 0068 Political Dept
　　　　2687 0062 Economic and
　　　　Commercial Dept
　　　　2687 0065 Press and Public Affairs
　　　　2687 0060 Visa Dept
　　　　2611 4603 Defence Dept
　　　　2611 6094 Consular Dept
　　　　2467 0234 Estates
　　　　2410 5783 International Pension
　　　　Service Officer
　　　　2687 9430 Global Procurement
Airtech:　　(00) (91) (11) 2611 4601
e-mail: postmaster.NewDelhi@fco.gov.uk
Office Hours (GMT): Mon – Fri 03 30 - 07 30 and
08 30 - 11 30
High Commissioner: Sir Michael A Arthur, KCMG
Minister and Deputy High Commissioner:
Mr Mark Runacres
Defence and Military Adviser:
Brigadier Ian D O Rees
Counsellor (Political): Mr Dominic Martin
Counsellor (Economic and Commercial):
Mr John Dennis
Counsellor: Mr Stuart Morley, OBE
Counsellor (Management): Mr Ian Kydd
Naval and Air Adviser:
Group Captain Ian M Draper, RAF
First Secretary (Medical Officer):
Dr John Llewellyn
First Secretary (Press and Public Affairs):
Mr Gerry McCrudden, MBE
First Secretary (Commercial): Mr Peter Stephenson
First Secretary (Political): Mr David Quarrey
First Secretary (Internal): Mr Peter Holland
First Secretary (Science and Technology):
Ms Sarah Bamber
First Secretary (Environment and Trade Policy):
Dr David McMahon
First Secretary (Immigration/Consular):
Mr Chris Dix, OBE

First Secretary (Estate Manager):
Mr Andrew Lelliott
First Secretary (Management):
Mr Michael Holmes, MVO
First Secretary (ALO Regional Manager):
Ms Janet Battersby
First Secretary (Defence Supply): Mr Lee Griffiths
First Secretary (Technical Management):
Mr Barry Vargas
First Secretary (Technical Works):
Mr Gavin Thomas
First Secretary (Consular): Mr Paul Baines
Assistant Defence Adviser:
Lieutenant Commander Duncan Foster, RN
Second Secretary (Political): Ms Emma Stanton
Second Secretary (Political):
The Hon. R William Stonor
Second Secretary (Political): Ms Katherine Jones
Second Secretary (Technical Management):
Mr Terence Watson
Second Secretary (Immigration):
Ms Margaret Partridge
Second Secretary (Immigration): Mr Steve Burns
Second Secretary (Commercial):
Mr Tom Marchbanks
Second Secretary (Commercial): Mr Neil Brigden
Second Secretary (Science and Technology):
Mr Thomas Mark Tomlinson
Second Secretary (Management): Mr Peter Carr
Second Secretary (Security Officer):
Mr Robbie Robinson
Second Secretary (Airline Liaison Officer):
Mr David Westgate
Third Secretary (Economic and Commercial):
Mr Danny Wells
Third Secretary (Commercial): Mr Alistair Elder
Third Secretary (Political): Mr Eric Taylor
Third Secretary (Political): Mr John Bradshaw
Third Secretary (Consular): Ms Susan Wilson
Attaché (International Pension Service Officer):
Ms Helen Ibbott

New Delhi
DFID (Department For International Development)
India
B-28 Tara Crescent
Qutab Institutional Area
New Delhi 110 016
FTN Code – 8772 + extn number
Telephone: (00) (91) (11) 26529123
Facsimile: (00) (91) (11) 26529296
Minister (Development) and Head, DFIDI:
Ms Charlotte Seymour-Smith
Deputy Head DFIDI: Mr Rick Woodham
First Secretary (Economic):
Mr Andrew Kenningham
First Secretary (Environment): Mr Ian Curtis
First Secretary (Social Development):
Dr Dennis Pain
First Secretary (Development): Mr Alex Kremer
First Secretary (Governance): Ms Judith Kent
First Secretary (Governance): Ms Sylvia Bluck
First Secretary (Development): Ms Sally Taylor
First Secretary (Development):
Ms Elizabeth Burgess
First Secretary (Economic): Mr Shan Mitra

First Secretary (Environment): Mr Sean Doolan
First Secretary (Education):
Mr Roger Cunningham
First Secretary (Social Development):
Mr Arjan De Haan
First Secretary (Management): Mr Peter Little
First Secretary (Contracts/Procurement):
Mr William Starbuck
First Secretary (Health): Mr Desmond Whyms
First Secretary (Health): Ms Joanna Reid
First Secretary (Urban Development):
Mr Peter Smith
First Secretary (Rural Livelihoods):
Mr Kevin Crockford
First Secretary (Rural Livelihoods):
Ms Catherine Arnold
First Secretary (Rural Livelihoods):
Mr Ken Desouza
First Secretary (Economic): Mr Phil Crook
Second Secretary (Management): Mr Neil McKie
Second Secretary (Development): Ms Anna Lake
Second Secretary (Development): Mr Steve Burton
Second Secretary (Development): Mr Colin Clark
Second Secretary (Economic):
Loga Gnanasambantham

British Council Division
17 Kasturba Gandhi Marg, New Delhi 110001
Telephone: (00) (91) (11) 23711401
Facsimile: (00) (91) (11) 23710717
e-mail: delhi.enquiry@in.britishcouncil.org
Minister (Cultural Affairs): Mr Edmund Marsden
Counsellor (Cultural Affairs): Dr Morna Nance
First Secretary (Resources Management):
Ms Rachel Hewitt
First Secretary (Education): Mr John Nance
First Secretary (Education Projects):
Ms Jacqui Allan
First Secretary (English Language Education):
Ms Alison Sriparam
First Secretary (Education Services):
Mr Mark Walker

Mumbai
Office of the British Deputy High Commissioner
Maker Chambers IV, 222 Jamnalal Bajaj Road,
(PO Box 11714) Nariman Point, Mumbai 400 021
FTN Code – 8413 + extn number
Telephone: (00) (91) (22) 5650 2222
Facsimile: (00) (91) (22) 2202 7940
e-mail: postmaster@bombay.mail.fco.gov.uk
Office Hours (GMT): 02 30 - 07 30 and 08 30 -
10 30
Deputy High Commissioner (ext 2240):
Mr Ian Hughes
First Secretary (Commercial) (ext 2232):
Ms Helen Deas
First Secretary (British Council Director):
Mr Paul Smith
First Secretary (Consular/Management) (ext 2219):
Ms Allison Marriott
First Secretary (Immigration) (ext 2143):
Mrs Mandy Ivemy
Second Secretary (Drug Liaison Officer) (ext 2238): Mr Simon Sutcliffe

Second Secretary (Inward Investment) (ext 2231):
Mr Mark Dolan
Second Secretary (Commercial) (ext 2250):
Ms Claire Tuhey
Second Secretary (Immigration) (ext 2145):
Ms Marie-Louise Archer
Second Secretary (Immigration) (ext 2111):
Mr Rafi Husain
Second Secretary (Airline Liaison Officer) (ext 2107): Mr Robert Smith
Third Secretary (Management) (ext 2218):
Mr Andy McFarlin
Attaché (Consular) (ext 2149): Mr Glyn Bottrell

Ahmedabad
British Trade Office
4th Floor, 404 Kaivanna Building
Near Ambawadi Circle
Panchwati
Ahmedabad 380 006
Telephone: (00) (91) (79) 6467138
Facsimile: (00) (91) (79) 6403537
e-mail: btoabad@icenet.net
Commercial Information Officer:
Milind Godbole

Pune
British Library
917/1 Fergusson College Road
Shivaji Nagar
Pune 411 004
Telephone:
Facsimile: (00) (91) (20) 5671580
e-mail: bicpune@vsnl.com
Commercial Officer: Mr Shantanu Parvati

Goa
British Tourists' Assistance Office
S-13/14, Dempo Towers
Ground Floor, Patto Plaza
Panaji, Goa 403 001
Telephone: (00) (91) (832) 243 8897 or 8734
Facsimile: (00) (91) (832) 564 1297
e-mail: bcagoa@goatelecom.com
British Liaison Officer: Mrs Shilpa Caldeira

Kolkata
British Deputy High Commission
1A Ho Chi Minh Sarani, Kolkata,
West Bengal 700071
Telephone: (00) (91) (33) 22885172, 22885173,
            22885174, 22885175, 22885176
            22885909 Deputy High Commissioner
            22883681 Press and Public Affairs
            22886536, 22882578
            (after office hours)
Facsimile: (00) (91) (33) 22883435 General
            22883683 Deputy High Commissioner
            22882515 Press and Public Affairs
            22883996 Visa Department
            22885177 Consular Department
Airtech: 22885010
e-mail: Postmaster.Calcutta@fco.gov.uk
Office Hours (GMT): 03 30 - 07 30 and 08 30 -
11 30
Deputy High Commissioner: Dr Andrew Hall
Second Secretary: Mr Paul Walsh

Third Secretary (Immigration and Consular):
Mr John Hamilton
Third Secretary (Immigration): Mr Gary Stilgoe

Chennai
Office of the British Deputy High Commissioner
in Southern India
20 Anderson Road, Chennai 600 006
FTN Code – 8578 + 1000 for switchboard
Telephone: (00) (91) (44) 52192151
52192308/2310 Visa Office
28525002 British Council Division
Facsimile: (00) (91) (44) 52192321/28269004
Commercial
52192322/28203790 Management/PPA
52192320/28275130 Visa
28523234 British Council Division
e-mail: bdhcchen@vsnl.com
Office Hours (GMT): 03 00 - 07 30 and 08 00 -
10 30
Deputy High Commissioner: Mr Stuart H Innes
*First Secretary (Cultural Affairs) (British Council
Division):* Ms Eunice Crook
First Secretary (Clerk of Works):
Mr Patrick Sullivan
Second Secretary (Commercial): Mr David Abbott
Second Secretary (Immigration): Mr Geoff Wood
*Second Secretary (Airline Liason Officer) (Resides
at Mumbai):* Mr Robert Smith
Third Secretary (Management/Consular):
Mrs Julia Campbell
Attaché (Immigration): Mr Simon Dadd
Attaché (Immigration): Mr Shashikant Patel
Attaché (Immigration): Mrs Rita Casserly
Attaché (Immigration): Mr Michael Murtagh
Attaché (Immigration): Mrs Susan Edghill
Attaché (Immigration): Mr Sean Hopkins

Bangalore
British Trade Office
Prestige Takt
23 Kasturba Road Cross
Bangalore 560 001
Telephone: (00) (91) (80) 2100200
Facsimile: (00) (91) (80) 2100400
e-mail: bto.bangalore@fco.gov.uk
Second Secretary: Mr Kelvin Green

Hyderabad
British Trade Office
H-3-6-322, Chamber 104, 1st Floor
Mahavir House, Basheerbagh
Hyderabad 300 029
Telephone: (00) (91) (40) 55669147/48
Facsimile: (00) (91) (40) 55669149
e-mail: hyd_btohyd@sancharnet.in
Senior Trade Promotion Adviser:
Mr M C Srinagesh

INDONESIA

Jakarta
British Embassy
Jalan M H Thamrin 75, Jakarta 10310
FTN Code – 8554 + extn number
Telephone: (00) (62) (21) 315 6264 (Switchboard)
Facsimile: (00) (62) (21) 314 1824 Development

315 4061 Commercial
390 7493 Management
392 6263 Chancery/Economic
390 2726 Defence
Office Hours (GMT): Mon - Thurs 00 45 - 09 00
and Fri 00 45 - 05 45

British Consulate General
Deutsche Bank Building, (19th Floor)
J1 Imam Bonjol 80
Jakarta 10310
Telephone: (00) (62) (21) 390 7484 – 87 (Visa
Section)
319 01314 (Consular Section)
Facsimile: (00) (62) (21) 316 0858
Office Hours (GMT): Mon - Thurs 00 45 - 09 00
and Fri 00 45 - 05 45
Ambassador: Mr Charles Humfrey, CMG
Deputy Head of Mission and Consul-General:
Mr Paul Speller
Counsellor (Political): Mr Seamus Tucker
Defence Attaché: Colonel Alan J Roberts
British Council Director: Mr Mike Hardy
First Secretary (Political/Economic):
Miss Rochelle Cohen
First Secretary (Commercial): Mr Mark Walmsley
First Secretary (Management): Mr Tim Fisher
First Secretary (Development): Mr Jim Carpy
First Secretary (Forestry): Mr Martin Dawson
DFID – Governance Adviser: Mr Bill Baker
DFID – Social Development Adviser: (Vacant)
DFID – Forestry Adviser: Mr Yvan Biot
Second Secretary (Consular): Mr Alan Marshall
Second Secretary (Political/Press):
Ms Eleanor Kiloh
Second Secretary (Political/Economic):
Mr Charles Morgan
Second Secretary (Political): Mr Simon Hall
Third Secretary (Immigration): Mr Dave Lovell
Third Secretary and Vice-Consul: Mr Daryl Crooks
Third Secretary (Management): Ms Nicola James

Medan
British Consulate
Jl Kap. Pattimura 459
PO Box 1286,
Medan 20153
Telephone: (00) (62) (61) 821 0559
Facsimile: (00) (62) (61) 821 0991
e-mail: psbaskett@attglobal.net
Office Hours (GMT): Mon-Fri 01 00 - 05 00
Honorary Consul: Mr Pat Baskett
Honorary Vice-Consul: Mrs Sue Baskett

Surabaya – (Vacant)

Bali
British Consulate
Jalan Mertasari No. 2,
Sanur
Denpasar 80227
Bali
Telephone: 0361 270 601
Mobile: 0812 3838844
Facsimile: 0361 270 601
e-mail: bcbali@dps.centrin.net.id
Office Hours (GMT): 01 30 - 09 00

Honorary Consul: Mr Mark Wilson, OBE

IRAN

Tehran
British Embassy
198 Ferdowsi Avenue, Tehran 11344
(PO Box No 11365-4474)
FTN Code – 8657 + extn number
Telephone: (00) (98) (21) 6705011-19 (8 lines)
Facsimile: (00) (98) (21) 6708021 Commercial
            6700720 Visa
            6710761 Management/Consular
e-mail: BritishEmbassyTehran@fco.gov.uk
visaenquiries.Tehran@fco.gov.uk
Consular.Tehran@fco.gov.uk
Commercial.Tehran@fco.gov.uk

British Council
Telephone: (00) (98) (21) 2001222, 2004060,
2546099, 2604905, 2618664
Facsimile: (00) (98) (21) 2007604
Office Hours (GMT): Sun – Thurs: (Sept-Mar) 04
00 - 11 00, (Apr-Aug) 03 00 - 10 00
Ambassador: Mr Richard J Dalton, CMG (2202)
Counsellor and Deputy Head of Mission:
Mr Matthew Gould, MBE (2205)
First Secretary (Commercial):
Mr Graeme Thomas (2260)
First Secretary (British Council Director):
Mr Michael Willson
First Secretary (Press and Public Affairs):
Mr Andrew Dunn (2210)
First Secretary (Political):
Miss Sarah Mannell (2211)
First Secretary (Management) and HM Consul:
Mrs Moira Stevenson (2280)
Second Secretary (Commercial):
Mr Chris Deardon (2262)
Second Secretary (Technical Management):
Mr Alex Bennett (2235)
Second Secretary (Immigration):
Mr James Gillman (2300)
Third Secretary (Political): Mr Rob Ellis (2220)
Third secretary(Commercial):
Mr Neil Wilson (2266)
Third Secretary (Management) and Vice-Consul:
Mr Colin Glen (2282)
Third Secretary (Immigration):
Mrs Olu Abayomi (2305)
Third Secretary (Immigration):
Mr Kevin Hennessy (2306)
Third Secretary (Immigration):
Mr Tommy Sanmoogan (2304)
Third Secretary (Immigration):
Mr Chris Taylor (2302)
Third Secretary (Immigration):
Mr Ian Walker (2307)
Third Secretary (Immigration):
Mr Stuart Wright (2308)
Third Secretary (Security Manager):
Mr Geoffrey McLaren-Oliver (2295)
Third Secretary: Mr Tim Hawley (2223)

IRAQ

Baghdad
British Embassy
International Zone
FTN Code – 8280 + extn number
Telephone: FTN 8280 1000 (Switchboard)
Facsimile: FTN 8280 2341
Office Hours (GMT): Sat – Wed: 08 00 – 16 00
and Thurs: 08 00 – 12 30
Ambassador: Mr Edward Chaplin, CMG, OBE
Counsellor and Deputy Head of Mission:
The Honourable Dominic Asquith
Defence and Military Adviser:
Colonel the Honourable Alastair Campbell
Counsellor (Political): Mr Simon Buckle
Counsellor (Political): Mr Richard Thompson
Counsellor (Political): Mr Peter Mason
Counsellor (Political): Mr Keith Green
First Secretary (Political): Mr Gareth Bayley
First Secretary (Political): Mr Simon Elvy
First Secretary (Political):
Mr Jeremy Birkbeck, MBE
First Secretary (Political): Ms Andrea Reidy
First Secretary (Political): Mr Paul Kennedy
First Secretary (Political): Mr Richard Etherington
First Secretary (Political): Ms Jo Cetti
First Secretary (Political): Mr James Watson
First Secretary (Legal): Mr Andrew Hood
First Secretary (Economic): Mr Christopher Brown
First Secretary (Energy): Mr Keith Scott
First Secretary (PPA): Ms Victoria Whitford
First Secretary (Commercial):
Mr Richard Hardiman
First Secretary (Commercial): Mr David Raines
First Secretary (Management):
Mr Steve Collier, MVO, RVM
First Secretary (Technical Management):
Mr Fred Roissetter
First Secretary (Development):
Mr Yusuf Samiullah
First Secretary (Development): Ms Lindy Cameron
First Secretary (Culture): Mr Adrian Chadwick
Second Secretary (Press): Ms Zeenat Khanche
Second Secretary (Political): Mr David McNaught
Second Secretary (Political): Mr Joshua Burch
Second Secretary (Political): Mr Matthew Nelson
Second Secretary (Political): Ms Maria Steel
Second Secretary (Political): Mr Jatinder Singh
Second Secretary (Political): Mr Brendan Hughes
Second Secretary (Management):
Ms Helen Brodie, MBE
Second Secretary (Security): Mr Rob McCallum
Second Secretary (Development): Mr Rob Ower
Third Secretary (Political/Administration):
Mr David Gale
Third Secretary (Political): Ms Sandra Robertson
Third Secretary (Commercial): Mr Jeffrey Williams
Third Secretary (Management):
Mr Stelios Kyriakides
Third Secretary (Management): Ms Jackie Connor
Third Secretary and Deputy Consul:
Mr John Walker
Third Secretary (Development): Ms Sara Fawcett
Third Secretary (Defence Attaché):
Mr Derek Vincent

Basra
Office of the British Embassy, Basra
Al Sarraji, Basra
FTN Code – 8357 + extn number
Telephone: (00) (964) 831 000 (Switchboard)
FTN 8357 1000
Facsimile: (00) (964) 832 344
FTN 8357 2344
Office Hours (GMT): Sat – Wed: 08 00 – 16 00
and Thurs: 08 00 – 12 30
*Head of British Embassy Office, Basra and Consul
General:* Mr Simon Collis
First Secretary and Deputy Consul General:
Mr Tom Dodd
First Secretary (Political): Mr Timothy Smart
First Secretary (Political): Mr Sean Holt
First Secretary (Political): Mr Simon Walters
First Secretary (Management): Mr John Dyson
First Secretary (Development): Mr Rod Matthews
Second Secretary (Political): Mr Jonathan Layfield
Second Secretary (Political): Ms Emma Walters
Second Secretary (Political): Ms Blaise Metreweli
Second Secretary (Commercial): Mr Ross Hunter
Second Secretary (Press): (Vacant)
Second Secretary (Security): Mr Ray Cunningham
Second Secretary (Technical Management):
Mr Rod Parker
Second Secretary (Development):
Mr James Golshetti
Second Secretary (Development):
Mr Dominic D'Angelo
Third Secretary (Political): Ms Yasmine Radi
Third Secretary (Political/Administration):
Ms Ann Murduck
Third Secretary (Management):
Ms Aspara Fernando
Third Secretary (Management):
Ms Julie Evans

Kirkuk
Office of the British Embassy, Kirkuk
North Oil Compound
Arafa, Kirkuk
Contact Details:-
OP Telic
BFPO 684
Kirkuk (via Baghdad)
Telephone: (00) (1) (281) 669 1673 extension 3108
(via USA)
(00) (964) (0)50 220715 (Government Offices,
Kirkuk)
Mobile: 07701 309695 (Noel Guckian)
07701 309675 (Philippa Bruckshaw)
e-mail: Noel.Guckian@fco.gov.uk or
njguckian@yahoo.co.uk
Philippa.Bruckshaw@fco.gov.uk or
philiraq@yahoo.co.uk
(NB: The Mobile telephones work in Kirkuk,
Suleimaniyah, Dohuk and Mosul Provinces, but
not in Arbil Province)
*Political Counsellor and HM Consul General for
North Iraq:* Mr Noel Guckian, OBE
First Secretary (Northern Iraq):
Ms Philippa Bruckshaw

IRELAND

Dublin
British Embassy
29 Merrion Road, Ballsbridge, Dublin 4
FTN Code – 8302 + extn number
Telephone: (00 353) (1) 205 3700
            (Main Switchboard)
            205 3775 (Commercial)
            205 3792 (Defence)
            205 3700 (Passport/Visa)
            205 3742 (Press and Public Affairs)
Facsimile: (00 353) (1) 205 3731 (Chancery)
            205 3880 (Commercial)
            205 3885 (Management)
            205 3890 (Consular/Passport/Visa)
            205 3893 (Press and Public Affairs)
            205 3878 (Defence)
e-mail: chancery.dublx@fco.gov.uk (Chancery)
defence.dublx@fco.gov.uk (Defence)
trade.dublin@fco.gov.uk (Commercial)
publicaffairs.dubli@fco.gov.uk (Press and Public
Affairs)
consular.dubli@fco.gov.uk (Consular)
visas.dubli@fco.gov.uk (Visas)
passports.dubli@fco.gov.uk (Passports)
management.dubli@fco.gov.uk (Management)
Website: www.britishembassy.ie
Office Hours (GMT): Mon-Thur 09 00 – 12 45 and
14 00 – 17 15. Fri 09 00 – 12 45 and 14 00 – 17 00
Ambassador: Mr Stewart Eldon, CMG, OBE
Counsellor and Deputy Head of Mission:
Mr Ted Hallett
Director of Trade and Investment:
Mr Martin McIntosh, OBE
Defence Attaché: Colonel Paul B G Cummings
First Secretary (EU/Economic): (Vacant)
First Secretary (Political): Mr Patrick Reilly
First Secretary (Management): Mr Ian Stevens, LVO
British Council Director: Mr Tony Reilly
Second Secretary (Press and Public Affairs):
Ms Sharon Ewart
Second Secretary (Immigration/Consular):
Mr Randolph Jones
Second Secretary (Commercial):
Mr Matthew Donnelly
Second Secretary (EU/Economic):
Mr Jayd Davies, MBE
Third Secretary (Management): Mr Roger Clarke
Third Secretary (Management): Mrs Sarah Howard
Attaché: Ms Valerie Brimfield
Attaché (Defence): Mr Peter Hodgett

ISRAEL

Tel Aviv
British Embassy
192 Hayarkon Street, Tel Aviv 63405
FTN Code - 8447 + extn number
Direct Dial: (00) (972) (3) 7251 + last three digits
of extn number (except where shown)
Telephone: (00) (972) (3) 725 1222 (switchboard)
Facsimile: (00) (972) (3) 524 3313
            Trade and Investment
            527 1572 Chancery
            527 8574 Management

510 1167 Consular
Airtech: (00) (972) (3) 725 1283
e-mail: webmaster.telaviv@fco.gov.uk
Website: www.britemb.org.il
Office Hours (GMT): Mon - Thur 06 00 - 14 00
Fri 06 00 - 11 30 (Aug/Sept-March/April)
Mon - Thur 05 00 - 13 00
Fri 05 00 - 10 30 (March/April-Aug/Sept)
Ambassador: Mr Simon McDonald, CMG (2245)
Counsellor, Consul-General and Deputy Head of Mission: Mr Peter Carter (2246)
Counsellor: Mr Andrew Gibbs (2261)
Defence and Military Attaché:
Colonel Alan K M Miller, OBE (2256)
Naval and Air Attaché:
Wing Commander Mike S Rafferty, RAF (2257)
Cultural Attaché (British Council Director):
Mr Kevin Lewis, OBE (direct 6113620)
First Secretary (Director, Trade and Investment):
Mr Peter Stephenson (2231)
First Secretary (Chancery): Mr Neil Wigan (2248)
First Secretary (Management): Mr Rick Lee (2260)
Second Secretary and Consul:
Mr Michael Hancock (3202 direct: 7251292)
Second Secretary (Chancery):
Mr Adam Sambrook (2266)
Second Secretary (Technical Management):
Mr John Walker (2265)
Assistant Cultural Attaché (British Council):
Ms Ruth Ur (direct 6113625)
Third Secretary and Vice-Consul:
Mr Paul Stokes (3205 direct 7251295)
Third Secretary (Chancery): Mr Mark Bell (2219)
Assistant Defence Attaché:
Staff Sergeant Brian Hogan (2259)

Tel Aviv
British Consulate-General
Migdalor Building (6 th Floor)
1 Ben Yehuda Street, Tel Aviv 63801
Telephone: (00) (972) (3) 7251222
Facsimile: (00) (972) (3) 5101167
Office Hours (GMT): Mon - Thur 05 30 - 13 00
Fri 05 30 - 11 30 (Aug/Sept-March/April)
Mon – Thur 04 30 - 12 30. Fri 04 30 - 10 00
(March/April-Aug/Sept)
Consul-General: Mr Peter Carter (2246)
Consul: Mr Michael Hancock (3202 or direct: 7251292)
Vice-Consul: Mr Paul Stokes (3205 or direct: 7251295)

Eilat
British Consulate
c/o Aqua Sport
Coral Beach
P.O. Box 300
Eilat 88102
Telephone: (00) (972) (8) 6326287
Honorary Consul: Mrs Dafna Budden

ITALY

Rome
British Embassy
Via XX Settembre 80a, 00187 Rome

FTN Code – 8350 + extn number or 8350 1000
(switchboard)
Telephone: (00) (39) 06 4220 0001
             06 478141 British Council
Facsimile: (00) (39) 06 4220 2347 Press and
             Public Affairs
             06 4220 2333 Chancery
             06 4220 2348, 4220 2363, 4220 2410 E
             and C Dept,
             06 4220 2335 Management
             06 4220 2334 Consular
             06 4220 2283 Defence
Airtech: 06 4220 2257
e-mail: info@rome.mail.fco.gov.uk
cons@rome.mail.fco.gov.uk
RomeCommEnq@fco.gov.uk
Management.Rome@fco.gov.uk
Website: www.britain.it
Office Hours (GMT): Sept-July: Mon-Fri 08 00 -
16 00, Aug: Mon-Fri 08 00 - 14 00
Ambassador: Sir Ivor A Roberts, KCMG
Deputy Head of Mission and Minister:
Mr Scott Wightman
Defence and Military Attaché:
Colonel Mike C D Montagu
Naval and Air Attaché:
Captain John H Hollidge, RN
Counsellor (Political): Mr Patrick J McGuinness
Counsellor (Economic and Commercial):
Mr Peter E Jones
Counsellor (British Council Director):
Mr Paul Docherty
First Secretary (Political, Press and Public Affairs): Mr Andrew Jackson
First Secretary (Economic): Mr James Bryce
First Secretary (Management):
Mrs Christine Dharwarkar
First Secretary (Agriculture and Environment):
Mr James P Howie
First Secretary (Social /Science andTechnology Affairs): Mr Ashley Prime
First Secretary (Consul): Mr Peter Jones
First Secretary (Political): Mr Andrew Whiteside
First Secretary (Political):
Mr Francis Martin-Xavier Campbell
Second Secretary (Management):
Mrs Jillian FitzGerald
Second Secretary (Energy/Commercial):
Mr Christopher Wigginton
Second Secretary: Mr Graham J Dempsey
Second Secretary: Mr Simon Grunwell
Second Secretary: Mr Mark C E Norman
Third Secretary: Mr Alexander E Madisons
Third Secretary (Political): Miss Claire Millington
Third Secretary (Vice-Consul): Mrs Sue Donegan
Vice-Consul: Mrs Angela T Sweeney, MBE

Rome United Kingdom Representation to the United Nations Food and Agriculture Agencies in Rome, see Missions and Delegations page 117

Florence
British Consulate
Lungarno Corsini 2,
50123 Florence

Telephone: (00) (39) 055 284133
    (00) (39) 055 289556 (Commercial)
Facsimile: (00) (39) 055 219112
Airtech: (00) (39) 055 2654354
e-mail: Consular.Florence@fco.gov.uk
Commercial.Florence@fco.gov.uk
Office Hours (GMT): Apr-Oct 07 00 - 11 00
and 12 00 - 15 00, Nov-Mar 08 00 - 12 00
and 13 00 - 16 00
Consul (also Consul-General for the Republic of San Marino): Mrs Moira A Macfarlane
Vice-Consul: Ms Jane H de C Ireland, MBE
Pro-Consul: Ms Diane L Johnson

Milan (SP – see page 120)
British Consulate-General
Via San Paolo 7, 20121 Milan
FTN Code – 8353 1000 (switchboard)
Telephone: (00) (39) 02 723001
Facsimile: (00) (39) 02 72020153 Commercial
   86465081 Consular, Management
   and PPA
(Visa and Passport work is centralized in Rome)
Office Hours (GMT): Apr – Oct 07 00 - 11 00 and
12 00 - 15 00, Nov – Mar 08 00 - 12 00 and
13 00 - 16 00
Director General for Trade and Investment and Consul-General: Mr Richard J Northern, MBE
Deputy Director General for Trade and Deputy Consul-General: Mr Brendan Doyle
Consul (Consular/Management): Mr David Wells
Consul (Press and Political Affairs):
Ms Joanne Yeadon
Second Secretary (Investment):
Ms Fiona Corby, LVO
Vice-Consul: Mrs Elizabeth Crosley, MBE
Pro-Consul: Mrs Julia Billingsley

Genoa
British Consulate
c/o Coeclerici Armatori S.p.A
Via di Francia, 28 16149 Genoa
Telephone: (00) (39) 010 416828
Facsimile: (00) (39) 010 416958
Office Hours (GMT): Apr-Oct: Mon - Thur 07 30
– 10 30, Nov-Mar: Mon - Thur 08 30 – 11 30
Honorary Consul: Mr Alexander Edmonds

Turin
British Consulate
Via Madama Cristina, 99
10126 Turin
Telephone: (00) (39) 011 6509202
Facsimile: (00) (39) 011 6695982
e-mail: bcturin@yahoo.com
Office Hours (GMT): Apr – Oct Mon and
Thurs: 07 00 - 10 00, Nov – Mar Mon and
Thurs: 08 00 - 11 00
Honorary Consul: Mr Tim R Priesack

Venice
British Consulate
Piazzale Donatori di Sangue 2/5
30171 Venice-Mestre
Telephone: (00) (39) 041 5055990
Facsimile: (00) (39) 041 950254
e-mail: britconvenice@tin.it

Office Hours (GMT): Apr-Oct Mon – Fri 08 00 –
11 00, Nov-Mar Mon – Fri 09 00 – 12 00
Honorary Consul: Mr Ivor N Coward
Pro-Consul: Mrs Lita Santin, MBE

Trieste
British Consulate
Via Dante Alighieri, 7
34122 Trieste
Telephone: (00) (39) 040 3478303
Facsimile: (00) (39) 040 3478311
e-mail: jododds@tin.it
Office Hours (GMT): Apr-Oct Tues: 08 00 – 10 00
Nov-Mar Tues: 09 00 – 11 00, Fri: 12 30 – 14 30
Fri: 13 30 – 15 30
Honorary Consul: Prof. John Dodds

Cagliari
British Consulate
Viale Colombo,160 Quartu S.E.
09045 Cagliari
Telephone: (00) (39) 070 828628 (Consular
   Enquiries)
   813412 (Business Phone)
Facsimile: (00) (39) 070 862293
e-mail: agraham@iol.it
Honorary Consul: Mr Andrew Graham, MBE

Naples
British Consulate
Via dei Mille 40, 80121 Naples
UK Postal Address: Consulate, BFPO 8 London
Telephone: (00) (39) (081) 423 8911
Facsimile: (00) (39) (081) 422 434
   422 419 (Commercial Section)
Airtech: (00) (39) (081) 423 8917
e-mail: info.naples@fco.gov.uk
Office Hours (GMT): August: 07 00 - 13 00
Winter: 08 00 - 12 00 and 13 00 - 16 00
Consul: Mr Michael Burgoyne, MBE
Commercial Officer: Mr Giuseppe Saraceno
Political and Public Diplomacy:
Mr Gerardo Kaiser
Vice-Consul: Mr Brian McKeever

Bari
British Consulate
David H Gavan and Sons Shipping SrL,
Via Dalmazia 127, 70121 Bari
Telephone: (00) (39) (080) 554 3668
Facsimile: (00) (39) (080) 554 2977
e-mail: gavan@tin.it
Honorary Consul: Mr David Gavan, MBE

Catania
British Consulate
Via G Verdi 53,
95129 Catania
Telephone: (00) (39) 095 715 1864
Facsimile: (00) (39) 095 715 1503
e-mail: consular@omnilog.com
Honorary Consul: Mr Richard Brown

Palermo
British Consulate
S Tagliavia and Co, Via Cavour 117
90133 Palermo
Telephone: (00) (39) 091 326412

Facsimile: (00) (39) 091 584240
e-mail: luigi@tagliavia.it
Honorary Consul: Mr Luigi Tagliavia

IVORY COAST (CÔTE D'IVOIRE)

Abidjan (SP – see page 120)
British Embassy
3rd Floor, Immeuble "Bank of Africa"
Angle Avenue Terrasson de Fougères
Plateau, Abidjan
Postal Address: 01 BP 2581, Abidjan 01
FTN Code – 8531 + extn number
Telephone: (00) (225) 20300800
Visa Section: (00) (225) 20300803
Facsimile: (00) (225) 20300834 Chancery
            20300821 Commercial
            20300828 Visa Section
Airtech: (00) (225) 20217036
e-mail: britemb.a@aviso.ci
Website www.britaincdi.com
Office Hours (GMT): Mon - Thur 08 30 - 13 00
and 13 45 - 16 00, Fri 08 30 - 13 00 and
13 30 - 15 00
Ambassador: Mr D Coates
*First Secretary (Commercial), Consul and Deputy
Head of Mission:* Mr J S Thornton
Defence Attaché (resides Accra):
Lieutenant Colonel J A F Howard
Second Secretary (Political/ Information):
Ms K Miller, MBE
Second Secretary (Management): Mrs S D Mitchell
Third Secretary Vice-Consul (Visas and Passports):
Ms E Mamet

JAMAICA

Kingston
British High Commission
PO Box 575, 28 Trafalgar Road, Kingston 10
FTN Code – 8602 + extn number or 1000
(switchboard)
Telephone: (00) (1) (876) 510 0700
Telegrams: UKREPKIN JA
Facsimile: (00) (1) (876) 510 0737 (Management)
            511 5304 (Commercial)
            511 5303 (Chancery)
            510 0738 (Immigration)
            511 5335 (Consular)
Airtech: (00) (1) (876) 510 0711
e-mail: bhckingston@cwjamaica.com
bhckingston@mail.infochan.com
Office Hours (GMT): Mon - Thu: 13 00 - 18 00
and 19 00 - 21 30, Fri: 13 00 - 18 00
High Commissioner:
Mr Peter J Mathers, LVO (3349/8)
Deputy High Commissioner:
Mr Phil Sinkinson (3732/1)
Defence Adviser:
Colonel Charles G Le Brun (3743)
First Secretary (Management):
Mr Dennis Carter (3727)
First Secretary (Chancery):
Mr Malcolm Bragg (3338)
First Secretary (Chancery): Mr Tony Ridout (3320)

First Secretary (Development):
Mrs Elizabeth Carriere (3708)
British Council Manager: (Vacant)
Second Secretary (Chancery):
Miss Clara Quantrill (3730)
Second Secretary (Consular):
Mr Mike Goodwin (3747)
Second Secretary (Immigration):
Mrs Amanda Ivemy (3710)
Second Secretary (Chancery):
Mr Keith Wiggins (3339)
Second Secretary (Chancery):
Mr Stewart Lister (3302)
Second Secretary (Chancery):
Mr Phil Powell (3832)
Second Secretary (Chancery):
Mr Andrew Bonsey (3833)
Second Secretary (Chancery):
Mr Paul Abbott (3334)
Second Secretary (Development):
Mr Gordon Saggers (3720)
Third Secretary (Chancery):
Mr Daniel Cook (3330)
Third Secretary (Management):
Mr Alex McCann (3312)
*Third Secretary (Chancery/Press and Public
Affairs):* Mr Mark Waller (3746)
Third Secretary (Immigration):
Mr Andrew Fennell (3841/8)
Third Secretary (Immigration):
Miss Karen Chang (3841/8)
Third Secretary (Immigration):
Ms Jo Halliday (3841/8)
Third Secretary (Immigration):
Mr Chris Kellar (3841/8)
Third Secretary (Immigration):
Mr Raj Annis (3841/8)
Third Secretary (Immigration):
Ms Wendy McMinn (3841/8)
Third Secretary (Commercial):
Mr Stewart Gorman (3718)
Attaché (International Pension Service Officer):
Mr Neil Kirk (3712)

Montego Bay
Telephone/Facsimile: (00) (1) (876) 912 6859
(Home)
(00) (1) (876) 954 6394/5 (Office Hours)
(00) (1) (876) 999 9693 (Cellular)
Honorary Consul: Mr John Terry

JAPAN

Tokyo
British Embassy
No 1 Ichiban-cho, Chiyoda-ku, Tokyo 102-8381
FTN Code – 8460 + extn number
Telephone: (00) (81) (3) 5211 1100
Facsimile: (00) (81) (3) 5275 3164 (All sections
            except those listed below)
            5211 1111 (Ambassador's Office)
            5211 1345 (Minister's Office)
            5211 1270 (Energy Section)
            3265 5580 (Commercial Section)
            5275 0346 (Consular and Visa Section)
            5211 1254 (Defence Section)

5211 1121 (Financial Section)
5211 1344 (Political Section)
3230 0624 (Press and Public Affairs)
3230 4800 (Science and Technology Section)
Airtech: 5211 1266
e-mail:
(General Enquiries) embassy.tokyo@fco.gov.uk
(Consular Section) consular.tokyo@fco.gov.uk
(Visa Section) visa.tokyo@fco.gov.uk
(Commercial Section) commercial-section.tokyo@fco.gov.uk
(Defence Section) defence.tokyo@fco.gov.uk
(Energy Section) energy.tokyo@fco.gov.uk
(Inward Investment Section) investukjapan.tokyo@fco.gov.uk
(Management Section) management.tokyo@fco.gov.uk
(Political Section) political.tokyo@fco.gov.uk
(Press and Public Affairs Section) ppas.tokyo@fco.gov.uk
(Trade Policy Section) trade-policy.tokyo@fco.gov.uk
(Science and Technology Section) science.tokyo@fco.gov.uk
Embassy Website: www.uknow.or.jp
Office Hours (GMT): 00.00 – 03.30 and 05.00 – 08.30
Ambassador: Mr Graham Fry
Minister: Mr Martin Hatfull
Defence Attaché: Captain Simon R L Chelton, RN
Counsellor (Political Affairs): Mrs Madelaine Alessandri
Counsellor (Management) and Consul-General: Mr Roger French
Counsellor (Cultural and Director, British Council): Mr Alan Curry
Counsellor (Science and Technology): Dr Mike G Norton
Counsellor (Financial): Mr Peter Green
Counsellor (Political): Mr Colin Roberts
Counsellor (Commercial): Ms Jane Owen
Counsellor (Trade Policy)/Director, Inward Investment: Mr Alastair Morgan
First Secretary (Political): Mr Giles Lever
First Secretary (Press and Public Affairs): Mrs Sue Kinoshita, OBE
First Secretary (Commercial): Mr Robin Ord-Smith
First Secretary (Inward Investment): Mr Simon Collier
First Secretary (Deputy Director, British Council): Mr Mike Winter, OBE
First Secretary (Science and Technology): Mr Brian Ferrar
First Secretary (Trade Policy): Mr Tom Goodwin
First Secretary (Science and Technology): Ms Philippa Rogers
First Secretary (Energy and Environment): Dr John Murton
First Secretary (Commercial): Mrs Camilla Roberts
First Secretary and Consul: Mr Alan Sutton
First Secretary (Management): Ms Gill Lever
Second Secretary (Political): Ms Marie-Claire Joyce

Second Secretary (Commercial): Mr Donald Spivey
Second Secretary (Political): Mr Dallas Windsor
Second Secretary (Financial): Mr Andrew King
Second Secretary (Political): Mr Tom Burn
Second Secretary (Commercial): Mr Simon Wood
Second Secretary (Technical Management): Mr Robin South
Third Secretary and Vice-Consul: Ms Louisa Noel
Third Secretary and Vice-Consul: Mr Matthew Prouten
Third Secretary (Political): Mr Mark Montaldo
Third Secretary (Press and Public Affairs): Mr Martin O'Neill
Third Secretary (PS to Ambassador): Ms Clare Allbless
Third Secretary (Management): Mr Shaun Clarke

British Consulate-General
No 1 Ichibancho, Chiyoda-ku Tokyo 102-8381
Telephone: (00) (81) (3) 5211 1100
Facsimile: (00) (81) (3) 5275 0346
Office Hours (GMT): 00:00 - 03:30 and 05:00 - 08:30
Consul-General: Mr Roger French
Consul: Mr Alan Sutton
Vice-Consul: Ms Louisa Noel
Vice-Consul: Mr Matthew Prouten

British Council:
2 Kagurazaka 1-chome Shinjyuku-ku Tokyo 162-8381
Telephone: (00) (81) (3) 3235 8031
Facsimile: (00) (81) (3) 3235 8040
e-mail: bctokyo@britishcouncil.or.jp
Website: www.uknow.or.jp
Office Hours (GMT): Monday-Friday 00 00-08 00
Director: Mr Alan Curry
Assistant Director: Mr Mike Winter, OBE

Sapporo
British Consulate
c/o Sapporo Nissan Motor Co Ltd
17-1-23 O-dori Nishi Chuo-ku
Sapporo-shi, Hokkaido 060-0042
Telephone: (00) (81) (11) 613 1123
Facsimile: (00) (81) (11) 613 4210
Office Hours (GMT): 00 00 – 08 20
Honorary Consul: Mr Y Kaneko

Osaka
British Consulate-General
Epson Osaka Building, 19F, 3-5-1 Bakuro-machi, Chuo-ku, Osaka 541-0059
Telephone: (00) (81) (6) 6120 5600
Consular enquiries: (00) (81) (6) 6120 5601
Facsimile: (00) (81) (6) 6281 1731
e-mail: bcgosaka@fco.gov.uk
bcgosaka@soleil.ocn.ne.jp
Consul-General and Director of Trade Promotion: Mr Neil K Hook, MVO
Deputy Consul General and Consul, Inward Investment: Mr David Smith
Consul (Commercial): Mr Paul Lynch
Consul: Ms Diane Lloyd

Nagoya
British Consulate
Nishiki Park Building 15F
2-4-3 Nishiki, Naka-ku
Nagoya 460-0003, Japan
Telephone: (00) (81) (52) 223 5031
Facsimile: (00) (81) (52) 223 5035
e-mail: bcon.nagoya@fco.gov.uk
bc.nagoya@crux.ocn.ne.jp
Consul: Mr Julian Miller

Fukuoka
British Trade Promotion Office (FCO Office - bag address)
Hakata Riverain 11F
3-1 Shimokawabatamachi
Hakata-ku
Fukuoka 817-0027
Telephone: (00) (81) (92) 262 0405
Facsimile: (00) (81) (92) 262 0374
e-mail: btpo.fukuoka@fco.gov.uk
btpo.fukuoka@crux.ocn.ne.jp
Head of British Promotion Office: Mr Richard Lyle
Commercial and Inward Investment Assistant:
Mr Koji Fujii

Honorary British Consulate
c/o The Nishi-Nippon Bank Ltd
1-3-6 Hakata-Ekimae
Hakata-ku, Fukuoka
Telephone: (00) (81) (92) 476 2154
Facsimile: (00) (81) (92) 476 2619
Office Hours (GMT): Mon – Fri 03 00 - 07 00
Honorary Consul: Mr S Koga

Hiroshima
Honorary British Consulate
c/o Hiroshima Bank Ltd, 3-8
1-Chome Kamiyacho
Naka-ku, Hiroshima
Telephone: (00) (81) (82) 247 5151
Facsimile: (00) (81) (82) 240 5759
Honorary Consul: Mr O Hashiguchi

JERUSALEM

Jerusalem
British Consulate-General
19 Nashashibi Street, Sheikh Jarrah Quarter
PO Box 19690 East Jerusalem, 97200
FTN Code – 8446 + extn number
Telephone: (00) (972) (2) 541 4100 (24 hour
        switchboard)
        (2) 532 8459/540 0451 (Development)
        (2) 628 2545 (British Council)
Facsimile: (00) (972) (2) 532 5629 (Chancery)
        (2) 532 2368 (Management and
        Commercial)
        (2) 672 9820 (Consular)
        (2) 628 3021 (British Council)
        (2) 541 4157 (Visa)
Airtech: (00) (972) (2) 541 4123
e-mail: britain.jerusalem@fco.gov.uk
Website: http://www.britishconsulate.org
Office Hours (GMT): Sept - Mar: Mon – Thurs 05
30 – 13 30 and Fri 05 30 – 11 30. Apr - Sept: Mon
– Thurs 06 30 – 14 30 and Fri 06 30 – 12 30

Consul-General: Dr John Jenkins, CMG, LVO
Deputy Consul-General:
Mr Piers Cazalet, OBE (541 4108)
Consul (Political): Mr Tom Hurd (541 4103)
Consul (Political):
Mr Andrew Whittaker (541 4109)
Consul (Development): Mr Jim Carpy (532 8462)
Vice-Consul (Management):
Mr Alasdair Hamilton (541 4130)
Vice-Consul (Consular/Immigration):
Mr Valentine Madojemu (541 4129)
Vice-Consul (Political):
Mr Rob Carrick (541 4115)
Vice-Consul (Political): Mr John Kane (541 4119)
Vice-Consul (Political):
Ms Lucy Rashbrook (541 4133)
Vice-Consul: Mr Keith Squibb (541 4139)
Attaché: Miss Julie McGregor (541 4112)
Attaché: Mr Steve Haines (541 4105)
Cultural Attaché (British Council Director):
Ms Sarah Ewans, OBE (628 2545)
*Assistant Cultural Attaché (British Council Deputy
Director):* Mr Martin Daltry (626 2545)

West Jerusalem
British Consulate General
Beit Ha'omot Building
1st Floor
101 Hebron Road
Jerusalem 93460
Telephone: (00) (972) (2) 671 7724
Facsimile: (00) (972) (2) 672 9820
e-mail: britain.jerusalem@fco.gov.uk
Office Hours (GMT): Sept - Mar: Mon - Fri 07 00
- 10 00. Apr - Sept: Mon - Fri 08 00 - 11 00

Gaza
British Information and Services Office
1st Floor, Al-Riyad Tower
Jerusalem Street
Al-Rimal South, Gaza
Telephone: (00) (972) (8) 283 7704
Facsimile: (00) (972) (8) 283 7734
e-mail: bisogaza@palnet.com
Office Hours (GMT) Sept - Mar: Sun – Wed 05 30
– 13 30, Thurs 05 30 – 11 30. Apr - Sept: Sun –
Wed 06 30 – 14 30, Thurs 06 30 – 11 30

JORDAN

Amman
British Embassy
(PO Box 87) Abdoun, 11118 Amman
FTN Code – 8486 + extn number or 1000
(Switchboard)
Telephone: (00) (962) (6) 5923100
Facsimile: (00) (962) (6) 5923759
        5923230 (Chancery)
e-mail: becommercial@nets.com.jo (Commercial)
Website: www.britain.org.jo (Information)
Office Hours (GMT): Sun - Mon 06 00 - 13 30
Tue - Thurs 06 00 - 13 00
Ambassador: Mr Christopher N R Prentice
*Counsellor, Consul-General and Deputy Head of
Mission:* Ms Pat Phillips
Counsellor: Mr Richard Potter

Defence, Naval and Military Attaché:
Colonel Richard W Currie
Air Attaché:
Wing Commander C Jim Lawrence, RAF
British Council Director: Mr Tim Gore
First Secretary (Political): Mr Charles Murdoch
Consul and First Secretary (Management):
Mr Michael Snell
First Secretary (Commercial): Mr Bill Preston
Second Secretary (Political): Mr Allen Hodgson
Second Secretary (Political/Economic):
Mr Richard Shaw
Second Secretary (Technical): Mr Pete Bishop
Second Secretary (ALO): Mr Bill Carmichael
Security Manager: Mr Graham Lindley
Third Secretary (Political): Ms Alexia Quail
Entry Clearance Officer: Mr Gerry Grant
Vice-Consul and Third Secretary (Management):
Ms Alison Banks
PA to Ambassador: Ms Alison Balfour
Attaché: Ms Rachel Cockayne
Attaché: Mr Dan Mantini

KAZAKHSTAN

Almaty (SP – see page 120)
British Embassy
U1 Furmanova 173, Almaty
FTN Code – 8721 + extn number
Telephone: (00) (73272) 506191, 506192, 506229
Facsimile: (00) (73272) 506260
e-mail: british-embassy@kaznet.kz
Opening Hours (GMT): Winter: Mon-Thurs 03 00
- 11 30; Fri 03 00 - 10 00. Summer: Mon-Thurs 02
00 - 10 30; Fri 02 00 - 09 00

Visa/Consular Section
158 Panfilova Street, Almaty
Telephone: (00) (73272) 508280
Facsimile: (00) (73272) 507432
e-mail: visa-british-embassy@nursat.kz
Opening Hours (GMT): Winter: Mon-Thurs 02.30
- 11.00; Fri 02 30 - 09 30. Summer: Mon-Thurs 01
30 - 10 00; Fri 01 30 - 08 30
Ambassador: Mr James L Sharp
Defence Attaché:
Lieutenant Colonel Graham J Sheeley, AFC
Cultural Attaché (British Council Director):
(Vacant)
Deputy Head of Mission: Ms Catherine Inglehearn
British Council Acting Director: Mr Jon Gore
Second Secretary (Management) and Consul:
Mr George Scott
Second Secretary (Commercial): Mr Shozey Jafferi
Third Secretary and Vice-Consul:
Mr Andrew Brand
Third Secretary (Political/Aid): Mr David Hinchon
Defence Assistant: Mr Kenny Macintosh

KENYA

Nairobi
British High Commission
Upper Hill Road, Nairobi, P.O. Box 30465 - 00100
Nairobi
Commercial Department: P.O. Box 30133 - 00100
Nairobi

Consular Department: P.O. Box 48543 - 00100
Nairobi
FTN Code – 8606 + extn number
Telephone: (00) (254) (20) 2844000 (15 Lines)
Facsimile: 2844033 Chancery
2844088 Management/Press and Public
Affairs
2844077 Commercial
2844239 Consular
2844296 UK Permanent Mission to
UNEP and UNHSP
2844003 Political Section
2844111 Visa
2844102 DFID(K)
2844325 Defence
2844413 DLO
2844069 ALO Fax
e-mail: Nairobi-Chancery@fco.gov.uk (Chancery
Section)
CommercialSection.nairobi@fco.gov.uk
(Commercial Section)
Comms.nairobi@fco.gov.uk (Communications
Section)
ConsularSection.nairobi@fco.gov.uk (Consular
Section)
ManagementSection.nairobi@fco.gov.uk
(Management Section)
PressandPublicAffairsection.nairobi@fco.gov.uk
(Press and Public Affairs Section)
UNSection.nairobi@fco.gov.uk (UN Section)
VisaSection.nairobi@fco.gov.uk (Visa Section)
(Individuals) FirstName.Surname@fco.gov.uk
Office Hours: Mon-Thur 07 00 – 17 00 and Fri 07
00 – 13 00 Local time. The office works Flexi-time
within these hours.
High Commissioner: Mr E Clay, CMG
Deputy High Commissioner: Mr R W Kyles
Counsellor: Mr N Syrett
Defence Adviser: Colonel A D K Inkster
British Council Director: Mr P Goodwin
First Secretary (Commercial): Mr R G Church
First Secretary (Political): Mr D H Evans
First Secretary (Management): Mr J B Greenlee
First Secretary (United Nations): Mr J P Virgoe
First Secretary (Communications):
Mr T P Bilimoria
First Secretary: Mr M Harding
First Secretary: Mr J F Prior
First Secretary: Mr C P Wools
First Secretary (Regional Conflicts Adviser):
Mr M W E McNulty
First Secretary (Human Rights Adviser):
Ms M Garling
First Secretary (Somalia Unit): Mr D G Bell
Second Secretary (Consular):
Mr D F Forbes-Batey
Second Secretary (Information/Press):
Mr M R Norton
Second Secretary (Political/Economic):
Mr I R Paterson
Second Secretary (Immigration/ECM):
Ms G Emmanuel
Second Secretary (Management):
Mr S G P Burns, MBE
Second Secretary (Regional): Mr R P Barker
Second Secretary: Mr J Greenfield

Second Secretary (Communications):
Mr F Hinchliffe
Second Secretary (Communications): Mr L Fennel
Third Secretary (Communications): Mr D Rees
Third Secretary (Immigration): Mrs S B Shaw
Third Secretary (Immigration): Ms J Farrar
Third Secretary (Immigration): Mrs L R Powell
Third Secretary (Immigration): Mr M Stovold
Third Secretary (Political): Mr D P Lloyd
Third Secretary: Mr J G Fairweather
Attaché: Mr P K Bart-Plange
Attaché: Mrs P E Hunter-Okulo
Attaché: Mr M A Bridgeman
Attaché: Mr D McLeod

**Department for International Development
Eastern Africa (Kenya)**
c/o British High Commission
Upper Hill Road
P O Box 30465, Nairobi
Telephone: (00) (254) (20) 2717609 (5 lines)
          (00) (254) (20) 2844000
Facsimile: (00) (254) (20) 2844102
Office Hours (GMT): Mon - Thur: 07 45 - 12 30
and 13 30 - 16 30, Fri: 07 45 - 13 00
*First Secretary (Development) and Head of DFID
(Kenya):* Mr S Bland
First Secretary (Senior Education Adviser):
Ms F Townsend
First Secretary (Senior Natural Resources Adviser):
Ms R Lambert
First Secretary (Senior Economist): Ms J Barugh
Second Secretary (Personnel/Office Manager):
Mr G Dixon
Second Secretary (Development): Mr E Rich
First Secretary (Governance Adviser): Ms S Lane
Second Secretary (Regional/IT Manager):
Mr I Rivers
Second Secretary (Health and Population Adviser):
Ms M McDonagh

**Nairobi United Kingdom for Human
Settlements (Habitat), See Missions and
Delegations page 116
Nairobi United Nations Environment
Programme, See Missions and Delegations
page 116**

Mombasa
Honorary British Consular Representative
1st Floor Cotts House, Moi Avenue
P O Box 85593, Mombasa
Telephone: (00) (254) (41) 313609/220023
Facsimile: (00) (254) (41) 312416
e-mail: Valerie@ikenya.com
jknight@africaonline.co.ke
Assistant Honorary Consular Representative in
Mombasa
c/o Mission to Seamen, Mogadishu Road,
PO Box 80424, Mombasa
Telephone: (00) (254) (41) 230027/8, 316502/3,
316486, 316285

Facsimile: (00) (254) (41) 230001
Honorary British Consular Representative:
Mr J W L Knight

*Assistant British Honorary Consular
Representative:* Mr J Attenborough

Watamu/Malindi
Watamu
PO Box 100,
Watamu
Telephone: 042 32154 (H) 042 32132/32571(O)
Mobile: 0733 625646
Facsimile: 042 32132/32482
e-mail: Captandy@swiftmalindi.com
Honorary Correspondent: Mr A D Thomas

Malindi
PO Box 162,
Malindi
Telephone: 042 21156 (H)
Honorary Correspondent: Mr I A D Robertson

KIRIBATI

Tarawa
British High Commission Office
PO Box 5, Bairiki
Tarawa
Telephone: (00) (686) 22501
Facsimile: (00) (686) 22505
Airtech: (00) (686) 22506
e-mail: ukrep@tskl.net.ki
britainkiribati@tskl.net.ki
Website:
http://www.britishhighcommission.gov.uk/fiji
Office Hours (GMT): Sun-Wed 20 15 – 01 00 and
02 00 – 05 00, Thurs 20 15 – 01 00
*High Commissioner: Mr Charles F Mochan
*Deputy High Commissioner: Mr Ian Powell
Resident Deputy High Commissioner:
Mr Peter Heigl
**Resides at Suva

KOREA (NORTH)

Pyongyang
British Embassy
Munsu Dong
Pyongyang
FTN Code – 8464 + extn number
Telephone (International): (00) (850) 2 381 7980-3
(4 lines)
Facsimile (International): (00) (850) 2 381 7985
Telephone (Within DPRK): 382 7980-2 (3 lines)
Facsimile (Within DPRK): 382 7983
Airtech: (00) (850) 2 381 7990
              (FTN 8464 2223)
Office Hours (GMT): Mon-Fri: 00 01 – 08 30
Ambassador (ext 2211): Mr David Slinn, OBE
Deputy Head of Mission (ext 2206):
Miss Lindsay Stent
Vice-Consul (ext 2210): Mr Jim Warren
AMO/Accountant/Archivist (ext2205):
Mr Reg Duncan

KOREA (SOUTH)

Seoul
British Embassy
Taepyeongno 40

4 Jeong-dong, Jung-gu
Seoul 100-120
FTN Code – 8492 + extn number
Telephone: (00) (82) (2) 3210 5500
Facsimile: (00) (82) (2) 725 1738
         722 7270 (Airtech)
         736 6241 Commercial Section
         3210 5653 Consular Section
         3210 5528 Defence Section
         733 8368 Defence Supplies
         738 2797 Economic Section and
         Science/Technology/Environment
         Section
         735 7473 Political Section
         720 4928 Press and Public Affairs
         Section
         736 3174 Residence
e-mail: bembassy@britain.or.kr
postmaster.seoul@fco.gov.uk
Website: www.uk.or.kr
Office Hours (GMT): Mon - Fri 00 00 - 08 30
Ambassador (5510/5511): Mr Warwick Morris
*Deputy Head of Mission and Consul General
(5517):* Mr Christopher Robbins
*Counsellor and British Council Director (3702
0600 ext 0677):* Ms Shoba Ponnappa
Defence and Military Attaché (5524):
Brigadier J H Harry O'Hara, OBE
Naval and Air Attaché (5525):
Group Captain K R Colin Greaves, OBE, RAF
First Secretary (Defence) (5520): Mr Chris Earl
*First Secretary (Science/Technology/Environment)
(5590):* Dr Jim Thomson
First Secretary (Political) (5530):
Dr Antony Stokes
First Secretary (Commercial) (5620):
Mr Dai Billington
First Secretary (Management and Consul) (5655):
Mrs Diana Fitch
*First Secretary (Education/British Council Deputy
Director) (3702 0622):* Mr Gavin Anderson
Second Secretary (Political/Public Affairs) (5560):
Mr Adrian Chapman
Second Secretary (Investment) (5610):
Miss Claudia Casey
Second Secretary (Political) (5537):
Mr Mike Cowin
Second Secretary (Economic) (5600): Mr Phil Ellis
Second Secretary (Commercial) (5621):
Ms Jacqueline Mullen
*Assistant Cultural Attaché (British Council) (3702
0633):* Mr Kevin McLaven
*Second Secretary (Technical Works Office) (resides
at Beijing):* Mr Carl Gray
*Second Secretary (Management/Consular)
(5560/5656):* Mr Dave Torrance
*Third Secretary (Technical Management Officer)
(resides Tokyo):* Mr Robin South

Pusan
Honorary Consul's Office
12th Floor
Yuchang Building, 25-2,
Chungang-Dong, 4-Ga
Chung-Gu,
Pusan, 600-014

PO Box No 75
Telephone: (00) (82) (051) 463 0041 and 463 4630
Facsimile: (00) (82) (051) 462 5933
Honorary Consul: Mr S E Wang, CBE
Honorary Vice-Consul: Mr H Guack

KUWAIT

British Embassy
Arabian Gulf Street
Postal Address: PO Box 2, Safat, 13001 Kuwait
Commercial Section Address: PO Box 300, Safat,
13003, Kuwait
FTN Code – 8607 + extn number
Telephone: (00) (965) 240 3334/5/6
Facsimile: 240 7395 Commercial
         242 6799 Chancery/Defence
         242 5778 Consular/Visa
         240 7633 Management
e-mail: general@britishembassy-kuwait.org
Office Hours (GMT): Sat - Wed: 04 30 - 11 30
Ambassador: Mr Christopher E J Wilton
Counsellor and Deputy Head of Mission:
Mr James N G Bowden, OBE
Defence Attaché: Colonel Steve O Thomas
First Secretary (Political): Mr Nicholas Watson
First Secretary (Management) and Consul:
Mr John Francis
First Secretary (Commercial): Mr Bernard Wilson
First Secretary (Defence Supply): Mr Keith Harper
First Secretary (British Council):
Mr Bob Steedman
*Second Secretary (Political/Press and Public
Affairs):* Mr Mark Ellam
Vice-Consul and Third Secretary (Management):
Mr Neil Frape
Third Secretary: Mr Kurt Sutherland
Third Secretary: Mr Phil Norris

KYRGYZSTAN

Bishkek
British Embassy
(All staff reside at Almaty)
Ambassador: Mr James L Sharp
Defence Attaché:
Lieutenant Colonel Graham J Sheeley, AFC
Cultural Attaché: Mr James Kennedy
Deputy Head of Mission: Mr Andrew Dinsley
Second Secretary and Consul: Mr George Scott
Second Secretary (Commercial): Mr Shozey Jafferi
Third Secretary (Political/Aid): Mr David Hinchon
Third Secretary and Vice-Consul:
Mr Andrew Brand

British Consulate
0soo Fatboys
Prospekt Chyl 104
Bishkek
Telephone: (00) (996 312) 584245
e-mail: fatboys@mail.kg
Honorary Consul: Mr Mike Atsoparthis

LAOS

Vientiane
British Embassy

(All staff reside at Bangkok)
PO Box 6626, Vientiane
Telephone: (00) (856) (21) 413606
Facsimile: (00) (856) (21) 413607
Ambassador: Mr David W Fall
Counsellor: Mr Andrew J Pearce
Counsellor (Commercial): Mr Martin Hill
First Secretary (Political): Mr Ian Proud
Consul and First Secretary (Management):
Mr Alan Mayland
First Secretary: Mr John Hector
Second Secretary (Immigration):
Mrs Jane F Lacey-Smith
Third Secretary: Mr Philip McKenzie

British Trade Office
Office Hours (GMT): Mon – Fri 01 00 – 05 00
and 06 00 – 09 30
Head of British Trade Office: Dr Robert Cooper

LATVIA

Riga (SP – see page 120)
British Embassy
5 J. Alunana Iela, Riga
LV 1010
Telephone: (00) (371) 777 4700
Facsimile: (00) (371) 777 4707
         Chancery/Information/Management/
         Consular
         777 4724 Commercial
Airtech: (00) (371) 777 4741
e-mail: british.embassy@apollo.lv
Website: www.britain.lv
Office Hours (GMT): 07 00 - 11 00 and 12 00 -
15 00
Ambassador: Mr H A P Tesoriere
Deputy Head of Mission and Consul:
Mr David Musgrave
Defence Attaché:
Lieutenant Colonel Glen A B Grant
First Secretary (British Council Director):
Ms Agita Kalvina
First Secretary (resides in Vilnius):
Mr Martin Thursfield
Second Secretary (Commercial):
Ms Jeanette Stevens
Third Secretary: Ms Helen Teasdale
*Third Secretary/Vice-Consul and Management
Officer:* Mrs Jackie White
Third Secretary (resides in Helsinki):
Mr Tim Goode
Attaché: Mr John Pond
Attaché: FS Joe Stansfield
Technical Works Supervisor: Mr Andrew Moore

LEBANON

Beirut
British Embassy
Serail Hill
Beirut Centre-Ville
PO Box 11-471 Beirut
FTN Code – 8690 + extn number
Telephone: (00) (961) (1) 990400
         (00) (961) (4) 417007 (24 hrs)
Facsimile: (00) (961) (1) 990420

Mobile: (00) (961) (3) 412448
e-mail: britemb@cyberia.net.lb
Website: www.britishembassy.org.lb
Office Hours (GMT): Mon-Thurs: 06 30 – 15 15
and Fri: 06 30 – 11 30
Ambassador: Mr James W Watt, cvo
Deputy Head of Mission: Mr Chris Poole, MBE
Defence Attaché:
Lieutenant Colonel Nigel R Forrestal
*First Secretary (Education Culture) (British
Council Director):* Mr Kenneth Churchill, OBE
First Secretary (Political): Mr James Baxendale
Second Secretary (Commercial):
Ms Karen Williams
Second Secretary (Management):
Mrs Karen Kavanagh
Second Secretary (ICLO): Mr Michael Roberts
Third Secretary (Management):
Miss Doris Vir Singh
Third Secretary (Chancery): Mr Darren James
Vice-Consul: Miss Nicolette Smith
Entry Clearance Officer: Miss Michelle Callus
Attaché: Ms Cathy Dennis

Mount Lebanon
Coolrite Building,
Beirut
Telephone: (00) (961) (4) 723 502
Honorary Consul: Mr William Zard, MBE

Tripoli
British Consulate
Daar Al Ain, Tripoli
Telephone: (00) (961) (6) 621320
Honorary Consul: Mr Anwar Arida, MBE

LESOTHO

Maseru (SP – see page 120)
British High Commission
PO Box 521, Maseru 100
FTN Code - 8608 + extn number
Telephone: (00) (266) 22313961
Facsimile: (00) (266) 22310120
Airtech: (00) (266) 22310387
e-mail: hcmaseru@lesoff.co.za
Website: www.bhc.org.ls
Office Hours (GMT): Mon-Thurs 06 00 - 11 00
and 11 45 - 14 30 Fri 06 00 - 11 00
High Commissioner (ext. 2202): Mr Frank Martin
Deputy High Commissioner (ext. 2203):
Mr Mark Watchorn
Defence Adviser (Resides at Pretoria):
Brigadier David H Keenan, OBE
*Third Secretary (Management and Consular) (ext.
2205):* (Vacant)

**Department for International Development
(DFID) Field Office**
Address as for British High Commission
Telephone: (00) (266) 22321601
Facsimile: (00) (266) 22321600
Office Hours: as for British High Commission
Head of Field Office/Programme Administrator:
Miss Diana Webster
(e-mail: d-webster@dfid.gov.uk)

LIBERIA

Monrovia
British Embassy
(Staff resident at Abidjan unless otherwise stated)
Ambassador: Mr D Coates
Defence Attaché (resides at Freetown):
Lieutenant Colonel D J A Bergin, OBE
Third Secretary (Chancery): Ms E Mamet

British Honorary Consul
Office of the European Commission
UN Drive, Mamba Point
Monrovia
Telephone: (00) (231) 22 74 68
Satellite Phone: (00) (874) 762 15 47 56
Facsimile: (00) (231) 22 62 74
Satellite Fax: (00) (874) 762 72 48 74
Mobile: (00) (37747) 55 39 88
e-mail: dpaidcoord@yahoo.com
Office Hours: Mon-Thurs: 08 00 - 17 00;
Fri 08 00 - 13 30
Honorary Consul: Mr Roy Chalkley

LIBYA

Tripoli
British Embassy
PO Box 4206
Tripoli
FTN Code – 8609 + extn number
Telephone: (00) (218) (21) 340 3644/5 (Chancery)
                335 1084 (Consular/Visa/Management)
Facsimile: (00) (218) (21) 340 3648 (Chancery)
                335 1425 (Consular/Management)
                335 1427 (Visa Section)
Office Hours (GMT): Sun – Thurs: 07 00 – 14 00
Ambassador: Mr Anthony M Layden
Deputy Head of Mission and Consul-General:
Mr Colin Crorkin, MBE
First Secretary (Political): Mr Justin Hustwitt
First Secretary (Management): Mr David Lusher
First Secretary (Commercial): Mr Graham Glover
*First Secretary (Education and British Council
Director):* Mr Carl Reuter
Second Secretary (Political): Mr Chris Rampling
Second Secretary (Commercial):
Mrs Joanne Finnamore-Crorkin
Second Secretary (Immigration): Mrs Jo Glover
Third Secretary (Management) and Vice-Consul:
Mr Steve Auld
Third Secretary (Immigration): (Vacant)
Third Secretary (Immigration): Mr Rob Winstanley
Attaché: Mrs Ann Stephen
Attaché: Mr Simon Beglin

LIECHTENSTEIN

Vaduz
Ambassador (resides at Berne): Mr Simon
Featherstone
Consul-General (resides at Berne):
Mr D G Roberts

LITHUANIA

Vilnius (SP – see page 120)
British Embassy
2 Antakalnio, 2055
Vilnius
FTN Code – 8327 + extn number
Telephone: (00) (370) (5) 246 2900
Facsimile: (00) (370) (5) 246 2901
Airtech: (00) (370) (5) 246 2922
Website www.britain.lt
Office Hours (GMT): Mon - Thur 0630 - 1000
and 1100 - 1500, Fridays 0630 - 1000 and
1100 - 1400
Ambassador (ext 2904): Mr Colin Roberts
Deputy Head of Mission and Consul (ext 2915):
Mr Keith Shannon
Defence Attaché:
Lieutenant Colonel Michael J Clements
First Secretary (Political) (ext 2911):
Ms Fiona MacCallum, MBE
First Secretary (British Council):
Ms Lina Balenaite
Third Secretary (Political) (ext 2903):
Mr David Giles
*Third Secretary (Political/Economic/Public
Affairs):* (Vacant)
*Third Secretary (Management) and Vice-Consul
(ext 2936):* Mr Ryan Griffin
Assistant Defence Attaché (ext 2926):
CPO(W) Paul Hutton
Attaché (ext 2902): Miss Judith Hitchings
MOD Attaché to Lithuanian Ministry of Defence:
Mr Graham Roberts

LUXEMBOURG

Luxembourg (SP – see page 120)
British Embassy
14 Boulevard Roosevelt, L-2450 Luxembourg
FTN Code – 8305 + extn number
Telephone: (00) (352) 22 98 64/65/66
Facsimile: (00) (352) 22 98 67 (Office)
                (00) (352) 22 98 68 (Residence)
Airtech: (00) (352) 22 98 64 (Ext. 2231)
e-mail: britemb@pt.lu
Website: webplaza.pt.lu/public/britemb
Office Hours (GMT): Summer 07 00 - 11 00 and
12 00 - 15 00. Winter 08 00 - 12 00 and
13 00 - 16 00
Ambassador and Consul-General: Mr James Clark
Counsellor (Commercial) (resides at Brussels):
Mr Matthew Rous
*First Secretary, Consul and Deputy Head of
Mission:* Mr John Beyer
Defence Attaché (resides at The Hague):
Captain A Robin Davies, RN
*Cultural Attaché (British Council Director) (resides
at Brussels):* Mr Stephen Kinnock
First Secretary (Commercial) (resides at Brussels):
Mr Guy Harrison
Third Secretary (Management) and Vice-Consul:
Mr Jason Lonsdale

MACEDONIA

Skopje (SP – see page 120)
British Embassy
Dimitrija Chupovski 4/26
Skopje 1000
FTN Code - 8386 +1000 for switchboard
Telephone: (00) (389) (2) 3299 299
Facsimile: (00) (389) (2) 3117 555
                3117 566 (Consular/Visa)
Airtech: (00) (389) (2) 3299 226
e-mail: BritishEmbassySkopje@fco.gov.uk
Website: www.britishembassy.org.mk
Office Hours (GMT): Summer: Mon-Thurs: 06 00
– 14 30; Fri 06 00 – 11 00, Winter: Mon-Thurs:
07 00 – 15 30; Fri 07 00 – 12 00
Ambassador:
Mr Robert Chatterton Dickson (2201)
Deputy Head of Mission: Mr Douglas Gray (2203)
First Secretary (Political):
Mr Charles Reeve (2262)
*First Secretary (Cultural, Director British
Council):* Mr Andrew Hadley
Defence Attaché: Lieutenant Colonel D Steve
English (2208)
*HM Consul and Second Secretary
(Management/ECM):*
Ms Christine Richardson (2245)
Second Secretary (Political):
Mr Tom Southern (2207)
Second Secretary (ILO) (Resident in Sofia):
Mr Adrian Barnard
Second Secretary (DLO) (Resident in Sofia):
Mr Lee Williams
Third Secretary (Immigration):
Ms Jill Mathieson (2250)
Attaché: Ms Sarah Feetam (2205)
Assistant *Defence Attaché:*
Sergeant Stephen Chase (2210)

Bitola
Honorary British Consulate
Marsal Tito 42
7000 Bitola
Telephone/Facsimile: (00) (389) (47) 22 87 65
e-mail: consulatebitola@britishembassy.org.mk
Honorary Consul: Mrs Lilijana Spirovska

MADAGASCAR

Antananarivo (SP – see page 120)
British Embassy
Lot II 164 Ter,
Alarobia – Amboniloha, BP 167
Antananarivo 101
FTN Code – 8726 + extn number
Telephone: (00) (261) (20) 22 49378/79/80
Facsimile: (00) (261) (20) 22 49381
e-mail: ukembant@simicro.mg
Office Hours (GMT): Mon-Wed: 04 30 – 09 00 and
09 30 - 13 00. Thur-Fri: 04 30 - 10 00
Ambassador: Mr B Donaldson
Deputy Head of Mission: Ms D Partridge
Defence Attaché (resides at London):
Lieutenant Colonel J J J Lemay
Commercial Officer: Mr Tsiry Wilkinson

Toamasina
British Consulate
Seal Tamatave
Telephone: (00) (261) (20) 5332548/5332569
Facsimile: (00) (261) (20) 5333937
e-mail: sealtmm@bow.dts.mg
Honorary Consul: Mr M Gonthier

MALAWI

Lilongwe
British High Commission
PO Box 30042, Lilongwe 3
FTN Code – 8610 + extn number
Telephone: (00) (265) 1 772 400
Facsimile: (00) (265) 1 772 657
Airtech: (00) (265) 1 772 153
e-mail: bhclilongwe@fco.gov.uk
Office Hours (GMT): Mon – Thurs: 05 30 – 10 00
and 1130 - 14 30. Fri: 05 30 - 10 30
High Commissioner: Mr David Pearey
Defence Adviser (resides at Harare):
Colonel Bob J Griffiths, MBE
British Council Director: Mr Brendan Barker
First Secretary (Regional Medical Adviser):
Dr Howard Friend
Second Secretary (Management/Consular):
Mrs Julie Bell
*Second Secretary (Political/Press and Public
Affairs):* Mr Chris Wraight
Third Secretary (Consular/Commercial):
Mr Shaun Earl

**Department for International Development
(DFID) Malawi**
*Head of DFID (Malawi) and Deputy High
Commissioner:* Mr Roger Wilson
Deputy Head of DFID (Malawi): Mr Joe Reid
Livelihoods Adviser: Dr Harry Potter, OBE
Livelihoods Adviser: Ms Leigh Stubblefield
Health Adviser: Mr Richard Cibulskis
Health Adviser: Ms Susan Mshana
Education Adviser: Ms Christine Wallace
Governance Adviser: Ms Jackie Peace
Infrastructure Adviser: Mr Jim Craigie
Infrastructure Adviser: Mr Joe Mumar
Economics Adviser: Mr Alan Whitworth
Economics Adviser: Ms Lindsay Mangham
Social Development Adviser: Ms Andrea Cook
Assistant Social Development Adviser:
Mr Peter Evans
Human Resources Manager: Mr Tom Cushnan
HIV/AIDS Adviser: Ms Anna de Cleene
Private Sector Adviser: Mr Rob Rudy

MALAYSIA

Kuala Lumpur
British High Commission
185 Jalan Ampang, 50450 Kuala Lumpur,
or PO Box 11030, 50732 Kuala Lumpur
FTN Code - (8) 611 2 + officer's three digit extn
number
Telephone: (00) (60) (3) 2170 2200 - Switchboard
Direct Dial: (00) (60) (3) 2170 2 + officer's three
digit extension number
Facsimile: (00) (60) (3) 2170 2370 Management

2170 2303 Political/Economic
2170 2285 Commercial
2170 2360 Consular/Visa
2170 2325 Public Diplomacy
2170 2309 Defence/ Defence Supply
Airtech:　　(00) (60) (3) 2170 2304
e-mail: political.kualalumpur@fco.gov.uk
(Political/Economic)
press.kualalumpur@fco.gov.uk (Public Diplomacy)
scholarships.kl@fco.gov.uk (Scholarships)
trade.kualalumpur@fco.gov.uk (Commercial)
defence.kualalumpur@fco.gov.uk (Defence Supply)
consular.kualalumpur@fco.gov.uk (Consular/Visa)
webmaster.kualalumpur@fco.gov.uk (IT)
Website: www.britain.org.my
Office Hours (GMT): Mon - Fri 00 00 - 04 30 and
05 15 - 08 30
High Commissioner (PA: 224):
Mr Bruce Cleghorn, CMG
Deputy High Commissioner (238; PA: 244):
Mr Mark Canning
*Counsellor (Commercial) and Director for Trade
and Investment (PA: 307):* Mr Gordon Reid
Counsellor (Political) (PA: 222):
Mr Richard Moore
Defence Adviser (226; PA: 206):
Colonel Jamie A Athill
*First Secretary (Political, Economic and Public
Diplomacy) (202):* Mr Edward Hobart
First Secretary (Defence Supply) (242; PA: 206):
Mr Rob Lingham
First Secretary (Trade and Investment) (232):
Mr Steven Green
First Secretary (Management) (258):
Mr Mike Dunn
First Secretary (resides at Bangkok):
Mr John Hector
Assistant Defence Adviser (228):
Lieutenant Commander Martin P Davis, RN
Second Secretary (Economic) (245):
Mr Jeremy Pilmore-Bedford
Second Secretary (Political) (301):
Mr Benjamin Conway
Second Secretary (Political): Ms Katherine Rowe
Second Secretary (Technical Management) (225):
Mr Ian Attwood
*Second Secretary (Immigration Attaché) (207; Asst:
308):* Mr Paul Feeney
*Second Secretary (Political/Public Diplomacy)
(209):* Mr Rob Noble
Second Secretary (Trade and Investment) (210): Mr
Neil Floyd
Second Secretary (Consular) (204):
Ms Julie Johnson
Third Secretary (Trade and Investment) (233):
Mrs Marion Guthrie
Third Secretary (Management) (254):
Miss Margaret Gallacher

Johor Bahru
Office of the Honorary British Representative
Lucas Automotive Sdn Bhd, PLO 17
Senai Industrial Estate
KB 105, 81400 Senai, Johor
Telephone: (00) (60) (7) 599 1301/2/3/4 Ext 111
Facsimile: (00) (60) (7) 599 4301

e-mail: john.w.bradbury@trw.com
Honorary British Representative:
Mr John Bradbury, MBE

Kota Kinabalu (Sabah)
Office of the Honorary British Representative
c/o Pekah Sdn Bhd
Suite 1-7-WS, 7th Floor, CPS Tower, Centre Point
Sabah
88000 Kota Kinabalu
Sabah
Telephone: (00) (60) (88) 253 333
Facsimile: (00) (60) (88) 267 666
e-mail: pmole@pc.jaring.my
Honorary British Representative: Mr Peter Mole

Kuching (Sarawak)
Office of the Honorary British Representative
1st and 2nd Floors
183 C/D/E Fortune Land Business Centre
Jalan Rock
Kuching, Sarawak
Tel/Fax: (00) (60) (82) 250 950
e-mail: valm@pc.jaring.my
Honorary British Representative:
Mrs Valerie Mashman

Miri (Sarawak)
Office of the Honorary British Representative
NJV Sarawak Shell Berhad
98100 Lutong
Miri Sarawak
Telephone: (00) (60) (85) 475 865/452 736
Facsimile: (00) (60) (85) 653 877
e-mail: smroddy@streayx.com
Honorary British Representative:
Mr Simon Roddy

Penang
Office of the Honorary British Representative
c/o Plantation Agencies Sdn Bhd
3rd Floor, Standard Chartered Bank Chambers
Beach Street, 10300 Penang
Telephone: (00)(60)(4) 262 5333
Facsimile: (00)(60)(4) 262 2018
e-mail: pasb@mailworld.net
Honorary British Representative:
Mr John West, MBE

MALDIVES

Malé
British High Commission
(All staff resident in Colombo except where
otherwise stated)
High Commissioner: Mr Stephen N Evans, CMG, OBE
Deputy High Commissioner: Mr Peter J Hughes
Defence Adviser:
Lieutenant Colonel Colin P G Martin
Cultural Attaché (British Council Director):
Mr Tony O'Brien
First Secretary (Economic and Commercial):
Mr Dave Waring
First Secretary (Management): Mr Mick Mitchell
First Secretary (Development): Miss Penny Thorpe
First Secretary (Development):
Ms Anthea Mulakala

Second Secretary (Chancery):
Miss Margaret Tongue
Second Secretary (Immigration/Consular):
Mrs Paula Peacock
Second Secretary (Immigration):
Mr Roger Goodall
Second Secretary (resides at Mumbai):
Mr Simon Sutcliffe
Deputy Cultural Attaché (British Council):
Ms Anna Searle
Third Secretary (Management): Mrs Rebecca Brett
Third Secretary (Chancery): Mr Colin Hicks
Attaché (Immigration): Miss Jo Ford
Attaché (Immigration): Mrs Yasmeen Rahman
Attaché (Immigration/Consular): Mr Ryan Griffin
Attaché (Immigration/Consular):
Mrs Sarah Downing
Attaché: Miss Julie Coleman
Attaché: Miss Jenny Jones
Attaché: Mr Mike Whyte
Attaché: Staff Sergeant Alistair Farrow
Attaché: Mr Tony Mason

MALI

Bamako
British Embassy Liaison Office (BELO)
(All staff resident in Dakar except where otherwise stated)
Enceinte Ambassade du Canada, sise à
L'hyppodrome sur la route de Koulikoro
BP. 2069 - Bamako
Telephone: (00) (223) 221 34 12 / 277 46 37
Facsimile: (00) (223) 221 34 12
e-mail: belo@afribone.net.ml
Office Hours (GMT): Mon-Thurs: 08 00 – 16 30,
Fri 08 00 – 12 30
Ambassador: Mr Peter Newall
Deputy Head of Mission and Consul:
Mr Derek Levoir
Vice-Consul/ECO: Ms Christine Johnson
Management Officer: Mr Nick Faulkner

BELO Staff:
Trade and Investment Officer/PPA: Ms Mariam
Traore (mobile: 223 674 82 08 / 674 98 29)
Consular Assistant: Mr Benjamin Tessougue
(mobile: 223 674 90 77 / 679 02 02)

MALTA

Valletta
British High Commission
Whitehall Mansions
Ta'Xbiex Seafront
Ta'Xbiex MSD 11
FTN Code – 8727 + extn number
Telephone: (00) (356) 2323 0000
Facsimile: (00) (356) 2323 2269 Management
                   2323 2226 Commercial
                   2323 2216 Chancery
                   2323 2234 Consular and Visa Section
e-mail: bhccomm@vol.net.mt (Commercial
Section)
Website: www.britishhighcommission.gov.uk/malta

Office Hours (GMT): Winter: Mon - Thur 07 00 -
15 45; Fri 07 00 - 12 15. Summer: Mon - Fri
05 30 - 11 30
High Commissioner: Mr Vincent Fean
*Deputy High Commissioner and First
Secretary (Commercial/Economic):*
Mr John Hillman
Defence Adviser (resides in Rome):
Captain John H Hollidge, RN
First Secretary (Political): Mr Jeremy Hart
British Council Director: Mr Ronnie Micallef
Second Secretary (Management/Consular):
Ms Jenny Fenton
Second Secretary (EU/Economic):
Ms Sue Elliott, MBE
Third Secretary (Political/Information/Cultural):
Ms Ravinder Hans
Third Secretary (Consular/Immigration):
Ms Elaine Marsh
Registrar: Mr Rory O'Brien

MARSHALL ISLANDS

Majuro
British Embassy
Ambassador (resides at Suva): Mr Ian Powell

MAURITANIA

Nouakchott
British Embassy
(All staff resident in Rabat)
Ambassador: Mr Haydon Warren-Gash
Deputy Head of Mission: Mr Kevin Lyne
Defence Attaché:
Lieutenant Colonel Simon J A Lloyd MBE
Second Secretary: Mr Steve Moore

Nouakchott
SOGECO
Route de l'Aeroport
B.P 351 Nouakchott
Telephone: (00) (222) 525 8331
(00) (222) 630 1217 (Mobile)
Facsimile: (00) (222) 525 3903
e-mail: sogeco@opt.mr or sab@opt.mr
Opening Hours: Sun-Thurs 08 00 – 16 00
Honorary Consul: Mr Sid' Ahmed Ould Abeidna

MAURITIUS

Port Louis
British High Commission
Les Cascades Building, Edith Cavell Street
Port Louis, PO Box 1063
FTN Code – 8612 + extn number or 1000
(switchboard)
Telephone: (00) (230) 202 9400
Facsimile: (00) (230) 202 9408
Airtech: (00) (230) 202 9448
Duty Officer: (00) (230) 252 8006 (Out of hours
emergency)
e-mail: bhc@intnet.mu (All sections)

Commercial Section:
Les Cascades Building,
Edith Cavell Street, Port Louis, PO Box 1063

Telephone: (00) (230) 202 9400
Facsimile: (00) (230) 202 9408
Consular and Immigration Section:
Les Cascades Building
Edith Cavell Street
Port Louis, PO Box 1063
Telephone: (00) (230) 202 9400
Facsimile: (00) (230) 202 9407
Office Hours (GMT): Mon - Thur 03 45 - 11 45.
Fri 03 45 - 09 30
High Commissioner (ext 2420):
Mr Anthony Godson
Deputy High Commissioner and First Secretary
(Commercial) (ext 2424): Mr Michael B G Plumb
Defence Adviser (resides at Pretoria):
Brigadier David H Keenan, OBE
British Council Director: Ms Rosalind Burford
Second Secretary (Chancery) (ext 2422):
Ms Ginny Silva
Third Secretary (Management) (ext 2428):
Mr Faruk Miah
Third Secretary (Immigration/Consular) (ext
2411): Mrs Sandra Belfitt

Rodrigues
British Honorary Consulate
Craft Aid
Camp du Roi
Rodrigues, Mauritius
Telephone: (00) (230) 831 1766
Facsimile: (00) (230) 831 2276
e-mail: pdraper@intnet.mu
Opening Hours: (local time) Mon – Fri: 07 00 –
16 00. Sat: 08 00 – 12 00
Honorary Consul: Mr Paul Draper, MBE

MEXICO

Mexico City
British Embassy
Rio Lerma 71, Col Cuauhtémoc
06500 Mexico City
FTN Code – 8457 + extn number
Telephone: (00) (52) (55) 5 242 8500
Facsimile: (00) (52) (55) 5 242 8517
e-mail: ukinmex@att.net.mx
Website: www.embajadabritanica.com.mx
Office Hours (GMT): Mon - Fri 14 30 - 21 30
(Winter). Mon - Fri 15 30 - 22 30 (Summer)
Ambassador: Mrs Denise Holt, CMG
Counsellor (Public Services) and Consul-General:
Mr Mark Kent
Counsellor (Political/Economic/Internal Services):
Mr Vijay Rangarajan
Counsellor (Cultural) (British Council Director)
(5263 1992): Mr Clive Bruton
Defence Attaché (resides at Guatemala City):
Colonel Ian C D Blair-Pilling, OBE
First Secretary (Political): Mr Jeremy Hobbs
First Secretary (Cultural) (British Council) (5263
1962): Mr Eric Lawrie
First Secretary (Global Issues): Ms Catherine Firth
First Secretary (Internal Services/Management):
Mr Steve James
First Secretary (Commercial):
Mr Andrew J F Ford, MVO

Second Secretary (Technical Management):
Mr Ian Taylor
Second Secretary (Commercial) and Consul:
Mr Andrew Morris
Second Secretary (Economic): Mr Gavin Tench
Second Secretary (Works) (Resides at Miami):
(Vacant)
Third Secretary (Internal Services/Management):
Ms Jane Atkinson
Attaché: Mrs Alison Diaz
Attaché: Mrs Kim Taylor
Attaché: Mr Allan Wilson

Mexico City
British Consulate
Embassy, Consular Section
Rio Usumacinta 30, Col Cuauhtémoc,
06500, Mexico DF
Telephone: as for Embassy
Facsimile: (00) (52) (55) 5242 8523
e-mail: consular.section@fco.gov.uk
Consul: Mr Andrew Morris
Vice-Consul: Ms Dawn Naughton

Acapulco
Honorary British Consulate
Centro Internacional Acapulco
Casa Consular
Costera Miguel Aleman
39851, Acapulco, Guerrero
Telephone: (00) (52) (744) 484 173
Facsimile: (00) (52) (744) 412 533 (ask for tone)
Honorary Consul: Mrs Lorraine E Bajos

Cancun
Honorary British Consulate
The Royal Sands
Blvd Kulkukan, Km 13.5
Zona Hotelera
77500 Cancun, Quintana Roo
Telephone: (00) (52) (998) 881 0100
Facsimile: (00) (52) (998) 888 229
Honorary Consul: Mr Mark Carney, OBE

Ciudad Juárez
Honorary British Consulate
Calle Fresno 185, Campestre Juárez
32460 Ciudad Juárez, Chihuahua
Telephone: (00) (52) (656) 616 7791/617 5088
Facsimile: (00) (52) (656) 887 351
Honorary Consul: Mr Rex Maingot

Guadalajara
British Trade Office
Aurelio Aceves 225, Local 40
Col. Vallarta Poniente
Guadalajara, Jal. 44110
Telephone: (00) (52) (333) 630 43 57/630
4385/630 4359
Facsimile: (00) (52) (333) 616 2159
Commercial Officer: Mr Eduardo Vega

Guadalajara
Honorary British Consulate
Jesus de Rojas No. 20
Colonia Los Pinos
Zapopan
Jalisco CP 45120

Telephone/Facsimile: (00) (52) (33) 3343 2296
Honorary Consul: Mr Simon Cohen, MBE

Monterrey
British Consulate
Ave. Ricardo Margain Zozaya 240
Colonia Valle del Campestre
C P 66225
San Pedro Garza Garcia
Nuevo Leon
Telephone: (00) (52) (818) 356 5359
Facsimile: (00) (52) (818) 356 5379
Consul: Mr Karl Burrows
Commercial Officer: Mr Horacio Licon

Oaxaca
Hotel Xestal
Blvd. Chahue
Lote 37, Mza. 4 Sector R
Bahias de Huatulco, Oaxaca
Telephone: (00) (52) (958) 587 2372 (leave a
message)
Facsimile: (00) (52) (958) 587 2373
Consular Correspondent: Mr Wolfgang Wilczek

Tijuana
Honorary British Consulate
Blvd Salinas No 1500, Fracc Aviación Tijuana
22420 Tijuana, BCN
Telephone: (00) (52) (664) 686 5320/681 7323
Facsimile: (00) (52) (664) 681 8402
Honorary Consul: Mr Eric M Baloyan

Veracruz
Honorary British Consulate
Independencia No 1349-1
Zona Centro (PO Box 724), 91700 Veracruz
Telephone: (00) (52) (229) 9311255
Facsimile: (00) (52) (229) 931285, (ask for tone)
Honorary Consul: Mr Luis Carbajal

MICRONESIA

Pohnpei
British Embassy
Ambassador (resides at Suva): Mr Ian Powell

MOLDOVA

Chisinau
British Embassy
ASITO Building, office 320
57/1 Banulescu-Bodoni St.
Chisinau 2005
Telephone: (00) (3732) 238 991 (General
           Enquiries)
           232 712 (Ambassador)
           233 018 (DHM)
           238 476 (DFID)
Facsimile: (00) (3732) 238 992
            238 478
Mobile: (00) (373) 910 4088/910 4443
Ambassador and Consul-General
(e-mail: bernardwhiteside@be.moldline.net):
Mr Bernard G Whiteside, MBE
Deputy Head of Mission: Mr Tony Kay
Defence Attaché (resides at Bucharest):
Colonel Anthony A A Beattie

MONACO (HC)

British Consulate
33 Boulevard Princesse Charlotte,
BP 265, MC 98005 Monaco CEDEX
Telephone: (00) (377) 93 50 99 54
Facsimile: (00) (377) 97 70 72 00
Consul-General (resides at Marseille):
Mr Simon Lever
Honorary British Consul: Mr Eric Blair

MONGOLIA

Ulaanbaatar (SP – see page 120)
British Embassy
30 Enkh Taivny Gudamzh (PO Box 703)
Ulaanbaatar 13
FTN Code – 8728 + 1000 for switchboard
Telephone: (00) (976) (11) 458133
Facsimile: (00) (976) (11) 458036
FTN Facsimile: 8728 2034
e-mail: britemb@magicnet.mn
Office Hours (GMT): Winter: Mon-Thurs 00 30 -
05 00 and 06 00 - 09 00. Fri 00 30 - 05 30
Summer: Mon-Thurs 01 30 - 06 00 and 07 00 -
10 00, Fri 01 30 - 06 30
Ambassador: Mr Richard J Austen, MBE
Deputy Head of Mission: Mr Justin Tait
Vice Consul and Management Officer:
Ms Lesley Beats, MBE
Defence Attaché (resides at Beijing):
Brigadier Archie J Miller-Bakewell

MOROCCO

Rabat
British Embassy
17 Boulevard de la Tour Hassan (BP 45), Rabat
FTN Code – 8387 + extn number
Telephone: (00) (212) (37) 72 96 96
Facsimile: (00) (212) (37) 70 45 31
            (Management/Consular)
            26 08 39 (Chancery)
Airtech: 72 99 62
e-mail: consular.rabat@fco.gov.uk
Website: www.britain.org.ma
www.fco.gov.uk
Office Hours (GMT): Winter: Mon – Thur 08 00 -
16 30; Fri 08 00 - 13 00. Summer: Mon – Thur 08
00 - 14 00, Fri 08 00 - 13 00
Ambassador: Mr Haydon Warren-Gash
Deputy Head of Mission: Mr Kevin Lyne
Defence Attaché:
Lieutenant Colonel Simon J A Lloyd MBE
Cultural Attaché (British Council Director):
Mr Steve McNulty
First Secretary and Consul: Mr Nick Collyer
First Secretary (Regional Affairs): Mr Mike Fox
Second Secretary (Political/Information):
Mr Matthew Hedges
Second Secretary (Commercial/Economic):
Mr Steve Moore
Vice Consul: Mrs Ann-Marie Teeuwissen
Attaché (Registry/Communications): Mrs Sue Kirk
Attaché (Chancery): Ms Erika Benning
Attaché (Military): Warrant Officer Iain Kennedy

Tangier
British Consulate
41 Boulevard Mohamed V, (BP 1203) Tangier
Telephone: (00) (212) (39) 94 15 57
Facsimile: (00) (212) (39) 94 22 84
e-mail: uktanger@mtds.com
Office Hours (GMT): Winter: Monday to Thursday
08 00 - 16 30. Summer: Monday to Thursday 08 00
- 14 00; Friday 08 00 - 13 00
Consul: Miss S L Sweet, MBE

Casablanca
British Consulate-General
43 Boulevard d'Anfa
(BP 13.762)
Casablanca
Telephone: (00) (212) 22 43 77 00
Facsimile: (00) (212) 22 43 77 04
(Commercial/Consular Section)
Visa Section Fax: (00) (212) 22 43 77 03
Airtech: (00) (212) 22 43 77 05
e-mail: consular.casablanca@fco.gov.uk
Office Hours (GMT): Winter: Mon – Thur 08 00 -
16 30; Fri 08 00 - 13 00. Summer: Mon – Thur 08
00 - 14 00; Fri 08 00 - 13 00
*Consul-General and Director, British Trade
Promotion:* Mr Denis Healy
Consul (Commercial): Mr Simon Williams
Vice-Consul (Commercial): Mr Driss Amal
Vice-Consul/Management Officer: Mr Ian Fox
Vice-Consul (Immigration): Mrs Kamla Taylor
Vice-Consul (Immigration): Mr Andrew Heseltine

Agadir
British Consulate
Complet Tours
Immeuble Oumlil
No. 26 3rd Floor
Avenue Hassan II
Agadir
Telephone: (00) (212) 48 823401, 823402
Facsimile: (00) (212) 48 823403
Honorary Consul: Ms Lesley Sanchez

Marrakech
British Consulate
55 Boulevard Zerktouni, Residence Taib,
Marrakech
Telephone: (00) (212) (44) 435095
Facsimile: (00) (212) (44) 439217
Honorary Consul: Mr Mohamed Zkhiri

MOZAMBIQUE

Maputo
British High Commission
Av Vladimir I Lenine 310, Caixa Postal 55
Maputo
FTN Code - 8614 + 1000 for switchboard
Telephone: (00) 258 1 320 111
Facsimile: (00) 258 1 321 666
Airtech: (00) 258 1 429 194
Office Hours (GMT): Mon - Thurs 06.00 10.30,
12.00 - 15.00; Fri 06.00 - 11.00
High Commissioner: Mr Howard Parkinson, CVO
Deputy High Commissioner and Consul:
Mrs Louise de Sousa

Defence Adviser (resides at Harare):
Colonel Bob J Griffiths, MBE
First Secretary (British Council Director):
Mr Simon Ingram-Hill
Second Secretary (Management/Consular):
Mr Chris Bowden, MBE
Third Secretary (Commercial):
Mr Jonathan Bamber
*Third Secretary (Vice Consul/Press and Public
Affairs):* Mrs Sarah Cassidy

**Department for International Development
(DfID) Mozambique**
37 Andar, Prédio JAT
Av 25 Setembro 420 , Caixa Postal 93
Maputo
Telephone: (00) 258 1 351400
Facsimile: (00) 258 1 351450
Head of Office: Eamon Cassidy
First Secretary, Senior Governance Adviser:
Caroline Rickatson
First Secretary, Senior Economic Adviser:
Nick Highton
First Secretary, Health and Education Adviser:
Dr Allison Beattie
First Secretary, Sustainable Livelihoods Adviser:
Julia Compton
First Secretary, Social Development Adviser:
Alicia Herbert
Second Secretary, Deputy Programme Manager:
John Hawkes
Second Secretary, Deputy Programme Manager:
Melanie Speight
Second Secretary, Head of Management Services:
Tom Jamieson
Third Secretary, IS Manager: Andy Galbraith
Third Secretary, Programme Officer: Sandra Grant
Second Secretary, Asst Governance Adviser:
Maja de Vibe
Third Secretary (Accountant): Ms Roma Nelson

Beira
British Honorary Consulate
Rua Paiva Couceiro 175, Caixa Postal 1401
Beira
Telephone: (00) 258 3 311 763
Facsimile: (00) 258 3 312 318
Honorary Consul: Mr Colin Cronin

NAMIBIA

Windhoek (SP – see page 120)
British High Commission
116 Robert Mugabe Avenue
Windhoek
Postal Address: PO Box 22202, Windhoek
FTN Code – 8616 + extn number
Telephone: (00) (264) (61) 274800
Facsimile: (00) (264) (61) 228895
Airtech: (00) (264) (61) 239004
e-mail: bhc@mweb.com.na Consular@fco.gov.uk
Visa@fco.gov.uk, Commercial@fco.gov.uk
Opening Hours: (April - September GMT+2) Mon-
Thurs 06 00 – 11 00; 12 00 – 15 00. Fri 06 00 –
10 00. (September - April GMT+1) Mon-Thurs 07
00 – 12 00; 13 00 – 16 00. Fri 07 00 – 11 00
High Commissioner: Mr Alasdair MacDermott

Deputy Head of Mission: Ms Sally Biskin
Defence Adviser (Resides at Pretoria):
Commander Peter Lankester, RN
Third Secretary (Management/Visa/Consular):
Mr Jim Couzens
Attaché: Ms Margaret Horsley
British Council
1-5 Peter Muller Street
Windhoek West
Windhoek
Postal Address: PO Box 13392
Telephone: (00) (264) (61) 226776
Facsimile: (00) (264) (61) 227530
e-mail: general.enquiries@bc-namibia.bcouncil.org
Website: www.britcoun.org/namibia
Opening Hours: same as British High Commission
Director: Ms P Mahlalela

Department for International Development (DFID) Field Office

11th Floor,
Sanlam Centre
Independence Avenue
Windhoek
Postal Address: 20689
Telephone: (00) (264) (61) 256294/5; 256251/17
Facsimile: (00) (264) (61) 256296
Opening Hours: same as British High Commision
Head of DFID Field Office/Programme
Administrator: Ms Rachel Malone
(e-mail: r-malone@dfid.gov.uk)

NAURU

Nauru

British High Commission
(All staff resident at Suva)
High Commissioner: Mr Charles F Mochan
Deputy High Commissioner: Mr Ian Powell

NEPAL

Kathmandu

British Embassy
Lainchaur, Kathmandu (PO Box 106)
FTN Code – 8397 + extn number
Telephone: (00) (977) (1) 4410583, 4411281,
4414588, 4411590
Facsimile: (00) (977) (1) 4411789, 4416723
e-mail: britemb@wlink.com.np (General)
ukconsular@wlink.com.np (Consular)
Office Hours (GMT) Mon-Thurs: 02 30 – 06 45
and 07 45 – 11 15; Fri 02 30 – 07 30
Ambassador: Mr Keith G Bloomfield
First Secretary and Deputy Head of Mission:
Mr David Ward
Defence Attaché: Colonel Peter R Sharland
First Secretary (Development) (Head of DFID-Nepal): Mr David Wood
First Secretary (Cultural) (British Council Director): Ms Barbara Hewitt
First Secretary (Political): Mr Andrew McCosh
First Secretary (Human Rights):
Mr Ben Schonveld
Assistant Defence Attaché: Major Peter Bullock
First Secretary (Resident in Mumbai):
Mr Chris Noon

Head of Management: Mrs Val Chamberlain
Clerk of Works: Mr Jeff Davies
Second Secretary, HM Consul/ECM, (Head, Consular and Immigration Services):
Mr John C Chick, MBE
Third Secretary (Chancery): Mr Jon Goddard
Third Secretary (Immigration): Mr Adrian Lewis
Vice Consul: Mr Oscar Castillo
Attaché: Ms Rosie Howes
Attaché: Ms Alison Garrity
Political Attaché and Information Officer:
Mr Mitra Pariyar
Commercial Attaché:
Mr Pradyumna G Karmacharya

Department For International Development, Nepal (DFID Nepal)

FTN Code – 8773 + extn number
Telephone: (00) (977) (1) 5542980/5542981
Facsimile: (00) (977) (1) 5542979
First Secretary (Head of DFID Nepal):
Mr David Wood
First Secretary (Deputy Head of DFID Nepal):
Mr Alex Harper
First Secretary (Deputy Head of DFID Nepal):
Mr Bob Smith
First Secretary (Senior Governance Adviser):
Mr Stephen Sharples
First Secretary (Economic Adviser):
Mr Andrew Hall
First Secretary (Rural Livelihoods Adviser):
Ms Helen Wedgwood
First Secretary (Senior Health and Population Adviser): Ms Susan Chapham
First Secretary (Engineering and Infrastructure Adviser): Mr Mark Harvey
First Secretary (Education Adviser) (based in Ministry of Education): Mr Mark Waltham
First Secretary (Statistics Adviser):
Ms Frances Harper
Second Secretary (Head of Finance):
Mr David Collingwood
Second Secretary (Head of HR and Office Services): Mr Jim Black
Deputy Programme Manager:
Ms Rebecca Goddard
Conflict Adviser: Mr Mark Segal
Social Development Adviser: Ms Rebecca Calder

British Council

Lainchaur, Kathmandu (PO Box 640)
Telephone: (00) (977) (1) 4410798, 4413003
Facsimile: (00) (977) (1) 4410545
Office Hours: Mon – Fri: 0245 – 0645 and 0745 -
1200
Director (British Council and Cultural Attaché):
Ms Barbara Hewitt
Assistant Director (British Council):
Mr Colin Earley

NETHERLANDS

The Hague

British Embassy
Lange Voorhout 10, 2514 ED, The Hague
FTN Code – 8307 + extn number
Telephone: (00) (31) (70) 427 0427

Facsimile: (00) (31) (70) 427 0345 General
0346 Commercial Section
0347 Ambassador's Office, DHM and
Political Section
Website: www.britain.nl
Office Hours (GMT): Mon - Fri 08 00 - 16 30
Ambassador: Sir Colin R Budd, KCMG
Deputy Head of Mission: Ms Jane Darby
Counsellor (Economic, Trade and Investment):
Ms Patricia R Phillips
Counsellor: Mr Tony Cowan
Defence Attaché: Captain A Robin Davies, RN
First Secretary and Head of Political Section:
Mr Andrew Price
First Secretary (Legal): Mr Dominic Raab
First Secretary (Chemical Weapons):
Mr Mark Matthews
First Secretary (Labour): Ms Gill Fraser
First Secretary (Trade and Investment):
Mr Tony Hennessy
First Secretary (Management):
Ms Monique Foulcer
Second Secretary (Labour): Mr Andrew Kirk
Second Secretary (Chemical Weapons):
Ms Gabrielle Kruger
Second Secretary (Economic):
Mrs Christine Lufkin
Second Secretary (Political): Mr David Burton
Second Secretary (Political): Mr Derek Tindell
Attaché: Mr Paul Harris
Attaché: Mr Keith Ditcham
Attaché: Mr Andrew Dean
Attaché: Mr Steve Cobbold
Attaché: Mr Kevin Field

Amsterdam (SP)
British Consulate-General
Koningslaan 44, Amsterdam
(PO Box 75488, 1070 AL Amsterdam)
FTN Code - 8306 + extn number
Telephone: (00) (31) (20) 676 43 43 (6 lines) for
extensions see individual officers
Facsimile: (00) (31) (20) 676 10 69
675 83 81 Consular Section
Airtech: (00) (31) (20) 676 4343 (Option 1,
2252#)
Telex: 15117 (a/b UKAMS NL)
e-mail: PassportEnquiries.amsterdam@fco.gov.uk
VisaEnquiries.amsterdam@fco.gov.uk
Office Hours (GMT): Mon-Fri 08 00 - 16 00
Consul-General (2209): Mr Bernhard Garside
British Council Director: Mr David Alderdice
Vice-Consul (Management) (2210): Ms Dawn Tok
Vice-Consul (Consular) (2222):
Mr Malcolm Mason, MBE
Vice-Consul (Immigration) (2216):
Mr Barry Wilde

Willemstad (Curacao)
British Consulate
Jan Sofat 38
(PO Box 3803)
Curacao
Netherlands Antilles
Telephone: (00) (599) (9) 747 3322
Facsimile: (00) (599) (9) 747 3330

e-mail: britconcur@attglobal.net (British
Consulate)
owersa@curinfo.an (Honorary Consul)
Office Hours (GMT): 12 00 - 16 00
Honorary Consul (see address above):
Mr Antony W Owers

Philipsburg (St Maarten)
(Netherlands Antilles)
British Vice-Consulate
(Temporarily closed)

NEW ZEALAND

Wellington
British High Commission
44 Hill Street, Wellington 1
Mailing Address: British High Commission
PO Box 1812, Wellington
FTN Code – 8480 + extn number
Telephone: (00) (64) (4)924 2888
Facsimile: (00) (64) (4)473 4982 Economic/Trade
Policy Section
924 2810 Passports
924 2822 Immigration
924 2831 Chancery
924 2809 Management
Airtech: (00) (64) (4)924 2836
e-mail: PPA.Mailbox@fco.gov.uk
bhc.wel@xtra.co.nz
Website: www.britain.org.nz
Office Hours (GMT): 20 45 – 05 00
High Commissioner (ext 2874):
Mr Richard T Fell, CVO
Deputy High Commissioner (ext 2859):
Mr Martin Bourke
Defence Adviser (ext 2875): Colonel Nigel Lloyd
*First Secretary (Economic/Trade Policy) (ext
2842):* Mr Paul D Noon
*First Secretary (Political/Press/Public Affairs) (ext
2861):* Mr Matthew K Forbes
*First Secretary (British Council Director) (ext
2853):* Ms Paula Middleton
First Secretary (Political/External) (ext 2881):
Ms A Ruth Walker
*First Secretary (Senior Technical Management
Officer) (resides at Canberra):* Mr Larry King
Second Secretary (Management) (ext 2871):
Mr Phil Hickson
Second Secretary (Political) (ext 2862):
Ms Sarah M Weeks
Second Secretary (Consular) (ext 2899):
Mr John D A Kenny
Third Secretary (Consular) (Ext 2891):
Mr Matthew R Simpson

Auckland
British Consulate-General
Level 17 IAG House, 151 Queen Street, Auckland 1
Mailing Address: British Consulate-General
Private Bag 92014, Auckland 1
Telephone: (00) (64) (9) 303 2973
Facsimile: (00) (64) (9) 303 1836
Airtech: (00) (64) (9) 358 4538
e-mail: trade_enquiries.auckland@fco.gov.uk
Website: www.uktradeinvest.co.nz
Office Hours (GMT): 20 45 - 05 00

Consular, Visa and Passport work is centralised in
Wellington
*Consul-General and Director of Trade
Development:* Mr Stephen E Turner
Deputy Consul-General: Mr Gary V Scroby
Trade Promotion Manager: Mrs Barbara Harris
Trade Promotion Manager: Mr Brian Murray
Pro-Consul (Management): Miss Deborah Clay
Press and Public Affairs Officer:
Ms Katharine Fenton-Wells

Christchurch
British Trade Office and Consulate
PO Box 13292, Christchurch 8031
Telephone: (00) (64) (3) 337 9933
Facsimile: (00) (64) (3) 337 9938
Office Hours (GMT): 21 00 - 05 00
Trade Representative and Honorary Consul:
(Vacant)

Cook Islands
Office of the Honorary British Consul
Muri Beach
PO Box 552
Rarotonga
Cook Islands
Telephone: (00) (682) 21080 (Office)
20444 (Home)
Facsimile: (00) (682) 21087
e-mail: mitchell@oyster.net.ck
Honorary British Consul: Mr Mike C Mitchell, MBE

NICARAGUA

Managua

British Embassy Closed
(Please refer to Costa Rica)

**Department for International Development,
Central American (CAM) Nicaragua**
PO Box C-194, Reparto Los Robles
#17-A Del Alke, 1 c. Oeste, 1½c. Sur
Managua
Telephone: (00) (505) (2) 702 985
Facsimile: (00) (505) (2) 702 988
*Head of Office and First Secretary to the British
Embassy:* Ms Penny Davies
Private Sector Adviser: Ms Geraldine Murphy
Violence Reduction and HIV/AIDS Adviser:
Ms Anne Christian Largaespada
Governance Adviser: Ms María José Jarquín

NIGER

Niamey
British Embassy
(All staff resident in Abidjan)
Ambassador and Consul-General: Mr D Coates
First Secretary (Commercial) and Consul:
Mr James Thornton
Second Secretary: Ms Karen Miller, MBE
*Third Secretary, (Visas/Passports) and Vice-
Consul:* Ms Emma Mamet

British Honorary Consulate
BP 10151, Niamey
Telephone: (00) (227) 725046

Honorary Consul: Mrs Susan Jarrett

NIGERIA

Abuja
British High Commission
Shehu Shangari Way (North)
Maitama, Abuja
FTN Code – 8495 + extn number
Telephone: (00) (234) (9) 413 2010, 2011, 2796,
            2880, 2883, 2887, 9817 (Chancery and
            Defence Sections)
Facsimile: (00) (234) (9) 413 3552 (Chancery and
            Defence Sections)
Airtech: (00) (234) (9) 413 2010
e-mail: Chancery.abuja@fco.gov.uk
Abujadefence@fco.gov.uk
Commercial.abuja@fco.gov.uk
Consular.abuja@fco.gov.uk
Management.abuja@fco.gov.uk
Visaenquiries.abuja@fco.gov.uk
Clinic.abuja@fco.gov.uk
Office Hours (GMT): 07 00 - 14 00

**Trade Development, Management, Consular and
Visa Sections:**
Dangote House, Aguyi Ironsi Street,
Maitama, Abuja
Telephone: (00) (234) (9) 413 4559-64,
0899,.0900, 3885-7, 3889
Facsimile: (00) (234) (9) 413 4565 (Visa Section)
(00) (234) (9) 413 3888 (Management, Trade
Development and Consular Sections)

Department for International Development
Plot 607
Bobo Street
Maitama, Abuja
FTN Code – 8771 + extn number
Telephone: (00) (234) (9) 413 7710-19
Facsimile: (00) (234) (9) 413 7400, 7398-99
Office Hours (GMT): Mon-Thurs: 07 00 – 15 30
Fri: 07 00 – 12 00

British Council
Plot 2935
IBB Way
Maitama, Abuja
Telephone: (00) (234) (9) 413 7870-7
Facsimile: (00) (234) (9) 413 7883, 0902
Office Hours (GMT): Mon-Thurs: 07 00 – 15 30
Fri: 07 00 – 12 00
*High Commissioner (also Ambassador non
–resident to the Republic of Benin):*
Mr Richard Gozney, CMG
Deputy High Commissioner:
Mr Martin Shearman, CVO
Defence Adviser: Colonel Neil J N Salisbury, OBE
Counsellor (Development): Mr William Kingsmill
Counsellor (Cultural): Dr John Richards
First Secretary (Political): Mr David Haines
First Secretary (Political): Ms Gillian Dare
First Secretary (Management): Mr Ken Clark
First Secretary (Cultural): Mr Peter Brown
First Secretary (Development): Ms Liz Gaere
First Secretary (Regional Medical Officer):
Dr Yinkori Toun

Second Secretary (Political): Mr Robert Paterson
Second Secretary (Political): Mr Colin Wells
Second Secretary (Economic): Vel Gnanendran
Second Secretary (Immigration): (Vacant)
Second Secretary (Technical Works):
Mr John Neale, MBE
*Third Secretary (Political/Press and Public
Affairs):* Mr Paul Edwards
Third Secretary (Management) and Vice Consul:
Mr Declan Byrne
Third Secretary (Security and Transport):
Mr Keith Rowland, MVO
Third Secretary (Immigration):
Mr Kingsley Magee
Third Secretary (Immigration): Mrs Dawn Neale
Third Secretary (Immigration):
Mr Dominic O'Callaghan
Third Secretary (Immigration):
Ms Sheila Underwood
Attaché (Defence Section Support Staff):
Staff Sergeant Terry Roberts

Lagos
British Deputy High Commission
11 Walter Carrington Crescent
Victoria Island, Lagos
(Private Mail Bag 12136)
FTN Code – 8326 + extn number
Telephone: (00) (234) (1) 2619531, 2619537,
2619541, 2619543, 2619566, 2619588, 2619592,
2619598
Facsimile: (00) (234) (1) 2614021
Office Hours (GMT): 0700 – 1400

Visa and Consular Sections
11 Walter Carrington Crescent
Victoria Island, Lagos
Telephone: (00) (234) (1) 2625930-7
Facsimile: (00) (234) (1) 2625940 Consular
(00) (234) (1) 2625941 Visa
Office Hours (GMT): 0630 – 1330
Deputy High Commissioner: Mr David Wyatt
Deputy Head of Mission: Mr Peter McCoy
Director Visa Services (Immigration):
Mr Chris Dix
First Secretary (Immigration): Mr Charles Molloy
First Secretary (Commercial): Mr John Williams
First Secretary (Technical Management):
Mr Ian Willsher
Second Secretary (Commercial): Mr John Wales
Second Secretary (Consular): Mr Maurice Harper
Second Secretary (Immigration):
Mr Stephen Brown
Second Secretary (Immigration): Mr John Mellor
Second Secretary (Immigration): Mr Kevan Clifton
Second Secretary (Immigration): Mr Jason Ivory
Second Secretary (Management): Mr Kevin Curran
Second Secretary (Political): Mr John King
Second Secretary (Technical Management):
Mr J Malcolm Lawrie, MBE
Third Secretary (Consular): Mr Tony Ward
Third Secretary (Management): Mr Steve Doust
Third Secretary (Management): Mrs Sarah Morris

Kano
2 Tsauna Close
Off Amadu Bello Way

PO Box 11872
Kano
Telephone: (00) (234) (64) 631 686
Facsimile: (00) (234) (64) 632 590
e-mail: bhc.kan@skannet.com
Honorary Consul: Mr Harold Blackburne, OBE

Warri
ABB Lummus Global
Unit 6, Jefia State
62 Enerhen Road
Delta State, Warri
Telephone/ Facsimile: (00) (234) (53) 245 523 or
                                                 255 929
Mobile: 080 3708 2048
e-mail: melhenthorn@hyperia.com
Honorary Consul: Mr Mel Henthorn

Kaduna
British High Commission Liaison Office
3 Independence Way, Kaduna
Telephone: (00) (234) (62) 243380/81
Facsimile: (00) (234) (62) 237267
e-mail: bhc@wwlkad.com
Liaison Officer: Ms Deborah Butterworth

Port Harcourt
British Commercial/Liaison Office
Plot 300, Olu Obasanjo Road, Port Harcourt,
Rivers State
Telephone: (00) (234) (84) 237173, 335104
Facsimile: (00) (234) (84) 237172
e-mail: bhcliaison@phca.linkserve.com

Ibadan
British Liaison Office
Rotimi Williams Avenue, Bodija, Ibadan
Telephone: (00) (234) (22) 810 4953
e-mail: blo.ibadan@skannet.com

Lagos
British Council Division
11 Alfred Rewane Road
Ikoyi, PO Box 3702
Lagos
Telephone: (00) (234) (1) 2692188-92, 261020,
                                                 2615047
Facsimile: (00) (234) (1) 2615047, 2622193
Office Hours (GMT): Mon-Thurs: 06 30 - 15 00
Fri: 06 30 – 11 30
First Secretary (Cultural): Mr Sam Harvey

British Council Division (Enugu, Ibadan and Kano)
Teachers House, Ogui Road, Enugu
Telephone: (00) (234) (42) 255577, 255677,
                                                 258456
Facsimile: (00) (234) (42) 250158
53 Magazine Road, PMB 5314, Jericho, Ibadan
Telephone: (00) (234) (22) 2410299, 2410678
Facsimile: (00) (234) (22) 2410796
10 Emir's Place Road, Kano
Telephone: (00) (234) (64) 646652, 643489
Director's Direct Line: (00) (234) (64) 643861
Facsimile: (00) (234) (64) 632500
First Secretary (Cultural and Aid, Kano):
Ms Gillian Belben

NORWAY

Oslo
British Embassy
Thomas Heftyesgate 8, 0244 Oslo
FTN Code – 8324 + extn number
Telephone: (00) (47) 23 13 27 00
Facsimile: (00) (47) 23 13 27 41 Management
27 89 Chancery
27 38 Consular/Visa Section
27 05 Trade, Investment and Economic
Department
27 27 Information Section
2797 Defence
Website: www.britain.no
Office Hours (GMT): Summer 06 30 - 14 00,
Winter 07 30 - 15 00
Ambassador (2701): Mrs Mariot Leslie
*Deputy Head of Mission and Consul-General
(2707):* Mr Ian Hay-Campbell, lvo
Counsellor (2716): Mr Keith Beaven
Defence Attaché (2711):
Lieutenant Colonel Steve J Hughes, rm
*First Secretary (Trade, Investment and Economic
Dept) (2752):* Dr Laurence Bristow-Smith
First Secretary (Management/Consul) (2751):
Mr Mark Forrester
British Council Director: Ms Sarah Prosser
*Second Secretary (Trade, Investment and Economic
Dept) (2759):* Mr Duncan Hoyland
*Second Secretary (Press and Public Affairs)
(2718):* Mr Charles H J Davies
Second Secretary (2719): Mrs Claire Evans
Second Secretary (2708): Mr Rufus Drabble
Vice Consul/DMO (2778): Mr Gerald Smith

Bergen
British Consulate
PO Box 7255, 5020 Bergen
VISITING ADDRESS:
Carl Konowsgate 34, 5161 Laksevåg
Telephone: (00) (47) 55 94 47 05
Telefax: (00) (47) 55 34 34 28
Honorary Consul: Mr R C Hestness (Norwegian)

Kristiansand
British Consulate
Post Box 479, 4664 Kristiansand
VISITING ADDRESS:
Tangen 10, 4610 Kristiansand
Telephone: (00) (47) 38 12 20 70
Facsimile: (00) (47) 38 12 30 71
Honorary Consul: Mr T Wiese-Hansen
(Norwegian)

Stavanger
British Consulate
PO Box 28, 4001 Stavanger
VISITING ADDRESS:
Prinsensgate, 12 4008 Stavanger
Telephone: (00) (47) 51 52 97 13
Facsimile: (00) (47) 51 53 83 01
Honorary Consul: Mr T Falck, Jnr (Norwegian)

Tromsø
British Consulate
c/o Mack's Ølbryggeri, 9291, Tromsø

VISITING ADDRESS:
c/o Mack's Ølbryggeri, Storgaten 5-13, 9291
Tromsø
Telephone: (00) (47) 77 62 45 00
Facsimile: (00) (47) 77 65 86 77
Honorary Consul: Mr H Bredrup (Norwegian)

Trondheim
British Consulate
Post Box 2521, 7413 Trondheim
VISITING ADDRESS:
Beddingen 8, 7037, Trondheim
Telephone: (00) (47) 73 60 02 00
Facsimile: (00) (47) 73 60 02 50
Honorary Consul: Mrs B Kjeldsberg (Norwegian)

Ålesund
British Consulate
Post Box 1301, 6001 Ålesund
VISITING ADDRESS:
Farstadgården, St Olav's Plass, 6001 Ålesund
Telephone: (00) (47) 70 12 44 60
Facsimile: (00) (47) 70 12 85 30
Honorary Consul: Mr S A Farstad (Norwegian)

Bodø
British Consulate
VISITING ADDRESS and POSTAL ADDRESS
Brggcon AS
Notveien 17
8013 Bodø
Telephone: (00) (47) 75 56 58 00
Facsimile: (00) (47) 75 56 58 01
Mobile: 950 29 769
e-mailkjell@byggcon.no
Opening Hours: 09 00 – 16 00
Honorary Consul: Mr Kjell Alf Nyvold
(Norwegian)

OMAN

Muscat
British Embassy
PO Box 185, Mina Al Fahal, Postal Code 116
FTN Code – 8449 + extn number
Telephone: (00) (968) 609000
609001 (Consular/Visa)
609002 (UK Trade and Investment)
609224 (Defence)
Facsimile: (00) (968) 609010 (General)
609011 (Consular)
609012 (UK Trade and Investment)
609013 (Chancery)
609014 (Defence)
e-mail: Enquiries.Muscat@fco.gov.uk (General)
UKTI.muscat@fco.gov.uk (UK Trade and
Investment)
Consular.Staff@fco.gov.uk (Visa and Consular)
Website: www.britishembassy.gov.uk/oman
Office Hours (GMT): Sat - Wed 03 30 - 10 30
Ambassador: Mr Stuart Laing
Counsellor and Deputy Head of Mission:
Mr Charles Hill
Defence and Military Attaché:
Brigadier Hugh C G Willing
Naval and Air Attaché:
Commander Bob P Thomas, rn

British Council Director: Mr Jim Scarth
First Secretary (Political): Mr Nicholas Diggle
First Secretary (Management) and Consul:
Mrs Clare Douglas
First Secretary (UK Trade and Investment):
Mr Malcolm Ives
First Secretary (Defence Equipment Co-operation):
Mr Jim Catchpole
Second Secretary (Chancery/Information):
Mr Alex Brown, MBE
Second Secretary (Political): Mr William Stringer
Third Secretary (UK Trade and Investment):
Mrs Janine Philpott
British Vice-Consul: Mrs Susan Ives

PAKISTAN

Islamabad
British High Commission
Diplomatic Enclave, Ramna 5,
PO Box 1122, Islamabad.
FTN Code – 8685 + extn number
Telephone: (00) (92) (51) 2822131/5, 2206071/5
Auto Direct Dial: (00) (92) (51) 2820941/47 + Ext
(only from a digital phone)
Direct Lines: (00) (92) (51) 2822996 High
Commissioner
(00) (92) (51) 2206056 Counsellor (Political)
Facsimile: (00) (92) (51) 2201109 Chancery
            2825299 Defence
            2823439 Management
            2826217 Commercial
            2279355 Commercial
            2206069 Immigration
            2824728 Immigration
            2279356 Consular
            2279351 Accommodation/TWG
            2277159 Clinic
            2823017 Development
            2271198 DLO
            2279350 DIFD
            2201172 PLO
Secure Facsimile: (00) (92) (51) 2822989
(Cryptek), 2279358 (Airtech)
Telegrams: Prodrome, Islamabad
e-mail: bhctrade@isb.comsats.net.pk (Commercial
Section)
bhcmedia@isb.comsats.net.pk (Media and Public
Affairs)
bhcdefence@isb.comsats.net.pk (Defence Section)
Office Hours (GMT): High Commission: Mon –
Thurs: 03 00 – 11 00, Fri: 03 00 – 07 00
Immigration/Consular Sections: Mon – Thurs: 02
30 – 09 30, Fri: 02 30 – 08 30
High Commissioner: Mr Mark Lyall Grant, CMG
Deputy High Commissioner: Mr Mark Sedwill
Counsellor (Political): Mr Peter Waterworth
Counsellor (Political): Mr David Cox
Counsellor (Regional Affairs): Mr Tim Clayden
Defence and Military Adviser:
Brigadier Andrew J M Durcan
Naval and Air Adviser: Colonel Mark W Bibbey, RM
First Secretary (Political): Mr Martin Cronin
First Secretary (Political): Mr Harvey Woods
First Secretary (Political): Mr Richard Seddon

First Secretary (Immigration/Consular):
Mr Colin Mulcahy
First Secretary (Management): Mr Peter Hardman
First Secretary (Works): Mr Alan McKerron
First Secretary (Technical Manager):
Mr Hugh Smith
Head of Development Section: Mr Gareth Aicken
*First Secretary (Health, Population and Women in
Development Adviser):* (Vacant)
First Secretary (Senior Governance Adviser):
Ms Jackie Charlton
First Secretary (MWD, Nursing Officer):
Ms Elizabeth McManus, MBE
Second Secretary (Political): Mr Adrian Scott
Second Secretary (Political): Mr Trevor Parker, MBE
Second Secretary (Political/External):
Mr Timothy Voase
Second Secretary (Political): Ms Caroline Jarrett
Second Secretary (Political): Mr David Birrell
Second Secretary (Development): (Vacant)
Second Secretary (Estates Manager):
Mr David Walters, MVO
Second Secretary (Technical Management):
Ms Debbie Cuthbertson
Second Secretary (Commercial): Mr David Oswald
Second Secretary (Drugs): Mr Eric Lane
Second Secretary (Works): Mr Gary Holmes
Second Secretary (Works): (Vacant)
Second Secretary (Immigration):
Mr Quinton Eyre Wilson
Second Secretary (Immigration): Ms Doris Davis
Second Secretary (Immigration):
Mr Adrian Loxton
Second Secretary (Immigration): Ms Kim Charman
Second Secretary (Management): Mr David Denyer
Second Secretary (Consular): Ms Cindy Parker
Second Secretary (Media and Public Affairs):
Mr Mark Korad
Third Secretary (Political): Mr Michael Halpin
Third Secretary (Political): Mr Kevin Jones
Third Secretary (Political): Ms Philippa Carnall
Third Secretary (Estates): Ms Caroline Gallagher
Third Secretary (Management): Ms Jean Tranter
Third Secretary (Management/Finance):
Mr Neil Scrambler
Third Secretary (Consular): Ms Lara Bryden

Lahore
British Trade Office
65 Mozang Road
PO Box 1679, Lahore
Telephone: (00) (92) (042) 6316589 - 90
Facsimile: (00) (92) (042) 6316591
Office Hours (GMT): Mon – Thurs 03 30 – 11 30,
Fri 03 30 – 07 30
Lahore Trade Promotion Adviser:
Mr Imran Masood Chaudhry

Karachi
British Deputy High Commission
Shahrah-e-Iran, Clifton, Karachi 75600
FTN Code - 8686 + 1000 for switchboard
Telephone: (92) (21) 5872431-6 (Landline)
Facsimile: (92) (21) 5874014 General
            5874328 Consular/Visa
Airtech: (92) (21) 5862316

e-mail: tradeuk@cyber.net.pk
Office Hours (GMT): Mon – Thurs: 03 30 – 11 00
Fri: 03 30 – 07 30
Deputy High Commissioner:
Mr Hamish St. Clair Daniel, OBE
Deputy Head of Mission: Mr Roger M S Sykes, OBE
British Council Director: Mr Charlie Walker
First Secretary (Political): Ms Gillian Wilson
Second Secretary (Management): Mr Paul A Tylor
Second Secretary: Mr Steve Lee-Jones
Second Secretary: Mr Allan Shearer
Third Secretary (Consular/Immigration):
Ms Susan Farrent
Third Secretary (Immigration): Mr Clive Spare
Third Secretary (Immigration): Ms Sue Voak
Third Secretary (Immigration): Mr Esmail Ansari
Security Manager: Mr William J Smith

PALAU

Koror
British Embassy
Ambassador (resides at Suva): Mr Ian Powell

PANAMA

Panama City (SP – see page 120)
British Embassy
Swiss Tower, Calle 53
P O Box 0816-07946 Panama City
FTN Code – 8458 + extn number
Telephone: (00) (507) 269 0866 (5 lines)
Facsimile: (00) (507) 223 0730
263 5138 (HMA's fax)
Airtech: (00) (507) 264 6846
e-mail: britemb@cwpanama.net
Office Hours (GMT): Mon – Thur 12 30 - 18 00
and 19 00 - 21 30, Fri 12 30 - 17 30
Ambassador and Consul-General:
Mr James I Malcolm, OBE
Deputy Head of Mission and First Secretary:
Ms Penny Walsh
First Secretary: Mr Alan Pamplin
Second Secretary: Mr Gary Foster
Defence Attaché (resides at Caracas):
Group Captain William G S Dobson, RAF
Second Secretary (Technical) (resides at Caracas):
Mr Colin Tully

PAPUA NEW GUINEA

Port Moresby (SP – see page 120)
British High Commission
Locked Mail Bag 212, Waigani NCD 131
Port Moresby
FTN Code – 8444 + extn number:- 2201
(Switchboard)
          2209 (PA to HC)
          2215 (Consular/Visa)
          2202 (Management)
          2208/2210 (PPA)
          2206 (Chancery/Registry)
Telephone: (00) (675) 3251643, 3251645,
          3251659, 3251677
Facsimile: (00) (675) 3253547
Airtech: (00) (675) 3253953
e-mail: bhcpng@datec.net.pg

Office Hours: Mon-Thurs: 07 45 – 16 20 (Local)
Fri: 07 45 – 12 10 (Local)
The High Commission will continue to be open
over lunch
High Commissioner (ext 2207):
Mr David S Gordon-MacLeod
Deputy High Commissioner (ext.2204):
Mr Alastair Dent
Defence Adviser (resides at Canberra):
Group Captain Steven Duffill, RAF

PARAGUAY

Asunción (SP – see page 120)
British Embassy
Avenida Boggiani 5848
c/ R.I. 6 Boquerón
Asunción
FTN Code – 8462 + extn number
Telephone: (00) (595) (21) 612611
Facsimile: (00) (595) (21) 605007
Airtech: (00) (595) (21) 612611 ext. 2131
e-mail: brembasu@rieder.net.py
Office Hours (GMT): 11 00 - 18 00
12 00 - 19 00 (roughly April-September inc)
Ambassador and Consul-General (ext 2110):
Mr Anthony Cantor
*First Secretary and Deputy Head of Mission (ext
2112):* Ms Christine Winterburn
Defence Attaché (resides at Buenos Aires):
Group Captain Ian Capewell RAF
First Secretary (resides at Brasilia):
Mr Frank Dick
Second Secretary (resides at Sao Paulo):
Mr Nick Freeman
Trade and Investment Officer (ext 2116):
Mr Joel Cano
Deputy Trade and Investment Officer (ext 2117):
Ms Diana Diaz de Espada
Aid/Press and Public Affairs Officer (ext 2114):
Mrs Sandra Melamed
Management Officer/Accountant (ext 2123):
Mrs Janine Spalding

PERU

Lima
British Embassy
Torre Parque Mar (Piso 22)
Avenida Jose Larco
1301 Miraflores
Lima
FTN Code - 8624 + extn number
Telephone: (00) (51) (1) 617 3000 Main
          617 3030 Commercial
          617 3050 Consular/Visa
          617 3060 British Council
          617 3070 DFID
Facsimile: (00) (51) (1) 617 3100 Main
          617 3001 Chancery
          617 3020 Management
          617 3040 Commercial
          617 3055 Consular/Visa
          617 3065 British Council
          617 3080 DFID
Airtech: (00) (51) (1) 617 3008

e-mail: belima@fco.gov.uk (General)
consvisa.lima@fco.gov.uk (Consular/Visa)
Office Hours (GMT): Mon – Thurs: 13 00 – 22 00;
Fri 13 00 – 18 00
Ambassador:
Mr Richard Peter Ralph, CMG, CVO (3002)
Deputy Head of Mission: Mr Ian Davies (3004)
Defence Attaché (Resides at Bogotá):
Colonel Mike E Wilcox (3085)
Cultural Attaché (British Council Director):
Mr Frank Fitzpatrick (3061)
First Secretary (Management) and HM Consul:
Mr Neil Storey (3016)
First Secretary: Mr Steve Jones (3013)
First Secretary (Commercial):
Mr Martin Lamport (3031)
First Secretary (Development, DFID):
Mr Mark Lewis (3071)
First Secretary (Health Sector, DFID):
Mr Carlos Santiso (3073)
*Second Secretary (Works) (resides at Buenos
Aires):* Mr Ronnie Clark
Second Secretary: Mr Mark Williams
Third Secretary (Chancery):
Mr Jonathan Clare (3005)
Third Secretary (Management) (resides at Bogota):
Mr Nick Moss-Norbury
*Third Secretary (Management/Immigration) and
Vice-Consul:* Mr Ian Swann (3051)
Vice-Consul/Immigration:
Mrs Nicola Standen (3054)

Arequipa
British Consulate
Tacna y Arica 156, Arequipa
Telephone: (00) (51) (54) 241 340
Facsimile: (00) (51) (54) 236 125
Office Hours (GMT): Mon - Fri 13 30 - 17 30 and
20 00 - 23 30
Honorary Consul: Mr J R G Roberts, MBE

Cusco
British Consulate
Av. Pardo 895
PO Box 606, Cusco
Telephone: (00) (51) (84) 22-6671/23-9974
Facsimile: (00) (51) (84) 23-6706
Office Hours (GMT): 16 00 - 17 00
Honorary Consul: Mr B Walker, MBE

Iquitos
British Consulate
Putumayo 182a
Iquitos
Telephone: (00) (51) (94) 22 2732
Facsimile: (00) (51) (94) 22 3607
Office Hours (GMT): 16 00 – 1700
Honorary Consul: Mr P Duffy

Piura
British Consulate
Huancavelica 223, Piura
Telephone: (00) (51) (74) 333 300/326 233
Facsimile: (00) (51) (74) 327 009
Office Hours (GMT): 14 00 - 18 00 / 21 00 - 23 59
Honorary Consul: Mr H E Stewart

Trujillo
British Consulate
Jesus de Nazareth No 312, Trujillo
Telephone: (00) (51) (44) 23 55 48
Facsimile: (00) (51) (44) 25 58 18
Office Hours (GMT): 14 00 - 22 00
Honorary Consul: Mr W Barber

PHILIPPINES

Manila
British Embassy
15th – 17th Floors LV Locsin Building
6752 Ayala Avenue cor Makati Avenue
1226 Makati
(PO Box 2927 MCPO)
FTN Code – 8688 + extn number
Telephone: (00) (63) (2) 816 7116 – switchboard
816 7271/2, 816 7348/9 – Visa and
Consular Sections
580 xxxx – direct inward dial; use
extensions shown beside name
Facsimile: (00) (63) (2) 813 7755 – Chancery
819 7206 – Management
815 4809 – Information
810 2745 – Visa
840 1361 – Consular
815 6233 – Commercial
Airtech: 894 3367
Telex: 63282 (a/b 63282 PRODME PN)
e-mail: uk@info.com.ph (Information Section)
uktrade@info.com.ph (Commercial Section)
Office Hours (GMT): Mon – Thurs: 00 00 – 08 30;
Fri: 00 00 – 06 00
Consular/Visa Office Hours: 00 00 – 05 00
Ambassador: Mr Paul Dimond (8300)
Deputy Head of Mission:
Mr Robert Fitchett (8301)
Defence Attaché: Colonel Martin K Stretch (8302)
First Secretary (Commercial):
Mr Eamonn Staunton (8303)
*First Secretary (Cultural) (British Council
Director):* Ms Gill Westaway (based at British
Council)
HM *Consul:* Mr John Fielder (8306)
First Secretary (Management):
Mr George Hodgson (8307)
Second Secretary (Commercial):
Mr Rob Walker (8305)
Second Secretary (Political):
Ms Katy Parker (8309)
Second Secretary (Immigration):
Mr Chris Stacey (8321)
Second Secretary (Development):
Ms Nicola Jens (based at ADB)
Second Secretary (Economic and Global Issues):
Ms Nicole Cadwallader (8311)
Third Secretary (Immigration):
Mr Graham Sykes (8316)
Third Secretary (Immigration):
Mr Nigel Greetham (8317)
Third Secretary (Immigration):
Mr Colin Coward (8319)
Third Secretary (Immigration):
Mr Michael McKibben (8315)
Attaché: Mr Gary Walker (8310)

Attaché: Ms Louise Freegard (8314)
Attaché: Ms Shiela Tunley (8313)
Attaché: Mr James Hopkins (8308)
Attaché: CPO Dennis Finch (8312)

Manila UK representation at the Asian Development Bank, see Missions and Delegations page 116

Cebu
British Consulate
Villa Terrace, Greenhills Road
Casuntingan, Mandaue City, Cebu
Telephone: (00) (63) (32) 346 0525
Facsimile: (00) (63) (32) 346 0269
e-mail: moke@gsilink.com
Honorary Consul: Mrs Moya Jackson

Angeles City
British Consulate
18-6 Concepcion Drive
Villa Teresa, Angeles City
Pampanga 2009
Tel/Fax: (00) (63) (45) 323 4187
Mobile: (00) (63) 917 918 1269
e-mail: dougalp@datelnet.net
Honorary Consul: Mr Douglas Paterson

Olongapo
British Consulate
Subic International Hotel
Subic Bay Freeport Zone
Olongapo, Zambales 2200
Telephone: (00) (63) (47) 252 2222
e-mail: sihgm@info.com.ph
Honorary Consul: Mr Michael Wilson

POLAND

Warsaw
British Embassy
Aleje Róz No 1, 00-556 Warsaw
FTN Code – 8627 + extn number
Telephone: (00) (48) (22) 311 0000
Facsimiles: (00) (48) (22) 311 0311
311 0313 (Management)
311 0315 (Chancery)
e-mail: britemb@it.com.pl
Commercial, Visa and Consular Sections:
Warsaw Corporate Centre, 2nd Floor
Ul. Emilii Plater 28, 00-688 Warsaw
Telephone: (00) (48) (22) 311 0000
Facsimile: (00) (48) (22) 311 0250
e-mail: Commercial@britishembassy.pl
(Commercial)
Consular@britishembassy.pl (Consular)
Visa@britishembassy.pl (Visa)
Website: www.britishembassy.pl
Office Hours (GMT + 1): 08 30 – 16 30
Ambassador (ext 4110): Mr Charles Crawford, CMG
Counsellor and Deputy Head of Mission (ext 4114): Mr Tim Simmons
Counsellor (ext 4282): Mr Guy Spindler
Director of Trade Promotion/Consul-General (ext 2201): Ms Julia Longbottom
Counsellor (Cultural) (695 5900 ext 20): Ms Susan Maingay OBE

Defence and Air Attaché (ext 4146):
Group Capain Tim J Williams, AFC, RAF
Naval and Military Attaché (ext 4141):
Lieutenant Colonel Stephen Croft
First Secretary (Political/Military) (ext 4148):
Mr Philip Barclay
First Secretary (Political) (ext 4159):
Mr Graham Horry
First Secretary (Management) (ext 4127):
Mr Roger Harmer
First Secretary (Commercial) (ext 2203):
Mr John Anderson
First Secretary (Education) (695 5900 ext 50):
Mr Robin Rickard
Second Secretary (Political) (ext 4140):
Miss Anna Jackson
Second Secretary (Consul/Commercial) (ext 2219):
Mr Niall Cullens
Second Secretary (Political) (ext 4118):
Miss Alexandra Davison
Second Secretary (LELO) (ext 4156):
Mr George Rakowski
Second Secretary (Commercial) (ext 2243):
Ms Emma Robinson
Second Secretary (Political) (ext 4167):
Mr James Lipsett
Second Secretary: Mr Guy Pinsent
Second Secretary (Management) (ext 4103):
Mr Simon Lochmuller
Third Secretary (Political) (ext 4117):
Mr Christopher Thompson
Third Secretary (Management) (ext 4153):
Mr Scott Melling
Attaché and Vice-Consul (2225): Ms Fiona Ogg
Attaché (ext 4111): Ms Elizabeth Rowe
Attaché (ext 4119): Ms Lorraine Findell

Gdansk
British Consulate
ul Grunwaldzka 102, 80-244 Gdansk
Telephone: (00) (48) (58) 341 4365, 346 1558
Facsimile: (00) (48) (58) 344 1608
e-mail: consul@abcc.com.pl
Office Hours (GMT + 1): 09 00 - 15 00
Honorary Consul: Mr Andrzej Kanthak

Katowice
British Consulate
ul PCK 10, 40-057 Katowice
Telephone: (00) (48) (32) 206 9801
Facsimile: (00) (48) (32) 205 4646
e-mail: honcon@silesia.top.pl
Office Hours (GMT + 1): 09 00 – 15 00
Honorary Consul: Mr Alan Stretton

Kraków
British Consulate
ul. Sw.Anny 9
31-008 Kraków
Telephone: (00) (48) (12) 421 7030
Facsimile: (00) (48) (12) 422 4264
e-mail: ukconsul@bci.krakow.pl
Office Hours (GMT + 1): 09 00 – 15 00
Honorary Consul: Mr Kazimierz Karasinski

Lódz
ul. Piotrkowska 85

90-423 Lódz
Telephone: (00) (48) (42) 638 8960, 630 3349
Facsimile: (00) (48) (42) 636 4116
e-mail: konsulatUK@klub.lodz.pl
Office Hours (GMT + 1): 09 00 – 15 00
Honorary Consul: Mrs Malgorzata Brzezinska

Lublin
British Consulate
ul. Beskidzka 9
20-869 Lublin
Telephone: (00) (48) (81) 742 0101
Facsimile: (00) (48) (81) 742 9130
e-mail: ukconsul@uren.com.pl
Office Hours (GMT + 1): 09 00 – 15 00
Honorary Consul: Mr Jan Danilczuk

Poznan
British Consulate
ul Wroclawska 6, 61-837 Poznan
Telephone: (00) (48) (61) 851 72 90 Hotel Poznan
Telephone: (00) (48) (61) 833 19 61
Facsimile: (00) (48) (61) 853 29 19
e-mail: ukcons@protea.pl
info@protea.pl
Office Hours (GMT + 1): 09 00 – 15 00
Honorary Consul: Mr Wlodzimierz Walkowiak

Szczecin
British Consulate
ul. Starego Wiarusa 32
71-206 Szczecin
Telephone: (00) (48) (91) 487 0302
Facsimile: (00) (48) (91) 487 3697
e-mail: gacszz@fnet.pl
Office Hours (GMT + 1): 09 00 – 15 00
Honorary Consul: Mr Ryszard Karger

Wroclaw
British Consulate
ul. Olawska 2, 50-123 Wroclaw
Telephone/Facsimile: (00) (48) (71) 344 8961
e-mail: consulate@kmc.com.pl
Office Hours (GMT + 1): 09 00 – 15 00
Honorary Consul: Mr Marek Grzegorzewicz

PORTUGAL

Lisbon
British Embassy
Rua de São Bernardo 33, 1249-082 Lisbon
FTN Code – 8368 + extn number
Telephone: (00) (351) (21) 392 4000
Facsimile: 4178 Chancery
4184 Defence
4185 Information
4186 Commercial
4187 Management
4188 Consular
e-mail: Chancery@Lisbon.mail.fco.gov.uk
Commercial@Lisbon.mail.fco.gov.uk
Consular@Lisbon.mail.fco.gov.uk
Management@Lisbon.mail.fco.gov.uk
Political2@Lisbon.mail.fco.gov.uk
PPA@Lisbon.mail.fco.gov.uk
Website: www.uk-embassy.pt

Office Hours (GMT): Summer 08 00 - 12 00 and
13 30 - 16 30. Winter 09 00 - 13 00 and
14 30 - 17 30
Ambassador: Mr John S Buck
Deputy Head of Mission: Mr Tim C Morris
Counsellor (Political): Mr Jamie Darke
Defence Attaché:
Commander Richard M Simmonds, OBE, RN
Counsellor (Cultural) (British Council Director):
Ms Rosemary Hilhorst, OBE
First Secretary (Head of Political Section):
Mr Ben Lyster-Binns
First Secretary (UK Trade and Investment):
Mr Mark Turner
First Secretary (Consul): Ms Elizabeth Dow
Second Secretary (Political/EU): Miss Julia Wright
Second Secretary (UK Trade and Investment):
Mr Paul Welsh
Second Secretary (Management):
Mr David Lingwood
Second Secretary: Mr Glen Pounder
Second Secretary: Mrs Laura Leavy
Third Secretary (Press and Public Affairs):
Mrs Deborah Alliaga
Third Secretary (Vice-Consul): Mr Steve Askham
Third Secretary (Management): Mr David Baugh
Attaché (PA to Ambassador): Mrs Patricia Fletcher

Oporto
British Consulate
Avenida da Boavista 3072,
4100-120 Oporto
Telephone: (00) (351) (22) 618 4789
Facsimile: (00) (351) (22) 610 0438
e-mail: All.oporto@fco.gov.uk
Consul: Mr Gordon Simpson
Pro-Consul: Mrs Zilda M N Gomes

Portimão
British Consulate
Largo Francisco A Mauricio 7-1,
8500 Portimão
Telephone: (00) (351) (282) 490 750
Facsimile: (00) (351) (282) 490 758
e-mail: portimao.lisbon@fco.gov.uk
Honorary Consul: Mr Roger Nuttall
Pro-Consul: Mrs Angela Morado

Funchal, Madeira
Honorary British Consulate
Avenida de Zarco 2, CP 417
9000 - 956 Funchal, Madeira
Telephone: (00) (351) (291) 21 2860 / 61 / 62 / 63
/ 64 / 65 / 66 / 67
Facsimile: (00) (351) (291) 21 2869
e-mail: brit.confunchal@mail.eunet.pt
Honorary Consul: Mr Colin H Gedge

Ponta Delgada, Azores
Honorary British Consulate
Rua Domingos Rebelo 43-A
9500-234 Ponta Delgada, Azores
Telephone: (00) (351) (296) 283 786
Facsimile: (00) (351) (296) 628 175
e-mail: amgm@net.sapo.pt
Honorary Consul: Mr Antonio Gomes de Menezes

QATAR

Doha
British Embassy
PO Box 3, Doha
FTN Code - 8630 + extn number (not Commercial or Visa Sections)
Telephone: (00) (974) 4421991
Facsimile: (00) (974) 4438692
e-mail: bembcomm@qatar.net.qa (Commercial Section)
consular_qatar@fco.gov.uk (Consular Section)
Office Hours (GMT): Sun - Thurs 04 30 - 11 30

Visa Section:
Ground Floor, AKC Building,
Al Saad Street
Telephone: (00) (974) 4364189
Facsimile: (00) (974) 4364139

Commercial Section:
8th Floor, Toyota Towers
Telephone: (00) (974) 4353543
Facsimile: (00) (974) 4356131
Ambassador (ext 2000): Mr David R MacLennan
First Secretary (Commercial) and Deputy Head of Mission (ext 2002): Mr Eric Mattey
Defence Attaché (ext 2004):
Wing Commander Paul Cottell, RAF
Second Secretary (Commercial):
Mr Peter Harrington
Second Secretary (Defence Sales) (ext 2005):
Mr Alec Gribble
Second Secretary (Chancery/Information) (ext 2008): Mr Mohammed Shokat
Second Secretary (Management) and Vice-Consul (ext 2011): Mr Dale Harrison
Third Secretary (Immigration): Mr Danny Woodier
Third Secretary (Commercial): Mrs Dorothy Harris
Attaché (ext 2010): Mrs Elizabeth McCormack
Military Assistant to Defence Attaché (ext 2006):
CPO Ian St. Paul, RN
Chaplain: The Rev. Ian Young

British Council
PO Box 2992, Doha
Telephone: (00) (974) 4426185
Facsimile: (00) (974) 4423315
Director: Mr Antony Jones

ROMANIA

Bucharest
British Embassy
24 Strada Jules Michelet, 70154 Bucharest
FTN Code – 8416 + extn number
Telephone: (00) (40) (21) 201 7200
Facsimile: (00) (40) (21) 201 7299 (Chancery)
              7315 (Management)
              7311 (Trade Development)
              7317 (Consular)
Airtech: (00) (40) (21) 201 7225
Office Hours (GMT): Apr - Oct: Mon - Thurs: 05 30 - 14 00; Fri 05 30 - 10 30. Nov - Mar: Mon - Thurs: 06 30 - 15 00; Fri 06 30 - 11 30
Ambassador: Mr Quinton Quayle
Counsellor and Deputy Head of Mission:
Mr Andrew Pearce

Defence Attaché: Colonel Anthony A A Beattie
Cultural Attaché (British Council Director):
Mr Stephan Roman
First Secretary (Head of Political/EU/Economic):
Ms Susan Laffey
First Secretary (Political): Mr Gideon Beale
First Secretary (DFID): Mr Bob Napier
First Secretary (Trade Development):
Mr James Halley
First Secretary: Mr Michael White
Deputy Defence Attaché:
Squadron Leader Keith A Marshall, RAF
British Council Deputy Director: Ms Karen Giblin
Second Secretary (Management):
Mr Kevin McCole
Second Secretary and Consul: Mr James Cameron
Second Secretary (Political/Information):
Mrs Margaret McCole
Second Secretary (Works) (resides at Budapest):
Ms Sandra Agnew
Second Secretary: Mr Tom Burns
Third Secretary (Management): Mrs Claire Healy
Third Secretary (Trade Development):
Mr Ian Marsden
Vice-Consul: Mr Gerard Healy
Vice-Consul: Mrs Anne Cheong
Assistant Defence Attaché: Mr Jim Osborne
Attaché (resides at Budapest): Mr Terry Wiltshire
Attaché (Works): Mr George Manson
Chaplain: The Revd James Ramsey

RUSSIA

Moscow
British Embassy
Smolenskaya Naberezhnaya 10
Moscow 121099
FTN Code - 8375 + 1000 or extn number
Telephone: (00) (7) (095) 956 7200 (Main Switchboard)
Facsimile: (00) (7) (095) 956 7201 General
              7480 Trade and Investment
              7466 DFID
              7328 Consular
              7264 Defence
              7442 Estates
              7438 LELO
              7443 Management
              7446 Medical Centre
              7364 Political
              7430 Press and Public Affairs
              7443 Science
              7444 TMS
              7441 Visas
              7394 Russian Resettlement Programme
              7237 Registry/Comms
              7420 Security
Airtech: (00) (7) (095) 956 7398
e-mail: moscow@britishembassy.ru (Press and Public Affairs)
consular.moscow@fco.gov.uk (Consular)
Cultural Department/The British Council
Library for Foreign Literature,
Nikoloyamskaya 1, Moscow 109189
Telephone: (00) (7) (095) 782 0200 (Switchboard)
Facsimile: (00) (7) (095) 782 0201

Office Hours (GMT): Winter: 06 00 – 10 00 and
11 00 – 14 00. Summer: 05 00 – 09 00 and
10 00 – 13 00
Ambassador: Mr Anthony Brenton, CMG (7234)
Minister and Deputy Head of Mission:
Mr Stephen Wordsworth, LVO (7206)
Defence and Air Attaché:
Air Commodore Wilson Metcalfe (7231)
Counsellor (Political):
Mrs Sian Macleod, OBE (7212)
*Counsellor (Economic, Trade and Investment and
Science):* Ms Deborah Bronnert (7450)
Counsellor (Political Affairs):
Mr Robert Campbell (7210)
Counsellor (Management) and Consul-General:
Mrs Jessica Hand (7385)
Counsellor (Post Security):
Mr Norman Trapé, OBE (7356)
*Counsellor (British Council Director) (Cultural
Affairs):* (Vacant)
Military Attaché: Colonel Colin A Bulleid (7239)
Naval *Attaché:* Captain Jon T Holloway, RN (7232)
First Secretary (Regional Medical Adviser):
Dr Iain McDonald (7269)
First Secretary (Development):
Mr Jim Butler (7496)
First Secretary (Political):
Mr Nigel Casey, MVO (7280)
First Secretary (Political): Mr Chris Bowers (7360)
First Secretary (Trade and Investment):
Mr David Goodwin (7452)
First Secretary (Science and Technology):
Ms Susannah Montgomery (7491)
First Secretary (Estate Management):
Mr Derek Evans (7258)
First Secretary (Technical Management):
Mr David Welsted (7222)
First Secretary (British Council Deputy Director):
Mr Christopher Baxter
*First Secretary (British Council Deputy
Director/Info and Regions):* Ms Ruth Addison
*First Secretary (British Council Deputy Director/
Operations):* Mr Simon Kay
First Secretary (Press and Public Affairs):
Mr Alan Holmes (7359)
First Secretary (Consular/Immigration):
Mr Peter Smith (7240)
First Secretary (Development):
Ms Dawn Lindsay (7483)
First Secretary (Management):
Mrs Carol Priestley (7257)
First Secretary (LELO): Mr Mark Bishop (7436)
First Secretary (Technical Management):
Mr Dai Pugh (7223)
First Secretary (Economic):
Mr Nigel Gould-Davies (7338)
First Secretary (British Council/ Asst Director):
Mr Paul Norton
Assistant Naval Attaché:
Lieutenant Commander Karen McTear (7233)
Assistant Military Attaché:
Major Alfonso C J Torrents (7238)
Assistant Air Attaché:
Squadron Leader Sean T O'Brien (7245)
Second Secretary (Political):
Ms Esther McHugh (7209)

Second Secretary (Political):
Ms Faye O'Connor (7367)
Second Secretary (Political): Mr Marc Doe (7355)
Second Secretary (Political): Mr Paul Knott (7215)
Second Secretary (Economic):
Mr Anjoum Noorani (7354)
Second Secretary (Trade and Investment):
Mr Nick Latta (7453)
Second Secretary (Trade and Investment):
Ms Sayida Husain (7476)
Second Secretary (Immigration):
Mr Lawrence Weldon (7267)
Second Secretary (Immigration):
Mr Kevin Williams (7433)
Second Secretary (Airline Liaison Officer):
Mr Richard Hooton (7410)
Second Secretary (Technical Management):
Mr Steve Tetlow (7226)
Second Secretary (Technical Management):
Mr Christopher Broadbent (7227)
Second Secretary (Technical Management):
Mr Kevin Hodnett (7225)
Second Secretary (Technical Management):
Mr Sanjay Shah (7224)
Second Secretary (Development):
Mr Mark Fitzpatrick (7462)
Second Secretary (Development):
Mr Alan Reid (7467)
Attaché (Chief Security Officer):
Mr Rick Willams (7366)
*Second Secretary (Russian Resettlement
Programme):* Squadron Leader Max Jardin (7394)
Head of Defence Secretariat:
Flight Lieutenant Peter Edwards, RAF (7229)
Third Secretary (Management):
Mrs Eram Qureshi-Hasan (7255)
Third Secretary (Visits): Mrs Gillian Roberts
(7204)
Third Secretary (Political Affairs):
Mr Mark Tluczek (7362)
Attaché Vice-Consul: Mr Neil Abbott (7321)
Attaché (Visas): Mr Sean Myers (7336)
Attaché (Visas): Mr Tim Van Der Eyken (7323)
Attaché (Visas): Mrs Melanie Morrison (7472)
Attaché (Visas): Mr Ian Marson (7396)
Attaché (Visas): Mr David Hall (7236)
Attaché (Visas): Ms Julie Stephenson (7336)
Attaché (Visas): Mr Christopher Ward (7236)
Attaché (Visas): Mr William Callf (7312)

NATO Military Liaison Mission
C/o Ulitsa Mytnaya 3
Moscow 117049
Telephone: (00) (7) (095) 775 0270
Facsimile: (00) (7) (095) 775 0280
Head of Mission (accredited to British Embassy):
Major General Peter Williams, OBE

St Petersburg
British Consulate General
PL Proletarskoy Diktatury 5, Smolninskiy Raion
191124 St Petersburg
FTN Code – 8376+ extn number
Telephone: (00) (7) (812) 320 32 00 Switchboard
                  320 32 39 Visa Reception
Facsimile: (00) (7) (812) 320 32 11 General

320 32 22 Commercial Section
320 32 33 Visa Section
320 32 44 Chancery (Airtech)
e-mail: bcgspb@peterlink.ru
dfid@peterlink.ru (DFID Russia)
management.stpetersburg@fco.gov.uk
commercial.stpetersburg@fco.gov.uk
consular.stpetersburg@fco.gov.uk
information.stpetersburg@fco.gov.uk
visa.stpetersburg@fco.gov.uk
Consul-General: Mr C G Edgar 3205
Deputy Head of Mission/Consul (Commercial):
Mr P Langham 3220
Consul (Cultural) (British Council Director):
Ms A Coutts
Consul (Consular/Management):
Mr M Woodham 3210
Vice-Consul (Immigration): Mr S McColm 3230
Vice-Consul (Immigration): Mrs K Cullen 3231
Attaché: Mr I Saunders 3214

British Council
Fontanki Reki Nab 46
191025 St Petersburg
Telephone: (00) (7) (812) 118 5060
Facsimile: (00) (7) (812) 118 5061

Yekaterinburg
British Consulate-General
15a Gogol Street,
620075, Yekaterinburg
Telephone: (00) (7) (343) 379 4931
355 9201 Visa Section
Facsimile: (00) (7) (343) 359 2901
Airtech: (00) (7) (343) 777 068
e-mail: brit@sky.ru (General Enquiries)
ekatevisaenquiries@fco.gov.uk (Visa Enquiries)
Website: www.britain.sky.ru
Consul General: Mrs L Cross, MBE
Vice Consul: Ms M Byrd

Novorossiysk
British Consulate
3a Fabrichnaya Street,
Novorossiysk, PO Box 85
Novorossiysk 353923
Telephone: (00) (7) (8617) 618100
Facsimile: (00) (7) (8617) 618291
e-mail: ecr@laroute.net
Honorary Consul: Mr E C Rumens

Vladivostok
British Consulate
5 Svetlanskaya Street, Vladivostok
Telephone: (00) (7) (4232) 411312
Facsimile: (00) (7) (4232) 410643
e-mail: tiger@ints.vtc.ru
Honorary Consul: Mr A M Fox

RWANDA

Kigali (SP – see page 120)
British Embassy
Parcelle No 1131
Boulevard de l'Umuganda
Kacyiru Sud
BP 576 Kigali

FTN Code – 8740 + extn number
Telephone: (00) (250) 585771, 585773, 584098, 586072
Facsimile: (00) (250) 582044, 511586
e-mail: ppao@rwanda1.com
Website: britishembassykigali.org.rw
Office Hours (GMT): Mon – Thurs 06 00 - 10.00
and 11 00 - 15 00, Fri 06 00 - 10.00
Ambassador: Mr J J Macadie
Deputy Head of Mission: Mr C W Frean
Defence Attaché (resides at Kampala):
Lieutenant Colonel C J A Wilton
Third Secretary (Political): Ms C Vaudrey

**Department for International Development
Programme Office (Rwanda)**
BP 576 Kigali
Telephone: (same as Embassy)
Facsimlie: (00) (250) 510588
e-mail: @dfid.gov.uk
Office Hours (GMT): Mon-Thur 06 00 - 10 00 and
11 00 - 15 00, Fri 06 00 - 10 00
Head of Office: Mr Colin Kirk
Social Development Adviser: Ms Judy Walker
Economic Adviser: Mr Simon Stevens
Education Adviser: Ms Jo Bourne

ST KITTS AND NEVIS

Basseterre
British High Commission
PO Box 483, Price Waterhouse Coopers Centre
11 Old Parham Rd
St John's, Antigua
Telephone: (00) (1) (268) 462 0008/9, 463 0010
Facsimile: (00) (1) (268) 462 2806
e-mail: britishc@candw.ag
Office Hours (GMT): Mon – Thurs: 12 00 - 20 00
Fri: 12 00 - 17 00 (only)
Open to the Public: Mon – Fri: 12 00 - 16 30
High Commissioner: Mr John White
Resident British Commissioner:
Miss Jean Sharpe, OBE
Deputy *Resident British Commissioner:*
Mr Paul Lawrence
Deputy High Commissioner: Mr Rob Holland
Defence Adviser: Captain Steve G Wilson, RN
First Secretary (Chancery): Mr Graham Honey
Second Secretary (Chancery): Mr Rick Gomez
Second Secretary (Management): Ms Ros Day
Second Secretary (Chancery/Information):
Mr Nick J Pyle, MBE
Third Secretary (Immigration): Mr Mark Harrison
*Resides at Bridgetown

British Consulate
Office of the Honorary British Consul
PO Box 559, Basseterre
Telephone: (00) (1 869) 466 5620
466 8888 Home
Facsimile: (00) (1 869) 466 8889
Honorary Consul: Mr Peter Allcorn

ST LUCIA

Castries (SP – see page 120)
British High Commission

Francis Compton Building
2nd Floor (P O Box 227), Waterfront
Castries
Telephone: (00) (1) (758) 45 22484/5
Facsimile: (00) (1) (758) 45 31543
e-mail: postmaster.castries@fco.gov.uk
britishhc@candw.lc
Airtech: (00) (1) (758) 45 22486
Office Hours (GMT): Mon- Thurs: 12 00 - 16 30
and 17 00 - 20 00, Fri: 12 00 - 17 00
Open to public: Mon-Fri: 12 00 – 16 30
* *High Commissioner:* Mr John White
Resident British Commissioner: Mr Douglas Rice
* *Deputy High Commissioner:* Mr Rob Holland
* *Defence Adviser:* Captain Steve G Wilson, RN
* *First Secretary (Chancery):* Mr Graham Honey
* *First Secretary (Management):* Ms Ros Day
* *Second Secretary (Chancery/Information):*
Mr Nick J Pyle, MBE
* *Second Secretary (Chancery):* Mr Andy Danton
** *Second Secretary (Technical Works):*
Mr David Holmes
* *Third Secretary:* Mr Phil Barker
* *Third Secretary (Immigration):*
Mr Mark Harrison
*Resides at Bridgetown **Resides at Mexico City

ST VINCENT

Kingstown (SP – see page 120)
British High Commission
Granby Street (PO Box 132)
Kingstown
Telephone: (00) (1) (784) 457 1701
Facsimile: (00) (1) (784) 456 2750
Office Hours (GMT): 12 30 - 20 00
* *High Commissioner:* Mr John White
Resident Acting High Commissioner:
Mr Terry Knight
* *Deputy High Commissioner:* Mr Rob Holland
* *Defence Adviser:* Captain Steve G Wilson, RN
* *First Secretary (Chancery):* Mr Graham Honey
* *First Secretary (Management):* Ms Ros Day
* *Second Secretary (Chancery/Information):*
Mr Nick J Pyle, MBE
* *Second Secretary (Chancery):* Mr Rick Gomez
* *Third Secretary:* Mr Phil Barker
Third Secretary (Immigration): Mr Mark Harrison
*Resides at Bridgetown

SAMOA

Apia
British High Commission (all staff resident in
Wellington)
FTN Code – 8480 + extn number
Telephone: (00) (64) (4) 924 2888
Facsimile: (00) (64) (4) 473 4982
High Commissioner: Mr Richard T Fell, CVO
Deputy High Commissioner: Mr Martin Bourke
First Secretary (External): Ms A Ruth Walker
First Secretary (Economic/Trade Policy):
Mr Paul D Noon
First Secretary (Political/Press and Public Affairs):
Mr Matthew K Forbes
Second Secretary (Political): Ms Sarah M Weeks

Second Secretary (Consular): Mr John D A Kenny
Third Secretary (Consular):
Mr Matthew R Simpson

Office of the Honorary British Consul
c/o Kruse Enari and Barlow
Barristers and Solicitors
PO Box 2029
2nd Floor, N.P.F. Building
Beach Rd, Central Apia
Telephone: (00) (685) 21895
Facsimile: (00) (685) 21407
e-mail: barlowlaw@keblegal.ws
Honorary British Consul:
Mr R M (Bob) Barlow, MBE

SAN MARINO

San Marino
British Embassy
Via XX Settembre 80/A
00187 Rome
Ambassador (resides at Rome):
Sir Ivor A Roberts, KCMG

British Consulate-General
Lungarno Corsini 2,
50123 Florence
Telephone: (00) (39) 055 284133
(00) (39) 055 289556 (Commercial)
Facsimile: (00) (39) 055 219112
Airtech: (00) (39) 055 2654354
e-mail: Consular.Florence@fco.gov.uk
Commercial.Florence@fco.gov.uk
Office Hours (GMT): Apr-Oct 07 00 - 11 00 and
12 00 - 15 00. Nov-Mar 08 00 - 12 00 and
13 00 - 16 00
Consul-General (Resides at Florence):
Mrs Moira A Macfarlane

SÃO TOMÉ AND PRINCIPE

São Tomé
British Embassy
(All staff resident in Luanda)
Ambassador: Mr John Thompson, MBE
Consul: Mr F J Martin
First Secretary: Mr D G Cox
Second Secretary (Aid): Mr E Rich

São Tomé
British Consulate
Residencial Avenida,
Avienda Da Independencia
CP 257, São Tomé
Telephone: (00) (239) (12) 21026/7, 22505 (Home)
Facsimile: (00) (239) (12) 21372
Honorary Consul: Mr J Gomes

SAUDI ARABIA

Riyadh
British Embassy
PO Box 94351, Riyadh 11693
FTN Code – 8418 + extn number
Telephone: (00) (966) (1) 488 0077
Facsimile: (00) (966) (1) 488 2373, 488 0623
                Management,

488 1209 Consular
488 3125 Chancery
Voicemail Numbers: see individual officers
e-mail: Officers firstname.surname followed by
@fco.gov.uk
Office Hours (GMT): Sat - Wed 05 00 - 12 00
Ambassador: Sir Sherard Cowper-Coles, KCMG, LVO
*Counsellor, Deputy Head of Mission and Consul
General (2204):* Mr Barry Lowen
*Director of Trade and Investment Promotion
(2240):* (Vacant)
Cultural Attaché (British Council Director):
Mr Alan Smart
Defence and Military Attaché (2230):
Brigadier John G Askew, OBE
Naval and Air Attaché (2234):
Wing Commander Mike J Cole, RAF
First Secretary (Political) (2217): Mr Ian Baharie
First Secretary (Economic/PPA) (2242):
Mrs Karen Bell
First Secretary (Political) (2208): Mr Sean Keeling
*First Secretary (Head of Commercial Section)
(2206):* Mr Gareth O'Brien
First Secretary and Consul (2271): Mr Ken Neill
Second Secretary (Political) (2265):
Mr Derek Cooper
Second Secretary (Management) (2261):
Mr Stuart Sadler
Second Secretary (Technical) (2220):
Mr Robert Chambers
Third Secretary (Political) (2212): Mr Barrie Peach
Third Secretary and Vice-Consul (2277):
Mrs Kerenza Holzman
Third Secretary and Vice-Consul (2272):
Mr Sean McLean
Attaché (Management) (2264): Mr David Lawrie
Overseas Security Manager: Mr Michael Lyall

Jeddah

British Consulate-General
PO Box 393, Jeddah 21411
FTN Code – 8417 + extn number
Telephone: (00) (966) (2) 622-5550, 5557, 5558
Facsimile: (00) (966) (2) 622-6249
Airtech: (00) (966) (2) 622-5551
e-mail: Officers first name.surname followed by
fco.gov.uk
Office Hours (GMT): Sat-Wed 05 00 - 12 00
Consul-General (2209): Mr Carsten O Pigott
*Consul (Commercial) and Deputy Head of Post
(2212):* Mrs Cecille El Beleidi
*Senior Management Officer/HM Consul/Entry
Clearance Manager (2237):* Mr William John Neil
Vice-Consul (Immigration) (2232):
Mr Ian F Hodges
Generalist/Deputy Management Officer (2201):
Mr Dawood Mayet

Al Khobar

British Trade Office
PO Box 1868,
Al Khobar 31952
Telephone: (00) (966) (3) 882 5300
Facsimile: (00) (966) (3) 882 5384
e-mail: btokhobar@hotmail.com

officers firstname.surname followed by
@ALKHOBAR.mail.fco.gov.uk
Office Hours (GMT): Sat –Wed: 05 00 - 12 00
Head of British Trade Office: Mr Mike Hurley
Second Secretary (Commercial): Mr Richard Wood
Vice-Consul/Commercial Officer:
Mr Abdalla Abdalla
Pro-Consul/Commercial Assistant: Maha Fariz
(Visa and Passport work for Eastern Province is the
responsibility of Riyadh)

SENEGAL

Dakar (SP – see page 120)

British Embassy
20 Rue du Docteur Guillet
(Boite Postale 6025), Dakar
FTN Code – 8636 + extn number
Telephone: (00) (221) 823 7392, 823 9971
Facsimile: (00) (221) 823 2766, 823 8415
e-mail: britemb@sentoo.sn
British Council e-mail:
postmaster@britishcouncil.sn
Office Hours (GMT): Mon - Thurs 08 00 - 16 30,
Fri 08 00 - 12 30
Ambassador: Mr Peter Newall
Deputy Head of Mission and Consul:
Mr Derek Levoir
Defence Attaché (Resides at Rabat):
Lieutenant Colonel Simon J A Lloyd, MBE
British Council Director: Mr Andrew McNab, MBE
Human Rights Adviser (West Africa):
Ms Carolyn Norris
Technical Works Supervisor (West Africa):
Mr George Manson
Vice-Consul/ECO: Ms Christine Johnson
Management Officer: Mr Nick Faulkner
Attaché: Mr Ivan Friday
Trade and Investment Officer: Mme Aissatou Fall

SERBIA AND MONTENEGRO

Belgrade

British Embassy
Resavska 46, 11000 Belgrade
FTN Code – 8663 + four digit extn number
Telephone: (00) (381) (11) 2645 055, 3060 900,
               3615 660
Facsimile: (00) (381) (11) 659 651
               3061 089 (Chancery)
               3061 072 (Consular/Visa)
               3061 059 (Commercial)
               3061 077 (Information)
               3060 930 (Management)
Airtech: 3061 020
e-mail: britemb@eunet.yu
ukembcom@eunet.yu (Commercial)
ukembbg@eunet.yu (Information)
Website: britemb.org.yu
Office Hours (GMT): Mon - Thurs: 07 00 - 15 30;
Fri: 07 00 - 12 00
Ambassador: Mr David Gowan
Deputy Head of Mission: Mr David McIlroy
Counsellor: Mr John O'Callaghan
Defence Attaché:
Colonel Witek Nowosielski-Slepowron

First Secretary (Management and HM Consul):
Mrs Caroline Slaymaker
First Secretary (Commercial): Mr David Webb
First Secretary (Development): Mr Brian Foy
Second Secretary (Political): Mr David Ashley
Second Secretary (Chancery): Mr Daniel Workman
Second Secretary (Immigration Liaison Office): Mr
Roger Britton
Second Secretary (Works): Mr Robert Pattison
Third Secretary (Vice-Consul): Mr Julian Lyon
Third Secretary (Management):
Mrs Kathryn Lindsay
Third Secretary (Immigration): Mr Philip Jones
Attaché: Mr Frederick Bennett

British Council
Terazije 8/I
11000 Belgrade
Telephone: (00) (381) (11) 3023 800
Facsimile: (00) (381) (11) 3023 898
Office Hours (GMT): Mon-Fri: 08 00 – 15 15
Library Hours: Mon-Fri: 10 00 – 17 00 and Sat: 09
00 – 14 00
Director: Mr Christopher Gibson

Podgorica - Montenegro
British Office
Trg Vektra, zgrada Cijevna Komerc II/3
81000 Podgorica
Telephone: (00) (381) (81) 205 461
Facsimile: (00) (381) (81) 205 460
Office hours (GMT): Mon-Thurs: 07 30 - 15 30
Fri: 07 30 - 11 30
Honorary Consul: Mr Dragan Vugdelic

Pristina, Kosovo
British Office
Ismail Qemajli 6
Arberi, Dragodan
Pristina
Telephone: (00) 381 38 249 559
Facsimile: (00) 381 38 249 799
Office Hours (GMT): Mon - Thurs: 07 30 - 16 00,
Fri: 07 30 - 15 30
Head of Office: Mr Mark Dickinson
*Deputy Head of Office/Second Secretary
(Political):* Mr Colin Parish
Second Secretary (Political): Ms Victoria Whitford
Second Secretary (Political): Ms Rebecca Sutton
Management Officer: Ms Kay Harris

SEYCHELLES

Victoria (SP – see page 120)
British High Commission
3rd Floor
Oliaji Trade Centre
PO Box 161, Victoria, Mahé
FTN Code – 8637 + extn number
Telephone: (00) (248) 283666
Facsimile: (00) (248) 283657
e-mail: bhcvictoria@fco.gov.uk
Office Hours (GMT): Mon – Thurs 04 00 - 12 00
Fri 04 00 - 11 00
High Commissioner: Ms Diana Skingle
Deputy High Commissioner:
Mrs Philippa Thompson

Defence Adviser (Resides in Nairobi):
Colonel Jock A D K Inkster
British Council Director (Resides in Port Louis):
Mrs Shoba Ponnappa, OBE

SIERRA LEONE

Freetown (SP – see page 120)
British High Commission
Spur Road, Freetown
FTN Code – 8638 + extn number
Telephone: (00) (232) (22) 232961, 232362,
232563-5
Facsimile: (00) (232) (22) 228169, 232070
Airtech: (00) (232) (22) 231824
e-mail: bhc@sierratel.sl
Office Hours (GMT): Mon-Thurs 08 00 - 16 30
Fri 08 00 - 13 00
High Commissioner: Dr John E Mitchiner
Deputy High Commissioner: Mr Frank Marshall
Counsellor (Regional Affairs): Mr Sean Holt
Defence Adviser:
Lieutenant Colonel Desmond J A Bergin, OBE
First Secretary (Development): Mr Ian Stuart
Second Secretary (PPA): Mr Derek Smith
Second Secretary (Senior Management Officer):
Mr Jem Convery
Third Secretary (Political): Mr Andy Bolger
Third Secretary (Deputy Management Officer):
Mr Danny E Foote
Third Secretary (Immigration/Consular):
Ms Julia Shand
Third Secretary (Development): Mrs Nancy Stuart
Attaché: Miss Tracey Coleman
Attaché: Staff Sergeant Pete King
Cultural Attaché (British Council Director):
Mr Rajiv Bendre, OBE
Deputy Director (British Council):
Ms Honor Flanaghan

SINGAPORE

Singapore
British High Commission
Tanglin Road, Singapore 247919
Commercial Section: Tanglin PO Box 19,
Singapore 247919
FTN Code – 8634 + extn number (For those direct
dialling in over the PSTN: dial +65 6424 followed
by the extension number)
Telephone: (00) (65) 6424 4200 (General)
6424 4244 (Commercial)
6424 4270 (Visa/Consular)
Facsimile: (00) (65) 6424 4218 (Chancery)
6424 4250 (Management)
6424 4356 (Commercial)
6424 4264 (Consular)
6424 4230/4263 (Defence)
e-mail: Commercial.Singapore@fco.gov.uk
(Firecrest)
Website: www.britain.org.sg
Office Hours (GMT): Mon - Fri 01 30 – 06 00 and
07 00 – 10 00
High Commissioner: Mr Alan Collins, CMG (4202)

*Deputy High Commissioner and Counsellor
(Economic/Trade and Investment):*
Mr David Campbell (4300)
Defence Adviser:
Group Captain Martin D Stringer, RAF (4227)
Head of Chancery: Mr Philip Malone (4204)
First Secretary: Mr William Brandon (4211)
First Secretary (Management):
Mr Gavin Marshall (4256)
First Secretary (Trade and Investment):
Mrs Rosemary P Clarke, MBE (4302)
First Secretary (Science and Technology):
Mr Brian Ferrar (4343)
First Secretary (Technical):
Mr Richard M Hardy (4224)
First Secretary (Estate): Mr John McLean (4254)
First Secretary (DESO):
Mr Peter G Wythe, MBE (4225)
Assistant Defence Adviser:
Commander Brian Boxall-Hunt, OBE (4229)
Second Secretary (Trade and Investment):
Miss Erica Ackerman (4310)
Second Secretary (Trade and Investment):
Mr Matthew Oakley, MVO, MBE (4358)
Second Secretary (Economic/Inward Investment):
Mr Colin Dick (4323)
Second Secretary (Defence):
Mr Neil Deeley (4209)
Second Secretary (Technical):
Mr Nick Folker (4221)
Second Secretary (Consular/ECM):
Mr Peter McGregor (4360)
Assistant Management Officer:
Mr Kevin Mowbray (4242)
Third Secretary (Trade and Investment):
Mrs Niki Wright (4303)
Third Secretary (Consular/Visa):
Mr Stephen Evans, MBE (4274)
Assistant Attaché (PA to High Commissioner):
Mrs Fiona Mowbray (4203)
Assistant Attaché: Mr Dale Heath (4222)
Assistant Attaché: Ms Elizabeth Sprague (4213)
Assistant Attaché (PA Senior Management Team):
Mrs Winnie Neyland (4205)
Administrative Officer (Defence):
Mrs Liz Brown (4235)
Pay and Pensions (Defence):
Warrant Officer Mark Hincks (4262)
Trade and Investment Officer:
Mrs Valsa Panicker (4311)
Trade and Investment Officer:
Mr Teo Chong Kee (4309)
Regional Training Officer:
Mr Brian Lawrence (4288)
Political Officer: Mrs Geraldine Hennelly (4248)
Communications and External Relations Officer:
Ms Elisabeth Brodthagen (4305)
Accountant: Mr Alan Yeong, MBE (4261)
Estate Manager: Mr Terlok Singh (4328)
Systems Administrator: Miss Serene Cheong (4308)
Webmaster: Miss Chloe Choong (4320)
Inward Investment Officer: Ms Evelyn Gui (4420)

The British Council
30 Napier Road
Singapore 258509

Telephone: (00) (65) 6473 1111
Facsimile: (00) (65) 6472 1010
DID: (00) (65) 64707 followed by the three digit
extension number
*Cultural and Educational Adviser (British Council
Director):* Mr Les Dangerfield (101)
*Deputy Cultural and Education Adviser (Director,
English Language Centre):* Mr Martin Hope (104)
*Assistant Cultural and Educational Adviser (British
Council Assistant Director):*
Mrs Errim Mahmoud (103)

SLOVAKIA

Bratislava (SP – see page 120)
British Embassy
Panska 16, 811 01 Bratislava
FTN Code – 8377 + extn number
Telephone: (00) (421) (2) 5998 2000
                  5998 2258 Visa Section
UK Duty Officer: 0905 601 741
Facsimile: (00) (421) (2) 5998 2237 General
                  2225 Management/Consular
                  2241 Defence Section
                  2240 Commercial Section
                  2210 Visa Section
Airtech: 2204
e-mail: bebra@internet.sk
Website: www.britemb.sk
Office Hours (GMT): Mon-Fri: 07 30 – 16 00
Ambassador (ext 2201): Mrs Judith Macgregor
Deputy Head of Mission (job share) (ext 2203):
Mr Tom Carter / Ms Carolyn Davidson
Defence Attaché (ext 2205):
Lieutenant Colonel Anthony W Sutherland
Second Secretary (Commercial) (ext 2217):
Mr Richard Beams
Second Secretary (Political) (ext 2230):
Mrs Wendy Roebuck
Second Secretary (EU) (ext 2234): Mr Ian Fox
*Second Secretary (Management/Consular) (ext
2254):* Mr Spencer P O'Neil
Assistant Defence Attaché (ext 2206):
Squadron Leader Lloyd F Barrett, RAF
*Cultural Attaché (British Council Director) (ext
5443 1074 or 1793):* Mr Huw Jones

SLOVENIA

Ljubljana (SP – see page 120)
British Embassy
4th Floor Trg Republike 3
1000 Ljubljana
FTN Code – 8639 + extn number
Telephone: (00) (386) (1) 200 3910 Main
                  Reception
                  200 3940 Commercial Section
Facsimile: (00) (386) (1) 425 0174 Chancery
                  425 9080 Commercial Section
e-mail: info@british-embassy.si
postmaster.ljubljana@fco.gov.uk
Website: www.british-embassy.si
Ambassador (ext 3921): Mr Hugh Mortimer, LVO
Deputy Head of Mission (ext 3922):
Mr James Setterfield

Defence Attaché (3950):
Lieutenant Colonel Lindsay R Wilson, MBE
Second Secretary and HM Consul (ext 3914):
Mr David Blogg
Second Secretary (DLO): Mr Willie McColl
Third Secretary (Political) (3928): Mr Neil Abbott
Cultural Attaché (Director, British Council):
Mr Stephen Green

SOLOMON ISLANDS

Honiara (SP – see page 120)
British High Commission
Telekom House, Mendana Avenue
Honiara
Postal Address: PO Box 676
Telephone: (00) (677) 21705, 21706
Facsimile: (00) (677) 21549
e-mail: bhc@welkam.solomon.com.sb
Office Hours (GMT): Mon - Fri 21 00 - 01 00 and
02 00 - 05 00
High Commissioner: Mr Richard J Lyne
Deputy High Commissioner: Mrs Caroline J Hall

SOMALIA

Mogadishu
British Embassy
Waddada Xasan Geedd Abtoow 7/8
(PO Box 1036), Mogadishu
Telephone: (00) (252) (1) 20288/9, 21472/3
Telex: 3617 (a/b PRODROME SM)
Staff withdrawn from post

SOUTH AFRICA

Pretoria
British High Commission
255 Hill Street, Arcadia 0002
FTN Code – 8690 + extn number
Telephone: (00) (27) (12) 421 7500
Facsimile: (00) (27) (12) 421 7555
e-mail: bhc@icon.co.za
Website: http://www.britain.org.za
Office Hours (GMT): Mon-Thurs: 06 00 - 15 00
Fri: 06 00 - 10 30
High Commissioner: Ms Ann Grant
Counsellor and Deputy High Commissioner:
Mr Andrew S Patrick
Counsellor (Political): Mr Phil N Shott
Defence and Military Adviser:
Brigadier David H Keenan, OBE
Air and Naval Adviser:
Commander Peter Lankester, RN
First Secretary: Ms Fiona Morrison
First Secretary (Management): Mr Alan K Bubbear
First Secretary (Technical Works): Mr Mark Jones
First Secretary: Mr Andrew Millar
First Secretary (PPA): Mr Nick Sheppard
First Secretary (Technical Management):
Mr Andrew McNair
Second Secretary: Mr Paul Anderson
Second Secretary (Management):
Mr Nicholas G Collier
Second Secretary (Technical Management):
Mr Phil Cullen

Second Secretary (Technical Management):
Mr Neil Roper
Second Secretary: Mr Tony A Tenger
Second Secretary: Ms Diane Sheard
Third Secretary: Mrs Sally Forrester

Consular Section
Liberty Life Place, Block B
256 Glyn Street, Hatfield 0083
Postal Address: P O Box 13611
and P O Box 13612
Hatfield, 0028, Pretoria
Telephone: (00) (27) (12) 421 7802 Visas
421 7801 Passports
Facsimile: (00) (27) (12) 421 7888 Visas
421 7877 Passports
e-mail: PTA.PassportEnquiries@fco.gov.uk
PTA.VisaEnquiries@fco.gov.uk
Office Hours (GMT): Mon-Thurs: 06 00-14 15
Fri: 06 00-11 30
(* Based at High Commission, Pretoria)
* *Consul-General:* Mr Andrew S Patrick
Consul: Mr Paul Seaby
Second Secretary (Immigration/ECM):
Mr Quintin Eyre-Wilson
Third Secretary (Consular): Mrs Yvonne Dimmock
Third Secretary (Immigration):
Mrs T Bernadette Connolly
Third Secretary (Immigration): Mr Matthew Player
Third Secretary (Immigration): Miss Sarah G Say
Third Secretary (Immigration):
Mr Martin Lawrence
Third Secretary (Immigration): Mr Alan Green

Pretoria
Department for International Development
Southern Africa
Sanlam Building
Cnr of Arcadia and Festival Street
Hatfield 0083, Pretoria, Gauteng
Telephone: (00) (27) (12) 431 2100
Facsimile: (00) (27) (12) 342 3429
Counsellor (Head of Office): Ms S Warne
First Secretary (Senior Education Adviser):
Ms B Payne
*First Secretary (Rural Sustainable Livelihoods
Adviser):* Ms P Chalinder
First Secretary (Senior Governance Adviser):
Dr R Thomas
*First Secretary (Regional Sustainable Livelihoods
Adviser):* (Vacant)
*First Secretary (Programme Manager BLSN and
Deputy Head of Division):* Mrs G B Wright
First Secretary (Economic Adviser): Mr D Pedley
First Secretary (Social Development Adviser):
Ms O Williams
First Secretary (Enterprise Development Adviser):
Mr H Scott
*First Secretary (Senior Health and Population
Adviser):* Mr T Martineau
First Secretary (Regional Environmental Adviser):
Ms B Arthy
First Secretary (Regional Conflicts Adviser):
Brigadier S Gordon Hughes, CBE
*First Secretary (Senior Regional Engineering
Adviser):* (Vacant)

First Secretary (Engineering Adviser):
Mr R Blakelock
First Secretary (HIV/AIDS and Health Adviser):
(Vacant)
First Secretary (Regional Humanitarian Adviser):
Mr T Kelly
First Secretary Programme Manager (RSA):
Mr J McAlpine
First Secretary (Senior Regional Statistics Adviser): Mr M Dyble
Second Secretary (Regional Trade and Integration Adviser): Ms H McLeod
Second Secretary - Office Manager: Mr D Fidler
Second Secretary (Programme Manager – BLSN):
Mr S Clarke
Deputy Programme Manager: RSA (SL): (Vacant)
Second Secretary (IT Manager): Mr S McBride
Second Secretary (Finance and Contracts Officer):
(Vacant)
Third Secretary (Assistant Programme Manager – SADC/Regional): (Vacant)

Cape Town
British Consulate General
15th Floor, Southern Life Building
8, Riebeeck Street
Cape Town, 8001
Postal address: PO Box 500, Cape Town, 8000
FTN Code – 8692 + extn number
Telephone: (00) (27) (21) 405 2400
              405 2433 Commercial Section
Facsimile: (00) (27) (21) 405 2448
              405 2477 Consular
              405 2456 Chancery
              405 2466 Commercial Section
Airtech: (00) (27) (21) 405 2419
Office Hours (GMT): Mon-Thurs: 06 00 - 10 30
and 11 15 - 14 30, Fri: 06 00 - 11 30
Consul-General (2428): Mr Mike Mayhew
Second Secretary (Political) (2467):
Mr James Barbour
Vice-Consul (Commercial) (2420):
Mr Colin Duncan
Vice-Consul (Management/Consular) (2421):
Mrs Caroline Scales
Vice-Consul (2432): Mr Iain D Bain
Vice-Consul (2413): Mrs Lisa Woolley

East London
British Consulate
c/o Price Waterhouse Coopers and Lybrand, Suite 7
Norvia House, 34 Western Avenue
Vincent 5247, East London
Postal Address:
P O Box 19537, Tecoma
East London 5214
Telephone: (00) (27) (43) 726 9380
Facsimile: (00) (27) (43) 726 9390
Honorary Consul: Mr John L Fletcher

Port Elizabeth
British Consulate
5th Floor 1st Bowring House
66 Ring Road, Greenacres
Port Elizabeth, 6045
Postal Address: PO Box 35098
Newton Park

Port Elizabeth, 6055
Telephone: (00) (27) (41) 363 8841
Facsimile: (00) (27) (41) 363 8842
Telex: 242326
Telegraphic Address: Britain, Port Elizabeth
Office Hours (GMT): 07 00 - 10 30
Honorary Consul: Mr Harry Marston

Johannesburg
Trade and Investment
Callers - Dunkeld Corner, 275 Jan Smuts Avenue
Dunkeld West, 2196
Postal Address:
P O Box 1082, Parklands 2121, Johannesburg
Telephone: (00) (27) (11) 537 7000 Commercial
                                              Services
Facsimile: (00) (27) (11) 537 7257
Public Information Line:
Telephone: (00) (27) (11) 537 7206
Facsimile: (00) (27) (11) 537 7253
Management:
Telephone: (00) (27) (11) 537 7241
Facsimile: (00) (27) (11) 537 7253
Office Hours: Mon- Thurs 06 00 - 14.30 Fri 06 00
- 11.30
Director of Trade and Investment:
Mr Michael Mowlam
Deputy Director for Trade and Investment:
Ms Judith M Leon
Trade Investment Adviser: Mr Gareth Seaborne
Trade Investment Adviser: Mr Donal Ahern
Management Officer: Mr Yemi Odanye

British Council
Suite 1, Sanlam Gables
1209 Schoeman Street (cnr Duncan Street)
Hatfield, Pretoria 0083
PO Box 11759
Telephone: (00) (27) (12) 431 2400
Facsimile: (00) (27) (12) 431 2415
Cultural Attaché (British Council Director):
Ms Rosemary Arnott

Durban
British Consulate
Suite 1901, 19th Floor, The Marine
22 Gardiner Street, Durban 4001
Postal Address: P O Box 1404
Durban, 4000
Telephone: (00) (27) (31) 305 3041
Facsimile: (00) (27) (31) 307 4661
Office Hours (GMT): Mon-Thurs: 06 00 - 15 00
Fri: 06 00 - 11 30
Acting Consul-General: Mr Clive Correa
Vice-Consul (Management): Mrs Jean Busch
Trade Development Adviser: Mr W Geoffrey Tyler

SPAIN

Madrid
British Embassy
Calle de Fernando el Santo 16
28010 Madrid
FTN Code – 8360 + extn number
Telephone: (00) (34) 91 700 82 00
Facsimile: (00) (34) 91 700 83 09 Chancery
                            83 07 Defence

83 29 EU/Economic
83 11 Commercial
82 72 Information
82 10 Management
Office Hours (GMT): Winter 07 00-15 30
Summer Mon - Thurs 06 30-13 00, Fri 06 30-12 30
Ambassador: Mr Stephen John L Wright, CMG
Deputy Head of Mission: Mr Nicholas Kay
*Counsellor (Commercial) and Director of Trade
Promotion:* Mr John Hawkins
Counsellor: Mr Peter Davies
Defence and Naval Attaché:
Captain Nigel J K Dedman, RN
Military and Air Attaché:
Colonel S Mark J Rollo-Walker
*Counsellor (Cultural Affairs) (British Council
Director):* Mr Chris Hickey
First Secretary (Head of Public Affairs and Press):
Mr Jon Davies
First Secretary and Consul-General:
Mr Jeffrey Thomas
First Secretary (Management):
Mr Michael H F Legg
First Secretary (Press Officer): (Vacant)
First Secretary (Agriculture):
Mr Anthony J Bastian
First Secretary (Political/Economic):
Mr Scott Livingstone
First Secretary (Labour): Mr Giles Dickson
First Secretary (Political/Economic):
Mr Christopher Sainty
First Secretary (Technical Management):
Mr Keith Ager
*First Secretary (Cultural Affairs) (British Council
Deputy Director):* Ms Christine Melia
British Council: Ms Margaret Douglas
Second Secretary: Mr David Sykes
Second Secretary: Mr Michael Keogh
Second Secretary: Mr Mark Cox
Second Secretary (Management):
Ms Karen Roskilly
Second Secretary (Commercial): Mr David J Chun
Second Secretary (Commercial):
Mr Trevor Cayless
Second Secretary (Political/Economic):
Ms Priya Guha
Second Secretary (Technical Management):
Mr Paul Oliver
Senior Economic Officer: Mr William Murray
Third Secretary (Press Attaché):
Ms Caroline Sprod
Third Secretary/Vice-Consul: Mr Steve Morgan
Attaché: Miss Georgina Fuss

Madrid
British Consulate-General
Paseo de Recoletos 7-9, 4ª
28004 Madrid
Telephone: (00) (34) 91 524 9700
Facsimile: (00) (34) 91 524 9730
Office hours (GMT): All year: 07.00-17.00
Consul-General: Mr J Thomas
Vice-Consul: Miss R Choudhury
Vice-Consul: Mr D Wickham
Pro-Consul: Mr B Ormston

Alicante
British Consulate
Plaza Calvo Sotelo 1-2
Apartado De Correos 564
03001 Alicante
Telephone: (00) (34) 96 521 60 22
Facsimile: (00) (34) 96 514 05 28
e-mail: enquiries.alicante@fco.gov.uk
Office Hours (GMT): Winter: 06 00-13 30
Summer: 06 00-12 30
Consul: Mr Russell Thomson
Vice-Consul: Mr George Outhwaite, MBE
Vice-Consul: Miss Elizabeth Bell
Honorary Vice-Consul (resides at Benidorm):
Mr John A Seth-Smith (e-mail: jass@ctv.es)

Andorra
Tel/Fax: (00) (34) 376 83 98 40
e-mail: britcoand@mypic.ad
Honorary Consul: Mr Hugh Garner

Las Palmas, Canary Islands
British Consulate
Edificio Cataluña
Calle Luis Morote 6-3
35007 – Las Palmas de Gran Canaria
(Postal address: PO Box 2020, 35080 - Las Palmas
de Gran Canaria)
Telephone: (00) (34) 928 262 508
Facsimile: (00) (34) 928 267 774
e-mail: laspalmasconsulate@ukinspain.com
firstname.surname@fco.gov.uk
Office Hours (GMT): 08 00 - 15 30
Consul: Mr Peter J Nevitt
Vice-Consul: Mrs Anita J Pavillard
Commercial Officer: Mrs Montse Clemente

Málaga
British Consulate
Edificio EUROCOM
C/Mauricio Moro Pareto, 2, 2
29006 Málaga
Telephone: (00) (34) (95) 235 2300
Facsimile: (00) (34) (95) 235 9211
e-mail: postmaster@malaga.mail.fco.gov.uk
Office Hours (GMT): Winter: 07 00-14 30
Summer: 06 00-12 30
Consul: Mr Bruce McIntyre, MBE
Vice-Consul: Mr Patrick Boyce
Vice-Consul: Ms Rosslyn D Crotty
*Commercial Officer (Tel/Fax: (00) (34) 95
4187032):* Mr Joseph Cooper
*Commercial Officer (Tel/Fax: (00) (34) 95
4915874):* Ms Caroline Gray

Santa Cruz de Tenerife (Canary Islands)
British Consulate
Plaza Weyler 8-1
Santa Cruz de Tenerife 38003
Telephone: (00) (34) 922 28 68 63, 28 66 53
Facsimile: (00) (34) 922 28 99 03
e-mail: tenerife.enquiries@fco.gov.uk
Office Hours (GMT): 08 00-15 30
July and August: 08 00-14 30
Consul: Mr David G Ward
Vice-Consul: Mrs Helen Diaz de Arcaya Keating
Pro-Consul: Mrs Christine Trujillo

Vigo
British Consulate
Serafín Avendaño 11, 3°, B
PO Box 49
36201 Vigo
Telephone: (00) (34) 986 43 71 33
Facsimile: (00) (34) 986 43 71 33 / 11 26 78
e-mail: vigoconsulate@ukinspain.com
Office Hours (GMT): 08 00 – 12 00
Honorary Consul: Mr James G Skinner

Barcelona
British Consulate-General
Edificio Torre de Barcelona
Avenida Diagonal
477-13o, 08036 Barcelona
Telephone: (00) (34) 93 366 6200 (6 lines)
Facsimile: (00) (34) 93 366 6221
Airtech: (00) (34) 93 366 6222
e-mail: bcon@cyberbcn.com
Website: www.ukinspain.com
Office Hours GMT: 07 00-16 00 April – June,
September and October. 08 00-17 00 November to
March. 06 30-12 30 July to August
*Consul-General (also Consul-General for
Co-Principality of Andorra):* Mr Geoff S Cowling
Deputy Consul General/Consul (Commercial):
Ms Yvonne E Cherrie
Director, The British Council: Mr Martin Fryer
Vice-Consul (Consular): Ms Roser Clavell
Vice-Consul (Commercial): Mr John V Hankin
Commercial Officer: Ms Eva Prada
Commercial Officer: Mr Mike Thom
Pro-Consul (Management): Ms Joan Millet
Pro-Consul: Ms Cecilia Bosch
Pro-Consul: Mr Adrian Cox

Bilbao
British Consulate-General
Alameda de Urquijo 2-8, 48008 Bilbao
Telephone: (00) (34) 94 415 76 00, 415 77 11, 415
77 22
Facsimile: (00) (34) 94 416 76 32
Airtech: (00) (34) 94 416 47 51
e-mail bcgbilbo@readysoft.es
Office Hours (GMT): 07 00 - 16 00 (Apr - Jun,
Sept and Oct), 08 00 - 17 00 (Nov - Mar),
06 30 - 12 30 (Jul - Aug)
Consul-General: Mr Ian Lewis
Vice-Consul: Mr Derek Doyle, MBE
Pro-Consul: Mrs Flora Dorronsoro
Commercial Officer: Mr Angel Beti

Santander
British Consulate
Paseo de Pereda 27, 39004 Santander
Telephone: (00) (34) 942 22 00 00
Facsimile: (00) (34) 942 22 29 41
e-mail: mpineiro@nexo.es
Office Hours (GMT): 07 00 - 11 00 and 13 30 - 16
00 (April to mid June, mid Sept to Oct). 08 00 - 12
00 and 14 30 - 17 30 (Nov- March). 06 00 - 12 30
(Mid Jun to mid Sept)
Honorary Consul: Mr Modesto Pineiro, MBE

Palma
British Consulate

Balearic Islands
Plaza Mayor 3D
07002 Palma de Mallorca
Balearic Islands
Telephone: (00) (34) 971 712445, 712085,
716048,718501,712696
Facsimile: (00) (34) 971 717520
e-mail: consulate@palma.mail.fco.gov.uk
Office Hours (GMT): Nov-March: 07 00 - 14 30.
Apr-Jun and Sep-Oct: 06 00 - 13 30. Jul-Aug:
06 00 - 12 30
Consul: Mr Michael K Banham
Vice-Consul: Mr Esteban Mas Portell

Ibiza
British Vice-Consulate
Avenida Isidoro Macabich
45-1, Apartado 307
07800 Ibiza
Telephone: (00) (34) 971 301818, 303816, 301058
Facsimile: (00) (34) 971 30 19 72
e-mail: ibizacons@worldonline.es
Office Hours (GMT): Nov-March: 07 00 - 14 30.
Apr-Jun and Sep-Oct: 06 00 - 13 30.
Jul-Aug: 06 00 - 12 30
Vice-Consul: Mrs Helen Watson, MBE
Pro-Consul: Miss Raquel de la Osa

Menorca
British Vice-Consulate
St Casa Nova, Cami de Biniatap 30
07720 Es Castell, Menorca
Telephone: (00) (34) 971 36 78 18
Facsimile: (00) (34) 971 35 46 90
e-mail: deborahhellyer@infotelecom.es
Honorary Vice-Consul: Mrs Deborah Hellyer, MBE

SRI LANKA

Colombo
British High Commission
190 Galle Road, Kollupitiya
(PO Box 1433)
Colombo 3
Telephone: (00) (94) (11) 2 437336/43
Facsimile: (00) (94) (11) 2 430308,
335803 Consular/Visa
e-mail: bhc@eureka.lk
Office Hours (GMT): Mon - Thurs: 02 00 - 11 00;
Fri: 02 30 - 07 30
Visa Hours (GMT): Mon - Thurs: 02 00 - 05 30;
Fri: 02 30 - 04 30
British Council: 49 Alfred House Gardens
(PO Box 753), Colombo 3
Telephone: (00) (94) (11) 581171/2, 587078,
580301,502487, 582449
Facsimile: (00) (94) (11) 587079
e-mail: enquiries@britishcouncil.lk
*High Commissioner (also High Commissioner to
the Republic of Maldives):*
Mr Stephen N Evans, OBE
Deputy High Commissioner: Mr Peter J Hughes
Defence Adviser:
Lieutenant Colonel Colin P G Martin
Cultural Attaché (British Council Director):
Mr Tony O'Brien
First Secretary (Commercial): Mr Dave Waring

First Secretary (Management): Mr Mick Mitchell
First Secretary (Development): Miss Penny Thorpe
First Secretary (Development):
Ms Anthea Mulakala
Second Secretary (Development):
Mr Jay Sellahewa
Second Secretary (Chancery):
Miss Margaret Tongue
Second Secretary (Immigration/Consular):
Mrs Paula Peacock
Second Secretary (Immigration):
Mr Roger Goodall
Second Secretary (resides at Mumbai):
Mr Simon Sutcliffe
Deputy Cultural Attaché (British Council):
Ms Anne Searle
Third Secretary (Chancery): Mr Colin Hicks
Attaché (Management): Mrs Rebecca Brett
Attaché (Consular): Miss Jo Ford
Attaché (Consular): Mrs Yasmeen Rahman
Attaché (Consular): Mr Ryan Griffin
Attaché (Consular): Mrs Sarah Downing
Attaché: Miss Julie Coleman
Attaché: Miss Jenny Jones
Attaché (Security): Mr Mike Whyte
Assistant Defence Adviser:
Staff Sergeant Alistair Farrow
Attaché (Technical): Mr Tony Mason

SUDAN

Khartoum
British Embassy
Off Sharia Al Baladia, Khartoum East
(PO Box No 801)
FTN Code – 8381 + extn number
Telephone: (00) (249) (11) 777105
Facsimile: (00) (249) (11) 776457
775562 (Consular/Visa)
Airtech: 775492
e-mail: british@sudanmail.net
Office Hours (GMT): Sun - Thurs: 05 00 – 12 00
Visa Office Hours (GMT): Sun - Thurs: 05 00 –
12 00
Ambassador: Mr William Patey
DHM/Consul General: Mr Ric Girdlestone
Defence Attaché (Resident in Addis Ababa):
Colonel David S Charters
First Secretary (Aid): Mr Matthew Baugh
First Secretary (British Council):
Mr Bob Steedman
First Secretary (External Affairs):
Mr Rupert Gaskin
Second Secretary (Management/Commercial):
Mrs Debbie Beynon
Second Secretary (Political/Information):
Mr Mark Bryson-Richardson
Third Secretary and Vice-Consul:
Mr Doug Tunn
Third Secretary Entry Clearance Officer:
Mr Jonathan Knight
Attaché (Security): Mr Roger Tomkins
Attaché (Technical Works): Mr Ted Stewart
Attaché: Mr Brian Mills
Attaché: Miss Natalie Gowers

SURINAM

Paramaribo
British Embassy
*Ambassador: Mr Steve J Hiscock
*Consul and Deputy Head of Mission:
Mr Malcolm Kirk
Defence Attaché (Resides at Bridgetown):
Captain Steve G Wilson, RN
* *Second Secretary (Political/Commercial/Public
Diplomacy):* Mr Richard Cox
* *Third Secretary (Immigration/Consular):*
Mr Neil Frape
* *Resides at Georgetown*

Paramaribo
British Consulate
c/o VSH United Buildings, Van't Hogerhuysstraat,
9-11
PO Box 1860, Paramaribo
Telephone: (00) (597) 402558,402870
Facsimile: (00) (597) 403515,403824
e-mail: united@sr.net
Office Hours (GMT): 11 00 - 20 15
Honorary Consul: Mr J J Healy, Jnr

SWAZILAND

Mbabane (SP – see page 120)
British High Commission
Callers: 2nd Floor, Lilunga House
Gilfillan Street
Mbabane
Postal: Private Bag, Mbabane
FTN Code – 8644 + extn number
Telephone: (00) (268) 404 2581/2/3/4
Facsimile: (00) (268) 404 2585
Airtech: (00) (268) 404 2105
e-mail: enquiries.mbabane@fco.gov.uk
Office Hours (GMT): Mon - Thurs: 06 00 - 11 00
and 12 00 - 14 45. Fri: 06 00 - 11 00
High Commissioner (ext 2101): Mr George Squires
Deputy High Commissioner (ext 2103):
Ms Liz Ripard
Defence Adviser (resides at Pretoria):
Brigadier David H Keenan, OBE
Attaché (ext 2102): Mrs Christine Costantini

SWEDEN

Stockholm
British Embassy
Skarpögatan 6-8, Box 27819
115 93 Stockholm
FTN Code – 8312 + extn number
Telephone: (00) (46) (8) 671 3000 Direct Dial - use
extensions below in brackets
Facsimile: (00) (46) (8) 662 9989 Management
671 3104 Chancery/Defence
671 3077 Commercial
661 9766 Consular/Visa
671 3100 Information
Airtech: 671 3137
Website: www.britishembassy.com
Office Hours (GMT): Winter: 08 00 -16 00
Summer 06 30 -14 30
Ambassador: (ext 3102): Mr Anthony J Cary, CMG

Counsellor (Economic and Commercial) (ext 3050): Mr John Tucknott, MBE
Counsellor (ext 3112): Mr John Macpherson, OBE
Defence Attaché (ext 3105):
Wing Commander Nigel J Phillips, RAF
Cultural Attaché (British Council Director) (ext 3082): Mr Jim Potts
First Secretary (Political) (ext 3119):
Mr Kevin McGurgan
First Secretary (Inward Investment) (ext 3067):
Mr Adrian Pinder
First Secretary (Management and Consul (ext 3070): Mr David Broomfield
First Secretary (Commercial) (ext 3053):
Ms Shirley Smith
Second Secretary (Political/Information) (ext 3108): Mrs Emma Sundblad
Second Secretary (Political/Economic) (ext 3115): Ms Claire Jeffery
Second Secretary (Media and Public Relations) (ext 3006): Mr Damion Potter
Second Secretary (Science and Technology Affairs) (ext 3117): Ms Alice Hague
Third Secretary (Political) (ext 3191):
Mr Steven Chandler
Vice-Consul (ext 3023): Ms Karen Farley
Entry Clearance Manager (ext 3022):
Mr Henry Hodge
Honorary Chaplain: The V Rev. Bruce Evenson

Gothenburg
British Consulate-General
Södra Hamngatan 23
S 41114 Göthenburg
Telephone: (00) (46) (31) 339 3300
Facsimile: (00) (46) (31) 339 3302
Consul-General (resides in Stockholm):
Mr John Tucknott, MBE

Sundsvall
British Consulate
SCA Graphic
Sundsvall AB
Ostrand Pulp Mill
861 81 Timra
Telephone: (00) (46) (60) 16 40 00
Facsimile: (00) (46) (60) 57 49 90
Honorary Consul: Mr Ola Hildingsson (Swedish)

SWITZERLAND

Berne
British Embassy
Thunstrasse 50, 3005 Berne
FTN Code – 8370 + extn number
Telephone: (00) (41) (31) 359 7700
Facsimile: (00) (41) (31) 359 7701 General
         359 7769 Political and Information
         Section
         359 7765 Management and Consular
         Sections
Internet Address:
http://www.britain-in-switzerland.ch
Office Hours (GMT): 07 30 - 11 30 and
12 30 - 16 00
Ambassador (also Ambassador to the Principality of Liechtenstein): Mr Simon Featherstone

Counsellor, Consul-General, Deputy Head of Mission and Director of Trade and Investment (also Consul-General to the Principality of Liechtenstein): Mr David Roberts
Counsellor: Mr Hugh Patterson
Defence Attaché:
Lieutenant Colonel Paddy H Bangham
British Council Director: Ms Caroline Morrissey
First Secretary (Political): Dr Simon Harkin
First Secretary (Management) and Consul (also Consul for the Principality of Liechtenstein):
Mr Tony Bates, MVO
First Secretary (Trade): Ms Susan Mortimer
First Secretary (Investment): Mr Brian Hamill
Third Secretary (Political): Mr Martin Webber
Vice-Consul (Trade): Mr Beat Haessig
Vice-Consul (Trade): Mrs Sharon Valdettaro
Vice-Consul (Trade): Mr Peter Mueller
Vice-Consul (Science and Technology):
Mr Bernhard Sander
Pro-Consul: Miss Wendy Page, MBE

Geneva
British Consulate General
37-39 Rue de Vermont (6th Floor)
1211 Geneva 20
FTN Code – 8371 + extn number
Telephone: (00) (41) (22) 918 2400
Facsimile: (00) (41) (22) 918 2322
Telex: 414195 (a/b 414195 UKGV CH)
Office Hours (GMT): Summer: 06 30 - 10 30 and
12 00 - 15 00. Winter: 07 30 - 11 30 and
13 00 - 16 00
HM Consul General (ext 2458):
Mrs Susan Gregory
HM Consul (ext 2417): Mr Alistair Church
British Vice-Consul (Immigration/Consular) (ext 2425): Ms Lynne Sowerby
Vice-Consul (Commercial) (ext 2421):
Mrs Eleanor Baha
Passport Officer (ext 2308):
Mrs Christine Kaczmarek
Pro-Consul (ext 2480): Ms Julia Murray
Pro-Consul (ext 2423): Mrs Elizabeth Long

Geneva
Joint Management Office
37-39 Rue de Vermont, 1211 Geneva 20
FTN Code – 8371 + extn number
Telephone: (00) (41) (22) 918 2300
Facsimile: (00) (41) (22) 918 2310
Telex: 414195 (a/b 414195 UKGV CH
Office Hours (GMT): Summer: 07 00 - 11 00 and
12 30 - 16 00. Winter: 08 00 - 12 00 and
13 30 - 17 00
First Secretary, Head of Joint Management Office (ext 2458): Mrs Susan Gregory
Deputy Head of Joint Management Office (ext 2452): Mr Ian McKinlay
Technical Management Officer (ext 2414):
Mr Matthew Smith
Deputy Management Officer (ext 2425):
Ms Lynne Sowerby

Montreux/Vevey
British Vice-Consulate
13 chemin de l'Aubousset

1806 St Légier, Vaud
Telephone and Facsimile: (00) (41) (21) 943 3263
Honorary Consul: Mrs S Darra, MBE

Valais
British Vice-Consulate
Rue des Fontaines
CH 3974 Mollens - Valais
Telephone: (00) (41) (27) 480 3210
457 5111 (Radio Pager)
Facsimile: (00) (41) (27) 480 3211
Honorary Vice-Consul: Mr A Bushnell

Geneva United Kingdom Mission to United Nations, see Missions and Delegations page
Geneva United Kingdom Permanent Representation to the Conference on Disarmament, see Missions and Delegations page

Zurich
British Vice-Consulate
Hegibachstrasse 47
CH- 8032 Zurich
Telephone: (00) (41) (1) 383 6560
Facsimile: (00) (41) (1) 383 6561
Honorary Consul: Mr A L T McCammon

Lugano
British Vice-Consulate
Via Sorengo 22,Third Floor
PO Box 184
6903 Lugano
Telephone: (00) (41) (91) 950 0606
Facsimile: (00) (41) (91) 950 0609
Office Hours (GMT): 10 00 - 12 00
Honorary Consul: Mr J Takield OBE

Basel
British Vice-Consulate
Innovation Centre
Gewerbestrasse 14
CH4123
Allschwill
Tel/fax: (00) (41) (61) 483 0977
Mobile: (00) (41) 763 789 987
Honorary Consul: Dr A Chalmers

SYRIA

Damascus
British Embassy
Kotob Building
11 Mohammad Kurd Ali Street
Malki, PO Box 37, Damascus
FTN Code – 8489 + extn number or 1000 (Switchboard)
Telephone: (00) (963) (11) 373 9241/2/3/7
Facsimile: (00) (963) (11) 373 1600 Management
373 9236 Visa and Consular
373 9472 Commercial
Office Hours (GMT): Sun - Wed 06 00 - 13 30;
Thurs 06 00 - 12 00
Ambassador: Mr Peter Ford
Counsellor and Deputy Head of Mission:
Mr Roddy Drummond, OBE
Defence Attaché: Colonel C Julian A Lyne-Pirkis
British Council Director: Mr Paul Doubleday

First Secretary (Political): Mr Anthony Ball
First Secretary (Management) and Consul:
Mr Frank J McGinley
Second Secretary (Commercial): Mr Seif Usher
Second Secretary (Economic): Mr Mark Taylor
Vice-Consul (Immigration/Consular):
Miss Kirsty Saunders
Third Secretary (Political/Information):
Miss Nicola Davies
Attaché: Mr Jason Wells
Attaché: Mrs Kathryn Richmond
Attaché: Miss Helen Ridley
Attaché: Miss Janice Lytle
Attaché: Mr Simon Marshall
Attaché: Mr Jim Hall

Aleppo
British Consulate
PO Box 199
Aleppo
Telephone: (00) (963) (21) 267 2200, 266 1206 (Office)
267 5033 (Home)
Facsimile: (00) (963) (21) 267 7640
Office Hours (GMT): Mon-Thurs and Sat: 07 30 - 11 30 and 15 00 - 18 30. Fri: 15 00 - 18 30
Honorary Consul: Mr Alexander Akhras

British Trade Office
P O Box 5547
Aleppo
Telephone: (00) (963) (21) 268 0502/3
Facsimile: (00) (963) (21) 268 0501
Senior Commercial Officer: Mr Zaher Abu Baker

Lattakia
British Consulate
13 Gabriel Saadeh Street
PO Box 828
Lattakia
Telephone: (00) (963) (41) 461 615
Facsimile: (00) (963) (41) 465 723
e-mail: albany@postmaster.co.uk
Opening Hours (GMT): 08 00 - 12 00 and 16 00 - 18 00
Honorary Consul: Mr Bassam Albany

TAIWAN

See Annex for details.

TAJIKISTAN

Dushanbe
British Embassy
43 Lutfi Street
Dushanbe
FTN Code – 8311 + extn number
Telephone: (00) 992 91 901 5079
(00) 870 762 856 221 (Satellite)
(00) 992 372 242 221/ 241 477/ 510 192/ 510 187
Facsimile: (00) 992 91 901 5078
e-mail: reception@britishembassy-tj.com
Website: www.britishembassy.gov.uk/tajikistan
Staff resident in Dushanbe
Ambassador (2322): Mr Graeme Loten

Deputy Head of Mission (2319):
Ms Margaret Belof
Defence Attaché (resides at Almaty):
Lieutenant Colonel G J Sheeley, AFC
British Liaison Officer (2311): Mr Peter Cornell
British Council Director (resides in Tashkent):
Mr Neville McBain
Third Secretary/Vice-Consul (2328):
Mr Shanjeev Thiruchelvam

TANZANIA

Dar es Salaam
British High Commission
Umoja House
Garden Avenue, PO Box 9200
Dar es Salaam
FTN Code – 8499 + extn number
Telephone: (00) (255) (22) 211 0101
Facsimile: (00) (255) (22) 211 0102 Chancery
         211 0112 Management
         211 0296 Consular
         211 0297 Visa
         211 0080 Commercial
e-mail: bhc.dar@fco.gov.uk
Office Hours (GMT): Mon-Fri 04 30 – 12 00
High Commissioner: Dr A Pocock
Deputy High Commissioner: Mr M Croll
Defence Adviser (resides at Nairobi):
Colonel A D K Inkster
British Council Director: Mr T Cowin
Second Secretary (Commercial/Consular):
Mr N Hammond
Second Secretary (Management): Ms S Oulmi
Second Secretary (Press and Public Affairs):
Mr A Massey
*Third Secretary (Political/Press and Public
Affairs):* Ms P Smith
Third Secretary (Consular/Immigration):
Mr I D Craig
Third Secretary (Immigration): Mr S Thornton
Third Secretary (Management): Mr A Darker

Department for International Development
Eastern Africa (Tanzania): DFIDEA (T)
5th Floor
Umoja House
Garden Avenue
PO Box 9200
Dar es Salaam
Telephone: (00) (255) (22) 2110141
Facsimile: (00) (255) (22) 2110130
Office Hours (GMT): Mon-Fri 05 00 – 12 30
Head of DFIDEA (T): Mr D Stanton
Deputy Head of DFIDEA (T): Ms L Campbell
Deputy Programme Manager (Corporate Group):
Ms J Knowlton
Programme Officer (Poverty Reduction Strategy):
Mr A Walker
Economic Adviser: Mr J Piper
Assistant Economic Adviser: Mr C Kalapesi
Social Sector Adviser: Ms P Bird
Governance Adviser: Ms A Gerry
Assistant Governance Adviser: M T MacArther
Human Resources and Administrative Manager:
Ms F Lawless

Poverty Policy Adviser: Mr G Howe
Statistics Adviser: Mr T Harris
Growth Policy Adviser: Mr K Quinlan

THAILAND

Bangkok
British Embassy
Wireless Road, Bangkok, 10330
FTN Code – 8419 + extn number
Telephone: (66) (2) 305 8333
Facsimile: (66) (2) 305 8372 or 8380 Chancery
       (66) (2) 305 8220 Defence
       (66) (2) 255 8619 Commercial/Press
       and Public Affairs
       (66) (2) 255 9278 Management
       (66) (2) 255 6051 Consular
       (66) (2) 254 9579 Immigration
Airtech: (66) (2) 305 8342
Website: www.britishemb.or.th
Office Hours (GMT): Mon-Thurs: 01 00 – 05 00
and 05 45 – 09 30
Fri: 01 00 – 06 00 (Duty Staff until 09 30)
Ambassador: Mr David W Fall (2301)
Counsellor and Deputy Head of Mission:
Mr Andrew J Pearce (2266)
Counsellor (Commercial): Mr Martin Hill (2319)
Defence Attaché:
Colonel Peter C Roberts, MBE (2222)
Counsellor (Political): Mr David Chambers (2288)
First Secretary (Political): Mr Ian Proud (2224)
Consul and First Secretary (Management):
Mr Alan Mayland (2239)
British Council Director: Mr Peter Upton
First Secretary: Mr John Hector (2232)
First Secretary (Technical):
Ms Teresa Hyman (2267)
Second Secretary (Political):
Mr Fergus Auld (2230)
Second Secretary (Commercial):
Mr Trevor Adams (2294)
Second Secretary (Immigration):
Mrs Jane Lacey-Smith (2245)
Second Secretary (Airline Liaison Officer):
Mr Derek Swanson (2362)
Second Secretary (Management):
Mr Malcolm Surman (2317)
Second Secretary and Vice Consul:
Mrs Angela Tokalau (2253)
Second Secretary (Technical):
Mr David Ellis (2369)
Third Secretary (Commercial):
Mr Andrew Stephenson (2350)
Third Secretary (Economic/Development):
Mr Philip McKenzie (2291)
Third Secretary and Vice-Consul:
Mrs Fiona Borisuth (2229)
Third Secretary (Immigration):
Mr Stephen Taylor (2363)
Third Secretary (Immigration):
Mr Kevin Newman (2352)
Third Secretary (Immigration):
Ms Margaret Graham-Moses (2329)
Third Secretary (Immigration):
Mrs Caroline Wright (2338)

Department for International Development (DFID SEA)
c/o British Embassy
Wireless Road, Bangkok, 10330
Telephone: (66) (2) 305 8333
Facsimile: (66) (2) 253 7124
Head of Division: Mr Mark Mallalieu (2250)
Senior Governance Adviser: Mr Peter Owen (2335)
Senior Rural Livelihoods Adviser:
Mr Simon Croxton (2261)
Senior Social Development Adviser:
Mr Richard Edwards (2272)
Senior Economic Adviser: Mr John Hoy (2227)
Social Development Adviser: Mr Tom Beloe (2214)
Economic Adviser: Mr Omar Bargawi (2247)
Senior Health and Population Adviser:
Mr Michael O'Dwyer (2325)
Programmes Manager: Mr Philip Marker (2202)
Programmes Manager:
Mr Robert Leverington (2204)
Human Resources Development Officer:
Mrs Karen Parsons (2383)
Deputy Programme Manager:
Mr Gopi Menon (2215)
Deputy Programme Manager:
Mr Liam Docherty (2295)
Programmes Officer: Mr Alan Sach (2280)

Chiang Mai
British Consulate
198 Bumrungraj Rd
Muang, Chiang Mai, 50000
Telephone: (00) (66) (53) 263 015
Facsimile: (00) (66) (53) 263 016
e-mail: ukconsul@loxinfo.co.th
Office Hours (GMT): Mon – Thurs: 0100 – 0500
and 0545 – 0930. Fri: 0100 – 0600
Honorary Consul: Mr David Hopkinson

TOGO

Lomé
British Embassy
(All staff resident in Accra)
Ambassador and Consul-General: Mr Gordon
Wetherell
Counsellor and Deputy Head of Mission:
Mr Robin Gwynn
Defence Attaché:
Lieutenant Colonel Jonathan A F Howard
First Secretary (Commercial): Mr Kevin Lynch
First Secretary (Political/External): Mr Mike Wood
First Secretary (Senior Management Officer):
Mr David Jones
First Secretary (Immigration): Mr Ken Simpson
*Second Secretary (Political, Press and Public
Affairs):* Mr Gregory Quinn
Second Secretary (Environment): Ms Farida Shaikh
Second Secretary and Vice-Consul:
Mrs Caroline Cross
Second Secretary (Immigration):
Mrs Margaret Brown
Second Secretary (Immigration): Mrs Gillian Elliot
Second Secretary (Airline Liaison Officer):
Mr Julian Kennett

Second Secretary (Technical Management Officer):
Mr Roger Russell
Third Secretary (Chancery): Mr Jonathan Saunders
Third Secretary (Deputy Management Officer):
Mr Bernie Andrews
Third Secretary (Commercial): Mrs Carol Turvill
Third Secretary (Immigration): Ms Stacey Nichols
Third Secretary (Immigration): Mr Simon Winter
Third Secretary (Immigration): Mrs Tracey Singh
Third Secretary (Immigration): Mr Ian Abbott
Third Secretary (Immigration): Mr Stuart Turvill
Third Secretary (Immigration): Mr Alan Green
Third Secretary (Immigration): Mrs Angela Walters
Third Secretary (Immigration): Mr Paul O'Neill
Third Secretary (Immigration): Mrs Fiona McPhail
Third Secretary (Immigration):
Mrs Karen Simpson
Third Secretary (Immigration): Mr Rob Dixon
Third Secretary (Immigration): Mr Tim Galvin

Lomé
British Consulate
British School of Lomé, BP 20050, Lomé
Telephone: (00) (228) 2264606
Facsimile: (00) (228) 2264989
e-mail: "For Mrs Jeni Sayer, British Consulate"
Admin@bsl.tg
Office Hours (GMT): Mon - Fri: 09 00 - 11 00
Honorary Consul: Mrs Jeni A Sayer

British Commercial Office
Concession OTAM, Zone Portuaire,
Port de Peche, BP 9224, Lomé-Port, Lomé, Togo
Telephone: (00) (228) 2271141, 2275054
Mobile: (00) (228) 042180
Facsimile: (00) (228) 2274207
e-mail: tom@netcom.tg
Commercial Officer: Captain R A M Jones

TONGA

Nuku'alofa (SP – see page 120)
British High Commission
PO Box 56, Nuku'alofa, Tonga
Telephone: (00) (676) 24285/24395
Facsimile: (00) (676) 24109
Airtech: (00) (676) 23922
e-mail: britcomt@kalianet.to
Office Hours (GMT): Sun - Wed: 19 15 - 23 30
and 00 30 - 03 45. Thurs: 19 15 - 00 15
*High Commissioner and Consul for American
Samoa:* Mr Paul Nessling
Management Officer: Mrs Kathryn Nessling
Defence Adviser (resides at Wellington):
Colonel Alec A Peebles

TRINIDAD AND TOBAGO

Port of Spain (SP – see page 120)
British High Commission
19 St Clair Avenue
St Clair, Trinidad
FTN Code – 8649 + extn number
Telephone: (00) (1) (868) 622 2748, 628 1234, 628
1068, 622 8985/86, 622 8960/61/62
Facsimile: (00) (1) (868) 622 4555 Management
622 9087 Commercial

628 3064 Consular/Immigration
628 8715 Chancery
Airtech: (00) (1) (868) 622 4533
e-mail: csbhc@opus.co.tt
Website: www.britain-in-trinidad.org
Office Hours (GMT): Mon – Thurs: 1130 – 1600
and 1700 – 2000. Fri: 1130 – 1630
High Commissioner: Mr Ronald Nash, CMG, LVO
Deputy High Commissioner: Mr Keith Allan
Defence Adviser (Resides at Bridgetown):
Captain Steve G Wilson, RN
First Secretary (Regional Affairs): Mr Rob Kelly
British Council Manager: Ms Harriet Massingberd
Second Secretary (Management/Consular):
Mr Bryan D Scarborough
Second Secretary (Chancery): Mr Tony Reader
Second Secretary (Commercial):
Miss Helen Tanner
Second Secretary (Regional Affairs):
Mr Stuart R Brough
Third Secretary (Chancery/Information):
Mr Philip Everest

TUNISIA

Tunis
British Embassy
Rue du Lac Windermere
Les Berges du Lac
Tunis 1053
FTN Code – 8328 + extn number or 1000
(Switchboard)
Telephone: (00) (216) 71 108 703
Facsimile: (00) (216) 71 108 703 Chancery
            71 108 749 Management
            71 108 769 Commercial
            71 108 779 Visa
            71 108 789 Consular
Airtech: (00) (216) 71 108 726
e-mail: british.emb@planet.tn
Website: www.britishembassy.gov.uk/tunisia
Office Hours (GMT): Mon - Thurs 07 00 – 11 00
and 12 00 - 15 30. Fri 07 00 – 12 00
Ambassador and Consul-General:
Mr Alan F Goulty, CMG
Deputy Head of Mission: Mr Phil Batson
Defence Attaché (resides in London):
Commander Matt P Briers, RN
Cultural Attaché (British Council Director):
Mr Joe Docherty, OBE
*Second Secretary (Commercial/Press and Public
Affairs):* Mrs Marie-Claire Joyce
Second Secretary (Management): Mr Jim Buglass
Second Secretary (HMC/ECM/Pol/Econ):
Mr Gordon Stein
Vice-Consul: Mrs Sidsel Ghehioeuche
Third Secretary (Immigration): Mrs Rachel Mease
Third Secretary (Immigration): Mr Dave Burrows
Attaché: Mrs Sharn Davison
Attaché: Mr Peter Botham

Sfax
Honorary British Consulate
55 Rue Habib Maazoun, 3000,
Sfax 3000, Tunisia
Telephone: (00) (216) (74) 223 971

Facsimile: (00) (216) (74) 299 278
Honorary Consul: Mr Moneef Sellami

TURKEY

Ankara
British Embassy
Sehit Ersan Caddesi 46/A
Cankaya, Ankara
FTN Code – 8652 + extn number
Telephone: (00) (90) (312) 455 3344
            455 + extension number
Facsimile: (00) (90) (312) 455 3351
            Commercial/Economic
            455 3353 Consular/Visa
            455 3386 Clinic
            455 3226 Defence
            455 3259 Drugs
            455 3356 Information
            455 3352 Management
            455 3350 Political
            455 3320 HMA
Airtech: 455 3240
e-mail: britembank@fco.gov.uk (check Firecrest
for individuals)
Website: www.britishembassy.org.tr

British Council
Karum Is Merkezi, Iran Cad No. 21 Kat 5
Room 437, Kavaklidere
Ankara, 06700
Telephone: (00) (90) (312) 455 3600
Facsimile: (00) (90) (312) 455 3636
Office Hours (GMT): Summer 05 45 - 10 00 and
11 15 - 14 30. July, August 05 45 - 10 00 and 11
15 - 14 30 (Mon - Thurs). 05 45 - 10 00 (Fri).
Winter 06 45 - 11 00 and 12 15 - 15 30
Ambassador:
Sir Peter J Westmacott, KCMG, LVO 3201
Counsellor and Deputy Head of Mission:
Mr Michael Roberts3203
Defence and Military Attaché:
Colonel Mark H Auchinleck 3221
*Counsellor (British Council Director, Cultural
Affairs):* Mr Chris Brown, OBE
Naval and Air Attaché:
Wing Commander Joe Gillan RAF 3223
*First Secretary (Head of Economic/Commercial
Section):* Mr Steven Smith 3241
First Secretary (Head of Political Section):
Mr Ajay Sharma 3210
First Secretary (Political/Military):
Mr William Blanchard, OBE, MVO 3207
First Secretary (Management) and Consul:
Mr Dominic Clissold, OBE3261
*First Secretary (British Council and Cultural
Affairs):* Mr Tony Lockhart
*First Secretary (British Council and Cultural
Affairs):* Ms Gillian Cowell
First Secretary (Drugs): Mr Gary Brown 3360
First Secretary (Technical Management):
Mr Paul Holmes 3214
Second Secretary (Economic):
Mr Stephen McCormick3244
*Second Secretary (Political/Press and Public
Affairs):* Mrs Christine Bradley 3209

Second Secretary (Political):
Mr Geoff Collier 3205
Second Secretary (Political): Mr Ben Angell 3329
Second Secretary (Drugs): Mr Warren Spivey3380
Second Secretary (Technical Management):
Mr Bruce Hallybone 3218
Second Secretary (Immigration Liaison Officer):
Mr Roger Tate 3325
Third Secretary (Political): Mr Paul Ardley 3219
Third Secretary (Political): Mr Ed Garrett 3213
Third Secretary (Management):
Ms Clarice Whiteside3262
Vice-Consul: Mrs Trudie Pak 3257
Security Officer: Mr Bob Lackenby 3216

Antalya
British Vice-Consulate
Fevzi Çakmak Cad
1314 Sokak No.6/8
Antalya
Telephone: (00) (90) (242) 244 5313
Facsimile: (00) (90) (242) 243 2095
e-mail: britconant@turk.net
Vice Consul: Mrs Jane Baz

Bodrum
British Consulate
Kibris Sehitleri Caddesi
Konacik Mevkii No 401/B
Bodrum
Telephone: (00) (90) (252) 319 0093-94
Facsimile: (00) (90) (252) 319 0095
e-mail: britconbod2@superonline.com
Honorary Consul: Mrs Fatma Nese Coskunsu

Izmir
British Consulate
1442 Sokak No 49
Alsancak
PK 300 Izmir
Telephone: (00) (90) (232) 463 5151
Facsimile: (00) (90) (232) 465 0858
e-mail: postmaster@izmir.mail.fco.gov.uk (check
Firecrest for individuals)
Consul: Mr Willie Buttigie

Marmaris
British Consulate
c/o Yesil Marmaris Tourism and Yacht Management
Inc.
Barbaros Caddesi 11, Marina
P O Box 8, 48700 Marmaris
Telephone: (00) (90) (252) 412 6486
Facsimile: (00) (90) (252) 412 5077
e-mail: brithonmar@superonline.com
Honorary Consul: Mr Adnan Dogan Tugay

Mersin Consulate - Closed

Istanbul
British Consulate-General
Mesrutiyet Caddesi No 34
Tepebasi, Beyoglu
PK 33 Istanbul 80050
Telephone: (00) (90) (212) 334 6400
Facsimile: 334 6401
Visa Section:
Telephone: (00) (90) (212) 315 6141

Facsimile: 334 6501 Visa
            334 6407 Consular
e-mail: bricons.istanbul@superonline.com
Website: www.britishembassy.org.tr
Office Hours (GMT): 06 30 - 11 00 and
11 45 - 14 45
*Consul-General and Director of Trade and
Investment Promotion:* Ms B L Hay, CMG, MBE
Deputy Consul-General: Mr Peter Cook
*Consul (British Council Director and Cultural
Affairs):* Mrs Sue Barnes-Bubic
Consul (Management): Mr Paul Ramsay
Consul (Political Affairs): Mr Quentin Phillips
Consul (Consular Affairs): Mr Martin Abel
Consul (Drugs): Mr Steve Wren
Consul (Drugs): Mr Kevin Grist
Consul (Drugs): Mr Andy Kellaway
Consul: Mr Graeme Wiskar
Consul (Immigration): Mr Myron Reid
Consul (Immigration): Mr Thomas Burke
Vice-Consul (Technical Works Officer):
Mr Mike Wood, OBE
Vice-Consul: Mr Shane Campbell, MBE
*Vice-Consul (British Council Assistant Director
and Cultural Affairs):* Mr Nic Humphries
Vice-Consul (Commercial): Mr Colin Barrett
Vice-Consul (Consular Affairs): Mr Thomas Reid
Vice-Consul (Press and Political Affairs):
Mr Chris Kealey
Vice-Consul (Management): Mr Les Jones
Vice-Consul (Immigration): Mr Alasdair Horner
Vice-Consul (Immigration): Ms Ciara Palmer
Vice-Consul (Immigration): Mr Gwyn Jones
Vice-Consul (Immigration): Mr Steve Jackson
Vice-Consul (Immigration): Ms Theresa Gecim
Vice-Consul (Immigration): Mrs Julie Gorasia
Chaplain: Canon Ian Sherwood

Bursa
British Honorary Consulate
Ressam Sefik Bursali Sokak
Basak Caddesi Zemin Kat
16010 Bursa
Telephone: (00) (90) (224) 220 25 34
Facsimile: (00) (90) (224) 220 88 01
Home Telephone: (00) (90) (224) 221 29 84
Honorary Consul: Mr E Kagitcibasi

TURKMENISTAN

Ashgabat (SP – see page 120)
British Embassy
3rd Floor, Office Building
Four Points Ak Altin Hotel
Ashgabat
FTN Code – 8752 + extn number
Telephone: (00) (993) (12) 363462, 363463,
363464, 363466, 363498
Facsimile: (00) (993) (12) 363465
Airtech: (00) (993) (12) 363463 x292
e-mail: beasb@online.tm (General)
beasbtrade@online.tm (Commercial)
beasbppa@online.tm (Press and Public Affairs)
Website: www.britishembassy.gov.uk/turkmenistan

Office Hours (GMT): Mon - Thurs: 04 00 - 08 00
and 09 00 - 12 30. Fri: 04 00 - 08 00 and
09 00 - 11 00
Ambassador: Mr Paul Brummell 2201
Deputy Head of Mission: Mr Stephen Rapp 2202
Defence Attaché (resides at Moscow):
Colonel Colin A Bulleid
Assistant Defence Attaché (resides at Moscow):
Major Alfonso C J Torrens
Cultural Attaché (resides at Tashkent):
Mr Neville McBain
Second Secretary: Mr Stuart O'Neill 2270
Third Secretary (Chancery): Ms Rosie Tapper 2206
Third Secretary (Management) and Vice-Consul:
Ms Jane Rowlands 2210

TUVALU

Funafuti
British High Commission
(All staff resident at Suva)
High Commissioner: Mr Charles F Mochan
Deputy High Commissioner: Mr Ian Powell

UGANDA

Kampala
British High Commission
10/12 Parliament Avenue,
PO Box 7070, Kampala
FTN Code – 8656 + extn number
Telephone: (00) (256) (31) 312000
Facsimile: (00) (256) (41) 257304
          (31) 312281 (Consular /Visa Section)
Airtech: (00) (256) (31) 312210
e-mail: bhcinfo@starcom.co.ug (Press and Public
Affairs Section)
bhccomm@starcom.co.ug (Commercial Section)
bhcimm@infocom.co.ug (Consular/Visa Section)
firstname.lastname@fco.gov.uk
Office Hours (GMT): Mon to Thurs: 05 30 - 10 00
and 11 00 - 14 00. Fri: 05 30 - 10 00
High Commissioner: Mr Adam Wood
Deputy High Commissioner: Mr Jon Elliott
Defence Adviser:
Lieutenant Colonel Christopher J A Wilton
First Secretary (Regional Affairs):
Mr Robert Watson
First Secretary (British Council Director):
Ms Kate Ewart-Biggs
First Secretary (Management): Mr John Heffer
First Secretary (British Council): (Vacant)
Second Secretary (Entry Clearance Manager):
Mr Stephen Powell
Second Secretary (Political External):
Mr Craig Fulton
Second Secretary (Consular/Commercial):
Ms Sarah Young
*Second Secretary (Political/Press and Public
Affairs):* Ms Lynda St. Cooke
Second Secretary: Mr Andrew McLean
Military Staff Assistant: Staff Sergeant Max Sexton
Third Secretary (Political): Mr Matt Caney
Third Secretary (Immigration):
Mr Orlando Ames-Lewis
Third Secretary (Immigration): Mr Clive Mead

Third Secretary (Security Manager):
Mr Andy Davis

**Department for International Development
Eastern Africa (Uganda)**
3rd Floor Rwenzori Courts
Plot 2 Nakasero Road
P O Box 7306, Kampala
FTN Code – 8770 + extn number
Telephone: (00) (256) (41) 348727/9 and 348730/7
Facsimile: (00) (256) (41) 348732
e-mail: initial-surname@dfid. gov.uk
Head of Office: Mr Eric Hawthorn
Deputy Head of Office: Ms Charlotte Pierre
Deputy Programme Manager: (Vacant)
Sustainable Livelihoods Adviser: Dr Alan Tollervey
Health and Population Adviser: Ms Ros Cooper
Assistant Health Adviser: Ms Angela Spilsbury
Statistics Adviser: Ms Kim Bradford Smith
Social Development Adviser:
Mr Arthur Van Diesen
Assistant Governance Adviser: Mr Tom Wingfield
Economic Adviser: Mr Jonathan Beynon
Economist: Mr Andrew Keith
Enterprise Development Adviser: Mr Adrian Stone
Enterprise Development Adviser: Mr Anthony Way
Emergencies Adviser: Mr Graham Carrington

British Council
Ground Floor, Rwenzori Courts
Plot 2 Nakasero Road
PO Box 7306
Kampala
Telephone: (00) (256) (41) 234 730/7, 254 927,
031-206508/9
Facsimile: (00) (256) (41) 254 853
e-mail: firtsname.lastname@britishcouncil.or.ug

UKRAINE

Kiev
British Embassy
01025 Kiev Desyatinna 9
FTN Code – 8658 3660 or extn number
Telephone: (00) (380) (44) 490 3660
Facsimile: (00) (380) (44) 490 3662
e-mail: ukembinf@sovamua.com
Consular/Visa Section/DFID Section:
4, Glybochytska Street,
Kiev 04050
Telephone: (00) (380) (44) 490 3400
          (00) (380) (44) 490 2403 (DFID)
Facsimile: (00) (380) (44) 490 3480
          (00) (380) (44) 490 2414 (Consular)
e-mail: britvisa.kiev@fco.gov.uk (Consular and
Visa Section)
Office Hours (GMT): Mon – Thur 07 00 – 15 30.
Fri 07 00 – 14 00

British Council:
040704 Kiev
4/12, Hryhoria Skovorody
Telephone: (00) (380) (44) 490 5600
Facsimile: (00) (380) (44) 490 5605
Ambassador: Mr Robert E Brinkley
Consul-General and Deputy Head of Mission:
Mr Martin F Harris

Defence Attaché: Captain Rob E Drewett, MBE, RN
Counsellor (Political): Mr Julian Coulter
First Secretary (Economic): Ms Ruth Allen
First Secretary (Commercial): Mr David Moore
First Secretary (Management):
Mrs Janice A Moore
First Secretary (British Council Director):
Ms Liliana Biglou, OBE
First Secretary (Development – DFID Ukraine):
Mr John Stuppel
Deputy Defence Attaché: Major Stuart I Mehers
Defence Resettlement Officer: Major Donald Smith
Second Secretary (Chancery/Information): (Vacant)
Second Secretary (Immigration): Mr Chris Lain
Second Secretary (Immigration/Consul):
Mr Jonathan Verney
*Second Secretary (Assistant Director, British
Council):* Mr Colin Earley
Third Secretary (Political): Mr Stuart J Brown
Third Secretary (Management):
Mr Barry Bobin-Martin
Third Secretary (Development): Mr Stuart Andrew
Third Secretary (Immigration/Vice-Consul):
Miss Karen Slater
Third Secretary (British Council):
Mr Tony Hubbard
Third Secretary (Immigration): Mr David Haxton
Third Secretary (Immigration): Ms Anne Furey
Third Secretary (Immigration):
Mr Andrew J Meighan
Defence Section Office Manager:
Flight Sergeant Chris C Swain
Registrar: Ms Rebecca Smith

UNITED ARAB EMIRATES

Abu Dhabi
British Embassy
PO Box 248, Abu Dhabi
FTN Code – 8487 + extn number
Telephone: (00) (971) (2) 6101100
             6101111 (Commercial)
Facsimile: (00) (971) (2) 6101518 (Chancery)
             6101585 (Commercial)
             6101586 (Consular/Management)
             6101587 (Visa Section)
             6101514 (Airtech)
e-mail: chancery.abudhabi@fco.gov.uk
Website: www.britain-uae.org
Office Hours (GMT): Sat - Wed 03 30 - 10 30
Ambassador: Mr Richard Makepeace
Counsellor and Deputy Head of Mission:
Mr Alistair McKenzie, MBE
First Secretary (Political): Mr Andrew Neil
Defence Attaché: Colonel Anthony V Malkin
*Counsellor (Cultural Affairs) (British Council
Director):* Mr Peter Ellwood OBE
First Secretary (Commercial): Mr John Gardner
First Secretary, Defence Sales: Mr Navin Patel, MBE
Second Secretary (Management/Consul/ECM):
Mr Steve Davis
*Second Secretary (Chancery/Press and Public
Affairs):* Mr Jason Smith
Second Secretary (Commercial): Mr Rahat Siddiqi
Third Secretary and Vice-Consul:
Mr Amias Moores

Third Secretary (Chancery/Consular):
Mr Simon Heggie
Third Secretary (ECO): Mrs Fiona O'Driscoll

Dubai
British Embassy
PO Box 65, Dubai
FTN Code - 8485 + extn number
Telephone: (00) (971) (4) 309 4444 Main
             Switchboard
             309 4228 Chancery
             309 4241 Management
             309 4445 Commercial
             309 4210 Consular
             309 4333 Visa
             309 4278 Communications
Facsimile: (00) (971) (4) 309 4301 Main
             309 4225 Chancery
             309 4302 Commercial
             309 4303 Visa
Office Hours (GMT): Sat - Wed 03 30 - 10 30
Consul-General and Counsellor: Mr John Hawkins
*First Secretary (Commercial) and Deputy Head of
Mission:* Ms Claire Evans
First Secretary (Political): Mr Alex Younger
Royal Navy Liaison Officer:
Commander Steve Bateman, RN
First Secretary (Technical): Mr Gary Ward
Aviation Security Liaison Officer:
Mr Rob Axworthy
Customs Liaison Officer: Mr Cameron Walker
Cultural Attaché (British Council Director):
Ms Jo Maher
*Second Secretary (Senior Management/Consul/
ECM):* Mrs Heather Reynolds
Airline Liaison Officer: Mr Steve Burns
Second Secretary (Commercial): Mr Mark Ellam
Second Secretary (Technical): Mr Steve Beard
Second Secretary (Press and Public Affairs):
Mrs Vicky Lee-Gorton
Second Secretary (Economic): Mr Thomas Sisum
Second Secretary (Political):
Mrs Anne Marriott, MBE
Second Secretary (Regional Affairs):
Ms Rachel Stewart
Third Secretary (Commercial): Mr Paul Smith
Third Secretary (Immigration): Mr Andy Palmer
Third Secretary (Immigration): Mr Noorel Haque
Vice-Consul: Mrs Suzanne Bastin

UNITED STATES

Washington
British Embassy
3100 Massachusetts Avenue, NW
Washington, DC 20008
FTN Code – 8430 + extn number
Telephone: (00) (1) (202) 588 6500 Embassy
             7800 Consular
             7830 British Council
Facsimile: (00) (1) (202) 588 7870 Chancery
             7866 Management
             7901 Trade
             7850 Consular
Office Hours (GMT): Winter: 14 00 - 22 30.
Summer: 13 00 - 21 30

Ambassador: Sir David G Manning, KCMG
Minister: Mr Alan Charlton, CMG
Minister (Economic): Mr Thomas Scholar
Defence Attaché and Head of British Defence Staff:
Rear Admiral Antony K Dymock, CB
Minister (Defence Material): Ms Shuna Lindsay
Naval Attaché and Commander British Naval Staff:
Commodore C Joe Gass, RN
*Military Attaché and Commander British Army
Staff:* Brigadier E Johnny Torrens-Spence
*Air Attaché and Commander British Air Force
Staff:* Air Commodore Jerry J Witts, RAF
Counsellor (Political and Public Affairs):
Mr Robert Peirce
Counsellor (Political/Military/Europe):
Mr Frank Baker
Counsellor (Trade and Transport):
Mr Antony J Phillipson
Counsellor: Mr Ian F McCredie, CMG, OBE
Counsellor (Management) and Consul-General:
Mr Warren D Townend
Counsellor (External Affairs):
Mr Sebastian Wood, CMG
*Counsellor (Science Technology, Environment and
Energy):*
Dr Peter Hayes
Counsellor: Dr Ruth Martin
Counsellor: Mr Tristram Riley-Smith
Counsellor (NIB): Mr Daniel McNeill
Counsellor (DST): Mr Adrian Baguley
Counsellor (Defence Equipment):
Mr Robert Regan
Counsellor (Head of NSD): Mr David Deardon
Counsellor (Economic): Mr Alex Gibbs
Counsellor: Mr Steve Rowton
Cultural Attaché (British Council Director):
Mr Andrew Mackay
First Secretary (Political): Mr John Casson
First Secretary (Chancery): Mr Colin Crooks
First Secretary (Chancery): Mr Carl Newns
First Secretary (Chancery): Mr St John Gould
First Secretary (Chancery): Ms Alison Blake
First Secretary (Chancery): Ms Joanne Adamson
First Secretary (Agricultural): Mr James Hughes
First Secretary (Energy and Environment):
Dr Christian Turner
First Secretary (Science and Technology):
Mr Christopher Pook
First Secretary (Economic): Mr Dermot Finch
First Secretary (Trade Policy): Mr Philip Budden
First Secretary (Transport): Mr Simon Knight
First Secretary (Press and Public Affairs):
Mr Peter Reid
First Secretary (Politico/Military):
Mr Marcus Winsley
First Secretary: Mr Alasdair Share
First Secretary (Political): Mr Steve Hill
First Secretary (Management): Mr Peter J Newman
*First Secretary (Technical Management/IT Co-
ordination):* Mr Keith Edwards
First Secretary (Technical Management):
Mr Simon R Drew
First Secretary (UK/US Technical Exchange):
Mr Chris Judge
First Secretary: Mr Peter Lewis

First Secretary (Scottish Affairs):
Ms Susan Stewart
First Secretary (Defence Equipment):
Mr Chris Cook
First Secretary (Trade Promotion):
Mr Alan Attryde
First Secretary (Technical Works Officer):
Mr John Miles
First Secretary (Consul): Mr Graeme Wise
First Secretary (Education): Ms Jenny A Scott
First Secretary (NIB): Mr Michael Gould
Attaché (Defence Equipment - Sea/Air):
Mr Tim Whitemore
Attaché (Defence Equipment - Land): Mr Jim Platt
Attaché (Defence Equipment - Legal):
Mr Graham Farnsworth
Attaché (Defence Equipment - Commercial):
Mr Mike Newman
Assistant Defence Attaché:
Colonel S Tim Chicken, OBE, RM
Assistant Naval Attaché:
Captain John H J Gower, OBE, RN
Head of BDILS (NA): Colonel Michael K Hill
Assistant Military Attaché:
Colonel Philip St. L Baxter
Assistant Air Attaché:
Group Captain Andrew J Barrett, RAF
First Secretary (Defence/Trade): Mr Tim Johnson
*First Secretary (Defence Supply - Land and Sea
Systems):* Mr Alan Nisbet
Second Secretary (PS to Ambassador):
Ms Kirsty Paton
Second Secretary (Technical Management):
Mr Jerry Harland
Second Secretary (Management):
Mr John E Burran
Second Secretary (Transport): Mr Carl Sutcliffe
Second Secretary (Chancery): Mr Peter Jones
Second Secretary (Chancery/External):
Miss Rachel J Laycock
Third Secretary (Management): Miss Paula Friston
Third Secretary: Mr Ian Allan
Third Secretary (Vice-Consul):
Mr Adam Radcliffe, MBE
Third Secretary (Technical Management):
Mr Martin Burn
Third Secretary (Technical Management):
Mr Matthew Ormond
Third Secretary (Technical Management):
Mr Barney Griffiths
Head of Defence Administration: Mr Phil Jones

**Washington United Kingdom Delegation to the
International Monetary Fund and International
Bank for Reconstruction and Development, see
Missions and Delegations page 116
Washington United Kingdom Representation at
the Inter-American Development Bank, see
Missions and Delegations page 116**

Atlanta
British Consulate-General
Georgia Pacific Center, Suite 3400
133 Peachtree Street NE
Atlanta, GA 30303
FTN Code – 8438 + extn number

Telephone: (00) (1) (404) 954 7700
Facsimile: (00) (1) (404) 954 7702
Airtech: (00) (1) (404) 522 7739
Voicemail Numbers: see individual officers
Office Hours (GMT): 13.00 - 23.00
e-mail - {officers first name.surname} followed by @fco.gov.uk
Consul-General (Ext 7716): Mr Michael Bates, OBE
HM Consul (Ext 7720): Ms Helen Arbon
Consul (Trade) (Ext 7737): Ms Marguerite Meyer
Vice-Consul (Consular) (Ext 7713):
Ms Linda Nassar
Vice-Consul (Trade) (Ext 7725): Mr Mark Borst
Vice-Consul (Trade) (Ext 7722):
Ms Christina Lynton
Vice-Consul (Investment) (Ext 7730):
Mr Glen Whitley
Vice-Consul (Investment) (Ext 7731):
Mr Ian Stewart
Vice-Consul (Press and Public Affairs) (Ext 7706):
Ms Jo Le Good
Vice-Consul (Science and Technology) (7738):
Mr David Muller

Miami
British Consulate
Suite 2800, Brickell Bay Office Tower
1001, Brickell Bay Drive
Miami, FL 33131
FTN Code – 8437 + extn number
Telephone: (00) (1) (305) 374 1522
Facsimile: (00) (1) (305) 374 8196
Consul: Mr Simon J Davey, MBE
Vice-Consul (Commercial): Mrs B George-Hoerber
Vice-Consul (Commercial): Mr J Wright
Vice-Consul (Customs): Mr B Foreman
Vice-Consul (OTRCIS): Mr L Covington

Nashville
British Consulate
c/o Nashville Area Chamber of Commerce
211 Commerce Street
Nashville, TN 37201
Telephone: (00) (1) 615 743 3061
Facsimile: (00) (1) 615 256 6982
e-mail: jbutler@nashvillechamber.com
Honorary Consul: Mr J Butler

Orlando
British Vice-Consulate
Suite 2110, SunTrust Center,
200 South Orange Avenue,
Orlando, FL 32801
Telephone: (00) (1) 407 426 7855 Consular
Facsimile: (00) (1) 407 426 9343
Vice-Consul: Mr H Hunter

Charlotte
British Consulate
One Wachovia Center
301 South College St.
NC 0748, 9th Floor
Charlotte, NE 28288-0748
Telephone: (00) (1) 704 383 4359
Facsimile: (00) (1) 704 383 6545
e-mail: mdteden@bellsouth.net
Honorary Consul: Mr Michael Teden, OBE

Puerto Rico
British Consulate
Torre Chardón
Suite 1236
350 Chardon Avenue
San Juan, PR 00918
Telephone: (787) 758 9828
Facsimile(787) 758 9809
Vice-Consul: Mrs P Martinez

Boston
British Consulate-General
One Memorial Drive, 15th Floor
Suite 1500
Cambridge, MA 02142
FTN Code – 8434 + extn number
Telephone: (00) (1) (617) 245 4500
Facsimile: (00) (1) (617) 621 0220
Airtech: (00) (1) (617) 679 0054
e-mail: British.Consulate@fco.gov.uk
Postmaster@fco.gov.uk
Officers first name.last name followed by @fco.gov.uk
Office Hours (GMT): 14 00 – 22 00
Consul-General (4502): Mr John J Rankin
Deputy Consul-General (4515): Mr Geoff Plant
Consul (Science and Technology) (4547):
Mr Mark Sinclair
Vice-Consul (Science and Technology) (4549):
Dr Stefan Winkler
Vice-Consul (Trade) (4503): Ms Marguerite Meyer
Vice-Consul (Trade) (4510): Mr John Shipala
Vice-Consul (Press and Public Affairs) (4513):
Mrs Terri Evans
Vice-Consul (Management) (4520):
Mrs Kathy M Tunsley, MBE
Vice-Consul (Investment) (4507): Ms Alice Sloan
Vice-Consul (Life Sciences and Healthcare US-wide) (4530): Mrs Alice Pomponio

Chicago
British Consulate-General
The Wrigley Building,
400 N Michigan Avenue, Suite 1300
Chicago, IL 60611
FTN Code – 8453 + extn number
Telephone: (00) (1) (312) 970 3800
Facsimile: (00) (1) (312) 970 3852
970 3855 (Investment)
970 3858 (Trade)
970 3854 Consular and Visa Sections only
Airtech: (00) (1) (312) 970 3818
Office Hours (GMT): 14 30 - 23 00
HM *Consul-General:* Mr Andrew Seaton
Deputy Consul-General: Mr Jonathan Darby
Consul (Trade): Mr Jeff Taylor
Consul (Investment): Mr Rafe Courage
Head of Public Affairs: Ms Caroline Cracraft, MBE
Head of Management: Mr Chris Shaw
Trade Officer: Mr Ray Pimental
Trade Officer: Mrs Reet Robinson
Trade Officer: Mr Frank Phillips
Trade Officer: Mr Richard Knox
Trade Officer: Mr Brian Shapiro
Investment Officer: Ms Caroline Preece

Investment Officer: Mr Jonathan Wood
Entry Clearance Manager/British Vice-Consul:
Mrs Janet Bershers, MBE

Minneapolis
British Consulate
2600 U.S Bancorp Centre,
800 Nicollet Mall, suite 2600
Minneapolis, MN 55402-7035
Telephone: (00) (1) (612) 338 2525
Facsimile: (00) (1) (612) 339 2386
Office Hours (GMT): 14 30 - 23 00
Honorary Consul: Mr W R McGrann

Kansas City
British Consulate
12109 Aberdeen Road,
Shawnee Mission, Kansas City, KS 66209
Telephone: (00) (1) (913) 469 9786
Facsimile: (00) (1) (913) 469 8597
e-mail: britconkswmo@hotmail.com
Office Hours (GMT): 14 30 - 23 15
Honorary Consul: Mr J Scott Brown

St Louis
British Consulate
2323 Manor Grove Drive
#8, Chesterfield, MO 63017
Telephone: (00) (1) (636) 227 1334
Honorary Consul: (Vacant)

Houston
British Consulate-General
Suite 1900, Wells Fargo Plaza
1000 Louisiana Suite 1900, Houston, TX 77002
FTN Code – 8436 + extn number
Telephone: (00) (1) (713) 659 6270
            659 6275 Commercial Department
Facsimile: (00) (1) (713) 659 7094
Airtech: (00) (1) (713) 659 5839
e-mail: bcg.houston@fco.gov.uk
Office Hours (GMT): 15 00 - 23 00
Consul-General (ext 2116): Ms Judith Slater
Deputy Consul-General and Consul (Trade) (ext 2114): Mr David Bull
Vice-Consul (Trade) (ext 2113): Mr Kornel Rost
Vice-Consul (Trade, Oil and Gas): Mr Brian Foy
Vice-Consul (Information) (ext 2117):
Ms Helen Mann
Consul (Investment) (2140): Mr Matthew Hobbs
Vice-Consul (Investment) (ext 2142):
Miss Kim Fairweather
Vice-Consul (Science and Technology) (ext 2134):
Dr May Akrawi
Vice-Consul (Consular) (ext 2120):
Miss Linda Kelly
Management Officer (ext 2126): Ms Anne Medlin

Denver
British Consulate
Suite 1030, World Trade Center
1675 Broadway
Denver, CO 80202
Telephone: (00) (1) (303) 592 5200 (General)
            5205 (Consul – direct)
            5212 (Trade Assistant – direct)
Facsimile: (00) (1) (303) 592 5209

e-mail: Mark.Stevens@britcondenver.com
info@britcondenver.com
Office Hours (GMT): 16 00 - 24 00
Consul (Trade): Mr Mark Stevens
Vice-Consul (Trade and Investment):
Mr Barrett Stillings
Business Development Associate: Ms Vicky Lea
Business Development Associate: Ms Sarah Dotson

Dallas
British Consulate
2911 Turtle Creek Blvd.
Suite 940, Dallas TX 75219
FTN Code – 8433 + extn number
Telephone: (00) (1) (214) 521 4090
Facsimile: (00) (1) (214) 521 4807
e-mail: bc@airmail.net
Office Hours (GMT): 15 00 - 23 00
Consul (Trade) (ext 2012): Mr Michael D Morley
Vice-Consul (Trade) (ext 2014):
Mrs Betty Schnaufer

New Orleans
British Consulate
10th Floor, 321 St Charles Avenue
New Orleans, LA 70130
Telephone: (00) (1) (504) 524 4180
Office Hours (GMT): Sat and Wed 04 30 - 11 30
Honorary Consul: Mr James Coleman Jr
Consular Assistant: Ms Wendy Roberts

Los Angeles
British Consulate-General
11766 Wilshire Boulevard, Suite 1200
Los Angeles, CA 90025-6538
FTN Code – 8452 + extn number
Telephone: (00) (1) (310) 481 0031 (for officers
            direct lines see below)
            481 2900 (Visa Enquiries)
Facsimile: (00) (1) (310) 481 2960
Airtech: (00) (1) (310) 481 2963
            481-2961 (Visas only)
e-mail: trade.losangeles@fco.gov.uk
invest.losangeles@fco.gov.uk
pppa.losangeles@fco.gov.uk
visas.losangeles@fco.gov.uk
firstname.lastname@fco.gov.uk
Website: www.BritainUSA.com
Office Hours (GMT): 16 30 – 01 00
Consul-General (310 481 2950):
Mr Peter Hunt, CMG
Deputy Consul-General/Consul Trade (310 996 3036): Mr Brian Conley
Consul Investment (310 996 3021):
Mr David Slater
Consul (Consular/Entry Clearance) (310 481 2919): Mr Jeff Mee
Vice-Consul (Press, Political and Public Affairs) (310 996 3028): Mr Angus Mackay
Vice-Consul (Management) (310 996 3020):
Mrs Nancy Bridi
Vice-Consul (Trade) (310 996 3030):
Mr Mike Rosenfeld
Vice-Consul (Investment) (310 996 3024):
Mr Andrew Lewis
Vice-Consul (Trade) (310 996 3031):
Mr Carlo Cavagna

Vice-Consul (Consular/Entry Clearance) (310 481 2903): Ms Barbara Morgan
Vice-Consul (Entry Clearance) (310 481 2912): Ms Francesca Dooley
Vice-Consul (Entry Clearance) (310 481 2915): Mr Des Brewer
Consul (Defence) (310 481 2989): Mr Tim Johnson
Vice-Consul (Science and Technology) (310 996 3023): Dr Malcolm McLean

Phoenix
Honorary Consul: (Vacant)
British Trade and Investment Office
2375 East Camelback Road,
5th Floor, Phoenix, AZ 85016
Telephone: (00) (1) (602) 387 5092
Facsimile: (00) (1) (602) 387 5001
e-mail: Hank@btiophoenix.com
Office Hours (GMT): 15 00 - 23 30
Director: Mr Hank Marshall

Salt Lake City
British Consulate
c/o MK Gold Company
Eagle Gate Tower, Suite 2100
60 East South Temple
Salt Lake City, UT 84111
Telephone: (00) (1) (801) 297 6922
Facsimile: (00) (1) (801) 297 6940
e-mail: ijourney@mkgold.com
Office Hours (GMT): 16 00 - 01 00
Honorary Consul: Mr G Frank Joklik

San Diego
British Consulate
7825 Fay Ave, Suite 200
La Jolla, CA 92037
Telephone: (00) (1) (619) 459 8231
Facsimile: (00) (1) (619) 459 9250
e-mail: wblack@san.rr.com
Office hours (GMT): 15.00-01 00
Honorary Consul: Mr William F Black

New York
British Consulate-General
(incorporating British Trade and Investment Offices)
845 Third Avenue, New York, NY 10022
FTN Code – 8450 + extn number
Telephone: (00) (1) (212) 745 0200 Consular/Visa
745 0495 Trade
745 0300 Investment
Facsimile: (00) (1) (212) 754 3062 Consular/Visa
758 4023 Management
745 0456 Trade and Investment
Airtech: (00) (1) (212) 745 0296
e-mail: publicenquiries@newyork.mail.fco.gov.uk
Website: www.BritainUSA.com
Office Hours (GMT): Summer: 13 00 – 21 00.
Winter: 14 00 – 22 30
Consul-General and Director-General of Trade and Investment: Sir Philip Thomas, KCVO, CMG
Deputy Consul General, Political, Press and Public Affairs and Deputy Head of Mission:
Mr Duncan J R Taylor, CBE
Deputy Consul-General and Director of Trade; USA: Mr Mike Cohen

Deputy Consul-General and Director of Investment: Mr Alastair Newton
Consul (Management): Mr Andrew Dimbleby
Consul (Investment): Ms Helen Gates
Consul (Press and Public Affairs, Northern Ireland): Mr Paul Johnston
Consul (Trade): Mr Clive V Thompson
Consul (Trade): Mr Colin Brazier
Consul and Director of Entry Clearance Issuing Posts: Mr Patrick Owens, OBE
Vice-Consul (Consular):
Mrs Jacqueline Cerdan, MBE
Vice-Consul (Immigration): Mr Stephen Thompson
Vice-Consul (Immigration): Mr Martin Southey
Vice-Consul (Political): Dr Ray Raymond, MBE
Vice-Consul (Trade): Mr Charles Picarelli
Vice-Consul (Trade): Mr Robert F Lomnicki
Vice-Consul (Trade): Mr Robert Cassidy
Vice-Consul (Trade): Mr Michael Formosa
Vice-Consul (Trade): Ms Christina Lynton
Vice-Consul (Investment): Ms Kerry Appleton
Vice-Consul (Investment): Mr Ian Baines
Vice-Consul (National Market Research Co-ordinator): Mrs Francine J Conran
Vice-Consul (Fairs and Promotions):
Ms Annie Wildey
Vice-Consul (Commercial Publicity):
Mr Dominic Varle
Visits Officer (For all British Government Offices in New York): Ms Louise Redmond, MBE
Press Officer: Mr Dewi Williams

New York
British Information Services
845 Third Avenue, New York, NY 10022
Telephone: (00) (1) (212) 745 0200
Public Inquiries: (00) (1) (212) 745 0277
Facsimile: (00) (1) (212) 745 0359
e-mail: public.enquiries@newyork.mail.fco.gov.uk
Office Hours (GMT): Summer: 13 00 - 21 30
Winter: 14 00 - 22 30
Counsellor (Political and Public Affairs) and Head of BIS (resides at Washington): Mr Robert N Peirce
Director, BIS and Consul: Mrs Judy Legg
Vice-Consul (Reference and Library):
Mr Kevin Nolan
Vice-Consul (Media and Marketing):
Ms Sarah Kendall
Vice-Consul (Internet): Mr Paul Clark

New York United Kingdom Mission to United Nations, see Embassies, High Commission, Deputy High Commissions and Consular Posts

Philadelphia
British Consulate
33rd Floor, 1818 Market St
Philadelphia, PA 19103
Telephone: (00) (1) (215) 557 7665
Facsimile: (00) (1) (215) 557 6608
Honorary Consul: Mr O St C Franklin

Pittsburgh
British Consulate
Buchanan Ingersoll
301 Grant Street
One Oxford Center, 20th Floor

Pittsburgh, PA 15219-1410
Telephone: (00) (1) (412) 562 8872
Facsimile: (00) (1) (412) 391 0910
Honorary Consul: Mr W Newlin

Pacific Islands
(American Samoa)
British Consulate
(US Territories South of the Equator)
Consul (resides at Nuku'alofa): Mr Paul Nessling

San Francisco
British Consulate-General
Suite 850, 1 Sansome Street
San Francisco, CA 94104
FTN Code – 8435 + extn number
Telephone: (00) (1) (415) 617 1300
Facsimile: (00) (1) (415) 434 2018 Group 3
Website: www.britainusa.com/sf
Office Hours (GMT): 16 30 - 01 00
Consul-General: Mr Martin Uden
Deputy Consul-General and Consul (Commercial):
Mr Peter Broom
Consul (Investment): Mr John Lindfield, MBE
Consul (Science and Technology):
Dr Sharima Rasanayagam
Vice-Consul (Information): Ms Emma Stevenson
Vice-Consul (Commercial): Mr Dale Smith
Vice-Consul (Commercial): Ms Nicole Patrick
Vice-Consul (Investment): Ms Helen Moore
Vice-Consul (Management/Consular):
Mrs Karen S Thomas
Vice-Consul (Commercial): Ms Carrie Ann Schiller
Vice-Consul (Commercial): Ms Shaan Katari
Vice-Consul (Science and Technology): Dr Henry
Mahncke

Anchorage
British Consulate
College of Arts and Sciences
University of Alaska Anchorage
3211 Providence Drive
Anchorage, AK 99508
Telephone: (00) (1) (907) 786 4848
Facsimile: (00) (1) (907) 786 4647
e-mail: afdh1@uaa.alaska.edu
Honorary Consul: Dr Diddy R M Hitchins

Portland
British Consulate
1300 SW Fifth Avenue
Suite 2300
Portland, OR 97201
Telephone (Direct Line): (00) (1) (503) 778 5337
                    227 5669 Consulate
Facsimile: (00) (1) (503) 778 5299
e-mail: iainlevie@dwt.com
Honorary Consul: Mr I Levie

San Jose
British Consulate
1139 Karlstad Drive
Sunnyvale
San Jose, CA 94089
Telephone: (00) (1) (408) 747 7140 x1200 or
                    x1400 (Assistant)
Facsimile: (00) (1) (408) 747 7198

e-mail: belder@genus.com
Honorary Consul: Dr W R Elder

Seattle
British Consulate
900 Fourth Avenue,
Suite 3001,Seattle, WA 98164
FTN Code – 8454 + extn number
Telephone: (00) (1) (206) 622 9255
Facsimile: (00) (1) (206) 622 4728
Airtech: (00) (1) (206) 336 4186
Office Hours (GMT): 16 30 - 01 30
Consul (Commercial) (ext. 4178):
Mr David Broom
Vice-Consul (Commercial) (ext. 4183):
Ms Kim Chio
Vice-Consul (Commercial) (ext. 4184):
Mr Dave Baron

URUGUAY

Montevideo (SP – see page 120)
British Embassy
Calle Marco Bruto 1073, 11300 Montevideo, PO
Box 16024
FTN Code – 8659 + extn number
Telephone: (00) (598) (2) 622 3630, 622 3650
Facsimile: (00) (598) (2) 622 7815
e-mail officers first
name.surname@mail.fco.gov.uk
Embassy e-mail address:
bemonte@internet.com.uy
Office Hours (GMT): Mid Mar - Mid Dec: 12 00 -
16 00 and 17 00 - 20 15. Mid Dec - Mid Mar:
11 00 - 17 00

For officers residing in Buenos Aires refer to e-
mail addresses in Argentina.
Ambassador: Mr John Everard
*Deputy Head of Mission, First Secretary and
Consul:* Mr James Waterton
Defence Attaché (resides at Buenos Aires):
Group Captain Ian Capewell, RAF
First Secretary (resides at Buenos Aires):
Mr Michael Cavanagh
Second Secretary (Management) and Vice-Consul:
Mr Guy Parkinson
Second Secretary (TMO) (resides at Buenos Aires):
Mr Stuart Moss

UZBEKISTAN

Tashkent (SP – see page 120)
British Embassy
Ul. Gulyamova 67, Tashkent 700000
FTN Code – 8333 + extn number
Telephone: (00) (99871) 1206451, 1206288,
                    1207852, 1207853, 1207854
Facsimile: (00) (99871) 1206549 (General)
                    1206430 (Consular/Visa)
e-mail: brit@emb.uz
Office Hours (GMT)
Winter: 04 00-07 30 and 08 30-12 00 (GMT + 5
hours). Summer: 05 00-08 30 and 09 30-13 00
(GMT + 4 hours)
Ambassador: (To be announced)
Deputy Head of Mission: Mr Carl Garn

Defence Attaché: Lieutenant Colonel Nick J Ridout
British Council Director: Mr Neville McBain
First Secretary (Political) (resides in Baku):
Mr David Proudfoot
Second Secretary (DLO) (resides in Ashgabat):
Mr Stuart O'Neill
Third Secretary (Political/PPA):
Mr Daniel Grzenda
Third Secretary (Vice Consul/MO/ECO):
Mr Steve Brown
British Council Deputy Director:
Mr Martin Seviour
Attaché/ECO: Ms Angela Clark

VANUATU

Port-Vila (SP – see page 120)
British High Commission
Port Vila, Vanuatu
PO Box 567, Port Vila
Telephone: (00) (678) 23100 (3 lines)
Facsimile: (00) (678) 27153 (Airtech)
23651 (General)
e-mail: bhcvila@vanuatu.com.vu
firstname.surname@vila.mail.fco.gov.uk
Office Hours (GMT): Mon, Tue, Thu and Fri: 20
30 - 00.45 and 02 00 - 05 30. Wed: 20 30 - 00 45
High Commissioner: Mr Michael T Hill
Deputy High Commissioner: Mr Joel Watson

VENEZUELA

Caracas
Torre La Castellana, Piso 11
Avenida La Principal de la Castellana
La Castellana
Caracas 1061
FTN Code – 8660 + extn number
Telephone: (00) (58) (212) 263 8411
Facsimile: (00) (58) (212) 267 1275 (Main)
          (00) (58) (212) 263 7604 (Chancery)
          (00) (58) (212) 266 3232 (Commercial)
          (00) (58) (212) 266 8279 (HMCandE)
Airtech: (00) (58) (212) 264 7983
e-mail: britishembassy@internet.ve
Website: www.britain.org.ve
Office Hours (GMT): Mon-Thurs: 12 00 – 20 30
Fri: 12 00 – 17 15
Consular Section Hours (GMT): Mon - Fri: 12 00
– 16 30. Wed (only): 17 30 – 20 00
Ambassador: Mr Donald A Lamont
Deputy Head of Mission: Mr Steven M Fisher
Counsellor: (Vacant)
Defence Attaché:
Group Captain William G S Dobson, RAF
British Council Director: Mrs Barbara Wickham
First Secretary: Mr Anthony Buckingham
First Secretary (Commercial):
Mr Steve J Seaman, MBE
First Secretary (Management) and Consul:
Mrs Julie M Foster
Second Secretary (Political): Mr Andrew Tate
Second Secretary: Mr R A Williams
Second Secretary: Mr J Nicholas Cox
Second Secretary (Technical): Mr Colin Tully
Second Secretary (Commercial): Mr John M Foster

Third Secretary (Management / Consular):
Miss Dawn Farr
Attaché: Mrs Janice Micallef
Attaché: Mr Lee Farnsworth
Attaché: Miss Joanne Morrison

Maracaibo
British Consulate
Inspecciones C.A., Avenida 9B con Calle 77
Edifcio Banco Industrial, Piso 4
Maracaibo, Estado Zulia
Telephone: (00) (58) (2) (61) 797 7003 (Master)
Facsimile: (00) (58) (2) (61) 798 3708
e-mail: alexp@inspecciones.com
nomination@inspecciones.com
Opening Hours: Mon-Fri 09 00 – 12 00
Honorary Consul:
Mr Alexander Kirk Podolecki

Margarita
British Consulate
Centro Comercial y Empresarial CCM
Entrada Lateral, No. 4, Piso 2
Ofc 211, Avenida Bolivar, Urb. Costa Azul
Porlamar, Estado Nueva Esparta
Telephone/Facsimile: (00) (58) (2) (95) 264 6993
e-mail: orlandomonton@hotmail.com
Opening Hours: Mon-Fri 09 00 – 17 30
Honorary Consul: Mr Orlando Peter Paul Monton

Mérida
British Consulate
Calle Los Caminos, Quinta Caminos 2
Pedregosa Media, La Pedregosa, Merida
Telephone: (00) (58) (2) (74) 266 4665 / 0416 626
          1546
Facsimile: (00) (58) (2) (74) 266 4665
Honorary Consul: Dr R G Kirby

San Cristobal
British Consulate
AVECO, Edificio Britannia House
Avenida Rotaria, Esquina Parque Exposición
La Concordia, San Cristobal
Telephone: (00) (58) (2) 346 0434 / 347 1872 /
          0416 676 7489
Facsimile: (00) (58) (2) 346 7307
Honorary Consul: Mr R Burnison

VIETNAM

Hanoi
British Embassy
Central Building
Floors 4 and 5
31 Hai Ba Trung
FTN Code – 8493 + 1000 for switchboard
Telephone: (00) (84) (4) 936 0500
          (00) (84) (4) 90340 4919 Duty Officer
          Mobile
Facsimile: (00) (84) (4) 936 0561
          Chancery/Commercial
          (00) (84) (4) 936 0562
          Consular/Management
e-mail: behanoi@fpt.vn
Website: www.uk-vietnam.org

Office Hours (GMT): Mon-Fri 01 30 - 05 30 and
06 30 - 09 30

British Council
40 Cat Linh Street
Hanoi
Telephone: (00) (84) (4) 843 6780
Facsimile: (00) (84) (4) 843 4962
e-mail: behanoi@britishcouncil.org.vn
Office Hours (GMT): Mon-Fri 01 30 - 05 00 and
06 30 - 10.00
Ambassador (2201): Mr Robert Gordon, CMG, OBE
Deputy Head of Mission (2204):
Mr Mac McLachlan
British Council Director and Cultural Attaché:
Mr Keith Davies
Defence Attaché (resides at Kuala Lumpur):
Colonel Jamie A Athill
British Council Deputy Director/Cultural Attaché:
Ms Soma Chakrabarti-Fezzardi
British Council Deputy Director/Cultural Attaché:
Mr Tim Hood
*First Secretary (Defence Supply) (resides at Kuala
Lumpur):* Mr Rob Lingham
Second Secretary (Political) (2205):
Mr Paul Gaskell
Second Secretary (Management) (2249):
Ms Sheila O'Connor
Second Secretary (Commercial) (2228):
Mr Kevin Ringham
Third Secretary - Vice Consul/ECO (2244):
Mrs Elaine Henry Plieger
Third Secretary (Chancery) (2210):
Mr Richard Ridout
Attaché (2202): Mrs Molly Bicker
Attaché (2203): (Vacant)

DFID
Central Building
7th Floor
Telephone: (00) (84) (4) 936 0555
Facsimile: (00) (84) (4) 936 0556
Office Hours (GMT): Mon-Thurs 01 00 - 05 00
and 06 00 - 09 30; Fri 01 00 - 06 30
Head of DFID Vietnam (2272): Ms Bella Bird
First Secretary (Development) (2269):
Ms Cathy Welch
First Secretary (Development) (2271):
Ms Jane Rintoul
First Secretary (Development) (2273):
Mr Steve Passingham
First Secretary (Development) (2268):
Mr Simon Lucas
First Secretary (Development) (2270):
Mr Alwyn Chilver
Second Secretary (Development) (2267):
Mr Angus Miller
Third Secretary (Development) (2254):
Mr Scott McArthur

Ho Chi Minh City (SP)
British Consulate General
25 Le Duan,
District 1, Ho Chi Minh City
FTN Code – 8424 + extn number or 1000 for
switchboard
Telephone: (00) (84) (8) 8298433

(00) (84) 91392 0991 (Duty officer
mobile)
Facsimile: (00) (84) (8) 8295257 (Visa/Consular)
8221971 (Commercial/Information)
e-mail: bcghcmc@hcm.vnn.vn
Website: www.uk-vietnam.org
Office Hours (GMT): Mon - Fri 01 30 – 05 00 and
06 00 – 09 30

British Council:
25 Le Duan,
District 1, Ho Chi Minh City, Vietnam
Telephone: (00) (84) (8) 8232862/3 (Main Office)
8256403/4 (Teaching Centre)
Facsimile: (00) (84) (8) 8222105 (Main Office)
8232861 (Teaching Centre)
e-mail: bchcmc@britishcouncil.org.vn
Office Hours (GMT): Mon-Fri: 01 30 - 05 00; 06
30 - 10 00
*HM Consul-General and Director, UK Trade and
Investment (Vietnam)(ext 2207):*
Mr Adrian Stephens
Consul (Trade and Investment) (ext 2205):
Mr Phil Wyithe
British Council Director (Tel: 825 6402):
Mr Duncan Wilson

YEMEN

Sana'a
British Embassy
129 Haddah Road, Sana'a
Postal address: PO Box 1287
Telephone: (00) (967) (1) 264081/82/83/84
Facsimile: (00) (967) (1) 263059
Office Hours (GMT): Sat - Wed: 04 30 - 11 30
Ambassador: Mr Michael Gifford
Deputy Head of Mission and Consul General:
Mr Andrew Goodwin
Defence Attaché (resides at Riyadh):
Brigadier Jim G Askew, OBE
British Council Director: Ms Elizabeth White
Second Secretary (Political): Mr Patrick Tobin
Second Secretary (Political): Mr Arthur Snell
Overseas Security Manager: Mr Darren Parnaby

Aden
British Consulate-General
20 Miswat Road
Postal address: P O Box 6304, Khormaksar, Aden
Telephone: (00) (967) (2) 232712-4
Facsimile: (00) (967) (2) 231256
Office Hours (GMT): Sat - Wed: 04 30 - 11 30
Consul General (resident in Sana'a):
Mr Michael Kerr
Vice-Consul (Commercial): Mr Mustafa Rajamanar

Hodeidah
British Consulate
Sanaa Road, KM7
P O Box 3337, Hodeidah
Telephone: (00) (967) (3) 238130/131, 238958
Facsimile: (00) (967) (3) 211533
238269
Office Hours (GMT): Mon - Wed: 08 00 - 13 00
Honorary Consul: Mr Abdul Gabbar Thabet

YUGOSLAVIA see SERBIA AND MONTENEGRO

ZAMBIA

Lusaka
British High Commission
5210 Independence Avenue
P.O.Box 50050
15101 Ridgeway, Lusaka
FTN Code – 8555 + extn number
Telephone: (00) (260) (1) 251133
Facsimile: (00) (260) (1) 253798
(Management/Press and Public
Affairs/Development)
251923 (Commercial)
252842 (Visa/Consular)
252848 (Chancery)
Airtech: (00) (260) (1) 253162
e-mail: BHC-Lusaka@fco.gov.uk
Office Hours (GMT): Mon - Thurs: 06 00 - 11 00
and 12 00 - 14 30. Fri: 06 00 - 11 00
High Commissioner: Mr Tim J David
Deputy High Commissioner: Ms Julia Painting, MBE
Defence Adviser (Resides in Harare):
Colonel Bob J Griffiths, MBE
Second Secretary (Management):
Mr Richard Fielder
Second Secretary: Mr Aidan Linnell
Second Secretary (Political/Press/Public Affairs):
Mr Ian Mason
Second Secretary (Consular/Commercial/ECM):
Mrs Lyn Shaw
Third Secretary (Immigration): Mr Steve Gordon
Overseas Security Manager: Mr Mark Wardle

Department of International Development: Zambia
(Address same as British High Commission)
FTN Code - 8555 + 4000 for DFID Switchboard
Telephone: (00) (260) (1) 251164
Facsimile: (00) (260) (1) 253580
e-mail: DFIDZambia@dfid.gov.uk
Individual e-mail addresses: initial-surname (e.g:
h-mealins@dfid.gov.uk)
Office Hours same as British High Commission
Head of DFID Zambia: Mrs Helen Mealins
Deputy Head of DFID Zambia:
Mr Richard Montgomery
Health and Population Adviser: Mr Tony Daly
Governance Adviser: Gift Madzonga
Economics Adviser: Mr Keith Wood
Private Sector Adviser: Ms Susan Barton
Education Adviser: Mr Richard Arden
Social Development Adviser:
Mr Bruce Lawson-McDowall
Engineering Adviser (Resides in Pretoria):
Mr Yusaf Samiullah
Statistics Adviser (Resides in Pretoria):
Ms Julia Bunting
Environmental Adviser (Resides in Pretoria):
Ms Beth Arthy
Deputy Programme Manager: Mr Steve Graham
Education Associate Professsional Officer:
Ms Tanya Zebroff

Policy, Poverty and Performance Programme
Officer: Ms Amisha Patel
Management Support Officer: Mr Robert Ower

ZIMBABWE

Harare
British Embassy
Corner House, 7th Floor
Samora Machel Avenue/Leopold Takawira Street
(PO Box 4490), Harare
FTN Code - 8498 + extn number
Telephone: (00) (263) (4) 772990,774700
Facsimile: (00) (263) (4) 774617
Airtech: (00) (263) (4) 774703
Website: www.britainzw.org
Office Hours (GMT): Mon-Thurs: 06 00 - 10 30
and 11 30 - 14 30. Fri: 06 00 - 12 00
High Commissioner: Dr Roderick Pullen (2201/2)
Deputy High Commissioner:
Ms Alison Blackburne (2203/4)
Counsellor: Mr Adrian Stones (2205)
Counsellor (Regional Director, British Council):
Mr David Martin
Defence Adviser:
Colonel Bob J Griffiths, MBE (2221)
First Secretary (Medical Officer) (resides in
Lilongwe): Dr Howard Friend
First Secretary (Management):
Mr Roger D Hazlewood (2225)
First Secretary (Director Operations, British
Council): Ms Louisa Waddingham
Second Secretary (Political):
Ms Sophia Honey (2207)
Second Secretary (Political):
Mr David Bellass (2222)
Second Secretary (Consular/Immigration):
Mr David Ashford (2265)
Second Secretary (Immigration):
Ms Linda Smith (2290)
Second Secretary (Technical) (resides in Lusaka):
Mr Alex Holey
Third Secretary (Management):
Mrs Tina Wicke (2226)
Third Secretary (Political/Press and Public
Affairs): Mr Jim Newman (2238)
Third Secretary (Chancery):
Mr William Sims (2206)
Third Secretary (Consular/Immigration):
Mr Wayne N Pagett (2332)
Third Secretary (Immigration):
Mr John Collins (2334)
Third Secretary (Immigration):
Mr Ken Arundel (2333)
Third Secretary (Immigration):
Ms Catherine Ings (2331)
Third Secretary (Immigration): (Vacant) (2330)
Assistant to Defence Adviser:
Warrant Officer Adam Moore (2223)

Department for International Development:
Zimbabwe
Corner House, 6th Floor Samora Machel
Avenue/Leopold Takawira Street
PO Box 1030 Harare
Telephone: (00) (263) (4) 774719-28

Facsimile: (00) (263) (4) 775695
e-mail addresses:- Initial-Surname@dfid.gov.uk
(eg: J-Barrett@dfid.gov.uk)
Office Hours (GMT): Mon-Fri: 06 00 – 14 30
Head of DFID Zimbabwe: Mr John Barrett (3302)
Economic Adviser: Mr Alex Ferrand (3310)
HIV and Health Adviser: Dr Marion Kelly (3313)
Social Development Adviser:
Dr Rachel Yates (3228)
Humanitarian Adviser: Mr Shaun Hughes (3375)
Rural Livelihoods Adviser: Mr Tom Barrett (3307)

PART II: MISSIONS AND DELEGATIONS

UNITED KINGDOM MISSION TO THE UNITED NATIONS

New York
One Dag Hammarskjold Plaza, 28th Floor
885 Second Avenue, New York, NY 10017
FTN Code – 8451 + extn number
Telephone: (00) (1) (212) 745 9250
Facsimile: (00) (1) (212) 745 9316
Airtech: (00) (1) (212) 745 9272
Postal address: PO Box 5238 New York, NY
10150-5238
e-mail: UKUN@UN.INT
Office Hours (GMT): Summer 13 00 - 22 00
Winter 14 00 - 23 00
*United Kingdom Permanent Representative to the
United Nations and United Kingdom
Representative on the Security Council (with
personal rank of Ambassador):*
Sir Emyr Jones Parry, KCMG
*Deputy Permanent Representative to the United
Nations (with personal rank of Ambassador):*
Mr Adam Thomson
Counsellor and Head of Chancery: Mr Julian King
*Counsellor (Economic, Social and Humanitarian
Affairs):* Mr Michael O'Neill
Counsellor (Political): Mr Eugene Curley, OBE
Counsellor (Legal Adviser): Mr Iain MacLeod
Counsellor (ACABQ): Mr Nick Thorne, CMG
Counsellor (Finance): Dr Richard Moon
Military Adviser to UK Permanent Representative:
Colonel Jonathan Lloyd
Deputy Military Adviser:
Lieutenant Colonel Jonathan Calder-Smith
First Secretary (Chancery): Ms Anna Clunes, OBE
First Secretary (Chancery): Mr Dominic Fortescue
First Secretary (Chancery/Press):
Ms Catherine Mackenzie
First Secretary (Economic): Mr James Kariuki
First Secretary (Chancery):
Mr Christophe McBride
*First Secretary (Senior Social Development
Adviser):* Mr Phil Evans
First Secretary (Chancery):
Miss Vanessa Howe-Jones
First Secretary (Human Rights): Mr Richard Wood
First Secretary (Finance): Mr Bill Longhurst
First Secretary (Environment): Ms Alice Walpole
First Secretary (Chancery): Mr Adam Bye
First Secretary (Management):
Ms Madeleine Campbell
First Secretary (Humanitarian Affairs):
Mr Tom Kelly
First Secretary (Children/Health):
Mr George Turkington
Assistant Legal Adviser: Ms Alice Burnett
Second Secretary (Chancery): Ms Charlotte Cutler
Second Secretary (Chancery): Ms Rosemary Davis
Second Secretary (Management):
Mr Melvin Bell, MBE
Second Secretary (Chancery): Ms Sarah Broughton
Second Secretary (Finance): Mr Simon Horner

Second Secretary (Chancery): Mr Adrian Pisa
Second Secretary (Chancery): Mrs Clare Risman
Second Secretary (Chancery):
Mr Gerard McGurk, MBE
Second Secretary (Chancery): Ms Anne Power
Second Secretary (Chancery): Mr Paddy Davie
Second Secretary (Social Affairs):
Mr Tom Woodroffe
Third Secretary (Elections/ECOSOC):
Ms Elizabeth Changai
Third Secretary (Humanitarian/ECOSOC):
Mr Robin Lake
Third Secretary (Chancery): Mr John Steven

United Kingdom Mission to the Management Office
One Dag Hammarskjold Plaza 27th Floor
885 Second Avenue, New York, NY 10017
Telephone: (00) (1) (212) 745 9291
Facsimile: (00) (1) (212) 745 9292
Head of Management Section:
Ms Madeleine Campbell
Management Officer: Mr Peter Collins
Second Secretary (Technical Management):
Mr Melvin Bell, MBE
Head of Accounts Section: Ms Hayley Kirkham

UNITED KINGDOM MISSION TO THE OFFICE OF THE UNITED NATIONS AND OTHER INTERNATIONAL ORGANISATIONS AT GENEVA

Geneva
37-39 rue de Vermont, 1211 Geneva 20
FTN Code – 8371 + extn number
Telephone: (00) (41) (22) 918 23 00
Facsimile: (00) (41) (22) 918 23 33 Main No
                       24 35 Chancery
                       24 44 Spec Agencies
                       23 77 WTO/Economic
                       23 10 Joint Management Unit
Telex: 414195 (a/b 414195 UKGV CH)
Office Hours (GMT): Summer: 07 00 - 11 00 and
12 30 - 16 00. Winter: 08 00 - 12 00 and
13 30 - 17 00
*United Kingdom Permanent Representative (holds
personal rank of Ambassador) (ext 2358):*
Mr N A Thorne, CMG
*Minister and Deputy Permanent Representative
(ext 2434):* Mr Neil McMillan, CMG
*Counsellor (Development/Specialised Agencies)
(ext 2370):* Dr Carole Presern
First Secretary (Human Rights) (ext 2363):
Ms Caroline Rees
First Secretary (UN, Press Officer) (ext 2371):
Mrs Elizabeth March
First Secretary (Legal Adviser) (ext 2367):
Mrs Susan McCrory
*First Secretary (Specialised Agencies and
Humanitarian) (ext 2376):*
Ms Helen Nellthorp, OBE
First Secretary (Management) (ext 2458):
Mrs Susan Gregory

First Secretary (WTO) (ext 2378):
Mr David Cairns
First Secretary (UNCTAD, ECE) (ext 2359):
Mrs Rebecca Fabrizi
Second Secretary (WTO) (ext 2379):
Mr Robin Twyman
Second Secretary (WTO) (ext 2369):
Miss Jo Lomas
Second Secretary (Specialised Agencies) (ext 2353): Mrs Pamela Tarif
Second Secretary (ECE, UNCTAD) (ext 2368):
Mr Robert Fairweather
Second Secretary (Human Rights) (ext 2360):
Mr Robert Dixon
Second Secretary (Management) (ext 2452):
Mr Ian McKinlay
Second Secretary (Technical) (ext 2414):
Mr Matthew Smith
Second Secretary (Humanitarian) (ext 2338):
Mr John Webster

Geneva Joint Management Office, UK Government Offices, see Embassies, High Commissions, Deputy High Commissions and Consular Posts

UNITED KINGDOM DELEGATION TO THE UNITED NATIONS EDUCATIONAL, SCIENTIFIC AND CULTURAL ORGANISATION (UNESCO)

Paris
1 Rue Miollis
75732 Paris
Cedex 15
Telephone: (00) (33) 1 45 68 27 84
Facsimile: (00) (33) 1 47 83 27 77
United Kingdom Permanent Delegate (holds personal rank of Ambassador):
Mr Timothy Craddock
United Kingdom Deputy Permanent Delegate:
Ms Christine Atkinson
Third Secretary: Mrs Hilary Izon

UNITED KINGDOM MISSION TO THE UNITED NATIONS IN VIENNA

Vienna
Jaurèsgasse 12, 1030 Vienna
FTN Code – 8310 + extn number
Telephone: (00) (43) (1) 716 130 or (43) (1) 71613 + extn number
Facsimile: (00) (43) (1) 71613 4900
e-mail: ukmis.vienna@fco.gov.uk
Office Hours (GMT): Winter: Mon - Fri 08 00 - 12 00 and 13 30 - 16 30. Summer: Mon - Fri 07 00 - 11 00 and 12 30 - 15 30
United Kingdom Permanent Representative (with personal rank of Ambassador) (4237):
Mr Peter R Jenkins
Deputy Permanent Representative (4232):
Mr Tim Andrews
First Secretary (IAEA) (4240): Mr Ben Whitby
First Secretary (CTBTO) (4296): Ms Tracy Roberts
First Secretary (UN) (4234): Mrs Alison Crockett
First Secretary (UN/UNIDO) (4297):
Mr Graham Clough

Second Secretary (CTBTO/UN/IAEA) (4298):
Mr Llywelyn Skidmore
Second Secretary (IAEA): Mrs Anna Ashby

Joint Management
First Secretary (Management) (2261):
Mr Eric Jones
Third Secretary (Management) (2260):
Miss Jan H Richardson

UNITED KINGDOM PERMANENT REPRESENTATION TO THE CONFERENCE ON DISARMAMENT

Geneva
37-39 rue de Vermont, 1211 Geneva 20
FTN Code – 8371 + extn number
Telephone: (00) (41) (22) 918 23 00
Facsimile: (00) (41) (22) 918 23 44
Telex: 414195 (a/b 414195 UKGV CH)
e-mail: ukdis.geneva2@fco.gov.uk
Office Hours (GMT): Summer: 07 00 - 11 00 and 12 30 - 16 00. Winter: 08 00 - 12 00 and 13 30 - 17 00
United Kingdom Permanent Representative: (holds personal rank of Ambassador) (ext 2321):
Dr John Freeman
Deputy Permanent Representative (ext 2328):
Mr Michael Clark
First Secretary (Legal Adviser) (ext 2367):
Mrs Helen Upton
First Secretary (ext 2469): Mr Andrew Freeman
Second Secretary (ext 2312): Mr Guy Pollard

Geneva Joint Management Office, UK Government Offices, see Embassies, High Commissions, Deputy High Commissions and Consular Posts

UNITED KINGDOM DELEGATION TO THE ORGANISATION FOR SECURITY AND COOPERATION IN EUROPE (OSCE) IN VIENNA

Vienna
Jaurèsgasse 12, 1030 Vienna
FTN Code – 8310 + extn number
Telephone: (00) (43) (1) 716130
71613 + extn number (for direct lines and voicemail)
Facsimile: (00) (43) (1) 71613 3900
Telegraphic address: UKDEL Vienna
e-mail: ukdel@netway.at
Office Hours (GMT): Summer: Mon - Fri 07 00 - 16 00. Winter: Mon - Fri 08 00 - 17 00
Head of Delegation (Personal rank of Ambassador) (PA 3302): Mr Colin Munro, CMG
Counsellor and Deputy Head of Delegation (PA 3304): Mr Ian A M Bond
Counsellor (Arms control) (PA 3318):
Mr Andrew Brentnall
Military Adviser (PA 3318):
Colonel George A Young
First Secretary (Political) (3319):
Ms Kate Knight-Sands
First Secretary (Political) (3318):
Mr Eric Penton-Voak

First Secretary (Arms Control) (PA 3336):
Mr Henry Bradley
Second Secretary (Political) (3306):
Mr Stuart Adam
Second Secretary (Political) (3307):
Mr David Townsend
Third Secretary (3320): Mr Grant Pritchard

Joint Management Office
First Secretary (Management) (2261):
Mr Eric Jones
Third Secretary (Management) (2260):
Miss Jan H Richardson

UNITED KINGDOM DELEGATION TO THE NORTH ATLANTIC TREATY ORGANISATION

Brussels
OTAN/NATO, Autoroute Bruxelles - Zaventem,
Evere
1110 Brussels
Telephone: (00) (32) (2) 707 7211
Facsimile: (00) (32) (2) 707 7596
Airtech: (00) (32) (2) 707 7212
e-mail: ukdelnato@csi.com
Office Hours (GMT): 08 00 – 17 00
United Kingdom Permanent Representative on the North Atlantic Council (holds personal rank of Ambassador): Mr Peter F Ricketts, CMG
Minister, United Kingdom Deputy Permanent Representative: (Vacant)
United Kingdom Military Representative:
Air Marshal Rob A Wright, AFC, RAF
Deputy United Kingdom Military Representative/COS: Brigadier Nigel St. J Hall
Counsellor (Political): Mr Paul Arkwright
Counsellor (Defence): Mr Nigel Brind
Counsellor (Budget and Infrastructure):
Mr John Cunningham
First Secretary (Political): Mr Sam Selvadurai
First Secretary (European Defence):
Mr Paul V Devine
First Secretary (Defence Equipment):
Mr John Mattiussi
First Secretary (Nuclear Cooperation):
Ms Gill Atkinson
Staff Officer Plans and Policy:
Colonel Chris J Rose
First Secretary (Defence Plans and Policy):
Mr Graham Muir
Staff Officer (Operations):
Wing Commmander Bob D Jenkins, RAF
Staff Officer (Operations/Plans):
Lieutenant Colonel James Stuart
First Secretary (Infrastructure and Military Budget): Mr Richard Ladd-Jones
Staff Officer Intelligence:
Wing Commander Paul Edwards, RAF
Staff Officer (Resources and Arms Control):
Commander Nick Garland
First Secretary (Infrastructure and Military Budgets): Ms Helena Akiwumi
Second Secretary (Political): Mr Ernie Manley
Second Secretary (Political): Miss Susan Crombie

Second Secretary (Operations and Exercises):
Mrs Tanya Collingridge
Second Secretary (Management): Mrs Susan Pavis
Second Secretary: (Vacant)
Attaché (Defence): Mr Andrew Collingridge
Attaché (Defence): Mr Scott Gallacher
Attaché (Budget and Infrastructure):
Mr Nathaniel Wapshere
Staff Officer (CIS):
Wing Commander Rob Munday
Staff Officer (Cooperation):
Wing Commander Jim Squelch, RAF
Staff Officer (CEU Policy):
Wing Commander Tony Leggett

UNITED KINGDOM DELEGATION TO THE WESTERN EUROPEAN UNION

Brussels
c/o UK Permanent Representation to the EU,
Avenue d'Auderghem 10
1040 Brussels
Telephone: (00) (32) (2) 287 8346
Facsimile: (00) (32) (2) 287 8396
United Kingdom Permanent Representative - (holds personal rank of Ambassador): (Vacant)
Military Delegate:
Air Marshal R D Wright, AFC, RAF
Deputy UK Military Representative:
Commodore N J R Harland, RN
Deputy Permanent Representative – First Secretary (Pol/Mil Affairs): Ms Jennifer Anderson
First Secretary (Defence): Mr Sandy Johnston
Staff Officer EU (Ops/Plans):
Lieutenant Colonel Max Houghton
Staff Officer EU (Capabilities):
Commander Phil Stonor
Staff Officer EU (Policy):
Wing Commander Tony Leggett
Third Secretary (WEAG/WEAO):
Mr Scott Gallacher
Assistant Military Delegate:
Ms Alison MacLauchlan

Brussels Joint Management Office for the four Missions, see Embassies, High Commissions, Deputy High Commissions and Consular Posts

UNITED KINGDOM DELEGATION TO THE ORGANISATION FOR ECONOMIC CO-OPERATION AND DEVELOPMENT

Paris
140 avenue Victor Hugo, 75116 Paris
Telephone: (00) (33) 1 53 70 45 70
Facsimile: (00) (33) 1 53 70 45 86
e-mail: uk-del.oecd@wanadoo.fr
Website: www.ukdeloecd.org
Office Hours (GMT): Nov-Mar 08 30 – 17 00
Apr-Oct 07 30 – 16 00
United Kingdom Permanent Representative (holds personal rank of Ambassador):
Mr David E Lyscom
Deputy United Kingdom Permanent Representative and Counsellor (Economic and Financial):
Mr David Moran
Counsellor (Management): Mr Richard White

First Secretary (Energy, Environment and Budget):
Mr Craig Jones
First Secretary (Economic and Development):
Mr David Bendor
First Secretary (Trade, Finance and Agriculture):
Mr Jonathan Knott
First Secretary (Education, Employment, Social Affairs, Public Governance, Science, Technology and Industry, Regional Development): Mr Andrew McHallam

OFFICE OF THE UNITED KINGDOM PERMANENT REPRESENTATIVE TO THE EUROPEAN UNION

Brussels
Ave d'Auderghem 10, 1040 Brussels
Telephone: (00) (32) (2) 287 8211
Facsimile: (00) (32) (2) 287 8398 (2 lines)
Telex: 24312 (a/b 24312 UKEC BR B)
e-mail: ukrep@fco.gov.uk
Website: http://ukrep.fco.gov.uk
United Kingdom Permanent Representative (holds personal rank of Ambassador):
Mr John Grant, CMG
Deputy UK Permanent Representative:
Miss Anne Lambert
Political Security Committee Representative:
(Vacant)
Counsellor (Political and Institutions):
Mr Michael Aron
Counsellor (Agricultural): Mr David Barnes
Counsellor (External Relations):
Dr Carolyn Browne
Counsellor (Justice and Home Affairs):
Mr Jonathan Sweet
Counsellor (Industry): Mr Anthony Vinall
Counsellor (Economics and Finance):
Mr Peter Curwen
Counsellor (Social Affairs, Environment, Regional Policy): Ms Shan Morgan
Counsellor (Legal Adviser): Mr Paul Berman
Counsellor (Development Policy):
Mr Peter Landymore
First Secretary (External Relations):
Mr Duncan Sparkes
First Secretary (External Relations):
Mr Hamish Cowell
First Secretary (External Relations):
Mr Geoff Cole
First Secretary (Development):
Mrs Maryam Teschke
First Secretary (Trade Policy): Mr Ian Vollbracht
First Secretary (External Relations):
Miss Karen Betts
First Secretary (External Relations):
Mr Ken O'Flaherty
First Secretary (External Relations):
Mr Sandy Johnston
First Secretary (External Relations):
Mr Giles Portman
First Secretary (Agriculture and Food):
Mr Roy Norton
First Secretary (Agriculture): Dr Katherine Riggs
First Secretary (Fisheries):
Mr Gareth Baynham-Hughes

First Secretary (Commercial): Mrs Joyce Martin
First Secretary (Economic and Finance):
Mr Edward Smith
First Secretary (Economic and Finance):
Mr Gary Roberts
First Secretary (Budget): Mrs Fabia Jones
First Secretary (Taxation): Mr James Robertson
First Secretary (Transport): Mr Michael Rossell
First Secretary (Energy): Mr Ian Holt
First Secretary (Industry): Mr Chris Barton
First Secretary (Internal Markets):
Mr Andrew van der Lem
First Secretary (Industry): Mr Benjamin Turner
First Secretary (Justice and Home Affairs):
Mr Neil Bradley
First Secretary (Justice and Home Affairs):
Miss Jane Ferrier
First Secretary (Justice and Home Affairs):
Mr Paul McKell
First Secretary (Legal Section):
Miss Hazel Cameron
First Secretary (Legal Section):
Mr Michael Addison
First Secretary (Antici): Miss Caroline Wilson
First Secretary (European Parliament):
Mrs Corin Robertson
First Secretary (Political): Mr Matthew Taylor
First Secretary (Press): Mr Jonathan Allen
First Secretary (Environment):
Mr Andrew Dalgleish
First Secretary (Environment):
Mr Lindsay Croisdale-Appleby
First Secretary (Regional Policy): Mr Tim Figures
First Secretary (Social Affairs): Mr Marc Holland
First Secretary (Management): Mr Phil May
First Secretary (TMO): Mr Stephen Roseblade
Second Secretary (Agriculture and Fish):
Mr Keith Morrison
Second Secretary (Agriculture):
Ms Andrea Pearson
Second Secretary (Food and Veterinary):
Mr Simon Stannard
Second Secretary (Commercial): Mr Paul Knott
Second Secretary (Budget): Ms Hannah Robinson
Second Secretary (Finance): Miss Rebecca Jones
Second Secretary (Customs): Miss Karen Parkes
Second Secretary (External Relations):
Mr Stephen Hickey
Second Secretary (External Relations):
Mr Damian Thwaites
Second Secretary (Trade Policy):
Miss Harriet Rodger
Second Secretary (Pol/Mil): Ms Serra Tezisler
Second Secretary (Enlargement): Ms Sarah Cullum
Second Secretary (Transport): Ms Johanna Keech
Second Secretary (Industry): Mrs Lynne Vallance
Second Secretary (Industry): Miss Jennifer Young
Second Secretary (Consumer Affairs):
Mr Nick Thompson
Second Secretary (Justice and Home Affairs):
Mr Ben Llewellyn-Jones
Second Secretary (Justice and Home Affairs):
Dr Rod McLean
Second Secretary (European Parliament):
Mr Scott Furssedonn
Second Secretary (Political): Mr David Chitty

Second Secretary (Political): Ms Sarah Bell
Second Secretary (EU Staffing):
Miss Hilary McFarland
Second Secretary (TMO): Mr Bob Bruton
Second Secretary (TMO): Mr Neil Sturgess
Second Secretary (Environment):
Mr Philip McMurray
Second Secretary (Health, Culture, Sport):
Mr Jonathan Orr
Second Secretary (Social Affairs): Mr Kevin Dench
Second Secretary (Youth, Education/Training):
Miss Jo Hawley

Strasbourg
(Office only open when the European Parliament is
in session in Strasbourg)
Offices 561/562 IPE 1 Building, Strasbourg
Telephone: (00) (333) 88 17 68 16
Facsimile: (00) (333) 88 35 41 30
First Secretary (European Parliament Team):
Miss Corin Robertson
Second Secretary (European Parliament Team):
Mr Scott Furssedonn

**Brussels Joint Management Office for the four
Missions, see Embassies, High Commissions,
Deputy High Commissions and Consular Posts**

**UNITED KINGDOM DELEGATION TO THE
COUNCIL OF EUROPE**

Strasbourg
18 rue Gottfried, 67000-Strasbourg
Telephone: (00) (333) (88) 35 00 78
Facsimile: (00) (333) (88) 36 74 39
*United Kingdom Permanent Representative to
Council of Europe (holds personal rank of
Ambassador):* Mr Stephen F Howarth
*Deputy United Kingdom Permanent
Representative:* Ms Pamela Mitchison
Second Secretary: Mr Terence F Robins
Third Secretary (Chancery/Management):
Mr John A Webster

**UNITED KINGDOM DELEGATION TO THE
INTERNATIONAL MONETARY FUND AND
INTERNATIONAL BANK FOR
RECONSTRUCTION AND DEVELOPMENT**

Washington
Room 11-120, International Monetary Fund,
700 19th Street, NW, Washington, DC 20431
Telephone: (00) (1) (202) 623 4562
Facsimile: (00) (1) (202) 623 4965
*United Kingdom Executive Director of the
International Monetary Fund and World Bank:*
- e-mail: tscholar@imf.org Mr T Scholar
Alternate Executive Director of the World Bank:
- e-mail: rstevenson@imf.org Ms R Stevenson
*Alternate Executive Director of the International
Monetary Fund:*
- e-mail: mbrooke@imf.org Mr M Brooke
Assistant (IMF/IBRD):
- e-mail: njoicey@imf.org Mr N Joicey
Assistant (IMF/IBRD):
- e-mail: bkelmanson@imf.org Mr B Kelmanson

Assistant (IMF/IBRD):
- e-mail: bmellor@imf.org Mr B Mellor
Assistant (IMF/IBRD):
- e-mail: dmerotto@imf.org Mr D Merotto
Assistant (IMF/IBRD):
- e-mail: astuart@imf.org Ms A Stuart
Assistant (IMF/IBRD):
- e-mail: dtaylor@imf.org Mr D Taylor

**UNITED NATIONS HUMAN SETTLEMENTS
PROGRAMME (HABITAT)**

Nairobi
United Kingdom Permanent Representative:
Mr Edward Clay, CMG
Alternate Permanent Representative:
Mr Ray W Kyles
Deputy Permanent Representative: Mr John Virgoe

**UNITED NATIONS ENVIRONMENT
PROGRAMME**

Nairobi
United Kingdom Permanent Representative:
Mr Edward Clay, CMG
Alternate Permanent Representative:
Mr Ray W Kyles
Deputy Permanent Representative: Mr John Virgoe

**UNITED KINGDOM REPRESENTATION AT
THE AFRICAN DEVELOPMENT BANK**

Abidjan
Rue Joseph Anoma, Abidjan
Postal Address: 01 BP 1387, Abidjan 01
Telephone: (00) 20 40 23, 20 43 43
Telex numbers: 22203/2202/27717/23263
Executive Director: Mr M Bauer (German)
Alternate Executive Director:
Mr W Bronkhurst (Dutch)
Assistant to the Executive Director:
Mr P R Williams (British)

**UNITED KINGDOM REPRESENTATION AT
THE ASIAN DEVELOPMENT BANK**

Manila
6 ADB Avenue, Mandaluyong City, Manila
Postal address: PO Box 789, 0980 Manila
Telephone: (00) (632) 632 6079
Facsimile: (00) (632) 636 2056
Director's Adviser: Mr Frank Black

**UNITED KINGDOM REPRESENTATION AT
THE INTER-AMERICAN DEVELOPMENT
BANK**

Washington
1300 New York Avenue, N W Washington, DC
20577
Telephone: (00) (1) (202) 623
                1059/1058/1773/1980
Facsimile: (00) (1) (202) 623 3610
Cable address: Intambanc, Washington, DC
Telex numbers: 64141, 44240
Executive Director: Mr Y Ueda (Japanese)

Alternate Executive Director:
Mr Stewart Mills (British)
Senior Counsellor:
Mr Kazuki Watanabe (Japanese)
Counsellor: Mr Nobuyuki Otsuka (Japanese)

UNITED KINGDOM PERMANENT REPRESENTATION TO THE UNITED NATIONS AGENCIES FOR FOOD AND AGRICULTURE IN ROME

Rome
Via di Monserrato, 48/1. 00186 Rome
Telephone: (00) (39) 06 6840 0901/2/3/4
Facsimile: (00) (39) 06 6819 2965
United Kingdom Permanent Representative (holds personal rank of Ambassador): Mr Matthew Wyatt
First Secretary (Humanitarian Affairs):
Mr Michael Ellis
First Secretary (Senior Rural Livelihoods Adviser):
Dr Peter Reid
First Secretary (Rural Livelihoods Adviser):
Ms Jo Yvon
I.T Network Manager: Ms Fiona Pryce
Office Manager: Ms Nicolette Ciorba
Management and Programme Support Officer:
Ms Elizabeth Nasskau
Executive Assistant: Ms Elizabeth Buratti

UNITED KINGDOM REPRESENTATIVE ON THE COUNCIL OF THE INTERNATIONAL CIVIL AVIATION ORGANISATION

Montreal
Suite 1415, 999 University Street
Montreal, Quebec
H3C 5J9
Telephone: (00) (514) 954 8302/3
Direct Line – see individual officers
Facsimile: (00) (514) 954 8001
Airtech: (00) (1) (514) 866 4867 (Located in British Consulate-General Offices)
e-mail: ndenton@icao.int
asayce@icao.int
Office Hours (GMT) 14 00 – 22 00
United Kingdom Representative:
Mr Nicholas Denton (00) (1) (514) 954 8326
Deputy United Kingdom Representative:
Mr Adrian G Sayce (00) (1) (514) 954 8327

ORGANISATION FOR THE PROHIBITION OF CHEMICAL WEAPONS

The Hague
United Kingdom Permanent Representative:
Sir C R Budd, KCMG
First Secretary: Mr D G Cole
First Secretary: Mr M E Rack

GOVERNORS & COMMANDERS-IN-CHIEF ETC. OF THE UK OVERSEAS TERRITORIES

Anguilla
Government House, Anguilla
Telephone: (00) (1) (264) 497 2621/2622
(Governor/EA)

497 3312/3313 (Deputy Governor)
497 3315 (Staff Officer)
Tel/Fax: 497 2292 (Residence)
Facsimile: (00) (1) (264) 497 3314 (Unclassified)
497 3151 (Airtech)
e-mail: govthouse@anguillanet.com
Office Hours (GMT): 12 00 – 16 00, 17 00 20 00
Governor: Mr Alan Huckle
Deputy Governor: Mr Mark Capes
Staff Officer: Ms Jackie Barlow
Defence Adviser (resides at Bridgetown):
Captain Steve G Wilson, RN
Executive Assistant to the Governor:
Ms Angela Finn

Bermuda
Government House, Hamilton
Telephone: (00) (1) (441) 292 3600
Deputy Governor's Office: (00) (1) (441) 292 2587
Facsimile: (00) (1) (441) 295 3823
e-mail Address: depgov@ibl.bm
Office Hours (GMT): Summer: 11 45 - 16 00 and 17 15 - 20 00. Winter: 12 45 - 17 00 and 18 15 - 21 00
Governor (e-mail: governor@gov.bm):
Sir John Vereker, KCB
Deputy Governor (e-mail: deputygovernor@gov.bm): Mr Nick Carter
Executive Officer (e-mail: registrar@gov.bm):
Mrs Charlotte Rickward

British Antarctic Territory
Foreign and Commonwealth Office
Overseas Territories Department
Telephone: 020 7008 2616
Commissioner:
Mr Tony Crombie, OBE (non-resident)
Administrator: Dr M G Richardson (non-resident)

British Indian Ocean Territory
Foreign and Commonwealth Office
Overseas Territories Department
Telephone: 020 7008 2890
Commissioner:
Mr Tony Crombie, OBE (non-resident)
Administrator:
Mr Charles A Hamilton (non-resident)

Diego Garcia, c/o BFPO Ships
Facsimile: (00) 246 370 3943
Commissioner's Representative:
Commander Chris Davies, RN

British Virgin Islands
Government House
Road Town, Tortola
British Virgin Islands
Telephone: (00) (1) (284) 494 2345/70
Switchboard
468 3508 PA
3503 Head of Governor's Office
3507 Staff Officer
Facsimile: 4490
Airtech: (00) (1) (284) 494 5582
e-mail: bvigovernor@gov.vg
Website: http://www.bvi.gov.vg
Office Hours (GMT): 12 30 – 20 30

Governor: Mr Tom Macan
First Secretary and Head of Governor's Office:
Mr Duncan Norman
Third Secretary and Staff Officer: Mr Stuart Smith
Defence Adviser (resides at Bridgetown):
Captain Steve G Wilson, RN
Personal Assistant: Mrs Claire Means

Office of the Deputy Governor
Government Administration Building
Road Town, Tortola
Telephone: (00) (1) (284) 468 0346
Facsimile: (00) (1) (284) 494 6481
Acting Deputy Governor: Mrs Lisa Penn-Lettsome

Royal Virgin Islands Police Force
Telephone: (00) (1) (284) 494 3822 (24 hrs)
Immigration Department
Telephone: (00) (1) (284) 494 3471

BVI Passport Office
Telephone: (00) (1) (284) 468 3701 ext 3035/3036

Cayman Islands
4th Floor, Government Administration Building,
Elgin Avenue
George Town, Grand Cayman,
Telephone: (00) (1) (345) 949 7900 Switchboard
5776 PA direct
0980 Staff Officer
0479 Social Secretary
244 2431 AMO/Accountant/Archivist
Facsimile: (00) (1) (345) 945 4131 Governor's
Office
Airtech: 949 6556
945 5537 Social Secretary
e-mail: staffoff@candw.ky
Office Hours (GMT): 13 30-18 00 and
19 00 - 22 00
Governor: Mr Bruce H Dinwiddy, CMG
Chief Secretary: Mr George McCarthy
Deputy Chief Secretary: Mr Donnie Ebanks, MBE
Defence Adviser (Resides at Kingston):
Colonel Charles G Le Brun
*Second Secretary and Staff Officer to the
Governor:* Ms Kate Joad
PA to the Governor: Mrs Alison Bach
AMO/Accountant/Archivist: Mrs Melenie Mylrea
Social Secretary: Mrs Jacqueline Hennings

Government Information Services
Telephone: (00) (1) (345) 949 8092
Facsimile: (00) (1) (345) 949 5936/946 0664

Immigration Department
Telephone: (00) (1) (345) 949 8344
Facsimile: 949 8486

Cayman Islands Passport Office
Telephone: (00) (1) (345) 244 2024
Facsimile: (00) (1) (345) 945 4355

Falkland Islands
Government House, Stanley,
Telephone: (00) (500) 27433 Office
22210 Residence
Facsimile: (00) (500) 27434
e-mail: gov.house@horizon.co.fk

firstname.lastname@fco.gov.uk
Office Hours (GMT): Winter: 11 00-15 15 and 16
30-19 30. Summer: 12 00-16 15 and 17 30-20 30
Governor: Mr Howard J S Pearce, CVO
First Secretary: Ms Harriet Hall
PA/Governor: Miss Annette G Moore
MO/Archivist: Mr Rob Kempsell

South Georgia and the South Sandwich Islands
Government House, Stanley
Falkland Islands
Telephone: (00) (500) 27433 Office
22210 Residence
Facsimile: (00) (500) 27434
e-mail: gov.house@horizon.co.fk
OfficeHours (GMT): Winter 11 00 - 15 15 and 16
30 - 19 30. Summer 12 00 - 16 15 and
17 30 - 20 30
Commissioner (Resides in Falkland Islands):
Mr Howard J S Pearce, CVO
Assistant Commissioner and Director of Fisheries:
Ms Harriet Hall

Gibraltar
Office of the Governor
The Convent, Main Street
Telephone: (00) (350) 45440 (Switchboard)
47828 (PA to the Governor)
Facsimile: (00) (350) 47823 (Unclassified)
47830 (Airtech)
e-mail: convent@gibnet.gi
Office Hours (GMT) 08 00 - 16 15 (Winter); 07 30
- 13 30 (Summer)
Governor and Commander-in-Chief:
Sir Francis N Richards, KCMG, CVO
Deputy Governor: Mr David G Blunt, CVO
Assistant Deputy Governor: Mr Chris Shute
Second Secretary (Convent Liaison Officer):
Mr John Woodruffe
Second Secretary (EU Affairs): Mr David Flint
Second Secretary (Management):
Mr David Harries, OBE
Third Secretary (Political): Mr Stewart Dee

Consular/Visa inquiries:
Civil Status and Registration Office
Telephone: (00) (350) 51727/59839/59840
Facsimile: (00) (350) 42706

Commercial inquiries:
Department of Trade and Industry:
Telephone: (00) (350) 52052
Facsimile: (00) (350) 71406

Montserrat
Lancaster House
Olveston
Telephone: (00) (1) (664) 491 2688/9 Office
6124 Governor's Residence
Facsimile: (00) (1) (664) 491 8867
Airtech: 4553
e-mail: govoff@candw.ag
monmedia@candw.ag (Information section)
Office Hours (GMT): 12 00 - 16 00 and
17 00 - 20 00
Governor: Mrs D E V Barnes- Jones

First Secretary and Head of Governor's Office:
Mr R T Jarvis
Personal Assistant to the Governor: Miss L Cox
Defence Adviser (resides at Bridgetown):
Captain S G Wilson, RN
Third Secretary and Staff Officer:
Mr E M Patterson

Pitcairn Henderson Ducie and Oeno Islands
British High Commission,
Wellington, New Zealand
Governor (non-resident): Mr R T Fell, CVO
Deputy Governor: Mr M Forbes
Pitcairn Islands Administration, Private Box
105696
Auckland, New Zealand
Telephone: (00) (9) (64) 366 0186
e-mail: pitcairn@iconz.co.nz
Website: http://www.government.pn
Commissioner (non resident):
Mr Leslie Jaques, OBE

St Helena
Governor's Office
The Castle, Jamestown
St Helena,
South Atlantic Ocean
Telephone: (00) (290) 2555 Office
           4444 Residence
Facsimile: (00) (290) 2598 Office
           4418 Residence
Airtech: 2476
e-mail: OCS@helanta.sh
joany@sainthelena.gov.sh
Office Hours (GMT): Mon-Fri: 08 30 – 12 30 and
13 00 – 16 00
Governor and Commander-in Chief:
Mr Michael Clancy
Staff Officer: Mr Amias Moores

Chief Secretary's Office
The Castle, Jamestown
St Helena, South Atlantic Island
Telephone: (00) (290) 4552 Residence
           2525 Office
Facsimile: (00) (290) 2598 Office
e-mail: OCS@helanta.sh
sandrab@sainthelena.gov.sh
Office Hours (GMT): Mon-Fri: 08 30 – 12 30 and
13 00 – 16 00
Chief Secretary: Mr John Styles

Ascension
The Administrator's Office, Georgetown
Ascension, South Atlantic Ocean, ASCN IZZ
Telephone: (00) 247 6311 Office
           4525 Home
Facsimile: (00) 247 6152
Airtech: (00) 247 6892
e-mail: administrator@atlantis.co.ac
Website: http://www.ascension-island.gov.ac
Office Hours (GMT): Mon-Fri: 08 30 - 12 30 and
13 30 - 16 30
*Governor and Commander-in-Chief (Resides in St
Helena):* Mr Michael Clancy
Administrator: Mr Andrew Kettlewell

Tristan da Cunha
The Administrator's Office
Edinburgh of the Seven Seas
Tristan da Cunha
South Atlantic Ocean, TDCU 1ZZ
Telephone: (00) (871) 682 087 155
           763 421 817
Facsimile: (00) (871) 682 087 158
           600 245 563
e-mail: hmg@cunha.demon.co.uk
Office Hours (GMT): Mon-Fri: 08 30 - 12 30 and
13 00 - 16 30
*Governor and Commander-in-Chief (Resides in St
Helena):* Mr Michael Clancy
Administrator: Mr Mike Hentley

Turks and Caicos Islands
Waterloo, Government House
Grand Turk
Telephone: (00) (1) (649) 946 2309
Facsimile: (00) (1) (649) 946 2903
Airtech: (00) (1) (649) 946 2766
e-mail: govhouse@tciway.tc
Governor: Mr Jim Poston, CBE
First Secretary: Mr David Brett
Second Secretary and Assistant to Governor:
Ms Barbara Moser-Andon
Personal Assistant: Ms Michelle Ridley

Chief Secretary's Office
Government Secretariat, Grand Turk
Telephone: (00) (1) (649) 946 2910
Facsimile: (00) (1) (649) 946 2886
Chief Secretary: Mrs C Astwood, MBE
Defence Adviser (resides at Kingston):
Colonel C G Le Brun
Office Hours (GMT): Winter: Mon-Thu: 13 00 -
17 30 and 19 00 - 21 30. Fri: 13 00 - 17 30 and
19 00 - 21 00
Summer: Mon-Thu: 12 00 - 16 30 and 18 00 -
20 30. Fri: 12 00 - 16 30 and 18 00 - 20 00

SMALL POSTS

SOVEREIGN
Abidjan
Algiers
Almaty
Antananarivo
Ashgabat
Asunción
Baku
Banjul
Belmopan
Bratislava
Castries
Dakar
Dili
Freetown
Gaborone
Georgetown, Guyana
Guatemala City
Holy See
Honiara
Kigali
Kingstown, St Vincent
Kinshasa
La Paz
Luxembourg
Ljubljana
Maseru
Mbabane
Minsk
Montevideo
Nassau
Nuku'alofa
Panama City
Phnom Penh
Port Moresby
Port of Spain
Port-Vila
Quito
Rangoon
Reykjavik
Riga
St George's, Grenada
San José
Santo Domingo
Skopje
Strasbourg
Suva
Tallinn
Tashkent
Tbilisi
Tirana
Ulaanbaatar
Victoria
Vilnius
Windhoek
Yerevan

SUBORDINATE
Al Khobar
Alexandria
Amsterdam

Atlanta
Auckland
Barcelona
Bilbao
Bordeaux
Boston
Brisbane
Cape Town
Casablanca
Chiang Mai
Chicago
Dallas
Denver
Durban
Frankfurt
Hamburg
Ho Chi Minh City
Houston
Kolkata
Kuching
Lille
Los Angeles
Lyon
Marseille
Melbourne
Miami
Milan
Montreal
Munich
Oporto
Palma
Perth
San Francisco
Seattle
Stuttgart
Sydney
Tarawa
Toronto
Vancouver
Yekaterinburg
Zurich

OVERSEAS TERRITORY
Anguilla
Georgetown, Ascension
Gibraltar
Grand Cayman, Cayman Islands
Grand Turk, Turks and Caicos Islands
Hamilton, Bermuda
Plymouth, Montserrat
Stanley, Falkland Islands
Jamestown, St Helena
Tortola, British Virgin Islands
Tristan Da Cunha

ANNEX: NON GOVERNMENTAL TRADE OFFICES

TAIWAN

Her Majesty's Government do not recognise Taiwan as a sovereign state and consequently have no diplomatic relations with it. However, there are non- governmental trade and cultural offices at the following addresses:

Taipei
British Trade and Cultural Office
8-10th Floor Fu Key Building
99 Jen Ai Road, Section 2,Taipei 100
FTN Code – 8308 + four digit extn number
Telephone: (00) (886) (2) 2192 7000
   2192 + extension (Direct Line)
Facsimile: (00) (886) (2) 2394 8673(Commercial)
   2397 3559 (Inward Investment)
   2393 1985 (Visa Handling Unit)
   2397 3609 (Management)
Airtech: 2322 3265
e-mail: firstname.lastname@fco.gov.uk
Internet Website: www.btco.org.tw
Office Hours (GMT): 01 00 - 04 30 and
05 30 - 09 00
Director General: Mr Derek Marsh, cvo (ext 7009)
Deputy Director General:
Mr Rod Bunten (ext 7001)
Head of Commercial Section:
Mr Mark Robinson (ext 7006)
Head of Inward Investment Section:
Mr David Percival (ext 7066)
Head of Political and Economic Section:
Mr Den Moore (ext 7055)
Head of Management Section:
Mr David Walters (ext 7002)
Head of Visa Handling Unit:
Mr Alan Dillon (ext 7040)
Science and Technology Officer:
Mr Chong-Loon Tai (ext 7074)
Press and Public Affairs Officer:
Ms Maggie Yeh (ext 7015)

Education and Cultural Section
British Council
2nd Floor, No. 106 Hsin-yi Road
Section 5, Taipei 110
Telephone: (00) (886) (2) 8722 1000
Facsimile: (00) (886) (2) 8786 0985
e-mail: firstname.lastname@britishcouncil.org.tw
Website: www.britishcouncil.org.tw
British Council Director:
Mr Gordon Slaven (ext 1007)

Kaohsiung
British Trade and Cultural Office (Kaohsiung
Section)
Unit D, 7th Floor, Fu Bon Commercial Building
95 Ming-Tsu 2nd Road, Kaohsiung 800
Telephone: (00) (886) 7238 1034/5
Facsimile: (00) (886) 7238 1032
Commercial Officer: Ms Anne Lai

Education and Cultural Section
Unit D, 7th Floor, Fu Bon Commercial Building
95 Ming-Tsu 2nd Road, Kaohsiung 800
Telephone: (00) (886) 7235 1715
Facsimile: (00) (886) 7238 0411
Branch Manager: Ms Fay Chen

Guide to places and countries
Embassies, High Commissions, Deputy High Commissions and Consular Posts

Note: There is no HMG representation in Bhutan.
It is therefore omitted from the List.

A
Aabenraa, Denmark
Aalborg, Denmark
Aarhus, Denmark
Abidjan, Ivory Coast
Abuja, Nigeria
Abu Dhabi, United Arab
Emirates
Acapulco, Mexico
Accra, Ghana
Addis Ababa, Ethiopia
Adelaide, Australia
Aden, Yemen
Agadir, Morocco
Ahmedabad, India
Akureyri, Iceland
Aland Island, Finland
Aleppo, Syria
Ålesund, Norway
Alexandria, Egypt
Algiers, Algeria
Alicante, Spain
Al Khobar, Saudi Arabia
Almaty, Kazakhstan
Amiens, France
Amman, Jordan
Amsterdam, Netherlands
Anchorage, AK, United
States
Angeles City, Philippines
Anguilla, Anguilla,
  See Page 117
Ankara, Turkey
Antalya, Turkey
Antananarivo, Madagascar
Antwerp, Belgium
Apia, Samoa
Arequipa, Peru
Ascension, St Helena
  See Page 119
Ashgabat, Turkmenistan
Asmara, Eritrea
Asunción, Paraguay
Athens, Greece
Atlanta, GA, United States
Auckland, New Zealand
Azores, Portugal

B
Baghdad, Iraq
Bahrain, Bahrain
Baku, Azerbaijan
Bali, Indonesia
Bamako, Mali
Bandar Seri Begawan,
Brunei
Bangalore, India
Bangkok, Thailand
Bangui, Central African
Republic

Banja Luka, Bosnia and
Herzegovina
Banjul, The Gambia
Barcelona, Spain
Bari, Italy
Basel, Switzerland
Basra, Iraq
Basseterre, St Kitts and
Nevis
Beijing, China
Beira, Mozambique
Beirut, Lebanon
Belém, Brazil
Belgrade, Serbia and
Montenegro
Belmopan, Belize
Belo Horizonte, Brazil
Bergen, Norway
Berlin, Germany
Berne, Switzerland
Biarritz, France
Bilbao, Spain
Bishkek, Kyrgyzstan
Bissau, Guinea Bissau
Bitola, Macedonia
Bodrum, Turkey
Bogotá, Colombia
Bordeaux, France
Boston, MA, United States
Boulogne-sur-Mer, France
Brasilia, Brazil
Bratislava, Slovakia
Brazzaville, Congo
Bregenz, Austria
Bremen, Germany
Bridgetown, Barbados
Brisbane, Australia
Brussels, Belgium
Bucharest, Romania
Budapest, Hungary
Buenos Aires, Argentina
Bujumbura, Burundi
Bursa, Turkey

C
Cagliari, Italy
Cairo, Egypt
Calais, France
Calgary, Canada
Cali, Colombia
Canberra, Australia
Cancun, Mexico
Cape Town, South Africa
Caracas, Venezuela
Casablanca, Morocco
Castries, St Lucia
Catania, Italy
Cayenne, French Guiana,
France
Cebu, Philippines

Charlotte, NC, United States
Chennai, India
Cherbourg, France
Chiang Mai, Thailand
Chicago, IL, United States
Chisinau, Moldova
Chongqing, China
Christchurch, New Zealand
Ciudad Juárez, Mexico
Clermont Ferrand, France
Colombo, Sri Lanka
Conakry, Guinea
Copenhagen, Denmark
Córdoba, Argentina
Corfu, Greece
Cotonou, Benin
Curitiba, Brazil
Cusco, Peru

D
Dakar, Senegal
Dallas, TX, United States
Damascus, Syria
Dar es Salaam, Tanzania
Denver, CO, United States
Dili, East Timor
Dhaka, Bangladesh
Djibouti, Djibouti
Doha, Qatar
Douala, Cameroon
Dubai, United Arab Emirates
Dublin, Ireland
Dubrovnik, Croatia
Dunkirk, France
Dushanbe, Tajikistan
Durban, South Africa
Düsseldorf, Germany

E
East London, South Africa
  Edinburgh of the Seven Seas,
  Tristan da Cunha, St Helena,
  See Page 119
Eilat, Israel
Esbjerg, Denmark

F
Faroe Islands, Denmark
Florence, Italy
Fort de France,
Martinique, France
Fortaleza, Brazil
Frankfurt, Germany
Fredericia, Denmark
Freetown, Sierra Leone
French Guiana, France
Fukuoka, Japan
Funafuti, Tuvalu
Funchal, Madeira

G

Gaborone, Botswana
Galápagos, Ecuador
Gaza
Gdansk, Poland
Geneva, Switzerland
Genoa, Italy
Georgetown, Ascension
Georgetown, Guyana
Ghent, Belgium
Gibraltar, See Page 118
Gothenburg, Sweden
Grand Canary, Spain
Grand Cayman, Cayman
Islands, See Page 118
Grand Turk, Turks and Caicos,
See Page 119
Graz, Austria
Guadalajara, Mexico
Guadeloupe, France
Guangzhou, China
Guatemala City, Guatemala
Guayaquil, Ecuador

H

Halifax, Canada
Hamburg, Germany
Hamilton, Bermuda,
  See Page 117
Hanoi, Vietnam
Hanover, Germany
Harare, Zimbabwe
Havana, Cuba
Helsinki, Finland
Heraklion, Crete, Greece
Herning, Denmark
Hiroshima, Japan
Ho Chi Minh City, Vietnam
Hobart, Tasmania, Australia
Hodeidah, Yemen
Holy See
Hong Kong, China
Honiara, Solomon Islands
Houston, TX, United States
Hyderabad, India

I

Ibadan, Nigeria
Ibiza, Spain
Innsbruck, Austria
Iquitos, Peru
Islamabad, Pakistan
Istanbul, Turkey
Izmir, Turkey

J

Jakarta, Indonesia
Jamestown, St Helena
Jeddah, Saudi Arabia
Jerusalem
Johannesburg, South Africa
Johor Bahru, Malaysia
Jyväskylä, Finland

K

Kabul, Afghanistan
Kaduna, Nigeria

Kampala, Uganda
Kano, Nigeria
Kansas City, KS, United
States
Kaohsiung, Taiwan
Karachi, Pakistan
Kathmandu, Nepal
Katowice, Poland
Khartoum, Sudan
Kiel, Germany
Kiev, Ukraine
Kigali, Rwanda
Kingston, Jamaica
Kingstown, St Vincent and the
Grenadines
Kinshasa, Congo (Democratic
Republic)
Kirkuk, Iraq
Kolkata, India
Kos, Greece
Kosovo, Serbia and
Montenegro
Kota Kinabalu, Malaysia
Kotka, Finland
Kraków, Poland
Kristiansand, Norway
Kuala Lumpur, Malaysia
Kuching, Malaysia
Kuopio, Finland
Kuwait, Kuwait

L

Lagos, Nigeria
Lahore, Pakistan
La Paz, Bolivia
La Réunion, France
Las Palmas, Grand Canary,
Spain
Lattakia, Syria
Le Havre, France
Leipzig, Germany
Libreville, Gabon
Liège, Belgium
Lille, France
Lilongwe, Malawi
Lima, Peru
Lisbon Portugal
Ljubljana, Slovenia
Lomé, Togo
Lorient, France
Los Angeles, CA, United
States
Luanda, Angola
Lublin, Poland
Lugano, Switzerland
Lusaka, Zambia
Luxembourg, Luxembourg
Luxor, Egypt
Lyon, France

M

Macao, China
Madeira, Portugal
Madrid, Spain
Majuro, Marshall Islands
Malabo, Equatorial Guinea

Málaga, Spain
Malamo, Sweden
Malé, Maldives
Malindi, Kenya
Managua, Nicaragua
Manáus, Brazil
Manila, Philippines
Maputo, Mozambique
Maracaibo, Venezuela
Margarita, Venezuela
Mariehamn, Aland Islands,
Finland
Marmaris, Turkey
Marrakech, Morocco
Marseille, France
Martinique, France
Maseru, Lesotho
Mbabane, Swaziland
Medan, Indonesia
Medellin, Colombia
Melbourne, Australia
Mendoza, Argentina
Menorca, Spain
Mérida, Mexico
Mérida, Venezuela
Minneapolis, MN, United
States
Mexico City, Mexico
Miami, FL, United States
Milan, Italy
Minsk, Belarus
Miri, Malaysia
Mogadishu, Somalia
Mombasa, Kenya
Monaco, Monaco
Monrovia, Liberia
Montego Bay, Jamaica
Monterrey, Mexico
Montevideo, Uruguay
Montpellier, France
Montreal, Canada
Montreux, Switzerland
Moroni, Comoros
Moscow, Russia
Mount Lebanon, Lebanon
Mumbai, India
Munich, Germany
Muri Beach, Cook Islands
Muscat, Oman

N

Nagoya, Japan
Nairobi, Kenya
Nantes, France
Naples, Italy
Nashville, TN, United States
Nassau, The Bahamas
Nauru
Ndjamena, Chad
New Caledonia, France
New Delhi, India
New Orleans, LA, United
States
New York, NY, United States
Niamey, Niger
Nice, France

Nicosia, Cyprus
Nouakchott, Mauritania
Novorossiysk, Russia
Nuku'alofa, Tonga
Nuremburg, Germany

O
Oaxaca, Mexico
Odense, Denmark
Olongapo, Philippines
Olveston, Monserrat,
  See Page 118
Oporto, Portugal
Orlando, FL, United States
Osaka, Japan
Oslo, Norway
Ottawa, Canada
Ouagadougou, Burkina
Oulu, Finland

P
Palermo, Italy
Palma, Spain
Panama City, Panama
Papeete, French Polynesia,
France
Paramaribo, Surinam
Paris, France
Patras, Greece
Perth, Australia
Philadelphia, PA, United
States
Phoenix, AZ, United States
Phnom Penh, Cambodia
Penang, Malaysia
Pittsburgh, PA, United
States
Piura, Peru
Philipsburg, St Maarten,
Netherlands Antilles
Podgorica, Serbia and
Montenegro
Pohnpei, Micronesia
Pointe- à-Pitre, Guadeloupe
Pori, Finland
Port-au-Prince, Haiti
Port Elizabeth, South Africa
Port Harcourt, Nigeria
Portimão, Portugal
Portland, OR, United
States
Port Louis, Mauritius
Port Moresby, Papua New
Guinea
Port of Spain, Trinidad and
Tobago
Port Vila, Vanuatu
Porto Alegre, Brazil
Poznan, Poland
Prague, Czech Republic
Praia, Cape Verde
Pretoria, South Africa
Pristina, Kosovo, Serbia and
Montenegro
Puerto Plata, Dominican
Republic

Puerto Rico, United States
Punta Arenas, Chile
Pusan, Korea (South)
Pyongyang, Korea (North)

Q
Quebec City, Canada
Quito, Ecuador

R
Rabat, Morocco
Rangoon, Burma
Recife, Brazil
Reykjavik, Iceland
Rhodes, Greece
Ribeira Grande, Azores,
Portugal
Riga, Latvia
Rio de Janeiro, Brazil
Rio Grande, Brazil
Riyadh, Saudi Arabia
Rodrigues, Mauritius
Rome, Italy
Roseau, Dominica
Rovaniemi, Finland

S
St George's, Grenada
St John's, Antigua and
Barbuda
St John's, Canada
St Louis, MO, United States
St Malo-Dinard, France
St Petersburg, Russia
Salt Lake City, UT, United
States
Salvador, Brazil
Salzburg, Austria
Sanaa, Yemen
San Cristobal, Venezuela
San Diego, CA, United
States
San Francisco, CA, United
States
San Jose, CA, United
States
San José, Costa Rica
San Marino
San Pedro Sula, Honduras
San Salvador, El Salvador
Santa Cruz de Tenerife,
Canary Islands, Spain
Santa Fe, Argentina
Santander, Spain
Santiago, Chile
Santo Domingo, Dominican
Republic
Santos, Brazil
São Paulo, Brazil
São Tomé, Sao Tome and
Principe
Sao Vincente, Cape Verde
Sapporo, Japan
Sarajevo, Bosnia and
Herzegovina
Saumur, France
Seattle, WA, United States

Seoul, Korea (South)
Sfax, Tunisia
Shanghai, China
Singapore
Skopje, Macedonia
Sofia, Bulgaria
Split, Croatia
Stanley, Falkland Islands,
  See Page 118
Stavanger, Norway
Stockholm, Sweden
Stuttgart, Germany
Suez, Egypt
Sundsvall, Sweden
Suva, Fiji
Sydney, Australia
Syros, Greece
Szczecin, Poland

T
Taipei, Taiwan
Tallinn, Estonia
Tampere (Tammerfors),
Finland
Tangier, Morocco
Tarawa, Kiribati
Tashkent, Uzbekistan
Tasmania, Australia
Tbilisi, Georgia
Tegucigalpa, Honduras
Tehran, Iran
Tel Aviv, Israel
The Hague, Netherlands
Thessaloniki, Greece
Tijuana, Mexico
Tirana, Albania
Toamasina, Madagascar
Tokyo, Japan
Toronto, Canada
Tórshavn, Faroe Islands,
Denmark
Tortola, British Virgin
Islands, See Page 117
Toulouse, France
Tours, France
Trieste, Italy
Tripoli, Lebanon
Tripoli, Libya
Tromso, Norway
Trondheim, Norway
Trujillo, Peru
Tunis, Tunisia
Turin, Italy
Turku, Finland

U
Ulaanbaatar, Mongolia

V
Vaasa (Vasa), Finland
Varna, Bulgaria
Vaduz, Liechtenstein
Valais, Switzerland
Valletta, Malta
Valparaíso, Chile
Vancouver, Canada
Venice, Italy

Veracruz, Mexico
Victoria, Seychelles
Vienna, Austria
Vientiane, Laos
Vigo, Spain
Vilnius, Lithuania
Vladivostok, Russia

W
Warri, Nigeria
Warsaw, Poland
Washington, DC, United
States
Watamu, Kenya
Wellington, New Zealand
Willemstad, Curacao
Netherlands Antilles,
Netherlands
Windhoek, Namibia
Winnipeg, Canada
Wroclaw, Poland

Y
Yaoundé, Cameroon
Yekaterinburg, Russia
Yerevan, Armenia

Z
Zagreb, Croatia
Zakynthos, Greece
Zurich, Switzerland

**Chronological Lists from 1984 onwards
of Secretaries of State,
Ministers of State,
Permanent Under-Secretaries of State,
British Ambassadors etc.,
High Commissioners,
Permanent Representatives
to International Organizations and
Governors and Commanders-in-chief
of Dependent territories**

*Reference should be made to the Foreign Office and
Commonwealth Relations Office Lists of 1965, to the
Colonial Office List of 1966 and to the Diplomatic Service
List 2004 and earlier Lists for previous lists of officers
holding these appointments.*

Part III: Chronological Lists

The Foreign and Commonwealth Office was formed in October 1968 by the merger of the former Foreign Office and the Commonwealth Office

SECRETARIES OF STATE FOR FOREIGN AND COMMONWEALTH AFFAIRS 1984-2004/5

1989 July25 The Rt Hon. John Major, MP
1989 Oct26 The Rt Hon. Douglas Hurd, CBE, MP (later Baron Hurd of Westwell)
1995 July6 The Rt Hon. Malcolm Rifkind, QC, MP (later the Rt Hon Sir Malcolm Rifkind)
1997 May2 The Rt Hon. Robin Cook, MP
2001 June8 The Rt Hon. Jack Straw, PC, MP

MINISTERS OF STATE FOR FOREIGN AND COMMONWEALTH AFFAIRS 1984-2004/5

1984 Sept11 Timothy Renton, MP (later the Rt Hon. Baron Renton)
1986 Jan13 Mrs Lynda Chalker, MP (later the Rt Hon. Baroness Chalker)
1986 Sept8 Christopher Patten, MP (later the Rt Hon. Christopher Patten)
1987 June16 The Lord Glenarthur
1987 June16 David Mellor, QC, MP (later the Rt Hon. David Mellor)
1988 July16 The Rt Hon. William Waldegrave, MP (later Baron Waldegrave)
1989 July25 The Hon. Francis Maude, MP (later the Rt Hon. Francis Maude MP)
1989 July25 The Lord Brabazon
1989 July25 The Hon. Timothy Sainsbury, MP (later the Rt.Hon Timothy Sainsbury)
1990 July23 Tristan Garel-Jones, MP (later the Rt Hon. Tristan Garel-Jones, MP)
1990 July23 The Rt Hon. The Earl of Caithness
1990 July23 The Hon. Mark Lennox-Boyd, MP (later the Hon. Sir Mark Lennox-Boyd)
1990 Nov1 The Hon. Douglas Hogg, QC, MP (later the Rt Hon. Douglas Hogg, QC, MP, (later Viscount Hailsham)
1992 The Rt Hon. Alastair Goodlad, MP
1994 July20, David Davis MP (later the Rt Hon. David Davis MP)
1995 July5, The Rt Hon. Sir Nicholas Bonsor (Bt), MP
1995 July5, The Rt Hon. Jeremy Hanley, MP (later the Rt.Hon Sir Jeremy Hanley)
1997 May5, Derek Fatchett, MP (later the Rt Hon. Derek Fatchett, MP)
1997 May5, Tony Lloyd, MP
1997 May5, Doug Henderson, MP

1998 July28, Ms Joyce Quin, MP (later the Rt Hon. Joyce Quin, MP)
1999 May17, Geoff Hoon, MP
1999 July29, Peter Hain, MP
1999 July29, John Battle, MP
1999 July29, Baroness Scotland
1999 Oct12, Keith Vaz, MP
2001 Jan25, Brian Wilson, MP
2001 June11, Peter Hain, MP
2001 June11, Baroness Symons
2001 June11, Ben Bradshaw, MP
2001 June11, Denis MacShane, MP
2001 June11, Baroness Amos
2002 May30, Mike O'Brien, MP
2001 Oct 28, Bill Rammell, MP
2003 June13, Chris Mullin, MP
2004 Sept9, Douglas Alexander, MP

PERMANENT UNDER-SECRETARIES OF STATE FOR FOREIGN AND COMMONWEALTH AFFAIRS AND HEAD OF HM DIPLOMATIC SERVICE 1984-2004/5

1986 June23, Sir Patrick (Richard Henry) Wright, GCMG (later Baron Wright of Richmond)
1991 June28, Sir David (Howe) Gillmore, KCMG (later Baron Gillmore)(Dec'd 20th March 1999)
1994 Aug1, Sir (Arthur) John Coles, KCMG (later GCMG)
1997 Nov13, Sir John (Olav) Kerr, GCMG
2002 Jan14, Sir Michael (Hastings) Jay, KCMG

CHRONOLOGICAL LIST OF BRITISH REPRESENTATIVES ABROAD INCLUDING COMMONWEALTH COUNTRIES 1984-2004/5

Afghanistan
1984 Charles David Stephen Drace-Francis, Chargé d'Affaires a.i. July18
1987 Ian Warren Mackley, Chargé d'Affaires a.i. Jan8
Staff temporarily withdrawn from post February 1989
1994 Sir Nicholas Barrington, amb. ex. and plen. Feb22
2002 Ronald Peter Nash, amb. ex. and plen. May16
2004 Rosalind Mary Marsden, amb. ex. and plen. Jan

Albania
1992 Sir Patrick Stanislaus Fairweather, amb. ex. and plen. July20
1996 Harcourt Andrew Pretorius Tesoriere, amb.ex. and plen. Jan21
1998 Stephen Nash amb. ex. and plen. May15
1999 Dr Peter January amb. ex. and plen. March1
2001 Dr David Maurice Landsman OBE, amb. ex. and plen. July16
2003 Richard Hugh Francis Jones, amb. ex. and plen. Oct16

Algeria
1984 Alan (later Sir A) Gordon Munro, amb. ex. and plen. Jan21
1987 Patrick Howard Caines Eyers amb. ex. and plen. April12
1990 Christopher Charles Richard Battiscombe amb. ex. and plen. March6
1994 Christopher Donald Crabbie amb. ex. and plen Aug2
1996 Peter James Marshall, amb. ex. and plen Jan6
1997 (Jean) Francois Gordon, amb. ex. and plen. Nov4
1999 William Baldie Sinton OBE, amb. ex. and plen. July16
2001 Richard John Smale Edis, amb. ex. and plen. Sept15
2002 Graham Stewart Hand, amb. ex. and plen. July1
2004 Brian Edward Stewart, amb. ex. and plen. May

Andorra
1994 Anthony David Brighty amb. ex. and plen. Aug25
1998 Peter (later Sir P) James Torry amb. ex. and plen. Sep2
2003 Stephen John Leadbetter Wright, amb. ex. and plen. May

Angola
1985 Patrick Stanislaus Fairweather, amb. ex. and plen. Oct2
1987 Michael John Carlisle Glaze, amb. ex. and plen. Nov18

1990 John Gerrard Flynn, amb. ex. and plen. May9
1993 Anthony Richard Thomas, amb. ex. and plen. April8
1995 Roger Dudley Hart, amb. ex. and plen. July24
1998 Caroline Elmes, amb. ex. and plen. Sept14
2002 John Thompson, amb. ex. and plen. Feb21

Antigua and Barbuda
HIGH COMMISSIONERS
1986 Kevin Francis Xavier Burns. Oct19
1991 Emrys Thomas Davies. Feb15
1994 Richard Thomas. Oct7
1998 Gordon Meldrum Baker Aug3
2001 (Charles) John Branford White. Aug11

Argentina
Diplomatic and Consular relations with the Argentine Republic were broken off with effect from 2 April 1982. Consular Relations were resumed on 19 October 1989 and Diplomatic Relations on 15th February 1990.
1989 Alan Charles Hunt, Consul General. Oct19
1989 Alan Charles Hunt, Chargé d'Affaires a.i. and Consul General. Feb15
1990 The Hon Humphrey John Hamilton Maud, amb. ex. and plen. July15
1993 Sir Peter Hall, amb. ex. and plen. Sept8
1997 William Marsden, amb. ex. and plen. July27
2000 Duncan Robin (later Sir R) Carmichael Christopher, amb. ex. and plen. Nov17
2004 Dr Edgar John Hughes, amb. ex. and plen. Nov

Armenia
1992 Sir Brian James Proetel Fall, amb. ex. and plen. July15
1995 David Ivimey Miller, amb. ex. and plen. July31
1997 John Edward Mitchiner, amb. ex. and plen. April1
1999 Timothy Aidan Jones, amb. ex. and plen. Nov13
2003 Thorhilda Mary Vivia Abbott-Watt, amb. ex. and plen. Jan

Australia
HIGH COMMISSIONERS
1984 Sir John Henry Gladstone Leahy. Oct13
1988 (Arthur) John (later Sir J) Coles. March22
1991 Brian (later Sir B) Leon Barder. April11
1994 Roger (later Sir R) John Carrick. July27
1997 Alexander Claud Stuart Allan. Nov16
1999 Sir Alastair Goodlad KCMG. May25.

Austria
1986 Robert James O'Neill, amb. ex. and plen. Sept2
1989 Brian Lee Crowe, amb. ex. and plen. May31
1992 Terence Courtney Wood, amb. ex. and plen. April30
1996 Anthony (later Sir A) St John Howard Figgis, amb. ex. and plen. Sept29
2000 Antony Ford, amb. ex. and plen. Sept1
2003 John Malcolm Macgregor, amb. ex. and plen. May

Azerbaijan
1992   Sir Brian James Proetel Fall, amb. ex. and plen. July14
1993   Thomas Nesbitt Young, amb. ex. and plen. Sept1
1997   Roger Thomas, amb. ex. and plen. July1
2000   Andrew Victor Gunn Tucker, amb. ex. and plen. Nov1
2003   Dr Lawrence Stanley Charles Bristow, amb. ex. and plen. Dec2

Bahamas
HIGH COMMISSIONERS
1986   Colin Garth Mays. Oct16
1991   Michael John Gore. July16
1992   Brian Attewell. Sept16
1996   Peter Michael Heppell Young. May1
1999   Peter Richard Heigl. July15
2003   Roderick Gemmell. March21

Bahrain
1984   Francis Sidney Edward Trew, amb. ex. and plen. Dec5
1988   John Alan Shepherd, amb. ex. and plen. April4
1992   Hugh James Oliver Redvers Tunnell, amb. ex. and plen. Feb16
1996   David Ian Lewty, amb. ex. and plen. Jan13
1999   Peter Ford, amb. ex. and plen. April18
2003   Robin David Lamb, amb. ex. and plen. Aug25

Bangladesh
HIGH COMMISSIONERS
1989   Colin (later Sir C) Henry Imray. Oct21
1993   Peter James Fowler. Sept21
1996   David Critchlow Walker. Sept15
2000   David Carter. Jan19
2004   Anwar Choudhury. May

Barbados
HIGH COMMISSIONERS
1986   Kevin Francis Xavier Burns. Oct19
1991   Emrys Thomas Davies. Jan13
1994   Richard Thomas. Oct7
1998   Gordon Meldrum Baker. March8
2001   (Charles) John Branford White. Aug11

Belarus
1992   Sir Brian James Proetel Fall, amb. ex. and plen. July27
1993   John Vivian Everard, amb. ex. and plen. Oct12
1996   Jessica Mary Pearce, amb. ex. and plen. Jan22
1999   Iain Kelly, amb. ex. and plen. April6
2003   Brian Maurice Bennett, ex. and plen. March14

Belgium
1985   Peter (later Sir P) Charles Petrie, amb. ex. and plen. July7
1989   Robert James O'Neill, amb. ex. and plen. May10
1992   Sir John Walter David Gray, amb. ex. and plen. June18
1996   David Hugh Colvin, amb. ex. and plen. Oct6

2001   Gavin Wallace Hewitt, amb. ex. and plen. Feb2
2003   Richard Kinchen, amb. ex. and plen. Nov15

Belize
HIGH COMMISSIONERS
1984   John Michael Crosby. Oct19
1987   Peter Alexander Bremner Thomson. Nov10
1991   David Patrick Robert Mackilligin. Feb13
1995   Gordon Meldrum Baker. March30
1998   Timothy James David. April15
2001   Philip John Priestley. July16
2004   David Alan Jones. Nov

Benin
1986   Martin (later Sir M) Kenneth Ewans, amb. ex. and plen. Aug8
1988   Brian (later Sir B) Leon Barder, amb. ex. and plen. Sept23
1991   (Alastair) Christopher (later Sir C) Donald Summerhayes MacRae, amb. ex. and plen. June17
1994   (John) Thorold Masefield, amb. ex. and plen. May14
1997   Graham (later Sir G) Stuart Burton, amb. ex. and plen. May2
2001   Philip (later Sir P) Lloyd Thomas, amb. ex. and plen. March5
2004   Richard Hugh Turton Gozney, amb. ex. and plen. June

Bolivia
1985   Alan White, amb. ex. and plen. March9
1987   Colum John Sharkey, amb. ex. and plen. Aug19
1989   Michael Francis Daly, amb. ex. and plen. June4
1991   Richard Michael Jackson, amb. ex. and plen. May15
1995   David Frederick Charles Ridgway, amb. ex. and plen. June1
1998   Graham Leslie Minter, amb. ex. and plen. Aug15
2001   William Baldie Sinton, amb. ex. and plen. Oct15

Bosnia and Herzegovina
1994   Robert William Barnett, amb. ex. and plen. April26
1995   Bryan Hopkinson, amb. ex. and plen. March30
When Yugoslavia broke up "The Republic of Bosnia and Herzegovina" emerged as a new country. At Dayton in 1995 it was agreed that the country should be renamed "Bosnia and Herzegovina". This took effect in 1996
1996   Charles Graham Crawford, amb. ex. and plen. July2
1998   Graham Stewart Hand, amb. ex. and plen. July25
2001   Ian Cameron Cliff, amb. ex. and plen. Oct19

Botswana
HIGH COMMISSIONERS
1986   Peter Albert Raftery. Feb21
1989   Brian Smith. Feb18
1991   John Coates Edwards. Nov19

1994   David Colin Baskcomb Beaumont. Dec19
1998   John Wilde. May17
2001   David Byron Merry. Aug18

Brazil
1984   John Burns Ure, amb. ex. and plen. Feb26
1987   Michael John Newington, amb. ex. and
       plen. Dec15
1992   Peter William (later Sir P) Heap, amb. ex.
       and plen. Aug4
1995   Donald Keith Haskell, amb. ex. and plen.
       May15
1999   Roger (later Sir R) Bridgland Bone, amb.
       ex. and plen. May20
2004   Peter Salmon Collecott, amb. ex. and plen.
       July

Brunei
HIGH COMMISSIONERS
1986   Roger Westbrook. Sept8
1991   Adrian John Sindall. April9
1994   Ivan (later Sir I)Roy Callan. July7
1998   Stuart Laing. July27
2002   Andrew John Forbes Caie. Jan16

Bulgaria
1986   John Harold Fawcett, amb. ex. and plen.
       Aug30
1989   Richard Thomas, amb. ex. and plen. May5
1994   Roger Guy Short, amb. ex. and plen. Sept29
1998   Richard Stagg, amb. ex. and plen. July 8
2001   (Samuel) Ian Soutar, amb. ex. and plen.
       Dec3
2004   Peter Jeremy Oldham Hill, amb. ex. and
       plen. Jan

Burkina
(Country re-named on 3August 1984)
1988   Veronica Evelyn Sutherland, amb. ex. and
       plen. Jan26
1990   Margaret Irene Rothwell, amb. ex. and plen.
       Dec17
1997   Haydon Boyd Warren-Gash, amb. ex. and
       plen. Oct7
2001   Jean Francois Gordon, amb. ex. and plen.
       June7
2004   David Coates, amb. ex. and plen. Aug

Burma
1986   Martin Robert Morland, amb. ex. and plen.
       Oct19
1990   Julian Dana Nimmo Hartland-Swann, amb.
       ex. and plen. May5
1995   Robert Anthony Eagleson Gordon, amb. ex.
       and plen. Sept6
1999   John Jenkins, amb. ex. and plen. April26
2002   Victoria Jane Bowman, amb. ex. and plen.
       Dec16

Burundi
1984   Nicholas Peter Bayne, amb. ex. and plen.
       Feb7
1985   Patrick Howard Caines Eyers, amb. ex. and
       plen. Sept23
1987   Robert Linklater Burke Cormack, amb. ex.
       and plen. June11
1994   Edward Clay, amb. ex. and plen. Sept19

1995   Kaye Wight Oliver, amb. ex. and plen.
       Dec11
1998   Graeme Neil Loten, amb. ex. and plen.
       May11
2001   Susan Elizabeth Hogwood, amb. ex. and
       plen. July26
2004   Jeremy James Macadie, amb. ex. and plen.
       Oct

Cambodia
1994   Paul Reddicliffe, amb. ex. and plen. June24
1997   Christopher George Edgar, amb. ex. and
       plen. July29
2000   Stephen John Bridges, amb. ex. and plen.
       Dec17
2005   David George Reader, amb. ex. and plen.
       Jan

Cameroon
AMBASSADORS
1984   Michael John Carlisle Glaze, amb. ex. and
       plen. July7
1987   Martin Reith, amb. ex. and plen. Oct15
1991   William Ernest Quantrill, amb. ex. and plen.
       April16
1995   Nicholas Melvyn McCarthy, amb. ex. and
       plen. April11
In 1995 Cameroon joined the Commonwealth.
HIGH COMMISSIONERS
1998   George Peter Richard Boon. Feb8
2002   Richard James Wildash. July15

Canada
HIGH COMMISSIONERS
1984   Sir Derek (Malcolm) Day. Aug1
1987   Sir Alan Bedford Urwick. Dec4
1989   Brian (later Sir B) James Proetel Fall. Oct5
1992   Nicholas (later Sir N) Peter Bayne. April7
1996   Anthony (later Sir A) Michael Goodenough.
       March6
2000   Sir (Robert) Andrew Burns. July7
2003   David Norman Reddaway. Aug15

Cape Verde
1986   John Esmond Campbell Macrae, amb. ex.
       and plen. June17
1990   Roger Campbell Beetham, amb. ex. and
       plen. Oct18
1993   Alan Edwin Furness, amb. ex. and plen.
       Oct13
1997   David Raymond Snoxell, amb. ex. and plen.
       April 26
2000   Edward Alan Burner, amb. ex. and plen.
       Aug10
2004   Peter Newall, amb. ex. and plen. May

Central African Republic
1985   Michael John Carlisle Glaze, amb. ex. and
       plen. Feb9
1987   (vacant)
1988   Martin Reith, amb. ex. and plen. July2
1991   William Ernest Quantrill, amb. ex. and plen.
1998   George Peter Richard Boon, amb. ex. and
       plen. Feb8
2002   Richard James Wildash, amb. ex. and plen.
       July15

Chad
1985 Michael Francis Daly, amb. ex. and plen.
      March20
1987 Maeve Geraldine Fort, amb. ex. and plen.
      March7
1990 Charlotte Susanna Rycroft, amb. ex. and
      plen. March19
1991 William Ernest Quantrill, amb. ex. and plen.
      June
1994 John Thorold Masefield, amb. ex. and plen.
      May14
1995 Nicholas Melvyn McCarthy, amb. ex. and
      plen. April11
1998 George Peter Richard Boon, amb. ex. and
      plen. Feb8
2002 Richard James Wildash, amb. ex. and plen.
      July15

Chile
1987 Alan White, amb. ex. and plen. July31
1990 Richard Alvin Neilson, amb. ex. and plen.
      Aug31
1993 Frank Basil Wheeler, amb. ex. and plen.
      Oct27
1997 Madelaine (later Dame M) Glynne Dervel
      Evans, amb. ex. and plen. June8
2000 Leo Gregory Faulkner, amb. ex. and plen.
      April1
2003 Richard Denys Wilkinson, amb. ex. and
      plen. June16

China
1984 Sir Richard Mark Evans, amb. ex. and plen.
      Jan19
1988 Alan (later Sir A) Ewen Donald, amb. ex.
      and plen. May14
1991 Sir Robin John Taylor McLaren, amb. ex.
      and plen. June5
1994 Sir Leonard Vincent Appleyard, amb. ex.
      and plen. Sept8
1997 Anthony (later Sir A) Charles Galsworthy,
      amb. ex. and plen. May21
2002 Christopher (later Sir C) Owen Hum, amb.
      ex. and plen. March19

Colombia
1987 Richard Alvin Neilson, amb. ex. and plen.
      Feb5
1990 Keith (later Sir K) Elliott Hedley Morris,
      amb. ex. and plen. Sept26
1994 (Arthur) Leycester (later Sir Leycester)
      Scott Coltman, amb. ex. and plen. Nov1
1998 Jeremy Walter Thorp, amb. ex. and plen.
      May,31
2001 Thomas (later Sir T) Joseph Duggin, amb.
      ex. and plen. Aug16

Comoros
1984 James Nicholas Allan, amb. ex. and plen.
      June7
1986 Richard Borman Crowson, amb. ex. and
      plen. Aug29
1989 Michael Edward Howell, amb. ex. and plen.
      Sept27
1991 Dennis Oltrieve Amy, amb. ex. and plen.
      May14
1992 Peter John Smith, amb. ex. and plen. Oct20

1996 Robert Scott Dewar, amb. ex. and plen.
      April14
1999 Charlie Mochan, amb. ex. and plen.
      March30
2002 Brian Donaldson, amb. ex. and plen. Oct10

Congo (Democratic Republic)
1985 Patrick Howard Caines Eyers, amb. ex. and
      plen. Feb24
1987 Robert Linklater Burke Cormack, amb. ex.
      and plen. June11
1991 Roger Westbrook, amb. ex. and plen. July30
1996 Marcus Laurence Hulbert Hope, amb. ex.
      and plen. Jan21
1998 Doug Scrafton CMG, amb. ex. and plen.
      June15
2000 James Oswald Atkinson, amb. ex. and plen.
      May3
2004 Andrew James Sparkes, amb. ex. and plen.
      July

Costa Rica
1986 Michael Francis Daly, amb. ex. and plen.
      June6
1989 William Marsden, amb. ex. and plen.
      April14
1992 Mary Louise Croll, amb. ex. and plen. July5
1995 Richard Michael Jackson, amb. ex. and
      plen. Sept1
1997 Alan Stanley Green, amb. ex. and plen.
      Sept10
1999 Peter Joseph Spiceley, amb. ex. and plen.
      Jan5
2002 Georgina Susan Butler, amb. ex. and plen.
      March8

Côte d'Ivoire - See Ivory Coast

Croatia
1992 Bryan Sparrow, amb. ex. and plen. July23
1994 Gavin Wallace Hewitt, amb. ex. and plen.
      June16
1997 Colin Andrew Munro, amb. ex. and plen.
      Aug8
2000 Nicholas Jarrold, amb. ex. and plen. Nov10

Cuba
1984 (Patrick) Robin (later Sir R) Fearn, amb. ex.
      and plen. Feb29
1986 Andrew Eustace Palmer, amb. ex. and plen.
      July15
1989 (Anthony) David Brighty, amb. ex. and plen.
      Jan22
1991 (Arthur) Leycester (later Sir Leycester)
      Scott Coltman, amb. ex. and plen. March3
1994 Philip Alexander McLean, amb. ex. and
      plen. Nov25
1998 David Frederick Charles Ridgway, amb. ex.
      and plen. July27
2001 Paul Webster Hare, amb. ex. and plen. July11
2004 John Anthony Dew, amb. ex. and plen. Oct

Cyprus
HIGH COMMISSIONERS
1988 The Hon. Humphrey Maud. Sept7
1990 David (later Sir David) John Michael Dain.
      July4
1994 David Christopher Andrew Madden. May14

1999   Edward Clay. March12
2001   Lyn Parker. Sept16

Czech Republic
1985   Stephen Jeremy Barrett, amb. ex. and plen. March8
1988   (Peter) Laurence O'Keeffe, amb. ex. and plen. Nov1
1991   (Anthony) David Brighty, amb. ex. and plen. July21
1994   Sir Michael St Edmund Burton, amb. ex. and plen. Sept19
1997   David Stuart Broucher, amb. ex. and plen. Oct1
2001   Anne Fyfe Pringle, amb. ex. and plen. Nov8
2004   Linda Joy Duffield, amb. ex. and plen. Dec

Denmark
1986   Peter William Unwin, amb. ex. and plen. July9
1989   Nigel Christopher Ransome Williams, amb. ex. and plen. Jan4
1993   Hugh James Arbuthnott, amb. ex. and plen. June6
1996   Andrew Philip Foley Bache, amb. ex. and plen. Nov8
1999   Philip Astley, amb. ex. and plen. June4
2003   Sir Nicholas Walker Browne, amb. ex. and plen. Aug18

Djibouti
1985   David Everard Tatham, amb. ex. and plen. Jan14
1988   Mark Anthony Marshall, amb. ex. and plen. Jan18
1993   (Robert) Douglas Gordon, amb. ex. and plen. March20
1994   Duncan Robin Carmichael Christopher, amb. ex. and plen. April1
1997   Gordon Geoffrey Wetherell, amb. ex. and plen. Sept11
2000   Myles Antony Wickstead, amb. ex. and plen. Nov9
2004   Robert Scott Dewar, amb. ex. and plen. March

Dominica
1986   Kevin Francis Xavier Burns. Oct19
1991   Emrys Thomas Davies. Feb20
1994   Richard Thomas. Oct7
1998   Gordon Meldrum Baker. March8
2001   (Charles) John Branford White. Aug11

Dominican Republic
1985   Michael John Newington, amb. ex. and plen. July7
1988   Giles Eden FitzHerbert, amb. ex. and plen. May11
1993   John Gerrard Flynn, amb. ex. and plen. April4
1995   Dick Thomson, amb. ex. and plen. Sept.15
1998   David Gordon Ward, amb. ex. and plen. Sept18
2002   Andrew Richard Ashcroft, amb. ex. and plen. July30

East Timor
BRITISH REPRESENTATIVES
New British Mission (Dili) was formally opened in January 2000
2000   Dominic James Robert Jermey, Brit. Rep. Jan5
2000   Jane Elizabeth Mary Penfold, Brit. Rep. Nov21
On the 20th May 2002 East Timor became independent. The British Mission is now an Embassy.
2002   Hamish St Clair Daniel, amb. ex. and plen. May20
2003   Tina Susan Redshaw, amb. ex. and plen. Jan

Ecuador
1985   Michael William Atkinson, amb. ex. and plen. June28
1989   Frank Basil Wheeler, amb. ex. and plen. Aug18
1993   Richard Douglas Lavers, amb. ex. and plen.Nov18.
1997   John William Forbes-Meyler, amb. ex. and plen. June27
2000   Ian Gerken, amb. ex. and plen. Feb4.
2003   Richard George Lewington, amb. ex. and plen. June1

Egypt
1985   Sir Alan Bedford Urwick, amb. ex. and plen. Feb15
1987   (William) James (later Sir J) Adams, amb. ex. and plen. Dec14
1992   Christopher William Long, amb. ex. and plen. April26
1995   David Elliott Spiby Blatherwick, amb. ex. and plen. April25
1999   Graham (later Sir G) Boyce, amb. ex. and plen. Feb10
2001   (Robert) John Sawers, amb. ex. and plen. Sept19
2003   Sir Derek John Plumbly, amb. ex. and plen. Sept16

El Salvador
1984   Bryan Oliver White, amb. ex. and plen. Dec5
1987   David Joy, amb. ex. and plen. Sept8
1989   Peter John Streams, amb. ex. and plen. Sept13
1991   Michael Henry Connor, amb. ex. and plen. Nov25
1995   Ian Gerken, amb. ex. and plen. July1
1999   Patrick Morgan, amb. ex. and plen. July5
2003   Richard Douglas Lavers, amb. ex. and plen. (Accredited) Aug

Equatorial Guinea
1985   Michael John Carlisle Glaze, amb. ex. and plen. April25
1987   Martin Reith, amb. ex. and plen. Nov26
1991   William Ernest Quantrill, amb. ex. and plen.
1998   George Peter Richard Boon, amb. ex. and plen. Feb8
2002   Richard James Wildash, amb. ex. and plen. July15

Eritrea
1994   Duncan Robin Carmichael Christopher, amb. ex. and plen. April29
1997   Gordon Geoffrey Wetherell, amb. ex. and plen. Sept11
2000   Myles Antony Wickstead, amb. ex. and plen. Nov9
2002   Michael Thomas Murray, amb. ex. and plen. March17

Estonia
1991   Brian Buik Low, amb. ex. and plen. Oct8
1994   Charles Richard Lucien de Chassiron, amb ex. and plen. Oct15
1997   Timothy James Craddock, amb. ex. and plen. Sept20
2000   Sarah Squire, amb. ex. and plen. Sept6
2003   Nigel Robert Haywood, amb. ex. and plen. Nov22

Ethiopia
1986   Harold (later Sir H) Berners Walker, amb. ex. and plen. April29
1990   Michael John Carlisle Glaze, amb. ex. and plen. March21
1994   Duncan Robin Carmichael Christopher, amb. ex. and plen. April18
1997   Gordon Geoffrey Wetherell, amb. ex. and plen. Sept11
2000   Myles Antony Wickstead, amb. ex. and plen. Nov9
2004   Robert Scott Dewar, amb. ex. and plen. March

Fiji
AMBASSADORS
†1988 Roger Arnold Rowlandson Barltrop, amb. ex. and plen. March1
1989   (Alexander Basil) Peter Smart, amb. ex. and plen. Aug19
1992   Timothy James David, amb. ex. and plen. March14
†From 1March 1988, the British High Commission became the British Embassy
1995   Michael John Peart, amb. ex. and plen. April14.
1997   Michael Alan Charles Dibben, amb. ex. and plen. Dec3
2000   Michael Anthony Price, amb. ex. and plen. Oct16
2002   Charles Francis Mochan, amb. ex. and plen. Nov16

Finland
1986   (Hubert Anthony) Justin Staples, amb. ex. and plen. Feb25
1989   (George) Neil Smith. Nov21
1995   David Allan Burns, amb. ex. and plen. March9.
1997   Gavin Wallace Hewitt, amb. ex. and plen. Sept15
2001   Alyson Judith Kirtley Bailes, amb. ex. and plen. Jan5
2002   Matthew John Lushington Kirk, amb. ex. and plen. July24

France
1987   Sir Ewen Alastair John Fergusson, amb. ex. and plen. June22
1993   Sir Christopher Leslie George Mallaby, amb. ex. and plen. Jan29
1996   Sir Michael Hastings Jay, amb. ex. and plen. July10
2001   Sir John Eaton Holmes, amb. ex. and plen. Oct16

Gabon
1985   Ronald Henry Thomas Bates amb. ex. and plen. Feb18
1986   Mark Aubrey Goodfellow, amb. ex. and plen. Feb3
1990   Philip John Priestley, amb. ex. and plen. Nov22
1994   William Ernest Quantrill, amb. ex. and plen. Aug12
1995   Nicholas Melvyn McCarthy, amb. ex. and plen. April11
1998   George Peter Richard Boon, amb. ex. and plen. Feb8
2002   Richard James Wildash, amb. ex. and plen. July15

Gambia, The
HIGH COMMISSIONERS
1984   John Donald Garner. Nov6
1988   Alec Ibbott. Feb20
1990   Alan John Pover. Oct12
1994   Michael John Hardie. Jan7
1995   John Wilde. Feb13
1998   Tony Millson. March13
2000   John Gayford Perrott. April1
2002   Eric Jenkinson. Oct1

Georgia
1992   Sir Brian James Proetel Fall, amb. ex. and plen. June22
1995   Stephen Thomas Nash, amb. ex. and plen. Oct15
1998   Richard Thomas Jenkins, amb. ex. and plen. Jan27
2001   Deborah Elizabeth Vavasseur Barnes Jones, amb. ex. and plen. Apr6
2004   Donald MacLaren, amb. ex. and plen.

Germany
1984   Sir Julian Leonard Bullard, amb. ex. and plen. Sept1
1988   Sir Christopher Leslie George Mallaby, amb. ex. and plen. March20
1993   Nigel Hugh Robert Allen Broomfield, amb. ex. and plen. Jan17
1997   Sir Christopher Meyer, amb. ex. and plen. March5
1997   Sir Paul Lever, amb. ex. and plen. Dec31
2003   Sir Peter James Torry, amb. ex. and plen. May1

German Democratic Republic
1984   Timothy John Everard, amb. ex. and plen. Aug21
1988   Nigel Hugh Robert Allen Broomfield, amb. ex. and plen. May10

1990   Patrick Howard Eyers, amb. ex. and plen.
       Jan26

On 3 October 1990 the German Democratic
Republic ceased to exist.

Ghana
HIGH COMMISSIONERS
1986   Arthur Hope Wyatt. Oct24
1989   Anthony Michael Goodenough. Oct16
1992   David Critchlow Walker. June14
1996   Ian Warren Mackley. July21
2000   Roderick Allen Pullen. Oct11
2004   Gordon Geoffrey Wetherell. March

Greece
1985   Sir Jeremy Cashel Thomas, amb. ex. and
       plen. June6
1989   Sir (Henry) David Alastair Capel Miers,
       amb. ex. and plen. May24
1993   (Richard) Oliver Miles, amb. ex. and plen.
       July19
1996   Michael (later Sir M) John Llewellyn Smith,
       amb. ex. and plen. April4
1998   David (later Sir D) Christopher Andrew
       Madden, amb. ex. and plen. Dec,8
2004   Simon Lawrence Gass, amb. ex. and plen.
       Dec

Grenada
HIGH COMMISSIONERS
1986   Kevin Francis Xavier Burns. Oct19
1991   Emrys Thomas Davies. Feb5
1994   Richard Thomas. Oct7
1998   Gordon Meldrum Baker. March8
2001   (Charles) John Branford White. Aug11

Guatemala
1987   Bernard Jonathan Everett, amb. ex. and
       plen. June25
1991   Justin Patrick Pearse Nason, amb. ex. and
       plen. March22
1995   Peter Marcus Newton, amb. ex. and plen.
       March28
1998   Andrew John Forbes Caie, amb. ex. and
       plen. July21
2001   Richard Douglas Lavers, amb. ex. and plen.
       Oct25

Guinea
1986   John Esmond Campbell Macrae, amb. ex.
       and plen. May6
1990   Roger Campbell Beetham, amb. ex. and
       plen. Nov29
1994   Alan Edwin Furness, amb. ex. and plen.
       April21
1997   David Raymond Snoxell, amb. ex. and plen.
       April4
2000   David Alan Jones, amb. ex. and plen. May4
2003   Helen Margaret Horn, amb. ex. and plen.
       Aug21

Guinea Bissau
1986   John Esmond Campbell Macrae, amb. ex.
       and plen. May30
1990   Roger Campbell Beetham, amb. ex. and
       plen. April12
1994   Alan Edwin Furness, amb. ex. and plen.
       Jan18

1997   David Raymond Snoxell, amb. ex. and plen.
       April4
2000   Edward Alan Burner, amb. ex. and plen.
       Aug10
2004   Peter Newall, amb. ex. and plen. May

Guyana
HIGH COMMISSIONERS
1985   John Dudley Massingham. April6
1987   David Purvis Small, July16
1990   (Robert) Douglas Gordon, Oct24
1993   David John Johnson, March22
1998   Edward Glover, Nov19
2002   Stephen John Hiscock, Aug29

Haiti
1984   (Harold) Martin Smith Reid, amb. ex. and
       plen. March9
1987   Alan Jeffrey Payne, amb. ex. and plen.
       Oct15
1989   Derek Francis Milton, amb. ex. and plen.
       June29
1995   Anthony Richard Thomas, amb. ex and
       plen. Oct15
1998   David Gordon Ward, amb. ex. and plen.
       Sept18
2002   Andrew Richard Ashcroft, amb. ex. and
       plen. May2

Holy See
1985   David Neil Lane, amb. ex. and plen. May16
1988   John Kenneth Elliott Broadley, amb. ex. and
       plen. May18
1991   Andrew Eustace Palmer, amb. ex. and plen.
       Aug21
1995   Maureen Elizabeth MacGlashan, amb. ex.
       and plen. May27.
1998   Mark Edward Pellew, amb. ex. and plen.
       Jan1
2002   Kathryn Frances Colvin, amb. ex. and plen.
       July16

Honduras
1984   Bryan Oliver White, amb. ex. and plen.
       Nov20
1987   David Joy, amb. ex. and plen. July17
1989   Peter John Streams, amb. ex. and plen.
       July30
1992   Patrick Morgan, amb. ex. and plen. Jan30
1995   Peter Rodney Holmes, amb. ex. and plen.
       Aug3
1998   David Allan Osborne, amb. ex. and plen.
       July31
2002   Kay Coombs, amb. ex. and plen. Sept2

Hong Kong Special Administrative Region
CONSULS-GENERAL
1997   (Robert) Francis Cornish. July1
1997   Sir (Robert) Andrew Burns. Nov 26
2000   Sir James William Hodge. Aug26
2003   Stephen Edward Bradley. Dec1

Hungary
1986   Leonard Vincent Appleyard, amb. ex. and
       plen. July30
1989   John (later Sir J) Allan Birch, amb. ex. and
       plen. Aug21

1995   Christopher William Long, amb. ex. and
       plen. June2.
1998   Nigel James Thorpe, amb. ex. and plen.
       Aprl7
2003   John Roland Nichols, amb. ex. and plen.
       Aug6

Iceland
1986   Mark Fenger Chapman, amb. ex. and plen.
       Oct8
1989   Richard (later Sir R) Radford Best, amb. ex.
       and plen. March15
1991   Patrick Francis Wogan, amb. ex. and plen.
       Sept16
1993   Michael Stuart Hone, amb. ex. and plen.
       June21
1996   James Rae McCulloch, amb. ex. and plen.
       May12
2001   John Howard Culver, amb. ex. and plen.
       Jan15
2004   Alper Mehmet, amb. ex. and plen. April16

India
HIGH COMMISSIONERS
1986   Sir (Arthur) David Saunders Goodall.
       April2
1991   Sir Nicholas Maxted Fenn. Nov13
1996   The Hon. David (later the Hon Sir D)
       Alwyn Gore-Booth. March9
1999   Sir (John) Rob(ertson) Young. Jan18
2003   Michael (later Sir M) Anthony Arthur.
       Oct16

Indonesia
1984   Alan Ewen Donald, amb. ex. and plen.
       May16
1988   (William) Kelvin Kennedy White, amb. ex.
       and plen. March9
1990   Roger John Carrick, amb. ex. and plen.
       Aug3
1994   Graham Stuart Burton, amb. ex. and plen.
       Aug18
1997   (Duncan) Robin Carmichael Christopher,
       amb. ex. and plen. April13
2000   (Richard) Hugh Turton Gozney, amb. ex.
       and plen. Aug16
2004   Charles Thomas William Humfrey, amb. ex.
       and plen. March

Iran
1988   Gordon Andrew Pirie, Chargé d'Affaires a.i.
       Dec4
1989   Nicholas Walker Browne, Chargé d'Affaires
       a.i. Feb1
1990   David Norman Reddaway, Chargé
       d'Affaires a.i. Oct28
1993   Jeffrey Russell James, Chargé d'Affaires a.i.
       Aug16
1997   Nicholas Walker Browne, Chargé d'Affaires
       a.i. Nov13
1999   Nicholas Walker Browne, amb. ex. and plen.
       May
1999   Richard Anthony Neil Crompton, Chargé
       d'Affaires a.i. May24
2002   Richard John Dalton, amb. ex.and plen. Nov

Iraq
1985   Terence Josph Clark, amb. ex. and plen.
       March18
1990   Harold (later Sir H) Berners Walker amb.
       ex. and plen. Feb9
1991   Embassy Staff Withdrawn.
Diplomatic relations with Iraq were broken off
with effect from 6 February 1991.
An Iraqi Interim Government endorsed by the UN
assumed authority for governing Iraq on 28 June
2004. Diplomatic relations were re-established on
that date and the new British Embassy was opened
in Baghdad.
2004   Edward Graham Mellish Chaplin, amb. ex.
       and plen. July1

Ireland
1986   Nicholas (later Sir N) Maxted Fenn, amb.
       ex. and plen. Dec7
1991   David Elliott Spiby Blatherwick, amb. ex.
       and plen. Sept10
1995   Veronica (later Dame V) Evelyn Sutherland,
       amb. ex. and plen. March29
1999   Ivor (later Sir I) Anthony Roberts, amb. ex.
       and plen. Feb20
2003   Stewart Graham Eldon, amb. ex. and plen.
       Apr14

Israel
1984   (Clifford) William Squire, amb. ex. and
       plen. Sept11
1988   Mark Elliott, amb. ex. and plen. June19
1992   Robert Andrew Burns, amb. ex. and plen.
       July12
1995   David Geoffrey Manning, amb. ex. and
       plen. Nov11
1998   Francis Cornish, amb. ex. and plen. Sept7
2001   Sherard Louis Cowper-Coles, amb. ex. and
       plen. Sept16
2003   Simon Gerard McDonald, amb. ex. and
       plen. Aug14

Italy
1987   Sir Derek Morison David Thomas amb. ex.
       and plen. Dec3
1989   Sir Stephen Loftus Egerton, amb. ex. and
       plen. Nov14
1992   Sir Patrick Stanislaus Fairweather, amb. ex.
       and plen. July5
1996   Thomas (later Sir T) Legh Richardson, amb.
       ex. and plen. July10
2000   John (later Sir J) Alan Shepherd, amb. ex.
       and plen. July26
2003   Sir Ivor Anthony Roberts, amb. ex. and
       plen. May5

Ivory Coast (Côte d'Ivoire)
1987   Veronica (later Dame V) Evelyn Sutherland,
       amb. ex. and plen. June27
1990   Margaret Irene Rothwell, amb. ex. and plen.
       Dec17
1997   Haydon Boyd Warren-Gash, amb. ex. and
       plen. Oct7
2001   Jean Francois Gordon, amb. ex. and plen.
       June7
2004   David Coates, amb. ex. and plen. Aug

Jamaica

HIGH COMMISSIONERS
1984 (Harold) Martin Smith Reid. March9
1987 Alan Jeffrey Payne. June23
1989 Derek Francis Milton. April13
1995 Anthony Richard Thomas. Oct1
1999 Anthony Smith. March29
2002 Peter James Mathers. July4

Japan

1984 Sir (Charles) Sydney Rycroft Giffard, amb. ex. and plen. March1
1986 Sir John Stainton Whitehead, amb. ex. and plen. Nov12
1992 Sir John Dixon Ikl Boyd, amb. ex. and plen. July7
1995 David John Wright, amb. ex. and plen. Jan1
1999 Stephen (later Sir S) John Gomersall, amb. ex. and plen. May28
2004 Graham Holbrook Fry, amb. ex. and plen. July

Jordan

1984 (Arthur) John (later Sir J) Coles, amb. ex. and plen. Nov4
1988 Anthony Reeve, amb. ex. and plen. Feb3
1991 Patrick Howard Caines Eyers, amb. ex. and plen. April27
1993 Peter Robert Mossom Hinchcliffe, amb. ex. and plen. Oct19
1997 Christopher Charles Battiscombe, amb. ex. and plen. April14
2000 Edward Graham Mellish Chaplin, amb. ex. and plen. May16
2002 Christopher Norman Russell Prentice, amb. ex. and plen. June1

Kazakhstan

1992 Sir Brian James Proetel Fall, amb. ex. and plen. Sept14
1993 Noel Stephen Andrew Jones, amb. ex. and plen. Oct26
1996 Douglas Baxter McAdam, amb. ex. and plen. March7
1999 Richard George Lewington. Feb7
2002 James Lyall Sharp. Oct1

Kenya

HIGH COMMISSIONERS
1986 John (later Sir J) Rodney Johnson, June15
1990 (William) Roger (later Sir R) Tomkys, Oct19
1992 Sir Kieran Prendergast, Oct19
1995 Simon Nicholas Peter Hemans. April14
1997 Jeffrey Russell James, July7
2001 Edward Clay. Dec16

Kiribati

HIGH COMMISSIONERS
1990 Derek Leslie White. Jan17
1993 Frank McDermott. April14
1994 Timothy James David. Sept1
1995 Michael John Peart. April14
1997 Michael Alan Charles Dibben. Dec3
2000 Michael Anthony Price. Oct16
2002 Charles Francis Mochan. Nov16

Korea, North

New British Embassy (Pyongyang) was formally opened in July 2001
2001 Dr James Edward Hoare, Chargé d'Affaires Feb
2002 David Arthur Slinn, amb. ex. and plen. Oct16

Korea, South

1986 Lawrence John Middleton, amb. ex. and plen. Oct7
1990 David John Wright, amb. ex. and plen. April9
1994 Thomas George Harris, amb. ex. and plen. March19
1997 Sir Stephen David Reid Brown, amb. ex. and plen. April4
2000 Charles Thomas William Humfrey CMG, amb. ex. and plen. July1
2003 Warwick Morris, amb. ex. and plen. Nov1

Kuwait

1985 Sir Peter James Scott Moon, amb. ex. and plen. Feb17
1987 Peter Robert Mossom Hinchcliffe, amb. ex. and plen. May30
1990 Michael (later Sir M) Charles Swift Weston amb. ex. and plen. March18
1992 William Hugh Fullerton, amb. ex. and plen. Aug3
1996 Graham Hugh Boyce, amb. ex. and plen. March17
1998 Richard Muir CMG, amb. ex. and plen. Dec14
2002 Christopher Edward John Wilton, amb. ex. and plen. Aug16

Kyrgyzstan

1992 Sir Brian James Proetel Fall, amb. ex. and plen. Oct26
1994 Noel Stephen Andrew Jones, amb. ex. and plen. Feb2
1996 Douglas Baxter McAdam, amb. ex. and plen. March7
1999 Richard George Lewington. Feb7
2002 James Lyall Sharp. Oct1

Laos

1985 (Hubert Anthony) Justin Staples, April25
1986 Derek Tonkin, amb. ex. and plen. June4
1990 (Michael) Ramsey Melhuish, amb. ex. and plen. Jan24
1992 (Charles) Christian Wilfrid Adams, amb. ex. and plen. March14
1997 Sir James William Hodge, amb. ex. and plen. Sept6
2000 Lloyd Barnaby Smith, amb. ex. and plen. March1
2003 David William Fall, amb. ex. and plen. July25

Latvia

1992 Richard Christopher Samuel, amb. ex. and plen. Feb2
1993 Richard Peter Ralph, amb. ex. and plen. Aug8
1996 Nicholas Robert Jarrold, amb. ex. and plen. Feb1

1999   Stephen Thomas Nash CMG, amb. ex. and
       plen. July16
2002   (Harcourt) Andrew Pretorius Tesoriere, amb.
       ex. and plen. March28.

Lebanon
1985   John (later Sir J)Walton David Gray, amb.
       ex. and plen. Nov28
1988   Allan John Ramsay, amb. ex. and plen.
       June16
1990   David Everard Tatham, amb. ex. and plen.
       April28
1992   Maeve (later Dame M) Geraldine Fort, amb.
       ex. and plen. July31
1996   David Ross MacLennan, amb. ex. and plen.
       Oct9
2000   Richard Kinchen, amb. ex. and plen. Dec16
2003   James Wilfrid Watt, amb. ex. and plen.
       Oct16

Lesotho
HIGH COMMISSIONERS
1984   Peter Edward Rosling. March5
1988   John Coates Edwards. May31
1992   James Roy Cowling. Feb1
1996   Peter John Smith. April1
1998   Kaye Oliver. Dec15
2002   Francis James Martin. April19

Liberia
1985   Alec Ibbott, amb. ex. and plen. April19
1988   Michael Edward John Gore, amb. ex. and
       plen. Feb2
1990   Margaret Irene Rothwell, amb. ex. and plen.
       Dec17
1997   Haydon Boyd Warren-Gash, amb. ex. and
       plen. Oct7
2001   Jean Francois Gordon, amb. ex. and plen.
       June7
2004   David Coates, amb. ex. and plen. Aug

Libya
1984   (Richard) Oliver Miles, amb. ex. and plen.
       Jan5
Diplomatic and Consular relations with Libya were
broken off with effect from 30 April 1984
1999   Richard John Dalton CMG, amb. ex. and plen.
       Nov30
2002   Anthony Michael Layden, amb. ex. and
       plen. Oct31

Liechtenstein
1991   Christopher William Long, amb. ex. and
       plen. Dec12
1992   David Beattie, amb. ex. and plen. May21
1997   Christopher Hulse, amb. ex. and plen.
       April1
2001   Basil Stephen Talbot Eastwood, amb. ex.
       and plen. Aug15
2004   Simon Mark Featherstone, amb. ex. and
       plen. March20

Lithuania
1991   Michael John Peart, amb. ex. and plen. Oct8
1995   Thomas Townley Macan, amb. ex. and plen.
       Jan1
1995   Christopher William Robbins, amb. ex. and
       plen. July28

2001   Peter Jeremy Oldham Hill, amb. ex. and
       plen. Sept16
2004   Colin Roberts, amb. ex. and plen. March

Luxembourg
1985   (Richard) Oliver Miles, amb. ex. and plen.
       Feb26
1988   Juliet Jeanne d'Auvergne Campbell, amb.
       ex. and plen. Feb24
1991   The Hon. Michael Pakenham, amb. ex. and
       plen. Oct19
1994   John Nicholas Elam, amb. ex. and plen.
       May23
1998   William Ehrman, amb. ex. and plen. Sept13
2000   Gordon Geoffrey Wetherell, amb. ex. and
       plen. Sept5
2004   James Frame Clark, amb. ex. and plen.
       March

Macedonia
1993   Tony Millson, amb. ex. and plen. Dec23
1997   Woodman Mark Lowes Dickinson, amb. ex.
       and plen. April14
2001   Christopher George Edgar, amb. ex. and
       plen. Sept28
2004   Robert Maurice French Chatterton Dickson,
       amb. ex. and plen. July

Madagascar
1984   (David) Malcolm McBain, amb. ex. and
       plen. Oct2
1987   Anthony Victor Hayday, amb. ex. and plen.
       Dec28
1990   Dennis Oldrieve Amy, amb. ex. and plen.
       April26
1993   Peter John Smith, amb. ex. and plen. Jan2
1996   Robert Scott Dewar, amb. ex. and plen.
       April14
1999   Charles Francis Mochan, amb. ex. and plen.
       July2
2002   Brian Donaldson, amb. ex. and plen. Oct10

Malawi
HIGH COMMISSIONERS
1987   Denis Gordon Osborne. Aug17
1990   (William) Nigel Wenban-Smith. Nov3
1993   John Francis Ryde Martin. Oct1
1998   George Finlayson. May15
2001   Norman Arthur Ling. Sept23
2004   David Dacre Pearey. Dec

Malaysia
HIGH COMMISSIONERS
1986   (John) Nicholas (later Sir N) Teague
       Spreckley Oct31
1992   Duncan Slater. March10
1994   David Joseph Moss. Aug15
1998   Graham Fry. June23
2001   Bruce Elliot Cleghorn. Nov17

†Maldives
†From 9July 1982 the British Embassy became a
High Commission
HIGH COMMISSIONERS
1984   John Anthony Benedict Stewart. Nov11
1987   David Arthur Stewart Gladstone. June29
1991   Edward John Field. Dec30
1996   David Everard Tatham, March31

1999 Linda Joy Duffield. Jan18
2002 Stephen Nicholas Evans. July16

Mali
1986 John Esmond Campbell Macrae, amb. ex. and plen. March21
1990 Roger Campbell Beetham, amb. ex. and plen. Nov6
1993 Alan Edwin Furness, amb. ex. and plen. Sept3
1997 David Raymond Snoxell, amb. ex. and plen. April4
2000 Edward Alan Burner, amb. ex. and plen. Aug10
2001 Graeme Neil Loten, amb. ex. and plen. Oct1
2003 Edward Alan Burner, amb. ex. and plen. (Re-accredited) June
2004 Peter Newall, amb. ex. and plen. May

Malta
HIGH COMMISSIONERS
1985 Stanley Frederick St Clair Duncan. May3
1988 Brian Hitch. Jan10
1991 Peter (later Sir P) Gordon Wallis. Oct29
1995 Graham Robertson Archer. Jan3
1999 Howard John Pearce. June14
2002 Vincent Fean. Sept16

Marshall Islands
1992 Derek Leslie White, amb. ex. and plen. July22
1996 Vernon Marcus Scarborough, amb. ex. and plen. July23
2000 Christopher Haslam, amb. ex. and plen. Jan15
2003 Ian Francis Powell, amb. ex. and plen. March1

Mauritania
1986 John Esmond Campbell Macrae, amb. ex. and plen. April24
1993 Sir Allan John Ramsey, amb. ex. and plen. April26
1996 William Hugh Fullerton, amb. ex. and plen. April17
1999 Anthony Layden, amb. ex. and plen. March16
2002 Haydon Boyd Warren-Gash, amb. ex. and plen. July11

Mauritius
HIGH COMMISSIONERS
1985 Richard Borman Crowson. Dec11
1989 Michael Edward Howell. Aug12
1993 John Clive Harrison. May5
1997 James Daly. May30
2000 David Snoxell. Sept21
2004 Anthony Godson. Nov

Mexico
1986 John (later Sir J) Albert Leigh Morgan, amb. ex. and plen. May21
1989 Michael (later Sir M) Keith Orlebar Simpson-Orlebar, amb. ex. and plen. July27
1992 Sir Roger Blaise Ramsay Hervey, amb. ex. and plen. March2
1994 Adrian John Beamish, amb. ex. and plen. Oct2

1998 Adrian Charles Thorpe CMG, amb. ex. and plen. Oct30
2002 Denise Mary Holt, amb. ex. and plen. June15

Micronesia
1992 Derek Leslie White, amb. ex. and plen. July22
1996 Vernon Marcus Scarborough, amb. ex. and plen. July23
2000 Christopher Haslam, amb. ex. and plen. Jan15
2003 Ian Francis Powell, amb. ex. and plen. March1

Moldova
1992 Sir Brian James Proetel Fall, Aug28
1995 Sir Andrew Marley Wood. July12
1999 Richard Peter Ralph. Aug27
2002 Bernard Gerrard Whiteside. April16

Mongolia
1984 Allan Geoffrey Roy Butler, amb. ex. and plen. Oct11
1987 Guy William Pulbrook Hart, amb. ex. and plen. March19
1989 David Keith Sprague, amb. ex. and plen. April20
1991 Anthony Bernard Nicholas Morey, amb. ex. and plen. May29
1994 Ian Christopher Sloane, amb. ex. and plen. Jan18
1997 John Clive Durham, amb. ex. and plen. March1
1999 Kay Coombs, amb. ex. and plen. July30
2001 Philip Terence Rouse, amb. ex. and plen. Dec15
2004 Richard James Austen, amb. ex. and plen. Feb27

Morocco
1985 Ronald Archer Campbell Byatt, amb. ex. and plen. Jan28
1987 John William Richmond Shakespeare amb. ex. and plen. Nov15
1990 John Esmond Campbell Macrae, amb. ex. and plen. June12
1992 Sir Allan John Ramsey, amb. ex. and plen. Dec21
1996 William Hugh Fullerton, amb. ex. and plen. April17
1999 Anthony Layden, amb. ex. and plen. March16
2002 Haydon Boyd Warren-Gash, amb. ex. and plen. July11

Mozambique
1984 Eric Victor Vines, amb. ex. and plen. Feb6
1986 James Nicholas Allan, amb. ex. and plen. Feb21
1989 Maeve (later Dame M) Geraldine Fort, amb. ex. and plen. Sept10
1992 Richard John Smale Edis, amb. ex. and plen. Aug10
1996 Bernard Jonathan Everett, amb. ex. and plen. Jan1

2000 Robert Scott Dewar, amb. ex. and plen. Aug4
2003 Howard Parkinson, amb. ex. and plen. Dec15

Namibia
HIGH COMMISSIONERS
1990 Francis Neville Richards. June4
1992 Henry George Hogger. Oct3
1996 Glyn Davies. Feb1
1999 Brian Donaldson. Jan17
2002 Alasdair Tormod MacDermott, April16

Nauru
HIGH COMMISSIONERS
1990 (Alexander Basil) Peter Smart. March15
1995 Michael John Peart. April14
1997 Michael Alan Charles Dibben. Dec3
2000 Michael Anthony Price. Oct16
2002 Charles Francis Mochan. Nov16

Nepal
1987 Richard Eagleson Gordon Burges Watson, amb. ex. and plen. March1
1990 Timothy John Burr George, amb. ex. and plen. Oct16
1995 Lloyd Barnay Smith, amb. ex. and plen. Dec9
1999 Ronald Nash, amb. ex. and plen. March26
2002 Keith George Bloomfield, amb. ex. and plen. June27

Netherlands
1984 John (later Sir J) William Denys Margetson, amb. ex. and plen. Nov30
1988 Michael Romilly Heald Jenkins, amb. ex. and plen. Jan23
1993 Sir (Henry) David Alastair Miers, amb. ex. and plen. July1
1996 Dame Rosemary Jane Spencer, 1999, amb. ex. and plen. Nov15
2001 Colin (later Sir C) Richard Budd, amb. ex. and plen. Apr4

New Zealand
HIGH COMMISSIONERS
1984 Terence Daniel O'Leary. July24
1987 Ronald Archer Campbell Byatt. Dec15
1990 David Joseph Moss. Sept27
1994 Robert Alston. Aug1
1998 Martin Williams OBE. Apr15
2001 Richard Taylor Fell. Dec10

Nicaragua
1986 Michael Francis Daly, amb. ex. and plen. July14
1989 William Marsden, amb. ex. and plen. April19
1991 Roger Hugh Brown, amb. ex. and plen. Dec3
1992 John Howard Culver, amb. ex. and plen. Nov25
1997 Roy Paul Osborne, amb. ex. and plen. July15
2000 Harry Wiles, amb. ex. and plen. Sept
2002 Timothy Patrick Brownbill, amb. ex. and plen. Nov1

Niger
1987 Veronica (later Dame V) Evelyn Sutherland, amb. ex. and plen. Oct16
1990 Margaret Irene Rothwell, amb. ex. and plen. July10
1997 Haydon Boyd Warren-Gash, amb. ex. and plen. Oct7
2001 Jean Francois Gordon, amb. ex. and plen. June7
2004 David Coates, amb. ex. and plen. Aug

Nigeria
HIGH COMMISSIONERS
1986 Sir Martin Kenneth Ewans. Feb28
1988 Brian (later Sir B) Leon Barder. July27
1991 (Alastair) Christopher Donald Summerhayes MacRae. March7
1994 (John) Thorold Masefield. May14
1997 Graham (later Sir G) Stuart Burton. May2
2001 Philip (later Sir P) Lloyd Thomas. March5
2004 Richard Hugh Turton Gozney. June

Norway
1987 John Adam (later Sir J) Robson, amb. ex. and plen. March9
1990 David John Edward Ratford, amb. ex. and plen. May7
1994 Mark Elliott CMG, amb. ex. and plen. June4
1998 Richard (later Sir R) Dales, amb. ex. and plen. July3
2002 Alison Mariot Leslie, amb. ex. and plen. Sept5

Oman
1986 Robert John Alston, amb. ex. and plen. June3
1990 Terence Joseph (later Sir T) Clark, amb. ex. and plen. Jan29
1994 Richard John Sutherland Muir, amb. ex. and plen. June5
1999 Sir Ivan Callan amb. ex. and plen. Feb15
2002 (John) Stuart Laing, amb. ex. and plen. April12

†Pakistan
AMBASSADORS
1984 Richard Alwyne Fyjis-Walker, amb. ex. and plen. Oct12
1987 Nicolas John (later Sir N) Barrington, amb. ex. and plen. July20
HIGH COMMISSIONERS
†1989 Nicholas (later Sir N) John Barrington. Oct1
1994 Sir (Alastair) Christopher Donald Summerhayes MacRae, May31
1997 David (later Sir D) John Michael Dain, May5
2000 Hilary Nicholas Hugh Synnott. Oct15
2003 Mark Justin Lyall Grant. May15
†From 30January 1972, the British High Commission became the British Embassy, then from 1October 1989 it reverted to the British High Commission

Palau
1996 Vernon Marcus Scarborough, amb. ex. and plen. July23

2000 Christopher Haslam, amb. ex. and plen. Jan15

2003 Ian Francis Powell, amb. ex. and plen. March1

Panama
1986 Margaret Bryan, amb. ex. and plen. April9

1990 John Grant MacDonald, amb. ex. and plen. Jan6

1992 Thomas Herbert Malcomson, amb. ex. and plen. Jan31

1996 William Baldie Sinton OBE, amb. ex. and plen. Jan19

1999 Robert Harold Davies, amb. ex. and plen. March15

2002 James Ian Malcolm, amb. ex. and plen. March16

Papua New Guinea
HIGH COMMISSIONERS
1986 Michael Edward Howell. Jan27

1989 (Edward) John Sharland. June11

1991 John Westgarth Guy. July12

1994 Brian Buik Low. Dec12

1997 Charles Drace-Francis. Dec16

2000 Simon Mansfield Scaddan. March1

2003 David Scott Gordon-Macleod. Nov1

Paraguay
1984 Bernard Coleman, amb. ex. and plen. Jan19

1986 John Grant MacDonald, amb. ex. and plen. May3

1989 Terence Harry Steggle, amb. ex. and plen. May31

1991 Michael Alan Charles Dibben, amb. ex. and plen. March2

1995 Graham John Campbell Pirnie, amb. ex. and plen. Aug31

1998 Andrew Neil George, amb. ex. and plen. Oct15

2001 Anthony John James Cantor, amb. ex. and plen. Nov16

Peru
1987 Adrian John Beamish, amb. ex. and plen. Dec16

1990 (Donald) Keith Haskell, amb. ex. and plen. Feb11

1995 John Illman, amb. ex. and plen. May5

1999 Roger Hart, amb. ex. and plen. June4

2003 Richard Peter Ralph, amb. ex. and plen. May1

Philippines
1985 Robin John Taylor McLaren, amb. ex. and plen. May15

1987 Keith Gordon MacInnes, amb. ex. and plen. April27

1992 Alan Everard Montgomery, amb. ex. and plen. July11

1995 Adrian Charles Thorpe, amb. ex. and plen. July8

1998 Alan Stanley Collins CMG, amb. ex. and plen. Dec31

2002 Paul Stephen Dimond, amb. ex. and plen. April1

Poland
1986 Brian (later Sir B)Leon Barder, amb. ex. and plen. May27

1988 Stephen (later Sir S) Jeremy Barrett, amb. ex. and plen. Aug20

1991 Michael John Llewellyn Smith, amb. ex. and plen. Sept20

1996 Christoper Owen Hum, amb. ex. and plen. May6

1998 John Macgregor, amb. ex. and plen. Sept7

2001 The Hon Michael (later the Hon. Sir M) Aidan Pakenham, amb. ex. and plen. Jan5

2003 Charles Graham Crawford, amb. ex. and plen. Dec

Portugal
1986 Michael Keith Orlebar Simpson-Orlebar, amb. ex. and plen. March15

1989 Hugh James Arbuthnott, amb. ex. and plen. Aug23

1993 (John) Stephen (later Sir S) Wall, amb. ex. and plen. May31

1995 Roger Westbrook, amb. ex. and plen. July24

1999 John (later Sir John) Holmes, amb. ex. and plen. June14

2001 Dame (Madelaine) Glynne Dervel Evans, amb. ex. and plen. Sept16

2004 John Stephen Buck, amb. ex. and plen. Sept

Qatar
1984 Julian Fortay Walker, amb. ex. and plen. Oct10

1987 Patrick Michael Nixon, amb. ex. and plen. June11

1990 Graham Hugh Boyce, amb. ex. and plen. Feb27

1993 Patrick Francis Michael Wogan, amb. ex. and plen. Oct23

1997 David Alan Wright OBE, amb. ex. and plen. June4

2002 David Ross MacLennan, amb. ex. and plen. June15

Romania
1986 Hugh James Arbuthnott, amb. ex. and plen. Nov14

1989 Michael William Atkinson, amb. ex. and plen. Sept4

1992 Andrew Philip Foley Bache, amb. ex. and plen. April15

1996 Christopher Donald Crabbie, amb. ex. and plen. June30

1999 Richard Peter Ralph, amb. ex. and plen. Aug27

2002 Quinton Mark Quayle, amb. ex. and plen. Nov2

Russian Federation
1992 Sir Brian James Proetel Fall, amb. ex. and plen. June3

1995 Sir Andrew Marley Wood, amb. ex. and plen. July12

2000 Sir Roderic Michael Lyne, amb. ex. and plen. Jan14

2004 Anthony Russell Brenton, amb. ex. and plen. Sept

Rwanda
1984   Nicholas Peter Bayne, amb. ex. and plen. Feb7
1985   Patrick Howard Caines Eyers, amb. ex. and plen. Aug20
1987   Robert Linklater Burke Cormack, amb. ex. and plen. June11
1991   Roger Westbrook, amb. ex. and plen. July30
1994   Edward Clay, amb. ex. and plen. Jan10
1995   Kaye Wight Oliver, amb. ex. and plen. Dec11
1998   Graeme Neil Loten, amb. ex. and plen. May11
2001   Susan Elizabeth Hogwood, amb. ex. and plen. July26
2004   Jeremy James Macadie, amb. ex. and plen. Oct

Saint Kitts and Nevis
HIGH COMMISSIONERS
1986   Kevin Francis Xavier Burns. Oct19
1991   Emrys Thomas Davies. Feb13
1994   Richard Thomas. Oct7
1998   Gordon Meldrum Baker. March8
2001   (Charles) John Branford White. Aug11

St Lucia
HIGH COMMISSIONERS
1986   Kevin Francis Xavier Burns. Oct19
1991   Emrys Thomas Davies. Feb13
1994   Richard Thomas. Oct7
1998   Gordon Meldrum Baker. March8
2001   (Charles) John Branford White. Aug11

St Vincent and the Grenadines
HIGH COMMISSIONERS
1986   Kevin Francis Xavier Burns. Oct19
1991   Emrys Thomas Davies. Feb11
1994   Richard Thomas. Oct7
1998   Gordon Meldrum Baker. March8
2001   (Charles) John Branford White. Aug11

Samoa
HIGH COMMISSIONERS
1984   Terence Daniel O'Leary. July24
1987   Ronald Archer Campbell Byatt. Dec15
1991   David Joseph Moss. Aug6
1994   Robert Alston. Aug1
1998   Martin Williams. Apr15
2001   Richard Taylor Fell. Dec10

São Tomé and Principe
1986   Patrick Staislaus Fairweather, amb. ex. and plen. June9
1988   Michael John Carlisle Glaze, amb. ex. and plen. March25
1990   John Gerrard Flynn, amb. ex. and plen. May22
1993   Anthony Richard Thomas, amb. ex. and plen. April27
1996   Roger Dudley Hart, amb. ex. and plen. Sept18
1999   Caroline Elmes, amb. ex. and plen. Sept14
2002   John Thompson, amb. ex. and plen. Feb21

Saudi Arabia
1984   Sir Patrick Richard Henry Wright, amb. ex. and plen. Sept4

1986   Stephen (later Sir S) Loftus Egerton, amb. ex. and plen. April20
1989   Alan (later Sir A) Gordon Munro, amb. ex. and plen. Aug16
1993   The Hon. David Alwyn Gore-Booth, amb. ex. and plen. April4
1996   Andrew (later Sir A) Fleming Green, amb. ex. and plen. March27
2000   Derek (later Sir D) John Plumbly, amb. ex. and plen. June15
2003   Sherard (later Sir S) Louis Cowper-Coles, amb. ex. and plen. Sept

Senegal
1985   John Esmond Campbell Macrae, amb. ex. and plen. Dec18
1990   Roger Campbell Beetham, amb. ex. and plen. July7
1993   Alan Edwin Furness, amb. ex. and plen. Aug24
1997   David Raymond Snoxell, amb. ex. and plen. April4
2000   Edward Alan Burner, amb. ex. and plen. Aug10
2004   Peter Newall, amb. ex. and plen. May

Serbia and Montenegro (formerly Yugoslavia)
2001   Charles Graham Crawford, CMG, amb. ex. and plen. Jan12
2003   David John Gowan, amb. ex. and plen. Sept14

Seychelles
HIGH COMMISSIONERS
1986   (Alexander Basil) Peter Smart. Sept30
1989   Guy William Pulbrook Hart. June22
1992   Edward John Sharland. Jan24
1995   Peter Alexander Bremner Thomson. Feb17
1997   John William Yapp. Nov1
2002   Fraser Andrew Wilson. May7
2004   Diana Skingle. July

Sierra Leone
HIGH COMMISSIONERS
1984   Richard Dennis Clift. Sept7
1986   Derek William Partridge. June6
1991   David Keith Sprague. May30
1993   Ian McCluney. Sept23
1997   Peter Alfred Penfold. March10
2000   David Alan Jones. May4
2003   Dr John Edward Mitchiner. Aug1

Singapore
HIGH COMMISSIONERS
1985   Sir (William Erskine) Hamilton Whyte. March16
1987   Michael (later Sir M) Edmund Pike. July13
1991   Gordon Aldridge Duggan. Jan12
1997   Alan Charles Hunt. Aug8
2001   Sir Stephen David Reid Brown. March1
2002   Alan Stanley Collins. Dec14

Slovakia
1993   David Brighty, amb. ex. and plen.
1994   Michael Charles Bates, amb. ex. and plen. July1
1995   Peter Gale Harborne, amb. ex. and plen. Feb20

1998 David Edward Lyscom, amb. ex. and plen. Oct15
2001 Damian Roderic Todd, amb. ex. and plen. Nov16
2004 Judith Anne Macgregor, amb. ex. and plen. June

Slovenia
1992 Gordon Mackenzie Johnston, amb. ex. and plen. Aug25
1997 David Andrew Lloyd, amb. ex. and plen. Feb21
2001 Hugh Roger Mortimer, amb. ex. and plen. Jan1

Solomon Islands
HIGH COMMISSIONERS
1986 John Bramble Noss. March17
1988 (David) Junor Young. Oct10
1991 Raymond Francis Jones. May12
1995 Brian Norman Connelly. Dec31
1998 Alan Waters. Sept1.
2001 Brian Paul Baldwin. May16
2004 Richard John Lyne. Dec

Somali Democratic Republic
1987 Jeremy Richard Lovering Grosvenor Varcoe, amb. ex. and plen. Feb15
1989 Ian McCluney, amb. ex. and plen. July9

South Africa
AMBASSADORS
†1984 Patrick (later Sir P) Hamilton Moberly, amb. ex. and plen. Oct8
†1987 Robin (later Sir R) William Renwick, amb. ex. and plen. July24
†1991 Anthony (later Sir A) Reeve, amb. ex. and plen. July1
HIGH COMMISSIONERS
1994 Sir Anthony Reeve. June1
1996 Maeve (later Dame Maeve) Geraldine Fort. Nov11
2000 Ann Grant. Oct1
†From 10 May 1961, the British High Commission became the British Embassy, then from 1June 1994 it reverted to the British High Commission.

Soviet Union now see Russian Federation
1985 Sir Bryan George Cartledge, amb. ex. and plen. July18
1988 Sir Rodric Quentin Braithwaite, amb. ex. and plen. Sept20

Spain
1984 Lord Nicholas Charles Gordon Lennox, amb. ex. and plen. July2
1989 (Patrick) Robin (later Sir R) Fearn, amb. ex. and plen. Nov23
1994 Anthony David Brighty, amb. ex. and plen. Sept1
1998 Peter (later Sir P) James Torry, amb. ex. and plen. Sept2
2003 Stephen John Leadbetter Wright, amb. ex. and plen. May

Sri Lanka
HIGH COMMISSIONERS
1984 John Antony Benedict Stewart. Nov11

1987 David Arthur Stuart Gladstone. June29
1991 Edward John Field. Nov22
1996 David Everard Tatham. March21
1999 Linda Duffield. Jan18
2002 Stephen Nicholas. Evans, July16

Sudan
1984 Sir Alexander John Dickson Stirling, amb. ex. and plen. Sept1
1986 John Lewis Beaven, amb. ex. and plen. Dec3
1990 Allan John Ramsay, amb. ex. and plen. June23
1991 Peter John Streams, amb. ex. and plen. Nov29
1995 Alan Fletcher Goulty, amb. ex. and plen. March23
1999 Richard Edward Makepeace, amb. ex. and plen. July13
2002 William Charters Patey, amb. ex. and plen. Sept1

Surinam
1985 John Dudley Massingham, amb. ex. and plen. July3
1987 David Purvis Small, amb. ex. and plen. July16
1991 (Robert) Douglas Gordon, amb. ex. and plen. April27
1993 David John Johnson, amb. ex. and plen. Feb19
1998 Edward Glover, Nov19
2002 Stephen John Hiscock, Aug29

Swaziland
HIGH COMMISSIONERS
1987 John Gerrard Flynn. May26
1990 Brian Watkins. May20
1993 Richard Hugh Turton Gozney. Aug8
1996 John Frederick Doble. Feb29
1999 Neil Kenneth Hook. Oct4
2001 David (George) Reader. Sept26
2004 George Thomas Squires, Nov3

Sweden
1984 Sir Richard Edmund Clement Fownes Parsons, amb. ex. and plen. July26
1987 Sir John Burns Ure, amb. ex. and plen. Dec7
1991 Robert Linklater Burke Cormack, amb. ex. and plen. June17
1995 Roger (later Sir R) Bridgland Bone, amb. ex. and plen. Sept1
1999 John Douglas Kelso Grant CMG, amb. ex. and plen. April6
2003 Anthony Joyce Cary, amb. ex. and plen. Oct2

Switzerland
1985 John Rowland Rich, amb. ex. and plen. May2
1988 Christopher William Long, amb. ex. and plen. July25
1992 David Beattie, amb. ex. and plen. May5
1997 Christopher Hulse, amb. ex. and plen. April
2001 Basil Stephen Talbot Eastwood, amb. ex. and plen. Aug15

2004 Simon Mark Featherstone, amb. ex. and plen. March20

Syria
The Syrian Republic severed Diplomatic and Consular Relations with the United Kingdom on 6June 1967 until 28May 1973
1984 (William) Roger Tomkys, amb. ex. and plen. Nov13

Diplomatic and Consular relations with the Syrian Arab Republic were broken off with effect from 31October 1986. They were resumed on 28November 1990
1991 Andrew (later Sir A)Fleming Green, amb. ex. and plen. Feb17
1994 Adrian John Sindall, amb. ex. and plen. May28
1996 Basil Stephen Talbot Eastwood, amb. ex. and plen. Sept30
2000 Henry George Hogger, amb. ex. and plen. June12
2003 Peter Ford, amb. ex. and plen. Sept5

Tajikistan
1994 Alexander Paul A'Court Bergne, amb. ex. and plen. Jan27
1995 Barbara Logan Hay, amb. ex. and plen. May15
1999 Christopher Ingham, amb. ex. and plen. Feb3
2002 Michael Forbes Smith, amb. ex. and plen. May26
2004 Graeme Neil Loten, amb. ex. and plen. June

Tanzania
HIGH COMMISSIONERS
Diplomatic Relations were broken off with Tanzania from 15December 1965 to 4July 1968
1986 Colin (later Sir C) Henry Imray. Jan6
1989 (John) Thorold Masefield. July22
1992 Roger Westbrook. Sept30
1995 Alan Everard Montgomery. July15
1998 Bruce Harry Dinwiddy. April22
2001 Richard Ian Clarke. Aug2
2003 Andrew John Pocock. Sept22

Thailand
1986 Derek Tonkin, amb. ex. and plen. Feb18
1989 (Michael) Ramsay Melhuish amb. ex. and plen. Nov7
1992 Charles Christian Wilfrid Adams, amb. ex. and plen. March14
1996 James (later Sir J) William Hodge, amb. ex. and plen. Sept6
2000 Lloyd Barnaby Smith, amb. ex. and plen. March1
2003 David William Fall, amb. ex. and plen. July25

Togo
1986 Arthur Hope Wyatt, amb. ex. and plen. Oct24
1989 Anthony Michael Goodenough, amb. ex. and plen. Dec5
1992 David Crithlow Walker, amb. ex. and plen. June16

1996 Ian Warren Mackley CMG, amb. ex. and plen. Jul7
2000 Roderick Allen Pullen, amb. ex. and plen. Oct 11
2004 Gordon Geoffrey Wetherell, amb. ex. and plen. March

Tonga
HIGH COMMISSIONERS
1984 Gerald Francis Joseph Rance. Jan4
1987 Andrew Paul Fabian. March7
1990 William Lawson Cordiner. April3
1994 Andrew James Morris. Nov8
1998 Brian Connelly. Aug20
2002 Paul William Downs Nessling. Jan14

Trinidad and Tobago
HIGH COMMISSIONERS
1985 Martin (later Sir M) Seymour Berthoud. April11
1991 Brian Smith. Nov11
1996 Leo Gregory Faulkner. July3
1999 Peter Gale Harborne. July15
2004 Ronald Peter Nash. Jan16

Tunisia
1984 (William) James Adams, amb. ex. and plen. Aug21
1987 Stephen Peter Day, amb. ex. and plen. Dec17
1992 Michael Logan Tait, amb. ex. and plen. July9
1995 Richard John Smale Edis, amb. ex. and plen. Dec4
1999 Ivor Rawlinson, amb. ex. and plen. Feb15
2002 Robin Andrew Kealy, amb. ex. and plen. Jan15
2004 Alan Fletcher Goulty, amb. ex. and plen. Oct

Turkey
1986 Timothy (later Sir T) Lewis Achilles Daunt, amb. ex. and plen. Nov1
1992 Peter John Goulden, amb. ex. and plen. Oct23
1995 Sir (Walter) Kieran Prendergast, amb. ex. and plen. March23
1997 David Brian Carleton Logan, amb. ex. and plen. March28
2002 Peter (later Sir P) John Westmacott, amb. ex. and plen. Jan15

Turkmenistan
1993 Sir Brian James Proetel Fall, amb. ex. and plen. Jan31
1995 Neil Kenneth Hook, amb. ex. and plen. Sept15
1998 Fraser Wilson MBE, amb. ex. and plen. July6
2002 Paul Brummell, amb. ex. and plen. Feb16

Tuvalu
HIGH COMMISSIONERS
1989 (Alexander Basil) Peter Smart. Nov29
1995 Michael John Peart. April14
1997 Michael Alan Charles Dibben. Dec3
2000 Michael Anthony Price. Oct16
2002 Charles Francis Mochan. Nov16

Uganda

HIGH COMMISSIONERS
Diplomatic Relations were broken off on 28July
1976 until 21April 1979
1986 Derek (later Sir D) Maxwell March. June29
1989 Charles Augustine Kaye Cullimore. Dec21
1993 Edward Clay. Oct1
1997 Michael Edgar Cook. April10
2000 Tom Richard Vaughan Phillips. May15
2002 Adam Wood. Oct14

Ukraine

1992 David Arthur Stewart Gladstone, Chargé
     d'Affaires. Jan17
1992 Simon Nicholas Peter Hemans, amb. ex. and
     plen. June4
1995 Roy Stephen Reeve, amb. ex. and plen.
     June5
1999 Roland Hedley Smith, amb. ex. and plen.
     May16
2002 Robert Edward Brinkley, amb. ex. and plen.
     Aug3

United Arab Emirates

1986 Michael Logan Tait, amb. ex. and plen.
     April27
1990 Graham Stuart Burton, amb. ex. and plen.
     Feb6
1994 Anthony Davis Harris, amb. ex. and plen.
     June25
1998 Patrick Michael Nixon, amb. ex. and plen.
     Nov1
2003 Richard Edward Makepeace, amb. ex. and
     plen. Feb21

United States

1986 Sir Antony Arthur Acland, amb. ex. and
     plen. Aug28
1991 Sir Robin William Renwick, amb. ex. and
     plen. Aug20
1995 Sir John Olav Kerr, amb. ex. and plen.
     Aug15
1997 Sir Christopher Meyer, amb. ex. and plen.
     Oct31
2003 Sir David Geoffrey Manning, amb. ex. and
     plen. Aug

Uruguay

1986 Eric Victor Vines, amb. ex. and plen.
     March14
1989 Colum John Sharkey, amb. ex. and plen.
     July14
1991 Donald Alexander Lamont, amb. ex. and
     plen. July14
1994 Robert Andrew Michie Hendrie, amb. ex.
     and plen. Sept1
1998 Andrew Murray, amb. ex. and plen. May23
2001 John Vivian Everard. ex. and plen. Sept4

Uzbekistan

1992 Sir Brian James Proetel Fall, amb. ex. and
     plen. Oct21
1993 Alexander Paul A'Court Bergne, amb. ex.
     and plen. Oct29
1995 Barbara Logan Hay, amb. ex. and plen.
     May15

1999 Christopher Ingham, amb. ex. and plen.
     Feb3
2002 Craig John Murray, amb. ex. and plen.
     Sept16

Vanuatu

HIGH COMMISSIONERS
1985 Malcolm Lars Creek. Aug27
1988 John Thompson. March25
1992 Thomas Joseph Duggin. Jan15
1997 Malcolm Geoffrey Hilson.
2000 Michael Thomas Hill. Nov16

Vatican City (see Holy See)

Venezuela

1985 Michael John Newington, amb. ex. and
     plen. April28
1988 Giles Eden FitzHerbert, amb. ex. and plen.
     Jan18
1993 John Gerrard Flynn, amb. ex. and plen.
     April4
1997 Richard Denys Wilkinson, amb. ex. and
     plen. May2
2000 Dr Edgar John Hughes, amb. ex. and plen.
     July22
2003 Donald Alexander Lamont, amb. ex. and
     plen. July31

South Vietnam

(Vietnam was formally unified in July 1976)

Vietnam

1985 Richard Gilbert Tallboys, amb. ex. and plen.
     June12
1987 Emrys Thomas Davies, amb. ex. and plen.
     May27
1990 Peter Keegan Williams, amb. ex. and plen.
     Oct27
1997 David William Fall, amb. ex. and plen.
     Apr25
2000 Warwick Morris, amb. ex. and plen. June16
2003 Robert Anthony Eagleson Gordon, amb. ex.
     and plen. Sept16

Yemen

1984 David Everard Tatham, amb. ex. and plen.
     Sept19
1987 Mark Anthony Marshall, amb. ex. and plen.
     Nov23
1993 (Robert) Douglas Gordon, amb. ex. and
     plen. March20
1995 Douglas Scrafton amb. ex. and plen.
     March4
1997 Victor Joseph Henderson CMG, amb. ex. and
     plen. Oct19
2001 Frances Mary Guy, amb. ex. and plen.
     March9
2004 Michael John Gifford, amb. ex. and plen.
     July

Yemen (People's Democratic Republic of)

1986 Arthur Stirling-Maxwell Marshall, amb. ex.
     and plen. Jan4
1989 (Robert) Douglas Gordon, amb. ex. and
     plen. Jan29

The People's Democratic Republic of Yemen and
the Yemen Arab Republic merged on 22May 1990
to become the Republic of Yemen

Yugoslavia (Federal Republic of) (now see Serbia and Montenegro)

1996   Ivor (later Sir I) Antony Roberts, amb. ex.
       and plen. May6
1997   Joseph Brian Donnelly, amb. ex. and plen.
       Nov17

Diplomatic Relations with The Federal Republic of
Yugoslavia were broken off with effect from 26
March 1999 and were restored on 17 November
2000.

2000   David Maurice Landsman, OBE, Chargé
       d'Affaires Nov17

Zambia

HIGH COMMISSIONERS

1984   (William) Kelvin Kennedy White. Sept10
1988   John Michael Wilson. Jan21
1990   Peter Robert Mossom Hinchcliffe. May19
1994   Patrick Michael Nixon. Feb1
1998   Thomas Nesbitt Young. Jan3
2002   Timothy James David. May16

Zimbabwe

HIGH COMMISSIONERS

1985   (Michael) Ramsay Melhuish. Feb20
1989   (Walter) Kieran (later Sir K) Prendergast.
       Aug10
1992   Richard Nigel Dales. Sept21
1995   Martin John Williams. Nov28
1998   Peter Longworth. Apr7
2001   Joseph Brian (later Sir B) Donnelly. June30

In December 2003 the British High Commission in
Zimbabwe bacame the British Embassy.

AMBASSADORS

2004   Dr Roderick Allen Pullen, amb. ex. and
       plen. July

CHRONOLOGICAL LIST OF BRITISH REPRESENTATIVES TO INTERNATIONAL ORGANISATIONS 1984-2004/5

UNITED KINGDOM MISSION TO THE UNITED NATIONS

New York

1987   Sir Crispin Charles Cervantes Tickell, Perm.
       Rep. and Rep. on the Security Council with
       personal rank of amb. May29
1990   Sir David Hugh Alexander Hannay, Perm.
       Rep. and Rep. on the Security Council with
       personal rank of amb. Sept7
1995   Sir (Philip) John Weston, Perm. Rep. and
       Rep. on the Security Council with personal
       rank of amb. July15
1998   Sir Jeremy Quentin Greenstock, Perm. Rep.
       and Rep. on the Security Council with
       personal rank of amb. Aug8
2003   Sir Emyr Jones Parry, Perm. Rep. and Rep.
       on the Security Council with personal rank
       of amb. July1

UNITED KINGDOM MISSON TO THE OFFICE OF THE UNITED NATIONS AND OTHER INTERNATIONAL ORGANISATIONS AT GENEVA

1985   John Anthony Sankey, Perm. Rep. with
       personal rank of amb. Dec17
1990   Martin Robert Morland, Perm. Rep. with
       personal rank of amb. July13
1993   Nigel Christopher Ransome Williams, Perm.
       Rep. with personal rank of amb. Sept15
1997   Roderic Michael Lyne, Perm. Rep. with
       personal rank of amb. May1
2000   Simon William Fuller, Perm. Rep. with
       personal rank of amb. Jan16
2003   Nicholas Alan Thorne, Perm. Rep. with
       personal rank of amb. Nov30

UNITED KINGDOM DELEGATION TO THE CONFERENCE ON DISARMAMENT (formerly the UK Delegation to the Conference of the 18-Nation Committee on Disarmament) Geneva

1987   Tessa Audrey Hilda Solesby, Leader of Del.
       with personal rank of amb. Oct10
1992   Sir Michael Charles Swift Weston, Leader
       of Del. with personal rank of amb. April6
1997   (Samuel) Ian Soutar, Leader of Del. with
       personal rank of amb. Aug8
2001   David Stuart Broucher, Leader of Del. with
       personal rank of amb. Oct1
2004   Dr John PatrickGeorge Freeman, Leader of
       Del. with personal rank of amb. Sept

UNITED KINGDOM DELEGATION TO THE NORTH ATLANTIC TREATY ORGANISATION

Brussels

1986   Michael (later Sir M) O'Donel Bjarne
       Alexander, Perm. Rep. on the North Atlantic
       Council with personal rank of amb. Aug30
1992   Sir (Philip) John Weston, Perm. Rep. on the
       North Atlantic Council with personal rank
       of amb. Jan25
1995   Peter John Goulden, Perm. Rep. on the
       North Atlantic Council with personal rank
       of amb. April1
2000   David (later Sir D) Geoffrey Manning,
       Perm. Rep. on the North Atlantic Council
       with personal rank of amb. Dec
2001   Dr Emyr Jones Parry, Perm. Rep. on the
       North Atlantic Council with personal rank
       of amb. Sept16
2003   Peter Forbes Ricketts, Perm. Rep. on the
       North Atlantic Council with personal rank
       of amb. July1

UNITED KINGDOM DELEGATION TO THE WESTERN EUROPEAN COUNCIL

Brussels

1993   Sir (Philip) John Weston, Perm. Rep. on the
       Permanent Council of the Western European
       Union with personal rank of amb. Jan1

UNITED KINGDOM DELEGATION TO THE ORGANISATION FOR ECONOMIC CO-OPERATION AND DEVELOPMENT

Paris

1985 Nicholas Peter Bayne, Perm. Rep. with personal rank of amb. Oct1

1988 John Walton David Gray, Perm. Rep. with personal rank of amb. July11

1992 Keith Gordon MacInnes, Perm. Rep. with the personal rank of amb. July1

1995 Peter William Medlicott Vereker, Perm. Rep. with the personal rank of amb. Sept1

1999 Christopher Crabbie, Perm. Rep. with the personal rank of amb. June11

2004 David Edward Lyscom, Perm. Rep. with the personal rank of amb. Jan1

OFFICE OF THE UNITED KINGDOM PERMANENT REPRESENTATIVE TO THE EUROPEAN UNION (formerly UK Delegation to the European Communities)

Brussels

1985 David (later Sir D) Hugh Alexander Hannay, Perm. Rep. with personal rank of amb. Oct14

1990 John (later Sir J) Olav Kerr, Perm. Rep. with personal rank of amb. Sept2

1995 John (later Sir S) Stephen Wall, Perm. Rep. with personal rank of amb. Aug15

2000 Nigel (later Sir N) Elton Sheinwald, Perm. Rep. with personal rank of amb. Aug31

2003 John Douglas Kelso Grant, Perm. Rep. with personal rank of amb. Aug1

UNITED KINGDOM DELEGATION TO THE COUNCIL OF EUROPE

Strasbourg

1986 Colin McLean, Perm. Rep. with personal rank of amb. Aug6

1990 Noel Hedley Marshall, Perm. Rep. with personal rank of amb. Sept6

1993 Roger Campbell Beetham, Perm. Rep. with personal rank of amb. Aug1

1997 Andrew Carter, Perm. Rep. with personal rank of amb. Aug1

2003 Stephen Frederick Howarth, Perm. Rep. with personal rank of amb. March1

UNITED KINGDOM MISSION TO THE INTERNATIONAL ATOMIC ENERGY AGENCY, THE UNITED NATIONS INDUSTRIAL DEVELOPMENT ORGANISATION AND THE UNITED NATIONS (VIENNA) (formerly UK Mission to the IAEA and to UN Organisations at Vienna)

Vienna

1987 Gerald Edmund Clark, Perm. Rep. with personal rank of amb. June3

1992 Christopher Hulse, Perm. Rep. with personal rank of amb. Nov26

1997 John Patrick George Freeman, Perm. Rep. with personal rank of amb. May2

2001 Peter Redmond Jenkins, Perm. Rep. with personal rank of amb. Aug9

UNITED KINGDOM DELEGATION TO THE CONFERENCE ON SECURITY AND COOPERATION IN EUROPE (OSCE)

Vienna

1989 (John) Michael Edes, Perm. Rep. with personal rank of amb. March6

1990 Paul Lever, Head of Del. with personal rank of amb. May7

1992 Terence Courtney Wood, Head of Del. with personal rank of amb. April4

1993 Simon William John Fuller, Head of Del. with personal rank of amb. Sept1

1999 John Robert de Fonblanque, Head of Del. with personal rank of amb. June16

2003 Colin Andrew Munro, Head of Del. with personal rank of amb. Dec21

CHRONOLOGICAL LIST OF GOVERNORS AND COMMANDERS-IN-CHIEF ETC. OF OVERSEAS TERRITORIES 1984-2004/5 (MEMBERS HM DIPLOMATIC SERVICE ONLY)

Anguilla

1985 Alistair Turner Baillie

1990 Brian George John Canty

1992 Alan William Shave

1995 Alan Norman Hoole

1997 Robert Malcolm Harris

2000 Peter Johnstone

2004 Alan Edden Huckle

Bermuda

1984 Viscount Dunrossil

1988 Major General Sir Desmond Langley

1992 The Rt Hon The Lord Waddington

1997 Thorold Masefield

2002 Sir John Vereker

British Indian Ocean Territory

1986 William Marsden

1988 Richard John Smale Edis

1991 Thomas George Harris

1994 David Ross MacLennan

1996 Bruce Dinwiddy

1999 John White

2001 Alan Edden Huckle

British Virgin Islands

1987 John Mark Ambrose Herdman

1992 Peter Alfred Penfold

1995 David Patrick Robert Mackilligin

1998 Francis Joseph Savage

2000 Thomas Townley Macan

Cayman Islands

1992 Michael Edward John Gore

1995 John Wynne Owen

1999 Peter Smith

2002 Bruce Harry Dinwiddy

Falkland Islands/British Antarctic Islands

1986 Gordon Wesley Jewkes

1989 William Hugh Fullerton

1993 David Edward Tatham

1996 Richard Peter Ralph

1999 Donald Lamont

2002 Howard John Stredder Pearce

Gibraltar
1992   Sir Hugo White
1997   The Rt Hon Sir Richard Luce
2000   David (later Sir D) Robert Campbell Durie
2003   Sir Francis Neville Richards

Montserrat
1985   Arthur Christopher Watson
1987   Christopher John Turner
1990   David Pendleton Taylor
1993   Francis Joseph Savage
1997   Anthony John Abbott
2001   Anthony James Longrigg
2004   Deborah Elizabeth Vavasseur Barnes-Jones

Pitcairn, Henderson, Ducie and Oeno Islands
1985   Terrence Daniel O'Leary
1988   Robert Archer Campbell Byatt
1991   David Joseph Moss
1994   Robert John Alston
1998   Martin Williams
2001   Richard Taylor Fell

St Helena (incl. Ascension and Tristan da Cunha)
1989   Robert Frederick Stimson
1991   Alan Norman Hoole
1995   David Leslie Smallman
1999   David James Hollamby

Turks and Caicos Islands
1987   Michael John Bradley
1993   Martin Bourke
1996   John Philip Kelly
2000   Mervyn Thomas Jones
2002   James Poston

CHRONOLOGICAL LIST OF NON GOVERNMENTAL TRADE OFFICES (ANNEX) 1992-2004/5

Taipei
1992   Philip Morrice
1995   Alan Stanley Collins, CMG
1999   David Coates
2000   Derek Richard Marsh, CVO

**Biographical Notes and
List of Staff**

ABBREVIATIONS

m	married
ptnr	partner
d	daughter
s	son
Diss	Dissolved
Dec'd	Deceased
AUSS	Assistant Under Secretary of State
BOTB	British Overseas Trade Board
CDA	Career Development Attachment
CDE	Conference on Confidence and Security- Building Measures and Disarmament in Europe
CENTO	Central Treaty Organisations
CFE	Negotiations on Conventional Armed Forces in Europe
CO	Cabinet Office
COI	Central Office of Information
CRO	Commonwealth Relations Office
CSBM	Negotiations on Confidence-and Security Building Measures
CSC	Civil Service Commission
CSCE	Conference on Security and Co-operation in Europe
CSD	Civil Service Department
CSO	Chief Security Officer
CSSB	Civil Service Selection Board
DoE	Department of Environment
DETR	Department for Environment, Transport and the Regions
DHC	Deputy High Commissioner
DoI	Department of Industry
DfID	Department for International Development
DS	Diplomatic Service
DSAO	Diplomatic Service Administration Office
DSS	Department of Social Security
DoT	Department of Trade
DTI	Department of Trade and Industry
DUSS	Deputy Under Secretary of State
ECGD	Export Credits Guarantee Department
ECSC	European Coal and Steel Community
ENA	Ecole Nationale d'Administration (Paris)
FCO	Foreign and Commonwealth Office
FO	Foreign Office
HCS	Home Civil Service
HMOCS	Her Majesty's Overseas Civil Service
HO	Home Office
IISS	International Institute for Strategic Studies
JSDC	Joint Services Defence College
MBFR	Mutual Reduction of Forces and Armaments (Vienna)
MECAS	Middle East Centre for Arab Studies
MoD	Ministry of Defence
MPBW	Ministry of Public Buildings and Works
MPNI	Ministry of Pensions and National Insurance
MPO	Management and Personnel Office
NATO	North Atlantic Treaty Organisation
OEEC	Organisation for European Economic Co-operation
OFTEL	Office of Telecommunications
OMCS	Office of the Minister for the Civil Service
POMEF	Political Office Middle East Forces
PRO	Principal Research Officer
RCDS	Royal College of Defence Studies
SEATO	South East Asia Treaty Organisation
SO	Security Officer
SOAS	School of Oriental and African Studies
SOWC	Senior Officers War Course
SRO	Senior Research Officer
SUPL	Special Unpaid Leave
UN	United Nations
UNHCR	United Nations High Commission for Refugees
WO	War Office

Part IV: Biographical List

Statement concerning the present appointments and some other particulars of the careers of established members of Her Majesty's Diplomatic Service.

A

Abayomi, Olufunke Adepeju; Third Secretary (Immigration) Tehran since June 2003; Born 09/04/65; FCO 1995; Transferred to the Diplomatic Service 2003; Band B3; m 1992 Olushola Abayomi (2d 1993, 2000).

Abbott, Belinda-Jayne (née Simmons); FCO since May 2001; Born 12/09/65; FCO 1988; Buenos Aires 1990; Phnom Penh 1996; Band B3; m 2000 Peter Douglas Abbott.

Abbott, David; Second Secretary (Commercial) Madras since September 2001; Born 06/06/64; FCO 1983; Singapore 1985; Africa/ME Floater 1989; Kaduna 1991; Abuja 1993; FCO 1994; Band C4; m 1990 Nor Hayati Binte Ibrahim (1d 1992; 1s 1993).

Abbott, Neil Middleton; FCO since 2004; Born 21/06/65; FCO 1987; Riyadh 1990; FCO 1994; Third Secretary (Chancery/Consular) Abu Dhabi 1996; Third Secretary Ljubljana 1999; Band B3; m 1990 Janet Probyn (diss 2003) (1s 1992; 1d 1995).

Abbott, Nicholas Robert John; First Secretary (Regional Expert, Arab World Projects) Cairo since January 2004; Born 25/04/63; FCO 1985; Language Training 1986; Third Secretary (Chancery/Information) Riyadh 1988; Brussels-Stagiare 1991; Third Secretary (Economic) Paris 1992; Second Secretary (Commercial) Doha 1995; FCO 1998; First Secretary (Economic) Riyadh 2000; m 1989 Marcelle Ghislaine Julienne Delvaux (2d 1995, 1996).

Abbott-Watt, Thorhilda Mary Vivia; HM Ambassador Yerevan since January 2003; FCO 1974; SUPL 1977; FCO 1978; Latin American Floater 1979; Paris 1981; Brussels (UKREP) 1984; Second Secretary FCO 1986; Second Secretary Bonn 1988; First Secretary FCO 1991; First Secretary (Commercial/Know How Fund) Kiev 1995; FCO/Home Office Joint Entry Clearance Unit 1999; ptnr, Reef Talbot Hogg.

Abel, Martin Jeremy; First Secretary Istanbul since December 2001; Born 30/04/51; MPBW 1969; FCO 1971; Paris 1974; Madras 1976; FCO 1978; Luxembourg 1979; Peking 1982; FCO 1984; Istanbul 1988; Wellington 1993; FCO 1997; Band C5; m (1) 1974 Lynne Diane Bailey (diss 1991) (1d 1978; 1s 1980); (2) 1992 Nilufer Fasiha Kantarci (1d 1984).

Abrahams, David William; Second Secretary FCO since August 1983; Born 14/07/53; FCO 1974; Geneva 1978; Brussels 1981; Band C4; m 1978 Susan Joy Denise Gibson (3d 1987, 1988, 1990).

Abrams, Christine Ann; World Wide Floater Duties since May 2002; Born 07/01/64; WRAC 1986-89; Derbyshire Police Force 1995-98; FCO 2000; Band A2.

Ackerman, Erica Alexandra (née Smith); Second Secretary (Commercial) Singapore since November 2001; Born 09/04/63; FCO 1983; Caracas 1985; SUPL 1989; FCO 1995; Third Secretary (Commercial/Aid) Manila 1998; SUPL 1998; Manila 1998; Band C4; m 1989 Robert Joseph Ackerman (dec'd 1992).

Adam, Stuart William; Second Secretary (Political) Vienna (UKDEL - OSCE) since May 2002; Born 20/03/71; FCO 1990; Bonn 1992; Peking 1995; Vienna (Embassy) 2000; Band C4; m 1996 Lesley Elizabeth Quate (1d 2000; 1s 2001).

Adams, Catherine Elizabeth; Assistant Legal Adviser FCO since February 2000; Born 29/11/65; Assistant Legal Adviser FCO 1994; First Secretary (Legal) Brussels (UKREP) 1997; Band D7.

Adams, Geoffrey Doyne, CMG (2003); Private Secretary to the Secretary of State, FCO since July 2003; Born 11/06/57; FCO 1979; Language Training 1980; Third later Second Secretary Jedda 1982; First Secretary ENA Paris 1985; FCO 1986; Private Secretary to the PUS 1987; First Secretary (Head of Political Section) Pretoria/Cape Town 1991; FCO 1994; On loan to (European Secrerariat) Cabinet Office 1996; Counsellor and DHM Cairo 1998; Consul-General Jerusalem 2001; m 1999 Mary Emma Baxter (1d 2003).

Adams, Gillian; FCO since September 2001; Born 10/06/65; MOD 1982; FCO 1984; Nicosia 1986; Africa/Middle East Floater 1989; FCO 1993; Language Training 1997; Brussels (JMO) 1998; Band B3.

Adams, Trevor Malcolm; Deputy Director for Trade and Investment Bangkok since August 2002; Born 16/04/51; FCO 1971; Paris 1973; Middle East Floater 1976; Bucharest 1977; JAO New York 1979; FCO 1982; Vientiane 1984; Rangoon 1985; HM Consul Casablanca 1988; FCO 1993; First Secretary (Press and Public Affairs) Hong Kong 1998; Band C5; m 1979 Linda Jane Burgess (1d 1985).

Adamson, Donald Snaith; FCO since January 2000; Born 03/04/49; Ministry of Social Security 1967; FCO 1968; Khartoum 1971; Brussels (EC) 1972; Wellington 1975; Dacca 1978; loan to ODA 1981; FCO 1983; Cape Town 1985; FCO 1988; Second Secretary (Consular) Islamabad 1992; Second Secretary FCO 1993; Abuja 1996; m 1970 June Alice Manson Hall (1s 1973; 1d 1977).

Adamson, Joanne; Washington since October 2002; Born 09/07/67; FCO 1989; Language Training Cairo 1991; Third later Second Secretary (Chancery/Comm) Jerusalem 1992; On secondment to UNWRA 1999.

Addiscott, Emily Margaret (née Dallas); Seconded to British Trade International later renamed UK Trade and Investment since August 2003; Born 27/05/72; FCO 1991; SUPL 1994; Kiev 1996; SUPL 1997; Band A2; m 1993 Fraser John Addiscott (2d 1997, 1999).

Addiscott, Fraser John; Seconded to British Trade International later renamed UK Trade and Investment since May 2002; Born 04/09/71; FCO 1990; Vice Consul Helsinki 1994; Third Secretary (Management) Kiev 1996; Third Secretary (Political) Singapore 1997; SUPL 2001; Band C4; m 1993 Emily Margaret Dallas (2d 1997, 1999).

Ager, Keith; FCO since September 2002; Born 25/06/48; FO 1965; Bonn 1975; FCO 1977; Lilongwe 1979; FCO 1982; Montevideo 1982; FCO 1985; Rome 1988; FCO 1991; Madrid 1998; Band D6; m 1969 Ann Simmons (2d 1974, 1978).

Ager, Martyn Eric; FCO since August 1993; Born 17/06/55; FCO 1972; Moscow 1982; FCO 1985; Amman 1990; Band C4; m 1981 Kathryn Margaret Pierson (2s 1984, 1992; 1d 1986; twins, 1s, 1d 1994).

Agnew, Gail Eileen; Second Secretary FCO since March 1995; Born 21/01/48; FCO 1966; Lisbon 1970; Peking 1973; Bonn 1974; Vientiane 1977; FCO 1980; Nicosia 1982; Budapest 1985; FCO 1988; Zagreb 1992.

Ahmad, Asif Anwar; Head of Commonwealth Coordination Department FCO since April 2002; Born 21/01/56; DTI Business Link 1996; First Secretary FCO 1999; Deputy Head of Resource Budgeting Department FCO 2000; m (1) (diss 1991); m (2) 1993 Zubeda Khamboo (1d 1975; 3s 1980, 1982, 1984).

Al-Qaq, Stephanie Jane (née Powell); FCO since March 2003; Born 03/03/76; Band C4.

Alcock, Caroline; Second Secretary (Political) Cairo since November 2003; Born 08/12/70; FCO 1993; Full-Time Language Training 1993; Third Secretary Bahrain 1996; Third Secretary Cairo 1999; SUPL 2002; Band C4; m 1996 Amir Waguih.

Alcock, Michael Leslie, MBE (1986); FCO since April 1999; Born 07/08/50; Ministry of Labour 1967; DSAO (later FCO) 1968; Bangkok 1971; Port of Spain 1975; Tehran 1977; FCO 1979; Second Secretary (Chancery) and Vice-Consul Addis Ababa 1984; Second later First Secretary (Comm/Econ) New Delhi 1987; First Secretary FCO 1991; First Secretary (Aid/Commercial) Kathmandu 1994; m 1971 Barbara Ann Couch (2s 1972, 1976).

Alderton, Clive; Consul-General Lille since January 2004; Born 09/05/67; FCO 1986; Vice-Consul Warsaw 1988; Third Secretary (External Relations) Brussels (UKREP) 1990; Second later First Secretary FCO 1993; Head of Chancery (DHM) Singapore 1998; m 1990 Catriona Mitchell Canning (1d 1998; 1s 2000).

Aldridge, Terence John; FCO since February 2000; Born 11/09/56; FCO 1980; Darwin 1982; FCO 1984; Tel Aviv 1987; FCO 1988; Rome 1997; Band C5; m 1988 Janet Lorna Shore (1d 1991; 1s 1994).

Alessandri, Madeleine Kay (née Hateley); Counsellor Tokyo since January 2004; Born 06/03/65; FCO 1988; Second Secretary (Chancery/Info) Vienna 1990; Second later First Secretary FCO 1993; Consul (Economic) Frankfurt 1996; Language Training 1999; FCO 2000; m 1990 Enrico Alessandri (1d 1993; 1s 1998).

Aliaga, Deborah Joy; Third Secretary (Press and Public Affairs) Lisbon since September 2002; Born 08/07/60; FCO 1979; Bonn 1980; La Paz 1983; Resigned 1986; Reinstated FCO 1987; Third Secretary (Man/VC/ECO) La Paz 1997; Band B3; m 1989 Kenny Aliaga (1d 1996; 1s 2000).

Allan, Duncan Brierton; Principal Research Officer FCO since August 1996; Born 22/11/61; FCO 1989; Moscow 1992; m 1994 Joanne Clare Youde.

Allan, Jane Alison (née Higgs); Bahrain since December 2002; Born 09/03/63; HCS 1981; FCO 1981; Washington 1984; FCO 1987; SUPL 1989; Peking 1990; SUPL 1991; FCO 1996; SUPL 1998; Band B3; m 1987 Ian Allan.

Allan, Justine Rachael Anne; Second Secretary FCO since January 2000; Born 15/07/69; FCO 1990; Cape Town/Pretoria 1993; Jedda 1996; Floater Duties 1998; Band C4.

Allan, Keith Rennie; Deputy High Commissioner Port of Spain since July 2003; Born 25/08/68; MOD 1986; FCO 1988; Gaborone 1990; Floater Duties 1993; FCO 1996; Deputy Head of Mission Tashkent 1997; FCO 2000; British Trade International 2002; Band D6; m 1996 Martha Harriette Medendorp (1s 2000; 1d 2001).

Allan, Lynne Fleming; SUPL since March 2002; Born 22/10/68; FCO 1989; Moscow 1993; FCO 1995; Ankara 1998; Band B3; m 1999 Marat Ucer (1s 2001).

Allan, Moira, MBE (2004); Second Secretary Bogotá since March 2000; Born 27/05/61; FCO 1983; Prague 1985; FCO 1987; Mexico City 1989; Santiago 1993; FCO 1996; Band C4.

Allan, Nicholas Edward; First Secretary FCO since March 2002; Born 03/08/65; FCO 1990; Brussels (UKREP) 1993; Africa/Middle East Floater Duties 1994; Language Training 1995; Third Secretary (Political) Brussels 1996; Third later Second Secretary FCO 1999; Assistant Private Secretary to Peter Hain later Brian Wilson and Baroness Symons 2001; Band D6; m 2001 Elizabeth Rosemary Waugh.

Allbless, Clare Brickley; Lilongwe since May 2004; Born 04/05/71; FCO 1997; Third Secretary (PPA) Tokyo 2000; Band B3; m Dan Lindfield.

Allen, Jonathan Guy; First Secretary (Information) Brussels (UKREP) since July 2003; Born 05/03/74; FCO 1997; Nicosia 1999; Band D6.

Allen, Keith; FCO since June 2003; Born 05/09/72; FCO 1992; New Delhi 1996; Full-Time Language Training 2000; Deputy Head of Mission San Salvador 2000; Band C4.

Allen, Ross Christopher Edward; Jerusalem since December 2003; Born 30/11/78; FCO 2001; Full-Time Language Training (Japanese) 2002; Band C4.

Allen, Ruth Alexandra; First Secretary Kiev since April 2004; Born 31/08/76; FCO 2000; Band C4.

Allen, Sylvia Ann; SUPL since January 2004; Born 08/08/60; FCO 1984; La Paz 1986; Tunis 1990; Floater Duties 1995; Hanoi 1999; T/D Abidjan 2003; Band A2.

Alloway, Terence Michael; FCO since October 1998; Born 18/05/59; FCO 1980; Budapest 1982; Tel Aviv 1983; FCO 1986; SE Asia Floater 1987; FCO 1988; Kuwait 1992; FCO 1994; Full-Time Language Training 1994; Third later Second Secretary (Chancery) Geneva (UKDIS) 1995; Band D6; m 1991 Christine Ann Carr.

Ambrose, Philip John; First Secretary seconded to the China Britain Business Council since 2003; Born 03/11/59; FCO 1978; Brussels (UKREP) 1980; Jedda 1983; Riyadh 1986; South-East Asia Floater 1987; Vice-Consul and AMO Buenos Aires 1990; Vice-Consul and MO Tehran 1991; FCO 1992; Deputy Head of Mission and Consul, Kinshasa - accredited non-resident Second Secretary and Consul, Brazzaville 1995; Second Secretary (Commercial) Beijing 1997; Deputy Consul-General and Consul (Commercial) Rio de Janeiro 2002; Band C5.

Amos, Rex; Third Secretary (Political/PPA) Athens since November 2002; Born 24/09/72; FCO 1999; Band B3; m 1999 Jacqueline Palin (1s 2002).

Anderson, Annabel Mary; FCO since October 2000; Born 15/07/50; FCO 1995; Paris 1998; Band B3.

Anderson, Henry Ian; Counsellor (Political) Santiago since July 2004; Born 20/08/52; HO 1974; Dhaka 1983; Second Secretary FCO 1987; Vice-Consul Munich 1989; Second Secretary FCO 1994; First Secretary Budapest 1997; First Secretary FCO 2001; Band D6; m 1976 Janice Irene Leeman (1s 1984; 1d 1987).

Anderson, Jennifer Elizabeth; First Secretary (Political/Military) Brussels (UKREP) since June 2001; Born 16/11/68; Second later First Secretary FCO 1997; m 1997 Stephen Ashworth.

Anderson, John; First Secretary (Commercial) Warsaw since January 2002; Born 25/08/49; FCO 1966; Abu Dhabi 1970; Peking 1974; Lagos 1975; FCO 1978; HM Consul Istanbul 1982; Second later First Secretary (Comm) Paris 1987; First Secretary FCO 1991; First Secretary (Management) Harare 1995; FCO 1998; m 1970 Jacqueline Thorburn (2d 1981, 1990; 1s 1983).

Anderson, Lorraine Michelle; FCO since May 1994; Born 29/12/63; FCO 1989; Damascus 1992; Band A2; m (1) 1988 Lawrence Malcolm Reginald Simpson (diss 1994); (2) 1999 Neil Barrowman (1s 2000).

Anderson, Paul James; Second Secretary (Political) Pretoria since August 2003; Born 25/09/78; FCO 2001; Band C4.

Anderson, Philip Brian; FCO since October 2001; Born 18/07/73; HCS 1993; FCO 1997; Nicosia 1999; Band A2; m 1997 Jennie Linda Willis (1s 1996).

Anderson, Steven Martin; Third Secretary (Management/VC) Helsinki since December 2000; Born 29/12/70; FCO Home Civil Service 1990; Dubai 1997; Moscow 1998; Band B3; m Eevamaija Sofia Laitinen (twins, 1s and 1d 2002).

Andrews, Francesca Therese; FCO since July 1989; Born 23/02/54; FCO 1973; Cape Town/Pretoria 1975; Moscow 1978; FCO 1980; Brussels (UKDEL) 1982; Port of Spain 1986; Band A2.

Andrews, Moira Fraser, TD (1992); Legal Counsellor FCO since June 2000; Born 22/03/59; DTI 1995; Assistant Legal Adviser FCO 1998; m 1989 Ian Andrews (1s 1989; 1d 1992).

Andrews, Timothy John; First Secretary (IAEA) Vienna (UKMIS) since September 2001; Born 01/08/55; FCO 1976; Dacca 1979; Stuttgart 1982; Bonn 1984; FCO 1987; Second Secretary (Chancery/Info) Lusaka 1990; Deputy Head of Mission Port Louis 1994; First Secretary FCO 1997; m 1987 Carolyn Mary Moffat (1d 1989; 1s 1991).

Angell, Ben Thomas; Second Secretary Ankara since August 2002; Born 27/12/76; FCO 2000; Band C4.

Angrave, Gillian Linda; FCO since October 1994; Born 16/04/45; FCO 1976; Manila 1976; Lima 1980; Guatemala City 1981; Santiago 1982; FCO 1985; Mexico City 1987; Budapest 1991; Band B3.

Ankerson, Dr Dudley Charles; Counsellor FCO since April 2002; Born 04/09/48; Second Secretary FCO 1976; Second Secretary Buenos Aires 1978; First Secretary FCO 1981; First Secretary Mexico City 1985; First Secretary FCO 1988; First Secretary FCO on secondment to the Private Sector 1991; FCO 1991; Counsellor Madrid 1993; FCO 1997; Counsellor Budapest 1998; m 1973 Silvia Ernestina Galicia (1d 1985; 1s 1986).

Anstead, Alan Roger Hugh; SUPL since April 2003; Born 06/02/62; FCO 1980; Moscow 1983; Monrovia 1985; Hamburg 1989; FCO 1991; On loan to the DTI 1993; Deputy Head of Mission Riga 1996; Bratislava 2000; Band C4; m 1986 Paula Marita Nikkanen (1s 1991).

Anthony, Ian Nicholas; First Secretary FCO since April 1997; Born 18/01/60; FCO 1985; Second later First Secretary Lisbon 1988; First Secretary FCO 1990; First Secretary (Political) Brasilia 1993; Band D6.

Anthony-Rigsby, Lisa; SUPL since September 2001; Born 01/04/65; FCO 1998; Full-Time Language Training 2000; Band A2.

Arbon, Helen Marie; Deputy Consul-General Atlanta since January 2004; Born 21/04/70; FCO 1988; Jakarta 1991; World-wide Floater 1995; SUPL 1998; T/D Montevideo 1998; SUPL 1999; FCO 1999; Second Secretary Chisinau 2001; SUPL 2003; Band C4; m 1998 Adolfo Pando Molina (diss); ptnr, Hugo Ellis (1d 2003).

Archer, Marie-Louise; Second Secretary (Immigration) Mumbai since July 2003; Born 27/10/61; FCO 1990; Third Secretary (Immigration) Karachi 1991; DHM Managua 1996; Seconded to London Chamber of Commerce and Industry 1999; SUPL 2001; Overseas Attachment Training Scheme Bangalore and New Delhi 2002; Band C4.

Archer, Nicholas Stewart, MVO (2001); Head of Near East and North Africa Dept FCO since May 2002; Born 24/12/60; FCO 1983; Third later Second Secretary (Chancery) Amman 1986; Second later First Secretary FCO 1989; PS/Minister of State 1992; Language Training 1995; First Secretary (Commercial) Oslo 1995; on loan to St James's Palace 1997; m 1999 Erica Margaret Power.

Arkley, David Ballantine; Third Secretary (PPA) Moscow since October 2000; Born 10/10/66; FCO 1986; Moscow 1988; Floater Duties 1990; MO/Vice Consul São Paulo 1992; FCO 1995; Third Secretary (Press and Public Affairs) Washington 1997; Band B3; m 1992 Melissa Lea Buchanan.

Arkwright, Paul Thomas; Counsellor (Political) Brussels (UKDEL NATO) since November 2001;

Born 02/03/62; FCO 1986; Second Secretary (Chancery) BMG Berlin 1988; First Secretary FCO 1991; First Secretary (Chancery) New York (UKMIS) 1993; Attachement to Quai d'Orsay 1997; First Secretary (Chancery) Paris 1998; m 1997 Patricia Anne Holland (1d 1999; 1s 2001).

Armour, Nicholas Hilary Stuart; Head Of North America Department FCO since November 2000; Born 12/06/51; Third Secretary FCO 1974; Language Training MECAS 1975; FCO 1976; Third later Second Secretary Beirut 1977; First Secretary FCO 1980; Head of Chancery Athens 1984; First Secretary FCO 1989; Counsellor and Deputy Head of Mission Muscat 1991; Counsellor on loan to the DTI 1994; Consul-General/Counsellor Dubai 1997; m 1982 Georgina Elizabeth Fortescue (2d 1985, 1987).

Armstrong, Catherine Fraser; HM Consul Brussels since September 2000; Born 16/07/53; FCO 1971; Paris 1974; Gaborone 1977; FCO 1980; Manila 1985; Athens 1989; FCO 1990; Full-Time Language Training 1994; Second Secretary (Consular/Management) Caracas 1995; Second Secretary FCO 1997; m 1981 Clive Paul Ranson (diss 1986).

Armstrong, Catherine Fraser; HM Consul Brussels since September 2000; Born 16/07/53; FCO 1971; Paris 1974; Gaborone 1977; FCO 1980; Manila 1985; Athens 1989; FCO 1990; Full-Time Language Training 1994; Consul (Management) Caracas 1995; FCO 1997; Band C4; m 1981 Clive Paul Ranson.

Armstrong, Mark Christopher; Third Secretary (Political and Press) Tirana since September 2001; Born 04/05/72; FCO 1997; Geneva (UKDIS) 1998; Band B3.

Arnold, Troy Zachary Moncur; Second Secretary (Economic) Nicosia since October 2000; Born 19/12/72; Second Secretary FCO 1997; Language Training 1999; Band C4.

Aron, Michael Douglas; Counsellor (Political) Brussels (UKREP) since September 2002; Born 22/03/59; FCO 1984; Conference Support Officer New York (UKMIS) 1985; on Secondment to European Commission 1986; Second later First Secretary FCO 1986; First Secretary Brasilia 1988; First Secretary FCO 1991; First Secretary (Political) New York (UKMIS) 1993; First Secretary later Counsellor FCO 1996; Deputy Head of Mission Amman 1999; m 1986 Rachel Ann Golding Barker (2d 1986, 1996; 2s 1990, 1994).

Aron, Dr Rachel Ann Golding (née Barker); SUPL since March 2004; Born 18/07/51; First Secretary FCO 1984; Head of Chancery Brasilia 1988; SUPL 1990; First Secretary FCO 1992; First Secretary (Political) New York (UKMIS) 1993; SUPL 1996; Counsellor on loan to RAS as CSSB Chairman 1997; SUPL (Amman) 1999; Counsellor (E-Guidance) remotely in Amman from 2000 and Brussels 2002; m 1986 Michael Douglas Aron (2d 1986, 1996; 2s 1990 1994).

Arroyo, James Jose-Maria, OBE (2003); First Secretary FCO since June 2002; Born 25/03/67; FCO 1990; Full-Time Language Training 1991; Full-Time Language Training Cairo 1992; Second Secretary (Political) Amman 1993; Cairo 1996; Consul (Political) Jerusalem 1999; Band D6; m 1992 Kerry Ann Louise Ford (1d 2001).

Arthur, Hilary Jane; Sofia since September 2001; Born 28/01/61; FCO 1984; Karachi 1987; Vice Consul (Consular) Düsseldorf 1991; Frankfurt 1993; T/D Islamabad 1994; FCO 1995; Second Secretary (Development) Lusaka 1998; Band C4.

Arthur, Sir Michael Anthony, KCMG (2004), CMG (1992); High Commissioner New Delhi since October 2003; Born 28/08/50; FCO 1972; New York 1972; FCO 1973; Second Secretary Brussels (UKREP) 1974; Second Secretary Kinshasa 1976; Second later First Secretary FCO 1978; PS to Lord Privy Seal 1980; PS to Minister of State 1982; First Secretary (Chancery) Bonn 1984; Counsellor FCO 1988; Counsellor (Political) Paris 1993; Director (Resources) and Chief Inspector 1997; Minister Washington 1999; m 1974 Plaxy Gillian Beatrice Corke (2d 1978, 1980; 2s 1982, 1985).

Ash, Elizabeth; On secondment to Buckingham Palace since July 1996; Born 31/07/52; FCO 1975; New Delhi 1976; Geneva (UKMIS) 1978; Peking 1980; FCO 1982; Kingston 1983; FCO 1987; East Berlin 1988; FCO 1990; Band B3.

Ashcroft, Andrew Richard; HM Ambassador Santo Domingo since July 2002; Born 28/05/61; FCO 1980; Muscat 1982; Tel Aviv 1987; Second Secretary 1989; FCO 1991; First Secretary Harare 1996; FCO 1999; m 2001 Dr Amanda Sives.

Ashdown, Julie Anne; FCO since July 2001; Born 31/08/57; FCO 1976; Amman 1978; Asunción 1982; Brasilia 1983; FCO 1985; Belgrade 1990; Second Secretary FCO 1993; Second Secretary (Aid) Quito 1996; on loan to the Cabinet Office 1999.

Ashford, Leslie David; Second Secretary (Consular) Harare since January 2002; Born 07/09/50; Royal Air Force 1967-96; FCO 1996; T/D Khartoum 2000; T/D Abu Dhabi 2000; Band C4; m 1971 Francetta Xavier Marie (1d 1973; 1s 1979).

Ashley, David William; Second Secretary (Political) Belgrade since May 2002; Born 09/01/68; FCO 1999; Band C4; m 1994 Sophari Mao (1s 2002).

Ashton, John; SUPL since October 2002; Born 07/11/56; FCO 1978; Language Training Hong Kong 1980; Third later Second Secretary Peking 1981; FCO 1984; First Secretary on loan to the Cabinet Office 1986; Rome 1988; First Secretary later Counsellor Deputy Political Adviser Hong Kong 1993; On secondment as Visiting Fellow, Green College Oxford 1997; Counsellor FCO 1998; m 1983 Kao Fengning (1s 1986).

Ashworth, Patrick; Deputy Consul-General and Deputy Director of Trade Promotion São Paulo since January 2001; Born 02/11/50; FCO 1968; Dar es Salaam 1971; Castries 1975; Moscow 1978; FCO 1980; Valletta 1983; Vice-Consul (Commercial) São Paulo 1987; Second Secretary (UNCED) Brasilia 1992; Second Secretary FCO 1992; First Secretary (Press and Public Affairs) The Hague 1995; Band D6; m 1973 Pauline Mary Harrison (1d 1982; 1s 1986).

Aske, Antonia Jane; FCO since February 2003; Born 01/08/72; FCO 1998; Floater Duties 2000; Band C4.

Askham, Denise Ann (née Vaughan); SUPL since January 1999; Born 15/10/64; FCO 1983; Bonn 1985; Vienna (UKDEL) CSCE 1988; Washington 1988; Berne 1991; FCO 1995; SUPL 1995; FCO 1998; Band B3; m 1998 Stephen David Askham (1d 1997; 1s 2000).

Askham, Stephen David; Lisbon since October 2000; Born 20/05/60; RAF 1976-84; FCO 1984; Bonn 1991; FCO 1994; FCO 1994; Bahrain 1999; FTLT 2000; Band B3; m 1988 Denise Ann Vaughan (1d 1997; 1s 2000).

Aspden, Susan Elizabeth; Stockholm since September 2002; Born 20/01/57; FCO 1980; Rabat 1981; Jakarta 1983; Havana 1987; FCO 1989; On loan to DTI 1996; Band C4.

Aspery, Kevin; Dhaka since January 2004; Born 05/04/52; Army 1968-92; Havana 1993; Moscow (MNEB) 1997; Colombo 1998; Hong Kong 1999; m Penelope Jane (1d 1973; 2s 1975, 1977).

Asquith, Hon Dominic Anthony Gerard; Deputy Head of Mission Riyadh since October 2001; Born 07/02/57; FCO 1983; Second Secretary and Head of Interests Section Damascus 1986; First Secretary (Chancery) Muscat 1987; First Secretary FCO 1989; PS/Minister of State 1990; Washington 1992; Minister and Deputy Head of Mission Buenos Aires 1997; m 1988 Louise Cotton (2d 1989, 1990; 2s 1992, 1994).

Astbury, Nicholas Paul; First Secretary FCO since April 1999; Born 13/08/71; FCO 1994; Second Secretary (Chancery) Colombo 1995; m 1995 Elayna Joanne Gutteridge (1s 1999).

Astill-Brown, Jeremy; First Secretary (Regional Conflict Adviser) Addis Ababa since May 2003; Born 14/03/67; FCO 1987; Kampala 1990; Addis Ababa 1993; FCO 1997; Second Secretary (Political/Development) Luanda 1999; Band D6; m 1991 Marie-Loiuse (Marisa) Alegria Gunner.

Astle, Marilia Silva; SUPL since April 2004; Born 14/04/68; FCO 1991; Vice-Consul later Press & Public Affairs Lisbon 1994; FCO 1998; Band D6; m 2000 Jonathan Jones (1s 2004).

Atkinson, Christine; Deputy Permanent Delegate Paris (UKDEL) UNESCO since June 2001; Born 05/07/57; British Museum 1979; COI 1986; FCO 1990; APS/Minister of State 1996; PS/PUSS DFID 1997.

Atkinson, James Oswald, CMG (2004); HM Ambassador to Democratic Republic of Congo and non-resident Ambassador to Republic of Congo (Brazzaville) since May 2000; Born 20/10/44; Board of Trade 1964; DSA 1966; Commonwealth Office (later FCO) 1967; Nicosia 1969; Gaborone 1972; Second Secretary (Commercial) Damascus 1976; FCO 1980; First Secretary (Commercial) Athens 1984; First Secretary (Chancery/Inf) Jakarta 1988; First Secretary FCO 1990; Deputy Head of Mission Kampala 1993; FCO 1997; m 1980 Annemiek van Werkum (1d 1981).

Atkinson, Jane; Mexico City since June 2003; Born 20/07/60; MOD 1978-87; FCO 1987; Quito 1988; Floater Duties 1992; FCO 1996; Port Louis 1999; Band B3.

Atkinson, Kim Louise (née Kemp); FCO since May 2003; Born 04/04/74; FCO 1992; Islamabad 1996; Warsaw 1999; Band B3; m 1999 Simon Manington Atkinson.

Atkinson, Simon Manington; FCO since August 2003; Born 11/05/71; FCO 1989; Oslo 1992; FCO 1995; Pro-Consul Islamabad 1995; ECO/Vice Consul Warsaw 2000; Band B3; m 1999 Kim Kemp.

Attryde, Alan Robert James; First Secretary (Commercial) New Delhi since December 2003; Born 21/08/47; Ministry of Labour 1966; DSAO 1967; Middle East Floater 1970; Washington 1971; Jakarta 1974; FCO 1978; Cairo 1980; on loan to DTI 1985; Second Secretary 1985; FCO 1987; Consul (Commercial) Shanghai 1987; Second Secretary (Man/Cons) Caracas 1990; Full-time Language Training 1992; First Secretary (Commercial) Al Khobar 1993; FCO 1997; T/D as First Secretary (Management) Washington 1999; First Secretary (Commercial) Washington 2000; Band D6; m 1992 Ana Maria Diaz Molina.

Attwood, Ian; Kuala Lumpur since March 2000; Born 14/04/62; FCO 1983; Hong Kong 1991; FCO 1992; Bangkok 1993; FCO 1996; Band C4; m 1987 Tina Louise (1d 1989; 1s 1991).

Augustine-Aina, Felicity; Abuja since August 2002; Born 10/07/56; FCO 1989; Lagos 1991; FCO 1994; Dublin 1998; Islamabad 2000; Band A2; m 1992 Henry Aina (2d 1995, 1999).

Auld, Fergus Stephen; Second Secretary (Political/PPA) Bangkok since June 2002; Born 17/02/73; FCO 1999; Full-Time Language Training (Thai) 2000; Band C4; m 2001 Amy Louise Auld (1s 2003).

Auld, Steven James; Management Officer Yaoundé since March 2004; Born 09/07/71; FCO 1990; Moscow 1993; Nuku'alofa 1995; FCO 1996; Third Secretary (Management) and Vice Consul Tripoli 2001; Band B3; m 2001 Andrea Baity.

Austen, Richard James, MBE (1996); HM Ambassador Ulaanbaatar since February 2004; Born 25/05/55; Inland Revenue 1972-77; SUPL 1974-77; FCO 1981; Dar es Salaam 1983; Third Secretary (Consular) Ottawa 1987; Second Secretary FCO 1990; Deputy High Commissioner Banjul 1993; First Secretary FCO 1996; Deputy High Commissioner Port Louis 2001.

Austin, David John Robert, OBE (1999); SUPL since February 2003; Born 07/10/63; FCO 1986; Third later Second Secretary Dhaka 1989; FCO 1992; First Secretary (Political/Information) Belgrade 1993; On secondment as Political Adviser to Carl Bildt, ICFY/OHR 1995; FCO 1997; Deputy Head of Mission Zagreb 1999; m 1990 Emma Jane Carey (1d 1995; 1s 1997).

Austin, Vanessa Anne; FCO since October 2003; Born 04/08/71; FCO 1994; Cairo 1996; Nairobi 2000; Band A2.

Axworthy, Michael George Andrew; SUPL since July 2000; Born 26/09/62; FCO 1986; Third later Second Secretary Valletta 1988; Second Secretary FCO 1991; Second Secretary (Political/Military) Bonn 1993; Second Secretary (Economic) Bonn 1996; First Secretary FCO 1998; m 1996 Sally Hinds (1d 1999).

Axworthy, Sally Jane, MBE; On loan to the Home Office since July 2001; Born 01/09/64; FCO 1986; Language Training 1988; Third Secretary Moscow 1989; Second Secretary Kiev 1989; First Secretary FCO 1993; First Secretary Bonn 1994; FCO 1998; SUPL 2000; m 1996 Michael G A Axworthy (1d 1999).

Ayre, Andrew; Second Secretary Vienna since December 2001; Born 30/04/66; FCO 1986; Warsaw 1988; Rio de Janeiro 1990; FCO 1991; Nicosia 1994; SUPL 1997; Third later Second Secretary Tel Aviv 1998; Band C4; m 1990 Bettina Moosberger (1s 1997).

B

Bach, Alison Helen (née Clews); Cayman Islands since May 2003; Born 04/11/65; ODA 1987; FCO 1990; Manila 1992; FCO 1994; T/D Sarajevo 1996; SUPL 1996; Bonn 1997; Reykjavik 2000; Brussels 2001; Band A2; m 1997 Anthony Gordon James Bach (1s 1998; 1d 2000).

Bagnall, Andrew William; FCO since June 2003; Born 28/02/48; GPO 1964-70; FCO 1970; Pretoria 1982; Second Secretary FCO 1985; Attaché Caracas 1987; Second Secretary Nairobi 1994; FCO 1997; Lagos 1999; m 1981 Margaret Christine Bromwich (1s 1981; 1d 1985).

Bah, Stephanie Marie (née Holmes); Geneva (UKDIS) since September 2002; Born 28/12/56; FCO 1997; Singapore 1999; Band A2; m 2004 Souleymane Bah.

Baharie, Ian Walter; Counsellor Riyadh since July 2003; Born 03/05/61; FCO 1982; Language Training SOAS 1983; Third later Second Secretary (Chancery) Cairo 1985; Second later First Secretary FCO 1987; First Secretary Abu Dhabi 1991; First Secretary FCO 1994; Consul Jerusalem 1996; First Secretary (Political) Abuja 1999; m 1991 Bonaventura Agatha Jasperina Buhre (3d 1991, 1998, 2001).

Bailey, Ian Peter; FCO since December 1998; Born 21/08/57; DTI 1985; FCO 1987; Language Training 1988; Third Secretary (Political) Muscat 1990; Second Secretary (Commercial) Seoul 1995; Band D6; m 1990 Teresa Weronika Maria Frosztega (2s 1998, 2001).

Bailey, Rosemarie Anne (née Edwards); SUPL since March 1998; Born 20/04/59; FCO 1979; Tokyo 1983; FCO 1986; SUPL 1988; Vice-Consul Singapore 1992; SUPL 1996; FCO 1997; Band C4; m 1982 Mark Adrian Stephen Bailey (2s 1996, 1999).

Bailey, Stephen; FCO since October 2003; Born 13/04/53; FCO 1971; Mexico City 1975; Gaborone 1977; Sana'a 1981; FCO 1983; Wellington 1987; Budapest 1990; FCO 1995; Madras 2000; Band B3; m 1975 Carol Joan Sterritt (1d 1980).

Baird, Jamie Peter; Athens since January 2003; Born 25/08/72; FCO 1997; Band A2.

Baird, Nicholas Graham Faraday; Head of European Union Department (Internal) FCO since February 2002; Born 15/05/62; FCO 1983; Third later Second Secretary Kuwait 1986; Second later First Secretary (Econ/Finance) Brussels (UKREP) 1989; Private Secretary to the Parliamentary Under Secretary of State FCO 1993; Counsellor and Deputy Head of Mission Muscat 1997; Counsellor (Justice/Home Affairs) Brussels (UKREP) 1998; m 1985 Caroline Jane Ivett (1s 1989; 2d 1990, 1992).

Baker, Catherine Margaret; FCO since January 1998; Born 11/09/68; FCO 1991; Third Secretary (Chancery/Information) Tel Aviv 1994; Band B3.

Baker, Denise; FCO since July 2003; Born 27/09/67; FCO 1987; Brussels 1991; Belgrade 1994; FCO 1997; Plymouth 1999; Band A2.

Baker, Francis Raymond, OBE (1997); Counsellor (Political/Military) Washington since July 2003; Born 27/01/61; FCO 1981; Panama City 1983; Third later Second Secretary Buenos Aires 1986; Second Secretary FCO 1991; First Secretary (Political/Military) Ankara 1993; First Secretary on secondment to State Department Washington 1996; First Secretary FCO 1997; Private Secretary to the Minister of State 1998; Head of Africa Department (Equatorial), 2000; m 1983 Maria Pilar Fernandez (1d 1989; 1s 1991).

Baker, Nigel Marcus; Deputy Head of Mission Havana since October 2003; Born 09/09/66; Third Secretary FCO 1989; Third later Second Secretary (Econ) Prague 1992; Second Secretary later DHM Bratislava 1993; Resigned 1995; Reinstated 1998; First Secretary FCO 1998; on loan to St James's Palace 2000; m 1997 Alexandra Cechova.

Baker, Piers Howard Burton; Deputy Head of Mission Vienna since January 2001; Born 23/07/56; Second Secretary FCO 1983; First Secretary (Chancery) Brussels 1985; First Secretary FCO 1988; First Secretary Brussels (UKREP) 1993; First Secretary FCO 1996; m 1979 Maria Eugenia Vilaincour (1s 1984).

Baker, Rodney Kelvin Mornington; FCO since November 1996; Born 24/03/49; FO (later FCO) 1966; Warsaw 1974; FCO 1975; Athens 1977; Ankara 1978; FCO 1981; Third Secretary Tokyo 1984; FCO 1986; Third later Second Secretary Madrid 1989; FCO 1992; On loan to MOD Rheindahlen 1994; Band D6; m 1971 Christine Mary Holt (2d 1979, 1983).

Baker, Russell Nicholas John; First Secretary FCO since April 2001; Born 06/10/53; FCO 1977; Language Training 1979; Prague 1979; Private Secretary to HMA Bonn 1982; Second Secretary FCO 1986; APS to Minister of State 1987; Second Secretary (Political/Info /Comm) Lima 1990; First Secretary (Head of Scott Inquiry Unit) FCO 1994; First Secretary (Commercial) Dublin 1996; Band D6; m 1996 Silvia Chavez Montoya.

Baker-Mavin, Alison Bertha (née Baker), BEM (1991); SUPL since April 2003; Born 09/05/62; FCO 1989; Algiers 1991; Banjul 1995; Third Secretary (Management/Commercial) Freetown 1998; SUPL 2001; FCO 2002; Band B3; m 1997 Graham J Mavin (1s 2001; 1d 2004).

Baldwin, Brian Paul; High Commissioner Honiara since May 2001; Born 07/12/44; Ministry of Transport 1964; Board of Trade 1965; FCO 1967; Johannesburg 1970; Belgrade 1973; FCO 1976; Vice-Consul (Pol) Johannesburg 1979; Second later First Secretary FCO 1983; First Secretary (Commercial) Muscat 1988; Deputy Head of Mission Port Moresby 1993; Tristan da Cunha Administrator 1998; m Elizabeth Mary Evans (3s 1969, 1970, 1973; 1d 1971).

Baldwin, Peter Graham; FCO since April 1998; Born 28/08/43; Paymaster General's Office 1962; CRO 1963; Lusaka 1964; Calcutta 1967; Vienna (BE) 1971; Second Secretary Brussels (UKREP) 1973; FCO 1977; Algiers 1981; Second Secretary FCO 1983; Second Secretary (Immigration/Consular) Colombo 1987; Second Secretary (Consular) Jakarta 1991; Second Secretary (Immigration) Islamabad 1995; m 1968 Patricia Joyce Carter (2d 1970, 1972; 1s 1980).

Bale, Caroline Margaret; FCO since June 1991; Born 25/07/57; FCO 1980; Geneva (UKMIS) 1981; Moscow 1983; Port Stanley 1986; Sofia 1987; Gaborone 1989; Band A2.

Balfour, Alison Hannah; Amman since March 2002; Born 13/05/61; Scottish Office 1980-87; FCO 1987; Mexico City 1989; Nicosia 1992; Rome 1995; FCO 1999; Band B3.

Ball, Anthony James; First Secretary Damascus since September 2003; Born 18/12/68; FCO 1989; Full-Time Language Training 1991; FCO 1993; Second Secretary (Economic) Kuwait 1994; FCO 1996; First Secretary (Political) Madrid 1999; Band D6; m 1995 Celia Garcia-Marugan Mino (1s 2001).

Ball, Stephen; FCO since September 2003; Born 06/09/79; Band C4.

Ballett, Sarah Elizabeth; SUPL since October 2002; Born 31/10/71; FCO 1990; Washington 1994; SUPL 1997; Washington 1997; FCO 2000; Band B3.

Balmer, Michael Anthony; First Secretary, Head of Management New York (UKMIS) since July 2004; Born 21/07/51; MOD (Navy) 1969; FCO 1971; Geneva (UKMIS) 1973; Attaché Moscow 1975; LA Floater 1977; Third Secretary (Administration) Jedda 1979; Second Secretary (Commercial) Warsaw 1981; Second later First Secretary FCO 1984; Language Training 1987; First Secretary, Head of Commercial Section Athens 1988; First Secretary FCO 1992; Language Training 1995; Deputy Consul-General Düsseldorf and Deputy Director-General (Trade and Investment Promotion) Germany 1996; Deputy Head of Security Strategy Unit, FCO 2000; Band D7; m 1982 Helen Charmian Burgoine (2d 1984, 1987).

Bamber, Jonathan James; Third Secretary (Commercial) Maputo since August 2001; Born 24/09/65; FCO 1994; ECO later Vice-Consul Bangkok 1997; FTLT 2000; Band B3; m 2001 Sarah Louise Cooke.

Bamber, Sarah Ann; First Secretary New Delhi since May 2004; Born 06/01/74; FCO 1996; Second Secretary New York (UKMIS) 1998; Second Secretary FCO 2001; Band C4.

Bamford, Victoria Jane; SUPL since March 2004; Born 23/12/67; FCO 1989; Moscow 1992; FCO 1995; Nicosia 1996; FCO 1999; SUPL 2001; FCO 2002; Band B3; ptnr, Paul McLennan (1s 2001).

Banham, Michael Kent; Consul Palma since September 2001; Born 20/09/44; FO 1963; Rawalpindi 1967; Quito 1970; FCO 1974; Tripoli 1976; Nairobi 1980; FCO 1983; Second Secretary (Commercial) Bombay 1987; Second Secretary (Management/Consular) Lima 1990; First Secretary (Management) Riyadh 1994; First Secretary (Management) Cairo 1998; m (1) 1965 Christine Scott (1s 1969; 1d 1971) (diss); (2) 1995 Marie Louise Smith.

Banks, Alison Elizabeth; Amman since April 2004; Born 10/01/70; FCO 1992; Canberra 1994; Peking 1998; FCO 2000; Band B3.

Banks, Jacinta Mary Catharine (née Cookson); FCO since August 2000; Born 25/11/57; FCO 1977; Paris 1980; Bombay 1983; FCO 1987; Nicosia 1990; Damascus 1994; Islamabad 1996; Band C4; m 1982 Jamie Paul Banks (1d 1992).

Banks, Jamie Paul; Consul (Investment) Sydney since February 2003; Born 09/06/57; FCO 1977; Paris (UKDEL OECD) 1980; Bombay 1983; FCO 1987; Nicosia 1990; Second Secretary (Commercial) Damascus 1994; Second Secretary (Development) Islamabad 1996; FCO 2000; Deputy Head, Asia Pacific, Invest UK 2001; Band C5; m 1982 Jacinta Mary Catharine Cookson (diss 2002) (1d 1992).

Banks, Janice Kathleen (née Robinson); Riyadh since February 2001; Born 28/09/56; FCO 1995; Bonn 1997; Jerusalem 1999; Band B3; m 2000 Fraser Banks.

Banks, Simon John; FCO since November 2002; Born 05/04/66; FCO 1988; Language Training 1990; Third later Second Secretary (Economic) Warsaw 1990; on secondment to DGIA EC Commission Brussels 1993; First Secretary FCO 1996; Deputy High Commissioner Dar es Salaam 1999; m 1989 The Hon Rowena Joynson-Hicks (3s 1994, 1996, 1999; 1d 2003).

Bannatyne, William Graeme; Abuja since February 2004; Born 05/03/67; FCO 1988; Canberra 1990; FCO 1993; Sofia 1993; FCO 1995; Full-Time Language Training 2000; Lima 2000; Band B3; m 1990 Caterina Prestigiacomo (1d 1995).

Banner, Nick; First Secretary (Information) Brussels since January 2002; Born 28/02/74; FCO 1999; First Secretary FCO 2000; Band D6; m 1999 Emma Reisz.

Bannerman, Alexander Campbell; T/D Sana'a since July 2002; Born 29/09/67; FCO 1988; Nicosia 1993; FCO 1995; Dubai 1998; Band B3; m 1998 Fiona Vari MacKillop.

Barclay, John Hamish; FCO since February 2003; Born 11/09/64; Royal Air Force 1983-92; Department of Transport 1993-95; FCO 1995; Abu Dhabi 1997; Jedda 2000; Band B3.

Barclay, Philip Jeremy; Warsaw since January 2003; Born 14/10/67; FCO 1999; Band D6; m 1996 Emma Robinson.

Barker, Caroline Susan; FCO since July 1999; Born 15/09/69; Language Training 1993; Second Secretary (KHF) Bratislava 1994; Second Secretary FCO 1995; SUPL 1997.

Barker, Philip John; Bridgetown since January 2004; Born 18/11/70; FCO 1989; Berlin 1998; FCO 2001; m 1998 Elizabeth Margaret Jean Hindle.

Barker, Rowland Gifford Palgrave; Second Secretary Nairobi since January 2004; Born 06/06/75; FCO 2000; Band C4.

Barklamb, Peter Richard; FCO since March 2003; Born 18/07/51; FCO 1970; Delhi 1973; Islamabad 1975; Geneva 1976; Brussels 1978; FCO 1981; Warsaw 1984; Second Secretary (Commercial/Aid) Bridgetown 1989; Second Secretary (Commercial) Riyadh 1991; FCO 1994; Consul (Head of Post) later Consul-General Amsterdam 1998; Band D6; m 1974 Jane Bosworth (2d 1979, 1981; 1s 1984).

Barlow, Andrew Watson; FCO since October 1987; Born 23/12/54; UKAEA 1977; FCO 1978; UKAEA 1981; Private Secretary to Chairman 1983-84; Band D7.

Barlow, Jacqueline; Anguilla since February 2002; Born 21/07/47; FCO 1969; Berne 1969; Baghdad 1971; Islamabad 1972; Moscow 1973; Phnom

Penh and Hanoi 1975; FCO 1976; Moscow 1977; Floater Duties 1980; FCO 1984; Tokyo 1987; FCO 1990; Vice-Consul Shanghai 1994; Third Secretary (Commercial) Kuwait 1997.

Barlow, Richard David; Second Secretary (Chancery) Brasilia since December 2002; Born 17/01/75; FCO 2000; Band C4; m 2001 Silvia Claudia da Graça-Barlow.

Barnard, Michael Trevelyan; FCO since October 1995; Born 15/12/61; FCO 1986; Dar es Salaam 1989; Bratislava 1993; Band B3; m 1993 Tracy Dawn Clifford.

Barnes, Catherine Eleanor; FCO since May 2001; Born 12/06/68; FCO 1995; Human Rights Officer Jakarta 1998; Band C4.

Barnes, Nicholas John; FCO since May 2004; Born 25/11/72; FCO 2000; First Secretary (Political) Tirana 2002; Band D6.

Barnes Jones, Deborah Elizabeth Vavasseur (née Barnes); Governor Montserrat since April 2004; Born 06/10/56; FCO 1980; Moscow 1983; First Secretary on loan to Cabinet Office 1985; Resigned 1986; Reinstated 1988; First Secretary (Chancery) Tel Aviv 1988; First Secretary FCO 1992; Deputy Head of Mission Montevideo 1996; HM Ambassador Tbilisi 2001; m 1986 Frederick Richard Jones (2d (twins) 1991).

Barnett, Robin Anthony; Head of Joint Entry Clearance Unit later UKVisas (FCO/HO) since January 2002; Born 08/03/58; FCO 1980; Third later Second Secretary Warsaw 1982; Second later First Secretary FCO 1985; First Secretary Vienna (UKDEL) 1990; First Secretary New York (UKMIS) 1991; First Secretary FCO 1996; Deputy Head of Mission Warsaw 1998; m (1) 1989 Debra Marianne Bunt (diss 1999) (1 step s 1987, 1s 1990), (2) Tesca Maria Osman (1 step d 1990; 1 step s 1990).

Barnsley, Pamela Margaret; FCO since September 2003; Born 02/06/57; FCO 1982; Second Secretary (Chancery) Brasilia 1983; First Secretary (Comm/Econ) Peking 1987; Trade Commissioner BTC Hong Kong 1989; SUPL 1990; First Secretary FCO 1995; SUPL 1999; Band D6; m 1986 Perry Neil Keller (1d 1999).

Barr, Richard Barclay; FCO since August 2001; Born 03/05/55; FCO 1975; Freetown 1977; FCO 1980; Prague 1981; Düsseldorf 1983; Accra 1988; FCO 1992; Second Secretary 1994; Full-Time Language Training 1997; Second Secretary (Press and Public Affairs) Buenos Aires 1997; m 1977 Jane Anne Greengrass (1s 1978).

Barras, Ian Alexander; FCO since March 1998; Born 27/04/50; FCO 1976; Geneva 1979; Peking 1981; Douala 1984; FCO 1986; Athens 1989; FCO 1990; Washington 1991; Third Secretary (Information/Visits) Islamabad 1994; Band B3.

Barratt, Colin Ernest; Third Secretary (Commercial) Istanbul since June 2003; Born 02/03/62; FCO 1995; Third Secretary

(Management/Vice-Consul) Banjul 1999; Band B3.

Barrett, Donna Alison; Floater Duties since June 2004; Born 14/01/63; FCO 1995; The Hague 1999; FCO 2002; Band B3; (1d 1981).

Barrett, Douglas Wilson; Second Secretary (Commercial) Shanghai since February 2001; Born 28/01/56; HCS 1976; FCO 1978; Brussels (UKREP) 1980; Havana 1983; Latin America Floater 1986; Islamabad 1988; T/D Manila 1992; T/D Geneva (UKDEL) 1993; FCO 1993; Second Secretary/Management Officer/HM Consul Bombay 1996; m 2000 Gayle Viegas.

Barrett, Janet Ceclyn; FCO since May 2000; Born 19/12/67; HCS 1988; FCO 1994; Geneva (UKMIS) 1997; Band A2.

Barrett, Jill Mary; Assistant Legal Adviser FCO since 1997; Born 06/07/58; Assistant Legal Adviser FCO 1989; First Secretary (Legal) New York (UKMIS) 1994.

Barrie, Patricia Ann (née Gallagher); FCO since October 1998; Born 17/04/65; FCO 1988; Athens 1991; Montevideo 1993; Band A2; m 1993 Alexander Barrie (1d 1995; 1s 1998).

Barros, Lesley Susan; Riyadh since August 2000; Born 02/05/60; FCO 1980; Brussels 1981; Havana 1982; Brasilia 1984; FCO 1987; Paris 1990; Tokyo 1993; Gibraltar 1996; Band B3; m 1989 José Barros Filho (2d 1991, 1994).

Barrow, Timothy Earle, LVO (1994) MBE (1993); Assistant Director of EU (External), FCO since April 2003; Born 15/02/64; FCO 1986; Language Training 1988; Second Secretary (Chancery) Moscow 1990; First Secretary FCO 1993; Private Secretary to Minister of State, FCO 1994; First Secretary Brussels (UKREP) 1996; Private Secretary to Secretary of State for Foreign and Commonwealth Affairs, FCO 1998; Head of Common Foreign and Security Policy Department FCO 2000.

Barry, Thomas John; T/D First Secretary Mexico City since November 2003; Born 25/12/78; FCO 2002; Band C4.

Barson, Jacqueline Anne, MBE (1995); FCO since October 2002; Born 26/05/59; FCO 1979; Prague 1981; Belgrade 1982; Abu Dhabi 1982; Brunei 1985; Geneva (UKMIS) 1986; FCO 1990; Copenhagen 1992; Brussels 1992; Athens 1993; Ottawa 1994; Olympic Attaché Sydney 1999; Seconded to the Organising Committee for Manchester Commonwealth Games 2001; Band D6.

Barter, Craig Alan Roger; FCO since July 2001; Born 24/07/69; HCS 1990; FCO 1996; Tehran 1999; Band A2; m 2000 Lilis Purhaniah.

Barton, Helen Mary; SUPL since October 1999; Born 05/12/65; FCO 1991; Second Secretary (Political) The Hague 1996; m 1996 Alastair Matthew Wright.

Barton, Philip Robert, OBE (1997); Deputy High Commissioner Nicosia since July 2000; Born 18/08/63; FCO 1986; Third later Second Secretary Caracas 1987; First Secretary on loan to the Cabinet Office 1991; First Secretary FCO 1993; First Secretary (Political) New Delhi 1994; On loan as Private Secretary to the Prime Minister at No. 10 1997; m (1) 1995 Sabine Friederike Schnittger (diss) (2) 1999 Amanda Joy Bowen (1d 2001; 1s 2003).

Bassnett, Stephen Andrew, MBE (1983); First Secretary FCO since July 1999; Born 24/01/49; Army 1967-86; FCO 1986; First Secretary (Chancery) Cairo 1991; First Secretary FCO 1993; First Secretary (Political) Bahrain 1997; Band D6; m 1980 Judith Christine Anne Whitty.

Bastin, Suzanne Sarah (née Baxter); Dubai since September 2000; Born 03/07/69; Home Office 1989; Bombay 1994; Home Office 1994; Peking 1996; FCO 2000; Band B3; m 1998 David Richard Bastin.

Bateman, Peter; On secondment (Commercial) since January 2003; Born 23/12/55; FCO 1984; Language Training Tokyo 1986; Second later First Secretary Tokyo 1987; First Secretary FCO 1991; First Secretary (Commercial) Berlin 1993; FCO 1997; Counsellor (Commercial) Tokyo 1998; FCO 2002; m 1985 Andrea Subercaseaux-Peters (2s 1987, 1990; 1d 1992).

Bates, Anthony Michael, MVO (1994); First Secretary (Management) and Consul Berne since August 2001; Born 12/11/58; FCO 1978; Islamabad 1980; Wellington 1982; FCO 1987; Language Training 1990; Private Secretary Bonn 1990; Cayman Islands 1993; Second Secretary FCO 1996; Band C5; m 1985 Colette Ann Stewart (2d 1988, 1992).

Bates, Michael Charles, OBE (1994); Consul-General Atlanta since June 2001; Born 09/04/48; DSAO later FCO 1966; Delhi 1971; Third Secretary Moscow 1974; Second Secretary FCO 1977; Second later First Secretary Singapore 1979; First Secretary (Inf/Chancery) Brussels 1983; On loan to No.10 Downing Street 1987; First Secretary FCO 1990; First Secretary Riga 1991; Chargé d'Affaires later HM Ambassador Bratislava 1993; First Secretary FCO 1995; Deputy High Commissioner Bombay 1996; m 1971 Janice Kwan Foh Yin (1d 1977; 1s 1978).

Bates, Vicki Louise; Floater Duties since July 2004; Born 07/12/71; FCO 2002; Band A2.

Batson, Philip David; Second later First Secretary FCO since October 1997; Born 26/06/68; FCO 1987; Bombay 1991; Third Secretary Paris 1995.

Battson, Andrew John; FCO since September 2001; Born 08/05/66; FCO 1984; Bombay 1991; Bonn 1995; Port of Spain 1997; SUPL 2000; Band C4; m 1993 Andrea Jaun.

Batty, Simon Robert; Second Secretary Athens since September 2000; Born 30/09/62; FCO 1982; New Delhi 1985; FCO 1989; Cairo 1990; Second Secretary FCO 1993; Second Secretary Bogotá 1997; Band C4; m 1991 Sharon Morris (1d 1996; 1s 1998).

Batty-Smith, Katharine Amelia Louise; FCO since April 2003; Born 19/08/64; FCO 1984; Budapest 1986; Brasilia 1988; Floater Duties 1992; On loan to DTI 1994; Vice-Consul Sana'a 1997; Prague 1999; Band C4.

Bavinton, Sharon Jayne (née Vince); FCO since January 1999; Born 17/12/58; FCO 1979; New York (UKMIS) 1981; FCO 1983; Canberra 1984; FCO 1987; Abu Dhabi 1989; FCO 1993; Overseas Inspectorate 1995; Band B3; m 1982 Russell Alexander Bavinton (diss 1992).

Baxendale, James Lloyd; First Secretary (Political) Beirut since February 2004; Born 23/02/67; FCO 1991; Language Training 1993; Language Training Cairo 1994; Second Secretary FCO 1995; First Secretary (Political) Amman 1997; First Secretary (Political) Brussels 1999; First Secretary FCO 2001; Band D6; m 1996 Valerie Nathalie Bouchet (1s 2001).

Baxter, Alison Jane; Beijing since February 2004; Born 15/05/67; FCO 1990; Islamabad 1992; Canberra 1993; SUPL 1996; FCO 1999; Full-Time Language Training 2002; Band C4.

Baxter Amade, Vicki Louise; FCO since September 2000; Born 18/03/63; FCO 1982; T/D Luxembourg 1983; Lisbon 1984; Maputo 1987; FCO 1990; Khartoum 1993; Canberra 1996; Band C4; m 1990 Amade Chababe Amade (diss 2000) (1s 1992).

Bayfield, Rachael (née Greenwood); SUPL since December 2003; Born 04/03/68; FCO 1993; Language Training 1994; Full-Time Language Training Tokyo 1995; Private Secretary Tokyo 1996; SUPL 2000; FCO 2003; Band C4.

Bayliss, Jill Elizabeth (née Hooper); Lagos since October 2002; Born 03/08/68; FCO 1989; Colombo 1995; Moscow 1998; Band B3; m 1994 (Buster) IHW Bayliss.

Beach, Louise Eleanor (née Horwood); FCO since July 1995; Born 27/03/68; FCO 1989; New York (UKMIS) 1991; Nicosia 1993; PA/DHM Athens 1995; Second Secretary (Political) The Hague 1996; FCO 1998; Band A2; m 1998 Charles Beach.

Beale, Gideon David; First Secretary Bucharest since August 2002; Born 09/07/62; FCO 1986; Third Secretary/ Vice-Consul Athens 1990; Second Secretary FCO 1994; First Secretary (Political) Lagos later Abuja 1995; First Secretary FCO 1999; Band D6.

Beats, Lesley, MBE (2004); Ulaanbaatar since November 2003; Born 01/04/65; Prague 1989; Brussels (UKREP) 1991; Phnom Penh 1994; Brussels (UKREP) 1996; FCO 1998; Band B3.

Beattie, Phoebe; FCO since January 2001; Born 25/11/59; FCO 1984; Bangkok 1985; Stanley

1988; Floater Duties 1989; FCO 1993; Jakarta 1994; Brussels 1998; Band B3.

Beaven, Keith Andrew; Counsellor Oslo since February 2004; Born 07/01/61; FCO 1983; Third later Second Secretary (Chancery) Mexico City 1986; First Secretary FCO 1988; First Secretary (Political) Pretoria 1993; First Secretary FCO 1997; m 1986 Jane Marion Wells (1s 1996; 1d 1999).

Beckett, Alison Joan; SUPL since May 2004; Born 01/07/61; FCO 1989; Third Secretary (Management/Cons) Kiev 1992; Paris (UKDEL OECD) 1996; Second Secretary (Political) Bucharest 1999; FCO 2001; Band C4.

Beckford, Charles Francis Houghton; FCO since July 2003; Born 04/11/63; FCO 1991; First Secretary (Political) Islamabad 1993; First Secretary FCO 1995; First Secretary (Political) Nicosia 1999; Band D6; m 1993 Clare Elizabeth Stourton (twin s 1997; 1d 1999).

Beckingham, Peter; Consul-General Sydney since August 1999; Born 16/03/49; BOTB 1974; Director New York (BIS) 1979; First Secretary FCO 1983; First Secretary (Commercial) Stockholm 1988; First Secretary later Head of Political Section Canberra 1992; Director Joint Export Promotion Directorate (FCO/DTI) 1996; m 1975 Jill Mary Trotman (2d 1980, 1982).

Bedford, Adrian Frederick; FCO since February 2004; Born 30/10/56; Land Registry 1975; FCO 1976; Islamabad 1978; Hanoi 1981; Johannesburg 1982; FCO 1985; Bogotá 1988; Second later First Secretary FCO 1992; Tehran 1996; First Secretary and Deputy Head of Mission Beirut 1999; Band D6; m (1) 1995 Alexandra Pamela Cole (diss 2001); (2) 2001 Sandra Eid (1d 2002; 1s 2003).

Bedingfield, Julian Peter; FCO since March 2004; Born 23/07/45; FO 1964; Language Training 1968; Scientific Attaché Moscow 1969; FCO 1971; Düsseldorf 1971; Bonn 1973; Second Secretary (Commercial) Dacca 1975; Ulaanbaatar 1977; FCO 1978; Second Secretary (Admin) and Consul Berne 1982; Second Secretary (Chancery/Inf) Rabat 1986; Second later First Secretary FCO 1992; First Secretary Brussels UKDEL NATO 1994; First Secretary and DHM Ljubljana 1999; Deputy Head of Mission Ljubljana 1999; m 1975 Margery Mary Jones Davies (2d 1979, 1984; 1s 1982).

Bee, Stephanie Louise, MBE; Third Secretary and Vice-Consul Yerevan since June 2001; Born 27/01/67; FCO 1986; Brussels (UKDEL) 1988; Warsaw 1988; Moscow 1992; FCO 1995; Hong Kong 1998; Band B3.

Beer, Nicholas James Gilbert; Counsellor FCO since 2002; Born 06/12/47; Second Secretary FCO 1976; Nairobi 1977; FCO 1979; First Secretary Madrid 1982; First Secretary FCO 1986; First Secretary later Counsellor (Political) The Hague 1992; FCO 1996; Counsellor (Regional Affairs) Buenos Aires 1999; m 1975 Diana Eva Brooke (diss 1996) (1d 1977; 1s 1980).

Beer, Nicola Geraldine (née Calvert); Second Secretary Dubai since January 2002; Born 21/06/67; FCO 1985; Nicosia 1988; Resigned 1990; Reinstated 1996; Band C4; m 1999 Andrew John Beer (1d 2000).

Beeson, Richard John; Second Secretary (Consular) Kathmandu since July 2004; Born 07/06/54; FCO 1973; East Berlin 1975; Damascus 1976; FCO 1977; Brussels (UKREP) 1978; Peking 1980; FCO 1983; Tripoli 1984; FCO 1986; Singapore 1988; Third Secretary (Management) and Vice Consul Hamburg 1991; Second Secretary FCO 1994; Full-time Language Training 1996; Taipei 1998; FCO 2001; m (1) 1978 Kim Margaret Cotter; (2) 1989 Elizabeth Ann Allin.

Begbie, James Alexander, OBE (2004); FCO since 2004; Born 10/12/53; FCO 1973; Bahrain 1975; Middle Eastern Floater 1979; FCO 1980; Tunis 1983; Shanghai 1986; Third later Second Secretary (Comm) Muscat 1989; FCO 1993; Deputy Consul-General Istanbul 1999; Band C5; m 1980 Janice Isobel Mills (1s 1984; 1d 1985).

Begbie, Janice Isobel (née Mills); FCO since October 2003; Born 18/04/51; FCO 1971; Lusaka 1973; FCO 1975; Middle East Floater 1977; FCO 1980; SUPL 1983; Muscat 1989; SUPL 1993; FCO 1994; Second Secretary 1996; SUPL 1999; Istanbul 1999; m 1980 James Alexander Begbie (1s 1984; 1d 1985).

Beggs, Katherine Elizabeth; FCO since March 2002; Born 25/06/76; Band B3.

Belcher, Patrick Fred; Havana since June 2004; Born 25/08/48; Royal Air Force 1965-90; LCD 1990-92; Prague 1992; Moscow 1994; World-wide Floater Duties 1996; Hong Kong 1998; Beijing 2002; Band B3; m 1971 Ann Carr (1s 1977).

Belfitt, Sandra Jane; Port Louis since April 2002; Born 14/03/65; HM Customs and Excise 1986-93; FCO 1996; Brasilia 1997; Band A2; m 1984 Andrew Belfitt (1d 1990; 1s 1993).

Belgrove, David Raymond; FCO since October 2002; Born 18/01/62; FCO 1982; Prague 1984; Kuwait 1986; FCO 1991; Third Secretary (Consular/Economic) Calcutta 1994; Second later First Secretary (MPA) Ottawa 1998; Band C4; m 1985 Mette Ofstad (2d 1986, 1989).

Bell, Alan Douglas; Phnom Penh since March 2001; Born 26/05/72; FCO 1995; Madrid 1997; Band A2.

Bell, Jeremy Paul Turnbull; FCO since January 2003; Born 04/01/52; FCO 1974; The Hague 1976; Bahrain 1981; Hanoi 1982; FCO 1985; Tokyo 1988; Third Secretary (Management/Cons) Gaborone 1992; Second Secretary FCO 1996; First Secretary (UN) Nairobi 1998; Band C5; m (1) 1978 Jane Dorron Lee (diss 1981) (2) 1991 Setsuko Yamamoto (1d 1995).

Bell, Julie Dawn (née Raines); Second Secretary (Management/Consular) Lilongwe since March 2001; Born 12/11/66; FCO 1989; Language Training 1990; Moscow 1991; Budapest 1994;

Belgrade 1995; Second Secretary FCO 1997; m 1991 Andrew Michael Bell (2d 1993, 1997).

Bell, Karen Ann (née Norris); First Secretary (Economic) Riyadh since November 2003; Born 22/04/66; FCO 1983; Strasbourg 1986; New Delhi 1988; FCO 1991; Ottawa 1996; Second Secretary (Commercial) Abuja 1999; Band C5; m 1987 Adrian Bell (2s 1993, 1996).

Bell, Kay Beverley; Colombo since January 2002; Born 11/06/57; FCO 1984; Bonn 1986; Floater Duties 1989; New York (UKMIS) 1993; Band A2.

Bell, Laura (née Page); SUPL since August 2002; Born 06/09/69; FCO 1995; Algiers 1997; Bridgetown 1998; SUPL 1999; FCO 2000; Band B3; m 1999 Ian McDonald Bell.

Bell, Mark Robert; Third Secretary (Political) Tel Aviv since April 2004; Born 04/05/71; FCO 1997; Full-Time Language Training Cairo 1999; Third Secretary (Political/Press) Damascus 2000; Band B3.

Bell, Melvin, MBE (2002); New York (UKMIS) since November 1999; Born 14/05/65; FCO 1984; Madrid 1987; FCO 1990; Third Secretary Mexico City 1993; FCO 1997; Band C4; m 1997 Maria Louisa Toxtle de Bautista.

Bell, Samantha Jane; FCO since June 2002; Born 01/10/71; FCO 1997; Athens 1999; Band B3.

Bellas, David Livingston; FCO since September 2000; Born 06/11/74; Band C4.

Bellham, Richard Anthony; FCO since 1998; Born 26/01/50; HM Forces (Army) 1968 -74; FCO 1976; Bangkok 1986; FCO 1989; Tokyo 1995; Band C5; m 1987 Chidphan Jaiprasat (1d 1989).

Belof, Margaret Mary; Dushanbe since December 2003; Born 06/09/61; FCO 1990; Third Secretary Bucharest 1994; Third later Second Secretary (Economic/EU) Athens 1998; Band C4.

Bendor, David Ian; First Secretary (Financial & Economic) Paris since March 1999; Born 14/03/66; Economic Advisers FCO 1991-96; T/D Paris 1993; On secondment to IMF (European Division) 1996-98; Band D6.

Benham, Gary Edward; Phnom Penh since August 2003; Born 07/03/69; Royal Air Force 1987-96; FCO 1997; Santiago 1998; ECO Tunis 2000; Band B3; m 1998 Amanda Marsden (1s 1999; 1d 2002).

Benham, Nancy, MBE (2003); SUPL since June 2004; Born 02/08/60; FCO 2003; Band A2; m 1986 Colin (2d 1988, 1991).

Benjamin, Jon; Head of Human Rights Policy Department FCO since January 2000; Born 19/01/63; ODA 1986; Third later Second Secretary Jakarta 1988; First Secretary FCO 1992; Private Secretary to Minister of State FCO 1993; Full-Time Language Training 1995; First Secretary and Head of Political Section Ankara 1996; SUPL 1999; Deputy Head of Drugs and International Crime Department FCO 2000.

Bennett, Alexander; Tehran since April 2003; Born 04/11/67; FCO 1987; Paris 1998; Band C4; m 1997 Deborah Karen Stirzaker (1d 2001).

Bennett, Brian Maurice; HM Ambassador Minsk since March 2003; Born 01/04/48; FCO 1971; Prague 1973; Helsinki 1977; Second Secretary FCO 1979; Second Secretary (Comm/Aid) Bridgetown 1983; Second later First Secretary Vienna (UKDEL) MBFR 1986; First Secretary (Chancery/Inf) The Hague 1988; First Secretary FCO 1992; Deputy Head of Mission Tunis 1997; m 1969 Lynne Skipsey (3s 1974, 1978, 1991).

Bennett, Frederick Michael; Belgrade since February 2002; Born 07/12/49; Royal Military Police 1967-92; Prague 1992; Floater Duties 1994; FCO 1997; Peking 1997; Band B3; m 1978 Lynne Louise Jane Russell (2d 1979, 1980).

Bennett, Marylyn; FCO (Hanslope Park) since August 2000; Born 16/12/48; New Delhi 1972; Monrovia 1974; FCO 1977; South America Floater 1979; FCO 1982; Floater Duties 1983; Panama City 1986; Third later Second Secretary FCO 1988; Deputy Head of Mission Asunción 1993; Second Secretary Lilongwe 1996.

Bennett, Stephen Paul; FCO since October 1997; Born 28/10/62; FCO 1982; Nairobi 1986; FCO 1990; SUPL 1993; FCO 1994; Moscow 1995; Band A2; m 1990 Stephanie Cattermole (1 step d 1986; 1s 1991).

Bennett-Dixon, Vanessa May (née Bennett); Paris since July 2001; Born 12/01/57; FCO 1975; Nairobi 1978; Havana 1981; Kuwait 1982; Montserrat 1988; Stanley 1992; Hanoi 1994; Luanda 1996; Band A2; m 1987 Ronald William Dixon.

Bensberg, Jacqueline Margaret (née Campbell); FCO since July 2000; Born 06/06/63; FCO 1983; Cape Town/Pretoria 1985; UKDEL CSCE 1987; Third Secretary UKDEL CFE 1989; FCO 1990; Accra 1994; FCO 1997; Third Secretary (Political) Brussels 1998; Band B3; m 1991 Mark Bensberg (1d 1999).

Bensberg, Mark; Deputy Head of Mission Kinshasa since June 2004; Born 19/07/62; FCO 1980; Paris 1982; Africa/ME Floater 1985; Vice-Consul Vienna 1988; FCO 1991; Accra 1994; Second Secretary (Political/Press & Public Affairs) Brussels 1997; FCO 2000; m 1991 Jacqueline Margaret Campbell (1d 1999).

Bentley, Sally (née Myers); Athens since October 1999; Born 13/08/68; FCO 1998; Band A2; m 2001 Paul Stephen Bentley.

Berg, Geoffrey, MVO (1976); Consul-General Toronto and Director Trade and Investment Canada since January 2002; Born 05/07/45; CRO 1963; DSA 1965; LA Floater Duties 1968; Bucharest 1970; Second Secretary 1970; FCO 1971; Second later First Secretary (Inf) Helsinki 1975; FCO 1979; First Secretary (Commercial) Madrid 1984; First Secretary FCO 1988; Counsellor on loan to the DTI 1990; Deputy Head of Mission Mexico City 1993; Deputy Consul General and Director of Trade New York 1997; m 1970 Sheila Maxine Brown (1s 1975).

Berman, Paul Richard; Legal Counsellor Brussels (UKREP) since August 2002; Born 23/11/64; Called to the Bar, Gray's Inn 1990; Assistant later Senior Assistant Legal Adviser FCO 1991; Seconded to the International Committee of the Red Cross, Geneva 1996; FCO 1998; Legal Counsellor on loan to the Attorney General's Chambers (LSLO) 2000.

Berry, Susanna Gisela; SUPL since September 1997; Born 06/09/62; FCO 1986; Second Secretary Vienna (UKDEL) 1989; Second Secretary (Economic) Vienna 1990; Full-Time Language Training FCO 1992; Full-Time Language Training Cairo 1993; FCO 1994; Band D6; m 1996 Paul Adams (1s 1999).

Bersin, Jacqueline; First Secretary (Management/Consular) Singapore since November 1999; Born 13/08/58; FCO 1977; SUPL 1978; Islamabad 1979; SUPL 1980; FCO 1981; Rome 1982; Warsaw 1983; FCO 1985; Port Louis 1988; Montserrat 1993; Second Secretary FCO 1995; Band C5; m 1990 Alan Maurice Bersin.

Bertie, Julie Karina (née Finnigan); SUPL since October 1999; Born 08/06/71; FCO 1990; Nairobi 1996; Band A2; m 1995 Stewart Valentine Bertie (2d 1998, 2000).

Best, Eleanor Marion; Seconded to UK Trade & Investment since May 2003; Born 28/04/63; MOD 1986-89; FCO 1996; Brussels 1997; Copenhagen 2000; Band A2.

Bethel, Samantha Claire Risby; ECO Islamabad since November 2000; Born 25/02/70; FCO 1990; Jakarta 1993; Pro Consul Düsseldorf 1997; Band B3.

Betterton, Judith Anne; Ankara since September 2002; Born 02/08/57; FCO 1983; Warsaw 1984; Lilongwe 1987; Bogotá 1989; Canberra 1991; FCO 1994; Amman 1998; Band B3.

Bevan, Howard James; Brussels since July 2003; Born 19/11/54; Royal Signals 1970-92; FCO 1995; Brussels (UKREP) 1997; Pro Consul Düsseldorf 2000; Band A2; m 1973 Christine (1d 1975; 1s 1986).

Bevan, James David; FCO since July 1998; Born 13/07/59; FCO 1982; Kinshasa 1984; Second later First Secretary Brussels (UKDEL) 1986; First Secretary FCO 1990; First Secretary Paris 1993; First Secretary (Political) Washington 1994; m 1984 Alison Janet Purdie (3d 1986, 1989, 1998).

Bevan, Terence Richard; First Secretary FCO since May 1992; Born 10/04/54; FCO 1970; Bonn 1977; FCO 1980; Second later First Secretary Oslo 1988; Band C5; m 1978 Gillian Margaret Francis (2d 1981, 1984).

Bewley, Sarah Margaret; Second Secretary FCO since May 1999; Born 05/08/73; FCO 1995; Kuala Lumpur 1997; Band C4.

Beyer, John Charles; Deputy Head of Mission Luxembourg since September 2002; Born 29/04/50; Director, China-Britain Business Council 1991-98; First Secretary FCO 1999; Band D6; m 1972 Letty Marindin Minns (1d 1977, 1s 1988).

Beynon, Debra Jane; Management/Commercial Officer Khartoum since May 2003; Born 22/07/62; Department of Transport 1978; Department of Employment 1979; FCO 1983; Berlin BMG 1985; Kingstown 1988; Dhaka 1989; FCO 1993; Second Secretary (Immigration/Consular) Dhaka 1995; Second later First Secretary (Immigration) Islamabad 1998; FCO 2002; Band C4; m 1985 Paul Ogwyn Beynon.

Bicker, David Allen; St Helena since May 2002; Born 25/10/48; Army 1966-88; Brussels (UKDEL) 1989; Cairo 1991; FCO 1994; Tirana 1996; Anguilla 1998; Band B3; m 1974 Molly Patricia (1d 1976; 2s 1978, 1983).

Bickers, Esméa Lillian; FCO since June 2000; Born 18/12/54; FCO 1988; Ottawa 1989; FCO 1992; The Hague 1997; Band A2.

Bielby, Richard Stephen; FCO since 1997; Born 18/09/65; FCO (HCS) 1989; FCO 1991; Islamabad 1993; Band B3; ptnr, Loy Foo Cheong.

Biggerstaff, Sarah Jane; SUPL since September 2002; Born 04/11/70; FCO 1997; Budapest 1998; FCO 2000; Band A2.

Bilimoria, Tehemton Pirosha; Second Secretary Nairobi since August 2000; Born 21/01/46; HM Forces (Army) 1964-70; PO 1970-76; FCO 1979; Washington 1984; FCO 1987; Paris 1992; Band C5; m 1980 Tayariez Dastoor (1d 1984; 1s 1986).

Billing, Victoria Elizabeth; FCO since January 2003; Born 31/05/75; FCO 1997; SOAS University of London 1998; Rangoon 1999; Band D6.

Binfield, Marella Jane; FCO since May 2002; Born 12/01/69; FCO 1995; Warsaw 1996; Band B3.

Binnie, Serena Clare; FCO since October 1990; Born 04/09/63; FCO 1986; Montevideo 1989; Band C4.

Birch, Ann Elizabeth (née Ridge); FCO since January 2000; Born 23/10/62; FCO 1990; New Delhi 1992; FCO 1995; Hanoi 1997; Band B3; m 1996 Paul David Birch.

Bird, Charles Philip Glover; First Secretary (Political) Abuja since August 2001; Born 08/10/54; Second Secretary FCO 1986; Language Training 1987; Language Training Cairo 1988; Second Secretary (Chancery) Abu Dhabi 1989; Second Secretary Belgrade 1992; Second later First Secretary FCO 1993; First Secretary (Political) Athens 1995; m 1975 Clare St. John (2s 1978, 1980; 1d 1982).

Bird, Christabel Helen; Second later First Secretary FCO since May 1993; Born 18/11/53; Tehran 1978; FCO 1979; Caracas 1980; FCO

1982; Second Secretary Geneva (UKMIS) 1989; Consul Geneva 1990; Band C5.

Bird, Juliette Winsome; FCO since September 2003; Born 04/10/63; FCO 1990; New Delhi 1992; Second later First Secretary FCO 1994; First Secretary (Political) Brussels 2001; Band D6; m 2002 Donald Peter Scargill (1s 2002).

Birks, Ian Martin; FCO since 2004; Born 03/06/52; FCO 1971; Canberra 1973; Belgrade 1976; Georgetown 1978; New York 1981; FCO 1984; Islamabad 1988; Second Secretary (Aid) Lagos 1992; Second Secretary FCO 1994; Second Secretary (Commercial) New Delhi 1997; First Secretary (Commercial) Lagos 2000; m (1) 1976 Sheridan Elizabeth Grice (diss 1997) (2d 1987, 1991); (2) Anny Bhatti 1997 (1d 1999).

Bishop, Peter George; FCO since January 2002; Born 23/11/55; Home Civil Service 1984; Bonn 1998; Band B3; m 1983 Fiona Christine Buchanan (2s 1988, 1992).

Biskin, Sally-Ann (née Peters); Deputy Head of Mission Windhoek since May 2003; Born 08/02/65; FCO 1983; Brussels 1985; Harare 1988; Maputo 1989; Lagos 1989; Istanbul 1990; FCO 1993; SUPL 1994; FCO 1994; SUPL 1997; FCO 1998; Second Secretary (Management) Islamabad 2001; Band C4; m 1991 Cneyt Cem Biskin (diss) (2d 1992, 1994).

Black, Janice Sarah; Second Secretary Canberra since June 2003; Born 11/08/66; FCO 1987; SUPL 1994; FCO 1995; Second Secretary (Immigration) Tehran 1998; FCO 2001; Band C4.

Blackburne, Alison; Deputy High Commissioner Harare since June 2003; Born 20/06/64; FCO 1987; Third later First Secretary (Chancery) Warsaw 1989; First Secretary FCO 1992; First Secretary New York (UKMIS) 1996; First Secretary (Political) Stockholm 2000.

Blacker, Catherine Louise; FCO since June 2003; Born 15/09/68; FCO 1989; Brussels (UKDEL) 1991; FCO 1997; T/D Islamabad 2000; Kabul 2002; Band B3.

Blackwell, Christopher Robert; Second Secretary FCO since May 1984; Born 11/08/58; FCO 1975; Geneva (UKMIS) 1978; FCO 1981; Aden 1983; Band C4; m 1982 Catherine Rose Gallagher (1d 1987; 1s 1989).

Bladen, John; Second Secretary FCO since February 1987; Born 08/07/44; FCO 1971; Bangkok 1973; FCO 1975; Accra 1976; FCO 1979; Kingston 1980; FCO 1983; Second Secretary Harare 1984; m 1969 Nina Shaw (1d 1972).

Blake, Michael David; Head of Technical Group (Implementation) FCO Services since October 2001; Born 19/01/55; FCO 1971; HCS 1976; FCO 1978; Washington 1979; FCO 1981; Ottawa 1981; FCO 1984; FCO Services 1999; m 1978 Audrey Layfield (1s 1983).

Blake, Michael John Warwick; FCO since May 2004; Born 05/03/75; FCO 1997; Full-Time Language Training Peking 1999; Consul (Political/Economic) Hong Kong 2000; Band C4.

Blake, Stanley Clement; Second Secretary (Consular) Canberra since November 2000; Born 14/07/44; FO 1964; UK delegation NATO Paris and Brussels 1966; Amman 1969; FCO 1970; Moscow 1974; Paris 1975; FCO 1978; Tunis 1981; Second Secretary 1984; Second Secretary (Admin) and Consul Muscat 1984; Second Secretary FCO 1988; Second Secretary (Management) Addis Ababa 1991; Second Secretary FCO 1992; Second Secretary (Consular/Immigration) Accra 1993; ECO Bangkok 1997; m (1) Marion Lesley Jelly (diss 1972) (1s 1968); (2) 1977 Lindsay Jane Townsend (1s 1981).

Blanchard, William Hume James, OBE (1997); MVO (1993); First Secretary FCO since November 2001; Born 08/01/67; FCO 1988; Second Secretary (Information) Budapest 1992; Second Secretary FCO 1995; SUPL 1997; First Secretary (Chancery) Islamabad 1998; Band D6; m 1998 Meriel Beattie (1s 2000).

Blogg, David John; HM Consul and Management Officer Ljubljana since April 2002; Born 08/09/48; FCO 1971; East Berlin 1973; Khartoum 1974; Dacca 1977; FCO 1979; Calcutta 1981; Baghdad 1982; Jedda 1983; Athens 1986; Second Secretary Tripoli 1989; Second Secretary FCO 1991; Second Secretary (Management/Consular) Sana'a 1993; Second Secretary Ulaanbaatar 1994; Second Secretary FCO 1995; Second Secretary Lima 1996; Consul (Management) St Petersburg 1997; Second Secretary FCO 1998; m 1973 Susan Robinia Meloy.

Bloomfield, Keith George; HM Ambassador Kathmandu since July 2002; Born 02/06/47; HCS 1969-80; Brussels (UKREP) 1980; First Secretary FCO 1985; Head of Chancery Cairo 1987; Counsellor, Consul-General and Deputy Head of Mission Algiers 1990; Counsellor (Political/Management) Rome 1994; Minister and Deputy Head of Mission Rome 1996; FCO 1998; m 1976 Geneviève Paule (3d 1979, 1982, 1985).

Blows, Glyn Christopher; Washington since March 2003; Born 27/08/70; FCO 1990; Nicosia 1995; FCO 1999; Band A2; ptnr, Jane Brewer (1d 2001).

Bloxham, Siân Landis; Bandar Seri Begawan since July 2000; Born 11/11/64; HCS 1990; FCO 1996; St Petersburg 1998; Band A2.

Blunt, David Graeme, LVO (1986); Deputy Governor Gibraltar since January 2002; Born 19/01/53; FCO 1978; Second later First Secretary Vienna 1979; First Secretary (External Affairs) Peking 1983; FCO 1987; First Secretary (Chancery) Canberra 1989; Counsellor FCO 1994; Deputy Head of Mission and Consul-General Oslo 1997; m 1975 Geirid Bakkeli (3s 1982, 1984, 1990).

Boam, Rachel Christine (née Wickens); SUPL since August 2003; Born 05/11/68; FCO 1988;

New York (UKMIS) 1991; PA/Deputy Head of Mission Athens 1995; FCO 1998; SUPL 1999; Language Training 1999; PA/Ambassador Berlin 2000; Band A2; M 1993 Jason Daniel Boam (1s 1999).

Boardman, Clarence Ronald; FCO since August 1998; Born 11/12/48; DSAO/FCO 1965; Algiers 1970; Ottawa 1972; Warsaw 1974; FCO 1977; MECAS 1978; Aden 1979; Riyadh 1982; Second Secretary FCO 1986; Consul (Commercial) Vancouver 1989; Deputy High Commissioner and Head of Mission Bandar Seri Begawan 1995; m 1973 Marion Lynn Fraser (1s 1991).

Boath, Arlene; Tirana since September 2002; Born 09/06/71; FCO 1988; Geneva (UKMIS) 2000; Band A2.

Boddy, Ben; FCO since February 2004; Born 31/10/75; Band B3; ptnr, Caroline Sharman.

Boffa, Sandra Jean (née Isaac); Tokyo since February 2003; Born 22/08/67; Ministry of Agriculture 1984-90; FCO 1990; Tokyo 1995; FCO 1998; Vienna 1999; Band A2; m 1992 Anthony Paul Vincent Boffa (1d 1993; 2s 1994, 1998).

Bolgar, Andrew Ben; Third Secretary Freetown since August 2003; Born 03/07/75; FCO 1999; Band B3.

Bond, Clare Elizabeth; Second Secretary FCO since October 2001; Born 17/01/75; FCO 1997; Second Secretary (Political) Kuala Lumpur 1999; Band C4.

Bond, Ian Andrew Minton; Deputy Head of Mission Vienna (UKDEL OSCE) since June 2000; Born 19/04/62; FCO 1984; Third later Second Secretary (Political) Brussels (UKDEL NATO) 1987; First Secretary FCO 1990; First Secretary (Political) Moscow 1993; First Secretary FCO 1996; m 1987 Kathryn Joan Ingamells (1d 1989; 2s 1993, 2000).

Bond, Simon; FCO since August 2003; Born 23/04/65; Home Office 1988-89; FCO 1989; Port of Spain 1993; Kampala 1997; FCO 1999; Dakar 2000; Band C4.

Bonnici, Gail Margaret; SUPL since December 1997; Born 11/12/60; FCO 1984; Madrid 1985; LA Floater 1988; Valetta 1989; FCO 1991; Riyadh 1992; Buenos Aires 1996; Band A2; m 1990 Martin Mario Bonnici (1s 1991).

Bonsey, Jennifer Elaine; FCO since April 2004; Born 23/12/46; MOD 1964; FCO 1981; Paris 1982; Tunis 1985; Brussels (UKREP) 1988; FCO 1989; Singapore 1997; Bucharest 2001; Band B3.

Booker, Jacqueline Alice; FCO since June 1997; Born 19/01/62; FCO 1982; Athens 1984; Hanoi 1987; LA Floater 1988; FCO 1992; Dar es Salaam 1995; Band D6.

Booth, Mark James; FCO since June 2002; Born 13/03/72; FCO 1991; Geneva (UKMIS) 1995; Hong Kong 1998; Band B3.

Booth, Susan Jane (née Corcoran); FCO since March 1996; Born 03/08/68; FCO 1986; New York (UNGA) (UKMIS) 1988; Cape Town/Pretoria 1989; Warsaw 1991; Rabat 1993; Band B3; m 1991 Rodney James Booth.

Borisuth, Fiona Jayne (née Lavender); Bangkok since January 2000; Born 12/06/70; FCO 1991; Tokyo 1992; La Paz 1996; Band B3; m 2001 Wasan (Aek) Borisuth (1 step d 1995, 1d 2003; 1s 2001).

Borland, David; SUPL since June 2004; Born 20/06/60; on loan to DTI; Second Secretary FCO 1991; T/D Second Secretary (Political) Maputo 1993; Second Secretary (Political) Caracas 1994; First Secretary (Political/Economic) Mexico City 1995; First Secretary Helsinki (EU) 2000; Band D6.

Borley, Salud Maria Victoria; On attachment to British Trade International since January 2003; Born 06/05/70; FCO 1989; Caracas 1992; Floater Duties 1996; FCO 1998; Band C4.

Bossley, Edward; New Delhi since January 2004; Born 22/09/71; FCO 1991; New York (UKMIS) 1994; Islamabad 1997; FCO 1999; Band C4; m 1994 Stefany Elizabeth Rocque (1d 1997).

Bossley, Stefany Elizabeth (née Rocque); FCO since April 1999; Born 28/07/66; FCO 1989; World-wide Floater Duties 1992; New York (UKMIS) 1994; Islamabad 1997; Band B3; m 1994 Edward Bossley (1d 1997).

Boswell, Clive Timothy; Washington since December 2001; Born 29/08/70; FCO 1996; Brussels (UKREP) 1998; Band A2.

Botha, Caroline Jane; SUPL since August 2003; Born 01/04/70; FCO 1996; Bratislava 1997; Attaché (Immig/Cons) Colombo 2000; Band B3; m 1993 Peter Bortha (1d 1994; 1s 1998).

Botham, Peter; Tunis since June 2004; Born 10/08/78; FCO 2003; Band A2.

Bottomley, Patricia Fiona; FCO since March 2004; Born 29/03/59; FCO 1983; (Second Secretary) 1985; Second Secretary and Vice Consul Havana 1986; First Secretary (Chancery) Mexico City 1988; First Secretary FCO 1991; Brussels 1994; FCO 1998; First Secretary (Political) Rome 2000; Band D6; m 1997 Arno Baecker (1s 1999).

Bouakaze-Khan, Najma (née Khan); Istanbul since December 1999; Born 11/06/67; FCO 1987; Addis Ababa 1989; Brussels (UKDEL NATO) 1993; FCO 1996; Full-Time Language Training 1999; Band B3; m 1992 Didier Bouakaze-Khan. (2s 1996, 1999).

Bourke, Martin; Deputy High Commissioner Wellington since May 2000; Born 12/03/47; Third Secretary FCO 1970; Brussels 1971; Second Secretary Singapore 1974; Second later First Secretary FCO 1975; First Secretary Lagos 1978; FCO 1980; On loan to DOT 1980; Consul (Comms) Johannesburg 1984; First Secretary FCO 1988; Governor Turks and Caicos Islands 1993;

Seconded to The Prince's Trust 1997; m 1973 Anne Marie Marguerite Hottelet (4s 1974, 1977, 1979, 1983).

Bowden, Christopher John, MBE (2004); Maputo since June 2001; Born 06/07/59; FCO 1977; Copenhagen 1979; Karachi 1982; Bucharest 1983; Paris 1985; FCO 1988; Calcutta 1991; Istanbul 1994; FCO 1998; Band C4; m 1983 Jane Susan Manville (1d 1986).

Bowden, James Nicholas Geoffrey, OBE (2002); Deputy Head of Mission Kuwait since May 2003; Born 27/05/60; Royal Green Jackets 1979-86; Second Secretary FCO 1986; Language Training 1988; Language Training Cairo 1989; Deputy, later Acting Consul-General Aden 1990; Second later First Secretary (Chancery) Khartoum 1991; First Secretary FCO 1994; First Secretary (Political) Washington 1996; First Secretary (Economic and Commercial) Riyadh 1999; First Secretary FCO 2000; m (1) 1985 Alison Hulme (diss) (1s 1993; 1d 1995); m (2) 1999 Sarah Peaslee (1d 2001; twin s 2003).

Bowe, Michael Henry; FCO since July 1999; Born 08/03/46; FCO 1971; Lagos 1974; New Delhi 1978; FCO 1981; Second Secretary (Commercial) Lilongwe 1982; Second Secretary (Comm) Gaborone 1986; Second Secretary FCO 1990; Second Secretary (Management) and Consul Maputo 1993; Second Secretary (Consular) Sarajevo 1997; m (1) 1970 Ann Frances Ballard (diss 1985) (1d 1976; 1s 1979); m (2) 1985 Sandra Jean Brown Lassale.

Bowes, Andrew Martin; Deputy Head of Mission Dili since June 2002; Born 10/08/74; FCO 1997; Third Secretary (Vice-Consul/Press and Public Affairs) Maputo 1999; m 2001 Isabel Filipa Oliveira Goncalves.

Bowes, Jacqueline; FCO since October 1990; Born 28/02/60; Inland Revenue 1976-90; Band A2.

Bowie, Nigel John Graydon; FCO since May 2002; Born 31/05/51; FCO 1975; Seoul 1977; Paris 1981; Athens 1983; Second Secretary FCO 1985; Second Secretary (Comm/Econ) Oslo 1988; First Secretary (Comm) Athens 1992; FCO 1997; First Secretary (Political) Abuja 1999; m 1977 Mildred Alice Sansom (2s 1979, 1984; 1d 1982).

Bowling, Nicola Carron (née Jackson); SUPL since May 2004; Born 01/12/67; FCO 1991; Third Secretary (Aid/Commercial) Maputo 1994; Second Secretary Kuala Lumpur 1998; Band C4; m 1996 David John Robinson Bowling (1s 2000).

Bowman, Victoria Jane (née Robinson); HM Ambassador Rangoon since December 2002; Born 12/06/66; FCO 1988; Third later Second Secretary Rangoon 1990; First Secretary FCO 1993; First Secretary (Information/Press) Brussels (UKREP) 1996; SUPL 1999.

Bowskill, Robert Colin; Kingston since November 2002; Born 21/09/43; Army 1959-77; Police 1977-84; Prague 1984; Lusaka 1987; Warsaw 1989;

New Delhi 1991; Bucharest 1995; Tel Aviv 1998; Band C4; m 1966 Jean Spencer (2s 1967, 1968).

Bowyer, Aileen Jane (née Gemmell); SUPL since January 1994; Born 10/09/62; FCO 1983; Belgrade 1985; SUPL 1987; Kaduna 1990; FCO 1990; Band A2; m 1987 Anthony Harvey Bowyer (1d 1992).

Bowyer, Anthony Harvey; FCO since August 2001; Born 21/11/62; FCO 1982; Belgrade 1984; Kaduna 1987; FCO 1990; Harare 1994; Dublin 1997; Band C4; m 1987 Aileen Jane Gemmell (2d 1992, 1999).

Bowyer, Joanne Louise; Toronto since June 2001; Born 30/03/68; FCO 1989; Bogotá 1991; Abuja 1994; FCO 1998; Band B3.

Boxer, Peter John; FCO since July 2003; Born 24/07/71; FCO 1995; Second Secretary (Political) Nicosia 1997; On secondment 2001; Band D6.

Boyd, Andrew Jonathan Corrie, OBE (1992); Counsellor FCO since June 1999; Born 05/05/50; Royal Navy 1968-80; FCO 1984; First Secretary (Econ) Accra 1981; FCO 1984; First Secretary (Chancery) Mexico City 1988; First Secretary FCO 1991; Counsellor Islamabad 1996; m 1979 Ginette Anne Vischer (2s 1985, 1987; 1d 1991).

Boyden, Simon Denis; First Secretary FCO since July 2002; Born 24/02/68; FCO 1997; Second Secretary (Commercial) Moscow 1999; Band C4; m 1998 Geraldine Gallagher (1s 1999; 2d 2001, 2003).

Boyles, Elizabeth; SUPL since September 2003; Born 28/08/67; FCO 1990; Third Secretary (Political) Brussels 1994; New York (UKMIS) 1996; DHM San Salvador 1997; Second Secretary (Trade Policy) Brussels (UKREP) 2000; First Secretary (Economic and Social Affairs) Brussels 2003; Band D6; m 1997 Patrick Dens (1s 2003).

Bradbury, Jonathan Edward; FCO since 2004; Born 16/12/67; HCS 1989-95; Nairobi 1997; Dublin 2000; Band A2; m 1994 Rebecca Clare Sebborn (2s 1998, 2000; 1d 2003).

Bradley, Guy; FCO since March 1989; Born 03/02/62; FCO 1981; New Delhi 1983; FCO 1987; Havana 1988; Band C5; m 1987 Andrea Stannard. (1s 1993; 1d 1994).

Bradley, Henry Alexander Jarvie; First Secretary Vienna (UKDEL) OSCE since May 2000; Born 23/07/52; HM Customs and Excise 1969; FCO 1971; Brussels (EC) 1975; Budapest 1978; Bahrain 1979; FCO 1982; Munich 1984; Third Secretary (AO/Vice-Consul) Maseru 1987; Second Secretary FCO 1992; Deputy Hign Commissioner Banjul 1996; Band C5; m 1979 Gabriella Maria Schwery.

Bradley, Joseph Maxwell; SUPL since October 2002; Born 14/02/60; FCO 1978; East Berlin 1981; Resigned 1983; Reinstated 1986; Lusaka 1987; Vienna (UKDEL) 1990; FCO 1993; Third Secretary (Information) Berlin 1995; Full-Time Language Training 1995; Second Secretary

Geneva (UKMIS) 1998; m 1987 Melanie Rose (2d 1988, 1992; 1s 1990).

Bradley, Stephen Edward; Consul-General Hong Kong since December 2003; Born 04/04/58; FCO 1981; Language Training 1982; Second later First Secretary Tokyo 1983; SUPL (Guinness Peat Aviation) 1987; Deputy Political Adviser Hong Kong 1988; SUPL (Lloyd George Investment Management) 1993; FCO 1995; Head of West Indian Atlantic Department FCO 1997; Director of Trade and Investment Paris 1999; Minister Beijing 2002; m 1982 Elizabeth Gomersall (1s 1985; 1d 1988).

Bradley, Timothy Gawin, OBE (1991); First Secretary FCO since May 1999; Born 03/06/59; FCO 1983; Language Training 1984; Second later First Secretary (Chancery) Kuwait 1986; First Secretary FCO 1989; Belgrade 1996; Band D6; m 1990 Kathleen Scanlon (3s 1993, 1995, 1997).

Bradshaw, John Vincent; New Delhi since November 2000; Born 19/08/64; FCO 1999; Band C4; m 1994 Doris Jungling (2s 1994, 1996).

Braidford, Lindsey; FCO since February 1988; Born 20/04/47; Jedda 1975; Belize 1976; The Hague 1979; Rangoon 1982; Pretoria/Cape Town 1984; Band B3.

Braithwaite, Julian Nicholas; Washington since September 2004; Born 25/07/68; Second Secretary FCO 1994; Seconded to ICFY, Zagreb 1995; Second Later First Secretary (Chancery) Belgrade 1996; On loan to No.10 Press Office 1998; Seconded to SHAPE 1999; Prime Minister's Speech Co-ordinator 2000; Sarajevo 2002; m 1999 Biljana Njagulj (1d 2000).

Bramley, Sheila Jane; Second Secretary FCO since February 2002; Born 25/10/63; FCO 1982; Tokyo 1984; Sofia 1987; SE Asia/FE Floater 1989; FCO 1991; Kuala Lumpur 1994; Canberra 1995; Islamabad 1998; Band C4.

Brammer, Geoffrey Ian; FCO since January 2002; Born 09/06/65; FCO 1985; Kaduna 1987; Nassau 1990; Tehran 1991; FCO 1992; Deputy Head of Mission Ashgabat 1995; Second Secretary (Management) Bridgetown 1998; Band C4; m 1991 Shelley Diane Chalmers.

Brandon, William Roland; First Secretary (Political) Singapore since April 2001; Born 07/06/64; FCO 1993; First Secretary (Economic) Vienna 1996; First Secretary FCO 1999; Band D6; m 1991 Polly Jennifer Nyiri (3d (twins) 1996, 1998).

Brannigan, Virginia (née Reynolds); SUPL since July 1999; Born 16/01/62; FCO 1985; San José 1986; Madrid 1990; FCO 1998; Band A2; m 1992 Stuart Patrick Brannigan.

Brant, Andrew; FCO since March 2001; Born 13/02/74; Band B3.

Brant, Astrid Lorita Sophia; FCO since August 2002; Born 27/02/53; DHSS 1980-91; FCO 1991; Tunis 1992; Floater Duties 1997; Band B3.

Braun, David Alan; FCO since February 2000; Born 27/02/71; FCO 1991; Madrid 1998; Band B3; m 1998 Susan Jane Robottom.

Brazier, Colin Nigel; Consul (Commercial) New York since September 2000; Born 31/10/53; FCO 1973; Warsaw 1976; Singapore 1977; Accra 1980; FCO 1982; Dhaka 1985; Third Secretary (Comm)later Second Secretary (Development) Kingston 1989; Second Secretary FCO 1992; Deputy High Commissioner Georgetown 1997; m 1975 Jane Ann Pearson (1d 1979; 1s 1983).

Brear, Andrew James; FCO since July 2003; Born 28/01/60; Army 1979-90; Second later First Secretary FCO 1991; First Secretary (Inf) Santiago 1994; First Secretary FCO 1997; First Secretary (Political) Stockholm 2000; Band D6; m 1986 Jane Susan Matthews (1d 1991; 1s 1993).

Breeze, Christopher Mark; First Secretary FCO since October 2001; Born 13/08/63; FCO 1985; Second Secretary (Chancery) Nicosia 1988; Second later First Secretary FCO 1991; First Secretary (Trade Policy) New Delhi 1994; First Secretary (Political) Ankara 1997; Band D6; m 1990 Janet Suzanne Champion (2d 1995, 1998).

Breeze, Christopher Mark; FCO since October 2002; Born 13/01/74; Band B3.

Breeze, Susan Jane (née Cockel); FCO since 1996; Born 09/03/66; FCO 1989; Language Training 1990; Full-Time Language Training Peking 1991; Third Secretary (Commercial) Peking 1992; On loan to China-Britain Trade Group 1995; T/D Moscow 1996; m 2002 Paul Stothart Breeze.

Brennan, Anthony Bradford; FCO since December 2002; Born 06/02/66; FCO 1994; Second Secretary (Economic/KHF) later First Secretary (EU/Economic) Prague 1996; FCO 2000; Seconded to Czech Foreign Service 2002.

Brenton, Anthony Russell, CMG (2001); HM Ambassador Moscow since September 2004; Born 01/01/50; FCO 1975; MECAS 1977; First Secretary Cairo 1978; FCO 1981; Presidency Liaison Officer Brussels 1982; FCO 1982; First Secretary (Energy) Brussels (UKREP) 1985; On loan to the European Commission 1986; Counsellor FCO 1989; CDA Harvard University 1992; Full-Time Language Training 1993; Counsellor (Economic/Aid/Scientific) Moscow 1994; Director FCO 1998; Minister Washington 2001; m (1) 1971 Susan Mary Blacker (diss 1978); (2) 1982 Susan Mary Penrose (1s 1984; 2d 1987, 1988).

Brenton, Jonathan Andrew; First Secretary (Media) Berlin since April 2003; Born 24/12/65; FCO 1994; Second Secretary (Commercial) later First Secretary (Economic) Moscow 1996; FCO 2000; Band D6; m 2001 Sayana Yakovlena Virt (1d 1988).

Brett, David Lawrence; SUPL since July 2003; Born 20/09/52; FCO 1978; Tehran 1980; Chicago 1983; FCO 1986; Second Secretary (Chancery) Kingston 1989; Consul-General Alexandria 1992;

First Secretary FCO 1996; Consul-General Algiers 2001; m 1984 Carol Sue Lane (2s 1986, 1991; 1d 1988).

Brett, Rebecca Louise (née Fenwick); Colombo since September 2000; Born 27/11/64; FCO 1984; Washington 1987; The Hague 1990; SUPL 1992; FCO 1994; Abu Dhabi 1996; Band B3; m 1987 Paul Brett (2d 1992, 1996; 1s 1994).

Brett, Russell Michael; FCO since January 1999; Born 14/09/69; FCO 1989; Athens 1995; Band B3; m 1999 Simone Walsh (1d 2000).

Brett Rooks, Bedelia, LVO; FCO since August 2001; Born 09/12/46; FCO 1969; On loan to SEATO Bangkok 1972; Copenhagen 1975; Rome 1976; Second Secretary FCO 1978; Second Secretary Accra 1983; Brussels (UKREP) 1986; First Secretary FCO 1987; First Secretary (Inf) Berlin (BMG) 1989; First Secretary FCO 1993; First Secretary Brussels 1996.

Brettle-Cockman, Lynda Elizabeth; SUPL since March 2003; Born 02/10/62; FCO 1980; Tokyo 1983; SE Asia Floater 1987; Islamabad 1988; SUPL 1992; FCO 1993; Second Secretary (Management) and Consul Caracas 1997; First Secretary (Management) Mexico City 2000; Band C5; m 1994 Michael Anthony Cockman (1d 1994; 1s 2001).

Brewer, Dr Jonathan Andrew; Counsellor FCO since January 2002; Born 20/03/55; FCO 1983; Second later First Secretary Luanda 1986; First Secretary FCO 1988; First Secretary (Chancery) Mexico City 1991; Counsellor FCO 1995; Counsellor (Political Affairs) Moscow 1998; m (1) 1978 Tessa Alexandra Swiney (diss 1990); (2) 1993 Angela Margarita Sosa Teran.

Brewer, Lesley Ann; FCO since July 2003; Born 29/07/57; FCO 1995; Prague 1997; Tripoli 2000; Band A2.

Brewer, Nicola Mary, CMG (2003); On loan as Director General (Regional Programmes) to DFID since June 2002; Born 14/11/57; FCO 1983; Second Secretary (Chancery) Mexico City 1984; First Secretary FCO 1987; First Secretary (Economic) Paris 1991; SUPL 1994; Counsellor FCO 1995; Counsellor New Delhi 1998; Director (Global Issues) FCO 2001; m 1991 Geoffrey Charles Gillham (1d 1993; 1s 1994).

Bridge, Heather Susan (née Brown); FCO since September 2002; Born 19/04/62; FCO 1985; Second Secretary Skopje 2000; Band C4; m 1986 Christopher Martin Gibbons Bridge (2d 1990, 1992).

Bridge, Karen Maria (née Chadbourne); Dhaka since July 2002; Born 03/09/70; FCO 1990; Brussels (UKREP) 1993; FCO 1995; Brussels (UKREP) 1996; FCO 1997; Riyadh 1999; Band A2; m 1992 Peter Charles Benson Bridge (2s 1998, 2000).

Bridge, Richard Philip; Counsellor Geneva since August 2004; Born 24/03/59; Second Secretary (Inf) Warsaw 1986; FCO 1988; First Secretary

(Chancery) Moscow 1989; FCO 1993; Counsellor New Delhi 1998; Counsellor FCO 2001; m 1994 Philippa Anne Leslie-Jones (2s 1995, 1997).

Bridges, Stephen John; HM Ambassador Phnom Penh since December 2000; Born 19/06/60; FCO 1980; Africa/ME Floater 1983; Luanda 1984; Third later Second Secretary (Comm) Seoul 1987; Second later First Secretary FCO 1992; First Secretary Kuala Lumpur 1996; m 1990 Yoon Kyung Mi.

Bridgwood, Alistair Charles Jeudwine; Second Secretary (Political) Sarajevo since February 2004; Born 12/05/73; FCO 2001; Language Training 2003; Band C4; m 2001 Rachel Beale.

Brier, Lucy Jane (née Richardson); FCO since October 2003; Born 18/03/69; FCO 1995; Kuala Lumpur 1997; SUPL 2000; Ulaanbaatar 2002; Band B3; m 1996 Simon Richard Brier.

Brier, Simon Richard; FCO since 2004; Born 15/09/67; FCO 1987; Prague 1989; SE Asia/Far East Floater Duties 1991; FCO 1994; Kuala Lumpur 1997; Deputy Head of Mission Ulaanbaatar 2001; m 1996 Lucy Jane Richardson.

Brierley, David Anthony; FCO since September 2002; Born 14/10/47; Royal Marines 1965; Budapest 1987; Madrid 1989; FCO 1991; Kuwait 1996; Tirana 1998; Band B3; (1s 1998).

Brigden, Neil Stephen; First Secretary (Commercial) The Hague since August 2004; Born 07/08/68; Colombo 1989; Bucharest 1992; Sana'a 1995; FCO 1996; Second Secretary (Commercial) New Delhi 2000; Band C5; m 1993 Joanne (1d 1996; 1s 1999).

Brigenshaw, David Victor; First Secretary FCO since April 1998; Born 01/06/56; FCO 1973; Nairobi 1976; FCO 1981; Kuala Lumpur 1983; Third Secretary (Commercial) Quito 1986; Second Secretary FCO 1990; m 1977 Yvonne Lesley Bush.

Briggs, Geoffrey; Second Secretary FCO since July 1997; Born 20/02/64; FCO 1988; Third Secretary (Econ/Aid) Cairo 1990; Second Secretary FCO 1992; Tirana 1995; Band C4.

Bright, Colin Charles; Consul-General Lyon since January 2004; Born 02/01/48; Second Secretary FCO 1975; First Secretary Bonn 1977; FCO 1979; On loan to the Cabinet Office 1983; Consul New York (BTDO) 1985; Counsellor and Head of Chancery Berne 1989; Consul-General Frankfurt 1993; FCO 1998; m (1) 1978 Helen-Ann Michie (diss 1990); (2) 1990 Jane Elizabeth Gurney Pease (1s 1992; 1d 1995).

Brimfield, Valerie; Dublin since August 2003; Born 27/07/49; FCO 1979; Tunis 1980; Tehran 1983; New Delhi 1985; Dhaka 1989; Ottawa 1992; FCO 1995; Tokyo 1996; Bucharest 1997; FCO 2001; Band B3.

Brind, Kevin James; Second Secretary (SMO/Consul) Santiago since February 2003; Born 05/10/59; FCO 1977; Bonn 1980; Khartoum

1982; Moscow 1986; FCO 1987; Canberra 1990; Third Secretary (Development) Kathmandu 1993; Second Secretary, Deputy Head of Mission Ulaanbaatar 1997; FCO 1998; m 1983 Jane Louise Burns.

Brinkley, Robert Edward; HM Ambassador Kiev since August 2002; Born 21/01/54; FCO 1977; Third Secretary UKDEL Comprehensive Test Ban, Geneva 1978; Language Training 1978; Second Secretary Moscow 1979; First Secretary FCO 1982; First Secretary (Political/Military) Bonn 1988; First Secretary later Counsellor FCO 1992; Counsellor (Political) Moscow 1996; Head of Joint Entry Clearance Unit (FCO/Home Office) 2000; m 1982 Frances Mary Webster (3s 1982, 1984, 1989).

Bristow, Dr Lawrence Stanley Charles; HM Ambassador Baku since January 2004; Born 23/11/63; FCO 1990; Full-Time Language Training 1991; Second Secretary (Chancery/Inf) Bucharest 1992; First Secretary FCO 1996; Private Secretary to Minister of State 1996; Full-Time Language Training 1998; Ankara 1999; CDA, NATO Defence College, Rome 2002; FCO 2003; m 1998 Fiona McCallum (1s 2000).

Bronnert, Deborah Jane; Counsellor (Commercial) Moscow since July 2002; Born 31/01/67; DOE 1989; Royal Commission on Environmantal Pollution 1990; Brussels (UKREP) 1991; DOE 1993; FCO 1994; On secondment to European Commission (Kinnock Cabinet) 1995; FCO 1999; Band D7.

Bronson, Rodney Charles; Canberra since October 1999; Born 09/08/46; FCO 1971; Brussels 1974; Moscow 1977; FCO 1977; Copenhagen 1980; Cairo 1984; Second Secretary FCO 1988; Second Secretary Singapore 1991; m 1968 Margaret Ann Williams (2d 1972, 1974).

Brook, John Edwin; FCO since November 1997; Born 21/03/45; FO 1964; Moscow 1967; Latin American Floater 1970; Calcutta 1972; Second Secretary FCO 1975; Second Secretary (Commercial) Moscow 1978; Second later First Secretary Berne 1981; First Secretary (Commercial) East Berlin 1984; First Secretary on attachment to JSDC 1988; First Secretary FCO 1989; Full-Time Language Training 1993; Consul-General Stuttgart 1993; m 1981 Moira Elizabeth Lands (1d 1983; 1s 1986).

Brookes, Carter, MBE (1990); On loan to the Cabinet Office since May 1997; Born 13/12/46; FCO 1971; Saigon 1973; FCO 1974; St Helena 1976; FCO 1978; Singapore 1980; FCO 1983; Moscow 1986; New Delhi 1989; Beirut 1991; FCO 1992; Band C4; m 1971 Margaret Jean Stewart (3s 1974, 1976, 1977).

Brookes, Diana Lorraine; SUPL since December 2003; Born 19/04/64; Solicitor 1989; Assistant Legal Adviser FCO 1989; First Secretary (Legal) Brussels (UKREP) 1995; FCO 1998; Legal Counsellor FCO 1999; m 1990 Gerald Blais (1d 1999).

Brookes, Maurice John; FCO since July 2001; Born 14/06/49; FCO 1968; Accra 1971; Aden 1972; Nairobi 1974; Karachi 1976; FCO 1978; Tehran 1981; FCO 1982; Kampala 1982; FCO 1985; Paris 1986; Warsaw 1989; FCO 1989; Abidjan 1993; Third Secretary (Immigration/Visa) Harare 1997; Band B3.

Brooking, Karen (née Moore); Second Secretary (Political) Copenhagen since September 2002; Born 15/07/64; FCO 1987; Peking 1990; FCO 1992; SUPL 1994; FCO 1995; Band C4.

Brooking, Stephen John Allan, OBE (2002); FCO since June 2004; Born 13/03/64; FCO 1986; Second Secretary (Economic) Peking 1989; Second Secretary FCO 1992; First Secretary (Political) Sarajevo 1994; FCO 1995; First Secretary (ESCAP) Bangkok 1998; First Secretary FCO 2001; Counsellor (Political) Kabul 2002.

Brooks, Helen Katherine; SUPL since July 2003; Born 21/06/67; FCO 1991; On loan to the Hong Kong Government 1994; Hong Kong 1997; SUPL 1998; First Secretary FCO 1999; Band PRO.

Brooks, Shelagh Margaret Jane; FCO since October 2002; FCO 1979; On loan to Hong Kong Government 1987; Legal Counsellor FCO 1991; Brussels (UKREP) 1998.

Broom, David Charles; Consul (Commercial) Seattle since November 1999; Born 17/09/54; FCO 1973; Islamabad 1975; FCO 1976; Brussels (UKREP) 1977; Baghdad 1981; Home Civil Service 1982; FCO 1983; Rome 1986; Paris 1989; FCO 1989; Second Secretary FCO 1993; Second Secretary (Commercial) Kuala Lumpur 1996; m 1976 Diana Josephine Hewer (1s 1978; 1d 1989).

Broom, Peter David; Consul (Commercial) San Francisco since February 2003; Born 07/08/53; FCO 1970; Oslo 1974; Jedda 1977; Islamabad 1979; FCO 1981; Mbabane 1984; New Delhi 1987; Second Secretary FCO 1989; Consul (Commercial) Brisbane 1991; First Secretary (Commercial), Consul and DHM Yaounde 1997; Consul-General Cape Town 2000; Band C5; m 1976 Vivienne Louise Pyatt (5d 1979, 1981, 1985, 1988, 1994).

Broomfield, David Norman; SMO Stockholm since October 2002; Born 21/05/54; FCO 1973; Banjul 1975; LA Floater 1978; Prague 1980; FCO 1983; Tripoli 1986; Second Secretary (Chancery/Inf) Lusaka 1987; Vice-Consul Naples 1991; First Secretary FCO 1995; Consul (Commercial) Barcelona 1998.

Brosnan, Sheryl (née Landman); Kampala since August 2002; Born 05/12/71; FCO 1991; Bangkok 1993; Istanbul 1997; Abidjan 2000; m 1994 Mark Paul Brosnan (2s 1998, 2000).

Broucher, David Stuart; UK Permanent Representative to the Conference on Disarmament in Geneva since October 2001; Born 05/10/44; FO 1966; Berlin 1968; Second Secretary on loan to the Cabinet Office 1972; First Secretary 1973; First Secretary Prague 1975; First Secretary

(ECOFIN) Brussels (UKREP) 1983; Counsellor (Comm/Aid) Jakarta 1985; Counsellor (Econ) Bonn 1989; Counsellor later AUSS FCO 1994; HM Ambassador Prague 1997; m 1971 Marion M Blackwell (1s 1972).

Brough, Stuart Richard; Second Secretary Port of Spain since January 2003; Born 24/06/65; FCO 1984; Second Secretary Bridgetown 2002; Band C4; m 1989 Delia Claire Hickman (1s 1992; 1d 1995).

Broughton, Sarah; FCO since 2004; Born 12/08/66; FCO 1984; Ottawa 1987; Lilongwe 1990; Floater 1992; FCO 1995; Second Secretary (Political) New York (UKMIS) 1999; Band C4.

Brown, Alexander Mark; FCO since May 2000; Born 21/07/64; DHSS 1986; FCO 1988; Lagos 1991; FCO 1992; Full-Time Language Training 1993; Hamburg 1994; Ashgabat 1997; Band C4; m 1997 A Gehrke.

Brown, Alexander Nicholas Seaton; Second Secretary (Political) Buenos Aires since March 2003; Born 31/07/72; FCO 2000; Band C4.

Brown, Andrew Paul; FCO since January 2002; Born 12/10/68; FCO 1987; New York (UKMIS) 1991; FCO 1994; Third Secretary Seoul 1998; Band B3; m 1998 Joanna Beresford.

Brown, Deirdre Rebecca (née Herdman), MBE (2002); SUPL since November 2002; Born 19/07/66; FCO 1986; Dhaka 1988; FCO 1992; Third Secretary (Political/Economic) Bangkok 1995; FCO 1998; Band C4; m 1991 Stephen William Brown (1d 1992; 1s 1994).

Brown, Edward James Murch, MBE (1991); On loan to DTI since June 2001; Born 27/08/59; FCO 1978; Bonn 1980; Prague 1983; Rabat 1985; FCO 1987; Düsseldorf 1992; FCO 1995; Second Secretary Geneva (UKMIS) 1996; m 1980 Hannah Jane Gibbons.

Brown, Gordon Williams; FCO since April 2004; Born 17/10/54; Inland Revenue 1975; FCO 1976; Guatemala City 1979; The Hague 1981; SE Asia Floater 1983; Kampala 1985; FCO 1988; Second Secretary (Man and Consul) Havana 1991; Second Secretary (Management) and HM Consul Muscat 1995; British Trade International 1998; First Secretary and HM Consul Cairo 2001; m 1985 Rosalind Patricia Harwood (2s 1992, 1993).

Brown, Herbert George, MBE (1981); FCO since February 2001; Born 02/01/43; FO 1964; Rawalpindi 1966; Kuala Lumpur 1969; FCO 1973; Barcelona 1975; Maseru 1978; FCO 1981; Second Secretary and Vice-Consul Baghdad 1982; On loan to DTI 1985; First Secretary (Commercial) Rio de Janeiro 1988; First Secretary FCO 1990; HM Consul later HM Consul-General Cape Town 1996; m 1975 Susan Atkin (1d 1977).

Brown, John Mark; World Wide Floater Duties since May 2002; Born 15/05/43; RAF 1962-84; Islamabad 1990; Belgrade 1993; Moscow 1996; Damascus 1999; Band B3; m 1965 Carole Elizabeth Thompson (2d 1966, 1970).

Brown, Kerry; FCO since April 2003; Born 13/06/67; FCO 1998; First Secretary Beijing 2000; Band D6; m 1995 Siqin Toya (1d 2000).

Brown, Linda; SUPL since October 2002; Born 24/12/55; FCO 1974; Bonn 1977; FCO 1980; Budapest 1980; Oslo 1982; FCO 1985; Rome 1992; Moscow 1996; FCO 2000; Band B3.

Brown, Richard Anthony; Brussels since April 2002; Born 29/10/72; FCO 1996; Band B3.

Brown, Rosalind Patricia (née Harwood); SUPL since May 2004; Born 08/01/59; FCO 1981; Bangkok 1982; Rome 1984; Kampala 1985; FCO 1988; Resigned 1989; Reinstated, FCO 1990; Havana 1991; Muscat 1995; Resigned 1996; Reinstated, Cairo 2003; Band B3; m 1985 Gordon William Brown (3s 1992, 1993, 2002).

Brown, Sir Stephen (David Reid), KCVO (1999); Group Chief Executive (Permanent Secretary) British Trade International since October 2002; Born 26/12/45; HM Forces 1964-76; FCO 1976; First Secretary Nicosia 1977; First Secretary (Commercial) Paris 1980; FCO 1985; T/D DTI 1989; Consul-General Melbourne 1989; Counsellor (Commercial) Peking 1994; HM Ambassador Seoul 1997; Pre Post Training FCO 2000; High Commissioner Singapore 2001; m 1966 Pamela Gaunt (1s 1965; 1d 1969).

Brown, Stephen Leonard; T/D Baghdad since November 2003; Born 07/03/56; Army 1974-96; FCO 1998; Riyadh 1999; FCO 2001; Tehran 2001; Chisinau 2003; Band B3; m 1978 Gaynor Ruth (2d 1974, 1982).

Brown, Stephen Michael; Third Secretary (Vice-Consul) Tashkent since February 2003; Born 09/06/63; Household Cavalry 1980-95; FCO 1997; Mostar 1997; Amman 1998; Third Secretary (Management) Almaty 2000; Bahrain 2002; Band B3; m 2001 Natalya Ryltseva (1d 2002).

Brown, Stuart James; Kiev since August 2001; Born 29/04/75; FCO 1994; Band B3; ptnr, Fiona Brougham.

Brown, Trevor Maurice; FCO since June 2003; Born 24/10/69; FCO 1996; Tirana 2000; m 2003 Laura Mooney.

Brownbill, Timothy Patrick; Full-Time Language Training (German) since May 2004; Born 06/02/60; FCO 1979; Lagos 1982; Madrid 1986; FCO 1989; Resigned 1990 (March), Reinstated 1990 (July); Language Training 1992; Deputy Head of Mission Vilnius 1992; Second Secretary 1994; Second Secretary (Commercial/Economic) Havana 1996; First Secretary FCO 1999; On loan to the DTI 2000; HM Ambassador Managua 2002.

Browne, Dr Carolyn; Counsellor (External) Brussels (UKREP) since June 2002; Born 19/10/58; FCO 1985; Language Training 1987; Second later First Secretary Moscow 1988; FCO 1991; First Secretary New York (UKMIS) 1993; FCO 1997; Counsellor FCO 1999; Full-Time Language Training FCO 2002.

Browne, Sir Nicholas Walker, KBE (2002), CMG (1999); HM Ambassador Copenhagen since August 2003; Born 17/12/47; Third Secretary FCO 1969; Tehran 1971; Second later First Secretary FCO 1975; On loan to the Cabinet Office 1976; First Secretary and Head of Chancery Salisbury 1980; First Secretary FCO 1981; First Secretary (Environment) Brussels (UKREP) 1984; Chargé d'Affaires Tehran 1989; Counsellor FCO 1989; Counsellor (Press and Public Affairs) Washington and Head of BIS New York 1990; Counsellor FCO 1994; Chargé d'Affaires Tehran 1997; HM Ambassador Tehran 1999; m 1969 Diana Marise Aldwinckle (2s 1970, 1980; 2d 1972, 1976).

Brownridge, Valerie (née Ewan), MVO; FCO since January 2003; Born 10/12/56; FCO 1979; Paris (ENA) 1980; Third Secretary Paris 1981; Third Secretary Rome 1985; Third Secretary Lagos 1986; Second Secretary FCO 1988; Second Secretary Berlin 1991; First Secretary FCO 1994; Deputy Consul-General Jerusalem 1999; Band D7; m 1999 John L. F. Brownridge.

Broyd, Laurence Paul; Deputy Head of Mission Sofia since July 2003; Born 12/11/60; FCO 1990; First Secretary (Economic) Moscow 1995; FCO 1999; Band PRO; m 1990 Catherine Mary Carslake (1s 1994; 1d 1998).

Brummell, Paul; HM Ambassador Ashgabat since February 2002; Born 28/08/65; FCO 1987; Third later Second Secretary (Chancery) Islamabad 1989; First Secretary FCO 1993; Full-Time Language Training 1994; First Secretary (Political/Inf) Rome 1995.

Bruton, Robert James; Brussels since August 1999; Born 01/01/57; FCO 1980; Band C4.

Bryant, John Edward; First Secretary FCO since 2000; Born 04/01/51; FCO 1970; Canberra 1972; Kingston 1975; FCO 1977; Bahrain 1978; Cairo 1979; FCO 1983; Nairobi 1986; FCO 1990; Dubai 1994; m 1972 Joyce Anne Barrie (1d 1975; 2s 1985, 1988).

Bryant, Richard John; FCO since June 1998; Born 22/09/53; DTI 1973; Department of Energy 1973; DOT 1975; DTI 1982; FCO 1984; Dhaka 1986; Brussels (UKREP) 1990; Brunei 1993; T/D Islamabad 1997; Floater Duties 1997; Band B3; m 1986 Rosalyn Louise Morris (diss 1991) (1s 1991).

Bryden, Lara-Jean; Floater Duties since November 2003; Born 15/10/71; Employment Service 1991-96; FCO 1996; Floater Duties 1997; Islamabad 2001; Band B3.

Bryson, Alan Robert; FCO since June 2002; Born 12/03/70; FCO 1991; Riyadh 1995; Bangkok 1998; Band B3.

Bryson-Richardson, Mark Edward; Second Secretary (Chancery) Khartoum since January 2003; Born 30/10/76; FCO 1999; Full-Time Language Training 2000; Full-Time Language Training Cairo 2001; Band C4.

Bubbear, Alan Keith; First Secretary (Management) Pretoria since June 2004; Born 14/09/64; FCO 1983; Moscow 1985; SUPL 1988; Johannesburg 1990; FCO 1992; Second Secretary (Commercial) Helsinki 1996; First Secretary FCO 2000; m 1988 Theresa Bernice Allen (3d twins 1992, 1995).

Bubbear, Theresa Bernice (née Allen); FCO since September 2000; Born 14/12/62; FCO 1985; Moscow 1987; Johannesburg 1990; FCO 1992 (Second Secretary) FCO 1993; Second Secretary (Political) Helsinki 1996; Band D6; m 1998 Alan Keith Bubbear (3d twins 1992, 1995).

Buchanan, Sarah Louise (née Allen); FCO since March 2000; Born 31/07/69; FCO 1991; Full-Time Language Training 1994; Vice-Consul Stockholm 1994; Full-Time Language Training 1997; Third Secretary (Political/Press) Tel Aviv 1997; Band B3; m 1995 Hamish Malcolm Robert Buchanan (1s 1998).

Buck, Anthony Adrian; Copenhagen since July 2003; Born 26/08/71; FCO 2001; Band A2.

Buck, John Stephen; HM Ambassador Lisbon since September 2004; Born 10/10/53; FCO 1980; Second Secretary Sofia 1982; First Secretary FCO 1984; Head of Chancery Lisbon 1988; FCO 1992; Counsellor on loan to the Cabinet Office 1994; Counsellor and Deputy Head of Mission Nicosia 1996; Head of Public Diplomacy Department FCO 2000; m 1980 Jean Claire Webb (1d 1985; 1s 1989).

Buckle, Simon James; Consul-General Baghdad since July 2004; Born 29/02/60; Second Secretary FCO 1986; MOD 1988; First Secretary FCO 1991; First Secretary Dublin 1994; Counsellor (Political) and Consul-General Seoul 1997; Bank of England 1998; Counsellor FCO 2003; m 1990 Rajeshree Bhatt (1d 1997).

Buckley, Laura Margaret (née Clegg); FCO since September 2003; Born 29/03/65; FCO 1989; Vice-Consul Bucharest 1994; Deputy Head of Mission Antananarivo 1997; FCO 1999; SUPL 2002; Band C4.

Buckley, Stephen; First Secretary (Commercial) Peking since July 2000; Born 18/06/53; Export Credit Guarantee Department 1972; FCO 1972; Amman 1975; Canberra 1978; FCO 1980; Dakar 1983; Third later Second Secretary (Commercial) Seoul 1987; Second later First Secretary FCO 1992; First Secretary (Commercial) Kuala Lumpur 1996; m 1974 Barbara Frances Yelcich.

Bucknell, Bruce James; First Secretary Madrid since December 2003; Born 15/04/62; FCO 1985; Third Secretary Amman 1988; Secondment to EBRD 1992; FCO 1992; HM Consul Milan 1995; FCO 1999; Band D6; m 1993 Henrietta Dorrington-Ward (2s 1994, 1996).

Budd, Sir Colin Richard, KCMG (2002), CMG (1991); HM Ambassador The Hague since April 2001; Born 31/08/45; FCO 1967; Assistant Private Secretary to Minister without Portfolio FCO 1968-

69; Warsaw 1969; Islamabad 1972; FCO 1976; Head of Chancery The Hague 1980; Assistant Private Secretary to the Secretary of State FCO 1984; Counsellor 1986; Cabinet Office 1987; Head of Chancery Bonn 1989; Chef de Cabinet to Sir Leon Brittan, European Commission 1993; DUS Cabinet Office 1996; DUS (EU and Economic) FCO 1997; m 1971 Agnes Antonia Maria Smit (1d 1979; 1s 1986).

Budd, Robin S; Dhaka since 2001; Born 19/03/68; FCO 1995; Abuja 1996; Maputo 1998; Band B3; m 1995 Grazyna Karwoska-Budd (2s 1996, 1999; 1d 2003).

Budden, Alexander James; FCO since September 2001; Born 18/04/68; FCO 1991; Third Secretary Kathmandu 1994; Third later Second Secretary Zagreb 1998; Band D6; m 1995 Diane Margaret Scott (1d 2000; 1s 2003).

Budden, Philip Marcus; First Secretary (Trade/Political) Washington since August 2002; Born 12/09/65; Second Secretary FCO 1993; First Secretary Vienna 1999; m 1992 Deborah Allen Tripp (1d 1997).

Buglass, Melvyn James; Management Officer Tunis since June 2002; Born 25/09/46; Army 1966-89; Rome 1989; Brussels (UKDEL/NATO) 1992; DSLC 1995; Vice-Consul Beirut 1998; Band B3; m 1973 Sandra Ann Whitehouse (1d 1974; 1s 1975).

Bull, David Thomas John; Deputy Consul-General and First Secretary (Trade) Houston since December 2002; Born 20/02/61; FCO 1982; Rio de Janeiro 1983; Lusaka 1986; FCO 1990; Third Secretary (consular /Passports) Kingston 1994; Second Secretary (Management) Kathmandu 1997; On loan to the DTI 2000; Band C5; m 1989 Aisling Maccobb (1d 1989).

Bulmer, Sandra Kay (née Ferguson); FCO since June 1998; Born 11/11/67; FCO 1986; Vienna 1989; FCO 1991; Ottawa 1995; Band A2; m 1995 Ian Bulmer (1s 1998).

Bundy, Rosalind (née Johnson); Moscow since July 1999; Born 25/01/45; FCO 1977; Paris 1977; Tripoli 1980; FCO 1983; Bonn 1985; FCO 1987; Algiers 1993; Ottawa 1995; Band B3; m 1984 David Alan Bundy.

Bunten, Roderick Alexander James; Deputy Director General Taipei since September 2002; Born 24/11/59; FCO 1984; SOAS 1985; Language Training 1986; Assistant Political Adviser Hong Kong 1987; SUPL 1990; First Secretary FCO 1991; First Secretary (Information) Canberra 1997; m 1990 Frances Jennifer Adamson (3d 1991, 1997, 2001; 1s 1995).

Burch, Andrew David; Second Secretary São Paulo since May 2002; Born 18/03/57; Department of the Environment 1972; FCO 1976; Nicosia 1980; New Delhi 1982; FCO 1986; Nairobi 1989; Budapest 1994; British Trade International 1998; On loan to DTI 1999; Band C4; m 1982 Sarah

Miranda Hodgson Clarke (2s 1989, 1991; 1d 1995).

Burch, Joshua; FCO since September 2003; Born 05/03/76; Band C4.

Burch, Stella Jane; Second Secretary (Economic) Vienna since February 2003; Born 30/05/76; FCO 2000; Second Secretary (Bilateral) Berlin 2002; Band C4.

Burges Watson, Claire Rosamund; FCO since March 2003; Born 26/04/71; Band C4.

Burke, Alison Jane (née Wickham), MBE (2003); SUPL since May 2003; Born 25/07/65; FCO 1983; Prague 1988; Canberra 1990; SUPL 1991; Bucharest 1992; SUPL 1995; FCO 1998; SUPL 1998; New Delhi 1999; Band A2; m 1992 Thomas John Burke (1d 1995; 1s 1996).

Burke, Thomas John; Istanbul since August 2003; Born 12/12/50; Treasury 1968; FCO 1974; Brasilia 1976; FCO 1979; Harare 1979; Islamabad 1983; FCO 1984; Canberra 1987; Vice-Consul Düsseldorf 1991; Vice-Consul and later Second Secretary Bucharest 1992; Second Secretary (Immigration) New Delhi 1998; m 1991 Alison Jane Wickham (1d 1995; 1s 1996).

Burke-Wood, Alison Carmen (née Ferry); Muscat since March 2002; Born 07/06/66; FCO 1996; Canberra 1997; Band A2; m 1997 Joseph Burke-Wood.

Burlison, Sharon (née Clarke); Cape Town since May 1999; Born 22/07/70; FCO 1993; Harare 1996; Band A2; m 1998 Andrew Burlison.

Burn, Thomas Francis Southerden (known as Tom); Second Secretary Tokyo since November 2002; Born 12/11/75; FCO 1999; Full-Time Language Training 2000; Band C4.

Burn, Thomas Joseph; FCO since October 2003; Born 03/12/79; Band C4.

Burner, Edward Alan; HM Ambassador Dakar since August 2000; Born 26/09/44; Commonwealth Office (later FCO) 1967; Sofia 1970; Bonn 1972; Second Secretary 1973; Second Secretary (Commercial) Bridgetown 1974; Second later First Secretary FCO 1979; Assistant Private Secretary to Minister for Overseas Development 1979; FCO 1981; First Secretary, Head of Chancery and Consul Sofia 1984; On loan to ODA 1987; FCO 1990; Counsellor (Comm) Lagos 1992; Consul-General Munich 1995; FCO 1999; m 1969 Jane Georgine Du Port (2d 1970, 1972; 1s 1977).

Burnett, Alice Margaret; SUPL since July 2004; Born 17/10/68; Senior Assistant Legal Adviser, called to the Bar, Middle Temple 1991; FCO 1994; First Secretary (Legal) New York (UKMIS) 2000; FCO 2003; Band D7; m 2002 Roberto Lacourt (1s 2002).

Burnhams, Robin Edward; FCO since January 1997; Born 10/12/42; CSC 1960; FCO 1967; Buenos Aires 1970; Moscow 1973; FCO 1974; Kingston 1978; Mbabane 1982; Second Secretary

FCO 1984; Second Secretary (Admin) and Consul Caracas 1987; Second Secretary FCO 1990; Second Secretary (Aid) Dar es Salaam 1992; T/D Bosnia Conference, Lancaster House 1996; m 1978 Hilda Charlotte Patricia Phibbs (1d 1985).

Burns, Lynda Edwards; Second Secretary (Political) Athens since April 2002; Born 19/07/75; FCO 1999; Full-Time Language Training FCO 2001; Band C4.

Burns, Nicholas John; FCO since October 2003; Born 20/03/62; FCO 1980; The Hague 1983; Kuala Lumpur 1984; Hanoi 1988; FCO 1989; Third Secretary (Management) Riyadh 1992; FCO 1995; Third Secretary and Vice-Consul Prague 2000; Band B3.

Burns, Sarah Elizabeth; SUPL since September 1998; Born 20/04/66; FCO 1988; Third later Second Secretary (Chancery) Vienna 1991; Second Secretary FCO 1995; Band C4.

Burns, Sean Gilbert Peter, MBE (2001); Second Secretary (Management) Nairobi since September 2000; Born 19/02/61; FCO 1978; Dar es Salaam 1983; Antigua 1987; FCO 1991; Dhaka 1993; Third Secretary (Management) and Vice Consul Dakar 1997; m 1983 Marina Higgins (1d 1989; 1s 1991).

Burran, John Eric; Washington since February 2001; Born 18/05/63; FCO 1982; Bucharest 1987; LA/Caribbean Floater 1989; Islamabad 1992; FCO 1995; On loan to DCMS 1998; Band C4; m 1999 Samantha Nash.

Burrell, Demelza Fiona; New York (UKMIS) since September 2002; Born 09/12/70; FCO 1994; Madrid 1996; FCO 1999; World-wide Floater Duties 2000; Band A2.

Burrett, Louise Victoria; SUPL since May 2000; Born 16/08/61; FCO 1978; Bridgetown 1981; Dublin 1984; Bombay 1987; FCO 1990; SUPL 1993; On loan to the DTI 1995; Third later Second Secretary (Commercial/Management) Khartoum 1997; Second Secretary (Management) Tripoli 1999; Band C4; m 1996 William Anthony Frederick Ridout (1s 2000; 1d 2002).

Burrows, Christopher Parker; FCO since 2001; Born 12/09/58; FCO 1980; East Berlin 1982; Africa/Middle East Floater 1985; Second Secretary Bonn 1987; Second Secretary FCO 1989; First Secretary (Political/External) Athens 1993; First Secretary FCO 1996; First Secretary (Political) Brussels 1998; m 1988 Betty Cordi (2d 1987, 1990; 1s 1992).

Burrows, Karl; Consul Monterrey since July 2000; Born 08/05/68; FCO 1988; Floater Duties 1990; Tegucigalpa 1992; FCO 1993; Panama City 1996; Band C4; m (1) 1991 Jane Marie O'Mahoney (diss 2001) (1d 1991); (2) 2001 Denise Victoria Vergara (1d 2002).

Burt, Nicola Jayne; Stockholm since July 2001; Born 06/02/67; FCO 1986; Moscow 1989; FCO 1992; Tel Aviv 1993; FCO 1996; Kuala Lumpur 1997; FCO 2000; Band A2.

Burton, David Stewart; The Hague since February 2003; Born 12/08/77; FCO 2001; Band C4.

Burton, Simon David; Third Secretary (Vice-Consul) Guangzhou since November 2002; Born 11/04/73; FCO 1998; Floater Duties 1999; Band B3.

Busby, George Benedict Joseph Pascal, OBE (1996); FCO since April 2004; Born 18/04/60; FCO 1987; Second later First Secretary (Chancery) Bonn 1989; First Secretary FCO 1991; First Secretary Belgrade 1992; First Secretary FCO 1996; Counsellor Vienna 2000; m 1988 Frances Hurll (3d 1989, 1994, 2000; 1s 1991).

Busvine, Nicholas John Lewis, OBE (1995); Counsellor (Regional Affairs) Bogotá since January 2002; Born 13/05/60; FCO 1982; Third later Second Secretary Kuala Lumpur 1985; FCO 1988; First Secretary Maputo 1991; First Secretary FCO 1995; m (1) 1991 Sarah Ann Forgan (diss 1996) (2) 1997 Madeleine Ann Lewis (2d 1999, 2001).

Butcher, Peter Roderick; SUPL since June 2003; Born 06/08/47; FCO 1974; Second Secretary Lima 1979; Second Secretary (Commercial) Bombay 1983; First Secretary FCO 1987; Deputy High Commissioner Maseru 1990; First Secretary FCO 1994; On secondment to DFID 1997; Maputo 2000; Band D6.

Bute, Paul Kenrick; FCO since October 2002; Born 18/05/73; FCO 1994; Full-Time Language Training 1995; Third later Second Secretary (Chancery) New Delhi 1996; First Secretary FCO 1999; MBA, Imperial College Business School 2001; Band D6.

Butler, Caroline Mary (née Whitehorn); Second Secretary FCO since 2002; Born 04/10/67; FCO 1990; Third Secretary Mexico City 1992; Second Secretary FCO 1996; Vice-Consul Buenos Aires 2001; Band C4; m 2003 Rupert James Butler.

Butler, Georgina Susan; HM Ambassador San José since February 2002; Born 30/11/45; FCO 1968; Paris 1969; Resigned on marriage 1970; Re-employed on contract FCO 1971; Reinstated in service 1972; SUPL (New York and Brussels UKREP) 1975; Seconded to European Commission, Brussels 1982; FCO 1985; Resigned (New Delhi/Brussels UKREP/Washington) 1987; Re-employed FCO 1999; m 1970 Stephen John Leadbetter Wright (diss 2000) (1d 1977; 1s 1979).

Butt, Simon John; Head of Eastern Department since April 2001; Born 05/04/58; FCO 1979; Third later Second Secretary Moscow 1982; Second Secretary Rangoon 1984; Second Secretary FCO 1986; First Secretary (External Relations) Brussels (UKREP) 1990; First Secretary FCO 1994; Deputy Head of Mission Kiev 1997.

Butt, Stephen; FCO since July 2003; Born 07/05/63; FCO 1981; Cairo 1986; Athens 1991; Third Secretary FCO 1992; Second Secretary (Chancery) Islamabad 1997; FCO 2000; First Secretary Athens 2001; Band C5.

Buttery, Richard; FCO since September 2003; Born 15/01/75; Band C4.

Bye, Adam William; First Secretary (Chancery) New York (UKMIS) since June 2002; Born 06/11/72; Customs and Excise 1994; FCO 1996; Second Secretary on Attachment to the European Commission 1997; FCO 1998; First Secretary FCO 1999; On loan to Cabinet Office 2000.

Byford, Rebecca (née Mills); Washington since November 1999; Born 30/08/69; FCO 1991; Athens 1995; FCO 1996; Band A2; m 1999 David Byford.

Byrd, Margaret (née Allen); Yekaterinburg since September 2002; Born 19/06/61; FCO 1987; Nairobi 1990; SUPL 1993; Washington 1994; Lagos 1998; Band B3; m 1993 Roger Anthony Byrd.

Byrde, Petronella Leonie Diana; First Secretary FCO since August 2001; Born 20/10/48; DSAO (later FCO) 1967; Gaborone 1971; Dacca 1974; FCO 1977; Second Secretary 1979; Tokyo 1981; First Secretary (Commercial) Colombo 1986; First Secretary FCO 1990; First Secretary (Aid/Economic) Kampala 1994; First Secretary (Consular) Cairo 1998.

Byrne, Declan Sean; Third Secretary (Management and Consular) Abuja since October 2001; Born 23/12/72; FCO 1995; Band B3.

Caie, Andrew John Forbes; High Commissioner Bandar Seri Begawan since January 2002; Born 25/07/47; FCO 1969; SRO (DS Gr.7) FCO 1972; Second Secretary Manila 1976; PRO (DS Gr.5) FCO 1980, First Secretary FCO 1983; First Secretary Head of Chancery and Consul Bogotá 1984; First Secretary later Counsellor FCO 1988; Deputy Head of Mission Islamabad 1993; On loan to CSSB 1996; FCO 1997; HM Ambassador Guatemala City 1998; m 1976 Kathie-Anne Williams (1s 1979; 1d 1987).

C

Cairns, Alison Marie; SUPL since June 2003; Born 03/12/72; FCO 1994; Tallinn 1996; Tehran 2000; FCO 2003; Band A2.

Cairns, David Seldon; First Secretary Geneva (UKMIS) since August 2002; Born 17/04/69; FCO 1993; Second Secretary Tokyo 1995; FCO 1999; Private Secretary to Baroness Scotland FCO 2000; m 1996 Sharon Anouk Aeberhard (1d 2000; 1s 2002).

Cairns, Donald Hunter; Consul-General Brisbane since October 2001; Born 29/10/46; Post Office 1967; FCO 1969; Anguilla 1972; Montevideo 1974; Abu Dhabi 1977; FCO 1980; Second Secretary (Commercial) Bogotá 1982; Second Secretary (Admin) and HM Consul Caracas 1984; First Secretary (Commercial) Canberra 1988; Deputy Consul-General (Comm) Melbourne 1990; First Secretary FCO 1992; Counsellor New York (UKMIS) 1992; British Trade International 1998; m 1972 Judy Francis Woods (1s 1977).

Cairns, Gina Stephanie (née Tart), MVO (1992); FCO(S) since January 2001; Born 21/09/65; FCO 1984; Bridgetown 1986; Bonn 1990; FCO 1993; Vice-Consul Amsterdam 1997; SUPL 2000; Band C4; m 1987 William John Cairns (1s 1995; 1d 1998).

Calder, Stanley Shearer; Deputy Consul-General Toronto since May 2001; Born 07/02/44; Immigration Service 1965; Islamabad 1972; Second Secretary Lima 1975; FCO 1980; Deputy High Commissioner Belmopan 1982; First Secretary Peking 1986; First Secretary FCO 1990; First Secretary (Commercial) Caracas 1994; First Secretary (Commercial) Paris 1996; m 1967 Isobel Masson Leith (1s 1968; 1d 1970).

Caldwell, Christine Bernadette; FCO since July 2000; Born 31/07/56; HCS 1973-77; FCO 1977; Warsaw 1979; Ankara 1979; Tripoli 1983; FCO 1984; SUPL 1986; Vice-Consul Johannesburg 1991; FCO 1993; SUPL 1995; Vice-Consul Vienna 1999; Band C4; m 1982 Clive David Wright (2d 1986, 1989).

Caley, Joanne; First Secretary New Delhi since May 2004; Born 13/08/65; FCO 1991; Second Secretary Maputo 1993; FCO 1996; First Secretary (Chancery) Geneva (UKMIS) 1999; Full-Time Language Training 2003; m 1991 Peter David Morgan (3s 1996, 1998, 2001).

Callow, Judith Elizabeth; Athens since May 2001; Born 27/12/48; FCO 1970; Tananarive 1971; Geneva (UKMIS) 1973; Belgrade 1974; Abidjan 1975; Brussels (UKREP) 1977; Dakar 1979; Madrid 1983; Paris 1985; Brussels (UKDEL) 1987; Ottawa 1990; FCO 1993; Stockholm 1996; Band B3.

Calvert, Andrew Paul; Third Secretary (Political) Vilnius since May 2002; Born 17/01/69; HCS Cadre FCO 1989; FCO 1992; Bonn 1994; Floater Duties 1999; Band B3; m 1994 Julie Louis (1d 1995).

Cambridge, Roger Alan, MVO (1985); Counsellor Brussels since January 2004; Born 12/09/52; FCO 1972; Africa Floater 1975; Stockholm 1977; Dar es Salaam 1979; Second Secretary (Chancery/Inf) Port of Spain 1983; Second later First Secretary FCO 1986; Consul (Commercial) New York (BTIO) 1990; First Secretary New York (UKMIS) 1993; FCO 1996; Deputy Head of Mission Helsinki 1999.

Cameron, Hazel; First Secretary (Legal) Brussels since September 2003; Born 14/02/75; Solicitor; Assistant Legal Adviser FCO 2000.

Cameron, James; Second Secretary and Consul Bucharest since January 2001; Born 21/04/50; Army 1966-90; FCO 1990; Peking 1990; Bucharest 1991; FCO 1993; Taipei 1994; Band C4; m 1977 Angela Jane Arnold (2d 1977, 1979).

Cameron, Lee; Second Secretary Brussels (UKDEL NATO) since October 2000; Born 01/09/76; FCO 1999; Band C4.

Campbell, Amanda Joan; SUPL since July 2002; Born 24/01/69; FCO 1990; Full-Time Language Training 1999; Floater Duties 2000; Band B3.

Campbell, Christopher John; Brussels (UKDEL NATO) since August 2003; Born 12/04/63; FCO 1982; Khartoum 1985; Dhaka 1988; Jakarta 1992; FCO 1995; Second Secretary (Commercial) Caracas 1999; Band C4; m 1989 Sharon Isabel Hale.

Campbell, David Ian; Deputy High Commissioner and Counsellor (Commercial/Economic) Singapore since August 2003; Born FCO 1981; Budapest 1984; Third later Second Secretary Georgetown 1985; Second Secretary FCO 1988; First Secretary (Humanitarian) Geneva (UKMIS) 1989; First Secretary (Political) Belgrade 1994; First Secretary FCO 1994; Deputy Head of Mission Manila 2000.

Campbell, Madeleine Bernadette; Head of Management Section, New York (UKMIS) since March 2000; Born 14/05/54; COI 1989; FCO 1991; Band D7; m 1999 Nicholas Edward Boreham.

Campbell, Robert Pius; Moscow since October 2003; Born 19/10/57; FCO 1980; Second Secretary Nairobi 1984; FCO 1985; First Secretary (Economic) Belgrade 1986; First Secretary FCO 1990; First Secretary (Political) Helsinki 1992; First Secretary (Political) Skopje 1994; First Secretary FCO 1997; Counsellor (ESCAP) Bangkok 2001; m (1) 1985 Amanda Jane Guy (diss 1992) (1s 1989) (2) m 1992 Ailsa Irene Robinson (1s 1999).

Campbell, Sharon Isabel (née Hale); First Secretary (Management) Brussels since August 2003; Born 12/02/62; FCO 1983; Warsaw 1985; FCO 1986; Dhaka 1988; Jakarta 1992; FCO 1995 later Second Secretary FCO 1996; Caracas 1999; SUPL 1999; SMO/Consul Caracas 2000; m 1989 Christopher John Campbell.

Campbell, Susan Margaret; Pretoria since January 2000; Born 28/07/64; FCO 1984; Harare 1986; FCO 1990; Brasilia 1991; Floater Duties 1993; FCO 1995; Band B3.

Canning, Mark; Deputy High Commissioner Kuala Lumpur since September 2001; Born 15/12/54; FCO 1974; Freetown 1976; FCO 1978; SUPL 1978; FCO 1981; Georgetown 1982; Chicago 1986; First Secretary FCO 1988; First Secretary (Commercial) Jakarta 1994; FCO 1998; m 1988 Leslie Marie Johnson (diss 2004); ptnr, Cecilia Kenny (1d 2004).

Cannon, Andrew Michael John; Brussels since September 2004; Born 03/02/73; Solicitor 1999; Assistant Legal Adviser FCO 2001.

Cannon, Nicholas, OBE (2002); on loan to No. 10 Downing Street since February 2003; Born 29/05/58; FCO 1988; Second Secretary Paris 1990; Second Secretary FCO 1992; Second Secretary (Political/Commercial) Nicosia 1994; Full-Time Language Training 2000; First Secretary

(Chancery) Islamabad 2000; Band D6; m 1982 Alice Cheung (2s 1992, 1993).

Cantor, Anthony John James; HM Ambassador Asunción since November 2001; Born 01/02/46; DSAO 1965; Rangoon 1968; Language Training Sheffield University 1971; Tokyo 1972; Second Secretary (Consular) Accra and Vice Consul Lomé 1977; Second Secretary FCO 1980; Consul (Commercial) Osaka 1983; Deputy Head of Mission Hanoi 1990; On loan to Invest in Britain Bureau DTI 1992; First Secretary (Commercial) Tokyo 1994; Consul (Commercial) later Deputy Consul-General Osaka 1995; T/D Hanover 2000; m 1968 Patricia Elizabeth Naughton (2d 1969, 1972; 1s 1980).

Capelin, Melanie Jane; Full-Time Language Training since October 2003; Born 19/12/65; FCO 1998; PA/DHC Bridgetown 2000; Band A2.

Capes, Mark Andrew; Deputy Governor Anguilla since August 2002; Born 19/02/54; FCO 1971; Brussels (UKREP) 1974; Lisbon 1975; Zagreb 1978; FCO 1980; Lagos 1982; Vienna 1986; Second Secretary FCO 1989; Deputy Chief Secretary Providenciales Turks and Caicos Islands 1991; First Secretary (Economic) Wellington 1994; First Secretary FCO 1999; m 1980 Tamara Rossmanith (2d 1985, 1988).

Carbine, Michael Julian; SUPL since March 2000; Born 16/01/56; FCO 1975; Budapest 1977; Khartoum 1979; FCO 1982; Budapest 1983; Second Secretary FCO 1986; Second Secretary (Visas) Düsseldorf 1990; Sofia 1995; On secondment to ICL 1998; Band C5; m 1975 Marian Parkinson (1s 1975).

Carey, Colin Paul; FCO 1990 later Second Secretary FCO since 1994; Born 21/09/57; FCO 1974; Bonn 1988; m 1981 Janet Coleman (1d 1984; 2s 1986, 1990).

Carey, Joanne Claire; SUPL since November 2003; Born 06/02/72; FCO 1991; Islamabad 1995; T/D Peking 1999; Second Secretary (Commercial) Guangzhou 2000; Band C4.

Carlin, Neal Daniel; FCO since 2004; Born 22/03/71; FCO 1990; Geneva (UKMIS) 1994; Vice-Consul Khartoum 1996; T/D Cairo 1999; Full-Time Language Training 2000; Second Secretary and Deputy Head of Mission Tegucigalpa 2000; Band C4; m 1994 Tracey Alison Rae (1s 2002).

Carlin, Tricia Jane; FCO since February 2003; Born 08/10/78; Band A2.

Carnall, Philippa Jane, MBE (1986); Islamabad since November 2002; Born 31/07/57; FCO 1980; Beirut 1983; Damascus 1984; FCO 1986; Hanoi 1988; Washington 1991; FCO 1993; Cairo 1997; FCO 2000; Band B3.

Carney, Jonathan Patrick; FCO since December 2002; Born 23/02/68; DHSS 1986; FCO 1989; Islamabad 1992; Riyadh 1995; Bahrain 1999; Band B3; m 1996 Rhonda Ann Fitzgerald (2d 1997, 1999).

Carr, Corrinne Sharon (née Cannard); SUPL since May 2002; Born 28/02/70; FCO 1991; Berne 1994; FCO 1996; SUPL 1999; FCO 1999; Band B3; m 1996 Darren Andrew Carr (1s 1999; 1d 2002).

Carr, Peter Douglas; Deputy Management Officer New Delhi since July 2002; Born 02/05/47; DSAO (later FCO) 1967; Kaduna 1969; FCO 1970; Delhi 1971; Bogotá 1974; FCO 1978; Kuwait 1981; FCO 1984; New York (JAO) 1985; Second Secretary FCO 1988; Second Secretary (Consular) Jakarta 1997; m 1972 Cynthia Jane Begley (1s 1975; 2d 1977, 1983).

Carr-Alloway, Christine Anne (née Carr); Second Secretary (Management) New York since September 2004; Born 13/02/60; FCO 1978; Paris 1980; Brussels (UKREP) 1983; FCO 1986; Kuwait 1992; FCO 1994; Full-Time Language Training 1994; Third later Second Secretary Geneva (UKMIS) 1995; FCO 1998; Band C5; m 1991 Terry Alloway.

Carrick, Aileen Margaret; Brasilia since December 2003; Born 21/02/69; FCO 1989; Rome 1992; Floater Duties 1995; Havana 1999; Band B3.

Carrick, Nicholas John, OBE (2002); First Secretary FCO since May 2002; Born 01/02/67; FCO 1990; Second Secretary (Political) Berlin 1993; Second later First Secretary FCO 1995; First Secretary Lagos 1999; Band D6.

Carrick, Robert Thomas; Jerusalem since March 2002; Born 05/05/64; FCO 1987; Damascus 1994; FCO 1997; SUPL 2000; Band B3; m 1997 Rachel Woodward.

Carroll, Heidi Amanda; FCO since September 2000; Born 09/05/68; FCO 1988; Brussels 1992; FCO 1995; Floater Duties 1998; Band B3.

Carroll, Jamie Russell; FCO since February 2003; Born 23/04/76; DETR 2000; DTI 2001; Band B3.

Carson, Christine; Riyadh since July 2004; Born 18/05/65; FCO 1990; Hong Kong (JLG) 1992; Lima 1995; Seoul 1998; Band B3.

Carter, Dr David, CVO (1995); High Commissioner Dhaka since January 2000; Born 04/05/45; FCO (Research Cadre) 1970; Second Secretary Accra 1971; FCO/Cabinet Office 1975; First Secretary 1977; First Secretary and Head of Chancery Manila 1980; FCO 1983; Deputy High Commissioner and Head of Chancery Lusaka 1986; Counsellor FCO 1990; Deputy Head of Mission, later Deputy High Commissioner (1994) Cape Town/Pretoria 1992; Minister and Deputy High Commissioner New Delhi 1996; m 1968 Susan Victoria Wright (1d 1975; 1s 1978).

Carter, Dennis Sidney; First Secretary and Senior Management Officer Kingston since October 2002; Born 12/06/47; Commonwealth Office 1964; DSAO (later FCO) 1966; Bogotá 1969; Moscow 1973; FCO 1974; Bonn 1978; Washington 1982; Harare 1984; Second Secretary FCO 1987; Second Secretary (Aid) Addis Ababa 1991; Second Secretary (Comm/Man/Vice Consul) Montevideo 1995; First Secretary (Management Officer) T/D Madrid 1998; First Secretary FCO 1999; m 1968 Catherine Rose (2s 1969, 1975).

Carter, Hannah Katharine; First Secretary (Political) Tehran since June 2003; Born 20/08/74; FCO 1998.

Carter, Kevin Robert; First Secretary FCO(S) since 2002; Born 26/08/55; OPCS 1972-76; Australian Government (AGRBO) 1977-78; Dar es Salaam (LE) 1979-82; FCO 1983; Warsaw 1984; Third Secretary (Consular) Valletta 1987; FCO 1989; Third Secretary Peking 1992; Full-Time Language Training 1994; Vice-Consul (Commercial) Düsseldorf 1995; Euro 2000 Football Attaché, T/D Amsterdam and Brussels 2000; FCO(S) 2000; Band D6; m 1976 Sandra Ann McHugh (2d 1985, 1986).

Carter, Nicholas Paul; Deputy Governor Bermuda since June 2003; Born 13/03/46; Commonwealth Office (later FCO) 1966; Belgrade 1970; Bombay 1972; Prague 1976; On loan to Midland Bank (International) 1980; FCO 1981; Second Secretary Bonn 1983; First Secretary (Commercial) Kuala Lumpur 1986; First Secretary FCO 1990; Consul-General Ho Chi Minh City 1994; Attached to the Department for International Development 1997; Deputy Head of Mission Riga 1999; Band D6; m (1) 1970 (2s 1971, 1978; 1d 1974); m (2) 1994 Andrea Helen Abrahams.

Carter, Peter Leslie; Counsellor, Consul-General and Deputy Head of Mission Tel Aviv since May 2001; Born 19/11/56; FCO 1984; Second later First Secretary (Chancery) New Delhi 1986; First Secretary FCO 1989; On Secondment as Principal Administrator CFSP Unit, EU Council Secretariat, Brussels 1994; Counsellor FCO 1998; m 1985 Rachelle Hays (1d 1991).

Carter, Thomas Henry; Full-Time Language Training since February 2003; Born 22/11/53; FCO 1976; Paris (ENA) 1978; Paris 1979; Vice-Consul later Second Secretary (Chancery) Bogotá 1983; Second Secretary FCO 1987; T/D Paris 1990; First Secretary (Environment) Bonn 1990; FCO 1995; Full-Time Language Training 1999; First Secretary (Head of Political Section) Bangkok 1999; m 1997 Carolyn Jayne Davidson (2s 1998, 1999).

Cartmell, Glyn Richard; Third Secretary Addis Ababa since December 2001; Born 23/02/69; British Army 1985-92 and 1996; FCO 1996; Royal Air Force 1997; Kiev 1997; FCO 1997; Kampala 1998; Band B3; ptnr, Vanessa Cathy Thom (1s 1992).

Cartwright, Peter John; Management Officer La Paz since December 2001; Born 23/03/55; FCO 1975; On loan to Masirah 1978; Athens 1979; Paris 1982; Kabul 1984; FCO 1986; UKDEL NATO 1990; Banjul 1992; FCO 1996; On secondment to Business Link , Shropshire, DTI 1999; Band B3; m 1984 Pamela Jane Edwards (2s 1988, 1992; 1d 1986).

Cartwright, Stephen Mark; Oslo since March 2000; Born 23/08/64; FCO 1985; East Berlin 1987; Bombay 1988; FCO 1993; Third Secretary (Aid) Gaborone 1996; Band C4; m 1988 Nicola Bjorg Joyce (1s 1991).

Carty, Helen Elizabeth (née Measures); SUPL since April 2004; Born 23/06/66; FCO 1992; Johannesburg 1994; Bonn 1998; Jedda 2000; Floater Duties 2001; Band B3.

Carver, Alice P H; FCO since November 2001; Born 16/09/76; Band B3.

Carwithen, Paul Ivor; Second Secretary FCO since January 1999; Born 18/02/64; FCO 1993; Copenhagen 1996; Band C4; m 1992 Ann Davies (2s 1994, 1996).

Cary, Anthony Joyce, CMG (1997); HM Ambassador Stockholm since October 2003; Born 01/07/51; FCO 1973; Third Secretary Berlin (BMG) 1975; Second later First Secretary FCO 1978; Harkness Fellow at Stanford Business School 1980; FCO 1982; PS to Minister of State FCO 1984; First Secretary and Head of Chancery Kuala Lumpur 1986; Deputy Chef de Cabinet to Sir Leon Brittan, European Commission 1989; Counsellor FCO 1993; Counsellor Washington 1997; Chef de Cabinet to Chris Patten, European Commission 1999; m 1975 Clare Louise Katharine Elworthy (3s 1978, 1980, 1983; 1d 1985).

Casey, Claudia; Second Secretary Seoul since July 2002; Born 05/10/67; FCO 1996; Third later Second Secretary (Political/Information) Addis Ababa 1998.

Casey, Nigel Philip, MVO (1995); First Secretary (Political/Military) Moscow since December 2002; Born 29/05/69; FCO 1991; Vice-Consul (Political/Aid/Information) Johannesburg 1993; Second later First Secretary Washington 1996; FCO 1998; Full-Time Language Training (Russian) 2002.

Cassidy, Sarah Jayne (née Gardner); SUPL since July 2004; Born 27/12/68; FCO 1986; Bangkok 1989; Lilongwe 1992; SUPL 1996; FCO 1998; Maputo 2002; Band B3; m 1995 Eamon Martin Cassidy.

Cassy, Grace Aldren; Second Secretary Islamabad since September 2000; Born 04/08/76; FCO 1998; Band C4.

Castillo, Oscar Luis; Kathmandu since December 2001; Born 05/08/69; FCO 1990; Islamabad 1993; FCO 1995; Floater Duties 1999; Band A2.

Caton, Dr Valerie; Head of Environment Policy Department, FCO since October 2002; Born 12/05/52; FCO 1980; Second later First Secretary (EC Affairs) Brussels 1982; First Secretary FCO 1984; First Secretary (Chancery) Paris 1988; Counsellor and Consul-General Stockholm 1993; Counsellor (Financial & Economic) Paris 1997; m 1987 David Mark Harrison (1d 1992; 1s 1994).

Catsaras, Zamir Nicholas; Second Secretary (Political) Budapest since September 2003; Born

19/02/73; Life Guards 1995-01; FCO 2001; Full-Time Language Training (Hungarian) 2002; Band C4; m 1999 Natasha Landell-Mills.

Caughey, Alan Marsh; SUPL since June 2004; Born 17/11/71; FCO 1990; Geneva (UKMIS) 1994; Bombay 1997; Third Secretary (Political/EU) Prague 2001; Band B3.

Caulfield, Tracy Ann; Düsseldorf since September 2001; Born 10/03/70; FCO 1988; Vienna (UKMIS) 1990; FCO 1993; Wellington 1994; FCO 1998; Band B3.

Cavagan, John Raymond; FCO since May 2001; Born 09/10/66; FCO 1990; Bogotá 1993; Madrid 1997; Band C4.

Cave, Dr Stephen James; Second later First Secretary FCO since January 2001; Born 30/01/73; FCO 2001; m 1993 Friederike Freiin von Tiesenhausen.

Cawdron, Thomas Andrew; FCO since April 2002; Born 27/05/78; Band C4.

Cayless, Trevor Martin; Second Secretary (Commercial) Madrid since August 2001; Born 18/05/66; DHSS 1985; FCO 1986; Third Secretary (Aid) Lusaka 1990; Full-Time Language Training 1993; Frankfurt 1994; Second Secretary FCO 1997; m 1989 Rosemary Anne Whiting (1s 1996; 1d 1999).

Cazalet, Piers William Alexander, OBE (2003); Deputy Consul-General Jerusalem since December 2002; Born 20/10/66; FCO 1991; Language Training 1994; Second Secretary (Political/Information) Nicosia 1995; First Secretary FCO 1999; m 1994 Alyana Sharafutdinova (1s 1990; 1d 1995).

Cetti, Joanne Martine; FCO since June 2002; Born 18/01/72; Second Secretary FCO 1997; Second Secretary (Economic) Kampala 2000; Band C4.

Chadwick, Janine Linda (née Laurence); Kiev since January 2003; Born 09/04/54; FCO 1983; Brasilia 1987; Vienna (UKMIS) 1991; Reykjavik 1994; FCO 1997; Khartoum 1999; Band A2; m 1985 Peter Guy Chadwick.

Chadwick, John Anthony; FCO since September 2003; Born 16/12/52; FCO 1971; Malta 1973; Manila 1976; FCO 1980; Islamabad 1983; São Paulo 1988; FCO 1992 later Second Secretary FCO 1994; Second Secretary (Commercial) Riyadh 1996; Second Secretary (Commercial) Damascus 2000; Band C5; m 1976 Jane Saliba (3d 1979, 1983, 1986; 1s 1981).

Chadwick, Nigel Spencer; FCO since January 2003; Born 17/09/52; FCO 1971; Berne 1973; Buenos Aires 1977; Dacca 1980; Lima 1981; FCO 1984; Bombay 1988; FCO 1992; Banjul 1996; Athens 1999; Band B3; m 1991 Michelle Marina Dunne (1d 1996).

Chalmers, Kathleen Corbett; SUPL since September 1997; Born 19/08/59; Brasilia 1981; FCO 1982; Hanoi 1983; FCO 1986; Rome 1987;

SUPL 1990; FCO 1991; Hong Kong 1994; Band A2.

Chalmers, Nicholas John Pender; First Secretary FCO since May 2002; Born 04/05/71; FCO 1988; FCO 1993; Second Secretary (Political) Islamabad 1995; First Secretary Pristina 2000; Band D6.

Chamberlain, Valerie Ann (née Crocombe); Kathmandu since April 2002; Born 16/07/62; FCO 1980; Washington 1984; Gibraltar 1987; Prague 1989; FCO 1991; Bombay 1998; SUPL 2001; Mumbai 2001; Band B3; m 1997 Martin Chamberlain (1s 2001).

Chambers, Dr David Ian; Counsellor (Political) Bangkok since August 2003; Born 04/12/47; Principal Research Officer FCO 1987; First Secretary and Consul Macao BTC Hong Kong 1994; FCO 1998; Band D6; m (1) 1978 Merilyn Figueroa (diss 1990); (2) 1991 Tharinee Plobyon.

Chandler, Julian; FCO since August 2003; Born 07/07/50; DSAO (later FCO) 1967; Istanbul 1971; Singapore 1976; Kuala Lumpur 1977; FCO 1979; Port Stanley 1982; Assistant Trade Commissioner Hong Kong 1984; First Secretary FCO 1989; Deputy High Commissioner Mbabane 1992; First Secretary (Commercial) Nairobi 1998; m 1998 Caroline Louise Parkinson (1d 1980; 3s 1982, 1992, 1994).

Chandler, Steven; Third Secretary (Chancery) Stockholm since March 2002; Born 27/01/71; FCO 1994; Ottawa 1994; SUPL 1999; T/D Belgrade 2000; Band B3; m 1996 Jenny Wieslander (1s 1997).

Chandler, Steven Clive; FCO since September 2003; Born 16/03/68; DHSS 1986; FCO 1987; Berlin (BMG) 1989; Dhaka 1992; Istanbul 1995; Sarajevo 1997; Third later Second Secretary FCO 1998; SUPL 2002; Band C4.

Chaplin, Edward Graham Mellish, CMG (2004), OBE (1998); HM Ambassador Baghdad since July 2004; Born 21/02/51; FCO 1973; MECAS 1974; Third Secretary Muscat 1975; Second Secretary Brussels 1977; Paris (ENA) 1978; Private Secretary to Lord President of the Council 1979; First Secretary FCO 1981; First Secretary and Head of Chancery Tehran 1985; First Secretary FCO 1987; Counsellor FCO on secondment to Price Waterhouse Management Consultants 1990; Deputy Permanent Representative and Head of Chancery Geneva (UKMIS) 1992; Counsellor FCO 1996; HM Ambassador Amman 2000; Director to Middle East Command FCO 2002; m 1983 Nicola Helen Fisher (2d 1984, 1989; 1s 1987).

Chapman, Adrian Paul; Second Secretary (Political/Public Affairs) Seoul since June 2001; Born 14/08/69; FCO 1988; Brussels (UKREP) 1990; Islamabad 1993; FCO 1996; On loan to DTI 1998; Band C4; m 1999 Fiona Witty (1d 2000; 1s 2003).

Chapman, Colin; FCO since September 2000; Born 12/01/58; Army 1974-79; FCO 1980; Bonn

1986; FCO 1988; Third Secretary Rome 1991; Second Secretary Ankara 1997; m 1983 Katherine Anne French (1d 1987).

Chapman, Yvonne Kay; Gibraltar since August 2003; Born 28/09/62; DETR 1987; FCO 1998; Geneva (UKMIS) 1999; Band A2; (1s 1991).

Chappell, Julie Louise Jo; T/D Washington since January 2004; Born 02/04/78; FCO 1999; Full-Time Language Training 2000; Second Secretary (Political/Economic) Amman 2000; Band C4.

Charlton, Alan, CMG (1996); Deputy Head of Mission Washington since May 2004; Born 21/06/52; FCO 1978; Language Training 1979; Second later First Secretary Amman 1981; First Secretary FCO 1984; First Secretary (Deputy Political Adviser) Berlin (BMG) 1986; On loan to the Cabinet Office 1991; Counsellor FCO 1993; Counsellor (Political) and then Minister and Deputy Head of Mission Bonn 1996; Minister and Deputy Head of Mission Berlin 1999; Director South East Europe FCO 2001; Director Human Resources FCO 2002; m 1974 Judith Angela Carryer (2s 1979, 1985; 1d 1981).

Chassels, Avril (née Syme); Beijing since September 2002; Born 13/04/65; FCO 1987; Dublin 1989; Addis Ababa 1992; FCO 1993; Brussels 1994; FCO 1998; Ottawa 2000; FCO 2001; Band B3; m 2001 Mr Mirrlees Chassels.

Chatfield, Louise Mary; FCO since March 2002; Born 28/04/71; FCO 1997; Mbabane 1999; Band B3.

Chatt, Paul Anthony; FCO since October 2003; Born 07/04/56; FCO 1975; Ottawa 1977; East Berlin 1979; Khartoum 1981; FCO 1984; Third later Second Secretary (Aid/Comm) Banjul 1987; Second Secretary (Man/Cons) Berne 1990; Second later First Secretary FCO 1995; First Secretary (Management) Warsaw 2000; Band C5; m (1) 1979 Delyth Hudson (diss 1988); (2) 1990 Tracie Cavell Heatherington (2d 1992, 1993).

Chatterton-Dickson, Robert Maurice French; HM Ambassador Skopje since July 2004; Born 01/02/62; FCO 1990; Second Secretary (Chancery/Information) Manila 1991; First Secretary FCO 1994; First Secretary (Press, later PS/HMA) Washington 1997; First Secretary FCO 2000; m 1995 Teresa Bargielska Albor (2d 1996, 1997, 1 step d 1982; 1 step s 1984).

Cherrie, Yvonne Elizabeth; Deputy Consul-General and Consul (Commercial) Barcelona since July 2002; Born 31/03/62; FCO 1980; Brussels (UKREP) 1982; Sana'a 1985; Bahrain 1988; FCO 1989; On secondment to Birmingham Chamber of Commerce 1991; Third Secretary (Commercial) Berlin 1993; Second later First Secretary (Pol/PPA) Mexico City 1997; Band C5; m 1996 William Theodore von Minden.

Chick, John Charles, MBE (2003); Second Secretary (HM Consul/ECM) Kathmandu since September 2000; Born 22/10/47; FCO 1971; Baghdad 1973; FCO 1975; Amman 1976; FCO

1979; Darwin 1980; FCO 1984; Hanoi 1985; FCO 1988; Third Secretary (Management) and Vice-Consul Quito 1990; Third Secretary (Comm/Chan/P&PA) Dhaka 1995; Second Secretary FCO 1999; m (1) 1971 Denese Irene Smalley (diss); (2) 1989 Tran Thi Thuy Duong (1s 1989; 1d 1994).

Chilcott, Dominick John; Director EU (Bilateral, Mediterranean and Resources) FCO since September 2002; Born 17/11/59; Royal Navy 1978-79; FCO 1982; Language Training 1984; Third later Second Secretary Ankara 1984; First Secretary FCO 1988; First Secretary Lisbon 1993; First Secretary FCO 1996; Counsellor Brussels (UKREP) 1998; m 1983 Jane Elizabeth Bromage (1d 1986; 3s 1988, 1991, 1995).

Childs, Marie-Louise; SUPL since April 2002; Born 23/03/66; FCO 1989; Vice-Consul Bangkok 1991; Quito 1995; Band B3; m 1997 Mr S O'Sullivan.

Chown, Christopher James; FCO since August 1996; Born 05/03/67; FCO 1988; Paris 1993; Band C5; (1s 1994).

Chrimes, Neil Roy; Counsellor (Trade/Economic) Ottawa since July 2001; Born 10/06/54; MAFF 1975; Harkness Fellow MIT 1977; MAFF 1979; Economic Adviser FCO 1981; IMF Research Dept. 1987; Senior Economic Adviser FCO 1989; Deputy Permanent Representative Paris (UKDEL OECD) 1994; Jakarta 1998; Head of African Department (Southern) 1999; m 1982 Anne (Henny) Barnes (1s 1988; 1d 1990).

Christie, Iain Robert; SUPL since October 2000; Born 07/12/65; Called to the Bar (Inner Temple) 1989; Assistant Legal Adviser FCO 1992; Senior Assistant Legal Adviser FCO 1995; Bridgetown 1998; m Katherine Ann Gillam (2d 1996, 1997).

Christie, Katherine Ann (née Gillam); FCO since January 2003; Born 25/01/69; FCO 1992; SUPL 1997; Band B3; m 1995 Iain Robert Christie (2d 1996, 1998).

Christopher, Sir Duncan Robin Carmichael, KBE (2000), CMG (1997); HM Ambassador Buenos Aires since November 2000; Born 13/10/44; FCO 1970; Second later First Secretary New Delhi 1972; First Secretary FCO 1976; Head of Chancery Lusaka 1980; First Secretary FCO 1983; On loan to Cabinet Office 1985; Counsellor (Comm) Madrid 1987; Counsellor FCO 1991; HM Ambassador Addis Ababa 1994; HM Ambassador Jakarta 1997; m 1980 Merril Stevenson (2d 1989, 1991).

Chubbs, Sylvia Sharon; Geneva (UKMIS) since July 2004; Born 09/05/58; FCO 1984; Paris 1986; Colombo 1989; Moscow 1993; Brussels (UKREP) 1995; FCO 1998; Budapest 2001; Band A2.

Chugg, Daniel Patrick; Vice-Consul (Political) Hong Kong since August 2001; Born 26/01/73; FCO 1998; Language Training FCO 1999; Language Training Hong Kong 2000; Band C4; m 1999 Alison Fiona Cubie.

Chun, David John; Deputy Consul-General Boston since August 2004; Born 04/04/64; FCO 1985; Lagos 1987; Moscow 1992; FCO 1996; Second Secretary (Commercial) Madrid 1999; Band C5; m 1987 Grace Fotheringham (1d 1994).

Chun, Grace (née Fotheringham); SUPL since August 1999; Born 24/07/66; FCO 1985; Lagos 1987; Moscow 1992; FCO 1996; Band B3; m 1987 David John Chun (1d 1994).

Church, Alistair John Bentley; FCO since July 2002; Born 23/08/63; FCO 1992; Kiev 1995; Second Secretary FCO 1998; SUPL 2000; Band C4; m 1990 Michelina Patrizia Forgione (1d 1997).

Church, Roger Gilbert; First Secretary (Commercial) Nairobi since July 2003; Born 01/06/46; FO 1965; Abu Dhabi 1968; Bonn 1970; East Berlin 1973; Lusaka 1974; FCO 1976; Madras 1979; Colombo 1980; Quito 1982; Second Secretary (Commercial) Madras 1983; Second Secretary FCO 1988; Deputy High Commissioner Nassau 1990; Deputy Head of Mission Lima 1994; FCO 1998; Jedda 2000; Band C5; m 1972 Kathleen Wilson Dryburgh (2s 1974, 1977).

Clare, Debbie Marie; T/D Algiers since August 2004; Born 21/03/69; FCO 1987; Resigned 1990; Reinstated (FCO) 1994; Berne 1996; Dar es Salaam 1997; Bonn 1998; Lusaka 1999; FCO 2000; Band C4.

Claridge, Susan Elisabeth; On loan to the Cabinet Office since October 2000; Born 10/05/60; FCO 1984; Brussels (UKREP) 1987; Geneva (UKDIS) 1990; FCO 1993; Bonn 1995; FCO 1998; Band B3.

Clark, Angela; Tashkent since February 2003; Born 22/11/67; FCO 1997; Kuala Lumpur 1998; Dubai 1999; SUPL 2000; Band A2; m 1998 Christopher Neil Walker (2s 1996, 1999).

Clark, Catherine Elizabeth (née Ferguson); SUPL since May 2000; Born 12/06/59; FCO 1979; Singapore 1981; Istanbul 1985; FE/SEA Floater 1988; Brussels (UKDEL NATO) 1991; Band C4; m 1990 Eldred Richard Wraighte Clark (2d 1994, 1996).

Clark, Christopher George; Tashkent since June 2004; Born 15/04/70; FCO 1990; T/D Mostar 1994; Santiago 1995; Floater Duties 1999; FCO 2001; T/D Suva 2003; Band B3.

Clark, Elizabeth; T/D Bucharest since March 2004; Born 18/03/61; FCO 2001; Band A2; m 1988 Roger Clark (dec'd).

Clark, James Frame; HM Ambassador Luxembourg since March 2004; Born 12/03/63; FCO 1988; Second Secretary 1989; Full-Time Language Training Cairo 1990; FCO 1990; Second Secretary (External Affairs) Brussels (UKREP) 1991; Second later First Secretary FCO 1993; On loan to German Foreign Ministry 1997; First Secretary (EU) Bonn 1998; Head of Conference and Visits Group, FCO(S) 1999; m 1990 Michele Taylor (diss 1998); ptnr, Anthony John Stewart.

Clark, Katherine Margaret (née Storey); FCO since June 1985; Born 18/03/50; FCO 1971; Muscat 1972; Budapest 1974; FCO 1975; Peking 1977; New York (UKMIS) 1978; Rio de Janeiro 1982; Band B3; m 1987 Richard William Clark.

Clark, Kenneth; Management Officer Abuja since January 2004; Born 18/08/49; Post Office Savings Department 1966; DSAO 1967; Kuwait 1971; Moscow 1974; Rio de Janeiro 1975; FCO 1978; New York 1981; Jedda 1983; Second Secretary FCO 1986; Second Secretary (Comm) Gaborone 1989; Second Secretary (Management) and Consul Lima 1994; FCO 1997; m 1970 Agnes Pearson Elder (3s 1971, 1974 1978).

Clark, Michael; First Secretary and Deputy Permanent Representative Geneva (UKDEL) since August 2003; Born 21/09/59; FCO 1979; Georgetown 1983; Stockholm 1986; Kuwait 1988; Montreal 1992; FCO 1996; Band D7; m 1983 Jacqueline Anne Wilkins (2s 1985, 1987).

Clark, Paul Nicholas; FCO since May 2001; Born 26/01/69; FCO 1988; Vienna 1992; Brussels (UKDEL NATO) 1993; Dhaka 1996; World Wide Floater Duties 2000; Band C4; m 1991 Katherine Walsh (diss 2002) (2s 1991, 1993).

Clark, Peter; SUPL since April 2002; Born 18/04/54; Principal Research Officer FCO 1982; First Secretary (Chancery) Peking 1988; First Secretary FCO 1992; First Secretary Canberra 1996; FCO 2001; m 1977 Alison Padgett (1d 1982; 1s 1984).

Clarke, Pauline Joyce; FCO since August 2002; Born 08/10/67; FCO 1987; Dhaka 1989; Floater Duties 1993; FCO 1996; Zagreb 1999; Band C4.

Clarke, Roger Colin; Dublin since May 2003; Born 01/10/52; Armed Forces 1969-92; FCO 1992; Moscow 1993; New Delhi 1996; Cairo 2000; Band C4; m (1) 1971 Linda (2s 1973) (diss 1998); (2) Maria Louise Wesstrom.

Clarke, Rosemary Protase, MBE (1992); First Secretary (Commercial) Singapore since July 2000; Born 13/02/50; FCO 1977; Port Louis 1978; FCO 1982; Manila 1984; Bahrain 1988; Second Secretary FCO 1991; Second Secretary (Immigration) Dhaka 1992; Band C5; m 1982 Daniel Sinassamy (1s 1984; 1d 1987).

Clarke, Sarah (née Hutson); FCO since May 2002; Born 28/01/61; FCO 1983; Accra 1985; Ankara 1988; FCO 1991; Islamabad 1993; FCO 1996; Vice-Consul (Political) Jerusalem 1998; Band C4; m 1993 Richard Henry Clarke.

Clarke, Shaun Jerome; Third Secretary (Management) Tokyo since July 2001; Born 07/11/67; Home Civil Service 1989-93; FCO 1993; Amman 1996; Valletta 1999; Band B3; m 1996 Karen Angela Evans.

Clarke Soper, Julie Linda; Vice-Consul Bogotá since April 2004; Born 13/01/64; FCO 1988; Moscow 1990; New York (UKMIS) 1993; Brasilia 1999; SUPL 2002; Band B3; m 2002 Gary Soper.

Clasen, Peter; FCO since March 2004; Born 02/12/74; FCO 1998; Vice-Consul Istanbul 2001; Band C4.

Clay, Edward, CMG (1994); High Commissioner Nairobi since December 2001; Born 21/07/45; Third Secretary FO (later FCO) 1968; Nairobi 1970; Second later First Secretary (Chancery) Sofia 1973; FCO 1975; First Secretary (Comm) Budapest 1979; First Secretary FCO 1982; Counsellor and Head of Chancery Nicosia 1985; Counsellor FCO 1989; High Commissioner Kampala 1993 additionally HM Ambassador Burundi and Rwanda 1994; FCO 1997; High Commissioner Nicosia 1999; m 1969 Anne Stroud (3d 1972, 1974, 1978).

Clay, Pamela (née Kendall); SUPL since April 2001; Born 26/11/62; FCO 1986; Moscow 1989; FCO 1990; Copenhagen 1992; FCO 1995; Helsinki 1997; The Hague 1998; Band A2; m 1998 Andrew Garry Clay (1d 2000).

Clayden, Dr Timothy, OBE (2000); FCO since August 2004; Born 28/03/60; Second later First Secretary FCO 1989; First Secretary (Info) Warsaw 1991; FCO 1994; Lagos 1995; First Secretary FCO 1999; Counsellor (Political) Islamabad 2001; Band D6; m 1984 Katharine Susan Jackson.

Clayton, Mark Darrell; First Secretary Kabul since January 2003; Born 12/06/73; FCO 1997; Third Secretary (Political) Moscow 1998; Band D6.

Clayton, Tamsin Mary Clare; Third Secretary (Political Press and Public Affairs) Bahrain since May 2001; Born 25/05/69; FCO 2000; Band B3.

Cleary, Anthony Shaun; FCO since February 2003; Born 27/10/65; FCO 1988; Third later Second later First Secretary (Chancery) Pretoria/Cape Town 1990; First Secretary FCO 1994; First Secretary (Energy) Paris (OECD) 1998.

Cleaver, Helen Louise; FCO since June 2001; Born 11/12/68; FCO 1989; Brussels 1996; FCO 1999; Stockholm 2000; Band A2.

Cleaver, Lucy Ann (née Humphreys); Beijing since June 2001; Born 17/06/72; FCO 1993; New York (UKMIS) 1996; SUPL 1999; FCO 2000; Band A2; m 2003 Michael Anthony Cleaver (1s 2002).

Clegg, Leslie David, MVO (1985); Deputy Head of Consular Division since March 2000; Born 12/10/49; FO (later FCO) 1967; Banjul (formerly Bathurst) 1971; Wellington 1974; FCO 1977; New Delhi 1980; Second Secretary Lisbon 1984; First Secretary FCO 1988; First Secretary (Commercial) Madrid 1992; First Secretary (Management) Nairobi 1996; FCO 2000; m 1970 Louise Elizabeth Straughan (3d 1973, 1976, 1984).

Clegg, Sarah Jane; FCO since November 2003; Born 27/12/74; Band B3.

Cleghorn, Bruce Elliot; High Commissioner Kuala Lumpur since November 2001; Born

19/11/46; Second Secretary FCO 1974; Second Secretary Geneva (UKDEL CSCE) 1974; Second Secretary FCO 1975; First Secretary Brussels (NATO) 1976; First Secretary New Delhi 1980; First Secretary FCO 1983; Counsellor Vienna (UKDEL CSCE) 1987; Deputy Head of Delegation Vienna (UKDEL CFE) 1989; Counsellor and Deputy High Commissioner Kuala Lumpur 1992; Head of Non Proliferation Dept FCO 1995; Minister and Deputy Permanent Representative Brussels (UKDEL NATO) 1997; m 1976 Sally Ann Robinson (3s 1978, 1981, 1986).

Cleland, Deborah Julia (née Caldow); Second Secretary FCO since February 1999; Born 08/09/67; FCO 1987; Accra 1990; FCO 1992; Oslo 1994; Band C4; m 1993 James Cleland.

Clements, Martin Hugh, OBE (2002); Counsellor Kabul since June 2004; Born 26/07/61; FCO 1983; Second Secretary (Chancery) Tehran 1986; FCO 1987; First Secretary (IAEA) Vienna (UKMIS) 1990; First Secretary FCO 1994; First Secretary Bonn 1998; Counsellor Berlin 1999; Counsellor FCO 2003.

Clemitson, Lynne Dawn; SUPL since November 2002; Born 04/05/61; FCO 1979; Washington 1982; Dhaka 1985; Wellington 1988; FCO 1991; Band C4; m 1983 Malcolm John Clemitson.

Clephane, James Cavin Alexander, OBE (1996); SUPL since November 1999; Born 03/02/54; FCO 1973; Budapest 1976; Seoul 1977; Jakarta 1980; FCO 1983; Third later Second Secretary Muscat 1986; Second later First Secretary Bandar Seri Begawan 1991; First Secretary (Defence Co-operation) Bandar Seri Begawan 1995; On loan to MOD 1998; Band D6; m 1974 Mary Buchanan Dorman.

Cliff, Ian Cameron, OBE (1991); HM Ambassador Sarajevo since October 2001; Born 11/09/52; FCO 1979; Language Training 1980; Second later First Secretary Khartoum 1982; First Secretary FCO 1985; First Secretary (Chancery) New York (UKMIS) 1990; Counsellor on loan to DTI 1993; Deputy Head of Mission Vienna 1996; m 1988 Caroline Mary Redman (1s 1989; 1d 1993).

Clifton, Emma Jane; FCO since September 2002; Born 03/11/79; Band C4.

Clissold, Sean Dominic, OBE (2004); First Secretary (Management) and Consul Ankara since November 2000; Born 06/04/58; FCO 1975; Geneva (UKMIS) 1978; Rabat 1981; Ankara 1983; Lagos 1987; FCO 1990; Third Secretary (Commercial) Istanbul 1993; Second Secretary (Consular) Warsaw 1997; Band C5; m 1986 Belgin Savaci.

Clough, Graham Ronald; Second Secretary Vienna (UKMIS) since March 2002; Born 13/05/55; FCO 1995; Second Secretary (Political) Dhaka 1998; Band B3; m 1995 Harvinder Kaur Sabharwal.

Cloughton, Stephen Paul; FCO since June 2000; Born 04/11/65; FCO 1986; Bangkok 1991; FCO

1994; Skopje 1996; Band B3; m 1997 Karen Dowen.

Clunes, Anna Louise, OBE (2003); First Secretary Brussels since January 2004; Born 12/03/73; FCO 1994; Full-Time Language Training 1996; Second Secretary Warsaw (KHF) 1996; First Secretary (Chancery) New York (UKMIS) 2000; Band D6.

Clyde, Dr Keane; SUPL since May 2004; Born 19/09/71; Senior Research Officer FCO 2002; Band C5; m 2000 Alistair Clyde.

Clydesdale, William Reginald; FCO since January 1997; Born 12/08/43; MOD 1960; FCO 1980; Lagos 1985; Third Secretary Sofia 1987; FCO 1990; Washington 1994; Band C5; m 1969 Noreen Foister (2s 1973, 1976).

Coates, David; HM Ambassador Abidjan and HM Ambassador non-resident to Liberia, Niger and Burkina Faso since August 2004; Born 13/11/47; Second later First Secretary FCO 1974; Language Training Hong Kong 1977; First Secretary (Commercial) Peking 1978; FCO 1981; First Secretary Geneva (UKMIS) 1986; Counsellor Peking 1989; Counsellor FCO 1993; Director-General of Trade Taipei 1999; FCO 2002; m 1974 Joanna Kay Weil (2d 1976, 1978).

Coates, Sally Ann (née Mawby); FCO since March 2003; Born 29/07/60; FCO 1979; Washington 1984; FCO 1987; Tortola 1988; Georgetown 1992; FCO 1992; Mbabane 1993; Beirut 1996; Accra 1998; Band A2; m 1995 Alan Roger Coates.

Cobden, Alan; Consul-General Alexandria since July 2003; Born 15/07/54; FCO 1970; Canberra 1975; Tehran 1977; African Floater 1978; Bombay 1980; FCO 1983; Third later Second Secretary Sofia 1986; Second Secretary (Agriculture/Environment) Dublin 1989; Second Secretary FCO 1994; Deputy Consul-General and Consul (Commercial) Los Angeles 1998; m 1982 Karen Anne Fawn (1s 1985; 1d 1987).

Cochrane-Dyet, Fergus John; Deputy Head of Africa Department (Southern) FCO since June 2002; Born 16/01/65; FCO 1987; Third later Second Secretary (Political) Lagos 1990; Second Secretary Abuja 1993; First Secretary FCO 1994; Head of BIS Tripoli 1996; First Secretary (Commercial) Jakarta 1998; Deputy Consul-General and Director of Trade and Investment Promotion Sydney 1998; Chargé d'Affaires Conakry 2001; T/D Kabul 2002; m 1987 Susan Emma Aram (3s 1990, 1991, 1996).

Codd, Steven; Deputy Consul-General Shanghai since December 2000; Born 19/05/61; FCO 1981; Baghdad 1982; FCO 1985; Beirut 1986; FCO 1988; Hanoi 1990; Lusaka 1993; Second Secretary FCO 1996; First Secretary (Management) Kuala Lumpur 1997; Band D6; m 1993 Ruth Brown Mulligan (diss 2001); ptnr, Jacqueline Vanessa Goodhew (1s 2001).

Codrington, Richard John; FCO since November 2004; Born 18/12/53; MOD 1975; FCO 1978;

Second later First Secretary Dar es Salaam 1980; FCO 1983; New Delhi 1985; First Secretary FCO 1989; On loan to SG Warburg & Co Ltd. 1992; Counsellor on loan to the Department of National Heritage 1994; Counsellor (Trade Promotion and Investment) Paris 1995; Deputy High Commissioner Ottawa 1999; Head of Online Communications Department, FCO 2003; m 1985 Julia Elizabeth Nolan (twin s 1991).

Cody, Anne Bridget; Brussels (UKDEL) since February 2003; Born 30/01/42; FCO 1995; Band A2; m 1964 Kevin Anthony Cody (1d 1968; 1s 1970).

Cogger, Darren Barry; Canberra since November 2001; Born 20/05/63; FCO 1984; Athens 1988; Belgrade 1991; New Delhi 1993; FCO 1996; Third Secretary (Management) Kiev 1997; Band B3; m 1986 Johanna Lesley Payne (1d 1989).

Coggles, Paul James; SUPL since March 2004; Born 24/06/66; FCO 1989; Third Secretary (Chancery) Sofia 1992; Third Secretary FCO 1995; Full-Time Language Training 1996; Second Secretary (Political) Prague 1997; First Secretary (Political) Prague 2000; Band D6.

Coglin, Gillian Joanna; First Secretary (Management) Tokyo since June 2002; Born 09/08/67; FCO 1989; Bucharest 1991; Bombay 1994; Second Secretary FCO 1997; SUPL 2000; SUPL (Japan) 2001; Band C4.

Colby, Sheila Joan, MBE (2001); Buenos Aires since January 2002; Born 07/05/56; FCO 1979; Lima 1980; FCO 1983; Floater Duties 1984; FCO 1988; Kuala Lumpur 1990; Madrid 1993; FCO 1996; Mexico City 1998; Band B3.

Cole, Alexandra Pamela; Second Secretary (Political) Sarajevo since July 2002; Born 02/06/70; FCO 1990; Tehran 1996; Full-Time Language Training 2000; SUPL 2001; Band C4; m 1995 Adrian Frederick Bedford.

Coleman, Julie; Colombo since June 2001; Born 13/03/67; Department of Employment 1989-95; FCO 1995; Addis Ababa 1997; Band A2.

Coleman, Richard Alan; First Secretary (Management/Consul) Prague since July 2000; Born 01/02/45; CRO (later FCO) 1963; Dacca 1968; FCO 1971; Salisbury 1972; FCO 1972; Freetown 1973; Tehran 1975; FCO 1979; Vientiane 1982; Kingston 1985; Second Secretary FCO 1988; Second Secretary (Consular) Peking 1991; Bridgetown 1995; Karachi 1999; FCO 1999; m (1) 1968 Susan Robertson (diss 1973) (1s 1969); (2) 1973 Celia Frances Burnett (1d 1986).

Coleman, Sandra Marie (née Duffy); The Hague since August 2001; Born 21/11/60; FCO 1984; Algiers 1985; Jerusalem 1987; Turks and Caicos Islands 1991; Dakar 1993; SUPL 1996; Washington 1997; Band B3; m 1995 Scott Stanley Coleman.

Coleman, Tracey; SUPL since April 2004; Born 23/01/71; FCO 1990; Ottawa 1992; World-wide Floater Duties 1995; Freetown 1999; Band A2.

Collard, Ian Frank; FCO since September 2002; Born 13/04/76; Band C4.

Collard, Timothy Michael; Consul-General Hamburg since May 2004; Born 21/03/60; FCO 1986; Language Training SOAS 1987; Language Training Hong Kong 1988; Second Secretary (Science and Technology) Peking 1989; First Secretary FCO 1993; First Secretary (Hong Kong) Peking 1995; FCO 2001; m 1985 Patricia Polzer (2s 1987, 1989).

Collecott, Dr Peter Salmon, CMG (2002); HM Ambassador Brasilia since July 2004; Born 08/10/50; Second Secretary FCO 1977; MECAS 1978; First Secretary 1979; First Secretary (Political) Khartoum 1980; First Secretary (Economic/Commercial/Agricultural) Canberra 1982; FCO 1986; Counsellor (Head of Political Section, later DHM) Jakarta 1989; Counsellor (EU and Economic) Bonn 1994; FCO 1998; Director Resources FCO 1999; Director General (Corporate Affairs, initially Chief Clerk) FCO 2001; m 1982 Judith Patricia Pead.

Collett, Robert James; FCO since October 2003; Born 22/05/80; Band C4.

Colley, Timothy John; Deputy Head of Mission Sofia since July 2000; Born 13/03/65; FCO 1989 (Second Secretary 1991); Full-Time Language Training 1991; Second Secretary (Political) Islamabad 1992; First Secretary FCO 1995; Full-Time Language Training 1999; Band D6; m 1993 Janet Mary Rodemark (1s 1997; 2d 1999, 2002).

Collier, Geoffrey Thomas Grey; Second Secretary (Political/PPA) Ankara since August 2002; Born 27/04/68; FCO 1990; Belgrade 1993; Dakar 1997; FCO 2000; Full-Time Language Training (Turkish) 2002; m 1999 Müge Elif Törüner.

Collier, Nicholas Gavin; Pretoria since January 2003; Born 10/02/69; FCO 1996; Third Secretary (Political/Economic) Vilnius 1998; Band C4; m 1999 Simona Gatti.

Collier, Stephen John, MVO (1991), RVM (1979); Deputy Consul-General and Consul (Commercial) Atlanta since October 1999; Born 11/01/52; DTI 1968; FCO 1969; Bonn 1972; Aden 1975; Lilongwe 1976; Lagos 1979; FCO 1983; Amman 1985; Second Secretary Windhoek 1989; Second Secretary FCO 1992; First Secretary (Commercial) Lima 1996; m 1987 Erica Mary Cholwill Wilson.

Collingridge, Andrew; Brussels (UKDEL NATO) since January 2002; Born 02/11/62; FCO 1985; Lagos 1990; FCO 1994; Bucharest 1998; FCO 2001; Band C4; m 1993 Tanya Suzanne Parsons (2d 1998, 2001).

Collingridge, Tanya Suzanne (née Parsons); Second Secretary Brussels (UKDEL NATO) since June 2002; Born 04/02/65; FCO 1984; Warsaw 1987; Vienna (UKDEL) 1989; Lagos 1991; FCO 1994; Full-Time Language Training 1997; Second Secretary (Political/Information) Bucharest 1998; FCO 2001; Band C4; m 1993 Andrew Collingridge (2d 1998, 2001).

Collings, Jane Lindsay; FCO since January 2003; Born 05/03/80; Band B3.

Collins, Alan Stanley, CMG; High Commissioner Singapore since December 2002; Born 01/04/48; Ministry of Defence 1970; Private Secretary to Vice Chief of the Air Staff 1973-75; FCO 1981; First Secretary and Head of Chancery Addis Ababa 1986; Counsellor (Commercial) and Deputy Head of Mission Manila 1990; Counsellor FCO 1993; Director of BTCO Taipei 1995; HM Ambassador Manila 1998; m 1971 Ann Dorothy Roberts (1d 1985; 2s 1988, 1995).

Collins, Helen Laura; FCO since January 2003; Born 15/11/70; FCO 1990; Washington 1994; Cairo 1998; Band B3.

Collins, James Robert; Bridgetown since November 2001; Born 09/11/63; FCO 1986; Strasbourg 1988; Moscow 1990; FCO 1993; Band B3; m 1987 Sheila Marie Barry.

Collinson, Martin; Dubai since January 2002; Born 07/09/66; FCO 1987; Band A2; m 1999 Sharon Particia Stillwell (2d 2000).

Collis, Simon Paul; Consul-General Basra since 2004; Born 23/02/56; FCO 1978; Language Training 1979; Third later Second Secretary Bahrain 1981; First Secretary FCO 1984; New York (UKMIS) 1986; FCO 1987; First Secretary and Head of Chancery Tunis 1988; FCO 1990; First Secretary (Political) New Delhi 1991; First Secretary FCO 1994; Counsellor and Deputy Head of Mission Amman 1996; On secondment to the BP Amoco, 1999; Consul-General Dubai 2000.

Colloms, Catherine; On loan to OHR, Sarajevo since October 2004; Born 18/08/76; FCO 1998; On loan to Coalition Information Centre 2001; T/D (Public Diplomacy) Gibraltar 2002; FCO 2002; Band D6.

Collyer, Neil Patrick; FCO since 2002; Born 28/05/66; ODA 1985-89; FCO 1991; Pretoria 1996; Lagos 1999; Abuja 2000; Band B3; m 1997 Sara-Louise Hall.

Collyer, Nicholas Edwin; First Secretary (Management/Consular) Rabat since May 2003; Born 15/09/52; Forestry Commission 1969; FCO 1971; Moscow 1974; Colombo 1975; Budapest 1979; FCO 1981; Geneva (UKMIS) 1983; FCO 1986; New Delhi 1987; Second Secretary FCO 1989; Second Secretary (Commercial) Seoul 1992; Second Secretary (Commercial/Consular) Port of Spain 1995; First Secretary FCO 1999; m 1973 Kathryn Dobson (2s 1978, 1983).

Collyer, Sara-Louise (née Hall); FCO since 2002; Born 28/10/73; FCO 1992; SUPL 1996; Pretoria 1997; Lagos 1999; Abuja 2000; Band A2; m 1997 Neil Patrick Collyer.

Colvin, Kathryn Frances, CVO; HM Ambassador Holy See since July 2002; Born 11/09/45; FO (later FCO) 1968; Principal Research Officer FCO 1980; UK Delegation to the Commission on Human Rights, Geneva 1980-90; First Secretary (Internal Political) T/D Rome 1988 and 1991; First

Secretary (Internal Political) T/D Paris 1992; Counsellor FCO 1998; Head of Protocol Division and Vice Marshal of the Diplomatic Corps FCO 1999; m 1971 Brian T Colvin.

Conley, Brian John; Consul (Commercial) Los Angeles since January 2003; Born 10/04/67; FCO 1986; Lusaka 1989; Third Secretary (Management) and Vice Consul Auckland 1993; FCO 1994; Second Secretary (Commercial/Information) Tunis 1999.

Conlon, Stephen Austin; FCO since November 1999; Born 01/11/75; Band C4.

Connolly, Peter Terence; First Secretary FCO since September 2000; Born 02/05/65; FCO 1988; Third Secretary Managua 1990; Brussels (UKREP) 1993; Second Secretary FCO 1994; Second Secretary (Political) Lisbon 1996; Band D6.

Connolly, Sarah Ann; FCO since January 2004; Born 19/04/79; Band C4.

Connor, Michael Leslie; On loan to the DTI since May 2000; Born 15/11/49; FCO 1971; Vienna (UKDEL) 1975; Moscow 1975; Tehran 1977; FCO 1980, APS to Minister of State 1982; Second Secretary Bonn 1983; Second later First Secretary (Commercial) Abu Dhabi 1987; First Secretary FCO 1991; First Secretary (Commercial) Prague 1995; m 1973 Linda Helen Woolnough (1d 1984).

Conroy, Anne Elizabeth, MVO (1991); FCO since February 2001; Born 30/08/63; FCO 1985; Third later Second Secretary (Chancery) Manila 1988; Second later First Secretary FCO 1992; Full-Time Language Training 1995; First Secretary (Political) Budapest 1996.

Contractor, Robert; Banja Luka since September 2003; Born 17/05/68; FCO 1989; Floater Duties 1992; FCO 1993; Warsaw 1995; FCO 1997; Second Secretary (Political) Skopje 2001; Full-Time Language Training (Serbian) 2003; Band C5.

Conway, Benjamin Simon; Singapore since November 2003; Born 19/09/78; FCO 2001; Band C4.

Conway, Nicholas Peter; FCO since September 2001; Born 25/06/78; Band C4.

Cook, Gavin Douglas; FCO since September 2002; Born 31/12/78; Band C4; m 2004 Elizabeth Carey.

Cook, Peter Duncan Gifford; First Secretary FCO since September 2001; Born 15/08/63; FCO 1982; Georgetown 1985; Doha 1989; Third later Second Secretary FCO 1992; Second Secretary (Political/Information) Bridgetown 1995; Second later First Secretary (Chancery) Copenhagen 1997; m 1993 Maureen Nanette Sharp (2s 1995, 1996).

Cooke, Ann; Hong Kong since March 2000; Born 26/02/66; DoT 1982; CCA 1989; FCO 1992; New York (UKMIS) 1996; Band A2; m 1986 Lloyd Norman Cooke (1d 1990).

Coombs, Nicholas Geoffrey; FCO since July 2003; Born 14/12/61; FCO 1984; Language

Training 1985; Second Secretary (Chancery) Riyadh 1987; Second later First Secretary FCO 1989; First Secretary Amman 1993; First Secretary FCO 1997; First Secretary (Political) Riyadh 2000; Band D6; m 1990 Julie Elizabeth Hardman (2d 1996, 1998).

Cooper, Amanda Jane; Vice-Consul Dhaka since February 2003; Born 02/03/60; HSE 1987-95; FCO 1995; Vilnius 1996; Shanghai 1999; Tokyo 2002; Band B3.

Cooper, Andrew George Tyndale; Counsellor FCO since May 1999; Born 13/12/53; Royal Navy 1974-82; FCO 1983; First Secretary Canberra 1984; FCO 1987; First Secretary (UN/Press) Geneva (UKMIS) 1988; Counsellor FCO 1992; Stockholm 1995; m 1981 Donna Mary Elizabeth Milford (2s 1988, 1996).

Cooper, Derek John William; Second Secretary (Political) Riyadh since July 2001; Born 07/01/68; FCO 1986; Islamabad 1989; FCO 1992; Zagreb 1994; FCO 1998; Band C4; m 1998 Sanja Vilus.

Cooper, Rachel Elizabeth; FCO since May 1999; Born 03/11/65; FCO 1989; Vice-Consul Copenhagen 1992; Deputy Head of Mission Bratislava 1995.

Cooper, Robert Francis, CMG (1997), MVO (1975); SUPL since April 2002; Born 28/08/47; Third Secretary FCO 1970; Sheffield University 1971; Tokyo 1972; Second Secretary 1973; First Secretary 1976; FCO 1977; Seconded to the Bank of England 1982; First Secretary (External Trade) Brussels (UKREP) 1984; Counsellor FCO 1987; Counsellor (Political) Bonn 1993; Minister Bonn 1996; Director FCO 1998; Head of Overseas Defence Section Cabinet Office 1999.

Cope, Brian Roger, MVO (2000); FCO since September 2003; Born 01/03/59; Inland Revenue 1975; FCO 1976; Paris 1979; Bucharest 1982; Islamabad 1984; FCO 1988; Third Secretary Colombo 1991; Second Secretary (Management) Accra 1995; Kampala 2000; Band D6; m 1982 Heather Margaret Frensham (1d 1990; 1s 1993).

Cope, John Charles; FCO since October 1998; Born 10/08/46; FO 1964; Paris 1968; Moscow 1971; Delhi 1972; Karachi 1974; FCO 1976; Dakar 1978; Warsaw 1981; FCO 1982; Hanoi 1985; FCO 1987; Second Secretary (Admin/Consular) Kathmandu 1988; Second Secretary FCO 1991; Second Secretary (Management/Consular) Prague 1995.

Copland, Joanne Catherine; SUPL since August 2000; Born 02/09/71; FCO 1990; Washington 1993; Peking 1996; On loan to the Cabinet Office 1999; Band B3.

Copleston, John de Carteret; Counsellor FCO since September 2000; Born 26/01/52; FCO 1971; Paris 1975; Third later Second Secretary FCO 1978; Second later First Secretary Islamabad 1980; First Secretary FCO 1983; First Secretary (Chancery) Jakarta 1987; First Secretary FCO 1990; Counsellor Abuja later Lagos 1993;

Counsellor FCO 1995; Counsellor (Multilateral) Canberra 1997; m 1987 Jane Marie Francesca Wilcox (4d 1988, 1991, 1993, 1997).

Copley, Caroline Helen (née Hall); SUPL since June 2001; Born 19/01/65; FCO 1987; Third later Second Secretary (Chancery) Oslo 1990; Floater Duties 1991; FCO 1992 (First Secretary 1994); First Secretary (Political) Paris 1997; SUPL 1999; First Secretary (Political) Paris 2000; Band D6; m 1996 John Richard Copley (1d 1999).

Coppin, Nicholas James; Seconded as Adviser, Bucharest since February 2004; Born 27/03/71; FCO 1992; Second Secretary (Pol/PPA) Bucharest 1995; First Secretary Skopje 1999; First Secretary FCO 1999.

Corbett, Hannah Kathleen Taylor; On loan to DFID since July 2002; Born 04/08/74; FCO 1997; On loan to HM Treasury 1998; Second later First Secretary (External) Brussels (UKREP) 1999.

Cordery, Andrew David; Counsellor FCO since June 1999; Born 02/05/47; Second Secretary FCO 1974; Nairobi 1975; First Secretary New York (UKMIS) 1977; FCO 1981; First Secretary (Economic) Lusaka 1984; First Secretary Berlin (BM) 1988; First Secretary later Counsellor FCO 1991; Counsellor Oslo 1995; m 1970 Marilyn Jean Smith (2d 1975, 1977).

Cormack, Ian Ronald; First Secretary - SMO/Consul Lima since June 2004; Born 20/11/56; FCO 1975; Nairobi 1978; Havana 1980; Latin America and Caribbean Floater 1982; Africa/Middle East Floater 1984; FCO 1986; Shanghai 1989; Third Secretary Stockholm 1992; FCO 1995; First Secretary (Commercial) Stockholm 1998; T/D Victoria 2003.

Corner, Diane Louise; SUPL since April 2004; Born 29/09/59; FCO 1982; Second Secretary (Chancery) Kuala Lumpur 1985; Second Secretary FCO 1989; SUPL 1989; First Secretary FCO 1989; On loan to the Cabinet Office 1991; Deputy Head of Mission and First Secretary (Pol) Berlin 1994; FCO 1998; NATO College, Rome 2000; Deputy Head of Mission Harare 2001; FCO 2003; m 1986 Peter Timothy Stocker (3d 1989, 1991, 1994).

Corrans, Paula Anne; Floater Duties since August 2001; Born 04/02/70; FCO 1995; Brussels (UKREP) 1997; São Paulo 1998; Band B3.

Correa, Clive Joel; Durban since August 2002; Born 05/11/64; FCO 1988; Transferred to Diplomatic Service 1989; Rangoon 1991; Full-Time Language Training 1995; Budapest 1996; FCO 1998; On loan to British Trade International 2000; Band C4; m 1990 Andrea Parker (2d 1993, 1996).

Corrigan, Rosalind Mary; FCO since May 2001; Born 07/12/66; FCO 1991; New York (UKMIS) 1993; Third Secretary (Chancery) Buenos Aires 1994; Vice-Consul Toronto 1998; Band C4.

Cotton, Susan Jayne; FCO since May 2003; Born 03/05/65; FCO 1998; Geneva (UKMIS) 1999; Band B3.

Cottrell, Cathy; First Secretary (Management) Kuwait since November 2003; Born 03/04/63; FCO 1991; Second Secretary (Commercial) Moscow 1999; Band C4; m 1984 Simon John (2d 1990, 1992).

Coulson, Andrew John, LVO (1984); Counsellor FCO since March 1998; Born 17/12/50; FCO 1973; Tel Aviv 1976; Tehran 1978; Second later First Secretary FCO 1980; First Secretary (Inf) Amman 1983; FCO 1986; First Secretary (Chancery) Harare 1989; First Secretary FCO 1991; First Secretary (Political) Muscat 1995; m 1978 Merope Jane Wilkinson (1d 1982; 1s 1986).

Coulson, Graham; Istanbul since June 2004; Born 11/10/46; Army 1962-86; Vienna 1988; New Delhi 1989; Sofia 1992; Floater Duties 1996; Kingston 1999; FCO 2000; Moscow 2003; Band B3; m 1971 Maureen Joyce Howard (diss 1994) (1s 1971; 1d 1974).

Coulter, Anthony Julian; Counsellor Kiev since January 2004; Born 01/11/61; FCO 1984; Second Secretary (Chancery) Ankara 1987; Second Secretary FCO 1990; First Secretary (Political) Amman 1994; FCO 1998; First Secretary (Chancery) Baku 1999; Band D6; m 1997 Munire Gulay Kilic (1d 2000).

Courage, Rafe Philip Graham; Consul Chicago since August 2002; Born 20/10/63; FCO 1986; Third Secretary Brussels 1989; Third Secretary Islamabad 1991; Second Secretary FCO 1995; Full-Time Language Training 1997; Second Secretary (Economic/Commercial) Ankara 1998; m 1988 Theresa Jayne Pile (4d 1990, 1992, 1996, 1997).

Court, Robert Vernon; Deputy High Commissioner Canberra since April 2001; Born 28/01/58; FCO 1981; Concurrently Third Secretary and Vice-Consul Chad; Second Secretary Bangkok 1984; First Secretary FCO 1986; Private Secretary to the Minister of State FCO 1988; First Secretary (Political) Brussels (NATO) 1990; First Secretary (Press/Information) Brussels (UKREP) 1993; On loan to Rio Tinto Plc 1996; SUPL 1997; m 1983 Rebecca Ophelia Sholl (3s 1986, 1988, 1990; 1d 1993).

Courtney, Victoria Glynis; Second Secretary (Political) Paris since July 2002; Born 04/12/76; FCO 2000; On secondment to Quai d'Orsay 2001; Band C4; ptnr, Marcus Dean.

Couzens, James McGeorge Dale; Third Secretary Windhoek since January 2001; Born 19/02/67; FCO 1990; Bridgetown 1995; Third Secretary Tunis 1997; Band B3; m 1993 Susan Ann Phillips (1d 1994; 1s 1996).

Cowan, Anthony Evelyn Comrie; The Hague since November 2003; Born 28/03/53; Third Secretary FCO 1975; Language Training Cambridge 1977; Language Training Hong Kong 1978; Second later First Secretary Peking 1980; First Secretary FCO 1982; First Secretary (Chancery) Brussels 1987; First Secretary FCO 1991; Consul (Political and Economic) Hong Kong 1996; Counsellor FCO 2000.

Cowell, (Andrew) (John) Hamish; First Secretary (External Relations) Brussels (UKREP) since July 2001; Born 31/01/65; FCO 1987; New York (UKMIS) 1988; Douala 1989; Third later Second Secretary Colombo 1989; First Secretary (Chancery) and Deputy Head of Mission Tehran 1992; First Secretary FCO 1994; Head of Political, Economic and Aid Sections Cairo 1996; FCO 1999; m 2000 Shadi Akhtar Khan Kasmai (2d 2000, 2002).

Cowell, Anita Ann; FCO since August 2003; Born 07/05/54; FCO 1993; Jakarta 2000; Band A2.

Cowling, Geoffrey Stanley; HM Consul General Barcelona since November 2002; Born 20/09/45; Board of Trade 1964; Colonial Office later Commonwealth Office (later FCO) 1966; Vice-Consul and Third Secretary Kabul 1970; Vice-Consul and Third Secretary Port Moresby 1974; Second Secretary (Tech Asst) Lima 1976; FCO 1979; First Secretary (Economic) Copenhagen 1982; First Secretary FCO 1982; Joint Service Defence College 1987; First Secretary FCO 1988; Deputy Consul-General São Paulo 1991; On loan to Rover International 1995; FCO 1996; Consul-General Rio de Janeiro 1999; m 1970 Irene Joyce Taylor (1s 1971; 2d 1975, 1980).

Cowper-Coles, Sir Sherard Louis, KCMG (2004), CMG (1997), LVO (1991); HM Ambassador Riyadh since September 2003; Born 08/01/55; FCO 1977; Language Training MECAS 1978; Third later Second Secretary Cairo 1980; First Secretary FCO 1983; Private Secretary to the Permanent Under-Secretary FCO 1985; First Secretary (Chancery) Washington 1987; First Secretary FCO 1991; On secondment to International Institute for Strategic Studies 1993; Counsellor FCO 1994; Counsellor (Political) Paris 1997; Private Secretary to the Secretary of State FCO 1999; HM Ambassador Tel Aviv 2001; m 1982 Bridget Mary Elliot (4s 1982, 1984, 1987, 1990; 1d 1986).

Cox, David George; Counsellor (Political/Military) Islamabad since October 2002; Born 07/12/61; FCO 1984; Third later Second Secretary (Chancery) Canberra 1986; Second later First Secretary (Econ) Islamabad 1989; FCO 1992; First Secretary (Political) Luanda 1995; First Secretary FCO 2000.

Cox, David Thomas; FCO since May 2001; Born 27/04/44; FO (FCO) 1967; Berlin 1970; FCO 1972; Prague 1974; Munich 1976; FCO 1979; Lusaka 1982; Second Secretary (Commercial) Budapest 1986; First Secretary FCO 1990; Copenhagen 1993; On loan to the DTI 1998; m 1975 Claudia Zeillinger (1s 1981; 1d 1989).

Cox, Jolyon Nicholas; Second Secretary Bogotá since July 2003; Born 21/09/61; FCO 1979; Bonn

1983; Sana'a 1985; FCO 1988; Second Secretary (Bilateral Relations) Bonn 1993; Second Secretary FCO 1998; Second Secretary (Political) Tehran 2000; Second Secretary FCO 2001; Band C4; m 1986 Francesca Ann Hindson (1s 1993).

Cox, Julie Ann, MVO (1996); New Delhi since January 2001; Born 10/07/62; FCO 1986; Peking 1988; Jerusalem 1990; Warsaw 1993; FCO 1996; Band B3.

Cox, Laura; FCO since January 2003; Born 25/08/80; Band A2.

Cox, Nigel John; Director (Asia Pacific) FCO since May 2003; Born 23/04/54; FCO 1975; Language Training Cambridge 1976; Language Training Hong Kong 1977; Second Secretary Peking 1978; Second later First Secretary FCO 1981; Paris (ENA) 1984; First Secretary Paris 1985; First Secretary FCO 1990; Counsellor Peking 1992; Counsellor FCO 1996; Minister Peking 2000; m 1992 Olivia Jane Paget.

Cox, Olivia Jane (née Paget); First Secretary FCO since February 2003; Born 31/07/57; FCO 1978; Mexico City 1980; FCO 1982; Third Secretary (Chancery) Paris 1987; Third later Second Secretary FCO 1990; SUPL 1992; FCO 1996; SUPL 1999; Band C5; m 1992 Nigel John Cox.

Cox, Richard James; Georgetown since September 2002; Born 07/08/67; FCO 1991; Addis Ababa 1993; Vice-Consul Hanoi 1997; Band C4.

Coyle, Janet Clare (née Usher); San Francisco since October 2003; Born 23/04/65; FCO 1983; Washington 1986; Prague 1989; Floater Duties 1991; FCO 1994; On loan to the DTI 1996; Cape Town 1999; Band C5; m 2002 Damian Coyle.

Crabtree, Joanne Elizabeth; Athens since October 2002; Born 26/09/68; FCO 1988; Mexico City 1990; Dubai 1993; Sana'a 1999; Band B3.

Craddock, Timothy James; On loan to DFID since October 2000; Born 27/06/56; FCO 1979; Vice-Consul (Information) Istanbul 1981; Second Secretary Ankara 1982; First Secretary FCO 1985; First Secretary Paris (UKDEL) 1990; First Secretary FCO 1995; HM Ambassador Tallinn 1997.

Craig, David Hamilton; First Secretary (Political) Ankara since August 2001; Born 05/12/61; FCO 1989; Language Training 1990; Second Secretary (Chancery) Nicosia 1991; Second later First Secretary FCO 1993; Full-Time Language Training 1994; Full-Time Language Training Cairo 1995; Consul Jedda 1996; First Secretary FCO 1999; Band D6; m 1994 Hala el-Kara (2s 1995, 1997; 1d 1999).

Craig, Deborah Louise (née Tyson); SUPL since July 2002; Born 01/01/72; FCO 1990; Nicosia 1995; FCO 1998; Islamabad 2000; Band A2; m 1995 Ian Douglas Craig (1d 1999; 1s 2000).

Craig, John Jenkinson; Second Secretary FCO since September 1979; Born 08/01/49; FCO 1972; Third Secretary Rome 1978; Band C5; m 1965

Glenys Menai Edmunds (2d 1977, 1984; 2s 1979, 1981).

Craig, Lesley, MBE (1995); FCO since January 2001; Born 13/05/67; FCO 1988; T/D Islamabad 1990; Vice-Consul Kathmandu 1991; Third Secretary (Chancery) Kampala 1994; FCO 1997; Tel Aviv 2000; Band D6.

Craig, Robyn Jean; FCO since September 1997; Born 09/03/65; FCO 1984; Moscow 1986; Oslo 1987; Rabat 1990; FCO 1993; Addis Ababa 1996; Band B3.

Cramman, Ian Pallister; Third Secretary Yerevan since September 2004; Born 11/03/70; FCO 1989; Khartoum 1992; Full-Time Language Training 1994; Düsseldorf 1995; Addis Ababa 2000; Band B3; m 1997 Ding Yu.

Craven, Stella Susan; Wellington since July 2001; Born 24/03/50; WRAF 1967-71; FCO 1972; Suva 1973; FCO 1975; Khartoum 1976; FCO 1977; Resigned 1978; Reinstated, FCO 1979; Islamabad 1981; FCO 1984; Harare 1986; FCO 1989; Band B3.

Crawford, Charles Graham, CMG; HM Ambassador Warsaw since December 2003; Born 22/05/54; FCO 1979; Second later First Secretary (Information) Belgrade 1981; First Secretary FCO 1984; First Secretary Cape Town/Pretoria 1987; First Secretary FCO 1991; Counsellor Moscow 1993; HM Ambassador Sarajevo 1996; Harvard University 1998; Deputy Political Director then Director South East Europe 1999; HM Ambassador Belgrade 2001; m 1990 Helen Margaret Walsh (2s 1991, 1993; 1d 1999).

Crawford, Fabiola Magdalena; SUPL since May 2000; Born 01/04/66; FCO 1987; Vienna (UKDEL) 1988; Damascus 1991; FCO 1994; Riyadh 1996; Band B3.

Crawford, Marilyn Elisabeth; FCO since July 1995; Born 16/08/47; FCO 1975; Brussels (UKDEL NATO) 1977; Antigua 1980; FCO 1982; Brussels (UKDEL) 1988; FCO 1991; Paris 1994; Band A2.

Crawford, Michael James; Counsellor FCO since September 2001; Born 03/02/54; FCO 1981; Second later First Secretary Cairo 1983; First Secretary Sana'a 1985; First Secretary Riyadh 1986; First Secretary FCO 1990; First Secretary (Political) Warsaw 1992; FCO 1995; Counsellor Islamabad 1999; m 1984 Georgia Anne Moylan (twins, 1s 1d 1986; 1s 1989).

Crees, Ian Alec; FCO since January 2004; Born 31/01/43; Air Ministry 1960; Passport Office 1961; CRO 1963; Nairobi 1963; Nicosia 1966; FCO 1968; Rawalpindi (later Islamabad) 1971; Vice Consul Strasbourg 1975; FCO 1978; Second Secretary (Political/Aid) Kinshasa, also accredited to Congo-Brazzaville, Rwanda and Burundi 1980; Second later First Secretary (Commercial) Seoul 1984; First Secretary FCO 1989; First Secretary (Comm/DHM) Bombay 1993; Conference Department (European Council) FCO 1998; T/D

Islamabad 1998; HM Consul General and Joint
Management Officer Geneva 1999; m 1963 Betty
Winifred Kelder (1d 1965; 1s 1967).

Cresswell, Jeremy Michael, CVO (1996); Deputy
Head of Mission and Head of Political and Public
Affairs Berlin since June 2001; Born 01/10/49;
FCO 1972; Third later Second Secretary Brussels
1973; Second Secretary Kuala Lumpur 1977; First
Secretary FCO 1978; Private Secretary to
Parliamentary Under-Secretary, then Minister of
State FCO 1981-82; Deputy Political Adviser
Berlin (BMG) 1982; First Secretary FCO 1986;
Counsellor and Head of Chancery Brussels
(UKDEL) 1990; Full-Time Language Training
1994; Deputy Head of Mission Prague 1995;
Counsellor FCO 1998; m 1974 Ursula Petra
Forwick (1d 1978; 1s 1985).

Creswell, Alexander John Peter; First Secretary
(Political) Kuwait since July 2001; Born 27/07/65;
FCO 1993; Second Secretary (Political) Pretoria
1995; Second Secretary FCO 1998; Band D6; m
1995 Katharine Louise Reid.

Crockard, Gavin; Third Secretary Ottawa since
June 2002; Born 11/02/68; FCO 1989; Bombay
1991; Pretoria 1995; FCO 1996; Floater Duties
1998; Band B3.

Crocker, Helen; Madrid since September 2000;
Born 24/10/67; FCO 1999; Band A2.

Crockett, Patricia Anne; FCO since January 1997;
Born 19/11/48; Tokyo 1974; Copenhagen 1977;
FCO 1980; Port Louis 1981; FCO 1983; Lusaka
1985; Peking 1989; FCO 1991; Nicosia 1993;
Band C4.

Croisdale-Appleby, Lindsay; First Secretary
(Environment) Brussels (UKREP) since August
2002; Born 12/05/73; FCO 1996; Second
Secretary (Political/PPA/Aid) Caracas 1998; Band
D6.

Crombie, Anthony Campbell, OBE (1997); FCO
since August 2003; Born 18/10/56; COI 1980;
FCO 1985; Second later First Secretary Havana
1987; First Secretary FCO 1990; Deputy Head of
Mission Belgrade 1994; SUPL 1997; Counsellor
(Political) Moscow 1999; m 1982 Jane Nicholls
Talbot (diss 1987).

Crombie, Susan Elizabeth; Second Secretary
Brussels (UKDEL NATO) since September 2001;
Born 08/03/72; FCO 1998; Second Secretary
Pristina 1999; Band C4.

Crompton, Angela Louise; Geneva (UKMIS)
since January 2004; Born 04/05/64; FCO 1990;
Oslo 1991; T/D Islamabad 1994; Brasilia 1995;
FCO 1998; Maputo 2001; Band A2.

Crompton, Richard Anthony Neil, CBE (2003);
Head of Iraq Policy Unit, FCO since June 2003;
Born 25/09/64; FCO 1995; Senior Research
Officer, First Secretary FCO 1997; Full-Time
Language Training 1998; Counsellor and Deputy
Head of Mission Tehran 1999; m 1996 Rosa
Zaragoza (1d 2000; 1s 2001).

Cronin, Martin Eugene; First Secretary (Political)
Islamabad since December 2002; Born 22/01/65;
DoE 1987; FCO 1988; Vice-Consul/AMO Sana'a
1990; FCO 1993; Second Secretary
(Political/Economic) Amman 1994; First Secretary
Stockholm 1999; Band D6.

Crooks, Colin James, LVO (1999); Washington
since June 2002; Born 18/02/69; FCO 1992; Full-
Time Language Training (Korean) 1993; Full-Time
Language Training (Korean) Seoul 1994; Seoul
1995; First Secretary FCO 1999; m 1996 Kim
Young-Kee (1s 1997).

Crooks, Daryl; Third Secretary and Vice-Consul
Jakarta since April 2003; Born 27/05/68; FCO
1991; ECO later Vice-Consul Dhaka 1998;
Transferred to Diplomatic Service 1999; Band B3;
m 1999 Dina R Napao (1d 2000).

Crorkin, Colin Wynn, MBE (1993); Deputy Head
of Mission Tripoli since March 2002; Born
31/01/57; FCO 1975; Rome 1977; Beirut 1980;
Brussels (UKREP) 1983; FCO 1984; Kinshasa
1987; Second Secretary BTIO New York 1992;
Second later First Secretary FCO 1993; First
Secretary (Management) later Deputy Head of
Mission Lagos 1997; m (1) 1978 Gillian Smith
(diss 1991), (2) 1991 Joanne Lynn Finnamore (1s
1985; 1d 1998).

Cross, Caroline Janice, MBE (1991); Second
Secretary (Immigration/Consular) Accra since
June 2001; Born 30/09/64; FCO 1984; Warsaw
1986; Floater Duties 1989; Third Secretary
(Chancery/Information) Kampala 1991; Third later
Second Secretary FCO 1994; SUPL 1999; Band
C4; m 1998 M Higgins.

Cross, Harriett Victoria Saltonstall; FCO since
January 2002; Born 25/09/74; FCO 1997; Second
Secretary (Political) Rabat 1998; Band C4; m 1999
Lieutenant Philip Saltonstall RN.

Cross, Linda Mary (née Guild), MBE (2004);
Consul-General Yekaterinburg since February
2001; Born 15/03/56; FCO 1978; Rabat 1978;
Prague 1981; Quito 1983; Paris 1985; FCO 1988;
Vienna 1991; Third Secretary (Political) New York
(UKMIS) 1994; T/D Tirana 1997; Deputy Head of
Mission Baku 1998; Band C5; m 1989 Michael
John Cross.

Crossland, Jennifer Patricia (née Brown); SUPL
since August 2001; Born 28/08/64; FCO 1988;
Brussels (UKREP) 1990; FCO 1993; SUPL 1995;
New Delhi 1996; Bangkok 1998; Band A2; m
1993 Dudley Stewart Crossland (diss 2000).

Crossman, Steven Nigel; Deputy High
Commissioner Georgetown since April 2001; Born
16/11/55; FCO 1975; Muscat 1977; Washington
1978; New Delhi 1984; FCO 1987; Third
Secretary (Aid) Dar es Salaam 1990; Hanoi 1995;
Deputy High Commissioner Freetown 1999; m
1998 Le Hoang Lan (1s 2000).

Crowder, Richard Lawrence Robert; FCO since
November 2002; Born 14/11/73; FCO 1996; Full-
Time Language Training (Russian) 1998; Second

Secretary (Economic) Moscow 1999; Band D6; m 2000 Hilary Jane Louise Scott.

Cruickshank, Diane (née Robinson); On loan to DFID since June 2002; Born 15/07/60; FCO 1981; Bogotá 1982; Jakarta 1985; FCO 1988; Lusaka 1990; SUPL 1992; Tehran 1994; New Delhi 1998; FCO 2001; Band B3; m 1994 Douglas Graham Cruickshank.

Cullen, Carol Dulceta (née Fisher); FCO since September 2002; Born 12/11/56; DOE 1975; FCO 1977; Paris 1979; Dublin 1982; FCO 1985; Nairobi 1988; SUPL 1992; FCO 1993; Bridgetown 1996; Lusaka 1999; Band C4; m 1979 Thomas Cullen (1d 1984; 1s 1988).

Cullens, Niall James David; Second Secretary Consul (Commercial) Warsaw since July 2000; Born 28/02/65; FCO 1986; Berlin (BMG) 1988; LA/Caribbean Floater 1990; FCO 1993; Rome 1996; Band C4; m 1998 Caroline Anne Stramik.

Culley, John Douglas; FCO since November 2001; Born 26/05/71; MOD 1997; Band C4; ptnr, Joanne Childs.

Culligan, Phillip David; First Secretary Brussels (UKDEL NATO) since September 2003; Born 27/02/61; FCO 1981; Tripoli 1982; Pretoria/Cape Town 1983; Düsseldorf 1986; FCO 1989; Full-Time Language Training 1992; Second Secretary (Commercial) Budapest 1993; Deputy High Commissioner Nassau 1997; on loan to the MOD 2001; m (1) (diss); (2) 1997 Elizabeth June Huggins (1d 1999).

Culshaw, Robert Nicholas, MVO (1979); Director (Americas and Overseas Territories) FCO since March 2003; Born 22/12/52; Third Secretary FCO 1974; Language Training MECAS 1975; Language Training 1976; Third Secretary Muscat 1977; Second Secretary Khartoum 1979; First Secretary Rome 1980; APS to the Secretary of State FCO 1984; First Secretary and Head of Chancery later Counsellor, Consul General and Deputy Head of Mission Athens 1989; Counsellor and Head of News FCO 1993; Minister-Counsellor (Trade and Transport) Washington 1995; Consul-General Chicago 1999; m 1977 Elaine Ritchie Clegg (1s 1992).

Culver, John Howard, LVO (2000); HM Ambassador Reykjavik since January 2001; Born 17/07/47; Board of Trade 1967; FO later FCO 1968; Latin American Floater 1971; FCO 1973; Third Secretary Moscow 1974; Second Secretary La Paz 1977; Second later First Secretary FCO 1980; First Secretary (Commercial) Rome 1983; Head of Chancery Dhaka 1987; First Secretary FCO 1990; HM Ambassador and Consul-General Managua 1992; Consul-General Naples 1997; T/D Rome 2000; Band D7; m 1973 Margaret Ann Davis (1d 1974; 2s 1978, 1981).

Cummins, John, MBE (1983); Counsellor Moscow since September 2001; Born 07/09/46; FO later FCO 1964; Budapest 1969; Luxembourg 1971; Tunis 1973; FCO 1976; Second Secretary 1978; Consul and Second Secretary (Admin)

Santiago 1980; First Secretary Libreville 1985; First Secretary FCO 1988; Full-Time Language Training 1991; First Secretary (Commercial) Prague 1992; First Secretary FCO 1995; m 1969 Gillian Anne Biss (2s 1970, 1972).

Cunningham, Duncan; FCO since September 2003; Born 11/05/78; Band C4.

Cunningham, Kevin Francis; FCO since September 2002; Born 08/03/63; Civil Aviation Authority/National Air Traffic Control Services 1982; Royal Navy 1987; FCO 1992; Gaborone 1995; Bangkok 1998; Band C4; (2d 1995, 1999).

Cunningham, Raymond Peter, MBE (2001); Havana since July 2003; Born 21/01/45; Army 1963-89; FCO 1989; T/D Helsinki 1989; Warsaw 1990; Floater Duties 1992; FCO 1994; Floater Duties 1997; Islamabad 2000; Band C4.

Cupac, Dawn (née Womersley); SUPL since July 2002; Born 02/02/64; FCO 1992; Belgrade 1995; Vienna 1999; SUPL 2000; Vienna 2000; Band A2; m 1997 Dkordje Cupac.

Curley, Eugene Gerard, OBE (1991); FCO since July 2004; Born 30/09/55; FCO 1981; Second later First Secretary Mexico City 1984; First Secretary FCO 1986; First Secretary later Counsellor Paris 1993; Counsellor FCO 1998; Counsellor New York (UKMIS) 2000; m 1982 Joanne England (diss 1991); (2) 1993 Jane Margaret Crosland (1d 1996; 1s 2000).

Curley, Jane Margaret (née Crosland); Second Secretary FCO since February 1998; Born 24/11/61; FCO 1989; Second Secretary (Political) Copenhagen 1992; SUPL 1993; Band C4; m 1993 Eugene Gerard Curley (1d 1996; 1s 2000).

Curotto, Francine Elene; FCO since November 1999; Born 29/08/63; FCO 1990; Copenhagen 1993; FCO 1995; Havana 1997; Band C4.

Curran, David; Counsellor Tehran since May 2001; Born 08/06/60; FCO 1987; Second later First Secretary Manila 1989; First Secretary (Chancery) New York (UKMIS) 1992; First Secretary FCO 1994; First Secretary (Political) Lusaka 1997; First Secretary FCO 2000; m 1989 Lesley Jane Thomas.

Currie, David James; Deputy Head of Mission Algiers since March 2003; Born 21/10/46; CRO (later FCO) 1963; Peking 1969; Helsinki 1971; FCO 1972; Hanoi 1975; Brussels 1976; Vice-Consul Manila 1978; Second Secretary FCO 1982; Second Secretary (Commercial) Algiers 1986; Assistant Trade Commissioner, later Trade Commissioner (China Trade) Hong Kong 1989; First Secretary FCO 1993; First Secretary (Commercial) Brussels 1998; Band D6; m (1) 1968 Valerie Kirk (diss 1975) (1s 1970) ; (2) 1977 Joyce Rosalie Deacon (1 step s 1970, 1 foster s 1970).

Currie, Jacqueline Ann; SUPL since March 2003; Born 08/02/67; FCO 1987; Baghdad 1989; FCO 1991; LA Floater 1992; Atlanta 1994; Kigali 1998;

Deputy High Commissioner Victoria 2001; Band C4.

Curry, Trudy Gay (née Hibbs); Third Secretary (Consular/Management) Berlin since June 2001; Born 09/12/57; FCO 1975; SUPL 1980; Canberra 1981; Brussels 1984; SUPL 1987; FCO 1992; Accra 1994; Doha 1997; Band B3; m (1) 1980 Peter Ian Webb (diss 1983); (2) 1983 Peter Lester Curry (1d 1987; 1s 1990).

Curtis, Penelope Ann; Kabul since July 2003; Born 24/06/68; FCO 1990; Mexico City 1992; Madrid 1996; FCO 2000; Band B3.

Cushing, Martyn David; FCO since July 2003; Born 18/09/80; Band A2.

Cuthbertson, Deborah Ann; Islamabad since November 2000; Born 07/04/72; FCO 1991; Band C4.

Cutler, Charlotte Margaret; FCO since December 2003; Born 16/10/72; FCO 1998; Second Secretary (Chancery) New York (UKMIS) 2001; Band C4.

Cutler, Giles Peter; FCO since August 2003; Born 09/10/79; Band B3; ptnr, Victoria Chapman.

D

Dacey, Alan Treharne; Third Secretary (Commercial/Immigration) Havana since January 2003; Born 10/04/70; FCO 1988; Brussels (UKDEL NATO) 1991; Floater Duties 1994; FCO 1998; Full-Time Language Training 2002; Band B3; m 1999 Salomé Maritz (diss 2003).

Dakin, Nigel John; FCO since June 2002; Born 28/02/64; FCO 1996; First Secretary New Delhi 1999; Band D6; m 1987 Amanda Louise Johnson (1d 1995).

Daley Goldsmith, Robyn Jean; SUPL since December 2003; Born 08/08/69; FCO 1990; World-wide Floater Duties 1993; Third Secretary Bombay 1995; Third later Second Secretary Belmopan 1998; FCO 2001; Band D6; m 1995 Simon Geoffrey Goldsmith (1s 2004).

Dallas, Andrew James; FCO since October 2002; Born 15/01/71; FCO 1990; Dublin 1995; Doha 1999; Band B3; m 2001 Sarah Gordon.

Dallas, Ian Michael; FCO since October 1999; Born 13/12/42; Board of Trade 1961; Commonwealth Office 1966; Peking 1969; Lagos 1971; Accra 1973; FCO 1975; Chicago 1978; Second Secretary FCO 1982; Second Secretary (Admin) Lusaka 1985; FCO 1988; Vice-Consul (Comm) Karachi 1989; First Secretary (Comm/Aid) Colombo 1993; First Secretary Dublin 1997; m 1968 Angela Margaret Moore (1s 1971; 1d 1976).

Dalton, Richard John, CMG (1996); HM Ambassador Tehran since November 2002; Born 10/10/48; Third Secretary FCO 1970; MECAS 1971; Second Secretary Amman 1973; Second later First Secretary New York (UKMIS) 1975; FCO 1979; First Secretary Head of Chancery and

Consul Muscat 1983; First Secretary FCO 1987; Counsellor on loan to MAFF 1988; Counsellor on CDA at Chatham House 1991; Counsellor FCO 1992; Consul-General Jerusalem 1993; Counsellor FCO 1998; HM Ambassador Tripoli 1999; m 1972 Elisabeth Keays (2s 1978, 1982; 2d 1973, 1979).

Daltrey, Christopher; Third Secretary Paris since October 2002; Born 21/09/68; FCO 1988; Rome 1990; FCO 1992; Third Secretary Hong Kong (BTC) 1993; Secondment to China - British Trade Group 1997; Third Secretary Tunis 1999; m 1991 Kim Rowena Newson (1s 1992; 3d 1993, 1995, 2002).

Damper, Carol Ann; Brussels (UKDEL NATO) since September 2003; Born 17/12/44; FCO 1975; Mogadishu 1975; Bonn 1977; Belmopan 1979; FCO 1982; Vienna 1984; FCO 1987; Athens 1988; Bucharest 1991; FCO 1993; Sofia 1997; FCO 2000; Band B3.

Daniel, Hamish St Clair, OBE (2004), MBE (1992); Deputy High Commissioner Karachi since January 2004; Born 22/08/53; FCO 1973; Algiers 1975; Prague 1977; Lisbon 1978; Islamabad 1980; FCO 1982; San Francisco 1985; Second Secretary Khartoum 1989; Second Secretary FCO 1992; Deputy Head of Mission and HM Consul Sana'a 1994; First Secretary (Political/Economic) Jakarta 1997; British Representative Dili 2001; HM Ambassador Dili 2002; m (1) 1975 Susan Brent (diss) (1d 1981; 1s 1985); (2) 2002 Heather Ann Bull.

Daniels, Malcolm; FCO since September 1986; Born 04/09/48; FCO 1965; Singapore 1980; Helsinki 1984; Band D6; m 1976 Jeannette Susan (2s 1977, 1980).

Daniels, Mark Ian; FCO since January 1994; Born 30/08/65; FCO 1982; New Delhi 1985; Washington 1989; Band C4; m 1989 Suzanne Jayne Woodworth (2s 1999, 2001).

Daniels, Suzanne Jane (née Woodworth); FCO since April 1989; Born 07/05/63; FCO 1983; New Delhi 1985; Band A2; m 1989 Mark Daniels (2s 1999, 2001).

Darby, Jane; Deputy Head of Mission The Hague since January 2002; Born 01/04/53; FCO 1984; Bonn 1990; HM Treasury 1994; Cabinet Office 1995; FCO 1996; Full-Time Language Training 2001; m 1984 Michael Reece (1s 1986; 1d 1988).

Darby, Jonathan; Deputy Consul-General Chicago since February 2002; Born 28/12/69; FCO 1999; Band D6.

Dare, Gillian Angela; First Secretary (Political) Abuja since March 2002; Born 07/07/48; Local Government 1987-99; FCO 1999; Band D6.

Darke, John Martin Jamie; Counsellor Lisbon since August 2003; Born 02/05/53; FCO 1975; MECAS 1977; FCO 1979; MBA London Business School 1981; Management Consultant HAY-MSL 1983; First Secretary FCO 1985; First Secretary (Chancery) Cairo 1988; First Secretary FCO 1991; First Secretary (Political) Dubai 1996; First

Secretary FCO 1999; m 1980 Diana Taylor (1d 1989; 1s 1991).

Darker, Aidan; Dar es Salaam since July 2002; Born 08/10/62; Royal Air Force 1983-95; FCO 1995; Hong Kong 1996; Bahrain 1999; m 1989 Angela Darker (1s 1999).

Darker, Angela; SUPL since February 1999; Born 12/02/68; Royal Air Force 1986-90; FCO 1995; Hong Kong 1996; m 1989 Aidan Darker (1s 1999).

Darroch, Nigel Kim, CMG; Director General (EU) FCO since April 2003; Born 30/04/54; FCO 1976; Third later Second later First Secretary Tokyo 1980; FCO 1985; Private Secretary to the Minister of State 1987; First Secretary (Economic) Rome 1989; First Secretary later Counsellor Secretary FCO 1993; Counsellor (External Relations) Brussels (UKREP) 1997; Counsellor FCO 1998; Director (EU) FCO 2000; m 1978 Vanessa Claire Jackson (1s 1983; 1d 1986).

Dart, Jonathan, MVO; FCO since December 2003; Born 14/07/64; FCO 1988; Third Secretary (Science and Technology) Bonn 1991; Third Secretary Pretoria 1994; Full-Time Language Training 1998; Second Secretary (Inward Investment/Financial Services) Seoul 1999; Band D6; m 1990 Claire Emma Juffs (2s 1992, 1994; 1d 1998).

Dauris, James Edward; FCO since May 2002; Born 15/01/66; FCO 1995; First Secretary (Commercial) Moscow 1999; Band D6; m 1995 Helen Claire Parker (2d 2000, 2002).

Davda, Sheetal Arun (née Kotak); FCO since September 1993; Born 27/08/69; FCO 1988; Madrid 1991; Band C4; m 2001 Shailesh J Davda.

Davenport, Michael Hayward, MBE (1994); Deputy Head of Mission Cairo since April 2004; Born 25/09/61; FCO 1988; Warsaw 1990; FCO 1993; First Secretary (Political) Moscow 1996; Consul-General and Director of Trade Promotion Warsaw 2000; Full-Time Language Training 2003; m 1992 Lavinia Sophia Elisabeth Braun (1s 1994; 1d 1996).

Davey, Denise; Second Secretary (Management) Beirut since August 2001; Born 08/05/69; HCS 1987; FCO 1989; Dubai 1990; FCO 1994; Mexico City 1994; Guatemala City 1995; FCO 1996; Band B3.

Davey, Simon James, MBE (1985); Consul (Commercial) Miami since November 2001; Born 01/02/47; Army 1965-68; FCO 1969; Latin American Floater 1972; Havana 1973; Second Secretary (Aid/Commercial) Kathmandu 1976; Second later First Secretary FCO 1980; Consul Durban 1983; First Secretary (Commercial) Prague 1988; First Secretary FCO 1992; First Secretary (Commercial) Bogotá 1995; First Secretary 1999; m 1992 Marcela Eva Dzurikova.

David, Timothy James (known as Tim); High Commissioner Lusaka since May 2002; Born 03/06/47; FCO 1974; Second later First Secretary Dar es Salaam 1977; FCO 1980; On loan to the

ODA 1983; First Secretary Geneva (UKMIS) 1985; First Secretary later Counsellor FCO 1988; HM Ambassador Suva, also non-resident High Commissioner to Kiribati, Nauru and Tuvalu 1992; Deputy High Commissioner Harare 1996; High Commissioner Belmopan 1998; m 1996 Rosemary Kunzel (1s 1998; 1d 2001).

Davidson, Barry Alexander; On loan to British Trade International since November 2002; Born 01/08/64; HCS 1985; Geneva (UKMIS) 1988; Freetown 1990; FCO 1994; Kathmandu 1997; FCO 2001; Band C4; m 1985 Elizabeth Helen Oxley (1s 1992; 2d 1994, 1999).

Davidson, Brian John; Deputy Head of Mission Vilnius since September 2001; Born 28/04/64; FCO 1985; Language Training 1986; Third later Second Secretary (Chancery/Inf) Peking 1988; First Secretary on loan to the Cabinet Office 1992; First Secretary FCO 1994; First Secretary (Political) Canberra 1996; Full-Time Language Training 2001.

Davidson, Carolyn Jayne; Deputy Head of Mission Bratislava since December 2003; Born 18/04/64; FCO 1986; Language Training 1987; Language Training Kamakura 1988; Tokyo 1989; European Commission 1993; Bonn 1993; Second later First Secretary FCO 1995; SUPL 2000; Full-Time Language Training 2003; Band D6; m 1997 Thomas Henry Carter (2s 1998, 1999).

Davidson, James Gerard; FCO since July 2003; Born 20/05/67; MOD 1985; FCO 1988; Budapest 1989; Lagos 1991; FCO 1994; Jerusalem 1997; Tripoli 2000; Band B3.

Davidson, Raymond John Bruce, MBE (1995); On loan to the DTI since August 2002; Born 24/12/62; FCO 1995; Paris 1997; Islamabad 1999; Band B3; m 1988 Shivaun Anne (2s 1991, 1994).

Davidson, Sarah Victoria (née Fox); Doha since January 2000; Born 08/10/65; FCO 1985; Warsaw 1987; Hamilton 1989; Budapest 1992; FCO 1994; SUPL 1999; Band C4; m 1997 Fraser Reid Davidson (1s 1999; 1d 2002).

Davidson, Susan; SUPL since August 2001; Born 13/12/57; FCO 1987; Tokyo 1990; FCO 1992; Bangkok 1996; FCO 1998; Band A2.

Davidson Harkins, Katherine Elizabeth (known as Kate); Belgrade since January 2003; Born 27/04/74; FCO 2002; Band A2.

Davies, Caroline Elizabeth; FCO since April 2002; Born 04/06/63; RAF 1983-88; FCO HCS 1991-99; Kuwait 1998; World-wide Floater Duties 2000; Band B3.

Davies, Deborah Ann (née Kidd); Seoul since December 2000; Born 23/09/70; FCO 1992; Islamabad 1996; FCO 1999; Band A2.

Davies, Elved Richard Malcolm; Deputy Consul-General Hong Kong since April 2000; Born 19/01/51; Army 1972-75; Third later Second Secretary FCO 1975; Language Training 1977; Second later First Secretary Jakarta 1977; FCO

1980; Athens 1984; FCO 1985; First Secretary (Chancery) Nairobi 1989; FCO 1991; First Secretary later Counsellor Oslo 1991; Counsellor FCO 1995; m 1976 Elizabeth Angela Osborne (1d 1981; 1s 1984).

Davies, Gerald Howard; FCO since January 2001; Born 24/04/48; HCS 1965; FCO 1968; Paris 1971; Karachi 1973; Ibadan 1977; FCO 1978; Vice-Consul (Consular) Warsaw 1981; FCO 1984; Vice-Consul (Consular/Management) Melbourne 1986; FCO 1988; Consul and Second Secretary (Man) Muscat 1990; Consul Brussels 1995; m 1972 Yvonne Arnold (2d 1984, 1988).

Davies, Griselda Christian Macbeth (née Todd); SUPL since October 1999; Born 20/02/59; Budapest 1981; FCO 1982; Buenos Aires 1983; FCO 1985; Damascus 1987; FCO 1988; SUPL 1989; FCO 1990; Riga and Vilnius 1993; FCO 1997; Band A2; m 1989 John Howard Davies (1s 2001).

Davies, Ian; Deputy Head of Mission Lima since April 2002; Born 01/08/56; FCO 1976; Moscow 1978; SUPL 1980; FCO 1983; Paris 1985; Third later Second Secretary Moscow 1988; Second Secretary FCO 1990; Second Secretary (Com/Con) and Deputy Head of Mission La Paz 1993; Consul-General Marseille 1997; m 1979 Purificacion Bautista Hervias (2d 1985, 1988).

Davies, Jennifer Ann Tudor; Second Secretary FCO since February 1995; Born 02/03/50; FCO 1969; Khartoum 1972; Valletta 1974; Singapore 1977; FCO 1979; Buenos Aires 1980; FCO 1982; New Delhi 1984; FCO 1987; Hong Kong 1992; Band C4.

Davies, John Howard; FCO since July 2003; Born 31/01/57; FCO 1980; Riyadh 1983; Second later First Secretary FCO 1985; First Secretary and Head of Interests Section Damascus 1987; First Secretary FCO 1990; First Secretary (Political) Riga and Vilinius 1993; First Secretary FCO 1997; First Secretary (Political) Sofia 1999; Band D6; m 1989 Griselda Christian Macbeth Todd (1s 2001).

Davies, Jonathan Mark; Counsellor Madrid since November 2000; Born 01/12/67; FCO 1990; Language Training Cairo 1992; Second Secretary (Political/Information) Kuwait 1993; On loan to the Cabinet Office 1996.

Davies, Maureen Kerr Stewart (née Paisley); Brussels (UKREP) since August 1994; Born 12/06/53; FCO 1984; Washington 1987; Kathmandu 1990; Band A2; m 1988 Maxim Philip Davies.

Davies, Nicola Claire (née Dixon); SUPL since December 1998; Born 10/07/68; FCO 1990; Third Secretary (Political) Singapore 1993; Third Secretary FCO 1996; Band C4; m 1996 Jonathan Mark Davies.

Davies, Patrick James; FCO since March 2003; Born 08/05/68; FCO 1993; Full-Time Language Training 1994; Second Secretary (Political/Press)

Rabat 1995; First Secretary FCO 1999; Private Secretary FCO 2000.

Davies, Paul Ronald; First Secretary FCO since May 2000; Born 30/03/53; FCO 1970; African Floater 1974; Dacca 1976; FCO 1979; Tripoli 1982; Kingston 1984; Third Secretary (Commercial) Peking 1988; Second Secretary FCO 1990; Second Secretary (Political/Commercial/Information) Lima 1993; Consul (Commercial/Economic/Press and Public Affairs) Shanghai 1996; Deputy Consul-General Shanghai 1997; m 1976 Fiona Avril Canning (1d 1979; 1s 1981).

Davies, Peter Brian; Counsellor Madrid since April 2003; Born 30/12/54; Third Secretary FCO 1977; Language Training Hong Kong 1980; Second Secretary FCO 1981; Second later First Secretary Rome 1983; First Secretary FCO 1987; First Secretary and Consul Peking 1988; First Secretary FCO 1992; Counsellor (Political) Jakarta 1996; Counsellor FCO 1999; m 1981 Charlotte Helena Allman Hall (1d 1984; 1s 1986).

Davies, Roger James; First Secretary (Management) Nicosia since June 2001; Born 23/09/47; HCS 1965; FO (later FCO) 1967; Moscow 1970; Kampala 1971; Islamabad 1973; Kathmandu 1974; FCO 1978; Baghdad 1981; Vice-Consul (Comm) Johannesburg 1985; Second Secretary FCO 1987; Second Secretary (Management/Consular) Doha 1991; Deputy Consul-General Melbourne 1994; FCO 1998; m (1) 1974 Catherine Yvonne Moorby (diss 1990) (1s 1982; 1d 1984); (2) 1990 Jean Thérésa Austin.

Davies, Samantha Jayne Elizabeth; FCO since June 2002; Born 27/11/79; Band A2.

Davies, Tracy Denise (née Chagnot); SUPL since March 2001; FCO 1986; Vancouver 1987; Rome 1988; Paris 1988; FCO 1990; SUPL 1991; FCO 1992; Bangkok 1993; SUPL 1997; FCO 1999; Band B3; m 1990 Mark John Henry Davies (1s 1991; 1d 1994).

Davis, Andrew Cornwall; Brussels (UKREP) since April 2003; Born 29/04/68; FCO 1995; ECMM Sarajevo 1997; Santiago 1999; Band A2.

Davis, Ashley James; FCO since July 1991; Born 23/02/59; FCO 1986; Islamabad 1987; Band B3; m 1988 Roberta Scott (1d 2000).

Davis, Doris; Second Secretary (Immigration) Islamabad since February 2003; Born 26/01/47; DSAO 1967; Baghdad 1968; Sofia 1970; FCO 1971; Kuala Lumpur 1972; Peking 1973; Washington 1975; FCO 1978; Cairo 1980; Cape Town/ Pretoria 1984; FCO 1988; Washington 1992; Third Secretary (Man) Rangoon 1995; Second Secretary (Commercial) Baku 1999; Band C4.

Davis, Kevin Roy; FCO since June 1998; Born 02/01/65; FCO 1981; Washington 1989; FCO 1991; SUPL 1997; Band C4; m 1991 Karen Roberts (1s 1994).

Davis, Rosemary; First Secretary (Chancery) New York (UKMIS) since July 2001; FCO 1987; Language Training 1988; Language Training Cairo 1989; FCO 1990; Brussels (UKREP) 1991; Third Secretary (Chancery) Damascus 1994; FCO 1998; Band D6.

Davis, Stephen Alexander James; Second Secretary (Management/Consul/ECM) Abu Dhabi since May 2001; Born 24/09/65; FCO 1983; Mexico City 1986; Warsaw 1990; FCO 1993; Third Secretary (Commercial) Accra 1997; m 1986 Maureen Patricia Oates.

Davison, Andrew James; Third Secretary (Commercial) Bucharest since February 2004; Born 11/08/70; FCO 1992; Kiev 1997; Third Secretary New Delhi 2000; FCO 2003; Band B3; m 1997 Lana Jane Sawa.

Davison, Brian William Edward; Islamabad since July 2003; Born 06/06/45; Royal Marines 1961; MOD Police 1985; HM Prison Service 1986; Lusaka 1988; Cairo 1992; Lagos 1995; Karachi 1999; Damascus 2002; Band C4; m 1966 Sandra June Thompson (2s 1970, 1971).

Davison, Nicole April; Full-Time Language Training (Mandarin) since May 2004; Born 06/08/68; FCO 1988; Pretoria/Cape Town 1990; Third Secretary Dhaka 1991; Third later Second Secretary FCO 1996; Second Secretary Kiev 2001; Band C4.

Dawbarn, John Nathaniel Yelverton; FCO since March 2002; Born 03/05/65; FCO 1987; Language Training 1990; Third later Second Secretary (Chancery/ Information) Belgrade 1990; Second later First Secretary FCO 1993; First Secretary T/D (Political/Information) Belgrade 1995; FCO 1996; First Secretary (Political) Bonn later Berlin 1998; m 1989 Katherine Sarah Urry.

Dawber, Mary Welsh (née Campbell); T/D New Delhi since June 2004; Born 04/04/56; FCO 1996; SUPL 1997; Moscow 1997; Ankara 2000; Band A2; m 1975 Philip Dawber (1d 1976).

Dawber, Philip; Ankara since March 2000; Born 01/04/54; Armed Forces 1971-94; FCO 1995; Band A2; m 1975 Mary Welsh Campbell (1d 1976).

Day, Mark Christopher; Belmopan since April 2003; Born 01/05/63; FCO 1994; Hong Kong 1996; Lusaka 1999; Band A2; m 2003 Carolyn Yetman.

Day, Martin Charles; First Secretary FCO since 2003; Born 04/11/65; FCO 1989; Language Training Cairo 1991; Second Secretary (Chancery) Cairo 1992; First Secretary FCO 1995; First Secretary (Commercial) Prague 2000; Band D6.

Day, Rosamund; Bridgetown since September 2001; Born 27/06/64; FCO 1983; Bonn 1985; Suva 1987; Africa/ME Floater 1989; FCO 1991; Second Secretary (Management) Colombo 1996; SUPL 1999; Band C5; m 1993 Nicholas John Pyle (2s 1996, 2001; 1d 1999).

de Chassiron, Charles Richard Lucien, CVO (2000); Head of Protocol Division and Vice Marshal of the Diplomatic Corps, FCO since May 2002; Born 27/04/48; FCO 1971; Third Secretary Stockholm 1972; First Secretary Maputo 1975; FCO 1978; First Secretary (Commercial) Brasilia 1982; First Secretary later Counsellor FCO 1985; Counsellor (Comm/Econ) Rome 1989; HM Ambassador Tallinn 1994; Consul-General Milan 1997; m 1974 Britt-Marie Sonja Medhammar (1d 1975; 1s 1976).

de Csillery, Patricia Katarina; Second Secretary FCO since April 1998; Born 30/04/69; FCO 1993; Second Secretary (Political) New York (UKMIS) 1996; Band D6; m 1993 Michael de Csillery (1d 2000; 1s 2002).

De Gier, Helen Majorie; FCO since July 2001; Born 19/02/59; HCS 1976-84; FCO 1984; Freetown 1986; FCO 1989; Peking 1998; Band A2; m 1992 Joseph Eugene O'Carroll.

de Jeune d'Allegeershecque, Susan Jane (née Miller); Deputy Head of Mission Bogotá since October 2002; Born 29/04/63; FCO 1985; Brussels (UKREP) 1987 (Second Secretary 1989); FCO 1990; Second Secretary (Economic/Information) Singapore 1992; First Secretary FCO 1995; Deputy Head of Mission Caracas 1999; m 1991 Stephane Herv Marie le Jeune d'Allegeershecque (2s 1993, 1995).

de Mink, Julie Maria (née Ingham); FCO since January 2003; Born 03/01/65; FCO 1984; Harare 1986; SUPL 1990; Dhaka 1991; SUPL 1994; FCO 1997; Cape Town 1997; Gaborone 1997; Pretoria 1999; SUPL 2002; Band B3; m 2002 Ian Paul de Mink (2s 1989, 1990; 1d 2003).

De Pauw, Amanda Jayne (née Rutter); SUPL since May 2002; Born 20/03/64; HM Land Registry 1984; FCO 1988; Brussels (UKREP) 1989; Yaoundé 1993; FCO 1996; Ottawa 1999; Band A2; m 1993 Luc Paul Solange Marie De Pauw (2d 1998, 2000).

De Ramos, Nicola Anne (née Smyth); SUPL since September 2002; Born 11/08/65; FCO 1988; Bucharest 1989; Quito 1992; Havana 1996; Mexico City 1999; Band A2; m 1994 Bryan Dubal Ramos Montero (2d 1995, 1997).

de Ridder, Kathryn Louise Carmel (née Peacock); FCO since September 2002; Born 16/07/60; FCO 1984; New Delhi 1985; Brussels (UKREP) 1988; FCO 1991; SUPL 1992; Lagos 1994; SUPL 1997; Tel Aviv 1998; Band B3; m 1992 Wouter de Ridder (1d 1993).

De Sousa, Louise Amanda (née Clark); Deputy High Commissioner Maputo since May 2003; Born 23/07/68; FCO 1991; Second Secretary (Political/Information/Aid) Brasilia 1993; First Secretary FCO 1997; SUPL 2000; FCO 2001; m 1994 Allan Rivail de Sousa (1s 1998; 1d 2001).

de Valencia, Michelle (née Lawler); Deputy Head of Mission Holy See since September 2001; Born 08/06/64; FCO 1987; Bogotá 1990; Third

Secretary (Commercial later Chancery) Stockholm 1993; Second Secretary FCO 1999; Band C4; m 1993 Jairo Alberto Valencia Diaz (1d 1996; 1s 1998).

De Vere Lane, Graham Vaughan, MBE (1991); FCO since July 1993; Born 05/05/45; FCO 1968; Singapore 1969; FCO 1971; Lusaka 1973; FCO 1975; Darwin 1976; FCO 1978; Amman 1979; FCO 1983; Khartoum 1984; FCO 1987; Moscow 1988; Pretoria 1990; Band C4; m 1964 Janet Pine (1s 1964; 2d 1967, 1979).

de Waal, James Francis; Deputy Head of Mission Santiago since April 2003; Born 18/12/68; FCO 1990; New York (UKMIS) 1992; Full-Time Language Training 1994; Second Secretary (Political/ Information) Berlin 1994; FCO 1998; Washington 2002; Full-Time Language Training (Spanish) 2002.

Dean, Amy Charlotte; FCO since March 2003; Born 12/08/78; Band C4.

Dean, Andrew John; Counsellor (Multilateral) Canberra since September 2000; Born 06/02/55; FCO 1982; Second Secretary (UNIDO/UN) Vienna (UKMIS) 1984; Second later First Secretary FCO 1986; First Secretary (Chancery) Hanoi 1990; First Secretary FCO 1992; São Paulo 1997; First Secretary FCO 1999; m 1989 Nicola Moreton (1s 1993).

Dean, Robert John; FCO since December 2003; Born 21/05/59; MOD 1977; FCO 1978; Second Secretary Copenhagen 1987; Second later First Secretary FCO 1992; On secondment to MOD 1994; FCO 1995; First Secretary (External) Wellington 1999; Band C5; m 1981 Julie Margaret Scott (2d 1986, 1988).

Deane, Geoffrey; HM Consul Munich since July 2001; Born 19/02/50; FCO 1976; Nairobi 1980; Second Secretary FCO 1984; First Secretary (Chancery) East Berlin 1988; FCO 1991; First Secretary FCO 1997; Band D6; m Karen Aileen Wallace (4d 1980, 1983, 1986, 1994).

Deane, Michael Boyd; FCO since March 2003; Born 01/08/72; Second Secretary FCO 1999; Second Secretary (Economic) Vienna 2001; Band C4; m 2001 Natalya Samantha Pilbeam.

Deane, Robert Edward; Full-Time Language Training (Arabic) since April 2004; Born 28/09/62; HM Treasury 1985; Bonn 1994; FCO 1998; Band D7; m 1993 Corinna Osmann (1s 1998; 2d 2000, 2003).

Deaney, Tina Marie; Floater Duties since June 2002; Born 18/04/72; FCO 1991; Islamabad 1995; Prague 1999; Band B3.

Dear, Robert Edward; First Secretary (Political/Economic) Budapest since October 2000; Born 19/02/55; FCO 1986; First Secretary 1987; First Secretary FCO 1992; Deputy Head of Mission Havana 1994; m 1982 Caroline Margaret Reuss.

Dearden, Christopher Robert; On loan to the DTI since April 2001; Born 07/12/59; FCO 1978; Wellington 1981; Ankara 1984; LA/Caribbean Floater 1987; FCO 1989; Athens 1993; Vice-Consul Warsaw 1997; FCO 2000.

Dearden, Janine Elaine (née Lawrence); SUPL since June 2001; Born 18/10/60; FCO 1982; Rome 1983; Nairobi 1985; SUPL 1988; FCO 1989; SUPL 1990; FCO 1998; Band A2; m 1985 Timothy John Dearden (2s 1987, 1989).

Dee, Pauline (née Thompson); SUPL since September 2000; Born 11/10/63; FCO 1987; Bridgetown 1989; FCO 1992; Peking 1993; Grand Turk 1996; Sarajevo 1998; Band A2; m 1998 Stewart Dee (1d 1999; 1s 2003).

Dee, Stewart; Third Secretary (Political) Gibraltar since November 2000; Born 12/08/69; FCO 1988; Bonn 1990; FCO 1993; SUPL 1996; Vice Consul Sarajevo 1998; Band B3; m (1) 1991 Claire Duggan (diss 1996); m (2) 1998 Pauline Thompson (1d 1999; 1s 2003).

Delaney, Michael; FCO since June 2002; Born 14/12/67; FCO 1988; Ankara 1989; Lagos 1990; Abuja 1992; Colombo 1995; Manila 1998; Band B3; m 1990 Zeliha Doganavsargil.

Deneiffe, Paul Michael; FCO since October 1998; Born 21/06/63; FCO 1982; Lagos 1984; Khartoum 1986; Cairo 1987; FCO 1989; Seconded to Belfast 1989; FCO 1993; Madrid 1995; Band C4.

Dening-Smitherman, Major Peter Clemens Henri; Queen's Messenger since 1990; Born 12/07/47; HM Forces 1967-90.

Dennis, Catherine Teresa; Beirut since August 2002; Born 20/05/70; FCO 1998; Vienna (UKDEL) 1999; Band A2; m 2004 Zahi Talal Srour.

Dennis, John David; Minister, Consul General and Deputy Head of Mission Beijing since October 2003; Born 06/08/59; FCO 1981; Hong Kong 1983; Peking 1985; Second later First Secretary FCO 1987; First Secretary Kuala Lumpur 1992; On secondment to Standard Chartered Bank 1997; Counsellor on loan to the DTI 1998; Counsellor (Economic and Commercial) New Delhi 2001; m 1989 Jillian Margaret Kemp (2s 1994, 1999).

Dennison, Simon Becher; FCO since November 2003; Born 01/02/80; Band B3.

Denny, Ross Patrick; Deputy Head of Mission Luanda since April 2002; Born 13/09/55; RN 1972-79; FCO 1979; Santiago 1980; Doha 1983; Warsaw 1985; FCO 1988; Second Secretary (Political) The Hague 1992; FCO 1997; São Paulo 1998; m (1) 1977 Barbara Harvard (diss 1996) (1d 1979; 1s 1981); (2) 2000 Claudenise De Lima.

Dent, Alastair Ross Möller; Deputy High Commissioner Port Moresby since January 2004; Born 07/02/54; DHSS 1972; FCO 1974; Brussels (UKREP) 1976; Moscow 1979; FCO 1981; LA Floater 1984; Third Secretary (Management) Mexico City 1986; FCO 1989; Second Secretary

(Commercial/Information) later Deputy High Commissioner Gaborone 1993; Second later First (Management) Manila 1997; Second Secretary FCO 2001; m (1) 1977 (diss 1983); m (2) 1985 (2s 1988, 1996).

Denwood, Judith Elizabeth; Second Secretary FCO since April 2000; Born 21/10/65; FCO 1986; Bridgetown 1988; FCO 1991; Third Secretary FCO 1993; T/D New Delhi, Accra, Damascus 1995; Third Secretary (Management) and Vice-Consul Bahrain 1997; Band C4.

Desloges, Christina Anne (née Sanders); Dhaka since December 2003; Born 30/11/63; FCO 1984; Lagos 1987; FCO 1991; Harare 1992; Bandar Seri Begawan 1996; Stanley 2000; Band A2; m 1989 Daniel Albert Joseph Desloges (1d 1990; 1s 1997).

Devine, John Joseph; Second Secretary FCO since November 2003; Born 03/07/70; FCO 1991; Floater Duties 1994; New Delhi 1996; Consul Tallinn 2000; Band C4.

Devine, Paul Graham; FCO since May 1995; Born 19/01/51; DHSS 1973; FCO 1981; Bonn 1983; Riyadh 1985; Suva 1988; Düsseldorf 1992; Band B3; m 1993 Losana Lewamoqe Di Lo Tuisawau.

Dew, John Anthony; HM Ambassador Havana since October 2004; Born 03/05/52; FCO 1973; Third Secretary Caracas 1975; Second later First Secretary FCO 1979; First Secretary Paris (OECD) 1983; First Secretary FCO 1987; Counsellor and Deputy Head of Mission Dublin 1992; Minister Madrid 1996; Head of Latin America and Caribbean Department FCO 2000; On secondment to Lehman Brothers 2003; m 1975 Marion Bewley Kirkwood (3d 1977, 1980, 1984).

Dewar, Robert Scott; HM Ambassador Addis Ababa since March 2004; Born 10/06/49; FCO 1973; Third later Second Secretary Colombo 1974; First Secretary FCO 1978; First Secretary (Comm) Head of Chancery and Consul Luanda 1981; First Secretary FCO 1984; First Secretary and Head of Chancery Dakar 1988; Deputy High Commissioner Harare 1992; HM Ambassador Antananarivo 1996; FCO 2000; High Commissioner Maputo 2000; m 1979 Jennifer Mary Ward (1d 1988; 1s 1995).

Dholakia, Nishi Rajendra; FCO since September 2002; Born 03/11/78; Band C4.

Diaz, Alison Jean; Mexico City since March 2002; Born 24/02/68; FCO 1991; Belgrade 1993; Lima 1995; Vienna (OSCE) 1999; Band B3; m 1998 Juan Carlos Diaz (2s 1998, 2001).

Diaz, Sharon Vanessa (née Gordon); FCO since October 2003; Born 28/09/69; FCO 1998; Caracas 1999; Band B3; m 1998 Tirso Diaz Garcia.

Dibble, Hilary Anne (née Light); FCO since June 1998; Born 17/07/51; FCO 1973; Moscow 1974; FCO 1975; Rome 1976; Kingston 1980; Islamabad 1983; FCO 1987; Moscow 1990; Third later Second Secretary (Consular) Canberra 1993; m 1980 Geoffrey Walter Dibble.

Dick, Colin John; Second Secretary (Economic and Inward Investment) Singapore since November 2001; Born 22/06/70; FCO 1990; World wide Floater Duties 1994; Third later Second Secretary FCO 1996; Band C4; m 2001 Elaine Hargreaves (1s 2003).

Dick, Paula Jayne; SUPL since August 2002; Born 20/06/69; FCO 1988; Amman 1990; Belmopan 1994; Cairo 1998; Band B3.

Dickerson, Nigel Paul; On loan to the DTI since May 2002; Born 25/04/59; FCO 1978; Bonn 1981; Warsaw 1984; FCO 1987; Second Secretary 1990; Second Secretary (Management) and Consul Santiago 1992; Deputy High Commissioner and Second Secretary (Aid) Windhoek 1995; FCO 2000; m 1984 Marianne Gaye Tatchell (2d 1992, 1994; 1s 1995).

Dickins, Nicholas William; FCO since January 2001; Born 15/11/56; FCO 1985; Tel Aviv 1991; FCO 1994; New York (UKMIS) 1997; SUPL 2000; Band C5; m 1991 Marina Papaspyrou.

Dickinson, Woodman Mark Lowes, OBE (2000); Head of Office Pristina since August 2002; Born 16/01/55; FCO 1976; Second Secretary Ankara 1979; First Secretary FCO 1983; First Secretary (Pol/Inf) Dublin 1987; First Secretary FCO 1991; First Secretary on loan to the Bank of England 1994; Full-Time Language Training 1996; HM Ambassador Skopje 1997; SUPL 2001; m (1) 1986 Francesca Infanti (diss 1991); (2) 1995 Christina Houlder.

Dickson, Susan Jane; Legal Counsellor FCO since May 2003; Admitted as Solicitor (Scotland) 1989; Assistant later Senior Assistant Legal Adviser FCO 1990; First Secretary (Legal) New York (UKMIS) 1997; First Secretary (Overseas Territories Legal Adviser) Bridgetown 2000.

Dickson, William Andrew; FCO since August 1998; Born 17/12/50; FCO 1969; SUPL to attend University 1970; FCO 1974; Cairo 1976; Nairobi 1980; Second Secretary FCO 1982; Second Secretary (Commercial) Budapest 1982; Second later First Secretary FCO 1986; First Secretary (IAEA) Vienna 1989; First Secretary (Information) Hong Kong 1994; Band D6; m 1981 Gillian Ann Hague.

Digby, Simon; FCO since October 2003; Born 04/08/55; Crown Agents 1977; FCO 1980; Tehran 1982; LA Floater 1986; FCO 1987; Third Secretary (Admin/Cons) Mbabane 1989; FCO 1991; Luanda 1997; Consul and Second Secretary (Commercial) Bratislava 1999.

Diggle, Wadham Nicholas Neston; First Secretary (Political) Muscat since July 2004; Born 07/11/69; FCO 2002; Band D6.

Dillon, Alan Steven; Taipei since June 2002; Born 25/10/69; Royal Marines 1988-00; FCO 2000; Band B3; m 1994 Nichola Jane Clark (2d 1999; 2001).

Dimbleby, Andrew Timothy; Consul (Management) New York since April 2002; Born

20/05/59; FCO 1979; Accra 1981; FCO 1985; Pretoria 1986; Third Secretary (Commercial/Information/Chancery) Dubai 1989; Language Training 1989; Second Secretary FCO 1993; Second Secretary (Commercial) Manila 1996; First Secretary New York (UKMIS) 2000; Band C5; m 1981 Susan Margaret Joy Irvine (1s 1988; 2d 1991, 1996).

Dimond, Paul Stephen; HM Ambassador Manila since March 2002; Born 30/12/44; FO 1963; DSA 1965; Language Training Tokyo 1966; Osaka 1968 (Consul - Comm 1970); Second Secretary Tokyo 1972; On loan to DTI 1973; Second Secretary FCO 1975; First Secretary (Economic) Stockholm 1977; First Secretary FCO 1980; First Secretary (Commercial) Tokyo 1981; First Secretary FCO 1986; on secondment to Smiths Industries Plc 1988; Counsellor (Commercial) Tokyo 1989; Deputy Head of Mission The Hague 1994; Consul-General Los Angeles 1997; m 1965 Carolyn Susan Davis-Mees (2s 1968, 1970).

Dinsdale, Ian McLean Taylor; Abuja since December 2003; Born 20/10/49; FCO 1969; Nairobi 1972; Colombo 1976; Second Secretary FCO 1979; Santo Domingo 1982; Maseru 1985; Riyadh 1986; FCO 1989; Islamabad 1993; Wellington 1996; FCO 1998; Second Secretary (Immigration) Lagos 2002; Band C4; m 1975 Elizabeth Ann Montaut.

Dinsley, Andrew; Bangalore since June 2004; Born 22/08/66; FCO 1990; Kiev 1992; FCO 1996; Deputy Head of Mission Almaty 2000; Band C4; m 2000 Larissa Kolomiyets (1s 1986; 1d 2002).

Dinwiddy, Bruce Harry, CMG (2003); Governor Cayman Islands since May 2002; Born 01/02/46; Second Secretary FCO 1973; First Secretary Vienna (UKDEL MBFR) 1975; FCO 1977; First Secretary and Head of Chancery Cairo 1981; First Secretary FCO 1983; Counsellor on loan to the Cabinet Office 1986; FCO 1988; Counsellor Bonn 1989; Deputy High Commissioner Ottawa 1992; High Commissioner Tanzania 1998; FCO 2001; m 1974 Emma Victoria Llewellyn (1d 1976; 1s 1979).

Dix, Christopher John, OBE (2003); First Secretary (Immigration/Consular) Lagos since March 2004; Born 30/09/64; FCO 1983; Geneva (UKMIS) 1985; Dhaka 1988; Second Secretary FCO 1993; Language Training 1995; Second Secretary (Commercial) Madrid 1995; First Secretary (Immigration/Consular) New Delhi 1999; Band D7; m 1988 Julia Milward (diss 2003) (1d 1991; 1s 1994); ptnr, Christina Fernandex.

Dixon, Debra Audrey (née Churchill); First Secretary (Commercial) Amman since September 2000; Born 06/04/58; FCO 1978; Washington 1980; Sana'a 1983; FCO 1986; Düsseldorf 1989; SUPL 1992; Lusaka 1993; FCO 1998; Band C4; m 1978 Russell Kenneth Dixon (2d 1985, 1992; 1s 1990).

Dixon, Hazel, MBE (2003); Maputo since May 2001; Born 19/08/49; HM Forces 1967-77; Ankara 1989; Peking 1992; Moscow 1999; Band B3.

Dixon, Russell Kenneth; First Secretary (Management) Amman since July 2000; Born 24/01/58; MOD 1976; FCO 1978; Washington 1980; Sana'a 1983; FCO 1985; Düsseldorf 1989; SUPL 1993; Second Secretary (Political/Information) Lusaka 1993; Band C5; m 1978 Debra Audrey Churchill (2d 1985, 1992; 1s 1990).

Dobson, Sharon Gail, MBE (2002); FCO since May 2002; Born 04/01/68; FCO 1991; Third Secretary (Chancery) Dakar 1995; Third Secretary Brussels (UKDEL NATO) 1997; FCO 1999; On loan to the DTI 2001; Band C4.

Docherty, Margaret Emily (née Taylor); On loan to the Cabinet Office since September 2003; Born 28/08/71; FCO 1994; Kathmandu 1995; FCO 1997; Band B3; m 2000 Stuart Docherty.

Docherty de Morell, Claire Elizabeth; Bucharest since March 2004; Born 30/07/68; FCO 1992; Santiago 1995; Havana 1999; Georgetown 2000; Band A2; m 2000 Raynol Morell Fernandez (1s 2000; 1d 2002).

Doe, Marc Gavin; Second Secretary (Political) Moscow since March 2004; Born 09/01/79; FCO 2001; Band C4.

Doherty, Emer Maria; SUPL since November 2002; Born 10/01/69; FCO 1990; Full-Time Language Training 1993; Geneva (UKMIS) 1993; Paris 1996; SUPL 2001; Paris 2001; Band C4.

Doidge, Mary Ellen; FCO since April 1995; Born 21/01/46; Bonn 1971; FCO 1974; Warsaw 1975; Tokyo 1977; FCO 1980; Floater Duties 1982; Moscow 1983; FCO 1985; Brussels (UKDEL NATO) 1988; On loan to the Home Office 1991; Band C4.

Doig, Michael David; FCO since April 2001; Born 28/05/54; FCO 1973; Tokyo 1975; Karachi 1979; Vienna 1982; Third Secretary (Consular/Visas) Kaduna 1983; FCO 1987; Third Secretary (Comm/Econ) Ottawa 1990; FCO 1993; Second Secretary (Press and Public Affairs) Cape Town 1998; m (1) 1983 Mary Walker McKinnie (diss 2000) (1d 1985); (2) 2002 Sarah Elizabeth Booker.

Donaldson, Brian; HM Ambassador Antananarivo since October 2002; Born 06/04/46; Ministry of Aviation 1963; DSAO (later FCO) 1965; Algiers 1968; La Paz 1971; FCO 1974; Lagos 1975; Luxembourg 1979; Second Secretary FCO 1982; APS to the Minister of State 1983; Second later First Secretary (Aid/Comm) Port Louis 1985; First Secretary (Comm) Head of Chancery and Consul Yaoundé 1989; First Secretary (Immigration/Consular) Dhaka 1992; FCO 1996; High Commissioner Windhoek 1999; m 1969 Elizabeth Claire Sumner (3s 1971, 1973, 1979).

Donaldson, Ian Martin; On loan to the Home Office since September 2003; Born 21/07/66; FCO 1988; Third later Second Secretary (Political)

Jakarta 1991; FCO 1995; First Secretary Geneva (UKDEL) 1999; m 1990 Elspeth Jane Chovil Maguire (2d 1996, 1997).

Donegan, Susan Peta (née McAllister); Rome since June 2002; Born 28/05/67; FCO 1985; Paris 1987; LA Floater Duties 1990; Caracas 1992; SUPL 1993; Accra 1994; SUPL 1997; Band B3; m 1993 James Edward Donegan.

Donnelly, Sir Joseph Brian, KBE (2003), CMG (1997); High Commissioner Harare since July 2001; Born 24/04/45; Second Secretary FCO 1973; First Secretary (ECOSOC) New York (UKMIS) 1975; First Secretary and Head of Chancery Singapore 1979; First Secretary FCO 1982; Counsellor on loan to the Cabinet Office 1985; Counsellor and Consul-General Athens 1988; RCDS Course 1991; Counsellor FCO 1992; Minister and Deputy Permanent Representative Brussels (UKDEL NATO) 1995; HM Ambassador Belgrade 1997; Director and Special Representative for South East Europe FCO 1999; On secondment to BP/Amoco 2000; m (1) 1966 Susanne Gibb (diss 1994) (1d 1970) (2) 1997 Julia Mary Newsome.

Donnelly, Marie Thérésa; SUPL since February 2003; Born 21/05/61; FCO 1996; Kathmandu 1997; Tehran 2001; Band A2.

Donnelly, Matthew; FCO since November 1999; Born 21/11/61; FCO 1981; Algiers 1985; Nassau 1988; FCO 1990; Lagos 1992; Third Secretary (Commercial) Buenos Aires 1996; Band C4; m 1988 Tracy May Basnett (2s 1989, 1993).

Donnelly, Tracy May (née Basnett); SUPL since May 1995; Born 26/03/62; FCO 1982; Berne 1983; Algiers 1985; SUPL 1988; T/D Lagos 1994; Band A2; m 1988 Matthew Donnelly (2s 1989, 1993).

Dorey, Gregory John; Deputy Head of Mission Hong Kong since July 2000; Born 01/05/56; MOD 1977; On loan at UKDEL NATO 1982; MOD 1984; First Secretary FCO 1986; First Secretary (Chancery) Budapest 1989; PS/Minister of State FCO 1992; Counsellor (Economic) and later Deputy High Commissioner Islamabad 1996; Seconded to Industry 2000; m 1981 Alison Patricia Taylor (1d 1990; 2s 1988, 1994).

Dorrian, Claire Hicks (née Jones); Nicosia since August 2003; Born 15/07/68; HCS 1987; DS 1989; Stanley 1992; Riyadh 1995; Kampala 1999; Band B3; m 1992 Stuart Forsyth Dorrian (1s 1996).

Douglas, Helen Clare; Consul/Management Officer Muscat since June 2004; Born 13/06/68; FCO 1987; Lagos 1990; FCO 1994; ECO/VC Bridgetown 1998; SUPL 2001; FCO 2002; Band C4; m (1) 1990 Michael Thomas Fallon (diss 1997) (2s 1991, 1992); (2) 1999 Paul Leslie Douglas (1d 2001, 1 step d 1983; 1 step s 1985).

Douglas, Janet Elizabeth; First Secretary FCO since June 2000; Born 06/01/60; FCO 1985; Language Training 1987; Second later First

Secretary (Chancery/Inf) Ankara 1988; First Secretary FCO 1991; First Secretary on loan to the ODA 1993; First Secretary (Political) Stockholm 1996.

Douglas, Paul Leslie; FCO since April 2002; Born 05/11/58; Army 1975-88; Hanoi 1998; SUPL 1999; Band A2; m 1993 Tina Marie Field.

Douglas-Hiley, Mark Charles Piers Quentin; Third Secretary (Consular/Management) Kinshasa since November 2001; Born 06/11/54; Department of Employment 1972; DHSS 1973; FCO 1974; Castries 1977; FCO 1979; Geneva (UKMIS) 1980; FCO 1983; Lagos 1987; New York (JMO) 1991; FCO 1994; FCO 1997; Sofia 1998; FCO 2000; Band B3.

Douse, Sarah Louise (née Ansell); FCO since March 1998; Born 08/04/70; FCO 1990; Rome 1992; Bonn 1995; Band B3; m 2001 Carl Anthony Douse.

Doust, Claire Heather (née Barlow); Lagos since October 2001; Born 07/03/72; FCO 1991; Brussels (UKDEL NATO) 1995; Third Secretary (Management) Islamabad 1998; Band B3; m 1998 Stephen Terence Doust.

Doust, Stephen Terence; Lagos since November 2001; Born 04/12/72; FCO 1992; Brussels (UKDEL NATO) 1995; Islamabad 1998; Band B3; m 1998 Claire Heather Barlow.

Dove, John Henry; FCO since October 1997; Born 10/03/65; HM Customs and Excise 1989; FCO 1990; Full-Time Language Training 1991; Deputy Head of Mission Tallinn 1992; Moscow 1993; Deputy Head of Mission Tashkent 1996; Band C4.

Dow, Elizabeth Anne; Consul Lisbon since July 2003; Born 09/03/58; FCO 1976; New Delhi 1978; Brasilia 1982; FCO 1984; New York (CG) 1988; Vice-Consul/MO Jerusalem 1991; FCO 1995; Consul Rabat 1999.

Downer, James Robert Stephen; FCO since September 1998; Born 09/07/68; FCO 1992; Full-Time Language Training 1993; Full-Time Language Training Cairo 1994; Sana'a 1995; Band D6; m 1998 Nicola Marguerite Neary (1d 2003).

Downing, Joanna Watson; FCO since September 2001; Born 17/12/71; FCO 1995; OHR - Bosnia 1997; Attaché Dakar 1998; Band B3.

Dowse, Timothy Michael; Counsellor FCO since 2001; Born 18/12/55; FCO 1978; Manila 1980; Second later First Secretary Tel Aviv 1982; First Secretary FCO 1986; Washington 1992; Counsellor, Cabinet Office 1997-98; On loan as Head of Defence, Diplomacy and Intelligence Spending to HM Treasury 1998-00; m 1989 Vivien Frances Life (2d 1991, 1994).

Dowsett, Moira; SUPL since May 1999; Born 06/11/61; FCO 1988; Brussels 1991; FCO 1993; Band A2; m 2001 Dominic O'Donnell (2s 1998, 2000).

Drabble, Rufus John; Second Secretary Oslo since February 2002; Born 12/02/70; FCO 1995;

Nairobi 1998; Band C4; m 1997 Stella Elizabeth Waldron (1d 2001).

Drake, David Allen; FCO since January 2001; Born 01/09/47; RAF 1967-75; FCO 1977; Lagos 1979; Kuwait 1982; Second Secretary 1984; Second later First Secretary FCO 1985; First Secretary (Civil Aviation) Bonn 1989; First Secretary (Commercial) Singapore 1991; Consul (Commercial) New York 1996; m 1972 Anne Veronica Paice.

Drake, Howard Ronald, OBE (2001); Assistant Director, Human Resources Directorate, FCO since December 2002; Born 13/08/56; FCO 1975; LA Floater 1979; Los Angeles 1981; Second Secretary 1982; Second Secretary FCO 1983; Second Secretary (Chancery/Info) Santiago 1985; First Secretary FCO 1988; First Secretary and Head of Chancery Singapore 1992; First Secretary FCO 1995; Deputy Consul General and Director of Investment New York 1997; m 1988 Gill Summerfield (1s 1992; 1d 1994).

Drayton, Frank Anthony; FCO since December 2002; Born 10/12/54; FCO 1974; Islamabad 1976; Cape Town 1979; Munich 1982; FCO 1985; Prague 1989; Vice-Consul Doha 1990; FCO 1994; FCO British Trade International 1997; Second Secretary (Commercial) Riyadh 2000; Band C4; m 1988 Fidelma Bernadette Tuohy.

Drew, Simon Richard; Hong Kong since January 2004; Born 07/05/65; FCO 1981; Pretoria/Cape Town 1989; FCO 1992; Ankara 1993; FCO 1997; First Secretary Washington 1999; m 1991 Katharine Chappell (1d 1995).

Drew, Thomas; FCO since February 2002; Born 26/09/70; FCO 1995; Second Secretary Moscow 1998; First Secretary (Economic) Moscow 2000.

Drew, Timothy James; FCO since July 2003; Born 02/04/65; FCO 1994; Geneva (UKMIS) 1996; FCO 1999; Riyadh 2000; Band B3; m 1991 Claire Melanie (2d 1998, 2002).

Dring, Sarah Anne Maxwell; First Secretary FCO since March 2000; Born 23/11/48; FCO 1974; Sofia 1975; Nicosia 1977; FCO 1979; South East Asia Floater 1983; Algiers 1985; FCO 1987 (Second Secretary 1989); Johannesburg 1991; FCO 1995; First Secretary (Management) Kampala 1997; Band D6.

Drummond, Roderick Ian; Deputy Head of Mission Damascus since June 2004; Born 07/09/62; FCO 1985; Language Training SOAS 1986; University of Jordan 1987; Second Secretary (Political/ Economic) Algiers 1988; First Secretary FCO 1992; Deputy Consul-General (Trade/Investment) Johannesburg 1996; First Secretary (External) Brussels (UKREP) 1998; Deputy Head of Mission Amman 2002; m 1985 Carolyn Elizabeth Elliott (1s 1986; 2d 1988, 1990).

Drury, Alan Hyslop; FCO since July 1998; Born 21/02/52; FCO 1970; Budapest 1973; Dacca 1975; LA Floater 1977; FCO 1980; Second Secretary

(Comm) Muscat 1983; Second later First Secretary FCO 1987; Resident Representative St. Georges 1989; Consul (Commercial) Barcelona 1994; m 1980 Joan Lamb (1d 1984; 1s 1986).

Dryden, Paul James; T/D Maputo since July 2004; Born 15/06/69; FCO 1990; Warsaw 1992; T/D Zagreb 1992; Ottawa 1993; Hamilton 1996; Ashgabat 1999; FCO 2002; Band B3.

Drysdale, Craig Morrison; First Secretary (Political) Muscat since April 2001; Born 22/03/56; FCO 1981; Full-Time Language Training 1994; Full-Time Language Training Cairo 1995; First Secretary FCO 1996; Band C5; m 1988 Clare Elizabeth (2d 1993, 1996).

Drysdale, Heather; FCO since August 2000; Born 02/06/56; Brussels (NATO) 1977; Tokyo 1980; FCO 1983; Reykjavik 1984; Floater Duties 1987; FCO 1988; Valletta 1993; Full-Time Language Training 1996; Warsaw 1997; Band C5.

Duckett, Keith Dyson; SUPL since January 2004; Born 11/04/58; FCO 1977; Kuala Lumpur 1979; Maputo 1983; Brasilia 1985; FCO 1986; Jakarta 1989; Third Secretary (Man) Paris 1993; Second Secretary (Man) Damascus 1995; SUPL/Temporary Duties 1997; FCO 2002; Band C4; m 1989 Diane Puckridge (1d 1990; 1s 1991).

Dudgeon, Denise Ann (née Holland); FCO since October 2001; Born 13/04/63; FCO 1986; Washington 1989; JLG Hong Kong 1991; FCO 1994; British Trade International 1997; On loan to DTI 1999; Band C4; m 2000 Anthony James Dudgeon.

Duff, Janet Nancy; FCO since October 1997; Born 03/12/67; FCO 1990; Language Training 1991; Chiang Mai 1992; Vice-Consul Bangkok 1993; Addis Ababa 1996; Band D6.

Duff, Julie Anne; Helsinki since July 2002; Born 17/06/79; FCO 1999; Band A2.

Duffield, Linda Joy, CMG; HM Ambassador Prague since December 2004; Born 18/04/53; DHSS 1976; Paris (ENA) 1986; First Secretary FCO 1987; First Secretary (Comm) Moscow 1989; First Secretary later Counsellor FCO 1992; Deputy High Commissioner Ottawa 1995; High Commissioner Colombo 1999; Director (Wider Europe) FCO 2002.

Duffin, David Robert; FCO since 1996; Born 04/11/53; FCO 1972; New Delhi 1979; FCO 1981; Singapore 1987; FCO 1990; Berlin 1995; Band C5; m (1) 1980 Angela Thicke (diss 1984); (2) Carole Susan Matthews (diss 1996).

Duffy, Martin Patrick; First Secretary (Counter Narcotics) Kabul since March 2004; Born 11/01/70; British Army 1986 - 94; FCO 1999; On loan to No. 10 Downing Street 2000; Assistant Private Secretary to the Permanent Under Secretary, FCO 2002; Band D6; ptnr, Siân McLean.

Duffy, Peter John; First Secretary (Management) Paris since April 2001; Born 20/06/50; Ministry of

Aviation (later Ministry of Technology) 1966; FCO 1967; Addis Ababa 1971; Maseru 1974; Khartoum 1977; FCO 1978; Yaoundé 1982; Johannesburg 1985; Attaché later Second Secretary Budapest 1989; Second Secretary FCO 1991; Second Secretary Amsterdam 1994; Second later First Secretary (Management) Kingston 1995; m 1971 Juliet Heather Woodward (1s 1972).

Duggin, Sir Thomas Joseph; HM Ambassador Bogotá since August 2001; Born 15/09/47; Commonwealth Office (later FCO) 1967; Oslo 1969; Bucharest 1973; Assistant Private Secretary to the PUSS, FCO 1977; Second Secretary Bangkok 1979; First Secretary FCO 1982; First Secretary (Commercial), Consul and Head of Chancery La Paz 1985; First Secretary and Head of Chancery Mexico City 1989; High Commissioner Vila 1992; Counsellor FCO 1995; m (1) 1968 (diss 1983) (2s 1973, 1975); (2) 1983 (diss 1996) (3) 1999 Janette Mortimer David.

Dun, Peter John; SUPL since November 2002; Born 06/07/47; FCO 1970; Third later Second Secretary Kuala Lumpur 1972; Second later First Secretary FCO 1976; First Secretary (External Relations) Brussels (UKREP) 1980; First Secretary New York (UKMIS) 1983; FCO 1987; Counsellor on secondment to RCDS 1989; Counsellor (Economic) Islamabad 1990; Foreign Policy Adviser to External Affairs Commissioner, EC Brussels 1993; Counsellor FCO 1996; On Commercial Secondment 2000; FCO 2001; m 1983 Cheng-Kiak Pang (2s 1987, 1989).

Duncan, Colin; Second Secretary (Commercial) Cape Town since July 2003; Born 03/03/70; DSS 1988; FCO 1989; Brussels (UKREP) 1992; Sofia 1995; Floater Duties 1998; FCO 2000; Band C4.

Duncan, John Stewart, OBE (1993); Counsellor (Commercial) Paris since April 2002; Born 17/04/58; FCO 1980; Paris 1982; Khartoum 1985; Second Secretary FCO 1988; APS to Minister of State on loan to ODA 1991; NATO Defence College Rome 1992; Chargé d'Affaires Tirana 1992; Brussels (UKDEL WEU/NATO) 1993; First Secretary FCO 1996; On loan to SACEUR 1998; m 1984 Anne Marie Jacq (1d 1990; 1s 1994).

Duncan, Rachel Mignonne Bridget (née Blanche); SUPL since June 2002; Born 17/01/74; FCO 1997; Vice-Consul (Political) Jerusalem 2000; FCO 2002; Band B3; m 2000 Stuart Duncan.

Duncan, Reginald Arthur; Pyongyang since July 2002; Born 23/08/45; HM Forces 1963-93; FCO 1995; Ankara 1997; Stanley 2000; Band A2; m 1967 Cecily Coleman (2d 1971, 1974).

Duncan-Smith, Louise-Marie Veronica; Kingston since April 2003; Born 16/12/62; FCO 1984; Ottawa 1986; Banjul 1989; FCO 1989; Victoria 1992; Language Training 1996; Berne 1996; SUPL 2000; Sana'a 2000; Band A2; m 1986 Brian David Smith (2d 1996, 1999).

Dunlop, Alexander James Macfarlane; FCO since January 2001; Born 14/06/48; FCO 1968; Ottawa 1971; Vientiane 1974; FCO 1977; Sana'a 1980;

Vienna 1983; FCO 1986; Second Secretary (Chancery/Info) Lilongwe 1989; First Secretary FCO 1994; First Secretary (Consular) Nairobi 1996; T/D Vienna (UKDEL OSCE) 2000; Band C5; m 1978 Ortrud Wittlinger.

Dunn, Andrew Patrick Rymer; Second Secretary (Press and Public Affairs) Tehran since October 2003; Born 14/09/69; FCO 2000; Band C4; m 1995 Caroline Nicola Cann (2s 1998, 2002).

Dunn, David Hedley; FCO since August 2001; Born 21/09/68; FCO 1989; Oslo 1992; LA/Caribbean Floater Duties 1995; Second Secretary (Environment) seconded to UNEP Nairobi 1998; Band D6.

Dunn, James Michael; FCO since May 2003; Born 07/01/59; FCO 1980; Washington 1984; FCO 1986; Paris 1990; Third Secretary Lagos 1993; Warsaw 1999; Band C4; m 1993 B C Boyle.

Dunn, Jonathan Michael; FCO since September 2003; Born 07/03/75; FCO 1997; SOAS University of London 1998; Full-Time Language Training Hanoi 1999; Second Secretary (Chancery) Hanoi 2000; Band D6; m 2003 Karen Rex.

Dunn, Michael George; Kuala Lumpur since October 2003; Born 08/11/48; FO (later FCO) 1966; New York 1971; Lima 1974; FCO 1976; Copenhagen 1980; Harare 1983; Caracas 1986; FCO 1989; Quito 1992; Bogotá 1997; FCO 2000; m 1983 Mercedes Josefina Fuguet-Sanchez (3d 1987, 1990, 1998).

Dunnachie, Hugh, MBE (1987); Consul-General Perth since March 2000; Born 07/12/44; MOD (Navy) 1961-65; DSAO 1965; Singapore (Political Adviser's office) 1967; Warsaw 1972; Vice-Consul Cairo 1973; Second Secretary FCO 1976; Second Secretary (Commercial) The Hague 1980; Consul and Head of British Interests Tripoli 1984; First Secretary FCO 1989; Deputy Consul-General Melbourne 1992; First Secretary (Economic/Agriculture) Canberra 1994; Deputy Head of Post and HM Consul Dubai 1996; m (1) 1963 Elizabeth Mosman Baxter (diss 1986) (3d 1964, 1971, 1980; 1s 1965); (2) 1986 (Doreen) Carole Cleaver.

Dunne, John Richard; Deputy Head of Mission Pyongyang since May 2002; Born 04/10/67; FCO 1992; Third later Second Secretary New York (UKMIS) 1996; SUPL 2000; First Secretary FCO 2001; Band D6; m 1997 Naomi Anita Scott.

Duranko, Elizabeth Jean (née Paris); SUPL since August 2000; Born 23/01/69; FCO 1993; Geneva 1996; SUPL 1998; Pretoria 1999; Band B3; m 1997 John Eric Duranko (1d 1998).

Durham, Anna Catherine; FCO since January 2004; Born 04/11/79; Band B3.

Duxbury, Julie Annette; SUPL since January 2004; Born 05/02/70; FCO 1988; Brussels (UKDEL NATO) 1990; FCO 1993; Full-Time Language Training 1995; Vice-Consul Athens

1996; Dubai 1998; Third Secretary (Immigration) Zagreb 2000; Band B3.

Dwyer, Michael John; FCO since October 2001; Born 29/12/55; DOE 1972-74; FCO 1974; Ottawa 1977; Belmopan 1979; FCO 1982; Warsaw 1982; Islamabad 1983; FCO 1986; Vice-Consul (Management/Commercial/Consular) Toronto 1990; Second Secretary (Commercial) Toronto 1991; Consul/ECM New York 1995; Consul and Director U.S Entry Clearance Issuing Posts, New York 1999; m 1982 Karen Leolin Meighan (2s 1983, 1985; 1d 1989).

Dyson, John Alva, MVO (1995); SMO Baghdad since August 2003; Born 15/04/49; DSAO (later FCO) 1966; Port of Spain 1970; Geneva 1973; Yaoundé 1976; FCO 1978; Nuku'alofa 1982; FCO 1985; Second Secretary (Commercial) Jedda 1987; Vice-Consul (Management Officer) Cape Town 1991; First Secretary FCO 1996; T/D Asmara 2001; Deputy High Commissioner T/D Suva 2002; Deputy High Commissioner T/D Bandar Seri Begawan 2003; m 1971 Deirdre Anne George (2s 1974, 1981).

E

Ead, Mark; Nicosia since March 2002; Born 20/04/76; FCO 1997; Band A2; m 2001 Victoria Swan.

Eager, Helen Christine (née Gillings), BEM (1991); SUPL since May 1998; Born 10/06/65; FCO 1985; SUPL 1986; FCO 1988; Baghdad 1988; FCO 1990; Bangkok 1993; FCO 1997; Band A2.

Eager, Nigel Dominic; First Secretary FCO since August 2002; Born 09/05/62; FCO 1981; Dublin 1986; Third Secretary/Vice Consul Baghdad 1988; FCO 1990; First Secretary (Political) Valletta 1998; Band C5; m (1) 1987 Helen Christine Gillings (diss 1993); (2) 1998 Catherine Thomas.

Eakin, Christopher Howard; SUPL since July 2000; Born 01/12/64; FCO 1984; East Berlin 1985; Paris 1987; FCO 1990; Vienna 1993; Grand Cayman 1996; Band C4.

Earl, Jane Ann (née Kerr); SUPL since February 2001; Born 15/06/68; FCO 1989; Luanda 1991; Islamabad 1995; SUPL 1998; Brussels 2000; Band B3; m 1991 Shaun Earl (1d 1997).

Earl, Shaun; SUPL since May 2004; Born 04/01/70; FCO 1989; Luanda 1991; Third Secretary Brussels (UKDEL) 1998; Lilongwe 2001; Band B3; m 1991 Jane Ann Kerr (1d 1997).

Easson, Hilary; FCO since February 2004; Born 10/01/68; FCO 1987; Kuwait 1990; Algiers 1991; FCO 1994; Bogotá 1995; FCO 1999; Vienna 2000; Band A2.

Easter, Christine Marie; FCO since July 1994; Born 22/11/44; FCO 1975; Cape Town 1975; FCO 1979; Luxembourg 1982; Anguilla 1985; Rangoon 1987; Budapest 1989; Washington 1991; Band B3.

Eatwell, Jonathan David; SUPL since July 2001; Born 08/11/67; FCO 1986; Lusaka 1988; FCO 1992; Dhaka 1995; FCO 1998; Jakarta 1998; Band B3; m 1991 Lisa Ann Brecknell (1d 1997).

Ebeling, Adrian Stanley Arthur; FCO since November 2000; Born 20/01/48; FCO 1984; Paris 1989; FCO 1992; Pretoria 1998; Band C4; m 1979 Laura Phipps (1s 1987).

Edgar, Christopher George; Consul-General St Petersburg since August 2004; Born 21/04/60; FCO 1981; Moscow 1983; Lagos 1986; FCO 1988; Resigned 1992; Reinstated, First Secretary FCO 1995; HM Ambassador Phnom Penh 1997; Full-Time Language Training 2001; HM Ambassador Skopje 2001; m 1994 Yelena Nagornichnykh (2d 1994, 1998).

Edge, Christopher James; FCO since August 2003; Born 30/08/53; FCO 1972; Kabul 1975; East Berlin 1977; Rome 1980; Kaduna 1981; FCO 1984; Beirut 1985; Third Secretary (Commercial) Mexico City 1987; Deputy Head of Mission Tegucigalpa 1988; Second later First Secretary (Commercial) Madrid 1992; FCO 1996; First Secretary (Commercial), San José and Director of Trade Promotion in Central America 1999; Deputy High Commissioner Port of Spain 2001.

Edghill, Susan Christine (née Cranwell); Chennai since April 2002; Born 14/07/58; FCO 1990; Paris 1993; Port Louis 1996; Manila 1998; Band A2; m 1996 Samuel Carlisle Edghill.

Edis, Rachel Pauline; Second Secretary (Political/Military) Washington since December 2002; Born 24/11/76; FCO 2001; Band C4.

Edusei, Charmaine (née Howe); SUPL since July 2003; Born 17/09/59; FCO 1988; Brussels (UKDEL NATO) 1991; FCO 1993; Valletta 1994; FCO 1997; Band B3; m 1989 Isaac Edusei (1d 1993).

Edwards, Carole Lilian (née Hellier); Brasilia since April 2002; Born 07/07/45; FCO 1973; Freetown 1973; Washington 1975; Prague 1978; Belgrade 1978; FCO 1979; Beirut 1980; Ottawa 1982; Moscow 1985; FCO 1986; Washington 1989; FCO 1992; Band B3.

Edwards, David Vaughan; Tehran since May 2001; Born 27/09/43; RAF 1961-89; Budapest 1989; Islamabad 1990; Kingston 1994; Moscow 1996; Riyadh 1998; Band B3; m 1967 Patricia Ann (2d 1968, 1969; 1s 1972).

Edwards, Gillian Rose; FCO since November 2003; Born 07/02/64; FCO 1983; Resigned 1987; Reinstated FCO 1988; World wide Floater Duties 1991; St Petersburg 1993; FCO 1994; Vice-Consul New York 1996; Dublin 2000; Band B3; m 1995 David Jonathan Mead.

Edwards, Keith Nigel; Washington since March 2001; Born 09/05/53; FCO 1969; Warsaw 1977; Athens 1978; FCO 1981; Hong Kong 1985; FCO 1988; Second Secretary Madrid 1992; Second Secretary FCO 1995; m 1975 Wendy Ann Carrington (2d 1980, 1982).

Edwards, Lucy Anne; Vienna since January 2003; Born 05/05/71; FCO 1993; Brussels (UKREP) 1995; FCO 1997; SUPL 1999; Nairobi 2000; Band A2; m 1997 Jason Edward Lambert (diss 2003).

Edwards, Paul Martin; Third Secretary (Political/PPA) Abuja since January 2002; Born 11/11/66; FCO 1996; Almaty 1998; Band B3; m 1990 Jane Baker (2d 1993; 2001; 1s 1999).

Edwards, Rose Catherine Amy; FCO since March 2004; Born 10/11/73; FCO 1998; Full-Time Language Training 1999; Second Secretary (Economic) Moscow 2001; Second later First Secretary (Economic) Kiev 2003; Band D6.

Eelbeck, Andrew; FCO since January 2002; Born 02/03/59; FCO 1979; Islamabad 1980; FCO 1982; Singapore 1982; FCO 1986; Third Secretary Prague 1988; Third Secretary Pretoria 1992; FCO 1995; Accra 1997; Band C5; m 1994 Miss F Botes (1s 1995).

Ehrman, William Geoffrey, CMG (1998); Director (International Security) FCO since September 2000; Born 28/08/50; Third Secretary FCO 1973; Language Training Hong Kong 1975; Third later Second Secretary Peking 1976; First Secretary (ECOSOC) New York (UKMIS) 1979; First Secretary Peking 1983; FCO 1985; On secondment as Political Adviser to the Governor in Hong Kong 1989; Counsellor FCO 1993; Principal Private Secretary to the Secretary of State for Foreign and Commonwealth Affairs 1995; On secondment to Unilever 1997; HM Ambassador Luxembourg 1998; m 1977 Penelope Anne Le Patourel (1s 1981; 3d 1977, 1979, 1986).

Eke, James Robert; FCO since June 2004; Born 28/06/78; Band B3.

El Beleidi, Cecille Maude (née Greaves); Consul (Commercial) Jedda since January 2003; Born 22/11/62; FCO 1982; Kuwait 1985; FCO 1986; Kathmandu 1989; Vice-Consul Casablanca 1992; APS/Baroness Symons FCO 1995; Second Secretary (Chancery) Riyadh 1999; SUPL 1999; Second Secretary (Chancery) Riyadh 2000; Full-Time Language Training 2002; Band C5; m 1987 Magdi El Beleidi (1d 1999).

El Ouassi, Sabine; FCO since 2003; Born 29/01/64; HCS 1990-93; FCO 1994; Riyadh 1995; Amman 1999; Band A2; m 1988 Mohamed El Ouassi (2s 1994, 2001).

El Roubi, Julie Anne (née Mooney); SUPL since August 2003; Born 21/04/71; Brussels (UKDEL NATO) 1991; Khartoum 1995; Lagos 1998; Abu Dhabi 2000; Band A2; m (1) 1992 Prince Felix Lewis (diss) (1d 1992); (2) 1999 Murtada Saad El Roubi (1s 2000).

Elder, Alistair Alexander; Third Secretary (Commercial) New Delhi since July 2001; Born 14/05/71; FCO 1989; Brussels (UKREP) 1992; FCO 1994; Vice-Consul Tel Aviv 1997; m 2001 Justine Elizabeth Pitts (2d 1992, 1995; 1s 2003).

Elder, Peter Edward; FCO since December 1997; Born 14/03/68; FCO 1989; Brussels 1992; FCO 1994; New Delhi 1994; Band C4; m 1994 Rosalind Anita Hall (1d 1997; 1s 2002).

Elder, Rosalind Anita (née Hall); SUPL since March 2002; Born 19/07/65; FCO 1990; Brussels (UKREP) 1992; New Delhi 1994; FCO 1997; Band A2; m 1994 Peter Edward Elder (1d 1997).

Eldon, Stewart Graham, CMG (1999), OBE (1991); HM Ambassador Dublin since April 2003; Born 18/09/53; New York (UKMIS) 1976; FCO 1976; Third later Second Secretary Bonn 1978; First Secretary FCO 1982; Private Secretary to the Minister of State FCO 1983; First Secretary (Chancery) New York (UKMIS) 1986; First Secretary FCO 1990; Counsellor on loan to the Cabinet Office 1991; Fellow, Center for International Affairs, Harvard University 1993; Counsellor (Political) Brussels (UKDEL NATO/WEU) 1994; Director (Conferences) FCO 1997; Deputy Permanent Representative (with the personal rank of Ambassador) New York (UKMIS) 1998; Visiting Fellow, Yale University 2002; m 1978 Christine Mary Mason (1d 1982; 1s 1985).

Elliot, Caroline Margaret (Carma), OBE (2004); Consul-General Chongqing since January 2000; Born 24/08/64; FCO 1987; Peking 1989; Brussels 1991; EC Presidency Liaison Officer Bonn, Paris and Madrid 1994; Second later First Secretary FCO 1996; (1d adopted 2002).

Elliot, Christopher Lowther; Second Secretary FCO since March 1997; Born 26/12/54; DNS 1974; DOE 1975; FCO 1975; Cairo 1979; Bridgetown 1982; FCO 1986; Islamabad 1990; Muscat 1993; m 1975 Julie Lorraine Inman (1s adopted 1975; 1d 1982).

Elliot, Jacqueline Mary; Second Secretary FCO since September 2002; Born 25/01/64; FCO 1984; Lima 1986; LA Floater 1989; San José 1991; FCO 1996; Caracas 1998; Band C4; (1d 1991).

Elliott, Hugh Stephen Murray; Counsellor Paris since July 2002; Born 31/08/65; FCO 1989; Third later Second Secretary (Chancery) Madrid 1991; FCO 1996; Buenos Aires 1999; m 1989 Toni Martin-Elena (1s 1993; 1d 1995).

Elliott, Jane Susan; First Secretary FCO since April 2002; Born 16/06/55; FCO 1980; Hong Kong 1991; FCO 1997; Consul-General Hong Kong 2000; Band D6.

Elliott, Jonathan Andrew; Deputy High Commissioner Kampala since March 2003; Born 03/09/66; FCO 1991; Full-Time Language Training 1993; Tokyo 1995; Second Secretary FCO 1999; First Secretary FCO 2001; Band D6.

Elliott, Robert David, LVO (2003); FCO since June 2004; Born 25/11/60; FCO 1980; Prague 1981; Peking 1982; Language Training 1983; Abu Dhabi 1984; Port Louis 1988; FCO 1993; HM Consul Jerusalem 1997; First Secretary (Management) Abuja 2000; Band C5; m 1998 Victoria Louise Holloway (2s 1988, 2004; 1d 2000).

Elliott, Stuart; FCO since January 2003; Born 15/04/75; HCS 1994; FCO 1997; Athens 1999; Athens 1999; Band A2; m 1999 Margaret Redmond.

Elliott, Susan Jayne, MBE (1991); Valletta since December 2003; Born 13/06/61; FCO 1978; SUPL 1980; SUPL 1982; Rome 1982; Cairo 1984; FCO 1985; Beirut 1988; Bombay 1992; FCO 1992; Second Secretary (Chancery) Bandar Seri Begawan 1999; Second Secretary (Political) Bucharest 2003; Band C4; m 1980 John Anthony Tucknott (diss 1992).

Elliott, William, OBE (2002); Deputy Head of Mission Tallinn since September 2002; Born 16/03/68; Second Secretary FCO 1993; Language Training 1994; Second Secretary (Political) Warsaw 1995; First Secretary FCO 1998; First Secretary (Political) Kabul 2001; Band D6; m 2003 Daria Anna Chrin (1d 2003).

Ellis, Alexander Wykeham; Madrid since October 2003; Born 05/06/67; FCO 1990; Third later Second Secretary (Political/Economic) Lisbon 1992; First Secretary (Economic) Brussels (UKREP) 1996; FCO 2001; m 1996 Maria Teresa Adegas.

Ellis, Amanda Jane; FCO since January 2003; Born 07/12/60; FCO 1987; Brussels 1989; FCO 1991; Jakarta 1995; Quito 1999; Band A2.

Ellis, David Edward; Second Secretary (Technical Management) Bangkok since June 2003; Born 07/03/67; FCO 1987; Lagos 1997; FCO 2001; Band C4; m 1996 Cherie Louise Wilson (1s 1997; 1d 2002).

Ellis, Hugo; SUPL since January 2004; Born 13/09/66; FCO 1988; Riyadh 1992; Strasbourg (UKDEL) 1995; FCO 1999; Band B3; ptnr, Helen Marie Arbon (1d 2003).

Ellis, John Arthur; First Secretary (Consul/MO) Sarajevo since July 2002; Born 27/03/52; DHSS 1969-71; FCO 1971; Wellington 1974; Khartoum 1976; Dar es Salaam 1979; FCO 1981; Islamabad 1982; Seoul 1986; Second Secretary FCO 1989; Second Secretary (Commercial/Aid) Cairo 1993; Second later First Secretary FCO 1996; m 1974 Law Kwai Chun (1s 1980; 1d 1983).

Ellis, Philip Donald; First Secretary FCO since October 1997; Born 09/05/57; FCO 1978; Brussels (NATO) 1981; Peking 1984; FCO 1987; New Delhi 1990; Vice-Consul São Paulo 1995; m 1981 Gail Teresa Drayton (1s 1997).

Ellis, Richard Anthony; Second Secretary (Economic) Nicosia since December 2002; Born 02/02/77; FCO 2000; Full-Time Language Training (Greek) 2002; Band C4.

Ellwood, Dr Sheelagh Margaret; FCO since October 1998; Born 21/02/49; FCO 1988; Assistant Deputy Governor Gibraltar 1995; Senior Principal Research Officer 1998.

Elvins, Christine Patricia (née Pettit); SUPL since February 1999; Born 04/06/60; FCO 1979; Bonn 1983; Pretoria 1986; FCO 1987; SUPL 1988; FCO 1993; Band C4; m 1988 Martyn Andrew Elvins.

Elvins, Martyn Andrew; FCO since August 2003; Born 13/02/58; FCO 1984; Warsaw 1988; Pretoria 1999; Band C5; m 1988 Christine P Pettit.

Elvy, Simon David, OBE; First Secretary Baghdad since April 2004; Born 08/12/61; FCO 1983; Baghdad 1985; Stockholm 1989; FCO 1992; Second Secretary (Political) Stockholm 1996; FCO 1997; On loan to the Cabinet Office 2001; FCO 2002; Band D6; m 1985 Lesley Jane (2s 1991, 1993).

Embleton, Robert Leitch; FCO since August 2003; Born 09/10/42; FO 1960; Leopoldville 1964; Bonn 1968; St Vincent 1969; FCO 1973; Stuttgart 1976; Prague 1979; Second Secretary FCO 1980; Second later First Secretary (Chancery) Washington 1984; Consul (Commercial) Düsseldorf 1989; First Secretary FCO 1993; First Secretary (Social/ Science) Rome 1998; m 1970 Ursula Biebricher (1d 1975).

Emery, Peter Michael; Lagos since October 2003; Born 25/11/72; FCO 1997; Helsinki 1999; Tokyo 2000; Band B3.

Empson, Jane Mary (née Silverwood); Montevideo since February 2002; Born 05/08/60; FCO 1985; Mexico City 1987; FCO 1991; T/D Montevideo 1993; Muscat 1994; SUPL 1998; Rome 1999; Band B3; m 1994 Richard Andrew Empson (1s 1996).

Enescott, Nicholas John; MO/VC Rangoon since March 2002; Born 06/12/51; FCO 1972; Cape Town 1975; Ankara 1977; Tripoli 1980; FCO 1983; Hanoi 1986; Third Secretary (Comm) and Vice-Consul Dakar 1989; Second Secretary (Management) Lilongwe 1991; Second Secretary FCO 1995; ECM Bombay 1998.

Engdahl, Denise Jean (née Sanders); Stockholm since March 2000; Born 19/09/60; FCO 1982; Wellington 1983; Colombo 1986; Mbabane 1989; FCO 1993; SUPL 1995; Kingston 1996; Band B3; m 1989 Geran Magnus Engdahl (1s 1991; 1d 1994).

Ennis, Alexandra Mary; FCO since September 2002; Born 18/05/79; Band A2.

Esling, Paul Francis; Warsaw since February 2004; Born 16/11/73; FCO 1996; Harare 1998; Lagos 2000; Band B3; m 1997 Lyndsey Jane Esling (1s 2000; 1d 2001).

Etherington, Richard David Ernest; FCO since 2002; Born 29/11/73; FCO 1999; T/D Dubai 2001; Band C4.

Etherton, Mark Roy; On loan to the House of Lords since September 2003; Born 17/03/58; FCO 1983; Second Secretary (Chancery) Paris 1988; First Secretary (Political/Economic) Warsaw 1991; First Secretary on loan to Cabinet Office 1994; FCO 1996; Deputy Permanent Representative Vienna (UKMIS) 1999; m 1991 Suzanne Margaret Miskin (2d 1994, 1996).

Evans, Carol Jeanette (née Kendall); SUPL since July 1997; Born 10/04/59; FCO 1982; Vienna (UKDEL) 1984; Warsaw 1987; FCO 1988; Band B3; m 1991 Keith Dennis Evans.

Evans, Claire Elizabeth; Deputy Head of Mission and First Secretary (Commercial) Dubai since April 2003; Born 02/11/61; FCO 1987; Jakarta 1989; Third Secretary (Commercial) Islamabad 1992; Second Secretary FCO 1996; First Secretary FCO 2000; Band D6.

Evans, Claire Margaret (née Bolland); Second Secretary Oslo since March 2002; Born 13/01/70; Second Secretary FCO 1994; Band C4; m 1996 David Howard Evans (2d 1997, 1999; 1s 2001).

Evans, David Hugh; First Secretary (Political) Nairobi since May 2001; Born 27/03/59; FCO 1985; Islamabad 1988; FCO 1989; First Secretary (Political) on loan to the US State Department Washington 1995; On secondment as Senior Policy Adviser, CBI 1999; Band D6; m 1988 Nirmala Vinodhini Chrysostom (2d 1996, 2001).

Evans, Derek John; First Secretary Moscow since July 2000; Born 04/06/56; DOE 1978; FCO 1984; Second Secretary Dubai 1985; Second Secretary Pretoria 1989; FCO 1994; m 1982 Dawn Marie Evans (1d 1984; 1s 1986).

Evans, Elizabeth Ann (née McNab); On loan to the MOD since October 2002; Born 26/07/61; FCO 1998; Third Secretary (Visits, Press and Public Affairs) Peking 1999; Band C4; m 1987 Laurance Bolton Evans (1s 1989).

Evans, Gayle Evelyn Louise (née Sperring); SUPL since April 1997; Born 01/09/62; FCO 1983; Accra 1984; Moscow 1986; FCO 1987; Floater Duties 1990; SUPL 1991; New York (UKMIS) 1992; FCO 1996; Band B3; m 1991 Julian Ascott Evans (2d 1997, 1999).

Evans, Gerald Stanley; FCO since October 2003; Born 26/10/51; FCO 1971; Havana 1973; Bonn 1974; Jedda 1977; FCO 1977; Third Secretary and Vice-Consul Dubai 1979; FCO 1983; Third Secretary (Commercial) Bogotá 1986; Third Secretary (Management) Athens 1990; Second Secretary FCO 1994; Deputy Head of Mission Asunción 1996; Second Secretary (Commercial) Montevideo 2000; m 1991 Graciela Elisa Casetta.

Evans, Gillian; Zagreb since June 2003; Born 01/09/59; FCO 1981; Berlin (BMG) 1982; Kinshasa 1984; Africa/Asia/ME Floater 1988; Zagreb 1992; Damascus 1996; Rabat 2000; Band A2.

Evans, Jennifer Louise; FCO since July 2001; Born 07/11/78; Band C4; ptnr, Nicholas Cole.

Evans, Jennifer Mary (née Lewis); SUPL since January 1995; Born 03/03/59; FCO 1978; Far East Floater 1981; SUPL 1983; Vienna 1984; SUPL 1985; Dhaka 1989; Second Secretary FCO 1993; m 1982 Wayne Evans (3d 1985, 1988, 1994; 1s 1997).

Evans, Julian Ascott; Deputy High Commissioner Ottawa since July 2003; Born 05/07/57; FCO 1978; Language Training 1980; Moscow 1982; Zurich 1985; Second Secretary FCO 1987; Second later First Secretary New York (UKMIS) 1991; First Secretary FCO 1996; Deputy High Commissioner Islamabad 2002; m 1991 Gayle Evelyn Louise Sperring (2d 1997, 1999).

Evans, Karen-Lane (née Williams); FCO since December 1999; Born 09/04/63; FCO 1989; Second Secretary (Chancery) The Hague 1992; Second Secretary FCO 1996; SUPL 1998; Band C4; m 1998 Paul Lawson Evans.

Evans, Kelly Jane (née Sage), MVO (1996); FCO since May 2002; Born 29/01/68; FCO 1989; The Hague 1992; Third Secretary (Visits/Information) Warsaw 1994; Third Secretary FCO 1996; SUPL 2000; Band C4; m 2000 David Evans.

Evans, Peter Dering; Deputy Head of Mission Quito since September 2003; Born 09/04/57; FCO 1976; Dhaka 1978; FCO 1980; Barcelona 1985; San Salvador 1988; Third Secretary (Management/Accounts) Caracas 1990; Third later Second Secretary FCO 1993; Deputy Head of Mission Reykjavik 1998; m 1985 Susan Elizabeth Parker (2s 1987, 1989).

Evans, Stephen Nicholas, CMG (2002), OBE (1994); High Commissioner Colombo since July 2002; Born 29/06/50; Third Secretary FCO 1974; Language Training SOAS 1975; Second Secretary FCO 1976; Head of Chancery and Consul Hanoi 1978; FCO 1980; Language Training Bangkok 1982; First Secretary Bangkok 1983; First Secretary FCO 1986; First Secretary (Political) Ankara 1990; Counsellor (Economic/Commercial/Aid) Islamabad 1993; Secondment to United Nations Special Mission to Afghanistan 1996; Counsellor FCO 1997; m 1975 Sharon Ann Holdcroft (2d 1981, 1984; 1s 1986).

Evans, Stephen Paul, MBE (2003); Third Secretary (Consular) Singapore since July 2002; Born 28/10/57; HM Forces (Army) 1975; Police Constable 1997; FCO 2000; Band B3; m 1986 Julie Spackman (1s 1988; 1d 1990).

Evans, Stephen Shane; FCO since July 2001; Born 07/12/54; FCO 1992; Second Secretary Zagreb 1998; Band C4; m 1995 Susan Jane (1d 1987).

Evans, Wayne; First Secretary (Political) The Hague since July 2000; Born 29/08/53; FCO 1971; Paris 1974; Maseru 1977; FCO 1979; Baghdad 1981; Vienna 1984; FCO 1987; Second Secretary (Aid) Dhaka 1989; Second later First Secretary FCO 1993; Deputy Head of Mission and Consul (Commercial) Jedda 1996; Band C5; m 1982 Jennifer Mary Lewis (3d 1985, 1988, 1994; 1s 1997).

Evans, William John Eldred; First Secretary (Political) Tallinn since July 2002; Born 13/04/71; FCO 1994; Language Training 1996; On loan to OHR Sarajevo 1997; Second Secretary (Political/Military) Sarajevo 1998; Second Secretary FCO 1999; Band D6.

Everard, John Vivian; HM Ambassador Montevideo since September 2001; Born 24/11/56; FCO 1979; Third later Second Secretary Peking 1981; Second Secretary Vienna 1983; Resigned 1984; Reinstated, Second later First Secretary FCO 1987; First Secretary (Commercial) Santiago 1990; HM Ambassador Minsk 1993; OSCE Mission to Bosnia-Herzegovina 1995; Counsellor FCO 1996; Counsellor Peking 1998; m 1990 Heather Ann Starkey.

Everard, Thomas James; Tehran since June 2001; Born 11/08/75; FCO 1998; Band A2.

Everest, Philip Ralph; Third Secretary (Political/PPA) Port of Spain since October 2002; Born 25/03/74; FCO 1999; Band B3.

Everett, Sara Gillian; First Secretary FCO since October 2002; Born 06/07/55; FCO 1979; Assistant Private Secretary to Minister of State 1980; Paris (ENA) 1981; Caracas 1983; Deputy Presidency Co-ordinator Brussels (UKREP) 1986; Second Secretary (Economic/Agriculture) Brussels 1987; First Secretary FCO 1991; Deputy later Director New York (BIS) 1996; m 1989 Christopher Ian Montague Jones (1s 1994).

Everitt, Oliver Hunter; FCO since January 2002; Born 28/12/71; FCO 1992; Vienna 1995; Third Secretary (Immigration) Lusaka 1999; Band B3.

Everson, Clare Elizabeth; SUPL since November 1999; Born 20/12/59; FCO 1981; Karachi 1983; SE Asia Floater 1988; FCO 1990; Deputy High Commissioner Vila 1994; Band D6.

Ewart, Sharon Linda (née Acheson); Third Secretary (Chancery) later Second Secretary (PPA) Dublin since July 2001; Born FCO 1992; Kuala Lumpur 1995; Third Secretary (Consular) Kingston 1997; Band C4; m 2002 Andrew Robert Ewart.

F

Fabrizi, Rebecca Jane (née Chesman); First Secretary (Trade and Development) Geneva (UKMIS) since October 2003; Born FCO 1994; Full-Time Language Training (Mandarin) 1995; Second Secretary (Economic/Commercial) later First Secretary (Political) Beijing 1997; SUPL 2002; Band D6; m 2001 Sem Fabrizi (1s 2002).

Fairley, Averil Margaret; Second Secretary (Management) Georgetown since March 2001; Born 18/06/67; FCO 1986; East Berlin 1988; Hanoi 1990; European Council Unit, Edinburgh 1992; Bombay 1993; FCO 1997; Band C4.

Fairweather, Maria Louise (née Latta); SUPL since November 2001; Born 25/05/67; MOD 1986; FCO 1988; Berne 1989; FCO 1992; Peking 1993; T/D Kiev 1995; FCO 1996; Band B3; m 1993 Robert John Fairweather.

Fairweather, Robert John; Second Secretary Geneva (UKMIS) since April 2002; Born 26/02/67; HMCE 1987-96; FCO 1996; Band C4; m 1993 Marie Louise.

Falconer, Lynne Marie; FCO since 2004; Born 27/09/67; HM Forces 1986-95; FCO 1995; Helsinki 1997; Lisbon 2000; Band A2.

Fall, David William; HM Ambassador Bangkok since July 2003; Born 10/03/48; Third Secretary FCO 1971; Language Training Bangkok 1973; First Secretary Bangkok 1976; On loan to Cabinet Office 1977; FCO 1979; First Secretary (Chancery) Pretoria/Cape Town 1981; First Secretary later Counsellor FCO 1985; Deputy Head of Mission and Counsellor (Commercial) Bangkok 1990; Deputy High Commissioner Canberra 1993; HM Ambassador Hanoi 1997; Estate Modernisation Manager, FCO 2000; m 1973 Margaret Gwendolyn Richards (3s 1976, 1977, 1980).

Falzarano, Assuntina; Second Secretary (Chancery) New York (UKMIS) since December 2000; Born 10/08/73; FCO 1998; Band C4.

Farish, Sandra Mary (née Olley); FCO since July 2002; Born 07/06/71; FCO 1995; Copenhagen 1996; Beirut 2000; Band B3; m 1996 Joseph Farish (1d 2001).

Farnham, Brian George; Paris since April 2000; Born 16/04/52; FCO 1968; Paris 1974; FCO 1977; Baghdad 1978; FCO 1980; Tokyo 1984; Hong Kong 1988; Second Secretary FCO 1991; Singapore 1995; FCO 1998; Band C5; m 1982 Emiko Ishida (2d 1985, 1990).

Farnsworth, Lee; Caracas since October 2002; Born 28/01/71; FCO 1998; La Paz 1999; Band A2; m 2001 Audrey Giovanna (née Vergara Rojas).

Farr, Charles Blanford, OBE (2003); First Secretary FCO since February 1995; Born 15/07/59; Second Secretary FCO 1985; Second Secretary Pretoria 1987; Second Secretary FCO 1990; First Secretary (Chancery) Amman 1992; Band D6.

Farr, Dawn Margaret; Caracas since October 2002; Born 05/07/70; FCO 1989; Nicosia 1992; Mostar 1995; Seoul 1996; Bogotá 1997; Band B3.

Farrand, John Percival Morey; First Secretary (Consul) Havana since July 2002; Born 04/06/54; HM Customs and Excise 1971; FCO 1972; Tokyo 1974; Mexico City 1977; Kuala Lumpur 1981; FCO 1985; San Francisco 1988; FCO 1990; Second Secretary FCO 1991; Deputy High Commissioner Nassau 1994; First Secretary (Management) Ottawa 1997; Band C5; m 1979 Sharon Anne Eddie (3d 1980, 1982, 1987).

Farrare, Jane; Jerusalem since September 2000; Born 05/02/72; FCO 1999; Band A2.

Farrell, Sarah Jane; SUPL since February 2003; Born 27/06/69; FCO 1991; Lisbon 1995; Istanbul Floater 1998; FCO 1999; Taipei 1999; SUPL 1999; Taipei 2000; Band A2.

Farrent, Susan Jennifer; Karachi since April 2004; Born 17/01/48; FCO 1986; Monrovia 1987; Port Moresby 1991; Port of Spain 1992; FCO 1995; Bangkok 1996; Dhaka 2000; Band B3.

Farrey, Sonia Louise; FCO since September 2001; Born 21/01/77; Band C4.

Farrington, Ian Francis; First Secretary FCO since December 1995; Born 21/08/63; FCO 1986; Third later Second Secretary (Econ) Athens 1989; Second later First Secretary FCO 1991; First Secretary Lagos 1993; Band D6.

Farrow, Stephen Alan; Islamabad since May 2003; Born 23/07/56; Armed Forces 1972-96; FCO 1996; Dar es Salaam 1997; FCO 2002; Band B3; m 1979 Linda Alexis Jeffrey (1s 1979; 1d 1981).

Faulkner, Nicholas Anthony; Dhaka since October 2003; Born 19/05/72; FCO 1991; Bonn 1994; Brussels 1997; Bangkok 2000; Band B3.

Fawcett, Christine Anne; T/D Freetown since January 2004; Born 17/08/50; FCO 1968; Dar es Salaam 1971; Lima 1973; Havana 1976; Freetown 1977; FCO 1979; SEA Floater 1982; Belgrade 1983; FCO 1986 (Second Secretary 1989); Second Secretary (Management/ Consular) Port of Spain 1991; Second Secretary FCO 1993.

Fay, Jacqueline Ann (née Builder); SUPL since August 2003; Born 22/09/61; FCO 1980; Dhaka 1983; Peking 1985; Vice-Consul New York 1987; SUPL 1991; FCO 1991; Third Secretary (Management/Consular) Bratislava 1995; Singapore 1998; Band B3; m 1987 Kevin Michael Fay (1s 1990; 1d 1994).

Fean, Vincent; British High Commissioner Valletta since September 2002; Born 20/11/52; FCO 1975; MECAS 1977; Third Secretary Baghdad 1978; Gaborone 1979; Second later First Secretary Damascus 1979; FCO 1982; First Secretary Brussels (UKREP) 1985; First Secretary FCO 1990; Counsellor Paris 1992; FCO 1996; Director Asia Pacific, International Group of Trade Partners UK 1999; m 1978 Anne Marie Stewart (2d 1979, 1981; 1s 1983).

Fear, Harriet; Second Secretary (PPA) Dublin since November 2002; Born 11/08/68; Department of Employment 1986; FCO 1987; Dakar 1989; World Wide Floater Duties 1992; T/D Phnom Penh 1994; FCO 1994; Prague 1997; Band C4.

Fearis, Timothy Rupert; FCO since July 1989; Born 05/02/58; FCO 1979; Accra 1982; FCO 1984; Attaché Islamabad 1987; Band B3.

Fearn, Thomas Daniel; Deputy Head of Mission Sarajevo since January 2001; Born 16/09/62; FCO 1991; Second Secretary (Political) Budapest 1992; First Secretary FCO 1996; Band D6.

Feasey, Susan Catherine; FCO since August 2000; Born 08/05/64; FCO 1983; Vienna (UKMIS) 1985; Dakar 1988; FCO 1990; Riga 1992; FCO 1993; Floater Duties 1998; Band C4.

Feather, Helen Mary; Islamabad since April 2004; Born 02/01/63; FCO 1982; Moscow 1985; Gaborone 1988; Latin American/Caribbean Floater 1990; Third Secretary Brussels (UKDEL WEU) 1993; Third Secretary FCO 1994; DTI 1996; Third Secretary (Immigration) Dar es Salaam 1999;

Second Secretary (Management) Dar es Salaam 2000; Band C4; m 1999 L. Ross Field.

Featherstone, Simon Mark; HM Ambassador, Berne additionally HM Ambassador (non-resident) Liechtenstein since March 2004; Born 24/07/58; FCO 1980; Language Training Hong Kong 1982; Second Secretary (Chancery) Peking 1984; First Secretary FCO 1987; On loan to the Cabinet Office 1988; First Secretary (Environment) Brussels (UKREP) 1990; HM Consul-General Shanghai 1994; Counsellor (Political and Economic) Peking 1996; Counsellor FCO 1998; m 1981 Gail Teresa Salisbury (2d 1985, 1992; 1s 1988).

Fehintola, Adebowale Bamidele; Copenhagen since May 2000; Born 14/11/67; FCO 1987; Copenhagen 1989; Sana'a 1992; Gaborone 1993; Band B3.

Fell, Richard Taylor, CVO (1996); British High Commissioner Wellington, also British High Commissioner (Non resident) Samoa, Governor (Non resident) of the Pitcairn, Henderson, Ducie and Oeno Islands since December 2001; Born 11/11/48; FCO 1971; Third Secretary Ottawa 1972; Second Secretary Saigon 1974; Vientiane 1975; Second later First Secretary FCO 1975; Chargé d'Affaires a.i. Hanoi 1979; Brussels (NATO) 1979; First Secretary and Head of Chancery Kuala Lumpur 1983; First Secretary FCO 1986; On secondment to Industry 1988; Counsellor (Comm/Econ) Ottawa 1989; Counsellor and Deputy Head of Mission Bangkok 1993; Counsellor FCO 1997; Consul-General T/D Toronto 2000; m 1981 Claire Peta Gates (3s 1983, 1987, 1990).

Felton, Ian; FCO since September 2003; Born 16/05/66; FCO 1986; Brussels 1987; Floater Duties 1990; FCO 1993; New York (ECOSOC)-(UKMIS) 1995-99; Deputy Head of Mission Phnom Penh 2000; Band D6.

Fenn, Robert Dominic Russell; Team Leader Emed, EU-Mediterranean, EUD FCO since September 2001; Born 28/01/62; FCO 1983; Third Secretary (Chancery) The Hague 1985; Second Secretary (Chancery) Lagos 1988; First Secretary FCO 1990; First Secretary New York (UKMIS) 1992; First Secretary (EU/Economic) Rome 1997; m 2002 Julia Lloyd Williams (1s 2003).

Fennell, Leigh; FCO since 2004; Born 13/12/60; FCO 1982; Darwin 1986; FCO 1988; Third Secretary Accra 1993; FCO 1997; Amman 2000; Band C4.

Fenner, Margaret Patricia Jean (née Watson); Kingston since November 1999; Born 29/01/66; Wellington 1986; Warsaw 1988; FCO 1988; Lagos 1990; Tehran 1993; Helsinki 1994; FCO 1995; Band B3; m 1989 Martin David Fenner (diss 1994) (1s 1990).

Fenning, Camilla Jane Vance (née Packman); SUPL since January 1998; Born 29/04/64; FCO 1985; Language Training 1986; Tokyo 1987; Second later First Secretary FCO 1990; SUPL

1992; FCO 1993; SUPL 1995; FCO 1995; m 1988 Richard John Fenning. (1s 1993; 1d 1995).

Fenton, Jennifer Muriel; Second Secretary (Consular) Muscat since June 2004; Born 30/12/57; Home Civil Service 1976; FCO 1977; Beirut 1980; Floater Duties 1982; Singapore 1984; SUPL 1986; FCO 1987; New Delhi 1989; Mbabane 1993; Second Secretary FCO 1996; Second Secretary (Management) Valletta 1999; (1d 1986).

Ferguson, Christine Julia; Deputy Head of Mission Vienna since July 2004; Born 05/10/57; FCO 1982; Language Training 1983; Second Secretary Cairo 1985; Second later First Secretary FCO 1987; First Secretary Geneva (UKDIS) 1990; FCO 1998; m 1990 Michael (later Sir Michael) Charles Swift Weston (1s 1993; 1d 1996).

Ferguson, Iain; FCO since July 2003; Born 18/02/70; FCO 1990; Lagos 1995; Vice-Consul Tokyo 1999; Band C4; m 1994 Helen Jane Lennie.

Ferguson, Jean McCauley; FCO since June 2002; Born 08/10/55; Department of Employment 1985; Inland Revenue 1988; FCO 1998; ECO/Vice-Consul Kathmandu 1999; Band C4; (1d 1975).

Fergusson, George Duncan; Cabinet Office since October 2003; Born 30/09/55; NIO 1978, Private Secretary to NIO Minister of State 1982-83; First Secretary Dublin 1988; Transferred to Diplomatic Service 1990; First Secretary FCO 1991; First Secretary (Political/Information) Seoul 1993; First Secretary FCO 1996; Counsellor FCO 1997; Consul-General Boston 1999; m 1981 Margaret Wookey (3d 1982, 1986, 1991; 1s 1984).

Fern, Deborah Jeanne (née Keith); Montreal since October 2000; Born 01/07/68; FCO 1988; Tokyo 1990; Floater Duties 1993; SUPL 1995; FCO 1996; Full-Time Language Training 2000; Band C4; m 1999 Steven Rennie Fern.

Ferrand, Simon Piers; Private Secretary to the Ambassador Berlin since August 2004; Born 05/03/68; FCO 1989; Kinshasa 1991; Paris 1996; BTI 1999; FCO 2002; Band C4; m 1995 Bettina Barbara Paustian (2s 1998, 2002).

Fewster, Miles Nicholas, MBE (1991); Second Secretary FCO since August 1999; Born 26/08/62; FCO 1982; Khartoum 1985; Riyadh 1989; FCO 1992; Second Secretary (Political) Nairobi 1996; Band C4; m 1986 Alexandria Fusco (3d 1992, 1993, 1998).

Fidler, Martin Alfred; FCO since January 2003; Born 10/12/53; DHSS 1972; FCO 1974; Belmopan 1977; Africa/ME Floater 1980; Havana 1981; Third Secretary New York (UKMIS) 1984; FCO 1987; Nuku'alofa 1989; Gibraltar 1992; FCO 1996; Deputy High Commissioner Belmopan 1999; Band C5; m 1981 Nicky Williams (2s 1982, 1985).

Field, Robert; Second Secretary FCO since November 1995; Born 04/01/53; FCO 1971; Karachi 1975; Far East Floater 1979; Second Secretary (Commercial) Harare 1982; Second

Secretary FCO 1987; Second Secretary (Management) Addis Ababa 1992.

Fielder, John; HM Consul/ECM Manila since July 2003; Born 27/06/47; CO (later Commonwealth Office) 1966; HM Forces 1967-73; FCO 1974; Accra 1976; Nassau 1977; Prague 1980; SE Asia/FE Floater 1982; FCO 1987; Second Secretary (Management/Consular) Maputo 1990; HM Consul Tel Aviv 1994; FCO 2002.

Fielder, Richard John; Second Secretary (Management) Lusaka since June 2002; Born 28/03/52; FCO 1971; Tokyo 1974; FCO 1975; Stockholm 1978; Khartoum 1981; FCO 1982; Dhaka 1985; Chicago 1988; Freetown 1990; FCO 1995; Second Secretary Ottawa 1997; m 1988 Samantha Louise Monton (3d 1988, 1993, 1996; 1s 1990).

Fieller, Daniel Richard Charles; FCO since September 2002; Born 14/07/78; Band B3; ptnr, Danielle Thomas.

Finch, Peter Leonard; FCO since November 1997; Born 01/01/58; FCO 1975; Geneva (UKMIS) 1978; Tel Aviv 1981; New Delhi 1983; FCO 1986; Tokyo 1991; Manila 1994; Band C4; m 1979 Mitsue Uchida (1d 1990).

Findlay, Matthew Ross; FCO since August 2002; Born 02/05/68; FCO 1996; Full-Time Language Training Bangkok 1998; Second Secretary (Political) Bangkok 1999; Band D6.

Fines, Barry John; FCO since April 2003; Born 13/09/69; FCO 1988; New Delhi 1991; FCO 1994; Lagos 1997; SUPL 2002; Band B3; m 1997 Monika Graf (1s 2002).

Finlay, Norah Ferguson Watson; Shanghai since January 2002; Born 13/04/70; FCO 1989; Singapore 1992; Islamabad 1995; Band A2.

Finlayson, Sharon Christine; FCO since June 2002; Born 04/05/58; Band A2; m 1976 (2d 1980, 1982).

Finley, Robert William; FCO since April 2002; Born 21/08/68; Band D6; m 1997 Claire Walker.

Finnamore Crorkin, Joanne Lynn; Second Secretary (Commercial) Tripoli since March 2002; Born 22/09/63; FCO 1982; Moscow 1984; Colombo 1985; Floater Duties 1989; SUPL 1992; Consulate-General New York 1992; FCO 1994; Second Secretary 1996; Lagos 1997; m 1991 Colin Wynn Crorkin (1d 1998).

Finnerty, Kevin John; FCO since February 2001; Born 01/02/49; FCO 1967; Kuwait 1970; Warsaw 1974; FCO 1976; Full-Time Language Training 1978; FCO 1979; Mogadishu 1983; Chicago 1985; Second Secretary FCO 1989; Full-Time Language Training 1992; Düsseldorf 1993; First Secretary and Consul Washington 1997; m (1) 1970 Sandra Tidy (diss 1982); (2) 1982 Norma Collins.

Firmstone, Imogen Joan; FCO since April 2004; Born 21/06/74; FCO 1999; Havana 2002; Band B3.

Firstbrook, Steven Paul; Deputy High Commissioner Nassau since February 2004; Born 22/02/70; FCO 1989; Helsinki 1992; World-Wide Floater Duties 1994; FCO 1996; Second Secretary (Commercial) Mumbai 2000; Band C4.

Firth, Catherine Alison Jane (née Readdie); SUPL since October 2003; Born 17/06/66; FCO 1990; Third Secretary (Chancery) Warsaw 1992; FCO 1994; Vice Consul Caracas 1995; FCO 1998; Full-Time Language Training 2001; First Secretary (Political) Mexico City 2001; Band C5; m 1994 Andrew Charleson Firth.

Fisher, Deborah Joan; Deputy Head of Mission Addis Ababa since April 2004; Born 04/03/62; FCO 1985; Second Secretary (Chancery) Dar es Salaam 1988; First Secretary FCO 1991; SUPL 1996; FCO 1997; Paris 2002; m 1992 William James Lodge.

Fisher, Deryck John; FCO since September 2003; Born 26/07/46; Inland Revenue 1961; Department of Technical Co-operation, ODA 1964; FCO 1973; Kinshasa 1975; Islamabad 1978; Second Secretary FCO 1980; Second Secretary (Consular) Accra 1983; First Secretary (Admin/Consul) Copenhagen 1987; First Secretary FCO 1991; First Secretary (Management) Dhaka 1996; First Secretary (Management) Bangkok 2000; Band D6; m 1973 Lynda Elizabeth Robinson (2d 1974, 1975; 3s 1976, 1979, 1983).

Fisher, Emily Caroline Gay (née Shapland); First Secretary (Political) Buenos Aires since October 2000; Born 05/05/72; FCO 1997; Lusaka 1998; Band D6; m 1998 Roland Barnabas Fisher.

Fisher, Gary John; Second Secretary (Euro 2004 Football Attaché) Lisbon since October 2003; Born 27/12/69; FCO 1989; Peking 1992; Third Secretary Düsseldorf 1996; Third Secretary (MO/VC) Bahrain 2000; Band C4; m 1992 Claire Louise White (1s 1998).

Fisher, John; Counsellor FCO since April 2003; Born 03/08/48; Third later Second Secretary FCO 1974; Language student SOAS 1975 and Bursar 1976; Second Secretary (Inf) Ankara 1976; First Secretary FCO 1979; Vienna (UKMIS) IAEA 1982; First Secretary FCO 1986; Counsellor Santiago 1993; Counsellor FCO 1997; Counsellor (Political) Jakarta 1999; m 1970 Lynette Joyce Corinne Growcott (1d 1978; 1s 1980).

Fisher, Miles Lyndon; SUPL since March 1999; Born 28/11/61; FCO 1981; Vienna 1995.

Fisher, Simon John; Director Trade Cairo since January 2002; Born 08/06/59; FCO 1983; Athens 1985; Language Training Kamakura 1989; Tokyo 1990; Osaka 1992; Second later First Secretary FCO 1996; Deputy Head of Mission Hanoi 1999 and 2001; On loan to the Population Council, Hanoi 2000; Band D6.

Fisher, Steven Mark; Deputy Head of Mission Caracas since July 2002; Born 07/02/65; FCO 1993; Second Secretary (Economic/Commercial) Singapore 1995; FCO 1998; Band D6; m 1990 Linda Westwood (3s 1993, 1995, 1997).

Fisher, Timothy Dirk Colomb; First Secretary (Management) Jakarta since June 2003; Born 23/08/47; FCO 1975; Moscow 1976; FCO 1977; Port Moresby 1978; Nairobi 1981; FCO 1985; Colombo 1987; Third later Second Secretary (Aid) Jakarta 1991; FCO 1995; Second Secretary (Management) Hanoi 1998; m 1992 Patricia-Jane Van Der Vooren (1d 1993; 1s 1994).

Fisher, Timothy Sinnett; Third Secretary (Political) Kigali since September 2000; Born 15/07/71; FCO 1998; Band B3; m 2000 Joanna Dinnen.

Fishman, Jason; SUPL since May 2001; Born 05/10/69; FCO 1990; Berlin 1994; Peking 1997; Band A2.

Fishwick, Nicholas Bernard Frank; Counsellor FCO since July 2004; Born 23/02/58; FCO 1983; Language Training 1986; First Secretary (Inf) Lagos 1988; First Secretary FCO 1991; Consul (Political Affairs) Istanbul 1994; First Secretary FCO 1997; Seconded to HM Customs and Excise 2001; m 1987 Susan Thérèsa Rouane Mendel (2s 1987, 1995; 1d 1989).

Fitch, Diana May (née Francis); Seoul since August 2002; Born 26/12/53; FCO 1975; Dar es Salaam 1976; Tortola 1977; FCO 1981; SE Asia Floater 1984; Singapore 1986; FCO 1988; Second Secretary Honiara 1995; FCO 1998; m Geoffrey William Fitch (1s 1988; 1d 1993).

Fitchett, Robert Duncan; Deputy Head of Mission Manila since August 2003; Born 10/06/61; FCO 1983; Dakar 1984; Second Secretary (Chancery) Bonn 1988; First Secretary FCO 1990; First Secretary on loan to the Cabinet Office 1993; Paris 1994; FCO 1998; m 1985 Adèle Thérèsa Hajjar (1s 1987; 2d 1988, 1993).

Fitton, David John, CMG (2004); Deputy Head of Mission Ankara since January 2001; Born 10/01/55; FCO 1980; Language Training Kamakura 1982; Second later First Secretary (Economics) Tokyo 1983; FCO 1986; First Secretary (Chancery) New Delhi 1990; First Secretary FCO 1994; Head of Chancery Tokyo 1996; m 1989 Hisae Iijima (1d 1996; 1s 1999).

Fitton-Brown, Edmund Walter; Counsellor Cairo since September 2003; Born 05/10/62; FCO 1984; Third later Second Secretary Helsinki 1987; Second Secretary FCO 1989; First Secretary 1991; Language Training Cairo 1991; First Secretary FCO 1992; First Secretary (Political) Cairo 1993; First Secretary FCO 1996; First Secretary (Political) Kuwait 1998; FCO 2001; m 1995 Julie Ann Herring (1d 1996; 1s 1998).

Fitton-Brown, Julie Ann (née Herring); SUPL since August 1994; Born 10/04/65; FCO 1984; Helsinki 1987; FCO 1989; SUPL 1993; Cairo 1994; Band B3; m 1995 Edmund Walter Fitton-Brown (1d 1996; 1s 1998).

FitzGerald, Jillian (née Lane); Second Secretary (Management) Rome since May 2002; Born 29/01/69; FCO 1989; Bonn 1992; Islamabad 1995; SUPL 1997; FCO 1998; Band B3; m 1998 Paul Edward FitzGerald (1s 1997; 1d 2000).

Fitzgerald-Prono, Antonia (née Fitzgerald); FCO since September 1999; Born 13/06/71; FCO 1990; Brasilia 1991; Brussels (UKDel WEU) 1995; Paris 1996; SUPL 1999; m 1999 Raphael Jacques Gerard Prono (1s 1999).

Flaherty, Shaun David; First Secretary (Management) Cairo since June 2001; Born 29/01/66; FCO 1984; Washington 1987; Ankara 1990; Lagos 1992; FCO 1996; Band C5.

Flear, Timothy Charles Fitzranulf, MVO (1989); FCO since May 2000; Born 22/01/58; FCO 1980; Third Secretary (Comm/Inf) Dubai 1982; Resigned and reinstated, FCO 1985; Third later Second Secretary Kuala Lumpur 1987; Second Secretary FCO 1991 (APS/Minister of State 1993); First Secretary (Economic) later First Secretary (Investment) subsequently First Secretary (Political) Seoul 1996; ptnr, Christopher Curtain.

Fleming De Luca, Wendy Alexandra; Second Secretary (Management) Osaka since April 2004; Born 11/05/70; FCO 1991; Jakarta 1995; Third Secretary (Commercial) Buenos Aires 1999; Full-Time Language Training (Japanese) 2003; Band C4; m 1995 Dino De Luca.

Flessati, Francesca Josephine Giovanna, OBE (2003); First Secretary (Political) Athens since April 1999; Born 27/10/58; FCO 1990; Language Training 1991; Third Secretary (Aid) Moscow 1992; FCO 1996; m 1985 Nicholas John Foster.

Fletcher, Patricia Anne (née Jones); Lisbon since August 2002; Born 12/05/70; FCO 1989; Bonn 1991; FCO 1993; Brasilia 1994; SUPL 1999; FCO 2000; Band B3; m 1993 Richard Fletcher (1s 1996; 1d 1999).

Fletcher, Patricia May; FCO since January 2002; Born 08/09/42; FCO 1983; Berlin (BMG) 1984; Tortola 1986; FCO 1988; Brussels (UKDEL) 1990; FCO 1991; Munich 1994; Tel Aviv 1997; Second Secretary (Management) Beirut 2000; Band C4; m 1974 Herbert Fletcher (dec'd 1986) (1s 1978).

Fletcher, Thomas Stuart Francis; Private Secretary to Baroness Amos later Chris Mullin FCO since 2002; Born 27/03/75; FCO 1997; Nairobi 1998; Band D6.

Fleurot, Tracey Marjorie (née Critoph); Gaborone since February 2002; Born 26/08/64; FCO 1988; Jakarta 1990; Port Louis 1994; FCO 1997; Bombay 1998; Band A2; m 1997 M J E Fleurot.

Flint, David Leonard; Liaison Officer Gibraltar since April 2001; Born 21/10/56; FCO 1975; Budapest 1979; Jedda 1980; FCO 1984; Athens 1986; Lagos 1990; Second Secretary FCO 1994; Deputy High Commissioner Gaborone 1997; m

1984 Mary Anne Elizabeth Goodale (3s twins 1986, 1988).

Flint, John David; Antigua since May 2001; Born 05/11/69; FCO 1996; Third Secretary (Political/PPA) Tallinn 1998; Band B3; m 1998 Sally Brazier.

Flisher, Nigel Frederick; FCO since December 1999; Born 20/04/53; FCO 1971; Singapore 1974; Vientiane 1978; Colombo 1979; FCO 1982; Islamabad 1984; Third Secretary (Passports/Visas) Dublin 1988; FCO 1991; Second Secretary 1994; Second Secretary (Immigration) Moscow 1996; m 1977 Valerie Tay Kim Heok (1d 1978; 1s 1980).

Floyd, Linda Vivienne (née Colvin); Kuala Lumpur since May 2002; Born 17/03/65; FCO 1987; New Delhi 1989; SUPL 1991; Georgetown 1994; SUPL 1997; FCO 1999; SUPL 2000; Band A2; m 1990 Neil Floyd (1d 1991; 2s 1993, 1995).

Floyd, Neil; Second Secretary (Commercial) Kuala Lumpur since September 2000; Born 20/05/67; FCO 1987; New Delhi 1989; Warsaw 1991; Georgetown 1993; FCO 1997; Band C4; m 1990 Linda Vivienne Colvin (1d 1991; 2s 1993, 1995).

Foakes, Joanne Sarah; SUPL since August 2001; Born 09/03/57; Called to the Bar, Inner Temple 1979; FCO 1984; Deputy Principal Crown Counsel Hong Kong 1991; Assistant Legal Adviser FCO 1994; SUPL 1995; Legal Counsellor 1997.

Foley, Victoria Beth Louise; FCO since December 1986; Born 23/06/60; FCO 1978; Budapest 1982; Paris 1984; Band B3.

Folker, Nicholas Mark; Singapore since October 2000; Born 20/05/67; FCO 1989; Band C4; m 1998 Laura Elizabeth Samm (1d 2000).

Folland, Richard Dudley; Deputy Consul General Düsseldorf and Deputy Director of Trade and Investment in Germany since August 2000; Born 10/03/61; FCO 1981; Moscow 1983; Third Secretary (Consular/Management) Gaborone 1985; FCO 1988; Second Secretary (Political/Inf) Stockholm 1991; First Secretary FCO 1996; On secondment to British Aerospace 1998; m 1985 Gwen Alison Evans (2s 1989, 1993).

Folliss, Tarquin Simon Archer; Counsellor Copenhagen since September 2001; Born 23/10/57; HM Forces 1981-86; Second Secretary FCO 1986; Second later First Secretary (Chancery) Jakarta 1989; First Secretary FCO 1992; First Secretary Bucharest 1995; First Secretary FCO 1998; Band D6; m 1991 Anne Mary Segar (1d 1996; 2s 1998, 1999).

Fontaine-Harvey, Joan; SUPL since August 2003; Born 03/10/67; FCO 1990; Dubai 2000; Band B3; m 1999 Christopher Antonio Harvey.

Foote, Daniel Edward; Third Secretary (Deputy Management Officer) Freetown since August 2001; Born 11/02/46; Royal Navy 1965-90; Moscow 1991; Lagos 1992; Abuja 1994; FCO

1996; Pretoria 1997; Band B3; m 1967 Carol Elizabeth Combe (2d 1970, 1971).

Forbes, Lachlan Pelly Ferrar; First Secretary Baku since December 2002; Born 24/04/70; Second Secretary FCO 1996; Second Secretary (Political) Nairobi 1998; FCO 2001; Band D6; m 1999 Melanie Fiona Knights (1s 2000).

Forbes, Matthew Keith; First Secretary (Political) Wellington since October 2002; Born 19/04/66; FCO 1987; Peking 1989; Colombo 1990; FCO 1995; Deputy High Commissioner Maseru 1999; Band C4; m 1988 Lydia Mary Bagg (2s 1989, 1991; 1d 1994).

Forbes, Melanie Fiona (née Knights); FCO since May 2001; Born 03/03/64; FCO 1996; Second Secretary (Political) Nairobi 1999; Band C4; m 1999 Lachlan Pelly Ferrar Forbes (1s 2000).

Forbes Batey, Darren Francis; Second Secretary (Consular) Nairobi since June 2003; Born 09/01/66; FCO 1984; Rabat 1987; Kampala 1990; FCO 1993; Third Secretary (Management) Dublin 1996; Third Secretary (Commercial) Dubai 2000; Band C4; m 1993 Sarah Frances Trevelyan (1d 1995, 1s 1998).

Ford, Andrew James Ford, MVO (1995); Second later First Secretary (Commercial) Mexico City since February 2000; Born 21/06/64; FCO 1987; Third Secretary (Chancery/Information/Consular) Georgetown 1990; Third Secretary (Political) Pretoria/Cape Town 1993; Second Secretary FCO 1996; m 1994 Claudeli Edna Dos Santos Silva (2 step d 1985, 1987).

Ford, Peter William; HM Ambassador Damascus since September 2003; Born 27/06/47; Third Secretary FCO 1970; MECAS 1971; Beirut 1973; Second later First Secretary Cairo 1974; First Secretary FCO 1977; ENA Paris 1980; First Secretary Paris 1981; First Secretary FCO 1985; Counsellor (Comm) Riyadh 1987; University of Harvard 1990; Counsellor Singapore 1991; Counsellor FCO 1994; HM Ambassador Bahrain 1999; m (1) 1975 Aurora Raquel Garcia Mingo (diss 1991), (2) 1992 Alganesh Haile Beyene.

Forman, Matthew; FCO since January 2004; Born 17/06/76; Band C5.

Forrester, Emma-Louise; FCO since October 2002; Born 22/03/80; Band A2.

Forrester, Mark Adrian; Second Secretary (Management) Oslo since October 2003; Born 29/06/59; FCO 1978; Geneva (UKMIS) 1980; Santiago 1983; Third Secretary FCO 1986; Dhaka 1989; Third Secretary (Management/Consular) Nuku'alofa 1992; Second Secretary FCO 1995; Second Secretary (Management) Hong Kong 1999; m 1982 Deborah Cannell (1d 1987; 1s 1990).

Forrester, Sally Joanne (née Watmough); Pretoria since April 2004; Born 22/05/64; FCO 1984; Belgrade 1987; FCO 1989; Buenos Aires 1990; FCO 1992; Vienna 1994; SUPL 1997; FCO 2000;

Band A2; m 1993 Guy Hamilton Forrester (1d 1995; 1s 1998).

Forrester, Stuart Russell; FCO since January 2003; Born 10/02/62; FCO 1983; Washington 1990; FCO 1994; Moscow 2000; Band C4; m 1990 Deborah Channon.

Forryan, Anne May; SUPL since November 1999; Born 03/08/66; FCO 1990; Düsseldorf 1993; Vice-Consul Madrid 1996 (SUPL 1997); Madrid 1997; Band B3; m 1996 Joaquin Rodriguez-Toubes Muniz.

Forsyth, Brian Gilbert; FCO since November 2003; Born 27/02/65; FCO 1984; Bucharest 1987; Dhaka 1989; FCO 1992; Third Secretary Cairo 1996; Third later Second Secretary (Political) Doha 1999; Band C4; m 1987 Marie Boyle (1s 1989; 1d 1992).

Forsyth, Marie (née Boyle); FCO since November 2003; Born 26/04/66; FCO 1984; Mexico City 1986; SUPL 1987; Dhaka 1990; FCO 1993; Cairo 1996; Management Officer/Vice Consul Doha 1999; SUPL 2000; Third Secretary (Commercial) Doha 2000; Band C4; m 1987 Brian Gilbert Forsyth (1s 1989; 1d 1992).

Fortescue, Dominic James Lewis; First Secretary New York (UKMIS) since July 2000; Born 09/10/66; FCO 1991; Second Secretary (Political) Pretoria 1993; Cape Town 1995; Second later First Secretary FCO 1996; Band D6; m 1990 Miriam Cathleen Rolls (2s 2001, 2003).

Fossaluzza, Lydia; Buenos Aires since September 1999; Born 12/03/64; FCO 1996; Band A2.

Foster, Hazel; FCO since May 1998; Born 10/04/69; FCO 1989; Ankara 1991; World Wide Floater duties 1996; Band B3.

Foster, Joelene; FCO since October 2002; Born 27/11/73; Band B3; ptnr, Peter Josse.

Foster, John Michael; Second Secretary (Commercial) Caracas since March 2003; Born 07/05/55; FCO 1989; New Delhi 1991; Third Secretary Tel Aviv 1994; FCO 1997; Band C4; m 1986 Julie Bearfoot.

Foster, Julie Maria (née Bearfoot); Consul/Management Officer Caracas since February 2003; Born 19/12/59; FCO 1978; Brussels (UKDEL NATO) 1981; Doha 1983; FCO 1987; Third Secretary New Delhi 1991; Tel Aviv 1994; On loan to the DTI 1997; Second Secretary FCO 1998; Band C5; m 1986 John Michael Foster.

Foster, Sarah Louise; Madrid since June 2003; Born 04/11/73; FCO 1992; Assistant to Lord Owen (International Conference on Former Yugoslavia) 1993; UKMIS later UKDEL later Chancery Vienna 1995; Tokyo 2000; Band B3.

Foulcer, Monique Antoinette (née Twigg); First Secretary (Management) The Hague since January 2003; Born 22/07/64; DTI 1985; FCO 1987; Kinshasa 1989; Third Secretary (Chancery) Geneva (UKDIS) 1992; FCO 1995; SUPL 1997; Second Secretary (Political) Paris 1998; SUPL

1999; FCO 2000; Band C5; m 1995 Kevin Andrew Foulcer (1s 1998).

Foulds, Sarah Ann; SUPL since September 1998; Born 10/08/57; FCO 1979; PRO (Band D6) 1987; First Secretary FCO 1992; First Secretary Geneva (UKMIS) 1995; m (1) 1981 (diss 1995) (1d 1985; 1s 1988), m (2) 1999 Peter Van Wulfften Palthe (3 step d).

Foulsham, Richard Andrew; Counsellor FCO since September 2003; Born 24/09/50; Second Secretary FCO 1982; First Secretary Badar Seri Begawan 1984; First Secretary (Chancery) Lagos 1986; First Secretary FCO 1990; Counsellor (Political) Rome 1995; Counsellor FCO 1999; Counsellor Ottawa 2001; m 1982 Deirdre Elizabeth Strathairn (1d 1984; 1s 1986).

Fowle, Angela Mary (née Hatcher), MBE (2004); Second Secretary (Management) and Consul Algiers since September 2001; Born 25/04/44; FO 1964; Bangkok 1966; Moscow 1968; Athens 1969; FCO 1972; Santiago 1974; FCO 1976; Geneva (UKMIS) 1980; FCO 1983; Düsseldorf 1986; FCO 1989; SUPL 1990; FCO 1995; Belgrade 1998; T/D Second Secretary (Management) Madrid 1999; Belgrade 2000; Band C4; m 1978 Leslie Thomas Fowle (1s 1983).

Fox, Alexander Norman Robson; Full-Time Language Training Cairo since September 2004; Born 20/09/77; FCO 2001; Band C4.

Fox, Christopher Roderick Henry; FCO since 2003; Born 19/09/70; FCO 1991; Ankara 2000; Band C4; m 2001 Leigh McCallum Forbes (1s 2001).

Fox, Ian David; Bratislava since November 2003; Born 02/06/66; FCO 1987; Peking 1988; Floater Duties 1991; FCO 1993; Secondment to London Chamber of Commerce 1995; Dubai 1997; Casablanca 2000; Band C4; m 1993 Alison Elizabeth Margaret Bain (1s 1998; 1d 2000).

Fox, John Frederick; First Secretary (Political) Beijing since September 2003; Born 09/04/75; FCO 1997; Brussels 1999; SUPL 1999; FCO 2000; Full-Time Language Training (Mandarin) 2002; Band C4.

Fox, Michael Roger; First Secretary (Regional Affairs) Rabat since March 2003; Born 09/07/58; FCO 1988; Consul Geneva 1993; FCO 1997; Band C5; m 1993 Charlotte Jane Gray.

Fox, Paul Leonard; FCO since April 1999; Born 24/07/62; FCO 1987; New Delhi 1990; Baku 1994; Bangkok 1996; Band D7; m 1991 Vicki Ann Rathbun (3d 1997, 1998, 2002).

Foxwell, Rachael Louise; FCO since September 2001; Born 29/10/59; FCO 1982; Africa/Middle East Floater 1984; Harare 1985; Third later Second Secretary Hanoi 1988; Second Secretary FCO 1991; Tunis 1992; First Secretary (Economic/Commercial) Wellington 1999; (1d 1991).

Francis, Catherine Joan, MBE (2004); Brussels since May 2003; Born 01/04/50; FCO 1972; Brussels 1972; Kuala Lumpur 1976; Bonn 1980; FCO 1980; Helsinki 1985; FCO 1987; Riyadh 1989; FCO 1991; Sofia 1993; Jakarta 1997; Band B3; m 1991 John Treharne Francis.

Francis, John Alexander; Baghdad since July 2004; Born 14/12/42; FO 1962; Athens 1964; Beirut 1964; Stockholm 1965; Seoul 1968; Malta 1971; Paris 1972; FCO 1972; Dacca 1975; Prague 1979; Kaduna 1981; Second Secretary FCO 1983; Consul Bangkok 1988; First Secretary (Management) Ankara 1992; First Secretary (Management/Consular) Seoul 1996; HM Consul Kuwait 1999; m 1981 Grace Engelen.

Francis, Lindsay (née Harvey); Washington since September 2001; Born 31/03/59; FCO 1984; Tehran 1986; Budapest 1987; Bridgetown 1988; FCO 1993; SUPL 1993; Grand Cayman 1997; Band B3; m 2001 Paul Richard Francis.

Franklin, Elizabeth Fay (née Bolton); SUPL since March 1995; Born 25/11/60; FCO 1981; Khartoum 1985; Valletta 1988; Dhaka 1992; Band B3; m 1994 John William Franklin.

Franklin, Joanna Mary Clare; SUPL since November 2000; Born 12/08/60; FCO 1978; Peking 1981; FCO 1982; Cairo 1986; Yaoundé 1989; FCO 1990; Beirut 1994; FCO 1997; Canberra 1998; Band C4; m 1988 Habib Elie Gouel.

Franklin-Brown, Alexander, MBE (2002); Second Secretary (Chancery) Muscat since November 2001; Born 30/03/72; FCO 1991; Full-Time Language Training 1996; Third Secretary (Chancery) Riyadh 1997; Third Secretary (Commercial) Al Khobar 1999; Band B3.

Fransella, Cortland Lucas; Counsellor FCO since September 1995; Born 09/09/48; Third Secretary FCO 1970; Language Training Hong Kong 1971; Assistant Trade Commissioner Hong Kong 1973; Second later First Secretary FCO 1975; Kuala Lumpur 1980; Santiago 1982; FCO 1986; Counsellor (Political) Rome 1991; m 1977 Laura Ruth Propper (2s 1979, 1981).

Frape, Neil Jeremy; ECO Georgetown since December 2004; Born 16/11/63; FCO 1984; Addis Ababa 1986; Paris 1990; FCO 1992; Full-Time Language Training 1995; Vice-Consul (Press and Public Affairs) Istanbul 1996; Kuwait 2000; Band B3; m 1987 Christine Mary Allen (1d 1989; 1s 1992).

Frary, Helen Elizabeth; SUPL since January 1999; Born 23/02/69; FCO 1988; New Delhi 1991; Third later Second Secretary (United Nations) Geneva (UKMIS) 1995; Band C4.

Fraser, James Terence; First Secretary (Commercial) Zagreb since May 2002; Born 12/04/49; GPO 1966; FCO 1967; Nicosia 1971; Johannesburg 1972; Prague 1974; Africa Floater 1975; FCO 1978; Vice-Consul (Information) Düsseldorf 1981; Language Training 1983;

Commercial Attaché Baghdad 1984; FCO 1988; Deputy Head of Political and Information Section later Head of Consular Section Ottawa 1993; First Secretary (Management) and HM Consul Copenhagen 1997; m 1988 Nada Babic (1s 1992; 1d 1995).

Fraser, Simon James; Director for Strategy and Innovation FCO since May 2002; Born 03/06/58; FCO 1979; Third later Second Secretary Baghdad 1982; Second Secretary (Chancery) Damascus 1984; First Secretary FCO 1986 (Private Secretary to Minister of State) 1989; First Secretary (Economic) Paris 1994; Counsellor on secondment to the EU Commission 1996; Deputy Chef de Cabinet of the Vice President of the EU Commission 1997; Counsellor (Political) Paris 1999; m 2003 Shireen Patel (1d 1993).

Frater, Charlene Adele; FCO since October 2002; Born 28/07/76; Band A2.

Frean, Christopher William; Deputy Head of Mission Kigali since November 2002; Born 31/07/64; HCS 1988; FCO 1990; Abidjan 1992; Third Secretary (Immigration) Karachi 1995; FCO 1997; Third later Second Secretary Abidjan 1999; Band B3; m 1994 Aya Esperance Gbakatchetche (2d 1995, 1996).

Freel, Philip John; FCO since December 1997; Born 24/12/55; FCO 1974; Paris 1976; Mogadishu 1979; Lisbon 1980; Addis Ababa 1983; FCO 1985; On loan to CAD, Hanslope Park 1986; Lagos 1987; Rome 1991; FCO 1992; Second Secretary (Management) Cape Town 1996; m 1977 Joan Winifred Hill (1d 1979; 1s 1986).

Freeman, Judith Louise; FCO since 2004; Born 24/03/61; FCO 1984; Berne 1985; East Berlin 1989; Floater Duties 1991; FCO 1994; Luxembourg 1996; T/D Berlin 1999; Geneva (UKMIS) 2000; Band A2.

Freeman, Timothy John; SUPL since July 2004; Born 24/04/65; FCO 1989; Paris 1992; Honiara 1996; Third Secretary (Aid/Chancery) Gibraltar 1997; Third Secretary (Passports/Visas) Dublin 2001; Band B3.

Freeman, Wendy Paula; SUPL since May 2003; Born 09/03/61; FCO 1980; Bonn 1982; Africa/ME Floater 1985; Abidjan 1988; FCO 1992; Kingston 1997; SUPL 1999; Second Secretary (Commercial) Beirut 2001; Band C4.

French, Roger; Counsellor (Management) and Consul-General Tokyo since July 2003; Born 03/06/47; FCO 1965; Havana 1970; Vice-Consul Madrid 1971; San Juan 1973; FCO 1977; Second later First Secretary (Chancery) Washington 1980; First Secretary (Commercial) Muscat 1985; Deputy Head North America Dept FCO 1988; Deputy Consul-General Milan 1992; Counsellor (Management) and Consul General Washington 1997; Acting Deputy High Commissioner Abuja 2001; Head of Information Management Group FCO 2001; m 1969 Angela Joyce Cooper (1d 1974; 1s 1980).

Friel, Nicola; FCO since April 2002; Born 08/03/70; FCO 1989; Washington 1992; Moscow 1995; Floater Duties 1998; Band B3.

Friis, Andrew Stuart; FCO since March 2002; Born 04/04/60; Metropolitan Police 1981; FCO 1982; Kuwait 1986; FCO 1988; Hong Kong 1997; Band C5; m 1989 Maria Carina Lumatan Reyes (1s 1991; 1d 1994).

Friston, Paula Jane; Washington since September 2002; Born 27/01/69; FCO 1992; Washington 1996; Algiers 1999; FCO 2001; Band B3.

Frizzel, Squadron Leader John Stewart; Queen's Messenger since 1989; Born 12/07/46; HM Forces 1966-89.

Frost, David George Hamilton; Head of European Union (Internal), FCO since June 2003; Born 21/02/65; FCO 1987; Third Secretary Nicosia 1989; Resigned 1990, reinstated 1992; First Secretary Brussels (UKREP) 1993; First Secretary New York (UKMIS) 1996; FCO 1998; Counsellor (EU/Economic) Paris 2001; m 1993 Jacqueline Elizabeth Dias (1d 1998).

Frost, Michael Reginald, OBE (2001); First Secretary (Political) Pretoria since June 2000; Born 02/12/52; FCO 1971; Prague 1974; Dar es Salaam 1976; Peking 1979; FCO 1982; Washington 1984; Consul (Political/Inf) Cape Town 1986; First Secretary (Aid/Comm) Kampala 1991; First Secretary FCO 1994; First Secretary (Political) Lagos 1996; Band D6; m 1973 Marie Thérésa McGlynn.

Frost, Simon Jaye; SUPL since February 2003; Born 24/05/70; FCO 1990; World-Wide Floater Duties 1993; T/D Mostar 1995; FCO 1996; Band B3.

Frost, Steven Alan; Second Secretary Stockholm since February 1999; Born 21/09/64; FCO 1987; Islamabad 1992; FCO 1996; Band C4; m 1993 Angela Elaine Morrissey.

Fry, Graham Holbrook; HM Ambassador Tokyo since July 2004; Born 20/12/49; FCO 1972; Third later Second Secretary Tokyo 1974; First Secretary on loan to DOI 1979; FCO 1981; First Secretary Paris 1983; FCO 1987; Counsellor (Chancery) Tokyo 1989; Counsellor FCO 1993; AUSS (Northern Asia and the Pacific) 1995; High Commissioner Kuala Lumpur 1998; Director General (Economic) FCO 2001; m (1) 1977 Meiko Iida (diss), (2) 1994 Toyoko Ando.

Fuguet Debarr, Margaret (née Debarr); FCO since March 1993; Born 02/01/48; Inland Revenue 1964; FCO 1967; Brussels (UKDEL EC) 1970; FCO 1972; Copenhagen 1974; FCO 1977; Harare 1982; FCO 1985; Dublin 1990; Band B3; m 1976 Juan Inocencio Fuguet Sanchez (1s 1977).

Fulcher, Michael Adrian; Counsellor FCO since April 2003; Born 15/10/58; FCO 1982; Second later First Secretary Athens 1985; First Secretary FCO 1989; First Secretary (Political) Sofia 1993; First Secretary FCO 1996; Counsellor Rome 1999; m 1983 Helen Parkinson (1s 1987; 1d 1988).

Full, Ian Francis; FCO since December 1997; Born 16/08/54; FCO 1972; Paris 1975; San José 1978; Jedda 1981; FCO 1986; Islamabad 1989; Suva 1994; Band C4.

Fuller, Eleanor Mary (née Breedon); First Secretary Geneva (UKMIS) since January 2000; Born 31/12/53; FCO 1975; ENA Course, Paris 1977 and 1978; Resigned 1980, reinstated FCO 1981; On loan to the ODA 1983; SUPL 1986; Second later First Secretary FCO 1990; SUPL 1993; UNRWA Vienna 1994-96; First Secretary Vienna (UKDEL) 1998; m 1984 Simon William John Fuller (3s 1986, 1988, 1991).

Fuller, Robert; FCO since September 2001; Born 19/09/74; Band C4; ptnr, Angela Richmond.

Fulton, Craig John; Second Secretary (Regional Affairs) Kampala since April 2002; Born 30/10/67; FCO 1987; Singapore 1990; Islamabad 1992; FCO 1996; Band C4.

Furssedonn, Scott; Second Secretary (Institutions) Brussels (UKREP) since October 2001; Born 13/02/78; FCO 2000; Band C4; ptnr, Elizabeth Wood.

Fussey, Lorraine Helen; FCO since February 2003; Born 30/01/67; FCO 1989; Bombay 1991; Tel Aviv 1995; FCO 1998; SUPL 2000; Band D6; m 1996 Alastair Walton Totty (2s 1997, 2001).

G

Gallacher, Ian Charles; Third Secretary (Consular) Paris since October 2001; Born 02/05/63; FCO 1983; Paris 1988; Peking 1990; FCO 1993; Band B3; m 1987 Diane Warren.

Gallacher, Margaret; Kuala Lumpur since July 2001; Born 05/12/63; MOD 1986-96; FCO 1996; Anguilla 1997; Band B3.

Gallagher, Tracy Anne; First Secretary (Political) Athens since June 2003; Born 22/01/58; FCO 1981; Language Training 1982; Third later Second Secretary (Comm) later First Secretary (Econ), Moscow 1983; First Secretary FCO 1988; First Secretary (Chancery) Dublin 1991; SUPL 1994; First Secretary FCO 1998; m 1986 Ian Robert Whitting (2d 1990, 1994).

Galvez, Elizabeth Ann (née Sketchley); Counsellor New York (UKMIS) since June 2003; Born 24/12/51; FCO 1970; SUPL to attend University 1970; FCO 1973; Helsinki 1974; Geneva (UKMIS) 1977; FCO 1981; Second Secretary Tegucigalpa 1981; Second Secretary FCO 1985; SUPL 1987; FCO 1988; First Secretary Vienna (UKDEL) 1989; First Secretary FCO 1994; Language Training (FT) 1997; Deputy Head of Mission Bucharest 1997; On secondment 2001; m 1985 Roberto Arturo Galvez Montes (1d 1987).

Gamble, Adrian Mark; Counsellor Vienna since July 2004; Born 30/03/61; FCO 1991; Second Secretary (EC Affairs) Brussels 1993; First Secretary FCO 1995; First Secretary (Political) Rome 1998; First Secretary FCO 2001; Band D6; m 1990 Jane Brison (2s 1991, 1993; 1d 1995).

Ganderton, Jennifer Louise; SUPL since September 1999; Born 15/06/70; Inland Revenue 1988; MOD 1988; FCO 1989; Stockholm 1992; World-Wide Floater 1995; Band B3.

Ganney, Sharon Ann (née Feeney); Vice-Consul (Management) Rio de Janeiro since March 2002; Born 11/10/70; FCO 1989; Warsaw 1992; Hamilton 1994; FCO 1996; T/D Doha 1997; Vice-Consul St Petersburg 1998; Band B3; m 1998 Mark William Ganney.

Garden, Alyson Margaret; Hong Kong since February 2004; Born 21/03/69; FCO 1988; Canberra 1991; FCO 1994; Warsaw 1996; FCO 1999; Band B3.

Gardiner, Judith Margaret (née Farnworth); First Secretary (Political) Prague since October 2000; Born 25/04/66; FCO 1991; Senior Research Officer 1992; Second Secretary (Chancery/Press and Public Affairs) Kiev 1996; m 1994 Christopher Gardiner.

Gardner, David Martin; First Secretary (Management) Bogotá since February 2001; Born 11/11/60; FCO 1978; Mexico City 1981; Tegucigalpa 1984; FCO 1988; Third Secretary (Chancery) Warsaw 1991; Vice-Consul Paris 1993; Second Secretary (Commercial) Mexico City 1996; Band C5; m 1983 Ana Luisa Dominguez Ortiz (1s 1992; 1d 1994).

Gardner, John Ewart; First Secretary (Commercial) Abu Dhabi since November 2000; Born 28/02/53; FCO 1971; Abu Dhabi 1974; Kinshasa 1978; Wellington 1981; FCO 1984; Lagos 1986; Los Angeles 1989; FCO 1992; Second Secretary 1994; Deputy Head of Mission and Consul La Paz 1996; Band C5; m 1975 Alexandra Marie Donald.

Gardner, Julie Ann (née Taylor); SUPL since June 1999; Born 15/02/67; FCO 1988; Peking 1990; Buenos Aires 1993; Karachi 1997; Band A2; m 1997 Stuart William Gardner (1d 1999).

Gardner, Stuart William; Brussels since August 2001; Born 10/03/70; FCO 1989; Buenos Aires 1993; Karachi 1999; Band B3; m 1997 Julie Taylor.

Gare, Berenice Veronica (née Erry); FCO since June 1984; Born 27/04/56; FCO 1975; Accra 1977; Cairo 1979; New Delhi 1980; Kuala Lumpur 1981; Band C4; m 2002 Adam Robert Gare.

Garn, Carl Raymond; Deputy Head of Mission Tashkent since September 2003; Born 17/10/56; Cabinet Office 1977; CSD 1979; FCO 1981; Dacca 1982; SEA Floater 1985; Vice-Consul Istanbul 1986; FCO 1990; Deputy Head of Mission Tallinn 1993; Tortola 1996; FCO 2000; Band C5; m 1987 Lisa Elaine Walter (1d 1995; 1s 1997).

Garner-Winship, Stephen Peter; First Secretary FCO since September 1994; Born 26/10/56; FCO 1989; Consul Rio de Janeiro 1991; First Secretary

(Political) Lisbon 1993; Band D6; m 1978 Mary Carmel (1s 1979; 1d 1982).

Garnham, Penelope Jane (née White); Pretoria since September 2000; Born 13/07/71; FCO 1989; Kingston 1992; Dubai 1996; Band B3; m 1993 Glen Joseph Garnham (1d 1999; 1s 2002).

Garnham, Sandra Jayne (née Hibbert); Kiev since July 2001; Born 15/09/68; FCO 1989; Rome 1992; FCO 1996; Islamabad 1998; Band B3; m 1992 Clive Julian Marcus Westbrook Garnham (diss).

Garrett, Charles Edmund; FCO since November 2001; Born 16/04/63; FCO 1987; Language Training 1988; Language Training Hong Kong 1989; Second Secretary Nicosia 1990; Second Secretary Hong Kong (UKREP JLG) 1991; First Secretary FCO 1993; First Secretary Berne 1997; m 1991 Véronique Frances Edmonde Barnes (2d 1992, 1993; 3s 1995, 1999, 2000).

Garrett, Martin, MVO (1996); Deputy Head of Mission Rangoon since March 2002; Born 21/02/54; FCO 1974; Governor's Office Honiara 1976; Paris 1979; BERS Masirah 1981; Tripoli 1982; FCO 1984; Stockholm 1990; Second Secretary (Commercial/Aid) Hanoi 1994; Bangkok 1996; Second Secretary FCO 1997.

Garrity, Alison; Kathmandu since January 2001; Born 19/10/71; FCO 1999; Band A2.

Garside, Bernhard Herbert; Consul-General Amsterdam since February 2003; Born 21/01/62; FCO 1983; Masirah 1986; Dubai 1987; Lagos 1990; FCO 1994; Havana 1999; Band C5; m 1989 Jennifer Susan Yard (2d 1992, 1998; 1s 1996).

Garth, Andrew John; First Secretary (Trade Development) Bucharest since April 2004; Born 28/09/69; FCO 1988; Warsaw 1990; South/South East Asia Floater Duties 1992; FCO 1996; On loan to the DTI 1998; Taipei 1999; FCO 2002; Band C5.

Garvey, Kevin Andrew; First Secretary (Deputy Head of Mission) and HM Consul Guatemala City since December 2001, also accredited non-resident San Salvador and Tegucigalpa since February 2004; Born 10/08/60; FCO 1978; Bangkok 1981; Hanoi 1985; Latin America Floater 1986; FCO 1988; Phnom Penh 1992; Second Secretary Turks and Caicos Islands 1993; FCO 1996; On loan to British Trade International 1999.

Gaskill, Katriona; FCO since September 2003; Born 07/02/80; Band C4.

Gaskin, Rupert John Addison; First Secretary (Political) Khartoum since August 2003; Born 19/06/74; FCO 1997; Second Secretary (Political) Cairo 1999; Second Secretary FCO 2001; Band D6; m 2003 Jacqueline Gartland.

Gass, Simon Lawrance, CVO (1999), CMG (1998); HM Ambassador Athens since December 2004; Born 02/11/56; FCO 1977; Lagos 1979; Second later First Secretary Athens 1984; First Secretary FCO 1987; APS to the Secretary of State 1990; Rome 1993; FCO 1995; Deputy High Commissioner Pretoria 1998; Director (Finance) FCO 2001; m 1980 Marianne Enid Stott (2s 1986, 1989; 1d 1995).

Gates, Helen Deborah; Consul New York since August 2002; Born 31/01/67; FCO 1990; Third Secretary (Political) Berlin 1993; World-Wide Floater Duties 1996; FCO 1997; Second Secretary Geneva (UKDIS) 1999; T/D Johannesburg 2001.

Gatward, William Henry Richard; Second Secretary (Political) Vienna since June 2003; Born 01/03/73; FCO 1999; Full-Time Language Training (German) 2002; Band C4; m 2003 Lynne Morrice.

Gay, Andrew Michael; First Secretary Bogotá since September 2002; Born 04/03/70; First Secretary FCO 1998; Band D6.

Gebicka, Anna Maria Teresa; Prague since July 2001; Born 27/01/64; FCO 1990; Tokyo 1992; Caracas 1995; T/D Stanley 1999; FCO 1999; Band B3.

Gecim, Thérésa Ellen; Istanbul since August 2003; Born 05/06/60; FCO 1977; Geneva (UKMIS) 1982; Belgrade 1984; Manila 1987; FCO 1990; SUPL 1993; FCO 1994; SUPL 1994; FCO 1998; Band B3; m 1985 Ali Gecim (1d 1993; 1s 1995).

Geddes, Jonathan Paul; FCO since June 2001; Born 03/09/65; FCO 1985; Rome 1987; Madras 1990; FCO 1994; Dhaka 1998; Band D6; m 1996 Susan Jane Fleming (1s 2000).

Geddes, Susan Jane (née Fleming); FCO since August 2002; Born 02/08/64; FCO 1984; Brussels (UKREP) 1985; Nassau 1988; FCO 1990; Dhaka 1998; SUPL 2001; Band C4; m 1996 Jonathan Paul Geddes (1s 2000).

Gedny, Philippa; SUPL since August 2000; Born 09/08/59; FCO 1977; Bonn 1979; Montevideo 1982; Antigua 1985; FCO 1987; APS to the PUS 1988; Lisbon 1992; Dubai 1995; FCO 1998; Band C4; (1d 1999; 1s 2000).

Gee, Alan Francis; First Secretary (Management) Canberra since October 2000; Born 02/12/43; FO 1960; Tokyo 1967; Blantyre 1970; Nicosia 1973; FCO 1975; JAO Brussels 1978; Lagos 1981; Second Secretary FCO 1984; Second Secretary (Admin) Sofia 1988; Second later First Secretary FCO 1992; First Secretary (Management) Brasilia 1997; m 1970 Wendy Rugman (1s 1973).

Gee, Mark Leonard; Guangzhou since July 2002; Born 27/06/70; FCO 1991; Moscow 1995; Pretoria 1999; Band B3; (1d 2000).

Gelling, William John; FCO since September 2001; Born 30/12/77; Band C4.

Gemmell, Roderick, OBE (2002); High Commissioner Nassau since March 2003; Born 19/08/50; POSB 1966; DSAO (later FCO) 1967; Bahrain 1971; Washington 1972; The Hague 1975; FCO 1979; Mbabane 1982; Stockholm 1984; Second Secretary (Comm/Econ) Ankara 1987; Second Secretary FCO 1991; First Secretary (Management) Kampala 1994; First Secretary

(Consular/Immigration) later Director of Entry Clearance Lagos 1998; m 1975 Janet Bruce Mitchell (1d 1981).

George, Andrew Neil; Assistant Director (Medical and Welfare) FCO since June 2003; Born 09/10/52; Third Secretary FCO 1974; Language Training SOAS 1975; Third later Second Secretary Bangkok 1976; Second later First Secretary FCO 1980; First Secretary Canberra 1984; First Secretary and Head of Chancery Bangkok 1988; First Secretary FCO 1993; HM Ambassador Asunción 1998; Counsellor (Commercial) Jakarta 2002; m 1977 Watanalak Chaovieng (1d 1979; 1s 1982).

George, Christopher Stephen; First Secretary (Commercial/Economic) Havana since June 2001; Born 08/05/62; Home Office 1982; FCO 1991; Band D6; m 1993 Susan Vince (1s 1999).

German, Robert Charles; First Secretary FCO since November 1999; Born 17/01/58; FCO 1978; Masirah 1985; FCO 1986; Third Secretary Kuala Lumpur 1990; Third Secretary FCO 1993; Second Secretary Tel Aviv 1997; m 1982 Penelope Jane Cooper (2s 1986, 1989; 1d 1996).

Gibbins, Ian Paul; First Secretary FCO since March 2001; Born 27/06/47; GPO 1963; FCO 1969; Washington 1975; later Third Secretary Brussels 1981; Third Secretary Prague 1984; Second Secretary FCO 1985; Second Secretary Bonn 1990; Second Secretary FCO 1992; Second Secretary Brussels 1995; Seconded to the Northern Ireland Office 1999; m 1975 Rose Elizabeth Devlin (2s 1978, 1980; 1d 1983).

Gibbs, Andrew Patrick Somerset, OBE (1992); Counsellor Tel Aviv since July 2002; Born 08/12/51; Third later Second Secretary FCO 1977; Vice-Consul later Consul (Econ) Rio de Janeiro 1979; First Secretary FCO 1981; Language Training 1983; First Secretary Moscow 1984; First Secretary FCO 1985; First Secretary (Inf) Pretoria 1987; First Secretary FCO 1989; SUPL 1991; First Secretary FCO 1993; Counsellor Lisbon 1994; Counsellor FCO 1998; m 1981 Roselind Cecilia Robey (2d 1982, 1986; 2s 1983, 1990).

Gibbs, Kristian Mark; FCO since August 2003; Born 12/05/74; FCO 1997; Caracas 2000; Band C4.

Gibbs, Timothy; FCO since September 1981; Born 20/10/48; FO (later FCO) 1967; Beirut 1974; FCO 1976; Paris 1978; Band C5; m 1978 Catherine MacDougall.

Gibson, John Stuart; FCO since November 2001; Born 15/03/48; Commonwealth Office 1967; FCO 1969; Moscow 1970; Bonn 1972; Berne 1974; Helsinki 1975; FCO 1977; Cairo 1979; Riyadh 1983; Düsseldorf 1984; Dhaka 1987; Second Secretary FCO 1991; Second Secretary (Consular/Management) Kathmandu 1994; Vice-Consul (Management) Maputo 1998; m 1972 Grete Sandberg (2d 1975, 1977).

Gibson, Pamela Ann (née O'Hanlon), MBE (2000); FCO since April 1996; Born 27/09/56; FCO 1975; Geneva (UKMIS) 1978; Kuwait 1981; FCO 1983; Copenhagen 1984; SUPL 1987; FCO 1990; Nairobi 1995; Band A2; m 1987 Graeme Robert Gibson (dec'd 1996).

Gibson, Robert Winnington; Deputy Head of Mission Dhaka since January 2002; Born 07/02/56; FCO 1978; Jedda 1981; Second Secretary UKREP Brussels 1984; Second Secretary (Chancery/Inf) Port of Spain 1986; Second later First Secretary FCO 1989; First Secretary (Political) UKDEL OECD Paris 1995; FCO 1999.

Gifford, Michael John; HM Ambassador Sana'a since July 2004; Born 02/04/61; FCO 1981; Language Training 1982; Third Secretary (Commercial) Abu Dhabi 1983; Second Secretary (Chancery) Oslo 1988; On loan to European Commission Brussels 1990; Second later First Secretary FCO 1991; First Secretary (Economic) Riyadh 1993; First Secretary FCO 1996; Deputy Head of Mission Cairo 2001; m 1986 Patricia Anne Owen (1d 1989; 1s 1991).

Gilbert, Juliet; SUPL since December 2002; Born 20/02/69; FCO 1998; New York (UKMIS) 1999; Band A2.

Gilbert, Mary Jean; Auckland since April 2002; Born 17/01/52; New Zealand Army 1979-94; FCO 1995; Jakarta 1999; Band B3.

Giles, Alison Mary; First Secretary FCO since September 2002; Born 15/09/64; FCO 1988; Third later Second Secretary Pretoria 1990; Second Secretary FCO 1993; First Secretary (IAEA) Vienna (UKMIS) 1998; Band D6.

Gill, Anne Frances; FCO since September 2001; Born 06/07/63; FCO 1988; East Berlin 1989; FCO 1990; Brussels (UKREP) 1992; Rangoon 1995; Tehran 1999; Band B3.

Gillett, Sarah, MVO (1986); Consul General Montreal since February 2002; Born 21/07/56; FCO 1976; SUPL 1978; FCO 1982; Washington 1984; Third later Second Secretary Paris 1987; Second Secretary on secondment to ODA 1990; Vice-Consul Los Angeles 1992; First Secretary FCO 1994; First Secretary (Economic), later Deputy Head of Mission Brasilia 1997.

Gillham, Geoffrey Charles; Assistant Director (EU-Mediterranean) FCO since April 2003; Born 01/06/54; FCO 1981; Second Secretary Caracas 1983; On loan to the Cabinet Office 1986; FCO 1988; First Secretary (Chancery) Madrid 1989; First Secretary (Economic) Paris (UKDEL OECD) 1991; First Secretary later Counsellor FCO 1995; Counsellor New Delhi 1998; Counsellor FCO 2001; m 1991 Dr Nicola Mary Brewer (1d 1993; 1s 1994).

Gillies, Duncan James (known as Jim); First Secretary (Works) Dubai since August 2001; Born 26/01/45; Royal Engineers 1964-85; PSA 1985-88; FCO 1988; Delhi 1990; Muscat 1993; St

Petersburg 1995; Nairobi 1997; Band C5; m (1) (diss 1985) (2d 1965; 1966); m (2) 1986 Barbara (Penny) Porter.

Gillman, James Samuel; FCO since June 2004; Born 30/09/73; FCO 1999; Second Secretary (Immigration) Tehran 2003; Band C4; m 2001 Samantha Jane Fisher (1d 2003).

Gingell, Colin John; Peking since September 2001; Born 05/03/45; Royal Marines 1966-88; Warsaw 1988; Madrid 1989; Bonn 1992; Kiev 1993; Khartoum 1995; Tehran 1999; Band C4; m 1964 Sandra Hall.

Girdlestone, John Patrick; Deputy Head of Mission and Consul-General Khartoum since November 2002; Born 26/09/46; FO 1964; Khartoum 1968; Mexico City 1971; Cairo 1974; FCO 1976; MECAS 1978; Doha 1979; Madrid 1983; Second Secretary and Consul Al Khobar 1986; Second Secretary FCO 1991; Chairman, Diplomatic Service Trade Union Side 1991; First Secretary (Commercial) Abu Dhabi 1994; Deputy Head of Mission Lima 1998; m 1975 Djihan Labib Nakhla (1d 1976).

Glackin, Clare Siobhan; Second Secretary (Chancery) Vienna since July 2002; Born 13/12/70; FCO 1999; Band C4.

Glass, Colin, MBE; FCO since October 1999; Born 06/02/55; FCO 1973; Paris 1975; Luanda 1977; Warsaw 1978; Luanda 1981; Stockholm 1985; FCO 1988; Vice-Consul Bahrain 1991; Deputy High Commissioner Freetown 1995; m 1981 Ruth Kathleen Elizabeth Pearce (1s 1986; 1d 1989).

Glen, Colin Ian; Third Secretary (Management) and Vice-Consul Tehran since April 2003; Born 11/03/60; FCO 1989; Beijing 1999; Band B3; m 2002 Luo Fan.

Glover, Esther Judith (née Hartless); FCO since February 2003; Born 17/10/76; Band A2; m 2004 Mark Glover.

Glover, Graham Dingwall; First Secretary (Commercial) Tripoli since December 2001; Born 14/08/68; FCO 1988; Peking 1989; FCO 1992; Warsaw 1993; Bangkok 1996; FCO 1996; Second Secretary (on loan to DfID), Kingston 1998; Band C5; m 1992 Joanne Ellen Whittle.

Glover, Joanne Ellen (née Whittle); Third later Second Secretary (Immigration) Tripoli since July 2002; Born 20/04/67; FCO 1987; Peking 1989; FCO 1992; Warsaw 1993; Bangkok 1996; FCO 1996; SUPL 1999; Kingston 2000; Band C4; m 1992 Graham Dingwall Glover.

Glynn, Christopher Barry; Deputy Consul-General Sydney since August 2001; Born 23/12/49; FO (later FCO) 1967; Bonn 1971; Abidjan 1973; FCO 1975; Alexandria 1978; FCO 1982; Canning House 1983; Vice-Consul (Commercial) São Paulo 1985; Second Secretary (Commercial) later First Secretary/Consul Lisbon 1988; First Secretary FCO 1992; First Secretary (Commercial) Manila 1994; Deputy Consul General and Deputy Director

of Trade Promotion São Paulo 1997; m 1988 Dr Wilma Sarino Ballat.

Goddard, Colette (née Boyd); Lagos since July 2002; Born 09/05/65; FCO 1995; Singapore 1997; Karachi 2000; Band B3; m 1997 Paul Anthony Goddard (1s 1995).

Goddard, Jonathan; Full-Time Language Training Amman since April 2004; Born 21/12/66; Home Office 1994; FCO 1997; Third Secretary (Chancery) Kathmandu 2000; Full-Time Language Training (Arabic) 2003; Band B3; m 1996 Hayley Morgan (2s 1998, 2000).

Godfrey, Ian David; FCO since July 1997; Born 02/10/60; FCO 1980; Washington 1987; FCO 1989; Third Secretary Islamabad 1993; m 1994 C Hochreiter (1s 1994).

Godson, Anthony; High Commissioner Port Louis since November 2004; Born 01/02/48; FCO 1966; Bucharest 1970; Third Secretary Jakarta 1972; Private Secretary to the High Commissioner Canberra 1976; FCO 1979; Second Secretary 1980; Second later First Secretary New York (UKMIS) 1983; First Secretary FCO 1988; Deputy Head of Mission Bucharest 1990; First Secretary Geneva (UKMIS) 1991; FCO 1996; Counsellor later Deputy Head of Mission and Consul General Jakarta 1998; Counsellor FCO 2002; m 1977 Marian Jane Margaret Hurst.

Goksin, Jill Elaine (née Cooke); Vienna since March 2002; Born 15/09/58; FCO 1982; Belgrade 1983; FCO 1986; Gaborone 1987; FCO 1989; Istanbul 1989; Colombo 1992; FCO 1996; Addis Ababa 1997; Band A2; m 1994 Cenk Bulent Goksin (2d 1996, 1997).

Gola, Elizabeth Ann; FCO since 2002; Born 04/07/61; FCO 1996; Havana 1998; Manila 2000; Band B3.

Golding, Terence Michael; Second later First Secretary FCO since October 2000; Born 26/07/49; FCO 1969; Washington 1973; Berne 1975; São Paulo 1978; FCO 1981; Budapest 1986; Kaduna 1988; FCO 1990; Second Secretary 1992; Second Secretary Singapore 1996; Band C5; m 1978 Irene Elizabeth Blackett.

Goldsmith, Simon Geoffrey; FCO since June 2001; Born 23/01/69; FCO 1990; Paris 1992; Bombay 1994; Third Secretary (On secondment to DFID) Belmopan 1998; Band B3; m 1995 Robyn Jean Daley (1s 2004).

Goldthorpe, Debra Kay, LVO (1999); First Secretary (Commercial) Budapest since November 2000; Born 30/01/58; FCO 1977; Africa Floater 1981; New York 1982; Second Secretary FCO 1985; Language Training 1989; Second Secretary Budapest 1989; First Secretary FCO 1993; HM Consul Durban 1996; Band D6; m 1989 Roger William Lamping.

Golland, Roger James Adam, OBE (1993); Counsellor FCO since January 2001; Born 08/05/55; FCO 1978; Third later Second Secretary Ankara 1979; FCO 1982; Language Training

1983; First Secretary Budapest 1984; FCO 1986; First Secretary Buenos Aires 1989; First Secretary FCO 1992; Counsellor (Political) Brussels 1998; m 1978 Jane Lynnette Brandrick (2s 1985, 1987).

Gomersall, Sir Stephen John, KCMG (2000), CMG (1997); HM Ambassador Tokyo since July 1999; Born 17/01/48; FCO 1970; Language Student Sheffield and Tokyo 1971; Third later First Secretary Tokyo 1972; FCO 1977; Private Secretary to Lord Privy Seal 1979; First Secretary Washington 1982; Counsellor (Economic) Tokyo 1986; Counsellor FCO 1990; Minister New York (UKMIS) 1994; m 1975 Lydia Veronica Parry (2s 1978, 1980; 1d 1982).

Goodall, David Paul; FCO since June 2003; Born 16/04/57; FCO 1976; Wellington 1978; Seoul 1981; SEA Floater 1985; FCO 1987; Third Secretary (Commercial) Accra 1990 (Second Secretary 1994); Second Secretary FCO 1994; Second Secretary (Management) Rome 1998; Band C5; m 1996 Diane Bainbridge.

Goodall, Diane (née Bainbridge); SUPL since November 2003; Born 07/10/58; FCO 1985; Ankara 1987; Accra 1991; FCO 1995; Rome 1998; FCO 2002; Band B3; m 1996 David Paul Goodall.

Gooderham, Peter Olaf; Director (Middle East/North Africa) FCO since October 2004; Born 29/07/54; FCO 1983; Second later First Secretary (Chancery) Brussels (UKDEL NATO) 1985; First Secretary FCO 1987; First Secretary (Economic) Riyadh 1990; First Secretary FCO 1993; New York (UKMIS) 1996; Counsellor (Political) Washington 1999; Brussels (UKREP) 2003; m 1985 Carol Anne Ward.

Gooding, Mark; Second Secretary (Commercial) Shanghai since December 2002; Born 17/12/74; FCO 1999; SUPL 2000; Full-Time Language Training Peking 2001; Band C4.

Goodman, James Henry Adam; FCO since February 2004; Born 31/12/65; FCO 1993; Full-Time Language Training 1995; Full-Time Language Training Cairo 1996; Second Secretary (Political) Riyadh 1997; Second Secretary FCO 1999; First Secretary (Political) Amman 2002; Band D6; m 1992 Andrea Dawn Wells (3s 1994, 1996, 1998).

Goodrick, Clair Isabella; Brussels since July 2003; Born 16/09/71; FCO 1993; Pretoria 1996; Zagreb 1999; Band A2.

Goodrick, Sophie Louise; Second Secretary (EU/Economic) Berlin since January 2001; Born 28/02/70; FCO 1997; On secondment to the German Federal Ministry of Economics 2000; Band C4.

Goodwin, Andrew John; Deputy Head of Mission Sana'a since March 2004; Born 22/03/59; FCO 1978; Hong Kong 1980; Dhaka 1982; Africa/ME Floater 1984; Aden 1987; Lagos 1992; FCO 1993 (Second Secretary 1995); Deputy Head of Mission and Consul Ulaanbaatar 1998;

Consul/Management Officer Tehran 2002; m 1997 (Carol) Louise Mottershead.

Goodwin, David Howard; First Secretary (Commercial) Moscow since April 2002; Born 16/08/46; FO (later FCO) 1964; Budapest 1969; Kinshasa 1970; Montevideo 1973; FCO 1975; Moscow 1978; San Francisco 1980; FCO 1983; Second Secretary (Immigration) New Delhi 1987; Second later First Secretary FCO 1990; First Secretary (Commercial) The Hague 1996; T/D Deputy Project Director Expo 2000 Hanover 2000; Band D6; m 1968 Dorothea Thompson (2d 1970, 1976).

Goodwin, Michael Roy; First Secretary (Management) Budapest since July 2004; Born 17/03/60; FCO 1981; Victoria 1983; FCO 1987; Dublin 1987; Third Secretary (Aid) Banjul 1990; FCO 1992; Ottawa 1995; Second Secretary (Immigration/Consular) Kingston 2001; Band C5; m 1983 Kerry Linda Graney (2d 1986, 1992).

Goodworth, Adrian Francis Norton; SUPL since January 2001; Born 06/07/53; FCO 1982; Third Secretary Seoul 1984; Third later Second Secretary Brussels (UKREP) 1988; FCO 1990; Second Secretary (Commercial) Jakarta 1992; First Secretary (Commercial) Caracas 1996; m (1) 1981 Caroline Ruth Steele (diss 1985), (2) 1987 Valerie Ann Chipcase (diss) (1s 1990; 1d 1992), (3) 1996 Susanti Djuhana (1s 1997).

Gordon, Alison Jill; FCO since April 2002; Born 02/02/72; Band D6.

Gordon, Claire Sandra; Kabul since November 2002; Born 19/11/76; FCO 1998; Lima 1999; New York (UKMIS) 2001.

Gordon, Emma Louise; FCO since April 2002; Born 25/05/74; Band C4.

Gordon, Jean Francois, CMG (1999); HM Ambassador Abidjan and HM Ambassador non-resident to Liberia, Niger and Burkina Faso since June 2001; Born 16/04/53; FCO 1979; Second later First Secretary Luanda 1981; First Secretary Geneva (UKDIS) 1983; First Secretary FCO 1988; First Secretary (Political) Nairobi 1990; First Secretary FCO 1992; HM Ambassador Algiers 1996; seconded to Royal College of Defence Studies 2000; m Elaine Margaret Daniel (2d 1984, 1988).

Gordon, Pamela Jane (née Taylor); SUPL since July 2003; Born 03/09/51; FCO 1973; Havana 1975; Brussels 1977; SUPL 1978; FCO 2001; m 1978 Robert Anthony Eagleson (2d 1980, 1981; 2s 1985, 1988).

Gordon, Robert Anthony Eagleson, CMG (1999), OBE (1983); HM Ambassador Hanoi since September 2003; Born 09/02/52; FCO 1973; Language Student 1974; Third later Second Secretary Warsaw 1975; Second later First Secretary (Head of Chancery) Santiago 1978; First Secretary FCO 1983; First Secretary (Economic) Paris (UKDEL OECD) 1987; Deputy Head of Mission Warsaw 1992; HM Ambassador Rangoon

1995; Counsellor FCO 1999; m 1978 Pamela Jane Taylor (2d 1980, 1981; 2s 1985, 1988).

Gordon-MacLeod, David Scott; High Commissioner Port Moresby since November 2003; Born 04/05/48; ODA 1973; Mbabane 1978; Second later First Secretary FCO 1983; First Secretary and Head of Chancery Maputo 1987; First Secretary FCO 1991; Full-Time Language Training 1994; Deputy Head of Mission Bogotá 1994; First Secretary (Economic) Athens 1998; m 1988 Adrienne Felicia Maria Atkins (2d 1989, 1992; 2s 1994, 1996).

Gotch, Chris; Second Secretary (Commercial) Baku since December 2002; Born 28/11/69; FCO 1996; Second Secretary (Political) Seoul 1997.

Gould, David Christopher; FCO then FCO Services since November 1990; Born 31/12/55; FCO 1976; Washington 1982; FCO 1985; On loan to Cabinet Office 1987; Band D7; m 1977 Susan Kensett (2d 1975, 1980).

Gould, John Richard William; Second Secretary FCO since April 2002; Born 28/11/73; FCO 1997; Second Secretary Sarajevo 2000; Band C4.

Gould, Matthew Steven, MBE (1998); Deputy Head of Mission Tehran since April 2003; Born 20/08/71; FCO 1993; Manila 1994; FCO 1997; T/D Islamabad 2002.

Gould, St. John Byrhtnoth; First Secretary (Political) Washington since July 2000; Born 12/08/68; FCO 1995; Band C5; m 1993 Siân Elizabeth Edwards.

Goulden, Katherine Lucy; FCO since May 2002; Born 20/06/67; FCO 1991; Third Secretary (Aid/Chancery) Port Louis 1994; Brasilia 1998; Band C4.

Goulty, Alan Fletcher, CMG (1998); HM Ambassador and Consul-General Tunis since October 2004; Born 02/07/47; Third Secretary FCO 1968; MECAS 1969; Third later Second Secretary Beirut 1971; Khartoum 1972; Second later First Secretary FCO 1975; On loan to Cabinet Office 1977; Washington 1981; First Secretary later Counsellor FCO 1985; Deputy Head of Mission Cairo 1990; HM Ambassador Khartoum 1995; Director Middle East 2000; UK Special Representative to Sudan 2002; m (1) 1968 Jennifer Wendy Ellison (1s 1970); (2) 1983 Lillian Craig Harris.

Gowan, David John; HM Ambassador Belgrade since September 2003; Born 11/02/49; Ministry of Defence 1970; Home Civil Service 1973; Second Secretary FCO 1975; Second later First Secretary (Comm) Moscow 1977; First Secretary FCO 1981; Head of Chancery and Consul Brasilia 1985; On loan to the Cabinet Office 1988; FCO 1989; Counsellor on loan to the Cabinet Office 1990; Counsellor (Commercial and Know How Fund) Moscow 1992; Counsellor and Deputy Head of Mission Helsinki 1995; Counsellor FCO 1999; On loan at St Antony's College Oxford 1999; Full-Time Language Training 2000; Minister and

Deputy Head of Mission Moscow 2000; m 1975 Marna Irene Williams (2s 1978, 1982).

Gowen-Smith, Stephen Donald; FCO since August 2000; Born 10/12/59; FCO 1984; Vice-Consul Geneva 1997; Band C4; m 1981 Janet Elizabeth (1s 1987; 1d 1991).

Gowers, Natalie Rachel; Khartoum since November 2002; Born 30/01/80; FCO 2001; Band A2.

Goya-Brown, Simon Nicholas; First Secretary (Financial) Beijing since February 2004; Born 19/07/73; FCO 1997; Full-Time Language Training 1998; Full-Time Language Training Kamakura 1999; Second Secretary Tokyo 2000; Band C4; m 2003 Yumiko.

Gozney, Richard Hugh Turton, CMG (1993); High Commissioner Nigeria, Ambassador (Non-resident) Benin since June 2004; Born 21/07/51; FCO 1973; Third Secretary Jakarta 1974; Second later First Secretary Buenos Aires 1978; First Secretary FCO 1981; Head of Chancery Madrid 1984; APS later PPS to Secretary of State FCO 1989; High Commissioner Mbabane 1993; Counsellor FCO 1996; On loan to the Cabinet Office (Chief of Assessment Staff) 1998; HM Ambassador Jakarta 2000; m 1982 Diana Edwina Baird (2s 1987, 1990).

Gracey, Colin; Guatemala City since June 2002; Born 25/03/47; FCO 1965; Anguilla 1969; Lima 1971; Bombay 1974; FCO 1976; La Paz 1979; FCO 1983; Geneva (UKMIS) 1986; Islamabad 1989; FCO 1992; Third later Second Secretary (Commercial) Caracas 1996; Consul (Commercial) Ho Chi Minh City 1999; Band C4; m 1972 Mercedes Ines Rosenthal (1d 1973; 1s 1977).

Graham, Alison Forbes; FCO since January 1994; Born 24/08/59; FCO 1980; East Berlin 1982; FCO 1984; Ottawa 1987; Paris 1990; Band C4.

Graham, David Frank; SUPL since October 2003; Born 27/06/59; FCO 1978; Vice-Consul (Commercial) Munich 1982; LA Floater 1985; Third later Second Secretary (Economic) Warsaw 1987; FCO 1991; Second Secretary (Commercial) Berlin 1992; First Secretary (Commercial) Seoul 1997; First Secretary (Head of Governor's Office) Montserrat 2000; m 1990 Anne Marie D'Souza.

Graham, Euan Somerled; FCO since January 2004; Born 21/06/68; Band C5.

Graham, Iain George; FCO since June 2001; Born 01/03/70; FCO 1989; Cairo 1991; Anguilla 1995; Islamabad 1998; Band C4; m 2003 Susanna Lickorish.

Graham, Steven; Second Secretary (Commercial) Luanda since May 2001; Born 08/07/68; FCO 1989; Islamabad 1993; Full-Time Language Training 1996; Vice-Consul (Commercial) Rio de Janeiro 1996; Band B3; m (1) 1991 Pauline Lannie (diss 1995), (2) 2000 Luisa Maria Satiago.

Grahame, David Aonghas Rees; FCO since September 2002; Born 21/02/79; Band C4.

Grainger, David Quentin; FCO since April 2000; Born 02/02/69; FCO 1990; Lusaka 1992; Kampala 1996; Band B3.

Grainger, John Andrew; Legal Counsellor later Deputy Legal Adviser, FCO since October 2001; Born 27/08/57; called to the Bar (Lincoln's Inn) 1981; Assistant Legal Adviser FCO 1984; First Secretary (Legal Adviser) BMG (later BM) Berlin 1989; Assistant Legal Adviser FCO 1991; Legal Counsellor FCO 1994; Legal Counsellor New York (UKMIS) 1997; m 1998 Katherine Veronica Bregou.

Grainger, Susan Carol; SUPL since January 2003; Born 17/06/67; FCO 1987; New York (UKMIS) 1989; Montserrat 1992; FCO 1996; Dublin 1997; FCO 2000; Band B3; m 1991 Angus Steele (diss 2001).

Grant, Ann; High Commissioner Pretoria/Cape Town since October 2000; Born 13/08/48; FCO 1971; Calcutta 1973; FCO 1975; Transferred to the Department of Energy 1976; First Secretary FCO 1979; Head of Chancery and Consul Maputo 1981; FCO 1984; First Secretary (Energy) Brussels (UKREP) 1987; Resigned 1989; Communications Director OXFAM 1989-91; Reinstated, FCO 1991; Counsellor (ECOSOC) New York (UKMIS) 1992; Counsellor FCO 1996; Director FCO 1999.

Grant, John Douglas Kelso, CMG (1999); Permanent Representative Brussels (UKREP) since August 2003; Born 17/10/54; FCO 1976; Stockholm 1977; Language Training 1980; Moscow 1982; FCO 1984; Resigned 1985; Reinstated, First Secretary FCO 1986; First Secretary (Press) Brussels (UKREP) 1989; First Secretary on loan to the Cabinet Office 1993; Brussels (UKREP) 1994; Principal Private Secretary to the Secretary of State for Foreign and Commonwealth Affairs 1997; HM Ambassador Stockholm 1999; m 1983 Anna Lindvall (2d 1987, 1988; 1s 1993).

Gray, Douglas Macdonald; Second Secretary (Political) Skopje since April 2003; Born 13/03/54; FCO 1975; Far East Floater 1978; Istanbul 1980; Second Secretary Yaoundé 1983; Second Secretary FCO 1986; First Secretary (Commercial) Seoul 1989; Deputy Head of Mission and Consul Quito 1994; Counsellor FCO 1997; m 1980 Alison Ann Hunter (1d 1985).

Gray, John Charles Rodger; Head of Middle East Department FCO since March 2002; Born 12/03/53; Third Secretary FCO 1974; Language Training 1975; Third later Second Secretary Warsaw 1976; FCO 1979; First Secretary FCO 1981; First Secretary Paris (UKDEL OECD) 1983; On loan to Cabinet Office 1987; First Secretary FCO 1989; Deputy Head of Mission Jakarta 1993; On secondment to Harvard University 1996; Washington 1997; FCO 2001; m 1988 Anne-Marie Lucienne Suzanne de Dax d'Axat (3s 1995, 1997, 2000).

Gray, Trudi Elisabeth Mary; Bogotá since July 2001; Born 19/07/47; FCO 1978; Buenos Aires 1979; Prague 1982; Port Stanley 1984; Nassau 1985; Lima 1988; Lisbon 1992; FCO 1995; Seoul 1997; Band A2.

Greatrex, Avril; Second Secretary FCO since February 1995; Born 17/04/47; DSAO (later FCO) 1967; Kuwait 1971; Lagos 1973; Latin America Floater 1976; FCO 1979; Second Secretary (Management) and Vice Consul Buenos Aires 1991.

Green, Andrew Philip; Third later Second Secretary FCO since August 1992; Born 12/05/58; FCO 1975; Moscow 1982; FCO 1984; Third Secretary Tokyo 1989; m 1982 Susan Mary Merry.

Green, Colin Harvey; Hong Kong since March 2001; Born 22/05/69; FCO 1989; New York (UKMIS) 1992; Abidjan 1995; Band B3; m 1997.

Green, Frances Moira; Moscow since February 2002; Born 29/04/48; Washington 1975; Georgetown 1977; The Hague 1981; FCO 1984; Maseru 1987; FCO 1991; Brussels (UKREP) 1993; Valletta 1997; Band A2.

Green, John Edward; Second Secretary (Management) Valletta since July 2004; Born 15/02/65; FCO 1983; Tehran 1991; World-Wide Floater Duties 1994; FCO 1996; Band C4; m 1994 Caroline Ann Hockings (1s, 1d (twins) 1999).

Green, Keith William; First Secretary (Regional Affairs) Santiago since August 2003; Born 14/02/64; FCO 1990; Second Secretary (Chancery) Buenos Aires 1992; Second Secretary FCO 1995; First Secretary Sarajevo 1998; First Secretary FCO 2001; Band D6.

Green, Kelvin Edward; Second Secretary Bangalore since January 2001; Born 19/01/63; Inland Revenue 1981; FCO 1982; Washington 1984; Kampala 1987; Lilongwe 1990; FCO 1993; Second Secretary (Commercial/Consular) Dar es Salaam 1997; Band C4; m 1984 Gillian Mary Lewis (2d 1991, 1993).

Green, Muriel Ruth (née Bailey); FCO since October 2002; Born 13/06/49; WRAF 1971-75; FCO 1975; Mexico City 1976; Islamabad 1982; FCO 1984; SUPL 1992; FCO 1993; On loan to the Cabinet Office 1999; Band A2; m 1981 William Charles Green (2s 1984, 1988).

Green, Noël Frank; First Secretary FCO since June 1996; Born 08/01/49; FCO 1968; Jedda 1971; Brussels (BE) 1974; Private Secretary to the Ambassador Brussels (UKDEL NATO) 1975; FCO 1977; Second Secretary 1977; Second Secretary (Commercial) Lagos 1981; Second Secretary (Admin) Moscow 1985; First Secretary FCO 1987; First Secretary (Management/Consular) Stockholm 1990; First Secretary (Commercial) Kuala Lumpur 1995; m 1984 Kerstin Anita Maria Höijer.

Green, Steven John; First Secretary (Commercial) Kuala Lumpur since August 2000; Born 17/05/55; HM Customs and Excise 1972-74; FCO 1974;

Peking 1976; Stockholm 1978; SUPL (Exeter University) 1980; FCO 1983; Third Secretary Lilongwe 1985; Third Secretary Geneva (UKDIS) 1989; Second Secretary FCO 1992; Full-Time Language Training 1995; Second Secretary (Commercial) Paris 1996; m 1978 Ulla Marianne Nilsson (1s 1980; twin d 1986).

Greenall, Elaine Linda; SUPL since April 2004; Born 04/10/77; FCO 2003; Band A2; (1d 1997).

Greene, Bernadette Theresa; Consul (Commercial) Monterrey since July 2004; Born 17/04/66; FCO 1988; Geneva (UKDEL) 1991; Maseru 1994; T/D Bosnia 1996; FCO 1997; On loan to the DTI 2000; T/D Port of Spain 2001; On loan to British Trade International later UK Trade & Investment 2002; Band C4.

Greengrass, John Kenneth, MBE (1999); First Secretary (Commercial) Paris since June 2000; Born 19/07/53; Ministry of Housing and Local Government 1970; FCO 1971; Brussels (UKREP) 1975; Washington 1978; Islamabad 1981; FCO 1983; Lagos 1986; Second Secretary Kuala Lumpur 1989; Second Secretary FCO 1993; Second Secretary (Consular) New Delhi 1996; Band C5; m 1975 Marian Cecilia Williams (3d 1981, 1983, 1986).

Greenlee, James Barry; First Secretary (Management) Nairobi since November 2002; Born 21/12/45; FO (later FCO) 1963; Vienna 1969; Tokyo 1971; FCO 1974; Calcutta 1979; Second Secretary (Admin) and Consul Budapest 1983; Second Secretary (Commercial) Lagos 1986; Second Secretary FCO 1989; First Secretary (Management) and Consul Seoul 1993; First Secretary (Management) Warsaw 1996; First Secretary (Management) Dhaka 2000; Band D6; m 1971 Amanda Jane Todd (2d 1979, 1981).

Greenslade, Natalie Samantha Juliet; SUPL since October 2000; Born 28/06/72; FCO 1993; Tokyo 1994; Floater Duties 1998; FCO 2000; Band B3.

Greenstock, Andrew John; Second Secretary FCO since December 2003; Born 26/10/72; Second Secretary FCO 1998; Full-Time Language Training 2000; Second Secretary (DFID/Public Diplomacy) Tehran 2001; Band C4; m 1999 Katherine Emma Gardner (1s 2003).

Greenstock, Sir Jeremy (Quentin), GCMG (2003), KCMG (1998), CMG (1991); FCO since July 2003; Born 27/07/43; Second Secretary FCO 1969; MECAS 1970; Second later First Secretary Dubai 1972; First Secretary (Private Secretary to the Ambassador) Washington 1974; FCO 1978; Counsellor (Comm) Jedda (later Riyadh) 1983; Head of Chancery Paris 1987; Deputy Political Director and AUSS (Western and Southern Europe) FCO 1990; Minister (Political) Washington 1994; DUS (Middle East/Eastern Europe) 1995; DUS (Political Director) 1996; UK Permanent Representative to United Nations, New York and UK Permanent Representative on the Security Council 1998; m 1969 Anne Ashford Hodges (2d 1970, 1975; 1s 1973).

Greenwood, Christopher Paul; On loan to the DTI since June 2003; Born 22/04/53; FCO 1973; Islamabad 1975; Moscow 1977; Manila 1980; FCO 1982; APS to Secretary of State 1982; Los Angeles 1985; Third later Second Secretary Budapest 1988; Second Secretary 1989; Second Secretary FCO 1992; Full-Time Language Training 1994; Second later First Secretary (Comm) Berne 1995; Consul-General Göthenburg 1999; m 1976 Dorothy Gwendolyn Margaret Hughes (1s 1983; 1d 1988).

Gregg, Sophie Catherine; FCO since September 2002; Born 17/04/72; FCO 1998; Full-Time Language Training 1999; Consul (Political/Economic) Hong Kong 2000; Band D6.

Gregson, Stuart Willens; Consul-General Paris since April 2000; Born 26/04/50; FO (later FCO) 1966; Cairo 1971; Yaoundé 1973; Islamabad 1976; FCO 1978; Gaborone 1982; Vice-Consul Johannesburg 1983; Second later First Secretary and Parliamentary Clerk FCO 1987; First Secretary (Information) Rome 1991; First Secretary FCO 1996; Full-Time Language Training 2000; Band D6; m 1976 Anne-Christine Wasser (1d 1976; 1s 1979).

Grennan, Gemma Brigid Anne; FCO since September 1986; Born 04/07/43; FO 1962; Vientiane 1967; Singapore 1969; Brussels 1971; Special leave 1973; Addis Ababa 1974; FCO 1977; Islamabad 1981; FCO 1983; Ottawa 1984; Band C4; m 1973 Christopher Roy Heaven (1s 1981).

Grey, Catherine Alice Jane; FCO since January 2003; Born 07/11/79; Band B3.

Grice, Sheridan Elizabeth; Third Secretary (Commercial) Cairo since June 1999; Born 14/07/54; FCO 1973; Canberra 1974; SUPL 1976; Belgrade 1976; Georgetown 1978; New York (UKMIS) 1981; FCO 1984; SUPL 1987; Islamabad 1988; Lagos 1992; Third Secretary FCO 1994; SUPL 1997; (2d 1987).

Griffin, Joseph Francis; On loan to the Cabinet Office since July 2002; Born 14/03/73; FCO 1996; Second Secretary Paris 1999; Band D6.

Griffin, Ryan John; Colombo since October 2003; Born 09/04/72; FCO 1991; Rome 1994; Vilnius 1999; Band B3.

Griffiths, Barney Mark; Washington since August 2001; Born 23/01/60; HM Forces 1977-00; FCO 2000; Band C4; m 1980 Beverley Jayne Morse (1d 1983).

Griffiths, Glyn Justyn; Hong Kong since March 2002; Born 11/07/61; FCO 1980; Darwin 1990; FCO 1993; Bonn 1996; FCO 1998; Band C4; m 1989 Susan Caroline Dover (1s 1995; 1d 1998).

Griffiths, Major David Allison; Queen's Messenger since 1990; Born 28/07/43; HM Forces 1966-90.

Griffiths, Nicholas Mark; FCO since January 2001; Born 20/11/58; FCO 1985; Second Secretary (Chancery) Moscow 1988; FCO 1990;

First Secretary (Trade Policy) later Deputy Permanent Representative Paris (UKDEL OECD) 1996.

Griffiths, Trudy Maureen; FCO since May 2002; Born 10/09/70; FCO 1991; Warsaw 1993; Lusaka 1996; Brussels (UKDEL NATO) 1999; Band B3.

Griggs, Kenneth John; FCO since August 2002; Born 02/09/61; FCO 1984; Washington 1985; FCO 1988; Athens 1989; FCO 1992; BTC Hong Kong 1993; FCO 1996; Bangkok 1999; Band C5; m 1986 Leisa Jayne (3d 1988, 1991, 1992; 1s ·1997).

Grime, Ann Kathleen (née Jenkins); Oslo since June 2003; Born 18/06/51; FCO 1975; Muscat 1976; FCO 1978; Moscow 1979; Brussels (UKREP) 1981; SUPL 1983; Bucharest 1988; Islamabad 1989; FCO 1990; Luxembourg 1990; Colombo 1993; FCO 1997; Budapest 1998; Band B3; m 1983 Stephen Howard Grime.

Grimes, Eleanor Claire; First Secretary FCO since September 1997; Born 22/08/63; Band D6; m 1998 Major Sean Robert Armstrong (1d 1999; 1s 2001).

Grimes, Susan (née Metcalfe); SUPL since March 2002; Born 02/10/65; DHSS 1984; FCO 1987; Copenhagen 1990; FCO 1993; Nairobi 1994; Colombo 1998; Band A2; m 1989 Jason Richard Grimes (1d 1993; twin s 1996).

Grinling, Scott MacKenzie; FCO since October 2001; Born 29/10/49; FCO 1991; Nairobi 1998; m 1974 Anita Fitzhugh.

Gristock, Frances Lorraine (née Alexander); SUPL since September 1998; Born 21/07/59; FCO 1981; SE Asia Floater 1983; FCO 1985; Third Secretary Quito 1986; FCO 1990; SUPL 1991; Second Secretary (Commercial/Consular) Victoria 1992; m 1986 Keith Gristock (1s 1994).

Groocock, Vicki; FCO since September 2003; Born 23/10/66; FCO 1988; Washington 1990; FCO 1993; Tokyo 1996; New Delhi 2000; Band A2.

Grover-Minto, Helen Katherine (née Grover); Harare since April 1999; Born 18/04/65; FCO 1986; Addis Ababa 1988; FCO 1991; Lagos later Abuja later Lagos 1992; FCO 1995; Band B3; m 1991 John Minto.

Groves, Eliot Sion; Management Officer Shanghai since July 2002; Born 17/07/69; FCO 1988; New York (UKMIS) 1994; Colombo 1997; New York 2000; Band B3; m 1996 Christine Ann Reynolds.

Growcott, Michael William; FCO since March 1998; Born 15/11/48; FCO 1968; Kampala 1972; Peking 1974; Pretoria 1975; FCO 1978; Assistant to Governor Port Stanley 1979; Second Secretary (Inf/Aid/Econ) Kuala Lumpur 1982; Second Secretary FCO 1986; Chairman Diplomatic Service Whitley Council Trade Union Side, FCO 1987; First Secretary (Management) Brussels 1990; Resident Acting High Commissioner

Castries 1994; m 1971 Avril Heather Kemp (2d 1972, 1976; 1s 1974).

Guckian, Lorna Ruth (née Warren); SUPL since July 1994; Born 18/06/63; FCO 1983; Port Stanley 1986; Düsseldorf 1987; Africa/ME Floater 1989; FCO 1990; Kuwait 1991; FCO 1992; Band B3; m 1990 Dr Noël Joseph Guckian (3d 1992, 1994, 2001; 1s 1997).

Guckian, Dr Noël Joseph, OBE (2001); Consul-General Kirkuk since July 2004; Born 06/03/55; FCO 1980; Consul (Commercial) Jedda 1984; Second Secretary FCO 1987; Paris 1988; Second later First Secretary FCO 1988; Deputy Head of Mission Muscat 1994; FCO 1997; Head of British Interests Section later Chargé d'Affaires and then Deputy Head of Mission Tripoli 1998; Deputy Head of Mission Damascus 2002; m 1990 Lorna Ruth Warren (3d 1992, 1994, 2001; 1s 1997).

Gudgeon, Jonathan Roy; FCO since May 1995; Born 09/05/64; GPO 1980-84; FCO 1984; Moscow 1988; Vienna 1992; Band C5; m 1988 Lisa Anne Forte (2s 1992, 1993).

Gudgeon, Simon Peter; FCO since August 2003; Born 08/02/66; FCO 1982; Lagos 1987; Moscow 1992; FCO 1996; On secondment to NIO, Belfast 1997; Second Secretary Tel Aviv 1999; Band C4; m 1994 Catherine Jane Stewart (2s 1999, 2003; 1d 2001).

Guha, Priya Victoria; FCO since September 2003; Born 21/09/73; FCO 1996; Second Secretary (EU) Madrid 1999; Band C4.

Gunn, Janet Frederica (née Podolier); FCO since June 1997; Born 04/10/48; Research Counsellor FCO 1970; SUPL 1976; FCO 1978; Moscow 1984; FCO 1985; Deputy Head of Mission Sofia 1994; (1s 1976).

Gunnett, Martin John; FCO since April 1999; Born 01/04/50; FO 1967; Darwin 1976; FCO 1978; Belgrade 1987; Second Secretary Prague 1990; Second Secretary FCO 1994; Second Secretary Peking 1995; m 1973 Linda Leah (1d 1979; 1s 1981).

Gurney, Tim; Deputy Head of Mission Kabul since September 2003; Born 28/04/55; FCO 1973; Istanbul 1976; Karachi 1979; Montreal 1982; Second Secretary FCO 1985; Second Secretary (Chancery/Inf) Accra 1989; Deputy Director and Consul (Inf) New York (BIS) 1991; First Secretary FCO 1996; Deputy Governor Bermuda 1998; m 1976 Denise Elizabeth Harker (1d 1984; 1s 1986).

Guthrie, Marion (née Whalley); Kuala Lumpur since August 2001; Born 04/03/69; FCO 1988; Paris 1990; Islamabad 1992; Belgrade 1994; FCO 1996; Yaoundé 1998; Band B3; m 1998 Robin Guthrie.

Gutierrez-Jones, Llinos Dawn; SUPL since September 2001; Born 27/03/68; FCO 1988; Kuwait 1989; Warsaw 1990; New York (UKMIS) 1992; Bandar Seri Begawan 1993; Santiago 1997; Band A2.

Guy, Frances Mary; HM Ambassador Sana'a since March 2001; Born 01/02/59; FCO 1985; Language Training 1987; Second Secretary (Chancery) Khartoum 1988; First Secretary FCO 1991; First Secretary and Head of Political Section Bangkok 1995; Deputy Head of Mission Addis Ababa 1997; m 1989 Guy Charles Maurice Raybaudo (2d 1991, 1996; 1s 1993).

Guymont, Sarah Jean (née Crouch); SUPL since October 2001; Born 08/08/52; FCO 1975; Islamabad 1976; FCO 1977; Moscow 1978; Resigned 1980; Reinstated, FCO 1982; Africa/ME Floater 1983; FCO 1987; Dar es Salaam 1989; SUPL (Cairo) 1992; Cairo 1993; SUPL 1996; Washington 1997; Band B3; m 1991 Frederick James Guymont.

Gwynn, Diana Caroline (née Hamblyn); SUPL since February 1997; Born 15/08/64; DOE 1986 - 89; FCO 1989; Third Secretary (Political/Information) Nairobi 1992; SUPL 1995; Third later Second Secretary FCO 1996; m 1988 Robert Charles Patrick Gwynn (1d 1995; 2s 1997, 2003).

Gwynn, Robert Charles Patrick (known as Robin); Deputy High Commissioner Accra since January 2002; Born 17/03/63; Department of Employment 1986 - 88; FCO 1988; Second Secretary (Chancery/Information) Nairobi 1992; First Secretary FCO 1995; Private Secretary to the Minister of State 2000; m 1988 Diana Caroline Hamblyn (1d 1995; 2s 1997, 2003).

H

Hackett, Anthony John; HM Consul Hamburg since July 2001; Born 19/12/55; FCO 1975; Muscat 1977; FCO 1981; Karachi 1981; FCO 1985; Manila 1988; Oslo 1992; FCO 1996; On loan to the DTI 1999; m 1983 Nilofer Akbar (1d 1986).

Haddock, Michael Kenneth; FCO since July 2001; Born 25/09/50; FCO 1973; Geneva (UKDEL) 1978; Moscow 1981; Kuwait 1983; Second Secretary Damascus 1986; Second Secretary (Commercial) Prague 1988; First Secretary (Commercial) Abu Dhabi 1991; First Secretary FCO 1995; First Secretary (Information) Moscow 1997; m 1972 Irene Doughty (1d 1979; 1s 1984).

Hadley, William Gerard; FCO since July 2002; Born 06/11/70; Customs and Excise 1989; MOD 1990; FCO 1991; Brussels (UKREP) 1994; FCO 1996; Full-Time Language Training 1997; Vice-Consul Paris 1998; Band B3; m 1996 Jacqueline Lillian Smart.

Hafele, Alec Graham; T/D Prague since June 2004; Born 10/05/50; FCO 1995; Bucharest 1999; Istanbul 2003; Band B3; m 1976 Brigitte Ann.

Hagart, Peter Richard; First Secretary (Management) Madrid since September 2003; Born 11/07/48; Department of Agriculture and Fisheries for Scotland 1966; FCO 1969; Bucharest 1972; Quito 1974; Bonn 1975; FCO 1977; FE Floater 1980; Hanoi 1982; Second Secretary

(Admin) and Vice-Consul Brasilia 1983; Second Secretary FCO 1986; Second later First Secretary (Commercial) Bombay 1990; Consul and Deputy Head of Mission Rangoon 1992; Consul (Commercial) Auckland 1994; FCO 1999; Full-Time Language Training (Spanish) 2003.

Hagger, Philip Paul; Consul Montreal since October 2001; Born 05/09/50; FCO 1970; Singapore 1973; FCO 1974; Washington 1975; Nicosia 1978; Casablanca 1981; Lagos 1982; Second Secretary FCO 1987; Second Secretary (Commercial) Riyadh 1989; Second Secretary (Consul) Caracas 1992; Second Secretary The Hague 1994; Second Secretary FCO 1995; Second Secretary (Commercial) Perth 1997; m (1) 1971 Janet Mary Milnes (dec'd 1975) (1s 1972); (2) 1976 Julie Elizabeth Eastaugh (diss 1988) (1d 1977); (3) 1990 Linda Mary Parmegiani (2s 1993, 1996).

Haggie, Paul; Counsellor FCO since October 2001; Born 30/08/49; Third Secretary FCO 1974; Second later First Secretary Bangkok 1976; FCO 1980; First Secretary (Economic) Islamabad 1982; First Secretary FCO 1986; First Secretary (Chancery) Pretoria 1989; First Secretary FCO 1993; Counsellor on loan to the Cabinet Office 1994; Counsellor FCO 1995; Counsellor Bangkok (ESCAP) 1998; m 1979 Deborah Frazer (1s 1984; 1d 1986).

Hague, John Keir; Consul (Management) Düsseldorf since June 2001; Born 26/03/47; CO (later FCO) 1966; Dakar 1970; Kuala Lumpur 1973; Munich 1975; Moscow 1977; FCO 1979; Houston 1983; Second Secretary Islamabad 1985; Second Secretary FCO 1989; Second Secretary (Commercial) Seoul 1992; First Secretary FCO 1995; m 1969 Julie Anne Knight (2d 1972, 1975).

Haigh, Trevor Denton; FCO since January 2000; Born 07/08/44; FCO 1982; Hong Kong 1985; FCO 1988; Moscow 1990; FCO 1993; Canberra 1997; m 1977 Freda Mary Porritt.

Hailey, Nicholas James; FCO since October 2003; Born 27/01/75; FCO 1997; Seconded to Ecole Nationale D'Administration, Paris 1999; Private Secretary to the Ambassador Berlin 2002; Band D6.

Haines, Dr David Michael; First Secretary (Political) Abuja since July 2003; Born 06/04/63; FCO 1989; Full-Time Language Training 1991; Full-Time Language Training Cairo 1992; First Secretary (Political) Tunis 1993; Consul (Political) Jerusalem 1994; First Secretary FCO 1996; First Secretary (Political) Damascus 2000; Band D6; m 1993 Susan Caroline Goodman (1d 1994; 1s 1996).

Haines, Stephen Andrew; Jerusalem since January 2003; Born 12/06/64; FCO 1997; Minsk 1999; Band A2; m 2003 Tatiana Vladimirovna Pilipchyk.

Haley, Anthony Peter; FCO since September 2001; Born 14/03/59; RAF 1979; FCO 1988; New Delhi 1991; Third Secretary FCO 1994; Mexico City

1997; m 1979 Elaine Cuthbertson (3s 1979, 1982, 1985).

Halksworth, Matthew Kenneth; T/D Kabul since September 2003; Born 21/02/75; FCO 2002; Band A2.

Hall, Alison Margaret; FCO since October 2002; Born 28/10/79; Band C4.

Hall, Amy Lea; FCO since March 2003; Born 27/08/77; Band A2.

Hall, Dr Andrew Rotely, OBE (1994); Deputy High Commissioner Kolkata since February 2003; Born 03/05/50; FCO 1980; First Secretary New Delhi 1984; FCO 1987; Deputy Head of Mission and Consul Kathmandu 1991; FCO 1995; Research Counsellor 2000; m 1973 Kathie Wright (2d 1973, 1978).

Hall, Caroline Jane (née Oakley); Deputy Head of Mission Honiara since October 2002; Born 16/09/64; FCO 1984; Santiago 1987; Floater Duties 1990; SUPL 1992; Karachi 1993; FCO 1996; Second Secretary (Immigration) Moscow 1998; Band C4; m 1992 James William Hall.

Hall, Harriet; First Secretary (Political) Stanley since July 2003; Born 24/12/69; FCO 1992; Full-Time Language Training FCO 1994; Full-Time Language Training Peking 1995; Second Secretary (Political) Peking 1996; FCO 1999.

Hall, James William David; First Secretary FCO since May 2003; Born 01/03/65; FCO 1987; Third later Second Secretary (Economic) Lusaka 1989; Second Secretary (Commercial) New Delhi 1991; Second Secretary FCO 1994; First Secretary Vienna 1999; First Secretary Pristina 2002; Band D6; ptnr, Jacqueline Ann Loveridge.

Hall, Margaret Ann; FCO since December 1991; Born 01/04/48; FCO 1975; on CDA at SOAS 1991; Band PRO; m 1974 Govind Anant Walawalkar (dec'd 2001).

Hall, Mary Eleanor (née Ford); Gibraltar since July 2000; Born 26/09/53; FCO 1978; Aden 1979; Geneva (UKMIS) 1980; Paris 1983; Ankara 1985; Warsaw 1988; Belgrade 1990; Lagos 1992; FCO 1995; Cape Town 1997; Band B3; m 1983 Peter Henry Hall.

Hall, Rebecca; FCO since December 2001; Born 29/09/72; FCO 1994; FCO 1996; Brussels (UKREP) 1997; Second Secretary (Political) Vienna (EU) 1999; Band D6; m 2000 Robert Page.

Hall, Russell David; SUPL since October 2003; Born 12/03/64; FCO 1984; Sofia 1996; Santiago 2000; Band A2; m 1985 Karen Hipkiss (1s 1985; 2d 1988, 1993).

Hall, Simon David; Second Secretary Jakarta since November 2003; Born 20/03/76; FCO 2000; Second Secretary Kabul 2002; Band C4.

Hall, Simon Lee; Second later First Secretary FCO since May 2000; Born 29/04/63; FCO 1982; Rome 1984; Hanoi 1986; Africa/Middle East Floater

1987; FCO 1990; Seconded to the DTI 1991; Ottawa 1993; Kingston 1996; Band C5.

Hall, Thomas Mark; FCO since December 1985; Born 15/09/47; HM Inspector of Taxes 1964; Commonwealth Office (later FCO) 1967; Tokyo 1970; FCO 1973; Milan 1979; Algiers 1981; Athens 1984; Band B3.

Hall Hall, Alexandra Mary; Seconded to the Private Sector since July 2002; Born 01/02/64; FCO 1986; Full-Time Language Training Bangkok 1989; Second Secretary 1989; First Secretary FCO 1993; On loan to the Cabinet Office 1995; Washington 1999; SUPL 2001.

Hallett, Edward Charles; Deputy Head of Mission Dublin since July 2003; Born 15/07/47; FCO 1971; Bonn 1972; FCO 1975; PRO (Band D6) 1979; Dublin 1984; FCO 1985; On loan to NIO 1988; FCO 1990; Senior Principal Research Officer FCO 1995; T/D Dublin 1996, 1997, 1998; m 1972 Audrey Marie Tobin.

Halliwell, Bernard, MBE (1981); First Secretary (Management)/Consul Budapest since November 1999; Born 31/01/45; FO 1963; Salisbury 1967; Bahrain Residency 1969; Muscat 1970; Ulaanbaatar, Geneva and Beirut 1973 - 74; FCO 1974; Addis Ababa 1975; FCO 1975; Hong Kong 1977; Peking 1978; Second Secretary (Chancery/Information) later (Admin/Cons) Bridgetown 1981; Second Secretary FCO 1985; First Secretary (Management) Bangkok 1988; First Secretary (Trade Promotion) Washington 1992; FCO 1996; Language Training 1999; m 1981 Vanessa Diane Brierley (3s 1984, 1986, 1989).

Hallsworth, Valerie; SUPL since March 2000; Born 09/11/48; FCO 1988; Band A2; m 1999 Yousif Rahhal.

Halperin, Claire Ruth; FCO since September 2002; Born 29/01/71; Band C4.

Halpin, Michael Christopher; Third Secretary (Political) Islamabad since March 2003; Born 04/09/75; FCO 1999; Floater Duties 2000; Band B3; ptnr, Adriana Auxtova.

Hamblett, Christine; New York (UKMIS) since January 2003; Born 08/12/60; FCO 1990; Rome 1992; Tel Aviv 1995; FCO 1998; Band B3.

Hamill, Brian William; Second Secretary (Investment) Berne since September 2001; Born 08/01/63; FCO 1981; Masirah 1983; Manila 1983; Budapest 1988; FCO 1989; Paris 1992; Third Secretary (Commercial) Berlin 1996; Second Secretary (Commercial) Düsseldorf 1998; Band C4; m 1987 Katrina Lacson Puentevella (1d 1991).

Hamilton, Alasdair Alexander; Jerusalem since August 2003; Born 13/04/71; FCO 1990; Kuala Lumpur 1993; Port Moresby 1997; Freetown 1998; Jakarta 1999; Band B3; m 1998 Erie Alu (1s 1999).

Hamilton, Amanda Zoe; FCO since September 2002; Born 08/08/80; Band B3.

Hamilton, Charles Allan; FCO since November 2001; Born 05/12/48; DSAO 1968; Vice-Consul Düsseldorf 1970; Third Secretary Prague 1973; Vice-Consul Phnom Penh 1974; Third later Second Secretary Cairo 1975; FCO 1979; Second Secretary Addis Ababa 1981; DHC and Head of Chancery Port Louis 1984; FCO 1988; Deputy Head of Mission Yaoundé 1992; Deputy Consul General Montreal 1997; m Mary Indiana Lazare.

Hamilton, John; Calcutta since July 2002; Born 28/09/68; FCO 1988; Brussels (UKDEL NATO) 1990; Windhoek 1993; FCO 1996; Third Secretary (Political) Abuja 1998; Band B3; m 1998 Maxine Jones (1d 1999).

Hamilton, Josephine Anne Temple, MBE (1989); FCO since February 1996; Born 15/06/45; FCO 1972; Georgetown 1974; FCO 1976; Ankara 1978; FCO 1982; Kingston 1986; FCO 1989; Rome 1993; Band B3.

Hancock, Janet Catherine; Deputy Head of Mission Tunis since July 2000; Born 05/01/49; FCO 1970; SRO 1975; PRO 1983; First Secretary FCO 1995; Full-Time Language Training 2000; Band D7; m 1973 Roger A Hancock (diss 1980).

Hancock, Michael John; Second Secretary and Consul Tel Aviv since December 2002; Born 21/10/62; FCO 1982; Bonn 1984; Belgrade 1987; Islamabad 1989; FCO 1991; Vice-Consul Rome 1995; Deputy Head of Mission Tbilisi 1995; Second Secretary Chancery Brussels (UKREP) 1998; Band C4; m (1) 1983 Elizabeth Alison Ormrod (diss 1999) (2s 1989, 1991; 1d 1987); (2) 1999 Rusudan Gachechiladze (2s 1992, 2001).

Hancon, John Anthony; FCO since July 1991; Born 05/01/48; GPO 1965; FCO 1969; Kuala Lumpur 1971; FCO 1973; Paris 1976; FCO 1978; Sofia 1982; FCO 1984; Nicosia 1988; Band C5; m 1970 Anne Lesley Hawke (1d 1975; 1s 1980).

Hand, Graham Stewart; HM Ambassador Algiers since July 2002; Born 03/11/48; HM Forces 1967-80; FCO 1980; Second later First Secretary Dakar 1982; First Secretary FCO 1984; Language Training 1987; First Secretary and Head of Chancery Helsinki 1987; Counsellor FCO 1992; Deputy High Commissioner Lagos 1994; on loan to the Royal College of Defence Studies 1997; Ambassador Bosnia Herzegovina 1998; m 1973 Anne Mary Seton Campbell (1s 1979; 1d 1984).

Hand, Jessica Mary (née Pearce); On secondment as Counsellor since January 2002; Born 01/09/57; FCO 1985; Second Secretary (Chancery) Dakar 1987; First Secretary FCO 1990; Full-Time Language Training 1994; HM Ambassador Minsk 1996; First Secretary FCO 1999; SUPL 2001; m 1999 Robert Wayne Hand.

Handley, Timothy Sean; T/D Islamabad since July 2003; Born 08/02/51; HCS 1969; FCO 1971; Abu Dhabi 1973; Stockholm 1976; Warsaw 1979; FCO 1981; Georgetown 1985; FCO 1986; Düsseldorf 1988; Tel Aviv 1991; FCO 1994; Band C4; m 1985 Julie Anne Russell (1s 1986; 1d 1989).

Hannah, Craig John; FCO since November 1999; Born 02/06/63; Department of Employment 1980; FCO 1983; Accra 1984; Sofia 1987; FCO 1990; Kuala Lumpur 1994; Vienna 1998; Band B3.

Hans, Ravinder; Third Secretary (Political/PPA/Culture) Valletta since September 2002; Born 17/03/74; FCO 1996; Buenos Aires 1997; Band B3.

Hansen, Caroline (née Thearle); SUPL since October 1999; Born 17/02/66; FCO 1984; Copenhagen 1987; SUPL 1990; Bangkok 1992; SUPL 1995; Dhaka 1996; Band B3; m 1989 Jakob Hansen.

Hanshaw, Danielle May; FCO since 2001; Born 11/02/71; MOD 1991-98; FCO 1998; Jakarta 2001; Band A2.

Hanson, Timothy Myles; Hong Kong since January 2004; Born 27/06/65; FCO 1984; Third Secretary (Chancery) Muscat 1987; Third Secretary (Aid) New Delhi 1991; Second Secretary FCO 1994; Second Secretary (Commercial) Kuala Lumpur 1997; First Secretary (Commercial) Sarajevo 2001.

Harborne, Peter Gale; High Commissioner Port of Spain since July 1999; Born 29/06/45; DHSS 1966; FCO 1972; Ottawa 1974; Mexico City 1975; Resigned 1979; Reinstated, First Secretary FCO 1981; First Secretary and Head of Chancery Helsinki 1983; Counsellor and Head of Chancery Budapest 1988; FCO Overseas Inspectorate 1991-94; HM Ambassador Bratislava 1995-98; m 1976 Tessa Elizabeth Henri (2s 1980, 1981).

Hardie, Alison; Lima since June 2002; Born 31/03/65; FCO 1988; Washington 1990; FCO 1992; Canberra 1994; FCO 1997; Floater Duties 1998; Yaoundé 2000; Band A2.

Hardman, Peter James William; SMO Islamabad since May 2003; Born 28/10/56; FCO 1974; SE Asia Floater 1978; Bombay 1979; Perth 1983; Bangkok 1986; Second Secretary on loan to the ODA 1988; Language Training 1990; Second Secretary Sofia 1991; First Secretary (Commercial) Bangkok 1996; Shanghai 2000; FCO 2001; Band D6; m 1983 Joelle Helene Schneider (1d 1984).

Hardy, Richard Martin; Singapore since July 2001; Born 07/10/50; FCO 1967; Brussels 1976; FCO 1978; Buenos Aires 1979; FCO 1982; Bridgetown 1986; Second Secretary FCO 1989; Paris 1993; FCO 1997; Band C5; m (1) 1975 Amanda Smith (diss 1981); (2) 1982 Astrid Posse (diss 1996); (3) 2001 Alison Jane Fossey.

Hare, Paul Webster, LVO (1985); Visiting fellow at the centre for International Affairs, Harvard University since August 2004; Born 20/07/51; FCO 1978; Second Secretary/PS to HMA Brussels (UKREP) 1979; First Secretary Lisbon 1981 (Head of Chancery 1983); FCO 1985; Consul (Investment) and Deputy Director Investment USA BTIO New York 1988; Deputy Head of Mission and later Counsellor (Commercial/Economic)

Caracas 1994; Counsellor FCO 1997; HM Ambassador Havana 2001; m 1978 Lynda Carol Henderson (3d 1979, 1982, 1994; 3s 1984, 1988, 1991).

Hargreaves, Roger John; First Secretary FCO since September 1999; Born 08/12/50; FCO 1968; Hong Kong 1973; FCO 1975; Sana'a 1976; FCO 1977; Second Secretary Hong Kong 1985; Second later First Secretary FCO 1990; First Secretary (Political) Wellington 1996; Band C5; m Andrea Margaret Kent (1s 1989; 1d 1992).

Harkin, Simon David; First Secretary (PPA) Berne since September 2001; Born 04/10/58; FCO 1989; New York (UKMIS) 1990; FCO 1991; Second Secretary (Political) Harare 1992; First Secretary FCO 1996; Full-Time Language Training 2000.

Harland, Amy Elizabeth; FCO since March 2003; Born 11/05/79; Band C4.

Harland, Jeremy; FCO since September 2003; Born 08/04/63; FCO 1983; Moscow 1988; FCO 1992; Bridgetown 1992; FCO 1996; Washington 1999; Band C5.

Harle, Roger William; FCO since August 1988; Born 04/02/59; FCO 1982; Darwin 1986; Band C4.

Harmer, Roger William; First Secretary (Management) Warsaw since July 2003; Born 05/01/53; FCO 1972; Bucharest 1974; La Paz 1976; Maseru 1978; FCO 1980; Third Secretary Muscat 1983; Ottawa 1986; FCO 1989; Riga 1992; Second Secretary FCO 1993; Geneva (Joint Management Office) 1998; m 1976 Cristobalina López Munoz (1d 1977).

Harper, Maurice Bertrand; Second Secretary (Consular) Lagos since December 2001; Born 03/12/46; FCO 1974; Bangkok 1976; East Berlin 1980; FCO 1981; Bombay 1984; Port Louis 1988; Second Secretary FCO 1993; HM Consul Bucharest 1996; FCO 2001; m (1) 1977 Susan Hayward (1s 1979); m (2) 1986 Veera Printer (1d 1987).

Harper, Monica Celia, CMG (2004); Consul-General Lille since September 1998; Born 18/08/44; FCO 1967; SEATO (Bangkok) 1969; ENA Paris 1972; BMG Berlin 1974; Second Secretary Bonn 1977; FCO 1979; Second Secretary Mexico City 1982; First Secretary Brussels (UKDEL NATO) 1984; First Secretary FCO 1989; Deputy Head of Mission Luxembourg 1994.

Harries, David George, OBE (1998), MBE (1990); Second Secretary (Management) Gibraltar since January 2003; Born 10/03/60; FCO 1980; BGWRS Darwin 1982; FCO 1984; Islamabad 1986; Beirut 1988; FCO 1991; Third Secretary (Consular/Management) Freetown 1993; Third Secretary (Commercial/Development) Maputo 1998; Second Secretary (Consular) BCG New York 2001; Band C4; m 1993 Carol Chammas (1d 2002; 1s 2004).

Harrington, Peter; Second Secretary (Commercial) Doha since August 2001; Born 29/09/62; FCO 1981; Baghdad 1984; Stockholm 1988; Georgetown 1990; FCO 1994; On loan to the DTI 1995; Madras 1997; Band C4; m (1) 1984 Angela Elizabeth Dent (diss); (2) 1993 Veronica Ann Clementson (1s 1993; 1d 1995).

Harris, Karina Lynn; FCO since September 2004; Born 28/02/62; FCO 1983; Cairo 1984; Tokyo 1988; FCO 1990; Vienna (UKMIS) 1993; Rabat 1997; T/D Jerusalem 2000; World Wide Floater Duties 2001; Band B3.

Harris, Kay; SMO Freetown since August 2004; Born 25/11/72; FCO 1992; Islamabad 1998; Pristina 2002; Band C4.

Harris, Martin Fergus; Deputy Head of Mission Kiev since December 2003; Born 17/05/69; FCO 1991; (CFE) UKDEL Vienna 1992; FCO 1997; Full-Time Language Training 1998; On loan to DFID as First Secretary (KHF), Moscow 1999; m 1993 Linda Margaret Maclachlan (1d 2001).

Harris, Peter Harold Charles; Counsellor FCO since September 2003; Born 25/01/50; FCO 1981; Second later First Secretary (Social and Agriculture) Lisbon 1981; FCO 1984; First Secretary Moscow 1985; FCO 1988; First Secretary Santiago 1990; FCO 1993; Counsellor Warsaw 1998; Counsellor Lisbon 2002; m 1976 Maria Judith Ocazionez (4s 1980, 1982, 1984, 1993).

Harrison, Caroline Margaret; First Secretary FCO since August 1999; Born 08/09/66; FCO 1989; First Secretary Helsinki 1997; Band C5.

Harrison, Charles Dale; Management Officer Doha since February 2003; Born 23/02/55; MOD 1971; FCO 1976; Accra 1978; Mbabane 1982; FCO 1985; Rome 1988; Islamabad 1991; FCO 1994; Second Secretary (Management) Brussels (UKREP) 1998; Band C4; m 1978 Lorraine Josie Richards (1d 1987; 1s 1990).

Harrison, Guy Andrew; First Secretary (Commercial) Brussels since June 2002; Born 30/05/64; FCO 1986; Language Training and later Third Secretary (Political) Seoul 1987; Munich 1992; Hanoi 1993; FCO 1995; Second Secretary (Economic) Seoul 1998; Band C5; m 1996 Ann Van Dyck (1d 1999).

Harrison, Mark Simon; Bridgetown since August 2002; Born 08/07/68; FCO 1989; Montevideo 1991; SUPL 1992; Jedda 1994; Nairobi 1996; Abidjan 2000; Auckland 2001; Band B3; m 1992 Roxane Miller (1s 2000).

Harrison, Paula Leslie; FCO since September 2000; Born 05/09/78; Band C4.

Harrison, Robert James; FCO since April 2002; Born 10/09/76; Band C4; ptnr, Andrea Robinson.

Harrison, Stephen Thomas, MBE (2000); On attachment as Assistant Private Secretary to the Duke of York, Buckingham Palace since June 2001; Born 14/08/64; FCO 1986; Language

Training SOAS 1987; Language Training Cairo 1988; Third Secretary (Chancery) Bahrain 1989; Full-Time Language Training (Russian) 1993; Moscow 1994; HM Consul-General Ekaterinburg 1998; FCO 2000; Band D6; m 1995 Philippa Capper (1d 1993; 1s 1998).

Harrison, Victoria Jane; Second Secretary (Political) Helsinki since August 2000; Born 31/10/74; FCO 1997; Full-Time Language Training 1999; Band C4.

Harrison, William Alistair, CVO (1996); Head of United Nations Department, FCO since June 2003; Born 14/11/54; FCO 1977; Third later Second Secretary Warsaw 1979; Second later First Secretary FCO 1982; Private Secretary to the Parliamentary Under Secretary 1984; First Secretary New York (UKMIS) 1987; First Secretary FCO 1992; Deputy Head of Mission Warsaw 1995; On loan as Foreign Policy Adviser to the European Commission 1998; Counsellor and Head of Chancery New York (UKMIS) 2000; m (1) 1981 Thérésa Mary Morrison (diss 1991); (2) 1996 Sarah Judith Wood (1d 1999).

Harrocks, Nicholas James Laurent; SUPL since September 2002; Born 16/04/73; FCO 1996; Full-Time Language Training 1998; Second Secretary (Political) Riyadh 1999.

Harrod, Jean (née Geary); First Secretary (Political) Canberra since October 2000; Born 28/04/54; FCO 1972; Geneva (CSCE) 1973; East Berlin 1975; Port Louis 1977; Peking 1980; SUPL 1983; FCO 1986; Third later Second Secretary (Chancery) Brussels (UKREP) 1992; Second Secretary and Consul Jakarta 1994; FCO 1997; m 1974 Jeffrey Harrod.

Harrod, Jeffrey; First Secretary (External Affairs) Canberra since October 2000; Born 01/04/54; FCO 1970; Geneva (CSCE) 1973; East Berlin 1975; Port Louis 1977; Vice-Consul (Commercial) and later Second Secretary Peking 1980; Consul (Commercial) Shanghai 1984; Second later First Secretary FCO 1986; First Secretary (Commercial) Brussels (UKREP) 1990; First Secretary (Political/Economic) Jakarta 1994; m 1974 Jean Geary.

Harrup, Christine Mary; FCO since August 2003; Born 18/04/49; FCO 1974; Baghdad 1974; Lagos 1977; FCO 1978; Dublin 1981; FCO 1985; Addis Ababa 1987; Colombo 1992; Budapest 1994; Kiev 1999; Kingston 2000; SUPL 2003; Band B3.

Harsent, Susan Elizabeth; FCO since November 2001; Born 16/06/49; FCO 1970; Bonn 1972; FCO 1975; Suva 1976; FCO 1978; Tel Aviv 1982; FCO 1984; Brussels (UKREP) 1989; Shanghai 1998; Band B3.

Harston, Stewart Ian; FCO since March 2000; Born 03/11/63; Singapore 1990; FCO 1994; Amman 1997; Band C5; m (1) 1990 Marianne Stallard (diss); (2) 1994 BG Carvello (2s 1995, 1998).

Hart, Graham Donald; FCO since January 2002; Born 25/10/46; FCO 1975; Tokyo 1977; Monrovia 1982; FCO 1985; JMO New York 1988; FCO 1992; New Delhi 1994; Canberra 1997; Band B3.

Hart, Jeremy Michael; First Secretary (Political) Valletta since September 2002; Born 24/02/57; FCO 1975; Paris 1978; FCO 1980; Second Secretary (Vice-Consul) Athens 1986; First Secretary FCO 1990; Band D6; m (1) 1979 Alison Jane Morrell (diss 1993) (1d 1984); (2) 1995 Penelope Helen Margaret Smyth (2d 1996).

Hart, Simon Charles; FCO since September 2003; Born 13/12/57; FCO 1975; Brussels 1978; Tehran 1981; LA Floater 1983; Bogotá 1985; FCO 1989; Third Secretary Panama City 1993; Brasilia 1997; Bandar Seri Begawan 2000; Band C4; m 1987 Amparo Meza (2s 1993, 1995; 1d 1996).

Harte, Josephine Moira (née Campbell); SUPL since August 2003; Born 17/11/67; FCO 1988; Prague 1990; FCO 1992; Full-Time Language Training 1994; Vice-Consul Berlin 1995; SUPL 1999; Brussels (UKDEL NATO) 2000; Seconded to the North West Development Agency 2003; Band C4; m 1996 Derek Thomas Harte (1s 1999).

Hartley, James Leslie; FCO since November 2003; Born 18/08/49; St Helena 1975; FCO 1977; Lusaka 1978; FCO 1980; LA Floater 1983; Khartoum 1985; Second Secretary and Head of Chancery Ulaanbaatar 1989; Second Secretary FCO 1992; Deputy Head of Mission Phnom Penh 1994; First Secretary and Consul Kuwait 1997; Deputy Head of Mission Algiers 1999; Conakry 2002; Band D6; m 1984 Ann Lesley Oakley.

Harvey, Christopher Paul Duncan; FCO since August 2003; Born 21/07/56; Second Secretary FCO 1986; Second Secretary Suva 1988; First Secretary (Chancery) Brussels 1990; First Secretary FCO 1995; UK Special Representative for Peace in Sierra Leone 1999; Deputy High Commissioner Nairobi 2000; m 1989 Anasaini Vesinawa Kamakorewa (1 step d 1987; 1 step s 1988).

Harvey, David; On loan to the DTI since July 2002; Born 10/11/57; FCO 1977; Dublin 1980; Kinshasa 1982; East Berlin 1986; FCO 1988; Guatemala City 1992; Second Secretary (WTO) Geneva (UKMIS) 1997; FCO 2001; m 1983 Bernadette Louise McMahon (1s 1987; 1d 1990).

Haslam, Christopher Peter de Landre; FCO since March 2003; Born 22/03/43; Admiralty and Ministry of Defence (Navy) 1960; DSAO 1966; Jakarta 1969; Sofia 1973; FCO 1974; Canberra 1978; Lagos 1981; Second Secretary FCO 1986; First Secretary (Commercial) Copenhagen 1989; First Secretary FCO 1993; First Secretary (Commercial) Colombo 1996; Deputy High Commissioner Suva and HM Ambassador (non resident) to Micronesia, Palau and Marshall Islands 2000; Band D6; m 1969 Lana Whitley (2s 1971, 1973).

Haslem, Michelle; FCO since November 2003; Born 18/02/74; FCO 1999; Second Secretary (Political) Kuala Lumpur 2001; Band C4.

Haslett, Matthew Frederick; Beijing since December 2001; Born 29/05/68; FCO 2000; Band A2.

Haswell, Charles Chetwynd Douglas; Director of Trade and Investment Promotion Beijing since November 2000; Born 18/02/56; FCO 1979; Language Training 1980; Beijing 1982; Second Secretary (Chancery) Ottawa 1986; First Secretary FCO 1989; First Secretary (Political) Vienna (UKDEL) 1994; First Secretary FCO 1996; Counsellor on loan to British Invisibles (now IFSL) 1998; m 1991 Sarah Caroline Folkes (1s 1994; 2d 1995, 1998).

Hatfield, Samuel Andrew Roland; FCO since November 2000; Born 15/01/63; FCO 1992; First Secretary (Political) Lagos 1995; First Secretary FCO 1996; SUPL 1999; Band D6; m 1995 Rachel Althea Rodney Pollaers (3d 1995, 1997, 2000).

Hatfull, Martin Alan; Deputy Head of Mission Tokyo since November 2003; Born 07/06/57; FCO 1980; Language Training 1982; Second later First Secretary Tokyo 1983; First Secretary FCO 1987; First Secretary Brussels (UKREP) 1991; First Secretary later Counsellor FCO 1995; Counsellor (Economic and Commercial) Rome 1998; full-Time Language Training (Japanese) 2003; m 1980 Phyllis Morshead (2s 1984, 1987).

Haveron, Monica; Tel Aviv since November 2001; Born 29/06/67; FCO 1987; Nicosia 1990; FCO 1993; Valletta 1995; FCO 1998; World Wide Floater 2000; Band A2.

Hawkes, Julie Anne (née Carr); SUPL since November 1996; Born 05/07/64; FCO 1990; Budapest 1992; FCO 1996; Band A2; m 1996 Edward Clifford Hawkes.

Hawkins, Carl McArthur; FCO since August 2001; Born 25/09/50; FCO 1967; HCS 1974; FCO 1977; Third Secretary Bangkok 1989; Second Secretary FCO 1992; First Secretary Singapore 1998; m 1987 Yuko Shibuya (1d 1988).

Hawkins, John Mark; Consul-General Dubai since June 2004; Born 30/04/60; FCO 1982; Third later Second Secretary (Chancery) Pretoria/Cape Town 1984; First Secretary FCO 1989; First Secretary (Commercial) New Delhi 1993; First Secretary later Counsellor FCO 1997; Counsellor (Commercial) Madrid and Director of Trade and Investment Promotion for Spain 2000; m 1991 Rosemarie Anne Kleynhans (2s 1993, 1996).

Hay, Barbara Logan, CMG (1998), MBE (1991); Consul-General Istanbul since 2004; Born 20/01/53; FCO 1971; Language Training 1974; Moscow 1975; Johannesburg 1978; Second Secretary FCO 1980; Vice-Consul (Commercial) Montreal 1985; First Secretary (Information) Moscow 1988; HM Consul-General St Petersburg 1991; First Secretary FCO 1992; Language Training 1994; HM Ambassador Tashkent and non-resident Dushanbe 1995; Language Training 1999; Consul-General St Petersburg 2000.

Hay, Charles John, MVO (1996); FCO since September 2003; Born 22/09/65; HM Forces (Army) 1987-93; FCO 1993; Second Secretary (Political/Information) Prague 1995; First Secretary FCO 1998; First Secretary (Economic/Finance) Brussels (UKREP) 1999; Band D7; m (1) 1992 Caroline Jane Windsor (diss 1997); (2) 2001 Pascale Sutherland.

Hay-Campbell, (Thomas) Ian, LVO (1994); Deputy Head of Mission Oslo since September 2001; Born 19/05/45; BBC 1972-84; First Secretary FCO 1984; First Secretary Head of Chancery and Consul Kinshasa 1987; First Secretary FCO 1990; Full-Time Language Training 1993; First Secretary (Press and Public Affairs Unit) Moscow 1994; Deputy High Commissioner Harare 1998; Full-Time Language Training 2001; m 1970 Margaret Lorraine Hoadley (4s 1973, 1974, 1977, 1979).

Haydon, Joanna Mary; SUPL since February 2003; Born 14/03/69; FCO 1992; Full-Time Language Training Bangkok 1995; Vice-Consul Bangkok 1995; FCO 1999; On loan to the Cabinet Office 2001; Band C4; m 1998 Peter L Spoor.

Hayes, Julie Patricia; FCO since September 2002; Born 22/07/59; FCO 1988; Hanoi 1991; FCO 1993; Harare 1996; FCO 1999; SUPL 2001; Band B3.

Hayes, Kirsty Isobel (née Paton); Private Secretary to the Ambassador Washington since January 2002; Born 02/02/77; FCO 1999; Vice-Consul (Political and Economic) Hong Kong 2000; Band C4; m 2002 Peter Richard Hayes.

Haywood, Ian; FCO since January 2003; Born 02/10/59; FCO 1978; Kampala 1981; Düsseldorf 1985; FCO 1989; Peking 1994; Full-Time Language Training 1997; Lisbon 1998; m (1) 1984 Angela Jane Kennedy (diss 1988); (2) 1991 June Sandra Tyler.

Haywood, Nigel Robert; HM Ambassador Tallinn since November 2003; Born 17/03/55; HM Forces (Army) 1977-80; FCO 1983; Second later First Secretary Budapest 1985; First Secretary FCO 1989; Deputy Consul-General Johannesburg 1992; Counsellor and Deputy Head of Delegation UKDEL OSCE Vienna 1996; Assistant Director, Personnel FCO 2000; m 1979 Mary Louise Smith (3s 1984, 1985, 1991).

Hazlewood, Roger Derek; First Secretary (Management) Harare since January 2001; Born 10/01/50; FCO 1968; Georgetown 1971; Bonn 1975; Paris 1977; FCO 1980; Cairo 1983; Brussels (JMO) 1987; FCO 1990; Second Secretary 1991; Full-Time Language Training 1993; Second Secretary (Commercial) Warsaw 1994; Second Secretary (Management) Dhaka 1997; m 1971 Yvonne Helen Betty Johnston McPhee (3s 1973, 1976, 1978).

Head, Ian; FCO since April 1993; Born 21/10/46; Home Civil Service 1987; Bonn 1990; Band C4; m 1992 S. Bigonesse-Caron.

Healy, Claire Louise (née Roche); SUPL since March 2004; Born 17/03/72; FCO 1991; Warsaw 1995; Floater Duties 1998; Bucharest 2001; Band B3; m 2001 Gerard Peter Healy (1s 2003).

Healy, Denis Terence; Consul-General Casablanca since February 2002; Born 18/11/43; FO 1963; DSAO 1965; Belgrade 1967; FCO 1970; Port of Spain 1974; Second Secretary 1975; Vice-Consul Douala 1976; FCO 1979; Second Secretary (Chancery/Aid) Bridgetown 1983; First Secretary (Commercial) Brussels (UKREP) 1985; First Secretary FCO 1990; First Secretary (Commercial) Ankara 1991; First Secretary FCO 1996; First Secretary (Commercial) Tokyo 2000.

Healy, Dora Claire Sarah; FCO since August 1998; Born 30/08/52; Principal Research Officer; FCO 1982; Language Training 1986; Second later First Secretary (Chancery/Information) Addis Ababa 1987; FCO 1991; First Secretary (Political) Nairobi 1995; m 1983 Nicholas Guttmann (2d 1976, 1983; 1s 1985).

Healy, Martin Frederick; FCO since October 2000; Born 21/10/55; FCO 1972; Moscow 1978; FCO 1979; Third Secretary Pretoria 1984; FCO 1987; Hong Kong 1990; Second Secretary FCO 1993; Second Secretary Nairobi 1997; m 1977 Jane Catherine Stacey (2d 1981, 1983).

Hearn, Natalie Louise; FCO since March 2002; Born 13/07/72; FCO 1992; Peking 1995; ECO/VC Düsseldorf 1998; On loan to the DTI 2001; Band B3.

Heaslip, Lisanne Marie; FCO since October 2003; Born 16/01/69; FCO 1988; Belgrade 1998; FCO 1999; Tokyo 2000; Band B3.

Heath, Gillian Carol; Suva since April 2001; Born 21/08/45; FCO 1969; Islamabad 1970; Kampala 1971; San Salvador 1973; Panama 1973; Kuala Lumpur 1975; Brunei 1976; FCO 1978; Havana 1980; Dar es Salaam 1981; Singapore 1984; Washington 1988; FCO 1989; Algiers 1990; FCO 1994; Cairo 1996; T/D Canberra 2000; Band B3.

Heatly, Charles Robert; Amman since January 2003; Born 07/08/70; FCO 1993; Full-Time Language Training Cairo 1995; Second Secretary (Political/Economic) Amman 1997; Second Secretary (Political/Economic) Sana'a 2000.

Hebden, Ian Mark; Washington since January 2001; Born 25/03/60; Royal Navy 1976-87; FCO 1987; Bonn 1990; Harare 1992; FCO 1996; Brussels (UKREP) 1997; Band A2; (1d 2002).

Hedges, Matthew James; Second Secretary (Political) Rabat since January 2002; Born 23/04/73; FCO 1999; T/D New York (UKMIS) 2000; Language Training 2001; Band C4.

Heffer, John William Charles; SMO Kampala since August 2003; Born 31/07/52; FCO 1971; Kampala 1973; FCO 1974; Victoria 1975; Bogotá 1977; Peking 1980; FCO 1981; Warsaw 1983; FCO 1984; Valletta 1988; Pretoria 1991; FCO 1994 (Second Secretary 1995); First Secretary (Management) Tripoli 2000; Band C5; m 1975 Lynne Ida Brown (2s 1977, 1980).

Hefford, Brian; Second Secretary (Consular) Bogotá since March 2003; Born 10/08/48; FCO 1969; Karachi 1972; Paris 1976; FCO 1979; Islamabad 1983; FCO 1986; Colombo 1989; Second Secretary Bangkok 1994; FCO 1997; m 1971 Susan Mary Gorman (1s 1975 (dec'd 1991)).

Helke, Jill Beynon (née Barker-Harland); SUPL since April 1999; Born 10/04/56; FCO 1978; Language Training Hong Kong 1981; Peking 1983; Second Secretary New York (UKMIS) 1986; First Secretary FCO 1990; SUPL 1990; New York (UKMIS) 1992; SUPL 1993; Geneva (UKMIS UN) 1993; m 1987 Heinz Michael Rudolf Juergen Helke (1s 1988; 1d 1990).

Hellen, Gary David; FCO since February 2003; Born 24/06/70; FCO 1990; Zagreb (ECMIS) 1992; FCO 1993; Dhaka 1995; Nicosia 1999; Band B3.

Helmer, Victoria Jane; Second Secretary FCO since July 2003; Born 19/10/75; FCO 1998; Full-Time Language Training 1999; Full-Time Language Training Cairo 2000; Second Secretary (Political) Amman 2001; Band C4.

Hemmings, Kathryn Louise; FCO since July 2003; Born 20/08/70; FCO 1991; New York (UKMIS) 1993; FCO 1996; Nairobi 1999; SUPL 1999; On loan to No.10 Downing Street 2002; Band B3.

Henderson, Andrew David Forbes; Consul-General São Paulo since September 2003; Born 12/07/52; FCO 1971; Latin America Floater 1975; Rio de Janeiro 1977; Second Secretary (Chancery) Oslo 1980; APS/Minister of State FCO 1985; Consul New York (CG) 1987; First Secretary Washington 1988; Consul and Deputy Head of Mission Luanda 1992; Cairo 1994; Head of Parliamentary Relations Department FCO 1998; Consul-General Jedda 2000; m 1987 Julia Margaret King (2d 1988, 1990).

Henderson, Christopher George; Vice-Consul (Commercial) Sydney since June 2004; Born 23/04/66; Metropolitan Police Office (Civil Staff) 1987; FCO 1990; Lilongwe 1993; FCO 1996; On T/D (Overseas) 1997 - 1999; Third later Second Secretary FCO 1999; Band C4.

Henderson, Matthew Magnus Murray; First Secretary FCO since March 1996; Born 19/07/60; Second Secretary FCO 1986; Second later First Secretary BTC Hong Kong 1988; First Secretary FCO 1990; First Secretary (External/Press) Peking 1992; Band D6.

Henderson, William Robert, LVO (1988); Director (Middle East/Africa), British Trade International since October 2001; Born 07/11/47; DSAO later FCO 1965; Moscow 1970; Sana'a 1971; Lima 1972; Rio de Janeiro 1973; FCO 1976; MECAS 1977; Dubai 1978; Second Secretary 1980; FCO

1983; First Secretary (Information) Madrid 1985; First Secretary FCO 1989; Deputy Head of Mission Abu Dhabi 1992; First Secretary FCO 1996; m 1969 Carol Mary Smith (1d 1973; 1s 1976).

Hendry, Carol Anne Walls; FCO since October 2002; Born 07/12/66; FCO 1985; Brussels (UKREP) 1987; Tokyo 1990; World Wide Floater Duties 1993; FCO 1995; On loan to the DTI 1999; FCO 2001; SUPL 2002; Band C4; ptnr, Roy Ireland (1s 2002).

Hendry, Ian Duncan, CMG (1996); Deputy Legal Adviser FCO since October 1999; Born 02/04/48; Assistant Legal Adviser FCO 1971; First Secretary (Legal Adviser) BMG Berlin 1982; Assistant Legal Adviser, later Legal Counsellor FCO 1986; Counsellor (Legal Adviser) Brussels (UKREP) 1991; Legal Counsellor FCO 1995; m (1) 1973 Elizabeth Anne Southall (1d 1975; 1s 1977); (2) 1991 Sally Annabel Hill.

Hennessy, Alexandra Mary (née Wintour); SUPL since September 2000; Born 25/03/66; Office of Fair Trading 1985; FCO 1987; New York (UKMIS) 1988; Vienna 1991; FCO 1995; SUPL 1996; T/D The Hague 2000; Band A2; m 1993 Anthony John Hennessy (1d 1996).

Hennessy, Anthony John; First Secretary (Commercial) The Hague since June 2000; Born 01/02/55; FCO 1980; Singapore 1981; FCO 1985; Second Secretary (Commercial) Riyadh 1987; Second Secretary (UN/UNIDO) Vienna (UKMIS) 1991; First Secretary FCO 1995; Band C5; m 1993 Alexandra Mary Wintour (1d 1996).

Henry, Elaine Monica; Hanoi since August 2001; Born 11/09/69; FCO 1989; New Delhi 1993; Maputo 1997; FCO 1999; T/D La Paz 2000; FCO 2001; Band B3; (1d 1991).

Henry, Mark; FCO since September 2003; Born 09/03/78; Band C4.

Hentley, Michael Joseph; Tristan da Cunha since April 2004; Born 13/07/46; CRO 1964; DSAO 1965; Benghazi 1969; Moscow 1972; Lagos 1973; Kaduna 1976; FCO 1978; Second Secretary (Commercial) Port of Spain 1982; Second Secretary FCO 1985; First Secretary (COCOM) Paris 1987; Deputy Head of Mission Dakar 1992; First Secretary FCO 1995; First Secretary and Consul Seoul 1999; First Secretary (Consular) Lagos 2002; m 1969 Janice Paterson (1s 1971; 2d 1973, 1979).

Herbert, David; Consul-General Madrid since July 2003; Born 13/07/47; CO 1966; Algiers 1969; Baghdad 1970; Tananarivo 1971; FCO 1974; Second Secretary Luxembourg 1977; Second Secretary (Commercial) Prague 1981; First Secretary FCO 1985; Consul (Commercial) Montreal 1988; First Secretary (Political/Economic) Abuja 1993; First Secretary FCO 1995; Deputy Head of Mission Luxembourg 1998; Full-Time Language Training (Spanish) 2002; m 1970 Maureen Violet Edmundson (2d 1976, 1978).

Herd, Theresa Ann; FCO since February 2002; Born 24/10/54; FCO 1972; Resigned 1974; Reinstated 1980; Lilongwe 1981; FCO 1984; Pretoria 1986; Cape Town 1987; LA/Caribbean Floater 1989; FCO 1991; Full-Time Language Training 1994; Luanda 1995; Second Secretary FCO 1996; Full-Time Language Training 1999; Deputy Head of Mission Kinshasa 1999; Band C4.

Heseltine, Lavinia Pauline; SUPL since July 2004; FCO 1974; Brussels 1975; Moscow 1979; Canberra 1981; Khartoum 1984; Lagos 1988; Dhaka 1992; SUPL 1995; FCO 1998; Peking 2000; Lagos 2002; Band B3; m 1990 Barry Heseltine.

Heseltine, Robert Andrew; ECO Casablanca since December 2002; Born 18/11/73; MAFF 1996-97; FCO 1997; St Petersburg 2000; Full-Time Language Training (French) 2002; Band B3.

Hetherington, Martin Duncan; FCO since July 2003; Born 22/02/74; DETR 1997; FCO 1998; T/D Second Secretary (Political) Islamabad 2002.

Hewer, Susan Jane; Floater Duties since April 2001; Born 18/09/61; FCO 1980; Washington 1982; FCO 1985; New Delhi 1985; Strasbourg (UKDEL) 1989; Kuwait 1991; FCO 1995; New York (UKMIS) 1997; Band B3.

Hewitt, Norman; FCO since January 1989; Born 12/09/46; FCO 1981; Washington 1985; Band C4; m 1968 Catherine Georgina Sahadeo (1s 1975; 2d 1970, 1983).

Heyn, Andrew Richard; FCO since August 2000; Born 14/01/62; DTI 1985 - 89; Second Secretary FCO 1989; Second Secretary (Chancery) Caracas 1991; First Secretary FCO 1994; First Secretary (Political) Lisbon 1996; m 1988 Jane Carmel (1d 1994).

Hickey, Katherine (née Blair); Third Secretary (Political) Ottawa since December 2002; Born 11/02/69; FCO 1988; Tokyo 1989; Colombo 1992; Peking 1993; Full-Time Language Training FCO 1997; Third Secretary (Vice-Consul/ECO) Tokyo 1998; Band B3; m 2000 Sean Patrick Hickey.

Hickey, Patricia Helen; FCO since September 1997; FCO 1975; Bangkok 1977; FCO 1979; Canberra 1981; FCO 1984; New York 1986; Berlin 1988; FCO 1991; Hong Kong 1995; Band C5.

Hickey, Stephen Benedict; Brussels (UKREP) since November 2003; Born 07/06/79; FCO 2001; Band C4.

Hicking, Nicola Jane (née Boyles); FCO since September 2002; Born 28/07/63; FCO 1983; Brasilia 1985; Lagos 1987; FCO 1988; Montevideo 1999; Band A2; m 1992 Robert Hicking (2s 1994, 1996).

Hicks, Colin Michael, MBE (2002); Third Secretary (Chancery) Colombo since November 2002; Born 04/03/74; MAFF 1993-96; FCO 1996; Dublin 1997; Islamabad 2001; Band B3; m 1998 (1s 1999).

Hickson, Philip John; FCO since February 1998; Born 21/03/65; FCO 1984; Kingston 1986; Floater Duties 1990; Tehran 1993; New Delhi 1996; Band C4; m 1992 Amanda Ruth Woolham (2s 1993, 1995).

Higginbottom, Sandra Patricia (née Wright); SUPL since October 2003; Born 03/03/65; FCO 1984; Brussels 1986; Dhaka 1989; FCO 1992; Tunis 1997; Lagos 2000; Band B3; m (1) 1989 Robert Freeman Walker (diss); (2) 1997 Andrew Higginbottom (1s 1996).

Higgins, Gillian (née Newbury); SUPL since July 2002; Born 23/03/63; FCO 1987; Budapest 1989; FCO 1991; Grand Cayman 1995; SUPL 1997; Grand Cayman 1997; FCO 1999; New York (UKMIS) 2002; Band B3; m 1995 Russell Mark Higgins (2d 1997, 2002).

Higham, Andrew Bolton; Cairo since November 2002; Born 28/10/59; FCO 1982; Singapore 1986; FCO 1988; Government Secretary Hong Kong 1993; FCO 1997; Band C4; m 1989 Veronica Jane Nazareth (1d 1990; 1s 1993).

Hildersley, Sarah Jane; On loan to the DTI since November 2002; Born 30/05/68; FCO 1987; Brussels (UKDEL NATO) 1988; FCO 1989; Third Secretary (Management) JMO Brussels 1990; Floater Duties 1991; FCO 1994; Deputy Head of Mission Santo Domingo 1998; SUPL 2002; Band C4; (1s 1996).

Hill, Charles Edward; First Secretary FCO since September 2000; Born 31/03/63; FCO 1990; Third Secretary (Chancery) Doha 1993; Deputy Head of Mission Almaty 1997; Band D6; m 1996 Suzanne Victoria Stock.

Hill, Duncan N; First Secretary (Trade & Investment) Santiago since October 2004; Born 08/12/68; FCO 1989; Berlin 1991; Full-Time Language Training 1994; Rio de Janeiro 1995; FCO 1997; Shanghai 2000; FCO 2002; T/D Basra 2004; Band C5; m 1992 Lisa Pegram (1d 2002).

Hill, Jeremy John Leonard; FCO since September 2002; Born 03/05/57; FCO 1975; SOAS 1978; Tokyo 1979; Jakarta 1982; FCO 1986; Harare 1990; Second Secretary FCO 1994; Sana'a 1996; Second Secretary (Commercial) Seoul 1998; m 1985 Roosnadia (Nana) Roesno (1s 1990; 1d 1992).

Hill, Kristina Maria; Nicosia since October 2003; Born 10/04/72; FCO 1999; Third Secretary (External Relations) Brussels (UKREP) 2000; Second Secretary FCO 2003; Band C4.

Hill, Martin Henry Paul; Counsellor (Trade and Investmentl) Bangkok since February 2002; Born 17/05/61; Ministry of Agriculture, Fisheries and Food 1983; Privy Council Office 1985; MAFF 1986; First Secretary Bonn 1993; FCO 1996; Deputy High Commissioner Colombo 1998; m 1985 Kim Lydyard (3d 1992, 1993, 1996).

Hill, Michael Thomas; High Commissioner Vila since November 2000; Born 02/01/45; FO 1963; New York (UKMIS) 1966; Vientiane 1969;

Kaduna 1970; FCO 1974; T/D Sana'a 1975; Second Secretary, DHM and Vice-Consul Ulaanbaatar 1978; Second Secretary (Cons/Immig/Aid) Port of Spain 1981; Second later First Secretary FCO 1985; Assistant to Deputy Governor Gibraltar 1988; First Secretary (Aid) Nairobi 1993; First Secretary FCO 1997; m 1977 Elizabeth Louise Carden (3s 1981, 1988, 1990; 1d 1983).

Hill, Peter Jeremy Oldham; HM Ambassador Sofia since January 2004; Born 17/04/54; FCO 1982; First Secretary (Legal Adviser) Bonn 1987; On loan to the Law Officers' Department 1991; Legal Counsellor Brussels (UKREP) 1995; Counsellor FCO 1999; HM Ambassador Vilnius 2001; m 1981 Katharine Hearn (1d 1987; 1s 1989).

Hill, Ruth; Copenhagen since April 2003; Born 30/06/71; FCO 2001; Band A2.

Hill, Sarah Margaret; First Secretary FCO since August 2000; Born 18/09/72; FCO 1995; Third Secretary (Aid) Belgrade 1996; Second Secretary (Political) Buenos Aires 1997; Band D6.

Hill, Simon Robert; SUPL since October 2000; Born 18/03/67; FCO 1994; Brussels 1996; FCO 1999; Band B3; m 1998 Carina Megia Abarca.

Hill, Steven John; First Secretary (Political) Washington since August 2001; Born 07/04/62; FCO 1984; Second Secretary (UNIDO/UN) Vienna (UKMIS) 1988; Second later First Secretary FCO 1990; First Secretary New York (UKMIS) 1996; First Secretary FCO 1999; Band D6; m 1998 Geraldine Steele (2d 1995, 2001; 1s 1998).

Hill, Suzanne Victoria (née Stock), MBE (2003); Second Secretary FCO since August 2000; Born 01/12/65; Home Office 1988-91; FCO 1991; T/D Accra 1993; Doha 1994; Third Secretary (Political/Aid) Almaty 1997; SUPL 1999; Band C4; m 1996 Charles Edward Hill.

Hillman, John; Deputy High Commissioner Valletta since July 2002; Born 30/05/48; FO (later FCO) 1967; Dhaka 1971; Budapest 1974; Calcutta 1975; Second Secretary (Commercial) Dublin 1979; Second Secretary FCO 1983; First Secretary and Consul Cairo 1988; Deputy Consul-General Sydney 1991; First Secretary FCO 1997; m 1978 Pushp Kanta Sahney (1d 1981).

Hilton, Christopher Charles Donald; FCO since November 2002; Born 07/11/69; FCO 1988; Budapest 1991; World Wide Floater Duties 1994; FCO 1997; Third Secretary (Chancery) Port of Spain 1999; Band C4.

Hilton, Margaret; FCO since September 1995; Born 09/08/53; FCO 1990; Strasbourg 1993; Band A2.

Hilton, Michael Anthony; FCO since October 1996; Born 07/03/50; Department of Employment 1973; FCO 1973; Manchester Business School 1975; Frankfurt 1977; FCO 1979; Second Secretary Ulaanbaatar 1981; Second later First Secretary FCO 1983; First Secretary (Dev/Comm)

Kathmandu 1987; Hanoi 1990; First Secretary (Commercial) Tehran 1992; m 1976 Janet Elizabeth Tyler.

Himmer, Melanie (née Read-Ward); SUPL since December 1997; Born 16/05/68; FCO 1989; Warsaw 1991; Tashkent 1994; Band B3; m 1993 Alan Keith Himmer.

Hinchley, Carol Ruth; Full-Time Language Training since March 2004; Born 09/04/59; FCO 1981; Gaborone 1983; Stockholm 1987; Second Secretary FCO 1991; Second Secretary (Chancery) Wellington 1994; FCO 1999.

Hinchon, David Alan; Third Secretary (Political) Almaty since September 2002; Born 15/04/67; FCO 2000; Band B3; m 2001 Anna Taylor (2s 1997, 1999).

Hines, Trevor John; First Secretary (Commercial) Tripoli since September 2004; Born 10/11/60; FCO 1979; Floater Duties 1982; Third Secretary (Consular) Jedda 1984; Riyadh 1985; FCO 1987; Third Secretary (Man/Cons) Belmopan 1990; Second Secretary (Commercial) Mexico 1995; Secondment to Fire Industry, 2000; On loan to British Trade International 2000; T/D First Secretary (Commercial) Bogotá 2002; On loan to Interchange-Partnership Sourcing Ltd. 2002; HLT 2004; Band C5; m 1985 Sandra Bradley (1s 1992; 1d 1994).

Hiscock, Stephen John; High Commissioner Georgetown and Ambassador Paramaribo since August 2002; Born 16/06/46; Inland Revenue 1963; FO 1965; Kuala Lumpur 1968; Lusaka 1972; FCO 1976; Second Secretary 1977; Islamabad 1978; First Secretary (Comm/Inf) Seoul 1982; First Secretary FCO 1986; Deputy High Commissioner Georgetown 1988; First Secretary FCO 1993; Consul-General Brisbane 1997; m (1) (diss 1982) (2s 1967, 1971); (2) 1983 Denise Mary Forster (1d 1986; 2s 1989, 1991).

Hitchens, Timothy Mark; Head of Africa Department (Equatorial), FCO since May 2003; Born 07/05/62; FCO 1983; Language Training Tokyo 1985; Second Secretary Tokyo 1986; Second later First Secretary FCO 1989; Private Secretary to the Minister of State 1991; First Secretary (Political/Info) Islamabad 1994; FCO 1997; On secondment to Buckingham Palace 1999; m 1985 Sara Kubra Husain (1d 1991; 1s 1993).

Ho, David Tat Lun; Stockholm since April 2003; Born 05/05/61; Home Civil Service 1989-1998; FCO 1998; Brussels (UKDEL NATO) 1999; Band A2.

Ho, Wai-Kit; FCO since November 2003; Born 25/11/75; Band B3.

Hoar, Gareth Keith; First Secretary (Commercial) Beijing since February 2002; Born 23/06/65; FCO 1984; Peking 1986; Santiago 1989; Washington 1991; FCO 1994; Language Training Guangzhou 1998; Consul (Economic) Guangzhou 1999; m 2000 Rebecca Xie.

Hoare, Michael John Antony; FCO since October 2003; Born 30/11/76; Band C4.

Hobart, Edward Andrew Beauchamp; Kuala Lumpur since May 2003; Born 30/11/71; FCO 1993; Third later Second Secretary Havana 1995; First Secretary FCO 1998; Band D7; m 1999 Suzanna Louise Massey (1s 2003).

Hobbs, Jeremy Alexander; First Secretary (Chancery) Mexico City since May 2003; Born 08/02/61; Senior Research Officer FCO 1991; Second Secretary (Political/Technical Co-operation) Bogotá 1995; Principal Research Officer FCO 1999; Band D6; m 1983 Ana Maria Erndira (1s 1990; 1d 1994).

Hodge, Christopher Martin; Brussels since June 2004; Born 29/08/73; MOD 1996; UK Delegation to NATO 1998; FCO 2000; Second Secretary (Political) Sana'a 2002; FCO 2003; Band D6; m 2000 Melanie Jean (1s 2002).

Hodges, Ian Foyle; Vice-Consul Jedda since April 2001; Born 30/10/67; FCO 1987; Budapest 1989; Paris 1990; FCO 1994; Third Secretary (Consular) Karachi 1994; Third Secretary FCO 1994; Third Secretary (Management) and Vice-Consul Tehran 1997; m 1991 Patricia Paule Andre Seguin (1s 1992; 1d 1993).

Hodges, Jeremy Andrew; FCO since April 2003; Born 16/07/67; FCO 1988; Floater Duties 1990; Peking 1992; Karachi 1994; Full-Time Language Training FCO 1998; Bucharest 1998; m 1992 Adele Bushnell.

Hodgetts, Susan Jacqueline; Second later First Secretary FCO since January 1995; Born 07/11/48; DSAO (later FCO) 1967; Lagos 1970; Warsaw 1973; Kathmandu 1973; Montevideo 1975; Madrid 1975; FCO 1978; Bridgetown 1981; FCO 1985; Vice-Consul Bucharest 1990; HM Consul Algiers 1993; Band D6.

Hodgson, Allen Richard; Second Secretary (Political) Amman since October 2003; Born 08/02/60; FCO 1977; Geneva (UKMIS) 1991; FCO 1995; Second Secretary (Regional Affairs) Cairo 1998; Second Secretary FCO 2001; Band C4; m 1989 Sally Maureen Cole-Hamilton (1d 1993; 1s 1997).

Hodgson, George Kenneth; First Secretary (Management) Manila since February 2001; Born 15/02/49; FCO 1969; Lagos 1971; Belgrade 1974; Berlin CG 1975; Reykjavik 1976; Karachi 1977; FCO 1979; DHSS 1980-84; FCO 1984; Colombo 1985; Luxembourg 1989; Second Secretary FCO 1992; Second Secretary Ulaanbaatar 1995; Second later First Secretary (Management) Nicosia 1997; m 1971 Jill Taylor (1s 1975; 2d 1978, 1980).

Hogarth, Philip; Consul-General Bilbao since August 2003; Born 10/05/55; FCO 1976; Damascus 1978; Accra 1982; FCO 1984; Tokyo 1988; Paris 1991; Second Secretary FCO 1995; Deputy Head of Mission/Consul La Paz 2000; Band C4; m 1978 Monique Marie Therese Morand.

Hogg, Rachel Ann; Vienna since January 2002; Born 20/05/77; FCO 2000; Band A2.

Hoggard, Robin Richard; FCO since September 2003; Born 26/11/56; FCO 1982; Language Training SOAS 1983; Kamakura 1984; Second later First Secretary (Commercial) then (Economic) Tokyo 1985; First Secretary FCO 1989; On loan to DTI 1991; First Secretary (Political) Brussels (UKDEL NATO/UKDEL WEU) 1994; Counsellor (Management/Con) Tokyo 1998; m 1988 Tonoko Komuro (1s 1995).

Hogger, Henry George; FCO since August 2003; Born 09/11/48; Third Secretary FCO 1969; MECAS 1971; Aden 1972; Second Secretary Caracas 1972; Second later First Secretary Kuwait 1975; FCO 1978; First Secretary, Head of Chancery and Consul Abu Dhabi 1982; FCO 1986; Counsellor and Head of Chancery Amman 1989; High Commissioner Windhoek 1992; Counsellor FCO 1996; HM Ambassador Damascus 2000; m 1972 Fiona Jane McNabb (2d 1979, 1982; 2s 1984).

Hogwood, Jonathan Felix; Second Secretary British Trade International since June 1998; Born 24/07/52; FCO 1971; Warsaw 1974; Islamabad 1975; Luanda 1978; FCO 1981; Dhaka 1986; Tokyo 1989; FCO 1992; SUPL 1995; Second Secretary (Commercial) Nairobi 1996; m 1978 Susan Elizabeth Farmer.

Hogwood, Susan Elizabeth (née Farmer), OBE (2003), MBE (1981); HM Ambassador Kigali since July 2001; Born 27/05/52; FCO 1971; Islamabad 1974; SUPL 1978; Second Secretary FCO 1982; Second Secretary (Aid) Dhaka 1986; Second later First Secretary (Consular) Tokyo 1989; First Secretary FCO 1992; First Secretary (Humanitarian) Nairobi 1994; FCO 1998; m 1978 Jonathan Felix Hogwood.

Holbrook, Andy David; FCO since July 2003; Born 18/06/74; Band B3; ptnr, Donna Michelle Hart.

Holder, Donald John; HM Consul Athens since October 2000; Born 16/08/50; FCO 1976; Bonn 1978; Islamabad 1981; FCO 1984; Auckland 1985; BMG Berlin 1987; FCO 1988; Second Secretary (Commercial) Bahrain 1990; Language Training 1994; Second Secretary (Info/Visits) Warsaw 1995; Consul (Immigration/Passports) Düsseldorf 1996.

Holdich, Patrick Godfrey Hungerford; FCO since September 1997; Born 19/09/56; Senior Research Officer; FCO 1985; Principal Research Officer 1990; First Secretary (Chancery) Ottawa 1992; m 1987 Ailsa Elizabeth Beaton (diss 1992).

Holifield, Martin; Sarajevo since September 2002; Born 08/09/61; FCO 1979; Islamabad 1986; FCO 1989; Kuwait 1991; FCO 1995; Luanda 1997; FCO 2001; Band B3; m (1) 1985 Morag Catherine Fraser (diss 1995); (2) 1996 Anna Maria Sandelin (1s 1998; 1d 2001).

Hollamby, David James; Governor St Helena, Ascension Island and Tristan da Cunha since June 1999; Born 19/05/45; CO 1961; DSAO 1964; Beirut 1967; Latin America Floater 1970; Asunción 1972; Second Secretary FCO 1975; Vice-Consul (Commercial) BTDO New York 1978; Consul (Commercial) Dallas 1983; First Secretary FCO 1986; First Secretary Rome 1990; First Secretary FCO 1994; m 1971 Maria Helena Guzman (2 step s 1961, 1964).

Holland, Henry Robert Cumber; Deputy Head of Mission Bridgetown since October 2002; Born 25/11/57; FCO 1984; Second Secretary (Chancery) Nairobi 1986; First Secretary FCO 1989; First Secretary (Political/Information) Canberra 1993; First Secretary FCO 1997; m 1983 Anne Elizabeth Wardle (2s 1987, 1990; 1d 1988).

Holland, Neil R; FCO since 2001; Born 07/08/71; Band D6; m 2000 (1d 2002).

Holland, Patricia Anne (Tricia); Counsellor on secondment to the European Commission since September 2002; Born 02/04/64; FCO 1986; Third Secretary (Chancery) Prague 1988; Second later First Secretary FCO 1989; First Secretary (Finance) New York (UKMIS) 1993; SUPL 1997; First Secretary (EU Affairs) Paris 1998; SUPL 2001; m 1997 Paul Thomas Arkwright (1d 1999; 1s 2001).

Holland, Stephen Peter; First Secretary (Internal) New Delhi since December 2000; Born 31/08/65; FCO 1999; Band D6; m Judith Kent.

Hollis, Ian Malcolm; Sofia since December 2003; Born 16/12/70; FCO 1989; Bonn 1994; Lisbon 1997; FCO 2000; Band B3; m 1997.

Holloway, Michael John; First Secretary Dhaka since July 2002; Born 14/01/57; FCO 1976; Dubai 1978; Bucharest 1979; Africa/Middle East Floater 1981; Mexico City 1983; FCO 1984; Barcelona 1988; FCO 1991; Second Secretary (Political/Information/Aid) Mexico City 1994; Deputy Consul-General Rio de Janeiro 1998.

Hollywood, Jane Christina Emma; FCO since June 2002; Born 07/03/66; FCO 1991; Second Secretary (Political) The Hague 1998; Band C4.

Holmes, Alan Thomas; Full-Time Language Training since December 2003; Born 25/09/53; FCO 1977; Brussels (UKDEL NATO) 1980; FCO 1982; Bridgetown 1986; Cairo 1989; FCO 1992; Full-Time Language Training 1996; Moscow 1997; FCO 1998; Second Secretary Sarajevo 2000; Band C4; m 1980 Helen Hook.

Holmes, Helen (née Hook); Second Secretary FCO since December 1998; Born 26/05/51; Department of Employment and Productivity 1969; FCO 1969; Bangkok 1973; Lagos 1975; FCO 1976; SUPL 1980; FCO 1982; Bridgetown 1986; Cairo 1989; FCO 1992; Moscow 1998; m 1980 Alan Thomas Holmes.

Holmes, John Dominic; FCO since May 1994; Born 18/08/59; Inland Revenue 1977; FCO 1978;

Paris 1984; FCO 1987; Warsaw 1989; The Hague 1991; Band C4.

Holmes, Sir John Eaton, GCVO (2004), KBE (1999), CVO (1998), CMG (1997); HM Ambassador Paris since October 2001; Born 29/04/51; Third Secretary FCO 1973; Language Training 1975; Third Secretary Moscow 1976; Second later First Secretary FCO 1978; First Secretary (Economic) Paris 1984; First Secretary FCO 1987; Counsellor 1989; On secondment to the De La Rue Company 1989; Counsellor and Head of Chancery (later Counsellor (Econ/Comm) New Delhi 1991; Head of European Union Department (External) FCO 1995; Private Secretary to the Prime Minister for Overseas Affairs 1996; Principal Private Secretary to the Prime Minister 1997; HM Ambassador Lisbon 1999; m 1976 Margaret Penelope Morris (3d 1981, 1982, 1985).

Holmes, Michael, MVO (1991); First Secretary (Management) New Delhi since October 2001; Born 03/04/54; FCO 1973; Belmopan 1975; Rio de Janeiro 1978; Baghdad 1981; FCO 1985; Third Secretary Harare 1988; Second Secretary (Cons/Comm) Melbourne 1992; Second Secretary later Consul (Comm) Casablanca 1994; FCO 1998; m 1980 Jennifer Margaret Lesley Pike (1d 1982; 1s 1985).

Holmes, Paul Barry; FCO since 1997; Born 15/11/54; FCO 1972; Warsaw 1978; Bonn 1980; FCO 1982; Third Secretary Accra 1986; Addis Ababa 1990; FCO 1993; Hong Kong 1995; Band C5; m (1) 1975 Elaine Down (diss) (2s 1981, 1983); (2) 1988 Sarah Penelope Briggs (1d 1989; 1s 1991).

Holmes, Timothy Charles; Consul-General Sydney since April 2004; Born 26/04/51; Third Secretary FCO 1974; Language Training SOAS 1975; Language Training Tokyo 1976; Second later First Secretary Tokyo 1977; On loan to the DOT 1981; First Secretary FCO 1983; First Secretary (Chancery) Islamabad 1986; First Secretary FCO 1990; Deputy Head of Mission and Counsellor (Commercial/Economic) Seoul 1994; Deputy Head of Mission and Consul-General The Hague 1997; On loan to the DTI 2002; m 1973 Anna-Carin Magnusson (1s 1977; 1d 1988).

Holt, Denise Mary (née Mills), CMG (2002); HM Ambassador Mexico City since August 2002; Born 01/10/49; Research Analyst FCO 1970; First Secretary (Political) Dublin 1984; SUPL 1987; FCO 1988; SUPL 1990; First Secretary (Political) Brasilia 1991; Deputy Head of Eastern Department FCO 1993; SUPL 1994; Deputy Director Personnel Management FCO 1996; Counsellor and Deputy Head of Mission Dublin 1998; Director (Personnel Command) FCO 1999; m 1987 David Holt (1s 1987).

Holt, Sean Christopher Eric, OBE (1999); Counsellor Freetown since November 2001; Born 18/12/49; HM Armed Forces (Army) 1968-78; FCO 1978; Second Secretary Havana 1979; First Secretary FCO 1980; Athens 1982; First Secretary

FCO 1984; First Secretary (Chancery) Khartoum 1987; First Secretary FCO 1990; First Secretary (Political) Accra 1991; First Secretary FCO 1994; Counsellor Bogotá 1995; Counsellor Luanda 1999; m (1) 1973 Jennifer Patricia Trevaskis (diss 1987) (1s 1974; 1d 1976); (2) 1987 Joyce Amanda Anderson (diss 1994); (3) 1999 Johanna Antonia Maria Rutten.

Homer, Richard David; Budapest since January 2001; Born 24/12/72; FCO 1992; Stockholm 1995; FCO 1997; Washington 1997; Band B3.

Honey, Sophie Margaret; First Secretary Harare since October 2001; Born 18/11/72; FCO 1999; Cabinet Office 2000; Band D6.

Hook, Neil Kenneth, MVO (1983); Consul-General Osaka since October 2001; Born 24/04/45; FCO 1968; Moscow 1971; FCO 1972; Language Training Sheffield University 1974; Tokyo 1975; Second Secretary (Aid) Dhaka 1980; First Secretary FCO 1984; On loan to DTI 1986; First Secretary (Commercial) Tokyo 1987; First Secretary FCO 1992; HM Ambassador Ashgabat 1995; High Commissioner Mbabane 1999; m 1973 Pauline Ann Hamilton (1d 1975; 1s 1977).

Hopkins, Kathleen Elizabeth; Bratislava since March 2003; FCO 1994; Vienna 1996; Language Training 1999; Paris 1999; Band A2.

Hopkins, Melanie; FCO since October 2002; Born 09/08/73; Band C4.

Hopkinson, Celia Lois; FCO since September 1995; Born 09/10/59; FCO 1979; New York (UKMIS) 1982; Sofia 1984; Paris 1986; FCO 1988; Lusaka 1992; Band B3.

Hopton, Nicholas Dunster; Counsellor (EU) Paris since July 2003; Born 08/10/65; FCO 1989; Second Secretary (Political/Information) Rabat 1991; First Secretary FCO 1995; First Secretary Rome 2000; m 1993 Maria Alejandra Echenique (2d 1998, 2000; 2s 2002, 2003).

Horder, Rebekah Elizabeth; FCO since September 2003; Born 28/09/79; Band B3.

Horine, Fern Marion; Strasbourg since September 2003; Born 28/07/69; FCO 1987; Vienna (UKDEL) 1990; FCO 1995; On loan to the DTI 1998; Second Secretary (Political) Baku 2000; Band C4.

Horne, Gordon; DMO Cairo since October 2002; Born 05/12/66; FCO 1986; Riyadh 1988; New York (UKMIS) 1992; FCO 1994; MO/VC/ECO Riga 1998; Band B3; m 1989 Susan Lisa Berry (2s 1991, 1993).

Horner, Katharine Sarah Julia; On loan to the Cabinet Office since May 2002; Born 15/08/52; FCO 1980; Moscow 1985; Senior Research Officer FCO 1987; PRO 1996; First Secretary (Political) (Internal) Moscow 1997; FCO 2000.

Horner, Simon; Second Secretary (Finance) New York (UKMIS) since June 2002; Born 10/12/69; DHSS 1987; FCO 1988; Nassau 1991; Floater Duties 1993; FCO 1995; Canberra 1998; Band C4;

m 1995 Katharine Jean Gallager (1d1998; 1s 2000).

Horton-Jones, Sarah Caroline; Second Secretary FCO since July 1998; Born 13/10/68; Lord Chancellor's Department 1991-93; FCO 1993; Second Secretary (Political) The Hague 1996.

Hoskin, Thomas David; FCO since March 2003; Born 08/12/75; FCO 1998; Second later First Secretary Dublin 1999; Band D6.

Hosking, Simon Paul; FCO since June 2004; Born 15/06/71; FCO 1993; Second Secretary Santiago 1997; First Secretary FCO 1999; First Secretary (Science and Technology) New Delhi 2001; Band D6; m 1995 Allison Jane Christou (2d 1998, 1999; 1s 2001).

House, Greg Stewart; FCO since April 2001; Born 03/06/68; FCO 1988; Lilongwe 1991; Lagos 1995; Floater Duties 1999; Band B3.

Houston, Sharon (Sher) Linda; SUPL since September 2002; Born 14/06/68; FCO 1989; Bridgetown 1991; Brussels (UKREP) 1995; Islamabad 1998; Band B3; m 1993 Steve Giovanni Campbell (diss 1997) (1s 1996).

Howard, (Charles Andrew) Paul; Second later First Secretary FCOS since November 1999; Born 23/09/60; FCO 1983; New Delhi 1985; Third Secretary Bridgetown 1989; FCO 1992; Third Secretary (Consular) Islamabad 1996; FCOS 1997; m 1984 Alayne Anne Whitehouse (2s 1987, 1988).

Howard, Alayne Anne (née Whitehouse); First Secretary FCOS since April 2000; Born 04/06/63; FCO 1982; New Delhi 1985; Third Secretary (Consular) Bridgetown 1989; SUPL 1992; Second Secretary FCO 1993; Second Secretary (Immigration) Islamabad 1996; FCOS 1997; Band C5; m 1984 Paul Howard (2s 1987, 1988).

Howard, Sarah Catherine (née Sullivan); Dublin since August 2003; Born 05/11/68; FCO 1987; Kingston 1989; Tehran 1993; FCO 1995; Harare 1998; Band B3; m 1989 Simon James Howard.

Howarth, Stephen Frederick; UK Representative with the Personal rank of Ambassador, to the Council of Europe at Strasbourg since March 2003; Born 25/02/47; FCO 1966; Vice-Consul Rabat 1971; Third later Second Secretary Washington 1975; Second later First Secretary FCO 1980; Seconded to ENA Paris 1982; First Secretary FCO 1984; Deputy Head of Mission Dakar 1984; First Secretary FCO 1988; Counsellor and Deputy Head of PUSD 1990; Head of Consular Department later Division 1992; Minister Paris 1997; m 1966 Jennifer Mary Chrissop (2d 1966, 1970; 1s 1974).

Howden, Yvonne Catherine Helen; Floater Duties since December 2003; Born 06/03/73; FCO 1997; Luanda 1998; FCO 1999; Prague 2000; Band B3.

Howe-Jones, Vanessa Jane; First Secretary (Political) New York (UKMIS) since September 2001; Born 23/06/65; FCO 1991; Full-Time Language Training 1992; Second Secretary

Budapest (KHF) 1993; First Secretary FCO 1996; T/D Brussels (UKREP) 2000.

Howel, Iwan Gruffydd; SUPL since October 2002; Born 05/01/68; FCO 1988; Washington 1991; Brasilia 1994; Beijing 1999; Band B3.

Howells, Julie (née Satchell); SUPL since July 2001; Born 03/06/64; FCO 1982; Brussels (UKDEL NATO) 1986; Seoul 1991; Dar es Salaam 1996; Band B3; m 1991 David Howells.

Howitt, Derrick; Istanbul since May 1999; Born 14/02/43; Royal Navy 1958 - 83; Moscow 1983; Paris 1985; Singapore 1988; Colombo 1991; Floater Duties 1995; Band B3; m 1966 Averil E Rose (1d 1968; 1s 1972).

Howlett, David John; Senior Principal Research Officer FCO since June 1982; Born 17/01/55; m 1979 Bridget Mary de Boer.

Howlett, Keith Raymond; FCO since 1998; Born 29/03/50; FCO 1968; Moscow 1980; FCO 1982; Tokyo 1986; Second Secretary FCO 1989; Second Secretary Caracas 1994; Band D6; m (1) (diss 1998); (2) 1998 Natasha Mota Hurtado (1 step d 1996, 1d 2002; 1s 2001).

Huckle, Alan Edden; Governor Anguilla since May 2004; Born 15/06/48; Civil Service Department 1971; On loan to Northern Ireland Office 1974; Civil Service Department 1975; On loan to Northern Ireland Office 1978; First Secretary FCO 1980; Executive Director British Information Services New York 1983; Head of Chancery Manila 1987; First Secretary FCO 1990; Counsellor and Deputy Head of Delegation Vienna (UKDEL CSCE) 1992; Head of Dependent Territories Regional Secretariat Bridgetown 1996; Head of OSCE/Council of Europe Department FCO 1998; Head of Overseas Territories Department FCO 2001; m 1973 Helen Myra Gibson (1s 1981; 1d 1985).

Huckle, Steven Allan; First Secretary Moscow since August 2000; Born 24/10/64; FCO 1981; Brussels (UKREP) 1989; FCO 1992; Sofia 1994; FCO 1997; Band C5; m 1987 Alison Elaine Porter (1s 1990; 1d 1991).

Hudman, Anne (née Lister); SUPL since December 2002; Born 01/09/62; FCO 1987; Helsinki 1989; FCO 1992; Bonn 1993; St Petersburg 1996; Third Secretary (Commercial) Vienna Embassy 1999; FCO 2002; Band B3; m 1991 Roger Grenville Hudman.

Hudson, James Alexander; Sarajevo since November 2003; Born 14/01/72; FCO 1994; Havana 1996; FCO 1998; Tirana 1999; T/D Budapest 2000; T/D Skopje 2000; St Petersburg 2000; Montserrat 2002; Band B3; m 1996 Sally Barrett (diss 1997) (1d 1995).

Huggins, Elaine Anne; Kuala Lumpur since July 2003; Born 04/05/59; WRAC 1978 - 82; MOD 1983 - 86; FCO 1997; Lisbon 1998; Band B3; m Michael James Huggins (1d 1988; 1s 1995).

Huggins, Elizabeth June; SUPL since July 2003; Born 25/06/70; DSS 1987; FCO 1989; Copenhagen 1992; FCO 1993; Budapest 1995; SUPL 1998; FCO 2001; Band B3; m 1997 Phillip David Culligan (1d 1999).

Hughes, Beverley Elizabeth (née Lewis); FCO since October 2002; Born 22/07/66; HCS 1985; FCO 1985; Karachi 1987; Africa/Middle East Floater 1991; FCO 1994; SUPL 1998; Band C4; m 1997 Peter John Hughes.

Hughes, Dr Edgar John; HM Ambassador Buenos Aires since November 2004; Born 27/07/47; FCO 1973; On secondment to Cabinet Office 1979; First Secretary CSCE Madrid 1981; FCO 1982; First Secretary and Head of Chancery Santiago 1983; First Secretary (Information) Washington 1985; First Secretary later Counsellor FCO 1989; Deputy Head of Mission Oslo 1993; Change Manager FCO 1997; On secondment to BAe Systems 1999; HM Ambassador Caracas 2000; Seconded to Shell as Vice President, International Relations 2003; m 1982 Lynne Evans (2s 1984, 1988).

Hughes, Geraldine Mary; FCO since November 2002; Born 24/03/76; Band A2.

Hughes, Ian Noel; Deputy High Commissioner Mumbai since October 2003; Born 05/12/51; FCO 1971; Latin America Floater 1974; Kabul 1976; Warsaw 1980; FCO 1982; Second Secretary and Vice-Consul Tegucigalpa 1985; First Secretary (Political) Berne 1988; First Secretary FCO 1993; First Secretary (Press/Information) New Delhi 1993; First Secretary FCO 1997; Deputy Head of Mission Mexico City 2000; m 1978 Teresa June Tinguely (2s 1979, 1981; 1d 1984).

Hughes, Peter John; Deputy Head of Mission Colombo since December 2001; Born 14/09/53; FCO 1976; Islamabad 1978; Rome 1980; Warsaw 1983; FCO 1985; Second Secretary 1987; Vice-Consul (Commercial) Sydney 1989; Second later First Secretary FCO 1994; Resident British Commissioner Castries 1998; m 1997 Beverley Elizabeth Lewis.

Hulands, Michael Robert; FCO since February 2000; Born 29/11/53; FCO 1970; Singapore 1976; Tel Aviv 1978; FCO 1981; Third Secretary Bangkok 1983; Addis Ababa 1986; FCO 1990; Second Secretary Bonn 1995; FCO 1998; North American IT Advisor Washington 1999; m 1979 Normah Binti Maznun (2d 1981, 1986).

Hulbert, Neil Peter; Oslo since August 2001; Born 21/06/63; FCO 1995; Berlin 1997; Band A2.

Hum, Sir Christopher Owen, KCMG (2003), CMG (1996); HM Ambassador Beijing since March 2002; Born 27/01/46; FO 1967; Hong Kong 1968; Peking 1971; Second later First Secretary/Private Secretary to Permanent Representative Brussels (UKREP) 1973; FCO 1975; First Secretary Peking 1979; First Secretary (Chancery) Paris 1981; First Secretary FCO 1983; Counsellor and Deputy Head of Falkland Islands Department FCO 1985; Counsellor FCO 1986;

Counsellor and Head of Chancery New York (UKMIS) 1989; AUSS (Northern Asia and the Pacific) FCO 1992; HM Ambassador Warsaw 1996; Chief Clerk 1998; m 1970 Julia Mary Park (1d 1974; 1s 1976).

Humfrey, Charles Thomas William, CMG (1999); HM Ambassador Jakarta since March 2004; Born 01/12/47; Third Secretary FCO 1969; Language Student Sheffield University 1970; Second Secretary Tokyo 1971; First Secretary FCO 1976; Private Secretary to Minister of State 1979; New York (UKMIS) 1981; First Secretary FCO 1985; Counsellor Ankara 1988; Tokyo 1990; Counsellor FCO 1994; Minister Tokyo 1995; HM Ambassador Seoul 2000; m 1971 Enid Wyn Thomas (2s 1975, 1983; 1d 1977).

Humphreys, Nita (née Saha); SUPL since June 2003; Born 23/12/69; FCO 1990; SUPL 1998; FCO 1998; Amman 2001; Band B3; m 1997 Phillip David Humphreys (1d 1998).

Humphries, Eric Henri Edward; Islamabad since March 2003; Born 11/10/59; FCO 1978; Islamabad 1982; Nairobi 1984; Victoria 1987; FCO 1990; Zagreb 1992; FCO 1993; Dhaka 1995; Jakarta 1998; FCO 2001; Band B3; m 1982 Sara Dorothy Watts (1d 1984).

Hunt, Peter Lawrence, CMG (2001); Consul-General Los Angeles since October 2001; Born 10/06/45; FO 1962; DSAO 1965; Africa Floater Duties 1967; Brussels 1969; Managua 1970; FCO 1973; Second Secretary (Commercial) Caracas 1978; First Secretary FCO 1982; Head of Chancery Montevideo 1987; FCO 1990; Deputy Head of Mission Santiago 1993; Consul-General Istanbul 1997; m 1971 Anne Langhorne Carson (2d 1972, 1976; 2s 1974, 1984).

Hunt, Sara Jennifer; FCO since January 2003; Born 29/10/67; FCO 1987; Bonn 1990; Full-Time Language Training 1993; Latin America/Caribbean Floater 1993; FCO 1995; Third Secretary (Political) Warsaw 1999; Band C4.

Hunt, Stephen Anthony; FCO since June 2003; Born 03/09/57; MOD 1977; FCO 1978; Lisbon 1981; Prague 1984; Gaborone 1986; Moscow 1988; FCO 1990; La Paz 1994; Full-Time Language Training 1997; Second Secretary (Political) Vienna 1999; Band C5; m 1984 Eileen Crossan (2s 1994, 1s 1996).

Hunt, Stephen Paul; First Secretary FCO Services since 1998; Born 13/01/61; FCO 1993; Brussels 1994; FCO 1997.

Hunter, David Eric; FCO since September 2001; Born 08/12/71; FCO 1989; Third Secretary (Political) Kiev 1998; Band B3; m 2000 Peta Leigh Brennan.

Hunter, Gordon Robert Peter; Ljubljana since February 2004; Born 11/01/80; FCO 2002; Band A2.

Hunter, Robert; Zagreb since September 2003; Born 10/08/47; HM Forces 1964 - 70; Merchant Navy 1973 - 74; FCO 1974; Darwin 1975; Beirut

1976; Peking 1977; FCO 1979; Lilongwe 1980; Jedda 1981; FCO 1984; Pretoria 1985; FCO 1988; Vice-Consul (Consular/Management) Suva 1989; Full-Time Language Training 1994; Deputy Head of Mission Antananarivo 1995; Second Secretary FCO 1997; Full-Time Language Training 2000; Second Secretary (Management) and Consul Sana'a 2000; Band C4; m 1981 Carol Mary Chorley.

Hunter Okulo, Paulette Elaine; Nairobi since August 2001; Born 17/10/65; FCO 1985; Lagos 1987; Peking 1990; Bridgetown 1993; FCO 1997; T/D Islamabad 1997; FCO 1998; Band B3; m 2003 Anthony Akelo Okulo.

Huntington, Janet Elizabeth (née Bull); SUPL since February 2003; Born 22/09/63; FCO 1986; Third later Second Secretary (Chancery) Managua 1988; Second Secretary (Chancery) Lisbon 1990; Second later First Secretary FCO 1993; First Secretary (Political) Caracas 1995; First Secretary (Trade Policy) New Delhi 1997; First Secretary FCO 2001; Band D6; m 1995 Daniel Peter Huntington (2d 1997, 1999).

Hurd, Thomas Robert Benedict; Consul (Political) Jerusalem since March 2002; Born 22/09/64; FCO 1992; Language Training 1994; First Secretary (Political) Warsaw 1995; First Secretary Amman 1998; Band D6; m 1994 Katherine Siân Aubrey (2s 1996, 1998; 1d 1997).

Hustwitt, Justin John; First Secretary Tripoli since April 2004; Born 08/09/67; FCO 1991; Full-Time Language Training 1992; Language Training Cairo 1993; Second Secretary (Political) Cairo 1994; Second Secretary (Commercial) Riyadh 1995; First Secretary FCO 1997; First Secretary (Regional Affairs) Kampala 2001; Band D6.

Hutchings, Nicholas Alexander; Second Secretary Kabul since July 2004; Born 29/02/80; FCO 2002; Band C4.

Hutchison, Jacqueline Margaret (née Wigzell); SUPL since August 2002; Born 12/05/65; FCO 1987; Third Secretary (Commercial) Berlin 1990; Third Secretary Port of Spain 1993; Third later Second Secretary FCO 1997; Band C4; m 1993 Ian James Hutchison (1s 1995; 2d 2000).

Hyde, Richard Damian; Second Secretary (Commercial) Jedda since October 2001; Born 18/09/69; FCO 1989; Hamilton 1991; Vice-Consul Paris 1995; Band C4; m 1994 Jacqueline Pearl Sadio.

Hyland, Mark; SUPL since December 2003; Born 03/07/69; HCS 1986; FCO 1990; Brussels (UKDEL NATO) 1993; T/D New York (UKMIS) 1995; Belgrade 1996; SUPL 1999; Sarajevo 2000; Band A2; m 1992 Deborah Jane Tomlinson.

Hyland, Susan Margaret; Private Secretary to the Permanent Under Secretary FCO since June 2001; Born 30/10/64; Second Secretary FCO 1990; Second Secretary (Political) Oslo 1992; New York (UKMIS) 1992; Second Secretary UKDEL OECD

1993; ENA Paris 1994; First Secretary FCO 1996; First Secretary (Political) Moscow 2000; Band D7.

Hyman, Teresa; First Secretary (Technical Management) Bangkok since July 2002; Born 11/09/65; FCO 1983; Band C5; (1d 1985; 1s 1994).

Hyne, Sarah Jean; New York (UKMIS) since August 2001; Born 20/04/74; FCO 1999; PA to Deputy Heads of Economic Policy 1999; Band A2.

I

Inglehearn, Catherine Mary; Deputy Head of Mission Almaty since October 2003; Born 15/05/65; FCO 1990; Rome 1992; Third Secretary Ljubljana 1996; FCO 2000; Full-Time Language Training (Russian) 2003; Band C5.

Ingold, Andrew Henrik; FCO since September 1994; Born 30/07/53; Customs and Excise 1972; FCO 1973; Valletta 1975; Monrovia 1978; Paris 1982; FCO 1984; Bombay 1987; Vice-Consul Abu Dhabi 1990; Band B3.

Ingram, Rachel Victoria; FCO since April 2001; Born 25/04/69; FCO 1994; Berne 1996; World Wide Floater Duties 1998; Band C4.

Inkster, Nigel Norman, CMG (2003); Counsellor FCO since January 1998; Born 11/04/52; Third Secretary FCO 1975; Language Student/Third Secretary Kuala Lumpur 1976; Third later Second Secretary FCO 1976; Second later First Secretary Bangkok 1979; FCO 1982; First Secretary and Consul Peking 1983; Buenos Aires 1985; First Secretary FCO 1989; Counsellor Athens 1992; Counsellor BTC Hong Kong 1994; m 1977 Leong Chui Fun (1d 1980; 1s 1981).

Innes, Stuart Harcourt; Deputy High Commissioner Chennai since June 2003; Born 30/10/55; FCO 1980; Doha 1983; Second Secretary Cairo 1986; First Secretary FCO 1989; Deputy Permanent Representative Vienna (UKMIS) 1993; Deputy Head of Mission Damascus 1999; m 1983 Susan Jane Wood (1s 1987; 2d 1989, 1992).

Innes-Hopkins, Christopher Randolph; Counsellor and Deputy Head of Mission Kuwait since August 2004; Born 26/11/53; FCO 1976; Third Secretary Georgetown 1979; Commercial Attaché Paris 1982; Second Secretary FCO 1985; HM Consul and Second Secretary (Commercial) Tunis 1988; Deputy Consul-General Jerusalem 1993; First Secretary FCO 1996; On secondment as Political Adviser to EU Special Envoy for the Middle East 1997; First Secretary (Commercial/Economic) Ankara 2001; m 1983 Soraya Dookie (1s 1986; 1d 1993).

Ireland, Jonathan Charles Wintour; FCO since April 2002; Born 02/07/72; Band A2.

Irens, Jules Marie Nigel; First Secretary (Political) Brussels since June 2004; Born 11/08/68; FCO 2002; Band D6; m 2002 Nicola Clare Charlton (1d 2004).

Ives, Malcolm Albert; First Secretary (Commercial) Muscat since August 2001; Born 10/03/47; MPNI 1964; FO (later FCO) 1966; Dacca 1969; FCO 1971; Sana'a 1973; Addis Ababa 1974; Warsaw 1976; FCO 1978; São Paulo 1981; Jakarta 1985; Second Secretary (Development) Amman 1987; Second Secretary FCO 1991; On loan to the DTI 1992; Second Secretary (Commercial) Riyadh 1994; First Secretary (Commercial) Accra 1997; m 1973 Susan Robertson (3s 1969, 1974, 1976).

Ives, Susan; Muscat since August 2001; Born 08/02/44; FCO 1992; Riyadh 1994; FCO 1997; SUPL 1997; Accra 1999; Band B3; m 1973 Malcolm Albert Ives (3s 1969, 1974, 1976).

Ivey, Peter Robert; Düsseldorf since September 2001; Born 25/05/58; FCO 1982; Bahrain 1983; Language Training 1987; Second Secretary (Information/Chancery) Helsinki 1988; On loan to the London Chamber of Commerce 1992; On loan to the DTI 1993; Full-Time Language Training 1995; First Secretary (Commercial) Zagreb 1996; FCO 1999; Band D6; m 1998 Sally Helen Elizabeth Hill (2s 1998, 2000).

Ivey, Sally Helen Elizabeth (née Hill); SUPL since September 1998; Born 25/10/65; FCO 1987; New Delhi 1988; FCO 1990; World Wide Floater Duties 1992; Full-Time Language Training 1995; Zagreb 1996; Band A2; m 1998 Peter Robert Ivey (2s 1998, 2000).

Ivins, Suzanne Gillian (née Parker); Second Secretary (Immigration) Shanghai since December 2000; Born 05/02/65; FCO 1983; Tokyo 1985; FCO 1988; Third Secretary (Consular) Ottawa 1992; Third Secretary Ho Chi Minh City 1996; Band C4; m 1988 James Browell Ivins (1d 1994).

Ivory, Jason; Lagos since May 2004; Born 04/08/70; Madrid 1991; Bombay 1994; FCO 1998; New Delhi 2000; Band C4; m 1992 Susannah Ruth Knowles (1s 1994; 1d 1995).

Izzard, Richard Brian George; FCO since March 2002; Born 04/01/69; Metropolitan Police 1987; FCO 1988; Sofia 1990; Accra 1992; World Wide Floater Duties 1993; FCO 1997; Luanda 2000; Band C4; m 2003 Ceinwen Mary Reeves.

J

Jack, Stuart Duncan Macdonald, CVO (1994); FCO since September 2003; Born 08/06/49; FCO 1972; Third later Second later First Secretary Tokyo 1974; FCO 1979; First Secretary and Press Attaché Moscow 1981; First Secretary FCO 1984; Bank of England 1984; First Secretary (Economic) Tokyo 1985; Counsellor FCO 1989; HM Consul-General St Petersburg 1992; FCO 1996; Minister Tokyo 1999; m 1977 Mariko Nobechi (2d 1980, 1982; 1s 1986).

Jackson, Anna Elizabeth; Second Secretary (EU) Warsaw since May 2001; Born 08/06/78; FCO 1999; Band C4.

Jackson, Clare Charlotte Mabel; Hong Kong since May 2004; Born 04/09/77; FCO 2003; Band C4.

Jackson, Freya; FCO since October 2003; Born 10/04/74; FCO 1997; Support Officer New York (UKMIS) 1999; Full-Time Language Training 2000; Second Secretary Buenos Aires 2000; Band D6.

Jackson, Helen; SUPL since September 1999; Born 27/01/62; FCO 1981; Stockholm 1983; Port of Spain 1986; Moscow 1990; Bridgetown 1993; FCO 1998; Band A2; (1d 1998).

Jackson, Lee Barry Thomas, MBE (2003); Deputy Head of Mission Dili since March 2004; Born 02/07/65; FCO 1996; Full-Time Language Training Hong Kong 1997; Vice-Consul (Consular) Hong Kong 2000; Band B3; m 1995 Vanda Morais-Jackson (diss 1999).

Jackson, Paul Michael, MBE (2000); FCO since August 2002; Born 05/04/63; FCO 1982; Islamabad 1985; FCO 1987; Washington 1991; FCO 1994; Belgrade 1997; Helsinki 1999; Band C5; m 1984 Cheryl Barrington (1d 1986; 1s 1988).

Jackson-Houlston, William Lester, OBE (1994); Berne since December 2003; Born 06/10/52; FCO 1979; Second Secretary Brussels (UKREP) 1980; Second later First Secretary FCO 1981; Buenos Aires (BIS) 1982; FCO 1986; First Secretary Belgrade 1990; First Secretary FCO 1993; Counsellor The Hague 1999; m 1985 Susana Olivia Fitzpatrick (twins, 1s and 1d 1989).

Jacobs, Lisa Claire; FCO since January 2000; Born 21/03/65; FCO 1986; Moscow 1988; Riyadh 1990; FCO 1993; Peking 1995; SUPL 1998; Band C4.

Jacobsen, Neil Marius; Counsellor FCO since August 2003; Born 16/06/57; Second Secretary FCO 1984; Second later First Secretary (Economics) Athens 1986; First Secretary FCO 1989; First Secretary (Political) Madrid 1992; First Secretary FCO 1996; First Secretary (Regional Affairs) Santiago 2000; Band D6; m 1982 Susan Clark (1d 1984; 2s 1988, 1990).

Jagoe, Neale David; FCO since January 2002; Born 11/06/68; Royal Hong Kong Police 1990 - 96; Second Secretary FCO 1996; Second Secretary (Political/Information) Manila 1997; Band D6; m 1992 Margarita Hanio (1d 1992).

Jagpal, Harjit Kaur; SUPL since March 2004; Born 08/10/68; FCO 1988; Lagos 1991; Abuja 1993; SUPL 1995; Moscow 1998; FCO 1999; Band B3; m 1996 Robin David Phillips (diss).

James, Darren Ian; Third Secretary (Political) Beirut since October 2001; Born 18/04/72; FCO 1998; Full-Time Language Training 2000; Band B3; m 2001 Clare Mallett.

James, Neill; Bangkok since December 2003; Born 06/07/71; FCO 1991; Dhaka 1994; Manila 1998; Sana'a 2001; Full-Time Language Training (Thai) 2003; Band B3; m 1997 Rangsiya Promsrisuk (1 step s 1990, 1s 1999; 1d 2001).

James, Nicola Patricia; Jakarta since April 2002; Born 29/09/60; FCO 1980; Peking 1983; Kuala Lumpur 1985; Bandar Seri Begawan 1988; FCO 1993; Band B3.

James, Stephen Anthony; First Secretary (Management) Mexico City since July 2003; Born 01/09/51; Customs and Excise 1968; FCO 1971; Saigon 1973; Peking 1975; Warsaw 1976; Manila 1977; Berne 1981; FCO 1984; Islamabad 1987; Third Secretary (Aid/Commercial) Mbabane 1990; Second Secretary FCO 1994; Second later First Secretary Tokyo 1996; m 1979 Nikki Jean Smith (2d 1980, 1982; 1s 1984).

Jamieson, Rachel Janet; FCO since May 2003; Born 31/05/68; FCO 1993; Full-Time Language Training 1995; ECO/VC Bucharest 1996; Second Secretary (Press) Islamabad 1999; Band C4.

Janjua, Nadeem Hameed; FCO since October 2002; Born 14/07/71; FCO 1999; Yaoundé 2001; Band B3; ptnr, Kathryn Whale (1d 2003).

January, Dr Peter; Head of OSCE/CoE Department FCO since July 2001; Born 13/01/52; FCO 1983; First Secretary (Commercial) Budapest 1985; First Secretary FCO 1988; Consul and Deputy Head of Mission Maputo 1991; First Secretary later Counsellor FCO 1993; HM Ambassador Tirana 1999.

Jardine, Martine; FCO since March 1999; Born 27/09/70; FCO 1990; Madrid 1993; Floater Duties 1997; SUPL 1998; Band C4.

Jarrett, Anne; FCO since March 2001; Born 26/01/60; FCO 1978; Moscow 1981; Africa/Middle East Floater 1984; Brussels (UKDEL NATO) 1986; Second Secretary FCO 1989; Second Secretary (Political) Peking 1993; Full-Time Language Training 1997; First Secretary (Economic) Bucharest 1997; Band D6.

Jarrett, Caroline Julia Rachel; Second Secretary (Political) Islamabad since August 2002; Born 07/09/76; FCO 1999; Band C4.

Jarrold, Nicholas Robert; HM Ambassador Zagreb since August 2000; Born 02/03/46; Third Secretary FCO 1968; Third later Second Secretary The Hague 1969; Dakar 1972; First Secretary FCO 1975; Nairobi 1979 (Head of Chancery 1983); FCO 1983; Counsellor and Deputy Head of Mission Havana 1989; CDA at St Antony's College Oxford University 1991; Counsellor (Commercial/Economic) Brussels 1992; HM Ambassador Riga 1996; m 1972 Anne Catherine Whitworth (2s 1976, 1979).

Jarvie, Carole Marina; ECO/Vice-Consul Addis Ababa since January 2004; Born 26/09/54; FCO 1984; The Hague 1986; Canberra 1989; Brussels (UKDEL) 1992; FCO 1998; ECO Istanbul 2000; Band B3.

Jarvis, Russell Thomas; Deputy Head of Mission Plymouth since October 2003; Born 27/09/47; Commonwealth Office (later FCO) 1964; Sofia 1969; EC Brussels 1972; Sana'a 1972; Islamabad 1973; FCO 1975; Second Secretary Dar es Salaam 1978; Vice-Consul (Commercial) BTDO New York 1982; First Secretary FCO 1986; First Secretary (Management) BTC Hong Kong 1990; First Secretary FCO 1994; Deputy Head of Mission Stanley 1997; m 1969 Joan Ann Wyard (2s 1971, 1986; 1d 1973).

Jay, Sir Michael Hastings, KCMG (1997), CMG (1992); Permanent Under Secretary of State and Head of the Diplomatic Service FCO since January 2002; Born 19/06/46; ODM 1969; UKDEL IMF/IBRD Washington 1973; ODM 1975; First Secretary (Development) New Delhi 1978; First Secretary FCO 1981; Private Secretary to Permanent Under Secretary of State FCO 1982; Counsellor on loan to Cabinet Office 1985; Counsellor (Finance/Commercial) Paris 1987; AUSS (European Community) FCO 1990; DUS (European and Economic Affairs) 1994; HM Ambassador Paris 1996; m 1975 Sylvia Mylroie.

Jeenes, Kelley Elizabeth; SUPL since May 2001; Born 23/02/71; FCO 1992; Nairobi 1995; FCO 1997; Band B3.

Jeffery, Claire Rachel; Second Secretary (Political) Stockholm since July 2002; Born 20/04/73; FCO 1997; Band C4.

Jeffrey, Frieda King (née Rolland); Bridgetown since April 2000; Born 17/10/63; FCO 1988; Brussels (UKREP) 1990; Manila 1993; FCO 1996; Uganda 1997; Band A2; m 1997 Bruce Jeffrey.

Jeffrey, John Peacock Reid; First Secretary FCO since September 2003; Born 04/04/53; FCO 1971; Jakarta 1974; Singapore 1975; Africa Floater 1977; FCO 1980; Mexico City 1982; Bucharest 1986; Second Secretary FCO 1988; Second Secretary (Commercial/Consular/Management) Montevideo 1992; Second Secretary FCO 1996; ECM/Consul Tunis 1998; Band C4; m 1980 Arlene Elizabeth Watson (1s 1991).

Jeffreys, Stella Ann; FCO since December 1999; Born 16/11/62; FCO 1990; Dar es Salaam 1992; Hanoi 1996; Band B3.

Jenkins, Dr John, CMG (2003), LVO (1989); Consul-General Jerusalem since July 2003; Born 26/01/55; Second Secretary FCO 1980; Second later First Secretary Abu Dhabi 1983; First Secretary FCO 1986; First Secretary and Head of Chancery Kuala Lumpur 1989; First Secretary FCO 1992; Deputy Head of Mission Kuwait 1995; SOAS, University of London 1998; HM Ambassador Rangoon 1999; m 1982 Nancy Caroline Pomfret.

Jenkins, Owen John; First Secretary (Political) Buenos Aires since June 2002; Born 21/08/69; FCO 1991; Full-Time Language Training 1993; Third later Second Secretary (Political/Information) Ankara 1994; FCO 1998; m 1998 Catherine Margaret Baker.

Jenkins, Paul David; On loan to the DTI since November 2000; Born 22/06/51; FCO 1968; Bonn 1972; FCO 1974; Prague 1974; Monrovia 1976; Kaduna 1978; FCO 1981; Nairobi 1984; Gaborone

1986; Second Secretary FCO 1990; Second Secretary (Commercial) Lagos 1992; First Secretary (Commercial) Islamabad 1996; Yaoundé 2000; m (1) 1972 Jennifer Whitmarsh (diss) (2s 1976, 1979); (2) 1987 Elaine Vera Walsh (née Avery).

Jenkins, Peter Redmond; UK Permanent Representative with Personal rank of Ambassador Vienna since August 2001; Born FCO 1973; Third later Second Secretary UNIDO/IAEA Vienna 1975; First Secretary FCO 1978; First Secretary and PS to HM Ambassador Washington 1982; First Secretary FCO 1984; First Secretary (Economic) Paris 1987; Minister/Counsellor, Consul-General and Deputy Head of Mission Brasilia 1992; Minister and Deputy Permanent Representative Geneva (UKMIS) 1996; m 1990 Angelina Chee-Hong Yang (1d 1992; 1s 1994).

Jenkinson, Eric, OBE (2003); High Commissioner Banjul since October 2002; Born 13/03/50; FO 1967; EC Brussels 1971; Islamabad 1973; Second Secretary (Commercial) Jedda 1978; Second Secretary FCO 1982; First Secretary (Economic) Bonn 1986; Consul and Deputy Head of Mission Bahrain 1992; First Secretary FCO 1995; First Secretary Tehran 1999; m 1973 Kathleen Forster (2s 1980, 1981).

Jenkinson, Gale Louise; FCO since September 2002; Born 24/11/63; FCO 1984; Islamabad 1986; Ottawa 1989; FCO 1992; Third Secretary (Management) and Vice-Consul Doha 1996; São Paulo 2000; Band C5; m 1990 Tony Takashi Baba (1d 1992).

Jennings, Kay (née Henderson); FCO since April 2004; Born 27/02/72; FCO 1993; Nicosia 2001; Band A2; m 2000 Richard Llewellyn Jennings.

Jennison, Vanessa Sandford; SUPL since July 2003; Born 25/02/64; FCO 1988; Third Secretary Geneva (UKMIS) 1990; FCO 1993; Vice-Consul Paris 1995; SUPL 1998; Vice-Consul Amsterdam 2000; m 1989 Geoffrey John Peck (2s 1993, 1997).

Jermey, Dominic James Robert, OBE (2001); Counsellor (Commercial) Madrid since May 2004; Born 26/04/67; FCO 1993; Full-Time Language Training 1994; Second Secretary (Political/Information) Islamabad 1995; First Secretary Afghanistan 1998; T/D Skopje 1999; T/D Dili 2000; FCO 2000; m 2003 Clare Judith Roberts (1s 2004).

Joad, Kate Louise; Cayman Islands since July 2003; Born 18/03/69; FCO 1990; Tokyo 1992; Floater Duties 1996; T/D Pretoria 1999; Second Secretary FCO 1999; Band C4.

Johansen, Laura Suzanne; FCO since January 2003; Born 05/04/77; Band B3.

Johns, Allison Marie; Damascus since August 2000; Born 20/11/66; FCO 1988; Washington 1991; Bonn 1993; FCO 1997; Band A2.

Johnsen, Emma Louise (née Williams); SUPL since September 1998; Born 23/02/66; FCO 1990;

Geneva (UKMIS) 1993; FCO 1996; Band C4; m 1992 Per-Arne Johnsen.

Johnson, Alison Jane (née Sindon); SUPL since May 2001; Born 16/11/63; FCO 1983; Mexico City 1985; Asunción 1988; FCO 1991; Sofia 1995; SUPL 1997; FCO 1999; Band B3; m 1997 Clive Andrew Johnson.

Johnson, Christine; Dakar since August 2001; Born 12/04/73; FCO 1997; Budapest 1998; Full-Time Language Training 2001; Band B3.

Johnson, Helen (née Matthews); SUPL since September 2000; Born 27/03/62; FCO 1981; Dhaka 1984; Moscow 1985; Tunis 1985; Berne 1988; FCO 1991; Islamabad 1994; San José 1998; Band B3; m (1) 1987 R B L Marzouk (diss 1999) (1s 1994); (2) 2000 Ridha Ben Larbi.

Johnson, Julie Michelle; Second Secretary (Consular) Kuala Lumpur since September 2000; Born 12/11/63; FCO 1983; Port Stanley 1985; FCO 1986; Vienna 1987; Hong Kong 1990; FCO 1991; Bombay 1993; FCO 1993; Third Secretary (Management) and Vice-Consul Guatemala City 1996; Band C4.

Johnson, Katrina; FCO since September 2001; Born 10/03/66; FCO 1985; Paris 1987; FCO 1990; SUPL 1992; Third Secretary (Institutions) Brussels (UKREP) 1993; On loan to the ODA/DFID 1996; SUPL 1998; Second Secretary (Economic/Trade Policy) New Delhi 1999; Band D6; m 1994 Richard Adam Noble (2s 1996, 1998).

Johnson, Matthew Alfred; FCO since October 2003; Born 11/06/70; FCO 1988; Cape Town/Pretoria 1990; FCO 1993; Osaka 1994; FCO 1996; Second Secretary 1998; On loan as Private Secretary to Head of Policy Unit, No 10 Downing Street 1999; Second Secretary (Social Policy Issues) New York (UKMIS) 2000; Band D6; m 1993 Heidi Suzanne Burton (1s 1997; 1d 1999).

Johnson, Simon William; FCO since December 1999; Born 26/05/64; FCO 1983; Budapest 1987; Istanbul 1989; FCO 1993; Third Secretary (Visits) Peking 1996.

Johnson, Stuart James; Second Secretary FCO since January 2002; Born 08/05/72; Second Secretary FCO 1998; Second Secretary (Pol/Mil) Banja Luka on secondment to MOD 2000; Band C4.

Johnston, Paul Charles; Counsellor FCO since November 2002; Born 29/05/68; MOD 1990-93; FCO 1993; Private Secretary to Lord Owen (International Conference on Former Yugoslavia) 1994; Second Secretary (PS/HMA) Paris 1995; Second Secretary (Political) Paris 1997; FCO 1999; Deputy Head of European Union Department (External) FCO 2001.

Johnstone, James; FCO since September 2002; Born 16/03/44; Army 1962 - 88; New York 1988; Peking 1991; Geneva (UKMIS) 1992; T/D Moscow 1995; Moscow 1996; Hong Kong 1998; Band B3; m (1) 1967 Patricia Anne Strong (1d

1968; 2s 1969, 1974) (diss 1983); (2) 1986 Rachel Baliti (1s 1991).

Johnstone, Lauren Clair (née Blagburn); SUPL since September 2002; Born 21/07/70; FCO 1989; SUPL 1992; Scottish Office 1992; FCO 1993; Gibraltar 1997; Band B3; m 1992 Andrew Johnstone (diss 1999).

Jones, Adrian Ellis; FCO since October 2002; Born 15/07/65; Home Office 1988; Brussels (UKREP) 1998; Band D6; ptnr, Stine Strømsnes (1s 2002).

Jones, Alison; Lagos since February 2003; Born 19/12/72; DSS 1995; FCO 1998; World Wide Floater Duties 1999; Band B3.

Jones, Amanda Louise; SUPL since June 2003; Born 16/03/69; FCO 1997; Kigali 1998; Baku 2001; Band A2.

Jones, Andrew; FCO since August 2000; Born 02/03/67; FCO 1988; Hong Kong 1997; Band C4; m 1989 Lisa Roberts (1d 1993; 2s 1997, 2000).

Jones, Andrew Martin; FCO since June 2003; Born 14/12/59; FCO 1980; Darwin 1981; FCO 1984; Singapore 1986; FCO 1989; Third Secretary Amman 1993; FCO 1997; Copenhagen 2000; Band C5; m 1985 Amanda Wainer (1s 1988; 1d 1990).

Jones, Dr Brian James; FCO since September 2003; Born 03/04/77; Band C4.

Jones, Caitlin Olga; FCO since December 2001; Born 03/06/67; FCO 1990; Nicosia 1993; Brussels (UKDEL) 1996; Guatemala City 1999; Band D6.

Jones, Catherine Helen Courtier, MBE (1999); SUPL since August 2000; Born 13/09/56; FCO 1976; Moscow 1979; Latin America Floater 1982; Bogotá 1984 (Second Secretary 1985); Second Secretary FCO 1989; Deputy Head of Mission Tirana 1997.

Jones, Ceinwen Jane; FCO since November 2002; Born 02/05/50; FCO 1976; Bangkok 1977; Moscow 1979; Geneva (UKDIS) 1981; FCO 1984; Banjul 1990; FCO 1992; Brussels (UKREP) 1995; Deputy Head of Mission Tallinn 1999; Band C5.

Jones, David Alan; High Commissioner Belmopan since November 2004; Born 26/10/53; Lord Chancellor's Department 1970; FCO 1971; Tehran 1975; Islamabad 1978; Second Secretary on loan to the MOD 1981; Second Secretary FCO 1983; First Secretary (Commercial) Cairo 1986; First Secretary FCO 1989; Full-Time Training 1993; Deputy Head of Mission/Consul Luanda 1993; Deputy High Commissioner Dar es Salaam 1996; High Commissioner Freetown and also non resident HM Ambassador to Republic of Guinea 2000; SUPL 2003; FCO 2004; m (1) 1975 Jennifer Anne Wright (diss 1992); (2) 1994 Daphne Patricia Foley (1d 2001).

Jones, David Stephen; First Secretary (Management) Accra since February 2003; Born 19/09/51; Public Record Office 1970-73; FCO 1976; Port of Spain 1978; Peking 1981;

Africa/Middle East Floater 1982; FCO 1984; Brasilia 1988; Tripoli 1991; Second Secretary on loan to the DTI 1994; Second Secretary FCO 1995; Deputy High Commissioner Honiara 1998; Band C5; m (1) 1973 Jane Martin (diss 1978) (2) 1997 Carole Banstead.

Jones, Eric Malcolm; First Secretary (Management) and Consul Vienna since November 2001; Born 07/10/45; Passport Office Liverpool 1963; DSAO 1966; Middle East Floater 1969; Düsseldorf 1970; Vice-Consul Peking 1973; FCO 1974; Third Secretary (Commercial) Kuwait 1976; Second Secretary FCO 1980; Second Secretary (Aid) later Second Secretary (Chancery) Dhaka 1982; Second Secretary (Commercial) later First Secretary (Development) Lilongwe 1985; First Secretary FCO 1990; First Secretary (Development) Jakarta 1994; First Secretary FCO 1998; m 1988 Sylvia Margaret Hayhurst (1s 1989).

Jones, Frank; First Secretary (Commercial) Athens since May 2001; Born 07/09/48; FO (later FCO) 1967; Kaduna 1970; Brussels (NATO) 1974; Sana'a 1977; FCO 1978; Ottawa 1982; FCO 1984; Second Secretary (Visa) Paris 1989; Second Secretary (Commercial) Kuala Lumpur 1994; FCO 1997; Band C5; m 1982 Elizabeth Mary Lendrum (1d 1985; 1s 1991).

Jones, Katherine; Second Secretary New Delhi since September 2002; Born 07/08/65; Home Office 1990-92; FCO 1992; SUPL 1998; FCO 2001; Band C4; m 1999 Richard Joseph David Perry (1d 1998).

Jones, Leslie Norman; FCO since June 2003; Born 26/05/48; Army 1964 - 88; Cairo 1988; Moscow 1991; Budapest 1993; FCO 1995; Language Training 1999; Berlin 2000; Band B3; m 1972 Dorothy Alma Tanner (1s 1977; 1d 1978).

Jones, Mark Hampton; First Secretary (Tehnical Works Officer) Pretoria since July 2003; Born 10/12/64; HCS 1982; Mexico City 1999; Miami 2001; Band C5; m 1999 Jennifer Tracy Cliffe.

Jones, Neale Robert; Copenhagen since December 2003; Born 20/02/63; FCO 1986; Islamabad 1989; Istanbul 1992; Dubai 1999; Band B3; m (1) 1992 Catherine Ingham (diss 1999) (2s 1993, 1995); (2) 2000 Ebru Jones (1 step d 1996; 1d 2000).

Jones, Peter; First Secretary Rome since April 2003; Born 23/07/57; FCO 1976; Port Stanley 1979; Madrid 1981; Kathmandu 1984; FCO 1986; Peking 1988; Luxembourg 1992; Third later Second Secretary FCO 1995; Second Secretary (Political) Washington 1997; m 1979 Elaine Frances Scott.

Jones, Peter Edward; Counsellor (EU/Economic/Commercial) Rome since October 2002; Born 28/08/61; FCO 1985; Second later First Secretary Vienna (UKDEL) 1989; First Secretary FCO 1992; First Secretary (Politico-Military) Bonn 1994; Assistant Director Personnel FCO 1998; m 1998 Sumita Biswas.

Jones, Phillip Roy; FCO since March 2000; Born 18/02/50; FO (later FCO) 1966; Washington 1976; FCO 1979; Attaché Muscat 1982; FCO 1985; Moscow 1996; Band C4; m (1) 1972 Lesley Pamela Goody (diss 1981) (2s 1973, 1978; 1d 1975); (2) 1982 Karen Patricia Lyle (2s 1985, 1995; 1d 1987).

Jones, Ralph Mahood; FCO since July 2002; Born 04/05/69; FCO 1989; Riyadh 1992; T/D New Delhi 1995; Karachi 1996; T/D Kuwait 1997; World Wide Floater Duties 1999; Band B3.

Jones, Randolph Thomas; Second Secretary (Consular) Dublin since April 2004; Born 12/09/56; FCO 1976; Islamabad 1978; Colombo 1982; FCO 1985; Peking 1989; Port of Spain 1989; Copenhagen 1993; Second Secretary FCO 1997; Second Secretary (Immigration) Pretoria 2000; Band C4; m 1980 Kathryn Rosemary Smith (2s 1984, 1987).

Jones, Rebecca Louise; Havana since September 2003; Born 18/10/74; FCO 1998; Cairo 2000; Band A2.

Jones, Richard Alexander Owen; Second Secretary Zagreb since September 2001; Born 19/04/71; FCO 1990; World Wide Floater Duties 1993; Third Secretary (Vice-Consul) Tashkent 1997; Band C4; m 2000 Madina H Sagindirova.

Jones, Richard Christopher Bentley; First Secretary FCO since March 2003; Born 22/03/53; Second Secretary FCO 1978; PS to HM Ambassador later Second Secretary Tokyo 1980; First Secretary FCO 1984; Deputy Head of Mission Suva 1988; First Secretary FCO 1992; First Secretary Tokyo 1998.

Jones, Richard Hugh Francis; HM Ambassador Tirana since October 2003; Born 28/09/62; FCO 1983; Third later Second Secretary Abu Dhabi 1986; Second later First Secretary FCO 1989; First Secretary (External Relations) Brussels (UKREP) 1994; First Secretary FCO 1998.

Jones, Robert Edward; First Secretary FCO since September 2002; Born 30/05/47; FCO 1966; Singapore 1973; FCO 1974; Belgrade 1978; FCO 1981; Attaché Prague 1985; FCO 1988; Second Secretary 1989; Second Secretary Budapest 1993; FCO 1994; Second later First Secretary Bonn 1998; First Secretary Berlin 2000; m 1972 Linda Joan Edith Watts (1d 1974; 1s 1977).

Jones, Siân; Second Secretary Amman since February 2003; Born 08/11/74; FCO 1999; Second Secretary (Pol/Mil) Nicosia 2000; Band C4.

Jones, Timothy Aidan; FCO since February 2003; Born 05/09/62; FCO 1984; Language Training 1986; T/D Vienna (UKDEL CSCE) 1987; Second Secretary (Chancery) The Hague 1988; First Secretary FCO 1992; T/D Mostar (EUAM) 1994; Full-Time Language Training 1995; Deputy Head of Mission Tehran 1996; HM Ambassador Yerevan 1999; m 2001 Christin Marschall.

Jones Parry, Sir Emyr, KCMG, CMG (1992); United Kingdom Permanent Representative to the United Nations at New York and the United Kingdom Permanent Representative on the Security Council since July 2003; Born 21/09/47; FCO 1973; Second later First Secretary (Political) later First Secretary (Economic) Ottawa 1974; FCO 1979; First Secretary (Energy) later First Secretary (Institutions) Brussels (UKREP) 1982; Counsellor on SUPL Brussels (EC) 1987; Counsellor FCO 1989; Deputy Head of Mission Madrid 1993; Deputy Political Director 1996; Director EU 1997; Political Director 1998; Permanent Representative Brussels (UKDEL NATO) 2001; m 1971 Lynn Noble (2s 1977, 1979).

Joseph, Nicholas Eli; FCO since April 2004; Born 12/01/71; FCO 2000; Second Secretary Geneva (UKMIS) 2002; Band C4.

Joshi, Bharat Suresh; Private Secretary to the Parliamentary Under-Secretary of State, FCO since April 2004; Born 23/08/69; FCO 1995; Third Secretary later Deputy High Commissioner Banjul 1999; Second Secretary FCO August 2001; Band C5; m 1997 Bhakti Oza (2d 2000, 2002).

Joy, Rupert Hamilton Neville; SUPL since May 2003; Born 05/09/63; FCO 1990; Full-Time Language Training 1991; Full-Time Language Training Cairo 1992; Second Secretary (Comm/Econ/Pol) Sana'a 1994; Second later First Secretary (Political) Riyadh 1995; First Secretary FCO 1996; Deputy Head of Mission Rabat 2000; Band D6.

Joyce, Lucy Rebecca; Second Secretary (Political/PPA) Brussels since April 2000; Born 11/12/69; FCO 1992; Third Secretary (Political) Sofia 1996; Band C4.

Joyce, Marie-Claire; Second Secretary (Economic) Tunis since March 2004; Born 04/05/69; FCO 1995; Full-Time Language Training 1997; Third Secretary (Commercial) later Second Secretary (Political) Tokyo 1998; Band C4; m Makoto Noguchi (1d 2001; 1s 2004).

Joynson-Squire, Richard James; Second Secretary FCO since April 2002; Born 11/09/74; FCO 1996; Full-Time Language Training 1998; Second Secretary (Political/External) Islamabad 1999; Band C4; m 1998 Rolla Khadduri.

Judd, Claire (née Rowswell); FCO since October 1988; Born 13/01/55; FCO 1979; Quito 1979; Brussels (UKREP) 1981; Moscow 1984; FCO 1985; Mexico City 1986; Band B3; m 1996 David Judd.

Judge, Christopher John; Washington since August 2001; Born 19/05/64; FCO 1980; Second Secretary Moscow 1996; FCO 2000; Band C5; m 1995 Fiona Jane (1s 2000).

Juleff, Andrew John Gerent; Second Secretary (Commercial) Rio de Janeiro since May 2000; Born 03/05/60; FCO 1986; Third Secretary (Aid/Comm) Kampala 1989; Vice-Consul CG New York 1991; Second Secretary FCO 1994; Band C5.

Jupp, Sheridan Arlene; SUPL since January 2002; Born 02/01/57; FCO 1990; Stockholm 1993; Band A2.

K

Kahlow, Bonita; SUPL since April 2004; Born 23/01/66; FCO 1989; Rome 1993; FCO 1996; Rome 1998; SUPL 2001; Rome 2002; Band A2.

Kana-Rupal, Sadhana (née Rupal); SUPL since September 2002; Born 31/05/66; FCO 1995; Band A2; m 1996 Animesh Kana.

Kane, Jacqueline; SUPL since August 2002; Born 25/03/67; FCO 1987; Athens 1990; FCO 1993; New Delhi 1994; FCO 1998; Band B3.

Kane, John Michael; Vice-Consul (Political) Jerusalem since November 2002; Born 23/12/72; FCO 1994; World Wide Floater Duties 2000; Band B3; m 2002 Camelia Sterescu.

Kariuki, James; New York (UKMIS) since September 2002; Born 06/05/71; FCO 1993; On secondment to UN Special Commission (UNSCOM) Baghdad 1994; Second Secretary (Political/Economic) Caracas 1995.

Karmy, Peter John; Head of Management Section Taipei since June 2001; Born 01/07/47; FO (later FCO) 1967; Benghazi 1969; San José 1970; Seoul 1973; Kuwait 1976; FCO 1977; Sofia 1980; FCO 1984; Second Secretary (Admin) and Consul Manila 1985; Second Secretary and Consul (later Second Secretary Commercial) Ankara 1989; Second Secretary FCO 1993; Bogotá 1998; m 1977 Eui Jong Han (2d 1979, 1981).

Kavanagh, Karen Jane (née Williams); SMO Beirut since March 2004; Born 28/04/70; FCO 1991; Brussels (UKDEL NATO) 1994; Bombay 1997; FCO 2000; Band C4; m 1996 Neil Richard Kavanagh.

Kavanagh, Neil Richard; SUPL since April 2004; Born 28/03/72; FCO 1992; Brussels (UKDEL NATO) 1995; Bombay 1997; FCO 2000; Band C4; m 1996 Karen Jane Williams.

Kay, Anthony Paul; Deputy Head of Mission Chisinau since November 2002; Born 29/06/72; FCO 1992; Hong Kong 1995; Third Secretary (Vice-Consul) later Second Secretary (Political) Bucharest 1999; Band C4; m 2004 Michelle Htun.

Kay, Martin Paul; FCO since February 2003; Born 21/03/68; FCO 1987; New York (UKMIS) 1989; Suva 1991; FCO 1994; Pretoria 1999; Band C4; m 2000 Sue Bradley.

Kay, Nicholas Peter; Counsellor and Deputy Head of Mission Madrid since December 2002; Born 08/03/58; First Secretary FCO 1994; First Secretary and Deputy Head of Mission Havana 1997; First Secretary FCO 2000; Deputy Head of Policy Planning Staff, FCO 2001; m 1986 Susan Wallace (1s 1987; 2d 1988, 1991).

Kay, Susan Pauline (née Bradley); FCO since February 2003; Born 16/05/62; FCO 1987; Pretoria 1999; Band B3; m 2000 Martin Paul Kay.

Kazer, Kathleen; Senior Principal Research Officer FCO since 1998; Born 01/06/47; FCO 1970.

Kealy, Robin Andrew, CMG (1991); HM Ambassador and Consul-General Tunis since February 2002; Born 07/10/44; Third Secretary FO 1967; MECAS 1968; Tripoli 1970; Second later First Secretary Kuwait 1972; First Secretary FCO 1975; Head of Chancery Port of Spain 1978; Political Advisor Belmopan 1978; First Secretary (Commercial) Prague 1982; First Secretary later Counsellor FCO 1986; Counsellor, Consul-General and Deputy Head of Mission Baghdad 1987; Counsellor, Director of Trade Promotion and Investment Paris 1990; Head of AMD FCO 1995; Consul-General Jerusalem 1997; m 1987 Annabel Jane Hood (2s 1989, 1992).

Keefe, Denis Edward Peter Paul; Head of Far Eastern Group, FCO since July 2004; Born 29/06/58; FCO 1982; Second Secretary (Chancery) Prague 1984; First Secretary FCO 1988; First Secretary (Political) Nairobi 1992; First Secretary FCO 1996; Counsellor and Head of ASEM Unit, FCO 1997; Deputy Head of Mission Prague 1998; On loan as Counter Terrorism Strategy Team Leader, Cabinet Office 2002; Head of China Hong Kong Department FCO 2003; m 1983 Catherine Ann Mary Wooding (3d 1985, 1993, 1996; 3s 1987, 1989, 1991).

Keegan, David Barclay; First Secretary FCO since May 2002; Born 04/04/63; FCO 1986; Vice-Consul (Economic) Rio de Janeiro 1989; Second Secretary FCO 1991; Washington 1995; First Secretary (Political) Accra 1999; Band D6; m 1987 Susan Amanda Line (1s 1994; 1d 1996).

Keeling, Alison Heather; Private Secretary to the Political Director FCO since January 2002; Born 29/08/72; FCO 1996; Geneva (UKMIS) 1997; Beirut 1998; Band C4; m 2002 Reuben Thorpe.

Keeling, Heather; Lilongwe since December 2001; Born 04/05/71; FCO 2000; Band A2.

Keen, Gillian; Bangkok since September 2001; Born 18/02/61; Home Office 1979; Cabinet Office 1987; FCO 1992; Hanoi 1993; Tokyo 1997; Band A2; m 1987 Raymond Keen.

Keller, Ciaran Joseph; SUPL since August 2002; Born 02/02/77; FCO 1998; New York (UKMIS) 1999; Full-Time Language Training Lisbon 2000; Second Secretary (Political/EU) Lisbon 2000; Band C4.

Kelly, Iain Charles MacDonald; FCO since March 2003; Born 05/03/49; FCO 1974; Language Training 1975; Moscow 1976; Kuala Lumpur 1979; FCO 1982 (Second Secretary 1984); Istanbul 1986; FCO 1988; Los Angeles 1990; First Secretary (Commercial) Moscow 1992; Consul Amsterdam 1995; HM Ambassador Minsk 1999; m 1981 Linda Clare McGovern (2s 1984, 1988).

Kelly, Mark Terence; Third Secretary (Chancery) Tel Aviv since May 2001; Born 17/09/71; GCO

1990; Amman 1994; World Wide Floater Duties 1996; Panama 1999; FCO 2000; Band B3.

Kelly, Paul John, MBE (1984); First Secretary Beijing since March 1999; Born 11/03/64; FCO 1982; Pretoria 1987; FCO 1989; Nicosia 1994; FCO 1997; Band C5; m 1993 V L Stone (1d 1993, 1s 1997).

Kelly, Robert Anthony, OBE (2003); First Secretary (Regional Affairs) Port of Spain since February 2003; Born 10/12/59; FCO 1986; Third later Second Secretary Hong Kong 1990; Second Secretary FCO 1994; Second Secretary and Vice-Consul later First Secretary Athens 1996; First Secretary FCO 2000; Band D6; m 1986 Heather Erica Christina Smith (1s 1992; 1d 1993).

Kelly, William Charles; Consul (Commercial) Düsseldorf since March 2002; Born 05/01/61; FCO 1980; Jedda 1982; Lisbon 1985; Warsaw 1988; FCO 1990; Private Secretary to the Ambassador Bonn 1993; Third Secretary (Commercial) Paris 1996; FCO 1999; Band C4; m 1983 Carol Ann Villis (4s 1985, 1987, 1990, 1992; 1d 2000).

Kendall, Louise Margaret (née Wood); FCO since September 2002; Born 16/01/63; FCO 1981; Prague 1984; Tel Aviv 1986; FCO 1988; Language Training 1991; Third Secretary (Commercial) Budapest 1992; Vienna 1996; SUPL 2000; Band C4; m 1988 Philip Gary Kendall (1d 1992).

Kendall, Philip Gary; FCO since July 2002; Born 28/04/65; FCO 1984; Tel Aviv 1986; FCO 1988; Budapest 1992; SUPL 1996; Vienna 1998; Band B3; m 1988 Louise Margaret Kendall (née Wood) (1d 1992).

Keningale, Jacqueline; SUPL since October 1999; Born 18/02/66; FCO 1986; Moscow 1987; SUPL 1990; Jedda 1992; FCO 1994; Damascus 1996; Band B3; m 1990 Paul Bevan Downing.

Kennedy, Paul Vincent; First Secretary FCO since August 2003; Born 18/04/57; FCO 1989; Second Secretary (Chancery) Riyadh 1991; FCO 1995; First Secretary (Political) Bahrain 1999; Band D6; m 1984 Najia Ben Salah (1d 1990).

Kennedy, Thomas John, LVO (2004); Consul-General Bordeaux since February 2002; Born 03/02/57; FCO 1992; Second Secretary (Aid/Information) Buenos Aires 1994; First Secretary FCO 1997; m 1985 Clare Marie Ritchie (1s 2000).

Kennedy, Trudi Michelle; FCO since July 2003; Born 17/02/75; Band B3.

Kenny, John David; Second Secretary (Consular) Wellington since September 2003; Born 07/06/55; FCO 1973; Vienna 1976; Georgetown 1978; East Berlin 1982; FCO 1984; Cairo 1987; Third Secretary Dublin 1991; FCO 1995; Colombo 1999; Band C4; m 1979 Pamela Bernadette Baptiste (1s 1981; 1d 1985).

Kent, Andrew Magnus; First Secretary FCO since January 2001; Born 30/11/65; FCO 1989; Second

Secretary (Commercial) Tehran 1992; Second Secretary FCO 1995; Consul Jedda 1999; Band D6; m 1991 Sarah Louise Mills (1s 1994).

Kent, Mark Andrew Geoffrey; First Secretary (Commercial) later Counsellor (Public Services) Mexico City since October 2000; Born 14/01/66; FCO 1987; Third later Second Secretary (Chancery/Information) Brasilia 1989; Second later First Secretary Brussels (UKREP) 1993; First Secretary FCO 1998; m 1991 Martine Delogne (1s 1992; 1d 1995).

Kent, Sarah Louise (née Mills); FCO since April 1996; Born 28/01/65; FCO 1983; Prague 1987; FCO 1989; SUPL 1992; Band B3; m 1991 Andrew Magnus Kent (1s 1994).

Kenwrick-Piercy, Theodore Maurice; Counsellor FCO since December 1998; Born 16/01/48; Third later Second Secretary FCO 1971; Second later First Secretary (Press) Brussels (UKREP) 1974; FCO 1977; Nicosia 1982; First Secretary FCO 1986; First Secretary (Chancery) The Hague 1988; First Secretary FCO 1992; Counsellor Athens 1994; m 1976 Elisabeth Kenwrick-Cox (1s 1981; 1d 1983).

Keogh, David John; On loan to the Cabinet Office since April 1998; Born 24/06/56; FCO 1979; Ankara 1980; Abu Dhabi 1981; FCO 1983; Islamabad 1984; FCO 1988; Khartoum 1988; FCO 1991; Band C4; m 1987 Carolyn Ann Connolly (diss 1990).

Kernohan, Neil Alexander, MBE (1997); Private Secretary to the Political Director, FCO since March 2003; Born 20/09/65; FCO 1989; Riyadh 1992; T/D Vice-Consul Sana'a 1994; Vice-Consul and Third Secretary (Management) BIS Tripoli 1995; Third Secretary (IAEA/UN) Vienna (UKMIS) 1997; FCO 2000; Band C4.

Kerr, Christine; Nicosia since July 2002; Born 07/04/60; FCO 1989; Cape Town/Pretoria 1991; Moscow 1994; FCO 1996; Lilongwe 1998; Band A2; m 1991 Andrew Tuck (diss 1996) (1d 1994).

Kerr, Douglas James; On secondment (Commercial) since January 2003; Born 04/11/58; FCO 1980; Bucharest 1982; Kampala 1984; Tel Aviv 1988; FCO 1991; First Secretary (Commercial) Lima 1999.

Kerr, Michael John; Deputy Head of Mission Sana'a since January 2003; Born 12/08/49; RAF 1969 - 73; FCO 1973; Islamabad 1975; FCO 1977; Dakar 1979; FCO 1983; Cairo 1985; Oslo 1989; Second Secretary FCO 1992; Jedda 1995; Second Secretary (Management) Prague 1998; FCO 2000; m 1975 Linda Ruth Campbell (2s 1982, 1984; 1d 1989).

Kerrison, Irene; FCO since November 2002; Born 09/02/65; FCO 1986; Peking 1988; FCO 1990; Nassau 1991; FCO 1995; Language Training 1998-99; Moscow 1999; Band B3.

Kerry, Catherine Anne; FCO since October 2001; Born 31/07/65; FCO 1988; Lagos 1991; Tortola 1998; Band B3.

Kershaw, Roger; FCO since September 2001; Born 18/03/58; FCO 1982; Language Training 1983; Second Secretary (Commercial) Tehran 1984; First Secretary FCO 1987; First Secretary (Economic) Bonn 1992; First Secretary FCO 1996; Deputy High Commissioner Lagos 2000; m 1983 Annick Marie Jeanne Réné Gourley (2d 1986, 1988; 1s 1993).

Kettle, Mark Brian, MBE (2002); SUPL since October 2003; Born 22/10/66; FCO 1985; Vienna (UKMIS) 1990; FCO 1993; Muscat 1995; Third later Second Secretary (Consular) Islamabad 1999; Band B3; m 1995 Justine Carey (diss 2001); ptnr, Yvonne Dimmock (1d 2003).

Khan, Karim-ullah Akbar; Assistant Legal Adviser FCO since August 2003; Born 22/06/68; Band D7.

Khoo, Lionel John; FCO since January 2004; Born 30/04/68; Northern Ireland Office 1991; FCO 1994; Bandar Seri Begawan 1997; Tallinn 2000; Band A2.

Khosla, Nick Mahindra; Consul (Science and Technology) Shanghai since February 2004; Born 10/09/50; m 1978 Harumi Ishiwata (2s 1981, 1984).

Kidd, John Christopher William; Deputy Permanent Representative Brussels (UKDEL NATO) since August 2004; Born 04/02/57; FCO 1978; Third later Second Secretary Nicosia 1980; Second Secretary and PS to HM Ambassador Paris 1984; First Secretary 1985; First Secretary FCO 1986; Deputy Head of Mission Addis Ababa 1990; First Secretary FCO 1993; Counsellor on secondment to European Commission 1996; Counsellor (Political) Bonn later Berlin 1998; Counsellor FCO 2001; m 1995 Carine Celia Ann Maitland (1 step d 1983; 1 step s 1986; twin d 1996).

Kidner, James Hippisley; On secondment as APS to HRH The Prince of Wales since April 2003; Born 26/02/61; FCO 1985; Second Secretary Kuala Lumpur 1987; First Secretary FCO 1990; On attachment to Privy Council Office as PS to Leader of the House of Commons 1992; First Secretary FCO 1993; First Secretary later Deputy Head of Mission Sofia 1996; FCO 2000; m 1987 Sally Baillie-Hamilton (3d 1996, 1998, 2002; 1s 2000).

Kilby, David James; First Secretary (Regional Affairs) Cairo since April 2003; Born 05/11/66; FCO 2000; First Secretary (Political) and Deputy Permanent Representative ESCAP Bangkok 2001; Band D6; m 1997 Alison Jean McKenna (2s 2002, 2004).

Kiloh, Eleanor Anne; Second Secretary (Political) Jakarta since March 2002; Born 20/04/77; FCO 1999; Band C4.

Kilvington, Sally Louise; FCO since July 1995; Born 20/02/67; FCO 1989; Santiago 1991; Band B3; m 2002 Harsharan Singh Nijjar.

Kinchen, Richard, MVO (1976); HM Ambassador Brussels since November 2003; Born 12/02/48;

Third Secretary FCO 1970; Temporary secondment to British Commission on Rhodesian Opinion 1972; MECAS 1972; Kuwait 1973; Second Secretary FCO 1974; Second later First Secretary Luxembourg 1975; First Secretary (Economic) Paris 1977; FCO 1980; PS/Parliamentary Under-Secretary of State 1982; First Secretary and Head of Chancery Rabat 1984; Counsellor (Finance) New York (UKMIS) 1988; Head of Dependent Territories Secretariat Bridgetown 1993; HM Ambassador Beirut 2000; m 1972 Cheryl Vivienne Abayasekera (1s 1976; 3d 1973 (dec'd 1980), 1979, 1982).

King, Alison Jane; SUPL since December 2002; Born 11/06/66; FCO 1984; Brussels (UKREP) 1987; Mexico City 1989; FCO 1993; Floater Duties 1996; FCO 1998; Band C4.

King, Alyson Ruth Grace; FCO since October 2003; Born 02/01/76; Admitted Practice (New York and England/Wales) 2000; Band C4; m 1999 Ayman Jarjour (1d 2001; 1s 2003).

King, Julian Beresford; Counsellor and Head of Chancery New York (UKMIS) since April 2003; Born 22/08/64; FCO 1985; Third later Second Secretary Paris (including ENA) 1987; Luxembourg and The Hague 1991; Second later First Secretary FCO 1992; Private Secretary to Permanent Under-Secretary of State FCO 1995; First Secretary later Counsellor (Enlargement) Brussels (UKREP) 1998; m 1992 Lotte Knudsen.

King, Larry; FCO since May 1998; Born 01/07/62; FCO 1982; Amman 1985; FCO 1988; Pretoria 1995; Band C5; m 1988 Elaine Margaret Neeve (2d 1992, 1996).

King-Smith, Alastair; FCO since March 2003; Born 27/09/74; FCO 1996; Full-Time Language Training (Arabic) 1997; Cairo 1998; Deputy Head of Interests Section later Acting Chargé d' Affaires Tripoli 1999; Head of Political/Information Sections Khartoum 1999; Band C4.

Kingdom, David George, OBE (2004); Istanbul since November 2003; Born 19/08/46; FCO 1986; Third Secretary Brussels 1992; First Secretary FCO 1994; Ankara 2000; Band C5; m 1968 Janice (2s 1972, 1981).

Kingford, Paul; Third Secretary Beijing since September 2003; Born 05/04/56; MOD 1987-98; FCO 1998; Tehran 2000; Band B3.

Kingston, Iain Conger; Management Officer Bahrain since August 2003; Born 30/05/50; DOE (PSA) 1975; FCO 1976; Cairo 1979; Lilongwe 1983; FCO 1985; Houston 1988; Maseru 1991; Second Secretary FCO 1995; Band C4; m 1978 Georgia Georgiou (2s 1982, 1983).

Kinoshita, Susan Margaret (née Copnell), OBE (2003); FCO since October 2003; Born 28/07/61; FCO 1983; Language Training Tokyo 1985; Tokyo 1986; FCO 1989; SUPL 1991; FCO 1992; SUPL 1993; Osaka 1996; First Secretary (Press and Public Affairs) Tokyo 1999; Band D6; m 1989 Makoto Kinoshita (1d 1991; 1s 1993).

Kirby, Diane (née Tallon); SUPL since April 1995; Born 25/01/67; FCO 1986; Muscat 1988; Gibraltar 1993; Band A2; m 1988 Sean William Kirby (1s 1991).

Kirk, Andrew Philip; Second Secretary (Economic) The Hague since September 1999; Born 26/02/54; FCO 1972; Yaoundé 1975; Havana 1979; FCO 1981; Vice-Consul Lisbon 1985; Aid Attaché Nairobi 1987; Second Secretary FCO 1991; BTIO New York 1994; FCO 1997; Vice-Consul (Investment) San Francisco 1997; Band C4; m 1978 Cheryl Jeanne Nichols (2d 1983, 1987).

Kirk, Anna Theresa (née Macey); FCO since July 2002; Born 01/06/59; FCO 1982; Language Training 1984; Third later Second Secretary Oslo 1984; First Secretary FCO 1988; First Secretary (Political) Paris 1992; First Secretary FCO 1997; Counsellor on loan as Resident Chair to Civil Service Selection Board 1999; m 1989 Matthew John Lushington Kirk (2d 1995, 1998).

Kirk, Malcolm Braidwood; Deputy High Commissioner Georgetown since July 2004; Born 10/04/59; FCO 1978; Nassau 1980; Dakar 1981; FCO 1984; Havana 1985; FCO 1987; Paris 1990; Deputy Head of Mission Tegucigalpa 1993; FCO 1997; Staff Officer later First Secretary (Head of Governor's Office) Tortola 2000; Band C5; m 1982 Linda Patricia Greenwood (1 step s 1980; 1s 1983).

Kirk, Matthew John Lushington; HM Ambassador Helsinki since August 2002; Born 10/10/60; FCO 1982; Language Training 1984; Third later Second Secretary (Political/Information) Belgrade 1984; Second later First Secretary FCO 1988; ENA Paris 1992; First Secretary (Political/Military) Paris 1993; Counsellor FCO 1997; Counsellor on loan to the Cabinet Office 1998; Counsellor FCO 1999; m 1989 Anna Thérèse Macey (2d 1995, 1998).

Kirk, Susan Mary; Rabat since September 2002; Born 28/04/46; FCO 1994; Nairobi 1996; Floater Duties 2000; Band A2; m 1969 (1s 1975).

Kirkpatrick, Andrew John; Second Secretary FCO since January 2002; Born 01/06/63; FCO 1988; Third Secretary (Chancery) Budapest 1990; Third Secretary FCO 1992; Third Secretary (Immigration) Islamabad 1995; Third Secretary FCO 1998; Second Secretary (Management) Lagos 1999; Band C5; m 1992 Sara Elizabeth Pickering.

Kitsell, Corinne Angela; FCO since August 1998; Born 18/10/69; FCO 1992; T/D New York (UKMIS) 1994; T/D Beijing 1995; Vice-Consul Beirut 1996; Band D6.

Kittmer, John; FCO since January 2003; Born 06/07/67; Department of Employment 1993; Department of Education and Employment 1995; Brussels (UKREP) 1998; Band D6.

Knapp, Maria Grace; Santiago since July 2002; Born 03/04/70; FCO 1989; Madrid 1992; FCO

1995; On loan to HM Customs and Excise at Caracas 1996; FCO 1999; Band B3.

Knewstubb, Rosemary Anne (née Urch); SUPL since June 2004; Born 26/10/68; FCO 1992; Ottawa 1995; Bucharest 1999; Brussels (UKREP) 2002; Band A2; m 1996 Mark Andrew Knewstubb.

Knight, Terence Ronald; Resident British Commissioner Kingstown since August 2002; Born 03/09/51; FCO 1973; Rabat 1976; Lima 1978; Islamabad 1981; FCO 1983; Oslo 1986; Third later Second Secretary (Chancery) Port of Spain 1989; Second Secretary FCO 1993; First Secretary (Management) Washington 1997; m 1971 Jane Willcocks (2d 1975, 1980; 2s 1977, 1982).

Knott, Graeme Jonathan; First Secretary (Trade and Investment) Paris (UKDEL OECD) since September 2000; Born 02/11/66; FCO 1988; Third later Second Secretary (Chancery) Havana 1991; First Secretary FCO 1995; First Secretary Mexico City 1996; Full-Time Language Training 2000; Band D6.

Knott, Paul Robert; Second Secretary (Commercial) Brussels (UKREP) since February 2001; Born 30/06/70; FCO 1989; Bucharest 1992; Dubai 1993; Full-time Russian language training 1997; Third Secretary (Chancery) Tashkent 1997; Second Secretary (Political) Kiev 2000; Band C4; m 2002 Mwana Lugogo.

Knowlton, Richard Jonathan; Counsellor Helsinki since October 2003; Born 25/03/50; Third later Second Secretary FCO 1973; Language Student FCO and Finland 1977; Second later First Secretary Helsinki 1978; First Secretary FCO 1981; Harare 1984; FCO 1989; First Secretary (Chancery/Economic) Dubai 1991; First Secretary later Counsellor FCO 1995; Counsellor (Regional Affairs) Bridgetown 1997; Counsellor FCO 2000; Counsellor Caracas 2002; m 1995 Evelina Ravarino.

Koizumi, Richard Akio; Tokyo since January 2004; Born 25/08/77; FCO 2002; Band B3.

Korad, Mark David; Second Secretary (Political/PPAO) Islamabad since March 2003; Born 19/06/69; FCO 1991; Bucharest 1994; Paris 1998; Band C4; m 1996 Corina Ioana Mantu (diss 2003).

Kraus, John Arthur; First Secretary (Political Internal) Berlin since August 2003; Born 07/05/66; FCO 1993; Second Secretary (Political) Bonn 1995; FCO 1998; Band D6; m 1995 Judith Mary Smakman (1s 1996).

Kruger, Gabrielle Lisa; Second Secretary - BCW The Hague since September 2003; Born 22/02/76; FCO 2001; Band C4.

Kuenssberg, Joanna Kate; First Secretary (EU Economic) Paris since January 2001; Born 06/02/73; Second Secretary FCO 1997; Attachment to Foreign Ministry, Budapest 1999; Attachment to Quai d'Orsay, Paris 2000; m 1997 Finbarr O'Sullivan.

Kydd, Ian Douglas; SMO New Delhi since February 2003; Born 01/11/47; CO 1966; DSAO (later FCO) 1966; New Delhi 1970; Second Secretary (Radio/TV) BIS New York 1975; FCO 1979; First Secretary on loan to No 10 Downing Street 1981; Language Training 1983; First Secretary (Chancery) Lagos 1984; First Secretary (Economic/Commercial) Ottawa 1988; First Secretary FCO 1993; Counsellor (Management) Moscow 1995; Consul-General Vancouver 1998; m 1968 Elizabeth Louise Pontius (1s 1971; 1d 1973).

Kyle, Michael Anthony; Counsellor FCO since February 1998; Born 20/07/48; FCO 1970; Third later Second Secretary Saigon 1972; Second later First Secretary FCO 1975; Washington 1978; FCO 1981; First Secretary (Political/Economic) Accra 1984; First Secretary (Chancery) Dar es Salaam 1988; First Secretary later Counsellor FCO 1991; Counsellor Berlin 1995; m 1976 Wendy Suzanne Sloan (1d 1979; 1s 1981).

Kyles, Raymond William; Deputy High Commissioner Nairobi since July 2003; Born 10/03/56; FCO 1980; Geneva (UKMIS) 1982; Second Secretary Brussels (UKREP) 1985; First Secretary FCO 1987; First Secretary (Chancery) Pretoria 1991; First Secretary FCO 1996; Deputy Permanent Representative Paris (OECD) 1998; Deputy Head of News Department FCO 2000; m 1981 Christine Jane Thompson.

L

Lacey-Smith, Jane Frances; SUPL since January 2004; Born 20/09/63; FCO 1984; East Berlin 1985; Dublin 1987; Algiers 1990; Vice-Consul/Management Frankfurt 1997; ECM Bangkok 2000; Band C4; m 1995 Martin Frederick Smith (1d 2001).

Ladd, Benjamin Dafydd Oswin; Second Secretary (Commercial) Beijing since November 2000; Born 18/02/76; FCO 1997; Full-Time Language Training 1998; Full-Time Language Training Beijing 1999; Band C4.

Ladd, Michael John; FCO since 1992; Born 23/10/54; FCO 1971; Washington 1980; FCO 1983; Baghdad 1986; Vienna 1990; Band D6; m 1979 Christine Jane Tate (1s 1983; 1d 1986).

Laffey, Susan; SUPL since August 2003; Born 09/10/61; FCO 1985; East Berlin 1987; Senior Research Officer (DS Band C4) 1987; Second Secretary (Chancery) Bucharest 1989; FCO 1992; UKDEL OSCE Budapest 1994; Principal Research Analyst FCO 1995; UKDEL OSCE Vienna 1996; FCO 1996; T/D Zagreb 1998; First Secretary (Political) Bucharest 2001; Band D6.

Laing, (John) Stuart; HM Ambassador Muscat since April 2002; Born 22/07/48; Third Secretary FCO 1970; MECAS 1971; Third later Second Secretary Jedda 1973; Second later First Secretary Brussels (UKREP) 1975; FCO 1978; First Secretary and Head of Chancery Cairo 1983; First Secretary FCO 1987; Deputy Head of Mission

Prague 1989; Counsellor and Deputy Head of Mission Riyadh 1992; Counsellor FCO 1995; DFID 1997; High Commissioner Brunei 1998; m 1972 Sibella Dorman (1s 1974; 2d 1979, 1985).

Laird, Alison Margaret; Second Secretary (Political) Buenos Aires since March 2003; Born 05/12/75; FCO 2000; Band C4.

Lake, Robin Duncan; Third Secretary New York (UKMIS) since January 2002; Born 15/12/70; FCO 1989; Berlin 1991; Ottawa 1994; FCO 1997; Third Secretary (Immigration) Tehran 1998; Band B3.

Lamb, Robin David; HM Ambassador Bahrain since August 2003; Born 25/11/48; FCO 1971; Language Training MECAS 1974; FCO 1977 Research Officer (DS Band C4); Second Secretary Jedda 1979; Principal Research Officer FCO 1982; First Secretary (Economic) Riyadh 1985; FCO 1988 PRO (Band D6); First Secretary (Head of Political Section) Cairo 1993; FCO 1996; Counsellor, on loan to the DTI 1999; Counsellor and Deputy Head of Mission Kuwait 2001; m 1977 Susan Jane Moxon (1d 1982; 2s 1986, 1996).

Lambert, Jason Edward; Cairo since April 2003; Born 27/09/71; FCO 1990; Brussels 1994; FCO 1997; Nairobi 1999; Band B3; m 1997 Lucy Anne Edwards (diss 2003).

Lamont, Donald Alexander; HM Ambassador Caracas since July 2003; Born 13/01/47; Second later First Secretary FCO 1974; First Secretary (UNIDO/IAEA) Vienna 1977; First Secretary (Commercial) Moscow 1980; First Secretary FCO 1982; Counsellor on attachment to IISS 1988; Counsellor and Head of Chancery BMG (later BM) Berlin 1988; HM Ambassador Montevideo 1991; Head of Republic of Ireland Department 1994; Chief of Staff, OHR Sarajevo 1997; Governor Stanley and Commissioner for South Georgia and Sandwich Islands 1999; m 1981 Lynda Margaret Campbell (1d 1983; 1s 1986).

Lampert, Sarah Jane; First Secretary (Political) New Delhi since September 2003; Born 08/11/65; FCO 1988; Language Training 1990; Third later Second Secretary (Chancery) Sofia 1991; First Secretary FCO 1995; SUPL 1996; First Secretary FCO 1997; SUPL 1999; Full-Time Language Training 2003; Band D6; m 1993 Andrew William Kenningham (2d 1996, 1998).

Lamport, Martin Henry; First Secretary (Commercial) Lima since July 2002; Born 22/11/52; HM Forces 1972; FCO 1975; SUPL 1976; FCO 1979; Tripoli 1980; Caracas 1983; FCO 1987; Third Secretary (Institutions) Brussels (UKREP) 1990; Deputy High Commissioner Belmopan 1993; FCO 1996; Deputy Head of Mission Sana'a 1999; Band C5; m 1990 Catherine Priscilla Maxwell (3d 1992, 1994, 1996).

Lancaster, Ian Francis Millar; Counsellor FCO since January 1995; Born 23/09/47; Second Secretary FCO 1974; Second later First Secretary and Consul Hanoi 1975; First Secretary FCO 1977; Prague 1978; First Secretary FCO 1981;

First Secretary (Chancery) Brussels 1983; First Secretary FCO 1987; First Secretary (Chancery) later Counsellor Ankara 1991; m 1972 Simone Daniel (1d 1978; 1s 1981).

Landsman, Dr David Maurice, OBE (2000); FCO since October 2003; Born 23/08/63; FCO 1989; Second Secretary (Economic) Athens 1991; FCO 1994; Deputy Head of Mission Belgrade 1997; FCO 1999; Head of British Embassy Office Banja Luka and concurrently First Secretary (Regional Affairs) Budapest 1999; Chargé d'Affaires Belgrade 2000; HM Ambassador Tirana 2001; m 1990 Catherine Louise Holden (1s 1992).

Lane, Bari Albert; FCO since May 1997; Born 06/05/48; Ministry of Technology 1965; FO, DSAO and FCO 1966; Vice-Consul Aden 1970; Warsaw 1973; Bombay 1974; FCO 1975; Second Secretary (Admin) Peking 1978; Vice-Consul (Commercial) Sydney 1980; Second later First Secretary FCO 1985; First Secretary (Management) Paris 1992; m 1971 Jacqueline Mary Chatt.

Langham, Elizabeth Jane (née Webb); SUPL since July 2001; Born 04/08/61; FCO 1984; Moscow 1986; Washington 1988; FCO 1991; SUPL 1992; Bahrain 1995; SUPL 1996; Second Secretary Stockholm 1997; m 1989 Peter Andrew Langham (2d 1992, 1994).

Langham, Peter Andrew; Consul (Commercial) St Petersburg since January 2003; Born 26/09/64; FCO 1983; Moscow 1985; Hamilton 1988; Washington 1990; FCO 1991; Bahrain 1994; Second Secretary Stockholm 1998; m 1989 Elizabeth Jane Webb (2d 1992, 1994).

Langman, Nicholas John Andrew; Counsellor Athens since April 2003; Born 01/11/60; FCO 1983; Second Secretary Montevideo 1986; Second later First Secretary New York (UKMIS) 1988; First Secretary FCO 1991; Paris 1994; First Secretary FCO 1998; m 1992 Sarah Jane Pearcey (2d 1994, 1995).

Langridge, Pauline Anne; Full-Time Language Training since January 2004; Born 17/08/63; FCO 1988; Madrid 1990; Guatemala 1993; FCO 1995; Havana 2000; Band A2.

Langrish, Sally (née Monk); SUPL since July 2003; Born 05/08/68; Called to the Bar Middle Temple 1991; Treasury Solicitors Department 1993; Assistant Legal Adviser FCO 1995; First Secretary (Legal) Brussels (UKREP) 2000; First Secretary (JHA) Brussels (UKREP) 2001; Band D7; m 1996 Richard Michael John Langrish.

Lankester, Rosalind Philippa (née Greig); SUPL since February 2001; Born 16/04/66; FCO 1989; Third Secretary Bangkok 1992; SUPL 1995; T/D Moscow 1996; FCO 1996; SUPL 1999; FCO 2000; Band B3; m 1997 Thomas Henry Gervase Lankester (1s 1999).

Lapsley, Angus Charles William; First Secretary (Political/Internal) later (Political/Military) Paris since April 2001; Born 16/03/70; Second Secretary

Department of Health 1991; Second Secretary Brussels (UKREP) 1994; Private Secretary Department of Health 1995; Private Secretary No 10 Downing Street 1996; First Secretary Head IGC Unit, EUD(I) FCO 1999; Band D6; m 1999 Georgina Maria Power (1s 2002).

Larden, Kendra Jane; FCO since May 2003; Born 07/03/71; FCO 1991; Paris 1993; Muscat 1996; Peking 2000; Band B3.

Larkins, Christopher Paul; FCO since March 2000; Born 02/10/63; FCO 1986; Warsaw 1991; FCO 1994; Hong Kong 1996; Band A2.

Larmouth, Helen Dorothy; Brussels (UKREP) since December 2002; Born 22/08/63; FCO 1989; Washington 1992; Lilongwe 1994; Rangoon 1998; Band A2.

Larner, Jeremy Francis; FCO since October 2002; Born 12/11/49; Inland Revenue 1967; FCO 1968; Cairo 1971; Benghazi 1972; Abu Dhabi 1972; Moscow 1975; Seoul 1975; Manila 1976; Monrovia 1977; FCO 1980; Third later Second Secretary (Commercial) Tunis 1983; Second Secretary (Commercial) Port Louis 1989; Second later First Secretary FCO 1992; Deputy Head of Mission and HM Consul Rangoon 1995; Deputy Director General BTCO Taipei 1999; Band D6; m 1975 Sally Dewhurst (2s 1978, 1980).

Lassman, Louise (née Mason); Strasbourg since September 2003; Born 30/08/63; FCO 1986; Gibraltar 1993; Hong Kong 1996; FCO 2000; Band B3; m 1993 Nigel Abraham Lassman.

Latham, Sarah Jane; FCO since July 2002; Born 24/06/70; FCO 1996; Ankara 1998; Band B3; m 2002 Firat Ucer.

Latham-Green, Tracey Lynne; SUPL since October 2003; Born 06/09/76; FCO 2002; Band B3; m 2001 Duncan Aaron.

Latta, Nicholas Karim; Second Secretary (Commercial) Moscow since May 2002; Born 02/09/71; FCO 1995; Full-Time Language Training 1996; Full-Time Language Training Cairo 1997; Second Secretary Muscat 1998; Band C4; m 1997 Susanna Mary Davis (1d 2000; 1s 2002).

Latter, Edwin John Scott; First Secretary FCO since August 1997; Born 16/02/68; FCO 1991; Vice-Consul Istanbul 1994; Band D6; m 1994 Rosemary Helen Fabre (1d 1996).

Lattin-Rawstrone, Howard; Deputy High Commissioner Belmopan since January 2003; Born 23/03/55; FCO 1975; Buenos Aires 1977; Maputo 1981; Brussels 1982; FCO 1984; Cairo 1988; Second Secretary (Commercial/Aid) Cairo 1991; Second Secretary Lilongwe 1993; FCO 1997; First Secretary (Commercial) Warsaw 1999; m 1987 Caroline Sarah Lattin (2 adopted d 1976, 1978; 1s 1987).

Lavers, Richard Douglas; HM Ambassador Guatemala City since October 2001, also accredited to San Salvador since August 2003 and Honduras since February 2004; Born 10/05/47;

Third Secretary FCO 1969; Buenos Aires 1970; Second later First Secretary Wellington 1973; FCO 1976; First Secretary (Political/Economic) Brussels 1981; On secondment to Guinness Mahon 1985; First Secretary FCO 1987; NATO Defence College Rome 1989; Deputy Head of Mission and Consul-General Santiago 1993; HM Ambassador Quito 1993; Counsellor FCO 1997; Head of Research Analysts FCO 1999; m 1986 Brigitte Anne Julia Maria Moers (2s 1988, 1989).

Lavery, Creena Christina Maureen; SUPL since November 2003; Born 17/05/62; FCO 1991; Brussels (UKDEL NATO) 1993; Presidency Liason Officer Luxembourg 1997; Bonn 1999; Consul (Consular/Immigration) Düsseldorf 2000; Band C4.

Lavery, Derek John; Baku since July 2002; Born 01/06/68; FCO 1987; Islamabad 1989; Bonn 1993; FCO 1996; Band B3; m 1992 Claire Ruth Haines.

Lavery, Sheena Anne; FCO since January 2003; Born 09/12/74; Band B3.

Lavocat, Amanda Joyce (née Thomas); SUPL since April 2003; Born 21/12/67; DHSS 1986; FCO 1987; Pretoria 1989; Algiers 1992; FCO 1994; Istanbul 1997; Dakar 2000; Band B3; m 1993 Frederic Paul Francis Lavocat (1s 1995).

Lawley-Woods, Claire Angela; HM Consul Guangzhou since July 2003; Born 14/06/62; FCO 1984; Rome 1985; SUPL 1988; Resigned 1989; Reinstated, FCO 1994; Ottawa 1996; Vice-Consul New Delhi 1999; FCO 2001; Band C4; m 2003 Roger Michael Woods (2s 1982, 1988; 1d 1985).

Lawrence, Joanne Louise (née Watson); FCO since March 2003; Born 30/04/68; FCO 1986; Wellington 1988; SUPL 1992; Stanley 1995; Islamabad 1998; FCO 2001; T/D Kabul 2002; Band C4; m 1991 Martin Lawrence (2d 1993, 1999).

Lawrence, Julie; Floater Duties since July 2002; Born 28/01/66; FCO 2000; Band A2; m 2004 Andy Allman.

Lawrence, Paul David; St John's since December 2002; Born 10/04/68; FCO 1989; New York (UKMIS) 1993; World Wide Floater Duties 1997; Kigali 2000; Band B3.

Lawrie, James Malcolm, MBE (1985); Second Secretary Lagos since November 2000; Born 01/06/44; FCO 1970; Jedda 1972; FCO 1973; Islamabad 1975; FCO 1977; Kuwait 1979; FCO 1983; Third Secretary Peking 1984; FCO 1986; Accra 1990; FCO 1993; Cairo 1995; FCO 1998; Band C4; m (1) 1971 Anne Margaret Martin (diss) (3s 1974, 1977, 1982); (2) 2000 Sheila Boxer.

Laxton, Rowan James; Deputy Head of Mission Kabul since September 2002; Born 19/02/61; FCO 1993; First Secretary (Chancery) Islamabad 1997; FCO 2000; Band D7; m 2000 Sonya L Laxton.

Laycock, Rachel Jane; Second Secretary (Chancery) Washington since May 2000; Born

20/05/71; FCO 1994; Band C4; m 2000 Owen Pengelly.

Layden, Anthony Michael; HM Ambassador Tripoli since October 2002; Born 27/07/46; Third Secretary FCO 1968; MECAS 1969; Second Secretary Jedda 1971; Second later First Secretary Rome 1973; FCO 1977; First Secretary and Head of Chancery Jedda 1982; First Secretary FCO 1982; Head of Chancery Muscat 1987; Counsellor (Commercial/Economic) Copenhagen 1991; Counsellor FCO 1995; HM Ambassador Rabat 1999; m 1969 Josephine Mary McGhee (3s 1973, 1974, 1977; 1d 1982).

Layfield, Jonathan Timothy Whitton; Second Secretary Basra since April 2004; Born 19/06/67; FCO 1997; Jedda 1999; Full-Time Language Training 2000; Amman 2001; m 1997 Rebecca Anne (2s 2001, 2003).

Leake, Nicholas Howard; On loan as Legal Adviser at HM Treasury since January 2003; Born 15/01/72; FCO 1994; Second Secretary (KHF) Budapest 1996; On loan to DFID 1998; First Secretary (Industry) Brussels (UKREP) 2000.

Lee, Adrian Jonathan; Second Secretary (Chancery) Luanda since February 2003; Born 24/10/68; FCO 1989; Full-Time Language Training Cairo 1991; Third Secretary (Commercial later Political) Riyadh 1992; British Vice-Consul and Management Officer São Paulo 1996; FCO 2000; Band C4.

Lee, Laurence John; First Secretary (Chancery) Kingston since July 2004; Born 03/08/69; Band D6; ptnr, Sarah Byrne (1s 1983).

Lee, Richard John Clifton; SMO Tel Aviv since September 2002; Born 26/09/51; FCO 1971; Copenhagen 1973; Addis Ababa 1976; Moscow 1979; FCO 1982; Accra 1984; Lusaka 1987; FCO 1989; Second Secretary (Commercial) Kuwait 1992; Jakarta 1994; Second Secretary FCO 1999; m 1973 Lesley Eleanor McConnell (1d 1980; 1s 1982).

Lee, Thomas David; Second Secretary FCO since May 2003; Born 09/05/63; FCO 1983; Nicosia 1987; Third later Second Secretary FCO 1990; SUPL 2002; Band C4.

Lee-Gorton, Victoria (née Lee); SUPL since August 2003; Born 05/03/70; FCO 1990; Full-Time Language Training 1992; Third Secretary Maputo 1993; Third Secretary EU Presidency Liason Officer Rome/Dublin/The Hague 1995; Third later Second Secretary FCO 1997; Full-Time Language Training FCO 2001; Second Secretary (Chancery/Information) Dubai 2002; Band C4; m 1992 Christopher John Gorton (1d 2001).

Legg, Judy; Director New York since May 2002; Born 29/04/67; FCO 1991; Full-Time Language Training 1992; Second Secretary 1993; Moscow 1994; First Secretary FCO 1995; SUPL 2000; Band D6; m 1994 Graham Barry Stanley (1d 1998; 1s 2003).

Legg, Rufus Alexander; Second Secretary FCO since October 2000; Born 13/03/68; FCO 1990; Third Secretary Port Moresby 1993; Third later Second Secretary and Deputy Head of Mission Tegucigalpa 1997; Band C4.

Legge, Jeremy John; First Secretary (Political) Paris since August 2001; Born 19/05/61; Second Secretary FCO 1985; Second Secretary Lusaka 1987; Second later First Secretary FCO 1989; First secretary on loan to the Cabinet Office 1989; Vienna (UKMIS) 1994; First Secretary FCO 1998; Band D6; m 1990 Melanie King (3s 1991, 1992, 1994).

Leigh, David John; Second later First Secretary FCO since August 1987; Born 03/07/48; Post Office 1964; FCO 1969; Lagos 1974; FCO 1975; Third Secretary Tokyo 1978; FCO 1981; Third Secretary Sofia 1984.

Leinster, Norman Kennedy; FCO since November 2003; Born 04/06/65; Band B3.

Leister, Helen Grace (née McCarthy); SUPL since February 2003; Born 01/02/64; FCO 1983; Paris 1985; Luxembourg 1988; Paris 1991; Kiev 1994; FCO 1996; Ottawa 1999; SUPL 2000; Ottawa 2000; Band B3; m 1991 Alan Leister.

Leith, Dennis, RVM (1975); Seattle since April 2004; Born 10/12/48; FCO 1967; Moscow 1971; Mexico City 1972; Sofia 1975; FCO 1976; Guatemala City 1979; Vienna 1982; Second Secretary FCO 1984; Second Secretary (Commercial) Bahrain 1987; On secondment to the London Chamber of Commerce 1991; Consul-General Ho Chi Minh City 1992; Second Secretary FCO 1995; First Secretary (Commercial) Sofia 1998; FCO 2003; m 1971 Barbara Mary Hum (1s 1974; 1d 1979).

Lelliott, David Patrick; Monrovia since October 2003; Born 13/09/66; FCO 1993; Third Secretary Doha 1996; Second Secretary (Commercial) Mexico City 2000; Band D6.

Lennard, Sarah Jill; First Secretary FCO since November 1998; Born 19/04/56; FCO 1981; Third Secretary Montevideo 1982; Second Secretary FCO 1983; Brussels (UKREP) 1983; First Secretary FCO 1985; Budapest 1994; Band D6; m 1987 Mark Kilroy (1s 1989; 1d 1992).

Leon, Judith Mary; Deputy Consul-General Johannesburg since June 2001; Born 17/07/63; Home Office 1984; FCO 1987; New York 1989; Bangkok 1992; FCO 1994; Second Secretary 1995; Second Secretary (Commercial) Bombay 1997.

Leslie, Alison Mariot (née Sanderson); HM Ambassador Oslo since August 2002; Born 25/06/54; FCO 1977; Singapore 1978; Bonn 1982; FCO 1986; Quai d'Orsay Paris 1990; Head of ESED 1992; Scottish Office 1993 - 95; Head of Policy Planning Staff FCO 1996; Deputy Head of Mission Rome 1998; m 1978 Andrew David Leslie (2d 1987, 1990).

Leslie, Thomas Gary; FCO since April 2003; Born 27/04/69; FCO 1989; Karachi 1991; FCO 1993; Tokyo 1994; Kamakura 1998; Tokyo 1999; Band C4; m 2001 Angela Burns.

Leslie-Jones, Philippa Anne; SUPL since July 2004; Born 19/07/59; FCO 1984; Second Secretary Warsaw 1986; First Secretary FCO 1989; First Secretary (Chancery) Moscow 1991; On loan to No. 10 Downing Street 1994; SUPL 1995; FCO 1995; SUPL 1996; On secondment Cabinet Office 2002; m 1994 Richard Philip Bridge (2s 1995, 1997).

Less, Timothy Garnham; FCO since January 2004; Born 26/07/73; Band C5.

Lever, Giles; SUPL since May 2004; Born 20/03/68; FCO 1990; Third later Second Secretary (Political) Hanoi 1993; First Secretary FCO 1997; Full-Time Language Training 2000; Tokyo 2001.

Lever, Simon Jeffrey; Consul-General Marseilles since September 2001; Born 04/01/63; FCO 1983; Doha 1985; SE Asia/FE Floater 1988; Full-Time Language Training FCO 1989; Language Training Hong Kong 1990; Third later Second Secretary Beijing 1991; On loan to the DTI 1996; FCO 1997; HM Consul Chiang Mai 1998; Peking 2000; Band C5; m 1993 Krisana Khumnuan (1d 2000; 1s 2002).

Levey, Joanna Claire (née Brewis); SUPL since November 2002; Born 22/09/60; FCO 1981; Kuwait 1983; Luanda 1986; FCO 1989; Copenhagen 1990; FCO 1992; Band A2; m 1997 Robert Edward Levey (1d 2000).

Levi, Andrew Peter Robert; Head of Aviation, Maritime and Energy Department, FCO since April 2003; Born 04/03/63; FCO 1987; Second Secretary 1989; Second Secretary (Chancery, subsequently Economic/EC) Bonn 1990; First Secretary FCO 1993; On secondment to the European Commission (EU enlargement) 1996; On secondment to OECD Secretariat (eastern European administrative reform) 1998; First Secretary (Political) Bonn 1998; Seconded to the EU Presidency CFSP Team at the German Foreign Office 1999; Seconded to Special Co-ordinator of the Stability Pact for South Eastern Europe (Deputy Chief of Staff) 1999; Deputy Head of Eastern Adriatic Department, FCO 2001; m 2002 Roswitha Elisabeth von Studnitz.

Levoir, Derek Charles; Deputy Head of Mission Dakar since June 2003; Born 08/08/46; DSAO 1965; Latin America Floater 1969; Rome 1971; FCO 1974; Second Secretary 1976; Asunción 1978; Lisbon 1982; Vice-Consul Naples 1986; FCO 1991; First Secretary (Consular) Nairobi 1999; m 1973 Liana Annita Ugo (2d 1975, 1976).

Lewington, Richard George; HM Ambassador Quito since June 2003; Born 13/04/48; DSAO (later FCO) 1968; Attached to Army School of Languages 1971; Ulaanbaatar 1972; Second Secretary (Chancery/Information) Lima 1976; FCO 1980; Second Secretary (Commercial) Moscow 1982; Second later First Secretary FCO

1983; First Secretary (Commercial) Tel Aviv 1986; First Secretary FCO 1990; EU Monitoring Mission Yugoslavia 1991; Deputy High Commissioner Valletta 1995; HM Ambassador Almaty and HM Ambassador (non-resident) Bishkek 1999; m 1972 Sylviane Paulette Marie Cholet (1s 1982; 1d 1984).

Lewis, Claire Samantha; SUPL since December 2002; Born 03/06/66; FCO 1990; Madras 1993; New Delhi 1998; FCO 2001; Band C4; m 2000 Ian David Booth (1s 2003).

Lewis, Harriet Catherine; FCO since October 2002; Born 13/06/79; Band B3.

Lewis, Dr John Ewart Thomas; Counsellor (Regional Affairs) Buenos Aires since October 2002; Born 05/11/55; FCO 1987; First Secretary (Chancery) Bonn 1991; Consul (Economic) Frankfurt 1993; First Secretary FCO 1996; Band D6.

Lewis, Joy Suzanne (née Spalding); SUPL since September 2002; Born 01/08/60; FCO 1980; Rio de Janeiro 1983; Buenos Aires 1986; FCO 1988; SUPL 1991; FCO 1998; Band C4.

Lewis, Marion Rachel (née Douche); SUPL since March 1999; Born 19/03/69; FCO 1991; SUPL 1996; Berlin 1997; Band B3; m 1994 Peter Robert Lewis (2s 1997, 1999; 1d 2001).

Lewis, Matthew Dafydd; FCO since October 2002; Born 04/10/78; Band C4.

Lewis, Peter Robert; First Secretary Washington since June 2003; Born 16/08/68; Second Secretary FCO 1994; Second Secretary Berlin 1997; First Secretary FCO 1999; Band D6; m 1994 Marion Rachel Douche (2s 1997, 1999; 1d 2001).

Lewis, Trevor James; FCO since October 2003; Born 08/10/60; FCO 1979; Brussels (UKREP) 1982; Accra 1984; FCO 1988; Washington 1991; Third Secretary (Commercial/Information) Dubai 1994; FCO 1997; Second Secretary (Commercial) Shanghai 2000; Band D6; m 1993 Claire Louise Hawthorne.

Ley, Graham John; First Secretary FCO since September 2003; Born 31/05/61; FCO 1984; Second Secretary Cairo 1987; Second later First Secretary FCO 1989; First Secretary (Chancery) Nicosia 1994; First Secretary FCO 1998; First Secretary (Regional Affairs) Cairo 1999; Band D6; m 1988 Carol Anne Buchan (1d 1991; 1s 1995).

Liddell, James; First Secretary and Consul-General Jakarta since July 2003; Born 20/06/45; FCO 1970; Buenos Aires 1973; Blantyre 1975; FCO 1977; Seoul 1980; Suva 1984; FCO 1988; Consul (Commercial) Perth 1992; Bridgetown 1997; Consul Harare 1999; m 1978 Jillian Stella Coventry (1d 1981; 1s 1985).

Liddle, Aidan Thomas; Second Secretary Brussels (UKREP) since August 2004; Born 06/07/79; DTI 2001; FCO 2003; Band C4.

Liddle, Johanna Mary; FCO since April 2002; Born 13/09/71; Band D6.

Life, Vivien Frances; Counsellor FCO since April 1999; Born 30/05/57; Civil Service Dept. 1979; HM Treasury 1981; FCO 1988; First Secretary Washington 1992; First Secretary FCO 1996; m 1989 Timothy Michael Dowse (2d 1991, 1994).

Lilley, George Arthur, MBE (1997); First Secretary (Works) Cairo since April 2003; Born 21/01/51; Tokyo 1987; Kuwait 1989; Wellington 1990; Dublin 1993; Canberra 1995; Lagos 1997; FCO 1999; Dar es Salaam 2001; Band D6; m 1996 Marjorie.

Lillie, Stephen; Counsellor New Delhi since August 2003; Born 04/02/66; FCO 1988; Full-Time Language Training 1989; Full-Time Language Training Hong Kong 1990; Second later First Secretary (Economic/Political) Peking 1992; FCO 1996; Consul-General Guangzhou 1999; m 1991 Denise Chit Lo (2s 1997, 1999).

Lillington, Leisa; FCO since November 2002; Born 23/01/65; Home Office 1985; FCO 1991; Vienna (UKDEL) 1992; FCO 1995; SUPL 2000; Band A2.

Lindfield, John Richard, MBE (1999); Consul (Investment) San Francisco since July 1999; Born 12/05/59; DHSS 1978; FCO 1978; Cairo 1981; Floater Duties 1984; Karachi 1985; FCO 1989; Second Secretary 1994; Vice-Consul (Commercial) Cape Town 1995; m 1985 Judith Christine Brown (2s 1988, 1990).

Lindley, Graham; Amman since April 2004; Born 18/03/46; Royal Navy 1964; HOPD 1982; Bucharest 1988; Prague 1990; Brussels 1992; Hong Kong 1996; Kampala 2000; FCO 2003; Band B3; m 1967 Anita Wood (1s 1969; 1d 1976).

Lindsay, Bridget Clare (née O'Riordan); SUPL since June 2003; Born 13/08/59; FCO 1980; Warsaw 1982; Tokyo 1984; SUPL 1986; Canberra 1987; FCO 1989; SUPL 1991; FCO 1992; SUPL 1994; Tokyo 1995; SUPL 1995; Second Secretary British Trade International 2001; m 1983 Iain Ferrier Lindsay (1s 1991).

Lindsay, Iain Ferrier, OBE (2002); Deputy Head of Mission Bucharest since August 2003; Born 09/03/59; FCO 1980; Warsaw 1982; Tokyo 1983; Third later Second Secretary (Political) Canberra 1986; Second Secretary FCO 1989; First Secretary (Political) Tokyo 1994; FCO 1999; m 1983 Bridget Clare O'Riordan (1s 1991).

Lindsay, Kathryn Hilary (née Buchanan); Belgrade since October 2002; Born 07/07/70; FCO 1989; T/D Moscow 1991; Brussels (UKREP) 1992; Dakar 1995; SUPL 1998; Band B3; m 1994 Douglas Tennant Lindsay (1d 1998; 1s 2000.

Lindsay, Richard Stephen; FCO since October 2001; Born 18/02/69; Second Secretary FCO 1996; Second Secretary Harare 1998; m 1997 Xanthe Critchett (2s 1998, 2003; 1d 2000).

Ling, Norman Arthur; High Commissioner Lilongwe since September 2001; Born 12/08/52; Second Secretary FCO 1978; Second Secretary Tripoli 1980; Second later First Secretary Tehran

1981; First Secretary FCO 1984; Deputy Consul-General Johannesburg 1988; Full-Time Language Training 1992; Deputy Head of Mission Ankara 1993; Counsellor FCO 1997; m 1979 Selma Osman.

Lingwood, David Michael; Second Secretary (Management) Lisbon since October 2002; Born 10/05/68; FCO 1989; Cairo 1991; Bonn 1994; FCO 1997; Yerevan 2000; Band C4; m 2003 Deborah Berns.

Link, Joan Irene (née Wilmot), LVO (1992); Counsellor FCO since August 1996; Born 03/03/53; FCO 1974; Third Secretary Bonn 1975; Third later Second Secretary FCO 1977; Second later First Secretary Geneva (UKDIS) 1980; First Secretary FCO 1983; First Secretary (Information) Bonn 1990; First Secretary FCO 1994; (2s 1977, 1985).

Linnell, Aidan John; FCO since March 2002; Born 13/04/60; FCO 1982; Canberra 1987; FCO 1989; Third Secretary Bonn 1993; FCO 1996; Second Secretary Caracas 1998; Band C4; m 2000 Zenaida Degadillo.

Lion, Stephanie Ann (née Smith); SUPL since August 2000; Born 16/02/65; FCO 1986; Madrid 1988; SUPL 1989; FCO 1992; Berne 1994; FCO 1997; Band A2; m 1997 Dominique Lion (1d 1999).

Lisbey, Lisa Marie (née Harrison); FCO since September 2003; Born 23/02/69; Customs and Excise 1992-95; FCO 1995; Belmopan 1996; New Delhi 2000; Band A2; m 1999 Nestor Lisbey (1s 2001).

Lister, Kirsten Fiona; Floater Duties since June 2002; Born 04/05/68; FCO 2001; Band A2.

Litman, Lee; FCO since September 2003; Born 11/09/72; Band D6.

Little, Alison Jane; FCO since September 2001; Born 03/04/68; FCO (HCS) 1986; FCO (DS) 1988; Lusaka 1990; FCO 1992; Maseru 1993; Tunis 1994; FCO 1997; On loan to the DTI 1999; Band C4.

Livesey, Timothy Peter Nicholas; SUPL since February 2002; Born 29/06/59; FCO 1987; Rabat 1988; FCO 1988; Second later First Secretary (Aid) Lagos 1989; FCO 1993; Head of Press and Public Affairs Section Paris Embassy 1996; On secondment to No. 10 Downing Street (Press Office) 2000; m 1986 Catherine Eaglestone (3d 1990, 1996, 1999; 2s 1992, 1997).

Livingston, Catherine Mary (née Bramley); Hong Kong since April 2002; Born 22/06/56; FCO 1975 (Resigned 1980); Cairo 1977; Reinstated, FCO 1982; Rome 1984; Muscat 1986; SUPL 1990; FCO 1991; SUPL 1991; FCO 1995; Hong Kong 1996; SUPL 2001; Band A2; m 1985 Richard Ian Livingston (1s 1990; 1d 1992).

Livingstone, Carolyn B; Management Officer Windhoek since June 2004; Born 04/11/48; FCO 1997; Abidjan 1999; Wellington 2000; Band B3; (1d 1974).

Livingstone, Scott, OBE (2002), MBE (Mil) (1995); First Secretary Madrid since September 2003; Born 28/11/65; First Secretary FCO 1996; First Secretary (Political) Islamabad 1998; First Secretary FCO 2000; Band D6; m 1996 Lorna Jane Pettipher (2d 1998, 2000).

Llewellyn, Huw; New York (UKMIS) since August 2004; Born 21/05/59; Assistant Legal Adviser FCO 1988; Legal Counsellor, FCO 1999; m 1990 Fiona Jane Boote (2d 1994, 1995).

Lloyd, Andrew, MBE (1995); Head of African Department (Southern), FCO since September 2003; Born 22/10/64; FCO 1982; Washington 1984; Kaduna 1987; FCO 1990; Second Secretary 1992; Second Secretary (Economic) Seoul 1993; Second later First Secretary (Political/Press) New York (UKMIS) 1995; Head of Post Pristina 2000; m (1) 1987 Sandra Leigh Craven (diss 1996) (1s 1990); (2) 1997 Tania Mechlenborg (1s 2003).

Lloyd, Diane Elizabeth; Osaka since January 2000; Born 27/02/68; FCO 1987; Warsaw 1989; Full-Time Language Training FCO 1989; Full-Time Language Training Tokyo 1990; Vice-Consul Tokyo 1991; Rabat 1995; T/D Japan 1999; Band C4; m (1) 1994 Souichiroh Saito (née Urushibara) (dec'd); (2) 2003 Takeshi Watanabe.

Lloyd, Susan Jacqueline; FCO since January 2003; Born 28/02/70; FCO 1989; Harare 1991; Montevideo 1998; St John's 2002; Band B3.

Lochmuller, Simon; Warsaw since January 2003; Born 26/07/70; FCO 1986; Bonn 1993; FCO 1996; Cairo 1998; Band C4; m 1998 Verena Mackenzie (1d 1995).

Lock, Jennifer Hazel; Auckland since May 2004; Born 09/07/59; FCO 1978; Jakarta 1982; Stockholm 1985; FCO 1988; Tunis 1991; Third Secretary (Management/Consular) Almaty 1994; Second Secretary (Immigration) Islamabad 1998; FCO 2001; Pitcairn 2003; Band C4.

Lockwood, Emma Constance, MVO (2000); Second Secretary (Press and Public Affairs) Brussels since April 2004; Born 01/01/71; FCO 1996; Language Training 1999; Third Secretary (Political) Rome 1999; FCO 2003; Band C4.

Lodge, Katherine Rosemary; SUPL since March 2003; Born 03/08/59; FCO 1984; Language Training Tokyo 1985; Third Secretary Tokyo 1986; FCO 1990; Second Secretary 1992; SUPL 1994; FCO 1998.

Lodge, Matthew James; Private Secretary to the PUS FCO since August 2004; Born 03/06/68; FCO 1996; Second Secretary (Political) Athens 1998; Second Secretary (PPS) Paris 2001; Second Secretary (Political/Military) Brussels (UKREP) 2001; First Secretary FCO 2003; m 2001 Alexia Ipirotis (2s 2002).

Logan, Marilla Joy Fiona (née Tandy); First Secretary FCO since April 1998; Born 12/09/53;

FCO 1974; Moscow 1977; FCO 1978; Düsseldorf 1980; FCO 1983; Second Secretary Kuala Lumpur 1992; FCO 1996; m 1986 Allan Robert Logan (1s 1994).

Lomas, Joanne; Second Secretary (WTO) Geneva (UKMIS) since July 2001; Born 07/09/70; FCO 1993; Full-Time Language Training 1995; Secondment to UNSCOM Baghdad 1997; Third Secretary (Political/Information) Damascus 1997; Band C4.

Lomax, Christopher Thomas; FCO since June 2004; Born 02/05/80; Band B3.

London, David Charles George; First Secretary (Political) Bahrain since July 2003; Born 24/01/66; FCO 1994; Second Secretary (Political) Bonn 1996; First Secretary (Political) Buenos Aires 1997; First Secretary FCO 2000; Band D6; m 1996 Monique Day (2s 1998, 2002; 1d 2000).

Long, Alastair Douglas; FCO since 2002; Born 06/08/77; Band B3.

Longbottom, Julia Margaret; Counsellor Warsaw since June 2003; Born 13/07/63; FCO 1986; Attachment to European Commission 1988; Language Training 1988; Second Secretary (Chancery) Tokyo 1990; First Secretary FCO 1994; First Secretary (Political) The Hague 1998; m 1990 Richard James Sciver (2d 1992, 1993; 1s 1995).

Longdon, Catherine Mary; SUPL since August 2000; Born 15/12/64; FCO 1990; Islamabad 1993; FCO 1997; SUPL 1997; FCO 1998; Band C4.

Longhurst, William Jesse; First Secretary (Finance) New York (UKMIS) since June 2001; Born 07/02/67; FCO 1990; Seoul 1992; Second Secretary 1992; First Secretary (Commercial) Tokyo 1995; On loan to the DTI 1998; m 1991 Eriko Niimi (2d 1991, 1993).

Lonsdale, Charles John; First Secretary FCO since February 2003; Born 05/07/65; FCO 1987; Vienna CSCE 1988; FCO 1989; Third later Second Secretary Budapest 1990; On loan to the Cabinet Office 1993; First Secretary FCO 1995; First Secretary (Political) Moscow 1998.

Lonsdale, Jason Peter; Third Secretary (Management/Consular) Luxembourg since August 2002; Born 27/11/67; HM Forces (Royal Navy) 1988 - 94; FCO 2000; Band B3; m 1999 Emma Sarah Vero.

Lorimer, Eamonn Barrington; Secondment (Commercial) since April 2003; Born 11/12/64; Home Civil Service 1985 - 88; Washington 1989; FCO 1993; Valletta 1994; FCO 1997; On loan to the DTI 2002; Band B3.

Loten, Graeme Neil; HM Ambassador Dushanbe since June 2004; Born 10/03/59; FCO 1981; Brussels (UKDEL NATO) 1983; Khartoum 1986; Second Secretary (Economic/Agriculture) The Hague 1988; Full-Time Language Training 1993; Second Secretary Almaty 1993; FCO 1997; HM Ambassador Bamako 2001.

Lott, Ann Veronica (née Lewis); Second Secretary FCO since November 1996; Born 22/11/55; FCO 1978; Algiers 1979; Montevideo 1982; FCO 1984; Latin America Floater 1987; FCO 1988; Canberra 1989; SUPL 1992; m 1989 Justin Karl Lott (1d 1993).

Louizos, Alexandra Emma; Full-Time Language Training Beijing since January 2004; Born 09/10/78; FCO 2001; Full-Time Language Training (Mandarin) 2003; Band C4.

Louth, Michael; FCO since July 1999; Born 21/05/63; FCO 1981; Lagos 1984; East Berlin 1988; FCO 1989; Third Secretary (Management/Commercial) Ljubljana 1992; Vienna 1994; Port of Spain 1996; m 1992 Carmen Elena Fuentes (1s 1994; 1d 1998).

Love, Darren Mark; Floater Duties since February 2001; Born 26/02/68; FCO 1988; Warsaw 1989; Accra 1991; FCO 1993; Colombo 1997; Band B3.

Love, Stephanie Cynthia; FCO since January 1993; Born 24/07/45; Bogotá 1969; Rio de Janeiro 1969; Cairo 1971; Antigua 1971; Manila 1973; New York (UKMIS) 1975; FCO 1978; Bahrain 1979; FCO 1984; Budapest 1986; Islamabad 1988; FCO 1990; Lisbon 1991; Band B3.

Loveday-Baugh, Christine; FCO since August 2001; Born 15/08/59; FCO 1984; Muscat 1986; Kingston 1989; FCO 1991; Rome 1994; New York (UKMIS) 1999; Band B3; m 1992 C. Anthony Baugh.

Lovett, Elizabeth Ann; Dar es Salaam since February 2004; Born 16/04/77; FCO 2002; Band A2.

Low, Nicholas David; Consul Algiers since June 2004; Born 14/12/57; Metropolitan Police 1982 - 92; FCO 1993; T/D Rabat 1994; Santiago 1995; Full-Time Language Training 1999; Brasilia 1999; FCO 2003; Band D6.

Lowen, Barry Robert; Counsellor (Commercial) Riyadh since August 2003; Born 09/01/64; FCO 1986; Language Training Cairo 1987; Third later Second Secretary (Chancery) Kuwait 1989; First Secretary FCO 1993; First Secretary (Economic) New York (UKMIS) 1997; FCO 2001; m 1989 Karin Rhiannon Blizard.

Lowes, Merrick John; First Secretary (Commercial) Mumbai since June 2001; Born 14/11/44; RAF 1962 - 74; FCO 1975; Vienna 1978; Maseru 1981; Vice-Consul Naples 1983; Second Secretary FCO 1986; First Secretary on loan to the Office of Fair Trading 1989; First Secretary (Commercial) Damascus 1991; Trade Commissioner Hong Kong and Consul Macao 1994; Deputy Consul-General Johannesburg and Head of Southern Africa Regional Commercial Hub 1998; m 1970 (Christine) Wendy Ralley (1s 1975; 1d 1978).

Loweth, Alan Robert; First Secretary later Counsellor FCO since May 1995; Born 12/12/52; FCO 1973; Language Training 1977; Copenhagen 1978; FCO 1981; Language Training 1984;

Second Secretary Moscow 1985; First Secretary FCO 1988; First Secretary Warsaw 1991; m 1986 Linda Susan Parr.

Lownds, Matthew John; Brasilia since August 2003; Born 06/08/65; FCO 1987; Dublin 1989; Düsseldorf 1990; Luanda 1992; Second Secretary FCO 1995; Second Secretary (Political) UKDEL OSCE Vienna 1996; First Secretary FCO 2000; Full-Time Language Training 2003; Band D6; m 1996 Rebecca Louise Allen (1s 1997; 1d 1999).

Lowson, Gillian (née Murray); FCO since October 2002; Born 18/09/69; FCO 1990; Language Training 1991; Paris 1992; Language Training 1994; Vienna 1995; Third Secretary Beijing 1999; Band B3; m 1999 Paul James Lowson (1s 2002).

Lucas, Stephen John; FCO since July 2000; Born 30/06/62; DTI 1986 - 90; FCO 1990; Third Secretary (Press/Information) Paris 1992; HM Consul Mexico City 1996; m 1994 Claudia Bautista Alfonso (1s 1998).

Lucey, Janette Margaret (née Mansley); SUPL since July 2003; Born 14/07/64; FCO 1983; New Delhi 1985; Luanda 1989; Suva 1992; Canberra 1997; FCO 2001; Band A2; m 1994 James Courtney Lucey.

Lucien, Valerie Linda; FCO since October 2003; Born 12/08/47; FCO 1977; Lagos 1978; Brussels (UKREP) 1981; Africa/Middle East Floater 1984; FCO 1987; Third Secretary Kingston 1990; Third Secretary (Cultural/Information) Valletta 1993; Second Secretary FCO 1996; Consul-General Mexico City 2000; Band C5.

Luckock, Ben; Third Secretary (Visa) Islamabad since June 2003; Born 03/11/77; FCO 2001; Band B3.

Luff, Jonathan James; FCO since September 2003; Born 19/04/73; FCO 1998; Full-Time Language Training 1999; Full-Time Language Training Cairo 2000; Second Secretary (Political) Riyadh 2001; Band C4.

Lufkin, Christine Anne (née Wilson), MVO; Second Secretary (Economic) The Hague since November 2000; Born 05/01/66; FCO 1988; Washington 1990; Kuwait 1994; Second Secretary FCO 1997; SUPL 2000; m 1996 David Jonathan Peter Lufkin (1d 1999).

Luke, Robert Haydon Vernon; Second Secretary Brasilia since August 2002; Born 09/09/74; FCO 2000; Band C4.

Lumsden-Bedingfeld, Ann; FCO since August 1997; Born 11/08/62; FCO 1985; East Berlin 1987; FCO 1989; Colombo 1990; FCO 1993; Floater Duties 1995; Band A2.

Lungley, Gareth Geoffrey; First Secretary Zagreb since October 2002; Born 08/01/71; FCO 1994; Full-Time Language Training 1996; Second Secretary (Commercial) Tehran 1997; Second Secretary FCO 1999; Band D6; m 1997 Suzanne Clare Smith (1s 2001).

Lunt, Iain Andrew; FCO since September 2001; Born 11/05/77; Band C4.

Lusher, David; First Secretary (Management) Tripoli since September 2002; Born 27/12/55; DOE 1973; FCO 1975; Belgrade 1977; Seoul 1978; Accra 1982; FCO 1984; Islamabad 1987; Vice-Consul Milan 1991; Second Secretary FCO 1994; Second Secretary (UN/UNIDO) UKMIS Vienna 1998; m 1978 Soon-Ja Chung (1s 1983).

Lusty, Gregor Malcolm; FCO since October 2001; Born 12/03/69; FCO 1991; Full-Time Language Training Cairo 1993; Third Secretary (Chancery) Amman 1994; Kinshasa 1998; Second Secretary on loan to the DTI 1999.

Luttrell, David Charles; FCO since August 2003; Born 03/06/72; FCO 1999; Freetown 2001; Band B3.

Lyall, Michael David; Riyadh since November 2003; Born 09/09/43; Royal Navy 1961-89; Moscow 1991; Warsaw 1992; Geneva (UKMIS) 1993; Moscow 1996; Peking 1998; Moscow 2002; Band B3; m 1967 Janet Haugh (1s 1969).

Lyall Grant, Mark Justin, CMG (2003); High Commissioner Islamabad since May 2003; Born 29/05/56; FCO 1980; Second Secretary Islamabad 1982; First Secretary FCO 1985; First Secretary (Chancery) Paris 1990; First Secretary FCO 1993; Counsellor on loan to the Cabinet Office 1994; Deputy High Commissioner Pretoria 1996; FCO 1998; Director (Africa) FCO 2000; m 1986 Sheila Jean Tresise (1s 1989; 1d 1991).

Lyall Grant, Sheila Jean (née Tresise); FCO since 1999; Born 16/12/60; FCO 1980; Islamabad 1982; FCO 1985; Vice-Consul Paris 1990; FCO 1993; SUPL 1997; Band C4; m 1986 Mark Justin Lyall Grant (1s 1989; 1d 1991).

Lycett, Nadine Claire; FCO since July 2000; Born 19/04/65; FCO 1984; Brussels (UKDEL NATO) 1986; FCO 1988; Washington 1992; Ankara 1997; Band A2.

Lynch, Paul Francis; Consul (Commercial) Osaka since May 2002; Born 18/08/63; Home Office 1991; Cabinet Office 1994; First Secretary (Science and Technology) Tokyo 1996; Full-Time Language Training 2000; Band D6; m 1992 Yoko Hirayama (1s 1997).

Lyne, Kevin Douglas; Deputy Head of Mission Rabat since April 2003; Born 06/11/61; Research Officer FCO 1988; Senior Research Officer FCO 1989; Second Secretary (Chancery) Santiago 1991; Principal Research Officer FCO 1995; First Secretary FCO 1996; First Secretary (Human Rights) Geneva (UKMIS) 1998; m 1988 Anne Francoise Dabbadie (2d 1989, 1995).

Lyne, Richard John; High Commissioner Honiara since December 2004; Born 20/11/48; FCO 1970; Belgrade 1972; Algiers 1974; Damascus 1977; FCO 1980; On loan to DTI 1981; Second Secretary (Commercial) New Delhi 1984; Second later First Secretary (Chancery/Information) Stockholm 1988; First Secretary FCO 1992;

Deputy High Commissioner Port of Spain 1996; FCO 2000; m 1977 Jennifer Anne Whitworth (1d 1982; 1s 1985).

Lyne, Sir Roderic Michael John, KBE (1999), CMG (1992); HM Ambassador Moscow since January 2000; Born 31/03/48; FCO 1970; Attached to Army School of Languages 1971; Moscow 1972; Second Secretary Dakar 1974; FCO 1976; Assistant Private Secretary to Secretary of State 1979; First Secretary New York (UKMIS) 1982; Chatham House (CDA) 1986; Counsellor (Head of Chancery) Moscow 1987; Counsellor FCO 1990; On loan as PS/Prime Minister at No 10 Downing Street 1993; On loan to British Gas 1996; UK Permanent Representative Geneva 1997; m 1969 Amanda Mary Smith (2s 1971, 1974; 1d 1981).

Lyon, Julian Edmund; Belgrade since August 2001; Born 20/10/65; FCO 1990; Transferred to Diplomatic Service 1999; Third Secretary and Vice-Consul Yerevan 1999; Band B3; (1d 2000).

Lyons, Benedict David; Second Secretary Algiers since November 2003; Born 15/02/72; FCO 1997; Third Secretary Madrid 2000; m Amanda Louise Crowhurst (2d 1996, 2000).

Lysaght, Stephen Peter; FCO since 1999; Born 17/05/70; FCO 1989; Washington 1992; Moscow 1995; Band C5.

Lyscom, David Edward; UK Representative for the Organisation for Economic Co-operation and Development, Paris since January 2004; Born 08/08/51; FCO 1972; Third later Second Secretary Vienna 1973; Second Secretary Ottawa 1977; Second later First Secretary FCO 1979; First Secretary 1980; First Secretary Bonn 1984; First Secretary (Economic) Riyadh 1988; First Secretary FCO 1990; Counsellor (Science and Technology) Bonn 1991; Counsellor FCO 1996; HM Ambassador Bratislava 1998; FCO 2002; m 1973 Nicole Jane Ward (2d 1983, 1987; 1s 1985).

Lyster-Binns, Benjamin Edward Noël; First Secretary (Political) Lisbon since September 2003; Born 19/10/65; FCO 1989; Third Secretary (Development) Lilongwe 1991; Third Secretary (Chancery/Information) Muscat 1995; Second later First Secretary FCO 1998; m 1995 Belinda Hunter Blair (2d 1999, 2000; 1s 2002).

Lytle, Janice; Damascus since July 2003; Born 17/06/62; FCO 2002; Band A2; m 2004 Ali Al-Shatti.

M

Macadie, Jeremy James; HM Ambassador Kigali since October 2004; Born 10/07/52; FCO 1972; Dakar 1975; Addis Ababa 1980; FCO 1981; Sana'a 1984; Antananarivo 1986; FCO 1991; Assistant Private Secretary to Minister of State for Europe 1995; Deputy Head of Mission Algiers 1997; FCO 2000; On loan to French MFA, Paris 2003; Band D6; m 1975 Chantal Andrea Jacqueline Copiatti (1d 1978).

Macaire, Robert Nigel Paul; Counsellor (Political) New Delhi since July 2004; Born 19/02/66; MOD 1987 - 90; FCO 1990; Second Secretary (Know How Fund) Bucharest 1992; FCO 1995; First Secretary Washington 1998; Head of Counter-Terrorism Policy Dept FCO 2002; m 1996 Alice MacKenzie (2d 1997, 1999).

Macan, Thomas Townley; Governor British Virgin Islands since October 2002; Born 14/11/46; FCO 1969; Third later Second Secretary Bonn 1971; Second later First Secretary Brasilia 1974; FCO 1978; First Secretary (Press and Information) Bonn 1981; First Secretary later Counsellor FCO 1986; Counsellor and Deputy Head of Mission Lisbon 1990; HM Ambassador Vilnius 1995; On loan to the BOC Group 1998; Minister New Delhi 1999; m 1976 Janet Ellen Martin (1s 1981; 1d 1984).

MacCallum, Fiona, MBE (1997); First Secretary (Political) Tallinn since July 2004; Born 25/06/62; FCO 1986; Moscow 1989; FCO 1992; Second Secretary Riga 1995; First Secretary (Political) Kiev 2000; First Secretary FCO 2003; Band D6.

MacDermott, Alastair Tormod; High Commissioner Windhoek since April 2002; Born 17/09/45; FO (later FCO) 1966; Kabul 1971; FCO 1973; Accra 1973; FCO 1977; Language Training Tokyo 1978; Second Secretary Tokyo 1979; Colombo 1983; First Secretary (Information) Tokyo 1986; First Secretary FCO 1991; Full-Time Language Training 1995; First Secretary (Commercial) Ankara 1995; m (1) 1968 Helen Gordon (diss 1992) (2d 1969, 1971); (2) 1994 Gudrun Geiling.

MacDonald, Catriona MacLeod; FCO since November 2000; Born 18/04/64; FCO 1988; Belgrade 1990; FCO 1992; Berlin 1993; FCO 1996; Vienna 1997; Band B3.

MacDonald, Michelle; SUPL since February 2002; Born 18/09/78; FCO 2000; Band A2.

MacDougall, David; T/D Basra since October 2003; Born 07/07/73; FCO 1991; Helsinki 1995; Tel Aviv 1997; T/D Kinshasa 1999; Guatemala City 1999; SUPL 2002; Band C4.

Mace, Andrew Stephen; FCO since January 2003; Born 31/12/73; FCO 1995; Brussels (UKREP) 1997; FCO 1999; Copenhagen 1999; Band D6.

Macgregor, John Malcolm, CVO (1992); HM Ambassador Vienna since May 2003; Born 03/10/46; FCO 1973; Second later First Secretary New Delhi 1975; First Secretary FCO 1979; Private Secretary to Minister of State 1981; Counsellor and Head of Chancery Prague 1986; Counsellor and Head of Chancery Paris 1990; Counsellor FCO 1993; Consul-General Düsseldorf 1995; HM Ambassador Warsaw 1998; Director Wider Europe FCO 2000; m 1982 Judith Anne Brown (1d 1984; 3s 1986, 1987, 1990).

Macgregor, Judith Anne (née Brown), LVO (1992); HM Ambassador Bratislava since June 2004; Born 17/06/52; FCO 1976; First Secretary

(Chancery/Information) Belgrade 1978; FCO 1981; SUPL 1986; First Secretary (Political/Information) Prague 1989; SUPL 1990; First Secretary (Chancery) Paris 1992; First Secretary FCO 1993; SUPL 1995; Counsellor (Head of Security Strategy Unit) FCO 2001; SUPL 2003; m 1982 John Malcolm Macgregor (1d 1984; 3s 1986, 1987, 1990).

Macintosh, Anne; SUPL since October 1997; Born 15/04/61; FCO 1980; Rome 1982; Havana 1985; FCO 1988; Third later Second Secretary (Commercial) Buenos Aires 1991; m 1993 Gustavo Javier Barreiro (1d 1996).

MacIntosh, Sarah; FCO since May 2002; Born 07/08/69; FCO 1991; Third Secretary (IAEA/UN) Vienna (UKMIS) 1994; Second Secretary (Economic/EU) Madrid 1996; First Secretary FCO 1997; First Secretary (Political/Development/Economic) New York (UKMIS) 2000; Band D7.

Maciver, Graham; Assistant Legal Adviser FCO since October 2001; Born 26/07/76.

Mackay, Gavin Anderson, MBE (1994); On loan to the Cabinet Office since September 2001; Born 01/11/49; FCO 1973; Wellington 1975; Suva 1978; Dhaka 1981; FCO 1983; Dubai 1986 (Second Secretary 1988); Second Secretary Nicosia 1989; FCO 1994; m 1975 Glenys Pickup (1d 1977; 2s 1980, 1984).

MacKenna, Roderic Hamish; Third Secretary (Political) later Second Secretary and Deputy Head of Mission Tbilisi since 2002; Born 15/08/58; FCO 2000; m 1991 Ayoma Indrani Nethsingha (2d 1992, 1993).

MacKenzie, Angela Susan (née Wright); SUPL since September 2003; Born 17/01/67; FCO 1985; Lilongwe 1989; SUPL 1993; FCO 1995; SUPL 1997; Jerusalem 2001; Band B3; m (1) 1988 Mohammed Ouassine (diss 1992); (2) 1997 Graham John MacKenzie.

MacKenzie, Catherine Louise Hay; SUPL since June 2004; Born 09/08/66; FCO 1989; Language Training FCO 1991; Language Training Tokyo 1992; Second Secretary 1992; Second Secretary (Chancery) Tokyo 1993; New York (UKMIS) 2000; Band D6; m 1992 John Page.

Mackenzie, Dorothy (née Byers); FCO since September 2001; Born 01/03/56; FCO 1974; The Hague 1976; Lusaka 1979; FCO 1982; Ottawa 1985; SUPL 1990; Singapore 1991; FCO 1993; SUPL 1999; Muscat 2000; Band C4; m 1978 Robert Mackenzie (1d 1987).

MacKenzie, Kenneth John Alexander; First Secretary FCO since July 2001; Born 09/09/49; FCO 1973; Brussels 1975; Second later First Secretary FCO 1978; Buenos Aires 1981; First Secretary FCO 1982; First Secretary (Economic) Bucharest 1985; First Secretary FCO 1988; First Secretary Vienna 1992; First Secretary FCO 1995; Consul Munich 1997; Band D6; m 1980 Alison Mary Linda Sandford (1d 1983; 1s 1987).

MacKenzie, Nina Ruth (née McBratney); Third Secretary (Political) Canberra since June 2003; Born 08/06/73; FCO 1999; Third Secretary (Political) Abidjan 2001; Band B3; m 2002 Scott MacKenzie.

MacKenzie, Robert (known as Rab); FCO since December 2001; Born 05/03/54; Dept of National Savings 1973; FCO 1974; The Hague 1976; Lusaka 1979; FCO 1982; Ottawa 1985; Second Secretary FCO 1988; Second Secretary (Commercial) Mexico City 1988; Second Secretary (Commercial) Singapore 1990; Second Secretary FCO 1993; First Secretary (Commercial) Muscat 1998; m 1978 Dorothy Byers (1d 1987).

MacKerras, Carl Anthony; Second Secretary (Consular/Management) Belmopan since April 2001; Born 13/11/69; Land Registry 1988 - 90; FCO 1990; St Petersburg 1995; Vice-Consul Copenhagen 1997; m 1997 Vera Ermolova (2d 1997, 2000).

Macklin, Diane Elaine (née Crowther); FCO since October 2002; Born 05/09/64; FCO 1981; SUPL 1995; FCO 1995; SUPL 1996; Band A2.

Maclean, Andrew Mark; Second Secretary Kampala since May 2004; Born 25/11/72; FCO 2002; Band D6.

MacLennan, David Ross; HM Ambassador Doha since June 2002; Born 12/02/45; FO 1963; DSAO 1965; MECAS 1966; Aden 1969; Civil Service College 1972; Second later First Secretary FCO 1972; First Secretary UKDEL OECD Paris 1975; First Secretary, Head of Chancery and Consul Abu Dhabi 1979; First Secretary FCO 1982; On secondment to European Commission 1984; Counsellor (Commercial) Kuwait 1985; Counsellor and Head of Chancery Nicosia 1989; HM Consul-General Jerusalem 1990; Counsellor FCO 1994; HM Ambassador Beirut 1996; m 1964 Margaret Lytollis (2d 1964, 1966).

MacLeod, Gordon Stewart; Nicosia since February 2002; Born 15/02/52; FCO 1971; Ankara 1973; Washington 1977; Dacca 1979; FCO 1982; Valletta 1985; Third later Second Secretary New Delhi 1988; Second Secretary FCO 1992; Consul (Commercial and Information) Casablanca 1998; m 1978 Susan Raggatt (2d 1981, 1984).

MacLeod, Iain; Counsellor (Legal Adviser) New York (UKMIS) since August 2001; Born 15/03/62; Assistant Legal Adviser FCO 1987; First Secretary (Assistant Legal Adviser) Brussels (UKREP) 1991; FCO 1995; Legal Secretariat to the Law Officers 1997; m 1988 Dr Alison Mary Murchison (2d 1991, 1995; 2s 1993, 1997).

MacLeod, Siân Christina, OBE (2002); On loan to the Cabinet Office since January 2002; Born 31/05/62; FCO 1986; Language Training 1987; Second Secretary (Chancery) Moscow 1988; Second later First Secretary FCO 1992; First Secretary (Political) The Hague 1996; FCO 2000; m 1987 Richard Anthony Robinson (2d 1991, 1994; 1s 1998).

MacMillan, Alison Flora; SUPL since February 2004; Born 22/08/61; FCO 1982; Mexico City 1983; Washington 1987; SUPL 1989; FCO 1990; Third Secretary Vice-Consul and Deputy Head of Mission Managua 1993; Second Secretary (EU) Gibraltar 1996; FCO 2001; m 1997 Julian Thomas Lee (1s 1997; 1d 1999).

Macpherson, John Bannerman, OBE (2004); Counsellor Stockholm since June 2003; Born 23/06/51; Third later Second Secretary FCO 1975; Language Training MECAS 1977; Second Secretary Khartoum 1979; Second later First Secretary Sana'a 1980; FCO 1983; Language Training 1985; First Secretary Sofia 1987; First Secretary FCO 1990; Counsellor Cairo 1993; Counsellor FCO 1996; m 1985 Monica Jane Lancashire (2s 1986, 1988; 1d 1992).

Macpherson, Kara Isobel; Second Secretary FCO since September 1998; Born 03/08/60; FCO 1981; Islamabad 1983; Prague 1986; Africa/Middle East Floater 1988; FCO 1992; T/D Khartoum 1994; FCO 1994; T/D New York (UKMIS) 1996; FCO 1997; Band C4.

MacQueen, Christine Ann; Counsellor Brussels since July 2002; Born 24/05/59; FCO 1982; Second Secretary (Economic) Brasilia 1984; Second later First Secretary FCO 1987; New York 1989; First Secretary and UNESCO Observer Paris 1990; First Secretary later Counsellor FCO 1995; m 1992 Bruno Pascal Castola (1d 1992; 1s 1994).

MacSween, Norman James; Counsellor FCO since October 1998; Born 22/01/48; FCO 1970; Third later Second Secretary Nairobi 1972; FCO 1975; Language Training SOAS 1976 and Shiraz 1977; First Secretary Tehran 1977; FCO 1979; First Secretary (Chancery) Bonn 1983; First Secretary FCO 1987; First Secretary later Counsellor Stockholm 1991; Counsellor Moscow 1995; m 1983 Julia Jane Reid (1s 1988; 1d 1990).

Madden, Sir David Christopher Andrew, KCMG (2003), CMG (1996); HM Ambassador Athens since May 1999; Born 25/07/46; Third Secretary FCO 1970; Third later Second Secretary BMG Berlin 1972; First Secretary on loan to Cabinet Office 1975; First Secretary Moscow 1978; First Secretary and Head of Chancery Athens 1981; FCO 1984; Counsellor, Head of Chancery and Consul-General Belgrade 1987; Counsellor FCO 1990; High Commissioner Nicosia 1994; m 1970 Penelope Anthea Johnston (1s 1972; 2d 1974, 1975).

Madden, Kevin Peter; Transferred to the Diplomatic Service since May 2002; Born 27/06/82; FCO (HCS) 2000; Band B3.

Madden, Paul Damian; Counsellor FCO since September 2003; Born 25/04/59; DTI 1980; PS/PUSS 1984; Language Training FCO/Kamakura 1987; First Secretary Tokyo 1988; First Secretary FCO 1992; First Secretary Washington 1996; Deputy High Commissioner and Counsellor (Commercial/Economic) Singapore 2000; m 1989 Sarah Pauline Thomas (2s 1991, 1992; 1d 1996).

Maddicott, David Sydney; First Secretary FCO since September 2000; Born 27/03/53; First Secretary FCO 1994; Full-Time Language Training 1996; On attachment to the Canadian Government 1996; First Secretary (Head of Pol/Info Section) Ottawa 1997; m 1980 Elizabeth Wynne (4s 1980, 1984, 1990, 1993; 1d 1982).

Maddinson, Paul Francis; First Secretary (Political) Moscow since November 2001; Born 16/05/72; FCO 1995; Second Secretary (Political) Nairobi 1996; Second Secretary FCO 1998; Full-Time Language Training 2000; Band D6; m 1996 Rebecca Anne Jackson (1s 2000; 1d 2002).

Madisons, Alexander Emil; Third Secretary Rome since October 1999; Born 09/11/62; FCO 1983; Peking 1990; Belgrade 1994; FCO 1997; Band C4.

Madojemu, Valentine Isi; Jerusalem since February 2003; Born 27/03/58; FCO 1998; Karachi 2000; Band B3; m 1989 Rita (1s 1992; 1d 1997).

Maguire, John; HM Consul Denver since January 2000; Born 04/06/49; FCO 1968; Moscow 1971; Belmopan 1972; New Delhi 1974; Tokyo 1978; FCO 1982; Alexandria 1985; Consul (Commercial) Perth 1988; FCO 1992; Deputy Head of Mission, Consul and First Secretary (Commercial) Doha 1995; FCO 1999; Band C5; m 1978 Mette Lucie Konow Monsen.

Maguire, Natalie (née Rule); Jerusalem since June 2004; Born 22/05/62; MOD 1985-00; FCO 2000; Bahrain 2001; Band A2; m 1981 Robin Maguire.

Maher, Heather Kirsten Maria; FCO since April 2003; Born 12/01/70; FCO 1988; Bangkok 1990; FCO 1993; Athens 1994; Kuwait 1995; Harare 1999; FCO 1999; Abidjan 2000; Kiev 2000; Band A2.

Major, Pamela Ann; Berlin since October 2002; Born 04/03/59; FCO 1982; Language Training SOAS 1983; Second Secretary (Chancery) Peking 1986; First Secretary FCO 1988; First Secretary Moscow 1993; First Secretary later Counsellor FCO 1996; SUPL 1998; On secondment 2001; m 1992 Robert Leigh Turner (1s 1992; 1d 1994).

Makepeace, Richard Edward; HM Ambassador Abu Dhabi since February 2003; Born 24/06/53; FCO 1976; Language Training MECAS 1977; Third later Second Secretary Muscat 1979; Second later First Secretary (Chancery) Prague 1981; FCO 1985; Private Secretary to the Parliamentary Under-Secretary of State 1986; First Secretary Brussels (UKREP) 1989; Counsellor FCO 1993; Cairo 1995; HM Ambassador Khartoum 1999; m 1980 Rupmani Catherine Pradhan.

Makin, John; Second Secretary (Commercial) Perth since March 2001; Born 13/01/64; DHSS 1984; FCO 1985; Kaduna 1987; Düsseldorf 1990; Floater Duties 1992; FCO 1996; Jakarta 1999; Band C4.

Makriyiannis, Lorraine Elizabeth (née Colhoun); SUPL since May 1999; Born 10/06/69; FCO 1991; Sofia 1993; Nicosia 1995; Band A2; m 1995 Michael Makriyiannis.

Malcolm, James Ian, OBE (1995); HM Ambassador Panama City since March 2002; Born 29/03/46; MPBW 1964; FO 1966; Brussels (UKDEL NATO) 1969; Rangoon 1972; FCO 1974; Nairobi 1977; Damascus 1980; Second Secretary (Commercial) Luanda 1983; Second Secretary FCO 1985; First Secretary (Political/Economic) Jakarta 1987; First Secretary FCO 1994; Deputy High Commissioner Kingston 1997; m 1967 Sheila Nicholson Moore (1s 1976; 1d 1980).

Malin, Carl Spencer; FCO since August 2002; Born 07/07/69; FCO 1987; Ottawa 1989; FCO 1992; Floater Duties 1993; FCO 1995; Vice-Consul Lagos 1996; SUPL 1998; Lilongwe 1999; Kathmandu 2000; Lusaka 2002; Band C4; m 1995 Kerstin Ruge (1d 2001).

Malin, Keith Ian; Counsellor FCO since November 1999; Born 11/12/53; FCO 1976; Third Secretary (Developing Countries) Brussels (UKREP) 1978; Second later First Secretary FCO 1979; First Secretary on secondment to HCS 1983; First Secretary (UN/Press) Geneva (UKMIS) 1984; FCO 1986; First Secretary (Chancery/Economic) Sofia 1990; First Secretary later Counsellor FCO 1993; Counsellor Peking 1996; m 1977 Gaynor Dudley Jones (2s 1985, 1992).

Mallion, Richard Julian; Addis Ababa since January 2001; Born 23/12/68; FCO 1999; Band A2.

Malone, Philip, MVO; Head of Chancery Singapore since April 2003; Born 03/12/61; FCO 1981; Buenos Aires 1983; Guatemala City 1986; FCO 1989; Third Secretary (Commercial/Information) Luxembourg 1992; Second Secretary (Chancery) Bandar Seri Begawan 1995; First Secretary FCO 1999; Full-Time Language Training (Mandarin) 2002; m 1999 Sarah Tan Yee Whey (1d 2001).

Mamet, Emma Kate (née Miller); ECO/Vice-Consul Abidjan since August 2003; Born 06/08/70; FCO 1991; Third Secretary (Chancery) Geneva (UKMIS) 1994; Port Louis 1995; Third Secretary (Economic) Ottawa 1999; FCO 2002; Band B3; m 2000 Anthony Roger Mamet.

Man, Kam Lon; FCO since April 2003; Born 16/06/72; FCO 1996; Islamabad 2000; Band A2.

Manley, Ernest George; Brussels (UKDEL NATO) since June 1999; Born 15/02/51; FCO 1970; Aden 1973; Milan 1975; East Berlin 1978; FCO 1980; Kuala Lumpur 1983; Consul Milan 1986; FCO 1990; Band C4; m 1973 Mary Catherine Whelan (1s 1975).

Manley, Philip Ernest; FCO since September 1999; Born 17/06/44; GPO 1960; FCO 1969; Washington 1971; FCO 1974; Amman 1975; FCO 1976; Attaché Moscow 1978; FCO 1980; Third Secretary Lagos 1981; FCO 1984; Second Secretary Bonn 1987; Second Secretary FCO 1990 (First Secretary 1993); Moscow 1996; Band D7; m 1967 Christine Anne Kellett (1s 1970; 1d 1972).

Manley, Simon John; FCO since September 2002; Born 18/09/67; FCO 1990; On secondment to the European Commission 1993; Second later First Secretary (Political) New York (UKMIS) 1993; On secondment to the EU Council Secretariat Brussels 1998; m 1996 Maria Isabel Fernandez-Utges (2d 2000, 2001).

Manley, Suzanne Marie Theresa; Moscow since April 2001; Born 12/12/64; FCO 1987; La Paz 1990; T/D Havana 1993; Santiago 1994; T/D Buenos Aires 1998; FCO 1998; Band B3.

Manning, Sir David Geoffrey, KCMG (2001), CMG (1992); HM Ambassador Washington since August 2003; Born 05/12/49; Third Secretary FCO 1972; Language Training 1973; Third later Second Secretary Warsaw 1974; Second later First Secretary New Delhi 1977; FCO 1980; First Secretary Paris 1984; Counsellor on loan to the Cabinet Office 1988; Political Counsellor Moscow 1990; Head of Eastern Department FCO 1993; UK Member of ICFY Contact Group for Bosnia 1994; Head of Policy Planning FCO 1994; HM Ambassador Tel Aviv 1995; Deputy Under-Secretary FCO 1998; Permanent Representative Brussels (UKDEL NATO) 2000; Foreign Policy Adviser to the Prime Minister 2001; m 1973 Dr Catherine Parkinson.

Manuel, Francesca Jane (née Lintner); Paris since August 2002; Born 05/04/72; FCO 1995; Washington 1997; FCO 2001; Band A2; m 1997 (1s 1998).

March, Shirley Elizabeth; First Secretary (UNPR) Geneva (UKMIS) since June 2000; Born 04/02/61; FCO 1984; Second Secretary (EC Affairs) Brussels 1988; First Secretary FCO 1990; Band D6; m 1984 Paul Louis March (2s 1990, 1992).

Marden, Nicholas; Counsellor Tel Aviv since January 1998; Born 02/05/50; Army 1971-74; Third later Second Secretary FCO 1974; Second Secretary Nicosia 1977; First Secretary FCO 1980; Warsaw 1982; FCO 1985; First Secretary Paris 1988; First Secretary FCO 1993; m 1977 Melanie Gaye Glover (2d 1980, 1982).

Mardlin, Robert Andrew; SUPL since July 2001; Born 13/01/65; FCO 1984; Lima 1986; Sofia 1990; Dhaka 1992; FCO 1996; Nairobi 1999; Band B3; m 1988 Amanda Karen Morall.

Marmion, Elisabeth Claire (née Terry); Hong Kong since May 1999; Born 09/07/72; FCO 1995; Band A2; m 1999 Nicholas Paul Marmion.

Marren, Marrena Ruby; Muscat since September 2002; Born 15/01/68; FCO 1987; Paris 1989; Prague 1992; Geneva 1994; FCO 1994; Brussels (UKREP) 1998; Band B3.

Marriott, Allison Mary, MBE (1997); Mumbai since April 2004; Born 31/03/66; FCO 1987; Vice-

Consul Amman 1990; Third Secretary Brussels (UKDEL) 1993; Copenhagen 1996; Second Secretary FCO 1997; First Secretary (Management) Addis Ababa 2000; Band C5.

Marriott, Anne Stewart Murray (née Corbett), MBE (2002); Second Secretary Dubai since June 2003; Born 29/10/57; FCO 1979; Brasilia 1982; FCO 1984; Abu Dhabi 1985; Bangkok 1988; FCO 1992; Amman 1997; FCO 2001; Band C4; m 1988 Paul James Marriott.

Marsden, Ian Thomas; SUPL since February 2004; Born 05/10/69; Department of Social Security 1989; FCO 1990; Colombo 1993; FCO 1996; Sarajevo 1997; On loan to the DTI 1998; T/D Pristina 1999; Third Secretary (Commercial) Bucharest 2002; Band B3.

Marsden, Rosalind Mary, CMG (2003); HM Ambassador Kabul since January 2004; Born 27/10/50; Third Secretary FCO 1974; Language Training SOAS 1975; Third, Second and later First Secretary Tokyo 1976; First Secretary FCO 1980; First Secretary (Economic) Bonn 1985; First Secretary FCO 1989; Counsellor on secondment to the National Westminster Bank 1991; Head of Chancery Tokyo 1993; Counsellor FCO 1996; Director (Asia Pacific) FCO 1999.

Marsh, Derek Richard, CVO (1999); Director-General of British Trade and Cultural Office Taipei since July 2002; Born 17/09/46; MOD 1968; DTI 1988; Seconded to the FCO 1997; Deputy Head of Mission and Consul-General Seoul 1997; m 1969 Frances Anne Roberts (1s 1972; 1d 1975).

Marsh, Elaine (née Skinner); Third Secretary Valletta since August 2002; Born 06/01/57; FCO 1976; Port of Spain 1978; Bucharest 1982; Valletta 1984; FCO 1987; New Delhi 1989; Third Secretary (Consular) Dar es Salaam 1992; Third Secretary FCO 1994; Washington 1998; Band B3; m 1985 Andrew Peter Marsh (diss 1989) (1s 1988).

Marshall, Alan John; Management Officer Bogotá since May 2004; Born 11/09/52; FCO 1971; Cairo 1973; Lilongwe 1975; Salisbury 1978; Sana'a 1980; FCO 1981; Islamabad 1983; Lisbon 1987; Luanda 1990; Second Secretary FCO 1993; Lisbon 1996; Consul Lisbon 1998; Second Secretary (Consular) Jakarta 2001; Band C5; (1s 1979; 1d 1986).

Marshall, Angela Rosemary; Brussels (UKREP) since July 2002; Born 22/08/60; FCO 1988; Maseru 1991; Kiev 1994; FCO 1997; Lisbon 2000; Band B3.

Marshall, Aurea Jane; Cairo since July 2003; Born 12/01/74; FCO 1999; Sofia 2000; Band A2.

Marshall, Bernard Alan; First Secretary FCO since January 2002; Born 23/03/48; FCO 1968; Bombay 1971; Islamabad 1971; Moscow 1973; Anguilla 1974; Bonn 1976; FCO 1978 (Second Secretary 1979); Vice-Consul (Commercial) Melbourne 1982; Second Secretary FCO 1986; First Secretary (Commercial) Bucharest 1989;

First Secretary FCO 1993; Full-Time Language Training 1995; Consul Munich 1995; Sarajevo 1997; First Secretary FCO 1998; T/D Tehran 1999; Second Secretary (Commercial) T/D Tripoli 2001; Band C5.

Marshall, Brian; Second Secretary FCO since April 1985; Born 13/12/51; FCO 1971; On loan to HCS 1974; FCO 1977; Second Secretary Muscat 1984; Band C4; m 1973 Susan Joyce Bishop (2d 1976, 1980).

Marshall, Francis James; Deputy High Commissioner Freetown since November 2002; Born 10/08/46; CRO 1963; Commonwealth Office (later FCO) 1965; Mogadishu 1969; Singapore 1971; FCO 1974; Port Louis 1977; Tripoli 1981; Addis Ababa 1983; FCO 1984; Vice-Consul Toronto 1987; Second Secretary (Management) JMO Brussels 1991; SUPL 1994; Deputy Head of Mission Rangoon 1999; m 1971 Clare Wray (1s 1972; 1d 1976).

Marshall, Jonathan Neil; On secondment since September 2003; Born 26/08/70; FCO 1992; Full-Time Language Training 1993; Athens 1994; SUPL 1999; FCO 2000; Band D6; m 1997 Maria Kontou (1s 1998; 1d 2001).

Marshall, Michael Gavin; First Secretary (Management) Singapore since June 2002; Born 13/09/60; FCO 1980; Moscow 1982; Baghdad 1983; Floater Duties 1988; FCO 1990; Second Secretary (Consul) St Petersburg 1992; Seoul 1995; Second later First Secretary FCO 1998; m 1993 Amanda Louise O'Connor (1d 1997; 1s 1999).

Marshall, Robert John; FCO since July 2003; Born 19/06/65; FCO 1988; Second Secretary Tokyo 1992; First Secretary FCO 1995; First Secretary Kuala Lumpur 2000; Band D7.

Martens, Alexandra Mary; Second Secretary Paris since May 2000; Born 20/10/57; FCO 1978; Johannesburg 1980; FCO 1981; Paris 1987; FCO 1987; Vienna 1989; FCO 1991; Band C4.

Martin, Alexander Benedict Lowry; First Secretary Prague since March 2004; Born 16/09/70; FCO 1996; Second Secretary (Economic) Jakarta 1999; Second Secretary FCO 2001; Band C4; m 1999 Nicola Barbara Hill.

Martin, Angus Charles Trench; FCO since June 2003; Born 27/12/71; FCO 1991; World Wide Floater Duties 1995; T/D Geneva (UKMIS) 1998; FCO 1999; World Wide Floater Duties 2001; Band B3.

Martin, Craig Keith; FCO since September 2001; Born 16/11/69; FCO 1988; Washington 1998; Band C4; m 1998 Natalie Jayne Wren.

Martin, Dominic David William; Washington since August 2004; Born 25/11/64; FCO 1987; Third later Second Secretary (Chancery) New Delhi 1989; First Secretary FCO 1992; First Secretary (Head of Political and Economic Section) Buenos Aires 1996; FCO 2000;

Counsellor (Political) New Delhi 2001; m 1996 Emily Rose Walter (3d 1996, 1998, 2001).

Martin, Frances Edith Josephine; First Secretary (Commercial) Brussels (UKREP) since March 2001; Born 20/02/48; MOD 1965; FCO 1973; Montevideo 1973; Peking 1976; Tehran 1977; Moscow 1979; FCO 1981; Washington 1987; Athens 1990; FCO 1993; Second Secretary Montreal 1996.

Martin, Francis James; High Commissioner Maseru since April 2002; Born 03/05/49; DSAO later FCO 1968; Reykjavik 1971; Stuttgart 1973; FCO 1976; Second Secretary 1978; Vice-Consul (Political/Information) Cape Town 1979; Second later First Secretary (Institutions) Brussels (UKREP) 1983; FCO 1988; Deputy High Commissioner Freetown 1988; First Secretary FCO 1991; On loan to the DTI 1992; Full-Time Language Training 1995; Deputy Head of Mission Luanda 1995; First Secretary (Commercial) Copenhagen 1998; m 1970 Aileen Margaret Shovlin (2s 1973, 1975; 2d 1976, 1978).

Martin, Neil Richard; T/D Managua since August 2003; Born 14/03/67; FCO 1987; Tunis 1989; Sofia 1991; Ho Chi Minh City 1994; On secondment to China Britain Trade Group 1996; FCO 1997; First Secretary and Deputy Head of Mission Asunción 2000; Band C4.

Martin, Nicholas Jonathan Leigh; Counsellor Regional Affairs Bridgetown since February 2000; Born 29/01/48; First Secretary FCO 1979; First Secretary (Chancery) Nairobi 1981; First Secretary FCO 1984; First Secretary (Chancery) Rome 1987; First Secretary FCO 1991; Counsellor Jakarta 1993; Counsellor FCO 1996; m 1980 Anna Louise Reekie (1s 1983; 2d 1985, 1987).

Martin, Siân Kurstin; Attaché Phnom Penh since July 2004; Born 05/01/76; FCO 2002; Band A2.

Martin, Simon Charles; Secondment (Commercial) since May 2003; Born 15/05/63; FCO 1984; Language Training 1986; Third later Second Secretary and Vice-Consul Rangoon 1987; Second later First Secretary FCO 1990; Full-Time Language Training 1995; First Secretary (Commercial) Budapest 1996; FCO 2001; m 1988 Sharon Margaret Joel (1s 1996; 1d 1998).

Martinek, Rachel Anne Emily; FCO since November 2002; Born 24/04/79; Band C4.

Martinez, Paul Lawrence; Consul Dallas since September 1999; Born 06/11/53; FCO 1972; Dublin 1975; Paris 1975; Kingston 1977; Chicago 1981; FCO 1984; Second Secretary (Chancery/Information) Lima 1986; Second Secretary FCO 1990; Assistant Private Secretary to Minister of State 1990; Second Secretary and HM Consul Mexico City 1993; First Secretary FCO 1996; m 1978 Ann Elizabeth Stokes (2d 1982, 1985).

Maryan-Green, Kerri-Lyn (née Miller); FCO since February 2000; Born 11/11/64; FCO 1987; Shanghai 1989; Port Louis 1990; SUPL 1994;

FCO 1996; SUPL 1998; Band B3; m 1992 James Richard Maryan-Green (2d 1993, 1998).

Mason, Colette Hazel, MBE (1999); SUPL since September 2001; Born 15/07/65; FCO 1987; Mogadishu 1989; Port of Spain 1991; FCO 1994; Peking 1996; Vice-Consul Maseru 1998; Band B3.

Mason, Edward Charles; Deputy Head of Mission Zagreb since August 2002; Born 11/05/68; FCO 1990; Third later Second Secretary Oslo 1992; Second later First Secretary FCO 1995; m 2002 Fiona Isabel Macleod.

Mason, Fiona Isabel (née MacLeod); SUPL since December 2003; Born 19/10/70; FCO 1992; Seoul 1994; T/D Belmopan 1996; FCO 1997; Zagreb 2002; Band B3; m 2002 Edward Charles Mason.

Mason, Ian David; Second Secretary (Political/Press/Public Affairs) Lusaka since May 2001; Born 26/10/67; FCO 1987; Mogadishu 1989; Floater Duties 1991; Phnom Penh 1993; FCO 1994; Third Secretary (Chancery) Buenos Aires 1997; Band C4; m 1992 Judith Caroline Elizabeth Owens (1s 1994; 3d 1996, 1998, 2000).

Mason, Judith Caroline Elizabeth (née Owens); SUPL since July 1994; Born 11/08/64; FCO 1984; Washington 1986; Warsaw 1988; Floater Duties 1990; Phnom Penh 1993; Band A2; m 1992 Ian David Mason (1s 1994; 3d 1996, 1998, 2000).

Massam, David Robert; FCO since July 2000; Born 02/10/70; Second Secretary FCO 1996; Second Secretary (IAIE) Vienna (UKMIS) 1998; Band C4; m 1996 Elisabeth Katharine Jenkinson (1d 1999).

Massey, Andrew Fraser; Second Secretary (Political) Dar es Salaam since January 2003; Born 24/07/63; FCO 1984; Bangkok 1987; Jedda 1989; FCO 1994; Bonn 1998; Band C4; m 1996 Patricia Elizabeth Parsons (1d 1997; 2s 2000, 2002).

Massingham, Andrea Sharron; Floater Duties since November 2002; Born 10/03/71; FCO 1990; SUPL 1992; Brussels (UKDEL NATO) 1992; FCO 1995; Kathmandu 1995; BTCO Taipei 1999; Band B3.

Mastin-Lee, Christopher Ernest; Legal Counsellor FCO since April 1995; Born 11/08/56; Assistant Legal Counsellor FCO 1990; m 1988 Katherine Louise Heron (2s 1994, 1996; 1d 1998).

Mathers, Peter James, LVO (1995); High Commissioner Kingston since July 2002; Born 02/04/46; HM Forces 1968-71; FCO 1971; SOAS 1972-73; Tehran (Commercial) 1973; Bonn (Chancery) 1976; FCO 1978; Copenhagen (Chancery and Information) 1981; Tehran (Commercial) 1986; FCO 1987; On secondment to UN Offices Vienna 1988; FCO 1991; Deputy High Commissioner Bridgetown 1995; Counsellor (Commercial and Economic) Stockholm 1998; m 1983 Elisabeth Hoeller (1s 1984; 1d 1986).

Mathews, Harriet Lucy; FCO since January 2003; Born 22/12/73; FCO 1997; On secondment Brazilian Diplomatic Academy (Instituto Rio

Branco) 1999; Second Secretary Brasilia 1999; Band D6.

Mathewson, Iain Arthur Gray, CMG (2004); Counsellor FCO since August 1996; Born 16/03/52; HM Customs and Excise 1974-77; DHSS 1977-80; FCO 1980; First Secretary New York (UKMIS) 1981; FCO 1985; Warsaw 1985; First Secretary FCO 1989; Counsellor Prague 1993; m 1983 Jennifer Bloch (1s 1984; 1d 1986).

Mathison, Beverley; Islamabad since January 2003; Born 28/09/69; Bonn 1999; Band A2.

Mattey, Eric; Deputy Head of Mission and Consul Doha since December 2003; Born 26/03/49; FCO 1968; Bucharest 1971; Rabat 1973; Moscow 1975; FCO 1977; Vienna 1980; Port Louis 1983; Second Secretary FCO 1985; Second later First Secretary (Commercial) Kuala Lumpur 1990; Consul Oporto 1995; FCO 2000; Band D6; m 1970 Janet Walker (1s 1971; 1d 1974).

Matthews, Andrew John; FCO since May 2001; Born 28/04/55; FCO 1974; Bonn 1976; Singapore 1979; FCO 1982; Dublin 1982; FCO 1985; Colombo 1988; Paris 1992; FCO 1995; Berlin 1998; Band B3; m (1) 1976 Carole Susan Thomson (diss 1986) (1d 1976; 1s 1978); (2) 1988 Denise Ann Mary Carroll (1d 1992).

Matthews, David Alan; FCO since October 2002; Born 09/10/72; Band B3; m 2002 Sara Blackall.

Matthews, Mark Julian; First Secretary (Chemical Weapons) The Hague since July 2003; Born 24/08/68; FCO 1990; Third Secretary (Defence) Brussels (UKDEL NATO) 1992; Full-Time Language Training (Arabic) 1996; Second Secretary (Political/Press and Public Affairs) Abu Dhabi 1997; Foreign Office Spokesman for the Middle East, 2000; m 1997 Shauna Rudge (1s 1998; 1d 2001).

Maxton, Fiona; FCO since November 2003; Born 19/12/67; FCO 1985; Bonn 1988; Third Secretary (Management) Rabat 1989; Third Secretary FCO 1993; Vice-Consul Kiev 1997; Zagreb 2000; Band C4.

Maxwell, Letitia Kelso; FCO since November 2003; Born 12/02/42; FCO 1977; Helsinki 1979; Doha 1981; FCO 1984; Copenhagen 1989; FCO 1992; Brussels (UKDEL NATO) 1995; FCO 1998; T/D Brussels (UKREP) 2002; T/D Rabat 2003; Band B3.

May, Philip; First Secretary (Management) Brussels (UKREP) since July 2001; Born 12/11/60; Ottawa 1982; Moscow 1985; Islamabad 1986; FCO 1988; Resigned later reinstated 1990; Tehran 1992; BTC Hong Kong 1994; Second Secretary FCO 1997; DSTUS Chairman 1998; Band C5; m 1985 Susan Ann Checketts (2d 1989, 1990).

May, Susan Ann (née Checketts); SUPL since June 2001; Born 18/08/56; FCO 1978; Peking 1980; Ottawa 1982; Moscow 1985; Islamabad 1986; SUPL 1989; FCO 1997; Band B3; m 1985 Philip May (2d 1989, 1990).

Mayhew, Michael John Ernest; HM Consul General Cape Town since December 2002; Born 06/11/46; DSAO (later FCO) 1966; Mexico City 1969; Algiers 1972; Tokyo 1974; FCO 1975; Prague 1978; Second Secretary (Information) Oslo 1981; Second Secretary FCO 1985; First Secretary (Commercial/Development) Bangkok 1987; First Secretary (Commercial) The Hague 1990; First Secretary FCO 1993; Deputy High Commissioner Bridgetown 1998; m 1976 Elizabeth Carol Owen (1d 1987).

Mayhew, Nicola Ann; Third Secretary (Management) Chisinau since July 2003; Born 14/08/66; WRAC 1985-88; Employment Services 1992; FCO 1998; Jakarta 2000; Band B3; m 1988 David Mayhew.

Mayland, Alan John; First Secretary (Management) Bangkok since July 2003; Born 05/11/46; FO 1965; Warsaw 1968; Cairo 1970; Brussels 1971; Calcutta 1974; Budapest 1975; FCO 1976; Paris 1981; Ottawa 1982; Second Secretary FCO 1986; Second Secretary (Admin) Colombo 1989; Bucharest 1993; Consul Rome 1999.

Mayne, Julie Ann; Mexico City since October 2003; Born 03/04/58; FCO 1989; Caracas 1992; Quito 1996; World Wide Floater Duties 1999; FCO 2002; Band B3.

McAllister, Andrew Thornton; Second Secretary (Commercial) Dhaka since June 2001; Born 30/11/67; FCO 1988; Karachi 1990; Seoul 1993; FCO 1998; Band C4; m 1995 Han Boon AE.

McAllister, Dominic James; First Secretary Caracas since June 2004; Born 12/02/64; FCO 1990; Full-Time Language Training 1992; Full-Time Language Training Cairo 1993; Third Secretary (Information) Riyadh 1995; Second Secretary (Management) Taipei 1998; FCO 2001; m 1993 (Nelly) Hei Yee Chan-McAllister (2d 1996, 1997; 2s 1999, 2002).

McAllister, Lesley (née Dorris); SUPL since July 2004; Born 04/04/72; FCO 1999; Peking 2001; Band A2; m 2000 Gordon McAllister (1s 2002).

McAree, Kevin Thomas; SUPL since December 2001; Born 27/06/52; FCO 1971; Caracas 1974; FCO 1974; Honiara 1974; Moscow 1977; Georgetown 1979; FCO 1983; Munich 1988; FCO 1989; Istanbul 1993; Brussels (UKDEL) 1997; FCO 1999; Band B3; m 1975 Susan Margaret Humphrey (2s 1980, 1984).

McAree, Patrick Sean; FCO since March 1991 (Second Secretary 1994); Born 30/12/53; FCO 1971; Cairo 1975; Calcutta 1978; FCO 1982; Tehran 1984; Düsseldorf 1988; Band C5; m 1975 Maureen Alexander.

McAree, Susan Margaret (née Humphrey); Bangkok since September 2001; Born 26/06/55; FCO 2000; Band A2; m 1975 Kevin Thomas McAree (2s 1980, 1984).

McBride, Christophe Charles Rene; First Secretary New York (UKMIS) since September

2003; Born 20/03/75; FCO 1997; Second
Secretary (Political) Abuja 1998; Second later First
Secretary FCO 2001; Band D6; m 2001 Caroline
Jane Davies.

McCafferty, Marie Claire; SUPL since May 2004;
Born 17/05/65; FCO 1988; Bonn 1990; Nairobi
1993; FCO 1996; Wellington 1998; New Delhi
2003; Band A2; m 2001 (1d 2002).

McCall, Gary; Abuja since March 2004; Born
08/02/69; FCO 1987; Bridgetown 1989; Dhaka
1993; Karachi 1997; ECO Sofia 2000; Band B3;
m (1) 1990 Patricia Ann Chin (diss 1993); (2)
1993 Sharon Anne Thomas (diss) (1s 1994); ptnr,
Puticha NaNongkai (1d 1998).

McCallum, Robert Campbell; Havana since April
2004; Born 04/11/45; Moscow 1989; New York
(UKMIS) 1991; Kiev 1993; Moscow 1997; T/D
Tripoli 2000; T/D Moscow 2001; Cairo 2001;
Band C4.

McCallum, Ruth Elizabeth (née Thomson); FCO
since April 1995; Born 12/11/63; FCO 1985;
Moscow 1988; FCO 1989; Ankara 1991; Band C4;
m 1997 Martin Douglas McCallum.

McCann, Alec; Kingston since May 2003; Born
04/11/70; FCO 1988; Rome 1991; Lisbon 1994;
Lagos 1997; Band B3.

McCarthy, Susan Margaret (née Hutton); FCO
since September 2003; Born 01/04/59; FCO 1984;
Khartoum 1985; Georgetown 1989; Tortola 1994;
SUPL 1998; Band B3; m 1990 Jonathan Paul
McCarthy (1d 1992; 1s 1996).

McCarthy, Tina Ann; FCO since December 1998;
Born 25/01/66; FCO 1984; Peking 1987; FCO
1988; Dar es Salaam 1990; FCO 1993; Budapest
1995; Band B3.

McCleary, William Boyd; Director Trade and
Investment in Germany and Consul- General
Düsseldorf since November 2000; Born 30/03/49;
HCS 1972; First Secretary (Agriculture later
Chancery) Bonn 1975; First Secretary FCO 1981;
First Secretary, Head of Chancery and Consul
Seoul 1985; First Secretary FCO 1988; Counsellor,
Deputy Head of Mission and Director of Trade
Promotion Ankara 1990; Counsellor (Economic)
Ottawa 1993; Head of Overseas Estate
Department, later Estate Strategy Unit FCO 1997;
m (1) 1977 Susan Elizabeth Williams (diss 1999)
(2d 1983, 1985); (2) 2000 Jenny Collier (1d 2001).

McCleery, Katherine Louise (known as Kate);
Assistant Legal Adviser, FCO since September
2002; Born 25/04/74; Band D6.

McCluskie, Matthew William; FCO since January
2001; Born 06/05/65; FCO 1984; Bonn 1986;
Prague 1988; Tunis 1990; FCO 1992; Warsaw
1997; Band B3.

McCole, Kevin John; Second Secretary
(Management) Bucharest since April 2002; Born
06/05/69; FCO 1989; The Hague 1992; Valletta
1995; FCO 1998; Band C4; m 2001 Margaret
Rose Howie.

McCole, Margaret Rose (née Howie); Second
Secretary (Political/PPA) Bucharest since May
2002; Born 07/03/66; FCO 1985; Tokyo 1988;
Stockholm 1990; FCO 1993; Rome 1994; Third
Secretary FCO 1997; m 2001 Kevin John McCole.

McColl, Lorraine Helen, RVM (1992); Tunis since
September 2000; Born 20/08/57; FCO 1989; Bonn
1990; Ottawa 1993; Berlin 1996; Band A2; m
1992 Alan McElroy (1d 1996).

McColm, Sean; St Petersburg since October 2002;
Born 10/07/72; FCO 1990; Copenhagen 1994;
Dhaka 1997; FCO 1998; Band B3.

McCooey, Geraldine Mary; Second Secretary FCO
since November 2001; Born 25/05/73; FCO 1996;
Second Secretary (Economic) Nicosia 1998; Full-
Time Language Training 2000; Band C4.

McCormack, Elizabeth (née McKenna); Doha
since May 2002; Born 28/06/66; Office of
Electricity Regulation 1991; FCO 1996; Brussels
(UKDEL NATO) 1997; Vienna 1999; Band A2; m
1986 Columbus McCormack (2s 1988, 1996; 1d
2001).

McCormick, Stephen; Second Secretary
(Economic/Commercial) Ankara since June 2002;
Born 05/09/67; FCO 1990; Bangkok 1993;
Istanbul 1993; Tbilisi 1997; Tokyo 1997; Full-
Time Language Training FCO 2001; Band C4; m
1996 Sevda Unalan (1d 1999).

McCosh, Andrew David; First Secretary (Political)
Kathmandu since March 2003; Born 06/01/72;
FCO 1994; Vice-Consul (Political) Istanbul 1997;
FCO 1999; Kabul 2002; Band D6; m 2002 Malika
Geraldine Browne.

McCoy, Peter Owen David; Deputy Head of
Mission Lagos since January 2002; Born 28/04/52;
FCO 1971; New Delhi 1974; Kaduna 1977; FCO
1981; Maseru 1984; AO/Vice-Consul/Comm
Montreal 1987 (later Second Secretary); Second
Secretary FCO 1990; Vice-Consul (Commercial)
Los Angeles 1992; Assistant Trade Commissioner
(China Trade) BTC Hong Kong 1993; First
Secretary (Commercial) Bombay 1996; m 1975
Sally Ann Lord (2d 1976, 1978; 1s 1982).

McCreadie, Katrina; Beijing since July 2003;
Born 10/05/73; FCO 2001; Band A2.

McCrory, Mark Frank; FCO since September
2003; Born 28/01/74; Band C4.

McCrory, Susan Margaret Therese; Legal Adviser
Geneva (UKMIS) since February 2001; Born
17/12/64; Solicitor; Legal Adviser MAFF 1992;
Assistant Legal Adviser FCO 1996; m 1990
Ignacio de Castro (1s 1998).

McCrudden, Patrick Gerald, MBE (1993); First
Secretary FCO since October 2003; Born
22/04/50; FCO 1969; Saigon 1971; Mexico City
1974; Bahrain 1976; FCO 1977; Tristan da Cunha
1980; Brussels 1981; Pretoria 1982; Second
Secretary FCO 1985; Second Secretary
(Chancery) Bridgetown 1988; First Secretary
(Somalia/Humanitarian) and Deputy Permanent

Representative UNEP/UNCHS Nairobi 1991; First Secretary FCO 1995; Director BIS and Deputy Consul General New York 1997; First Secretary (Press and Public Affairs) New Delhi 2000; Band D6; m 1973 (diss 1989) (1s 1974; 2d 1974, 1976).

McCurrie, Marianne Linzi Claire; FCO since November 2003; Born 19/03/79; Band B3.

McDonald, David Christopher; Washington since September 2003; Born 12/05/64; FCO 1984; Washington 1990; FCO 1993; Band C4.

McDonald, Simon Gerard, CMG (2004); HM Ambassador Tel Aviv since August 2003; Born 09/03/61; FCO 1982; Language Training SOAS 1983; Third later Second Secretary Jedda (later Riyadh) 1985; Second Secretary (Economic) Bonn 1988; First Secretary FCO 1990; Private Secretary to Permanent Under-Secretary 1993; First Secretary (Chancery) Washington 1995; Counsellor and Deputy Head of Mission and Consul-General Riyadh 1998; Private Secretary to the Secretary of State for Foreign and Commonwealth Affairs 2001; m 1989 The Hon. Olivia Mary Wright (2s 1990, 1994; 2d 1992, 1996).

McDuff, Nicholas Frederic; Second Secretary FCO since March 1995; Born 22/07/50; MOD (Navy) 1967; FCO 1970; Muscat 1972; Brussels (UKDEL NATO) 1972; BMG Berlin 1975; Karachi 1978; Islamabad 1980; FCO 1982; Athens 1983; Brussels (UKDEL NATO) 1984; Bandar Seri Begawan 1987; On loan to the DTI 1990; Second Secretary Casablanca 1992; m 1978 Jennifer Mary Cain (3s 1981, 1985, 1986).

McEvoy, Edward James; Consul Tokyo since July 2004; Born 06/02/46; CRO (later FO) 1962; Belgrade 1968; Mbabane 1970; FCO 1972; Aden 1975; Luxembourg 1977; Addis Ababa 1979; On loan to Home Office 1982; Second Secretary (Immigration) Dhaka 1985; Second Secretary (Commercial) Manila 1989; Vice-Consul (Commercial) Cape Town 1990; FCO 1995; First Secretary Manila 1997; First Secretary FCO 2001; m 1967 Patricia Gibbs (diss 1991) (1s 1972).

McEwen, Christine Elizabeth; HM Consul and First Secretary (Management) Buenos Aires since April 2001; Born 04/10/58; FCO 1978; BMG Berlin 1981; Peking 1984; Bombay 1987; FCO 1990; Rome 1994; Deputy Head of Mission Guatemala City 1997; FCO 2000; Band C5.

McFarlane, David Andrew; First Secretary (Political) Beijing since November 2003; Born 20/10/77; FCO 1999; T/D Beijing 2002; Band D6.

McFarlane, Jacqueline (née Stewart); Mumbai since January 2001; Born 01/11/67; FCO 1986; Manila 1988; FCO 1992; Damascus 1994; Islamabad 1997; Band B3; m 1988 Neil Ross McFarlane (1s 2001).

McFarlane, Neil Ross; Mumbai since January 2001; Born 26/03/69; FCO 1991; Damascus 1994; Islamabad 1997; Band B3; m 1988 Jacqueline Stewart (1s 2001).

McFarlin, Andrew John; Mumbai since February 2002; Born 30/08/70; FCO 1990; Vienna 1993; Floater Duties 1996; Georgetown 1998; Band B3; m 1999 Juanita Adrian.

McGee, Annie (née Brown); Vice-Consul Madrid since January 2003; Born 14/10/68; HCS FCO 1987; FCO 1994; Tunis 1996; FCO 1999; Full-Time Language Training (Spanish) 2002; Band B3; m 1996 W M V McGee (1s 1999).

McGill, Clive John; FCO since February 2003; Born 09/10/58; FCO 1978; Belmopan 1982; Stockholm 1985; FCO 1988; Karachi 1991; Baku 1995; Deputy Head of Mission Ashgabat 1999; Band C4; m (1) 1983 Thelma Garcia; (2) 1988 Angela Raw.

McGinley, Francis John; First Secretary (Management) Damascus since August 2001; Born 12/01/49; FCO 1971; Brussels (NATO) 1974; Nairobi 1977; FCO 1980; Banjul 1982; Second Secretary (Information) Oslo 1984; Second Secretary FCO 1989; Second Secretary (Commercial) Zagreb 1992; First Secretary (Management/Consular/Immigration) Kiev 1995; Full-Time Language Training 2001; m 1994 Neriman Kreso.

McGlone, Andrea Lynne (née Webb); Assistant Private Secretary to the Permanent Under Secretary, FCO since August 2002; Born 27/03/66; FCO 1985; The Hague 1987; FCO 1990; Harare 1995; Riyadh 1999; Band C4; m 1993 Kevin McGlone (2d 1994, 1997).

McGregor, Julie; Islamabad since June 2004; Born 23/06/80; FCO 1999; Jerusalem 2001; Band B3.

McGregor, Peter; Singapore since January 2003; Born 30/05/50; FCO 1970; Jedda 1972; Lusaka 1976; FCO 1979; Damascus 1982; Port of Spain 1986; New Delhi 1989; Second Secretary FCO 1992; Second Secretary Peking 1994; HM Consul Tel Aviv 1998; m (1) 1972 Vanessa Avril Utteridge (dec'd 1989) (1s 1980); (2) 1991 Alexandra Davenport Gillies (1d 1991).

McGregor-Bell, Sharon Ann (née McGregor); FCO since December 2001; Born 23/06/71; FCO 1990; Brussels 1993; FCO 1996; SUPL 1998; Tel Aviv 1999; Band C4; m 1995 Kevan Watson Bell.

McGuinness, Cheryl Vinetta (née Lynch); New Delhi since August 2003; Born 04/11/66; FCO 1988; Peking 1991; Abidjan 1994; SUPL 1997; Band A2; m 1996 Mark John McGuinness.

McGuinness, Mark Andrew, MBE (2004); FCO since August 2003; Born 25/08/67; FCO 1988; Islamabad 1990; FCO 1992; Doha 1996; Abidjan 1999; Band B3; m 2001 Elizabeth Krauk (1d 2003).

McGuinness, Patrick Joseph, OBE (1997); Counsellor Rome since September 2003; Born 27/04/63; FCO 1985; Language Training 1986; Second Secretary (Chancery) Sana'a 1988; Second Secretary FCO 1991; First Secretary (Political) Abu Dhabi 1994; First Secretary Cairo 1996; First

Secretary FCO 1999; m 1994 Susannah Imogen Mills (1d 2001).

McGurgan, Kevin; First Secretary (Political) Stockholm since October 2003; Born 31/05/71; FCO 1990; Floater Duties 1992; Brussels (UKREP) 1994; Sarajevo 1996; Third later Second Secretary (Chancery) New York (UKMIS) 1997; FCO 2000; Band D7; m 1997 Victoria Ann Harrison.

McGurgan, Victoria Ann (née Harrison); SUPL since August 2003; Born 13/08/71; FCO 1994; New York (UKMIS) 1997; FCO 2000; SUPL 2002; FCO 2002; Band A2; m 1997 Kevin McGurgan (1s 2002).

McGurk, Gerard, MBE (2000); Second Secretary (Chancery) New York (UKMIS) since August 2000; Born 22/12/70; FCO 1988; Athens 1991; Floater Duties 1994; Deputy Head of Mission and Vice-Consul Skopje 1996; Band C4; m 1998 Sonja Kurcieva (1d 2002).

McHugh, Esther Phoebe; Second Secretary (Political) Moscow since December 2002; Born 08/09/75; FCO 2000; Band C4.

McHugh, Susan Mary; Second later First Secretary FCO since November 1994; Born 12/02/44; FCO 1971; On loan to SEATO Bangkok 1974; New Delhi 1977; SUPL 1980; Victoria (Seychelles) 1981; Second Secretary FCO 1983; Second Secretary Nicosia 1994; Band C5.

McIntosh, Margaret Claire; FCO since August 2001; Born 31/05/63; FCO 1995; Brussels (UKREP) 1997; World Wide Floater Duties 1999; Band C4.

McIntosh, Martin Howard, OBE (1994); Counsellor (Commercial) later Director of Trade and Investment Dublin since April 2001; Born 26/12/47; FO (later FCO) 1966; Jakarta 1970; Tokyo 1970; Moscow 1972; Beirut 1973; FCO 1976; Madrid 1979; Second Secretary Bogotá 1982; Second later First Secretary (Commercial) Nairobi 1984; First Secretary FCO 1989; First Secretary (Commercial) Buenos Aires 1990; First Secretary (Commercial) Mexico City 1994; On loan to the DTI 1997; m 1970 Erika Wagner (2d 1983, 1985).

McIver, Damian John; First Secretary FCO since April 1999; Born 02/11/61; HM Customs and Excise 1986; FCO 1986; Third Secretary (Political) Belgrade 1987; Second Secretary FCO 1991; Political Adviser ECMIS Zagreb 1992; FCO 1993; Second Secretary (KHF) Bucharest 1995; First Secretary (Political) Belgrade 1998; Band D6; m 1998 Raluca Vasiliu.

McKee, Tracey Anne; World Wide Floater Duties since March 2004; Born 03/06/77; FCO 2000; Kigali 2000; Band B3.

McKell, Paul Leo; Brussels (UKREP) since September 2001; Born 01/09/66; Assistant Legal Adviser FCO 1997; m 2001 Elizabeth C Hanlon.

McKelvey, Diane Elizabeth; FCO since July 2001; Born 06/07/67; FCO 1989; Third Secretary (Political) Copenhagen 1992; FCO 1994; Second Secretary (Political/Press and Public Affairs) Lusaka 1998.

McKen, Dawn; First Secretary FCO since January 2000; Born 23/07/66; FCO 1995; Second Secretary (Political) Moscow 1996; m Matthew Edward Sparrowhawk (1d 2003).

McKendrick, Ian; Full-Time Language Training Beijing since January 2004; Born 04/10/70; FCO 1991; BTC Hong Kong 1995; Floater Duties 1998; FCO 2000; Full-Time Language Training (Mandarin) 2003; Band C4.

McKenzie, Alistair William, MBE (1980); Counsellor and Deputy Head of Mission Abu Dhabi since July 2001; Born 19/02/45; DSAO 1965; Budapest 1967; Singapore 1969; Brasilia 1972; FCO 1975; San Salvador 1978; San José 1980; Commercial Attaché Madrid 1982 (Second Secretary 1983); Second Secretary FCO 1984; Deputy High Commissioner and Head of Chancery Banjul 1986; Consul-General Bilbao 1990; First Secretary (Immigration/Consular) Lagos 1995; British Trade International 1998; m 1968 Margaret Emily Young (2s 1970, 1974).

McKenzie, Hilary (née Grace); Second Secretary (Commercial) Johannesburg since August 1999; Born 01/03/59; FCO 1980; Islamabad 1982; Oslo 1984; Bombay 1987; Amsterdam 1989; FCO 1992; Vice-Consul Helsinki 1996; Band C4; m 1989 Ian James McKenzie (1d 1999).

McKenzie, Philip; Third Secretary (Political/Economic) Bangkok since September 2001; Born 26/04/65; FCO 1986; Lusaka 1987; San José 1991; FCO 1993; BTC Hong Kong 1996; Band B3.

McKenzie Smith, Justin James; First Secretary New York since February 2004; Born 04/02/69; FCO 1994; Full-Time Language Training 1995; Second Secretary (Political) Moscow 1996; First Secretary FCO 1999.

McKeogh, Fiona (née Sutherland), MBE (1993); Paris since February 2003; Born 17/09/59; FCO 1983; Bonn 1984; Cape Town 1987; Brussels (UKREP) 1989; FCO 1993; SUPL 1993; FCO 1995; Moscow 1997; New York (UKMIS) 1999; Band B3; m 1992 Paul Nicolas McKeogh.

McKerron, Alan; Islamabad since June 2003; Born 20/03/65; Scottish Office 1981-99; FCO 1999; Band C5; m 2002 Susan Road-Night.

McKerron, Susan Catherine (née Road-Night); SUPL since July 2004; Born 13/03/67; FCO 1991; Kiev 1992; Full-Time Language Training 1995; Mexico City 1995; FCO 1999; Islamabad 2003; Band B3; m 2002 Alan McKerron.

McKerrow, Elizabeth Mary (née Foot); FCO since August 1991; Born 18/01/67; FCO 1986; Buenos Aires 1990; Band B3; m 1991 Ian Bernard Harry McKerrow (1s 1998; 1d 2000).

McKie, Margaret Stevenson; Brussels (UKREP) since May 2001; Born 07/08/62; FCO 1988; Prague 1991; Cairo 1993; FCO 1996; Floater Duties 1998; Full-Time Language Training 2001; Band A2.

McKinlay, Ian Leonard; Second Secretary (Management) Geneva since August 2002; Born 17/09/58; FCO 1978; Geneva (UKMIS) 1980; Tehran 1983; FCO 1986; Addis Ababa 1989; Dakar 1992; FCO 1997; m 1984 Ann Hugoline Cameron (1s 1989; 2d 1991, 1993).

McLachlan, Malcolm Orde; Deputy Head of Mission Hanoi since September 2001; Born 10/09/63; FCO 1981; Karachi 1984; Guatemala City 1988; FCO 1993; Second later First Secretary (Political) Nairobi 1998; m 1989 Maricruz Mendia Moynes (1d 1995).

McLaren, Marilynn, MBE (1993); SUPL since January 1998; Born 20/07/47; Scottish Office 1963; FCO 1981; Dacca 1981; Tehran 1985; Lisbon 1987; FCO 1989; Tehran 1990; Washington 1994; Band B3.

McLaren-Oliver, Geoffrey Harold; Tehran since November 2003; Born 11/06/48; HM Forces 1965-88; Moscow 1989; Madrid 1991; World Wide Floater Duties 1993; Moscow 1998; Khartoum 2000; Band B3.

McLean, Sean Nicholas; Vice-Consul Riyadh since August 2002; Born 07/10/70; FCO 2000; Band B3; m 1999 Parimala Chandramohanadas.

McLean, Siân Alexis; First Secretary (Economic) Peking since July 2001; Born 12/09/69; FCO 1993; Full-Time Language Training Peking 1996; Consul (Economic) Hong Kong 1997; Band D6.

McLuskie, Karen-Louise; FCO since September 2003; Born 21/06/78; Band C4.

McMahon, Brian Patrick; FCO since December 2002; Born 26/03/46; CRO and DSAO 1963; Prague 1968; Bonn 1969; Kabul 1972; FCO 1975; Islamabad 1978; Geneva (UKMIS) 1981; Second Secretary FCO 1984; Second Secretary (Immigration/Consular) Colombo 1990; HM Consul Rome 1994; FCO 1999; British Trade International 1999; m 1967 Eileen Conroy (1d 1970; 1s 1975).

McMahon, Dr David John Hugh; SUPL since August 2004; Born 04/05/65; FCO 1991; Second Secretary (Political/Information) Dhaka 1993; FCO 1997; First Secretary (Environment and Trade Policy) New Delhi 2001; Band D6; m 1994 Kay Taylor Lacey.

McMahon, Ian Irvine; Counsellor FCO since October 2001; Born 08/06/55; Army 1973-83; Second Secretary FCO 1983; Second later First Secretary (Chancery) Islamabad 1985; First Secretary FCO 1987; First Secretary (Chancery) New Delhi 1989; First Secretary later Counsellor FCO 1992; Counsellor Copenhagen 1997; m 1979 Anne Elizabeth Baker (diss 2002) (1d 1981).

McMahon, Keith David, MBE (1998); First Secretary (Management) Athens since April 2003; Born 10/03/68; FCO 1988; Lusaka 1990; SE Asia/Middle East Floater Duties 1993; Deputy Head of Mission Yerevan 1995; FCO 1998; Band C5; m 2000 Melissa Schwartz.

McManus, John Andrew; First Secretary (Political) Brussels since January 2001; Born 20/05/55; FCO 1977; Paris 1980; Algiers 1983; FCO 1985; Language Training FCO 1987 (Second Secretary 1987); Second Secretary Moscow 1988; Second Secretary Brussels (UKREP) 1992; Second later First Secretary (Information) Berne 1993; FCO 1997; Band D6.

McMinn, Wendy Lily Alexandra; Kingston since May 2003; Born 07/07/71; MOD 1991; FCO 1999; Canberra 2001; Band B3.

McMurrie, Jane Patricia (née Hannah); FCO since June 1997; Born 23/09/70; FCO 1989; Athens 1991; Floater Duties 1995; Band B3.

McNair, Richard Andrew; First Secretary Pretoria since June 2003; Born 18/02/59; FCO 1979; Lagos 1980; FCO 1982; Ankara 1984; FCO 1987; Cairo 1991; FCO 1995; Band C5; m 1978 Julie Elaine Stephen (1d 1981; 1s 1983).

McNeill, Alasdair Morrell; FCO since February 1999; Born 13/11/67; FCO 1988; Istanbul 1992; FCO 1995; Moscow 1997; Band B3; m 1994 Elizabeth Hall (1s 2000; 1d 2003).

McNeill, Christine Mary; First Secretary (Commercial) Sofia since December 2002; Born 12/03/62; FCO 1979; Cairo 1983; Suva 1987; Second Secretary FCO 1991; Madras 1995; Deputy High Commissioner Mbabane 1999; m 1982 Scott Robertson McNeill (1d 1994; 1s 1998).

McPhail, Dr Alastair David; FCO since September 2000; Born 02/03/61; FCO 1994; Language Training 1995; second later First Secretary (Political/Military) Ankara 1996; m 1989 Pamela Joanne Davies (2s 1992, 1994).

McPhail, Pamela Joanne (née Davies); First Secretary FCO since August 2000; Born 03/12/62; FCO 1990; Third Secretary (Press and Public Affairs) Moscow 1992; FCO 1995; SUPL 1996; Band C5; m 1989 Alastair David McPhail (2s 1992, 1994).

McQuibban, Peter James, OBE (2003); Counsellor Paris since July 2004; Born 07/11/55; Third later Second Secretary FCO 1981; Second Secretary (Economic) Brasilia 1982; First Secretary FCO 1985; First Secretary (Political) Warsaw 1988; First Secretary on loan to the Cabinet Office 1992; Counsellor FCO 1995; Counsellor on sabbatical at Copenhagen University 1996; SUPL at the Danish School of Public Administration 1997; Counsellor FCO 2002; Counsellor on loan to the Cabinet Office (Civil Contingencies Secretariat) 2002; Band D6; m (1) 1982 Susan Jennifer Magdalen Hitch (diss 1996); (2) 1996 Annegrethe Felter Rasmussen (1d 1996; 2s 1998, 2002).

McQuilton, Patricia Bernadette (née Edwards); Athens since March 2002; Born 15/03/69; Home Civil Service 1988; FCO 1996; Nicosia 1998; Band B3; m 1999 Craig McQuilton.

McVey-Dobson, Andrea; SUPL since August 1997; Born 28/01/64; FCO 1988; Paris 1991; Luxembourg 1993; FCO 1996; Band A2.

Meacock-Bashir, Danaë Miranda; FCO since September 2002; Born 22/07/74; Band C4.

Means, Claire Stewart (née Hunter); Tortola since October 2001; Born 02/03/69; FCO 1990; Kuala Lumpur 1993; SUPL 1994; T/D Suva 1997; New York (UKMIS) 1997; Band A2; m 1994 Thomas E Means.

Mearns, Stuart; FCO since June 2003; Born 21/11/58; FCO 1982; Khartoum 1985; FCO 1989; Paris 1995; FCO 1998; Addis Ababa 2000; Band C4; m 1983 Andrea Chapman (2s 1993, 1996).

Mease, Rachel Elizabeth (née Tunn); Tunis since October 2003; Born 28/05/68; FCO 1989; Bucharest 1991; Hanoi 1993; New York (UKMIS) 1995; T/D Croatia 1996; FCO 1997; Dublin 1999; Band B3; m 1994 Paul Mease.

Meath Baker, William John Clovis, OBE (2002); Counsellor FCO since October 2002; Born 11/05/59; FCO 1985; Second later First Secretary (Chancery and Information) and Consul Kabul 1988; FCO 1989; First Secretary and Consul Prague 1989; First Secretary FCO 1993; Consul (Political) Istanbul 1997; First Secretary FCO 2000; Counsellor Kabul 2002; m 1985 Elizabeth Diana Woodham-Smith (4d 1988, 1990, 1992, 1995).

Meconi, Anne-Marie; Brussels (UKREP) since February 2003; Born 14/01/61; Transferred from the Scottish Office 1997; FCO 1997; Hanoi 1999; Band A2.

Mee, Jeffery Bryan; Second Secretary (Consular) Los Angeles since July 2003; Born 08/07/56; Passport Office 1975; FCO 1976; Kathmandu 1978; FCO 1980; Khartoum 1982; Peking 1985; Vancouver 1987; FCO 1987; Vice-Consul Vienna 1991; Lisbon 1994; Second Secretary FCO 1997; (1s 1990; 1d 1993).

Meehan, Sean Patrick; Lisbon since November 2003; Born 15/07/73; FCO 1995; Sarajevo 1998; SUPL (Sarajevo) 1999; Budapest 2000; Band A2; m 2000 Mirela Krajnc (1s 2003).

Mehmet, Alper, MVO (1990); Ambassador and Consul-General Reykjavik since April 2004; Born 28/08/48; Immigration Service 1970; Lagos 1979; FCO 1983; Second Secretary 1986; Bucharest 1986; Second Secretary (Head of Chancery) Reykjavik 1989; FCO 1993; First Secretary (Information) Bonn 1999; m 1968 Elaine Susan Tarrant (2d 1969, 1971).

Mehta, Nikesh A; Second Secretary (Regional-Multilateral) Kampala since May 2004; Born 07/04/77; FCO 2002; Band C4.

Meiklejohn, Dominic Francis; FCO since April 2003; Born 14/11/67; HM Customs and Excise 1989 - 90; FCO 1990; Full-Time Language Training 1993; Second later First Secretary (EU/Public Affairs) Warsaw 1993; Band D7; m 1997 Anna Iwona Reichel.

Melbourne, Sean; Baku since September 2002; Born 09/12/68; FCO 1988; Maputo 1990; Tashkent 1994; FCO 1998; Band C4; m 1997 Elmira Vakkasova.

Melling, Scott Richard; Third Secretary (Commercial) Düsseldorf since April 2004; Born 10/05/72; FCO 1990; Madrid 1994; FCO 1997; World Wide Floater Duties 1998; FCO 1999; Third Secretary (Management) Warsaw 2000; Band B3; (1d 2002).

Mellor, John; Lagos since October 2003; Born 09/02/52; Department of National Savings 1968; FCO 1971; Belgrade 1973; Middle East Floater 1975; Dar es Salaam 1977; FCO 1979; Strasbourg 1980; FCO 1982; Washington 1987; Ankara 1990; FCO 1993; Jakarta 1997; Sana'a 2002; Band C4; m 1987 Mary Bridget Ann McGettigan.

Meredith, Richard Evan; First Secretary FCO since August 1998; Born 31/01/61; FCO 1983; Third Secretary Bridgetown 1985; Second Secretary Managua 1987; Second later First Secretary FCO 1989; Bonn 1995; Band D6; m 1986 Louisa Jane Oriel (2d 1992, 1995).

Merritt, Christopher; FCO since October 2003; Born 25/02/81; Band C4.

Merry, David Byron, CMG (2000); High Commissioner Gaborone since August 2001; Born 16/09/45; Ministry of Aviation 1961; CRO (later Commonwealth Office, later FCO) 1965; Bangkok 1969; Second Secretary (Information) Budapest 1974; Second later First Secretary FCO 1977; First Secretary (Civil Air Attaché) Bonn 1981; Head of Chancery East Berlin 1985; First Secretary FCO 1989; Deputy Head of Mission Manila 1993; Deputy High Commissioner Karachi 1997; FCO 2000; m 1967 Patricia Ann Ellis (2d 1969, 1972; 1s 1971).

Mesarowicz, Anthony David; Algiers since June 2003; Born 28/07/70; FCO 1991; Paris 1995; Guatemala City 1999; Band B3.

Metcalfe, Julian Ross; Head of Estate Strategy Unit, FCO since September 2000; Born 24/02/56; Economic Adviser FCO 1983; First Secretary Cairo 1987; First Secretary FCO 1991; Full-Time Language Training 1994; Deputy Head of Mission Zagreb 1995; First Secretary FCO 1997; m 1985 Rachel Mai Jones (1d 1997).

Metreweli, Blaise Florence; FCO since March 2003; Born 30/07/77; FCO 1999; Second Secretary (Economic) Dubai 2000; Band C4.

Miah, Faruk; Third Secretary (Management) Port Louis since February 2002; Born 18/12/70; FCO 1990; Singapore 1994; Dar es Salaam 1997; FCO 1998; Band B3; m 1993 Nilufa Yasmin (3d 1996, 2001, 2004).

Micallef, Janice Pauline (née Roughley); Caracas since May 2000; Born 15/01/66; FCO 1993; New Delhi 1996; SUPL 1999; Band A2; m 1996 Mark Antoine Micallef (2d 1999, 2002).

Michael, Alan Rhys; FCO since July 2002; Born 02/01/48; FCO 1971; MECAS 1973; Jedda 1975; Jedda/Riyadh 1976; FCO 1978; Second Secretary Geneva (UKMIS) 1982; First Secretary (Commercial) Kuwait 1986; First Secretary FCO 1988; Brussels (UKREP) 1994; Consul-General Casablanca 1999; m 1973 Anita Ruth Ford (1s 1973; 1d 1977).

Middel, Julie; SUPL since May 2003; Born 26/04/58; DHSS 1976; FCO 1979; Copenhagen 1982; Floater Duties 1985; Sofia 1986; Brussels 1987; FCO 1990; SUPL 1990; Karachi 1994; FCO 1994; On loan to the DTI 1996; FCO 1999; Band B3; m 1988 Wolfgang Middel.

Middlemiss, Matthew, MBE (1991); First Secretary FCO since January 2004; Born 11/01/62; First Secretary FCO 1998; First Secretary (Humanitarian) Geneva (UKMIS) 2001; Band D6; m 2001 Phyllida Alison Cheyne (1d 2000).

Middleton, David Farquharson; Counsellor FCO since August 2001; Born 21/11/53; FCO 1982; Language Training Kamakura 1984; First Secretary Tokyo 1985; First Secretary FCO 1988; First Secretary Lusaka 1991; First Secretary FCO 1994; Counsellor Amman 1998; m 1984 Georgina Mary Housman (1s 1987; 2d 1989, 1992).

Middleton, William Alexander; FCO since September 2002; Born 03/01/78; Band C4.

Miles, Joanne Denise, MBE (1993); SUPL since January 2003; Born 10/06/57; FCO 1980; Prague 1982; FCO 1984; Bandar Seri Begawan 1986; Guatemala City 1988; San José 1991; FCO 1992; Caracas 1994; FCO 1997; Second Secretary (Political) Nairobi 1999; Band C4.

Miles, John; First Secretary Washington since October 2000; Born 30/10/46; Nepal 1972; Germany 1974; Home Civil Service 1978; Hong Kong 1980; New Delhi 1984; FCO 1988; Moscow 1995; Band D6; m 1968 Lynda Patricia Frances McNair (1d 1972; 1s 1974).

Millar, Andrew James; First Secretary (Economic/Political) Pretoria since September 2000; Born 13/07/65; Office of Gas Supply 1994; FCO E/Advs 1996; FCO 1999; Band D6; m 1996 Catherine Jo Russell Davis.

Millar, Lindsey; SUPL since December 2000; Born 18/06/67; Scottish Office 1984 - 90; FCO 1991; Berlin 1993; The Hague 1997; Band A2.

Miller, Andrew John; FCO since December 2003; Born 29/05/66; FCO 1985; Munich 1991; FCO 1995; Abu Dhabi 1998; Second Secretary Muscat 2002; Band C4; m 1991 Coral Annabel (1d 1997; 1s 1999).

Miller, David; FCO since July 2004; Born 19/05/66; Second Secretary FCO 1997; First Secretary (Chancery) Bogotá 2000; Band D6; m 1993 Carmen Delgado.

Miller, David Roland; First Secretary FCO since February 2003; Born 01/11/52; FCO 1972; Bucharest 1975; Tripoli 1976; Rome 1979; FCO 1982; Kuala Lumpur 1985; Second Secretary FCO 1989; Deputy High Commissioner Vila 1990; Second later First Secretary FCO 1994; Resident Acting High Commissioner Grenada 1998; Band D6; m 1976 Gillian Mary Cornthwaite (2s 1980, 1983).

Miller, Jamie Jonathan, MBE (1999); First Secretary (Political) Freetown since November 2000; Born 01/05/72; FCO 1996; Second Secretary (Chancery) Islamabad 1998; Band D6.

Miller, Julian Peter; HM Consul Nagoya since October 2002; FCO 1987; Language Training 1989; Language Training Kamakura 1989; Tokyo 1990; San José 1994; FCO 1998; m 1993 Yasuko Yanai (2s 1995, 1998).

Miller, Julie; FCO since September 1998; Born 21/11/70; FCO 1988; Jakarta 1991; FCO 1994; Buenos Aires 1995; Band C4.

Miller, Nicholas Michael; FCO since September 2001; Born 10/10/62; FCO 1982; Bangkok 1984; Peking 1987; FCO 1990; Tehran 1993; Full-Time Language Training 1996; Hamburg 1997; m 1995 Raquel Evangelina Varela (2d 1994, 1999).

Miller, Pablo; FCO since August 2002; Born 27/02/60; FCO 1990; First Secretary (Political) Abuja later Lagos 1992; First Secretary FCO 1995; First Secretary Tallinn 1997; Band D6; m 1989 Elke Schmidt (3d 1991, 1994, 1996).

Miller, Penelope Helen; FCO since November 2001; Born 18/03/70; FCO 1995; Language Training Kamakura 1997; Second Secretary (Commercial) Tokyo 1998; Band D6.

Miller, Shirley; Vienna since June 2002; Born 06/12/56; FCO 1976; Reykjavik 1981; Geneva (UKDIS) 1984; Port Stanley 1987; FCO 1988; Brussels (UKREP) 1992; Helsinki 1995; FCO 1998; Band A2; m 1997 Martin Corcoran.

Millett, Peter Joseph; Head of Security Strategy Unit, FCO since December 2002; Born 23/01/55; FCO 1974; LA Floater 1976; Caracas 1978; Doha 1981; Second Secretary FCO 1985; First Secretary (Energy) Brussels (UKREP) 1989; Counsellor FCO 1993; Deputy Head of Mission Athens 1997; FCO 2001; m 1981 June Harnett (3d 1984, 1987, 1991).

Millington, Claire; Third Secretary (Political) Rome since January 2003; FCO 1999; Band B3.

Mills, Anwen Eluned (née Rees); SUPL since April 1999; Born 22/07/64; FCO 1991; T/D New York (UKMIS) 1992; Resigned 1993; Reinstated 1994; Cape Town 1995; Band A2; m 1993 (William) Gary Mills (1s 1997).

Mills, Beverley; FCO since March 2003; Born 09/05/69; FCO 1990; Brussels 1995; FCO 1997; Washington 1999; Band A2.

Mills, David Paul; Pristina since February 2004; Born 02/10/67; FCO 1987; Cairo 1989; FCO 1992; Addis Ababa 1993; HO 1999; Dar es Salaam 2000; Band B3.

Mills, Emma, MBE (2001); SUPL since September 2003; Born 27/02/69; FCO 1988; Baghdad 1990; Peking 1991; Bogotá 1994; FCO 1997; Pristina 1999; Second Secretary (Political/Information) Athens 2001; FCO 2002; Band C4.

Milne, Carole Lesley; SUPL since August 2001; Born 01/10/66; FCO HCS 1989; FCO 1994; Executive Assistant Lusaka 1996; Staff Officer Montserrat 1998; FCO 1999; Band B3.

Milne, Hilary Taylor; SUPL since August 2001; Born 07/06/65; FCO 1984; Rome 1985; Freetown 1988; FCO 1990; FCO 1991; Windhoek 1994; Moscow 1998; Band B3; m 2001 John Burton.

Milton, Kirstie Jane (née Levitt); FCO since July 1997; Born 04/07/69; FCO 1988; Cairo 1991; FCO 1992; The Hague 1995; Band A2; m 2000 Jonathan Milton.

Minshall, Heidi Jane; First Secretary FCO since May 1997; Born 02/03/67; FCO 1990; Full-Time Language Training Cairo 1993; Second Secretary (Political/Information) Abu Dhabi 1995.

Minshull, Simon Peter; Deputy Head of Mission Reykjavik since April 2003; Born 21/11/68; FCO 1988; Moscow 1990; Islamabad 1992; FCO 1996; Vice-Consul Bridgetown 1999; Band C4; m 1991 Hrefna Dis Luthersdottir (2d 1991, 1994).

Minter, Graham Leslie, LVO (1983); Deputy Head of Economic Policy Department, FCO since June 2002; Born 04/01/50; FCO 1968; Anguilla 1971; Latin America Floater 1973; Asunción 1975; FCO 1978; First Secretary (Economic/Political) Mexico City 1979; First Secretary FCO 1984; First Secretary (Economic/Trade Policy) Canberra 1990; First Secretary later Counsellor FCO 1994; HM Ambassador La Paz 1998; m 1975 P Anne Scott (1s 1978).

Mir, Wasim Ullah; First Secretary FCO since April 2001; Born 11/08/71; Department of Education 1994; European Commission 1997; Second Secretary (EU/Economic) Brussels 1998; First Secretary (Political) Brussels (UKREP) 2000.

Mistry, Hemlata; FCO since September 2001; Born 07/06/62; FCO Home Civil Service 1988; FCO 1990; Floater Duties 1992; FCO 1994; Mumbai 1998; Band B3.

Mitchell, Andrew Jonathan; Counsellor FCO since September 2002; Born 07/03/67; FCO 1991; Second Secretary (Political) Bonn 1993; First Secretary FCO 1996; Deputy Head of Mission Kathmandu 1999; m 1996 Helen Sarah Anne Magee (2s 1998, 2000; 1d 2001).

Mitchell, Carole, RVM (1990); Budapest since December 2002; Born 07/06/57; Scottish Office 1975; FCO 1987; Reykjavik 1988; The Hague

1991; Geneva (UKDIS) 1994; FCO 1999; Sarajevo 2000; Band A2.

Mitchell, Helen Sarah Anne (née Magee); SUPL (c/o Kathmandu) since May 1999; Born 18/10/67; FCO 1990; Second Secretary (EU) Bonn 1993; First Secretary FCO 1997; m 1996 Andrew Jonathan Mitchell (2s 1998, 2000).

Mitchell, John Steven; Second Secretary (Management) Beijing since April 2003; Born 28/11/67; FCO 1985; Tokyo 1988; Stockholm 1990; T/D Riga 1991; FCO 1992; Dhaka 1995; Riyadh 1999.

Mitchell, Jonathan Kenneth Milton; First Secretary Bucharest since June 1998; Born 18/12/59; Second Secretary FCO 1987; Second later First Secretary (Information) Amman 1989; First Secretary FCO 1990; First Secretary (Chancery) Harare 1991; First Secretary FCO 1994; Band D6; m 1986 Joyce Ann Henderson (2d 1990, 1993).

Mitchell, Marcia Julia; Full-Time Language Training since January 2004; Born 22/11/77; FCO 1999; Brussels (UKREP) 2000; Band A2.

Mitchell, Michael James, MVO (1989); First Secretary (Management) Colombo since October 2002; Born 07/08/54; HM Customs & Excise 1980; FCO 1985; Third Secretary (Aid) Kampala 1986; Third Secretary (Chancery) Singapore 1989; Full-Time Language Training 1993; Deputy Head of Mission Guatemala City 1993; Second Secretary FCO 1997; First Secretary (Management) Karachi 1999; Band C5; m 1982 Dominique Steggle (1d 1994).

Mitchell, Sheilah Dawn (née Bramley); Second Secretary (Management) Abidjan since October 2003; Born 15/04/59; FCO 1979; Brussels (UKDEL NATO) 1980; Maputo 1982; Floater Duties 1987; FCO 1990; Third Secretary (Management)/Vice-Consul Jerusalem 1994; SUPL 1998; Seconded to Bacon & Woodrow, Cardiff 2000; Islamabad 2002; Band C4; m 1994 Alan Stuart Mitchell.

Mitchell, Simon Andrew; Dhaka since April 2001; Born 27/11/64; PSA DoE 1987; The Court Service 1995; FCO 1999; Band A2.

Mitchiner, Dr John Edward; High Commissioner Freetown since August 2003; Born 12/09/51; FCO 1980; Language Training 1981; Third later Second Secretary Istanbul 1982; Second Secretary FCO 1985; Second Secretary (Development) New Delhi 1987; Second later First Secretary (Political) Berne 1991; First Secretary FCO 1995; HM Ambassador Yerevan 1997; Deputy High Commissioner Calcutta 2000; m 1983 Elizabeth Mary Ford.

Mitchison, Pamela Denise; Deputy Head of Mission Strasbourg since September 2003; Born 28/12/58; FCO 1978; Far East Floater 1981; Moscow 1982; Paris 1985; Second Secretary FCO 1988; APS Minister of State 1989; First Secretary (Chancery) Washington 1991; First Secretary FCO 1995; SUPL 1996; First Secretary FCO 1997;

SUPL 1997; m 1996 Ian Richard Whitehead (1d 1996).

Mititelu, Alexandra Marie; FCO since April 2004; Born 15/09/76; FCO 1999; Full-Time Language Training 2001; Second Secretary (Political) New Delhi 2002; Band C4.

Mochan, Charles Francis; High Commissioner Suva since November 2002; Born 06/08/48; MOD (Navy) 1966; FCO 1967; Port Elizabeth 1970; Kingston 1972; FCO 1974; Second Secretary 1975; Seoul 1977; FCO 1980; Second later First Secretary (Commercial) Helsinki 1981; First Secretary FCO 1984; Deputy High Commissioner and Head of Chancery Port Louis 1988; First Secretary FCO 1991; Consul-General Casablanca 1995; HM Ambassador Antananarivo 1999; m 1970 Ilse Sybilla Carleon Cruttwell (1d 1971; 1s 1974).

Monck, Anthony; FCO since October 2003; Born 14/04/79; Band C4.

Monckton, The Honourable Anthony Leopold Colyer; Counsellor Belgrade since March 2001; Born 25/09/60; HM Forces 1979-87; Second Secretary FCO 1987; Second later First Secretary Geneva (UKDEL) 1990; First Secretary FCO 1992; First Secretary (Political) Zagreb 1996; British Embassy Banja Luka Office 1998; First Secretary FCO 1999; Band D6; m 1985 Philippa Susan Wingfield (1s 1988; 1d 1989).

Monk, Rachel; British Trade International since April 2002; Born 12/09/69; FCO 1994; Chennai 2000; Band B3.

Montagnon, Giles; Full-Time Language Training Beijing since January 2004; Born 08/12/77; FCO 2001; Full-Time Language Training (Mandarin) 2003; Band C4.

Moody, Patrick Thomas Robert; FCO since December 2002; Born 17/03/66; FCO 1988; Third later Second Secretary (Political/Information) Mexico City 1990; First Secretary FCO 1994; First Secretary (Political) Brussels (UKDEL NATO) 1998; m 1996 Atalanta Sturdy (1s 1998; 1d 2000).

Moon, Dorian Lawrence; FCO since March 1993; Born 02/01/59; HCS 1985; BEMRS Cyprus 1986; HCS 1989; FCO 1990; Moscow 1992; Band C4; m 1989 Joanne Ashley (1d 1989; 1s 1991).

Moon, Michael Yelland; Consul (Inward Investment) Toronto since July 2003; Born 19/08/59; FCO 1977; Brussels (UKREP) 1979; Khartoum 1982; Africa/Middle East Floater 1986; FCO 1990; Third Secretary (Aid/Information) Mbabane 1993; Consul Brussels 1995; Second Secretary Bandar Seri Begawan 1996; British Trade International 1999; On loan to the DTI 2001; Band C5; m 1997 Christine Jo-Anne Florendo.

Moon, Nancy Patricia (née Handyside); SUPL since March 2003; Born 27/08/51; Islamabad 1984; Kampala 1988; Khartoum 1991; Sana'a 1995; Bucharest 1998; Brussels (UKREP) 1999; Band A2.

Moon, Dr Richard John; New York (UKMIS) since March 1999; Born 03/01/59; FCO 1983; Second Secretary Jakarta 1985; First Secretary FCO 1988; First Secretary (Political) Rome 1993; FCO 1997; m 1987 Sandra Sheila Francis Eddis (1s 1990; 1d 1993).

Moon, Sandra Sheila Francis (née Eddis), MVO (1984); SUPL since January 1994; Born 11/03/56; FCO 1980; Washington 1982; Jakarta 1984; FCO 1988; Band C4; m 1987 Richard John Moon (1s 1990; 1d 1993).

Mooney, Laura; FCO since June 2003; Born 30/04/73; MOD 1989 - 96; FCO 1996; Wellington 1997; World Wide Floater Duties 2001; Band B3.

Moore, Charles Jonathan Rupert; FCO since April 2002; Born 14/04/63; FCO 1982; Harare 1984; Masirah 1987; Gaborone 1987; FCO 1991; Third Secretary (Commercial) Jakarta 1995; Second Secretary (UN/UNIDO) Geneva (UKMIS) 1998; Band C5; m 1988 Deborah Mary Ford (1s 1989; 1d 1992).

Moore, David; First Secretary (Commercial) Kiev since April 2002; Born 18/06/59; HO 1977; FCO 1978; Moscow 1980; Wellington 1982; FCO 1986; Vice-Consul Osaka 1990; FCO 1992; Second Secretary 1994; Full-Time Language Training 1996; Second Secretary (Commercial) Madrid 1996; Full-Time Language Training 2001; m (1) 1981 Annette May Gardner (diss) (1d 1982; 1s 1985); (2) 1996 Janice Ann Bell.

Moore, Deborah Mary (née Ford); SUPL since August 1998; Born 15/04/63; FCO 1982; Muscat 1985; SUPL 1988; FCO 1991; SUPL 1993; Jakarta 1995; Band B3; m 1988 Charles Jonathan Rupert Moore (1s 1989; 1d 1992).

Moore, Fiona Charlotte; SUPL since April 2004; Born 15/08/59; FCO 1981; Third later Second Secretary Warsaw 1983; Second later First Secretary FCO 1987; First Secretary (Chancery) Athens 1991; CDA, Imperial College London 1995; First Secretary FCO 1995; Counsellor FCO 2000.

Moore, Janice Ann (née Bell); Kiev since March 2002; Born 06/10/64; FCO 1984; Accountant Nairobi 1986; Vice-Consul Budapest 1989; Resigned 1991; Reinstated, FCO 1992; Second Secretary 1994; Second Secretary Madrid 1996; Band C5; m 1996 David Moore.

Moore, Jason Richard Alexander; Second Secretary (Press and Public Affairs/Programmes) Budapest since September 2000; Born 06/04/73; FCO 1998; Full-Time Language Training 1999; m 2000 Rebecca Marie Letts.

Moore, Richard Peter; Counsellor (Political) Kuala Lumpur since November 2001; Born 09/05/63; Second Secretary FCO 1987; Second Secretary Ankara 1990; Consul (Information) Istanbul 1991; First Secretary FCO 1992; Islamabad 1995; First Secretary FCO 1999; m 1985 Margaret Martin (1s 1989; 1d 1992).

Moore, Sarah Jane; Assistant Legal Adviser FCO since January 1995; Born 20/09/66; Band D7.

Moore, Stephen Lawrence; Rabat since March 2002; Born 22/07/68; Paris 1991; FCO 1993; Islamabad 1994; FCO 1997; On loan to DTI 1999; Band C4; m 1992 Carolyn Andrea (1d 1998; 1s 2001).

Moore, Trevor Charles; FCO since June 2001; Born 19/01/58; FCO 1980; Belgrade 1982; Vice-Consul New York 1986; Second Secretary Washington 1987; Second later First Secretary FCO 1989; First Secretary (CTBT) Vienna (UKMIS) 1997; m 1991 Diane Elizabeth Burns (3s 1994, 1997, 1999).

Moores, Amias Steven; St Helena since August 2004; Born 31/03/71; FCO 1990; Geneva (UKMIS) 1994; Abu Dhabi 1997; FCO 1997; Third Secretary and Vice-Consul Abu Dhabi 2001; Band C4; m 2000 Lindsey Cave (1s 2002).

Moorhead, Michelle Anne; Tel Aviv since August 2002; Born 02/02/70; FCO 1988; Washington 1991; Accra 1995; FCO 1998; SUPL 2000; FCO 2001; Band B3; m 1990 Ian William Moorhead (1s 2000; 1d 2002).

Moran, David John; Deputy Permanent Representative UKDEL OECD Paris since January 2001; Born 22/08/59; DTI 1985; ODA 1985; Second Secretary (Programmes Adviser) British Development Division in Eastern Africa Nairobi 1988; First Secretary ODA/FCO 1991; First Secretary (Know How Fund) Moscow 1993; First Secretary FCO 1996; m 1993 Carol Ann Marquis.

Moran, Karen (née Pinkney); FCO since September 2003; Born 02/03/65; National Savings Department 1984; FCO 1984; Washington 1986; Seoul 1989; FCO 1993; Third Secretary (Management) Hong Kong 1996; Deputy Head of Mission Tashkent 2000; Band C4; m 1986 Sean Moran (diss 1995).

Moran, Lindy Jane (née Preston); SUPL since July 2000; Born 09/10/58; FCO 1981; Caracas 1982; Grand Turk 1986; FCO 1989; Warsaw 1990; Nairobi 1992; Band B3; m 1995 Eamon Andrew Moran.

Moran, Sean; Second Secretary FCO since March 2001; Born 06/03/64; Inland Revenue 1984; FCO 1984; Washington 1986; Seoul 1989; FCO 1993; On secondment to DTI 1996; World Wide Floater Duties 1998; Band C4; m 1986 Karen Pinkney (diss 1995).

Morgan, Angela Merril; Consul Shanghai since July 2004; Born 14/03/68; FCO 1989; Warsaw 1991; FCO 1992; Riga 1993; FCO 1994; New Delhi 1995; FCO 1996; Third Secretary (Political) Suva 1997; SUPL 2000; Suva 2000; Second Secretary (Consular) Bangkok 2001; Band C4; m 2001 Sainivalati Tokalau (1d 2000).

Morgan, Charles Edward William; Second Secretary Jakarta since March 2004; Born 24/08/73; FCO 2001; Band C4.

Morgan, John Philip Arwyn; World Wide Floater Duties since June 2001; Born 17/12/71; FCO 1999; Band B3.

Morgan, Karen; Lisbon since August 2002; Born 11/08/71; FCO 2000; Band A2.

Morgan, Linda; SUPL since June 2003; Born 09/07/72; FCO 2002; Band A2; ptnr, Stephen Watson.

Morgan, Mark Scott Thomas, MBE (1997); First Secretary Budapest since July 2001; Born 26/04/58; FCO 1976; Geneva 1984; FCO 1986; Second Secretary and Vice-Consul Aden 1988; Second Secretary FCO 1990; Second later First Secretary Valletta 1994; First Secretary FCO 1998; Band C5; m 1998 Samantha Thompson.

Morgan, Richard de Riemer; First Secretary (PPA) Paris since September 2000; Born 09/05/61; FCO 1984; Language Training Tokyo 1986; Second Secretary (Commercial) Tokyo 1987; First Secretary FCO 1991; First Secretary (Political/Aid) Pretoria 1995; m 1987 Susan Carolyn McGaw (1s 1992; 1d 1994).

Morgan, Steven Leonard; Second Secretary (Political) Bogotá since August 2002; Born 14/01/65; Department of Employment 1983; FCO 1984; Budapest 1986; FCO 1987; Paris 1988; Guatemala City 1990; Mexico City 1993; FCO 1994; Madrid 1999; Band C4; m 1995 Maria del Carmen Toledo Municio.

Morgan, Stuart John; FCO since December 1990; Born 02/12/63; FCO 1983; Khartoum 1988; Band B3; m 1993 Milla Heidi Susan Chapman (1s 2000).

Morgan, William Donovan; Second later First Secretary (Political) Peking since October 2000; Born 02/06/71; Second Secretary FCO 1996; Full-Time Language Training 1998; Full-Time Language Training Peking 1999; Band D6; m 1992 Lucy Bullock (2s 1992, 1995).

Morley, David John; First Secretary FCO since September 2001; Born 23/10/54; MAFF 1972; FCO 1973; Geneva (UKMIS) 1975; Port Stanley 1978; Kuala Lumpur 1980; FCO 1981; Kaduna 1984; FCO 1988; Second Secretary (Management) Moscow 1991; Second Secretary FCO 1994; Deputy High Commissioner Mbabane 1995; First Secretary (Information) Brussels (UKDEL NATO) 1999; Band C5; m 1978 Jacqueline Ann Wells.

Morley, Ian Robert; Zagreb since October 2000; Born 24/07/71; FCO 1992; New York (UKMIS) 1996; Luanda 1999; Band A2.

Morley, Jacqueline Ann (née Wells), MBE (1991); FCO since November 2001; Born 20/07/55; FCO 1973; New York (UKMIS) 1974; FCO 1975; Geneva (UKMIS) 1975; Port Stanley 1978; SUPL (Kuala Lumpur) 1980; Kuala Lumpur 1981; FCO 1981; SUPL (Kaduna) 1984; Kaduna 1987; FCO 1988; Moscow 1991; FCO 1994; SUPL (Mbabane) 1995; FCO 1999; SUPL (Brussels) 1999; Brussels (UKDEL NATO) 2000; Band B3; m 1978 David John Morley.

Morley, Michael Donald; HM Consul Dallas since February 2004; Born 18/02/53; FCO 1973; Moscow 1975; Kuala Lumpur 1977; Latin America Floater 1981; Beirut 1983; FCO 1984; Third later Second Secretary La Paz 1987; Second Secretary (Commercial) Santiago 1991; FCO 1995; First Secretary (Management) Athens 1999; m 1983 Carmen Gloria Del Prado (2s 1987, 1989).

Morley, Stuart Richard, OBE (2002); First Secretary FCO since April 1999; Born 26/01/59; Second Secretary FCO 1988; Second later First Secretary (Chancery/Information) San José 1989; First Secretary (Chancery) Bridgetown 1990; First Secretary FCO 1992; First Secretary (Chemical Weapons) The Hague 1996; Band D6; m 1987 Janet Henry (3d 1990, 1993, 1998; 1s 1996).

Morrell, Susan Mary; First Secretary and Consul Peking since September 2001; Born 07/11/50; FCO 1977; New York (UKMIS) 1978; Budapest 1981; Khartoum 1982; Islamabad 1985; Moscow 1988; Brussels (UKREP) 1989; FCO 1992; Sofia 1996; Band C5.

Morris, Jill; Second Secretary (Political) Nicosia since August 2001; Born 14/08/67; FCO 1999; Band C4.

Morris, Neil Andrew; FCO since November 2003; Born 05/11/64; Home Office 1988.

Morris, Richard Charles; First Secretary later Counsellor FCO since February 2000; Born 01/11/67; New York (UKMIS) 1993; Third Secretary (Political) Ottawa 1993; Second Secretary (Political) Bridgetown 1996; m 1992 Alison Jane Waring (1d 1996; 2s 1998, 2003).

Morris, Richard Peter; FCO since October 2002; Born 08/09/64; FCO 1983; Dhaka 1985; Bucharest 1988; FCO 1991; Full-Time Language Training 1995; Vice-Consul Rome 1995; Second Secretary (Management) Colombo 1999; m 1990 Diane Jacqueline Harvey.

Morris, Sara Joanne; FCO since May 1995; Born 19/10/62; FCO 1983; Mexico City 1987; FCO 1991; Floater Duties 1993; Band A2.

Morris, Timothy Colin; Deputy Head of Mission Lisbon since January 2003; Born 17/09/58; FCO 1981; SOAS 1982; Language Training Tokyo 1983; Second Secretary (Commercial) Tokyo 1984; First Secretary FCO 1987; On loan to the DTI 1989; First Secretary (Head of Political Section) Madrid 1991; First Secretary FCO 1996; Counsellor (Trade and Investment) Tokyo 1998; m 1996 Patricia Tena Garcia (3s 1998, 1999, 2001).

Morris, Warwick; HM Ambassador Seoul since November 2003; Born 10/08/48; FCO 1969; Paris 1972; Language Training Seoul 1975 (Second Secretary 1977); FCO 1979 (PS to Deputy PUS 1979 - 80); First Secretary 1982; First Secretary (Commercial) Mexico City 1984; First Secretary and Head of Chancery Seoul 1988; First Secretary later Counsellor FCO 1991; Counsellor (Commercial/Economic) New Delhi 1995; Career Development Attachment Royal College of

Defence Studies 1999; HM Ambassador Hanoi 2000; m 1972 Pamela Jean Mitchell (1s 1976; 2d 1978, 1982).

Morrison, Alan; Hong Kong since December 2002; Born 04/01/70; FCO 1989; Islamabad 1992; FCO 1995; Ottawa 1997; Band B3; m 1997 Lynne Jean Gregory.

Morrison, Fiona Margaret; First Secretary (Political) Kabul since September 2002; Born 23/01/67; FCO 1989; Third Secretary (Chancery) Brussels (UKDEL) 1991; FCO 1994; Third Secretary (Commercial) Oslo 1995; Third Secretary (Chancery/PPA) Kingston 1996; Second Secretary FCO 2000; Band D6.

Morrison, Ian Kenneth; First Secretary (Commercial) Tel Aviv since July 1999; Born 27/12/54; Inland Revenue 1974; FCO 1977; Budapest 1979; Islamabad 1981; Madrid 1983; FCO 1986; Third Secretary Accra 1988; Vice-Consul (Political/Information) Cape Town 1991; FCO 1996; Band D6; m (1) 1978 Gillian Winifred Turk (diss) (1d 1982); (2) 1994 Jean MacAlpine Kerr (2s 1995, 1998).

Morrison, Jonathan James Howard; Counsellor FCO since 2002; Born 31/12/67; Home Office 1989 - 91; Third later Second later First Secretary Brussels (UKREP) 1994; FCO 1999; Private Secretary to Minister for Europe 2000; m 1994 Helen Louisa Pope (3d 1996, 1998, 2002).

Morrison, Melanie Kathryn (née Girling); Moscow since January 2002; Born 18/03/62; FCO 1995; Wellington 1997; Band B3; m 1997 John Morrison.

Morrison, Thérésa Mary; Vienna (UKDEL) since April 2001; Born 07/01/55; Copenhagen 1976; Warsaw 1978; FCO 1982; Resigned 1983; Reinstated 1991; Montevideo 1992; FCO 1993; Budapest 1998; Band B3; m 1981 William Alastair Harrison (diss 1991).

Morrissey, Gillian Lesley (née Worrall); FCO since February 1990; Born 02/02/60; FCO 1979; Helsinki 1981; Doha 1984; Bonn 1988; Band C4; m 1984 Patrick John Morrissey (1d 1993).

Mortimer, Hugh Roger, LVO (1992); HM Ambassador Ljubljana since January 2001; Born 19/09/49; FCO 1973; Rome 1975; Singapore 1978; FCO 1981; Second later First Secretary New York (UKMIS) 1983; First Secretary FCO 1987; On attachment to the Auswärtiges Amt 1990; First Secretary (Chancery) Berlin 1991; Counsellor FCO 1994; Royal College of Defence Studies (RCDS) 1996; Deputy Head of Mission Ankara 1997; m 1974 Zosia Cecylia Rzepecka (2d 1976 (dec'd 1993), 1980).

Morton, David Stanley Thomas; First Secretary (Management) Copenhagen since January 2002; Born 06/12/45; FO 1963; Kinshasa 1967; Cairo 1967; Wellington 1969; Brussels (UKREP) 1972; FCO 1975; Beirut 1977; Washington 1979; Dacca 1982; Second Secretary FCO 1985; Second Secretary (Commercial) Baghdad 1990; Second

Secretary (Commercial) Nairobi 1991; Second Secretary FCO 1995; Consul (Management) Istanbul 1998; m (1) 1972 Judith Anne Amies (diss 1983) (1s 1973); (2) 1987 Beverley Anne Sheppard (2s 1988, 1991).

Morton, Ralph Christopher; Consul (Commercial/CCU) Düsseldorf since July 2001; Born 13/12/55; FCO 1979; Khartoum 1982; Brussels (UKDEL NATO) 1984; Third later Second Secretary (Chancery) East Berlin 1987; Second Secretary FCO 1991; Second Secretary (Commercial/Consular) Kampala 1992; Second Secretary (Commercial) Johannesburg 1995; Second Secretary FCO 1996; Second Secretary (Political) Vienna Embassy 1998.

Moseley, Simon Arthur; Peking since July 2002; Born 11/02/72; FCO 1989; Band C4; m 1999 Aleesha.

Moser-Andon, Barbara; Grand Turk since December 2002; Born 04/08/47; FCO 1991; Damascus 1993; FCO 1996; Kathmandu 1997; Tehran 2000; Band B3.

Moss, Kerry May (née Ford); Buenos Aires since April 2002; Born 04/05/67; Home Office 1990-93; FCO 1994; Hanoi (T/D) 1996; The Hague (T/D) 1996; Hong Kong 1997; FCO 2000; SUPL 2001; Full-Time Language Training (Spanish) 2001; Band A2; m 2001 Stuart Moss.

Moss, Kylie Joanne; FCO since May 2003; Born 22/10/71; FCO 1990; Amman 1993; Tbilisi 1999; T/D Kinshasa 2002; Band A2.

Moss, Stuart; Second Secretary (Technical) Buenos Aires since March 2001; Born 14/06/67; FCO 1987; Washington 1994; FCO 1996; Band C4; m 2001 Kerry May Ford.

Moss-Norbury, Nicholas Adam; Bogotá since May 2003; Born 12/05/72; FCO 1991; Third Secretary Peking 1997; FCO 2000; Band C4.

Mott, Alan Lawrence; FCO since November 1999; Born 05/10/65; FCO 1984; Washington 1989; FCO 1991; Bridgetown 1996; Band C5; m 1988 Tina Michaela.

Mowbray, Fiona (née Roberts); Singapore since October 2003; Born 08/11/63; FCO 1983; Washington 1984; Addis Ababa 1986; Nassau 1990; Ankara 1991; SUPL 1994; FCO 1996; Grand Cayman 1999; Band B3; m 1986 Kevin Lewis Mowbray (1s 1993).

Mowbray, Kevin Lewis; SUPL since August 2003; Born 05/04/59; FCO 1977; Brussels (UKREP) 1979; Africa/Middle East Floater 1982; FCO 1984; Addis Ababa 1986; Nassau 1990; Second Secretary (Chancery/Consular) Ankara 1991; FCO 1996; SUPL 1999; Grand Cayman 2000; m 1986 Fiona Roberts (1s 1993).

Muir, David John; FCO since March 2003; Born 22/05/58; FCO 1995; Floater Duties 1996; Attaché Tashkent 1999; Third Secretary (Vice-Consul) Tashkent 2000; Band B3; m 1999 Deborah Okey.

Mulcahy, Colin Paul Peter, OBE (2000); First Secretary (Consular) Islamabad since July 2000; Born 21/06/44; CRO 1963; Freetown 1966; DSAO (later FCO) 1968; Attaché (Consular) Bombay 1972; Second Secretary (Chancery) Wellington 1976; Second Secretary FCO 1981; Second Secretary (Commercial) Damascus 1984; Vice-Consul later Consul (Commercial) Toronto 1985; First Secretary (Management) and Consul Khartoum 1989; Consul Warsaw 1992; First Secretary FCO 1993; First Secretary (Consular/Immigration) New Delhi 1996; m 1969 Josephine Ann Molly Smyth (2s 1973, 1976).

Mulheirn, Gregory; FCO since October 2003; Born 16/11/75; Band C4.

Mullee, Patrick; Deputy Head of Mission Quito since August 2000; Born 08/10/54; FCO 1974; Prague 1976; Caracas 1977; Africa Floater 1980; Latin America Floater 1983; FCO 1985; Third later Second Secretary San José 1988; Second Secretary (Chancery/Information) Bridgetown 1991; Second later First Secretary FCO 1995; Full-Time Language Training 2000; Band C5; m 1987 Joanna Louise Johnson (2d 1989, 1994).

Mullender, Andrea; Moscow since March 2004; Born 16/08/73; FCO 1999; Dar es Salaam 2001; Band A2.

Mulvaney, Isabella Maria; Bahrain since July 2001; Born 18/03/68; FCO 1986; Brussels (UKDEL) 1988; Karachi 1991; FCO 1994; Lusaka 1998; Band C4; m 2000 Dean Ashley Horton.

Mulvein, Helen Jane; Assistant Legal Adviser FCO since April 2000; Born 04/12/70.

Muncie, Heather; SUPL since March 2001; Born 19/08/67; FCO 1992; Jakarta 1994; Paris 1998; Band A2.

Munks, Robert John; FCO since January 1997; Born 14/02/72; Band C4.

Munro, Colin Andrew, CMG (2002); Head of UK Delegation to OSCE Vienna since December 2003; Born 24/10/46; Inland Revenue 1968; Third Secretary FCO 1969; Bonn 1971; Second later First Secretary Kuala Lumpur 1973; FCO 1977; Private Secretary to Minister of State 1979; First Secretary and Head of Chancery Bucharest 1981; First Secretary FCO 1983; Counsellor East Berlin 1987; HM Consul-General Frankfurt 1990; Counsellor FCO 1993; HM Ambassador Zagreb 1997; Deputy High Representative Mostar (Bosnia ang Herzegovina) 2001; On secondment to the Royal College of Defence Studies 2002; m 1967 Ehrengard Maria Heinrich (2s 1967, 1978).

Murdoch, Charles Edward; First Secretary Amman since April 2004; Born 02/11/66; FCO 2002; Band D6; m 2001 Jocelyn Drew.

Murduck, Ann Victoria; Third Secretary (Political) Basra since May 2004; Born 11/08/77; FCO 2003; Band B3.

Muronen, Victoria Evelyn (née Foster); SUPL since September 2003; Born 28/12/72; FCO 1990; Geneva (UKMIS) 1994; FCO 1997; Band C4.

Murphy, John Matthew; FCO since January 2004; Born 10/03/70; HCS 1990 - 93; Moscow 1995; Vice-Consul Beijing 1999; Band B3.

Murphy, Jonathan Philip; FCO since October 2003; Born 20/01/77; FCO 1999; Second Secretary (Chemical Weapons) The Hague 2001; Band C4.

Murphy, Sandra; FCO since March 2003; Born 09/04/50; FCO 1968; Brussels (UKREP) 1972; Resigned 1975; Reinstated, FCO 1978; Harare 1981; Second Secretary FCO 1984; Second Secretary (Aid) Kingston 1987; Second Secretary (Commercial) Addis Ababa 1991; Second Secretary (Commercial) Caracas 1993; First Secretary FCO 1996; Resident Acting High Commissioner St John's 1999; Band D6.

Murray, Craig John; HM Ambassador Tashkent since August 2002 – October 2004; Born 17/10/58; FCO 1984; Second Secretary (Commercial) Lagos 1986; First Secretary FCO 1990; Full-Time Language Training 1993; First Secretary (Political/Economic) Warsaw 1994; FCO 1998; Deputy High Commissioner Accra 1999; m 1984 Fiona Anne.

Murray, Iain Richard, OBE (1991); Consul-General Houston since January 2001; Born 13/08/44; CRO 1963; SUPL at University 1965; Commonwealth Office (later FCO) 1968; Accra 1970; Second Secretary Addis Ababa 1972; Vice-Consul (Commercial) Rio de Janeiro 1975; Consul Oporto 1979; First Secretary on loan to No. 10 Downing Street 1983; First Secretary FCO 1985; Chargé d'Affaires San Salvador 1987; First Secretary FCO 1992; Counsellor (Commercial/Economic) Kuala Lumpur 1994; Consul-General and Director of Trade Promotion in Brazil São Paulo 1997; m (1) 1967 Victoria Crew Gee (diss 1983) (1d 1969; 1s 1971); (2) 1993 Norma Agnes Wisden (née Hummel).

Murray, June; FCO since March 2003; Born 09/06/50; FCO 1986; Tegucigalpa 1988; Johannesburg 1990; Moscow 1992; FCO 1995; Ankara 1998; Band B3.

Murray, Michael Thomas; HM Ambassador Asmara since March 2002; Born 13/10/45; FO DSAO 1964; Prague 1967; Vienna 1971; Vice-Consul (Commercial) Frankfurt 1973; Second Secretary (Development) Khartoum 1977; FCO 1980; First Secretary and Head of Chancery Banjul 1983; First Secretary FCO 1987; First Secretary (Development/Economic) Lusaka 1995; On loan to DFID at Lusaka 1998; Deputy Consul-General Chicago 1999; Band D6; m 1968 Else Birgitta Margareta Paues (1s 1974; 1d 1981).

Murray, William Richard; FCO since March 2003; Born 09/04/72; Band C4.

Murray, Winston Anthony; FCO since April 1999; Born 04/07/64; OFT 1985; FCO 1985; Bonn 1991;

Bahrain 1994; Band B3; m 1990 Judith Muponda (1s 1992).

Murtagh, Michael Louis; Chennai since October 2001; Born 12/02/53; RAF Flt Lt 1981-97; Defence Attaché's Office, Moscow 1995-97; Moscow, New Embassy Project 1997-00; FCO 2000; Band B3; m 1988 Diana Morford (2s 1980, 1983).

Murton, John Evan; SUPL since January 2004; Born 18/03/72; FCO 1997; Full-Time Language Training Tokyo 1998; Second Secretary (Global Issues) later First Secretary (Energy and Environment) Tokyo 2000; Band D6; m 1998 Sarah Elizabeth Harvey (1s 2002).

Murton, Sarah Elizabeth; SUPL since October 2002; Born 06/04/76; FCO 2001; Third Secretary (PS/HMA) Tokyo 2001; Band B3; m 1998 John Murton (1s 2002).

Musgrave, David William; Deputy Head of Mission and Consul Riga since November 2002; Born 12/05/53; FCO 1983; Second later First Secretary Copenhagen 1985; First Secretary FCO 1989; First Secretary (Political/Information) Lagos 1994; First Secretary (Political) Abuja 1995; First Secretary FCO 1998; m 1978 Madeleine Nnomo Assembe (2d 1979, 1991; 1s 1981).

Mustafa, Jon; Third Secretary (Immigration) New Delhi since May 2003; Born 22/12/61; FCO 1988; Band B3; m 1995 Marilyn Melanie Mongal (1s 1999; 1d 2001).

Mustard, Simon; Third Secretary (Chancery) Belmopan since May 2002; Born 03/08/71; FCO 2000; Band B3; m 2003 Mary Roberton.

Myers, Sharon Theresa; Copenhagen since January 2001; Born 19/04/65; FCO 1987; Moscow 1988; Bogotá 1991; FCO 1995; Band B3; m 1993 Manuel Bolano (diss 2003) (2s 1996, 2002).

N

Nailard, Allison Mary (née Abbott); Abu Dhabi since February 2004; Born 03/07/73; FCO 1999; Moscow 2000; Band A2; m 1999 Michael Nailard.

Nalden, Philip Nigel; Floater Duties since September 2002; Born 30/03/45; Army (CRMP) 1963-88; Moscow 1988; Lagos 1989; Peking 1993; Dhaka 1994; FCO 1997; Belgrade 1998; Colombo 1999; Band B3; m 1982 Heather McIntosh.

Nandi, Mark Debal; FCO since December 2003; Born 02/02/72; Band C5.

Napthen, Florence Wilson; FCO since November 2000; Born 25/10/61; Crown Office, Edinburgh 1978; FCO 1986; Wellington 1988; FCO 1991; Washington 1993; Addis Ababa 1996; Band B3; m 1990 Stephen Kenneth Napthen (1s 1997).

Nash, Ronald Peter, CMG (2004), LVO (1984), MVO (1983); High Commissioner Port of Spain since January 2004; Born 18/09/46; FCO 1970; Second later First Secretary Moscow 1974; First Secretary Vienna (UKDEL) 1976; FCO 1979;

New Delhi 1983; First Secretary FCO 1986; Counsellor and Head of Chancery Vienna 1988; Deputy High Commissioner Colombo 1992; Counsellor FCO 1996; HM Ambassador Kathmandu 1999; HM Ambassador Kabul 2002; m 1976 Annie Olsen (3s 1979, 1981, 1983).

Naughton, Dawn Karen; HM Consul Mexico City since February 2003; Born 22/08/69; FCO 1988; Brussels (UKDEL) 1990; Maputo 1993; Lagos 1997; Jerusalem 2000; Band B3; m 1993 Steven John Horsup.

Neale, Dawn Teresa; SUPL since May 2004; Born 13/08/60; FCO 1996; Abuja 1998; Band B3; m 1995 John Harry Albert.

Needham, David Brent; Jakarta since May 2003; Born 22/02/51; Royal Marines 1968-91; Moscow 1992; Kingston 1996; Brussels (UKDEL NATO) 1999; Floater Duties 2002; Band B3; m 1992 Karen Dawn Ackers (2s 1993, 1995).

Neely, Maxine Lorna (née Hunter); SUPL since September 2001; Born 09/12/64; FCO 1988; Washington 1989; Bangkok 1992; FCO 1995; Tokyo 1997; British Trade International 1999; Band B3; m 2000 Peter Gordon Neely.

Neil, Andrew Alasdair; First Secretary (Political) Abu Dhabi since April 2001; Born 11/06/68; FCO 1991; Second Secretary (Political) Nairobi 1994; Second Secretary FCO 1996; Band D6; m 1998 Amanda Lewis (2s twins 2000).

Neil, William John; Jedda since January 2002; Born 23/05/67; FCO 1988; T/D Sofia (CSCE Conference) and East Berlin 1989; Brussels (UKDEL NATO) 1990; Brussels (UKREP) 1990; Baku 1993; Bombay 1995; Vice-Consul (Visas) Shanghai 1999; Band C4.

Neill, Kenneth Andrew; HM Consul Riyadh since July 2001; Born 06/11/44; FO 1961; Tripoli 1967; Moscow 1970; Vientiane 1970; FCO 1974; Hanoi 1977; Karachi 1979; Second Secretary (Chancery/Information) Lilongwe 1982; Second Secretary FCO 1986; Second later First Secretary Honiara 1988; First Secretary (Commercial/Consular) Lusaka 1992; First Secretary FCO 1996; Deputy Head of Mission T/D Yaoundé 2000; m 1977 Julie C Brown (2s 1981, 1991; 2d 1987, 1993).

Neilson, James George Lovie; Floater Duties since February 2004; Born 27/07/44; Army 1965-88; Geneva 1988; Moscow 1991; Budapest 1992; Pretoria 1994; Peking 1997; Ankara 2000; Band B3; m 1967 Lorraine (1d 1968; 1s 1971).

Nellthorp, Helen Rosemary, OBE (2002); First Secretary (Specialised Agencies) Geneva (UKMIS) since September 2001; Born 10/05/62; FCO 1980; Athens 1984; Floater Duties 1987; Third Secretary (Commercial) Washington 1989; Second Secretary (Commercial) Prague 1991; Second later First Secretary FCO 1994; Band D6.

Nelson, Diana June (née Gordon); FCO since September 1997; Born 17/06/58; FCO 1981; Paris 1984; Algiers 1987; Second Secretary FCO 1989;

SUPL 1991; FCO 1992; SUPL 1995; m 1985 Miles Christopher Nelson (diss 2002) (2d 1991, 1993).

Nelson, Matthew Charles; FCO since March 2004; Born 19/06/74; FCO 2000; Full-Time Language Training FCO 2002; Full-Time Language Training, Amman 2003; Band C4.

Nelson, Philip Raymond; First Secretary later Counsellor FCO since April 1994; Born 07/04/50; FCO 1972; Third later Second Secretary (Commercial) Budapest 1974; Second later First Secretary Paris 1976; FCO 1979; Rome 1980; First Secretary FCO 1983; First Secretary (Chancery) Manila 1989; First Secretary Budapest 1991; m (1) 1971 Cynthia Elson (diss 1978); (2) 1992 Lyndsay Ann Halper (2s twins 1992).

Nessling, Paul William Downs; High Commissioner Nuku'alofa since January 2002; Born 26/09/45; Chicago (From BOT) 1971; Bahrain (From DOI) 1975; Second Secretary FCO 1979; Lisbon 1981; Warsaw 1982; First Secretary (Aid) Nairobi 1984; T/D Aden 1984; FCO 1987; First Secretary (Commercial) Harare 1989; First Secretary (Commercial) Muscat 1993; First Secretary Sarajevo 1996; FCO 1997; Deputy High Commissioner Lusaka 1998; m 1975 Kathryn Freeman.

Nethersole, Jonathan Sebastian; FCO since 2001; Born 07/11/69; FCO 1988; Pretoria/Cape Town 1990; Sana'a 1993; FCO 1995; EU Presidency Liaison Officer Bonn, Helsinki, Lisbon, Paris 1999-00; Band C4.

Nettleton, Catherine Elizabeth, OBE (1999); Counsellor (Political/Economic) Peking since October 2000; Born 13/03/60; FCO 1983; Language Training 1984; Peking 1987; Second Secretary 1988; Second Secretary FCO 1989; First Secretary (Political/Economic) Mexico City 1991; First Secretary FCO 1995; Counsellor FCO 1999.

Nevin, Michael Patrick; FCO since August 2003; Born 13/01/69; FCO 1993; Osaka 1996; Second Secretary (Chancery) Lilongwe 1999; Band C4; m 1997 Sawako (1 step d 1989; 1s 1998).

Newall, Peter; HM Ambassador Dakar since May 2004; Born 20/03/47; DSAO (later FCO) 1966; Tehran 1970; Delhi 1972; FCO 1976; Second Secretary (Commercial) Belgrade 1979; First Secretary (Commercial) Kuwait 1982; FCO 1986; HM Consul Marseilles 1989; First Secretary (Management) Geneva (UKMIS) 1990; FCO 1995; Counsellor, Head of Joint Management Office Brussels 1999; m 1969 Marina Joy McHugh (2d 1972, 1973; 1s 1976).

Newell, Clive Dare; Ottawa since December 2003; Born 22/12/53; FCO 1976; Third Secretary (Commercial) later Second Secretary Tehran 1979; FCO 1980; Second later First Secretary Kabul 1982; FCO 1984; First Secretary Addis Ababa 1986; FCO 1990; First Secretary on secondment to the Ministry of Defence 1992; FCO 1993; First Secretary on loan to the Cabinet Office 1993; Counsellor (Political) Ankara 1994; Counsellor

FCO 1998; Counsellor Moscow 2001; m 1997 Gamze Ozen (1s 1999; 1d 2002).

Newlands, Andrew; Deputy Consul-General Vancouver since August 2003; Born 10/02/68; DHSS 1984; FCO 1988; Bonn 1990; FCO 1992; Manila 1993; T/D Hong Kong 1996; FCO 1997; Deputy Head of Mission Panama City 2000; Band C4; m 1989 Eileen Mitchell (1s 1993; 1d 1996).

Newman, James Michael; Third Secretary (Political) Harare since September 2002; Born 31/03/70; Metropolitan Police 1989; FCO 1990; Cairo 1992; Cape Town 1996; FCO 1999; Band B3; m 2000 Sarah Louise.

Newman, Kevin Paul; Bangkok since September 2002; Born 31/07/73; Home Office 1994; FCO 1995; Abuja 1998; T/D Harare 2001-02; Band B3.

Newman, Peter James; First Secretary (Management) Washington since September 2001; Born 29/05/46; FO 1963; Muscat 1968; Bahrain Residency 1970; Tokyo 1971; FCO 1975; Dacca 1978; Second Secretary UKDEL MBFR Vienna 1980; Second Secretary (Economic) Oslo 1983; First Secretary FCO 1987; Deputy High Commissioner and Head of Chancery Gaborone 1989; First Secretary (Commercial) Nicosia 1992; First Secretary FCO 1996; Deputy Head of Mission Abuja 1998; m 1966 Kathryn Yvonne Alcock (1d 1969; 1s 1972).

Newns, Carl Edwin Francis; First Secretary (Chancery) Washington since March 2000; Born 30/06/68; FCO 1989; Third later Second Secretary (Political) The Hague 1992; First Secretary FCO 1996; Private Secretary to the Parliamentary Under-Secretary of State 1997; Band D6; m 1999 Christina Klaassen.

Newson, Gavin Erskine Walter; Second Secretary FCO since April 2001; Born 20/07/71; FCO 1996; Second Secretary (Financial/Economic) Tokyo 1998; Band C4.

Newsum, Wendy Elizabeth; FCO since June 2004; Born 11/05/78; Band B3.

Newton, Alastair Dan Barr; Head of IUK USA New York since July 2002; Born 08/01/54; FCO 1985; Second later First Secretary Kinshasa 1986; First Secretary FCO 1989; First Secretary Paris (UKDEL) 1992; On secondment as Economic Adviser to Lehman Bros 2000; m 1988 Vivienne Jane Ivanich (2d 1979, 1980).

Nicholas, Barry Stewart; FCO since March 2003; Born 01/11/62; FCO 1981; East Berlin 1984; Dubai 1986; Warsaw 1988; FCO 1991; Cairo 1995; Second Secretary (Commercial) Port of Spain 1999; m 1989 Susan Jane Parker (1s 1992; 1d 2002).

Nicholas, Susan Jane (née Parker); SUPL since May 2003; Born 17/09/62; FCO 1981; Warsaw 1984; Bonn 1987; Düsseldorf 1988; Warsaw 1989 (Second Secretary 1991); FCO 1993; SUPL 1995; Cairo 1996; SUPL 1999; Port of Spain 2000; m 1989 Barry Stuart Nicholas (1s 1992; 1d 2002).

Nicholas, Suzanne Elizabeth; FCO since March 2000; Born 14/08/70; FCO 1995; Second Secretary (Political) Warsaw 1999; Band C4.

Nicholls, Gary Patrick; Second Secretary (Chancery) Accra since October 2003; Born 04/10/68; FCO 1988; Tokyo 1990; Islamabad 1993; FCO 1998; HM Consul Guangzhou 2000; Band C4; m 1993 Helen Marie Glanfield (diss 1998) (1s 1994; 1d 1997).

Nichols, John Roland; HM Ambassador Budapest since August 2003; Born 13/11/51; Third later Second Secretary FCO 1977; Second later First Secretary Budapest 1979; FCO 1982; First Secretary (Commercial) Brasilia 1985; First Secretary FCO 1989; Counsellor and Deputy High Commissioner Dhaka 1993; Consul-General Geneva 1995; Deputy Head of Mission and Director of Trade Promotion Berne 1997; On secondment to British Invisibles 2000; m 1983 Angela Suzanne Davies (1s 1987; 1d 1989).

Nichols, Martin Christopher; On loan to the Cabinet Office since May 1998; Born 04/05/62; FCO 1981; Tel Aviv 1984; FCO 1987; Darwin 1988; FCO 1990; New Delhi 1991; FCO 1994; Band C4; m 1983 Julie Marie Wilkins (2s 1983, 1988; 1d 1992).

Nicholson, Emma Jane (née Woodward); Attaché Shanghai since December 2001; Born 06/06/70; FCO 1996; BTCO Taipei 1997; BCG Jerusalem 2000; Band A2.

Nicholson, Karen Jayne (née Baudains); FCO since June 2003; Born 29/09/55; FCO 1977; Mexico City 1979; South East Asia Floater Duties 1983; Second Secretary FCO 1985; First Secretary (Commercial) Lisbon 1992; FCO 1994; On loan to British Trade International 1998; Seconded to the Private sector 2002; m 1994 David J Nicholson.

Nickels, Tina; FCO since March 2002; Born 15/06/78; British Trade International 2002; Band A2.

Nicolopulo, Evangelo Paul; First Secretary FCO since January 2000; Born 14/01/50; FCO 1969; Lourenço Marques 1972; Saigon 1973; FCO 1974; Kingston 1977; Madrid (CSCE) 1980; Alexandria 1982; Second Secretary FCO 1985; Vice-Consul (Commercial) Montreal 1988; First Secretary FCO 1993; First Secretary (Political) Copenhagen 1995; m 1981 Kareen Elizabeth Sun.

Nithavrianakis, Elizabeth Rosemary (née Hingston-Jones); FCO since April 2002; Born 27/06/63; FCO 1983; Peking 1985; Kuala Lumpur 1986; FCO 1990; Moscow 1990; FCO 1992; T/D Riyadh 2001; Band B3; m 1992 Michael Stephen Nithavrianakis (1s 1996; 1d 2000).

Nithavrianakis, Michael Stephen, MVO (2000); FCO since January 2002; Born 30/04/67; FCO 1984; Kuala Lumpur 1987; Moscow 1990; FCO 1992; Second Secretary (Chancery) Accra 1997; First Secretary (Commercial) Riyadh 2000; Band D6; m 1992 Elizabeth Rosemary Hingston-Jones (1s 1996; 1d 2000).

Noakes, Stephen Martin, OBE (1993); First
Secretary FCO since August 2000; Born 06/02/57;
Home Civil Service 1979-88; Second Secretary
FCO 1988; First Secretary (Chancery) Luanda
1990; First Secretary FCO 1993; First Secretary
New York (UKMIS) 1996; Band D6; m 1989
Hazel Clarke.

Nobes, Paula Louise; Deputy Head of Mission
Baku since September 2002; Born 01/08/69; FCO
1988; Language Training 1990; Third Secretary
(Chancery) Belgrade 1991; APS Lord Owen,
Peace Conference on Former Yugoslavia, Geneva
1993; Kiev 1994; Zagreb 1995; Second Secretary
FCO 1998; Band C5.

Noble, Andrew James, LVO (1995); Deputy Head
of Mission Hong Kong since December 2004;
Born 22/04/60; FCO 1982; Third Secretary
(Chancery/Information) Bucharest 1983; On
attachment to Auswärtiges Amt, Bonn 1986;
Second Secretary (Chancery) Bonn 1987; First
Secretary FCO 1989; First Secretary (Political)
and Head of Political Section Pretoria/Cape Town
1994; FCO 1998; Deputy Head of Mission Athens
2001; m 1992 Helen Natalie Pugh (2s 1995, 1996;
2d 2000, 2003).

Noble, Helen Natalie (née Pugh); SUPL since May
1994; Born 17/07/66; FCO 1988; On secondment
to Auswärtiges Amt 1989; Third later Second
Secretary Bonn 1990; Second Secretary FCO
1992; Second Secretary on loan to the ODA 1993;
m 1992 Andrew James Noble (2s 1995, 1996; 2d
2000, 2003).

Noble, Richard Adam; T/D HM Ambassador
Tashkent since September 2003; Born 09/06/62;
FCO 1987; Third later Second Secretary
(Chancery) Moscow 1987; Second later First
Secretary FCO 1989; First Secretary The Hague
1993; FCO 1995; First Secretary (Political) New
Delhi 1998; Head of Research Analysts FCO
2001; Counsellor (Political) Moscow 2003; m
1994 Katrina Johnson (2s 1996, 1998).

Noble, Robert Antony; Second Secretary
(Political) Kuala Lumpur since September 2002;
Born 24/08/66; FCO 1984; Lisbon 1986;
Islamabad 1989; FCO 1992; Rio de Janeiro 1995;
FCO 1999; Band C4; m 1997 Elisabeth Patrice
Wilkinson.

Noël, Louisa Veronica; Tokyo since June 2003;
Born 24/04/62; FCO 1988; Kuala Lumpur 1989;
Amman 1993; FCO 1996; Bangkok 1999; Band
B3.

Nolan, Julia Elizabeth; SUPL since June 1997;
Born 02/01/59; FCO 1983; Bangkok 1984; SUPL
1986; New Delhi 1987; Second Secretary FCO
1989; First Secretary FCO 1993; SUPL 1994; First
Secretary (Political) Paris 1995; m 1985 Richard
John Codrington (twin s 1991).

Noon, Paul David; First Secretary (Trade)
Wellington since September 2001; Born 01/06/68;
FCO 1989; Damascus 1991; Bonn 1995; FCO
1998; Band C5; m 1990 Karren Lesley Robson
(1d 1993; 1s 1998).

Noorani, Anjoum Aziz; Second Secretary
(Economic) Moscow since December 2002; Born
06/04/79; FCO 2000; Band C4.

Norburn, Jonathan Edward; Second Secretary
FCO since March 2002; Born 16/08/76; FCO
1999; Second Secretary (Chancery) Bridgetown
2001; Band C4.

Norman, Duncan Charles, MBE (2000); Tortola
since March 2004; Born 12/10/71; FCO 1990;
Riyadh 1994; Yerevan 1998; FCO 2000; m 1997
Kerry Jones (1d 2000).

Norman, Paul Stephen Raymond; First Secretary
(Political) Brussels since July 2002; Born
04/05/56; FCO 1992; Consul Hong Kong 1995;
First Secretary FCO 2000; Band D6; m 1989
Felicity Shan Abram (1s 1991; 2d 1993, 1998).

Norman, Sarah Caroline; SUPL since October
2000; Born 16/12/70; FCO 1990; New Delhi
1991; FCO 1992; SUPL 1994; FCO 1998; Band
C4.

Norris, George E P; FCO since September 2002;
Born 24/02/76; Band C4; m 2003 Ching-Yi Yang.

Norris, Peter James; FCO since September 2000;
Born 22/12/55; FCO 1982; First Secretary Lagos
1985; FCO 1988; Deputy Head of Mission and
Consul Guatemala City 1990; First Secretary FCO
1993; First Secretary (Political) Jakarta 1997;
Band D6; m 1982 Dilvinder Kaur Dhaliwal (2d
1986, 1990; 2s (twins) 1993).

Norsworthy, Sean Francis; FCO since April 2003;
Born 18/04/68; FCO 1987; Islamabad 1989; Tunis
1992; FCO 1996; Brussels (UKREP) 2001; Paris
2001; Band A2.

Northern, Richard James, MBE (1982); Consul-
General Milan since September 2001; Born
02/11/54; FCO 1976; MECAS 1978; Language
Training FCO 1978; Riyadh 1980; Second later
First Secretary (Chancery) Rome 1983; First
Secretary FCO 1987; First Secretary
(Economic/Commercial) Ottawa 1992; Deputy
Consul-General and Deputy Director
Trade/Investment Toronto 1994; Counsellor
(Commercial/Economic) Riyadh 1997; Counsellor
FCO 2000; m 1981 Linda Denise Gadd (2s 1983,
1986; 1d 1992).

Norton, Mark Rolffe; Head/Press and Public
Affairs Nairobi since September 2001; Born
03/01/55; Customs and Excise 1974; Immigration
Service 1983; On secondment to Kaduna 1987;
FCO 1992; On secondment to ICFY/Observer
Mission to Serbia and Montenegro 1994; Addis
Ababa 1995; Copenhagen 1996; Ottawa 1996;
Georgetown 2000; m 1995 Gelila Assefa Wedajo
(2d 1996, 1998).

Norton, Redmond; FCO since October 2002; Born
30/04/46; Board of Trade 1962; FCO 1969; Rio de
Janeiro 1972; Caracas 1975; Dacca 1977; FCO
1980; Second Secretary (Admin) Tripoli 1984;
Second Secretary Quito 1985; Second later First
Secretary (Commercial) Helsinki 1988; First
Secretary FCO 1992; Consul (Commercial)

Houston 1994; Deputy Head of Mission Montevideo 1999; Band D6; m 1969 Jean McGarrigle (1d 1974; 1s 1979).

Nye, Alison Claire (née Edwards); SUPL since March 2001; Born 18/12/64; FCO 1983; SUPL 1985; Vienna 1986; Algiers 1987; Third Secretary Karachi 1990; FCO 1993; Third later Second Secretary (Development) Lilongwe 1997; Band C4; m 1985 Richard Paul Nye (1s 1999).

Nye, Richard Paul; On loan to British Trade International, later UK Trade & Investment since October 2002; Born 29/02/64; FCO 1982; Vienna 1984; Algiers 1987; Third Secretary Karachi 1990; FCO 1994; Second Secretary 1996; Second Secretary Lilongwe 1997; SUPL (Private Sector) 2001; Band C4; m 1985 Alison Claire Edwards (1s 1999).

O

O'Brien, Gareth David; First Secretary (Commercial) Riyadh since November 2001; Born 27/07/65; FCO 1982; Copenhagen 1985; Warsaw 1988; Africa/Middle East Floater 1990; FCO 1991; Belmopan 1995; Consul (Commercial) Jedda 1998; Band C5; m 1991 Lisa Margaret Donagher (2s 1997, 1999).

O'Brien, Julie Ann Valentine; FCO since October 2001; Born 20/03/61; FCO 1994; Moscow 1996; Kuwait 1999.

O'Brien, Lisa Margaret (née Donagher); SUPL since June 1997; Born 30/10/66; FCO 1984; BMG Berlin 1986; Floater Duties 1989; FCO 1991; Belmopan 1995; Band B3; m 1991 Gareth David O'Brien (2s 1997, 1999).

O'Brien, Patrick Thaddeus Dominic, MBE (1995); Head of Media and Public Affairs Ottawa since August 2002; Born 03/11/49; Post Office 1966; FCO 1968; Lagos 1971; Georgetown 1975; FCO 1978; JAO Brussels 1982; Abidjan 1984; Second Secretary FCO 1988; Brussels 1993; First Secretary and Deputy Head of Mission Dakar 1998; Seconded to the Spanish Foreign Service, Madrid 2001; m 1970 Maureen Mortimer (3d 1970, 1971, 1979; 1s 1973).

O'Callaghan, Dominic Paul Hutton; Islamabad since May 2004; Born 26/01/46; FCO 1998; Third Secretary (Immigration) Abuja 2001; Band B3.

O'Callaghan, John Matthew; Counsellor Belgrade since July 2004; Born 27/04/66; FCO 1990; Second Secretary (Information) Santiago 1992; Second Secretary FCO 1994; First Secretary (Political) Moscow 1998; First Secretary FCO 2001; First Secretary Stockholm 2003; m 1996 Sophie Dauchez (2d 1998, 2001).

O'Connell, Charles; FCO since October 2003; Born 02/11/77; Band C4.

O'Connell, Ruairí; Second Secretary (Political) Pristina since August 2003; Born 22/02/77; FCO 2001; Band C4.

O'Connell, Terence; SMO Algiers since June 2004; Born 19/09/58; MOD 1976; FCO 1978; Stockholm 1980; Tripoli 1983; FCO 1984; Santiago 1984; Bombay 1987; FCO 1990; Full-Time Language Training 1995; Mexico City 1996; Full-Time Language Training 2000; Peking 2000; Band C4; m 1991 Valerie Anna-Maria Gonsalves.

O'Connor, Christopher Paul; Head of Political Section Ottawa since August 2000; Born 18/12/68; Third later Second Secretary FCO 1993; Full-Time Language Training Cairo 1995; Riyadh 1996; First Secretary Brussels (UKDEL NATO) 1999; On secondment to the Canadian Government 1999-00; m 2001 Martha Nelems (1d 2002).

O'Connor, Faye Emily; Second Secretary (External) Moscow since November 2002; Born 04/04/74; FCO 2001; Band C4.

O'Connor, Paul Vincent; Berlin since May 2003; Born 29/06/56; FCO 1975; Jedda 1977; Washington 1980; Floater Duties 1983; FCO 1985; Istanbul 1987; Second Secretary (Aid/Commercial) Maseru 1991; On loan to the DTI 1995; Language Training 1998; Deputy Head of Mission and Consul (Commercial) St Petersburg 1999; m 1985 Georgina Louise Jayne (2s 1987, 1989; 1d 1991).

O'Connor, Sheila Mary; SMO Hanoi since January 2003; Born 28/12/60; FCO 1982; Brussels (UKREP) 1983; Yaoundé 1986; Rangoon 1989; Prague 1991; FCO 1993; OSCE Sarajevo 1996; Third Secretary (Chancery/Development) Kathmandu 1997; FCO 2000; Band C4.

O'Donnell, Patricia (née Daubeney); On secondment as Press Officer, Attorney General's Chambers since October 2003; Born 22/12/68; FCO 1991; Warsaw 1994; Moscow 1997; FCO 2000; Band C5; m 1993 Simon Tristan O'Donnell.

O'Donnell, Sara Jane (née Sharp); SUPL since September 2001; Born 24/12/67; FCO 1991; Third Secretary Brussels (UKDEL WEU) 1994; Yaoundé 1996; m 1996 Francis Joseph O'Donnell.

O'Flaherty, Kenneth James; First Secretary (External Relations) Brussels (UKREP) since July 2000; Born 04/03/72; FCO 1996; Secondment to French Foreign Ministry 1998; Second Secretary (Political) Paris 1999; m 1997 Maria de los Reyes Lopez Garcia (diss 2000) (1d 1998).

O'Flaherty, Stephen John, CMG (2003); First Secretary later Counsellor FCO since August 1992; Born 15/05/51; Third Secretary FCO 1975; Language Training India 1977; Second Secretary New Delhi 1978; First Secretary FCO 1980; Prague 1981; First Secretary FCO 1984; First Secretary (Chancery) Vienna 1988; m 1975 Sarah Louise Gray (2d 1979, 1987; 1s 1983).

O'Hagan, Mark; Second Secretary Bogotá since July 2002; Born 25/10/67; FCO 1996; Band C4.

O'Henley, Andrew Alexander; FCO since October 2001; Born 07/08/76; FCO 1998; Cape Town 1999; Freetown 2001; Band C4.

O'Mahony, Angela Millar (née Lindsay); SUPL since June 2000; Born 17/08/66; FCO 1989; Paris 1991; Kampala 1994; Stockholm 1996; FCO 1996; Band B3; m 1994 Daniel Lawrence O'Mahony.

O'Neill, Martin Gerard Francis; Third Secretary and Vice-Consul Abu Dhabi since June 2004; Born 10/06/71; FCO 2001; Third Secretary (Press and Public Affairs) Tokyo 2002; Band B3; m 2002 Sachiko Suzuki.

O'Neill, Michael Angus; Counsellor (Economic) New York (UKMIS) since July 2002; Born 25/05/65; MOD 1988; Second Secretary UKDEL NATO/WEU 1991; FCO 1994; First Secretary (Political) Washington 1998; m 1991 Claire Bannerman (1d 1994; 3s 1996, 1998, 2001).

O'Reilly, Mark Carne; Third Secretary (Political) Brussels since May 2001; Born 08/06/73; FCO 1999; Band B3.

O'Rourke, Peter Vincent; FCO since April 2000; Born 26/09/60; FCO 1980; Maputo 1981; Lisbon 1984; Rabat 1987; FCO 1990; Yaoundé 1993; Third later Second Secretary (Management) Beirut 1997; Band C4; m 1999 Louise Karen.

O'Shaughnessy, Jonathan Edward; ECO/Vice-Consul Vienna since August 2002; Born 07/10/71; FCO 1991; Bonn 1995; Gibraltar 1998; ECO Islamabad 2000; Band B3; m 1997 Lisa Diane.

Oakden, Edward Anthony; Director (International Security) FCO since November 2002; Born 03/11/59; FCO 1981; Third later Second Secretary (Chancery) Baghdad 1984; Second Secretary (Chancery) Khartoum 1985; First Secretary and Private Secretary to HM Ambassador Washington 1988; First Secretary FCO 1992; Private Secretary to Prime Minister (Overseas/Defence) 1995; Counsellor FCO 1997; Counsellor Madrid 1998; Deputy Head of Mission and Minister Madrid 2000; Head of Security Policy Department, FCO 2002; m (1) 1999 (diss) (1d 1995); m (2) Ana Romero.

Oakley, Matthew Edward, MVO (1999), MBE (2003); Second Secretary (Commercial) Singapore since June 2000; Born 19/07/65; FCO 1983; Athens 1985; Pro-Consul Jedda 1988; Vice-Consul Riyadh 1990; Third Secretary FCO 1992; Third Secretary (Political) Cape Town 1996; Band C4.

Oertle-Hurt, Jane Michelle; SUPL since February 1995; Born 13/09/65; HCS 1987-89; Rome 1990; Africa/Middle East Floater 1994; Band B3; m 1995 Horst Dietrich Oertle.

Ogg, Fiona; Warsaw since April 2003; Born 25/07/70; FCO 1989; Warsaw 1992; Paris 1994; FCO 1996; Lagos 1999; Band B3.

Oliphant, Jeremy Craig; Principal Research Officer FCO since April 1999; Born 04/04/56; MOD 1989-99; NATO 1992-94; OSCE 1996-99; Band D6; m 1983 Eithne Grant (2d 1985; 1989).

Oliver, Matthew Keith; Second Secretary FCO since June 2003; Born 16/08/51; Blantyre 1973; Washington 1975; Belgrade 1978; FCO 1979; Tehran 1980; Bombay 1980; Warsaw 1983; FCO 1984; Auckland 1986; Istanbul 1989; Second Secretary FCO 1993; Baku 1996; Second Secretary (Management) The Hague 1999; m 1993 Hatice Iker Urgen (dec'd 1999).

Oliver, Paul John; Madrid since July 2000; Born 11/02/74; FCO (Hanslope Park) 1996; Band C4.

Oman, Magnus Paul; On loan to the DTI since November 1999; Born 05/08/68; FCO 1989; Valletta 1991; Doha 1994; FCO 1998; Band B3; m 1998 Ms S Broderick.

Ord-Smith, Robin Jeremy, MVO (1998); First Secretary (Commercial) Tokyo since July 2003; Born 08/10/65; FCO 1989; Vice-Consul Bucharest 1991; Third Secretary (Political/Information) Kuala Lumpur 1994; Second Secretary (State Visit) Kuala Lumpur 1998; Seconded to Auswärtiges Amt 1999; Second Secretary FCO 1999; Full-Time Language Training 2000; Seconded to Bae Systems Japan 2001; Full-Time Language Training 2002; Band D6; m 1995 Tania Jane Vallis (2s 1996, 1998).

Ormiston, Ewan Kenneth; On secondment to TPUK, British Trade International since November 2002; Born 27/08/68; FCO 1989; Brussels 1992; Luanda 1995; Third Secretary Lima 1996; Third later Second Secretary Kampala 1999; Band C4; m 1994 Gillian Keating (1s 1997; 1d 2000).

Ormiston, Gillian (née Keating); on secondment to TPUK, British Trade International since 2003; Born 01/06/66; FCO 1988; Brussels (UKREP) 1991; Luanda 1995; Lima 1996; Kampala (SUPL) 1999; later ECO Kampala 2001; Band A2; m 1994 Ewan Kenneth Ormiston (1s 1997; 1d 2000).

Ormond, Matthew John; Washington since January 2001; Born 23/04/73; FCO 1991; Band C4.

Osborn, Andrew Robert; Third Secretary (Management/Consular/Immigration) Suva since February 2004; Born 13/02/64; FCO 1982; Lagos 1987; Budapest 1990; Moscow 1992; FCO 1994; Vice-Consul Dar-es-Salaam 1997; Third Secretary (Consular/Management) Maseru 2001; Band B3; m 1988 Karyn Lindsay Heraty (2d 1993, 1997).

Osborn, Karyn Lindsay (née Heraty); SUPL since July 1997; Born 12/02/66; FCO 1986; Lagos 1988; Budapest 1990; Moscow 1992; FCO 1994; Band B3; m 1988 Andrew Robert Osborn (2d 1993, 1997).

Osborne, Christopher Wyndham; Deputy Head of Protocol Division and Assistant Marshal of the Diplomatic Corps, FCO since November 2001; Born 18/06/46; CO 1964; Commonwealth Office (later FCO) 1966; Lusaka 1968; Kampala 1970; Bridgetown 1973; FCO 1976; Second Secretary Dacca 1979; Second Secretary (Commercial) Caracas 1982; First Secretary FCO 1986; First Secretary (Information) BTC Hong Kong 1989; First Secretary FCO 1994; First Secretary T/D BTC Hong Kong 1996; Deputy Head of Mission

Luanda 1998; m 1967 Gillian Mary (3s 1967, 1974, 1979).

Osborne, Roy Paul; Deputy Head of Overseas Territories Department, FCO since February 2001; Born 13/07/51; FCO 1970; Oslo 1972; Islamabad 1974; Vice-Consul Rome 1978; Second Secretary FCO 1981; Second Secretary (Commercial/Development), later First Secretary, Head of Chancery and Consul Yaoundé 1985; First Secretary (Chancery/Information) Madrid 1989; First Secretary FCO 1993; HM Ambassador Managua 1997; m 1977 Vivienne Claire Gentry (2d 1983, 1984).

Ostler, Malcolm Thomas; FCO since November 2003; Born 20/09/66; FCO 1988; Bonn 1997; Berlin 1999; Hamilton 2002; Band A2.

Oswald, David; Second Secretary (Commercial) Islamabad since December 2001; Born 15/06/46; FO 1965; Amman 1968; Zomba 1970; Blantyre 1971; Tokyo 1973; FCO 1976; Gaborone 1978; FCO 1982; Jedda 1986; Second Secretary FCO 1990; Second Secretary (Management) Dhaka 1993; Consul (Commercial/Economic) Shanghai 1997; m 1972 Jane Avril Bennett Edmunds (2d 1974, 1977).

Oughton, Carolyn Ann; FCO since September 2003; Born 23/06/81; Band A2.

Oulmi, Sally Teresa (née Cashman); Consul (Management) Dar es Salaam since January 2004; Born 04/10/52; FCO 1974; Brussels (UKREP) 1975; Abidjan 1979; Strasbourg 1983; FCO 1986; Ottawa 1987; Stockholm 1990; FCO 1993; Second Secretary (Management) Dhaka 1996; Band C4; m 1976 Hocine (Frank) Oulmi (dec'd) (2s 1993, 1994).

Owen, Amy Grace; Vice-Consul Hong Kong since October 2002; Born 29/08/75; FCO 1999; Full-Time Language Training 2000; Full-Time Language Training Peking 2001; Band C4.

Owen, Caroline Jane; Jakarta since October 2001; Born 29/10/66; FCO 1986; Washington 1990; FCO 1992; Bombay 1994; Dhaka 1998; Band A2.

Owen, Gareth Wynn; SUPL since September 2002; Born 24/11/69; FCO 1989; Prague 1992; FCO 1993; Warsaw 1994; Lusaka 1996; Baku 1999; FCO 2001; Band B3.

Owen, Helen Patricia; FCO since August 1987; Born 09/04/49; FCO 1974; Sana'a 1974; FCO 1976; Bandar Seri Begawan 1981; Manila 1982; Madrid 1984; Band B3.

Owen, Jane Caroline; Counsellor (Commercial) Tokyo since May 2002; Born 15/04/63; FCO 1987; Language Training (Japanese) 1988; Second Secretary (Commercial) Tokyo 1989; First Secretary DTI Exports to Japan Unit 1993; FCO 1996; Deputy Head of Mission Hanoi 1998; SUPL 1999; Deputy High Commissioner Hanoi 2000; m 1998 David Donnelly.

Owen, Kara Justine (née Palmer); Private Secretary to the Foreign Secretary since February

2003; Born 27/05/71; FCO 1993; Vice-Consul later Vice-Consul (Political) Hong Kong 1996; Second Secretary FCO 2000; Assistant Private Secretary to Minister of State 2001; First Secretary FCO 2002; Band D6; m 1995 Craig Sterling Owen.

Owen, Philip Haydn, MBE; Second Secretary (Political) Berlin since May 2003; Born 03/03/66; FCO 1997; Islamabad 1998; Band C4; m 1996 Elizabeth Jane Knight (1s 2003).

Owen, Richard Lloyd; Counsellor FCO since January 1998; Born 21/04/48; Second Secretary FCO 1975; Language Training 1976; Language Training MECAS 1977; First Secretary Abu Dhabi 1978; Beirut 1980; FCO 1981; San José 1983; BMG Berlin 1986; First Secretary FCO 1988; Counsellor Copenhagen 1993; m 1985 Eva Maria Steller (2d 1986, 1988).

Owens, Patrick Eldred, MBE (1998); HM Consul New York since July 2001; Born 20/04/53; FCO 1972; Muscat 1974; Bucharest 1977; Algiers 1979; FCO 1981; Jakarta 1984; Third later Second Secretary Riyadh 1988; Second Secretary FCO 1994; First Secretary (Information) Madrid 1997; m 1978 Merle de Ceuninck van Capelle (1d 1980; 2s 1982, 1985).

Owens, Ruth Mary; FCO since August 2002; Born 28/03/67; FCO 1987; Nairobi 1989; FCO 1992; Moscow 1995; Antananarivo 1999; Band B3.

P

Packer, Deborah (née Wilde); SUPL since November 2003; Born 10/05/66; FCO 1985; NEDO 1986; Tokyo 1994; Bridgetown 1997; Tokyo 2000; Band A2; m 1990 Philip Anthony Packer (2s 1995; 2001; 1d 2003).

Page, Alexander Simon; FCO since July 2003; Born 20/10/64; FCO 1987; Dhaka 1989; Warsaw 1989; FCO 1993; Valletta 1996; Third Secretary (Management) Mexico City 1999; Band B3; m 1989 Isabella Lynn Marshall (1s 1996).

Page, Andrew John Walter; First Secretary (Chancery) Paris since September 2000; Born 17/09/65; FCO 1990; Full-Time Language Training 1991; Second Secretary Kiev 1992; Second Secretary FCO 1996.

Page, Brian Ronald; FCO since January 2000; Born 05/03/49; FCO 1968; Helsinki 1971; Doha 1973; Cape Town 1976; FCO 1978; Muscat 1979; Singapore 1983; FCO 1986; Second Secretary 1988; Dubai 1992; Second Secretary (Consular/Immigration) Accra 1997; m 1973 Susan Frances Vinall (2s 1975, 1979).

Page, Derek Alan; On loan to the DTI since August 2002; Born 29/09/50; FCO 1975; Pretoria 1977; Bombay 1979; FCO 1981; Frankfurt 1984; Montevideo 1987; FCO 1990 (Second Secretary 1992); Second Secretary Taipei 1994; Second Secretary (Commercial) Abu Dhabi 1998; FCO 2001; m 1972 Inger Merete Ebbesvik (2s 1977, 1981).

Page, Isabella Lynn (née Marshall); SUPL since May 2004; Born 06/01/64; FCO 1981; Kuala Lumpur 1984; Prague 1987; SUPL 1989; Warsaw 1989; Dhaka 1990; FCO 1993; Third Secretary (Political/Information) Valletta 1996; Third Secretary (Political) Mexico City 1999; FCO 2003; m 1989 Alexander Simon Page (1s 1996).

Page, Simon Graham; Second Secretary FCO since September 2001; Born 22/11/61; FCO 1979; Kuala Lumpur 1983; Floater Duties 1987; Dublin 1988; FCO 1990; Third Secretary (Chancery) New Delhi 1992; FCO 1996; Second Secretary (Political) Riyadh 1998; Band C4; m 1985 Sharon Ann Murphy (2s 1990, 1995; 1d 2000).

Pagett, Christopher Robert Geoffrey, OBE (1990); Counsellor FCO since September 2000; Born 13/06/52; Third Secretary FCO 1975; Second Secretary Havana 1978; Second later First Secretary (Economic) Lusaka 1979; First Secretary FCO 1984; First Secretary (Chancery) Maputo 1988; First Secretary FCO 1991; Counsellor New York (UKMIS) 1997; m (1) 1974 Anne-Marie Roberts; (2) 1988 Diane Brown (1s 1993).

Pagett, Ian William; FCO since February 1995; Born 19/09/69; FCO 1988; Khartoum 1989; FCO 1992; Warsaw 1993; Band B3.

Pagett, Wayne Norman; Third Secretary (Consular/Immigration) Harare since March 2001; Born 26/03/67; FCO 1988; New Delhi 1990; Tel Aviv 1994; FCO 1997; Band B3; m 1990 Kay Louise Clements (1d 1994).

Paginton, David Alan; Management Officer São Paulo since December 2000; Born 01/04/51; Board of Inland Revenue 1968; FCO 1971; Istanbul 1973; Brussels (UKREP) 1976; Sofia 1979; FCO 1981; São Paulo 1984; Islamabad 1988; FCO 1991; Second Secretary (Commercial) Dar es Salaam 1994; HM Consul Buenos Aires 1998; m 1986 Marcia Rosana Antonio (1s 1986; 1d 1987).

Pain, Warren David; Vice-Consul (Political/Economic) Hong Kong since February 2000; Born 17/05/71; FCO 1992; Peking 1995; World Wide All-Rounder 1998; m 2000 Armine Ghevondyan.

Painter, Anthony Clifford; FCO since December 2002; Born 20/03/59; FCO 1994; Paris 1996; Hanoi 1999; Band A2; m 1984 Lisa Nelson (1d 1984).

Painting, Julia, MBE (1993); Deputy Head of Mission Lusaka since October 2001; Born 24/04/60; FCO 1981; Prague 1983; Africa/Middle East Floater 1985; South East Asia Floater 1987; FCO 1989; Tallinn 1991; FCO 1992; Milan 1994; HM Consul Naples 1995; Second Secretary FCO 1997; First Secretary FCO 1998.

Pakes, Stuart Murray; FCO since June 2002; Born 08/05/49; FO 1967; FCO 1968; Aden 1970; Anguilla 1973; Reykjavik 1973; East Berlin 1976; FCO 1977; Madrid 1981; Cairo 1984; FCO 1987;

Second Secretary 1989; Accra 1990; Abu Dhabi 1994; First Secretary 1998; Islamabad 1998; Band C5; m 1972 Linda Anne Rawlings (2d 1977, 1981; 1s 1984).

Palmer, Andrew David; ECO Dubai since July 2003; Born 21/01/76; FCO (HCS) 1994; Transferred to Diplomatic Service 2000; World Wide Floater Duties 2000; Band B3.

Pankhurst, Donia Lee; Floater Duties since July 2002; Born 27/05/65; House of Commons 1991-97; FCO 1997; Geneva (UKMIS) 1998; Band B3.

Parfitt, Alan Frank, MBE (1997); SUPL since October 1998; Born 06/08/66; Senior Research Officer FCO 1989; Vienna (UKDEL) 1994.

Parham, Philip John; FCO since September 2003; Born 14/08/60; FCO 1993; Private Secretary to the Parliamentary Under-Secretary of State 1995; First Secretary (Chancery) Washington 1996; Director Trade and Investment Promotion, Riyadh 2000; m 1985 Kasia Giedroyc (2d 1986, 1994; 5s 1988, 1989, 1990, 1992, 1996).

Parish, Colin; Pristina since September 2002; Born 27/11/43; Royal Navy 1961-70; FCO 1970; Phnom Penh 1973; Accra 1974; SUPL 1978; FCO 1982; Belgrade 1986; Consul (Commercial) Jedda 1990; Second Secretary FCO 1995; Budapest 1997; m (1) 1966 Carole Grace (diss 1978); (2) 1978 Fairrolaigh Janet Lee Syme (2s 1985, 1989).

Parish, Paul Edward; FCO since March 2002; Born 10/08/63; FCO 1983; Vienna 1986; FCO 1989; SUPL 1992; Second Secretary FCO 1995; Second Secretary (Bilateral) Bonn 1998; Second Secretary Berlin 1999; Band C4.

Parker, Cindy; Third Secretary (Consular) Islamabad since March 2003; Born 01/02/72; FCO 1997; T/D Third Secretary Tashkent 2000; Vice-Consul Bogotá 2000; Band C4.

Parker, Katherine Clare (known as Katy); Manila since December 2001; Born 14/07/70; FCO 1988; Band C4; ptnr, Steve Dolan.

Parker, Lyn; British High Commissioner Nicosia since September 2001; Born 25/11/52; FCO 1978; Second later First Secretary Athens 1980; FCO 1984; Counsellor on loan to the Cabinet Office 1989; Counsellor and Head of Chancery New Delhi 1992; Counsellor (Political) Brussels (UKREP) 1995; Counsellor FCO 1999; m 1991 Jane Elizabeth Walker (2d 1993, 1996).

Parker, Nigel Denis; Legal Counsellor FCO since February 2001; Born 25/08/61; Called to the Bar, Middle Temple 1985; Assistant Legal Adviser FCO 1988; Legal Adviser Bridgetown 1995; Assistant Legal Adviser FCO 1998.

Parker, Nigel Graham; Geneva (UKMIS) since April 2000; Born 13/09/56; FCO 1982; Kingston 1985; FCO 1988; Budapest 1990; Band C4; m 1983 Paula Northwood (1s 1987; 1d 1991).

Parker, Rod; Baghdad since October 2003; Born 14/11/60; FCO 1996; Peking 2000; Band C4; m 1981 Bernadette Corr (2d 1987, 1991).

Parker, Susan Caroline; FCO since June 1993; Born 01/07/63; FCO 1985; Brussels (UKREP) 1987; FCO 1988; Vienna 1990; Band A2.

Parker-Brennan, Michael; Abuja since March 2004; Born 30/05/52; Royal Corps of Transport 1967-92; FCO 1992; Helsinki 1992; Bucharest 1993; Pretoria 1996; Moscow 1997; FCO 1999; Band B3; m (1) 1982 Catherine Mary Parker (diss); (2) 1988 Carmen Dorina.

Parkins, David Alan; FCO since August 1997; Born 07/05/64; GPO 1980 - 84; FCO 1984; Third Secretary Nairobi 1989; FCO 1993; Third Secretary Bucharest 1994; Band C5; m 1991 Diane Reed (2s 1992, 1994).

Parkinson, Guy Paul; Second Secretary (Commercial) Montevideo since April 2002; Born 05/06/70; FCO 1989; Budapest 1992; Moscow 1995; Floater Duties 2000; Band B3; m 2002 Romina Rodriguez del Puerto.

Parkinson, Howard, CVO (1998); High Commissioner Maputo since December 2003; Born 29/03/48; BOT 1967; FCO 1969; LA Floater 1972; Tegucigalpa 1974; Buenos Aires 1975; Second Secretary 1977; Maputo 1978; Second later First Secretary FCO 1981; First Secretary (Commercial) Lisbon 1985; First Secretary on loan to British Gas 1989; First Secretary FCO 1991; Consul-General and Counsellor (Management) Washington 1994; Counsellor (Commercial) Kuala Lumpur 1997; Deputy High Commissioner Mumbai 2001; m 1974 Linda Wood (1d 1979; 1s 1982).

Parsons, Alexander Colin; First Secretary (Political) Nicosia since June 2003; Born 26/03/73; FCO 1997; Second Secretary (Political) Santiago 1999; Second Secretary FCO 2001; Band D6.

Parsons, Sarah Anne Pascale; FCO since November 2002; Born 22/10/74; Band C4.

Parton, Charles William, OBE (1995); Counsellor (Political) Nicosia since December 2003; Born 23/03/56; FCO 1979; Language Training Hong Kong 1982; Second Secretary FCO 1983; First Secretary (Economic) Peking 1985; First Secretary FCO 1987; First Secretary Joint Liaison Group Hong Kong 1990; Counsellor FCO 1994; Counsellor Kabul 2002; m 1983 Charmian Constance Denman (1d 1987; 1s 1990).

Partridge, Andrew Warren; Third Secretary (Economic/Commercial) New Delhi since August 2003; Born 26/04/68; FCO 1986; Islamabad 1989; Moscow 1992; FCO 1995; SUPL 1997; Third Secretary Vienna 2000; SUPL 2003; Band B3; m 1988 Margaret Robertson (1s 1996; 1d 1998).

Partridge, Colin Douglas; Counsellor Seoul since June 2000; Born 12/12/55; FCO 1978; Third later Second Secretary (Chancery) New Delhi 1980; Second later First Secretary FCO 1983; Language Training 1986; Head of Chancery and Consul Hanoi 1987; First Secretary FCO 1989; First Secretary Hong Kong 1994; Language Training 1998; m (1) 1983 Gita Sahgal (diss 1989); (2) 1993 Helena June Beattie (1d 1996).

Partridge, Diane Freda; Deputy Head of Mission Antananarivo since June 2002; Born 29/11/44; OECD Paris 1966; Yaoundé 1969; Lagos 1970; Rio de Janeiro 1971; FCO 1972; Antananarivo 1974; FCO 1976; Buenos Aires 1977; FCO 1979; Brasilia 1981; FCO 1985; Third Secretary (Aid) Belmopan 1989; Third Secretary ATTC Taipei 1993; FCO 1995; Second Secretary (Commercial) Luanda 1999; T/D Durban 2001; Band C4.

Partridge, Margaret (née Robertson), MBE (1995); Second Secretary (Immigration) New Delhi since February 2003; Born 03/03/66; FCO 1986; Islamabad 1989; Vice-Consul Moscow 1992; FCO 1995; Vice-Consul Muscat 1997; SUPL 2000; Band C4; m 1988 Andrew Warren Partridge (1s 1996; 1d 1998).

Pasquill, Derek James; FCO since November 2001; Born 11/01/59; HCS 1984; FCO 1986; Kampala 1988; Maseru 1990; FCO 1993; Vice-Consul Abu Dhabi 1997; m 2002 Nony Verioti.

Patel, Shofiya; FCO since January 2004; Born 03/02/69; DSS 1988; FCO 1990; Canberra 1992; FCO 1995; Riga 1996; Floater Duties 2000; Dushanbe 2002; Band B3.

Patel, Vaishali; FCO since March 2003; Born 28/03/74; Home Office 2000; Band B3; ptnr, Bruce McMahon.

Paterson, Annabel Christina Mary; FCO since March 2003; Born 19/05/79; Band C4.

Paterson, Fiona; First Secretary (Political) Lisbon since November 1999; Born 06/04/51; FCO 1977; Bogotá 1979; Ottawa 1983; Second Secretary FCO 1987; Second Secretary (Chancery/Information) Bangkok 1989; Second Secretary (Information) later First Secretary (Science and Technology) Paris 1990; First Secretary FCO 1994; Band D6.

Paterson, Ian Robert; Second Secretary (Political/Economic) Nairobi since April 2002; Born 22/09/62; FCO Communications 1986; FCO 1996; Third Secretary (Political) Berne 1998; Band C4; m Diane (2d 1992, 1997).

Paterson, Lynne Kathryn; Wellington since September 2001; Born 22/05/63; FCO 1999; Band A2.

Paterson, Robert Ralston; Second Secretary (Political/Economic) Abuja since December 2002; Born 31/01/74; FCO 2000; Band C4.

Paterson, William Neil Carlton; Consul-General Frankfurt since April 2001; Born 19/10/50; FCO 1978; Sofia 1980; FCO 1981; Düsseldorf 1983; Second Secretary (Commercial/Aid) Yaoundé 1986; Second Secretary FCO 1989; Consul (Commercial) Montreal 1992; Consul-General Stuttgart 1997; m 1975 Margaret Christine Schmidt-Feuerheerd (1s 1976; 3d 1978, 1981, 1983).

Patey, William Charters; HM Ambassador Khartoum since September 2002; Born 11/07/53;

FCO 1975; MECAS 1977; Abu Dhabi 1978;
Second Secretary (Commercial) Tripoli 1981; First
Secretary FCO 1984; First Secretary (Chancery)
Canberra 1988; First Secretary later Counsellor
FCO 1992; Deputy Head of Mission Riyadh 1995;
Head of Middle East Department, FCO 1999; m
1978 Vanessa Carol Morrell (2s 1987, 1991).

Patrick, Andrew Silas; Deputy Head of Mission
Pretoria since February 2004; Born 28/02/66; FCO
1988; Third later Second Secretary (Chancery)
Nicosia 1991; First Secretary T/D Brussels
(UKDEL) 1995; FCO 1996; Assistant Private
Secretary to Secretary of State FCO 1998; FCO
2000.

Patrick, Claire Mary Angela; FCO since March
2003; Born 17/11/78; Band C4.

Patterson, Ernest Mark; Plymouth since
November 2003; Born 22/02/69; FCO 1989;
Vienna 1989; Addis Ababa 1996; Floater Duties
1998; Sarajevo 2000; Band B3.

Patterson, Hugh William Grant; FCO since
August 2004; Born 17/10/50; FCO 1979; First
Secretary BMG Berlin 1980; First Secretary FCO
1984; First Secretary (Head of Chancery) and
Consul Guatemala City 1987; First Secretary FCO
1990; First Secretary later Counsellor Caracas
1992; Counsellor FCO 1995; Counsellor Berne
2000; m 1981 Philippa Anne Colbatch Clark (1d
1986; 1s 1997).

Pattison, Stephen Dexter; On secondment to
Harvard since September 2003; Born 24/12/53;
FCO 1981; Nicosia 1983; FCO 1986; First
Secretary (Chancery) Washington 1989; FCO
1994; Director of Trade Promotion and Consul-
General Warsaw 1997; Head of United Nations
Department, FCO 2000; m 1987 Helen Andrea
Chaoushis 1987 (1d 1993).

Patton, Geoffrey Joseph Laurence; FCO since
January 2003; Born 26/04/62; MOD 1985 - 86;
FCO 1986; Warsaw 1989; Floater Training 1991;
Floater Duties 1991; Colombo 1994; FCO 1998;
T/D Bombay 2000; Plymouth, Montserrat 2000;
Band C4.

Paver, James Edward Luke, MVO (1994); First
Secretary FCO since September 2001; Born
02/10/63; FCO 1991; Third Secretary (Press and
Public Affairs) Moscow 1994; Second Secretary
FCO 1997; Second Secretary (Political) Brussels
(UKDEL) 1998; m 1992 Rebecca Jane Ash (3d
1993, 1995, 1997).

Pavis, Susan Mary (née Hartland); Brussels
(UKDEL NATO) since August 1999; Born
16/04/64; FCO 1983; Washington 1986; Riyadh
1988; FCO 1991; Vice-Consul Singapore 1995;
Band C4; m (1) 1985 Neil Cronin (diss 1994) (1s
1993); (2) 2002 Christopher Pavis (1d 2003).

Paxman, Timothy Giles, LVO (1989); Minister
Paris since June 2002; Born 15/11/51; Department
of Environment/Transport 1974; First Secretary
Brussels (UKREP) 1980; FCO 1985; First
Secretary and Head of Chancery Singapore 1989;

Counsellor on loan to the Cabinet Office 1992;
Full-Time Language Training 1994; Counsellor
(Commercial/Economic) Rome 1994; Counsellor
(Political) Brussels (UKREP) 1999; m 1980
Segolene Claude Marie (3d 1982, 1984, 1988).

Peacock, Paula Geraldine (née Hackett); SUPL
since May 2004; Born 01/01/65; FCO 1990; Third
Secretary Nairobi 1993; Full-Time Language
Training 1996; Vice-Consul Prague 1997; FCO
2000; SUPL 2002; Second Secretary
(Immigration) Colombo 2003; Band C4; m 1997
David Laurance Peacock (1d 2002).

Peake, Philippa Jane; SUPL since December
2000; Born 30/03/64; FCO 1990; Moscow 1993;
UKDEL NATO 1996; FCO 1999; Band A2; m
1997 Dominic Alister Stephens.

Pearce, Andrew John; Counsellor and Deputy
Head of Mission Bangkok since December 2003;
Born 07/10/60; FCO 1983; Language Training
1984; Third later Second Secretary Bangkok 1986;
First Secretary FCO 1988; First Secretary
(Chancery) Tel Aviv 1992; First Secretary
(Economic) Pretoria 1996; Counsellor and Deputy
Head of Mission Bucharest 2000; m 1986 Pornpun
Pathumvivatana (1s 1989; 1d 1994).

Pearce, David Avery; FCO since April 2003; Born
17/02/52; FCO 1971; New York (UKMIS) 1973;
Rome 1976; FCO 1979; Dhaka 1982; FCO 1986;
Second Secretary Paris 1987; Second Secretary
and Deputy Head of Mission Libreville 1990;
Consul Douala 1991; Deputy Head of Mission and
Consul-General Sana'a and Aden 1996; HM
Consul-General Durban 2000; m (1) 1973 Anne
Matthews (dec'd 1986) (1d 1980; 1s 1984); (2)
1988 Virginia Martin (diss 2001) (2d 1991, 1995;
1s 1993); (3) 2001 Randa Al Harazi (1d 2001).

Pearce, Howard John Stredder, CVO (1993);
Governor Stanley and Commissioner for South
Georgia and Sandwich Islands since December
2002; Born 13/04/49; FCO 1972; Buenos Aires
1975; First Secretary FCO 1978; First Secretary
and Head of Chancery Nairobi 1983; First
Secretary later Counsellor FCO 1987; Language
Training 1990; Deputy Head of Mission Budapest
1991; On loan at Harvard University 1994; Head
of Central European Department 1996; British
High Commissioner Valletta 1999.

Pearey, (Dorothy) Jane, MBE (1980); FCO since
September 1999; Born 31/05/45; OECD Paris
1969; Moscow 1972; FCO 1973; Belgrade 1977;
FCO 1980; New York (UKMIS) 1983; Seconded
to NATO 1984; Seconded to 21st Century Trust
1988; FCO 1989 (Second Secretary 1991); Second
Secretary (Aid) Harare 1995; On secondment to
DFID (Harare) 1998.

Pearey, David Dacre; High Commissioner
Lilongwe since December 2004; Born 15/07/48;
On secondment from MOD to Ankara 1979; First
Secretary FCO 1983; First Secretary and Head of
Chancery Kampala 1987; First Secretary later
Counsellor FCO 1990; Counsellor
(Commercial/Economic) Lagos 1995; Deputy

High Commissioner Karachi 2000; m 1996 Susan Anne Knowles (1d 2000).

Pearson, Frances; Prague since October 2002; Born 17/07/54; FCO 1987; Washington 1988; Brussels (UKREP) 1991; Moscow 1994; FCO 1996; Buenos Aires 1998; Band B3.

Pearson, John Anthony; FCO since September 2002; Born 28/04/68; FCO 1990; Madrid 1992; FCO 1994; Brasilia 1996; FCO 2000; SUPL 2001; Band D6; m 2002 Leyla-Claude Werleigh.

Pearson, Julian Christopher; Tirana since December 2001; Born 08/07/69; FCO 1990; Third Secretary Prague 1992; Third Secretary Kinshasa 1995; FCO 1998; Minsk 1998.

Pearson, Ruth Alexandra (née Stephens); SUPL since February 2002; Born 30/01/71; FCO 1993; Full-Time Language Training 1995; Budapest 1996; Second Secretary (Political) Brussels (UKREP) 1999; Band C4; m 1996 Simon Mark Pearson (1s 2000; 1d 2002).

Peart, Christopher John Stuttle; Moscow since January 2002; Born 23/08/75; FCO 1998; Band A2.

Pease, Simon Robert Hellier; Assistant Director, Personnel Management FCO since September 2001; Born 20/02/52; FCO 1972; Ibadan 1975; SUPL 1978; FCO 1981 (Second Secretary 1982); Second later First Secretary UKDEL CDE Stockholm 1984; First Secretary FCO 1986; First Secretary and Head of Chancery Rabat 1988; First Secretary later Counsellor FCO 1992; Deputy Head of Mission and Consul-General Tel Aviv 1997; m 1975 Catherine Elizabeth Bayley (1d 1981; 1s 1983).

Peate, David James, OBE (1989); First Secretary Turks and Caicos Islands since July 2001; Born 02/07/44; FO 1964; DSAO 1965; Delhi 1967; Warsaw 1971; Second Secretary Lomé 1972; FCO 1975; Melbourne 1978; FCO 1983; First Secretary Brussels 1984; First Secretary (Commercial) East Berlin 1989; First Secretary FCO 1993; Deputy Consul-General Milan 1996; m 1971 Siri Jean Jessica Elizabeth Zetter (2d 1973, 1990; 2s 1975, 1986).

Peers, Gary Clive; Madrid since July 2002; Born 06/12/58; FCO 1985; Third Secretary Bonn 1990; Third Secretary Pretoria 1995; FCO 1997; Band C5; m 1979 Pamela Jane Tailby (1d 1981; 2s 1983, 1985).

Peers, Tracy Ann (née Rose); Taipei since September 2002; Born 29/11/63; FCO 2000; Band A2; m 2004 David Peers.

Peirce, Robert Nigel; Counsellor Washington since October 1999; Born 18/03/55; FCO 1977; Language Training Cambridge 1978; Language Training Hong Kong 1979; Second later First Secretary (Chancery) Peking 1980; First Secretary FCO 1983; On loan to the Cabinet Office 1985; On secondment as Deputy Political Adviser to Hong Kong Government 1986; Assistant Private Secretary to the Secretary of State 1988; First

Secretary (Chancery) New York (UKMIS) 1990; Political Adviser Hong Kong 1993; On secondment to the Royal College of Defence Studies 1998; Secretary to the Independent Commission on Policing for Northern Ireland 1998; m (1) 1978 Christina Anne Skipworth Davis (1s 1986; 1d 1988); (2) 2000 Robin Lynn Raphel (2 step d 1986, 1990).

Pendered, Jo; FCO since October 2002; Born 02/11/65; FCO 1984; Bombay 1987; Santiago 1990; FCO 1992; Athens 1996; Cape Town 1999; Dili 2001; Band C4.

Penfold, Jane Elizabeth Mary (née Govier); FCO since June 2002; Born 21/03/62; FCO 1984; Language Training 1986; Third Secretary (Commercial) Peking 1987; Vice-Consul (Management) Istanbul 1990; Presidency Liaison Officer Luxembourg 1990 (Second Secretary 1991); T/D Bangkok 1991; Second Secretary FCO 1992; Full-Time Language Training 1994; Second Secretary (Political) Sofia 1995; FCO 1998; First Secretary Dili 2000; m 1997 Nigel John Penfold.

Pengelly, Rachel Jane (née Laycock); Second Secretary (Chancery/External) Washington since May 2000; Born 20/05/71; FCO 1994; Band C4; m 2000 Owen Pengelly.

Penrith, Alan Paul; FCO since 2001; Born 24/05/58; Inland Revenue 1977; FCO 1978; Mexico City 1980; Yaoundé 1983; FCO 1985; Third later Second Secretary (Political/Information) Ottawa 1988; Assistant to Governor British Virgin Islands 1993; Second later First Secretary FCO 1996; On loan to the DTI 1999; m 1982 Karen Cooper (2s 1987, 1991).

Penton-Voak, Martin Eric; First Secretary Vienna (UKDEL) since May 2001; Born 09/11/65; Third later Second Secretary FCO 1991; Moscow 1995; First Secretary FCO 1998; Band D6; m 1994 Lucy Katrina Howarth.

Percy, Michael Vivian; First Secretary FCO since July 2002; Born 09/08/50; DSAO (later FCO) 1968; Paris 1972; Brasilia 1975; Vice-Consul Budapest 1977; FCO 1980; Third Secretary (Commercial) Quito 1983; Third Secretary (Management) Warsaw 1987; FCO 1989; Second Secretary 1991; Deputy Head of Mission Riga 1993; Second Secretary FCO 1994; Second Secretary British Trade International 1998; Band C5; m 1972 Susan Roslyn Penrose (2d 1974, 1981; 1s 1977).

Perkins, Jacqueline Louise (née Gage); Bahrain since October 2003; Born 03/10/64; FCO 1989; Second Secretary 1990; Language Training Cairo 1991; Second Secretary (Chancery/Information) Abu Dhabi 1992; First Secretary FCO 1995; SUPL 1996; First Secretary Cairo 1999; SUPL 2001; First Secretary Cairo 2001; m 1991 Stuart Blair Perkins (1s 1996; 1d 2001).

Perks, Adam Cecil; Second Secretary (Immigration) Moscow since September 2002; Born 03/05/66; FCO (HCS) 1984; Kuwait 1988; FCO 1991; Third Secretary (Consular) Ottawa

1991; Third Secretary FCO 1994; Vice-Consul Luxembourg 1998; Band C4; m 1990 Nicola Rose Wardle (2s 1992, 1996; 1d 1998).

Perrin, Geoffrey Gordon; Second later First Secretary FCO since October 1978; Born 12/08/49; FCO 1971; Geneva 1975; Band C5; m 1977 Heather Beryl Robson (2s 1979, 1984).

Perry, Christopher Ian; Lagos since June 2002; Born 27/05/70; FCO 1990; Brussels (UKREP) 1993; Paris 1995; New Delhi 1999; Band B3; m (1) 1992 Charlotte Dawson (diss 1995) (1d 1992); (2) 1995 Lesa Jayne Elliot (3d 1996, 1997, 1998).

Perry, Susan; Management Officer Bratislava since November 2000; Born 07/03/44; HCS 1965; FCO 1977; Havana 1979; Tunis 1980; Warsaw 1983; Kathmandu 1986; FCO 1990; Kampala 1993; Vice-Consul Shanghai 1997; Band C4.

Perry, Thomas Ian; Consul/Management Officer Bratislava since August 2004; Born 29/03/55; MOD 1972; FCO 1974; New York (UKMIS) 1976; Africa/Middle East Floater 1979; T/D Dubai 1979; Jakarta 1981; FCO 1983; The Hague 1986; FCO 1988; T/D Warsaw 1990; T/D Dar es Salaam 1990; Islamabad 1991; FCO 1995; Jerusalem 1998; T/D Kabul 2001; FCO 2001; Band C4; m 1982 Jeannie Bell (2s 1992, 1995).

Persighetti, Stephen Victor; FCO since March 2002; Born 31/03/56; FCO 1975; Moscow 1977; Beirut 1978; Tokyo 1981; Floater Duties 1983; On loan to the ODA 1985; Third Secretary (Aid) Jakarta 1988; Second Secretary FCO 1991; Second Secretary (Political/Aid) Cape Town 1996; SUPL 1998; Band C5; m 1992 Rozany Deen.

Pert, David John; Kiev since March 2001; Born 21/01/68; Royal Navy 1987-94; FCO 1994; Third Secretary (Political) Sofia 1996; m 1990 Christine Walsh (2s 1991, 1994).

Petch, Eleanor; Prague since August 2001; Born 26/01/77; FCO 1998; Full-Time Language Training 2000; Band C4.

Peters, Mark Crispin; FCO since November 2000; Born 07/06/64; Royal Engineers 1987-94; FCO 1994; Second Secretary (Chancery) Oslo 1996.

Peters, Siobhan; SUPL since April 2004; Born 27/06/70; FCO 1996; Full-Time Language Training 1998; Second Secretary (Economic) later First Secretary (Environment) Beijing 1999; FCO 2003; Band D6; m Mark Davies (1d 1999; 1s 2001).

Petherbridge, Richard Sydney; FCO since January 1996; Born 23/08/55; DHSS 1975; FCO 1980; Nicosia 1982; Seoul 1985; FCO 1987; Prague 1990; Riyadh 1992; Band A2; m 1982 Pauline Joan Mulvey (1s 1984; 1d 1986).

Pethick, Mark Julian; FCO since January 2001; Born 03/04/68; FCO 1990; Karachi 1993; Deputy Head of Mission Minsk 1997; Band C5.

Pettigrew, Marina, MVO (2004); Third Secretary (Visits) Paris since April 2001; Born 17/01/64; FCO 1984; Berne 1986; Budapest 1989; Tel Aviv 1991; Floater Duties 1997; Band B3; m 1999 Mark Pettigrew (1d 2000).

Phillips, Alison Jane (née Francis), OBE (1991); SUPL since January 2001; Born 18/04/56; FCO 1974; New York (UKMIS) 1981; Second Secretary FCO 1982; First Secretary Paris 1986; First Secretary FCO 1990; Band D6; m 1978 Richard Charles Jonathan Phillips, QC.

Phillips, Linda Ann; SUPL since August 2003; Born 17/01/56; FCO 1995; Accra 1997; Washington 2000; Band A2.

Phillips, Patricia Ruth; Deputy Head of Mission Amman since June 2004; Born 11/03/62; MAFF 1984; First Secretary (Trade Policy/Agriculture) Washington 1992; First Secretary FCO 1997; Counsellor (Economic/Trade/Investment) The Hague 2002.

Phillips, Quentin James Kitson; Consul (Political Affairs) Istanbul since January 2004; Born 20/10/63; FCO 1986; Second Secretary (Information) Budapest 1989; Second later First Secretary FCO 1992; First Secretary (Political) Moscow 1995; First Secretary FCO 1996; First Secretary (Political) Kiev 1997; First Secretary FCO 2000; Band D6; m 1989 Gillian Lynne Murray (2d 1993, 1996; 1s 1999).

Phillips, Russell James; FCO since February 2001; Born 24/02/64; FCO 1983; Georgetown 1985; Khartoum 1988; FCO 1991; Bombay 1995; Abuja 1998; Band C4.

Phillips, Tom Richard Vaughan, CMG; UK Special Representative for Afghanistan, August 2002 and Director (South Asia) since January 2003; Born 21/06/50; DHSS 1977; FCO 1983; First Secretary Harare 1985; First Secretary FCO 1988; Counsellor, Consul-General and Deputy Head of Mission Tel Aviv 1990; Counsellor (External) Washington 1993; Counsellor FCO 1997; High Commissioner Kampala 2000; m 1986 Anne Renee Marie de la Motte (2s 1987, 1989).

Phillpotts, Claire Louise; FCO since September 2003; Born 15/07/81; Band C4.

Philpott, Hugh Stanley; Deputy Head of Mission Muscat since October 2001; Born 24/01/61; FCO 1980; Oslo 1982; Budapest 1985; Language Training 1987; Third Secretary (Commercial) Baghdad 1988; FCO 1990 (Second Secretary 1992); Second Secretary (Political/Military) Washington 1993; On loan to DFID 1997; First Secretary FCO 1999; Band D6; m 1984 Janine Frederica Rule (1d 1998).

Philpott, Janine Frederica; Third Secretary (Commercial) Muscat since October 2001; Born 30/01/60; FCO 1980; Brussels (UKDEL NATO) 1982; Budapest 1985; FCO 1986; Baghdad 1988; FCO 1990; Third Secretary (Press) Washington 1993; FCO 1998; Band C4; m 1984 Hugh Stanley Philpott (1d 1998).

Pickering, Helen Mary; FCO since January 2004; Born 10/07/64; FCO 1986; Moscow 1988; Algiers 1989; Geneva 1990; FCO 1993; Second Secretary

(EU) Warsaw 1997; FCO 2001; SUPL 2003; Band D6; m 1996 James Owen (1d 2003).

Pickering, Sara Elizabeth; FCO since January 2002; Born 22/04/67; FCO 1988; Vice-Consul Budapest 1991; FCO 1992; Islamabad 1995; Second Secretary (Commercial) Lagos 1998; Band C5; m 1992 Andrew John Kirkpatrick.

Pickett, Jane Louise (née Houghton), MBE (1994); SUPL since August 2003; Born 05/12/64; FCO 1984; Santiago 1987; FCO 1991; Bogotá 1993; FCO 1995; Band C5; m 1998 Peter Derek Pickett.

Pickup, Lawrence; FCO since October 2003; Born 10/09/52; FCO 1976; Dar es Salaam 1980; Dubai 1982; Floater Duties 1986; On loan to the DTI 1989; FCO/DTI 1991; Consul Warsaw 1993; Deputy Head of Mission Phnom Penh 1997; Deputy Head of Mission Khartoum 2000; T/D Amman 2003; Band C5.

Pierce, Karen Elizabeth; Head of Eastern Adriatic Department, FCO since November 2002; Born 23/09/59; FCO 1981; Language Training 1984; Tokyo 1985; FCO 1987; Private Secretary to the Ambassador Washington 1991 (First Secretary 1994); FCO 1996; Counsellor FCO 2001; m 1987 Charles Fergusson Roxburgh (2s 1991, 1997).

Pigott, Carsten Orthöfer; Consul-General Jedda since June 2003; Born 31/05/53; FCO 1972; Lagos 1975; Language Training MECAS 1977; Language Training FCO 1978; Third Secretary (Commercial) Khartoum 1979; Second Secretary (Commercial) Tripoli 1982; Second Secretary FCO 1984; First Secretary (Chancery) Peking 1987; First Secretary FCO 1991; Deputy Head of Mission Addis Ababa 1993; First Secretary (Chancery) New Delhi 1997; Counsellor FCO 1998; Full-Time Language Training 2002; m 1976 Susan Kathlyn Pugh (1d 1981; 1s 1983).

Pike, Andrew Kerry; Consul New York since December 2003; Born 06/06/64; Dept of Transport 1982; FCO 1984; Sana'a 1985; Warsaw 1990; FCO 1993; Second Secretary (Chancery and Information) Dublin 1998; SUPL 2002; Band D6.

Pilmore-Bedford, Jeremy Patrick; FCO since July 2004; Born 22/08/67; FCO 1990; Singapore 1993; Full-Time Language Training 1995; Third Secretary (Aid) Moscow 1995; FCO 1998; Second Secretary (Economic) Kuala Lumpur 2001; Band D6; m Amanda Joanne West (1d 1997; 1s 1999).

Pinsent, Guy Hume; Second Secretary Warsaw since February 2003; Born 07/03/76; FCO 2000; Full-Time Language Training 2002; Band C4.

Pinson, David Richard; Second Secretary Kabul since May 2003; Born 07/05/77; FCO 2000; Full-Time Language Training FCO 2002; Band C4.

Pinto, Alison Louise (née Johnson); FCO since January 2004; FCO 1989; Vice-Consul Tokyo 1992; Third Secretary (Chancery) Berlin 1995; FCO 1997; SUPL 2002; Band D6; m 2001 Andrew Pinto (1d 2003).

Pisa, Adrian; FCO since September 2004; Born 13/03/72; FCO 2001; Second Secretary New York (UKMIS) 2002; Band C4.

Pitchford, Wendy (née Tivey); Tirana since November 2003; Born 20/07/61; FCO 1995; Copenhagen 1997; Accra 2000; Band A2; m 1999 Colin Pitchford.

Pitts, Barbara Anne, MVO (1989); Copenhagen since October 2000; Born 26/01/54; FCO 1975; Lagos 1975; Moscow 1977; FCO 1979; Nairobi 1981; FCO 1984; Kuala Lumpur 1987; FCO 1990; New Delhi 1997; Band B3.

Plank, John; FCO since January 2003; Born 03/10/64; FCO 1986; Second Secretary (Political) Pretoria 2000; Band C4; m 1997 Corinne Lambshead (1s 2001).

Plant, Michael Geoffrey; Deputy Consul-General Boston since May 2000; Born 12/10/46; Post Office 1964; DSAO 1966; Moscow 1969; Rabat 1970; Peking 1973; Brussels (JAO) 1975; FCO 1978; Banjul 1980; Los Angeles 1984; Second Secretary FCO 1987; Second Secretary (Commercial/Consular) Al Khobar 1990; First Secretary (Management) Yerevan, Tbilisi and Ashgabat 1995; FCO 1998; Band C5; m 1971 Hayfa Theodora Massouh (2d 1972, 1975).

Plater, Stephen James; Consul-General Munich since December 2003; Born 23/01/54; FCO 1976; Second Secretary Tokyo 1978; Second later First Secretary FCO 1982; First Secretary and Head of Chancery Vienna (UKDEL MBFR) 1987; First Secretary Vienna (UKDEL CACN) 1989; First Secretary (Commercial) Tokyo 1990; First Secretary FCO 1995; m 1980 Keiko Kurata (1d 1990).

Platt, David Watson; New Delhi since October 2001; Born 09/04/54; Inland Revenue 1972; FCO 1973; Beirut 1977; Brasilia 1980; Sofia 1981; FCO 1983; Dhaka 1985; Bridgetown 1988; FCO 1992; Dubai 1997; Band B3.

Platt, Janet Elizabeth (née Howells); SUPL since July 2001; Born 26/03/61; Brussels (NATO) 1982; Washington 1985; FCO 1987; Anguilla 1988; FCO 1991; Brussels (UKREP) 1992; Band A2; m 1988 Philip Charles Platt (2s 1987, 1990; 1d 1997).

Plumb, Michael Barry George; Deputy High Commissioner Port Louis since January 2003; Born 16/05/45; DSAO 1965; Kampala 1968; Lahore 1971; FCO 1975; Washington 1977; Canberra 1979; Baghdad 1982; FCO 1986; Jakarta 1990; FCO 1995; Deputy High Commissioner Port Moresby 1997; T/D Jakarta 2001; Management Officer Kuala Lumpur 2002; m 1968 Linda Wills Gledhill (1s 1972; 1d 1975).

Plumbly, Sir Derek John, KCMG (2001), CMG (1991); HM Ambassador Cairo since September 2003; Born 15/05/48; FCO 1972; Reporting Officer New York 1972; FCO 1973; MECAS 1973; Second later First Secretary Jedda 1975; First Secretary Cairo 1977; FCO 1980; First Secretary (Commercial) Washington 1984;

Counsellor and Head of Chancery Riyadh 1988; Counsellor and Head of Chancery New York (UKMIS) 1992; AUS FCO 1996; HM Ambassador Riyadh 2000; m 1979 Nadia Youssef Gohar (1d 1983; 2s 1985, 1987).

Pocock, Dr Andrew John; High Commissioner Dar es Salaam since September 2003; Born 23/08/55; FCO 1981; Second later First Secretary (Commercial) Lagos 1983; First Secretary FCO 1986; First Secretary (Chancery) Washington 1988; First Secretary FCO 1992; Counsellor on loan to the Royal College of Defence Studies 1996; Deputy High Commissioner Canberra 1997; Head of African Department (Southern) FCO 2001; m (1) 1976 Dayalini Pathmanathan (diss); (2) 1995 Julie Eyre-Wilson.

Polatajko, Mark Alexander; FCO since June 2002; Born 16/10/70; FCO 1991; Cairo 1995; New Delhi 1998; Band C4; m 1998 Chloe Robson (1d 2000; 1s 2003).

Poll, Christopher John; FCO since May 2002; Born 29/06/57; Army 1972-84; FCO 1984; Brussels (UKREP) 1988; FCO 1991; Canberra 1994; Deputy High Commissioner Vila 1997; Band C4; m 1988 Gillian Anne Smith (1d 1994; 1s 1998).

Poll, Gillian Anne (née Smith); FCO since September 2002; Born 30/04/58; HCS 1976; FCO 1985; Brussels 1987; Brussels (UKREP) 1990; FCO 1991; SUPL 1994; Band A2; m 1988 Christopher John Poll (1d 1994; 1s 1998).

Pollard, Guy Sephton; SUPL since June 2003; Born 03/06/71; FCO 1991; Islamabad 1995; Third later Second Secretary (Political) Bratislava 1998; Band C4; ptnr, Catherine Louise Nicol (1d 2000; 1s 2002).

Pond, John; Riga since January 2003; Born 22/05/52; Armed Forces 1969-92; FCO 1995; Brussels (UKDEL NATO) 1997; Band A2; m 1973 Catherine Herbert (1s 1971).

Ponsonby, Gareth James; FCO since May 2000; Born 25/05/70; FCO 1991; Islamabad 1996; Band B3; m 1995 Natalie Lalanie Beverley Yeo (1d 2000).

Poole, Christopher George Robert; Deputy Head of Mission and Consul La Paz since June 2003; Born 19/04/52; FCO 1970; Algiers 1973; Brasilia 1974; Rio de Janeiro 1976; Freetown 1978; Paris 1981; Kinshasa 1984; FCO 1988; Third later Second Secretary Antananarivo 1991; Vice-Consul (Commercial/Information) São Paulo 1995; FCO 1998; T/D Second Secretary (Political) Freetown 2000; FCO 2000; Band C5; m 1977 Maria Madalena Gomes Ferreira.

Poole, Christopher James, MBE (1987); Deputy Head of Mission Beirut since July 2003; Born 24/12/46; CRO 1964; FCO 1968; Georgetown 1969; Africa Floater 1969; St Lucia 1971; Bridgetown 1973; FCO 1976; Munich 1979; FCO 1982; Second Secretary Beirut 1985; Second Secretary Luxembourg 1987; EC Monitor Mission

Former Yugoslavia 1992; Deputy Head of Mission Zagreb 1993; Deputy Head of Mission Jerusalem 1995; First Secretary FCO 1996; First Secretary (Commercial) Sarajevo 1998; SUPL (OSCE Albania) 2001; T/D Deputy Head of Mission Tirana 2002; m (1) 1973 Lillian Hodgson (diss) (2d 1979, 1980); (2) 1987 Marilyn Kathleen Povey (diss 1996); (3) 1996 Lynne Diana Merrin.

Pooley, Nigel Arthur, CMG; FCO since August 2001; Born 12/11/61; FCO 1991; Third later Second Secretary (Chancery) Vienna 1994; First Secretary FCO 1998; On secondment to Oxfam 2000; m 1985 Helena Falle (3s 1986, 1991, 1994; 1d 1988).

Porter, Gillian Sarah; FCO since August 2003; Born 07/04/66; FCO 1988; Moscow 1991; Manila 1993; New York (UKMIS) 2000; SUPL 2002; Band A2.

Porter, Neil David; FCO since February 2003; Born 14/04/63; FCO 1982; Riyadh 1985; Budapest 1989; FCO 1992; Third Secretary Johannesburg 1996; Valletta 1999; Band B3; m 1986 Gajetana Dominica Maria de Wit (3s 1988, 1992, 1997; 1d 1989).

Portman, Giles Matthew; First Secretary (External) Brussels (UKREP) since March 2003; Born 25/05/71; Department of Transport 1994; FCO 1995; Second Secretary (Political/Information) Prague 1998; FCO 2002; Band D6.

Poston, James, CBE (2002); Governor Turks and Caicos Islands since November 2002; Born 19/06/45; Third Secretary FCO, Concurrently Third Secretary and Vice-Consul HM Embassy to Chad 1970; Second Secretary and Private Secretary to Head of UKDEL EC Brussels 1971; First Secretary Tel Aviv 1973; FCO 1978; First Secretary (Commercial) Lagos 1982; FCO 1985; Counsellor and Head of Chancery Pretoria 1988; Counsellor FCO 1992; Consul-General Boston 1995; FCO 1999; m (1) 1976 Anna Caroline Bos (diss 1980); (2) Rosemary Fullerton (2d 1987, 1988; 1s 1991).

Potter, Richard William; Counsellor Amman since July 2004; Born 22/05/60; FCO 1983; Third later Second Secretary Riyadh 1985; Second Secretary FCO 1988; First Secretary (Information) Nicosia 1990; First Secretary FCO 1994; First Secretary Sarajevo 1995; FCO 1998; First Secretary Skopje 1999; First Secretary FCO 2002; Band D6.

Potter, Rupert James; On loan to the Cabinet Office since April 2002; Born 14/11/68; FCO 1992; Amman 1995; Third Secretary (Political) Stockholm 1999; Band C4; m 1995 Juliette Wilcox (1s 1998).

Powell, David Herbert; Assistant Director (Personnel Services) FCO since September 2002; Born 29/04/52; MOD 1974; FCO 1984; First Secretary Tokyo 1988; First Secretary FCO 1992; Counsellor on loan to the Cabinet Office 1995; Political Counsellor UKDEL NATO/WEU

Brussels 1997; m 1984 Gillian Mary Croft (1d 1994).

Powell, Hugh Eric; FCO since 2003 October; Born 16/02/67; FCO 1991; Second Secretary Paris 1993; First Secretary FCO 1998; Full-Time Language Training 2000; First Secretary Political (Internal) Berlin 2000; Band D6; m 1993 Catherine Claire Young (2s 1996, 1997).

Powell, Ian Francis, OBE (1995); Deputy High Commissioner Suva and HM Ambassador (non-resident) to Federal States of Micronesia, Palau and Marshall Islands since March 2003; Born 30/12/47; Commonwealth Office (later FCO) 1966; Freetown 1970; Havana 1973; FCO 1975; Stockholm 1978; Dublin 1981; Second Secretary 1983; Second Secretary FCO 1986; First Secretary 1988; First Secretary (Management/HM Consul) Kingston 1989; Deputy Head of Mission Sana'a 1994; First Secretary FCO 1995; Assistant Deputy Governor Gibraltar 1998; m 1969 Priscilla Ann Fenton (2d 1974, 1980).

Powell, Martin; FCO since April 1998; Born 21/10/46; FCO 1969; Warsaw 1973; FCO 1974; Brussels 1982; FCO 1985; Second Secretary Singapore 1988; FCO 1991; Dubai 1994; m (1) 1972 Susan Kay Bower (diss); (2) 1982 Patricia Helen Scruby (1d 1985; 1s 1987).

Powell, Richard Stephen; Deputy Head of Mission Helsinki since June 2003; Born 19/10/59; FCO 1981; Third later Second Secretary Helsinki 1983; First Secretary FCO 1988; First Secretary (Science) Tokyo 1992; CDA Imperial College London 1996; FCO 1997.

Power, Anne Maria; New York since March 2002; Born 14/08/65; FCO 1989; Strasbourg UKDEL 1992; Consulate-General Geneva 1993; Strasbourg UKDEL 1993; SUPL 1996; FCO 1999; Band C4.

Power, Carmel Angela; Copenhagen since September 2001; Born 30/10/63; FCO 1990; Third Secretary (Political) Vienna (UKDEL) 1992; Vice-Consul (Commercial) Damascus 1995; FCO 1997; Band D6.

Prentice, Christopher Norman Russell; HM Ambassador Amman since June 2002; Born 05/09/54; FCO 1977; Language Training MECAS 1978; Third later Second Secretary Kuwait 1980; First Secretary on loan to the Cabinet Office 1983; First Secretary Washington 1985; First Secretary FCO 1989; Deputy Head of Mission Budapest 1994; Counsellor FCO 1998; m 1978 Marie-Josephine (Nina) King (2s 1981, 1988; 2d 1982, 1985).

Preston, James David; Copenhagen since May 2003; Born 21/04/68; FCO 1987; Helsinki 1994; FCO 1997; Band C4; m 1992 Kim Dickinson (2s 1995, 1997).

Preston, Joseph Raymond; Deputy Head of Mission Tirana since March 2003; Born 01/06/61; FCO 1980; Dhaka 1983; Kathmandu 1985; Nicosia 1989; FCO 1993; Third Secretary (Commercial) Islamabad 1995; FCO 1999; On loan to BTI (Institute of Export) 1999; Band C5; m 1993 Sandra Elizabeth Cook.

Preston, Sandra Elizabeth (née Cook); Tirana since June 2003; Born 12/06/64; FCO 1987; Nicosia 1990; FCO 1992; Islamabad 1996; FCO 1999; Full-Time Language Training (Albanian) 2002; Band B3; m 1993 Joseph Raymond Preston.

Preston, William Edward Johnston, LVO (2004); First Secretary FCO since August 2000; Born 07/07/47; FCO 1965; Ankara 1969; Kinshasa 1972; FCO 1974; Rabat 1976; Oslo 1979; Second Secretary (Admin) Moscow 1983; Second Secretary FCO 1985; Second Secretary (Commercial) Port of Spain 1988; First Secretary (Commercial) Bucharest 1992; First Secretary Nicosia 1996; m 1969 Anne Kathleen Smith (1s 1974).

Price, Adrian James; Port of Spain since August 2003; Born 25/04/65; FCO 1982; Ekaterinburg 1999; FCO 2001; Band A2; m 2000 Tatyana Arkhipova (1d 2002).

Price, Andrew Haydn; First Secretary (Political) The Hague since July 2002; Born 09/11/63; MAFF 1985; FCO 1997; On attachment to Netherlands Foreign Ministry 2002; Band D6; m 1993 Amanda Kirby (2s 1995, 1998; 1d 2000).

Price, Denis Charles; Berlin since January 2002; Born 20/04/52; Royal Electrical and Mechanical Engineers 1973-95; FCO 2000; Band C4; m 1977 Jane Ann (1s 1978).

Price, Kenneth George; FCO since August 2002; Born 12/04/65; FCO 1983; Bonn 1985; Accra 1988; FCO 1991; Third Secretary (Political/Aid) Almaty 1994; World Wide Floater Duties 1997; Second Secretary FCO 1998; Deputy Head of Mission Kinshasa 2001; Band C4.

Price, Sarah Helena; FCO since April 2004; Born 04/06/66; FCO 1990; Second Secretary Helsinki (UKDEL CSCE) 1992; Second Secretary (Economic/KHF) Prague 1993; First Secretary FCO 1996; Secondment to the EU Secretariat of the Finnish Ministry for Foreign Affairs 1999; Full-Time Language Training 2000; Deputy Head of Mission Belgrade 2000.

Price, Siân Rhyannon; Assistant Private Secretary to Minister of State FCO since August 2001; Born 17/02/76; FCO 2000; Band C4.

Price, Tristan Robert Julian; Head of Resource Budgeting Department, FCO since April 2003; Born 24/11/66; Economic Assistant 1993; Economic Adviser 1995; SUPL 1999; m 1988 Judith Ann Torrance (1d 1996; 1s 1998).

Priest, Timothy Ian; Counsellor FCO since October 2003; Born 27/10/47; FCO 1972; Vienna 1975; First Secretary (Chancery) Helsinki 1981; FCO 1985; First Secretary (Chancery/Information) Athens 1989; Counsellor FCO 1993; Counsellor (Political) Helsinki 1999; m Teresa Jean Bagnall (2d 1975, 1980; 2s 1978, 1987).

Priestley, Andrew Howard James; FCO since March 2003; Born 10/12/76; Band C4.

Priestley, Carol Ann (née Edwards); First Secretary (Management) Moscow since July 2003; Born 11/11/53; FCO 1974; Paris 1976; Düsseldorf 1979; Kathmandu 1980; FCO 1982; Dhaka 1985; Auckland 1989; Second Secretary FCO 1993; Second Secretary (Management) later HM Consul Washington 1997; m 1976 Lawrence Minton Priestley.

Priestley, Philip John, CBE (1996); High Commissioner Belmopan since July 2001; Born 29/08/46; FCO 1969; Third Secretary Sofia 1971; Third later Second Secretary Kinshasa 1973; First Secretary FCO 1976; Head of Chancery Wellington 1979; First Secretary FCO 1984; Counsellor (Commercial) Manila 1987; HM Ambassador Libreville 1990; CDA Harvard University 1991; Consul-General Geneva 1992; Head, North America Department FCO 1996; m 1972 Christine Rainforth (1d 1976; 1s 1978).

Prime, Ashley Walter John; First Secretary Rome since March 2003; Born 06/08/59; FCO 1978; Bonn 1980; Kingston 1983; Peking 1986; FCO 1989; Full-Time Language Training 1993; Milan 1993; Rome 1995; Full-Time Language Training 1996; Deputy Consul-General Guangzhou 1996; On loan to Invest UK 1999; FCO 2001; Band D6; m 1997 Silvia Ardizzone (1s 1999).

Pring, Alison June; First Secretary (Commercial) Berne since October 1999; Born 18/06/61; FCO 1983; SUPL 1983; FCO 1984; Third Secretary Brussels 1986; Third later Second Secretary Caracas 1989; Second Secretary FCO 1991; Full-Time Language Training 1995; Second Secretary (Commercial) and Deputy Head of Mission St Petersburg 1996; Band C5.

Pring, Mary; FCO since January 1999; Born 29/06/60; FCO 1991; Full-Time Language Training 1993; Language Training Cairo 1994; Jerusalem 1995; Band B3.

Pringle, Anne Fyfe, CMG (2004); Director for Strategy and Information FCO since September 2004; Born 13/01/55; FCO 1977; Moscow 1980; San Francisco 1983; Second Secretary Brussels (UKREP) 1986; Second later First Secretary FCO 1987; First Secretary on secondment to European Political Cooperation Secretariat 1991; First Secretary later Counsellor FCO 1994; Full-Time Language Training 2001; HM Ambassador Prague 2001; m 1987 Bleddyn Glynne Leyshon Phillips.

Pringle, Julia Margaret Georgina (née Wright); Luxembourg since June 2004; Born 28/03/48; FCO 1966-71; Metropolitan Police 1971; FCO 1991; SUPL 1993-98; Bogotá 1998; Band A2; m 1971 Raymond Elliot Pringle (diss 2003) (1d 1981).

Pringle, Raymond Elliott; SUPL since July 2004; Born 28/11/51; Department of Employment 1968-69; FCO 1970; Brussels (UKREP) 1972; Quito 1975; FCO 1978; Bilbao 1981; Barcelona 1983; Second Secretary (Chancery/Information) Lilongwe 1986; Second later First Secretary FCO 1989; Deputy Consul-General and Consul (Commercial) San Francisco 1993; SUPL 1999; First Secretary (Management) Washington 1999; First Secretary (Trade & Investment) Copenhagen 2001; m (1) 1971 Julia Margaret Georgina Wright (diss 2003) (1d 1981); (2) 2003 Mary Ellen Sullivan Murphy.

Pritchard, Grant; Pitcairn since March 2004; Born 02/06/70; FCO 1990; Peking 1994; Third Secretary (Management) and Vice-Consul Kuwait 1997; Third Secretary Vienna (OSCE) 2000; m 1996 Rebecca Louise Williams (diss 2001).

Proctor, Jacqueline (née Jones); FCO since April 2002; Born 03/10/71; FCO 1991; Athens 1993; SUPL 1996; Geneva (UKDis) 1996; Kampala 1999; Band B3; m 1996 Matthew Joel Proctor (1d 2003).

Proctor, Matthew Joel; FCO since May 2002; Born 16/07/71; FCO 1991; SUPL 1993; Geneva (UKMIS) 1996; Kampala 1999; Band B3; m 1996 Jaqueline Jones.

Prodger, David Wilce; First Secretary (Commercial) Buenos Aires since March 2002; Born 28/09/66; FCO 1999; Band D6; m 1993 Tiffany Darwent (2s 1997, 2000).

Proudfoot, David Owen; Baku since August 2002; Born 15/04/71; HCS 1991; FCO 1995; Sarajevo 1998; FCO 2001; Band B3.

Prouten, Matthew David, MBE (1996); Tokyo since October 2002; Born 10/03/69; FCO 1988; Tokyo 1992; FCO 1996; Third Secretary (Political) Vilnius 1997; FCO 2000; Full-Time Language Training FCO 2000; Band B3; m 1994 Akino Matsumoto (1s 1997; 1d 2000).

Pruce, Daniel Robert; On loan to No. 10 Downing Street since January 2002; Born 24/07/66; FCO 1990; Brussels (UKREP) 1993; FCO 1996; First Secretary (Information) Brussels (UKREP) 1999; Band D6.

Pryce, Andrew William; Second Secretary (Political) Helsinki since December 2003; Born 09/02/70; FCO 1988; Washington 1991; FCO 1993; Karachi 1994; FCO 1997; Band C4; m 1993 Corienne Marie Madden.

Publicover, Ralph Martin; FCO since January 2003; Born 02/05/52; FCO 1976; Language Training MECAS 1977; Second later First Secretary Dubai 1979; First Secretary (Economic) Ottawa 1981; First Secretary on loan to the Cabinet Office 1985; FCO 1987; First Secretary (Chancery) Washington 1989; First Secretary FCO 1992; Full-Time Language Training 1994; Bucharest 1994; Deputy Head of Mission Lisbon 1999; m 1973 Rosemary Sheward (2d 1979, 1988; 1s 1983).

Pugh, David Evan; FCO since July 2000; Born 26/04/51; FCO 1982; Pretoria 1983; FCO 1985; Cairo 1988; FCO 1991; Tokyo 1992; FCO 1995; Vienna 1997; Band C5; m (1) 1976 Bethan Jones (diss 1989) (4d 1980, 1982, 1984, 1986); (2) 1992 Sally Anne Jones.

Pullen, Roderick Allen; HM Ambassador Harare since July 2004; Born 11/04/49; MOD 1975; Second Secretary Brussels (UKDEL NATO) 1978; MOD 1980; First Secretary Madrid (UKDEL CSCE) 1981; FCO 1982; DHC Suva 1984; First Secretary FCO 1988; Counsellor (Technology) Paris 1990; Deputy High Commissioner Nairobi 1994; Deputy High Commissioner Lagos 1997; FCO 2000; High Commissioner Accra 2000; m 1971 Karen Lesley Sketchley (1d 1975; 4s 1978, 1989, twins 1994).

Purdon, Michael; FCO since October 2003; Born 01/05/80; Band C4.

Purdy, Samantha Louise, MVO (1996); First Secretary FCO since July 1999; Born 22/08/71; FCO 1992; Full-Time Language Training FCO 1994; Full-Time Language Training Bangkok 1995; Second Secretary (Political/Information) Bangkok 1996.

Purves, Michael; First Secretary (Management) Berlin since March 2004; Born 03/11/57; FCO 1975; New Delhi 1978; ME Floater 1982; Mogadishu 1983; FCO 1986; Third later Second Secretary (Economic/Aid) Kuala Lumpur 1989; Second Secretary (Management) Colombo 1992; First Secretary FCO 1996; First Secretary (Commercial) and Deputy Head of Mission Doha 2000; m 1985 Ruth Joan Goodwin (1d 1986; 1s 1990).

Puryer, Stuart John; Consul Copenhagen since May 2004; Born 03/06/67; FCO 1987; Copenhagen 1990; Ljubljana 1993; FCO 1996; DFID 1997; FCO 1998; Band D6.

Pyle, Nicholas John, MBE (1999); SUPL since May 2004; Born 09/12/60; FCO 1981; Geneva (UKMIS) 1984; Kabul 1986; Jedda 1990; FCO 1992 (Second Secretary 1995); Second Secretary (Immigration) Colombo 1996; Second Secretary Bridgetown 2000; Band C4; m 1993 Rosamund Day (2s 1995, 2001; 1d 1999).

Pyper, Alan; Berlin since June 2001; Born 13/06/62; DSS 1990-97; FCO 1999; Band A2; m 1995 Patrocinia Haban.

Q

Quantrill, Clara Jane; Second Secretary (Political/Economic) Kingston since December 2002; Born 06/08/68; FCO 1999; Band C4.

Quarrey, David; FCO since October 2003; Born 06/01/66; FCO 1994; Second Secretary (Political) Harare 1995; First Secretary (Political) New Delhi 2000.

Quayle, Quinton Mark; HM Ambassador Bucharest since November 2002; Born 05/06/55; FCO 1977; Language Training 1978; Third Secretary (Chancery) Bangkok 1979 (Second Secretary 1981); FCO 1983 (First Secretary 1984); ENA Paris 1986; First Secretary Paris 1987; First Secretary FCO 1991; First Secretary seconded to

Price Waterhouse 1993; Counsellor FCO 1994; Deputy Head of Mission Jakarta 1996; Director British Time International 1999; International Group Director Trade Partners UK 1999; m 1979 Alison Marshall (2s 1982, 1985).

Quinn, James Gregory; Deputy Head of Mission Minsk since February 2004; Born 16/06/71; Second Secretary FCO 1999; Language Training 1999; Second Secretary (Political/PPA) Accra 2000; Band C4; m 1995 Wendy Ann Dackombe.

Quinn, Jean Margaret (née Leiper); FCO since May 2003; Born 21/03/53; FCO 1975; Abidjan 1978; Brasilia 1982; Second Secretary FCO 1984; SUPL 1990; FCO 1994; Second Secretary (Commercial/ECM) Tunis 1996; Second Secretary (Commercial/Management) Riga 2000; Band C4; m 1985 Peter Nugent Quinn (1d 1987; 1s 1989).

Quinn, Lorraine; New Delhi since April 2004; Born 25/06/66; FCO 1991; Bonn 1993; Gibraltar 1997; Helsinki 2000; FCO 2002; Band B3; m (1) 1986 Martin Quinn (diss 2000) (1s 1988); (2) 2000 Stephen Andrew Pettigrew.

R

Raab, Dominic; First Secretary (Legal) The Hague since March 2003; Born 25/02/74; Assistant Legal Adviser FCO 2000.

Raby, Charlotte Jane; FCO since May 2002; Born 05/05/72; HCS FCO 1992; FCO 1996; Peking 1998; Band A2.

Rack, Martin Elliott; Second Secretary FCO since May 2001; Born 30/12/73; FCO 1997; Second Secretary (Political) The Hague 1999; Band C4.

Radcliffe, Adam, MBE (2002); Third Secretary (Consular) Washington since June 2002; Born 10/06/67; FCO 1988; Geneva (UKMIS) 1990; Istanbul 1993; FCO 1996; Band B3; m 1992 Julie Anne Nichols (1s 1994; 2d 1995, 1996).

Rae, Karen (née Hooper); FCO since August 2002; Born 28/05/60; FCO 1980; Port Stanley 1983; Berne 1984; Cairo 1987; FCO 1990; Third Secretary (Consular) Islamabad 1993; Language Training 1997; Second Secretary (Commercial) Prague 1997; Band C5; m 1984 Thomas Park Rae (1d 1993).

Raine, John Andrew, OBE (2003); Counsellor FCO since April 2004; Born 12/07/62; FCO 1984; Language Training 1986; Second Secretary (Information) Kuwait 1988; First Secretary FCO 1991; First Secretary (Political) Damascus 1994; First Secretary Riyadh 1997; FCO 2000; Counsellor Baghdad 2003; Band D6.

Raine, Sarah Emily; FCO since March 2004; Born 16/07/76; FCO 1999; Full-Time Language Training 2001; Second Secretary (Political) Sarajevo 2002; Band C4.

Rajguru, Harish L; FCO since April 2003; Born 23/04/61; HCS cadre of the FCO 1989; FCO 1990; Sofia 1992; Kiev 1994; FCO 1996; Floater

Duties 1999; Ekaterinburg 2001; SUPL 2002; Band B3.

Rakestraw, Mark Andrew; Consul Cairo since April 2004; Born 30/11/67; FCO 1988; Athens 1990; FCO 1993; Full-Time Language Training 1996; Vice-Consul Lisbon 1997; Second later First Secretary FCO 2001; Band C5; ptnr, Lorna Wood.

Ralph, Richard Peter, CMG (1997), CVO (1991); HM Ambassador Lima since May 2003; Born 27/04/46; Third Secretary FCO 1969; Third later Second Secretary Vientiane 1970; Second later First Secretary (Information) Lisbon 1974; First Secretary FCO 1977; First Secretary and Head of Chancery Harare 1981; First Secretary later Counsellor FCO 1985; Counsellor Washington 1989; HM Ambassador Riga 1993; HM Governor Stanley 1996; HM Ambassador Bucharest 1999; m (1) 1970 (diss 2001) (1s 1970; 1d 1974); (2) 2002 Jemma Victoria Elizabeth Marlor.

Ram, Sutnam; ECO New Delhi since December 2001; Born 12/02/61; FCO 1999; Band B3; m 1987 Reeta Vaish (2d 1987, 1998).

Rampling, Christopher Maxwell; Second Secretary (Political/PPA) Tripoli since May 2002; Born 08/10/73; FCO 1999; Full-Time Language Training (Arabic) 2000; Band C4.

Ramsay, Paul Andrew, MBE (1988); First Secretary FCO since April 2000; Born 10/10/55; FCO 1975; East Berlin 1977; Istanbul 1979; Brussels (UKDEL NATO) 1981; Tehran 1984; FCO 1987 (Second Secretary 1990); Second Secretary Madrid 1992; First Secretary (Management) Singapore 1997; m 1980 Carey-Jane Lambert (1d 1987; 2s 1989, 1993).

Ramscar, Michael Charles; Counsellor FCO since December 2000; Born 26/02/48; Second Secretary FCO 1975; Second Secretary (Economic) Lagos 1977; First Secretary (Economic) Brasilia 1979; First Secretary FCO 1982; Madrid 1986; San José 1989; First Secretary FCO 1991; Counsellor Madrid 1997; m 1970 Janis Lemon (2s 1976, 1981).

Ramsden, Sir John (Charles Josslyn), Bt; FCO since April 2003; Born 19/08/50; FCO 1975; Third later Second Secretary Dakar 1976; First Secretary Vienna (UKDEL MBFR) 1979; First Secretary, Head of Chancery and Consul Hanoi 1980; First Secretary FCO 1982; On loan to HM Treasury 1988; First Secretary FCO 1988; Counsellor and Deputy Head of Mission East Berlin later British Embassy Berlin Office 1990; Counsellor FCO 1993; Deputy Head of Mission Geneva (UKMIS) 1996; Head of Central and North West European Department FCO 1999; m 1985 Jane Bevan (2d 1987, 1989).

Ramsey, Patricia Anne; FCO since February 2004; Born 09/01/48; FO 1967; Brussels (UKDEL EEC) 1969; Rio de Janeiro 1972; FCO 1974; Athens 1980; Geneva (UKMIS) 1983; FCO 1986; Paris 1987; SUPL 1991; FCO 1992; SUPL 1997; Second later First Secretary (Political) Berlin 1998; SUPL 2003; Band D6; m 1990 Paul Lever.

Rangarajan, Francis Vijay Narasimhan; Deputy Head of Mission Mexico City since September 2003; Born 22/09/69; FCO IGC Unit, EUD(I) 1995; Second later First Secretary (Trade Policy and Antici) Brussels (UKREP) 1997; Private Secretary to Permanent Under-Secretary of State 1999; FCO 1999; m 2000 Rosie Francis Cox.

Rankin, John James; Consul-General Boston since November 2003; Born 12/03/57; Assistant, later Senior Legal Adviser FCO 1988; Legal Adviser Geneva (UKMIS & UKDIS) 1991; Legal Counsellor FCO 1995; First Secretary FCO 1996; First Secretary Dublin 1998; Counsellor and Deputy Head of Mission Dublin 1999; m 1987 Lesley Marshall (2d 1989, 1991; 1s 1993).

Rapp, Stephen Robert; Deputy Head of Mission Ashgabat since December 2002; Born 09/03/52; Home Office 1986; FCO 1986; Accra 1988; Hanoi 1992; FCO 1994; Vice-Consul Jedda 1996; Ekaterinburg 1999; Vice-Consul Lahore 2001; Band C4; m 1978 Judy Elizabeth Flewett.

Ratcliffe, Deborah; FCO since September 2001; Born 06/04/62; FCO 1980; Geneva (UKMIS) 1982; Harare 1985; ECO Manila 1988; Third Secretary - VC/ECM Hanoi 1995; Third Secretary (Management) Kingston 1997; Second Secretary (Management) T/D Islamabad 2001; Band C4.

Ratcliffe, Yvonne; FCO since December 2003; Born 18/06/62; FCO 1988; Athens 1989; Peking 1992; FCO 1994; Prague 1996; T/D Khartoum 1999; Singapore 2000; Band B3.

Raven, Martin Clark; On loan to the DTI since May 2001; Born 10/03/54; FCO 1976; Third Secretary Lagos 1978; FCO 1979; Third later Second Secretary New Delhi 1979; Second later First Secretary FCO 1983; First Secretary New York (UKMIS) 1988; First Secretary FCO 1993; Counsellor FCO 1996; Counsellor Stockholm 1998; m 1978 Philippa Michaela Morrice Ruddick (2s 1982, 1984).

Rawbone, Jane Lynn; FCO (Wilton Park) since January 2003; Born 21/03/53; FCO 1976; Vienna (UKDEL MBFR) 1977; Helsinki 1980; FCO 1982; Mexico City 1984; New York (UKMIS) 1988; Madrid 1991; FCO 1993; Kuala Lumpur 1996; Canberra 2000; Band B3.

Rawlings, Menna Frances; Private Secretary to the Permanent Under Secretary, FCO since September 2002; Born 16/09/67; FCO 1989; Third later Second Secretary (Institutions) Brussels (UKREP) 1991; Second Secretary (Economic/Environment) Nairobi 1993; FCO 1997; SUPL 1998; First Secretary Tel Aviv 1998; m 2000 Mark John Rawlings (2d 1998, 2000).

Rawlins, Helen Catherine; FCO since July 2002; Born 31/07/64; FCO 1986; Bonn 1988; Manila 1991; Second Secretary FCO 1994; Second Secretary (Consular) Kampala 1998.

Rawlins, Isabel May; FCO since September 2003; Born 24/07/79; Band B3.

Rawlinson, Colin James; Consul-General Vancouver since November 2002; Born 21/02/46; FCO 1967; Reykjavik 1968; Nicosia 1971; Hamburg 1973; Second Secretary FCO 1976; Copenhagen 1979; Second Secretary (Commercial) New Delhi 1981; First Secretary FCO 1984; New York (UKMIS) 1993; FCO 1994; Consul-General Bordeaux 1998; m 1966 The Hon Catharine Julia Trend (2d 1967, 1969).

Rawlinson, Ivor Jon, OBE (1988); FCO since March 2002; Born 24/01/42; FO 1964; Warsaw 1966; Bridgetown 1969; Second Secretary FCO 1971; Assistant Private Secretary to Minister of State FCO 1973; Second Secretary (Economic) Paris 1974; First Secretary FCO 1978; First Secretary (Commercial) Mexico City 1980; Consul Florence 1984; First Secretary later Counsellor FCO 1988; Royal College of Defence Studies 1993; Consul-General Montreal 1993; HM Ambassador Tunis 1999 - 2002; m 1976 Catherine Paule Caudal (1s 1980; 2d 1977, 1983).

Rawlinson, Timothy Simeon; First Secretary FCO since May 2000; Born 12/01/62; Second Secretary FCO 1988; Second later First Secretary (Information) Lagos 1991; First Secretary FCO 1993; First Secretary (Political) Stockholm 1996; Band D6; m 1998 Janet Mary Cooper.

Rayner, Robert Alan; Deputy Consul-General and Director (Trade and Investment) Hong Kong since October 2003; Born 14/12/50; FCO 1968; Islamabad 1972; Language Training 1974; Tokyo 1975; DOT 1979; FCO 1981; Second Secretary (Chancery/Information) and Vice-Consul Lima 1984; FCO 1987; Consul (Commercial) Osaka 1989; First Secretary (Press and Public Affairs) Tokyo 1995; First Secretary FCO 1999; Counsellor (Atomic Energy) Tokyo 2000; m 1984 Dawn Carol Richards (1d 1991).

Rea, Elizabeth Rose, MBE (1993); FCO since May 1996; Born 31/10/54; FCO 1976; Luxembourg 1978; Lima 1981; Washington 1984; FCO 1987; Brussels (UKREP) 1992; Band C4.

Read, Rachel Frances; Pretoria since January 2003; Born 23/10/65; FCO 1989; Cairo 1991; Sofia 1995; Grand Turk 1998; Band B3.

Reader, David George; HM Ambassador Phnom Penh since January 2005; Born 01/10/47; CRO, DSAO and FCO 1964; Warsaw 1969; Paris 1972; Bucharest 1974; FCO 1976; Kinshasa 1979; Kathmandu 1982; Second Secretary FCO 1984; Vice-Consul (Commercial) Brisbane 1987; First Secretary (Management) and Consul Belgrade 1992; First Secretary FCO 1996; First Secretary Cairo 1998; High Commissioner Mbabane 2001; m 1969 Elaine McKnight (1s 1975; 1d 1980).

Rebecchi, Silvano Marco Raffaele; Second Secretary (Commercial) Helsinki since August 2000; Born 14/08/52; Department of Education and Science 1972; FCO 1975; Baghdad 1977; Valletta 1981; Dhaka 1984; FCO 1986; Paris 1990; Amman 1992; Cairo 1992; Second Secretary FCO

1996; Full-Time Language Training 2000; m 1984 Eileen Zammit (2s 1985, 1987).

Reddaway, David Norman, CMG (1993), MBE (1980); High Commissioner Ottawa since August 2003; Born 26/04/53; FCO 1975; Language Training SOAS 1976; Language Training Iran 1977; Third later Second Secretary (Commercial) Tehran 1977; Second later First Secretary (Chancery) Tehran 1978; First Secretary (Chancery) Madrid 1980; First Secretary FCO 1985; Private Secretary to Minister of State 1986; First Secretary (Chancery) New Delhi 1988; Chargé d'Affaires a.i. Tehran 1990 (Counsellor 1991); Minister and Deputy Head of Mission Buenos Aires 1993; FCO 1997; Director, Public Services 1999; UK Special Representative for Afghanistan, with personal rank of Ambassador and Visiting Fellow at Harvard University 2002; m 1981 Roshan Taliyeh Firouz (2s 1983, 1996; 1d 1987).

Redden, Michael James; Management Office Gaborone since January 2002; Born 22/02/70; DHSS 1987; FCO 1990; Khartoum 1994; FCO 1997; Colombo 1998; Band B3; m 1995 Nicola Jane Elizabeth Sharp (1d 1997).

Reddicliffe, Paul, OBE; Senior Principal Research Officer FCO since August 1997; Born 17/03/45; FCO 1977; First Secretary Canberra 1985; First Secretary FCO 1989; HM Ambassador Phnom Penh 1994; Band D7; m 1974 Wee Siok Boi (2s 1977, 1979).

Redshaw, Tina Susan; HM Ambassador Dili since January 2004; Born 25/01/61; FCO 1999; First Secretary (Political) Beijing 2000; Band D6; (1d 2001).

Reed, Pamela Karen (née Williams); FCO since August 1999; Born 10/05/70; HCS 1989; FCO 1994; Brasilia later São Paulo 1997; Band A2; m 1997 Antony Jason Reed.

Reeve, Charles Michael Campbell; First Secretary Skopje since September 2002; Born 12/07/71; Second Secretary FCO 1997; Second Secretary (Political/Military) Banja Luka 1999; Full-Time Language Training 2001; First Secretary (Political) Zagreb 2001; Band D6.

Reeve, Richard Robert; Counsellor FCO since June 2000; Born 28/07/48; FCO 1971; Third later Second Secretary Singapore 1973; Language Training Cambridge University 1975; Language Training Hong Kong 1976; Trade Commissioner Hong Kong 1977; First Secretary FCO 1981; First Secretary Hong Kong 1983; First Secretary FCO 1987; Counsellor Berne 1996; m 1971 Monique Marie-Louise Moggio (2s 1974, 1977).

Reeves, Ceinwen Mary; FCO since September 2001; Born 09/06/57; FCO 1976; SUPL 1976; FCO 1979; Bonn 1982; Lilongwe 1984; Paris 1987; FCO 1989; Vice-Consul Sofia 1993; Second Secretary (Commercial) Beijing 1995; FCO 1998; SUPL 2000; m 2003 Richard Brian George Izzard.

Regan, Michael John; Counsellor FCO since September 1998; Born 17/08/55; FCO 1983; Second later First Secretary Kabul 1986; FCO 1988; First Secretary (Chancery/Economic) Dubai 1989; First Secretary FCO 1991; Bangkok 1995; m 1986 Carolyn Gaye Black (2s 1987, 1989).

Rehal, Opinder Kumar; FCO since February 1995; Born 15/09/48; FCO 1979; Bonn 1982; FCO 1985; Islamabad 1989; FCO 1990; Canberra 1992; Band C5; m 1974 Jagdeep Nandra (1s 1975 (dec'd 1990); 1d 1978).

Reid, Gordon Bryden; Counsellor (Commercial) Kuala Lumpur since May 2003; Born 09/05/56; FCO 1980; Second Secretary Budapest 1982; First Secretary FCO 1985; First Secretary (Chancery) Santiago 1988; First Secretary (Chancery) Islamabad 1990; First Secretary FCO 1994; Deputy Head of Mission Budapest 1998; m 1979 Marinella Ferro (2s 1982, 1988; 1d 1984).

Reid, Norma Fraser; FCO since December 2000; Born 19/08/43; Saigon 1968; Rome 1970; Bucharest 1971; FCO 1973; HCS 1975; Latin America Floater 1977; Peking 1979; FCO 1980; Moscow 1983; FCO 1984; Rome 1986; FCO 1988; Bucharest 1993; Third Secretary (Consular) Nicosia 1997.

Reid, Robert Lloyd; Washington since December 2002; Born 12/06/59; FCO (HCS) 1995; Kingston 1999; Band A2; m 1997 Janet Manning (1s 1989; 1d 1996).

Reid, Thomas Samuel; Vice-Consul Istanbul since June 2003; Born 28/12/76; FCO 2000; T/D Second Secretary Harare 2002; Band C4.

Reidy, Andrea Jane; First Secretary (International Liaison) Baghdad since July 2004; Born 24/11/58; FCO 1995; Second Secretary (KHF) Bratislava 1997; Deputy High Commissioner Freetown 2000; FCO 2003; (1d 1981).

Reilly, Julian; FCO since June 2000; Born 03/02/71; FCO 1993; Full-Time Language Training 1994; Full-Time Language Training Cairo 1995; Second Secretary (Chancery) Khartoum 1996; Nairobi (Khartoum Unit) 1998; Deputy Head of Mission Khartoum 1999; Band D6.

Reilly, Michael David; Head of South East Asia Department since February 2003; Born 01/03/55; FCO 1978; Language Training Seoul 1979; First Secretary FCO 1984; First Secretary Paris (UKDEL OECD) 1988; First Secretary (Political) and Consul Seoul 1991; First Secretary FCO 1994; Deputy Head of Mission Manila 1996; Head of Cultural Relations Department FCO 2000; m 1981 Won-Kyong Kang (1d 1987; 1s 1992).

Reilly, Michael Patrick; First Secretary (Political/Economic) Bucharest since March 2003; Born 30/07/66; FCO 1984; Bonn 1987; Bombay 1990; FCO 1991; Third Secretary (Development) Lilongwe 1994; FCO 1997; Band D6; m 1991 Andrea Louise Bradley.

Reilly, Patrick; First Secretary (Political) Dublin since January 2002; Born 03/11/70; FCO 1995;

Second Secretary (Political) Cape Town 1997; FCO 2000; Band C4.

Reilly, Richard John; Peking since March 2002; Born 17/09/73; FCO 1999; Band A2; m 2001 Angela Forsyth.

Reilly, Thomas Saul Anthony; FCO since September 2003; Born 17/11/70; Second Secretary FCO 1998; Second Secretary (Political) Buenos Aires 2001; Band C4.

Remmington, Gillian Elizabeth; FCO since January 2004; Born 26/02/56; FCO 1984; Quito 1985; Berne 1988; World Wide Floater Duties 1991; FCO 1993; Nicosia 1997; Hong Kong 2000; Band B3.

Rennie, Alexander Thomson Inglis; Brasilia since February 2004; Born 03/03/53; FCO 1998; Bangkok 2000; Full-Time Language Training 2003; Band A2.

Rennie, Nadia Jane; FCO since October 2002; Born 30/09/71; FCO 1990; Brussels (UKDEL NATO) 1994; Kiev 2000; Band C4.

Rennie, Paul Joseph Gordon; Second Secretary (Chancery) Brasilia since August 2003; Born 10/02/78; FCO 2001; Band C4.

Rennie, Piers Damian Lee; FCO since March 2003; Born 20/04/74; Band C4.

Reuter, Alan; Consul Milan since February 2000; Born 05/07/51; FCO 1970; Bucharest 1972; Kaduna 1974; Frankfurt 1978; Gaborone 1980; FCO 1982; Tel Aviv 1986; Third Secretary (Commercial) Kuala Lumpur 1988; Second Secretary FCO 1992; Second Secretary (Consular/Immigration) Lagos 1995; Nairobi 1998; FCO 1999; Band C4; m (1) 1973 Christine Caton; (2) 1982 Brenda Yvonne Mary Neumann (1s 1983; 1d 1985).

Rey, Rosemary; SUPL since April 1996; Born 14/03/55; FCO 1974; Cayman Islands 1976; FCO 1978; Gibraltar 1979; Bogotá 1981; FCO 1986; Bogotá 1988; Caracas 1990; Band A2; m 1983 Alvaro Rey Romero (2s 1991, 1995).

Reynolds, Colin; Washington since August 2004; Born 03/07/71; FCO 1990; Nicosia 1992; Africa/Middle East Floater 1995; Assistant Private Secretary to Minister of State, FCO 1999; First Secretary 2000; Board Chair and Head of Professional Development Operations Team, FCO 2003.

Reynolds, Gillian Marjorie; FCO since October 1993; Born 16/10/50; FCO 1976; New Delhi 1977; Budapest 1979; Mbabane 1981; FCO 1984; Singapore 1987; Peking 1991; Band B3.

Reynolds, Heather (née Turnbull); Dubai since March 2003; Born 30/05/54; FCO 1973; Moscow 1975; FCO 1976; Brasilia 1977; Bridgetown 1980; SUPL 1983; Kuala Lumpur 1984; FCO 1986; Prague 1988; SUPL 1990; FCO 1991; New Delhi 1993; FCO 1997; Moscow 1999; Band C4; m 1982 Keith James Reynolds (1s 1990).

Reynolds, Leslie Roy; FCO since January 2003; Born 22/09/59; DTI 1978; Passport Office 1979; HO 1984; FCO 1984; Wellington 1986; Islamabad 1988; FCO 1992; Dublin 1997; FCO 2000; Bucharest 2002; Band B3; m 1982 Tracey Sapsford (3s 1986, 1989, 1991).

Reynolds, Martin Alexander Baillie; FCO since January 2002; Born 05/06/69; FCO 1997; Second Secretary (Economic/Commercial) Singapore 1998; Band D6.

Rhodes, Ian Peter; Second Secretary FCO since September 1998; Born 12/04/60; Second Secretary FCO 1986; Nicosia 1995; Band C4.

Rice, Douglas; Resident British Commissioner Castries since May 2001; Born 28/01/46; FO 1964; Jedda 1968; Paris 1970; Sana'a 1972; Sofia 1973; FCO 1974; Full-Time Language Training 1977; Doha 1978; Düsseldorf 1982; Second Secretary (Consular/Passports) Singapore 1983; Second later First Secretary FCO 1986; First Secretary (Press and Public Affairs) Madrid 1993; FCO 1998; m (1) 1969 Christine Elizabeth Chisholm (diss) (1d 1973; 1s 1977); (2) 1995 Allison Denise Hay.

Rice, John Gordon; FCO since October 2001; Born 06/01/46; Home Office 1962; Commonwealth Office DSAO and FCO 1967; Ankara 1969; Paris 1972; FCO 1976; Seoul 1978; Assistant Trade Commissioner (Second Secretary) Hong Kong 1980; Parliamentary Clerk FCO 1985; First Secretary (Commercial) and Head of Chancery Doha 1988; Deputy High Commissioner Windhoek 1992; First Secretary FCO 1995; Deputy Head of Mission Lilongwe 1997; m 1972 Gail Marjorie Pearce (2s 1975, 1979; 1d 1976).

Richards, Sir Francis Neville, KCMG (2002), CMG (1994), CVO (1991); Governor Gibraltar since May 2003; Born 18/11/45; Army 1967-69; Third Secretary FCO 1969; Moscow 1971; Second later First Secretary Vienna (UKDEL MBFR) 1973; First Secretary FCO 1976; Counsellor (Commercial/Economic) New Delhi 1985; Counsellor FCO 1988; High Commissioner Windhoek 1990; Minister Moscow 1992; AUS (Central and Eastern Europe) FCO 1995; Director (Europe) 1996; DUSS (Defence and Intelligence) 1998; Head of GCHQ Cheltenham 1998; m 1971 Gillian Bruce Nevill (1s 1975; 1d 1977).

Richards, Ian; FCO since January 2002; Born 07/10/62; FCO 1993; Full-Time Language Training 1994; Consul (Commercial) Shanghai 1996; First Secretary (Political) Beijing 2000; Band D6.

Richards, Owen Jeremy; Second Secretary (Political) Addis Ababa since July 2001; Born 28/06/66; FCO 1988; Bombay 1991; Third Secretary (ECE/UNCTAD) Geneva (UKMIS) 1995; On loan to the DTI 2000; Band C4.

Richards, Steven Thomas; Second Secretary (Commercial) Dublin since July 2000; Born 29/01/58; FCO 1978; New Delhi 1980; Beirut 1982; Europe Floater 1985; FCO 1987; Warsaw 1988; FCO 1988; Vice-Consul Moscow 1990; FCO 1993 (Second Secretary 1994); Second Secretary (Management/Consular) Valletta 1996; Band C4; m 1989 Tracey Lee Barnett (1d 1995).

Richardson, Christine Lynn; Skopje since August 2003; Born 04/10/67; FCO 1987; Brussels (UKREP) 1989; Africa/Middle East Floater 1992; On loan to DTI 1997; Baku 1998; Band C4.

Richardson, Michael John; Second Secretary (Regional Affairs) Seoul since November 2001; Born 16/05/66; FCO 1985; Warsaw 1988; FCO 1991; Attaché Cairo 1993; FCO 1996; Band C4; m 1989 Audrey Zena Fairall (1s 1994).

Richmond, Alan Thomas; Second Secretary (Economic) Ottawa since July 1999; Born 22/04/55; Department of Education 1973; FCO 1975; Maputo 1977; Lima 1981; FCO 1983; Islamabad 1985; Singapore 1988; FCO 1991; Full-Time Language Training 1994; Abidjan 1995; Band C4; m 1976 Iseabal MacLean Graham (1d 1986).

Richmond, David Frank, CMG (2004); FCO since August 2003; Born 09/07/54; FCO 1976; Language Training MECAS 1977; Third later Second Secretary Baghdad 1979; Second later First Secretary FCO 1982; First Secretary (External Trade) Brussels (UKREP) 1987; Deputy Head of NENAD FCO 1991; Head of Economic Relations Department 1994; Head of Chancery New York (UKMIS) 1996; Political and Security Committee Representative and Permanent Representative to the Council of the WEU Brussels (UKREP) 2000; m 1990 Caroline Florence Pascale Matagne (1s 1992; 1d 1994).

Rickerd, Martin John Kilburn, OBE (2004), MVO (1985); Team Leader for North America, Americas Directorate FCO since August 2003; Born 17/08/54; FCO 1972; Brussels (UKDEL NATO) 1975; Wellington 1978; Assistant Private Secretary to Parliamentary Under Secretary of State 1980; Bridgetown 1982; Consul (Information) Milan 1986; First Secretary FCO 1991; Head of Chancery Singapore 1995; On secondment to the Standard Chartered Bank 1998; FCO 2000; Deputy Head of Mission Abidjan 2000; Band D7; m 1976 Charmain Gwendoline Napier (2s 1986, 1988).

Ricketts, Peter Forbes, CMG (1999); Permanent Representative Brussels (UKDEL NATO) since July 2003; Born 30/09/52; FCO 1974; New York 1974; FCO 1975; Third Secretary Singapore 1975; Second Secretary Brussels (UKDEL NATO) 1978; First Secretary FCO 1982; APS to Secretary of State 1983; First Secretary (Chancery) Washington 1986; First Secretary later Counsellor FCO 1989; Counsellor (EC/Finance) Paris 1994; Deputy Political Director FCO 1997; Director International Security FCO 1999; On loan as Chairman of the Joint Intelligence Committee to the Cabinet Office 2000; Political Director and Deputy Under-Secretary FCO 2001; m 1980 Suzanne Julia Horlington (1s 1982; 1d 1987).

Rickitt, Clare Louise; On loan to the Department of Health since December 2002; Born 20/09/64; FCO 1991; Full-Time Language Training 1992; Second Secretary (Economic Trade Policy) Brasilia 1993; First Secretary FCO 1996; On loan to HM Treasury 2001.

Rickward, Charlotte Lucy; Hamilton since November 2003; Born 12/05/72; FCO 1997; Manila 2000; Band B3; m 1994 Jarlath Ambrose.

Ridley, Michelle; Grand Turk since August 2002; Born 22/01/63; DHSS 1986-87; FCO 1987; Kaduna 1990; Peking 1993; New York (UKMIS) 1997; Band A2.

Ridout, Anthony Robert; Second Secretary (Political) Kingston since June 2001; Born 31/03/66; FCO 1986; New Delhi 1989; Paris 1992; FCO 1995; Second Secretary Cairo 1996; Second Secretary FCO 1998; Band C4; m 1989 Karen Marie Hendy (1d 1991).

Ridout, Richard William; Third Secretary (Political) Hanoi since July 2002; Born 19/11/67; FCO 1986; Moscow 1990; FCO 1993; Third Secretary Riyadh 1994; FCO 1998; Band B3; m 1992 Sarah Beth Evans (1d 1996).

Ridout, William Anthony Frederick; HM Consul Hong Kong since July 2001; Born 27/04/50; MOD 1970; FCO 1974; Islamabad 1976; Stuttgart 1979; Bridgetown 1982; FCO 1982; Bombay 1984; Second Secretary (Commercial) East Berlin 1988; Consul Milan 1990; FCO 1995; Deputy Head of Mission Khartoum 1997; Head of Khartoum Unit, Nairobi 1998; First Secretary (Commercial) Tripoli 1999; m 1996 Louise Victoria Burrett (2s 1986, 2000; 1d 2002).

Riley, John Lawrence; FCO since September 2003; Born 13/08/61; FCO 1982; Cairo 1984; FCO 1986; Ankara 1986; Hanoi 1991; FCO 1992; New Delhi 1995; Third Secretary (Aid) Gaborone 1999; m (1) 1982 Caroline Peacock (diss); m (2) 1990 Ayce Birergin.

Rimmer, Ronald Stanley; Deputy High Commissioner Banjul since December 2001; Born 24/02/54; Royal Air Force 1972-95; FCO 1995; Lagos 1998; Band C4.

Ringham, Christine Mary; SUPL since October 2002; Born 11/12/61; FCO 1988; Brussels (UKDEL) 1991; Prague 1995; FCO 1998; SUPL 2000; FCO 2001; Band B3; m 1998 Kevin P Ringham (2d 2000, 2002).

Ripard, Elizabeth Anne (née Auld); Deputy High Commissioner Mbabane since March 2002; Born 27/06/57; FCO 1976; Madrid 1979; SE Asia Floater 1982; San José 1984; FCO 1988; Third Secretary Valletta 1991; Third later Second Secretary FCO 1994; Language Training 1998; Second Secretary Abidjan 1998; m 1992 Nicholas Charles Ripard (diss).

Ritchie, Joseph Battle; Lilongwe since April 2004; Born 13/07/44; RAF 1961-91; FCO 1998; New York 1999; Band A2; m Paula May (1d 1975; 1s 1980).

Ritchie, Paul John, OBE (1994); Counsellor FCO since December 2003; Born 26/03/62; FCO 1983; Second Secretary (Chancery) Nicosia 1986; Second later First Secretary FCO 1988; First Secretary New York (UKMIS) 1991; First Secretary FCO 1996; Counsellor Nicosia 1999; m 1991 Jane Risely (1d 1997; 1s 2002).

Rixon, Margaret Carol; FCO since August 2003; Born 16/02/57; FCO 1976; Castries 1978; Washington 1980; Peking 1982; FCO 1983; Vienna (UKMIS) 1984; East Berlin 1987; Kingston 1988; FCO 1991; Dublin 1999; Band B3.

Robbins, Christopher William; Deputy Head of Mission and Consul-General Seoul since November 2001; Born 16/06/46; First Secretary FCO 1984; First Secretary (Chancery) New Delhi 1987; First Secretary FCO 1990; Counsellor on loan to the DTI 1991; Counsellor (Commercial) The Hague, later also Consul-General Amsterdam 1994; HM Ambassador Lithuania 1998.

Roberts, Amanda Claire; FCO since May 2000; Born 06/09/67; FCO 1989; Santiago 1996 (Second Secretary 1997); Band C4.

Roberts, Camilla Frances Mary (née Blair); SUPL since May 2004; Born 23/11/66; FCO 1988; Full-Time Language Training 1990; Third later Second Secretary Prague 1991; First Secretary FCO 1994; m 2000 Colin Roberts (1s 2002).

Roberts, Catherine Mary; SUPL since July 2002; Born 05/10/68; FCO 1995; Washington 1997; Band A2.

Roberts, Colin; HM Ambassador Vilnius since March 2004; Born 31/07/59; Called to the Bar 1986; FCO 1989; Second Secretary (Economic) later First Secretary (Political) Tokyo 1990; First Secretary FCO 1995; First Secretary (Political/Military) Paris 1997; Counsellor FCO 1998; Counsellor (Political) Tokyo 2001; m 2000 Camilla Frances Mary Blair (1s 2002).

Roberts, David Eric; FCO since September 2003; Born 15/08/54; Customs and Excise 1971; FCO 1973; Lagos 1977; Doha 1979; FCO 1983; Washington 1986; Helsinki 1989; On loan to London Chamber of Commerce 1993; HM Consul Jedda 1995; Vancouver 1999; m 1979 Kim Louise Fyleman (3d 1990, 1992, 1993).

Roberts, David George; Deputy Head of Mission, Director of Trade and Investment and Consul-General for Switzerland and Liechtenstein at the British Embassy in Berne since August 2000; Born 11/04/55; FCO 1976; Third later Second Secretary (Chancery) Jakarta 1977; Second Secretary (Chancery) Havana 1981; First Secretary FCO 1984; First Secretary (Economic) Madrid 1988; First Secretary (Financial/EC) Paris 1991; FCO 1994; First Secretary FCO 1994; Deputy Head of Mission Santiago 1996; m 1985 Rosemarie Rita Kunz (1d 1990; 1s 1992).

Roberts, Gareth Daniel; FCO since September 2003; Born 07/09/77; Band C4.

Roberts, Gillian (née Phenna); Moscow since June 2002; Born 03/12/68; FCO 1986; Cape Town/Pretoria 1988; Buenos Aires 1992; FCO 1995; Third Secretary (Passports) Paris Embassy 1998; Band B3; m 1993 Michael John Roberts.

Roberts, Sir Ivor Anthony, KCMG (2000), CMG (1995); HM Ambassador Rome since May 2003; Born 24/09/46; Third Secretary FCO 1968; MECAS 1969; FCO 1970; Paris 1970; Second Secretary 1971; Second later First Secretary FCO 1973; First Secretary (Chancery) later First Secretary (Economic/Commercial/Agriculture) Canberra 1978; First Secretary FCO 1982; Counsellor FCO 1986; Minister Madrid 1989; Chargé d'Affaires and HM Consul-General later HM Ambassador Belgrade 1994; On loan to St Antony's College, Oxford 1997; HM Ambassador Dublin 1999; m 1974 Elizabeth Bray Bernard Smith (2s 1976, 1979; 1d 1982).

Roberts, Michael John Wyn; Deputy Head of Mission Ankara since July 2004; Born 04/07/60; Second Secretary FCO 1984; Second later First Secretary (Chancery) Athens 1987; First Secretary FCO 1991; First Secretary (Institutions) Brussels (UKREP) 1995; Head of Division Cabinet Office (European Secretariat) 1999; FCO 2003; m 1985 Margaret Anne Ozanne (2d 1989, 1991; 1s 1993).

Roberts, Peter Raymond; FCO since June 2002; Born 09/02/62; Band B3; m 1992 Diane Margaret.

Roberts, Philip John Barclay; Counsellor FCO since June 1999; Born 04/12/49; FCO 1973; Third later Second Secretary Islamabad 1977; First Secretary FCO 1980; Head of Chancery and Consul Hanoi 1982; First Secretary Tokyo 1984; First Secretary FCO 1987; First Secretary (Chancery) later Counsellor Lisbon 1991; Counsellor Bogotá 1994; Counsellor FCO 1995; Counsellor Vienna 1997; m 1996 Amparo Jimenez Avilan (1d 1997).

Roberts, Tracy Melissa Renata Juliet (née Dodge); First Secretary (UKMIS) since May 2001; Born 31/01/62; HM Customs and Excise 1985; FCO 1998; On loan to CSSB 2000; Band D6; m 1993 David William (1s 1999).

Roberts-Gurr, Anne Catherine; FCO since November 1997; Born 07/05/63; FCO 1985; Bucharest 1988; FCO 1990; Floater Duties 1991; FCO 1993; Athens 1995; Band B3; m 2001 Andrew William George Gurr.

Robertson, Corin Jean Stella (née Leatherbarrow); First Secretary (Institutions) Brussels (UKREP) since December 2002; Born 15/01/72; FCO 1994; Full-Time Language Training 1995; Second Secretary (Trade Policy) Tokyo 1997; First Secretary Vienna 2001; Band D6; m 1996 James Francis Robertson.

Robertson, Emma Jane; FCO since September 2002; Born 25/12/71; FCO 1997; Third Secretary (Economic) Damascus 2000; Band B3.

Robertson, William Smellie; FCO since March 2004; Born 05/03/66; FCO 1984; Dublin 1986;

Riyadh 1989; On loan to the ODA 1992; Third Secretary (Aid/Information) Harare 1996; Second Secretary (Consular) Wellington 2001; Band C4; m 1986 Catherine Elizabeth McGregor (1d 1992; 2s 1995, 2002).

Robins, Terence Frederick; FCO since September 2003; Born 15/10/66; FCO 1989; Vice-Consul Algiers 1991; Victoria 1995; Second Secretary (Chancery) Strasbourg 1999; Band C5; m 1994 Wassila Kerri (1s 1998).

Robinson, Carole May (née Davis); SUPL since August 1999; Born 26/03/59; FCO 1994; Washington 1996; Band A2; m 1995 Miles Gordon Robinson.

Robinson, Julie Anne (née Whitehead); FCO since September 1995; Born 02/08/63; FCO 1984; Washington 1985; Bahrain 1988; FCO 1991; SUPL 1993; Band B3.

Robinson, Kathleen Julia Anne (known as Julia); FCO since January 2004; Born 24/09/50; FCO 1995; The Hague 1996; New York (UKMIS) 2000; SUPL 2003; Band A2.

Robinson, Philip Andrew; First Secretary (Management) Beijing since July 2001; Born 18/09/51; FCO 1970; Warsaw 1973; Jedda 1974; FCO 1977; Wellington 1978; Islamabad 1980; FCO 1982; Johannesburg 1985; Moscow 1987 (Second Secretary 1988); Second Secretary FCO 1991; HM Consul Hong Kong 1996; Band D6; m 1972 Elizabeth Andrina Mathieson Riding (2d 1976, 1980).

Robinson, Tanya Mari; Beijing since June 2004; Born 07/04/81; FCO 2000; Transferred to DS 2001; Band A2; ptnr, Mickel Braithwaite (1d 2002).

Robinson, William; New Delhi since August 2003; Born 26/11/44; RAF Regiment 1962; Islamabad 1987; Moscow 1991; Pretoria 1992; Amman 1996; Dublin 2000; Band C4; m 1966 Cynthia Margaret Pugh (2s 1966, 1969).

Robson, Elizabeth Carol; Deputy Head of Mission Copenhagen since March 2002; Born 14/01/55; FCO 1977; Latin America Floater 1981; FCO 1982; Moscow 1984; Second Secretary FCO 1985; Second later First Secretary (Chancery) Geneva (UKMIS) 1988; Counsellor FCO 1993; Counsellor (Political) Stockholm 1996.

Roche, Shaun Martin; Nairobi since April 2001; Born 23/01/68; FCO 1992; Band C4; m 2001 Rebecca Louise York.

Rocks, Lynne; FCO since September 2003; Born 28/10/79; Band A2.

Rodemark, Janet Mary; SUPL since January 2002; Born 28/05/65; FCO 1988; Islamabad 1992; Second Secretary FCO 1995; SUPL 1997; FCO 1998; SUPL 1999; Sofia 2001; Band C4; m 1993 Timothy John Colley (1s 1997; 2d 1999, 2002).

Roden, Joel Charles; FCO since April 2002; Born 24/02/77; Band C4; m 2000 Camila Miranda.

Rogan, Janet Elizabeth; FCO since April 2001; Born 19/12/62; FCO 1986; Language Training 1988; Language Training Hong Kong 1989; Second later First Secretary (Chancery) Peking 1991; On loan to the Cabinet Office 1994; First Secretary FCO 1995; Deputy Head of Mission Sarajevo 1998.

Rogers, Diana Caroline; SUPL since November 2001; Born 30/07/74; FCO 1998; World Wide Floater Duties 2000; Band B3.

Rogers, Jonathan Mark; FCO since September 2004; Born 04/04/74; MOD 1999; FCO 1999; World Wide Floater Duties 2002; Band B3.

Rogers, Michael Roy; SUPL since August 2000; Born 14/12/48; FCO 1967; Tunis 1973; Bridgetown 1975; Pretoria/Cape Town 1976; FCO 1978; Bahrain 1981; Wellington 1984; Resigned 1989; Reinstated, Second Secretary FCO 1990; Second Secretary (Management) JMO New York 1995; m 1970 Elaine Anne Stewart (2s 1980, 1986).

Röhsler, Caron Amanda; FCO since January 2000; Born 28/08/72; Band C4; ptnr, David Mingay.

Roissetter, Frederick Charles; Second later First Secretary FCO since June 1998; Born 09/10/50; Army 1966-77; FCO 1978; Cabinet Office 1979-81; Paris 1982; FCO 1984; Third later Second Secretary Tel Aviv 1989; FCO 1992; Athens 1995; Band C5; m 1979 Kay Jacqueline (2d 1981, 1984; 1s 1986).

Rolt, Colette; FCO since February 2001; Born 10/08/71; FCO 1989; Washington 1997; Band C4.

Rooney, Kay (née Smith); FCO since July 2003; Born 01/07/68; FCO 1990; Vienna 1993; FCO 1996; Vice-Consul Frankfurt 1996; SUPL 1998; Band B3; m 2000 Sean Michael Rooney.

Rooney, Sean Michael; FCO since June 2003; Born 17/02/72; FCO 1991; Vienna (UKDEL) 1995; Dhaka 1996; Düsseldorf 2000; Band B3; m 2000 Kay Smith.

Roper, Martyn Keith; FCO since October 2003; Born 08/06/65; FCO 1984; Tehran 1986; Maputo 1988; Vice-Consul Kuwait 1990; Third Secretary (Political/Aid) Karachi 1991; FCO 1994; First Secretary 1996; First Secretary (Development/Economic) Paris (UKDEL OECD) 1999; Band D7; m 1989 Elisabeth Melanie Harman Watson (1s 1992; 1d 1995).

Roper, Neil Gregson; Second Secretary (Technical Management) Pretoria since August 2000; Born 27/11/65; FCO 1987; Madrid 1993; FCO 1995; Band C4.

Roskilly, Karen Elizabeth; Second Secretary (Management) Madrid since September 2001; Born 18/10/65; FCO 1990; Amsterdam 1991; Gibraltar 1994; SUPL 1998; Band C4; m 1995 Antonio Gonzalez Saugar (1d 1997; 1s 2000).

Ross, Carne William; SUPL since June 2002; Born 24/08/66; FCO 1989; Third later Second Secretary (Political) Bonn 1992; First Secretary FCO 1995; New York (UKMIS) 1997.

Ross, William Lawson; First Secretary (Consular) Dhaka since July 2003; Born 13/09/53; FCO 1973; New York (UKMIS) 1975; CG New York 1977; Tunis 1978; Kinshasa 1981; FCO 1984; Nassau 1985; Warsaw 1988; FCO 1991 (Second Secretary 1993); HM Consul and Second Secretary (Commercial) Al Khobar 1995; Full-Time Language Training 2000; First Secretary (Commercial) Nicosia 2000; Band C5; m 1978 Mary Margaret Delaney (1d 1980; 1s 1982).

Ross McDowell, Amanda (née Ross); Vice-Consul (Commercial) Sydney since June 1999; Born 25/11/62; FCO 1981; 10 Downing St 1985; Cape Town 1988; Zurich 1991; Second Secretary FCO 1994; Second Secretary (Commercial) Addis Ababa 1997; m 1987 Christopher McDowell (1d 1990; 1s 1992).

Rossiter, Lynne; Copenhagen since July 2002; Born 10/08/50; FCO 1990; Tel Aviv 1992; Floater Duties 1995; Band B3.

Rothery, James Peter; FCO since September 1985 (Second Secretary 1993); Born 15/04/51; FCO 1975; Masirah 1977; Washington 1982; Band D6; m 1996 Agnes Maria Smith.

Rous, Matthew James; Deputy Head of Mission and Consul-General Brussels Embassy since February 2002; Born 29/06/64; FCO 1991; Full-Time Language Training SOAS 1992; Full-Time Language Training Peking 1993; Second later First Secretary (Chancery) Peking 1994; First Secretary (Commercial) Tokyo 1998; m 1989 Beryl Ann Scott (2d 1992, 1998; 1s 1994).

Rowbottom, Major Kenneth John; Queen's Messenger since 1988; Born 04/03/47; HM Forces 1966-86.

Rowe, David Ian; FCO since July 2000; Born 16/06/66; FCO 1985; Addis Ababa 1987; Bucharest 1991; FCO 1992; Manila 1996; Band C4; m 1993 Nancy Elizabeth Vince.

Rowe, Elizabeth Jane; Warsaw since January 2003; Born 19/01/71; FCO 1997; Sarajevo 1998; Floater Duties 2001; Band B3.

Rowe, Jane Victoria; SUPL since June 2004; Born 20/05/73; FCO 2001; Paris 2003; Band B3.

Rowe, Katherine Jane; Second Secretary Kuala Lumpur since May 2004; Born 30/01/78; FCO 2002; Band C4; ptnr, Robert Long.

Rowe, Victoria Helen (née Goodwin); Vice-Consul Geneva since July 2000; FCO 1995; Band C4; m 1996 Richard David Rowe.

Rowett, Caroline Sarah; FCO since September 1999; Born 16/09/58; FCO 1990; Jakarta 1992; Paris 1996; Band C4; m 1992 Joseph Spurgeon (1d 1998).

Rowland, Keith Irving, MVO (2004); Kabul since February 2004; Born 09/11/46; Royal Navy 1963-88; Islamabad 1988; Moscow 1992; New York

1993; FCO 1996; Attaché (Management) Abuja 2001; Band A2; m 1971 Helena Sloan (1s 1972).

Rowlands, Jane Ellen; Third Secretary (Management) and Vice-Consul Ashgabat since August 2001; Born 16/03/67; FCO 1987; Mexico City 1989; Seoul 1993; Third Secretary FCO 1997.

Rowlandson, Peter Roderick Saxby; FCO since January 1997; Born 22/09/49; FCO 1970; Georgetown 1972; FCO 1976; Brussels 1978; Moscow 1981; FCO 1982; Brussels 1984; Madrid 1985; New Delhi 1988; FCO 1991; Dhaka 1995; Band B3; m (1) 1973 Nancy Lee Townsend (1d 1974); (2) 1989 Jillian Roberts (1s 1990; 1d 1992).

Rowney, Michael Ernest, MBE (1991); FCO since January 2001; Born 23/06/53; FCO 1972; Warsaw 1975; Kinshasa 1976; Hamilton 1979; Bahrain 1982; FCO 1985; Vice-Consul Monrovia 1988; Lisbon 1991; FCO 1994; First Secretary Security Officer Moscow 1998.

Rowton, Alastair Clifford; FCO since January 1998; Born 28/11/46; FCO 1979; Gaborone 1981; FCO 1982; Darwin (BGWRS) 1984; FCO 1986; Second Secretary Budapest 1994; Band C5; m 1976 Jean Margaret Cowie (2d 1982, 1986).

Royal, Caroline Patricia; New York (UKMIS) since February 2001; Born 22/01/57; MOD 1973; FCO 1990; Lisbon 1992; FCO 1995; Sana'a 1998; Band A2.

Royle, Catherine Jane; Deputy Head of Mission Buenos Aires since September 2003; Born 17/08/63; FCO 1986; Third later Second Secretary (Chancery) Santiago 1988; First Secretary FCO 1991; First Secretary (EU/Economic) Dublin 1997; FCO 2001; m 1991 Marcelo Enrique Camprubi Valledor (1s 2000).

Rudge, Peter Alan; FCO since November 2003; Born 05/09/73; Second Secretary FCO 1999; Second Secretary (Political) Rome 2001; Band C4.

Runacres, Mark Alastair; Minister New Delhi since July 2002; Born 19/05/59; FCO 1981; Third later Second Secretary New Delhi 1983; Second later First Secretary FCO 1986; First Secretary (Chancery) Paris 1991; First Secretary FCO 1995; On loan to the DTI 1998; Counsellor (Economic) New York (UKMIS) 1999; m 1989 Shawn Reid (1s 1994; twins 1s/1d 2000).

Ruse, Lynne Elaine (née Gerrish); SUPL since December 1997; Born 15/05/58; FCO 1988; Paris 1991; FCO 1995; Band A2; m 1996 Howard Michael Ruse (1d 1998; 1s 1999).

Ruskin, Peter Jonathan; Full-Time Language Training (Norwegian) since December 2003; Born 29/11/76; FCO 2002; Band C4.

Russell, Andrew John; Second later First Secretary later Counsellor FCO since April 1987; Born 12/08/48; FO (later FCO) 1967; Bonn 1972; Berlin 1973; FCO 1975; Second Secretary Vienna 1982; m 1972 Marilyn Elizabeth Turp (2d 1974, 1984; 1s 1982).

Russell, Gerard Simon Joseph, MBE (2002); FCO since October 2001; Born 11/07/73; FCO 1995; Full-Time Language Training (Arabic) 1996; Cairo 1997; Consul (Political) Jerusalem 1998; Band D6.

Russell, Malcolm Arthur; FCO since May 2001; Born 27/02/54; FCO 1973; Kuala Lumpur 1976; FCO 1980; Frankfurt 1983; Tehran 1985; Third Secretary Nuku'alofa 1988; Peking 1989; FCO 1992; Suva 1999; Band C4; m 1982 Jean Frances Matthews (1d 1987; 1s 1992).

Russell, Neil; SUPL since April 2001; Born 18/02/69; FCO 1989; Abu Dhabi 1992; Brasilia 1994; Full-Time Language Training 1998; Third Secretary (Information) Warsaw 1998; Band B3; m 1993 Trudie Helen Denby (1d 1995).

Russell, Roger; Accra since November 2001; Born 14/05/54; FCO 1970; Brussels 1983; FCO 1986; Canberra 1989; FCO 1999; Band C4; m 1983 Teresa Mary McGeough.

Rutherford, John, OBE (2003); SUPL since December 2002; Born 02/01/59; FCO 1978; Nairobi 1980; Jedda (later Riyadh) 1983; Second Secretary Warsaw 1990 (Second Secretary 1988); Los Angeles 1994; Regional Director, Invest in Britain Bureau Hong Kong 1998; m 1989 Karen Chapman (1s 1991).

Rutherford, Karen (née Chapman); FCO since November 2002; Born 19/02/59; FCO 1977; Rome 1979; Floater Duties 1982; FCO 1986; Warsaw 1990; SUPL 1992; Band B3; m 1989 John Rutherford (1s 1991).

Ryan, Elizabeth Jane Karen; Zagreb since August 2003; Born 02/02/61; FCO 1998; Bratislava 1999; Band B3; m 1993 Chaeil Ok-soon (1d 1994).

Ryan, Robert Christopher; Bucharest since January 2002; Born 21/02/72; HCS 1991; FCO 1994; New Delhi 1997; FCO 2001; Band A2.

Rycroft, Matthew John; Private Secretary to the Prime Minister for Foreign Affairs, No.10 Downing Street since February 2002; Born 16/06/68; FCO 1989; Third Secretary Geneva (UKDIS) 1990; Third later Second Secretary (Chancery) Paris 1991; First Secretary FCO 1995; First Secretary (Political) Washington 1998; m 1997 (2d 1998, 2000).

Ryder, Michael; FCO since July 2003; Born 13/11/53; FCO 1984; Second later First Secretary BMG Berlin 1986; First Secretary FCO 1988; First Secretary Brussels (UKREP) 1993; First Secretary FCO 1996; Counsellor (Head of Security Policy Department) FCO 1997; Special Representative for International Drugs Issues and Head of Drugs and International Crime Department FCO 1998.

S

Sadler, Stuart Roger; Second Secretary (Management) Riyadh since October 2002; Born 22/12/70; FCO 1990; Pretoria 1994; Moscow 1998; Karachi 2001; Band C4; m 1995 Wendy Jane Hoole (1d 1997; 2s 2000, 2003).

Sadler, Tiffany Alexandra (née White); FCO since August 2003; Born 10/06/71; FCO 1994; Language Training 1995; Third later Second Secretary (Political and Economic) Rangoon 1996; FCO 1999; Economics Training 2001; m 2002 Stephen Paul Sadler (1d 2003).

Sagar, Rebecca Ann; Kabul since December 2003; Born 09/09/76; FCO 1999; Second Secretary (Political) Islamabad 2001; Band D6.

Sainty, Christopher James; First Secretary (Political/EU) Madrid since March 2000; Born 29/03/67; FCO 1989; Language Training FCO 1991; Third later Second Secretary (Chancery) New Delhi 1992; First Secretary FCO 1996; Language Training FCO 1999; Band D6; m 1993 Sarah Helen Norris (1s 1996; 2d 1998, 2000).

Salkeld, Peter Charles; FCO since May 1993; Born 31/08/53; FCO 1969; Bonn 1980; FCO 1983; New Delhi 1989; m 1978 Carol Elizabeth Anne Dent (2s 1985, 1988).

Salt, Richard André; First Secretary (Commercial) Sarajevo since August 2003; Born 30/07/62; FCO 1980; Brussels (UKREP) 1983; Algiers 1985; Banjul 1988; FCO 1990; New Delhi 1993; Second Secretary (Commercial) Damascus 1996; On secondment to Petrofac UK Ltd 2000; Band C5; m 1992 Karen Baden Davies (1s 1995).

Salter, Leigh Audra; SUPL since June 2002; Born 16/03/69; FCO 1988; Wellington 1991; Windhoek 1994; Floater Duties 1998; Band B3.

Salvesen, Charles Hugh; FCO since August 2000; Born 10/09/55; Second Secretary FCO 1982; First Secretary BMG Berlin 1984; First Secretary Bonn 1985; FCO 1988; Head of Political Section Buenos Aires 1993; Counsellor and Deputy High Commissioner Wellington 1996; m 1983 Emilie Maria Ingenhousz (2s twins 1987; 1d 1990 (dec'd 1995)).

Sambrook, Adam John; Full-Time Language Training Jerusalem since January 2004; Born 01/02/78; FCO 2001; Full-Time Language Training (Hebrew) 2003; Band C4.

Sampson, Jerome; FCO since September 2002; Born 11/11/74; Band A2.

Sampson, William; FCO since October 2003; Born 17/02/80; Band C4.

Samuel, Edwin Douglas Lincoln; Private Secretary to the Ambassador, Berlin since December 2003; Born 08/08/72; FCO 2001; Band C4.

Sancar, Kim (née Neilson); SUPL since July 2002; Born 30/09/71; FCO 1991; Islamabad 1995; Third Secretary (Immigration) Tehran 1998; Third Secretary (Commercial) and Vice-Consul Al Khobar 2001; Band B3; m 1997 Rizkul Oktay Sancar.

Sanderson, Michael John; First Secretary FCO since July 1995; Born 21/01/48; FO 1967; Cairo 1972; FCO 1976; New York (UKMIS) 1979; Second Secretary (Chancery) Oslo 1984; Second Secretary FCO 1988; First Secretary Hong Kong 1993; Band C5; (1d 1979; 1s 1985).

Sandover, William Geoffrey; Counsellor Islamabad since August 2004; Born 07/04/55; FCO 1979; Third later Second Secretary Vienna (UKMIS) 1981; First Secretary FCO 1984; First Secretary (Chancery) Dublin 1986; First Secretary FCO 1987; First Secretary (Chancery) Buenos Aires 1992; First Secretary FCO 1996; Counsellor Paris 2002; Band D6; m (1) 1981 Sharman Winsome Knight (diss 1985); (2) 1992 Beatrice Martin.

Sargeant, Ian Charles; Consul Shanghai since July 2004; Born 24/04/52; FCO 1971; Language Training SOAS 1974; Bangkok 1975; LA Floater 1979; FCO 1982; Manila 1986; Deputy Economic Adviser Berlin 1990; Vice-Consul (Commercial) Düsseldorf 1991; FCO 1995; First Secretary and HM Consul Manila 1998; FCO 2003; m 1988 Mari Grace Eddun (diss 1999) (1d 1989).

Satheesan, Sujeevan; Paris since June 2003; Born 25/03/77; FCO 2001; Band C4.

Sattaur, Christopher; FCO since August 2003; Born 25/04/71; FCO 1991; Athens 1996; Amman 2000; Band A2.

Saunders, Caroline Ann; Deputy Consul-General Brisbane since October 2000; Born 28/09/60; FCO 1983; New Delhi 1986; FCO 1988; Third Secretary (Chancery) Kuala Lumpur 1991; Second Secretary FCO 1995; Second Secretary British Trade International 1998; m 1989 Rhodri Christopher Kevin Meredith (1s 1993; 1d 1996).

Saunders, Ian David; St Petersburg since April 2002; Born 20/01/67; COI 1989-99; FCO 2000; Band A2.

Saunders, Kirsten Mary Margaret; Vice-Consul Damascus since November 2003; Born 08/10/68; FCO 1995; Bangkok 1997; Third Secretary (Immigration) Dhaka 2000; Band B3.

Saunders, Liane, OBE (2004); On attachment to the Coalition Provisional Authority, Northern Iraq since April 2003; Born 24/10/68; FCO 1993; Full-Time Language Training FCO 1994; Full-Time Language Training Cairo 1995; Second Secretary Kuwait 1996; First Secretary (Chancery) Ankara 2000; Band D6; m 1994 Andrew Stewart Smith (1d 1998).

Saunderson, Lesley Margaret; SUPL since February 2003; Born 18/11/69; FCO 1991; New Delhi 1993; St Petersburg 1994; Dar es Salaam 1997; On loan to DFID 1998.

Savill, Margaret Ann; First Secretary FCO since April 1995; Born 06/04/46; FCO 1968; Third Secretary Georgetown 1972; Geneva 1975; Second Secretary Rio de Janeiro 1975; FCO 1980; Second later First Secretary (Information) Berne 1984; First Secretary FCO 1989; First Secretary (Information/Management) Brussels (UKDEL NATO) 1993.

Saville, John Donald William; Deputy Head of Mission Havana since July 2000; Born 29/06/60; FCO 1981; Third later Second Secretary Jakarta 1983; FCO 1985; Second later First Secretary (Information) Warsaw 1988; First Secretary FCO 1991; First Secretary (Political) Vienna 1995; FCO 1998; Full-Time Language Training 2000; Band D6; m 1992 Fabiola Moreno de Alboran (1d 1993).

Sawers, Robert John, CMG (1996); DUS (Political), FCO since July 2003; Born 26/07/55; FCO 1977; Sana'a 1980; SUPL 1980; Language Training 1981; Second Secretary Damascus 1982; First Secretary FCO 1984 (PS to Minister of State 1986); First Secretary Pretoria/Cape Town 1988; Head of European Union Department (Presidency) 1991; Principal Private Secretary to the Secretary of State for Foreign and Commonwealth Affairs 1993; Career Development Attachment Harvard University 1995; Counsellor (Political/Military) Washington 1996; Foreign Affairs Private Secretary to the Prime Minister 1999; HM Ambassador Cairo 2001; m 1981 Avril Helen Shelley Lamb (2s 1983, 1985; 1d 1987).

Say, Sarah Gillian; Pretoria since July 2003; Born 02/04/59; FCO 1986; Paris 1988; Washington 1991; Havana 1993; FCO 1994; Mexico City 1996; T/D Helsinki 1999; Brussels (UKREP) 2000; Band B3.

Sayle, Lorraine Mary; SUPL since August 2003; Born 22/09/72; FCO 1990; Brussels (UKDEL NATO) 1994; Lilongwe 1996; SUPL 1998; Lilongwe 1998; Luanda 2001; Band B3; (1s 1998).

Scales, Caroline Ann (née Smyth), MBE (1999); Cape Town since April 2002; Born 02/06/61; FCO 1980; Moscow 1982; Strasbourg 1983; Peking 1987; FCO 1989; Washington 1993; Tripoli 1997; FCO 1998; Band C4; m 2001 Michael Scales.

Scales, Martin Milner; Vice-Consul Oslo since April 2001; Born 31/01/65; FCO 1997; Band B3; m 2001 Caroline Smyth.

Scanlon, Edward Joseph; FCO since February 2003; Born 18/05/70; HCS 1990-93; FCO 1993; Peking 1995; Istanbul 1999; Band B3; m 2002 Jenni Williams.

Scanlon, Jenni (née Williams); FCO since March 2003; Born 21/12/70; FCO 1990; Peking 1995; FCO 1999; Istanbul 1999; Band B3; m 2002 Edward Scanlon.

Scantlebury, Ian Patrick; FCO since July 2003; Born 12/09/60; FCO 1978; Georgetown 1981; SE Asia Floater 1985; Calcutta 1987; FCO 1991; Third Secretary (Commercial) Accra 1994; Second Secretary Lima 1997; FCO 2001; On secondment (Commercial) 2002.

Scarborough, Bryan David; Consul (Management) Port of Spain since January 2003; Born 19/01/45; FCO 1973; Warsaw 1975; Douala 1976; Delhi 1979; Freetown 1983; FCO 1985; Lilongwe 1988; Third Secretary (Commercial) Jakarta 1991; FCO 1995; Consul (Commercial)

Shanghai 1999; m 1969 Kathleen Mary Johnston (1s 1980).

Scarborough, Vernon Marcus; Resident Deputy High Commissioner Tarawa, Kiribati since March 2001; Born 11/02/40; Passport Office 1958; CRO 1961; Dacca 1962; CRO 1964; Karachi 1965; Vice-Consul Brussels 1969; Third Secretary Banjul 1971; Second Secretary FCO 1977; Second Secretary (Commercial) Muscat 1980; First Secretary (Admin) Kuala Lumpur 1984; First Secretary FCO 1987; Consul (Commercial) Auckland 1990; Deputy Head of Mission Suva and concurrently HM Ambassador (non-resident) to Palau, Micronesia and the Marshall Islands 1995; T/D Suva 2000; m 1966 Jennifer Bernadette Keane (3d 1970, 1972, 1980).

Scarratt, Claire Rebecca; Hong Kong since May 2003; Born 07/02/75; HCS 1997; FCO 1999; Stockholm 2000; Band A2.

Schofield, Nigel; FCO since 2001; Born 17/04/70; FCO 1990; Bonn 1993; FCO 1993; Lagos 1994; On loan to the DTI 1999; Floater Duties 2000; Band C4; m 1994 Rebecca Imogen.

Scholes, Elizabeth Marian; SUPL since September 1998; Born 28/04/66; FCO 1987; Third later Second Secretary (Chancery) Buenos Aires 1990; Second later First Secretary FCO 1993; First Secretary (Chancery) Tel Aviv 1996; m 1998 Richard Wrigley.

Schroeder, Dominic Sebastian; FCO since October 2001; Born 13/11/65; FCO 1988; Third later Second Secretary Kinshasa 1989; Second Secretary FCO 1992; Second Secretary New York (UKMIS) 1993; Second later First Secretary FCO 1994; First Secretary (Commercial) Berlin 1997; m 1997 Susan Caroline Kerr (1s 2001).

Schroeder, Susan Caroline (née Kerr); SUPL since September 1999; Born 09/04/69; FCO 1988; Prague 1990; Rabat 1992; FCO 1994; On loan to the DTI 1996; Third Secretary (Political) Berlin 1998; Band B3; m 1997 Dominic Sebastian Schroeder (1s 2001).

Schulz, Lynne; Pretoria since April 2002; Born 16/11/66; HCS 1997; SUPL 1998; FCO 2000; SUPL 2001; Band A2; m 1994 Sven Schulz (1s 1998; 1d 2001).

Schumann, Carol Ann (née Hill); Consul/MO Frankfurt since June 2000; Born 18/07/46; FCO 1976; Paris 1977; FCO 1980; Washington 1981; FCO 1987; The Hague 1988; Bonn 1991; FCO 1995; SUPL 1996; Third Secretary (Finance) Bonn 1997; Band C4; m 1980 Jürgen Klaus Dieter Schumann (2s 1981, 1983).

Scott, Gavin David; Private Secretary to the Group Chief Executive British Trade International since January 2002; Born 26/06/60; FCO 1978; Paris 1981; Beirut 1983; Washington 1985; FCO 1988; Third Secretary (Commercial) Bogotá 1991; Third Secretary FCO 1995; Bridgetown 1995; Band C4; m 1992 Julie Ann Owen (1s 2003).

Scott, George; Almaty since July 2002; Born 11/10/56; FCO 1981; East Berlin 1982; Luxembourg 1984; Lagos 1986; FCO 1991; Kigali 1995; Tirana 1999; Band C4.

Scott, Julie Ann (née Owen); FCO since January 1999; Born 18/07/68; DSS 1986; FCO 1989; World Wide Floater Duties 1990; SUPL 1992; Bridgetown 1997; Band C4; m 1992 Gavin David Scott (1s 2003).

Scott, Keith John; FCO since July 2002; Born 19/02/69; FCO 1991; Abuja 1994; Second Secretary FCO 1995; SUPL 1998; On loan to the DTI 1999; Band D6.

Scott, Victoria; FCO since October 2003; Born 04/03/81; Band C4.

Scott-Dunne, Naomi Anita; SUPL since April 2002; Born 25/09/68; FCO 1990; Geneva (UKMIS) 1995; SUPL 1997; FCO 2001; Band A2; m 1997 John Richard Dunne.

Scroby, Gary Vance; Counsellor (Commercial) Auckland since July 2003; Born 15/07/69; FCO 1988; Brussels (UKREP) 1989; Floater Duties 1992; FCO 1994; Deputy Head of Mission Managua 1999; Band C4; m 1999 Lisa Marie Dowell (1d 2000; 1s 2003).

Seaby, Paul Robert; HM Consul Pretoria since August 2002; Born 24/05/56; FCO 1975; Warsaw 1978; Masirah 1978; Ottawa 1979; Floater Duties 1982; Port Moresby 1984; Third Secretary (Commercial) Muscat 1991; Second Secretary (Management) Lusaka 1994; First Secretary (Management) and Consul Tehran 1999; Band C5; m 1984 Lynette Margaret Heffernan (1d 1995).

Sealy, Amanda Sarah (née Franklin); Gaborone since September 2003; Born 03/01/59; FCO 1980; Peking 1982; Pretoria/Cape Town 1984; Warsaw 1986; FCO 1988; Windhoek 1991; Jakarta 1995; FCO 1999; Band C4; m 1989 Dominic John Sealy (1s 1992; 1d 1995).

Seaman, Michael William; First Secretary (Political) Tbilisi since May 2002; Born 01/11/55; FCO 1975; Jakarta 1977; Bombay 1981; FCO 1984; Second Secretary (Chancery) The Hague 1988; Second Secretary FCO 1992; On loan to the MOD 1992; First Secretary FCO 1994; Athens 1999; Full-Time Language Training 2001; Band C5; m 1978 Jane Lesley Stockwell (2d 1984, 1987).

Seaman, Stephen James, MBE (1991); First Secretary (Commercial) Caracas since October 2000; Born 04/12/55; DOT 1975; Copenhagen 1979; Salisbury 1980; DOT 1980; FCO 1982; Vice-Consul Bucharest 1983; FCO 1986; Second Secretary and Deputy Head of Mission Monrovia 1988; Second Secretary (Commercial) Lilongwe 1991; Second Secretary (Management) Nicosia 1993; First Secretary FCO 1997; m (1) 1980 Katherine Ann Barker (dec'd 1996); (2) 2001 Magda Guillermina.

Searight, Pauline Mabel; SUPL since August 1999; Born 27/06/55; FCO 1988; Banjul 1990;

Karachi 1993; Kuala Lumpur 1996; Band A2; m 1991 Graham Kenneth Denham (1d 1997).

Seaton, Andrew James; Consul-General Chicago since August 2003; Born 20/04/54; FCO 1977; Third later Second Secretary Dakar 1979; Trade Commissioner (China) BTC Hong Kong 1981; First Secretary FCO 1987; Trade Counsellor BTC later Deputy Consul-General and Trade Counsellor Hong Kong 1995; Head of China Hong Kong Department FCO 2000; m 1983 Helen Elizabeth Pott (3s 1989, 1992, 1995).

Seddon, Christine; Floater Duties since October 2001; FCO 1988; Brasilia 1990; Wellington 1994; FCO 1998; Band A2.

Seddon, David William; Deputy Consul-General Melbourne since February 2003; Born 30/05/48; FO (later FCO) 1966; Bonn 1970; FCO 1971; Port of Spain 1973; Vila 1977; FCO 1981; Milan 1983; Vice-Consul later Consul Douala 1987; Second Secretary FCO 1991; Kampala 1995; First Secretary (Commercial) Harare 1999; m 1972 Monica Elisabeth Josefina van Loon (1s 1976).

Seddon, Richard Charles Leslie; First Secretary (Political) Islamabad since June 2003; Born 25/09/68; FCO 1992; Second Secretary (Political) New Delhi 1994; First Secretary FCO 1997; First Secretary Washington 1999; Band D6; m 1999 Alice Kim Fugate.

Sedwill, Mark Philip; Counsellor and Deputy High Commissioner Islamabad since February 2003; Born 21/10/64; FCO 1989; Language Training 1990; Second Secretary Language Training Cairo 1991; Second Secretary (Political/External) Cairo 1992; First Secretary FCO 1994; First Secretary (Political) Nicosia 1998; First Secretary FCO 1999; Private Secretary to the Foreign Secretary, 2000; m 1999 Sarah-Jane Lakeman.

Seedhouse, Richard; FCO since September 2003; Born 23/08/79; Band A2.

Segar, Christopher Michael John, CMG (2004); Head of British Office, Baghdad since April 2003; Born 25/11/50; FCO 1973; Language Training MECAS 1974; Third later Second Secretary (Commercial) Dubai 1976; First Secretary FCO 1979; First Secretary (Commercial) and Head of Chancery Luanda 1984; First Secretary Paris (UKDEL) 1987; Counsellor, Consul-General and Deputy Head of Mission Baghdad 1990; On loan to the MOD 1991; Counsellor (Commercial) Riyadh 1994; Counsellor (Commercial) Peking 1997; Head of Aviation, Maritime and Energy Dept FCO 2001.

Self, Andrew Paul; Second Secretary FCO since December 1998; Born 02/04/64; FCO 1982; Hong Kong 1986; FCO 1988; Third Secretary (Information) Sana'a 1992; Third Secretary FCO 1993; Tehran 1996; Band C4; m (1) 1987 Michele Carmichael Crouch (diss 1995); (2) 1997 Andrea Louise Carter (2s 1998, 2001).

Selvadurai, Louise Mary (née McCallum); SUPL since September 2002; Born 26/04/69; FCO 1990;

Vienna (UKDEL) 1992; Full-Time Language Training 1995; Third Secretary Moscow 1996; FCO 1999; Band C4; m 2000 Samuel Selvadurai (1s 2002).

Selvadurai, Samuel Dayalan; First Secretary Brussels (UKDEL NATO) since January 2003; Born 01/10/70; FCO 1993; Full-Time Language Training 1994; Second Secretary (KHF) Moscow 1995; First Secretary FCO 1998; Band D6; m 2000 Louise Mary McCallum (1s 2002).

Sen-Gupta, Millie Sharmila; Second Secretary (Press and Public Affairs) Dhaka since July 2003; Born 13/06/76; FCO 2001; Band C4; ptnr, David McDevitt.

Senior, Major Michael Roger; Queen's Messenger since 1987; Born 15/11/45; HM Forces 1964-87.

Setterfield, (James) Robert; Deputy Head of Mission Ljubljana since February 2004; Born 06/05/47; DSAO (later FCO) 1967; Bombay 1969; New Delhi 1971; FCO 1973; Second Secretary (Aid/Information) Rangoon 1976; Assistant Secretary (Political) Vila 1980; Vice-Consul Stuttgart 1980; Vice-Consul (Commercial) Düsseldorf 1982; First Secretary FCO 1985; First Secretary (Chancery) Wellington 1987; FCO 1992; First Secretary Helsinki 1995; Full-Time Language Training 2000; Deputy Head of Mission Bratislava 2000; Band D6; m 1980 Margaret Jean McMahon (1s 1983; 1d 1985).

Seymour, Irene Frances (née McDonagh); SUPL since September 1995; Born 02/12/64; FCO 1984; San José 1987; FCO 1990; Band A2; m 1991 Peter James Seymour.

Seymour, Peter James; First Secretary FCO since March 2001; Born 10/02/62; FCO 1984; Second Secretary (Chancery/Information) and Vice-Consul San José 1987; Second Secretary FCO 1989; SUPL 1990; First Secretary FCO 1991; Berlin 1995; First Secretary Vienna 1999; Band D6; m 1991 Irene Frances McDonagh.

Shackell, Robin John; SUPL since March 2004; Born 04/02/63; HCS 1983; FCO 1985; Vienna 1987; T/D Munich 1989; Doha 1990; Management Officer/Vice-Consul La Paz 1991; FCO 1995; Quito 1999; Band C4; m 2002 Lezlie Lynae Van Hiel (1s 1991; 1d 2003).

Shackleton, Richard David; Second Secretary (Economic) Sofia since January 2004; Born 26/05/68; FCO 1990; Third Secretary (Political) New York (UKMIS) 1992; Third Secretary (Commercial) Bogotá 1995; SUPL 1998; Band C4.

Shaikh, Farida; Second Secretary (Environment/Human Rights) Accra since June 2002; Born 16/10/65; FCO 1990; Third Secretary (Chancery/Information) Harare 1992; Third Secretary (Chancery) Singapore 1996; SUPL 1997; FCO 1998; University College London 2001; m 1997 Emil Levendoglu.

Shand, Ian, LVO (2000); FCO since September 2003; Born 17/01/54; FCO 1973; Accra 1975;

Munich 1979; FCO 1982; Bonn 1985; Islamabad 1988; FCO 1991; Language Training 1994; Santiago 1995; Second Secretary (Press and Public Affairs) Milan 1999; m 1975 Lyndsey Elizabeth Hall (2d 1983, 1985).

Shanmuganathan, Krishna; First Secretary FCO since August 2003; Born 14/02/74; FCO 1995; Second Secretary (Political) Pretoria 1998; Athens 2000; Band D6.

Shannon, Keith; Deputy Head of Mission and HM Consul Vilnius since November 2004; Born 17/09/66; FCO 1988; Third Secretary (Aid/Commercial) Maputo 1991; Second Secretary (Technology) Paris 1995; FCO 1999; m 2002 Kate Levesley.

Shapcott, William James; SUPL (Counsellor to Dr Javier Solana, EU High Representative for the CFSP, Brussels) since October 1999; Born 25/07/61; HM Forces 1983-88; Second Secretary FCO 1988; Second Secretary Bonn 1990; First Secretary FCO 1993; First Secretary Washington 1995 (Counsellor 1999); m 1986 Shelley Mary Harrison (twin s 2001).

Shapland, Anthony Gregory; FCO since July 1992; Born 17/12/49; PRO (Band D6) ; FCO 1979; On loan to the Cabinet Office 1990; m (1) 1973 Margaret Elizabeth Moriarty (diss); (2) 1982 Leonora Alexandra Hebden (1s 1983).

Sharma, Ajay; First Secretary (Economic) Ankara since September 2003; Born 07/05/70; FCO 1995; Full-Time Language Training 1996; Second Secretary (Political/Information) Ankara 1997; Seconded to HM Treasury 2000; Full-Time Language Training 2001; First Secretary (Economic) Moscow 2002; m 2000 Evren Birdal.

Sharman, Edwin; FCO since April 2002; Born 03/10/80; Lord Chancellors Office 2000; Band A2; ptnr, Derek Cox.

Sharp, David Stewart; Floater Duties since March 2003; Born 19/01/71; FCO 1989; New York (UKMIS) 1992; Gibraltar 1995; FCO 1999; Band B3.

Sharp, Gemma Goulding; FCO since September 2002; Born 07/08/72; Second Secretary FCO 1995; Second Secretary (Political) Copenhagen 1998; Band C4.

Sharp, James Frederick Bailey; FCO since December 2003; Born 01/04/72; FCO 1994; SUPL 1998; New Delhi 2000; Band A2.

Sharp, James Lyall; HM Ambassador Almaty and HM Ambassador (non-resident) Bishkek since October 2002; Born 12/04/60; Second Secretary FCO 1987; Language Training Cairo 1988; Second Secretary Cairo 1989; First Secretary FCO 1992; First Secretary Vienna (UKDEL) 1996; FCO 1998; m 1992 Sara Essam el-Gammal (2s 1998, 2002).

Sharp, Jonathan Dinsdale; Second Secretary (Political) Lagos since August 2000; Born 31/03/67; FCO 1988; Karachi 1990; Paris 1991; LA/Caribbean Floater 1994; FCO 1997; Third

Secretary (Political) Tunis 1997; m 1995 Tracey Ennis.

Sharp, Paul John Gibson; Second later First Secretary FCO since April 1993; Born 24/09/48; FCO 1967; New Delhi 1975; FCO 1976; Rome 1978; FCO 1981; Attaché Ankara 1981; FCO 1985; Attaché Moscow 1987; Second Secretary FCO 1989; Second Secretary Pretoria 1990; Band D6; m (1) 1969 Anita Tsang (2s 1972, 1976) (diss 1986); (2) 1996 J Tuckey.

Sharp, Richard; First Secretary (Management) Ottawa since February 2002; Born 08/03/49; FO (later FCO) 1967; Karachi 1971; Canberra 1972; Port Moresby 1974; Santiago 1975; Jakarta 1977; FCO 1980; Cairo 1984; Second Secretary (Admin) Moscow 1987; Second Secretary FCO 1990; Second Secretary and Vice-Consul Luanda 1993; First Secretary (Management) New Delhi 1997; m 1974 Patricia Anne Whitby (1s 1979; 1d 1983).

Sharpe, Jean Cynthia, OBE (1994); Resident British Commissioner St John's since November 2002; Born 18/10/47; CO 1964; DSAO 1965; The Hague 1970; Kingston 1973; FCO 1974; Dubai 1974; FCO 1975; Freetown 1978; JAO Brussels 1981; Second Secretary FCO 1984; On loan to the DTI 1986; Second Secretary (Commercial) Nairobi 1988; First Secretary and Consul Bangkok 1991; First Secretary FCO 1996; Trade Commissioner Hong Kong 1998.

Sharpe, Rosemary Helen; Counsellor FCO since April 2003; Born 11/03/56; Second Secretary FCO 1982; Second Secretary (Information) New Delhi 1985; First Secretary Brussels (UKREP) 1987; First Secretary FCO 1988; First Secretary (Economic) Berlin 1991; First Secretary FCO 1996; Counsellor Madrid 2000.

Sharpless, Fiona Ure (née McGowan); SUPL since October 2002; Born 23/02/65; FCO 1988; Brussels (UKREP) 1989; SUPL 1992; Kathmandu 1993; SUPL 1994; Lagos 1998; SUPL 1999; Dhaka 2001; Band B3; m 1990 Kristian Sharpless (1d 1993; 1s 1995).

Sharpless, Kristian; FCO since April 2003; Born 17/06/67; Dept of Employment 1985; FCO 1987; Brussels 1989; Kathmandu 1992; FCO 1995; Lagos 1996; FCO 1999; Dhaka 2001; Band C4; m 1990 Fiona Ure McGowan (1d 1993; 1s 1995).

Shaughnessy, Kevin John; Deputy Head of Mission Santo Domingo since January 2002; Born 10/11/64; FCO 1983; Tehran 1986; Kingston 1988; Bonn 1991; Second Secretary FCO 1994; Second Secretary (Commercial) Bahrain 1998; m 1997 Elizabeth Ann Churchill (2d 1998, 2001).

Shaw, Alan John; Second Secretary (Political/Information) Dhaka since January 2002; Born 09/06/66; FCO 1987; Washington 1989; Peking 1992; FCO 1995; Bangkok 1998; Prague 1999; Band C4; m 1989 Claire Louise Morgan.

Shaw, Andrew John; FCO since November 2003; Born 03/03/70; FCO 1989; Bonn 1991; Tehran 1994; FCO 1996; Prague 2000; Band C4; m 1995 Sarah Gosling (2s 1996, 1999).

Shaw, Andrew William; Harare since June 2002; Born 31/03/50; FCO 1997; Band A2; m 1981 Ruth Heeps (s 1984, 1989; 1d 1990).

Shaw, Claire Louise (née Morgan); Second Secretary (Immigration/Consular) Dhaka since November 2001; Born 18/06/68; FCO 1987; Washington 1989; FCO 1992; Peking 1993; FCO 1995; Bangkok 1998; Band C4; m 1989 Alan John Shaw.

Shaw, Philip; First Secretary (Commercial) Paris since December 1999; Born 22/05/45; CRO 1963; DSAO 1965; Khartoum 1966; Language Training 1969; Ulaanbaatar 1970; Nairobi 1973; FCO 1978; Seconded to the DTI 1980; São Paulo 1982; Brussels 1985; FCO 1990; Lisbon 1991; First Secretary FCO 1997; m (1) 1970 Christine Goodwin (diss) (1d 1974; 1s 1976); (2) 1992 Marthe Vercammen.

Shaw, Samantha; Nicosia since October 2001; Born 31/03/67; FCO 1999; Band A2.

Shaw, Sarah Elaine (née Gosling); FCO since April 2001; Born 29/07/69; FCO 1990; Bonn 1992; FCO 1994; Tehran 1994; FCO 1996; SUPL 1997; Band B3; m 1995 Andrew John Shaw (2s 1996, 1999).

Shaw, Sharon Beverley (née Dolan); Nairobi since October 2002; Born 28/11/66; MAFF 1991; FCO 1993; Peking 1994; MO/VC Guangzhou 1998; ECO Pretoria 1999; Band B3; m 2001 Andrew Shaw.

Shead, Robert John; Second Secretary (Commercial) Shanghai since July 2002; Born 14/04/50; FCO 1969; Bonn 1973; Seoul 1976; FCO 1977; Paris 1978; Damascus 1982; FCO 1985; Damascus 1986; FCO 1987; Nairobi 1988; Second Secretary Manila 1992; FCO 1997; Second Secretary Guangzhou 1998; m (1) 1981 Carol Ann Bostock (diss 1987); (2) 1987 Fayha Sultan (1s 1987).

Shearing, Sally Louise; FCO since August 1995; Born 20/04/66; FCO 1985; Budapest 1988; FCO 1990; Sofia 1992; Band A2.

Shearman, Martin James, CVO (2004); Deputy High Commissioner Abuja since July 2003; Born 07/02/65; Third later Second Secretary FCO 1989; Language Training 1991; Full-Time Language Training Tokyo 1992; Second Secretary (Commercial) Tokyo 1993; First Secretary (Commercial) Tokyo 1994; On loan to the DTI 1996; On loan to the Cabinet Office 1998; NATO Secretariat 1999; FCO 1999; m 1996 Miriam Elizabeth Pyburn (1s 2004).

Shearman, Miriam Elizabeth (née Pyburn); SUPL since November 2003; Born 11/06/65; FCO 1990; Full-Time Language Training 1990; Tokyo 1992; APS/PUS 1996; T/D Brussels (UKREP) 2000; FCO 2000; SUPL 2001; FCO 2002; Band D7; m 1996 Martin James Shearman (1s 2004).

Sheikh, Soraya Zia; SUPL since June 2003; Born 03/07/72; FCO 1998; Brussels 2000; Band A2.

Sheinwald, Sir Nigel Elton, KCMG (2001), CMG (1999); Foreign Policy Adviser to the Prime Minister, No. 10 Downing Street since August 2003; Born 26/06/53; FCO 1976; Moscow 1978; Second later First Secretary FCO 1979; First Secretary (Chancery) Washington 1983; First Secretary later Counsellor FCO 1987; Counsellor and Head of Chancery Brussels (UKREP) 1993; Head of News Department FCO 1995; Director FCO (European Union) 1998; Permanent Representative Brussels (UKREP) 2000; m 1980 Julia Dunne (3s 1984, 1985, 1987).

Shelly, Simon Richard; Full-Time Language Training (French) since November 2003; Born 05/07/60; HM Customs & Excise 1981-83; FCO 1983; Kabul 1986; Paris 1988; FCO 1991; Ankara 1995; FCO 1998; m 1991 Monique Marie Renée Le Roux (1d 1995; 1s 1996).

Shepherd, Daniel James Owen; First Secretary New Delhi since August 2004; Born 05/11/71; FCO 1994; Full-Time Language Training 1995; Third later Second Secretary (Political/PPA) Hanoi 1996; New York (UKMIS) 2000; First Secretary FCO 2001; Band D6; m 2001 Marina Naomi Yanai (1 step s 1991, 1s 2003).

Shepherd, Wendy Elizabeth; Peking since September 2000; Born 03/07/71; OFFER 1993; FCO 1996; Port of Spain 1997; Band B3.

Sheppard, David Anthony; Second later First Secretary FCO since November 1995; Born 06/07/51; HCS 1968; Hong Kong 1977; FCO 1980; Baghdad 1983; Tel Aviv 1986; FCO 1989 (Second Secretary 1992); Second Secretary Brussels 1993; Band D6; m 1988 Bonita Dorsman (dec'd).

Sheppard, Jane Louise (née McMullin); Tel Aviv since April 2001; Born 19/07/70; FCO 1997; Ottawa 1998; SUPL 2000; Band A2; m 1998 William John Crean Sheppard (1d 2000).

Sheppard, Nicholas Ugo; First Secretary (Media and Public Affairs) Pretoria since June 2001; Born 02/06/56; DTI 1973; FCO 1974; Paris (UKDEL OECD) 1977; Islamabad 1980; FCO 1982; Aden 1983; Canberra 1986; Second Secretary FCO 1989; Second Secretary (Commercial) New Delhi 1992; First Secretary (Commercial) Bucharest 1995; First Secretary FCO 1998; Band C5.

Sherar, Paul Desmond; Second later First Secretary FCO since May 1995; Born 24/02/53; FCO 1970; Brussels 1973; Africa Floater 1976; Georgetown 1978; FCO 1981; Vice-Consul (Commercial) New York (BTDO) 1986; Second Secretary (Commercial/Aid) Luanda 1991.

Shercliff, Simon; Baghdad since September 2003; Born 23/12/72; FCO 1998; Full-Time Language Training 1999; Second Secretary Tehran 2000; Band D6; m 2002 Emma Louise.

Sheriff, Philip Mark; First Secretary Bogotá since June 2004; Born 30/11/71; FCO 2002; Band D6.

Sherman, Sheila Ann (née Baker); FCO since April 1993; Born 06/06/60; FCO 1984; Peking 1985; FCO 1988; Nicosia 1990; Band A2; m 1995 Christopher Sherman.

Sherrin, Barrie Robert; FCO since May 2001; Born 20/07/44; Royal Marines 1961-84; Baghdad 1989; Moscow 1991; Lisbon 1992; Dublin 1996; New Delhi 2000; Band B3; m 1967 Kathleen Mary.

Sherrington, Simon Richard; SUPL since June 2000; Born 27/05/55; FCO 1980; Language Training Kamakura 1982; Tokyo 1983; Second Secretary FCO 1987; Second Secretary (Chancery/Admin) Johannesburg 1987; Second Secretary FCO 1989; First Secretary on loan to the DTI 1994; Deputy Consul-General Boston 1996; Band D6.

Sherry, Daniel Thomas; FCO since March 2002; Born 01/02/72; Cabinet Office 1999; Band B3.

Shield, William George Rupert; FCO since March 2003; Born 18/12/78; Band C4.

Shingler, Michael John; First Secretary FCO since April 2003; Born 31/01/47; Post Office 1963; DSAO 1965; Manila 1969; Prague 1973; Dacca 1975; FCO 1979; Dar es Salaam 1981; Consul (Commercial) Casablanca 1984; FCO 1988; Consul (Management) Istanbul 1991; Deputy Consul-General Atlanta 1995; First Secretary FCO 1999; On loan to No. 10 Downing Street 2002; m 1969 Katina Janet Wall (1d 1972; 1s 1975).

Shipster, Michael David, OBE (1990); Counsellor Washington since July 2004; Born 17/03/51; Second later First Secretary FCO 1977; First Secretary (Chancery) Moscow 1981; First Secretary FCO 1983; New Delhi 1986; First Secretary (Chancery) Lusaka 1990; Consul Johannesburg 1991; First Secretary later Counsellor FCO 1994; m 1974 Jacquelynne Mann (2d 1981, 1982; 1s 1987).

Shirodkar, Dr Justin; FCO since March 2003; Born 30/10/73; Band C4.

Shivers, Marie Louise (née Stone); New York (UKMIS) since September 2002; Born 27/08/74; FCO 1992; Singapore 1996; FCO 1999; Band A2; m 1999 Gavin John Shivers

Shokat, Mohammed; Amman since September 2003; Born 07/11/75; FCO 2001; Full-Time Language Training 2002; Band C4.

Short, James Walter; Dhaka since September 1999; Born 19/10/66; FCO 1986; Calcutta 1989; Shanghai 1991; Third Secretary Tehran 1994; FCO 1997; Band B3; m 1990 Stephanie Sanjukta Ghosh (1s 1998).

Shorter, Hugo Benedict; FCO since August 2001; Born 11/08/66; FCO 1990; Second Secretary on attachment to ENA Paris 1992; Second later First Secretary Brussels (UKDEL NATO) 1994; FCO 1998; Private Secretary to Minister of State 2000; m 2001 Laura Mercedes Lindon (1d 2002).

Shott, Philip Nicholas; Counsellor Pretoria since November 2001; Born 27/11/54; Second Secretary FCO 1980; First Secretary Lagos 1983; First Secretary FCO 1986; First Secretary (Chancery) Nicosia 1987; First Secretary FCO 1991; First Secretary (Political) Lusaka 1994; First Secretary FCO 1997; m 1981 Lesley Ann Marsh (1s 1986; 1d 1987).

Shrimpton, Katy Emma; FCO since November 2002; Born 27/07/78; Band A2.

Shute, Christopher David; Gibraltar since December 2002; Born 08/10/49; HMIT 1968; FCO 1969; Middle East Floater 1972; Lagos 1974; Cairo 1975; FCO 1979; Rome 1983; Second Secretary FCO 1986; Second Secretary (Commercial) Warsaw 1987; Second Secretary FCO 1990; First Secretary (Chancery) Wellington 1995; FCO 1999; First Secretary FCO 2000; Band D6; m 1975 Peta Ann Dewhurst (2s 1987, 1990).

Sidebottom, Jane Louise; FCO since September 2003; Born 12/11/79; Band B3.

Sidnell, Gail Marilyn, MBE; FCO since August 1999; Born 09/04/53; FCO 1974; Addis Ababa 1975; Monrovia 1977; Gibraltar 1981; FCO 1982; Prague 1983; FCO 1985; Nairobi 1989; FCO 1993 (Second Secretary 1994); Second Secretary (Commercial) Jakarta 1996; SUPL 2001.

Silva, Ginny Anne (née Kesterton); SUPL since January 2004; Born 09/07/63; Immigration Service 1985; FCO 1987; Seoul 1989; Luxembourg 1994; FCO 1998; Port Louis 2002; Band C4; (1d 1993).

Simcox, Paul Alan; FCO since March 2003; Born 19/06/65; Band C4.

Simmons, Ian Paul; Counsellor FCO since February 2003; Born 05/09/55; FCO 1983; Second Secretary (Information) New Delhi 1987; First Secretary FCO 1989; Full-Time Language Training Point Cook, Melbourne 1992; First Secretary (Political) Hanoi 1992; First Secretary (Regional Affairs) Bangkok 1993; FCO 1996; Counsellor Nairobi 1999; m 1999 Elisabeth Jozina van de Ree (1d 2002).

Simmons, Timothy Michael John; Deputy Head of Mission Warsaw since November 2001; Born 08/04/60; FCO 1982; Third later Second Secretary Warsaw 1985; First Secretary FCO 1987; First Secretary Geneva (UKMIS) 1993; Seconded to Price Waterhouse Coopers MCS 1997; Assistant Director FCO 1999; m 1989 Caroline Mary Radcliffe (2s 1990, 1993).

Simon, Susannah Kate; On loan to the Home Office since September 2003; Born 07/06/64; FCO 1988; Third later Second Secretary Bonn 1989; Second Secretary Almaty 1992; FCO 1994; First Secretary (Political) Bonn 1999; m 1994 Mikhail Mnaidarovich Kubekov (1s 1996).

Simpson, Brian; Third Secretary (Visits) Hong Kong since May 2003; Born 08/05/67; FCO 1986; Warsaw 1988; Lagos 1991; FCO 1995; Vice-Consul Budapest 1999; Band B3.

Simpson, Faye Marie; Paris since June 2004; Born 03/06/78; FCO 2003; Band A2.

Simpson, Georgina Felicity (née Little); FCO since September 1999; Born 23/02/64; FCO 1986; Language Training 1987; Second Secretary Amman 1989; SUPL 1991; Second Secretary (Commercial/Economic/Political) Sana'a 1991; FCO 1994; SUPL 1999; m 1991 Dominic Mark Simpson (1d 1996).

Simpson, Gordon Grant; HM Consul Oporto since June 2003; Born 25/08/46; FO 1964; Peking 1968; Lisbon 1970; Ibadan 1972; FCO 1975; Bucharest 1978; Nairobi 1979; Lisbon 1982; Second Secretary FCO 1985; Second Secretary (Commercial) Luanda 1987; Second Secretary (Immigration) Islamabad 1990; First Secretary FCO 1992; Deputy Consul-General Rio de Janeiro 1994; Deputy Consul-General and HM Consul (Commercial) San Francisco 1998; m 1970 Jenny Frances Parker (1d 1974; 2s 1975, 1982).

Simpson, Louise Jane; FCO since 2002; Born 24/06/66; FCO 1986; Lima 1988; SUPL 1990; FCO 1992; Moscow 1993; FCO 1996; Kampala 1998; Band C4.

Simpson, Matthew Richard; Third Secretary (Consular) Wellington since February 2004; Born 04/05/72; FCO 1999; Floater Duties 2001; Band B3; m 2003 Anita Angela Krishna.

Simpson, Scott; FCO since May 2003; Born 28/03/70; FCO 1991; Bangkok 1995; Lima 1999; Band B3.

Simpson, Timothy John; FCO since September 1998; Born 14/09/60; FCO 1988; Third Secretary (Political) Budapest 1994; Band B3; m 1985 Lise Margaret Finlay (3d 1986, 1992, 1995).

Sims, Christopher Julien Bouyer; Second Secretary (Political) Seoul since November 2001; Born 08/05/78; FCO 1999; Full-Time Language Training 2000; Band C4.

Sinclair, Fiona Louise; FCO since October 2003; Born 13/01/71; FCO 1993; Full-Time Language Training 1995; Third Secretary (Political) Strasbourg 1996; Third Secretary (Political) Zagreb 1999; Band C4.

Sinclair, Robert Nelson Gurney; On loan to the DTI since November 1999; Born 10/12/52; FCO 1972; Dacca 1975; Algiers 1978; East Berlin 1980; CG Berlin 1981; FCO 1984; Third later Second Secretary Jakarta 1987; FCO 1991; Second Secretary (KHF) Sofia 1996; Band C5; m 1975 Diana Sawyer (1s 1986; 1d 1988).

Singh, Jatinder Jit; FCO since September 2001; Born 08/09/75; Band C4.

Singh, Mala; SUPL since August 2003; Born 01/01/73; FCO 1996; Buenos Aires 2000; Band A2.

Singh, Tracey Michelle (née Chapman); SUPL since April 2004; Born 30/10/68; FCO 1988; New Delhi 1990; FCO 1994; Dubai 1996; SUPL 1999; FCO 2000; Third Secretary (Immigration) Accra

2001; Band B3; m 1995 Jasminder Singh (2d 1999, 2002).

Sinkinson, Philip Andrew; Deputy Head of Mission Kingston since September 2001; Born 07/10/50; Inland Revenue 1967; FCO 1970; Warsaw 1973; FCO 1974; East Berlin 1974; Rome 1975; FCO 1976; Rio de Janeiro 1978; Quito 1978; Prague 1979; FCO 1981; Blantyre 1982; Lilongwe 1985; FCO 1986; Second Secretary (Commercial) São Paulo 1991; Olympic Attaché Atlanta 1995; First Secretary (Commercial) Lisbon 1996; m 1971 Clare Maria Catherine Jarvis (1s 1974).

Sinton, William Baldie, OBE (1999); HM Ambassador La Paz since October 2001; Born 17/06/46; Third Secretary FCO 1968; Third later Second Secretary (Commercial) Prague 1970; Second later First Secretary Brussels (UKDEL NATO) 1973; First Secretary FCO 1977; First Secretary (Commercial) Algiers 1981; First Secretary FCO 1985; HM Ambassador Panama City 1996; HM Ambassador Algiers 1999; m 1995 Jane S B Aryee.

Sisum, Thomas George; FCO since September 1999; Born 16/10/73; Band C4; m 2002 Sophie Katherine Devonshire.

Sizeland, Paul Raymond; Director (Consular Services), FCO since July 2003; Born 19/02/52; FCO 1980; Brussels (UKDEL NATO) 1981; Doha 1985; Second Secretary FCO 1986; First Secretary (Chancery/Aid) Lagos 1988; Private Secretary to the Chairman of EC Conference on Yugoslavia 1991; First Secretary later Counsellor FCO 1991; Deputy Head of Mission Bangkok 1996; Consul-General Shanghai 2000; m 1976 Vasantha Jesudasan (2d 1981, 1982).

Skidmore, Jonathan Richard Llywelyn; Second Secretary Vienna (UKMIS) since October 2001; Born 06/01/70; FCO 1998; Band C4.

Skilton, Christopher Paul; FCO since June 2003; Born 07/04/54; Bonn 1974; Santiago 1976; FCO 1980; Buenos Aires 1983; Madrid 1986; Resigned 1991; Reinstated, FCO 1993; Madrid 1996; FCO 1998; Deputy High Commissioner Kampala 2001; m 1978 Kathleen Jane (1d 1982; 1s 1980).

Skingle, Diana; High Commissioner Victoria since July 2004; Born 03/05/47; Commonwealth Office (later FCO) 1966; Kampala 1970; FCO 1972; Abidjan 1974; Vila 1975; Prague 1977; Casablanca 1979; Second Secretary FCO 1982; Second Secretary (Aid/Commercial) Georgetown 1985; Second Secretary (Development) Bridgetown 1986; First Secretary (Information) Brussels (UKDEL NATO) 1988; First Secretary FCO 1993; Deputy Head of Mission Addis Ababa 2001; ptnr, Christopher John Marshall Carrington.

Skinner, Dawn Emma; Bucharest since June 2002; Born 18/05/65; FCO 1985; Prague 1987; Brussels (UKREP) 1989; Anguilla 1991; FCO 1993; World Wide Floater Duties 1995; SUPL 1996; Sarajevo 1997; FCO 1998; Band B3.

Skinner, Gillian (née Smith); SUPL since August 2002; Born 09/01/57; FCO 1976; SUPL 1978; Beirut 1980; SUPL 1980; Beirut 1982; FCO 1982; Brussels 1983; FCO 1984; Kinshasa 1987; FCO 1988; Second Secretary 1992; Band C4; m (1) 1978 Colin Wynn Crorkin (diss 1991) (2s 1985, 1992); (2) 1996 Graeme John Skinner.

Skyring, Andrea; SUPL since July 2002; Born 01/08/66; FCO 1998; Dar es Salaam 1999; Band A2.

Slater, Angela (née Caldwell); SUPL since July 2002; Born 09/03/67; FCO 1986; Washington 1988; Floater Duties 1992; Third later Second Secretary FCO 1994; SUPL 1999; Second Secretary (Consular) New Delhi 2000; Band C4; m 1998 David John Slater (1d 1999; 1s 2001).

Slater, David John; HM Consul (Investment) Los Angeles since August 2002; Born 02/03/68; FCO 1987; Abu Dhabi 1989; Third Secretary Accra 1991; Third later Second Secretary FCO 1995; Second Secretary (Commercial) New Delhi 1999; Band C5; m 1998 Angela Caldwell (1d 1999; 1s 2001).

Slater, Gina Michelle (née Lambert); Second Secretary FCO since March 1996; Born 29/07/54; FCO 1974; Port Stanley 1976; SUPL 1978; Lisbon 1982; FCO 1986; Dhaka 1988; Harare 1992; m 1976 Gordon Slater (diss) (1d 1981).

Slater, Jacqueline (née Brewitt); SUPL since January 2002; Born 02/08/65; FCO 1985; Dublin 1989; FCO 1989; Beirut 1992; Bonn 1996; Band B3; m 1997 Steven Haigh Slater.

Slater, Judith Mary; Consul-General Houston since August 2004; Born 26/06/64; FCO 1988; Third later Second Secretary (Political) Canberra 1989; New York (UKMIS) 1992; First Secretary FCO 1993; Private Secretary to Minister of State 1994; First Secretary (Press and Public Affairs) New Delhi 1997; Assistant Director, Personnel Policy FCO 2001; SUPL 2003; Full-Time Language Training 2004; m 1998 Philip Frederick de Waal (1d 2000; 1s 2003).

Slater, Karen Elizabeth Sunley; Kiev since August 2002; Born 07/03/70; FCO 1988; Lagos 1991; Anguilla 1995; Tunis 1999; Band C4.

Slaymaker, Caroline Frances (née Grigg); Belgrade since August 2001; Born 14/10/64; FCO 1983; Düsseldorf 1986; Third Secretary (Aid) Khartoum 1988; FCO 1990; Vice-Consul Addis Ababa 1992; Third Secretary (Political/Information) Bratislava 1997; m 1996 Michael William Slaymaker.

Slinn, David Arthur, OBE (2000); HM Ambassador Pyongyang since October 2002; Born 16/04/59; FCO 1981; Geneva (UKDIS) 1983; Language Training 1986; Second Secretary and Head of Chancery Ulaanbaatar 1987; Second Secretary (Information/Aid) Pretoria/Cape Town 1990; Second Secretary FCO 1993; Chargé d'Affaires T/D Tirana 1995; First Secretary (Commercial) later (Chancery) Belgrade 1996;

Head of British Government Office Pristina 1999; On loan to MOD 2001; T/D Belgrade 2001; T/D Skopje 2001; m 1982 Melody Sarah Hesford.

Sloan, Kevin Joseph Carnegie; Counsellor FCO since October 2002; Born 31/08/58; HM Forces 1976-84; FCO 1984; Second later First Secretary (Chancery) Islamabad 1987; First Secretary FCO 1990; First Secretary Phnom Penh 1992; First Secretary (Economic) Kuala Lumpur 1993; First Secretary FCO 1997; Counsellor New Delhi 2001; m 1991 Christine Ruth Lowson (2d 1993, 1994).

Small, Susan Jane Rosemary; FCO since November 2002; Born 23/01/49; FCO 1985; Banjul 1986; Brussels (UKDEL NATO) 1989; New York (UKMIS) 1992; FCO 1994; Brussels 1995; Prague 1999; Band B3.

Smart, Christopher David Russell; Second Secretary (Consular) Ottawa since December 2001; Born 22/05/52; FCO 1971; Paris (UKDEL OECD) 1974; Bridgetown 1977; Lilongwe 1980; Third Secretary FCO 1983; Port Moresby 1987; Kingston 1991; Second Secretary FCO 1995; Second Secretary (Commercial) Nairobi 1998; m 1980 Patricia Margaret King (2 adopted d 1993, 1998).

Smart, Melanie Jane; Sofia since August 2002; Born 12/04/67; MOD 1986 - 2000; FCO 2000; Band A2; m 1989 David Michael Smart (4d 1991, 1993, 2001, 2002).

Smart, Simon James; Islamabad since July 2003; Born 29/04/71; FCO 2002; Band B3.

Smart, Timothy Spencer; First Secretary (Political) Basra since July 2004; Born 17/09/74; FCO 1999; Second Secretary (Political) Tel Aviv 2001; Band D6.

Smith, Andrew Dominic Charles; FCO since January 2002; Born 01/06/67; FCO 1990; Bangkok 1992; Full-Time Language Training 1992; Third Secretary (Economic) Warsaw 1993; Third Secretary (Political) Bonn 1996; SUPL 2001; Band D6.

Smith, Carol Ann; On secondment to Greater Merseyside Enterprise since January 2003; Born 11/11/63; FCO 1987; Pretoria/Cape Town 1989; Budapest 1992; Moscow 1995; FCO 1997; Khartoum 1999; SUPL 2000; Band B3.

Smith, Claire Helen (née Stubbs); FCO since July 2004; Born 23/12/56; FCO 1979; Language Training Hong Kong 1981; Second Secretary Peking 1983; First Secretary FCO 1985; SUPL 1990; On secondment to German MFA Bonn 1994; Bonn 1997; Counsellor (Political/Aid) Islamabad 1999; On loan to the Cabinet Office 2001; m 1986 Michael Forbes Smith (1d 1989; 1s 1992).

Smith, Colin Anthony; FCO since February 2001; Born 19/09/69; FCO 1995; Secondment to European Commission Brussels 1997; Second Secretary FCO 1998; Second Secretary (Political) Sofia 1998; On loan to DFID Sofia 1999; Band D6; m 2000 Suzanne Hunnewell (1s 2002).

Smith, David Joseph; HM Consul Osaka since February 1998; Born 12/01/51; FCO 1969; Tokyo 1972; Kuwait 1977; Warsaw 1979; FCO 1981; Osaka 1984; Second later First Secretary (Assistant Trade Commissioner) BTC Hong Kong 1989; First Secretary to T/D Taiwan 1994; First Secretary FCO 1994; First Secretary (Commercial) Tokyo 1996; m 1975 Hitomi Takahashi (2d 1978, 1982).

Smith, Deborah Ann (née Connor); SUPL since January 1999; Born 10/02/64; FCO 1992; New Delhi 1994; Amman 1998; Band B3; m 1997 (1d 1987).

Smith, Derek Moir; Second Secretary Freetown since February 2001; Born 12/09/67; Department of Employment 1986; FCO 1987; Riyadh 1989; Latin America/Caribbean Floater 1993; SUPL 1995; FCO 1996; Band C4.

Smith, Gerald Dominic; Oslo since June 2004; Born 04/04/70; FCO 1988; Islamabad 1992; Luanda 1996; FCO 1998; Bratislava 2002; Band B3; m 1992 Penelope Jane Clifford (1d 1996; 1s 1999).

Smith, Hugh Maxwell Spencer; Islamabad since January 2003; Born 04/04/59; FCO 1981; Brussels 1985; FCO 1988; New York 1992; FCO 1995; Tokyo 1998; FCO 2002; Band C5.

Smith, Jason R; Second Secretary (Political) Abu Dhabi since December 2000; Born 20/11/70; FCO 1989; Sofia 1991; Dar es Salaam 1993; FCO 1998; Band C4; m 1994 Andreana Vlaeva (1s 1994).

Smith, John Lawrence; Deputy High Commissioner Gaborone since November 2000; Born 15/10/65; FCO 1988; Vice-Consul Chicago 1990; Third Secretary Nairobi 1993; Second Secretary FCO 1997; m 1990 Gillian Monsen (2s 1993, 1997).

Smith, John Stephen; Head of South Asian Department FCO since February 2002; Born 28/03/57; Third Secretary FCO 1979; Third later Second Secretary (Commercial) Seoul 1980; Second Secretary FCO 1985; Second later First Secretary (Chancery) New York (UKMIS) 1987; First Secretary FCO 1990; First Secretary (Political/Internal) Bonn 1994; Deputy Head of Mission Brussels Embassy 1999; m 1984 Wanda Won Min Kim.

Smith, Justine Mary (née Bunn); SUPL since June 2003; Born 02/10/64; FCO 1983; Budapest 1986; Doha 1987; FCO 1991; Bangkok 1995; Durban 1999; SUPL 2001; Durban 2002; FCO 2002; Band C4; m 2000 Stephen Thomas Smith (1d 2001).

Smith, Katherine Jane; SUPL since April 1999; Born 21/05/67; FCO 1990; Third Secretary (Information) Istanbul 1993; T/D Suva 1997; Band B3.

Smith, Katherine Lucy; FCO since September 2001; Born 10/01/64; FCO 1987; Full-Time Language Training 1990; Second Secretary

(Chancery/Inf) Athens 1991; First Secretary FCO 1994; New York (UKMIS) 1997.

Smith, Lynne Marie; Bucharest since September 2003; Born 17/02/63; FCO 1982; Peking 1984; Ankara 1987; FCO 1990; SUPL 1994; Istanbul 1999; Band C4; m 1989 Ahmet Kalaycio Fglu.

Smith, Mairi (née Dyer); Helsinki since March 2001; Born 03/03/71; FCO 1991; SUPL 1995; FCO 1996; Canberra 1997; Band A2; m 1997 Daniel Beaton Smith (1d 2001; 1s 2003).

Smith, Nicolette Jane; Beirut since July 2001; Born 30/04/70; FCO 1989; Kuala Lumpur 1992; SUPL 1995; FCO 1997; Band B3.

Smith, Peter; First Secretary (Consular/Immigration) Moscow since November 2001; Born 06/08/51; FCO 1971; Canberra 1974; East Berlin 1976; Khartoum 1978; FCO 1982; Dhaka 1983; Manila 1988; Washington 1989; FCO 1991 (Second Secretary 1994); New Delhi 1994; Muscat 1996; m 1974 Cynthia Angela Shearn (1d 1975).

Smith, Shirley Kathleen (née Sandford); First Secretary (Trade Development) Stockholm since December 2002; Born 05/01/56; FCO 1974; Bonn 1977; Karachi 1979; FCO 1981; Nicosia 1984; Manila 1987; FCO 1991; Dublin 1994; m 1978 Roland Berkeley Smith (diss 1993) (1s 1988).

Smith, Simon John Meredith; Head of North East Asia and Pacific Dept FCO since July 2002; Born 14/01/58; Department of Employment 1981; Second Secretary FCO 1986; Language Training FCO/Kamakura 1987; Second later First Secretary (Economic) Tokyo 1989; FCO 1992; Counsellor (Commercial/Economic/S&T) Moscow 1998; m 1984 Siân Rosemary Stickings (2d 1989, 1993).

Smith, Stephen Jeremy; First Secretary (Management) and HM Consul Kabul since February 2002; Born 25/10/44; FO later DSAO 1964; Baghdad 1968; Sofia 1973; FCO 1974; Vice-Consul Sydney 1977; Assistant Parliamentary Clerk FCO 1982; Second Secretary (Admin) and HM Consul Algiers 1983; FCO 1986; On secondment to the Birmingham Chamber of Industry and Commerce 1989; Second Secretary (Commercial) Dar es Salaam 1991; First Secretary, Deputy Consul-General and Consul (Commercial) Shanghai 1994; First Secretary FCO 1998; Band D6; m 1969 Delyth Morris (dec'd 2002) (2d 1973, 1977; 2s 1975, 1978).

Smith, Stuart Harris; Floater Duties since February 2004; Born 24/04/48; Nicosia 1989; Belgrade 1991; World Wide Floater Duties 1993; Moscow 1996; Kiev 1998; Band B3; m 1969 Carol Ann (1s 1971; 1d 1974).

Smith, Stuart Vaughan; Tortola since June 2002; Born 05/07/72; FCO 1991; New Delhi 1995; Rio de Janeiro 1999; Band B3.

Smith, Susan Lesley; FCO since January 2000; Born 29/12/63; FCO 1983; New Delhi 1985; T/D Belgrade 1988; Kathmandu 1989; FCO 1992; Pretoria 1996; T/D Casablanca 1999; Band C4.

Smith, William John; Karachi since April 2002; Born 20/02/48; Royal Marines 1964-88; Bonn 1988; Floater Duties 1993; Sofia 1994; Peking 1998; Band B3; m 1971 Doreen (1s 1973; 2d 1971, 1976).

Snee, Nicholas James Michael; Vice-Consul Moscow since June 2001; Born 10/07/65; HM Forces Army 1982-94; FCO 1996; Windhoek 1998; Band B3; m 2000 Valerie Johr.

Snell, Arthur Gordon; Second Secretary (Political) Sana'a since October 2003; Born 30/10/75; FCO 1998; Second Secretary (Political/Economic) Harare 2000; Second Secretary (Political/Economic) Abuja 2001; Full-Time Language Training (Arabic) 2003; Band C4.

Snell, Michael George, MVO (1980); Management Officer Muscat since August 2001; Born 09/06/47; FCO 1972; Darwin 1973; FCO 1975; Rome 1978; Banjul 1981; FCO 1982; Sofia 1983; Second Secretary FCO 1985; Second Secretary Washington 1988; Jakarta 1994; FCO 1998; m (1) 1973 Diana Mary Powell-Williams (diss 1992) (2d 1977, 1979; 1s 1982); (2) Victoria B Curry (1s 1996).

Snook, Andrew John; FCO since August 2002; Born 18/07/72; FCO 1992; World Wide Floater Duties 1995; Full-Time Language Training 1997; Rio de Janeiro 1998; Band C4; m 1999 Priscila de Medeiros Ivo Santos (1d 2000).

Snowdon, Susan Carol (known as Sue); FCO since 2000; Born 12/07/65; MOD 1983; FCO 1985; Brussels 1987; Manila 1989; FCO 1993; Accra 1997; Band B3.

Snoxell, David Raymond; High Commissioner Port Louis since September 2000; Born 18/11/44; FCO 1969; Islamabad 1972; Geneva (UKMIS) 1976; Second later First Secretary FCO 1984; Executive Director and Consul (Information) New York (BIS) 1986; First Secretary FCO 1991; HM Ambassador Cape Verde, Dakar, Guinea, Guinea Bissau and Mali 1997; m 1971 Anne Carter (2s 1972, 1977; 1d 1973).

Sommerlad, Alistair Martin; First Secretary (Political) Sarajevo since July 2001; Born 15/10/65; FCO 1996; Lagos 1996; First Secretary FCO 1999; Band D6.

Soothill, Deborah Jane; FCO since October 2001; Born 22/05/69; FCO 1992; Full-Time Language Training Peking 1995; Second Secretary (Chancery/External) Peking 1996; Second Secretary FCO 1999; SUPL 2000; Band C4; m 1996 Brendan Paul Mahoney da Madariaga.

Soper, Andrew Keith; Deputy Head of Mission Brasilia since June 2001; Born 06/07/60; FCO 1985; Second later First Secretary (Chancery) Mexico City 1987; First Secretary FCO 1990; First Secretary Washington 1995; FCO 1999; m 1987 Kathryn Garrett Stevens (1s 1991; 1d 1993).

Southern, Thomas Andrew Oliver; Second Secretary (Political) Skopje since January 2002; Born 15/01/75; FCO 2000; Band C4.

Sowerby, Karen Dorothy Howell; Rangoon since November 2002; Born 14/06/46; FCO 1991; La Paz 1993; Yaoundé 1997; Luanda 2000; Band A2.

Sowerby, Lynne; Geneva since June 2002; Born 17/09/67; FCO 1988; East Berlin 1990; Ankara 1993; FCO 1997; Band B3.

Sparkes, Andrew James; HM Ambassador Kinshasa since July 2004; Born 04/07/59; FCO 1982; Second Secretary (Chancery) Ankara 1985; First Secretary FCO 1988; First Secretary (Political) Bangkok 1992; First Secretary later Counsellor FCO 1995; On loan to the DTI 1997; Deputy Head of Mission Jakarta 1999; Deputy High Commissioner Pretoria 2001; m 1985 Jean Mary Meakin (1s 1988; 1d 1992).

Sparrow, Rosalyn Louise (née Morris), MVO (1999); SUPL since June 2001; Born 15/05/61; FCO 1983; Dhaka 1986; Brussels (UKDEL) 1989; Second Secretary (Economic) Brussels 1991; Second Secretary (Commercial) Singapore 1993; Second Secretary Seoul 1998; m (1) 1986 Richard John Bryant (diss) (1s 1991); (2) David John Sparrow.

Spearman, Richard David; First Secretary FCO since August 2001; Born 30/08/60; FCO 1989; Consul Istanbul 1992; First Secretary FCO 1994; First Secretary (Political) Paris 1997; Band D6; m 1987 Caroline Jill Scoones (1s 1992; 2d 1995, 1998).

Speller, Paul Anthony; Deputy Head of Mission Jakarta since January 2002; Born 21/01/54; FCO 1983; Second later First Secretary Bonn 1986; First Secretary FCO 1989; Private Secretary to the Parliamentary Under Secretary of State 1991; First Secretary (External Relations) Brussels (UKREP) 1993; FCO 1996; Deputy Governor Gibraltar 1998; m 1998 Jane Hennessey.

Speller, Susan Barbara (née Arnold); FCO since October 2001; Born 22/10/56; FCO 1984; Vice-Consul (Commercial) Munich 1987; Vice-Consul (Information) Düsseldorf 1988; FCO 1990; Second Secretary FCO 1992; On loan to the ODA 1994; Second later First Secretary (PPA/Management) Bonn 1996; First Secretary (Public Relations) Berlin 1999.

Spellman, Antoinette Marie (née Mills); FCO since June 2002; Born 24/05/65; FCO 1988; Brussels (UKDEL NATO) 1991; Abuja 1993; Kuwait 1996; Islamabad 1999; Band A2; m 1990 Garry James Spellman (2s 1993, 1998).

Spencer, David Paul, MBE (1988); First Secretary FCO since July 2002; Born 04/04/59; FCO 1978; Kuala Lumpur 1981; FCO 1983; Aden 1985; First Secretary FCO 1988; First Secretary (Political) Stockholm 1992; FCO 1996; First Secretary (Political) Dubai 1999; Band D6; m 1988 Patricia Anne McCullock (2s 1990, 1993).

Spencer, Elaine Joan; FCO since March 1976; Born 24/03/49; FO 1966; DSAO 1966; FO (later FCO) 1967; Bonn 1972; Khartoum 1975; Band A2.

Spencer, Sarah; FCO since June 2003; Born 31/05/68; FCO 1988; Kathmandu 1990; FCO 1993; Bucharest 1995; Cairo 1999; Band B3; m 1997 Mark Anthony James Hamilton (1s 2000; 1d 2003).

Spicer, Haden Richard; Consul (Commercial) Guangzhou since February 2002; Born 18/06/62; FCO 1985; Abu Dhabi 1989; Moscow 1992; FCO 1995; Second Secretary (Commercial) Bandar Seri Begawan 1999; Band C4; m 1988 Carole E Pymble.

Spindler, Guy David St. John Kelso; Counsellor (Political) Warsaw since August 2002; Born 09/06/62; Second Secretary FCO 1987; Second later First Secretary (Commercial) Moscow 1989; First Secretary FCO 1992; First Secretary (Political) Pretoria 1997; First Secretary FCO 2000; Band D6; m 1999 Laura Jane Brady (1d 2000; 1s 2001).

Spires, David Mark, MVO (1992); Second Secretary (Commercial) Beijing since November 2001; Born 18/11/61; FCO 1980; Warsaw 1982; Lima 1985; FCO 1986; Islamabad 1987; Paris 1991; Full-Time Language Training 1993; San Salvador 1993; Belgrade 1997; Second Secretary (Management) Dublin 1999; Band C4; m 1987 (2s 1986, 1996; 1d 1990).

Spivey, Donald; Colombo since June 2004; Born 12/04/68; FCO 1989; Tokyo 1992; FCO 1995; Kamakura 1998; Tokyo 1999; Band B3.

Spoor, Peter Logan; Full-Time Language Training (Spanish) since November 2003; Born 04/11/68; FCO 1992; Full-Time Language Training 1994-96; Third Secretary (Commercial) Bangkok 1996; Second later First Secretary FCO 1999; Band D6; m 1998 Joanna M Haydon (1s 2002).

Sprod, Caroline; FCO since June 2002; Born 02/03/71; FCO 1993; T/D Kiev 1995; Full-Time Language Training 1995; Third Secretary Hong Kong 1996; Full-Time Language Training 2000; Madrid 2000; Band C4.

Sprunt, Patrick William; Counsellor FCO since January 2004; Born 13/04/52; Third Secretary FCO 1975; Language Training SOAS 1976; Second later First Secretary Tokyo 1978; FCO 1982; Brussels (UKREP) 1982; First Secretary Bonn 1983; First Secretary FCO 1986; First Secretary Tokyo 1987; First Secretary (ECOSOC) New York (UKMIS) 1992; First Secretary FCO 1996; Counsellor (Political Affairs) Tokyo 1999; m 1979 Haang Ai-Yuan Wong (1s 1985; 1d 1989).

Squibb, Keith Norman; Jerusalem since November 2002; Born 02/09/49; Prague 1989; Tel Aviv 1991; Warsaw 1993; Moscow 1995; Lagos 1998; Cairo 1999; Band B3; m 1974 Brigitte Pronier (3s 1974, 1978, 1984).

Squire, Richard James; First Secretary Pristina since May 2003; Born 11/09/74; FCO 1996; Full-Time Language Training 1998; Kabul 2002; Band D6.

Squires, George Thomas; High Commissioner Mbabane since November 2004; Born 20/10/48; FCO 1968; Dacca 1971; Antigua 1973; Warsaw 1975; Jakarta 1976; FCO 1979 (Second Secretary 1983); Vice-Consul later Consul and Administration Officer Sydney 1985; First Secretary (Commercial/Development) Bangkok 1990; First Secretary FCO 1993; First Secretary (Management) Peking 1997; On loan to the DTI 2002; m 1979 Helen Mary Thomas (2s 1983, 1985).

Squires, Helen (née Thomas); FCO since June 2000; Born 18/10/51; FCO 1973; Third Secretary (Commercial) Jakarta 1976; Third Secretary FCO 1979; SUPL 1983; Vice-Consul Bangkok 1990; FCO 1993; Second Secretary (Management) Peking 1997; m 1979 George Thomas Squires (2s 1983, 1985).

Stacey, Christopher Robin; ECM Manila since September 2002; Born 09/12/47; RAF 1965-74; FCO 1974; Islamabad 1976; Budapest 1980; Singapore 1983; FCO 1984; Manila 1988; Nicosia 1992; FCO 1995; New Delhi 1999; Band C4; m 1977 Coral Jane Chargé (2s 1981, 1987).

Stafford, Andrew Jeremy; Counsellor FCO since June 2003; Born 01/02/53; Third Secretary FCO 1975; Stockholm 1977; FCO 1979; Second Secretary Accra 1979; Second later First Secretary FCO 1981; First Secretary and Consul Prague 1984; First Secretary FCO 1987; First Secretary (Chancery) Brussels 1991; FCO 1994; Counsellor (Political) Stockholm 1999; m (1) 1977 Felicity Joanna Maria Kelly; (2) 1983 Elizabeth Rosemary Kempston (2d 1985, 1992; 1s 1988).

Stafford, Nina Jeanne; SUPL since February 2001; Born 28/09/71; FCO 1991; Buenos Aires 1997; The Hague 2000; Band A2.

Stafford, Rosemary Anne Jane (née Fish); SUPL since June 2002; Born 28/08/49; Ankara 1974; Honiara 1976; Bogotá 1978; FCO 1979; Far East Floater 1980; FCO 1982; On loan to DTI 1984; Second Secretary (Commercial) Rio de Janeiro 1986; FCO 1988; SUPL 1992; Second Secretary (Commercial) Singapore 1994; On loan to the DTI 1999; m 1987 Anthony John Stafford (1s 1991; 1d 1993).

Stagg, Charles Richard Vernon, CMG (2001); Director General (Corporate Affairs) FCO since December 2003; Born 27/09/55; FCO 1977; Third later Second Secretary Sofia 1979; The Hague 1982; First Secretary FCO 1985; Brussels (UKREP) 1987; First Secretary FCO 1988; First Secretary (Information) Brussels (UKREP) 1991; First Secretary FCO 1993; HM Ambassador Republic of Bulgaria 1998; Director (Information) FCO 2001; m 1982 Arabella Clare Faber (3s 1984, 1985, 1990; 2d 1992, 1997).

Standbrook, Timothy William; Second Secretary (Commercial) Shanghai since May 2003; Born 08/06/63; FCO 1988; Language Training Seoul 1990; Third Secretary (Political) Seoul 1992; FCO 1994; Peking (ECO) 1995; Karachi 1997; FCO

1997; On loan to British Trade International 2000; m 1997 Jia Lei (1d 2000).

Stanton, Emma Jane Elizabeth; Second Secretary (Political) New Delhi since June 2002; Born 21/04/78; FCO 2000; Band C4.

Stanton, Karen Jane (née Owen); First Secretary (Commercial) Prague since August 2003; Born 25/01/62; FCO 1984; Language Training Kamakura 1986; Vice-Consul Tokyo 1987; Third Secretary (Chancery) Rome 1991; Second Secretary FCO 1994; First Secretary FCO 1996; First Secretary (Commercial) Tokyo 1999; m 1990 Graham Stanton.

Stanton, Louise Jane; FCO since April 1999; Born 14/08/68; FCO 1990; Language Training (Japanese) SOAS 1991; Full-Time Language Training Kamakura 1993; Third Secretary (Commercial) Tokyo 1993; World Wide Floater Duties 1997; Band C4.

Stanyer, Julie Grace (née Robins); FCO since February 2000; Born 15/03/48; FCO 1984; Bridgetown 1985; Brussels (UKDEL NATO) 1989; FCO 1992; Oslo 1994; Brussels (UKDEL NATO) 1997; Band B3; m 1988 Patrick Julian Serville (diss 1995).

Staples, Graham Raymond; FCO since March 2001; Born 24/01/69; FCO 1988; Dublin 1989; Warsaw 1992; FCO 1994; Vice-Consul and Third Secretary Windhoek 1997; Band B3; m 1994 Sarah Kathleen Paterson (1d 1998).

Starkey, Nicholas Andrew; FCO since January 2003; Born 20/12/52; FCO 1972; SE Asia Floater 1975; Warsaw 1977; Bridgetown 1979; FCO 1981; Kuwait 1985; Second Secretary (Consular) Lagos 1989; Second Secretary FCO 1992; Second Secretary (Management) Bucharest 1995; Senior Management Officer Islamabad 1999; Band C5; m 1981 Rhodora Corrales Maroto (2s 1983, 1999; 1d 1985).

Staunton, Andrew James; Head of Political Section, Ottawa since September 2003; Born 07/08/67; FCO 1987; Peking 1989; Third Secretary (Chancery/Management) Strasbourg 1991; Third Secretary (Economic) Bucharest 1994; Second later First Secretary FCO 1997; Seconded to the Canadian Department for Foreign Affairs and International Trade, Ottawa 2002; Band D6; m 1990 Rebecca Anne Nixon (1s 1991; 1d 1993).

Stead, Michael; FCO since April 2002; Born 19/01/58; British Library 1976; FCO 1979; Jedda 1981; Riyadh 1982; LA Floater 1985; Rio de Janeiro 1988; FCO 1991; Second Secretary (Political) Addis Ababa 1994; Second Secretary (Commercial) Lisbon 1997.

Steel, Diane Elizabeth; On loan to No.10 Downing Street since December 1999; Born 02/08/60; FCO 1978; Brussels (UKREP) 1982; Dar es Salaam 1985; Doha 1989; St Petersburg 1992; FCO 1995; Band B3.

Steele, Christopher David; First Secretary FCO since September 2002; Born 24/06/64; FCO 1987;

Second Secretary (Chancery) Moscow 1990; Second later First Secretary FCO 1993; First Secretary (Financial) Paris 1998; Band D6; m 1990 Laura Katharine Hunt (2s 1996, 1998; 1d 2000).

Steen, Barry John; FCO since June 2002; Born 10/12/75; Benefits Agency 1997; Inland Revenue 1998-02; Band A2.

Steers, John Leonard; First Secretary (Technical Management) Washington since December 2003; Born 20/10/58; FCO 1988; Third Secretary (Technical Management) Washington 1996; FCO 1999; Band C5; m 1995 Claire Margaret Bullock (1s 1999; 1d 2000).

Stein, Gordon; ECM Tunis since July 2002; Born 20/02/69; FCO 1989; Geneva (UKMIS) 1991; Rabat 1994; Third Secretary Peking 1998; Band C4; m 1994 Deborah Anne Hooper.

Stent, Lindsay Samantha; Deputy Head of Mission Pyongyang since October 2004; Born 26/09/70; FCO 1996; First Secretary 2001; Full-Time Language Training 2002; On loan to the Cabinet Office 2003; Band D6.

Stephen, Ann (née Barbour); Tripoli since April 2002; Born 02/04/66; FCO 1988; Paris 1991; Freetown 1993; Banjul 1998; Brussels (UKDEL NATO) 1999; Band A2; m 1992 Robert Stephen (1s 1995).

Stephens, Adrian Charles; Consul-General Ho Chi Minh City since January 2001; Born 19/03/46; DSAO (later FCO) 1964; Karachi 1968; Colombo 1970; Budapest 1972; FCO 1974; Islamabad 1976; FCO 1978 (Second Secretary 1979); Bangkok 1982; Consul Berlin 1986; First Secretary FCO 1990; Seoul 1993; First Secretary (Commercial) Mexico City 1997; m 1968 Susan Jane Everitt (1d 1971; 1s 1973).

Stephens, Moira Elizabeth (née Hopkinson); SMO Tehran since June 2004; Born 28/08/59; FCO 1980; Copenhagen 1982; Peking 1985; Islamabad 1986; FCO 1990; Beirut 1992; FCO 1994; SUPL 1997; On loan to the DTI 2002; Band C4.

Stephenson, John Edmund; Counsellor New York since July 2004; Born 19/12/60; FCO 1986; Second later First Secretary (Information) Santiago 1989; First Secretary FCO 1992; First Secretary Havana 1994; First Secretary FCO 1998; Band D7; m 1986 Jacqueline Denise Clayton (3s 1990, 1992, 1993).

Sterling, Janice Aeyesha Odanna; FCO since August 2002; Born 08/08/69; FCO 1997; New York (UKMIS) 2000; Band A2; m 1994 Dwight Sterling.

Steven, John Young; Third Secretary (Political) New York (UKMIS) since December 2002; Born 21/05/68; FCO 1988; Moscow 1989; Washington 1992; FCO 1995; Floater Duties 2000; Band B3.

Stevens, Ian James; First Secretary (Management) Dublin since June 2002; Born 15/05/66; FCO 1985; Brussels (UKDEL NATO) 1989; New Delhi

1992; FCO 1996; First Secretary (Management/Consul) Oslo 1998; Band C5; m 1987 Adele Oliver (1d 1989; 1s 1991).

Stevens, Jill Frances; FCO since December 1992 (Second Secretary 1996); Born 10/03/57; FCO 1977; Damascus 1979; Bridgetown 1982; FCO 1984; Dar es Salaam 1987; FCO 1989; Moscow 1990; Band C4.

Stevens, Mark; First Secretary & Consul Denver since May 2004; Born 05/07/49; DSAO 1966; FCO 1968; Georgetown 1970; Madrid 1973; East Berlin 1976; FCO 1978; Kingston 1982; New Delhi 1985; Second Secretary FCO 1988; Second Secretary (Management) and Vice-Consul Tunis 1992; FCO 1995; Consul-General Alexandria 1999; m 1970 Pauline Elaine Graber (2d 1973, 1976).

Stevens, Paul David; FCO since September 2003; Born 08/09/59; MOD 1977; FCO 1981; Geneva (UKMIS) 1983; Kampala 1985; Washington 1988; FCO 1991; Full-Time Language Training 1994; Second Secretary Los Angeles 1999; Band C4; m 1985 Faye Jaqueline Brand (1s 1992; 1d 1995).

Stevenson, William Michael; First Secretary (Management) Dhaka since October 2002; Born 04/09/51; FCO 1971; Brussels (UKDEL NATO) 1973; Luxembourg 1977; Addis Ababa 1979; Moscow 1983; FCO 1985; Khartoum 1988; Second Secretary Ankara 1993; FCO 1997; Band C5; m 1982 Laura Birse Stirton (2s 1986, 1987).

Stew, Timothy David, MBE (1996); First Secretary (Political/Economic) Cairo since August 2003; Born 08/10/66; FCO 1988; Language Training 1989; Language Training Cairo 1990; Third Secretary (Chancery) Riyadh 1991; Sarajevo 1995; Deputy High Commissioner Belmopan 1996; FCO 2000; Band D6; m 1991 Michelle Louise Mealor (1d 1996; 1s 1998).

Stewart, Brian Edward; HM Ambassador Algiers since May 2004; Born 04/02/50; Third Secretary FCO 1972; MECAS 1973; Third later Second Secretary Amman 1975; On loan to the Cabinet Office 1978; First Secretary 1979; FCO 1980; First Secretary and Head of Chancery Singapore 1982; Head of Chancery Tunis 1986; First Secretary FCO 1989; Deputy Head of Mission Damascus 1993; Counsellor FCO 1996; Deputy Head of Mission and Counsellor Kuwait 1998; FCO 2002; On loan to Royal College of Defence Studies 2003; m 1975 Anne Elizabeth Cockerill.

Stewart, Iain Jamieson; Sofia since June 2003; Born 03/12/71; Geneva (UKDIS) 1994; World Wide Floater Duties 1999; Full-Time Language Training (Bulgarian) 2002; Band C4.

Stewart, Rachel Lovett; Second Secretary Dubai since June 2004; Born 09/02/79; FCO 2002; Band C4.

Stewart, Roderick James Nugent; SUPL since July 2000; Born 03/01/73; FCO 1995; Second Secretary (Economic) Jakarta 1997; Second

Secretary British Embassy Office Banja Luka 1999; Band C4.

Stirling, Sonia Louise; SUPL since June 2000; Born 17/06/74; FCO 1994; Paris 1996; Band A2.

Stitt, (Thomas) Clive Somerville; British Trade International since May 1999; Born 01/01/48; Third Secretary FCO 1970; Language Training Tehran 1972; Kabul 1972; Third later Second Secretary New Delhi 1974; First Secretary FCO 1977; Geneva (UKMIS) 1982; First Secretary later Counsellor FCO 1986; Counsellor New York (UKMIS) 1992; m 1977 Margaret Ann Milward (2d 1982, 1984).

Stokes, Antony, LVO (1996); First Secretary (Political) Seoul since April 2000; Born 21/01/65; FCO 1994; First Secretary and Head of Political Section Bangkok 1996; Full-Time Language Training 1999; Band D6.

Stokes, Karen Ann (née Chambers); FCO since February 2003; Born 18/12/67; FCO 1987; Bonn 1989; FCO 1991; Vienna 1993; FCO 1996; Tel Aviv 1999; m 1998 Paul Terence Stokes.

Stokey, Tracey Joanne Tudor; Brussels (UKDEL) since September 2002; Born 10/03/65; FCO 1988; Bonn 1990; Luxembourg 1993; Band A2; m 1988 Brendan Stokey (2s 1996, 1998).

Stokoe, Kay; FCO since 1997; Born 23/06/69; FCO 1989; Madrid 1992; Floater Duties 1995; Band B3.

Stollery, Mark Thomas; SUPL since May 2003; Born 08/10/60; Royal Navy 1978-88; Second Secretary FCO 1988; On loan to EU Commission 1989; Second Secretary (EC Affairs) Brussels 1990; First Secretary FCO 1993; First Secretary (Political) Islamabad 2002; First Secretary FCO 2002; Band D6; m 1990 Denise Jekyll (1s 1995; 1d 1998).

Stone, Jemma Catherine; Riyadh since March 2002; Born 08/01/70; FCO 1991; Bonn 1994; Moscow 1998; Band A2.

Stones, Adrian; First Secretary later Counsellor Harare since October 2000; Born 16/10/60; FCO 1986; Second later First Secretary (Information) New Delhi 1989; First Secretary FCO 1991; First Secretary (Chancery) Washington 1992; First Secretary FCO 1995; m 1990 Gillian Ruth Millman (2s 1992, 1994; 1d 1998).

Stonor, Ralph William Robert Thomas; Second Secretary New Delhi since April 2004; Born 10/09/74; FCO 2002; Band C4.

Storey, Neil William; First Secretary (Management) Brasilia since June 2004; Born 10/09/61; FCO 1982; Third Secretary Brasilia 1994; FCO 1998; First Secretary (Management) and HM Consul Lima 2000; Band C5; m 1992 Oyami Azevedo (2d 1992, 1996; 1s 1999).

Stott, Adam Paul; FCO since June 2003; Born 26/03/71; FCO 1993; Geneva (UKMIS) 2000; Band A2.

Stoves, Margaret; FCO since October 1999; Born 03/07/45; FCO 1987; Lisbon 1990; Almaty 1992; Brussels (UKDEL NATO) 1995; Band A2.

Strain, Scott Robert; Second Secretary FCO since June 2003; Born 04/10/70; FCO 1989; Attaché Pretoria/Cape Town 1991; Attaché later Third Secretary Vice-Consul Peking 1995; Consul-General Chongqing 2000; Band C4; m (1) 1995 Caroline Joanne Ewing (diss 2000); (2) 2001 Liu Xiao Meng.

Stubbings, Graham James; FCO since November 1999; Born 17/09/57; DHSS 1974; FCO 1976; New York (UKMIS) 1979; Kingston 1982; FCO 1986; New Delhi 1989; Johannesburg 1996; Pretoria 1996; Band B3; m 1989 Kirsty Alexander (2s 1987, 1994).

Stucley-Houghton, Nicholas John Knight; FCO since June 1996; Born 03/10/54; Inland Revenue 1974; Santiago 1976; Mbabane 1979; Warsaw 1982; FCO 1983; Kathmandu 1986; FCO 1988; Copenhagen 1989; Johannesburg 1992; Band C4; m (1) 1976 Beatriz Elvira Sierra-Galindo (1s 1978; 1d 1980) (diss 1990); (2) 1993 Susanna Elisabeth Watkins-Pitchford (diss 1996).

Sturgeon, Christopher Charles Alexander; FCO since October 2001; Born 15/03/68; FCO 1988; Floater Duties 1990; Colombo 1993; Sana'a 1996; Islamabad 1998.

Sturgeon, Mary Nicol, MBE (2004); Basra since November 2003; Born 27/05/48; FCO 1973; Bangkok 1974; Kuwait 1976; Suva 1978; Khartoum 1980; FCO 1982; Resigned 1985; Reinstated 1988; Nicosia 1991; Amman 1994; FCO 1998; Brussels (UKDEL NATO) 2001; Band B3.

Sturgess, Neil Christopher; Brussels since July 2003; Born 13/05/62; FCO 1980; Helsinki 1991; FCO 1994; Band C4; m 1988 Wendy Alison (1d 1995).

Styles, Graham Charles Trayton; FCO since August 1998; Born 16/04/58; FCO 1977; SUPL 1978; FCO 1981; Port Louis 1985; Paris 1989; FCO 1992; Vienna (UKDEL) 1995; Band D6; m 1984 Rachael Jane Hopkins (2d 1989, 1991).

Styles, Rachael Jane (née Hopkins); FCO since February 2000; Born 14/05/62; FCO 1980; Port Louis 1985; SUPL 1988; Paris 1989; SUPL 1990; Band B3; m 1984 Graham Charles Trayton Styles (2d 1989, 1991).

Sullivan, Janet Ann; Havana since July 2004; Born 15/02/58; FCO 1977; Kuala Lumpur 1980; Montevideo 1984; Tel Aviv 1988; Floater Duties 1992; FCO 1996; Floater Duties 1999; On loan as Director to the DTI 2002; Band C4.

Summers, David; FCO since May 2003; Born 13/11/64; FCO 1983; Islamabad 1985; Lisbon 1988; FCO 1991; Lagos 1994; Third Secretary (Management) Ankara 1997; Abidjan 2001; Band C4; m 1987 Anita Cecilia Marsh (2d 1991, 1999).

Summers, Timothy Andrew; Chongqing since July 2004; Born 17/02/72; FCO 1994; Full-Time Language Training 1995; Consul Hong Kong 1997; On loan to the Cabinet Office 2001; Full-Time Language Training (Mandarin) 2003; Band D7.

Sundblad, Emma Louise; SUPL since May 2004; Born 28/10/75; FCO 1999; Second Secretary (Political/PPA) Stockholm 2001; Band C4; m 1998 Morgan Sundblad (2s 1994, 1997).

Surman, Derek Malcolm; Bangkok since September 2001; Born 20/06/47; Commonwealth Office/DSAO 1967; Kinshasa 1969; FCO 1970; Madrid 1971; Dacca 1974; Stuttgart 1976; Beirut 1977; Durban 1978; Salisbury 1980; Khartoum 1982; FCO 1985; Canberra 1990; Second Secretary (Immigration) Bombay 1994; Prague 1999; FCO 1999; m 1982 Frances Louise Stapelberg.

Sutcliffe, Nicholas Derek; First Secretary FCO since September 2001; Born 09/12/57; FCO 1985; Second Secretary (Economic) Brasilia 1990; Second Secretary FCO 1993; First Secretary (Commercial) Havana 1998; Band D6; m 1985 Carole Ann Hunter (4s 1990, 1992, 1994 (twins)).

Sutherland, Julia Marie Ludmila (née Haworth); FCO since January 2002; Born 09/09/73; FCO 1995; Language Training 1996; Beijing 1998; Band D6; m 2003 Dr Duncan Sutherland.

Sutton, Janet (née Christie); FCO since February 1996; Born 25/03/64; Department of Employment 1983; FCO 1984; Abidjan 1987; Paris 1990; FCO 1991; SUPL 1994; Band C4; m 1986 Andrew Richard Sutton (2s 1987, 1995).

Sutton, Rebecca Claire; Second Secretary (Political) Pristina since August 2002; Born 25/09/73; FCO 1999; Full-Time Language Training 2001; Band C4.

Swainson, Emma Mary Dillwyn; Second Secretary Amman since August 2003; Born 28/12/75; FCO 2000; Full-Time Language Training FCO 2002; Band C4.

Sweeney, Carole Mary (née Crofts); FCO since October 1999; Born 24/06/59; MOD 1985; FCO 1987; Second Secretary Bonn 1989; Second Secretary East Berlin 1990; Second later First Secretary FCO 1991; First Secretary (Economic) Oslo 1997; m 1988 Paul Martin Sweeney (1d 1990; 1s 1992).

Sweeney, Ian John; First Secretary Vienna since July 2001; Born 01/07/49; Second Secretary Bankok 1984; Second later First Secretary Lagos 1989; FCO 1993; First Secretary Washington 1996; FCO 2000; m 1975 Mairead Aine Condron (2d 1977, 1988; 2s 1978, 1988).

Sweet, Kay (née Rose); Brussels (UKREP) since January 1997; Born 11/11/63; FCO 1984; Budapest 1985; Paris 1987; Floater Duties 1991; Brussels (UKREP) 1993; Paris 1995; SUPL 1996; Band B3; m 1996 Jonathan Charles Sweet (1d 2002).

Sweid, Janice Ann Townsend (née Oldfield); FCO since January 2004; Born 13/06/50; FCO 1970; On loan to the Cabinet Office 1973; FCO 1974; Accra 1977; FCO 1979; Washington 1984; Second Secretary (Management) Tel Aviv 1987; FCO 1992; First Secretary (Management) JMO Brussels 1998; m 1980 Youda Yomtob Sweid.

Swift, Elined Clare (née Evans); First Secretary FCO since April 2001; Born 22/02/60; FCO 1988; Second later First Secretary (Economic) Buenos Aires 1990; First Secretary FCO 1993; First Secretary Geneva (UKDIS) 1997; First Secretary (Regional Affairs) Washington 1999; Band D6; m 1999 Hans Eric Swift.

Swift, Hans Eric; Counsellor FCO since April 2001; Born 14/05/58; FCO 1980; New Delhi 1982; Second Secretary FCO 1986; Second later First Secretary (Chancery) Stockholm 1988; FCO 1991; First Secretary (Political) Washington 1998; m (1) 1981 Susan Mary Brown (diss 1995) (1d 1988; 1s 1991); (2) 1999 Elined Clare Evans.

Sykes, Christopher Rowland Charlesworth; Counsellor and Deputy Consul-General Hong Kong since September 2004; Born FCO 1986; Second later First Secretary Hong Kong 1987; SUPL 1990; Resigned 1991; Reinstated, FCO 2003; First Secretary FCO 2004; m 1981 Sandra Ross (1d 1983; 1s 1985).

Sykes, Graham Leslie; Manila since July 2003; Born 20/09/60; FCO 1987; New Delhi 1992; FCO 1995; Pretoria 1995; Sana'a 1999; Band B3; m 1995 Wei Li Ming.

Sykes, Roger Michael Spencer, OBE (2002); Deputy Head of Mission Karachi since February 2002; Born 22/10/50; FCO 1968; Caracas 1971; Freetown 1972; Karachi 1976; Valletta 1978; Lagos 1982; Port Vila 1986; Second Secretary FCO 1990; Amman 1993; First Secretary and Head of British Trade Office Al Khobar 1997-01; Band D6; m 1976 Anne Lesley Groves-Gidney (3s 1977, 1980, 1988).

Sylvester, Robert Anthony; Vice-Consul Nicosia since December 2002; Born 29/12/56; FCO 1996; Johannesburg 1999; Band B3; m 1976 Jacqueline Lovely (1d 1986).

Syposz, Shelley Liann (née Mayman); SUPL since May 2001; Born 02/05/70; FCO 1991; New Delhi 1993; FCO 1995; Prague 1998; Band A2; m 1996 Julian Jeremy Syposz.

Syrett, Mark Robert; Second Secretary FCO since June 2002; Born 09/04/69; FCO 1993; Second Secretary (Political) Oslo 1998; Band C4.

Syrett, Nicholas Simon; Counsellor Nairobi since February 2003; Born 07/12/60; FCO 1989; First Secretary (Political) Luanda 1993; First Secretary FCO 1996; First Secretary (Political) Bogotá 1998; First Secretary FCO 2000; m 1993 Elena Fircks (1s, 1d 1997 (twins)).

T

Tandy, Arthur David; Second later First Secretary FCO since May 1989; Born 16/08/49; HO 1974-85; FCO 1985; Second Secretary Riyadh 1987; Band C5; m 1973 Hilary Denise Watson (1s 1978; 1d 1982).

Tansley, Anthony James Nicholas; Counsellor and Deputy Head of Mission Muscat since November 1998; Born 19/07/62; FCO 1984; Language Training 1986; Second Secretary (Chancery) Riyadh 1988; Second Secretary (Chancery) Baghdad 1989; First Secretary FCO 1991; Dublin 1994; m 1998 Blaithin Mary Curran (1s 2002).

Tarif, Pamela (née Neave); Second Secretary Geneva (UKMIS) since January 2003; Born 03/06/65; FCO 1985; Lagos 1988; Ottawa 1992; FCO 1994; Quito 1997; Second Secretary Yaoundé 2000; m 1988 Nacer Tarif (1d 1992; 1s 1995).

Tarry, Stephen Norman; Second Secretary (Political) Suva since July 2001; Born 21/01/54; FCO 1971; Washington 1974; Damascus 1977; Brussels 1981; FCO 1983; Islamabad 1983; FCO 1988; Warsaw 1991; Dublin 1993; Vilnius 1997; Band C5; m (1) 1981 Julie Christine Lawrence (dec'd 1985) (1d (adopted) 1984); (2) 1992 Elzbieta Jaskaczek (1s 1997).

Tarshish, Daniel Morton; First Secretary (Political) Athens since August 2003; Born 14/10/69; FCO 1994; Second Secretary New York (UKMIS) 1998; Second Secretary FCO 2000; Band D6; m 1999 Pamela Goddard (1d 1999).

Tatham, Michael Harry; Deputy Head of Mission Prague since July 2002; Born 02/07/65; FCO 1987; Third later Second Secretary (Chancery) Prague 1990; First Secretary FCO 1993; Deputy Head of Mission and HM Consul Sofia 1997; On loan to 10 Downing Street 1999; Band D6.

Tauwhare, Richard David, MVO (1983); Assistant Director (Training) FCO since April 2002; Born 01/11/59; FCO 1980; Third later Second Secretary (Chancery/Information) Nairobi 1982; Second later First Secretary Paris (UKDEL OECD) 1986; First Secretary FCO 1989; First Secretary Geneva (UKDIS) 1994; FCO 1999; m 1985 Amanda Jane Grey (2d 1991, 1998; 1s 1994).

Taylor, Andrea Lynn (née Reid); Asmara since April 2002; Born 06/02/70; FCO 1989; Lagos 1992; Banjul 1995; Abuja 1999; Band B3; m 1996 Charles Richard Taylor.

Taylor, Duncan John Rushworth, CBE (2002); Deputy Consul General (Political, Press and Public Affairs) New York since April 2000; Born 17/11/58; FCO 1982; Third later Second Secretary Havana 1983; First Secretary FCO 1987; Language Training 1991; First Secretary (Commercial) Budapest 1992; On loan to Rolls Royce Plc 1996; Counsellor FCO 1997; m 1981 Marie-Béatrice (Bébé) Terpougoff (3 step d 1972 (twins), 1973; 2s 1984, 1986).

Taylor, Emma Louise; SUPL since March 2004; Born 02/01/82; FCO 2000; Abu Dhabi 2002; Band A2; ptnr, John Galbraith.

Taylor, Eric Raymond; Second Secretary FCO since August 2004; Born 09/01/69; FCO 1994; Deputy Head of BIS Tripoli 1999; Vice-Consul BE Tripoli 1999; Third Secretary (Political) New Delhi 2001; Band C4; m 1998 Lynn Dudley (1s 2001).

Taylor, Hugh Mackay; Consul (Commercial) Munich since November 1999; Born 15/05/54; FCO 1972; Brussels (UKREP) 1975; Brunei 1978; FCO 1981; Munich 1985; Second Secretary (Chancery/Information) Lisbon 1988; Second Secretary FCO 1993; Warsaw 1996; m 1977 Christine Caggie.

Taylor, Ian Stewart; Mexico City since August 2001; Born 27/01/70; FCO 1986; Cairo 1994; FCO 1998; Band C4; m 1998 Kim Catherine Higgins (2s 2001, 2003).

Taylor, Jeffrey; First Secretary (Commercial) Chicago since January 2002; Born 15/08/57; FCO 1976; BMG Berlin 1979; Lusaka 1982; Moscow 1984; FCO 1985; Melbourne 1988; Canberra 1990; Second Secretary (Commercial) Helsinki 1992; Second Secretary FCO 1997; Second Secretary British Trade International 1999; m 1981 Janette Anne Hunt (diss) (2s 1987, 1990).

Taylor, Karen Ruth (née Nelms); FCO since July 2000; Born 23/06/57; FCO 1978; New Delhi 1978; Peking 1982; Washington 1983; FCO 1985; Port Louis 1992; SUPL 1996; Band B3; m 1991 Nigel David Muir Taylor (1d 1993; 1s 1995).

Taylor, Kenneth James; FCO since November 2003; Born 06/09/79; Band B3.

Taylor, Kim Catherine (née Higgins); Mexico City since July 2002; Born 14/10/66; FCO 1987; Lagos 1989; FCO 1993; Cairo 1994; FCO 1998; SUPL 2000; Band A2; m 1998 Ian Stewart Taylor (2s 2001, 2003).

Taylor, Louis Charles; FCO since August 2003; Born 10/03/54; Home Office 1973; Dhaka 1980; Home Office 1984; Second Secretary Lagos 1990; FCO 1994; Second Secretary (Economic and Trade Policy) New Delhi 1996; Consul Oporto 2000; Band D6; m 1977 Margaret Ann Price (2s 1984, 1987).

Taylor, Louise Elizabeth; Third Secretary (Pol/PPA) Tirana since March 2004; Born 30/11/75; FCO 2000; Third Secretary (Management) Tanzania 2002; Band B3.

Taylor, Mark Christopher; Second Secretary (Political) Damascus since October 2002; Born 04/06/76; FCO 2000; Band C4.

Taylor, Matthew John; First Secretary Brussels (UKREP) since September 2002; Born 27/08/72; FCO 1995; Second later First Secretary New York (UKMIS) 1997; Private Secretary to the Minister of State FCO 2001; Band D6.

Taylor, Nigel David Muir; On loan to the DTI since July 2002; Born 21/04/61; FCO 1981; Kaduna 1982; Africa/Middle East Floater 1986; FCO 1989; Port Louis 1992; Second Secretary Grand Turk 1996; Second Secretary FCO 1999; Band C4; m 1991 Karen Ruth Nelms (1d 1993; 1s 1995).

Taylor, Robert James; SUPL since October 2000; Born 07/04/57; HCS 1987; FCO 1989; Prague 1990; Havana 1992; FCO 1993; Buenos Aires 1996; Band A2.

Taylor, Stephen Andrew; Bangkok since January 2002; Born 15/09/66; FCO 2000; Band B3.

Teale, Ian Robert McKinnon; Islamabad since May 2003; Born 28/02/71; FCO 1991; The Hague 1995; Kingston 1996; Sana'a 1999; T/D Antigua 2000; FCO 2000; Band B3.

Tebbit, Sir Kevin Reginald, KCMG (2002), CMG (1997); On secondment to the Ministry of Defence since July 1998; Born 18/10/46; MOD 1969-79; UKDEL NATO 1979; First Secretary FCO 1982; First Secretary and Head of Chancery Ankara 1984; On secondment as Directeur du Cabinet, Cabinet of the Secretary-General of NATO, Brussels 1987; Counsellor (Political/Military) Washington 1988; Counsellor FCO 1992; m 1966 Alison Tinley (1d 1972; 1s 1975).

Telford, Sarah Elizabeth; FCO since January 2003; Born 15/06/75; Band A2.

Teller, Linda Margaret (née Campbell); SUPL since June 1995; Born 12/04/61; FCO 1991; Prague 1993; Band A2; m 1995 Nicholas Roy Richard Teller (2s 1997, 1999).

Temple, Tracey Joy; FCO since September 2000; Born 09/08/65; FCO 1993; Buenos Aires 1995; Helsinki 1998; Band A2.

Tench, Gavin Andrew; Mexico City since May 2003; Born 29/08/68; FCO 1995; Second Secretary (Commercial) Kingston 1999; Band B3.

Terrett, Nicola; FCO since May 2003; Born 02/09/66; HCS 1985; FCO 1994; Havana 1999; Band B3.

Tesoriere, Harcourt Andrew Pretorius; HM Ambassador Riga since March 2002; Born 02/11/50; Royal Navy 1969-73; FCO 1974; Language Training SOAS and Iran 1975; Oriental Secretary Kabul 1976; Nairobi 1979; Second Secretary Abidjan 1981; FCO 1985; First Secretary and Head of Chancery, later Chargé d'Affaires a.i. BIS Damascus 1987; First Secretary FCO 1991; SUPL on secondment as UNOCHA Head of Field Operations (Afghanistan) 1994; HM Ambassador Tirana 1996; Head of UN Special Mission Afghanistan 1998; Full-Time Language Training 2001; Chargé d'Affaires a.i. Kabul 2001; m 1987 Dr Alma Gloria Vasquez.

Tett, Tracey Joanne (née Holland); FCO since September 2000; Born 16/07/66; FCO 1990; Language Training 1991; Full-Time Language

Training Tokyo 1992; FCO 1993; SUPL 1996; Band C4.

Thain, Robert; First Secretary FCO since December 2002; Born 09/09/52; FCO 1975; Warsaw 1977; Rabat 1979; Zagreb 1982; FCO 1984; Canberra 1986; FCO 1990; Vice-Consul Helsinki 1992; Second Secretary FCO 1994; HM Consul Pretoria 1997; m 1977 Susan Mary Nice (1s 1989; 1d 1992).

Thakrar, Paresh; FCO since October 2003; Born 31/01/75; Band C4.

The MacLaren of MacLaren, Donald; HM Ambassador Tbilisi since 2004; Born 22/08/54; FCO 1978; Third later Second later First Secretary BMG Berlin 1980; Language Training 1983; First Secretary and Press Attaché Moscow 1984; First Secretary FCO 1987; Deputy Head of Mission Havana 1991; First Secretary FCO 1994; Consul-General and Deputy Head of Mission Kiev 2000; m 1978 Maida-Jane Aitchison (3s 1980, 1981, 1984; 2d 1987, 1994).

Thiel, Ann Bernadette; Second Secretary FCO since May 1997; Born 02/08/52; FCO 1971; Moscow 1973; Kuwait 1975; Düsseldorf 1978; FCO 1981; Floater Duties 1984; Moscow 1986; FCO 1988; Second Secretary FCO 1991; HM Consul Johannesburg (later Pretoria) 1995.

Thom, Dr Gordon; SUPL since September 1998; Born 18/05/53; DOE 1978; FCO 1979; Second later First Secretary Tokyo 1981; FCO 1985; First Secretary (Commercial) New Delhi 1989; Counsellor (Economic) Tokyo 1994; m 1977 Margaret Pringle (1s 1982; 1d 1986).

Thomas, Dr Catherine Clare Mitchell; First Secretary Washington since August 2004; Born 03/02/58; FCO 1987; Senior Research Officer (DS Band C4) later Principal Research Officer (Band D6); m 1989 Martin Brian Howe (2d 1990, 1994).

Thomas, Colin Ronald; Third Secretary FCO since October 1987; Born 27/03/49; Board of Trade 1967; FCO 1969; Dacca 1971; Havana 1974; Maputo 1975; FCO 1979; Geneva 1984; Rio de Janeiro 1987.

Thomas, David Lloyd; FCO since July 2003; Born 04/08/70; FCO 1996; Lagos 1997; Pretoria 2000; Band D6; m 2003 Lauren Sarah Hill (1d 2004).

Thomas, Graeme Gordon; First Secretary (Commercial/Economic) Tehran since November 2002; Born 26/09/48; FCO 1968; Africa Floater 1971; Sana'a 1975; Jedda 1976; Far East/South East Floater 1977; FCO 1980; Victoria 1982; FCO 1986; Consul Warsaw 1987; Second Secretary FCO 1988; Riyadh 1992; Full-Time Language Training 1996; First Secretary (Commercial) Athens 1997; FCO 2001; m 1981 Penelope Ann Richmond.

Thomas, Jeffrey, MBE (1995); Consul-General Paris since May 2004; Born 13/07/47; CO 1964; FO (later FCO) 1966; Manila 1969; Berlin 1973; FCO 1975; Ibadan 1978; Kaduna 1980; Second Secretary FCO 1984; Second Secretary

(Admin/Consular) Muscat 1987; Consul Oporto 1991; First Secretary FCO 1996; HM Consul-General Madrid Embassy 1999; m 1969 Lesley Anne Wishart (3s 1973, twins 1975).

Thomas, Katherine Louise; FCO since September 2002; Born 17/06/76; Band A2.

Thomas, Lauren Sarah (née Hill); SUPL since January 2004; Born 14/02/73; FCO 1992; Conference Officer Brussels (UKREP) 1995; World Wide Floater Duties 1997; Johannesburg 1999; FCO 2003; Band C4; m 2003 David Lloyd Thomas (1d 2004).

Thomas, Penelope Ann (née Richmond); Tehran since November 2002; Born 17/02/50; FCO 1973; Brussels (UKREP) 1974; Caracas 1977; FCO 1979; Victoria 1982; SUPL 1987; FCO 1988; Riyadh 1992; FCO 1996; SUPL 1997; Athens 1997; FCO 2001; Band B3; m 1981 Graeme Gordon Thomas.

Thomas, Peter James; FCO since January 2002; Born 04/05/74; Band B3.

Thomas, Sir Philip Lloyd, KCVO (2004), CMG (2001); Consul-General New York since 2004; Born 10/06/48; FCO 1972; Second Secretary Belgrade 1974; Second later First Secretary FCO 1977; First Secretary (Commercial) Madrid 1981; FCO 1984; First Secretary (Press) Brussels (UKREP) 1987; Counsellor on loan to the Cabinet Office 1989; Counsellor (Political/Military) Washington 1991; FCO 1996; Consul-General Düsseldorf 1999; High Commissioner Nigeria, Ambassador (Non-resident) Benin 2001.

Thomas, Ryder Hugh; FCO since June 2002; Born 24/05/73; Band B3.

Thomas, Simon D; First Secretary on loan to the Cabinet Office since April 2002; Born 24/05/75; FCO 1997; Second Secretary (Political) Warsaw 1998; Band D6.

Thompson, Christopher Colin; Third Secretary (Political) Warsaw since December 2002; Born 18/05/69; FCO 1989; Floater Duties 1992; Tokyo 1995; On loan to the Football Association 1999; Port Moresby 2000; Full-Time Language Training 2002; Band B3.

Thompson, Clive Vincent; First Secretary (Commercial) and Deputy Director of Trade New York since October 1999; Born 03/04/47; FCO 1973; MECAS 1975; Islamabad 1976; Tunis 1978; Stuttgart 1981; Second Secretary FCO 1983; Second Secretary (Consul) Moscow 1987; Second Secretary FCO 1990; Consul later First Secretary (Commercial) Munich 1990; First Secretary FCO 1996; Acting Deputy Head of Mission T/D Zagreb 1999; m 1969 Carol Knight (2d 1973, 1974).

Thompson, Jan; First Secretary later Counsellor FCO since March 2000; Born 25/08/65; FCO 1990 (Second Secretary 1991); Second Secretary Bonn 1991; First Secretary FCO 1994; First Secretary New York (UKMIS) 1997.

Thompson, John, MBE (1975); HM Ambassador Luanda since February 2002; Born 28/05/45; FO 1964; DSA 1965; Vice-Consul Düsseldorf 1966; Abu Dhabi 1969; Phnom Penh 1972; Management Studies Polytechnic of Central London 1974; Second Secretary on loan to DOT 1975; FCO 1977; First Secretary and Head of Chancery Luanda 1979; Consul (Commercial) São Paulo 1981; First Secretary FCO 1985; High Commissioner Vila 1988; Counsellor and Director of Trade Promotion BTIO New York 1992; Counsellor FCO 1997; m 1966 Barbara Hopper (1d 1967).

Thompson, Lindsy; Third Secretary Brussels (UKREP) since September 2004; Born 06/12/75; FCO 2003; Band B3.

Thompson, Lynne Diana; Floater Duties since January 2003; Born 20/08/59; FCO 1981; Warsaw 1982; Bandar Seri Begawan 1983; FCO 1986; Vienna 1987; FCO 1988; Istanbul 1996; FCO 2000; Band B3.

Thompson, Philippa Ann (née Hadley); Deputy High Commissioner Victoria since March 2004; Born 03/08/62; FCO 1980; Brussels 1983; Bridgetown 1985; FCO 1989; Ottawa 1991; Second Secretary Brussels (UKREP) 1994; FCO 1995; ENA Paris 1998; Second Secretary (PPA) Paris 1999; SUPL 2003; m 2000 Alphaeus Randolph Thompson (2s 2001, 2003).

Thompson, Richard Paul Reynier, OBE (2001); First Secretary FCO since January 2001; Born 17/08/60; FCO 1989; Second later First Secretary Stockholm 1991; First Secretary FCO 1993; First Secretary Geneva (UKMIS) 1996; Band D6; m 1991 Louisa Halliday-Yates (1d 1992).

Thomson, Adam McClure; New York (UKMIS) since August 2002; Born 01/07/55; FCO 1978; Third later Second Secretary Moscow 1981; Second later First Secretary Brussels (UKDEL NATO) 1983; FCO 1986; On loan to the Cabinet Office 1989; First Secretary (Chancery) Washington 1991; Counsellor (Head of Chancery) New Delhi 1995; Counsellor FCO 1998; m 1984 Fariba Shirazi (2d 1991, 1993; 1s 1996).

Thomson, Andrew Robert Hay; Second Secretary FCO since September 2002; Born 23/06/75; FCO 1998; Second Secretary (Political) Pristina 2000; Band C4.

Thomson, Jonathan Hiroshi Stewart; FCO since June 2001; Born 13/05/72; FCO 1996; Full-Time Language Training 1997; Second Secretary Tokyo 1998.

Thorne, Nicholas Alan, CMG (2002); Permanent Representative Geneva (UKMIS) since November 2003; Born 31/03/48; FO (later FCO) 1965; Yaoundé 1971; Brussels (UKREP) 1974; Second Secretary FCO 1977; Central London Polytechnic 1977; FCO 1978; Second later First Secretary New York (UKMIS) 1980; First Secretary and Head of Chancery Manila 1983; First Secretary FCO 1987; On secondment to Thorn EMI 1989; Counsellor (Commercial) and Deputy Head of Mission

Helsinki 1991; Counsellor (Financial) New York (UKMIS) 1995; m 1974 Ann Margaret Boorman (1s 1978; 1d 1980).

Thornton, James Sebastian; Deputy Head of Mission Abidjan since August 2003; Born 02/11/64; UKAEA 1986-89; FCO 1989; Second Secretary (Commercial/Information) Algiers 1992; Second later First Secretary FCO 1994; First Secretary (Chancery) Mexico City 2000; Band D6; m 1999 Anne Scrase.

Thornton, John Norris; Beijing since January 2003; Born 06/07/59; FCO 1978; BGWRS Darwin 1980; FCO 1982; Beirut 1983; FCO 1984; Third Secretary Tehran 1986; FCO 1987; Third Secretary Geneva 1991; FCO 1993; Third Secretary Berlin 1996; FCO 1999; Band C5; m 1980 Angela Dawn Clarke (1d 1989; 1s 1994).

Thornton, Patricia Ann; First Secretary FCO since February 1995; Born 11/01/52; FCO 1971; Tehran 1973; Lima 1976; New Delhi 1979; FCO 1982; Guatemala City 1984; FCO 1987; Second Secretary (Commercial) Santiago 1988; Consul Johannesburg 1991.

Thornton, Sarah; New Delhi since May 2004; Born 05/06/72; FCO 1992; Rome 1995; SUPL 1999; FCO 2000; Band B3.

Thurlow, John Robert; FCO since December 2003; Born 28/08/67; HCS 1984; FCO 1988; Algiers 1990; Bridgetown 1992; FCO 1995; On loan to the DTI 1998; Second Secretary (Commercial/Industrial Relations) Rome 2000; Band C4; m 1992 Joanna Welch (1d 1988).

Thursfield, Martin Robert; First Secretary (Political) Vilnius since December 2000; Born 08/06/67; FCO 1989; Full-Time Language Training Peking 1991; Second Secretary (Information) BTC Hong Kong 1993; First Secretary FCO 1995; Band D6; m 1996 Ingrid Katharina Corbyn Hale (1s 1997; 1d 2000).

Thurston, Brenda Pauline; Yaoundé since June 2002; Born 09/11/49; DHSS 1980; FCO 1984; Damascus 1986; Port Louis 1987; Karachi 1990; Pretoria 1994; Abuja 1998; Band A2; m 1974 John Anthony Thurston.

Tibber, Peter Harris; On loan to British Trade International since September 2000 (Director of Business Group 2002); Born 07/09/56; Second Secretary FCO 1984; Second later First Secretary Paris 1986; First Secretary FCO 1989; PS to the Minister of State 1990; Full-Time Language Training 1992; First Secretary (Political) Ankara 1993; Deputy Head of Mission Mexico City 1996; m 1983 Eve Levy-Huet (3s 1986, 1988, 1992).

Tiffin, Sarah Anne; SUPL since April 2004; Born 05/11/65; FCO 1988; ENA Paris 1989; Third later Second Secretary Paris 1990; Second later First Secretary 1993; First Secretary (Political) New Delhi 1997; On secondment to the Irish Department of Foreign Affairs 2000; Dublin 2001; m 2000 Pádraig Francis (1s 2002).

Tillson, Clare Nicola (née Studham); SUPL since February 2003; Born 29/06/58; FCO 1977; Washington 1979; FCO 1982; Floater Duties 1983; Brasilia 1984; FCO 1988; Second Secretary (ECOSOC) New York (UKMIS) 1994; Consul Tokyo 1996; FCO 2000.

Timsit, Milli (née Abbott); Consul/MO Munich since August 2000; Born 11/06/56; FCO 1975; Washington 1977; Africa/Middle East Floater 1981; FCO 1982; Islamabad 1984; Tokyo 1986; FCO 1988; Tel Aviv 1991; Casablanca 1995; Band C4; m 1992 Uzi Timsit (1s 1995; 1d 1997).

Tindell, Derek Graham; Second Secretary The Hague since April 2002; Born 11/08/69; FCO 1987; Oslo 1989; Moscow 1992; FCO 1995; Band C4; m 1993 Gail Joyce Brodie (1s 1999).

Tiney, Michael Charles; Floater Duties since March 2002; Born 12/09/66; HCS 1989-92; Bucharest 1993; Kampala 1996; Kathmandu 1998; Band B3.

Tinline, Robert John; First Secretary FCO since January 2003; Born 13/08/76; FCO 1997; Second Secretary Bogotá 1999.

Tissot, Philip Marius Arthur; Trade Commissioner Hong Kong since September 2002; Born 10/02/60; FCO 1978; Africa Floater 1981; Lagos 1983; FCO 1986; Vice-Consul Toronto 1988; Second Secretary 1989; Second Secretary (Chancery) New York (UKMIS) 1990; FCO 1994; Deputy High Commissioner Valletta 1999; m (1) 1985 Julie Anne Grant (diss 1999) (1s 1989; 1d 1990); (2) 2001 Caroline Victoria Agius (1d 2002).

Tluczek, Karl Shaun Paul; Third Secretary Sofia since April 2002; Born 05/01/72; FCO 1991; Prague 1998; Band B3.

Tluczek, Mark Joseph; Moscow since October 2001; Born 22/03/67; HCS FCO 1987; FCO 1996; Abuja 1998; Band B3; m 1991 Joanne Lindley.

Tobin, Patrick Michael; Second Secretary (Political/Press/Aid) Sana'a since January 2003; Born 21/04/71; FCO 2000; Full-Time Language Training 2001; Full-Time Language Training (Amman) 2002; Third Secretary (Political) Cairo 2002; Band C4.

Todd, Damian Roderic; Director (Finance) FCO since 2004; Born 29/08/59; FCO 1980; Third later Second Secretary Pretoria/Cape Town 1981; Second Secretary FCO 1984; First Secretary and Consul Prague 1987; First Secretary FCO 1989; First Secretary (Economic) Bonn 1991; HM Treasury 1995; FCO 1997; On secondment as Head of EU Co-ordination and Strategy Team at HM Treasury 1998; HM Ambassador Bratislava 2001; m 1987 Alison Mary Digby (1s 1989; 2d 1992, 1999).

Tolfree, Alison (née Oxenford); Washington since December 2003; Born 17/02/66; FCO 1985; Belgrade 1992; FCO 1995; Lusaka 1999; FCO 2002; Band B3; m 1991 Mark Tolfree (1d 1997; 1s 2000).

Tollyfield, Caroline Leslie (née Brewer); Second Secretary FCO since September 1998; Born 20/06/61; FCO 1994; Second Secretary (Political) Vienna 1995; Band C4; m 1995 Andrew John Tollyfield (1s 2000).

Tomkins, Michael Paul; FCO since October 2003; Born 23/12/50; FCO 1970; Honiara 1972; Aden 1976; Kingston 1977; Wellington 1980; Warsaw 1982; FCO 1983; Dhaka 1986; Geneva (UKMIS) 1989; FCO 1992 (Second Secretary 1994); Second Secretary (Commercial) Dubai 1996; First Secretary (Management) Jakarta 2000; m 1979 Eleanor Michelle Ritch (1d 1986; 1s 1989).

Tomkins, Roger James; Khartoum since May 2003; Born 30/06/48; Royal Navy 1966-88; Prison Service 1988-90; Budapest 1990; Islamabad 1992; Lagos 1994; Moscow 1998; Band B3; m 1971 Pauline Bennett (1s 1974; 1d 1976).

Tomlinson, Deborah Jane, MVO (1996); Deputy Head of Mission Kinshasa since January 2003; Born 16/02/63; FCO 1981; Islamabad 1984; Jakarta 1986; FCO 1990; Third Secretary (Visits) Brussels (UKREP) 1993; Third Secretary Belgrade 1996; Second Secretary (KHF) Sarajevo 1998; SUPL 2000; Band C5; m 1992 Mark Hyland.

Tomlinson, Thomas Mark; Second Secretary (Science and Technology) New Delhi since August 2002; Born 02/02/63; Third Secretary (Management) and Vice Consul Maputo 1995; Jedda 1998; Second Secretary (Chancery) Belgrade 2001; Band C4.

Tonge, Simon David; FCO since June 2002; Born 18/09/69; FCO 1996; New York (UKMIS) 1997; Jakarta 1998; Band D6.

Tongue, Margaret Lee; Second Secretary (Political) Colombo since April 2002; Born 19/09/74; FCO 2000; Band C4; ptnr, Paul Thomas Griffiths.

Tonkin, Ramsey Harris; First Secretary (Management) Berlin since May 2001; Born 17/04/44; FO 1964; Ankara 1966; Bonn 1969; FCO 1972; Tehran 1975; Second Secretary (Commercial) Port of Spain 1978; Second Secretary FCO 1982; Second later First Secretary (Admin/Consul) Bombay 1987; First Secretary (Management) Oslo 1989; First Secretary FCO 1995; First Secretary Bangkok 1997; Full-Time Language Training 2000; m 1966 Valerie Anne Duff (2d 1967, 1969).

Toothe, Adrian Gerald; Counsellor FCO since August 2004; Born 07/01/52; FCO 1972; Jedda 1976; Second Secretary FCO 1980; Geneva (UKMIS) 1985; First Secretary later Counsellor FCO 1989; Seconded to the Home Office 2001; m 1976 Diane Whitehead (2s 1982, 1985).

Toovey, Rebecca; Dublin since November 2003; Born 28/05/81; FCO 2001; Band A2.

Topping, Dr Patrick Gilmer; First Secretary FCO since August 1998; Born 05/09/59; FCO 1986; Second later First Secretary (Chancery) Kuala Lumpur 1990; First Secretary FCO 1991;

Washington 1994; Band D6; m 1985 Indira Annick Coomaraswamy (1s 1992; 1d 1993).

Torlot, Timothy Achille; On loan to DTI since January 2002; Born 17/09/57; FCO 1981; Muscat 1984; Second Secretary (Chancery) Wellington 1987; Second later First Secretary FCO 1992; First Secretary (Commercial) Santiago 1997; m 1986 Bridie Morton (1d 1990).

Torrance, David John Baillie; Seoul since December 2001; Born 29/02/56; FCO 1975; Bangkok 1978; LA Floater 1982; Doha 1984; FCO 1987; Third Secretary and Vice-Consul San Salvador 1990; Third later Second Secretary FCO 1994; Second Secretary (Commercial) Muscat 1998; Band C4.

Torry, Sir Peter James, KCMG (2003); HM Ambassador Berlin since May 2003; Born 02/08/48; FCO 1970; Third Secretary Havana 1971; Second Secretary (Economic/Commercial) Jakarta 1974; First Secretary FCO 1977; First Secretary (Chancery) Bonn 1981; First Secretary later Counsellor FCO 1985; Counsellor Washington 1989; Counsellor later AUSS (Personel and Security) FCO 1993; HM Ambassador Madrid 1998; m 1979 Angela Wakeling Wood (3d 1980, 1982, 1985).

Totty, Alastair Walton; FCO since January 2003; Born 24/07/69; FCO 1988; Abu Dhabi 1991; Jerusalem 1994; SUPL 1997; FCO 1998; Rangoon 2000; Band C4; m 1996 Lorraine Helen Fussey (2s 1997, 2001).

Towe, Sheila; Second Secretary (Commercial) Toronto since August 1999; Born 26/07/62; FCO 1981; East Berlin 1983; FCO 1985; Baghdad 1987; FCO 1990; On loan to the DTI 1992; Vice-Consul Jedda 1994; On loan to the DTI 1996; Band C4.

Towner-Evans, Louise; Floater Duties since June 2001; Born 12/08/71; FCO 1994; Jakarta 1996; FCO 2000; Band A2.

Townsend, David John; Second Secretary (Political) Vienna (UKDEL) since June 2001; Born 31/05/57; ECGD 1984-89; FCO 1989; Vienna 1991; Language Training 1994; Vice-Consul Prague 1995; FCO 1997; Band C4; m 1993 Sarah Ann Garry (2s 1994, 1997).

Townsend, Stephen Thomas; Second Secretary (Commercial) Cairo since March 2002; Born 10/07/61; FCO 1980; Caracas 1982; Kinshasa 1986; FCO 1990; Full-Time Language Training 1992; Madrid 1993; FCO 1997; Band C4; m 1996 Fiona Maria Kilpatrick.

Townson, Jennifer Caroline; FCO since June 2002; Born 22/02/68; FCO 1989; On loan to the ODA 1991; Third Secretary (Chancery) Paris 1992; Vice-Consul Port Louis 1995; FCO 1999; On secondment (Commercial) 2001; Band C4.

Towsey, Erica Pamela (née Filder), MBE (2003); Washington since November 2003; Born 05/06/53; FCO 1974; Rabat 1975; Dhaka 1976; Resigned 1978; Reinstated, FCO 1992; T/D Lagos 1992;

Abuja 1993; FCO 1994; On loan to the Prime Minister's Office 2001; Band B3; m 1976 Malcolm John Towsey (diss 2003) (1s 1979; 1d 1981).

Towsey, Malcolm John; First Secretary FCO since August 2003; Born 06/05/47; MOD 1963; FO (later FCO) 1965; Baghdad 1969; Warsaw 1972; Rabat 1973; Dhaka 1976; FCO 1979; Maseru 1982; Second Secretary FCO 1984; Second Secretary (Commercial) Dublin 1986; Second Secretary FCO 1990; First Secretary (Management) Lagos 1991; First Secretary (Management/Consular) Abuja 1993; First Secretary FCO 1994; First Secretary (Commercial) Helsinki 1999; m 1976 Erica Pamela Filder (diss 2003) (1s 1979; 1d 1981).

Traylor, Owen John; FCO since January 2004; Born 26/09/55; FCO 1977; Language Training Tokyo 1980; Second Secretary (Economic) Tokyo 1981; First Secretary FCO 1985; First Secretary (Chancery) Berlin 1990; First Secretary FCO 1994; Consul Istanbul 2000; Band D6; m (1) 1981 Angela Carmel Webb (1d 1985) (diss 1989); (2) 1991 Carola Wangerin.

Treadell, Alan; SUPL since March 2003; Born 08/11/51; FCO 1971; Stockholm 1973; Sana'a 1976; FCO 1977; Islamabad 1979; FCO 1983; Kuala Lumpur 1985; FCO 1990; British Trade International 1999; Band C4; m 1985 Victoria Marguerite Jansz.

Treadell, Victoria Marguerite (née Jansz), MVO (1989); First Secretary British Trade International since March 1998; Born 04/11/59; FCO 1978; Islamabad 1981; FCO 1983; Kuala Lumpur 1985; FCO 1990 (First Secretary 1998); Band D6; m 1985 Alan Treadell.

Treherne, Susan Elizabeth (née Morton); SUPL since April 1998; Born 25/02/62; FCO 1986; First Secretary (Chancery) Peking 1992; First Secretary FCO 1995; m 1996 Simon Grant Treherne.

Trevelyan, Sarah Frances; SUPL since December 1995; Born 06/02/65; FCO 1983; Lisbon 1987; Kampala 1990; FCO 1993; Band A2; m 1993 Darren Francis Forbes-Batey (1d 1995, 1s 1998).

Trott, Angela Christine; FCO since June 2002; Born 23/06/66; FCO 1990; Manila 1999; Band C4; m 1996 Jannick Pierre Michel Charpentier.

Trott, Christopher John; FCO since April 2003; Born 14/02/66; FCO 1991; Second Secretary 1992; Consul and Deputy Head of Mission Rangoon 1993; First Secretary (Commercial) later First Secretary (Political) Tokyo 1996; Band D7; m 1992 Sunna Park.

Truelove, Andrew John; FCO since April 2001; Born 03/04/64; FCO 1991; New Delhi 1997; Band C4; m 2003 Helen Todd.

Truman, Gary Douglas; FCO since March 1994; Born 15/10/63; Home Civil Service 1981; FCO 1990; Bonn 1993; Band A2.

Tucker, Andrew Victor Gunn; Counsellor FCO since January 2004; Born 20/12/55; Joint Technical Language Service 1978-81; FCO 1981; Second Secretary Dar es Salaam 1982; First Secretary on loan to the Cabinet Office 1985; First Secretary Moscow 1987; FCO 1991; First Secretary on loan to the German Ministry of Foreign Affairs 1993; First Secretary Bonn 1994; Deputy High Commissioner Nairobi and concurrently Alternate Permanent Representative to UNEP and UNHCS (Habitat) 1997; HM Ambassador Baku 2000; m 1986 Judith Anne Gibson.

Tucker, Ernest; Harare since May 2004; Born 16/03/45; Army 1963-91; Warsaw 1991; Moscow 1993; Lagos 1996; Amman 1999; Band B3; m 1965 Ute Elli Wilkelmine (1s 1978).

Tucker, James Philip, OBE; Counsellor (Political) Jakarta since April 2003; Born 10/01/66; FCO 1990; Second Secretary (Political) Prague 1993; Second Secretary (Political) Bratislava 1994; Second Secretary FCO 1996; First Secretary (Political) Islamabad 2001; First Secretary FCO 2002; m 1991 Susie Elizabeth Betts (2d 1994, 1995).

Tucknott, John Anthony, MBE (1990); Director Trade and Investment Development Stockholm since May 2002; Born 02/01/58; DOE 1975; FCO 1977; Rome 1980; Cairo 1982; FCO 1985; Second Secretary (Admin) later Deputy Head of Mission Beirut 1988; FCO 1993; First Secretary 1994; New York (UKMIS) 1995; FCO 1998; Counsellor 2000; m 2000 Riitta-Leena Irmeli Lehtinen (1s 2001).

Tuhey, Claire Elizabeth; Second Secretary (Commercial) Mumbai since May 2002; Born 07/02/57; FCO 1976; SUPL 1976; FCO 1979; Paris 1982; Africa/Middle East Floater 1985; Vice-Consul New York 1987; FCO 1991; Dublin 1994; On temporary duty secondment to the Glencree Centre 1997; FCO 1998; T/D Suva 2000; Band C4.

Tuke, Sarah Frances; SUPL since August 2000; Born 08/03/63; FCO 1982; Cape Town/Pretoria 1984; Jakarta 1987; Floater Duties 1990; Peking 1993; New York (UKMIS) 1996; SUPL 1999; FCO 2000; Band B3.

Tully, Colin Nigel; Caracas since March 2002; Born 15/07/58; FCO 1980; Amman 1982; FCO 1985; New Delhi 1987; FCO 1991; Buenos Aires 1995; FCO 1997; Band C4; m 1983 Wendy Joyce Ogden (1s 1985; 1d 1989).

Tunn, Douglas Charles; Khartoum since May 2003; Born 18/02/68; FCO 1987; New York (UKMIS) 1989; Port Moresby 1992; Jakarta 1998; Tehran 2000; Band B3; m 1996 Cecilia Rosemary Tokilala.

Tunney, Davina; Brussels since January 2004; Born 31/07/67; Home Civil Service 1987-89; FCO 1998; Washington 1999; FCO 2003; Band A2.

Biographical List

Tunnicliffe, Christopher John Robin; Second Secretary (Chancery) Port Louis since May 1999; Born 11/11/69; FCO 1989; Prague 1991; FCO 1993; Full-Time Language Training 1994; FCO 1995; Riyadh 1995; Band C4; m (1) 1991 Veronica Mary Walters (1d 1989; 1s 1992) (diss 1995); (2) 1996 Zara Louise Chapman.

Turnbull, David Robert; On secondment to British Trade International since July 2002; Born 25/08/55; MOD 1976; Ankara 1980; FCO 1983; Maputo 1984; The Hague 1988; Third later Second Secretary FCO 1991; Second Secretary (Commercial) Beirut 1995; Second Secretary (Finance) New York (UKMIS) 1997; Band D6; m 1987 Eva Marianne Persson.

Turnbull, Jane; FCO since February 2004; Born 25/05/76; Band A2; ptnr, Nathan Dorrington.

Turnbull, Nicholas Piers, MBE (1999); First Secretary Tirana since May 2004; Born 23/09/62; FCO 2002; Band D6.

Turner, Alan Roger; FCO since October 1995; Born 09/04/48; Royal Air Force 1965-68; Caracas 1992; Band C5; m 1974 Caroline Grace.

Turner, Andrew Williams; FCO since August 2001; Born 08/12/63; FCO 1986; Language Training 1987; Third later Second Secretary (Chancery) Muscat 1989; Second Secretary (Chancery) Damascus 1992; Second later First Secretary FCO 1994; First Secretary (Political) Pretoria 1998; Band D7; m 1992 Angeline Marie Biegler (1d 2001).

Turner, David Harvey; First Secretary FCO since October 1993; Born 17/02/45; FO 1966; Bonn 1968; Lagos 1970; Brasilia 1973; FCO 1975; Maputo 1978; Vice-Consul São Paulo 1981; Second later First Secretary FCO 1985; First Secretary (Commercial) Lisbon 1989; m 1966 Janet Mary Field (1s; 1d 1975).

Turner, Mark Robin; First Secretary (Commercial) Lisbon since April 2001; Born 23/08/55; FCO 1975; Budapest 1977; Maseru 1979; Islamabad 1982; FCO 1984; Los Angeles 1988; Second Secretary FCO 1991; Consul and Second Secretary (Management) Buenos Aires 1994; First Secretary FCO 1998; m 1981 Patricia Louise Brown (2d 1984, 1987).

Turner, Richard Patrick; First Secretary (Press and Public Affairs) Moscow since June 2001; Born 19/01/63; FCO 1981; Brussels (UKREP) 1984; Dar es Salaam 1986; Third Secretary (Admin) Strasbourg (UKDEL) 1988; FCO 1991 (Second Secretary 1993); São Paulo 1996; Full-Time Language Training 2000; Band C5.

Turner, Robert Leigh; SUPL since October 2002; Born 13/03/58; Department of Transport 1979; PSA 1980; DOE 1981; HM Treasury 1982; FCO 1983; Second Secretary (Chancery) Vienna 1984; First Secretary FCO 1987; Language Training 1991; First Secretary (Economic) Moscow 1992; First Secretary FCO 1995; Counsellor FCO 1997; Counsellor (EU/Economic) Bonn (later Berlin)

1998; m 1992 Pamela Ann Major (1s 1992; 1d 1994).

Turner, Stephen Edward; Consul-General and Director Trade Development Auckland since April 2002; Born 25/03/46; CRO 1963; DSAO 1965; Jakarta 1968; DTI 1972; Third Secretary (Commercial) Kuala Lumpur 1972; Second Secretary FCO 1976; Valletta 1978; Second Secretary (Commercial) Jakarta 1983; First Secretary (Economic) Jakarta 1986; First Secretary FCO 1988; Consul (Commercial) Seattle 1990; Deputy Head of Mission and Consul-General Hanoi 1995; Deputy High Commissioner and Commercial Counsellor Dhaka 1999; m 1966 Maureen Ann Dick (2s 1969, 1971; 2d 1973, 1982).

Turney, Nicholas; FCO since September 1984; Born 31/03/53; FCO 1971; Washington 1981; Band C4.

Turunc, Susan Kay (née Powell); Canberra since April 2003; Born 27/03/49; FCO 1968; Peking 1970; FCO 1971 (Resigned 1972); Home Civil Service 1975-79; Reinstated, FCO 1989; Istanbul 1990; Seoul 1994; FCO 1997; Cairo 1999; Band B3; m 1991 Gokhan Turunc (1 step d 1984).

Turvill, Carol May (née Massingham); SUPL since June 2004; Born 17/06/66; FCO 1985; Pretoria/Cape Town 1988; Havana 1990; FCO 1992; SUPL 1995; Islamabad 1995; FCO 1998; Accra 2000; FCO 2003; Band B3; m 1994 Stuart Graham Turvill.

Turvill, Stuart Graham; FCO since October 2003; Born 18/02/71; FCO 1991; Islamabad 1995; FCO 1998; Accra 2000; Band B3; m 1994 Carol May Massingham.

Twigg, Mark Paul; Consul-General Stuttgart since October 2001; Born 01/03/56; FCO 1975; Beirut 1979; FCO 1980; Harare 1981; Düsseldorf 1983; Tripoli 1987; FCO 1989 (Second Secretary 1991); Full-Time Language Training 1994; Second Secretary (Commercial) Prague 1994; First Secretary British Trade International 1999.

Twyman, Robin Edward; Second Secretary Geneva (UKMIS) since March 2001; Born 27/08/68; FCO 1987; Harare 1989; Africa/Middle East Floater 1993; FCO 1996; Band C4.

Tylor, Paul Andrew; Third Secretary (Immigration later Management) Karachi since April 2002; Born 22/09/64; RAF 1985-95; FCO 1995; Peking 1997; Band B3; m 1988 Yvonne Margaret Wilson.

U

Uden, Martin David; Consul-General San Francisco since September 2003; Born 28/02/55; FCO 1977; Seoul 1978; Second later First Secretary FCO 1982; First Secretary Bonn 1986; First Secretary FCO 1990; Counsellor (Political) and Consul-General Seoul 1994; Counsellor (Trade/Economic) Ottawa 1997; Director International Invest UK 2001; m 1982 Fiona Jane Smith (2s 1986, 1990).

Underwood, Sheila Bridget; SUPL since January 2004; Born 26/11/70; HCS 1995; FCO 1995; World Wide Floater Duties 1999; Band B3; m 2001 Neil Francis McConnell.

Upton, Helen Margaret; First Secretary (Legal) Geneva (UKMIS) since September 2004; Born 05/10/74; Called to the Bar, Lincoln's Inn 1998; Assistant Legal Adviser FCO 2000; m 2001 John Dominic Upton.

Upton, Michael John; Deputy Consul-General Toronto since February 2004; Born 28/10/51; RAF 1970-76; FCO 1976; Havana 1978; Aden 1982; FCO 1982; Bogotá 1984; Second Secretary New York (UKMIS) 1986; Vice-Consul (Inward Investment) Los Angeles 1990; First Secretary FCO 1992; HM Consul (Commercial) Seattle 1995; FCO 2000; m 1978 Susan Marshall (1s 1981; 1d 1983).

Usher, Judith; FCO since June 1999; Born 14/10/69; FCO 1988; Peking 1991; Zagreb 1993; Lagos 1995; Band B3.

Usher, Seifeldin; Second Secretary (Commercial) Damascus since May 2003; Born 27/06/69; FCO 1987; Vienna (UKMIS) 1989; New Delhi 1991; Khartoum 1994; FCO 1997; Accra 1999; Band C4; m 1995 Nihad Elnujumi (3s 1997, 1999, 2002).

V

Vallat, Joanna Clare; FCO since September 2003; Born 17/06/74; Band D6; m 2002 Jurgen Lootens.

Van Der Plank, Ian Derrick; FCO since October 1999; Born 21/08/56; Royal Navy 1972-77; FCO 1981; Paris 1987; Third Secretary Lagos 1990; Third Secretary FCO 1992; Second Secretary Islamabad 1997.

van-de-Cappelle, Clair Louise; FCO since November 2002; Born 24/05/77; Band C4.

Vargas, Emlyn Barry; First Secretary (Technical Management) New Delhi since January 2000; Born 02/02/46; HM Forces 1964-86; FCO 1986; Caracas 1989; Helsinki 1992; FCO 1997; Band C5; m 1991 Carmen Rafaela Velazquez.

Vaygelt, Robin (née Maitland); FCO since June 2000; Born 14/06/61; FCO 1984; Rio de Janeiro 1986; FCO 1988; Johannesburg 1993; Paris 1996; Band A2; m 1992 Marek Stephen Fernyhough Vaygelt.

Venn, Robert Lawrence; First Secretary FCO since August 2001; Born 15/04/65; FCO 1992; Second Secretary (Economic) Jakarta 1994; First Secretary (Political) Peking 1997; Band D6; m 1990 Wendy Ann Wightman (1s 1994; 1d 1996).

Vereker, Sir John, KCB (1999), CB (1992); Governor Hamilton since April 2002; Born 09/08/44; ODM 1967; World Bank 1970; ODA/ODM 1972; Prime Minister's Office 1980; ODA 1983; DES 1988; Permanent Secretary ODA/DFID 1994-02; m 1971 Judy Rowen (1d 1973; 1s 1975).

Verma, Neeras; SUPL since April 2000; Born 21/11/62; FCO 1982; Brussels (UKDEL NATO) 1984; Luanda 1988; FCO 1992; Vienna 1996; Düsseldorf 1999; Band B3; m 1985 Sarah-Jane Dodman (diss 1996).

Very, Donna (née Grant); Berne since October 2003; Born 27/07/69; FCO 1988; SUPL 1992; FCO 1994; Tehran 1996; FCO 1999; Band A2; m 1994 Steve Jason Very (1s 1997; 1d 1999).

Vickers, David Victor Edwin; First Secretary FCO since March 2003; Born 01/05/53; FCO 1973; Lusaka 1975; Kathmandu 1979; Sofia 1983; FCO 1984; Islamabad 1985; Ankara 1989; FCO 1992; Deputy Head of Mission Tallinn 1996; Grand Turk 1999; Band C5; m 1983 Pamela Barron (née Scott).

Villamizar, Bernadette Teresa (née Edwards); Ottawa since February 2003; Born 02/03/63; FCO 1983; Brussels (UKREP) 1985; Shanghai 1987; Rio de Janeiro 1988; FCO 1992; Madrid 1993; Caracas 1996; FCO 2000; Band B3; m 1999 Igor Antonio Villamizar Rivas (1d 2000; 1s 2001).

Vineall, Katherine Patricia (née Jenkins); SUPL since January 1999; Born 07/11/63; FCO 1987; Second Secretary 1989; Second Secretary (Chancery) Madrid 1991; Second Secretary FCO 1992; SUPL 1995; First Secretary FCO 1995; m 1992 Nicholas Edward John Vineall (1s 1995).

Vir Singh, Doris Nefertiti; Beirut since November 2003; Born 03/02/64; FCO 1993; Geneva (UKMIS) 1996; Paris 2000; FCO 2002; Band B3.

Virgoe, John; Deputy Permanent Representative to UNEP and UN-HABITAT and First Secretary (Environment) Nairobi since November 2002; Born 01/09/69; FCO 1991; Full-Time Language Training 1994; Jakarta 1995; FCO 1999; m 1999 Tuti Suwidjiningsih (1d 2004).

Voak, Susan; Karachi since June 2004; Born 02/06/69; FCO 1999; Lilongwe 2001; Band B3.

Vosper, Alistair John; FCO since January 2000; Born 09/04/70; FCO 1989; Islamabad 1992; Manila 1996; Band C5; m 1995 Lucy Jane Medforth (2s 2001, 2004).

Vowles, John Philip, MBE (1994); Hong Kong since September 2003; Born 13/08/47; Royal Marines 1962-87; Moscow 1987; Pretoria/Cape Town 1989; Tehran 1991; Kampala 1995; Havana 1999; Band C4; m 1968 Maureen Cann.

Vowles, Richard; FCO since October 2003; Born 16/11/76; Band C4; m 2003 Kelly Susanne.

W

Waddington, Jane Caroline; Tripoli since July 2004; Born 12/10/64; HO 1988; FCO 1998; Stockholm 2000; FCO 2001; Abu Dhabi 2003; Band A2.

Wade, Emma Lesley; FCO since January 2002; Born 15/09/73; FCO 1995; Second Secretary (Political) Santiago 1998; Band D6.

Wadvani, Sanjay Mark; Deputy Consul-General and Head of Commercial Section Guangzhou since May 2002; Born 06/12/66; FCO 1987; Peking 1989; Damascus 1991; FCO 1995; Santiago 1998; Band C5.

Wahab, Mohammed Toafiq; Third Secretary (Visa) Lagos since December 2001; Born 02/04/75; HM Customs & Excise 1993-94; FCO 1997; Islamabad 1998; Band B3; m 1996 Rozmina Muhammad Anwar (2s 1998, 2000).

Wain, Geoffrey William; British Trade International since August 2003; Born 10/05/65; FCO 1983; Islamabad 1986; Istanbul 1989; FCO 1992 (Second Secretary 1994); Maseru 1995; Second Secretary (Commercial) Manila 2000; Band C5; m 1985 Kathleen Anne Lowe (1d 1992).

Wain, Kathleen Anne (née Lowe); FCO since August 2003; Born 11/02/63; FCO 1982; Addis Ababa 1984; FCO 1985; Islamabad 1986; Istanbul 1989; FCO 1992; SUPL 1995; Third Secretary (Immigration) Manila 2000; Band C4; m 1985 Geoffrey William Wain (1d 1992).

Waite, Timothy Matthew; FCO since August 2003; Born 21/07/62; PSA 1988-91; FCO 1991; Jedda 1994; MO/Consul/ECM St Petersburg 1999; Band C5.

Wales, Lee Anne; Brussels since February 2002; Born 07/01/67; FCO 1996; Canberra 1998; Band A2.

Walker, Alisdair James; FCO since March 1999; Born 14/09/65; FCO 1989; Third Secretary (Chancery) Islamabad 1991; FCO 1995; Assistant Management Officer Moscow 1995; Band C4; m 1992 Susan Mary Ireland (2s 1996, 2000; 1d 1998).

Walker, Angela Ruth; First Secretary Wellington since October 2003; Born 07/05/54; FCO 1980; The Hague 1983; Vice-Consul Rio de Janeiro 1986; FCO 1989; On secondment to the MOD 1997; Band C4.

Walker, Derek Leonard; Second Secretary JMO Brussels since July 1999; Born 28/11/44; FCO 1971; Tripoli 1974; Bucharest 1976; Ottawa 1978; FCO 1980; JAO Brussels 1984; Vice-Consul later Second Secretary (Immigration) Lagos 1988; FCO 1992; Tunis 1995; m 1965 Janice Ann Gamble-Beresford (2d 1968, 1970).

Walker, Helen Mary; First Secretary Brussels (UKDEL NATO) since November 2003; Born 23/07/69; FCO 1991; Full-Time Language Training 1993; Athens 1994; First Secretary FCO 1999.

Walker, Ian Michael; Third Secretary (Immigration) Tehran since May 2002; Born 06/03/71; FCO (HCS) 1990; Transferred to the DS 2002; Band B3; m 1996 Nargis (2d 1999, 2001).

Walker, John Frank; Tel Aviv since August 2003; Born 10/02/64; Royal Engineers 1980-85; FCO 1987; Buenos Aires 1991; Budapest 1998; On loan

to the Northern Ireland Office 2002; Band C4; m 1990 Caroline Jane Masters (2s 1985, 1991).

Walker, John Ronald; Senior Research Officer FCO since March 1985; Born 04/05/60; Band D6.

Walker, John Stanley; Baghdad since June 2004; Born 20/10/66; FCO/HCS 1984; FCO 1988; Bucharest 1989; Doha 1991; FCO 1994; Hong Kong 1997; T/D Bombay 1999; Vice-Consul Damascus 1999; Band B3.

Walker, June (née Erwin); FCO since June 1997; Born 01/06/59; FCO 1992; Dar es Salaam 1996; Band A2; m 1996 Vincent Charles Walker (1s 1997).

Walker, Neil; On loan to the DTI since January 2003; Born 29/04/63; Royal Navy 1979-89; FCO 1997; Washington 1998; Band B3; m 1992 Angela Seatter (2d 1995, 1997).

Walker, Patricia Arlow; SUPL since May 1997; Born 29/09/63; FCO 1988; Berlin 1990; Ankara 1993; Band A2; m 1998 Paul A Bertrand.

Wall, Eric Simon Charles; Counsellor FCO since September 2001; Born 04/09/57; Royal Navy 1976-86; Second Secretary FCO 1986; Second later First Secretary Geneva (UKMIS) 1988; First Secretary FCO 1991; First Secretary (Political) Kampala 1994; First Secretary FCO 1995; Counsellor Harare 1998; m 1983 Elizabeth Anne Gibson (2s 1988, 1990; 1d 1994).

Wallace, David Malcolm; FCO since September 2002; Born 09/10/80; Band C4.

Wallace, Euan; Second Secretary FCO since June 1999; Born 15/06/63; FCO 1981; Paris 1984; Moscow 1986; Resigned 1988; Reinstated, FCO 1990; New York (UKMIS) 1993; Vice-Consul New York 1994; Brussels (UKDEL) 1996; m 1987 Gillian Whittaker (1d 1996; 1s 2000).

Wallace, Gillian (née Whittaker); SUPL since November 1996; Born 14/11/63; FCO 1983; Paris 1985; Moscow 1987; FCO 1988; New York (UKMIS) 1993; Band B3; m 1987 Euan Wallace (1d 1996; 1s 2000).

Waller, Mark; Kingston since July 2003; Born 29/09/67; FCO 1987; Kingston 1989; FCO 1992; Abuja 1995; Third Secretary (Political) Almaty 1999; Band B3.

Walley, Martin; Deputy High Commissioner Bandar Seri Begawan since July 2003; Born 11/06/58; HMIT 1977; FCO 1978; Ankara 1980; Mexico City 1984; FCO 1984; Budapest 1985; Dhaka 1987; FCO 1990; Third Secretary (Commercial) Manila 1992; Bangkok 1995; Second Secretary FCO 1996; On loan to DFID 1997; Second later First Secretary (Management) Moscow 1999; m 1981 Dilek Sule (2s 1991, 1995).

Wallis, Victor Charles; Resident British Commissioner Grenada since October 2002; Born 06/02/47; CO 1963; Commonwealth Office (later FCO) 1966; Bermuda 1969; Accra 1972; FCO 1975; Second Secretary Helsinki 1979; Vice-

Consul (Commercial) Sydney 1985; First
Secretary FCO 1989; Deputy Consul-General Los
Angeles 1994; First Secretary FCO 1999; m 1971
Jacqueline Wadhams (1s 1979).

Walmsley, Alan; FCO since July 1998; Born
06/09/61; FCO 1981; Abu Dhabi 1984; FCO 1988;
Washington 1996; Band C5; m 1992 C Richardson
(1d 1999).

Walmsley, Mark Ronan; First Secretary
(Commercial) Jakarta since October 2001; Born
17/06/58; FCO (HCS) 1978; FCO 1980; Bucharest
1981; Africa/Middle East Floater 1983; FCO
1984; Nicosia 1987; Second Secretary (Consular)
Bombay 1990; Second Secretary FCO 1994; Head
of Inward Investment Section Taipei 1997; m 1986
Andrea Elizabeth (1s 1995; 1d 1997).

Walpole, The Hon Alice Louise; New York
(UKMIS) since August 2001; Born 01/09/63; FCO
1985; Third later Second Secretary (Developing
Countries) Brussels (UKREP) 1987; Language
Training 1990; Second Secretary Dar es Salaam
1991; First Secretary FCO 1994; First Secretary
UKDEL NATO 1998; SUPL 1999; Brussels
(UKREP) 2000; m 1990 Angel Carro Castrillo
(diss 2002) (3d 1990 (twins), 1993; 3s 1996, 1999
(twins)).

Walsh, Nicola Jane; FCO since July 1996; Born
24/01/61; FCO 1980; Bahrain 1982; Bridgetown
1985; Kingston 1986; LA/Caribbean Floater 1988;
Bridgetown 1993; Band C4.

Walsh, Paul Richard; Consul (Management)
Calcutta since April 2002; Born 15/03/69; DHSS
1987; FCO 1988; Berlin 1990; FCO 1990;
Islamabad 1991; Third Secretary (Commercial)
Warsaw 1995.

Walsh, Paula Ellen; First Secretary FCO since
June 2003; Born 21/12/66; FCO 1998; Second
Secretary (Commercial) Buenos Aires 1999; Band
D6; m 1995 Nicholas Gibson.

Walsh, Penelope Ruth (known as Penny); Deputy
Head of Mission Panama since July 2003; Born
19/12/66; FCO 1990; Third Secretary (UN)
Geneva (UKMIS) 1991; Third Secretary Tirana
1994; T/D Rome (UKMIS) 1996; Consul Naples
1996; Consul and Second later First Secretary
(Management) Sana'a 1998; FCO 2000; Band C4;
m 1998 Primo Grilli.

Walter, Emily Rose; SUPL since August 2001;
Born 18/05/67; FCO 1992; Second Secretary
(Political) Buenos Aires 1995; First Secretary FCO
2000; Band D6; m 1996 Dominic William Martin
(3d 1996, 1998, 2001).

Walters, Alison Jane (née Lund); SUPL since
February 1996; Born 28/08/57; FCO 1976;
Yaoundé 1978; FCO 1982; Sofia 1985; Paris 1987;
SUPL 1988; Third later Second Secretary
(Information/Chancery) Islamabad 1989; SUPL
1991; FCO 1995; m 1978 Robert Leslie Walters
(2s 1987, 1994).

Walters, David Anthony, MVO (1985); Islamabad
since March 2000; Born 03/01/57; NSB 1975;

FCO 1977; Tehran 1979; Bonn 1980; Port of Spain
1982; FCO 1986; Dhaka 1988; Vice-Consul
Atlanta 1991; FCO 1994; T/D Abuja 1998; T/D
Bogotá 1998; T/D Tirana 1999; Band C4; m 1980
Janis Anne McPhail (3s 1982, 1984, 1991).

Walters, Helen Elizabeth; FCO since September
2001; Born 27/03/80; Band C4; ptnr, Andrew
Coolen.

Walters, Robert Leslie; SUPL since October 2000;
Born 23/01/50; FCO 1970; Havana 1972; Kaduna
1973; Valletta 1976; Masirah 1977; FCO 1977;
Yaoundé 1978; FCO 1982; Sofia 1985; Paris 1987;
Third Secretary (Commercial) Islamabad 1989;
Second Secretary FCO 1993; T/D Shanghai 1993;
Second Secretary FCO 1994; Vice-Consul
(Commercial) Brisbane 1996; Band C4; m (1)
1973 Mary Elaine Lee (diss 1978); (2) 1978
Alison Jane Lund (2s 1987, 1994).

Walters, Simon Christopher; Second Secretary
FCO since October 2001; Born 03/07/71; FCO
1995; Full-Time Language Training 1997; Full-
Time Language Training 1998; Second Secretary
Riyadh 1999; Band C4.

Walton, Derek Antony Ruffel; Senior Assistant
Legal Adviser later Legal Counsellor FCO since
October 2001; Born 21/07/66; Called to the Bar
(Lincoln's Inn) 1989; Assistant Legal Adviser FCO
1991; First Secretary (Legal) Geneva (UKMIS)
1997; m 1994 Claire Margaret Hughes (2s 1996,
2004; 1d 2000).

Walton, Gillian Mary (née Booth); First Secretary
FCO since November 1994; Born 16/08/54; FCO
1975; Second Secretary Moscow 1987; Second
Secretary FCO 1989; First Secretary Oslo 1992;
Band C5; m 1979 (diss 1986).

Walwyn, David Scott; SUPL since June 2001;
Born 14/04/59; FCO 1985; Second later First
Secretary (Chancery) Bangkok 1987; First
Secretary FCO 1990; Paris (UKDEL OECD)
1995; FCO 1999; m 1988 Fiona Cassels-Brown
(1s 1997).

Ward, Anthony John; Washington since December
2002; Born 08/05/47; Royal Marines 1964-88;
Brussels (UKREP) 1988; Moscow 1991; Paris
1992; FCO 1995; Port Louis 1998; Band B3; m
1996 Penelope Joan Walter (3s 1974, 1975, 1977).

Ward, Christine (née Gray); SUPL since May
1997; Born 25/12/59; FCO 1978; Budapest 1980;
Istanbul 1982; SUPL 1986; Paris 1988; Manila
1992; Band B3; m 1986 Michael John Ward.

Ward, Christopher Edwin; Attaché (Visa) Moscow
since April 2003; Born 11/05/75; FCO 1995;
Dhaka 2000; Band B3; m 2001 Donna Michelle
Perry (1s 2002).

Ward, Christopher James; FCO since May 2001;
Born 04/01/78; FCO 1997; Gibraltar 1999; Band
A2.

Ward, David; Deputy Head of Mission
Kathmandu since April 2002; Born 11/06/68; FCO
1992; Tokyo 1994; FCO 1998; Band D6.

Ward, Gareth Edward; FCO since January 2003; Born 17/01/74; FCO 1996; Second Secretary (KHF) Moscow 1998.

Ward, Katherine Georgina Louise (Cathy), LVO (2004); First Secretary (Political/Internal) Paris since October 2002; Born 07/04/65; Research Officer FCO 1994; Senior Research Officer 1995; Second Secretary Havana 1998; First Secretary FCO 2001; On secondment to Quai d'Orsay 2002; Band D6.

Ward, Michael David; FCO since July 1989; Born 01/06/63; FCO 1983; New Delhi 1986; Band C4.

Ward, Michael John; Deputy Head of Mission Budapest since August 2002; Born 25/12/58; FCO 1982; Istanbul 1985; Third Secretary (Commercial) later Second Secretary (Science and Technology) Paris 1988; Second later First Secretary FCO 1993; First Secretary Brussels (UKREP) 1997; Seconded to the European Commission 2000; m 1986 Christine Gray (2d 1990, 1995; 1s 1991).

Wardle, Mark Thomas; Lusaka since October 2003; Born 22/11/62; Royal Navy 1979-89; Police 1990-95; FCO 1995; Kuala Lumpur 1997; Pretoria 2000; Band B3; m 1994 Julie Anne Russell (1d 1999; 2s 2001, 2002).

Wardle, Mark William; Second Secretary (Chancery) Vienna since May 2000; Born 25/02/75; FCO 1997; Band C4.

Wardle, Sharon Anne; On loan to British Trade International since January 2003; Born 02/03/65; FCO 1985; Moscow 1987; FCO 1989; Ex-Floater Duties 1990; Vice-Consul Beirut 1991; On loan to British Trade International 1996; Secondment to Private Sector 2000; Band D6; m 2002 Peter Nicholas Millman.

Ware, Jillian Angela; SUPL since February 1999; Born 17/12/62; FCO 1982; New York (UKMIS) 1984; Africa/Middle East Floater 1988; FCO 1990; Amman 1994; Band B3; m 1990 David Edward Ware (2d 1991, 1995).

Waring, Lynn Elizabeth (née Cuthbert); Reinstated FCO since January 2003; Born 16/01/53; FCO 1973; Bonn 1978; Kuwait 1981; Resigned 1985; Band B3; m 1974 David Waring (1s 1987, 1d 1990).

Warr, Martyn John; FCO since December 1997; Born 01/05/59; FCO 1981; Language Training 1983; Jedda 1984; FCO 1988 (Second Secretary 1989); Second Secretary (Commercial) Lisbon 1993; Band D7; m 1992 Sarah Jane Thompson Warr (2d 1993, 1996; 1s 2001).

Warren, David Alexander; Director, Business Group, Trade Partners UK since April 2000; Born 11/08/52; Third Secretary FCO 1975; Language Training (Japanese) 1976-78; Second Secretary and Private Secretary to the Ambassador Tokyo 1978; Second later First Secretary (Economic) Tokyo 1979; First Secretary FCO 1981; Head of Chancery Nairobi 1987; FCO 1990; Counsellor on loan to the Science and Technology Secretariat, later Office of Science and Technology at the Cabinet Office 1991; Counsellor (Commercial) Tokyo 1993; Head of Hong Kong Department, later China Hong Kong Department 1998; FCO 1998; m 1992 Pamela Pritchard.

Warren-Gash, Haydon Boyd; HM Ambassador Rabat and (non-resident) to Mauritania since July 2002; Born 08/08/49; FCO 1971; Language Training London University 1972; Third Secretary Ankara 1973; Second later First Secretary (Chancery) Madrid 1977; First Secretary FCO 1981; First Secretary (Commercial) Paris 1985; First Secretary FCO 1989; Deputy High Commissioner Nairobi 1991; Counsellor FCO 1994; HM Ambassador Abidjan and HM Ambassador non-resident to Liberia, Niger and Burkina Faso 1997; FCO 2001; m 1973 Caroline Emma Bowring Leather (1s 1975; 1d 1977).

Warrington, Guy Murray; FCO since September 2001; Born 23/09/63; FCO 1986; Third later Second Secretary (Economic/Information) Singapore 1988; Second Secretary New York (UKMIS) 1992; First Secretary FCO 1993; Geneva (UKMIS) 1997.

Warwick, Sharon Joy; SUPL since April 2002; Born 31/01/57; FCO 1979; Rangoon 1980; Kuala Lumpur 1982; FCO 1983; Band B3; m 1983 Aiden Eustace Warwick.

Watchorn, Kenneth Graham; First Secretary FCO since April 2000; Born 20/09/54; FCO 1971; Washington 1979; FCO 1982; Vienna 1984; FCO 1987; Riyadh 1987; Second Secretary FCO 1992; Paris 1997; Band D6; m 1980 Rossalyn Keen (2s 1983, 1985).

Watchorn, Mark; Deputy High Commissioner Maseru since July 2002; Born 28/07/65; FCO 1984; Cape Town/Pretoria 1987; Africa/Middle East Floater 1990; FCO 1992; On loan to DTI 1996; Band C4; m 1996 Christine Jacqueline Holding (1s 1998; 1d 2001).

Waterhouse, Christine; FCO since November 2002; Born 15/09/67; FCO 1987; Nairobi 1991; FCO 1994; Athens 1998; Band B3.

Waterhouse, Peter Laurance; Addis Ababa since June 2003; Born 03/02/58; FCO 1975; Bonn 1987; FCO 1990; Nicosia 1991; FCO 1994; Warsaw 1996; NIO 1999; Band C4; m 1985 Clare Rachel Dewar (2d 1993, 1999).

Waterton, James, LVO (1995); Deputy Head of Mission Montevideo since May 2002; Born 25/04/49; FCO 1968; Havana 1970; Valletta 1972; Bonn 1974; FCO 1977; Wellington 1981; Second Secretary and Vice-Consul Montevideo 1984; Second Secretary FCO 1987; HM Consul later First Secretary Durban 1991; Deputy Consul-General Istanbul 1996; First Secretary FCO 1999; m 1994 Judith Kerwin.

Waterworth, Peter Andrew; Counsellor (Political) Islamabad since March 2003; Born 15/04/57; Assistant later Senior Legal Adviser FCO 1987; First Secretary (Legal Adviser) Bonn 1990; First

Secretary FCO 1994; First Secretary (Political/External) Rome 1996; Head of Political Affairs Division NIO (Belfast) 2000; m 1994 Catherine Finnigan.

Watkinson, Barry; FCO since April 2000; Born 22/08/44; FCO 1984; Brussels 1988; FCO 1991; Moscow 1996; Band C4; m 1988 Patricia Rose.

Watson, David James; First Secretary FCO since August 1999; Born 04/03/57; FCO 1988; Second later First Secretary Harare 1989; First Secretary FCO 1992; First Secretary (Political) Madrid 1996; Band D6; m 1989 Sheelah McKeown (2d 1989, 1991).

Watson, Gavin Christopher; First Secretary (Legal) New York (UKMIS) since July 2003; Born 21/07/70; Solicitor; Legal Assistant Home Office 1995; Assistant Legal Adviser FCO 2000.

Watson, James Spencer Kennedy; First Secretary FCO since October 2000; Born 30/11/64; FCO 1988; Second Secretary (Economic) Kuwait 1991; Second Secretary FCO 1994; First Secretary (Political) Damascus 1997; Band D6.

Watson, Joel Aaron; Deputy High Commissioner Vila since February 2002; Born 14/09/69; FCO 1989; Belmopan 1991; Islamabad 1994; FCO 1998; Band C4; m 1990 Victoria Jane Baxter (1s 1999).

Watson, Nicholas Henry Lewis; First Secretary (Political) Kuwait since October 2003; Born 12/06/71; FCO 1995; Full-Time Language Training 1997; Full-Time Language Training Cairo 1998; Second Secretary (Political) Amman 1999; Second Secretary FCO 2001; Band D6; m 1997 Catriona Ann (1s 2000).

Watson, Robert Emmerson; First Secretary (Regional Affairs) Kampala since March 2004; Born 10/08/70; FCO 1996; Second Secretary Tel Aviv 1998; FCO 2001; Band C4; m 2002 Cerys Anwen Evans.

Watson, Stephen; Chairman DSTUS FCO since July 2001; Born 18/06/57; HO 1975; FCO 1976; Jedda 1979; Hong Kong 1982; Brasilia 1986; FCO 1988; Band C5.

Watson, Terence Paul; Second Secretary (Technical Management) New Delhi since April 2001; Born 07/12/48; HM Forces 1964-76; FCO 1988; Band C4; m 1969 Jennifer Margaret (2s 1970, 1972).

Watt, James Wilfrid, CVO; HM Ambassador Beirut since October 2003; Born 05/11/51; FCO 1977; MECAS 1978; Second later First Secretary Abu Dhabi 1980; FCO 1983; First Secretary (Chancery) New York (UKMIS) 1985; First Secretary FCO 1989; Deputy Head of Mission Amman 1992; Deputy Head of Mission Islamabad 1996; SOAS 1999; Head of Consular Division 2000; m 1980 Elizabeth Ghislaine Villeneuvre (dec'd) (1s 1981; 1d 1986).

Wattam, John; Second Secretary (Political) Geneva (UKDIS) since August 1998; Born

11/05/63; FCO 1982; Bonn 1984; Karachi 1987; FCO 1991; Third Secretary (Commercial) Lagos 1994; Third Secretary (Political/Information) Lagos 1995; Full-Time Language Training 1998; m 1991 Anne Michelle Watson (2d 1993, 1998; 1s 1995).

Watts, Elizabeth Helen; SUPL since September 2003; Born 22/03/79; OFTEL 1997; FCO 1999; Bucharest 2000; Band A2.

Waugh, Linda Alison; FCO since October 1999; Born 20/03/65; MOD 1984; FCO 1992; Athens 1996; Band A2.

Waugh, Lisa Helen (née Maley); FCO since August 2000; Born 28/08/67; FCO 1988; Brussels 1990; FCO 1992; Hong Kong 1993; Istanbul 1996; FCO 1999; SUPL 2000; Band C5; m 1995 Graeme Stewart Waugh (1d 1998; 1s 2000).

Webb, Robert, OBE (2000); FCO since July 2000; Born 06/06/50; Montserrat; DSAO (later FCO) 1966; Singapore 1971; Guatemala City 1974; FCO 1978; Floater Duties 1982; Hanoi 1984; Second Secretary and Consul Mexico City 1985; Second Secretary FCO 1989; Deputy Head of Mission Georgetown 1993; First Secretary Plymouth 1997; m 1989 Maria Del Carmen Colin Irieta (1s 1994).

Webb, Sarah Jane; FCO since July 2002; Born 02/12/66; FCO 1987; Budapest 1990; FCO 1992; Kuala Lumpur 1994; FCO 1997; Floater Duties 2000; Band A2.

Webber, Barbara Ann (née Leatherbarrow); FCO since July 1995; Born 06/03/66; FCO 1987; Peking 1992; Band B3; m 1996 Martin George Webber (1s 1998; 1d 2001).

Webber, Martin George; Third Secretary (Political) Berne since March 2002; Born 19/10/60; HO 1979-81; FCO 1989; Geneva (UKMIS) 1990; FCO 1992; Peking 1993; FCO 1995; Third Secretary (Management) Quito 1998; Band B3; m 1996 Barbara Ann Leatherbarrow (1s 1998; 1d 2001).

Webster, John Auld; Geneva (UKMIS) since July 2003; Born 06/09/68; FCO 1988; Nicosia 1990; FCO 1992; Port Louis 1996; Strasbourg 1999; Band C4.

Weeks, Alan Richard; First Secretary FCO since November 2000; Born 29/07/48; FCO 1965; Tripoli 1970; Sofia 1972; Beirut 1974; Innsbruck 1976; FCO 1979; Second Secretary (Development) New Delhi 1984; Second Secretary (Admin) and Consul East Berlin 1987; First Secretary FCO 1991; Deputy Head of Mission and Consul Quito 1997; Band D6; m 1971 Penelope Dibb (2s 1974, 1976).

Weeks, Sarah Marguerite; Second Secretary (Chancery) Wellington since July 2002; Born 15/10/68; FCO 1987; Abidjan 1990; Floater Duties 1993; Paris 1995; FCO 1998; Band C4.

Weinrabe, Stephen Michael; First Secretary (Management) Brasilia since January 2001; Born 13/06/50; FO (later FCO) 1967; Bucharest 1971;

Paris 1972; Dublin 1973; Tehran 1975; FCO 1977; Nicosia 1981; Bangkok 1984; Second Secretary (Admin) Lagos 1988; Second Secretary FCO 1991; Second Secretary (Commercial) Canberra 1994; Second Secretary (Commercial) Sydney 1994; Assistant Personal Secretary to the Minister of State 1999; Full-Time Language Training 2000; Band C5; m 1973 Eugenia Del Transito Poppescov Lazo (2s 1975, 1995).

Weldin, Jonathan Michael; First Secretary FCO since December 2001; Born 23/02/59; FCO 1982; Second later First Secretary (Chancery) Sana'a 1986; First Secretary FCO 1988; First Secretary (Chancery) Tunis 1990; First Secretary FCO 1993; First Secretary (External) Athens 1996; Band D6; m 1984 Fiona Jean Nesbitt (1s 1987; 1d 1989).

Weldon, Lawrence John, MVO (1980); Second Secretary Moscow since January 2002; Born 06/03/50; FCO 1972; Attaché (Development) Bangkok 1975; Attaché (Commercial) Tunis 1978; FCO 1981; British Vice-Consul Johannesburg 1983; Second Secretary FCO 1986; Second Secretary (Commercial) Caracas 1989; SUPL 1992; Second Secretary FCO 1995; Convent Liaison Officer Gibraltar 1997; m 1984 Sarah Helen Burn (1d 1989; 2s 1991, 1999).

Weldon, Paul; Athens since August 2000; Born 03/04/59; FCO 1975; Pretoria 1987; FCO 1989; Band C4; m 1986 Karen Louise Ritchie (2s 1988, 1992).

Wells, Andrew Justin; Second Secretary (Commercial) Prague since June 2002; Born 08/03/68; FCO 1988; Floater Duties 1991; Zagreb 1993; FCO 1995; Language Training Cairo 1997; Third Secretary Amman 1998; Band C4; m 1994 Juliette Swain (2s 1996, 1999; 1d 2001).

Wells, Colin Neil; Second Secretary (Political) Abuja since August 2001; Born 29/09/67; FCO HCS 1987; DS 1990; Bridgetown 1992; Geneva (UKMIS) 1996 (Second Secretary 1997); FCO 1999; Band C4; m 1997 Rebekah Wells (2d 1993, 1995; 1s 1997).

Wells, Daniel; Accra since April 2004; Born 21/07/70; FCO 1989; Bucharest 1992; FCO 1994; Lagos 1995; FCO 1998; New Delhi 2000; Band B3.

Wells, David John; HM Consul Milan since May 2004; Born 29/06/63; FCO 1982; New Delhi 1988; FCO 1990; Vice-Consul Moscow 1995; FCO 1998; Deputy High Commissioner Nassau 2000; Band C5; m 1994 Helen Paula McCarron (1d 1996; 1s 1999).

Wells, Helen Paula (née McCarron); SUPL since September 2000; Born 29/06/68; FCO 1986; New Delhi 1989; Geneva (UKMIS) 1992; Moscow 1995; FCO 1998; Band B3; m 1994 David John Wells (1d 1996; 1s 1999).

Wells, Juliette Elizabeth (née Swain); SUPL since August 1994; Born 12/06/67; FCO 1986; Zagreb 1993; Band A2; m 1994 Andrew Justin Wells (2s 1996, 1999; 1d 2001).

Welsh, Jolyon Rimmer; FCO since August 2002; Born 22/12/67; FCO 1990; Second Secretary (Chancery/Information) Colombo 1992; First Secretary FCO 1995; New York (UKMIS) 1998; m 1999 Susan Lynley Welsh (1d 2002).

Welsh, Patricia Angela (née Sherry); SUPL since July 2003; Born 23/08/64; FCO 1985; Madrid 1989; FCO 1992; Brasilia 1994; SUPL 1997; FCO 1999; Oslo 2000; Band A2; m 1993 James Ormsby Welsh (2d 1996, 1998).

Welsh, Paul Anthony; Second Secretary (Commercial) Lisbon since March 2002; Born 12/10/67; FCO 1986; Harare 1988; Floater Duties 1992; FCO 1994; Deputy Head of Mission Tbilisi 1998; Band C4; m (1) 1988 Ann McCoy (diss 1993); (2) 1994 Emel Elif Icbilen.

Welsted, David Curtis; Moscow since May 2003; Born 17/10/52; FCO 1969; Attaché Warsaw 1975; FCO 1976; Tehran 1978; FCO 1978; Nairobi 1980; FCO 1983; Attaché Amman 1984; FCO 1987; Washington 1992; First Secretary FCO 1995; m 1974 Gillian Mary Harris (1s 1978; 1d 1982).

Wenban, Mark; Lima since July 2001; Born 29/05/67; FCO 2000; Band A2.

West, Brian William; HM Consul Paris since January 2002; Born 04/01/48; FCO 1968; Moscow 1971; Kampala 1972; Strasbourg 1975; FCO 1977; Port Louis 1980; Second Secretary (Commercial) Abidjan 1984; Second Secretary FCO 1988; T/D Athens 1990; Second Secretary (Commercial) Paris 1991; T/D New Delhi 1996; T/D Guangzhou 1997; Second Secretary (Commercial) Beirut 1997; m 1976 Marie-Odile Gilbert (2s 1977, 1980).

West, Peter Bernard; Consul-General Melbourne since July 2004; Born 29/06/58; FCO 1977; Ankara 1978; Buenos Aires 1980; Auckland 1984; Second later First Secretary FCO 1986; First Secretary (Political/Information) Copenhagen 1992; First Secretary FCO 1997; Deputy Head of Mission Bangkok 2000; FCO 2003; m 1980 Julia Anne Chandler (1d 1993; 2s twins 1995).

Westcott, Nicholas James, CMG (1998); Head of IT Strategy Unit, FCO since June 2002; Born 20/07/56; Second Secretary FCO 1982; Seconded to European Commission, Brussels 1984; First Secretary (Agriculture/Finance) Brussels (UKREP) 1985; First Secretary FCO 1989; Deputy Head of Mission Dar es Salaam 1993; Counsellor FCO 1996; Minister-Counsellor for Trade and Transport Policy Washington 1999; m 1989 Miriam Pearson (1d 1996; 1s 2000).

Westgarth, Nicholas Philip; On loan to the Cabinet Office since December 2002; Born 25/11/56; FCO 1980; Third Secretary (Economic) Athens 1981; Second Secretary FCO 1984; Language Training 1985; First Secretary Hong Kong 1986; First Secretary FCO 1989; First Secretary (Chancery) Nicosia 1991; First Secretary FCO 1995; Counsellor Peking 1999; RCDS 2002; m 1988 Kate Judith Sykes (2s 1989, 1992).

Westmacott, Sir Peter John, KCMG (2003), LVO; HM Ambassador Ankara since January 2002; Born 23/12/50; FCO 1972; Third later Second Secretary Tehran 1974; FCO 1978; Seconded to EC Commission Brussels 1978; First Secretary Paris 1980; FCO 1984; PS to Minister of State 1984; Head of Chancery Ankara 1987; Counsellor on secondment as Assistant Private Secretary to TRH the Prince and Princess of Wales at Buckingham Palace 1990; Head of Chancery Washington 1993; Director (Americas) 1997; DUS (Wider World) 2000; m (1) 1972 Angela Margaret Lugg (diss 1999) (2s 1975, 1979; 1d 1977); m (2) 2001 Susie Nemazee.

Wetherell, Gordon Geoffrey; High Commissioner Accra since March 2004; Born 11/11/48; FCO, concurrently Third Secretary Vice-Consul British Embassy, Chad 1973; Third later Second Secretary East Berlin 1974; First Secretary FCO, concurrently First Secretary UKDEL CTB at Geneva 1977; First Secretary UKDEL CTB Geneva 1979; New Delhi 1980; First Secretary FCO 1983; On loan to HM Treasury 1986; FCO 1987; Counsellor and Deputy Head of Mission Warsaw 1988; Counsellor (Political/Military) Bonn 1992; Counsellor FCO 1994; HM Ambassador Addis Ababa and (non-resident) Djibouti and Asmara 1997; HM Ambassador and Consul-General Luxembourg 2000; m 1981 Rosemary Anne Myles (4d 1982, 1985, 1987, 1989).

Whaanga-Jacques, Lorna (née Jacques); Santiago since April 2003; Born 15/09/59; FCO 1985; Vienna (UKDEL CSCE) 1988; Rangoon 1988; Phnom Penh 1992; SUPL 1993; FCO 1997; Muscat 1999; Band A2; m 1994 Dean Tamaku Whaanga.

Whale, Geoffrey; FCO since March 2001; Born 03/07/52; FCO 1983; Peking 1988; FCO 1990; Berlin 1998; Band C5; m 1985 Ingrid Moore (1s 1987).

Whanstall, Lisa Caroline Rachel; FCO since March 2003; Born 20/09/69; FCO 1995; Brasilia 1999; Band C4.

Whatley, Malcolm George; Beijing since October 2003; Born 05/09/52; FCO 1973; Washington 1975; Kuwait 1978; Budapest 1982; Dhaka 1984; FCO 1985; Muscat 1986; FCO 1989; Rio de Janeiro 1992 (Second Secretary 1995); Second Secretary (Commercial) Hong Kong 1999; Band C4; m 1975 Mary Elizabeth Niven (2s 1979, 1985; 1d 1983).

Whawell, Peter Gerald Maber; FCO since March 2003; Born 19/01/69; Band C4.

Wheeler, Fraser William; FCO since July 2000; Born 23/03/57; FCO 1980; Accra 1982; FCO 1984; Geneva (UKMIS) 1985; FCO 1988; Language Training 1990 (Second Secretary 1991); Second Secretary (Commercial) Moscow 1991; Deputy Consul-General Vancouver 1994; SUPL 1999; Band D6; m 1988 Sarah Humphreys (1d 1990; 1s 1993).

Whipp, Kathryn Sarah; SUPL since January 2001; Born 01/03/67; FCO 1988; Kiev 1992; FCO 1995; New Delhi 1998; FCO 2000; Band A2.

Whitaker, Giles David Humphrey; FCO since September 2000; Born 05/03/62; HM Forces 1980-88; Second Secretary FCO 1988; Second Secretary (Chancery) Brussels (UKDEL NATO) 1990; First Secretary FCO 1994; Deputy Head of Mission Berlin 1998; First Secretary (Political) Berlin (on attachment to Auswärtiges Amt) 1999; m 1990 Lucy Phyllida Whately Anderson (2s 1992, 1998; 2d 1994, 1996).

Whitby, John Benjamin; First Secretary Vienna since August 2002; Born 21/02/67; FCO 1990; Language Training 1993; Second Secretary (Political) Tokyo 1994; First Secretary FCO 1997; Band D6; m 1992 Ruth Alexander (1s 1995; 1d 1997).

White, (Charles) John (Branford); High Commissioner Bridgetown since August 2001; Born 24/09/46; Government of Botswana 1968; ODM 1971; Economic Advisers 1977; ODM 1982; CDA at UCL (London) 1983; FCO 1986; First Secretary Lagos 1990; Counsellor, Consul-General and Deputy Head of Mission Tel Aviv 1993; Commissioner for the British Antarctic Territory, Commissioner for the British Indian Ocean Territory and Counsellor FCO 1997; m 1975 Judy Margaret Lewis.

White, Anthony William; Bridgetown since October 1999; Born 29/12/54; FCO 1973; Peking 1980; FCO 1982; Lilongwe 1985; FCO 1988; Third Secretary Kuala Lumpur 1993; FCO 1996; Band C4; m 1996 Rahani Mat Tahir.

White, Benjamin Matthew; Second Secretary Kabul since January 2004; Born 02/01/79; FCO 2001; Band C4.

White, Debra; Bangkok since January 2003; Born 28/05/75; FCO 1996; Colombo 1998; Paris 2001; Band A2.

White, Jacqueline Denise (née Hill); Riga since October 2002; Born 24/05/64; FCO 1987; Dar es Salaam 1989; FCO 1993; New York (UKMIS) 1993; SUPL 1996; New York (UKMIS) 1996; SUPL 1997; FCO 2000; Grand Turk 2000; Band B3; m 1990 Jerry Lee White (3s 1996, 1998, 2002).

White, Kate Georgina; FCO since September 2003; Born 24/01/73; FCO 1995; Full-Time Language Training 1996; Full-Time Language Training, Beijing 1997; Hong Kong 1998; Taipei 2000; Band C4.

White, Richard Michael, MBE (1983); Counsellor (Management) Paris since June 2003; Born 12/07/50; FCO 1969; UKDEL (later UKREP) EC Brussels 1971; Language Training SOAS and Yazd 1974; Tehran 1975; Second Secretary 1978; APS to the Minister of State 1978; APS to the Lord Privy Seal 1979; FCO 1979; Second Secretary (Commercial/Admin) and Consul Dakar 1980; First Secretary (Technology) Paris 1984; First

Secretary FCO 1988; Deputy High Commissioner Valletta 1992; First Secretary FCO 1996; Counsellor, Head of Migration and Visa Division 1997; Assistant Director, Personnel Services 2000; m 1979 Deborah Anne Lewis (1s 1984; 1d 1986).

Whitecross, Andrew Ronald; First Secretary FCO since July 2001; Born 14/04/49; Army 1964-76; FCO 1976; Private Industry 1978; FCO 1980; Sana'a 1981; Baghdad 1985; Second Secretary FCO 1989; First Secretary (Political) Muscat 1998; Band C5; m 1980 Nancy-Jane Evans (dec'd 1994).

Whiteford, Kathryn Elizabeth; Pretoria since May 2004; Born 05/08/78; FCO 2002; Band A2.

Whitehead, Laurence Jeremy; First Secretary FCO since June 2002; Born 17/04/61; FCO 1984; Second Secretary Jakarta 1987; Second later First Secretary FCO 1990; First Secretary (Political) Vienna 1995; First Secretary (Political) Tirana 1999; Band D6; m 1995 Marjella Djorghi.

Whitehead, Roger; First Secretary FCO since January 2002; Born 22/05/54; FCO 1976; Lagos 1979; Kathmandu 1982; FCO 1984; Third Secretary (Management/Consular) Rangoon 1988; Third Secretary (Management/Consular/Commercial) Toronto 1991; Second Secretary FCO 1994; Second Secretary (Commercial) Singapore 1997; Band D6; m 1979 Diane Mann (1s 1987; 1d 1989).

Whiteley, Richard John Clive; Third Secretary (Management) Ankara since June 2001; Born 29/07/67; MOD 1984; FCO 1994; Band B3; m 2001 Louise Carol (1s 1989; 1d 2003).

Whiten, Peter Frank, MBE (1991); FCO since August 1998; Born 05/12/51; FCO 1974; SE Asia Floater 1976; Brussels (UKDEL NATO) 1978; Port of Spain 1981; Second Secretary FCO 1986; Second Secretary (Commercial) Madras 1991; Consul Chiang Mai 1995; m 1987 Antonia Ramsaroop (3s 1989, 1991, 1993; 1d 1994).

Whiteside, Andrew John; First Secretary (Political) Rome since February 2002; Born 21/09/68; FCO 1991; Language Training 1994; Second Secretary (Political) Budapest 1995; First Secretary FCO 1997; Band D6; m 1994 Fiona Elizabeth Bradley (1d 1999; 1s 2001).

Whiteside, Bernard Gerrard, MBE (1994); HM Ambassador Chisinau since April 2002; Born 03/10/54; FCO 1979; Moscow 1983; Geneva (UKDIS) 1986 (Second Secretary 1988); Second Secretary FCO 1989; Second Secretary (Chancery/Aid) Bogotá 1991; First Secretary FCO 1995; First Secretary on loan to DFID 1999.

Whiteway, Paul Robin; Director (International) Invest UK since July 2003; Born 01/12/54; FCO 1977; Third later Second Secretary Dublin 1980; First Secretary FCO 1984; First Secretary Stanley 1986; First Secretary FCO 1987; Seconded to MOD (Navy) 1988; Deputy High Commissioner Kampala 1990; First Secretary FCO 1993; Counsellor and Deputy Head of Mission

Damascus 1996; Counsellor and Deputy Head of Mission Santiago 2000; m 1996 Maha Georges Yannieh (1s 1998).

Whitford, Victoria; First Secretary (Press and Public Affairs) Baghdad since November 2003; Born 06/06/74; FCO 1999; Second Secretary (Political) Pristina 2001; Band D6.

Whittaker, Andrew Mark; Consul (Political) Jerusalem since October 2001; Born 22/06/76; FCO 1998; Full-Time Language Training (Arabic) 1999; Cairo 2000; Band C4.

Whitting, Ian Robert; First Secretary (Economic) Athens since July 2003; Born 02/04/53; FCO 1972; Moscow 1975; Tunis 1976; Athens 1980; Second Secretary 1981; FCO 1983; Second Secretary (Chancery) Moscow 1985; Second Secretary FCO 1988; Second Secretary (Chancery) Dublin 1990; First Secretary (Economic) FCO 1997; m 1986 Tracy Anne Gallagher (2d 1990, 1994).

Whittingham, Nick; Beijing since January 2004; Born 06/04/64; FCO 1995; Language Training 2000; Consul (Economic) Guangzhou 2001; Band C4; m 1999 Yuehping Yen.

Whittingham, Stephen Arthur; FCO since September 1990; Born 29/01/56; FCO 1972; Brussels 1981; FCO 1983; Hong Kong 1988; Band C5; m 1977 Christine Mary Ruth Hodgson (1d 1978).

Whittle, Lesley Elizabeth; SUPL since July 1999; Born 04/07/58; FCO 1980; Amman 1981; Cairo 1984; FCO 1987; Paris 1990; Islamabad 1994; Band B3; m 1986 Simon FD Mallett (1s 1995).

Whomersley, Christopher Adrian; Legal Counsellor FCO since 1997; Born 18/04/53; Assistant Legal Adviser FCO 1977; Legal Counsellor FCO 1991; Legal Secretariat to the Law Officers 1994; m 1977 Jeanette Diana Szostak (1s 1991; 2d 1993, 1998).

Whyte, Michael James; Colombo since October 2002; Born 24/03/42; Royal Navy 1958-89; Bucharest 1992; Peking 1994; Cairo 1998; Band B3; m 1979 Karen Nina Renée Walters.

Wicke, Tina (née Thackstone); Third Secretary (Political/Information) later (Management) Harare since August 1999; Born 05/02/61; HM Treasury 1980; FCO 1982; Stanley 1983; Kingston 1984; Peking 1986; FCO 1989; Harare 1993; SUPL 1997; Band B3; m 1996 Jürgen Manfred Wicke (1s 2003).

Wickenden, Peter James; Second Secretary (Political/Press) Prague since October 2003; Born 04/09/63; Second Secretary (Political/Economic) Taipei 1999; FCO 2000; Full-Time Language Training 2002; m 1989 Wendy Wang (2s 1991, 2000; 1d 1993).

Wicks, Genevieve Harriot-Jane; Brussels (UKREP) since March 2003; Born 29/06/54; FCO 1973; Geneva (UKMIS) 1974; Islamabad 1977; Peking 1979; Karachi 1981; FCO 1983; Victoria

1986; SUPL 1988; Band A2; m 1978 Graham Wicks (2s 1988, 1989).

Wicks, Graham; Second Secretary (Russia/Partnership) Brussels (UKDEL) since July 2003; Born 02/07/55; FCO 1974; Luxembourg 1976; Islamabad 1976; Peking 1979; Karachi 1981; FCO 1983; Victoria 1986; Vice-Consul Sofia 1990; Third later Second Secretary FCO 1992; Second Secretary (Commercial) Bombay 1995; FCO 1997; Second Secretary (Aid) Khartoum 2000; m 1978 Genevieve Harriot-Jane McCrossan (2s 1988, 1989).

Wicks, Joanna Ruth (née Collett); Second Secretary FCO since November 1995; Born 09/05/56; FCO 1978; Warsaw 1981; FCO 1982; SUPL 1984; Second Secretary FCO 1986; SUPL 1989; Second Secretary FCO 1992; SUPL 1994; Band C4; m 1984 Nigel Earl Wicks (2d 1989, 1994).

Wickstead, Myles Antony; HM Ambassador Addis Ababa, also HM Ambassador (non-resident) Djibouti since November 2000; Born 07/02/51; Ministry of Overseas Development 1976; APS to Lord Privy Seal FCO 1979; Assistant to UK Executive Director IMF/IBRD 1980; Principal ODA 1984; Private Secretary to Minister for Overseas Development 1988; Head of ODA European Community and Food Aid Development 1990; Head of British Development Division in East Africa (BDDEA) 1993; UK Alternate Executive Director World Bank and Counsellor (Development) Washington 1997; m 1990 Shelagh Paterson (1s 1996; 1d 1999).

Wigginton, Christopher James; Second Secretary (Immigration/Consular) Bogotá since November 2000; Born 23/05/60; FCO 1982; Language Training 1984; Tehran 1984; Stockholm 1988; FCO 1991 (Second Secretary 1992); Islamabad 1994; FCO 1997; Full-Time Language Training 2000; Band C4.

Wightman, Andrew Norman Scott; Deputy Head of Mission Rome since January 2002; Born 17/07/61; FCO 1983; Full-Time Language Training 1984; Second Secretary Peking 1986; First Secretary FCO 1989; On loan to the Cabinet Office 1989; First Secretary FCO 1991; On secondment to Quai d'Orsay 1994; First Secretary Paris 1995; Assistant Director Personnel Policy 1998; m 1988 Anne Margaret Roberts (2d 1993, 1997).

Wilbourn, Lillian; Kuwait since August 2002; Born 27/07/47; FCO 1985; Madrid 1987; Brasilia 1990; Maputo 1994; Buenos Aires 1998; Band A2.

Wilcox, Juliette Sarah (née Hannah); On loan to the Cabinet Office since June 2003; Born 29/06/66; FCO 1988; Full-Time Language Training Taiwan 1991; Second Secretary (Chancery) Peking 1992; First Secretary FCO 1995; First Secretary later British Representative, (JLG) Hong Kong 1996; FCO 2000; Band D6; m 1996 Wayne Philip Wilcox (1 step s 1984; 2s 1999, 2002).

Wildash, Elizabeth Jane (née Walmsley), MVO (1997); SUPL since September 2001; Born 17/10/58; FCO 1978; East Berlin 1980; FCO 1981; Abidjan 1983; FCO 1984; SUPL 1987; FCO 1988; Harare 1989; FCO 1992; Third Secretary (Chancery) New Delhi 1994; SUPL 1998; Second Secretary (Economic) Kuala Lumpur 1999; m 1981 Richard James Wildash (2d 1987, 1996).

Wildash, Richard James, LVO (1997); High Commissioner Yaoundé since July 2002; Born 24/12/55; FCO 1977; East Berlin 1979; Abidjan 1981; FCO 1984; Language Training 1986; FCO 1986; Harare 1988; FCO 1992; New Delhi 1994; Deputy High Commissioner Kuala Lumpur 1998; m 1981 Elizabeth Jane Walmsley (2d 1987, 1996).

Wildman, Richard Hugh; FCO since January 2002; Born 18/08/54; FCO 1983; Bridgetown 1989; FCO 1992; Brasilia 1999; Band C4; m (1) 1989 Fay Dawn Reid (1d 1983); (2) 1994 S E Odle.

Wiles, Celia Imogen; First Secretary Rome since February 2004; Born 23/04/63; FCO 1986; Language Training Kamakura 1988; Third Secretary (Commercial) Tokyo 1989; SUPL 1993; FCO 1995; On loan to the European Commission 1998; FCO 1999; SUPL 2000; FCO 2001; First Secretary (Economic and Public Affairs) Canberra 2001; Band D6; (1s 2000).

Wilkes, Jennifer Siobhan; FCO since February 2003; Born 06/09/75; Band A2.

Wilkinson, Richard Denys, CVO (1992); HM Ambassador Santiago since June 2003; Born 11/05/46; FCO 1972; Second later First Secretary Madrid 1973; FCO 1977; First Secretary (Economic/Commercial) Ankara 1983; Counsellor and Head of Chancery Mexico City 1985; Counsellor (Info) Paris 1988; Counsellor FCO 1993; HM Ambassador Caracas 1997; Director (Americas) FCO 2000; m 1982 Maria Angela Morris (2s 1983, 1986; 1d 1991).

Wilks, Jonathan Paul; Deputy Head of Mission Baghdad since April 2003; Born 30/09/67; FCO 1989; Full-Time Language Training Cairo 1992; Second Secretary (Political/Information) Khartoum 1993; First Secretary (Economic) Riyadh 1996; SUPL 1999; Band D7.

Willasey-Wilsey, Timothy Andrew; Counsellor FCO since April 2002; Born 12/09/53; Second Secretary FCO 1981; First Secretary (Chancery) Luanda 1983; First Secretary, Head of Chancery (later Deputy Head of Mission) and Consul San José 1986; First Secretary FCO 1989; Counsellor Islamabad 1993; Counsellor FCO 1996; Counsellor (UN Affairs) Geneva (UKMIS) 1999; m 1983 Alison Middleton Mackie (3s 1986, 1988, 1989).

Williams, Alexander Patrick; Rome since January 2004; Born 13/02/69; FCO 1986; Bangkok 1996; FCO 2000; Band C4.

Williams, Curtis; FCO since October 2002; Born 07/01/77; Band A2.

Williams, David John; Deputy Head of Mission Yaoundé since September 2001; Born 06/06/67; FCO 1986; Geneva (UKMIS) 1988; Bombay 1990; Second Secretary FCO 1995; m 1989 Denise Nowak (1d 1991; 1s 1995).

Williams, Deborah Mary; FCO since August 2002; Born 30/10/64; FCO 1985; Tokyo 1987; Buenos Aires 1990; FCO 1993; Vice-Consul Rome 1998; Band B3.

Williams, Douglas James; FCO since September 2001; Born 09/02/55; FCO 1978; Suva 1981; Brussels (UKREP) 1984; New Delhi 1987; FCO 1991; Bridgetown 1994; Second Secretary (Commercial) Madras 1998; Band C5; m 1981 Susan Anwen Jones (1s 1984; 1d 1986).

Williams, George (aka Rick), BEM (1975); Moscow since July 2003; Born 06/02/43; HM Forces 1962-84; Prague 1984; Singapore 1985; Moscow 1987; Washington 1988; Dhaka 1991; Colombo 1995; Lagos 1998; New Delhi 2001; Band C4 (CSO); m 1965 Eileen (2s 1965, 1968).

Williams, John; Deputy Director (Trade & Investment) Lagos since January 2004; Born 17/06/59; FCO 1978; Moscow 1981; Rabat 1982; FCO 1985; Masirah 1985; LA Floater 1986; FCO 1988; Vice-Consul Johannesburg 1992; Second Secretary (Political) Gibraltar 1996; On loan to the DTI 1997; Consul (Inward Investment) Toronto 1999; m 1994 Cheryl Ann Sim.

Williams, Karen Lesley, MBE (2001); Second Secretary (Commercial) Beirut since August 2002; Born 28/06/63; FCO 1987; Riyadh 1988; New York (UKMIS) 1991; World Wide Floater Duties 1993; FCO 1995; Rangoon 1999; Band C4.

Williams, Laura Kate Elizabeth; Second Secretary (Political/Information) Addis Ababa since April 2001; Born 03/04/74; FCO 1998; First Secretary Paris Embassy 1999; First Secretary Brussels (UKREP) 2000; Full-Time Language Training 2000; T/D Second Secretary (Political) Brussels (UKREP) 2000; Band C4.

Williams, Paul; First Secretary (Political) Berlin since October 2001; Born 25/11/48; Immigration Service 1969; Islamabad 1977; Dhaka 1982; Lagos 1987; Second later First Secretary Muscat 1996; First Secretary Houston 1998; m 1969 Barbara Jane Briggs (2s 1975, 1979).

Williams, Philip George; FCO since July 1988; Born 26/07/54; FCO 1972; Nairobi 1985; Band D6; m 1987 Susan Traise McAlden.

Williams, Prue, RVM; SUPL since November 2001; Bonn 1978; Moscow 1980; FCO 1981; Port of Spain 1983; FCO 1985; Bangkok 1996 (State Visit); The Hague/Luxembourg (Presidency) 1997; FCO 1998; Band B3.

Williams, Rebecca Louise; SUPL since July 2004; Born 17/08/71; FCO 1989; Geneva (UKMIS) 1991; Peking 1994; PA/HMA Kuwait 1997; Berne 2000; Band A2; m 1996 Grant Pritchard (diss 2001).

Williams, Dr Rhodri Huw; FCO since July 2004; Born 14/05/59; FCO 1990; First Secretary (Economic) Vienna 1992; First Secretary FCO 1996; Counsellor Amman 2001; m 1986 Hilary Clair Wakeham (1s, 1d (twins) 1991; 1s 1994).

Williams, Roger Gordon; Cairo since March 2004; Born 28/07/48; Army 1963-89; Prague 1989; Washington 1991; Cairo 1993; T/D Cairo 1997; Belgrade 1997; Lagos 1997; Jakarta 1999; Kabul 2003; Band C4; m 1974 Anne Elizabeth (1d 1974; 2s 1978, 1980).

Williams, Simon John; Casablanca since January 2002; Born 22/08/60; FCO 1979; Manila 1981; Mbabane 1984; Kaduna 1986; FCO 1992; Full-Time Language Training 1995; Third Secretary (Commercial) Riyadh 1995; Second Secretary (Commercial) Doha 1998; Band C5; m 1987 Rosemarie Caguntas Williams (1s 1989).

Williams, Stephen Michael; Head of Latin America and Caribbean Department FCO since September 2003; Born 20/07/59; FCO 1981; Third later Second Secretary Sofia 1984; Second later First Secretary FCO 1987; On loan to Barclays Bank 1990; First Secretary (Commercial/Economic) Oslo 1991; First Secretary (External Relations) Brussels (UKREP) 1995; Counsellor FCO 1998; Full-Time Language Training 2001; Counsellor and Deputy Head of Mission Buenos Aires 2001; m 1983 Fiona Michele Hume (2d 1986, 1989; 1s 1991).

Williams, Steven; First Secretary FCO since July 2003; Born 30/04/69; FCO 1987; Brussels 2000; Band C5; m 2000 Leah Victoria Cox.

Williams, Tony Scott; Second Secretary (Management) Sofia since August 2000; Born 12/09/62; FCO 1981; Brussels (UKDEL NATO) 1984; Prague 1986; Dhaka 1988; FCO 1989; Athens 1993; Third Secretary (Commercial) New Delhi 1996; m 1985 Denise Tilbrook (1s 1992).

Williamson, George Moray; FCO since September 2001; Born 25/02/74; Band C4.

Williamson, Martin Charles; Deputy High Commissioner Wellington since November 2004; Born 28/01/53; FCO (HCS) 1977; Economic Adviser FCO 1981; IMF Research Department 1984; Economic Adviser FCO 1987; Cabinet Office 1989; OECD Secretariat, Paris 1991; Senior Economic Adviser and Joint Head of Economic Advisers FCO 1994; Deputy Head of Economic Policy Department 1999; Head of Resource Budgeting Department 1999; Prism Team 2003; m 1978 Elizabeth Michelle Darvill (2s 1984, 1987).

Williamson, Morven Jane; Maputo since April 2004; Born 16/04/71; FCO 1991; Hanoi 1994; Jedda 1999; Band B3.

Willis, Iain Edward; FCO since January 2003; Born 25/05/71; FCO 1991; T/D Karachi 1995; Vice-Consul Tokyo 1996; Third Secretary (Political) Valletta 1999; Band B3.

Willis, Ruth Valerie (née Coward); FCO since June 2002; Born 18/09/60; FCO 1985; New Delhi

1988; Mexico City 1991; The Hague 1996; FCO 1999; SUPL 2001; Band C4; m 2000 Barry Willis.

Willmer, Nigel Stuart; FCO since September 2000; Born 03/07/65; FCO 1983; Madrid 1990; FCO 1993; Lusaka 1997; m 1985 Jackie Mann (diss 2001) (1d 1986).

Willmott, Emily Margaret; Assistant Legal Adviser FCO since October 2001; Born 02/11/72; Solicitor 1998; m 1999 Simon Nathan Willmott.

Willock, Oriel; San José since August 2001; Born 23/04/68; FCO 1988; Amman 1990; Floater Duties 1994; FCO 1997; T/D Islamabad 1999; T/D Ekaterinburg 2000; Band B3.

Wills, Jane Stirling; First Secretary FCO since January 2001; Born 12/12/46; Commonwealth Office (later FCO) 1964; Prague 1969; Copenhagen 1971; Vienna (UKDEL MBFR) 1973; Bombay 1976; FCO 1980; Prague 1983; Ankara 1986; Second Secretary FCO 1989; Deputy Head of Mission Reykjavik 1995; Deputy Head of Mission Bratislava 1999.

Wills, Ruth Margaret; Second later First Secretary FCO since December 1991; Born 07/11/54; FCO 1977; Rio de Janeiro 1980; Paris 1984; Second Secretary (Press/Information) Bonn 1989.

Willsher, Ian Robert; Lagos since June 2003; Born 14/04/47; Washington 1974; Vienna 1977; FCO 1979; Accra 1982; Geneva 1985; FCO 1988; Nairobi 1990; FCO 1994; British Forces Germany 1996; Brussels 1998; m 1976 Amanda Jane (2s 1978, 1979; 1d 1985).

Wilson, Allan Richard James; Mexico City since August 2001; Born 11/05/77; FCO 1999; Band A2; m 2003 Yessica Reyes Guisa.

Wilson, Caroline Melanie Cherry (née Meath); SUPL since July 2003; Born 16/09/69; FCO 1990; Canberra 1992; Moscow 1995; SUPL 1998; FCO 1999; Band B3; m 1993 James Jeffrey Wilson.

Wilson, Elizabeth Claire; Second Secretary (Political) Peking since November 2002; Born 20/09/74; FCO 1998; Full-Time Language Training 2000; Full-Time Language Training Peking 2001; Band C4.

Wilson, Fraser Andrew, MBE (1980); High Commissioner Victoria (Seychelles) since May 2002; Born 06/05/49; Commonwealth Office (later FCO) 1967; Havana 1970; SE Asia Floater 1971; Seoul 1973; Salisbury 1977; Second Secretary FCO 1980; Language Training 1983; Second Secretary (Commercial) Moscow 1984; Second Secretary (Commercial) and Vice-Consul (later First Secretary (Commercial) Rangoon 1986; First Secretary FCO 1990; Deputy Consul-General São Paulo 1994; Full-Time Language Training 1998; HM Ambassador Turkmenistan 1998; m 1981 Janet Phillips (2s 1982, 1985).

Wilson, Gillian Grace; SUPL since October 2002; Born 19/04/65; ODA 1981; FCO 1989; T/D Dhaka 1991; Accra 1991; Third Secretary (Chancery) Nairobi 1995; FCO 1998; Band C4.

Wilson, Harry Kenneth, BEM (1991); Buenos Aires since January 2003; Born 07/05/52; RAF 1971-97; FCO 1998; Madrid 1999; Band A2; m 1979 Elaine Carrick (1s 1981; 1d 1983).

Wilson, Ian Laurence; FCO since July 2002; Born 19/06/44; FO 1962; Moscow 1966; Colombo 1967; FCO 1971; Brussels (UKDEL NATO) 1974; Banjul 1977; FCO 1981; Canberra 1983; FCO 1987; Second Secretary (Consular/Admin) Calcutta 1987; Second Secretary (Management) Bucharest 1992; First Secretary FCO 1995; Consul and First Secretary (Management) Tehran 1997; HM Consul Riyadh 2000; HM Consul Beijing 2001; Band C5; m (1) 1970 (1d 1974; 1s 1976) (diss 1999); (2) 1999 Monica Dorri (1s 2000).

Wilson, James Jeffrey (Jeff); First Secretary New Delhi since July 2003; Born 07/08/67; FCO 1988; Canberra 1992; Moscow 1995; Ekaterinburg 1997; FCO 1999; Band D6; m 1993 Caroline Melanie Meath.

Wilson, Michael George; FCO since January 2002; Born 10/12/70; FCO 1989; Dhaka 1991; World Wide Floater Duties 1995; ECO Delhi 1998; Band B3.

Wilson, Peter Michael Alexander; FCO since January 2003; Born 31/03/68; FCO 1992; Full-Time Language Training 1993; Full-Time Language Training Peking 1994; Second Secretary (Commercial) Peking 1995; SUPL 1999; First Secretary (Institutions) Brussels (UKREP) 1999; Band D7; m 2001 Mónica Roma (1d 2002).

Wilson, Robert Thomas Osborne; FCO since January 2002; Born 28/01/52; Senior Research Officer; FCO 1982; First Secretary and Head of Chancery Abu Dhabi 1989; Principal Research Officer FCO 1993; Deputy Head of Mission, HM Consul Bahrain 1998; m 1979 Susan Ann Watson (2d 1985, 1988).

Wilson, Roy Andrew; Deputy Head of Mission Yerevan since September 2002; Born 03/12/59; HCS 1978; FCO 1979; Karachi 1982; Seoul 1985; FCO 1987; Bombay 1990; Zurich 1994; First Secretary Banja Luka 2000; Band C4.

Wilson, Sarah Elizabeth; Ankara since July 2002; Born 08/03/70; FCO 2000; Band A2.

Wilson, Simon Charles Hartley; Deputy Head of Mission and Head of Political Section Bahrain since November 2001; Born 09/08/57; FCO 1975; Johannesburg 1978; Helsinki 1981; FCO 1984; Tehran 1987; Riyadh 1987; Second Secretary (Chancery/Information) Lisbon 1992; Second later First Secretary FCO 1997; m 1984 Heather Graine Richardson (2s 1990, 1994).

Wilson, Simon Jules, OBE (1996); First Secretary Budapest since February 2002; Born 13/03/66; FCO 1988; Third later Second Secretary (Economic) Athens 1991; Second later First Secretary (Political) Zagreb 1993; First Secretary FCO 1996; First Secretary New York (UKMIS) 1999; FCO 2000; Band D6.

Wilson, Susan Jean; Vice-Consul New Delhi since January 2002; Born 01/02/70; FCO 1989; Bangkok 1994; Istanbul 1997; Band B3; m 2001 Ahmet Cikit.

Wilton, Christopher Edward John; HM Ambassador Kuwait since September 2002; Born 16/12/51; FCO 1977; MECAS 1978; Second later First Secretary Bahrain 1979; FCO 1981; First Secretary (Chancery) Tokyo 1984; On loan to the Cabinet Office 1988; Counsellor (Commercial) Riyadh 1990; Consul-General Dubai 1994; Counsellor FCO 1998; m 1975 Dianne Hodgkinson (1d 1981; 1s 1984).

Wiltshire, Terence Keith; Second Secretary (Technical Management) Budapest since February 2001; Born 24/12/57; FCO 1981; New Delhi 1983; FCO 1987; Lagos 1994; FCO 1997; Band C4.

Windle, William James; Counsellor Washington since August 2002; Born 03/07/52; FCO 1972; On loan to the MOD 1975; FCO 1977; Second Secretary (Commercial) Muscat 1980; Second later First Secretary FCO 1984; First Secretary (Chancery) Washington 1989; First Secretary later Counsellor FCO 1992; Band C5; m 1974 June Constance Grimmond (3s 1980, 1982, 1985).

Windsor, Dallas Frederick; Tokyo since October 2003; Born 24/04/74; FCO 2001; Language Training 2003; Band C4; m 2001 Kiyoe Higashi.

Winnington-Ingram, Charles Pepys; FCO since 2000; Born 06/10/55; Barrister 1977; Export Credits Guarantee Department 1979; FCO 1980; Third Secretary (Commercial) Tokyo 1981; Second Secretary FCO 1985; Second Secretary (Chancery/Information) Oslo 1989; HM Consul (Commercial) and Deputy Head of Mission St Petersburg 1995; HM Consul and Deputy Head of Mission Jerusalem 1996.

Winsley, Marcus Justin; First Secretary (Political) Washington since June 2002; Born 01/09/67; ODA 1993; First Secretary Moscow 1996; FCO 2000; Band D6; m 1996 Claire Underwood.

Winter, Douglas; First Secretary (Management) Addis Ababa since March 2004; Born 21/01/51; FCO 1969; Mogadishu 1972; Antigua 1974; FCO 1978; Bangkok 1981; Zagreb 1984; Warsaw 1985; Second Secretary FCO 1987; Second Secretary (Commercial) Abu Dhabi 1990; FCO 1994; Second Secretary (Consular/Management) Sarajevo 1999; m 1972 Linda Margaret Harmer (1s 1975; 1d 1978).

Winter, Simon; ECO Accra since November 2000; Born 10/04/68; FCO 1990; Tokyo 1995; Budapest 1999; Band B3; m 1993 Alyson Barnett (1s 1994; 2d 1997, 2001).

Winterburn, Christine Catherine (née Lowrie); Deputy Head of Mission Asunción since July 2003; Born 20/04/67; FCO 1986; Copenhagen 1987; FCO 1989; Kaduna/Abuja 1992; Lima 1996; Sofia 1999; Band C4; m 1989 (diss 2002) (2s 1995, 2000).

Wise, Graeme Michael; HM Consul Washington since June 2002; Born 17/06/64; FCO 1984; Addis Ababa 1985; Lagos 1988; Floater Duties 1991; FCO 1992; Second Secretary (Commercial) Buenos Aires 1997; SUPL 1999; FCO 2001; First Secretary (Management) Dublin 2001; Band C5.

Wise, Patricia (née Donnelly); Nicosia since March 2000; Born 24/02/58; FCO 1982; Port Stanley 1983; Lusaka 1983; Rome 1987; Cape Town/Pretoria 1990; FCO 1993; SUPL 1994; Helsinki 1994; SUPL 1996; FCO 1997; Band B3; m (1) 1985 Edward Meredith Leighton (diss 1991); (2) 1992 David Wise (dec'd 1999) (1d 1994).

Wisker, Rita; Berlin since February 2003; Born 15/09/51; FCO 1972; Tokyo 1973; FCO 1975; Washington 1977; Brussels (UKREP) 1980; BMG Berlin 1983; New York (UKMIS) 1984; FCO 1985; Brussels (UKDEL) 1992; FCO 1996; Band B3.

Withers, John Walter Charles; FCO since August 1994; Born 24/11/47; FCO 1975; Moscow 1979; FCO 1982; Lagos 1982; FCO 1985; Ottawa 1986; New York 1987; FCO 1989; Third later Second Secretary Bucharest 1991; m 1970 Vivienne Chater (1d 1976; 1s 1986).

Withers, Matthew Robert; Third Secretary (Political) Buenos Aires since January 2001; Born 14/10/67; FCO 1987; Kuala Lumpur 1988; Kathmandu 1992; Lagos 1994; FCO 1998; Band B3; m 1992 Leigh Cooper (2d 1994, 1996).

Witting, Lisa Marie; Vienna (UKMIS) since January 2000; Born 22/02/69; FCO 1988; Dublin 1989; FCO 1993; Berlin 1995; Band A2.

Wolstenholme, Jonathan David; FCO since December 2002; Born 15/01/60; FCO 1980; Baghdad 1982; Moscow 1984; Harare 1986; FCO 1990 (Second Secretary 1992); Second Secretary (Management) Brussels (UKREP) 1994; Second Secretary (Chancery) Wellington 1998; Band C5; m 1986 Karen Suzanne Vivian (2d 1989, 1994; 1s 1992).

Wolstenholme, Karen Suzanne (née Vivian); FCO since March 2003; Born 16/10/62; FCO 1980; Language Training 1983; Moscow 1984; FCO 1985; Harare 1986; Second Secretary FCO 1990; SUPL 1992; Second Secretary FCO 1993; Brussels (UKREP) 1994; Second later First Secretary Wellington 1998; Band D6; m 1986 Jonathan David Wolstenholme (2d 1989, 1994; 1s 1992).

Wong, Josephine; FCO since September 2001; Born 17/12/72; Band D6.

Wong, Lillian Paterson (née Walker); FCO since February 1976; Born 16/02/44; Senior Principal Research Officer; FCO 1970; Second Secretary (Information/Aid) Yaoundé 1973; Band D7; m 1979 Robert Puck Keong Wong.

Wood, Christopher Terence; Consul-General Guangzhou since July 2003; Born 19/01/59; FCO 1981; Hong Kong 1983; FCO 1987; Department

of Environment 1992; Department of
Environment, Transport & the Regions 1997;
Cabinet Office 1998; Office of the Deputy Prime
Minister 2002.

Wood, Ian David; SUPL since August 2001; Born
14/09/69; FCO 1992; Third later Second Secretary
UKDEL OECD 1994; Second Secretary (Political)
New Delhi 1996; UKDEL NATO 1996; FCO
1998.

Wood, James Sebastian Lamin, CMG (2002);
Counsellor Washington since July 2001; Born
06/04/61; FCO 1983; Language Training 1984;
Second Secretary Bangkok 1986; Second later
First Secretary FCO 1989; Full-Time Language
Training Taiwan 1991; First Secretary and Consul
for Macau BTC Hong Kong 1992; First Secretary
UKREP JLG Hong Kong 1994; FCO 1996; On
loan to the Cabinet Office 1998; Seconded to
Harvard 2000; m 1990 Sirihat Penguam (3d 1992,
1993, 1995).

Wood, Sir Michael Charles, KCMG (2004), CMG
(1995); Legal Adviser FCO since December 1999;
Born 05/02/47; Called to the Bar, Grays Inn 1968;
Assistant Legal Adviser FCO 1970; Legal Adviser
Bonn 1981; Legal Adviser later Legal Counsellor
FCO 1984; Counsellor (Legal) New York
(UKMIS) 1991; Legal Counsellor FCO 1994;
Deputy Legal Adviser 1996.

Wood, Michael John Hemsley; FCO since August
2003; Born 16/09/48; FCO 1972; Third later
Second Secretary Athens 1974; FCO 1976; First
Secretary Harare 1980; Language Training 1983;
First Secretary and Head of Chancery and Consul
Hanoi 1984; First Secretary FCO 1987; Counsellor
(Political) Helsinki 1993; Counsellor FCO 1997;
Counsellor Lusaka 2000; Counsellor (Regional
Affairs) Accra 2002; m (1) 1975 Susan Christine
Langford; (2) 1983 Wendy Mary Smith.

Wood, Dr Peter Gilruth; Counsellor Peking since
September 2002; Born 02/11/53; FCO 1982;
Language Training 1983; Taiwan 1984; First
Secretary (Economic) Peking 1986; First Secretary
FCO 1989; Counsellor 1994; Kuala Lumpur 1995;
Counsellor FCO 1998; m 1998 Pamela Sue
Shookman.

Wood, Richard John; First Secretary (Economic)
New York (UKMIS) since August 2002; Born
27/08/67; FCO 1991; Cape Town/Pretoria 1993;
First Secretary FCO 1998.

Wood, Richard Lewis; Second Secretary
(Consular) Al Khobar since February 2004; Born
07/06/61; FCO 1982; Sofia 1984; Bandar Seri
Begawan 1986; FCO 1989; Vice-Consul Riyadh
1992; Third Secretary (Commercial) Johannesburg
1996; FCO 1999; m 1994 Frances Anne Curley (2s
1995, 1998).

Wood, Simon Andrew; Second Secretary
(Commercial) Tokyo since October 2001; Born
25/02/73; FCO 1998; Language Training
(Japanese) 2000; Band C4; m 1998 Philippa
Hargrave (1s 2003).

Woodcock, Andrew; Second Secretary FCO since
February 2000; Born 18/09/65; FCO 1988; Vice-
Consul Baghdad 1990; AMO/Vice-Consul Brasilia
1991; Third Secretary (Science and Technology)
Bonn 1995; Third Secretary (Economic/Political)
Mexico City 1996; Band C4.

Woodham, Mark John; Consul St Petersburg since
July 2003; Born 18/11/67; FCO 1988; Helsinki
1991; Islamabad 1994; Bangkok 1998; Band C4;
m 1993 Sari Hannele Hakkarainen.

Woodier, Daniel Robert; Third Secretary
(Immigration) Doha since February 2004; Born
02/09/65; FCO 1996; Third Secretary (External
Affairs) Canberra 2000; Band B3; m 1989 Sarah
Harmer (2s 2000, 2001).

Woodrow, John Peter Gayford; FCO since
February 2002; Born 21/11/47; FCO 1972;
Barcelona 1975; Quito 1976; FCO 1979; La Paz
1983; Consul Istanbul 1988; FCO 1992; Consul
Oslo 1995; Second Secretary (Consular) Helsinki
1997; m 1977 Yvonne Leffmann.

Woodruffe, John Michael; Second Secretary
(Political) Gibraltar since August 2001; Born
26/06/57; FCO 1986; Dublin 1989; Amman 1992;
FCO 1995; Shanghai 1998; Band C4; m 1989
Marian Barrett.

Woods, David John; Counsellor (Political) Berlin
since August 2002; Born 04/08/51; Third later
Second Secretary FCO 1976; Second later First
Secretary (UNIDO & IAEA) Vienna 1978; FCO
1981; First Secretary (Economic) Bucharest 1981;
First Secretary FCO 1985; Counsellor Harare
1992; Counsellor FCO 1995; Counsellor (Political)
Pretoria 1997; m 1972 Rachel Haydon White (1s
1977; 1d 1979).

Woods, Harvey John; First Secretary Islamabad
since March 2002; Born 29/10/70; FCO 1999;
Full-Time Language Training 2001; Band D6.

Woods, Ian Alexander; Counsellor Sofia since July
2003; Born 10/06/51; Third Secretary FCO 1976;
Second Secretary New York (UKMIS) 1977; First
Secretary FCO 1980; BMG Berlin 1984; Bonn
1986; First Secretary later Counsellor FCO 1989;
Warsaw 1995; Counsellor FCO 1998; m 1978
Stephanie Flett (2s 1982, 1986).

Woodward, Amanda Jane; Rome since June 2002;
Born 29/04/56; FCO 1978; Brasilia 1979; New
Delhi 1982; Moscow 1985; FCO 1988; Lisbon
1989; FCO 1991; Kuala Lumpur 1993; Muscat
1997; Band B3.

Woodward, Barbara Janet, OBE; Counsellor
(Political) Beijing since December 2003; Born
29/05/61; FCO 1991; Second Secretary Moscow
1994; FCO 1998.

Woodward, Gillian Yvonne (née Aplin); SUPL
since November 1996; Born 20/12/46; DSAO
(later FCO) 1966; Paris (UKDEL OECD) 1969;
Yaoundé 1972; FCO 1974; Lagos 1979; SUPL
1981; Helsinki 1984; FCO 1987; Mexico City
1990; FCO 1993; Band B3; m 1977 Roger Charles
Woodward.

Woodward, Roger Charles; First Secretary (Management) and HM Consul Helsinki since October 2001; Born 15/03/48; Commonwealth Office (later FCO) 1967; Dacca 1970; Caribbean Floater 1972; Doha 1973; FCO 1976; Lagos 1979; Helsinki 1982 (Second Secretary 1984); FCO 1987; Second Secretary (Commercial) Mexico City 1990; Second Secretary FCO 1993; First Secretary (Management) Paris 1997; m 1977 Gillian Yvonne Aplin.

Wooten, Sarah Elisabeth; FCO since October 2002; Born 04/02/68; FCO 1989; Third Secretary (Consular) Valletta 1992; Full-Time Language Training 1994; Full-Time Language Training Tokyo 1995; Osaka 1996; Consul (Commercial and Investment) Nagoya 1999; Band C4.

Wootton, Adam Nicholas; FCO since September 1996; Born 19/05/60; FCO 1983; Baghdad 1985; FCO 1988; Nairobi 1993; Band C5; m 1984 Adele Wright (2s 1989, 1991; 1d 1993).

Wordsworth, Stephen John, LVO (1992); Minister and Deputy Head of Mission Moscow since May 2003; Born 17/05/55; FCO 1977; Third later Second Secretary Moscow 1979; FCO 1981; First Secretary (Economic/Commercial) Lagos 1983; On loan to the Cabinet Office 1986; First Secretary FCO 1988; First Secretary (Political) Bonn 1990; Counsellor (Deputy International Affairs Adviser) SHAPE Mons 1994; Head of Eastern Adriatic Dept FCO 1999; m 1981 Ellyse Nichole Mingins (1s 1987).

Worham, Paul Andrew; FCO since 2002; Born 15/12/66; HCS 1988; FCO 1997; Moscow 1999; Band A2; m 1999 Elizabeth Mary Smith.

Workman, Daniel John; Second Secretary (Chancery) Belgrade since August 2003; Born 11/09/78; FCO 2000; Band C4.

Worster, Paul Anthony; FCO since September 2002; Born 14/05/62; FCO 1983; Warsaw 1985; Washington 1986; Helsinki 1989; FCO 1992; Tehran 1996; Third Secretary (Consular) Singapore 1999; Band B3.

Worthington, Ian Alan, OBE (1999); First Secretary (Commercial) Berlin since October 2001; Born 09/08/58; FCO 1977; Language Training 1978; Moscow 1980; Lusaka 1982; Second Secretary FCO 1985; Second Secretary (Commercial) Seoul 1988; Second Secretary (Chancery) Kingston 1992; Head BETO later Consul-General Ekaterinburg 1995; FCO 1998; Band D6.

Wotton, Rosaleen Mary (née McManus); FCO since September 2003; Born 15/01/62; FCO 1987; Oslo 1988; Brussels 1991; FCO 1992; T/D Geneva 1993; Berne 1993; FCO 1996; SUPL 1998; ECO Nicosia 2000; Band B3; m 1997 Alan Leslie Wotton (1s 1998).

Wragg, Ann Desson (née Traill); FCO since August 1992; Born 20/03/65; FCO 1983; Paris 1985; FCO 1988; New York (UKMIS) 1989; Band C5; m 1988 John Wragg.

Wraight, Dr Christopher David; Second Secretary (Chancery) Lilongwe since July 2003; Born 19/11/75; FCO 2001; Band C4.

Wright, Carol; FCO since October 2003; Born 27/06/62; FCO 1988; Pretoria 1992; Johannesburg 1993; FCO 1996; Third Secretary (Management) Baku 2001; Band B3.

Wright, Christopher David; FCO since September 2003; Born 25/10/74; Band C4.

Wright, Clive David, MBE; FCO since September 2000; Born 14/01/58; Royal Marines 1976; FCO 1977; Ankara 1980; Tripoli 1983; FCO 1984; Doha 1986 (Second Secretary 1989); Vice-Consul (Political/Admin) Johannesburg 1989; Second later First Secretary FCO 1993; First Secretary Vienna (UKDEL OSCE) 1996; m 1982 Christine Bernadette Caldwell (2d 1986, 1989).

Wright, David Alan, OBE (1984); FCO since August 2002; Born 27/05/42; FO 1965; APS to Minister of State FO 1966; MECAS 1968; Baghdad 1971; Second Secretary (Commercial) and Vice-Consul Doha 1973; On loan to the DHSS 1976; Second later First Secretary FCO 1978; Consul and Head of Post Durban 1980; First Secretary (Commercial) Baghdad 1984; First Secretary later Counsellor FCO 1987; HM Consul-General Atlanta 1992; HM Ambassador Doha 1997; m 1966 Gail Karol Mesling (4s 1966, 1968, 1971, 1983; 1d 1978).

Wright, David Stephen; FCO since January 2003; Born 04/02/63; FCO 1989; Second Secretary (Chancery) Mexico City 1991; First Secretary FCO 1993; First Secretary (Political) Bogotá 2000; Band D6; m 1992 Tania Victoria Gessinger (2d 1999, 2001).

Wright, Julia Helen; Second Secretary (Political) Lisbon since May 2002; Born 06/02/65; FCO 1991; Amsterdam 1994; Oslo 1997; Band C4.

Wright, Nicola (née Daubney); Singapore since July 2001; Born 31/01/70; FCO 1989; Peking 1992; FCO 1993; Zagreb 1996; FCO 1999; Band B3; m 1998 Alan David Wright.

Wright, Stephen John Leadbetter, CMG (1997); HM Ambassador Madrid since May 2003; Born 07/12/46; Third Secretary FCO 1968; Havana 1969; Second later First Secretary FCO 1972; Director of Policy and Reference Division and Consul (Information) New York (BIS) 1975; Brussels (UKREP) 1980; First Secretary FCO 1984; Counsellor 1985; On loan to the Cabinet Office 1985; Counsellor and Head of Chancery New Delhi 1988; Counsellor (External Relations) Brussels (UKREP) 1991; Director (EU Affairs) FCO 1994; Minister Washington 1997; Director (Wider Europe) FCO 1999; Deputy Under-Secretary FCO 2000; m (1) 1970 Georgina Susan Butler (diss 2000) (1d 1977; 1s 1979); (2) 2002 Abbey Rosemont.

Wurr, Adam; Second Secretary FCO since January 2002; Born 14/12/71; Second Secretary

FCO 1995; Second Secretary Geneva (UKMIS) 2000; Band C4.

Wyatt, David; Deputy High Commissioner Lagos since October 2001; Born 18/04/46; DSAO 1965; Lusaka 1968; SOAS 1971; Bangkok 1972 (Second Secretary 1975); Second Secretary Yaoundé 1976; Second later First Secretary FCO 1977 (First Secretary 1979); National Defence Course Latimer 1980; First Secretary (Commercial) Athens 1981; First Secretary and Head of Chancery Bangkok 1984; First Secretary FCO 1988; Deputy High Commissioner Accra 1994; FCO 1998; Counsellor (Commercial) Bangkok 1999; m 1969 Rosemary Elizabeth Clarke (1s 1972; 1d 1974).

Wye, Roderick Francis; FCO since 1999; Born 13/09/50; Research Officer FCO 1973; PRO 1983; Peking 1985; First Secretary FCO 1988; First Secretary (Chancery) Peking 1995; m 1989 Katelin Rebecca Teller (1s 1994).

Wyithe, Philip Leslie; Second Secretary (Commercial) Ho Chi Minh City since March 2002; Born 30/12/64; FCO 1983; Moscow 1987; Floater Duties 1990; Third Secretary (Consular) Sana'a 1992; Third Secretary (Immigration) Valletta 1994; FCO 1995; Second Secretary (Management/Consular) Seoul 1997; Band B3; m 1992 Gina Olofernes Daniel (1d 1994).

Wylde, Richard Norman Gordon; First Secretary Kabul since June 2003; Born 18/10/58; FCO 1985; Second later First Secretary (Chancery) and Deputy Permanent Representative ESCAP Bangkok 1989; First Secretary FCO 1992; First Secretary (Political) Rome 1996; First Secretary FCO 2000; Band D6; m 1987 Lesley Tennison (1d 1991; 1s 1995).

Wyver, Wendy Anne; Copenhagn since August 2004; Born 26/10/64; FCO 1993; Full-Time Language Training 1995; Second Secretary (Political) Tokyo 1996; First Secretary FCO 1999; m 1995 Jakob Windfeld Lund (1s 2001).

Y

Yaghmourian, Paul Barkef; Consul-General Rio de Janeiro since March 2002; Born 14/02/58; FCO 1984; Second later First Secretary Lisbon 1986; First Secretary FCO 1989; First Secretary (Political) Brasilia 1993; Secondment to British Aerospace 1997; Counsellor and Deputy Head of Mission Copenhagen 1997.

Yamauchi, Mara Rosalind (née Myers); First Secretary FCO since December 2002; Born 13/08/73; FCO 1996; Language Training FCO 1997; Language Training Kamakura 1998; Second Secretary (Political) Tokyo 1999; Band D6; m 2002 Shigetoshi Yamauchi.

Yapp, John William; FCO since October 2002; Born 14/01/51; FCO 1971; Islamabad 1973; Kuala Lumpur (Consular) 1975; APS to Minister of State FCO 1978; Dubai (Commercial) 1980; Second Secretary (Economic/Commercial) The Hague 1984; First Secretary FCO 1988; First Secretary (Information/Political) Wellington 1991; Deputy

Head of North America Department FCO 1995; High Commissioner Victoria (Seychelles) 1998; m (1) 1973 (1d 1975); (2) 1979 (1s 1981; 2d 1983, 1987); (3) 1997 Petra Jodelis (1d 1998).

Yarrow, Jon William; Second Secretary Dubai since August 2003; Born 29/01/69; FCO 1987; Washington 1989; Berne 1992; FCO 1995; Third later Second Secretary (Political/Information) Dubai 1998; Second Secretary (Economic) Tunis 2002; m (1) 1989 Helen Mugridge (1d 1992; 1s 1995) (diss 1995); (2) 1999 Katherine Anne Short.

Yarrow, Katherine Anne (née Short); Baghdad since February 2004; Born 19/02/70; FCO 1992; Berne 1994; FCO 1996; SUPL 1998; FCO 2003; Band A2.

Yarunina, Maggie; SUPL since June 2004; Born 08/07/72; FCO 2000; Prague 2003; Band B3; m 1999 Alexandre (Sasha) V Yarounine.

Yeadon, Joanne Mary; Second Secretary (Press and Public Affairs) Milan since May 2003; Born 01/08/65; FCO 1983; Washington 1986; Gibraltar 1989; FCO 1992; Budapest 1996; FCO 1999; Band C4.

Yearsley, Sara Elizabeth; Kigali since January 2004; Born 16/02/76; FCO 2002; Band A2.

York, Jennifer Ann; FCO since April 2000; Born 01/11/60; FCO 1980; BMG Berlin 1982; Africa/Middle East Floater 1985; Mogadishu 1988; FCO 1989; Vice-Consul Durban 1992; Second Secretary (Management) Nairobi 1996; Band C5; m 1988 Murray Rex Clarkin (diss 1996).

Young, Amanda Elizabeth (née Mitchell); SUPL since December 2002; Born 03/06/59; FCO 1977; Paris 1979; Cayman Islands 1982; FCO 1986; Riyadh 1987; Muscat 1989; FCO 1994; SUPL 1995; Dubai 1999; Band B3; m 2000 Murray Andrew James Young.

Young, Andrew John; SUPL since February 2000; Born 02/04/60; Assistant Legal Adviser FCO 1990; Solicitor 1988 (Northern Ireland) and 1990 (England and Wales); Seconded as Deputy Principal Crown Counsel to Hong Kong Government 1994; Assistant Legal Adviser FCO 1997; Legal Counsellor FCO 1999; m (1) 1991 Lucy Stojak (diss 1996); (2) 1997 Annette Lee (1d 1997).

Young, Helena; FCO since September 1982 (First Secretary 1989); Born 08/10/60; Band D6.

Young, Marianne; FCO since October 2001; Born 08/08/71; Band D6; m 2002 Barry Young (1d 2003).

Young, Sarah Louise (née Boxall); Second Secretary (Consular) Kampala since June 2002; Born 16/09/63; FCO 1984; Lisbon 1987; FCO 1989; Cape Town 1997; Band B3; m 1990 Alan Young (2d 1991, 1992) (diss 1995).

Young, Thomas Richard; Second Secretary (Political) Kabul since June 2003; Born 26/04/77; FCO 2001; Band C4.

Younger, Alexander William; First Secretary (Political) Dubai since August 2002; Born 04/07/63; Second Secretary FCO 1991; First Secretary (IAEA) Vienna (UKMIS) 1995; First Secretary FCO 1998; Band D6; m 1993 Sarah Hopkins (1d 1994; 2s 1996, 1998).

Younis, Fouzia; SUPL since April 2004; Born 08/07/78; FCO 2000; Islamabad 2001; Band B3; m 2001 Haroon Suleman.

Yu, Tsui-Ling; FCO since October 2003; Born 20/07/79; Band A2.

Z

Ziaullah, Suman Rafique; FCO since March 2003; Born 27/10/76; FCO 1999; Second Secretary (Political/Economic) Jakarta 2001; Band C4.

Printed in the United Kingdom by The Stationery Office
ID 174779 19585 12/04 992140